P9-CFJ-845

The second edition of
**The Federal Income Tax
Its Sources and Applications**
incorporated the drastic changes of
the Tax Reform Act of 1969. The
1972 supplement covered relevant
changes created by the Revenue Act
of 1971. Now, in one volume, this
Third Edition incorporates the original
coverage of those two statutes.

This new edition also cites or quotes
from new regulations, rulings, and
court decisions which have come
down from late 1970 through mid-
1973.

**Every one of the twenty chapters
has been revised, updated, or
changed. These changes are various:**

- Changes in the law and the related
  interpretative regulations (increased
  personal exemptions, increased social security taxes, new Class Life
  Asset Depreciation Range System,
  the revitalized investment credit,
  and the new reverse corporate statutory merger, to mention a few).

- New court decisions.

- New rulings.

- Updating of examples in the text
  and of the questions at the end of
  each chapter plus additional new
  questions.

The individual income tax return
problem in the Appendix, although
similar to the one that appeared in
prior editions, has been revised and
updated to reflect new changes in the
tax law.

3rd
edition

THE FEDERAL INCOME TAX

Its Sources

and Applications

CLARENCE F. McCARTHY
A.B., J.D., C.P.A.
Retired Partner
Arthur Andersen & Co.

CLARENCE F. McCARTHY, A.B., J.D., DePaul University, is a Certified Public Accountant and a member of the Illinois Bar. A retired partner of Arthur Andersen & Co., he is now an instructor at the Northwestern University Graduate School of Management and the University of Chicago Graduate School of Business.

Prentice-Hall, Inc., Englewood Cliffs, New Jersey

CARNEGIE LIBRARY
LIVINGSTONE COLLEGE
SALISBURY, N. C. 28144

Library of Congress Cataloging in Publication Data

McCARTHY, CLARENCE F
   The Federal income tax.

   The 1968 ed., by C.F. McCarthy and others, is entered under title: The Federal income tax.
   Includes bibliographical references.
   1.–Income tax–United States–Law. I.–Title.
KF6369.M3 1974   343'.73'052   73–11479
ISBN 0–13–308817–0

© 1974, 1971, 1968 BY CLARENCE F. MCCARTHY

All rights reserved. Printed in the United States of America.

10 9 8 7 6 5 4 3 2

PRENTICE-HALL INTERNATIONAL, INC., *London*
  PRENTICE-HALL OF AUSTRALIA, PTY. LTD., *Sydney*
PRENTICE-HALL OF CANADA, LTD., *Toronto*
  PRENTICE-HALL OF INDIA PRIVATE LIMITED, *New Delhi*
PRENTICE-HALL OF JAPAN, INC., *Tokyo*

CARNEGIE LIBRARY
LIVINGSTONE COLLEGE
SALISBURY, N. C. 28144

CONTENTS

PREFACE ... vii

1

HISTORY OF TAXATION
AND THE
LEGISLATIVE PROCESS ... 1

2

SURVEY OF
THE SYSTEM ... 14

3

COMPONENTS OF
INDIVIDUAL
RETURNS ... 40

4

ELEMENTS
OF OTHER
RETURNS ... 90

96770

5

GROSS
INCOME ... 105

6

EXCLUSIONS
FROM
GROSS INCOME ... 157

7

DEDUCTIONS
IN GENERAL ... 195

8

DEPRECIABLE
AND DEPLETABLE
PROPERTY ... 245

9

LOSSES
AND
BAD DEBTS ... 315

10

OTHER DEDUCTIONS
ALLOWED WHETHER
BUSINESS OR PERSONAL ... 357

11

SALES AND OTHER
DISPOSITIONS OF
PROPERTY ... 396

12

CAPITAL GAINS
AND LOSSES ... 447

13

ACCOUNTING
PERIODS ... 506

14

CASH METHOD
OF ACCOUNTING ... 516

15

ACCRUAL METHOD
OF ACCOUNTING ... 534

16

OTHER ACCOUNTING
METHODS, CHANGES,
AND CLAIM OF RIGHT ... 582

17

DEFERRED
COMPENSATION ... 616

18

PARTNERSHIPS ... 642

19

CORPORATIONS ... 663

20

TRUSTS
AND ESTATES ... 719

Appendix

INDIVIDUAL
INCOME TAX RETURN
PREPARATION PROBLEM ... 736

TABLE OF CASES ... 744

FINDING LIST OF CODE
SECTIONS, REGULATIONS,
FORMS, AND RULINGS ... 751

SUBJECT INDEX ... 757

PREFACE

The first edition of this textbook was published in 1968, the second in 1971, and a supplement on May 1, 1972. The Congress, the Internal Revenue Service, and the Courts continue to churn out changes in our income tax law, but, thankfully, the concepts remain basically the same. The second edition reflected the major provisions of the Tax Reform Act of 1969. This third edition reflects not only some interpretations of that statute made by new regulations, but primarily it incorporates the changes made by the Revenue Act of 1971 (most of which were also covered in the May 1, 1972 supplement) and the new important rulings and court cases which have been published through mid-1973.

There is not a single chapter without updating changes. Perhaps the most important new matter consists of the explanation in Chapter 8 of the new Class Life Asset Depreciation Range system, and in that same chapter, of the revitalized investment credit.

As in the two prior editions, the goal of this textbook is to teach in pleasantly readable form the principles of the U.S. system of income taxation. Concepts and original source materials are stressed. The background reasons for many provisions of the Internal Revenue Code are given. Certainly there are rules within these concepts and principles, but this is not a rule book.

To aid understanding, there are three types of examples interspersed throughout the text. First and foremost are digests of or extracts from court cases involving "real life" people and circumstances. Secondly, there are official examples quoted verbatim from the regulations. Finally, there are the customary theoretical examples.

The method of presentation in this book is based upon the assumption that each student will also have his own paperback copy of the Code. A copy of the Regulations will be helpful but not required, because pertinent extracts are quoted in the text. The instructor and the serious student also will find it useful to have access to reporter volumes containing the texts of court cases, the *Cumulative Bulletins* of the Internal Revenue Service containing published rulings, and either CCH's *Standard Federal Tax Reporter* or Prentice-Hall's *Federal Taxes*. The last two are multi-volume, loose-leaf services.

By the end of the course, the student will have learned the most frequently applied provisions of the income tax law. He will be familiar with original source materials, will have learned the importance of tax planning in financial matters, will have prepared an individual income tax return for the proprietor of a small business, and will be capable of preparing a corporation income tax return. Hopefully, and most importantly, the student will have learned how to find the answers to tax problems, no matter how often the Internal Revenue Code may be further amended during the balance of his lifetime.

In writing and editing the first edition of this book, I was greatly assisted by my partners and associates in Arthur Andersen & Co.: Byrle M. Abbin, William H. Gregory, John P. Lindgren, and Billy M. Mann. The second edition saw me relying again on William H. Gregory and Billy M. Mann. For this third edition I have consulted with my partners, Nicholas T. DeLeoleos and Henry G. Wisniewski, on selected subjects. There also is a beautiful young lady, my secretary Judith Foreman, who did yeoman work on both the second and this third edition.

CLARENCE F. McCARTHY

HISTORY OF TAXATION AND THE LEGISLATIVE PROCESS

HISTORY OF TAXATION IN THE UNITED STATES . . . 2

    Customs Duties and Excise Taxes . . . 3
    Birth of the Income Tax . . . 3
    Estate Taxes . . . 6
    Gift Taxes . . . 7
    Employment Taxes . . . 7

TAXATION AND ECONOMICS . . . 9
THE TAX LEGISLATIVE PROCESS . . . 10

    How a Bill Becomes Law . . . 12
    Committee Reports . . . 13

HISTORY OF TAXATION IN THE UNITED STATES

1.1   The story of taxation in the United States centers primarily around the income tax, consistent with the pattern of taxation in almost any highly developed country. The first step in the growth of the typical tax system is the direct head tax (or poll tax). Though simple to understand and relatively easy to collect, this tax ignores the element of "ability to pay" and is somewhat limited in the amounts of revenue that it can produce. The second step is usually the tariff or customs duty on imports, which is even easier to collect and often has the added advantage of protecting growing domestic industries against foreign competition. The third stage is usually the excise tax, which can be imposed selectively upon a multitude of products, occupations, or transactions.

1.2   Sooner or later in the development of a highly industrialized nation, the fourth and most sophisticated step is taken, with the adoption of an income tax. In the United States, the income tax assumed a prominent role in 1913 with the adoption of the Sixteenth Amendment. Present financial requirements of the federal government make the income tax essential.

1.3   The income tax is usually followed or shortly preceded by the levy of succession taxes—death duties and gift taxes. Finally, social security taxes make their appearance. These are taxes imposed upon wages to provide old age assistance (charity distributed on the basis of need), old age benefit insurance, unemployment benefit insurance, and medical care assistance or insurance.

1.4   For thirteen years after the Declaration of Independence the former colonies were, to a major extent, separately autonomous and only loosely confederated. Not until March 4, 1789, when the Constitution began to operate, did the federal government have general taxing power, derived from Art. 1, Sec. 8, Cl. 1:

> The Congress shall have power to lay and collect taxes, duties, imposts and excises, to pay the debts and provide for the common defence and general welfare of the United States; but all duties, imposts and excises shall be uniform throughout the United States.

On direct taxes, Art. 1, Sec. 2, Cl. 3 imposed the restriction "... direct taxes shall be apportioned among the several States ..." according to population. Art. 1, Sec. 9, Cl. 4 amplified this restriction by providing "No capitation, or other direct, tax shall be laid, unless in proportion to the census."

1.5   The founding fathers were probably aware that, although then uncommon, throughout history various types of taxes on income had been levied; but if they had foreseen the future importance of an income tax, they would have mentioned it specifically in the Constitution. That document certainly gave Congress the power to impose such a tax; but if it is a direct tax, then the amount levied had to be apportioned among the several states in accordance with the population of each.

Customs Duties and Excise Taxes

In the early years of the Republic, the deep controversy between a growing national government and states jealous of their independence helped keep federal taxation to a minimum. The years from 1789 to the Civil War were a period of almost complete reliance upon customs receipts from imports, but a few miscellaneous excises were imposed from time to time. In 1791, taxes were levied on distilled spirits and carriages. A little later there were added levies on sugar, salt, snuff, proceeds of auction sales, legal instruments, and bonds.

1.6

Levying and collecting taxes requires administrative personnel. In 1792, for the first time, a Commissioner of Internal Revenue was appointed, and that office continued in existence until 1802. In those years from 1792 to 1802, less than $6 million in revenue[1] was collected, but this was the first era of the Internal Revenue Service, then called the Bureau of Internal Revenue.

1.7

A short history of the Internal Revenue Service published in 1930 comments that internal revenue taxation has gone hand in hand with the nation's wars.[2] The War of 1812 started the trend and inaugurated the second era of internal revenue. In 1813 the office of Commissioner was reintroduced along with a wide assortment of taxes designed to help pay for the war. Excise or stamp taxes were imposed on retail liquor dealers, retailers of foreign merchandise, bank notes, legal instruments, distilled spirits, manufactured articles, household furniture, watches, gold, silver and plated ware, and jewelry. Although this era lasted only about five years, it produced almost $26 million in revenues, over four times the amount collected in the first era, even though the second period was only half as long.

1.8

Birth of the Income Tax

The Civil War brought the first income tax, along with the third appearance of the Commissioner of Internal Revenue, this time with a bureau that has remained alive and active for more than 100 years. The income tax of 1864 taxed incomes from $600 to $5,000 at 5 percent; from $5,000 to $10,000 at 7½ percent; and incomes in excess of $10,000 at 10 percent.[3] This infant income tax, however, had little

1.9

1. *History of the Internal Revenue Service 1791–1929* (Washington: Government Printing Office, 1930). For additional historical material see Randolph Paul, *Taxation in the United States* (Boston: Little, Brown and Company, 1954), containing a detailed description of events to 1952, and R. G. and G. M. C. Blakey, *The Federal Income Tax* (New York: Longmans, Green & Co., Inc., 1940), covering the period from 1909 to 1939.

2. *History of the Internal Revenue Service 1791–1929.*

3. Boris Irving Bittker, *Federal Income, Estate and Gift Taxation*, 3rd ed. (Boston: Little, Brown and Company, 1964), p. 4.

vitality, and it expired after the war. By 1894, mounting pressures for revenue led to the adoption of another income tax.

1.10   When the income tax of 1894 appeared on the national scene, one Mr. Pollock quickly sued the Farmers' Loan & Trust Co., in which he held stock, asking that it be enjoined from paying this unconstitutional tax. On April 8, 1895, the Supreme Court handed down a decision that the portion of the tax imposed upon the income from real estate was unconstitutional since it was a direct tax, and that the portion of the tax imposed upon interest derived from state and municipal bonds was unconstitutional as a violation of the basic constitutional principles of separation of powers.[4] Rehearing brought a second decision on May 20, 1895, striking down the entire tax statute on the theory that the invalid provisions were inseparable and therefore the whole statute must fall.[5]

1.11   But this was only a temporary setback. The financial needs of the government and pressures from all sides to convert those needs into legislative action eventually resulted in another income tax in 1909, which political compromise confined to corporate incomes. The act of August 5, 1909, levied a tax of 1 percent "... upon the entire net income over and above five thousand dollars received by ... [certain corporations] from all sources during such year, exclusive of amounts received ... as dividends upon stock of other corporations ... subject to the tax hereby imposed. ..."

1.12   While the Revenue Act of 1909 was under consideration in Congress, doubt was expressed about its constitutionality in view of the Supreme Court decision of 1895. There was also a realization of need for a broader tax base. As a result, even before that act became law, a congressional resolution was sent to the states on July 12, 1909, calling for an enabling constitutional amendment. From 1909 to 1913, one state after another ratified the proposed constitutional amendment until the required number of three-fourths was reached. This Sixteenth Amendment laid the foundation for the basic framework of our modern tax; and whether it was right or wrong, the *Pollock* decision was nullified. This amendment, effective February 25, 1913, states broadly and explicitly:

The Congress shall have power to lay and collect taxes on incomes, from whatever source derived, without apportionment among the several States, and without regard to any census or enumeration.

Following this expression of authority, Congress quickly tapped the newly sanctioned source of revenue. The corporation income tax of 1909 was discontinued, and corporations as well as individuals became subject to the new income tax introduced in 1913.[6]

1.13   The first income tax act was followed in the next quarter century by

4. Pollock v. Farmers' Loan & Trust Co., 157 U.S. 429 (1895), 3 AFTR 2557.
5. Pollock v. Farmers' Loan & Trust Co. *et al.*, Hyde v. Continental Trust Co. of City of New York *et al.*, 158 U.S. 601 (1895), 3 AFTR 2602.
6. Tariff Act of October 3, 1913.

a series of revenue acts which, in the beginning, represented complete reenactments of the entire tax law with whatever current changes were desired. As the tax law grew in size and complexity, this procedure became cumbersome. In 1939, the entire federal tax law was codified into what was called the Internal Revenue Code.[7] Thereafter, additional revenue acts had only to amend the desired code provisions, rather than to reenact the entire tax law. By the 1950s, tax changes had been so numerous and complex, reflecting the most severe period of war that the world has ever known, that studies were begun to simplify and rearrange the 1939 Code. The result was the Internal Revenue Code of 1954, which, as amended from time to time, is the fundamental tax law in force today.[8]

1.14 The period since 1913 has seen the expansion and development of the federal income tax to a point that surely was never foreseen by its early advocates. World War I prompted the first excess profits tax. The need for revenue in World War II in the 1940s caused its reenactment.[9] For a third time it was repeated (though in a somewhat different form) a decade later, at the time of the conflict in Korea.[10] One of the most important features of the United States tax law was adopted in 1943. Without it, collection of the heavy wartime individual income taxes at best would have been a monumentally difficult task. We refer to what is known, euphemistically, as *pay-as-you-go*. Withholding income tax at the source from wage payments[11] was combined with the individual's obligation to declare, *during* the taxable year, his estimated income tax liability for that year and to make advance payments thereon.[12] Withholding and estimated tax have become the twin pillars supporting the efficient administration of the United States income tax.

1.15 The income tax, of course, did not replace all other forms of taxation. Even the old-fashioned excise taxes (with new and modern targets) survived. In recent years, there have been retailers' excise taxes and manufacturers' excise taxes, "luxury" taxes, taxes on marijuana and machine guns, taxes on telephone service, and other communication facilities. Several of these have been levied primarily for regulatory purposes; raising revenue is incidental.

1.16 Once any tax emerges upon the national scene, to eliminate it becomes very difficult. Some of the excise taxes were adopted in the 1940s as wartime emergency taxes, and yet twenty-five years elapsed before they were repealed. The Excise Tax Reduction Act of 1965 had barely become effective before some of its provisions were canceled. Scheduled reductions in the excise taxes on automobiles and telephone services were halted abruptly by the Tax Adjustment Act of

7. Title 26 of the United States Code, later known as the Internal Revenue Code of 1939.
8. Title 26 of the United States Code.
9. Second Revenue Act of 1940.
10. Excess Profits Tax Act of 1950.
11. Revenue Act of 1943.
12. Current Tax Payment Act of 1943.

1966 and were altered again, first by Public Law 90–285, next by the Revenue and Expenditure Control Act of 1968 (P.L. 90–364), and then by the Tax Reform Act of 1969. The propriety of continuing to tax items commonly considered to be modern necessities may be questionable, but the effectiveness of the excise tax as a revenue measure is attested to by its use in helping to pay for armed conflicts.

Estate Taxes

1.17   The first United States "death" tax had its own early death: enacted 1797, repealed 1802. The next such tax appeared in Civil War years and was repealed in 1870. Offering another example of the close association between war and taxes, the Revenue Act of 1898 adopted a tax on legacies or, more precisely, a tax on "Legacies and Distributive Shares of Personal Property," which had many characteristics in common with the present-day federal estate tax. The rates were progressive and amounts below a certain dollar limit ($10,000) were exempt. In 1900, the United States Supreme Court upheld the constitutionality of the tax, pointing out that some form of death tax was an ancient type of governmental levy and that in this case it was *not* a direct tax (requiring apportionment) but rather an excise tax that satisfied the uniformity requirements of the Constitution (previously held to require only geographical uniformity).[13] The "legacy" tax of 1899 was repealed in 1902. The Revenue Act of 1916 is responsible for the creation of the present estate tax, which, however, has been subject to many modifications during the intervening years.

1.18   Under the present federal estate tax law there is an exemption of $60,000, a tax on the balance of a decedent's estate at rates ranging from 3 percent of the first $5,000 to 77 percent of the excess over $10 million, and then a credit against such tax for state death taxes paid.[14] Probably the most important feature of the estate tax is the "marital deduction," adopted in 1948, to permit decedents in common-law states to achieve the tax benefits usually available to those in states with community property laws.[15] Briefly, amounts passing to a decedent's spouse (or which already may have so passed) are allowed as deductions for federal estate tax purposes up to a maximum of 50 percent of the "adjusted gross estate." One practical effect of the marital deduction is to double the size of the maximum estate that can be left tax-free by a decedent, without recourse to deductible charitable bequests; for example, an estate up to $120,000 can be left tax-free if at least $60,000 passes to the decedent's spouse in such a way that it will qualify for the marital deduction, and the $60,000 exemption offsets the balance.

1.19   The amounts of revenue raised by the estate tax are, as might be expected, much smaller than the grand sums generated by the income tax. The estate tax, however, is much more an instrument of social

13. Knowlton v. Moore, 178 U.S. 41 (1900), 3 AFTR 2684.
14. Code Sec. 2001.
15. Code Sec. 2056.

policy than a revenue producer. Whether it successfully redistributes wealth may be debatable, but unquestionably some of its side effects are more significant than the amount of revenue it produces. Since charitable bequests are deductible, many schools and hospitals are grateful to the estate tax, and many art collections that would have remained concealed are now available for public enjoyment.[16]

Gift Taxes

The gift tax made its first brief appearance in 1924, only to be repealed in 1926. It was reenacted in 1932 and has remained an apparently permanent feature of our federal tax system. The tax rates are progressive and range from $2\frac{1}{4}$ percent to $57\frac{3}{4}$ percent as they increase in orderly steps through 25 brackets in the tax table.[17] Incidentally, the rate in any gift tax bracket is exactly three-fourths of the rate in the corresponding estate tax bracket. Attracted by this happy circumstance and the even more significant fact that a gift during the donor's lifetime "comes off the top" of his estate for estate tax purposes, but goes into his gift tax schedule at the bottom of the brackets (assuming few or no prior gifts), many a wealthy person has become persuaded of the advantages of lifetime gifts so that his beneficiaries may enjoy his property now, rather than waiting for his death.

1.20

The gift tax is cumulative in that each year's gifts are added to those made previously and the tax is recomputed on the total gifts made in all years, with credit for all prior payments. There is a $30,000 specific lifetime exemption as well as an "annual exclusion" of the first $3,000 of gifts to each donee. These limits may be effectively doubled by a provision permitting husband and wife to treat gifts made to third parties by either one as being made one half by each spouse. There is also a marital deduction for one-half the value of a gift to the donor's spouse.[18]

1.21

Employment Taxes

The modern tendency of government to take on greater responsibilities toward its citizens is illustrated by the development of social security legislation within the last thirty-eight years. Starting with the basic Federal Social Security Act approved August 14, 1935, benefits of the following kinds have been provided by now:

1.22

Retirement benefits
Widows' allowances
Death benefits
Unemployment benefits

16. See the article in *Horizon*, Vol. 8, No. 1 (Winter 1966), by Jerome S. Rubin, entitled "Art and Taxes," starting on p. 5.

17. Code Sec. 2502.

18. The gift tax is contained in Sections 2501 to 2524, inclusive, of the Internal Revenue Code of 1954.

Hospitalization insurance
Insurance against other medical expenses

These are financed, at least partly, by payroll taxes on employers as well as by contributions from employees. The taxing provisions are known by the following names and are found in the indicated sections of the Internal Revenue Code:

ACT	CODE SECTIONS
Federal Insurance Contributions Act	3101 to 3126
Railroad Retirement Tax Act	3201 to 3233
Federal Unemployment Tax Act	3301 to 3309

1.23   The taxes imposed by the Federal Insurance Contributions Act are commonly called Social Security taxes. They are levied at the same rates separately on employers and employees. In addition (see Chapter 3) there is a Self-Employment tax. For the calendar years 1973 through 1977, with exceptions as to types of employment and wages that will not be detailed here, Social Security taxes amount to 5.85 percent of the wage base paid to each employee (i.e., in total 11.70 percent of the wage base). This rate is imposed by Sections 3101 and 3111 of the Code and consists of 4.85 percent for old-age, survivors, and disability insurance plus 1.0 percent for hospital insurance (the Medicare program). The wage base under Code Section 3121(a)(1) for 1973 is $10,800 and for 1974 is $12,600. For 1975 and subsequent years, the wage base is "the contribution and benefit base (as determined under Section 230 of the Social Security Act)." The tax imposed on the employee is withheld from his wages, and an equivalent amount is paid by the employer. The tax is on the gross amount of the wage base paid in a calendar year; there are no deductions for personal exemptions or business expenses.

1.24   Every employer of one or more employees is also subject to an unemployment tax. Each state has its own unemployment tax and benefit law, so that benefits are available for a limited period to employees who lose their jobs. The major portion of the tax is levied by the states, and a minor portion is levied by the federal government, allegedly to cover administrative expenses of supervising the state benefit insurance programs. For the calendar year 1973, the federal rate is 3.28 percent of the first $4,200 of each employee's wages, but the employer is allowed a credit (not to exceed 90 percent of the first 3 percent of the federal tax) for amounts paid by him to the states toward the cost of state sponsored but federally approved programs of unemployment compensation.[19] Actually, the credit allowable to an employer for state tax may be greater than the amount paid to the state if his state contributions have been reduced by a favorable experience rating: This rating is based upon the ratio of his employees whose services have for any reason terminated to the total number of his employees. An employer with a favorable employee retention experience usually will pay less tax to the state than the normal amount, but he is allowed to use the normal amount as a credit

19. Code Sec. 3301 and 3302.

against the federal tax. In most states, an employer with an unfavorable employee retention experience will pay a tax higher than the normal amount. The normal amount in most states is computed at the rate of 2.7 percent on the first $4,200 of each employee's wages. This federal tax for purposes of providing unemployment compensation benefits is levied only upon employers and not upon employees. A few states, however, require employees also to contribute to their state programs.

TAXATION AND ECONOMICS

Although our attention will be devoted primarily to understanding 1.25 the United States income tax system as it exists today, rather than analyzing it from an economic standpoint, it certainly cannot be understood without some awareness of the underlying economic factors. Adam Smith, writing in 1776—by a nice coincidence the year of United States independence—set forth four maxims in the light of which a tax could be evaluated to determine whether it is a "good" tax or not:

1. Equality—in the sense that each taxpayer enjoys fair treatment by paying taxes in proportion to the revenue he enjoys.
2. Certainty—which might better be called predictability, the advance knowledge of when, where, and how a tax will be levied.
3. Convenience of payment, from the taxpayer's standpoint.
4. Economy in collection, for the government's benefit.[20]

Today's federal income tax stands up well when measured by these 1.26 maxims of almost 200 years ago. Although the Internal Revenue Code becomes increasingly complex, the fact that the tax has been codified and supported by regulations and rulings has gone a long way to dispel the ancient fear of the tax collector and to create the "certainty" that Adam Smith sought. So far as convenience is concerned, payment of taxes will hardly ever be considered convenient by taxpayers, but the withholding of tax from wages and the system of estimated tax payments may be construed as modern methods of satisfying the "convenience" maxim. As for economy of collection, the Commissioner of Internal Revenue has stated that the department's collection costs amount to less than one-half of one percent of revenues collected.[21] Even if it costs somewhat more to produce income tax collections as compared to other forms of internal revenue, the costs still seem surprisingly negligible.

Does the income tax satisfy Adam Smith's first maxim, that a good 1.27 tax has the attribute of equality or fairness? One of the key features of the individual income tax is the system of progressive or graduated rates, and at first glance this seems somewhat inconsistent with strict equality—taxing individuals in proportion to their respective in-

20. *The Wealth of Nations* (New York: Random House, Inc., Modern Library, Inc., 1937), pp. 777–79, contains an introduction to the four maxims.
21. Annual Report for 1968 of Commissioner of Internal Revenue.

comes. Ability to pay, however, has become accepted as a yardstick by which equality (in the sense simply of fairness) may be measured.[22] Certainly an individual with a very large income is better able to pay his income tax, even under a system of progressive rates, than a man with a modest income, so long as the rates do not become shamefully confiscatory. Measured by these standards and viewed broadly, the United States income tax system must be considered a fair one.

1.28   Through the years, there has been a gradual shift in the government's attitude toward its own tax structure. The earliest view of our taxing system regarded it simply as a revenue-producing mechanism. As the tax base grew wider and the rates higher, the effects upon the entire economy of the country became so apparent that they could not be ignored, and timid efforts began to use the tax structure as a method of effectuating government policy. An example of this is the punitive tax laid upon machine guns or marijuana, to discourage socially undesirable activities. Another example is the use of the estate tax to effect some redistribution of large estates.

1.29   Current thinking goes far beyond these early, relatively minor efforts to use taxation as a positive instrument of government policy. To encourage the modernization of American industry, a direct credit against income tax payable was granted in 1962 in the form of a percentage of new investment in certain tangible property. Rate reductions and increases have been used alternately to stimulate or dampen the economy.[23] In 1964 there was an across-the-board reduction in individual income tax rates to speed up economic growth, followed in 1968 by the imposition of a 10 percent surcharge on all taxpayers to retard inflation.

1.30   Whatever the appraisal of the federal income tax system, or however it may be used by the government to carry out social or economic policies, the fact remains that the ever-increasing responsibilities assumed by the federal government in the last thirty years or so make it almost certain that the income tax will remain as the major permanent revenue-producing measure. The accompanying chart gives some idea of the extent to which the income tax has developed since its early days and its vast impact upon our lives.

THE TAX LEGISLATIVE PROCESS

1.31   The study of United States income taxes should begin with an appreciation of the process whereby tax legislation is created. If there is one all-important fact to fix firmly in mind, it is this:

22. Richard Goode, *The Individual Income Tax* (Washington, D.C.: The Brookings Institution, 1964).

23. For further consideration of these and other topics see Roy Blough, *The Federal Taxing Process* (Englewood Cliffs, N.J.: Prentice-Hall, Inc., 1952) and Lewis H. Kimmel, *Taxes and Economic Incentives* (Washington, D.C.: The Brookings Institution, 1950).

TAXES ARE IMPOSED BY LAW!

The key word here is *law*. Taxation proceeds from a statutory origin, an act of Congress. It must be analyzed and considered in the light of that origin, whether the purpose of the study is to support the law, attack it, or simply to understand it. The present tax law, the Internal Revenue Code of 1954 (Title 26 of the United States Code) contains

INTERNAL REVENUE COLLECTIONS

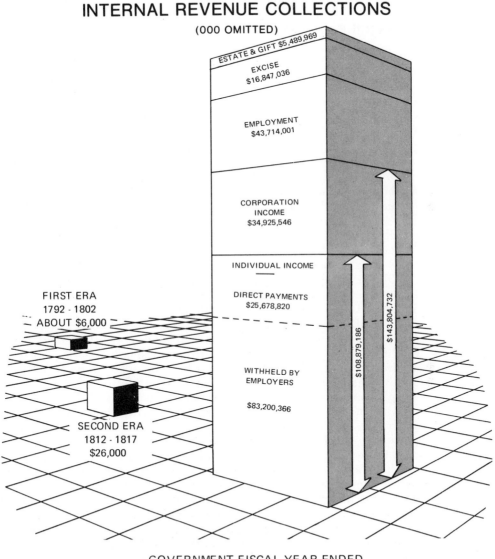

(000 OMITTED)

ESTATE & GIFT $5,489,969

EXCISE
$16,847,036

EMPLOYMENT
$43,714,001

CORPORATION
INCOME
$34,925,546

INDIVIDUAL INCOME

DIRECT PAYMENTS
$25,678,820

WITHHELD BY
EMPLOYERS

$83,200,366

$108,879,186

$143,804,732

FIRST ERA
1792 - 1802
ABOUT $6,000

SECOND ERA
1812 - 1817
$26,000

GOVERNMENT FISCAL YEAR ENDED
JUNE 30, 1972
$209,855,737

12

thousands of sections, painfully assembled and reassembled by legis-
lators over the last half century. Although it is hard to believe at times,
the Code has a definite pattern. It is recommended strongly that as a
first step in studying the subject of federal income taxes, the student
should scan the Code's table of contents, particularly the portions
dealing with income taxes. Familiarity with the basic structure of the
compiled tax law is certain to make the rest of the learning process
smoother.

How a Bill Becomes Law

1.32   The next step is to study how tax law is created. The House of Representatives has the constitutional responsibility for initiating revenue
bills.[24] A particular bill may come about in any one of many different
ways. A major proposal may be made by the president in his annual
budget message to Congress or his message on the state of the Union.
Very likely there is nothing in the form of a bill at this point; the
president's message simply may recommend action by Congress in a
given field. The proposal will be turned over to the Ways and Means
Committee of the House of Representatives. The Senate counterpart
of the Ways and Means Committee is the Senate Finance Committee. There also exists another committee, known as the Joint Congressional Committee on Internal Revenue Taxation, which consists
of important members from both the House Ways and Means Committee and the Senate Finance Committee.

1.33   As a tax proposal moves through the Ways and Means Committee,
it will be considered carefully by the members (usually through a sub-
committee) aided by their staff. Frequently, representatives of the
Treasury Department and of the staff of the Joint Congressional Committee will also be invited to assist in the deliberations. On any significant proposal, some stage in the proceedings will be marked by
public hearings at which witnesses from any segment of the economy
are free to testify. When the hearings have been concluded, the Ways
and Means Committee will retire into executive session from which
the public is excluded. The result will be a proposed bill that will be
reported to the entire House of Representatives, usually under a rule
providing that amendments from the floor may not be offered. If
passed by the House, the bill goes to the Senate, where it is turned
over to the Finance Committee for consideration.

1.34   The Ways and Means Committee procedure is generally repeated
by the Senate Finance Committee. The bill, with any amendments,
will then be presented on the floor of the Senate. There, further
amendments ordinarily may be offered freely. The final bill as passed
by the Senate may be quite different from the bill passed by the
House. If so, a Conference Committee consisting of members from
both Houses will be named to reach a compromise. The final version
will then be voted upon by both Houses and if adopted, sent to the

24. United States Constitution, Art. I, Sec. 7, Cl. 1.

president for approval. Under the Constitution, the president has ten days (excluding Sundays) from the day it is presented to him, within which to sign the bill into law. If he vetoes the bill during that period, it is returned to Congress where it may be passed, over his veto, by a two-thirds majority in both Houses. If he takes no action during the ten-day period, it becomes law without his signature unless Congress adjourns in the meantime, in which event the bill dies by the so-called pocket veto.

Committee Reports

When a bill is sent to the floor of a particular chamber by the appropriate committee, it will usually be accompanied by a committee report, intended to acquaint the members of that chamber with the significant facts behind the bill, the reason for its enactment, and its effect upon the revenues of the government as well as upon taxpayers. A Conference Committee will also issue a public report of its actions, although in many cases this contains little more than a numerical key enabling particular changes to be traced back to their origin. The reports of the Ways and Means Committee and the Senate Finance Committee are public documents and frequently invaluable in understanding tax legislation, especially in searching for that often nebulous concept called Congressional intent.[25]   1.35

It should not be assumed that all tax bills progress in exactly this fashion. This is simply the typical procedure, particularly in connection with a major tax proposal effecting many important changes in the Internal Revenue Code.   1.36

Whatever the origin, the result is a tax law reflected in a new or a changed portion of the Internal Revenue Code. Its enactment will be noted immediately by organizations engaged in publishing tax material. Information of its passage will be disseminated quickly throughout the country, and the next step in the tax process will begin: interpreting, understanding, and applying the law. The truly monumental job of collection and administration falls upon the executive branch of the government represented by the Internal Revenue Service. This function will be discussed in the next chapter, along with the tax duties of the third branch of government, the judiciary, which frequently has the last word in a tax controversy.   1.37

Hardly anyone these days can hope to avoid confronting the income tax, either as a significant factor in his business career or as an individual citizen helping to bear the costs of government. The income tax may be the price of our civilization, as Justice Holmes suggested.   1.38

25. See chapter 2 for a further discussion of the significance of committee reports and where they may be found.

2

SURVEY OF
THE SYSTEM

INTRODUCTION ... 15
SELECTED TAX TERMS ... 15

    Gross Income ... 15
    Capital Gains and Losses ... 16
    Section 1231 Gains and Losses ... 17
    Basis ... 17
    Tax Liability ... 18

TYPES OF TAXPAYERS ... 18
TAX-EXEMPT ORGANIZATIONS ... 19
THE INTERNAL REVENUE SERVICE ... 21
THE CHRONICLE OF AN INCOME TAX CASE ... 24

    Revenue Agents' Examinations and Administrative Remedies ... 24
    Judicial Remedies ... 28

LIMITATION PERIODS ... 29
PENALTIES ... 30
SOURCES OF TAX LAW ... 31

    Tax Reporter Services ... 32
    Cumulative Bulletins ... 33
    Court Decisions ... 33
    Texts, Treatises, and Articles ... 34
    Special Purpose Publications ... 34

THE WEIGHT OF AUTHORITY ... 34

INTRODUCTION

This chapter presents a bird's-eye view of the entire income tax 2.1
system. It starts with some brief definitions of selected tax terms, next
discusses the categories of taxpayers, particularly "tax-exempt" organizations, describes the functions of the governmental agency in
charge of administering and collecting the tax, presents a chronicle
of what happens or may happen to a tax return after it is filed, and con-
cludes with a discussion of sources of tax law and the weight of
authority.

SELECTED TAX TERMS

The foundation of the United States income tax system is self- 2.2
assessment. Each year, every person or entity having taxable income
files a form called a return, on which he reports the details of his
taxable income. Every return form calls for the listing of types of gross
income and then for a listing of the types of permitted deductions.

Gross Income

To determine the taxable base, the Internal Revenue Code starts 2.3
with the concept of "gross income"; and the definition is the same for
all taxpayers—individuals, corporations, partnerships, estates, and
trusts. Code Sec. 61(a) provides a "shotgun" clause that defines gross
income as ". . . all income from whatever source derived." Regulation
1.61–1(a) provides this more complete definition:

Gross income means all income from whatever source derived, unless excluded by law. Gross income includes income realized in any form, whether
in money, property, or services. Income may be realized, therefore, in the
form of services, meals, accommodations, stock, or other property, as well as
in cash.

Section 61 also lists specific benefits included in income: 2.4

Compensation for services, including fees, commissions, and similar items
Gross income derived from business (gross receipts in the case of a ser-
vice or transportation business; but gross sales less cost of goods sold in
the case of a manufacturer, wholesaler, or retailer)
Gains derived from dealings in property
Interest
Rents
Royalties
Dividends
Alimony and separate maintenance payments
Annuities

Income from life insurance and endowment contracts
Pensions
Income from discharge of indebtedness
Distributive share of partnership gross income
Income in respect of a decedent
Income from an interest in an estate or trust

Section 61 points out that these items are included in gross income, but gross income is not limited to them. Code sections 71 through 81 deal more specifically with some of these items plus a few other items included in income that will be discussed later in chapter 5. Code sections 101 through 122 cover items specially excluded from gross income. These will be covered in detail in chapter 6.

Capital Gains and Losses

2.5   That portion of gross income that consists of a capital gain is separately treated; so also are capital losses. A capital gain or loss results from the sale or taxable exchange of a capital asset. Capital assets are defined in Code Sec. 1221 and roughly consist of investment property such as securities and nonbusiness property such as a personal residence or jewelry. Capital gains and losses are either long-term or short-term. If the asset was owned for six months or less before its sale or taxable exchange, the resulting gain or loss is short-term. If it was owned for more than six months, the gain or loss is long-term. All short-term gains and short-term losses are combined to determine the net short-term capital gain or loss. Likewise, all long-term gains and losses are combined to determine the net long-term capital gain or loss. The net short-term gain or loss and the net long-term gain or loss are then algebraically added.

2.6   An excess of a short-term gain over any net long-term loss is taxed in full as ordinary income. On the other hand, an excess of a net long-term capital gain over any net short-term capital loss is taxed at lower rates. Individuals pay no more than 25 percent on the first $50,000 of such excess, and on any additional amount no more than $29\frac{1}{2}$ percent (disregarding the $2\frac{1}{2}$ percent surcharge) for 1970, $32\frac{1}{2}$ percent for 1971, and 35 percent for 1972 and later years. Corporations pay no more than 28 percent (disregarding the $2\frac{1}{2}$ percent surcharge) for 1970 and 30 percent for 1971 and later years. For an example of the application of the tax to a net long-term capital gain realized by an individual, see paragraph 3.23.

2.7   If the result of adding net short-term gains and losses and net long-term gains and losses is a loss, the tax treatment depends upon whether the taxpayer is a corporation or an individual. A corporation cannot deduct a net capital loss, whether short-term or long-term, from ordinary income. Instead, it is allowed to first carry it back for three years and then forward for five years to offset any net capital gains in those years. An individual is allowed a deduction each year to the extent of $1,000 from ordinary income. To the extent that a net loss consists of a net short-term capital loss, 100 percent of it is taken into account for that purpose; but, to the extent that a net loss consists of a net long-term capital loss, only one-half of it can be used to reduce ordinary income. In other words, for every $2 of a net long-term capital loss only $1 can be used as a deduction from ordinary income up to a maximum deduction of $1,000 per year. Any unused capital loss of an individual can be carried forward, but not backwards, for the balance of his life, using it first to offset short- or long-term capital gains of those years and then to reduce ordinary income. In determining the amount of the net long-term capital loss that carries forward, it must be reduced, not by the exact amount used as a deduction from ordinary income in the year in which the net loss was incurred, but by twice that amount.

Taxpayer's only capital transactions consisted of a short-term loss of $200 and a long-term loss of $2,700. His $1,000 current deduction from ordinary income comes first from the short-term loss of $200. The remaining $800 represents 50% of $1,600 out of the long-term loss. Thus the carry-over is $1,100 ($2,700 − $1,600).

EXAMPLE 1

Now assume that in the following year, taxpayer's only capital transaction shows a $700 gain (either short- or long-term). The $1,100 loss carry-over first is used to offset the gain in full. The remaining $400 must be reduced by 50%, resulting in an ordinary deduction of $200.

EXAMPLE 2

Capital gains and losses are discussed in depth in chapter 12.

Section 1231 Gains and Losses

Realized and recognized gains and losses on the sale or exchange of depreciable property and real property that are used in a trade or business and are held for more than six months are also accorded special treatment. A net gain is treated as a long-term capital gain, except to the extent of ordinary income resulting from recapture of depreciation. On the other hand, a net loss is an ordinary loss. These subjects are covered more fully in chapter 12.

2.8

Basis

On every sale or taxable exchange, whether of a capital, a Section 1231, or an ordinary asset, the gain or loss realized is the difference between the sales price, in the case of a sale, or the fair market value of the property received in an exchange, and the "adjusted basis" of the property given up. Every asset has a basis. The word *basis* used alone means the unadjusted basis, usually its original cost. The "adjusted basis" is the amount of such original cost increased by improvements and other capitalized charges and reduced by any depreciation, amortization, or depletion allowed or allowable in that and prior years.

2.9

EXAMPLE   A factory building located on an acre of land was acquired a number of years ago for a lump-sum price of $100,000. Upon acquisition, $20,000 was determined to be the cost of the land and $80,000 the cost of the building. During the intervening ten years, $20,000 was claimed and allowed as depreciation on the building. The adjusted cost of the land and building at this point, then, is $80,000 ($100,000 minus $20,000). If the land and building are then sold for $70,000, the loss sustained is $10,000. If the building is completely destoyed by fire, the loss sustained is $60,000 ($80,000 original cost minus the reserve for depreciation of $20,000).

The subject of basis is discussed in greater detail in chapter 11.

Tax Liability

2.10   The tax base is called "taxable income." It consists of gross income less permitted deductions. To the amount so determined are applied the appropriate tax rates. The result is the amount of income tax. From this are deducted credits, the principal of which are income tax withheld by an employer during the year, any payments of estimated tax, any foreign tax credit for income taxes paid to a foreign country, and any investment credit. The balance is the remaining amount of tax liability.

2.11   At this point scan the rate tables appearing in the front of your paperback copy of the Internal Revenue Code. Note that for individuals the rates range up to 70 percent, but that the brackets of income to which the specific rates are to be applied vary depending upon whether the individual is single, an unmarried head of a household, married and filing a separate return, or married and filing a joint return with his spouse. As to corporations, the first $25,000 of taxable income is taxed at 22 percent and the balance at 48 percent.

TYPES OF TAXPAYERS

2.12   The Internal Revenue Code defines the word taxpayer as "... any person subject to any internal revenue tax." The term "person" includes "an individual, a trust, estate, partnership, association, company, or corporation." The regulations are even broader:

> The term "person" includes an individual, a corporation, a partnership, a trust or estate, a joint-stock company, an association, or a syndicate, group, pool, joint venture, or other unincorporated organization or group. Such term also includes a guardian, committee, trustee, executor, administrator, trustee in bankruptcy, receiver, assignee for the benefit of creditors, conservator, or any person acting in a fiduciary capacity.[1]

A partnership includes "... a syndicate, group, pool, joint venture, or other unincorporated venture, through or by means of which any business, financial operation, or venture is carried on and which is

1. Reg. 301. 7701–1(a).

not ... a trust or estate or a corporation ..." The term corporation is not defined but is stated to include "... associations, joint-stock companies, and insurance companies."[2]

A proper classification of taxpayers is essential in determining the type of tax return to be filed. Individuals have little trouble choosing the right tax return, but problems often arise with artificial entities such as trusts, estates, partnerships, corporations, and associations. Chapters 18, 19, and 20 discuss some of these problems of classification.

2.13

Taxpayers are usually classified according to the type of tax return that they are required to file. Excluding most information returns, which are not tax returns in the strict sense of the term, and returns for organizations exempt from income tax, almost all tax returns will fall into one of the following four categories:

2.14

TYPE OF RETURN	FORM	FILED BY
Individual	1040	Every natural person with income in excess of statutory minimum
Corporation	1120	Corporations, including organizations taxed as corporations
Fiduciary	1041	Trusts and estates with income in excess of statutory minimums
Partnership	1065	Partnerships or joint ventures (Note: information return only)

Married persons can file either separate returns or joint returns. In a joint return they combine their income and deductions and claim the personal exemptions for themselves and their dependents. Because of the structure of the rate tables, it is usually cheaper for them to file a joint return.

2.15

TAX–EXEMPT ORGANIZATIONS

Ever since the Corporation Excise Tax Act of 1909, there have been provisions in the income tax law exempting from income taxation nonprofit corporations and trusts that are engaged in charitable, educational, religious, or scientific endeavors. Through the years other types of organizations have been added, so that today there are some twenty separate, loosely described categories of organizations enumerated in Section 501 that can qualify for exemption. In addition, qualified employees' pension and profit-sharing trusts are exempt, farmers' cooperatives are fully or partially exempt,[3] and shipowners' protection and indemnity associations are partially exempt.[4]

2.16

A corporation is said to be a nonprofit one if it is organized under the laws of a state pertaining to nonprofit corporations. Similarly a

2.17

2. Sec. 7701—also contains many other definitions.
3. Sec. 521.
4. Sec. 526.

trust is said to be of a nonprofit type if the permitted activities designated in the instrument creating it are directed primarily towards the good of the public. However, both types of entities can and do realize income from investments and other sources.

2.18   The most widely discussed types of organizations exempt from income tax are described in Section 501(c)(3) and include community chests, public and private foundations, churches, hospitals, and schools. Almost all of the organizations therein described also are included within the types of entities to which charitable contributions can be made and deducted under Section 170 in computing taxable income.

2.19   The term "private foundation" is important and is described in Section 509 in negative fashion. In general terms, it is every organization described in Section 501(c)(3) other than:

1. A church, school, hospital, or medical research organization;
2. An organization normally receiving more than one-third of its annual support from members and the general public and not more than one-third of its annual support from investment income, such as symphony societies, garden clubs, alumni associations, Boy Scouts, and parent-teacher associations.
3. An organization created and operated exclusively for the benefit of one or more of the organizations described above, provided that it is controlled by the latter, such as religious organizations other than churches, and organizations created and operated for the benefit of a specific school and also controlled by that school, such as university presses.
4. Organizations created and operated exclusively for testing for public safety.

2.20   Since 1970, private foundations are subjected to special excise taxes. There is a revenue raising annual excise tax of four percent on net investment income. In addition, punitive excise taxes are imposed for acts of self-dealing between the foundation and its contributors, failure of the foundation to distribute its income for exempt purposes, excessive foundation holdings in unrelated business enterprises, speculative investments that jeopardize the foundation's exempt purposes, and lobbying and other foundation activities that tend to influence elections and legislation. Some of these punitive excise taxes in designated instances are also imposed on large contributors and foundation managers. All of the provisions are complex and are to be found in Sections 4940 through 4945.

2.21   Prior to 1970 only private foundations and just a few other types of tax-exempt organizations were subjected to tax on their net income from an unrelated trade or business.[5] The Tax Reform Act of 1969, however, extended this liability under Section 511. Since 1970 this potential liability applies, among others, to both public and private foundations, churches, hospitals, schools, medical research organizations, civic leagues, social clubs, fraternal benefit societies, employees' beneficiary associations, benevolent life insurance companies, mutual irrigation companies, mutual telephone companies,

5. Sec. 512.

credit unions, farmers' cooperatives, certain small insurance companies, and qualified pension and profit-sharing trusts. A special exception was granted to churches so that many unrelated businesses
acquired before May 27, 1969, will not be taxed until 1976.

Generally speaking, an unrelated trade or business is one the conduct of which is not substantially related, aside from the need of such
organization for income or funds, to the exercise or performance by
such organization of its charitable, educational, or other purpose or
function constituting the basis for its exemption.[6] For example, a side
venture by an exempt employees' trust in leasing machinery to the
corporation that formed it was held to be unrelated business.[7] Also,
rental income from certain business leases is treated as unrelated
business taxable income.[8] Net income from an unrelated trade or
business is taxed at corporate rates to most entities, whether the tax-
exempt organization was created as a corporation or a trust.

2.22

THE INTERNAL REVENUE SERVICE

In beginning a study of federal income taxes, it is helpful to start
with some understanding of tax procedure. The federal income tax
is administered by the Internal Revenue Service, formerly known
as the Bureau of Internal Revenue, which operates as a branch of the
Treasury Department. This agency, now more than 100 years old,
has had a number of significant reorganizations through the years.
Its chief officer is the Commissioner of Internal Revenue, appointed
by the president of the United States. The Internal Revenue Service,
frequently called the IRS or the Service, partitions the country into
seven regions, each of which in turn is divided into a number of
districts. Each region is supervised by a Regional Commissioner, and
each district by a District Director of Internal Revenue. In each
region there is a data-processing Service Center. The most frequent
contact between taxpayer and IRS is with the local District Director's
office, which accepts hand-carried returns for filing and audits returns.
All returns that are mailed must be filed with the applicable regional
Service Center.

2.23

The headquarters of the IRS is the national office in Washington,
D.C. Taxpayer contact with this office is usually limited to requests
for IRS rulings on the tax effect of prospective transactions.[9] If a taxpayer's request for such a ruling also asks for a hearing, he will be
allowed one, and he will see at least a small portion of the operations
outlined on the top part of the IRS organization chart.

2.24

6. Sec. 513.

7. Cooper Tire & Rubber Co. Employees' Retirement Fund v. Com., 306 F.2d 20
(6th Cir. 1962), 10 AFTR2d 5366.

8. Sec. 514.

9. Rev. Proc. 72–3 outlines the procedures involved in seeking rulings. Rev. Proc.
69–6 specifies various areas in which rulings will not be issued and those in which
rulings ordinarily will not be issued.

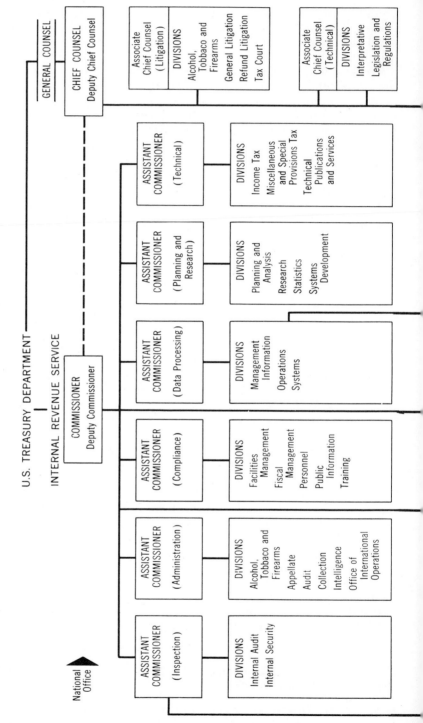

INTERNAL REVENUE SERVICE ORGANIZATION

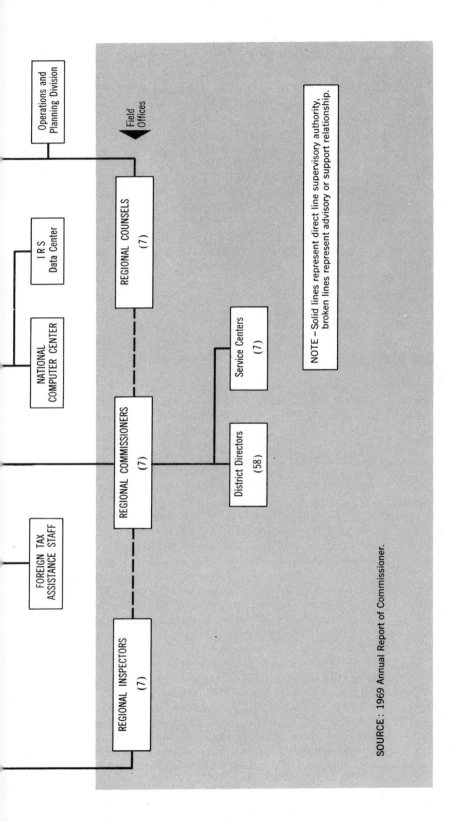

Operations and Planning Division

I R S Data Center

NATIONAL COMPUTER CENTER

FOREIGN TAX ASSISTANCE STAFF

Field Offices

REGIONAL COUNSELS (7)

REGIONAL COMMISSIONERS (7)

REGIONAL INSPECTORS (7)

Service Centers (7)

District Directors (58)

NOTE – Solid lines represent direct line supervisory authority, broken lines represent advisory or support relationship.

SOURCE : 1969 Annual Report of Commissioner.

THE CHRONICLE OF AN INCOME TAX CASE

2.25   At some point after the return has been filed it will be checked for mathematical accuracy. If mathematical errors have been made, any additional tax due will be billed to the taxpayer without the usual procedural limitations [Code Sec. 6213(b)(1)]. If correction of clerical mistakes results in an overpayment, a refund may occur at the instigation of the District Director's office or the regional Service Center, although there seems to be no specific statutory requirement.

2.26   After a return is filed, the taxpayer still has a prescribed time within which to file a claim for refund, and the IRS also has time to make an examination—or further examination—of the return and to assert that additional tax, a "deficiency," is due. The "period of limitations" is the technical term given to the provisions of law that define the rights both of the taxpayer and the government ultimately to consider a given tax year finally closed and settled. The rules will be outlined later in this chapter.

Revenue Agents' Examinations and Administrative Remedies

2.27   As every student will soon learn, there are many gray areas in the tax law, and subjective opinion is often the basis for applying rules to factual situations. Consider, for example, an expenditure to alter part of a building. Is it a deductible repair expense or a capitalizable improvement? The test is whether or not the work or item prolonged the life of the building. That is a matter of opinion. And such circumstances result in a fairly substantial number of controversies with IRS. By far the largest number are settled at the administrative level, others are settled after a case is docketed in court; only a relatively few are actually tried, but these few still constitute a fairly large volume of litigation with resulting published court opinions.

2.28   Filing a tax return on time and paying whatever balance of tax then may be due does not necessarily discharge completely a taxpayer's obligation. Any sense of security he feels at this point may prove to be unfounded. The American system of income taxation may be based on self-assessment and voluntary compliance—in the sense that the taxpayer files his own return—but a certain amount of enforcement is necessary to protect the revenue and to insure that each taxpayer bears his fair share.

2.29   Thus, the IRS will examine some tax returns. Testing procedures are used to select the returns to be examined, or classified for examination as the IRS refers to it. Since 1967 computers are used for this purpose. In 1969 a "discriminant function" technique was introduced in the selection of certain individual returns for audit. Under this technique, "proven" mathematical formulas are programmed into computers to identify and to select returns for examination. According to the Service, this system, by weighing significant return characteristics, permits the ranking of selected returns by greatest potential tax error.[10]

A revenue agent's examination is the start of a tax case. It can end in a settlement with the agent, at a higher level in settlement with a conferee, or in a decision of a court. The administrative and judicial avenues of recourse are depicted in the accompanying chart. If a taxpayer's return is selected for examination and his return is relatively simple, it will be given an "office audit," and he will be instructed by letter from the District Director's office to send or bring all his records and supporting information to the Director's office at a prescribed date and time. Many cases are begun and completed at the same meeting. If agreement is not reached with the examining officer, the taxpayer has the right to a district conference, formerly called an informal conference, with a district conferee to see if a settlement can be worked out. If the amount of the tax in controversy is $2,500 or more, the taxpayer must file a written "protest," i.e., a formal statement of his position and arguments, in order to attend a district conference. If the amount involved is less than $2,500, he need not file a written protest before going to the conference.   2.30

If a tax return is relatively complicated and reflects business operations, many types of income, or intricate financial transactions, the IRS examination will be conducted not as an office audit, but as a "field audit." As the term indicates, this simply means that the examining officer makes his examination at the taxpayer's office, place of business, or home. Otherwise, the procedure is generally the same as in the case of an office audit. If no agreement is reached with the examining agent on the amount of a proposed deficiency, the agent will write up his report, called a Revenue Agent's Report and frequently referred to as an RAR. He submits that report to his group chief, and the latter in turn submits it to his superiors in the district office of IRS. Shortly afterwards a "30-day letter" accompanied by a copy of the report will be mailed to the taxpayer. This letter notifies the taxpayer that within the next thirty days, he has two alternatives to comply with: (1) submit a written protest (if the proposed deficiency is more than $2,500) and ask for a conference with a district conferee or (2) sign an attached waiver Form 870 agreeing to the proposed deficiency. If the taxpayer ignores the 30-day letter and does nothing, an official notice of the proposed assessment of the deficiency, called a "90-day letter," will be sent to him. If he files a protest, has a conference with the district conferee, and cannot reach a settlement, he has a right to ask that the case be referred to the appellate division of the Regional Commissioner's office. In lieu of filing a protest with the district conferee in compliance with the 30-day letter, the taxpayer also has a right to bypass that level of administrative settlement procedure and ask that the case be transferred directly to the appellate division.[11]   2.31

10. 1968 Annual Report of Commissioner, p. 20.
11. Rev. Proc. 67–27.

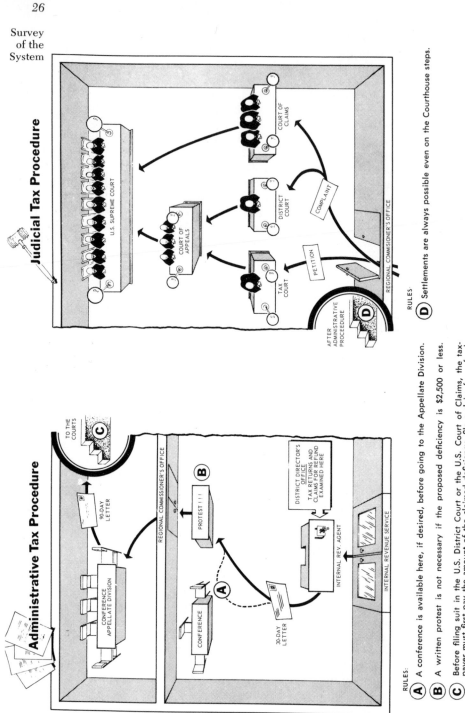

Judicial Tax Procedure

U.S. SUPREME COURT

COURT OF APPEALS

TAX COURT

DISTRICT COURT

COURT OF CLAIMS

PETITION

COMPLAINT

AFTER ADMINISTRATIVE PROCEEDURE

REGIONAL COMMISSIONER'S OFFICE

RULES:

(D) Settlements are always possible even on the Courthouse steps.

Administrative Tax Procedure

TO THE COURTS

90-DAY LETTER

CONFERENCE APPELLATE DIVISION

REGIONAL COMMISSIONER'S OFFICE

PROTEST !!!

CONFERENCE

30-DAY LETTER

DISTRICT DIRECTOR'S OFFICE
TAX RETURNS AND CLAIMS FOR REFUND EXAMINED HERE

INTERNAL REV. AGENT

INTERNAL REVENUE SERVICE

RULES:

(A) A conference is available here, if desired, before going to the Appellate Division.

(B) A written protest is not necessary if the proposed deficiency is $2,500 or less.

(C) Before filing suit in the U.S. District Court or the U.S. Court of Claims, the tax-payer must first pay the amount of the claimed deficiency, file a claim for refund, and wait until the earlier of six months or the date of denial of the claim.

At both the revenue agent and the district conference level, if the taxpayer agrees to a proposed deficiency, he will be asked to sign a Form 870. This bears the imposing title "Waiver of Restrictions on Assessment and Collection of Deficiency in Tax and Acceptance of Overassessments." If the taxpayer signs, he waives the right to formal notification of the proposed deficiency (by the statutory "90-day letter") and the right to appeal the matter to the United States Tax Court; however, he gains quick termination of the period for which he is obligated to pay interest on the agreed deficiency, since this period will stop within 30 days after the signing of the Form 870.[12] Both parties are in agreement, and the matter will be closed for the time being, at least. The IRS ordinarily will send the taxpayer a bill for the amount of the proposed deficiency plus interest, to be paid within ten days unless the taxpayer submits his payment along with the waiver. Despite the fact that a taxpayer signs a waiver Form 870 and the government accepts it, *neither party is ordinarily prohibited from taking further action.* This form is not a binding acceptance or closing agreement. The taxpayer can still file a claim for refund; and subject to rules concerning harassment, the Commissioner can assert an additional deficiency. Ordinarily the Commissioner will close his files on the return after receipt of the Form 870 and payment of the agreed deficiency, unless the taxpayer thereafter files a claim for refund. The only type of binding agreement at the administrative level is a closing agreement as authorized by Code Sec. 7121. These are rarely entered into. 2.32

At neither a district nor an appellate conference need the taxpayer himself be present. He can be represented by any tax practitioner authorized to practice before the Treasury Department. All certified public accountants and attorneys automatically have that right.[13] 2.33

The last administrative level available for settlement of a proposed deficiency is the appellate division. If the conferee there reaches a decision that the taxpayer accepts as favorable, the matter is ended; if the decision is unfavorable, he may concede or pursue further remedies. If he decides to call a halt to the proceedings, he will be asked to sign a "waiver" Form 870-AD, which appears deceptively similar to Form 870, but with important differences: 2.34

1. Form 870 is effective with the signature of the taxpayer, but Form 870-AD requires the acceptance and signature of a properly authorized representative of the IRS in order to become effective.
2. Form 870 does not bar the taxpayer from later filing a claim for refund (within the period of limitations), nor does it bar the IRS from future assertion of a deficiency if timely. Form 870-AD purports to bar the taxpayer from later filing a claim for refund, although the issue is not free from doubt. A court possibly may sustain a taxpayer who claims he can still file a refund claim after executing a waiver on Form 870-AD, but he will have to go to court to prove his point.

12. Sec. 6213(d) and 6601(d).
13. P.L. 89–332, enacted in 1965.

3. The printed terms of Form 870-AD are frequently modified by inser-
tions or changes that, if sponsored by the IRS, should be reviewed carefully by the taxpayer lest he bargain away valuable rights.

Judicial Remedies

2.35   After the taxpayer has exhausted his statutory right of appeal to the
appellate divison, if he is not satisfied and has not signed Form
870-AD, he may go to the courts to seek redress. The appellate division will send to him, by registered or certified mail, a statutory notice
of the proposed assessment of a deficiency pursuant to Section 6212.
This so-called 90-day letter gives him a period of 90 days (150 days if
he is outside the country) within which to file an appeal with the
United States Tax Court. When originally founded this court was
called the Board of Tax Appeals. In 1942 its name was changed to the
Tax Court of the United States. Until December 30, 1969, it was not
technically a court but an independent agency of the executive branch
of the government. The Tax Reform Act of 1969 established the Tax
Court as a court under Article I of the Constitution, dealing with the
legislative branch, and changed its name to the United States Tax
Court. Its sixteen judges are appointed by the president with the advice and consent of the Senate. The term of office is fifteen years. The
judges sometimes come from the ranks of high officials of the IRS, and
they are usually well acquainted with tax matters. Further, the chief
judge may appoint a commissioner to hear testimony, make findings,
and recommend to the court the type of decision to be rendered in
any case.

2.36   The jurisdiction of the Tax Court covers all fifty states. From it, appeals go to the eleven United States Circuit Courts of Appeal. The
appeal must be made to the court of the judicial circuit that covers the
geographical area where the corporate taxpayer has its principal
place of business or the individual taxpayer has his residence.

2.37   There is also a Small Claims Division within the Tax Court (Section 7463). Where the amount of the deficiency proposed by the
service is no more than $1,000[13A] and any counterclaim by the tax-
payer for a refund is for no more than $1,000,[13A] the taxpayer may re-
quest that the case be heard before this Division. Its proceedings are
informal and its decisions (1) are not precedents for any other case
and (2) are not reviewable by any higher court.

2.38   At this point in the procedure, the taxpayer should pause for serious
thought and consultation with his representatives, for here the road
forks. The jurisdiction of the Tax Court is limited to cases involving
proposed deficiencies in a tax yet unpaid. If the taxpayer pays the
proposed deficiency and files a claim for refund that is denied or not
acted upon within six months, he will be able to pursue a different
course by suing for a refund either in a federal district court or in
the Court of Claims in Washington, D.C.

2.39   Numerous important considerations in choosing the court to which
to carry a tax case are beyond the scope of this book. An attorney who

13A. The amounts are $1,500 starting January 1, 1974.

is skilled in tax practice is essential to the taxpayer in electing the
court in which he is most likely to win. Briefly, the following points
are among those to be considered:

1. Tax Court judges are relatively more experienced in tax matters than
   judges in the district courts or Court of Claims; the latter must be
   familiar with many subjects other than taxation.
2. Trial by jury is available only in the district courts. Although somewhat
   unusual in civil tax cases, jury trials are becoming more common there.
3. Appeal from decisions of the Tax Court or the district courts may be
   taken to the circuit courts of appeal and from there to the Supreme Court
   (if certiorari is granted); from the Court of Claims, the only recourse is
   directly to the Supreme Court.
4. Perhaps the most significant factor is the attitude of a particular court
   as expressed in its prior decisions on similar fact situations.

Settlements are frequently worked out between the opposing attor-   2.40
neys before trial actually takes place. The United States does not reimburse even a victorious taxpayer for fees and expenses of attorneys
and expert witnesses in his litigation, although since 1966, statutory
amounts of court costs can be awarded to successful taxpayers. Trials
are expensive for the government as well. These facts are strong in-
ducements to settlement of tax controversies, right up to the moment
of trial.

LIMITATION PERIODS

The principle of limitations is an old one in Anglo-American law   2.41
and has an important place in United States tax law. Unless there were
a stopping point beyond which neither party normally could carry a
tax dispute, many controversies would come up for consideration and
decision long after the taxable year involved. In general, the following
periods of limitation apply to income tax returns:

1. If *no return* or *a fraudulent return* is filed, the tax year remains open
   without limitation [Section 6501(c)].
2. If a significant amount (*more than 25 percent*) is omitted from gross
   income, the period of limitations is *six years* [Section 6501(e)].
3. In the *normal situation,* not covered by the two prior rules, the period of
   limitation is *three years* [Section 6501(a)].

Generally, these limitation periods begin to run from the later of the
date of filing of the tax return or the due date of the return. They apply
both to the taxpayer and to the government, limiting claims for refund
as well as assessment of additional tax. These are the general rules
only; there are many special rules.   2.42
Despite the sound purpose of limitations, equity, too, imposes
limits. Rigid and inflexible periods of limitation can work hardships
and produce results as inequitable as the absence of any limitations.

Sections 1311 to 1314, "Mitigation of Effect of Limitations and Other Provisions," were therefore added to the Internal Revenue Code in 1938, to permit the statute of limitations to be pushed aside in order to correct certain errors. Under these provisions, in certain specific situations, opening of a closed period is permitted when otherwise either the taxpayer or the government would reap an unconscionable benefit from a rigid application of the statute of limitations. Ironically, these sections are more complex than the purpose for which they were enacted, although they can be helpful.

PENALTIES

2.43   The consequences of failure to comply with the income tax laws are many, and range all the way from a simple interest charge to imprisonment, depending upon the seriousness of the offense. Interest is deductible as such in computing taxable income of the year when paid or accrued, but a penalty is an addition to the tax and is not deductible.

INTEREST.   Any underpayment of tax (except estimated tax) calls for interest at the rate of 6 percent per year, i.e., one-half of one percent per month for the period of underpayment. As calendar year individuals are required to pay any balance of tax due on April 15 after the end of the taxable year, interest commences to run on that date regardless of whether an extension of time is secured within which to file the return. Corporations and estates have the privilege of paying any balance of tax in installments. If that privilege is elected and timely payments are made of the amounts due, no interest is payable on the second or subsequent installments of the tax liability shown on the return. If later the return is amended to show a larger amount of tax, or if upon examination of the return the Service assesses a deficiency, interest accrues from the due date of the return on the additional amount due (Section 6601).

PENALTY FOR FAILURE TO PAY.   In addition to interest on any underpayment of tax, a penalty is imposed for failure to pay an amount of tax when due, unless it is shown that such failure is due to reasonable cause and not due to willful neglect. The penalty is computed at the rate of one-half of one percent a month up to a maximum of 25 percent on the unpaid balance. In the case of amounts shown on returns as due, the penalty commences to accrue with the date prescribed for payment of such tax, taking into account any extensions of time granted for payment but not for filing the return. If later a deficiency is assessed, the penalty commences to run at the end of ten days after the date of the notice and demand. Just as in the case of interest, this penalty does not apply to underpayments of estimated tax [Sections 6651(a)(2) and (3)].

PENALTY FOR UNDERPAYMENT OF ESTIMATED TAX.   The penalty for underpayment of estimated tax required to be paid by an individual or corporation is 6 percent per year for the period of underpayment (Sections 6654 and 6655).

DELINQUENCY PENALTY.   Failure to file a return, unless such failure was due to reasonable cause and not due to willful neglect, results in a penalty of

5 percent a month while the delinquency continues, up to a maximum of 25 percent. The percentage is applied to the balance of tax liability, that is, the amount of tax shown on the return when eventually filed plus any deficiency assessed and less any amounts of income tax withheld for the year, payments of estimated tax made before the due date of the return, and any other payment made on or before the date prescribed for payment of the tax[14] [Section 6651(a)(1)].

NEGLIGENCE PENALTY. Negligence or "intentional disregard of rules and regulations" that results in an underpayment of tax calls for a penalty of 5 percent of the underpayment [Code Sec. 6653(a)]. The word "rules" has not been authoritatively defined, but quite probably does not embrace either published or private rulings, because these by law are not binding even upon the Commissioner. If a regulation is held to be invalid by a court, its disregard will not result in a penalty.

FRAUD PENALTY. The civil penalty for fraud is 50 percent of a resulting underpayment—in place of, and not in addition to, the negligence penalty [Code Sec. 6653(b)].

CRIMINAL PENALTIES. Numerous acts or omissions are defined as crimes under the tax law, and conviction is punishable by the usual criminal penalties of fines or imprisonment or both. For example, a willful attempt to evade or defeat the tax is considered a felony, and conviction calls for a fine up to $10,000 or imprisonment for up to five years, or both.[15]

This list simply outlines the penalty structure of the Code. In addition, there are many specific penalties for particular violations.[16]

SOURCES OF TAX LAW

The primary sources of tax information are the pronouncements of the three branches of government; namely, legislative, executive, and judicial.   2.44

LEGISLATIVE SOURCES

The United States Constitution
Treaties with other countries
The Internal Revenue Code of 1954—the tax law itself
Committee reports of the Ways and Means Committee of the House of Representatives, the Senate Finance Committee, and Conference Committees of the two houses of Congress

ADMINISTRATIVE SOURCES

Regulations promulgated by the Internal Revenue Service to explain and interpret the law

14. Fischer, 50 T.C. 164 (1968); Sec. 6651(b)(1).
15. Code Sec. 7201. See also Code Sec. 7202 to 7215. Code Sec. 7206 and 7207 cover specific items of criminal fraud.
16. See chaps. 68 and 75 of Subtitle F of the Code.

Rulings issued by the IRS—public rulings published in the Internal Revenue Bulletins

Private rulings in response to letter requests from taxpayers (unpublished)

Procedural rulings issued by the IRS and generally published as Revenue Procedures in the Internal Revenue Bulletins

COURT DECISIONS

Decisions of the Tax Court, the United States district courts, United States Court of Claims, the United States circuit courts of appeal, and the United States Supreme Court

When this information has been sorted, classified, compiled, and edited, it appears in one or more of the following:

Tax reporter services
Cumulative Bulletins
Volumes of court decisions
Textbooks, treatises, and articles
Other specialized publications

Almost all tax research requires the use of most of these publications.

Tax Reporter Services

2.45   The usual tax reporter service consists of a series of loose-leaf volumes containing substantive material on various tax topics, indexed, and frequently arranged in such a way that the editorial discussion of a particular topic will be found in the same volume and at the same place as the appropriate sections of the Internal Revenue Code and the related regulations. Included are annotations of recent developments, rulings, and court decisions. Common to all tax services is the fact that they are kept current, at frequent intervals, by the issuance of new matter to replace obsolete pages or cross-indexed in such a way that it can be located easily.

2.46   The most widely used tax reporter services are *Federal Taxes*, in ten volumes, published by Prentice-Hall, Inc., and the *Standard Federal Tax Reporter* published by Commerce Clearing House, Inc. They are comprehensive and thorough, supplemented regularly by a large quantity of current material, and are necessary working tools for someone seriously studying income taxes. Callaghan & Company publishes another federal tax reporter service that has become a classic. This is Mertens' *Law of Federal Income Taxation,* perhaps the most scholarly approach to the subject. Its thorough treatment of any subject and its painstaking research have won many citations as an authority in court decisions. In addition, there are a number of other tax services such as Rabkin and Johnson's *Federal Income Gift and Estate Taxation* in seven volumes, published by Matthew Bender & Co., Inc., the *Federal Tax Coordinator* published by Research Institute of America, and the *Tax Management Portfolios* published by the Bureau of National Affairs, Inc.

Cumulative Bulletins

Announcements and decisions of the Internal Revenue Service are reported in the weekly *Internal Revenue Bulletins,* compiled semi-annually into bound volumes entitled *Cumulative Bulletins* and abbreviated as C.B., an essential source of significant governmental actions in the field of internal revenue taxation. The bulletins include texts of revenue rulings (except private rulings) and revenue procedures as they are issued, sometimes the text of new tax laws, and frequently the complete texts of congressional committee reports.

2.47

From time to time, one volume of the series of *Cumulative Bulletins* will gather together the congressional committee reports relating to a number of tax statutes. For example, *Cumulative Bulletin* 1939–1 (Part 2) contains committee reports for all income tax acts from the original statute of October 3, 1913 up to the Revenue Act of 1938, inclusive. Similarly, collections of tax laws and committee reports appear in the volumes of the *Cumulative Bulletins* numbered 1958–3, 1962–3, and 1964–1 (Part 2).

2.48

Court Decisions

The Government Printing Office publishes *U.S. Tax Court Reports,* bound volumes of selected decisions of the Tax Court. Prior to 1942, when the Tax Court was known as the U.S. Board of Tax Appeals, similar reports were published as *U.S. Board of Tax Appeals Reports.* Many Tax Court decisions, referred to as memorandum decisions, are not published by the Government Printing Office, usually because of lengthy facts or because their holdings are considered not to establish any new precedents. They are available, however, since both Prentice-Hall, Inc. and Commerce Clearing House, Inc. compile these memorandum decisions in a series of bound volumes. Both publishers also have loose-leaf Tax Court services through which printed copies of all Tax Court decisions, both memorandum and regular, are quickly made available to subscribers.

2.49

Tax decisions of all other federal courts are available weekly in the various reporter services. Later, at regular intervals, these cases are compiled into bound volumes by two tax publishers. Prentice-Hall's volumes are called *American Federal Tax Reports,* now in a second series, which is cited as *AFTR 2d.* Commerce Clearing House case reports are entitled *U.S. Tax Cases* and are cited as *USTC.* These decisions are also published in the official reporter volumes containing all types of cases heard by the federal courts. The principal reporter series are Federal (now in the second series and abbreviated "F. 2d"), Federal Supplement (abbreviated "F. Supp."), and the United States Supreme Court Reports (abbreviated "U.S.").

2.50

Texts, Treatises, and Articles

2.51   Tax practitioners and teachers are developing a growing body of texts, treatises, and articles on taxes. Some of the writers are leading authorities in a particular area of taxation. Published papers from tax institutes and forums, usually under university sponsorship, have resulted in many valuable contributions, among them the exceptionally helpful works of the annual Institute of Federal Taxation sponsored by New York University.

Special Purpose Publications

2.52   There are a number of special purpose publications, which can be classified roughly into two groups:

1. Those dealing with the *history* of the tax law, which enable it to be traced with relative ease, such as Seidman's *Legislative History of Federal Income Tax Laws, 1938–1861* and a two-volume loose-leaf service entitled *Cumulative Changes in Internal Revenue Code of 1954 and Tax Regulations Under the Code*, both published by Prentice-Hall, Inc.
2. Citators enabling a researcher to trace the history of a court decision and to find each subsequent case or ruling that cited the given case. Such a service is invaluable in appraising the authority of a particular court decision or ruling as a precedent and to determine that it has not been overruled after the date on which it was issued. The only complete tax service of this kind is the *Citator* published by Prentice-Hall in the form of several bound volumes plus one loose-leaf volume for current periodic supplements.

THE WEIGHT OF AUTHORITY

2.53   The most difficult part of tax study is evaluating the relative importance to be assigned various precedents. Consideration of what the "authorities" have held in prior cases similar to the one at issue is an old principle of the common law and Anglo-American jurisprudence. Actually, the field of federal income taxation is so interwoven with administrative regulations, rulings, and releases of many kinds, as well as court decisions, that the problem of appraising the weight to be given to a particular item is extremely difficult.[17] The principle of *stare decisis*, "let the decision stand," continues to have validity, as the courts—within limits—respect opinions of other courts. The United States district court must follow Supreme Court decisions and the principles of law laid down by the United States circuit court of appeals of its own judicial circuit.

17. See Mitchell Rogovin, "The Four R's: Regulations, Rulings, Reliance, and Retroactivity—A View from Within" Taxes—*The Tax Magazine*, Vol. 43 (December, 1965), 756–76.

The fact that cases are heard in many separate jurisdictions through- 2.54
out the country results in many complications, one being the precise
degree of respect that a particular district court should give to the
opinion of a court of appeals in another judicial district.[18] Another
similar problem is the attitude to be adopted by the Tax Court (which
tries cases around the country) toward decisions of the federal courts
in various districts and circuits.[18A] These conflicts frequently form the
basis for the Supreme Court's order granting a petition for the issuance of a writ of certiorari. The United States Supreme Court, unlike the circuit courts of appeal, need not hear every appeal of a tax
case that it is asked to take; it exercises its own discretion. If it decides
to hear an appeal, it issues a writ of certiorari; if it does not, it denies
certiorari.

Many times the various courts will differ on what the law means as 2.55
applied to substantially identical sets of facts. Further, the Internal
Revenue Service frequently will adopt an official position at odds with
a court decision or a whole series of them. The only court decisions
that it *must* follow are those of the United States Supreme Court. If
a taxpayer wins in the Tax Court, the IRS will hardly choose to appeal
if the particular circuit court of appeals, through prior decisions, has
adopted a position contrary to the contentions of the Service.

The weight of authority to be given to administrative rulings and 2.56
pronouncements is also uncertain. The degree of reliance that a taxpayer can place on an administrative ruling depends largely upon the
prospects of its retroactive withdrawal or alteration. Note the language in the introduction to each issue of the Internal Revenue
Bulletins:

It is ... the policy to publish all rulings and statements of procedures which
supersede, revoke, modify, or amend any published ruling or procedure.
Except where otherwise indicated, published rulings and procedures apply
retroactively. ...

As the IRS itself says, succinctly:

A ruling, except to the extent incorporated in a closing agreement, may be
revoked or modified at any time in the wise administration of the taxing
statutes.[19]

Revocations are retroactive unless the Commissioner exercises his 2.57
discretionary power under the Code to limit their effect.[20] The IRS,
however, does not make them retroactive indiscriminately, particularly private rulings issued to particular taxpayers:

Except in rare or unusual circumstances, the revocation or modification
of a ruling will not be applied retroactively with respect to the taxpayer to

18. See Stacey Mfg. Co. v. Com., 237 F.2d 605 (6th Cir. 1956), 51 AFTR 356.
18A. For present attitude, see Golsen, 54 T.C. 742 (1970).
19. Rev. Proc. 62–28, 1962–2 C.B. 496, 504.
20. Code Sec. 7805(b).

whom the ruling was originally issued or to a taxpayer whose tax liability was directly involved in such ruling if—

(1) There has been no misstatement or omission of material facts,

(2) the facts subsequently developed are not materially different from the facts on which the ruling was based,

(3) there has been no change in the applicable law,

(4) the ruling was originally issued with respect to a prospective or proposed transaction, and

(5) the taxpayer directly involved in the ruling acted in good faith in reliance upon the ruling and the retroactive revocation would be to his detriment.[21]

2.58   Despite this language, the fact remains that the IRS position sometimes is amended retroactively, and a taxpayer's outrage may receive little judicial sympathy. For example, two tax cases decided by the United States Supreme Court in 1965 and one case decided by the Court of Claims early in 1966 gave no relief to taxpayers who relied on the Commissioner's acquiescence in 1944 to a Tax Court decision —a position changed to nonacquiescence eleven years later![22] The hard truth is summed up in one sentence from the opinion in one of these cases:

> ... The Commissioner's rulings have only such force as Congress chooses to give them, and Congress has not given them the force of law. ...[23]

2.59   In addition to issuing both published and private rulings, the IRS from time to time will announce its acquiescence or nonacquiescence in the result of a particular regular Tax Court decision. It does not do so in the case of Tax Court memorandum decisions, nor in the case of decisions of the district courts, the Court of Claims, or the circuit courts of appeal. Naturally, it makes no such announcement in the case of United States Supreme Court decisions, because those are the law of the land for everyone. An announcement of acquiescence or nonacquiescence merely represents the attitude of IRS at the time. Such announcements are sometimes revoked or changed. Further, the absence of such an announcement has no necessary significance.

2.60   Regulations are more authoritative than rulings as support in a tax controversy. Congress has given the Treasury Department a broad grant of power "... to prescribe all needful rules and regulations for the enforcement of the Internal Revenue Code, including all those necessary by reason of any alteration of law in relation to internal revenue."[24] Ordinarily, the courts are reluctant to overturn regulations that represent the official explanation and interpretation of the tax law by those charged with the duty to administer it. They are carefully written and reviewed, usually released originally in the form of

21. Rev. Proc. 72–3.

22. U.S. v. Midland-Ross Corporation, 381 U.S. 54 (1965), 15 AFTR2d 836; Dixon v. U.S., 381 U.S. 68 (1965), 15 AFTR2d 842; Kehaya v. U.S., 355 F.2d 639 (Ct. Cl., 1966), 17 AFTR2d 171.

23. Dixon v. U.S., 381 U.S. 68 (1965), 15 AFTR2d 842, 844.

24. Code Sec. 7805(a).

proposed regulations subject to public hearing, and finally adopted in the form of Treasury Decisions (TD's). Regulations, proposed or final, are published in the *Federal Register* and are disseminated widely by the tax reporter services to interested parties.

Yet even the regulations are vulnerable and may be stricken down if they run contrary to the law in the opinion of a court. Taxpayers can, do, and should challenge the validity of a regulation that goes beyond the intended scope of the statute. If regulations are inviolable, our tax system might become one imposed by decree. Before blithely ignoring a regulation when completing a return, however, the taxpayer should keep in mind the 5 percent negligence penalty for intentional disregard of regulations.

2.61

The ultimate authority in any tax problem is the law, but rarely is a problem solved by a simple reference to the statute. Tax laws are becoming more and more complicated.[25] Even after reading the regulations, which are supposed to explain and clarify the law, a statute may still seem ambiguous. In some cases, regulations may not even be available. After the enactment of the 1954 Code, years passed before regulations were issued for many important sections of the law. The place to look for the intent of Congress is in the congressional committee reports. Their members are fully aware of this use of the reports and frequently comment very specifically about the purpose of the legislation. Committee reports are extremely useful in helping to interpret tax legislation, particularly in areas where there are no regulations.

2.62

In summary, it should be noted that "authority" is only relative: the weight of one authority or list of authorities as opposed to another has to be determined on a problem-by-problem basis. But the general rules are these:

2.63

1. The law is the prime authority, but it may take considerable study to determine the meaning of a particular section.
2. Regulations are strong authorities; issued as Treasury Decisions, they represent carefully considered administrative opinion.
3. Court decisions are strong precedents; generally, the higher the court, the stronger the precedent.
4. An IRS published ruling is always subject to retroactive change, although official policy is to avoid such changes.
5. Published announcements of acquiescence or nonacquiescence in a particular Tax Court decision indicate the attitude of the Internal Revenue Service at that moment of time. In many instances the IRS has subsequently withdrawn an acquiescence and substituted nonacquiescence.

Some further observations are these:

2.64

1. Little reliance will be placed by any IRS conferee, and almost none by any court, on text material appearing in the loose-leaf reporter services. The Mertens service is the only exception.

25. See, for example, Code Sec. 341(e), which almost defies rational analysis.

2. Private rulings from the national office of the IRS are helpful to the tax-payers who secure them, but taxpayers must be careful that the facts in their request for ruling are accurate and that a prospective transaction covered by a favorable ruling is actually carried out in accordance with these facts. Otherwise, the ruling may not be controlling even in the case of the taxpayer who secured it.

3. A private ruling can be relied upon only by the taxpayer who obtained it, not by anyone else, even though another person may also have been a party to the transaction covered by the ruling.

QUESTIONS AND PROBLEMS

1. An unmarried individual investor had the following gains and (losses) from sales of securities purchased this year:

DATE PURCHASED	DATE SOLD	SECURITY	GAIN OR (LOSS)
February 1	June 10	A	$ 500
January 15	August 1	B	1,300
February 15	November 1	C	(4,000)

His ordinary net income after deducting personal exemptions was $30,000.

(a) What is the amount of his taxable income?

(b) Is any part of it taxed at long-term capital gain rates?

(c) Is there any effect on a prior or subsequent year and, if so, what?

2. A private foundation, a non-profit corporation, had net investment income this year of $10,000 and $40,000 of net income from the operation of an unrelated business. What is its tax liability, if any?

3. If an IRS examination resulted in a proposed deficiency against you for a particular year, what administrative and judicial remedies would be available to you? Give a detailed discussion.

4. What is a Form 870? A Form 870-AD? How do they differ?

5. Can a taxpayer pay an additional assessment of tax resulting from a revenue agent's examination, file a claim for refund, and then initiate a suit for refund in the (a) Tax Court, (b) United States district court, (c) state court, (d) Court of Claims, (e) state court of appeals, (f) United States circuit court of appeals, (g) United States Supreme Court?

6. What is the meaning of the term period of limitation? How do these limitations benefit taxpayers? How the federal government?

7. For the year 1972, an individual files his return on January 31, 1973. Within what period can he file a claim for refund and within what period can the government assert a deficiency?

8. In his return for 1972, an individual does not include in his income $20,000 in graft payments. For how long can the government make an assessment of additional tax?

9. The United States tax system has been described as self-assessing. What is meant by this? Do you think this is a proper description in view of the enforcement penalties assessable against violators?

10. A taxpayer dislikes a particular regulation and decides to ignore it when preparing and filing his return. What risk, if any, does he run?
11. An individual has $10,000 in salary income and $8.00 interest income on a savings account. He properly reports his salary income and deductions, but intentionally does not report the interest income. What penalty, if any, does he risk? What is the period of limitations on additional assessment?
12. An individual prepares his 1972 return and finds that he owes a balance of $5,000. He does not have that much cash on hand and does not wish to borrow it at a rate of perhaps 8 percent. What should he do? Discuss.
13. In researching a tax question, you find that the law as applied to your facts is not clear: the regulations do not specifically cover the problem, and there is no United States Supreme Court case in point. The Tax Court has held against you in two cases involving other taxpayers, but the Seventh and Ninth Circuit Courts of Appeal, respectively, have reversed the Tax Court in those two cases. The IRS also has outstanding a published ruling against you. Your employer or client files in the Eighth Judicial District. What is the weight of authority, and what advice would you give?
14. How would you proceed in researching to determine whether the sum of $5,000 payable annually by a corporation to the widow of an officer for the rest of her life is taxable income to her? Do not give your opinion as to what the answer is, but list the steps you would take and the order in which you would take them.

3

COMPONENTS OF INDIVIDUAL RETURNS

RETURN FORMS 1040 and 1040A . . . 42
STEPS TO DETERMINE THE TAX . . . 42
GROSS INCOME . . . 44
ADJUSTED GROSS INCOME . . . 47

Introduction and Summary of Deductions . . . 47
Business Expenses . . . 48

NONEMPLOYEES . . . 48

NET OPERATING LOSS DEDUCTIONS . . . 49
PENSION CONTRIBUTIONS OF THE SELF-EMPLOYED . . . 49

EMPLOYEES . . . 50

Forfeitures by Shareholder Employees of Subchapter S Corporations . . . 51
Long-Term Capital Gains . . . 51
Losses from Sales or Exchanges of Property . . . 53
Expenses Attributable to Rents and Royalties . . . 53
Depreciation and Depletion Deductions of Life Tenants and Income Beneficiaries . . . 54

SUMMARY OF ITEMIZED DEDUCTIONS . . . 54
STANDARD DEDUCTION . . . 55

Percentage Standard Deduction . . . 56
Low-income Allowance . . . 56
Limitation for Unearned Income of Dependents . . . 56
Separate Returns of Married Persons . . . 58
Election . . . 59
Considerations in Making Election . . . 59

PERSONAL EXEMPTIONS . . . 60

    Spouse . . . 61
    Dependents . . . 61

        RELATIONSHIP . . . 62
        SUPPORT TEST . . . 63

            CHILDREN OF DIVORCED OR SEPARATED PARENTS . . . 63

        GROSS-INCOME TEST . . . 64

CHOOSING THE RIGHT INDIVIDUAL TAX RATE TABLE . . . 65

    Joint Returns . . . 65
    Heads of Households . . . 67
    Optional Tax Tables . . . 68

INCOME AVERAGING . . . 68
MAXIMUM TAX ON EARNED INCOME . . . 71
CREDITS AGAINST THE TAX . . . 73

    Income Tax Withheld and Estimated Tax Payments . . . 74
    Excess Social Security Taxes . . . 74
    Retirement Income . . . 74
    Foreign Taxes . . . 75
    Excise Taxes on Nonhighway Use of Gasoline and Lubricating
      Oil . . . 77
    Investment Credit . . . 77
    Political Contributions . . . 78

SELF-EMPLOYMENT TAX . . . 78
MINIMUM TAX ON TAX PREFERENCES . . . 79
WHO MUST FILE RETURNS . . . 81
WHEN AND WHERE TO FILE . . . 82
DECLARATION OF ESTIMATED TAX . . . 83

RETURN FORMS 1040 AND 1040A

3.1   The United States individual income tax return form for citizens and resident aliens is numbered 1040. It is probably the most familiar government form in the country. For more than twenty years its format differed little from year to year. For 1969 and later years, however, this was changed, probably because the Service started using electronic computers a few years earlier. Form 1040 for 1972 is a single sheet of paper consisting of two pages, and to it there must be attached, where applicable, supporting schedules, the most common of which are:

Schedules A&B (combined)—Itemized Deductions AND
                                    Dividend and Interest Income
Schedule C—Profit (or Loss) From Business or Profession
Schedule D—Capital Gains and Losses
Schedules E&R (combined)—Supplemental Income Schedule AND
                                    Retirement Income Credit Computation
Schedule F—Farm Income and Expenses
Schedule G—Income Averaging
Schedule SE—Computation of Social Security Self-Employment Tax

A copy of page 1 of Form 1040 is on the accompanying page.

3.2   For 1972 there is also available Short Form 1040A for use by individuals and married couples when most of their income is from wages and they did not pay any estimated tax. Itemized deductions and credits cannot be claimed on it.

STEPS TO DETERMINE THE TAX

3.3   The chart on p. 45 shows how an individual using Form 1040 computes his income tax under present law, starting with his gross income. First he subtracts from gross income certain designated business and other expenses that are deductible to determine "adjusted gross income."[1] At this point he has a choice of going in different directions. The path to the left leads to itemized deductions. To follow this path, he lists certain personal expenses that, by statute, individuals are permitted to claim as deductions for tax purposes. These itemized deductions include such major items as charitable contributions, medical expenses, interest paid, and state and local taxes. The resulting figure in the chart is called "net income," a term that is not used in the Code in defining the steps taken in arriving at taxable income, but through the years it frequently has been used in the tax return forms. The taxpayer is then allowed to claim further deductions for "personal exemptions." These are statutory allowances for himself, his wife, his children, and any other dependents he may have, with additional allowances if he is over sixty-five or blind. The amount for each ex-

1. Code Sec. 62.

| Form **1040** | US | Department of the Treasury / Internal Revenue Service **Individual Income Tax Return** | 🏛 **1972** |

For the year January 1–December 31, 1972, or other taxable year beginning ...., 1972, ending ...., 19 ....

Please print or type

First name and initial (If joint return, use first names and middle initials of both) | Last name | Your social security number (Husband's, if joint return)

Present home address (Number and street, including apartment number, or rural route) | Wife's number, if joint return

City, town or post office, State and ZIP code | Occupation — Yours / Wife's

Filing Status—check only one:

1 ☐ Single
2 ☐ Married filing joint return (even if only one had income)
3 ☐ Married filing separately. If wife (husband) is also filing give her (his) social security number and first name here.
4 ☐ Unmarried Head of Household
5 ☐ Widow(er) with dependent child (Enter year of death of husband (wife) ▶ 19)

Exemptions   Regular / 65 or over / Blind   Enter number of boxes checked ▶

6 Yourself . . . . ☐ ☐ ☐
7 Wife (husband) . . . ☐ ☐ ☐
8 First names of your dependent children who lived with you _____

9 Number of other dependents (from line 32) . . . ▶   Enter number ▶
10 Total exemptions claimed . . . . ▶

Income (Please attach Copy B of Form W-2 here)

11	Wages, salaries, tips, and other employee compensation. (Attach Form W-2 to front. If unavailable, attach explanation) ·	11
12a	Dividends (see pages 6 and 13 of instr.) $ .... 12b Less exclusion $ .... Balance . ▶	12c
	(If gross dividends and other distributions are over $200, list in Part I of Schedule B.)	
13	Interest income. [If $200 or less, enter total without listing in Schedule B / If over $200, enter total and list in Part II of Schedule B] · ·	13
14	Income other than wages, dividends, and interest (from line 45) . . . . . . ·	14
15	Total (add lines 11, 12c, 13 and 14)	15
16	Adjustments to income (such as "sick pay," moving expenses, etc. from line 50) .	16
17	Subtract line 16 from line 15 (adjusted gross income)	17

● **Caution:** If you have unearned income and you could be claimed as a dependent on your parent's return, see boxed instruction on page 7, under the heading "Tax-Credits-Payments." Check this block ☐. ● If you do not itemize deductions and line 17 is under $10,000, find tax in Tables and enter on line 18. ● If you itemize deductions or line 17 is $10,000 or more, go to line 51 to figure tax.

Tax, Payments and Credits

18	Tax, check if from: ☐ Tax Tables 1–12, ☐ Schedule D / ☐ Tax Rate Schedule X, Y, or Z ☐ Schedule G or ☐ Form 4726	18
19	Total credits (from line 61)	19
20	Income tax (subtract line 19 from line 18)	20
21	Other taxes (from line 67)	21
22	Total (add lines 20 and 21)	22
23	Total Federal income tax withheld (attach Forms W-2 or W-2P to front) . . . . [23]	
24	1972 Estimated tax payments (include amount allowed as credit from 1971 return) . . . . . [24]	
25	Amount paid with Form 4868, Application for Automatic Extension of Time to File U.S. Individual Income Tax Return . . . . . [25]	
26	Other payments (from line 71) . . . . [26]	
27	Total (add lines 23, 24, 25, and 26)	27

Bal. Due or Refund

28	If line 22 is larger than line 27, enter BALANCE DUE IRS Pay in full with return. Make check or money order payable to Internal Revenue Service ▶	28
29	If line 27 is larger than line 22, enter amount OVERPAID . . . . . . ▶	29
30	Line 29 to be **REFUNDED TO YOU** . . . . ▶	30
31	Line 29 to be credited on 1973 estimated tax	31		

Foreign Accounts

Did you, at any time during the taxable year, have any interest in or signature or other authority over a bank, securities, or other financial account in a foreign country (except in a U.S. military banking facility operated by a U.S. financial institution)? . . . . ▶ ☐ Yes ☐ No
If "Yes," attach Form 4683. (For definitions, see Form 4683.)

Note: Be sure to complete Revenue Sharing (lines 33 and 34) on next page.

Sign here

Under penalties of perjury, I declare that I have examined this return, including accompanying schedules and statements, and to the best of my knowledge and belief it is true, correct, and complete. Declaration of preparer (other than taxpayer) is based on all information of which he has any knowledge.

▶ Your signature | Date | ▶ Preparer's signature (other than taxpayer) | Date

▶ Wife's (husband's) signature (if filing jointly, BOTH must sign even if only one had income) | Address (and ZIP Code) | Preparer's Emp. Ident. or Soc. Sec. No.

Write soc. sec. no. on Check or Money Order. Attach here

16—82010-1

emption is $750 for 1972 and later years.

3.4   At this point, taxable income is reached. The actual tax computation is now begun by applying to taxable income the rates found in the proper table. There are separate rate tables for married persons filing joint returns, persons qualifying for special status as "head of the household," and for single individuals (or married persons filing separate returns). It would be logical to assume that applying the tax rate to taxable income would reveal the tax for the year; however, the tax so computed may be reduced by one or more of a half dozen tax credits, including a deduction for income tax that has been withheld from wages and a deduction for any payments made previously with respect to the taxpayer's declaration of estimated tax, if he was required to file one. The amount of estimated income tax paid is not defined as a "credit" in the Code but has the same effect because of Section 6315.

3.5   If the taxpayer does not choose the path of itemized deductions, he may use the alternate route of the standard deduction, an arbitrary amount designed to replace certain personal expenditures. The term is defined in Section 141 as consisting of the larger of the "percentage standard deduction" or the "low income allowance." These amounts are described later in this chapter. From this point on, the two paths are the same until the point of computing the credits against the tax. Taxpayers electing the standard deduction, as shown by the chart, must forego the benefits of several of the tax credits.

3.6   There are two basic differences between the two paths. First, the standard deduction route offers the convenience of using a fixed or easily determinable amount instead of classifying, analyzing, listing, and proving the specific deductions allowable under the other method. Second, some credits against the tax are not allowed if the standard deduction is elected.

3.7   The example on page 46 is based upon the law applicable to the year 1972 and illustrates the method of computing the taxable income and the tax payable for a corporation, an individual claiming itemized deductions, and the same individual claiming the standard deduction. The individual is married, has two children, operates a retail store as a proprietor, and files a joint return with his wife. The example further illustrates that there is a difference between deductions and credits. Deductions are subtracted from gross receipts, gross income, or adjusted gross income; credits are deducted directly from the tax liability itself.

GROSS INCOME

3.8   In calculating the tax liability of an individual or a married couple, the first step is to list all items of taxable gross income. See paragraphs 2.3 and 2.4 for a definition of taxable gross income; also note the first page of Form 1040 on page 43. In chapter 5 the subject is covered in depth.

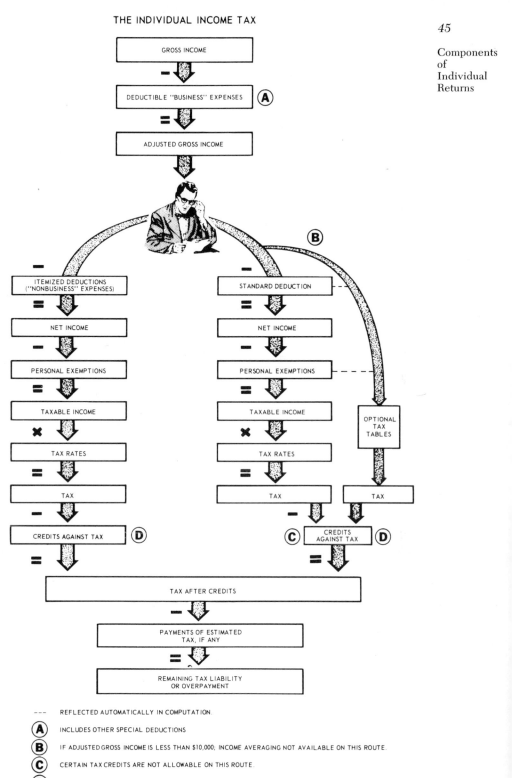

THE INDIVIDUAL INCOME TAX

GROSS INCOME

− DEDUCTIBLE "BUSINESS" EXPENSES (A)

= ADJUSTED GROSS INCOME

(B)

− ITEMIZED DEDUCTIONS ("NONBUSINESS" EXPENSES)

= NET INCOME

− PERSONAL EXEMPTIONS

= TAXABLE INCOME

× TAX RATES

= TAX

− CREDITS AGAINST TAX (D)

=

− STANDARD DEDUCTION

= NET INCOME

− PERSONAL EXEMPTIONS

= TAXABLE INCOME

× TAX RATES

= TAX

OPTIONAL TAX TABLES

TAX

− (C) CREDITS AGAINST TAX (D)

=

TAX AFTER CREDITS

− PAYMENTS OF ESTIMATED TAX, IF ANY

= REMAINING TAX LIABILITY OR OVERPAYMENT

--- REFLECTED AUTOMATICALLY IN COMPUTATION.

(A) INCLUDES OTHER SPECIAL DEDUCTIONS

(B) IF ADJUSTED GROSS INCOME IS LESS THAN $10,000; INCOME AVERAGING NOT AVAILABLE ON THIS ROUTE.

(C) CERTAIN TAX CREDITS ARE NOT ALLOWABLE ON THIS ROUTE.

(D) INCLUDES TAX WITHHELD.

EXAMPLE

	CORPORATION	INDIVIDUAL CLAIMING ITEMIZED DEDUCTIONS	INDIVIDUAL CLAIMING STANDARD DEDUCTION
Gross receipts from business	$70,000	$70,000	$70,000
Less — Cost of goods sold	40,000	40,000	40,000
Gross income from business	$30,000	$30,000	$30,000
Less — Expenditures attributable to the business, such as wages, rent, utilities advertising, and depreciation on selling facilities	$ 8,000	8,000	8,000
Adjusted gross income		$22,000	$22,000
Less —			
Charitable contributions	500	$ 500	$ —
Nonbusiness expenditures, such as real estate taxes on home, medical expenses, and interest on home mortgage	—	1,800	—
Standard deduction (15% of adjusted gross income but not more than $2,000) [See Note 1]	—	—	2,000
Personal exemptions (4 at $750) [See Note 2]	—	3,000	3,000
Totals	$ 8,500	$ 5,300	$ 5,000
Taxable income	$21,500	$16,700	$17,000
Tax liability —			
$21,500 at 22%	$4,730	$ —	$ —
Tax on first $16,000 ($3,260) plus 28% on balance up to total of $20,000	—	3,456	3,540
Less credits — estimated tax paid with respect to declaration filed a year ago.	—	3,200	3,200
Balance of tax payable	$4,730	$ 256	$ 340

ADJUSTED GROSS INCOME

Introduction and Summary of Deductions

To determine the amount of income subject to tax, the starting point, 3.9
as just stated, is "gross income" and the final amount is called "taxable income." In between the beginning and ending figure, for individuals but not for corporations or other types of taxpayers, is the stage "adjusted gross income." The purpose of this intermediary step is to allow the individual taxpayer deductions principally for certain business and income-producing expenses, whether or not he claims a "standard deduction." These business and income-producing expenses and other deductions are allowed as a reduction of gross income in computing this intermediary step of adjusted gross income. Beyond this point, the taxpayer may then claim either the standard deduction or itemize personal deductible items, whichever provides the lesser amount of taxable income. Thus, the concept of adjusted gross income merely carves out special treatment for certain of the deductions allowed by the Internal Revenue Code, but does not create any new deductions.

Section 62 of the Internal Revenue Code defines adjusted gross 3.10
income as gross income minus certain specified deductions. That section enumerates not the deductions replaced by the standard deduction, but those *not* replaced—those still available whether a taxpayer itemizes his deductions or not. The deductions listed in Section 62 that are deductible from gross income in determining adjusted gross income are:

1. Any *trade or business expenses* of a *nonemployee* (a proprietor or partner), including his payments into a pension plan for his own benefit as a self-employed person, provided the payments are deductible under Section 404 and Section 405(a).
2. Certain *trade or business expenses* of an *employee,* to the following extent:
    (a) Expenses for which he is reimbursed by his employer, or for which he receives an expense allowance.
    (b) His travel expenses (including meals and lodging) while he is away from home in connection with his employment.
    (c) His transportation expenses while he is on his employer's business.
    (d) *Any* of his trade or business expenses if he is an outside salesman.
    (e) His moving expenses to the extent they are deductible under Section 217.
3. A forfeiture by a shareholder employee of amounts paid into a qualified pension or profit-sharing plan for his benefit by a Subchapter S

Notes to the Example

(1) For 1972 and later years, the percentage is 15% and the ceiling $2,000.
(2) For 1972 and later years, the exemption is $750.

corporation and which forfeiture is deductible by him under Section 1379(b)(3).

4. Other deductions allowed to all individuals:
    (a) The deduction allowed under Section 1202 for 50 percent of the net long-term capital gain (in excess of net short-term capital loss).
    (b) Any losses arising from sales or exchanges of property or that are treated as if they arose from a sale or exchange, *and* that are deductible under Sections 165 or 166(d).
    (c) Expenses attributable to property held for the production of rents or royalties, including depreciation and depletion.
    (d) Any depreciation or depletion deduction allowable under Sections 167 or 611 to individuals who are life tenants or income beneficiaries of trusts or estates.

It should be repeated that Section 62 by itself does not allow any item as a deduction for tax purposes. It merely tells the taxpayer which of his allowable tax deductions are deductions for the purpose of computing adjusted gross income. The fact that a particular deduction is mentioned in Section 62 and is also mentioned elsewhere in the Code does not serve as an authority for deducting the same item twice.

3.11   The concept of adjusted gross income and the provision allowing elective use of a standard deduction originated in the Individual Income Tax Act of 1944. The Committee Reports[2] accompanying that act called the deductions allowable in determining adjusted gross income "business" deductions, even though, as in the case of employees, not all business type expenses are deductible and even though some nonbusiness types of deduction are also permitted. In turn, the standard deduction was designed to replace an individual's *nonbusiness* deductions such as charitable contributions, interest on personal indebtedness, medical expenses, and the like. Another way to categorize the amounts that are subtracted from gross income in determining adjusted gross income is to call them deductions *for* or *toward* adjusted gross income.

3.12   The amount of adjusted gross income can be significant to any individual taxpayer. To taxpayers who itemize their personal nonbusiness deductions, rather than claim the standard deduction, it seems at first glance that it would be unimportant whether particular deductions were claimed *in arriving at* adjusted gross income or *from* adjusted gross income. The difference would seem to be no more than one of presentation on the tax return. Actually, the difference is substantial. Statutory limitations on the amounts allowable as deductions for charitable contributions, medical expenses, and child care are all based upon the amount of adjusted gross income.[3]

Business Expenses

3.13   **Nonemployees.** By reason of Section 62(1) an individual engaged in a

---

2. H.R. Comm. Rep. 1365, 78th Cong., 2d sess., 1944, pp. 2–3, 1944 C.B. 821, 822.
3. Code Sec. 170(b)(1), 213, and 214.

business (including a profession) as a proprietor, independent con- tractor, or partner is entitled to deduct all of his expenses "which are attributable to a trade or business carried on by" him. They must be directly and not remotely connected with that business in determining adjusted gross income.[4] As was noted in paragraph 2.4, cost of goods sold is deductible from gross receipts in arriving at gross income. The business expenses which are deductible *for* adjusted gross income are discussed in later chapters, but, in summary, principally consist of compensation paid or accrued, supplies consumed, repairs, operating expenses of autos and trucks used in the business, advertising and other selling expenses, casualty insurance premiums, rentals, association dues, travel and entertainment expenses, employee fringe benefits, depreciation and depletion (to the extent not deducted in determining cost of goods sold), bad debts, casualty and other losses pertaining to business property, interest on business indebtedness, property taxes, and theft or embezzlement losses incurred in the business. In other words, all of the ordinary and necessary business expenses are deductible, except that charitable contributions are treated as a personal type itemized deduction and there are some restrictions on the amounts and types of deductions. For example, payments of fines and penalties incurred in contravention of public policy are not deductible at all in determining taxable income. The deductible business expenses are reported on Schedule C of Form 1040 by a proprietor or independent contractor.

A partner reports his distributable share of the firm's taxable income 3.14 or net operating loss on Schedule E of Form 1040, except that he separately accounts for, reports on other schedules, and treats as if directly received by him: his share of capital gains and losses, gains and losses on sales or exchanges of Section 1231 business property, charitable contributions, dividends received, and a few other items enumerated in Section 702(a). Accordingly, through Schedule E an individual's share of the business expenses of his partnership become deducted in determining adjusted gross income.

NET OPERATING LOSS DEDUCTIONS. As discussed in chapter 9, 3.15 a net operating loss incurred in a business (plus personal type casualty and theft losses), less wages, dividends, interest, and other nonbusiness type net income received, can be carried back three years and then forward five years to offset any type of income. Such a net operating loss carry-back or carry-over is taken as a deduction in determining adjusted gross income under Section 62(1) because it is or was attributable to a trade or business.[5]

PENSION CONTRIBUTIONS OF THE SELF-EMPLOYED. The pro- 3.16 prietor of his own business or member of a partnership is entitled, within limits, to set up his own retirement fund and deduct for tax purposes his contributions for that purpose [Section 404(e)]. Any

4. Reg. 1.62–1(d).
5. Godfrey M. Weinstein, 29 T.C. 142 (1957); Reg. 1.172–5(a), example (2).

such deductible contribution is a proper deduction under Section 62(7) in arriving at adjusted gross income.

3.17 **Employees.** Unlike persons in business for themselves, an employee may not treat *all* of his trade or business expenses as deductible for purposes of computing adjusted gross income. As stated in the regulations, "… the performance of personal services as an employee does not constitute the carrying on of a trade or business, except as otherwise expressly provided."[6] Thus, for purposes of computing adjusted gross income, the employee is limited to specifically defined travel, transportation, and moving expenses, unless he happens to be an "outside salesman," in which event all of the business expenses related to that occupation may be claimed.

> … an outside salesman is an individual who solicits business as a full-time salesman for his employer away from his employer's place of business. The term "outside salesman" does not include a taxpayer whose principal activities consist of service and delivery. For example, a bread driver–salesman or milk driver–salesman would not be included within the definition. However, an outside salesman may perform incidental inside activities at his employer's place of business such as writing up and transmitting orders and spending short periods at the employer's place of business, make and receive telephone calls, without losing his classification as an outside salesman.[7]

3.18 The fact that an employee is limited to certain of his trade or business expenses in computing adjusted gross income ordinarily does not cause any difficulties in preparing his federal income tax return. A problem can arise, however, in considering the relationship between a flat expense allowance and the deduction under Code Sec. 62 for "… expenses paid or incurred by the taxpayer, in connection with the performance by him of services as an employee, under a reimbursement or other expense allowance arrangement with his employer." It is simple enough to include the total amount of the expense allowance in gross income, but a problem of allocation arises in determining what portion of the expenditures on behalf of the employer's business are properly deductible in computing adjusted gross income.

EXAMPLE   John Q. Image is a vice-president of his company in charge of promotion and civic affairs. He receives an annual expense allowance of $5,000, which is intended to cover all of his business expenses incurred on behalf of the company, including travel and entertainment. He makes proper accounting to his employer for his expenses, which generally exceed the amount of his allowance. In preparing his tax return for the current year, his records indicate that he spent $4,000 for out-of-town travel including meals and hotels and another $2,000 for entertainment expenses. Mr. Image has been reimbursed a total of $5,000, which, of course, does not cover his $6,000 actual expenses. It may be assumed that the reimbursement applies ratably to the different categories of expenses that he has incurred. Accordingly, he would have

6. Reg. 1.62–1(d).
7. Reg. 1.62–1(h).

been reimbursed 5/6 of his travel expenses of $4,000 or a total of $3,333. Since travel expenses, however, are specifically deductible in computing adjusted gross income, Mr. Image is allowed $4,000, the actual amount of his expenditures for this purpose. On the other hand, entertainment expenses are not specifically deductible in computing adjusted gross income. He may treat 5/6 or $1,667 as deductible under the heading of "reimbursed business expenses." Thus, his total deduction under Section 62 in arriving at adjusted gross income is $5,667.[8] On his tax return, Mr. Image reports $5,000 in gross income and deducts $5,667 in arriving at adjusted gross income. The balance spent of $333 ($6,000 − $5,667) is deductible *from* adjusted gross income if the standard deduction is not elected.

3.19   Except for this problem of allocation in the case of reimbursed expenses of employees, Section 62 presents no new or novel problem as to trade or business expenses of an employee.

Forfeitures by Shareholder Employees of Subchapter S Corporations

3.20   A Subchapter S corporation is an ordinary business corporation having few stockholders. Under conditions discussed in chapter 19, it can elect to be treated somewhat like a partnership so that its net income or losses will flow through to the shareholders. Under Section 401, but subject to the limitations of Section 1379(a), it can set up a non-discriminatory tax-exempt pension or profit-sharing plan for its employees including shareholder-employees. If it does so, the amounts so paid are deductible by the corporation, and so in effect by its shareholders. If the amount paid into the fund for the benefit of a shareholder-employee exceeds the lesser of 10 percent of his compensation or $2,500, such excess, although deductible by the corporation, must be included in the gross income of that shareholder-employee. Later, if he leaves the employ of the corporation before retirement and forfeits his right to receive such taxed excess, Section 1379(b)(3) grants him a deduction for such forfeited amount. By Section 62(9), the deduction is taken in determining adjusted gross income.

Long-Term Capital Gains

3.21   A "net long-term capital gain" is defined in Section 1222 as the excess of long-term capital gains over long-term capital losses. And a "net short-term capital loss" is defined as the excess of short-term capital losses over short-term capital gains. The required holding periods were discussed in paragraph 2.5. If the amount of the net long-term capital gain exceeds the amount of the net short-term capital loss, if any, such excess is called a "net Section 1201 gain."

3.22   The Code presently provides that the maximum tax rate on the first $50,000 of the full amount of a net Section 1201 gain cannot exceed

---

8. See also the example in Reg. 1.62–1(f)(2).

CARNEGIE LIBRARY
LIVINGSTONE COLLEGE
SALISBURY, N. C. 28144

25 percent and that for 1971 the balance of the full amount of the net Section 1201 gain cannot be taxed at more than 32.5 percent. For 1972 and later years, the ceiling is 35 percent.

3.23   Section 1202 of the Code allows a taxpayer, other than a corporation, a deduction equal to 50 percent of a net Section 1201 gain, and this deduction is allowable in determining adjusted gross income. Accordingly, the amount of a net Section 1201 gain that is includible in taxable income is one-half of the amount actually realized. As a result, the ceiling on the first $25,000 (1/2 of $50,000) of the includible amount is 50 percent, and the ceiling for 1971 on the balance of the includible amount is 65 percent (2 times 32.5 percent). For 1972 and later years it is 70 percent. When these ceilings apply, the result is called the alternative tax. The subject of capital gains and losses is discussed in more depth in chapter 12.

EXAMPLE 1   John Smith has the following capital gains and losses for the taxable year.

Long-term capital gain	$6,000
Long-term capital loss	(4,000)
Short-term capital gain	300
Short-term capital loss	(1,800)

The aggregation required by Section 1202 is made as follows:

Net long-term gain ($6,000 — $4,000)	$2,000
Net short-term loss ($1,800 — $300)	(1,500)
Net Section 1201 gain	$ 500
Deductible under Section 1202 — 50%	$ 250

Code Sec. 62 allows this $250 to be deducted from gross income in determining adjusted gross income. The $250 remaining amount of net long-term capital gain is then added on top of ordinary taxable net income and taxed at the rate applicable to the bracket. If the bracket is 40 percent, the effective tax rate on the full $500 of net long-term capital gain is 20 percent (40 percent of 50 percent).

EXAMPLE 2   Mr. Brown, a married taxpayer, filed a joint return for 1972. His gross income consisted of salary, dividends, interest, and a net includible Section 1201 gain of $100,000 (one-half of the full gain of $200,000). From this he subtracted deductions (either itemized or the percentage standard) plus personal exemptions. The result was taxable income of $200,000.

His tax liability computed in the regular way pursuant to Section 1(a) is $110,980. However, his tax computed under the alternative method is only $106,430, and that is his liability:

Tax on ordinary income of $100,000 ($200,000 taxable income less $100,000 net long-term capital gain) is		$ 45,180
Tax on first $25,000 of the includible amount of net long-term capital gain (1/2 of $50,000) at 50%		12,500
Regular tax on full taxable income of $200,000	$110,980	
Less — Regular tax on $125,000 ($100,000 of ordinary taxable income plus first $25,000 of includible amount of net long-term capital gain)	60,780	
Tax on the $75,000 remaining amount of includible net long-term capital gain ($100,000-$25,000)	$ 50,200	
Total tax under alternative method		$107,880

Part VI, Schedule D, Form 1040, for the year 1972, uses 14 lines to arrive at the same result.

Losses from Sales or Exchanges of Property

By reason of the provisions of Section 62(4), all losses sustained by individuals on the sale or exchange of property, if deductible at all, are deductible in determining adjusted gross income. In addition, other losses that are treated *as if* they resulted from sales or exchanges are also deductible in determining adjusted gross income. Included in this category are losses from worthless securities under Section 165(g), and nonbusiness bad debts under Section 166(d). A loss on the sale of a personal residence or an automobile used solely for personal purposes is not deductible, because there is no provision in the Code allowing it. The subject is covered more fully in chapter 9. 3.24

The individual income tax return Form 1040 has a supporting Schedule D on which to report gains and losses from sales or exchanges of capital assets and other property. Part I, page 2, of Form 1040, not reproduced, calls for the insertion of the amount of the net gain or loss from Schedule D. This is the mechanical means by which a loss or net loss from the sale or exchange of property is deducted in determining adjusted gross income. 3.25

Expenses Attributable to Rents and Royalties

If the taxpayer owns property of a kind that produces income in the form of rents or royalties, all expenses attributable to such property are deductible in arriving at adjusted gross income, even if there is a deficit from operations. For example, all the operating expenses of a building held for the production of rental income are deductible at this point in the tax computation. This would include interest, prop- 3.26

erty taxes, depreciation, utilities, and maintenance. The word *at-tributable* in the phrase "attributable to property held for the pro-duction of rents or royalties" requires some careful distinctions to be drawn in determining whether certain expenses are deductible in arriving at adjusted gross income. For example, interest paid on an unsecured loan incurred to purchase rental property would be a proper deduction in computing adjusted gross income,[9] but interest paid on a loan, even though secured by a mortgage on such rental property, does not pass the "attributable" test where the proceeds are not used to purchase, construct, improve, or repair the property.[10]

Depreciation and Depletion Deductions
of Life Tenants and Income Beneficiaries

3.27   Property interests are of all types and descriptions and in many cases amount to less than complete outright immediate ownership. For an individual taxpayer who has less than a 100 percent interest in depreciable property or property subject to depletion, Code Sec. 167(h) (as to depreciation) and 611(b) (as to depletion) spell out what portion, if any, of the allowable deductions he is entitled to claim upon his tax return. Generally the one entitled to receive the income from the property is also entitled to the deductions for depreciation or depletion, either in whole or in part, proportionate to his interest in the income. Whatever the deduction is, Section 62(6) tells him that it is allowable as a deduction from gross income in determining adjusted gross income.

SUMMARY OF ITEMIZED DEDUCTIONS

3.28   After computing adjusted gross income during the course of prepar-ing his federal income tax return, the individual taxpayer is standing at a major fork in the road. Turning in one direction means itemizing his personal nonbusiness deductions. Turning in the other direction means choosing the route of the standard deduction, designed to replace the itemized deductions, at the option of the taxpayer.

3.29   The most common types of items deductible *from* adjusted gross in-come in determining taxable income are listed below. Most of these are discussed in chapters 7, 9 and 10.

Interest on personal indebtedness.

Taxes—property, foreign income, state and local income, state and local general retail sales and use taxes, state and local gasoline taxes, and state transfer taxes on the sale of securities.

Casualty and theft losses to the full extent of property used in a transaction entered into for profit and to the extent of the excess over the first $100 loss

9. Koshland, 19 T.C. 860 (1953), affirmed 216 F.2d 751 (9th Cir. 1953), 46 AFTR 1091.

10. U.S. v. Wharton, 207 F.2d 526 (5th Cir. 1953), 53–2 USTC ¶9597, 44 AFTR 512.

on each casualty or theft of property that is personal in nature.

Wagering losses to the extent of wagering gains (a professional gambler deducts the losses in determining adjusted gross income).

Charitable contributions to the extent of 50 percent of adjusted gross income for contributions to "public" types of organizations and to the extent of 20 percent of adjusted gross income for all other types.

Medical, dental, and hospital expenses in excess of 3 percent of adjusted gross income.

Medical and hospital insurance premiums to the extent of one-half thereof, but not in excess of $150 (the balance goes into the pot of general medical expenses mentioned above).

Deductible by employees:
  Fees paid in obtaining employment
  Labor union dues
  Cost of consumable small tools
  Cost of maintenance of uniforms

Nonbusiness expenses for production of income:
  Investors' expenses
  Proxy contest expenses
  Legal expenses (if not personal or capital in nature)
  Real estate investment expenses where the property in the year did not produce gross rental income (if it did, then the expenses are deductible in determining adjusted gross income)

Fees paid to accountants and attorneys for preparation of tax returns and tax advice
Alimony payments

STANDARD DEDUCTION

As mentioned earlier, the standard deduction came into existence 3.30 with the Individual Income Tax Act of 1944. The purpose behind its birth was to achieve a measure of simplification, particularly for the small taxpayer. In that year a $500 standard deduction was enacted as Section 23(aa) of the 1939 Code.[11] In subsequent years, a number of changes were made in the standard deduction. In 1948, the maximum amount of $500 became $1,000 to reflect the inauguration of income splitting by husband and wife through the vehicle of joint returns; and the principle was adopted, in the case of husband and wife filing separate returns, that if one elected the standard deduction, both had to use it. At the same time, the deduction became 10 percent of adjusted gross income, but not in excess of $1,000 for all single individuals and married couples filing joint returns (a $500 limit, nevertheless, in the case of a separate return of a married person). In 1951 the standard deduction was further liberalized by giving

11. Individual Income Tax Act of 1944. See also H.R. Comm. Rep. 1365, 78th Cong., 2d sess., 1944, 1944 C.B. 821.

the taxpayer some right to change his mind (within the period of limitations) after filing his return; the election of the standard deduction was no longer irrevocable.[12]

3.31   The biggest change in the standard deduction, however, occurred twenty years after its adoption. In 1964 the minimum standard deduction made its appearance in order to remove 1.5 million taxpayers from the tax rolls. The announced purpose was to give a tax reduction only to lower-income taxpayers and not to the middle class and the wealthy.[13] In 1969 the Tax Reform Act changed the name of the minimum standard deduction to the "low-income allowance" and made other changes in its amount so as to remove more poverty-level taxpayers from the tax rolls.

3.32   Since 1970 the term "standard deduction" means the *larger*, not *both*, of the "percentage standard deduction" or the "low-income allowance." These and other terms and conditions are set forth in Sections 141 through 144 of the Code.

Percentage Standard Deduction

3.33   The percentage standard deduction is a percentage of adjusted gross income but with a ceiling on the amount that can be claimed. For 1972 and later years, the percentage standard deduction is 15 percent but with a ceiling of $2,000.

Low-Income Allowance

3.34   Starting with 1972 the low-income allowance is a flat $1,300 regardless of family size or the amount of adjusted gross income. The amounts are built into the optional tax tables together, of course, with the allowances for personal exemptions. For 1972 and later years, a single person can have $2,050 ($1,300 low-income allowance plus $750 exemption) of income before becoming subject to tax.

Limitation for Unearned Income of Dependents

3.35   A popular tax planning device has been for a parent to transfer income-bearing securities to a child or other dependent either under a ten-year trust (see Code Section 673 and paragraph 20.46) or under the Uniform Gifts to Minors' Act (see paragraph 5.44). Because of the low-income allowance, the personal exemption available to the dependent himself, and the fact that any income in excess of the sum of those two amounts would normally be taxed in lower brackets than those of the donor, little or no taxes resulted. Starting with 1972, there is still a saving, but a smaller one. Section 141(e) has been inserted in the Code to deny such dependent on his own return any low-income allowance

12. Sections 308(a), (b), and (c) of the Revenue Act of 1951.
13. H.R. Comm. Rep. 749, 88th Cong., 1st sess., 1964–1 C.B. pt. 2:148.

or percentage standard deduction to reduce investment income; but he is still entitled to his own personal exemption even though the parent or other person upon whom he is dependent claims a similar exemption for him. The dependent's low-income allowance cannot exceed the amount of his *earned* income, if any. Further, the percentage standard deduction is computed solely by reference to his earned income. If the limitation applies, the optional tax tables prescribed under Code Section 3 (see paragraph 3.74) cannot be used.

The aforedescribed limitation on the standard deduction applies whenever the person with unearned income *can* be claimed as a dependent of another taxpayer. It does not matter that the other taxpayer does not, in fact, claim the exemption. Thus, the limitation will apply to a child who is 18 or a student, if more than 50 percent of the child's support is supplied by the parent (see paragraph 3.52). However, the limitation will not inhibit support arrangements, such as through a ten-year trust, for the benefit of persons who are not children if the unearned income is more than $750. As pointed out in paragraph 3.52, a person, other than a child who is under 19 or a student, cannot qualify as the dependent of another if, starting with 1972, he has more than $750 of gross income. For example, if an aged parent has $800 in interest income from banks plus perhaps tax-exempt Social Security benefits, income paid to the parent by the trustee of a ten-year trust can be reduced by the standard deduction in the return of that parent. 3.36

The origin of the dependent's unearned income is immaterial. It may come from interest or dividends on (a) savings from his own earnings, (b) cash or securities received as outright gifts, or (c) trust principal. 3.37

For 1972, a college son with the following indicated amounts of gross income and no itemized deductions would have taxable income of $350: EXAMPLE

| | INCOME | | |
	EARNED	UNEARNED	TOTAL
Gross income—			
Summer employment	$1,000	$ —	$1,000
Interest on savings account	—	300	300
Income from savings account in name of mother as custodian under a Uniform Gifts to Minors Act	—	800	800
Totals	$1,000	$1,100	$2,100

Deductions—
Standard deduction (the
higher of low-income
allowance of $1,300

limited to earned income of $1,000 or the percentage standard deduction equal to 15% of the $1,000 earned income)	$1,000	$ —	$1,000
Personal exemption			750
Total			$1,750
Taxable income			$ 350

Separate Returns of Married Persons

3.38   To prevent a husband and wife from claiming on separate returns more than they could obtain from filing a joint return, there are a number of restrictions and limitations on the use and the amounts of the standard deduction that are allowable on separate returns:

1. If one spouse itemizes deductions, both must do so; the standard deduction is not available
2. If both claim the standard deduction, (a) the ceilings on the amounts allowable under the percentage standard deduction are cut in half, and (b) the low-income allowance for 1972 and later years is $650.
3. If one spouse claims the percentage standard deduction on a separate return, the other spouse cannot claim the low-income allowance, even though it is larger than the percentage standard deduction. Conversely, however, both may claim the low-income allowance as long as one is entitled to it.

3.39   However, these restrictions and limitations do not apply where a family is abandoned by one parent. In other words, the abandoned spouse, even though filing separately, will receive the full benefit of the higher of the regular percentage standard deduction or the low-income allowance, without regard to whether the deserter spouse itemizes deductions or claims a different form of the standard deduction. The abandoned spouse is deemed not to have been married during that year. To have this relief the principal conditions are that he or she furnish more than half the support of a household that for more than half the year is the principal abode of a dependent child, and that the other spouse during the entire year is not a member of the household. Although the Committee reports speak of an "abandoned" spouse, Section 143(b) can apply even where the spouses have separated by mutual agreement. This concept is new in the tax law and applies only to the standard deduction and the right to use the "head-of-household" tax rates (see paragraph 3.71).

3.40   For instances other than abandonment, Section 143(a) contains two rules to determine marital status. First, the determination of marital status is made as of the end of the taxable year of the individual, or at the date of death of the spouse if this occurs earlier during the taxable year. Second, an individual is not regarded as married if he is legally separated from his spouse under a decree of separate maintenance.

Election

The standard deduction is optional, and a taxpayer must make an affirmative election to use it. He does this simply by preparing and filing his tax return on that basis. The amount of the standard deduction to be claimed is inserted in the proper place on Form 1040, and Schedule A for itemized deductions is not used.   3.41

If the adjusted gross income is less than $10,000, the taxpayer can compute his tax under the optional tables authorized by Section 3. Those tables are based upon use of the standard deduction, so that using the tables constitutes electing the standard deduction.   3.42

In the case of single persons and married couples filing joint returns, an election made in a return claiming either the standard deduction or itemized deductions can be changed at any time within the statutory period for filing claims for refund, usually three years.[14] If a married couple files separate returns, one spouse may make the desired change only if the other agrees to a consistent change and both agree to the assessment of any deficiency caused by the change in election and that otherwise would be barred by the statute of limitations or any other rule of law.[15]   3.43

Considerations in Making Election

As mentioned previously, the election of the standard deduction precludes itemizing the usual personal or nonbusiness deductions listed earlier. Further, as indicated on the chart at the beginning of this chapter, an election of the standard deduction prevents the use of the following credits against the tax: 3.44

1. Foreign tax credit
2. Credit for taxes withheld at the source on certain tax-free covenant bonds
3. Credit for partially tax-exempt interest

Whether or not to elect the standard deduction is usually decided by considerations more practical than mere convenience. Undoubtedly, it is easier for an individual to prepare his tax return by using the standard deduction or the optional tax table than by assembling his records for the entire year in order to collect the information necessary to itemize his deductions. More important, however, is determination of which method will produce the lesser tax. There are many   3.45

14. Code Sec. 144(b); reg. 1.144–2(a).
15. Code Sec. 144(b); reg. 1.144–2(b).

factors affecting this determination, but the most satisfactory method is actually to compute the tax *both* ways.

3.46   A few guideposts are found in the IRS booklet, *Your Federal Income Tax:*

> It will ordinarily be to your advantage to itemize your deductions if you are a homeowner paying interest and taxes, or if you make large contributions to qualified charities, have unusually large medical expenses during the year, pay alimony, or incur a major casualty loss.

3.47   Because most individuals use the cash method of accounting, and itemized deductions are available only for the years in which paid, many individuals have a measure of control over the year in which to make payment. There is only one day's difference between December 31 and January 1, but there is a whole year for tax purposes. By proper timing of payments, some persons can maximize deductible amounts by claiming itemized deductions in one year and the standard deduction in the following year. As an illustration, a person whose standard deduction normally exceeds his itemized deductions may be able to deter a planned, large, charitable contribution until a year in which he plans to itemize. Thus, he will be able to take advantage of an extra deduction in the current year measured by the excess of the standard deduction over his regular itemized deductions. Even homeowners with regular, large, annual amounts of real estate taxes and mortgage interest, which seem to commit them fully to the method of itemized deductions, have been known to attempt planning for increased overall deductions through intermittent use of the standard deduction.

PERSONAL EXEMPTIONS

3.48   In computing taxable income, individuals, trusts, and estates are entitled to deduct "exemptions" from net income. Here the discussion pertains to the exemptions allowed individuals.

3.49   The present system of deductions for personal exemptions is contained in Code Sec. 151, 152, and 153. Section 151 states the provision, Section 152 defines dependents, and Section 153 contains the rules relating to the determination of marital status, the perennial problem of U.S. individual income tax law. Personal exemptions fall into three major classes: allowances for (1) the taxpayer, (2) the taxpayer's spouse, and (3) dependents. Each exemption is worth $750 for 1972 and later years. The mathematics become simply a matter of determining the total number of exemptions to which the taxpayer is entitled and multiplying that number by the proper dollar amount for the year in order to determine the amount to be deducted on the tax return. One exemption is allowed for the taxpayer himself, one additional exemption if he has attained the age of sixty-five before the end of his taxable year, and another exemption if he is "blind" within the meaning of Sec. 151(d)(3).

Spouse

Exemptions in the second class correspond exactly to those in the first class except that they relate to the spouse of the taxpayer. If a joint return is filed (discussed starting at paragraph 3.65), all of the exemptions of both spouses are claimed in the return. If an individual files a separate return, then exemptions applicable to his spouse are deductible upon his return only if she has no gross income and is not claimed as a dependent upon the tax return of some other taxpayer.

3.50

Marital status is determined as of the end of the taxpayer's taxable year, except that if his spouse dies during the year, he will still be considered married during the entire year. Taxpayers are treated as unmarried if they are legally separated at the close of the taxable year under a decree of divorce or even under a decree of separate maintenance.[16] However, if a husband and wife are merely living apart, they are still married. If a divorce is obtained by the husband in a jurisdiction other than the marital domicile, such divorce is later declared void by a court in the state of the marital domicile, and the husband remarries, the courts are not in agreement as to whether the husband can file a joint return with his second "wife." The Tax Court says he cannot;[17] the Second Circuit says he can,[18] primarily in order to have uniform application of the tax laws. However, if the divorce is nullified by a court of the state which granted it, both the Tax Court[19] and the Second Circuit[20] agree that the second "wife" is not such for tax purposes.

3.51

Dependents

The third class of personal exemptions comprises the exemptions allowed for the dependents of the taxpayer. For an individual to qualify as the dependent of a taxpayer, three requirements must be satisfied:

3.52

1. A prescribed relationship by blood or by marriage must exist between the dependent and the taxpayer, with a single exception (see paragraph 3.53).
2. The taxpayer must furnish over one-half of the support of the dependent, with a single exception relating to multiple-support agreements described in paragraph 3.56.
3. The dependent must have less than $750 for 1972 and later years of gross income for the year unless he is a child of the taxpayer and either under nineteen years of age *or* a student.

16. Code Sec. 153.
17. John J. Unterman, 38 T.C. 93 (1962).
18. Estate of Herman Borax v. Com., 349 F.2d 666 (2nd Cir. 1965), 65–2 USTC ¶9592, 16 AFTR2d 5427.
19. Estate of Daniel Buckley, 37 T.C. 664 (1962).
20. *Supra* fn. 3.

3.53 **Relationship.** Code Sec. 152(a) lists ten categories into at least one of which an individual must fit in order to qualify as a dependent. The first eight categories describe more or less conventional relationships. The ninth category does not mention any degree of blood relationship or affinity, but simply requires that the individual be a member of the taxpayer's household and make the taxpayer's home his principal place of abode during the taxpayer's taxable year; however, under Section 152(b)(5) no dependency deduction is allowed in the case of an illicit relationship. The tenth category lists the situation of the so-called "institutionalized cousin." To be a dependent within the meaning of this provision requires that the individual be a descendant of a brother or sister of the father or mother of the taxpayer, who was formerly a member of the taxpayer's household, and who, during the taxable year, received institutional care for physical or mental disability. These categories, impressively genealogical in the statute, can be regrouped and classified somewhat as follows:

1. Relatives by blood:
   Ancestors—parents, grandparents, and others
   Aunts or uncles
   Brothers or sisters, including those of the half blood
   Children, grandchildren, and their descendants
   Nephews or nieces
   Institutionalized cousins
2. Relatives by marriage:
   Father-in-law or mother-in-law
   Stepfather or stepmother
   Brother-in-law or sister-in-law
   Stepchildren
   Son-in-law or daughter-in-law
3. Any person (except a spouse), including a foster child, who is a member of the taxpayer's household and makes the taxpayer's home his principal place of abode.

3.54 The foregoing lists only the bare outlines of the dependency provisions of the Code. There are many special rules, some of which apply to fairly narrow situations. Legally adopted children are considered to be children by blood, and even children not yet adopted but who have been placed in the taxpayer's home by an authorized placement agency pending adoption may also qualify as dependents.

3.55 Oddly enough, though divorce will terminate the bonds of marriage, the relationship of mother-in-law and father-in-law is evidently terminated only by death. The Regulations provide:

... the relationship of affinity once existing will not terminate by divorce or the death of a spouse. For example, a widower may continue to claim his deceased wife's father (his father-in-law) as a dependent provided he meets the other requirements of Section 151.[21]

21. Reg. 1.152–2(d).

Support Test. Although the general rule requires that the taxpayer 3.56
furnish over one-half of the support of the dependent, there is one
significant exception. This is the "multiple-support agreement." If
a group of persons furnish over one-half the support of a particular
person, but no one individual furnishes that much, any one individual
who furnishes over 10 percent of the support will be allowed the
exemption if all other individuals, each of whom likewise furnishes
over 10 percent of the support, consent in writing. This consent is
called a multiple-support agreement.[22] If this provision had not been
added to the tax law, many exemptions would have been lost by those
who share support of their parents.

A dependent's total support is the entire amount of support he re- 3.57
ceives from all sources, including amounts he contributes to his own
support. Amounts he contributes are counted, even though they
come from exempt income such as social security benefits.

The mere fact that a dependent has income of his own available 3.58
for his support is not controlling. Such income is counted as a contribution to his own support only if he uses it for that purpose. For
example, if a child has investment income which is not used for his
support, the amount is not taken into account; nor are scholarships
counted that are received by children who are students.[23]

A major problem presented by the support test is the determina- 3.59
tion of exactly what constitutes support. A hint of the many problems in this area is found in the following excerpt from the Regulations:

The term "support" includes food, shelter, clothing, medical and dental
care, education, and the like. Generally, the amount of an item of support will
be the amount of the expense incurred by the one furnishing such item. If
the item of support furnished an individual is in the form of property or lodging, it will be necessary to measure the amount of such item of support in
terms of its fair market value.[24]

CHILDREN OF DIVORCED OR SEPARATED PARENTS. Code Sec. 3.60
152(e) was added to the law in 1967 to settle controversies between
divorced or separated parents as to who is entitled to exemptions
for their children. The summary portion of the Senate Finance Committee Report accompanying the bill explained subsection (e) as
follows:[24A]

H. R. 6056 [enacted as P.L. 90–78] would amend the provision of the Internal Revenue Code of 1954 relating to the $600 [now $750] deduction for
dependents as it applies with respect to the children of divorced or separated
partners. ... The bill provides rules designed to facilitate the determination of
which parent is entitled to the deduction in these cases.

The new rules apply only if the combined support furnished by the

22. Code Sec. 152(c).
23. Code Sec. 152(d).
24. Reg. 1.152–1(a)(2)(i).
24A. See also Reg. 1.152–4.

parents amounts to more than one-half of the total support of the child for the year, and only if the child is in the custody of either or both of his parents for more than one-half of the year. In these cases the bill provides as a general rule that the parent having custody of a child for the longer period of time during the year is entitled to the $600 [now $750] deduction for personal exemption.

The bill contains exceptions to this general rule under which the parent not having custody (or having custody for the shorter period) becomes entitled to the deductions. Under these exceptions that parent is entitled to the deduction:

(1) If he contributes at least $600 toward the support of the child and the decree of divorce or separate maintenance, or a written agreement between the parents, provides that he is to receive the deduction; or

(2) If he provides more than $1,200 of child support (regardless of the number of children) and the parent having custody for the longer period does not clearly establish that he provided a greater amount of support.

In determining the amount of support provided by each parent for purposes of these exceptions, amounts expended for child support are to be considered as received from the parent not having custody to the extent he provides amounts for this purpose.

In cases where the parent not having custody contributes more than $1,200 of support and claims the deduction with respect to the child, or children, and the parent having custody claims to have provided a greater amount of the support, the bill provides that each parent is entitled to receive an itemized statement of the expenditures upon which the other bases his claim.

3.61 **Gross-income Test.** The gross-income test may cause as many problems as the support test. In determining whether the dependent has $750 gross income during the taxable year, we must first determine what is income. Note that the term referred to is *gross income*, which means gross income in a tax sense. A taxpayer with tax-free income may discover that he is actually someone else's dependent for the taxable year, provided the support and the relationship tests are also met. A typical example of this situation is the parent receiving social security benefits. These amounts are disregarded for purposes of the gross-income test, but they are taken into consideration in determining whether the amount spent for the support of the dependent parent by his son or daughter is more than one-half of the total spent for that purpose by all persons, including the parent.

3.62 The gross-income test does not apply to children, including foster children, under nineteen or those of any age who are students, but the support test does. Teenagers can earn a little money during their summer vacations without being disqualified as dependents in their fathers' income tax returns. Thus, a teenager of eighteen with summer vacation earnings can qualify as an exemption twice, once on his own return to recover any tax that has been withheld from his wages, and second, on his father's return. The same rule applies to a child of a taxpayer who is nineteen or over, provided he is classified as a student, which is defined very carefully in the Code and the regulations and means, in general, being a full-time student (for at least five months out of a year) at a recognized educational institution.

The income of a minor child is reported on his own return, if one is required, and is not the taxable income of his parents, regardless of any local law that the earnings of a minor child belongs to the parents.[25] 3.63

CHOOSING THE RIGHT INDIVIDUAL TAX RATE TABLE

The deduction of the allowance of personal exemptions from net income is the last step in the computation of taxable income for an individual. He then selects the applicable tax rate table to determine the amount of his tax liability, although he may be able to reduce that computed amount of tax by certain credits. The tax liability of an individual not only varies with the amount of his taxable income but also depends upon his marital status and whether, if single, he is the head of a household or a surviving spouse. The number of rate tables for 1972 and later years, the types of individuals to which they apply, and the relative sections are these: 3.64

1. Married persons filing joint returns and surviving spouses: Section 1(a).
2. Single persons who are heads of households (including an abandoned spouse as discussed in paragraph 3.39); Section 1(b).
3. Single persons who are not heads of households: Section 1(c).
4. Married persons filing separate returns (but not an abandoned spouse): Section 1(d).
5. Optional tax tables where the adjusted gross income is less than $10,000 and itemized deductions are not claimed: Section 3 and the regulations thereunder.

Reproductions of these rate tables are to be found in the front of the paperbound copies of the Code published by Prentice-Hall, Inc.

Joint Returns

A married couple may file a joint return including their combined incomes (Code Sec. 6013), or each spouse may file a separate return reflecting his or her income only. Joint returns were introduced in 1948 to permit husbands and wives to split their combined incomes for tax purposes, to equalize the situation of persons in common-law states with those in states following the laws of community property. In community property states (Arizona, California, Idaho, Louisiana, Nevada, New Mexico, Texas, and Washington) the income of one spouse, if from community property, belongs to both. Earnings from personal services are considered to be community earnings. Thus, even before 1948, a wife residing in one of these states with no income of her own nevertheless could file a separate tax return reporting her 3.65

25. Code Sec. 73.

share of her husband's income and relieving his return of an equivalent amount of taxable income. This may still be done in community property states, but it is frequently more advantageous and easier to file one joint return, the effect of which is to split the combined income into two equal parts, apply the graduated rate tables to each half, and then combine the two taxes. Note that a joint return may be filed and the splitting device may be used even if the wife has no income. The subject of community property income is again discussed starting with paragraph 5.42.

3.66   If a joint return is filed, the following procedures are observed:

Only one return is filed
Income and deductions of both spouses are combined
Personal exemptions, and exemptions for dependents to which either
    spouse is entitled, are combined
Both spouses sign the return
Liability for the tax is joint and several

3.67   If a joint return is filed, the general rule is that both spouses are jointly and severally liable for any deficiency in tax, interest, and penalties. However, P.L. 91–679 enacted January 12, 1971, provides relief for an innocent spouse and was retroactive to all open years. That law added subsection (e) to Section 6013 pertaining to joint returns and amended subsection (b) of Section 6653 pertaining to the 50 percent fraud penalty.

3.68   Under Section 6013(e) if there is an omission of gross income in excess of 25 percent of the amount of gross income stated in the return and if one spouse did not know of the omission and did not significantly benefit from the omitted gross income, then such innocent spouse is not liable for any deficiency, interest, or penalties.

3.69   Under amended Section 6653(b), a spouse will not be liable for a fraud penalty applicable to a joint return unless some part of the underpayment was due to her fraud, and the Service has the burden of proof. If the fraud arises from an omission of more than 25 percent of gross income, either Section 6013(e) or Section 6653(b) can be availed of by the innocent spouse. If the fraud arises from other circumstances, such as claiming an improper deduction, only Section 6653(b) is available.

3.70   The privilege to file joint tax returns is also extended to "surviving spouses." In addition to the right to file a joint return for the year in which a spouse died, a taxpayer whose spouse died in either of the two years preceding the taxable year, and who has not remarried, may file a joint return provided he maintains as his home a household that is the principal place of abode for a dependent child or stepchild for whom he is entitled to a deduction for an exemption under Section 151 and provided that over half of the cost of maintaining such household is furnished by the surviving spouse.

Heads of Households

In recognition of the fact that unmarried individuals who maintain 3.71 households for dependents incur many of the same expenses as married couples, the special status of "head of a household" was enacted into law in 1951. A special tax rate table was adopted which then provided, for qualified individuals, roughly one-half the benefits of income splitting available to married couples through the use of joint returns. Starting with the year 1971 the rates were further reduced. To qualify as head of a household, for tax purposes, a taxpayer must be either (1) an abandoned spouse as defined in paragraph 3.39 or (2) unmarried and furnish over one-half the cost of maintaining a household that is the principal place of abode of a person falling in one of the following four classes:

1. An unmarried child, stepchild, or descendant of a child of a taxpayer, whether or not such person is a dependent of the taxpayer under Section 151.
2. A person described in paragraph 1, if married, but then only if such person qualifies as a dependent under Section 151.
3. Any relative of the taxpayer (except an "institutionalized cousin") qualifying for dependency status under Section 151 by reason of such relationship.
4. Father or mother of the taxpayer, provided that such parent is the taxpayer's dependent under Section 151.

In the first three situations described above, the individual who qualifies the taxpayer for status as head of a household must actually be a member of the taxpayer's own household. Dependent parents, however, may have their own household separate and apart from that of the taxpayer provided, of course, that the taxpayer meets the requirement of furnishing over one half of the cost of maintaining such household. Even if the payment of maintenance is to a rest home where the parent resides, head-of-household status has been held proper.[26]

As in the case of most Code provisions granting special status, there 3.72 are a number of limitations and restrictions. A nonresident alien taxpayer cannot claim the benefits of head-of-household status, but a taxpayer who is a citizen may qualify, even though married, if his wife is a nonresident alien. A taxpayer does not qualify if he is a "surviving spouse" and entitled to file a joint return for the year. A dependent relative who is a dependent only by reason of a multiple-support agreement cannot qualify a taxpayer for head-of-household status. Finally, although a taxpayer may secure dependency exemptions under Code Sec. 152(a)(9) for unrelated persons living in his household, they cannot qualify him for head-of-household status. Only relatives serve this purpose, except institutionalized cousins [Code Sec. 152(a)(10)].

26. John Robinson, 51 T.C. 520 (1968), aff'd 70-1 USTC ¶9310 (9th Cir., 1970); Rev. Rul. 70-279.

3.73　　　To qualify as head of a household the taxpayer must furnish more than one-half of the cost of maintaining the household. The Regulations [27] offer some help in determining whether this test is met:

> ... the cost of maintaining a household shall be the expenses incurred for the mutual benefit of the occupants thereof by reason of its operation as the principal place of abode for such occupants for such taxable year. The cost of maintaining a household shall not include expenses otherwise incurred. The expenses of maintaining a household include property taxes, mortgage interest, rent, utility charges, upkeep and repairs, property insurance, and food consumed on the premises. Such expenses do not include the cost of clothing, education, medical treatment, vacations, life insurance, and transportation. In addition, the cost of maintaining a household shall not include any amount which represents the value of services rendered in the household by the taxpayer or by a person qualifying the taxpayer as a head of a household.

Optional Tax Tables

3.74　　　The optional tax tables are constructed from the rates shown in Code Sec. 1 and also take into account the standard deduction. Under Code Sec. 4(c), married persons filing separately would compare the tax shown on the tables utilizing respectively the percentage standard deduction and the low-income allowance, and pay the lesser of the two taxes. As mentioned in the discussion relating to the standard deduction, however, one spouse cannot claim the percentage standard deduction and the other the low-income allowance. The same rules apply here.

3.75　　　The optional tax tables are not available to:

> Individuals and married couples filing jointly whose adjusted gross income is $10,000 or more
> Nonresident aliens
> Citizens with income from possessions of the United States
> Returns for a short taxable period resulting from a change in accounting periods
> Estates or trusts
> Individuals electing to use income averaging

INCOME AVERAGING

3.76　　　So far, computing income tax has been discussed with reference to a normal situation. In most cases, taxable income for a given year is traced into one of the regular tax rate schedules or one of the optional tax tables, and the result becomes the tax for the year. Now we come to a measure designed to alleviate hardship suffered by an individual whose taxable income fluctuates widely from year to year. Because of the graduated rates, he may, over a period of years, pay

27. Reg. 1.1–2(d).

income taxes considerably higher in the aggregate than those of another individual whose total income is not lower, but constant. The Revenue Act of 1964 gave some recognition to this problem by adopting a limited form of income averaging; the Tax Reform Act of 1969 both liberalized and simplified the provisions effective for 1970 and later years.

3.77 Code Sec. 1301 to 1304 present this system of what is somewhat inaccurately called "income averaging." No recomputation of tax for any earlier or later year is involved. The impact of graduated rates on exceptionally high income is partially overcome, instead, by taxing only one-fifth of the extraordinary or exceptional income at graduated rates. The remaining four-fifths, instead of being taxed at graduated rates, is taxed at the same rates applicable to the "normal" portion without escalating the income into higher brackets.

3.78 The technique involves determining the "average base period net income" and subtracting 120 percent of that amount from taxable income of the current year. The base period consists of the four taxable years preceding the current year. Each of these four years is called a "base period year," and the current year is called the "computation year." Averaging relief is available only when current year income is more than $3,000 greater than 120 percent of the average income of the preceding four years, and the income of each of the five years, for the purpose of this computation, is subject to a few adjustments for unusual types of income. After this qualifying test is met, the amount by which current year income is in excess of 120 percent of the average income of the preceding four years is called "averageable income."

3.79 Solely for the purposes of determining whether averageable income exists in the computation year and of calculating the amount of tax relief, adjustments of income are required:

Income from Foreign Sources. Code Sec. 911 excludes from taxable income of United States citizens income up to $20,000 or $25,000 per year earned abroad while the citizen resided in a foreign country for at least seventeen out of eighteen months or was a bona fide foreign resident. Further, Sections 931 to 934 exclude from income certain amounts received from sources within possessions of the United States. All such excluded income, less any deductions allocable to it, must be restored to all base period years and to the computation year. The effect of inclusion in the computation year is to produce tax on this otherwise exempt income. Inclusion in the base years does not increase tax in those years, but does cut down relief in the computation year.

Premature Distributions from Keogh Plans. Under Section 401 self-employed persons and partners can set up a qualified retirement plan and within limits obtain deductions for contributions to it, as discussed in Chapter 17. If during the computation year the owner-employee receives a premature or excessive distribution from the plan within the meaning of Section 72(m)(5), such amount is not subject to averaging and must be deducted from otherwise averageable income of the computation year. However, any such amount received in a base year must remain in base period net income for that year.

Accumulation Distributions from Trusts. Income accumulated by a trust for future distribution is taxed to the trust as earned; then later, when the accumulated income is distributed, the beneficiary is taxed, but he is given a credit for taxes paid in prior years by the trust. Special averaging rules are contained in Sections 665 to 669 to minimize the effect of bunching the accumulated distribution income into one year. If a taxpayer receives an accumulation distribution, he must exclude it from both the base period and computation years.

3.80   Income averaging is elective, and every citizen or resident of the United States may take advantage of it except an individual who has the status of nonresident alien during either the current computation year or one of the base years. There are elaborate provisions designed to prevent a young person who is coming into the working force for the first time from averaging his entire income for his first working year simply because he had a negligible amount of income during his base period years, mainly because they were educational years.[28] Under these provisions, an individual is not eligible if he (or his spouse) furnished less than one-half of his support during any base period year. Again, there are relief provisions to these exceptions.[29]

3.81   If a taxpayer elects averaging, the 50 percent (60 percent for 1971) maximum tax on earned income does not apply. Also the alternative capital gains tax on a net long-term capital gain is not applicable, but one-half of the net long-term capital gain continues to be excluded from taxable income. Finally, he cannot use the optional tax tables, but he can use the standard deduction.

3.82   If averageable income exists, a special computation is made for the current year in order to determine the amount of tax attributable to the averageable income. To do this, the income for the current year, in effect, is structured into two tiers or layers. Because graduated rates are applicable, the first or bottom layer is subject to the lower rates of taxation, and the subsequent or higher layer is subject to higher rates. The first layer consists of an amount equal to the amount of nonaverageable income. The top layer is one-fifth of the amount of averageable income. From the total tax computed on both layers a tax computed on the nonaverageable income is then subtracted. The remainder represents the tax attributable to one-fifth of the averageable income. The tax attributable to 100 percent of the averageable income is then determined simply by multiplying by five. The actual tax for the year is the total of the tax on the nonaverageable income plus the tax attributable to the averageable income.

EXAMPLE   Mr. Brown, a married taxpayer filing a joint return, has taxable income for 1972 of $200,000. The gross income consisted of salary, dividends, interest, and a net includible Section 1201 gain of $100,000 (one-half of the full gain of $200,000). From this he subtracted itemized deductions and personal exemptions.

28. Code Sec. 1303(c) and (d).
29. Code Sec. 1303(c)(2)(A), (B), and (C).

For the base period years 1968 through 1971 his average taxable income was $40,000 and there was included in the years in which realized one-half of the full amounts of net long-term capital gains.

His tax computed in the regular way for 1972 is $110,980. His tax under the alternative method applicable to long-term capital gains is $106,430 as shown in Example 2 in paragraph 3.23. As a result of income averaging, however, his tax liability is reduced to $97,820, a saving of $8,610 over the alternative tax:

Tax on 120% of average base period net income of $40,000, namely $48,000		$16,060
Tax on averageable income — One-fifth of averageable income ($200,000 − $48,000 = $152,000 ÷ 5)	$30,400	
Tax on $78,400 ($48,000 + $30,400)	$32,412	
Less tax on $48,000	16,060	
Tax applicable to 1/5th of averageable income	$16,352	
Tax on averageable income (5 x $16,352)		81,760
Total tax on 1972 income with averaging		$97,820

MAXIMUM TAX ON EARNED INCOME

3.83 Professional men, executives, professional athletes, artists, and entertainers who derive a substantial portion of their income from personal services, have a new benefit starting with 1971. Code Section 1348 limits the tax on their "earned taxable income" to 60 percent for 1971 and 50 percent for 1972 and later years.

3.84 The amount of earned taxable income to which the ceiling rate applies is determined by, first, ascertaining what is gross earned income, second, reducing it by deductions for adjusted gross income that are attributable to the earned income, third, by allocating a part of the itemized deductions and exemptions to the adjusted gross earned income, and, fourth, by reducing the amount of the tentative "earned taxable income" so ascertained by excessive "tax preferences," if any.

3.85 Gross earned income includes all personal service earnings, such as salary and bonuses, fees of professional individuals, distributable share of the net income of a professional partnership, and royalties of an author. If the taxpayer is a proprietor or partner in a business where both personal services and capital are material income producing factors, earned income is a reasonable allowance as compensation for personal services rendered but not in excess of 30 percent of his share of the net profits. Finally, earned income for this purpose does not include most forms of deferred compensation, i.e., pensions and other amounts received under any kind of a plan in years subsequent to the years in which the compensation was earned. But a bonus received, for example, in 1972 for services rendered in 1971 based on a percentage of profits earned in 1971 is not considered to be deferred compensation; it is current income taxable to the recipient in 1972 and deductible by an accrual basis employer in 1971.[30]

3.86   From the amount of gross earned income then are subtracted deductions allowed in arriving at adjusted gross income to the extent that such deductions pertain to the earned income. The resulting amount is called "earned net income" in Section 1348(b)(2).

3.87   The next step is to determine "earned taxable income." The initial step is derived by applying this formula:

$$\frac{\text{Earned net income}}{\text{Adjusted gross income}} \times \text{Taxable income}$$

The ratio of earned net income to adjusted gross income cannot be more than 100 percent. If earned net income equals or exceeds adjusted gross income, then the taxable income is all earned taxable income. The effect of this formula, of course, is to reduce the amount of the earned net income by a portion (or all) of the itemized deductions and personal exemptions. From the amount so determined, the final step is to deduct the greater of (1) the individual's tax preferences (see paragraph 3.112) in excess of $30,000 in the current year, or (2) the excess of the individual's *average* of tax preferences for the current and prior four years, over $30,000. Because the concept of a tax preference first became effective in 1970, the average to be used for 1972 returns is one-third of the tax preference items for 1970, 1971, and 1972. The final step just described results in "earned taxable income."

3.88   The statutory computation of the ceiling requires separating the total taxable income into three tiers:

EXAMPLE   For 1972 a married individual's joint return shows taxable income of $105,000 composed of gross earned income of $110,000, interest and dividend income of $30,000, deductions of $15,000 in arriving at adjusted gross income of $125,000 (and of the $15,000 the amount of $10,000 is attributable to the gross earned income), and itemized deductions of $20,000 including personal exemptions. His tax preferences are less than $30,000.

Tier One: The amount of tax on the lowest amount of the taxable income on which the top tax rate would exceed 50%, namely $52,000.01 $18,060

30. Reg. 1.404(b)–1; Rev. Rul. 55–446, 1955–2 C.B. 531.

Tier Two: Determine the amount of earned
taxable income:

Gross earned income	$110,000	
Business expense deductions	10,000	
	————	
Earned net income	$100,000	
	════	

Earned taxable income ($100,000 earned net income/$125,000 adjusted gross income × $105,000 taxable income)	$ 84,000	
Less income taxed in first tier	52,000	
	————	
Balance of earned taxable income	$ 32,000	
	════	
Tax at 50% of $32,000		16,000
Tier Three: Tax at regular rates on total taxable income of $105,000	$ 48,280	
Less tax at regular rates on total earned taxable income of $84,000	35,660	
	————	
Balance of tax		12,620
		————
Tax payable		$46,680
		════

The limitation saves the taxpayer $1,600 ($48,280 regular tax on $105,000 less the tax payable of $46,680).

3.89   The benefit of the maximum tax on earned income is not available to a married person filing a separate return or to any individual electing income averaging.

CREDITS AGAINST THE TAX

3.90   Part IV of Subchapter A in Chapter 1 of the Code contains a list of a number of credits allowable directly against the tax. A tax credit can be more significant than a deduction of an equal amount, since an allowable deduction produces a tax benefit only to the extent of the effective tax rate in the taxpayer's top bracket multiplied by the amount of the deduction. Tax credits, on the other hand, are applied directly against the tax and reduce it dollar for dollar.

The principal types of credits are for:

Income tax withheld from wages
Excess social security taxes
Retirement income
Foreign taxes

Excise taxes paid on purchases of gasoline and lubricating oil to the extent
such fuel and oil was consumed in nonhighway use
Investment in certain depreciable property

Income Tax Withheld and Estimated Tax Payments

3.91   Each January, every employer is required to give each employee
two copies of Form W-2 showing the total amount of compensation
paid to him during the past year, the amount of income tax withheld,
and the amount of the employee's portion of the social security tax
withheld. The amount of the income tax shown on this form as having
been withheld is deductible as a credit from the computed amount of
the total tax shown on Form 1040 or Form 1040A and a copy of Form
W-2 itself is then attached to the tax return.

3.92   As discussed starting in paragraph 3.124, each year many individuals as they earn their income make "quarterly" payments of their
estimated income tax liability for that year. The total of these advance
payments is then deducted from the computed liability when return
Form 1040 (but not on Form 1040A) is filed after the close of the year.
These payments are not enumerated in the aforementioned Part IV
of Subchapter A in Chapter 1 of the Code as a tax credit, but have the
same effect because of Section 6315.

Excess Social Security Taxes

3.93   Each employer is required to withhold social security taxes from the
first $9,000 of wages paid to each employee in 1972. For 1973 the
amount is $10,800. However, each individual is subject to social
security tax only on total wages in those amounts received by him in
those calendar years. If he has more than one employer in a year,
social security taxes may be withheld on aggregate wages of more
than $9,000 or $10,800. A refund of the excess withholding can be
obtained by claiming the amount as a credit against his income tax
computed on Form 1040, not Form 1040A. The social security tax
rates are given in paragraph 1.23.

Retirement Income

3.94   The retirement income credit contained in Section 37 of the Code
was added to the tax law with the enactment of the 1954 Code. It is
available to all individuals sixty-five years of age or more and to individuals of any age receiving pensions or annuities from a public
retirement system of a governmental body. The purpose of the credit
is to benefit persons who do not receive the maximum primary social
security benefits but do have designated types of passive income
up to a maximum amount.[31] This maximum amount approximates
the maximum primary amount of social security benefits, the latter

31. S. Rep. 2202, 87th Cong., 2d sess., 1962–3 C.B. 1238.

being tax-free. The maximum amount of passive income, however, must be reduced by any social security benefits received, varying portions of earned income received before age seventy-two, and a few other types of income. Only the net amount qualifies for the credit at the rate of 15 percent. *The small amount of credit gained is sometimes not worth the time spent in computing it.*

3.95 Almost all types of income commonly considered to be passive income qualify, such as pensions, annuities, interest, rent, and dividends. The maximum amount of the total of these items taken into account for an unmarried individual is $1,524. For married couples, both sixty-five or over, who file a joint return and each of whom have passive income, the combined limit is $2,286. From these respective maximum amounts there then must be deducted any social security, railroad retirement, military retirement, or other pension excluded by law from gross income; but military disability pensions, private disability pensions, workmen's compensation payments, and the nontaxable return of capital portion of annuities need not be deducted. Further, the respective amounts of passive income are subject to reduction for earned income. If the person is seventy-two or more, there is no reduction. If he is sixty-five or over, but not yet seventy-two, there is no reduction for the first $1,200 of earnings but a reduction of 50¢ for every $1 of earnings between $1,200 and $1,700 and a reduction of $1 for each $1 of earnings in excess of $1,700.

3.96 In order to qualify for the retirement income credit, an individual must have received earned income in excess of $600 in each of any ten calendar years before the taxable year. A surviving spouse is deemed to have received earned income if the deceased husband or wife met this test. Similarly, if both spouses are sixty-five or over and file a joint return, each spouse is deemed to have received earned income if one of them meets the test.

3.97 The credit is not available to the following types of persons:

Individuals receiving social security or railroad retirement benefits in excess of $1,524
Individuals having earned income of $2,974 if less than seventy-two years of age
Nonresident aliens

Foreign Taxes

3.98 Each year a taxpayer has an option to either deduct or claim the credit for foreign income, war profits, and excess profits taxes. The election can be made or changed at any time within the period of limitations applicable to filing a claim for refund. The deduction is allowed by Section 164 and the credit by Section 33. If a credit is elected, individuals should compute its amount on Form 1116. This form is then attached to the related return.

3.99 Subject to certain limitations, citizens and domestic corporations are allowed credit for "... any income, war profits, and excess profits taxes paid or accrued during the taxable year to any foreign country or any possession of the United States." [32] Special provisions apply to resident aliens and Puerto Rico.

3.100   To be eligible for credit, the foreign tax must be imposed upon income or profits or, under Code Sec. 903, must be a tax imposed "in lieu of" such an income or profits tax. Ordinarily, property or excise taxes would not qualify under this test but might nevertheless be deductible under Sec. 164, as a business expense under Sec. 162, or under Sec. 212 as an expense incurred in the production of income.

3.101   Some foreign taxes are withheld in foreign countries from remittances of dividends, interest, royalties, or other investment income. If such taxes are of the proper type, they will qualify for the foreign tax credit as well as taxes upon foreign earnings paid directly, rather than by withholding.

3.102   Although a taxpayer may deduct or claim a credit for foreign taxes, he may not make a separate choice for each foreign tax. All must be treated as deductions, or all must be used as a credit.[33] The taxpayer also has the choice of handling his foreign taxes for credit purposes on either the cash or the accrual basis; but if he elects the accrual method, his decision is binding for future years. Even a cash basis taxpayer can use the accrual method in computing his foreign tax credit. Because of the mechanics of the limitation formula on the amount of a foreign tax credit (see paragraph 3.103), it is usually better to use the accrual method.

3.103   One of the most significant features of the foreign tax credit, and one that seems to cause a great deal of confusion and difficulty, is the provision limiting the foreign tax credit to a certain proportion of the taxpayer's United States income taxes.[34] The proportion is found by multiplying the United States tax by a fraction, the numerator of which consists of the taxpayer's income from foreign sources to the extent that it is includible on his United States income tax return, and the denominator of which is the taxpayer's total United States taxable income. As a result, if a taxpayer is using the cash method in claiming a foreign tax credit and if in a particular year he paid foreign taxes but had no foreign source income, the numerator of the fraction would be zero, and no credit would be available. In determining what is income from foreign sources, the rules in sections 861 to 865 are used.

3.104   This limitation may be computed, at the taxpayer's option, on either a "per country" basis or on an "overall" basis. If a taxpayer has income from more than one foreign country, he may compute the limitation separately for each country, using as the numerator of the limiting fraction only the income from sources in that country. On the other hand, he may elect to use the overall limitation and include in the numerator of the limiting fraction his total income from foreign

32. Code Sec. 901(b)(1).
33. Reg. 1.901–1(c).
34. Code Sec. 904.

sources. If he elects the overall limitation, he may not switch back and forth between the per country limitation and the overall limitation; election of the latter is binding for future years.

The purpose of the foreign tax credit is to eliminate double taxation, but the choice of a mechanical formula as a limiting factor results in a system that does not always work perfectly to fulfill that purpose. A correlation between the foreign taxes paid or accrued, and for which a foreign tax credit is sought, and the income from foreign sources which appears in the numerator of the limiting fraction need not exist. Where there is no such correlation, and where there is quite a difference between the United States tax rate and the foreign tax rate, a taxpayer may receive a benefit in excess of mere elimination of double taxation or, on the other hand, may suffer double taxation, at least to some extent. **3.105**

A taxpayer who is a United States citizen lives and works in country A. **EXAMPLE** His total income, $20,000, is $10,000 in salary from an employer in country A and $10,000 from property also in that country. This $20,000 is taxable in country A, and he pays a total tax of $2,000 on the amount. The effective rate is thus 10 percent. His $10,000 salary is exempt from United States income tax under Code Sec. 911. Since he is a United States citizen, however, his income from property in country A is fully taxable in the United States. Thus, he has total taxable income of $10,000 for United States tax purposes. If he pays a tax of $2,000 in the United States on this amount, his total effective rate in the United States is 20 percent. Based upon these facts—and the assumption that the taxpayer has no other income from foreign sources—his foreign tax credit will be the entire $2,000 paid to country A. Because the foreign tax rate is lower than the United States tax rate, he is, in effect, crediting against his United States tax the entire amount of a foreign tax, 50 percent of which is based upon income *not* taxable in the United States. The numerator of the limiting fraction is $10,000, the amount of United States taxable income from sources in country A, and the denominator of the limiting fraction is also $10,000, being his entire amount of taxable income in the United States. Thus, 100 percent of the total taxes of $2,000 paid to country A may be credited against the United States tax.

Excise Taxes on Nonhighway Use of Gasoline and Lubricating Oil

The Excise Tax Reduction Act of 1965 added Code Sec. 39, primarily to give farmers a more convenient way to secure refunds for gasoline tax paid on gasoline used for farming. Prior to the addition of Section 39, farmers claimed this refund by filing a special form. The present method of tax credit is available also to those who use gasoline or lubricating oil for off-highway purposes such as operating a boat or a local transit system. **3.106**

Investment Credit

A direct credit against tax is provided by Sections 38 and 46 through 48. The amount is usually 7 percent of the cost of certain tangible depreciable property used in a trade or business or in any operation **3.107** entered into for profit. The subject is quite technical and is discussed in chapter 8.

Political Contributions

3.108   Commencing with the calendar year 1972, there is available a small credit or deduction for political contributions paid [Section 41 added by the Revenue Act of 1971]. Each taxpayer each year has an option to claim a maximum credit of $25 on joint returns ($12.50 on other returns) or a maximum deduction of $100 on joint returns ($50 on other returns), but not both. The credit is one-half of the total contributions to one or more candidates for public office, but not in excess of the aforementioned ceiling of $25 or $12.50. The deduction is for the full amount of the contribution to one or more candidates, but subject to the ceiling previously mentioned of $100 or $50. The full cost of a ticket to a political dinner, subject to the maximum limitations, ordinarily will qualify as a political contribution, but the purchase price of a raffle ticket will not [Proposed Reg. 1.41–1].

SELF–EMPLOYMENT TAX

3.109   In 1950 a law was enacted imposing a tax on "self-employment income," in order to provide social security benefits for the self-employed. The tax is now found in Internal Revenue Code Sections 1401 to 1403. As originally enacted, a substantial number of occupations, primarily the liberal professions, were exempted from its application. Through the years, however, these exemptions have gradually been removed; the only significant remaining exemption applies to ministers who, nevertheless, may elect to be covered by the law, provided that they make the necessary application for its benefits. Since amendments in 1965, a member of a religious faith that does not sanction insurance benefit programs may make application to be left out of the program. If his application is approved, he must also waive any social security benefits.

3.110   As it now stands, the tax is applied to the first $9,000 for 1972, ($10,800 for 1973, and $12,600 for 1974) of defined net earnings from self-employment reduced by the amount of any wages subject to social security taxes. If such net earnings amount to less than $400, the tax does not apply. Farmers are given special treatment by being permitted to make a simpler determination of net earnings from self-employment in relation to the gross income of farm operations.

3.111   As presently scheduled, the tax rate applied to self-employment income is set at 7.5 percent for 1972 and at 8.00 percent for 1973 and 1974. These rates cover not only the old-age, survivors, and disability insurance program of the social security system, but also the cost of hospital insurance. For collection purposes, the tax is treated as if it were an income tax. It is computed on the taxpayer's income tax return and paid with whatever balance of income tax is due. Self-employment tax is taken into account along with income tax when a taxpayer files a declaration of estimated tax.

MINIMUM TAX ON TAX PREFERENCES

There are many provisions in the Code that grant favored treatment to certain types of income or large deductions for certain types of expenses. As a result, in years prior to 1970 it was possible for tax-conscious wealthy individuals to pay little or no tax, even though they had large amounts of economic income. The Treasury reported that for 1966 there were at least 154 returns showing adjusted gross incomes of $200,000 or more but no tax liability.[35] Primarily to obtain some tax from these few hundred individuals, the concept of a "minimum tax on tax preferences," was proposed in the House of Representatives in 1969. In the form in which the Tax Reform Act of 1969 passed the House, the tax would have applied only to individuals, estates, and trusts, but as enacted it also applies to corporations. The provisions are in Code Sections 56 through 58 and apply to 1970 and later years. 3.112

The annual rate of tax is a flat 10 percent and is applied to the total of nine enumerated "tax preference" items reduced by: 3.113

(1) A flat $30,000 exemption;
(2) The income tax imposed for the same taxable year after reduction by any foreign tax, retirement income, investment, work incentive program, and political contribution credits.

Further, there is a carryover for seven years of unapplied income taxes. If for 1970 or any later year a taxpayer is not liable for the minimum tax on tax preferences, then his income tax liability for that year, to the extent not applied to offset tax preference income, can be carried forward for seven years to offset tax preference income of those years. In other words, if for 1970 a taxpayer had no tax preference income but paid income taxes of $40,000, then the $40,000 (but not any part of the $30,000 exemption) can be carried forward one by one to each of the seven subsequent years to offset preference income of those respective years which is in excess of the annual $30,000 exemption.

The items of tax preference are listed in Section 57. Only one of them at this point in the book will be familiar to the student. This is the deduction allowed by Section 1202 for 50 percent of the excess of a net long-term capital gain over any net short-term capital loss. That deduction, allowed in computing the regular or alternative income tax, is a tax preference for purposes of the minimum tax. 3.114

Interest received on municipal bonds continues to be exempt from the regular income tax and also from the minimum tax. 3.115

35. Summary of H.R. 13270, Tax Reform Act of 1969, November 18, 1969, prepared by the Staff of the Joint Committee on Internal Revenue Taxation for the use of the Committee on Finance, p. 40.

3.116   There will be relatively few instances in which there will be any 10 percent minimum tax payable and most of those that do occur will result from net long-term capital gain income. Contrary to press releases issued at the time of the congressional hearings, the minimum tax is certainly no bar to middle- and upper-bracket taxpayers who seek investments that produce tax-exempt income, or tax shelter for ordinary income or means of converting ordinary income into capital gain. However, if most of such a taxpayer's income is from personal services, the new tax ceiling on earned income (60 percent for 1971 and 50 percent for 1972 and later years) ordinarily will render some of the devices no longer attractive. A venture producing current deductions and possible long-term capital gain later, but which has a high degree of risk, is not desirable when the tax benefit from the deductions is only 50 percent and any resulting long-term capital gain above $50,000 can be taxed at 35 percent.

EXAMPLE

TAXABLE INCOME	1971	1972
Salary	$40,000	$40,000
Dividend and interest income	10,000	—
Net rental income	20,000	20,000
Long-term capital gain on sale of investment land, a Section 1231 asset, full amount $60,000 and includible amount	—	30,000
Totals—adjusted gross income	$70,000	$90,000
Itemized deductions and exemptions	10,000	10,000
Taxable income	$60,000	$80,000
Income tax (Joint returns)	$22,300	$32,150

MINIMUM TAX ON TAX PREFERENCES

	1971	1972
Tax preference items-		
Excess of accelerated depreciation claimed in determining net income from rental property over straight-line depreciation	$25,000	$22,000
Excess of fair market value on date of exercise of qualified stock options over price paid	15,000	26,000
Untaxed one-half of net long-term capital gain	—	30,000
Totals	$40,000	$78,000
Less-		
Exemption	$30,000	$30,000
Income tax of current year	22,300	32,150
Carry-over	—	12,300
Totals	$52,300	$74,450

Excess of $22,300 income tax for 1971 over tax preference items exceeding $30,000 ($40,000 − $30,000)	$12,300	
Net preference income		$ 3,550
Minimum tax at 10%	$ —	$ 355
TOTAL TAXES		
Income tax	$22,300	$32,150
Minimum tax on tax preferences	—	355
Totals	$22,300	$32,505

Note: There was no carryover of unapplied income tax for 1970 because a minimum tax on tax preferences was paid for that year.

WHO MUST FILE RETURNS

The obligation to file a return depends upon both the amount of gross income and marital status in the year. For 1972 and later years, Section 6012 requires a return to be filed under the following circumstances: 3.117

(1) Single person — gross income of at least $2,050 if under sixty-five and $2,800 if sixty-five or over.
(2) Single person who can be claimed as a dependent on parents' return and who has unearned investment income — gross income of at least $750.
(3) Married persons — combined gross income of at least $2,800 if both spouses are under sixty-five; $3,550 if one is sixty-five or over; and $4,300 if both are sixty-five or over.

The gross income amounts for married persons apply only if (1) they have the same household as their home at end of taxable year (or at date of death of husband or wife), (2) they file jointly, and (3) neither is the dependent of another taxpayer, such as a newly married child could be. If any one of these conditions does not apply, the filing requirement is $750 even if the taxpayer was sixty-five before the end of the tax year. Even if the aforementioned gross income requirements are not met, a return nevertheless must be filed if an individual had earnings from self-employment of $400 or more.

These return filing requirements apply to every citizen of the United States, whether he resides here or abroad, and to every alien resident in the United States, and in each instance whether an adult or a minor.   3.118

WHEN AND WHERE TO FILE

3.119   Individual returns are due on the fifteenth day of the fourth month following the end of the taxable year, with two major exceptions. Since most individuals file their tax returns on the basis of the calendar year, the following comments are expressed in terms of a calendar year taxpayer. Appropriate adjustments of dates should be made for fiscal year returns. The calendar year return is due by April 15 of the following year, with these two exceptions:

1. If the taxpayer resides or is traveling outside the United States (and Puerto Rico) on April 15, he has an automatic extension to June 15.
2. If he has filed a declaration of estimated tax, he can elect *not* to pay the fourth installment due January 15, provided he files his return by January 31.

3.120   An automatic extension of time for two months beyond April 15 can be obtained by an individual taxpayer by filing a properly signed Form 4868 with the office of the Service in which his return must be filed [Reg. 1.6081–4]. He is required to make a tentative estimate of his tax for the year just ended and to pay any balance of such tentative tax when filing this form. If, when the final return is later filed, there is any unpaid balance, the amount bears interest at 6 percent per annum from the original due date of April 15 to the date of payment. The late payment penalty of one-half of 1 percent a month up to a maximum of 25 percent on the unpaid balance (described in the second indented subparagraph of paragraph 2.43) will apply unless there is reasonable cause. Reasonable cause will be deemed to exist if the balance due on return Form 1040 when filed does not exceed 10 percent of the amount shown as total tax and such balance due is remitted with the 1040 return. Returns are mailed to the Internal Revenue Service Center having jurisdiction over the area in which the taxpayer lives, but a hand-carried return may be filed in the office of the local District Director.

3.121   Since 1966, Section 7502 has treated timely mailing as timely filing: an individual return due April 15 will be treated as filed on time if mailed on April 15. Furthermore, when the regular due date falls on Saturday, Sunday, or a legal holiday, the law postpones the due date until the next succeeding business day (Section 7503).

3.122   If the Form 1040 shows an unpaid balance after credits for tax withheld from wages and prepayments in connection with a declaration of estimated tax, the amount must be remitted with the return. If the return reflects an overpayment, the taxpayer indicates on the return whether he wants the excess refunded or credited on his declaration of estimated tax for the current year. If he elects to take a refund, his return may be examined by the IRS before the refund is allowed, particularly if the amount of the refund is large. Assuming that a refund is requested and that there is no examination (or that an examination results in no changes in the figures), the IRS will issue a refund check without further action by the taxpayer. If the refund occurs within forty-five days after the due date of the return or the date it is actually filed, whichever is later, the IRS need not pay interest on the amount of the overpayment; a later refund carries interest at the rate of 6 percent per year or one-half of one percent a month.[36]

Every return must be signed by the taxpayer, and, if it is a joint return, both spouses must sign it. An unsigned return is no return. In *Peter Vaira* [37], a timely filed return was accompanied by a signed check for the balance of tax shown to be due, but the taxpayer "overlooked" signing the return. A delinquency penalty (see paragraph 2.43) was imposed at the rate of 25 percent of a later assessed deficiency, because "overlooking" the signing of a return does not constitute reasonable cause.

3.123

DECLARATION OF ESTIMATED TAX

The income tax liability is on a "pay as you go" basis. There is withholding on wages and a requirement that many individuals also file a declaration of estimated tax for the current year. Section 6015, as amended by the Revenue Act of 1971, requires a declaration to be filed if the taxpayer's gross income from all sources can "reasonably be expected to exceed" $20,000 in the case of a single person, head of household, surviving spouse, or a married couple entitled to file an estimate jointly provided that only one spouse works. If both work, the income level is $10,000. A married individual not entitled to file jointly, such as where one of the spouses is a nonresident alien, must file a declaration if gross income exceeds $5,000. Further, in any case, a declaration must be filed and payments made if gross income from nonwage sources exceeds $500. But no declaration is required where estimated tax liability (after credits, including withholding) is expected to be less than $100. Generally, a declaration must be filed by April 15, and the balance of estimated tax shown due thereon (after credit for withholding from wages,) is to be paid in equal installments on April 15, June 15, September 15, and January 15 of the following year. However, a farmer need not file any declaration until January 15 after the close of the year and can omit it completely if he files his return Form 1040 by March 1 accompanied by payment of the full amount of tax.

3.124

The amount of the estimated tax includes both the regular income tax and any self-employment tax, but does not include the 10 percent minimum tax on tax preferences.

3.125

The declaration form is numbered 1040–ES and since 1969 is entitled "Estimated Tax Declaration—Voucher for Individuals." It calls only for insertion of the taxpayer's name, address, social security number, amount of total estimated tax for the year, and the amount of

3.126

36. Code Sec. 6611(a) and (e).
37. 52 T.C. 986 (1969) (Acq.)

the payment attached. No computation of the estimated tax need be filed.

3.127   A nondeductible penalty at the rate of 6 percent per annum is imposed by Section 6654 upon the amount of underpayment of estimated tax for the period of underpayment. With exceptions to be found in Section 6654(d), an underpayment exists if the amount of the installment required to be paid is less than an amount based upon 80 percent (66⅔ percent in the case of farmers and fishermen) of the tax after credits shown on the return for the year. In other words, an individual who is required to make a payment of estimated tax on April 15 must pay on or before that day at least one-fourth of 80 percent of the amount of tax after credits that will be shown on his return for that year and make similar payments on the following June 15, September 15, and January 15. The period of underpayment runs from the due date of the installment to the earlier of (a) the date upon which the deficiency in amount is paid or (b) the due date of the return, namely, April 15 for most individuals. The penalty can be avoided by having an employer withhold an extra amount in December. Amounts withheld at any time during the year are aggregated and one-fourth of the total is subtracted from the required payments of estimated tax due on the four dates.

QUESTIONS AND PROBLEMS

1. Indicate whether each of the following items is directly deductible: in determining gross income; from gross income to determine adjusted gross income; or from adjusted gross income to determine taxable income:
   (a) Purchases of inventory by a proprietor
   (b) Salaries paid sales clerks by a proprietor
   (c) Contributions to a church
   (d) Purchase price of a real estate broker's advertisement in a printed program for a play sponsored by, and put on to raise funds for: (1) the athletic department of the local public high school, (2) a church, (3) a hospital, (4) an opera association, (5) local businessmen's association. In each instance the advertisement showed the broker's name, address, and occupation.
   (e) Medical expenses
   (f) Automobile expense of an outside salesman
   (g) Utility bills of a store owner
   (h) Nonreimbursed entertainment expense of an employee
   (i) State income taxes paid by a partner on his share of partnership net income

2. Tom Goeasy, age fifty, does not bother to separate his allowable deductions into those allowed in arriving at adjusted gross income and those deductible from adjusted gross income. Tom feels that since he always elects to itemize, anyway, the classification of his expenses should not be of any concern to the Internal Revenue Service.

Among his deductions this year are $10,000 in charitable contributions and $3,500 in medical expenditures.

Is Tom correct in his attitude?

3. An unmarried individual has adjusted gross income of $6,500. During the year he sustained a casualty loss that he claimed was in the amount of $2,000. As a result, he claimed itemized deductions totaling $2,300 on his return. Upon examination of his return, the IRS disallowed the full amount of the claimed casualty loss. Other than appealing the decision of IRS, what can this taxpayer do about the amount of his deductions?

4. For 1973 a husband has adjusted gross income of $12,000 and his wife $5,000.

   (a) What amount of standard deduction is available on a joint return?

   (b) What amounts are available on separate returns?

5. A wife is separated from her husband during the entire year 1972 and maintains a home for herself and two children under nineteen. For the year she had adjusted gross income of $8,000 and also received $2,000 from her husband for the support of the children. Such amount constituted 75 percent of their entire support. Assuming she files a separate return, what amount of standard deduction can she claim and what rate table can she use?

6. Mr. O'Keefe, a sixty-six-year-old widower, furnished chief support for three children, all under nineteen years of age, and his ninety-year-old father. One of the children earned $760 in summer employment. Mr. O'Keefe's father received $765 in social security benefits, but had no other income. How many exemptions are allowable to Mr. O'Keefe?

7. State the number of exemptions allowable to the taxpayers in each of the following cases, assuming the persons supported are citizens or residents of the United States:

   (a) Husband and wife, the taxpayers, live together during the entire year and file a joint return. The wife has no income. Their son, aged twenty-three, is away at college, and more than half of his support is furnished by the father, who also furnishes the entire support for their son's wife, aged twenty-one. The son's wife has no income of her own. The son earns $800 per year during summer employment.

   (b) The taxpayer, a son, furnishes the entire support of his widowed mother, aged sixty-seven, who has no income of her own.

   (c) The three taxpayers, who are sisters, support their widowed mother, who has no income of her own. Each sister contributes one-third of the mother's total support.

   (d) The taxpayer, a widower, sixty-six years of age, maintains a home where he supports the daughter (aged fifteen) of a deceased friend. She has no other means of support. The taxpayer is the guardian of the person supported but is not related to her by blood, marriage, or adoption.

   (e) H and W were married on July 1. W had $300 income for the year. H had gross income of $5,000. To what exemptions is H entitled if he files a separate return?

   (f) The taxpayer entirely supported his blind father, who died at age sixty-two on September 1. What exemption, if any, is the taxpayer entitled to for his deceased father for the calendar year in which he died?

8. In 1973, John and his sister Mary supported their widowed mother, who had no income of her own. The mother lived in a separate apartment. During the period January 1 to August 31, 1973, John provided $800 toward the general support of his mother. He also paid $1,600 during the year for rent on the apartment and other expenses of maintaining the mother's home. During the period September 1, 1973 to December 31, 1973, Mary provided $800 toward general support of her mother and paid $1,700 extraordinary medical expenses that her mother incurred in a sudden illness.

(a) Who is entitled to claim the dependency deduction for 1973 for the mother? Explain.

(b) May a multiple-support agreement be entered into, whereby either John or Mary can claim the credit for their dependent mother? Explain briefly.

(c) May either Mary or John use the head-of-household rates? Explain briefly.

9. Mrs. Jones, a widow since January 30, 1969, maintained a home for her infant son until she remarried on February 12, 1973. What type of returns are or were due from her for each of the years 1969, 1970, 1971, 1972, and 1973?

10. May any of the following be a head of a household? Why, or why not?

(a) An unmarried individual living in Philadelphia but maintaining a home for a dependent child in Knoxville, Tennessee.

(b) An unmarried individual who maintains a home that is the principal abode of a dependent cousin.

(c) An individual who is legally separated from his spouse under a decree of divorce and who, while living in Chicago, maintains a home for his dependent mother in Boston.

(d) An unmarried individual who maintains a home that is the principal abode of his married daughter who filed jointly with her husband.

(e) An unmarried individual who maintains a home that is the principal abode of his dependent father. The father has less than $750 in income. The taxpayer furnished one-third of the support of the father but claims the father as a dependent under a "multiple-support agreement."

11. To qualify as head of household, one must pay more than half the cost of its maintenance. Indicate which of the following expenses do not constitute maintenance for this purpose: (a) domestic help, (b) mortgage interest, (c) insurance on dwelling, (d) medical treatment, (e) food consumed in the home.

12. For the preceding calendar year a married couple had the following income and expenses:

	HUSBAND	WIFE
Salary and bonus	$120,000	$ —
Interest received on —		
Corporate bonds	—	300
Savings account	—	100
Municipal bonds	1,000	—
Net long-term capital gain	60,000	—
Net short-term capital (loss)	(4,000)	—
Real estate taxes on home	(2,500)	—

Charitable contribution to church and local community fund	(2,000)	—	of
Investment counsel fee	(200)	—	Individual
Fee paid C.P.A. for preparation of return	(150)	—	Returns
State income tax	(5,000)	—	

The husband became sixty-five years of age on December 1 of that year and the wife is sixty. They have an unmarried invalid daughter, age twenty-three, living at home who had $800 of investment income and also have a twenty-five-year-old unmarried son, who attends medical school. The son earned $1,600 during the summer and had $400 of dividend income. During the year he spent $500 for clothes and banked the balance. The son had a nontaxable scholarship of $3,000 and the father paid $1,000 towards his support.

For the four preceding taxable years, the joint returns of the husband and wife showed taxable income of $40,000, $50,000, $60,000, and $70,000.

What is the minimum amount of tax liability? Show all calculations.

13. Is each of the following statements true or false? An individual, otherwise qualified, is entitled to the retirement income credit when he:
    (a) elects to file a joint return with his spouse who earned more than $3,000 during the year.
    (b) is sixty-six years of age and his only income is from the operation of rental property, managed by an agent, from which he reports net profits of $4,500 for the year.
    (c) is an author, sixty-six years of age, and his only gross income consisted of royalties of $3,600.

14. During the taxable year, a married citizen of the United States had $1,000 taxable income from Country X, $1,000 from Country Y, and a total adjusted gross income of $58,000. He itemized $1,000 deductions and had $57,000 taxable income reported in his joint U.S. return. Assume a tentative United States tax of $20,710, a tax of $150 to Country X, and a tax of $400 to Country Y. What is the maximum foreign tax credit on a per country basis? On an overall limitation basis?

15. Zip Cody, as a hobby, develops automobile engines and tests them on his own property. During the taxable year, he spent $4,500 on gasoline for testing the engines. Of that amount $900 constituted federal gasoline taxes.

    Zip was told that federal taxes generally are not deductible, and he has not considered deducting the taxes when filling out his tax return. Is he correct?

16. In the above problem, assume that Zip was in the business of developing automobile engines. The federal gasoline tax would then be an expense deductible in computing adjusted gross income. Should Zip include the tax in the amounts deductible in computing adjusted gross income? Assume that all income is from the business and Zip takes the standard deduction.

17. Arthur Guthrie, who is sixty-nine years of age, operates a small watch repair shop. In 1970, he had gross income of $1,500 and business expenses of $400. Is he liable for any self-employment tax?

18. Jack Fainman works as a TV repairman for the Orbit TV stores. During his off-hours, he repairs television sets as a separate business of his own. Last year, Fainman earned $10,000 from Orbit and was

subject to social security and withholding taxes. He also earned $3,500 from his own TV repair business. Is Fainman subject to the self-employment tax?

19. George Rathman received a salary of $45,000 as an actor in 1972 and had a taxable income of $42,000. Taxable income for the four preceding years was $6,000, $10,000, $14,000, and $18,000, and the gross income from which these amounts of taxable income were derived consisted entirely of salary. For income averaging in 1972, Rathman's averageable income is (select one):
   (a) $30,000
   (b) $26,000
   (c) $24,000
   (d) $18,000
   (e) None of the above

20. Peterson is a partner in a large public accounting firm. He is married, under 65, and for all years under consideration has filed joint individual income tax returns. As pointed out in Chapters 4 and 18, he is taxable each year on his share of the partnership's income whether distributed to him or not. Further, as required by the particular partnership agreement, he is required to pay his own expenses for luncheon club dues, lunches for clients, and professional society dues. These are called nonreimbursed business expenses and are deductible. For 1973 his taxable income consisted of the following elements:

Partnership ordinary income (his share)	$105,000
Less nonreimbursed business expenses	10,000
Net	$ 95,000
Dividend and interest income	2,000
Net long-term capital gain (full amount $40,000)	20,000
Adjusted gross income	$117,000
Less itemized deductions and personal exemptions	20,000
Taxable income	$ 97,000

For the four preceding taxable years, his taxable income was as follows:

1969	$ 40,000
1970	100,000
1971	80,000
1972	70,000

   (a) Compute the amount of his 1973 tax liability (1) in the ordinary manner, (2) using the alternative tax on net long-term capital gains, (3) using income averaging, and (4) using the maximum tax on earned income.
   (b) Can Peterson use income averaging plus any reduction resulting from the alternative tax on net long-term capital gains?
   (c) Can he use income averaging plus any reductions resulting from the maximum tax on earned income?

21. For the calendar year 1972 an individual filed his U.S. Individual

Income Tax Return, Form 1040, on June 15, 1973, pursuant to an automatic extension of time obtained by filing Form 4868 on April 10, 1973. At the time of filing Form 4868, he made the following calculations and representations:

Tentative total U.S. income tax for the year	$30,000
Less:—	
Withholding by employer	15,000
Additional payments from 4-15-72 through 1-15-73 on vouchers for declaration of estimated tax	2,000
	$17,000
Balance due 4-15-73	$13,000

He paid the amount of $13,000 on April 10, 1973, when he filed Form 4868. On June 15, 1973, he filed his return and it disclosed:

Total U.S. income tax for the year	$35,000
Less:—	
Withholding by employer	$15,000
Additional payments from 4-15-72 through 1-15-73 on vouchers for declaration of estimated tax	2,000
Payment on 4-10-73	13,000
	$30,000
Balance of tax due and paid 6-15-73	$ 5,000

The payment of estimated tax on the declaration vouchers were "no penalty" types because they were based on last year's tax liability. (a) Does this individual on 6-15-73 owe any interest? (b) Any penalty? (c) How much, if any of each? No fraud or negligence is involved.

22. Using the same facts as in Problem 21 and under the general rule: Until what date can he file a claim for refund and until what date can the government assert a deficiency?

4

ELEMENTS
OF OTHER
RETURNS

CORPORATIONS . . . 91

    Return Form 1120 . . . 91

        DUE DATE, PAYMENTS, AND EXTENSIONS . . . 91

    Taxable Income . . . 94
    Dividends Received Deduction . . . 94
    Dividends Paid . . . 95
    Foreign Tax Credit . . . 95
    Other Credits . . . 96
    Tax Rates . . . 96
    Payments of Estimated Tax . . . 97

        PENALTY . . . 97

PARTNERSHIPS . . . 98

    Information Return Form 1065 . . . 98
    Taxable Income . . . 99
    Pass Through of Special Items . . . 99

TRUSTS AND ESTATES . . . 100

    Form 1041 . . . 100
    Taxation of Trust and Estate Income in General . . . 101
    Trust or Estate Income Taxable to Beneficiaries . . . 102

MINIMUM TAX ON TAX PREFERENCES . . . 102

CORPORATIONS

Most of the basic rules concerning gross income and deductions 4.1
discussed in other chapters apply to corporations; however, a number
of additional rules apply exclusively to corporations. A corporation
is a taxable entity separate and apart from its owners or stockholders.
It incurs its own income tax liability on its own taxable income. However, there is a special type of corporation, known as a "Subchapter S
Corporation," that to *some* extent is treated like a partnership. Its
income or loss flows through to the individual stockholders. They
must be few in number and adhere to stringent rules about electing
and preserving that status. The subject is discussed in chapter 19.
Here, we are talking only about the ordinary business corporation.

Return Form 1120

On accompanying pages there are reproduced copies of page one 4.2
and Schedules J, M–1, and M–2 of the return form. Another important schedule not reproduced is Schedule L, comparative balance
sheets as of the beginning and end of the year.

Due Date, Payments, and Extensions. The corporation income tax 4.3
return must be filed by the fifteenth day of the third calendar month
following the end of the taxable year.[1] An automatic extension of
ninety days may be secured simply by filing Form 7004 properly
filled out and paying at least one-half of the balance of tax liability
shown on that form.[2] Additional extensions (up to a total of six months
including the automatic ninety-day period) may be granted upon
written request,[3] ordinarily by filing Form 7005.

Regardless of extensions, one-half of any balance of tax due (after 4.4
credit for previous payments of estimated tax) must be paid by the
normal due date, and the other half three months later.[4] As explained
in paragraph 2.43 any underpayment of tax, whether or not shown on
the return, incurs interest at the rate of 6 percent per annum; and any
underpayment of an amount *shown on a return* also results in a nondeductible penalty of one-half of one percent a month up to a maximum of 25 percent. Return Form 1120, if filed by mail, must be mailed
to the Internal Revenue Service Center designated in the instructions
accompanying the form. If hand-delivered, it can be filed with the
local District Director. However, payments must be made by deposits

1. Sec. 6072(b).
2. Sec. 6081(b).
3. Reg. 1.6081–1(a).
4. Sec. 6152.

U.S. Corporation Income Tax Return

Form 1120

Department of the Treasury
Internal Revenue Service

For calendar year 1972 or other taxable year beginning

.... , 1972, ending .... , 19 ....
(PLEASE TYPE OR PRINT)

1972

Check if a—

A Consolidated return ☐

B Personal Holding Co. ☐

C Business Code No. (See page 7 of instructions.)

Name

Number and street

City or town, State, and ZIP code

D Employer Identification No.

E County in which located

F Enter total assets from line 14, column (D), Schedule L (See instruction R)

$

IMPORTANT—Fill in all applicable lines and schedules. If the lines on the schedules are not sufficient, see instruction N.

$

GROSS INCOME

1 Gross receipts or gross sales .... **Less:** Returns and allowances	1	
2 **Less:** Cost of goods sold (Schedule A) and/or operations (attach schedule)	2	
3 Gross profit	3	
4 Dividends (Schedule C)	4	
5 Interest on obligations of the United States and U.S. instrumentalities	5	
6 Other interest	6	
7 Gross rents	7	
8 Gross royalties	8	
9 (a) Net capital gains—(separate Schedule D)	9(a)	
(b) Ordinary gain or (loss) from Part II, Form 4797 (attach Form 4797)	9(b)	
10 Other income (see instructions—attach schedule)	10	
11 TOTAL income—Add lines 3 through 10	11	

DEDUCTIONS

12 Compensation of officers (Schedule E)	12	
13 Salaries and wages (not deducted elsewhere)	13	
14 Repairs (see instructions)	14	
15 Bad debts (Schedule F if reserve method is used)	15	
16 Rents	16	
17 Taxes (attach schedule)	17	
18 Interest . . . . , . .	18	
19 Contributions (not over 5% of line 28 adjusted per instructions—attach schedule) . . .	19	
20 Amortization (attach schedule)	20	
21 Depreciation (Schedule G)	21	
22 Depletion	22	
23 Advertising	23	
24 Pension, profit-sharing, etc. plans (see instructions)	24	
25 Employee benefit programs (see instructions)	25	
26 Other deductions (attach schedule)	26	
27 TOTAL deductions—Add lines 12 through 26	27	
28 Taxable income before net operating loss deduction and special deductions (line 11 less line 27) .	28	
29 **Less:** (a) Net operating loss deduction (see instructions—attach schedule) 29(a)		
(b) Special deductions (Schedule I) . . . . 29(b)		
30 Taxable income (line 28 less line 29)	30	

TAX

31 TOTAL TAX (Schedule J)	31	
32 **Credits:** (a) Overpayment from 1971 allowed as a credit . . .		
(b) 1972 estimated tax payments		
(c) Less refund of 1972 estimated tax applied for on Form 4466 . ( )		
(d) Tax deposited with Form 7004 (attach copy)		
(e) Tax deposited with Form 7005 (attach copy)		
(f) Credit from regulated investment companies (attach Form 2439)		
(g) U.S. tax on special fuels, nonhighway gas and lubricating oil (attach Form 4136) . .		
33 TAX DUE (line 31 less line 32). See instruction G for depositary method of payment . . .	33	
34 OVERPAYMENT (line 32 less line 31)	34	
35 Enter amount of line 34 you want: Credited to 1973 estimated tax ▶ Refunded ▶	35	

Under penalties of perjury, I declare that I have examined this return, including accompanying schedules and statements, and to the best of my knowledge and belief it is true, correct, and complete. If prepared by a person other than the taxpayer, his declaration is based on all information of which he has any knowledge.

The Internal Revenue Service does not require a seal on this form, but if one is used, please place it here.

Date .... Signature of officer .... Title ....

Date .... Signature of individual or firm preparing the return Preparer's address .... Emp. Ident. or Soc. Sec. No. ....

Schedule J—TAX COMPUTATION

1 Taxable income (line 30, page 1). (If DISC inter-company pricing rules (section 994(a)) apply, check here ☐, attach a computation of taxable income under section 994(a), and enter the recomputed taxable income here) . . . .

2 Surtax exemption—Enter line 1 or $25,000, whichever is lesser. (Component members of a controlled group—see page 6 of instructions and enter your surtax exemption or line 1, whichever is lesser.) . . . .

3 Line 1 less line 2 . . . .

4 (a) 22% of line 1 . . . .

  (b) 26% of line 3 . . . .

  (c) If multiple surtax exemption is elected under section 1562, enter 6% of line 2 . .

5 Income tax (line 4, or alternative tax from separate Schedule D, whichever is lesser) . . . .

6 (a) Foreign tax credit (attach Form 1118) . . . .

  (b) Investment credit (attach Form 3468) . . . .

  (c) Work incentive (WIN) credit (attach Form 4874) . . . .

7 Total of lines 6(a), (b), and (c) . . . .

8 Line 5 less line 7 . . . .

9 Personal holding company tax (attach Schedule 1120 PH) . . . .

10 Tax from recomputing a prior year investment credit (attach Form 4255) . . . .

11 Minimum tax on tax preference items (see page 6 of instructions). Check here ☐ if Form 4626 is attached . . .

12 Total tax—Add lines 8 through 11. Enter here and on line 31, page 1 . . . .

Schedule M-1—RECONCILIATION OF INCOME PER BOOKS WITH INCOME PER RETURN

1 Net income per books . . . .

2 Federal income tax . . . .

3 Excess of capital losses over capital gains . .

4 Taxable income not recorded on books this year (itemize) _____

5 Expenses recorded on books this year not deducted in this return (itemize) _____

6   Total of lines 1 through 5 . . . . . .

7 Income recorded on books this year not included in this return (itemize)

  (a) Tax-exempt interest _____

8 Deductions in this tax return not charged against book income this year (itemize) _____

9   Total of lines 7 and 8 . . . . .

10 Income (line 28, page 1)—line 6 less line 9

Schedule M-2—ANALYSIS OF UNAPPROPRIATED RETAINED EARNINGS PER BOOKS (line 24 above)

1 Balance at beginning of year . . . . . .

2 Net income per books . . . .

3 Other increases (itemize) _____

4   Total of lines 1, 2, and 3 . . . . . .

5 Distributions out of current or accumulated earnings and profits: (a) Cash . . . .

                 (b) Stock . . . .

                 (c) Property . . .

6 Current year's undistributed taxable income or net operating loss (total of lines 8 and 9, Schedule K) . . . .

7 Other decreases (itemize) _____

8   Total of lines 5, 6, and 7 . . . . .

9 Balance at end of year (line 4 less line 8) .

Elements
of Other
Returns

with a Federal Reserve bank or authorized commercial bank accompanied by Form 503, "Federal Tax Deposit, Corporation Income Taxes." If a taxpayer mails his tax deposit *two or more days before* the due date and it is actually received, the payment is timely even though the deposit is received after the due date.[5] In contrast, if the return form itself is mailed *on* the due date, it is deemed to be timely filed.[6]

4.5   At least for the purpose of calculating interest, Form 7004 has been held to be a return.[7] Thus, if Form 7004 shows a smaller amount of remaining tax liability than the return Form 1120 later filed, before deducting the payment made with Form 7004, the excess draws interest from the normal due date of the return. Only the amount shown on Form 7004, and only if timely paid, does not incur interest.

Taxable Income

4.6   The taxable income of a corporation is equal to its gross income minus deductions allowed by the Code. Subject to certain exceptions, gross income and deductions of a corporation are determined in much the same way as those of an individual. However, the concept of *adjusted gross income* is not used in the taxation of corporations, and certain deductions of a personal nature allowable to individuals are not applicable to corporations. Examples of these deductions are medical and dental expenses, expenses for care of certain dependents, personal exemptions, and the standard deduction.

Dividends Received Deduction

4.7   The taxable income of a corporation is taxed to the corporation. Then the income remaining after payment of the corporate tax is again taxed to the shareholders when and to the extent distributed as dividends. Using a tax rate of 50 percent both for a corporation and its shareholders, every $100 of net income earned by a corporation and distributed by it after payment of its tax would bear a total tax of $75 ($100 − $50 corporate tax = $50 × 50% = $25 shareholder tax; $50 + $25 = $75 total tax). Where dividends are paid by corporations that are members of a chain of corporations, the total tax could pyramid to almost 100 percent of the original net income. The double tax and pyramid problem have been the subject of considerable discussion in connection with our federal tax policies.

4.8   Discussed more fully in paragraphs 6.69 to 6.71, a small amount of relief is given shareholders who are individuals, estates, or trusts. Section 116 grants an exclusion of $100 per year to such shareholders. Each such person or entity can deduct up to $100 per year from the

5. Sec. 7502(e).
6. Sec. 7502(a).
7. Lorillard Co. v. U.S., 338 F.2d 499 (2nd Cir. 1964) 64–2 USTC par. 9876, 14 AFTR2d 5982.

total amount of dividends received from domestic corporations that are included in gross income.

Corporate shareholders are granted a special deduction by Section 243 with respect to dividend income from domestic corporations that are themselves subject to the normal tax and surtax. Ordinarily, this special deduction is equal to 85 percent of the dividends received. The deduction is limited to 85 percent of the taxable income computed without regard to such deduction; however, the limitation does not apply if the corporation has a net operating loss for the taxable year after allowance of the dividends received deduction in full. Further, the dividends received deduction of a member of an affiliated group of corporations can be equal to 100 percent of the dividends received from other members of the group provided that all members of the group elect the 100 percent deduction, as discussed in chapter 19.   4.9

Dividends Paid

In determining taxable income, a corporation receives no deduction for dividends paid, although the amount is quite important in determining the penalty surtaxes imposed on personal holding companies and corporations that accumulate income beyond the reasonable needs of the business. These two types of penalty surtaxes are discussed in chapter 19. However, investor-owned public utilities are entitled to a limited deduction for dividends paid on certain preferred stock. The deduction is allowed by Section 247.   4.10

Foreign Tax Credit

Just as in the case of an individual, each year a domestic corporation can either deduct or claim a credit for foreign income, war profits, and excess profits taxes. The deduction is allowed by Section 164 and the credit by Sections 33, 901 through 905, and 960. If a credit is elected, the amount is computed on Form 1118 and the latter is then attached to the return.   4.11

A United States corporation will directly pay foreign taxes if it has an operating branch in a foreign country or receives dividends from a foreign corporation. In the first instance, the branch will file income tax returns in the foreign country, and in the second, foreign tax will have been withheld by the foreign corporation from the amount of the dividend.   4.12

In addition to being able to take a credit for foreign income, war profits, and excess profits taxes directly paid or imposed upon it, a United States corporation in many instances can also claim a credit (but not a deduction) for taxes "deemed" to have been paid by it. If a domestic corporation owns at least 10 percent of the voting stock of a foreign company and in the taxable year receives a dividend from that foreign company, it is "deemed" to have paid a proportionate share   4.13

of the taxes actually paid by the foreign company. Further, if the foreign company in turn owns at least 50 percent of the voting stock of another foreign corporation and receives dividends from it in the taxable year, the first foreign corporation will be deemed to have paid a proportionate part of the income, war profits, and excess profits taxes paid by the second foreign corporation.

4.14   The techniques for computation of the deemed foreign tax credit are complex and vary depending upon whether the foreign corporation is located in a "developed" or "less-developed" country. As for directly paid or imposed foreign taxes, the comments made in paragraphs 3.98 to 3.105 are equally applicable to corporations.

Other Credits

4.15   The *investment credit* mentioned in paragraph 3.107 and discussed in chapter 8 is applicable to all types of taxpayers, and is of particular importance to corporations. Further, the *credit for excise taxes* paid on nonhighway use of gasoline and lubricating oil mentioned in paragraph 3.106 is also available to corporations.

Tax Rates

4.16   The income tax of a corporation is not determined by the graduated rates applicable to individuals. Instead, the corporation income tax is actually made up of two taxes, a normal tax and a surtax, both computed at flat rates. The normal tax is 22 percent of the corporation's taxable income, and the surtax is 26 percent of the taxable income in excess of $25,000 [Section 11]. In other words, the combined rate is 22 percent on the first $25,000 of taxable income and 48 percent on the balance. The exemption of the first $25,000 of corporation taxable income in calculating the surtax is known as the surtax exemption [Section 11(d)].

4.17   The computation of the corporate income tax for 1972 is illustrated as follows:

EXAMPLE 1

Taxable income		$100,000
Normal tax (22% of $100,000)		$ 22,000
Surtax —		
Taxable income	$100,000	
Less: Surtax exemption	25,000	
	$ 75,000	
26% of $75,000		19,500

Total tax before credits		$ 41,500
Less:		
Investment credit	$ 1,500	
Foreign tax credit	600	2,100
Tax liability		$ 39,400
Less: Payments of estimated tax		37,000
Balance of tax payable		$ 2,400

Payments of Estimated Tax

4.18 Corporations whose "estimated tax" reasonably can be expected to be $40 or more are required to make payments of "estimated tax" as the year progresses. The payments are made in equal installments on the fifteenth day of the fourth, sixth, ninth, and twelfth months of the taxable year. The term "estimated tax" means the excess of a corporation's expected income tax liability over credits and any applicable exemption. Prior to 1968 there was a $100,000 exemption, so that, if a corporation was expected to have a tax liability of not more than $100,000, it did not need to make any payments of estimated tax. Effective with that year, the $100,000 exemption commenced being phased out over two consecutive five-year periods.[8] For the calendar year 1971 most corporations expecting to have a tax liability of $100,000 or more after deducting credits had an exemption of $24,400. If the expected tax liability was less than $100,000, the exemption was less. As to subsequent calendar years, most corporations expecting a tax liability of $5,500 or more after deducting credits, have the following amounts of exemptions:

1972	$5,500
1973	4,400
1974	3,300

4.19 Since 1968, corporations no longer file declarations of estimated tax. Payments of estimated tax are deposited with a Federal Reserve bank or an authorized commercial bank accompanied by Form 503 showing the corporation's identifying number.

Penalty. Looking only at Section 6154, it would seem that a corporation 4.20 is required to pay its full estimated tax in installments during the year of liability. But this is not true. As a practical matter, because of the exceptions contained in Section 6655, imposing a 6 percent per annum penalty on underestimation of tax, the maximum estimated tax which needs to be paid in equal quarterly installments during the taxable

8. Sec. 6154.

year is no more than 80 percent of the final tax liability for the year after deducting tax credits and any applicable estimated tax exemption. Further, there are other exceptions to the imposition of the 6 percent penalty. The one most frequently applied is in Section 6655(d)(1). It provides that there will be no 6 percent underestimation penalty if the estimated tax declared and paid for the current year is at least as much as the tax liability paid for the preceding year. This exception has acquired the appellation of a "safe declaration." There is a similar "safe declaration" for individuals provided in Section 6654(d)(1).

PARTNERSHIPS

Information Return Form 1065

4.21   A partnership occupies a unique position in the scheme of federal income taxes. It is not a taxpaying entity; however, it is an entity for the calculation of taxable income. It is required to file an information tax return, Form 1065, on or before the fifteenth day of the fourth month after the end of its taxable year. This return shows the partnership's taxable income and each partner's distributable share of such income. Each partner then reports his share of the partnership's taxable income in his own income tax return and pays his own tax thereon. He is taxed on his share of such income whether or not distributed to him. The full amount of such distributable share is taxable in an individual's taxable year in which the last day of the partnership's taxable year falls. For example, if both a partner and the partnership use the calendar year, all of the partner's income from the partnership is taxed in the same calendar year, and it does not matter that the firm distributes some or all of the partnership's income to him in the following year. If the partnership has a January 31 fiscal year, the partner's share becomes taxable in his particular taxable year in which January 31 falls. Stated another way: a partnership can have a taxable year different from that of its members (although, as discussed in paragraph 18.17, there are limitations wherever there are "principal" partners), and every partner has *no* income from his firm until that one day which marks the end of the firm's fiscal year.

EXAMPLE   Assume that a partnership has a fiscal year ending March 31 and that all of the partners use the calendar year as their taxable year. In year one, a partner draws $1,000 a month against anticipated income of the firm for its fiscal year ending March 31 in year two. During January, February, and March of year two he continues to draw $1,000 a month. During April of year two it is determined that his share of the partnership net income for its fiscal year ended March 31, in year two, was $22,000. Since he had already drawn $12,000 (12 × $1,000), the balance due him is $10,000 ($22,000 − $12,000). This amount is then distributed to him in four equal installments of $2,500 each in April, August, and November of year two and in January of year three. The full amount of $22,000 is taxable to him in calendar year two.

Some items of partnership income, gain, loss, deduction, or credit 4.22
are affected only by rules applied at the partnership level. Other items
are affected by rules applied at the level of the partners. Thus, for
some tax purposes the partnership is treated as a separate entity; for
other tax purposes it is treated as an aggregate of the interests of the
partners.

Subchapter K of the Code contains a comprehensive set of rules 4.23
concerning partnerships. Some of these rules recognize the "entity"
concept; others recognize the "aggregate" concept. The merging of
these two concepts causes some tax aspects of partnerships to be
extremely complex.

Page one of Form 1065 calls for the insertion on separate lines of 4.24
the elements entering into the computation of ordinary income of the
firm as a whole. Gross income items are first entered. Next, the deductions are listed: salaries and wages (other than to partners), salaries
and interest paid to partners, rent, interest, taxes, bad debts, repairs,
depreciation, amortization, depletion, payments to employee retirement plans, payments to employee benefit programs, and other deductions. Page two calls for the details of capital gains and losses;
however, the totals are not entered on page one but rather on Schedule K. This schedule lists, item by item, the aggregate amounts of the
firm's income, deduction, and loss items which must be reported by
the individual partners on their own returns. On page 104 there is a
reproduction of Schedule K. Then a Schedule K-1 must be prepared
for each partner showing his individual share of the items listed on
Schedule K.

Taxable Income

Under Section 703(a) partnership taxable income is calculated in 4.25
general in accordance with the rules applicable to individuals. A
partnership, like a corporation, is not a natural person; consequently,
it is not allowed to deduct items of a strictly personal nature allowable
to individuals. Also, since a partnership's income or loss is taken into
account by its partners in determining their annual income taxes,
the partnership is not allowed a deduction for net operating loss carry-
overs and carry-backs. In chapter 18 we shall see that some elements
of partnership taxable income flow through to the respective partners
and must be stated separately in the partnership return. Nevertheless, all determinations of partnership income and its various elements must first be made at the partnership level in accordance with
the partnership's own taxable year, its own methods of accounting,
and elections made by the partnership.

Pass Through of Special Items

Sections 702 and 703 of the Code and the Regulations thereunder 4.26
set forth a number of items that, after being calculated at the partner-

ship level, are required to be allocated to partners separately from the remainder of partnership taxable income. These items represent elements of income and deductions requiring special treatment or with special tax significance at the partner level, and items subject to separate limitations at the partner level.

4.27   Net long-term capital gains or losses and net short-term capital gains or losses must be allocated separately to partners. Each partner must then combine such gains and losses with other similar gains and losses realized by him during his taxable year to determine his deduction for 50 percent of the excess of net long-term capital gains over net short-term capital losses.

4.28   Each partner's share of the partnership's gains and losses from sales or exchanges of property subject to Section 1231 also must be allocated separately, so that the partner can combine his share of such gains and losses with other gains and losses from similar property to determine whether those gains or losses should be treated as ordinary or capital. Since the limitations on charitable contributions are determined by reference to each individual taxpayer's adjusted gross income, each partner's share of the partnership's charitable contributions must be separately allocated.

4.29   Income taxes paid or accrued to foreign countries and to possessions of the United States are subject to an election to be taken as deductions or credits by each taxpayer (see paragraphs 3.98 to 3.105); therefore, any of such taxes paid by a partnership must be separately allocated to partners, so that each partner may make his own election. Dividends and partially tax-exempt interest also require special attention in the tax return of each taxpayer, and they must be separately allocated to partners.

TRUSTS AND ESTATES

Form 1041

4.30   Annual tax returns required for trusts and decedents' estates are filed on Form 1041, using the individual income tax rates applicable to separate returns of married individuals. Estate income tax returns are filed by the executor or administrator. In the case of trusts, the trustee is responsible for preparing and filing the return. Persons acting in behalf of those under a legal disability, such as conservators of incompetent persons, or guardians of minors, are fiduciaries, but not to the extent of filing fiduciary income tax returns on Form 1041. Individual tax returns on Form 1040, instead, are required in the names of the incompetents or the minors [Code Sec. 6012(b)(2)].

4.31   Trusts and estates are not subject to the requirement of filing declarations of estimated tax. Estates, however, may elect to pay the tax in quarterly installments.[9] Trusts may not. Returns in both

9. Sec. 6152(a)(2).

cases are due on the fifteenth day of the fourth month after the end of the taxable year.[10]

Taxation of Trust and Estate Income in General

The taxation of income of trusts and estates requires consideration of three or more possible taxpayers, the grantor of the trust or the decedent of the estate, the trust or estate represented by the fiduciary, and one or more beneficiaries. Subchapter J of the Code sets forth a comprehensive plan for the taxation of trust and estate income. This overall plan contemplates that all taxable income of trusts and estates will be taxed one time and one time only, but this one tax may be borne by any one or in part by all of these possible taxpayers. The allocation of the taxable income of a trust or estate among the possible taxpayers is one of the primary problems dealt with in Subchapter J.

In some instances, the grantor of a trust retains such dominion and control over part of the income and property of the trust that he is treated for tax purposes as its substantial owner. In these cases, the grantor is taxable on the income of that part of the trust, and the tax rules otherwise applicable to trusts never come into play with respect to such income (Section 671). Where the grantor is not considered a substantial owner, the trust income is taxed either to the trust or to the beneficiaries.

The income of an estate consists of two types: "income in respect of a decedent" and income earned by the estate itself. In the final return of a decedent there is reported all gross income realized by him prior to his death under his established method of accounting. As stated in Reg. 1.691(a)–1(b), "the term 'income in respect of a decedent' refers to those amounts to which a decedent was entitled as gross income but which were not properly includible in computing his taxable income for the taxable year ending with the date of his death or for a previous taxable year under the method of accounting employed by the decedent." It includes all accrued income and income to which the decedent had a contingent claim at the time of his death. Some items of income in respect of a decedent will be received by the estate and other items by his heirs. Each such amount is taxable to the estate or person who acquires a right to receive it and must be reported in the year when actually received [Section 691(a); Reg. 1.691(a)–2(a)]. If any estate tax was paid on the value of the right to receive this income at the date of decedent's death, the estate or other person reporting the gross income is allowed a deduction for the estate tax attributable to such value [Section 691(c)].

The allocation of taxable income between a trust or estate and the beneficiaries is accomplished by treating all gross income attributable to trust or estate property as gross income of the trust or estate and then granting to it a deduction for amounts taxable to the beneficiaries.

10. Sec. 6072(a).

By this overall plan, all taxable income of the trust or estate is taxed once, but only once, to the parties in the trust or estate arrangement.

4.36   Tax rates applicable to trusts and estates are the same as those applicable to married individuals filing separate returns [Section 641(a)]. In determining taxable income, as noted in chapter 1, trusts and estates are allowed deductions for personal exemptions. An estate is allowed $600; a trust that is required to distribute all its income currently is allowed $300; and all other trusts are allowed a deduction of $100 [Section 642(b)].

Trust or Estate Income Taxable to Beneficiaries

4.37   Trusts and estates are treated to some extent as conduits for tax purposes. Just as the trust or estate is allowed a deduction for its distributable net income that is distributed or required to be distributed currently, the beneficiaries of the trust or estate are required to treat their respective shares of such distributable net income as their own gross income [Sections 652(a) and 662(a)]. Each beneficiary includes his share of the distributable net income of the trust or estate in his gross income for his taxable year with which, or within which, the taxable year of the trust or estate ends.

4.38   The conduit theory of trust and estate taxation also applies in determining the nature of the beneficiary's gross income. The nature of each beneficiary's share of trust or estate income is determined by the nature of the various income items making up distributable net income [Sections 652(b) and 662(b)]. Thus, if distributable net income includes tax-exempt interest or long-term capital gains that are distributed to beneficiaries, the amounts received by the beneficiaries are considered to include a part of the tax-exempt interest or long-term capital gains. Unless the governing instrument or local law allocates income in a particular way, each beneficiary's share is considered to be composed proportionately of all items of distributable net income. To determine the makeup of distributable net income for this purpose, all deductions of the trust or estate are allocated to the various kinds of income entering into the determination of distributable net income. Deductions directly related to particular income items are allocated to those items. All other deductions, along with any excess of the deductions previously allocated over the income to which they are related, are then allocated to income items in a manner selected by the fiduciary. The fiduciary is free to allocate these deductions to any items of income he chooses, except that a proportionate part of such deductions must be allocated to any tax-exempt income. In the absence of any specific allocation of these deductions by the fiduciary, they are allocated proportionately to all items of income included in the distributable net income of the trust or estate [Reg. 1.652(b)–3].

Minimum Tax on Tax Preferences

4.39   As mentioned in paragraph 3.112, the 10 percent minimum tax on tax preferences also applies to corporations, trusts, and estates.

QUESTIONS AND PROBLEMS

1. What amounts are deductible from gross income in determining the adjusted gross income of: a corporation? a partnership? a trust?
2. A corporation estimates in March, 1972, that for the calendar year 1972 it will have taxable income of $300,000, and installment payments each for one-fourth of the estimated tax based on such amount of income are paid on April 15, June 15, and September 15. In early December a revised estimate shows probable taxable income of $400,000, and a final payment based on such amount was made on December 15. Another computation is made late in February of the following year, showing taxable income was probably $425,000, and Form 7004 was filed on March 15 accompanied by the required payment. The final return filed June 15 shows taxable income of $450,000, but the final installment due on that date was not paid until September 15, because the corporation was short of cash. Assume that there was no foreign tax credit or investment credit available and that none of the exceptions in Section 6655(d) applies. Compute the amounts of tax, penalties, and interest due on September 15, 1973.
3. The president of a corporation is in Europe on March 15. Is the corporation entitled to an automatic extension of time to June 15, within which to file its return for the preceding calendar year?
4. Return Form 1065 of a calendar year partnership for two equal partners shows aggregate taxable income of $50,000. At the end of its taxable year, only $30,000 had been distributed to the partners. Is the remaining $20,000 taxable to the partnership for that year, to the partners for that year, or to no one until distributed?
5. Partnership AB has taxable net income for calendar year 1972 made up of the following items. All items are shared 50 percent by Partner A and 50 percent by Partner B. Show Partner A's share of partnership taxable net income and other items he should report on his personal tax return.

Gross income from sales	$40,000	
Interest on savings deposits	200	
Gain on sale of building		
(subject to Section 1231)	10,000	
Total income		$50,200
Expenses—		
Selling expenses (all deductible)	$20,000	
General and administrative expenses (all deductible)	25,000	
Charitable contributions	1,500	
Total expenses		46,500
Net income		$ 3,700

Schedule K—PARTNER'S SHARES OF INCOME, CREDITS, DEDUCTIONS, ETC.

Enter the total distributive amount for each applicable item listed below. Note: Each partner's distributive share of partnership items will be entered on Schedule K–1.

List the number of partners in the partnership . . . .

Partnership's distributive share items	Total
1 Salary, interest, and ordinary income (loss) (total of lines 14 and 26, page 1)	
2 Additional first-year depreciation (line 1, Schedule J)	
3 Dividends qualifying for exclusion (attach list)	
4 Net short-term capital gain (loss) (line 3, Schedule D)	
5 Net long-term capital gain (loss) (line 7, Schedule D)*	
6 Net gain (loss) from involuntary conversions due to casualty and theft under section 1231 (line 2, Form 4797) . . .	
7 Net gain (loss) from sale or exchange of property used in trade or business and certain involuntary conversions under section 1231 (line 4, Form 4797)	
8 Net earnings from self-employment (line 9, Schedule N)	
9 Contributions (attach list)	
10 Expense account allowance	
11 Foreign taxes (attach schedule)	
12 Taxes paid by regulated investment companies on undistributed capital gains (attach schedule)	
13 Payments by partnership to retirement plan on behalf of partners	

14 Investment in property:

Property	Life years		Total
New property (enter basis)	**(a)** 3 or more but less than 5	. . . .	
	(b) 5 or more but less than 7	. . . .	
	(c) 7 or more	. . . .	
Used property (enter cost)	**(d)** 3 or more but less than 5	. . . .	
	(e) 5 or more but less than 7	. . . .	
	(f) 7 or more	. . . .	

15 Other (specify) _____

_____

_____

_____

_____

_____

	Total
16 Specially allocated items (attach schedule):	
(a) Short-term capital gain (loss)	
(b) Long-term capital gain (loss)*	
(c) Ordinary gain (loss)	
(d) Other	
17 Tax preference items:	
(a) Accelerated depreciation on real property	
1. Low-income rental housing (section 167(k))	
2. Other real property	
(b) Accelerated depreciation on personal property subject to a net lease	
(c) Amortization of certified pollution control facilities	
(d) Amortization of railroad rolling stock	
(e) Amortization of on-the-job training facilities	
(f) Amortization of child care facilities	
(g) Reserves for losses on bad debts of financial institutions	
(h) Depletion	
(i) Capital gains (losses):	
1. Short-term (total of lines 4 and 16(a))	
2. Long-term (total of lines 5 and 16(b))	

*Each partner must be notified as to the amount of his distributive share of long-term capital gains that may qualify as "subsection (d) gains," see section 1201(d).

5

GROSS
INCOME

WHAT IS INCOME? . . . 108

    Economic . . . 109
    Financial . . . 109
    Taxable . . . 110

        DEFINITION . . . 110
        CONCEPTS OF INCLUDIBLE GROSS INCOME . . . 111

            FORM OF BENEFIT . . . 111
            SOURCE OF BENEFIT . . . 112

        EXCLUSIONS . . . 114

            BY THE CONSTITUTION . . . 114
            BY STATUTE . . . 115
            BY DEFINITION —CAPITAL INFLOWS . . . 115

            Realization Doctrine — Its Effect on the Difference
              between Capital and Income . . . 116

            ADMINISTRATIVE CONVENIENCE . . . 118

DETERMINING THE TAXPAYER . . . 119

    Agents and Nominees . . . 119
    Property Concepts . . . 119

        JOINT TENANTS AND TENANTS IN COMMON . . . 119
        COMMUNITY PROPERTY INCOME . . . 119
        GIFTS TO MINORS . . . 120

Corporation v. Shareholders . . . 120

DUMMY REAL ESTATE CORPORATIONS . . . 122

The Fruit and the Tree . . . 124
Allocation of Income between Controlled Taxpayers . . . 126
Dividends . . . 127
Interest on Bonds Sold between Payment Dates . . . 129

SPECIFIC TREATMENT OF CERTAIN ITEMS . . . 130

Gains from Illegal Activity . . . 130
Prizes and Awards . . . 130
Scholarship and Fellowship Grants . . . 131
Treasure Finders . . . 133
Receipts in Kind . . . 133
Gain on Cancellation of Indebtedness . . . 134

PURCHASE BY THE ISSUER OF HIS OWN OBLIGATIONS . . . 135
GIFTS . . . 136
INSOLVENCY . . . 136
REDUCTION OF PURCHASE PRICE . . . 137
NO PERSONAL LIABILITY . . . 138
ELECTION TO EXCLUDE FROM GROSS INCOME . . . 138

Alimony and Separate Maintenance Payments . . . 139

PAYMENTS TO SUPPORT MINOR CHILDREN . . . 142
PROPERTY SETTLEMENTS . . . 142
INDIRECT PAYMENTS OF ALIMONY . . . 143

Annuities . . . 143

EXCLUSION RATIO . . . 144
ANNUITY STARTING DATE . . . 144
AMOUNT RECEIVED AS AN ANNUITY . . . 145
INVESTMENT IN CONTRACT . . . 145
ADJUSTMENT FOR REFUND FEATURE . . . 147
EXPECTED RETURN . . . 148
EMPLOYEE ANNUITIES . . . 150
REFUNDS AND LUMP-SUM PAYMENTS . . . 150

Dividends on Life Insurance and Endowment Policies . . . 151

Services of a Child . . . 151

Social Security Benefits . . . 151

Damages . . . 151

TAXABLE DAMAGES . . . 152

COMPENSATION FOR LOSS OF PROFITS . . . 152
ANTITRUST AND SIMILAR ACTIONS . . . 152

Nontaxable Damages . . . 152

  Loss of Personal Rights . . . 152
  Damage to Goodwill . . . 153
  Return of Capital . . . 153

WHAT IS INCOME?

5.1   Definition depends, to a large extent, upon the use we make of the term. Trying to define income—an artificial concept in that it cannot be derived from, or verified by, a study of immutable laws—one finds himself in the position of Alice talking to Humpty Dumpty.

> "When I use a word," Humpty Dumpty said, in rather a scornful tone, "it means just what I choose it to mean—neither more nor less." "The question is," said Alice, "whether you can make words mean so many different things." "The question is," said Humpty Dumpty, "which is to be master—that's all."

5.2   Humpty Dumpty's logic accepts different definitions—not necessarily "right" or "wrong"—but different. Economists, psychologists, and sociologists approach their respective definitions with essentially subjective concepts; drafters of federal income tax laws and accountants concentrate upon definitions that are objectively measurable. Each discipline has its individual definition and internal divergencies, but all are concerned with definition of income. A measure of objectives for economic endeavor, income is a motivating force that influences moral, social, cultural, and economic development of societies.

5.3   Two broad categories of definition will be referred to as (1) the equity concept and (2) the realization concept. The equity concept, generally advocated by economists, calls for a valuation at the close of each accounting period, with income being defined as the change in equity during the period. The realization concept reflects financial usage, including that of accountants.

5.4   Federal income tax law generally adheres to the "realization" principle in its income recognition requirements. The "realization" concept calls for the recognition of income at time of sale or exchange; income does not accrue either during production or as a result of simply holding assets as their prices rise.

5.5   It is not appropriate to delve into all possible definitions of income here, but we may briefly examine some of those commonly used.[1]

1. Several publications are devoted to the question "What is income?" A few of these are: Norton M. Bedford, *Income Determination Theory: An Accounting Framework* (Reading, Mass.: Addison-Wesley Publishing Co., Inc., 1965); Sidney Alexander, *Five Monographs on Business Income* (New York: AICPA, 1950); Edgar O. Edwards and Philip W. Bell, *The Theory and Measurement of Business Income* (Berkeley and Los Angeles: University of California Press, 1961); Irving Fisher, *The Nature of Capital and Income* (London: Macmillan & Co., Ltd., 1906); G. Edward Phillips, "Income Concepts," in *Contemporary Thought on Federal Income Taxation*, ed. Charles J. Gaa (Belmont, Calif.: Dickinson Publishing Company, Inc., 1969) pp. 106–25; Bert N. Mitchell, "A Comparison of Accounting and Economic Concepts of Business Income," (*New York C.P.A.*, October, 1967, p. 762); Dan Throop Smith, *Tax Factors in Business Decisions* (Englewood Cliffs, N.J.: Prentice-Hall, Inc., 1968), p. 78.

Economic

The English economist J. R. Hicks is often quoted to explain in- 5.6
come as the maximum value a person can consume during a given
period and still expect to be as well-off at the end of the period as he
was at the beginning.[2] This definition reflects the equity concept
based upon a valuation of wealth. It is subjective, whether based on
future expectations or past occurrences, and even economists admit
that it is not susceptible to objective measurement.

Although income tax laws do not profess to embody perfect eco- 5.7
nomic theory,[3] it is a questionable practice to tax unreal income (inflationary gain), as is frequently the situation under present law. If
tax law recognized the "well-off" concept of Hicks' definition in "real
income" terms, inflationary gains would be excluded from the tax
definition.

The courts have refused to enter into the refinements of econo- 5.8
mists and their complex theories, which appear to be in conflict with
a workable, practicable system of producing revenues.[4] The courts'
attitude is understandable in view of the problem of quantifying
income using economic definitions.

Financial

In financial usage, income means any realized benefit, other than 5.9
additional investment, that increases the owner's equity in an enterprise. It includes gains and profits from any source, including gain
from the sale of assets. But it excludes, for example, unrealized appreciation of assets, the imputed value of one's own services to himself, and other forms of imputed income, and it is, therefore, too
narrow for some economists.

Not even within the accounting profession, however, is there com- 5.10
plete uniformity in the methods to apply to determine the amount of
net income. All too often alternative procedures are permissible even
within the same industry. However, in recent years a greater degree
of uniformity is being achieved through the pronouncements of the
Accounting Principles Board of the American Institute of C.P.A.'s.

Income in a broad sense under the tax law follows the financial defi- 5.11
nition.[5] But there are major statutory differences as well as differences
in interpretation, because courts will accept accounting principles and
absorb them into law only if they are reasonably well settled and only
if acceptance aids the court in its interpretation of the statute.[6]

2. J. R. Hicks, *Value and Capital*, 2nd ed. (1946), p. 172.
3. Weiss v. Wiener, 279 U.S. 333 (1929), 7 AFTR 8865.
4. Merchants Loan & Trust Co. v. Smietanka, 255 U.S. 509 (1921), 1 USTC ¶42,
3 AFTR 3102.
5. Eric Louis Kohler, A *Dictionary for Accountants*, 3rd ed. (Englewood Cliffs,
N.J.: Prentice-Hall, Inc. 1963), p. 258.
6. See Old Colony R. Co. v. Com., 284 U.S. 552 (1932), 3 USTC ¶880, 10 AFTR 786.
For a negative view on the desirability of uniformity between financial and tax ac-

Taxable

5.12   In paragraph 1.12, the text of the Sixteenth Amendment to the Constitution was quoted. And in paragraphs 2.3 and 2.4 the provisions of the Code and regulations pertaining to the definition of gross income were covered. Please read these paragraphs again.

5.13   **Definition.** Neither the Sixteenth Amendment nor the Code completely defines income. The first attempt of a court to develop a definition was made by the United States Supreme Court in *Eisner* v. *Macomber*.[7] It there stated that income is the "gain derived from capital, from labor, or both combined, provided it be understood to include profit gained through sale or conversion of capital assets." In later years the Supreme Court abandoned any attempt to write an all-inclusive definition of income and adopted its 1918 philosophy, expressed in *Towne* v. *Eisner*,[8] that the meaning of the term can vary. The often quoted statement there is:

A word is not a crystal, transparent and unchanged; it is the skin of a living thought and may vary greatly in color and content according to the circumstances and the time in which it is used.

5.14   Thirty-five years later the Eighth Circuit Court of Appeals in *Helvering* v. *Edison Bros. Stores, Inc.*,[9] made this authoritative observation: "the meaning of the word 'income' in the Sixteenth Amendment and in the acts of Congress pursuant to the amendment is that given it in common speech and everyday usage." In other words, the theories of economists and some of the rules of accountants are to be disregarded unless the "public" knows of and agrees with those theories and rules. The natural result of this premise, developing on an accelerated scale in recent years, is that "income" and permitted deductions are being subjected to legalistic concepts developed by judges who, more frequently than not, have little background in accounting.

5.15   Finally, the meaning of the word "income" is not controlled by the regulations of another administrative agency. Many enterprises are subject to governmental regulatory bodies—for example, the Federal Power Commission (investor-owned electric and gas utility companies), Federal Communications Commission (telephone and broadcasting companies), Comptroller of the Currency (banks), Civil Aeronautics Board (airlines), Interstate Commerce Commission (railroads and interstate trucking companies), and public utility commissions in each of the fifty states. Each of these agencies prescribes

counting principles see Harold E. Arnett, "Taxable Income vs. Financial Income: How Much Uniformity Can We Stand?" *The Accounting Review*, vol. XLIV, No. 3 (July, 1969), 482–94.

7. 252 U.S. 189 (1920), 1 USTC ¶32, 3 AFTR 3020.
8. 245 U.S. 418 (1918), 1 USTC ¶14, 3 AFTR 2959.
9. 133 F.2d 575 (8th Cir. 1943) 30 AFTR 940, 944.

its own uniform chart of accounts and the method of presentation of financial statements to be filed with them. The courts have held that "the ruling of one administrative department of the government concerning income accounting [cannot] control that of another department made for an entirely different purpose under another act of Congress." [10] In other words, if a regulatory body requires the treatment of a financial transaction to be booked in a particular manner, such treatment is not binding upon the Internal Revenue Service.

Based upon court decisions,[11] a definition of taxable gross income [the authors'] may be this: **5.16**

> Gross income means all inflow of wealth except that which is exempt from tax by the Constitution, statute, or definition. It includes realized gains and profits from any source, including gain from the sale of capital assets. It is not a gain accruing to capital, not a growth or increment in value of an investment; but a gain, a profit, something of exchangeable value proceeding from the capital.

In determining gains and losses, a constant value is used for the dollar; inflation and deflation are disregarded.

Concepts of Includible Gross Income. Before proceeding to a study of the inclusions listed in Section 61, the opening "shotgun" clause of that section, "... gross income means all income from whatever source derived," should be understood. Its scope will be more meaningful if thoughts are referenced within the following factors: **5.17**

1. The *form* of a benefit
2. The *source* of a benefit

FORM OF BENEFIT. What is the significance of the form of the benefit received in deciding whether or not it should be included in income? Prior to the 1954 Code, the definition of gross income was "all income of whatever kind and in whatever form paid." [12] The reference to the form paid was eliminated in the drafting of Section 61 of the 1954 Code. There was no significance to this omission of the phrase. The committee report [13] explained: **5.18**

> Section 61(a) provides that gross income includes "all income from whatever source derived." This definition is based upon the Sixteenth Amendment and the word "income" is used as in Section 22(a) [§61's predecessor

10. *Supra*, fn. 9.

11. Com. v. Glenshaw Glass Co., 348 U.S. 426 (1955), 55–1 USTC ¶9308, 47 AFTR 162 (see extract from opinion at 5.20; General American Investors Co., Inc. v. Com., 348 U.S. 434 (1955), 55–1 USTC ¶9309, 47 AFTR 167; Eisner v. Macomber, 252 U.S. 189 (1920), 1 USTC ¶32, 3 AFTR 3020 (see extracts of court opinion at 5.13 and 5.33.)

12. 1939 Code Sec. 22(a).

13. S. Rep. 1622, 83d Cong., 2d sess., 1954, p. 168.

in the old Code] in its constitutional sense. It is not intended to change the concept of income that obtains under Section 22(a). Therefore, although the Section 22(a) phrase "in whatever form paid" has been eliminated, statutory gross income will continue to include income realized in any form.

Note that the committee refers to income realized. Form standing alone will not generally immunize a benefit from the reach of the shotgun clause. If, however, the benefit has not yet been realized, then there will be no income.

5.19   The question of the significance of form was considered in *Old Colony Trust Company, Executors v. Com.*[14] In this case the employer contracted to pay an employee an annual salary and, in addition, to pay separately and directly to the government the entire amount of the employee's income taxes. The Supreme Court, in its opinion, stated:

> ... The payment of the tax by the employers was in consideration of the services rendered by the employee and was a gain derived by the employee from his labor. The form of the payment is expressly declared to make no difference. ... It is therefore immaterial that the taxes were directly paid over to the government. The discharge by a third person of an obligation to him is equivalent to the receipt by the person taxed.

5.20   SOURCE OF BENEFIT. Regulation 1.61–1(a) states that "gross income means all income from whatever source derived, unless excluded by law." For a time some realized benefits not otherwise expressly made nontaxable by the statute were nevertheless deemed by lower courts to be beyond the reach of the then existing shotgun clause, but in 1955 the Supreme Court in *Com. v. Glenshaw Glass*[15] attributed a different and more sweeping meaning to the shotgun clause. In that case, Glenshaw Glass Company sued a manufacturer, claiming exemplary damages for fraud and treble damages for injury to its business by reason of the manufacturer's violation of the antitrust laws. An out-of-court settlement was reached, and Glenshaw received some $324,000 as punitive damages for fraud and antitrust violation in addition to actual damages for injury to its business. The case of another taxpayer, William Goldman Theatres, Inc., involving the same issue, was consolidated for hearing, argument, and decision. This operator of motion picture houses sued a film distributor, alleging violation of the antitrust laws and seeking treble damages. The court found that Goldman had suffered a loss of profits of $125,000 and awarded treble damages of $375,000. Both taxpayers admitted that the amounts received attributable to loss of profits constituted taxable income, but contended that the punitive damages were not within the scope of 1939 Code Sec. 22(a). The Tax Court and the Third Circuit Court of Appeals held for the taxpayers, but the United States Supreme Court reversed. The latter court held that "Congress

14. 279 U.S. 716 (1929) 1 USTC ¶408, 7 AFTR 8875.
15. 348 U.S. 426 (1955), 55–1 USTC ¶9308, 47 AFTR 162.

applied no limitations as to the source of taxable receipts, nor restrictive labels as to their nature." An extract from the Court's opinion follows:

This Court has frequently stated that this language [the Court is referring to the shotgun clause of the 1939 Code] was used by Congress to exert in this field "the full measure of its taxing power." ... Respondents contend that punitive damages, characterized as "windfalls" flowing from the culpable conduct of third parties, are not within the scope of the section. But Congress applied no limitations as to the source of taxable receipts, nor restrictive labels as to their nature. And the Court has given a liberal construction to this broad phraseology in recognition of the intention of Congress to tax all gains except those specifically exempted. ... Thus, the fortuitous gain accruing to a lessor by reason of the forfeiture of a lessee's improvements on the rented property was taxed in *Helvering* v. *Bruun*, 309 U.S. 461. ... Such decisions demonstrate that we cannot but ascribe content to the catchall provision of § 22(a), "gains or profits and income derived from any source whatever." The importance of that phrase has been too frequently recognized since its first appearance in the Revenue Act of 1913 to say now that it adds nothing to the meaning of "gross income."

.   .   .

Here we have instances of undeniable accessions to wealth, clearly realized, and over which the taxpayers have complete dominion. ... It would be an anomaly that could not be justified in the absence of clear congressional intent to say that a recovery for actual damages is taxable but not the additional amount extracted as punishment for the same conduct which caused the injury. And we find no such evidence of intent to exempt these payments. ... We would do violence to the plain meaning of the statute and restrict a clear legislative attempt to bring the taxing power to bear upon all receipts constitutionally taxable were we to say that the payments in question here are not gross income. ...

5.21 Although the shotgun clause of the 1939 Code was changed in the 1954 Code to include only the single word *income*, the congressional committee report[16] indicates that this elimination was not relevant to the meaning of the word *income*. An extract from the committee report follows:

This section corresponds to Section 22(a) of the 1939 Code. While the language in existing Section 22(a) has been simplified, the all-inclusive nature of statutory gross income has not been affected thereby. Section 61(a) is as broad in scope as Section 22(a).

Section 61(a) provides that gross income includes "all income from whatever source derived." This definition is based upon the Sixteenth Amendment and the word "income" is used as in Section 22(a) in its constitutional sense. It is not intended to change the concept of income that obtains under Section 22(a).

The Supreme Court cited the above report in *Glenshaw Glass Company* as a reason for its opinion that they would reach the same result under either the 1939 Code or 1954 Code.

16. S. Rep. 1622, 83d Cong., 2d sess., 1954, p. 168.

5.22   What if a taxpayer receives an amount earmarked for use by him in a certain manner and from which he receives no economic benefit? These amounts are not income. A pathologist asked the question about a research grant he received from the local county heart association. The funds were to be expended for the salary of a part-time laboratory technician and for certain supplies and equipment, with any unexpended portion to be returned to the grantor. Title to any permanent equipment purchased with such funds remained with the grantor. Revenue Rul. 59–92[17] held that the amounts were not includible in the pathologist's income. The situation is changed considerably if the amounts are diverted to personal use. Amounts diverted to personal use are includible in income.[18]

5.23   How about money mistakenly paid to a taxpayer in excess of an agreed amount? Initially, the excess is not income to the taxpayer, because he has a legal obligation to return the money.[19] The amount may be income, however, if it is impossible to find its owner, even though the overpayment is kept in a separate fund.[20]

5.24   **Exclusions.** All inflow of wealth (money or property rights) is within the scope of taxation except that excluded by (1) the Constitution, (2) statute, or (3) definition. In addition, some inflows of wealth have not been taxed for reasons of administrative convenience.

5.25   BY THE CONSTITUTION. As mentioned in chapter 1, the Sixteenth Admendment to the Constitution was adopted effective February 25, 1913, to nullify the 1895 United States Supreme Court decision in *Pollock* v. *Farmers' Loan & Trust Co.* The Court there held that an income tax had to be apportioned among the several states according to population; that requirement appears in Section 2 and in Section 9, Clause 4, of Article 1 of the Constitution of the United States. The Sixteenth Amendment did not define income, enlarge the taxing power of the federal government, nor restrict the kinds of income to be taxed, but merely removed the necessity of apportioning income taxes.

5.26   The power of the federal government to tax is derived from the original Constitution and embraces every conceivable form of taxation. Although an income tax need no longer be apportioned among the several states, every provision in such a law: (a) must be geographically uniform in its application throughout the United States,[21]

17. 1959–1 C.B. 111.
18. Arthur M. Godwin, 34 BTA 485 (1936) (Acq.).
19. O.D. 14, 1 C.B. 67.
20. Chicago, R.I. & P. Ry. Co. v. Com., 47 F.2d 990 (7th Cir. 1931), 9 AFTR 1040, 2 USTC ¶696; National Ry. Time Service Co., 88 F.2d 904 (7th Cir. 1937), 19 AFTR 212, 37–1 USTC ¶9123.
21. Article 1, Sec. 8, Clause 1 of the United States Constitution; Bromley v. McCaughn, 280 U.S. 124 (1929), 8 AFTR 10251. However, variations in state law, particularly in property concepts, properly may result in differences in tax consequences from state to state. Com. v. Stern, 357 U.S. 39 (1958), 1 AFTR 2d 1899; 58–2 USTC ¶9594.

(b) must not deprive a person of "life, liberty, or property without due process of law,[22] and (c) by reason of our dual form of federal and state governments cannot impose an undue burden upon a sovereign state.[23]

Through the years there have been many attempts to have a particular provision of a revenue act held unconstitutional. However, with few exceptions the courts have upheld the validity of the challenged provisions.[24] In two notable instances provisions were stricken down. In *Pollock* v. *Farmers' Loan & Trust Co.*, referred to above, a subsidiary issue was the power of the federal government to tax the income from municipal bonds. The Supreme Court unanimously held that it had no such power, and said such a tax is unconstitutional because it bears directly on the exercise of the borrowing power of the states and their political subdivisions. To restrict or hinder the borrowing power of a sovereign state is to limit its sovereignty. Interest on municipal bonds is now specifically excluded from income by Section 103(a)(1). The second instance was the 1918 holding in *Towne* v. *Eisner*,[25] two years later followed by *Eisner* v. *Macomber*,[26] that a stock dividend of common on common at a time when only common was outstanding does not constitute income and accordingly cannot constitutionally be taxed. Code Section 305(a) now expressly excludes the value of most stock dividends from taxable income.

BY STATUTE. The principal statutory exclusions are explained in chapter 6 and consist of life insurance proceeds; employee death benefits; gifts; inheritances; interest on local government securities; compensation for injuries or sickness; recoveries of bad debts, prior taxes, and delinquency amounts where the prior year deduction did not result in a tax benefit; limited dividend exclusion for individuals; contributions to capital of corporations; and meals or lodging furnished for the convenience of the employer.

BY DEFINITION—CAPITAL INFLOWS. Receipts of amounts that substitute for capital, or replace capital, are not included in gross income.

A merchant inventories his merchandise at cost and then sells an item costing $65 for $100. The cost of the item, $65, is not included in gross income.

EXAMPLE 1

Mr. R., an investor, sells common stock costing $200 for $500. Mr. R's gross income includes only the gain of $300.

EXAMPLE 2

22. Fifth Amendment to United States Constitution.
23. Collector v. Day, 78 U.S. 113 (1870); Mertens, *Law of Federal Income Taxation*, ¶8.13.
24. See Mertens, *Law of Federal Income Taxation*, ¶4.13.
25. 245 U.S. 418 (1918), 1 USTC ¶14, 3 AFTR 2959.
26. 252 U.S. 189 (1920), 1 USTC ¶32, 3 AFTR 3020. Also see para. 5.13 and 5.33.

5.30   Gross income from a business is defined by Reg. 1.61–3(a):

> In a manufacturing, merchandising, or mining business, "gross income" means the total sales, less the cost of goods sold, plus any income from investments and from incidental or outside operations or sources. Gross income is determined without subtraction of depletion allowances based on a percentage of income, and without subtraction of selling expenses, losses, or other items not ordinarily used in computing cost of goods sold. The cost of goods sold should be determined in accordance with the method of accounting consistently used by the taxpayer.

5.31   Referring to gains from dealings in property, Reg. 1.61–6(a) provides:

> Gain realized on the sale or exchange of property is included in gross income, unless excluded by law. ... Generally, the gain is the excess of the amount realized over the unrecovered cost or other basis for the property sold or exchanged. ...

5.32   Do not confuse substitutes for capital with substitutes for income.

EXAMPLE   X leased a building to Y for three years at an agreed rental of $50,000 per annum. At the end of one year, Y, the lessee, decided to cancel the lease, but X insisted that Y pay $50,000 for the privilege of canceling the lease. Y agreed to this. X did not include the $50,000 in his gross income in the year in which he received it.

A situation similar to this was settled in 1941 by the Supreme Court in *Hort v. Com.*,[27] where it was held that "the amount received by petitioner for cancellation of the lease must be included in his gross income in its entirety." The Court reasoned:

> The consideration received for cancellation of the lease was not a return of capital. We assume that the lease was "property," whatever that signifies abstractly. ... Simply because the lease was "property" the amount received for its cancellation was not a return of capital, quite apart from the fact that "property" and "capital" are not necessarily synonymous in the Revenue Act of 1932 or in common usage. Where, as in this case, the disputed amount was essentially a substitute for rental payments which § 22(a) [now § 61] expressly characterizes as gross income ... it is immaterial that for some purposes the contract creating the right to such payments may be treated as "property" or "capital". ...

5.33   *Realization doctrine—its effect on the difference between capital and income.* The Supreme Court decision in *Eisner v. Macomber* was mentioned earlier. The Court held that the concept of income required the *realization* of gain. In that case, the government sought to tax a stockholder on a dividend of common stock received

27. 313 U.S. 28 (1941), 41–1 USTC ¶9354, 25 AFTR 1207.

on her common stock, no other types of stock being outstanding. The Court, in deciding that the stock dividend was not taxable, set forth the doctrine of "realization," also referred to as the "severance theory." Here there was no realization because the stockholder was no richer after the dividend. She owned the same proportionate interest in the corporation's assets. All that she had were additional pieces of paper (additional stock certificates) representing that interest. The Court stated:

> After examining dictionaries in common use (Bouv. L.D.; Standard Dict.; Webster's Internat. Dict.; Century Dict.) we find little to add to the succinct definition adopted in two cases arising under the Corporation Tax Act of 1909 ... "Income may be defined as the gain derived from capital, from labor, or from both combined," provided it be understood to include profit gained through a sale or conversion of capital assets. ...
>
> Brief as it is, it indicates the characteristic and distinguishing attribute of income essential for a correct solution of the present controversy. The Government, although basing its argument upon the definition as quoted, placed chief emphasis upon the word "gain," which was extended to include a variety of meanings; while the significance of the next three words was either overlooked or misconceived. *"Derived-from-capital"; "the-gain-derived-from-capital,"* etc. Here we have the essential matter; *not* a gain *accruing* to capital, not a *growth* or *increment* of value *in* the investment; but a gain, a profit, something of exchangeable value *proceeding from* the property, *severed from* the capital however invested or employed, and *coming in*, being *"derived,"* that is, *received* or *drawn by* the recipient (the taxpayer) for his separate use, benefit and disposal;—*that* is income derived from property. Nothing else answers the description.
>
> The same fundamental conception is clearly set forth in the Sixteenth Amendment—"incomes, *from* whatever *source derived"*—the essential thought being expressed with a conciseness and lucidity entirely in harmony with the form and style of the Constitution.

The *Macomber* decision was issued in 1920. In the Revenue acts applicable to the years from 1921 through 1935, stock dividends were expressly exempted from tax. Nevertheless, many cases arising in those years were presented to the courts. The reason was that the Regulations provided for an allocation of basis between the new stock dividend shares and the old shares, and taxpayers were disputing the validity of those regulations. These decisions to a major extent narrowed the applicability of the *Macomber* rule, particularly where there were two classes of stock outstanding at the time of the stock dividend or as a result thereof. The Revenue Act of 1936 in Sec. 115(f)(1) removed the previous blanket exemption of stock dividends:

5.34

> *General Rule.*—A distribution made by a corporation to its shareholders in its stock or in rights to acquire its stock shall not be treated as a dividend to the extent that it does not constitute income to the shareholder within the meaning of the Sixteenth Amendment to the Constitution.

5.35

As a result, another flood of litigation started, to determine just what types of stock dividends constitutionally were not income.

To resolve the controversy, the 1954 Internal Revenue Code in Section 305 again restored the exemption from tax of most stock dividends and stock rights. However, the Tax Reform Act of 1969 added circumstances under which certain stock dividends will be taxable, as discussed in chapter 19.

5.36

In *Helvering* v. *Bruun*,[28] the severance theory was again presented. Here Bruun was a lessor of property on which the lessee built a building. Was the building income to Bruun in the year the lease was terminated? Bruun argued "no" because there had not been a severance. The Supreme Court distinguished this case from the stock dividend cases. The Court stated:

> He [the taxpayer] emphasizes the necessity that the gain be separate from the capital and separately disposable. These expressions, however, were used to clarify the distinction between an ordinary dividend and a stock dividend. They were meant to show that in the case of a stock dividend, the stockholder's interest in the corporate assets after receipt of the dividend was the same as and inseverable from that which he owned before the dividend was declared. We think they are not controlling here. ...
>
> Here, as a result of a business transaction, the respondent received back his land with a new building on it, which added an ascertainable amount to its value. It is not necessary to recognition of taxable gain that he should be able to sever the improvement begetting the gain from his original capital. If that were necessary, no income could arise from the exchange of property; whereas such gain has always been recognized as realized taxable gain. [However, the Code does provide a number of instances in which gain, though realized, is not recognized.]

After this case was decided, the Revenue Act of 1942 added Section 22(b)(11) to the 1939 Code, which is now Section 109 of the 1954 Code. It excludes from gross income the value of any improvements erected by a lessee and passed to a lessor on termination of a lease.

5.37

ADMINISTRATIVE CONVENIENCE. Through the years, the Internal Revenue Service has issued rulings stating that certain types of receipts do not constitute taxable gross income. In most of these instances, the rulings were issued to prevent administrative problems in enforcement; in others, it would seem that it was carrying out a directive from the particular governmental administration then in office. These rulings, of course, are based upon an interpretation (sometimes rather broad, particularly in the case of older rulings, as to what constitutionally is "income") that particular types of receipts or benefits do not constitute taxable income because excluded by the Constitution, statute, or definition. Many of such rulings are listed in *Arnold* v. *U.S.*[29] As stated there, the validity of these rulings has never been tested, because if a taxpayer takes advantage of them and

---

28. 309 U.S. 461 (1940), 40–1 USTC ¶9337, 24 AFTR 652.
29. 289 F. Supp. 206 (D.C., N.Y., 1968), 22 AFTR2d 5661.

the Service follows its own pronouncements, no controversy can arise.

DETERMINING THE TAXPAYER

When we discuss gross income, we ask "Who is taxed?" and our answer depends on several factors. It depends on the nature of the entity receiving the income; i.e., individual, trust, estate, or corporation. It also may depend on the legal relationship. Let us look at these and other determining factors. 5.38

Agents and Nominees

A basic rule is that a taxpayer does not include in his income amounts received as an agent or nominee for someone else. For example: the profit from a sale of property is not income to the seller if evidence shows that it was purchased and sold for the account of someone else.[30] 5.39

Property Concepts

Joint Tenants and Tenants in Common. Property of all kinds can be owned by two or more persons either as joint tenants with the right of survivorship or as tenants in common. In both instances, each living party owns an undivided interest in the whole. If there are two owners, each owns an undivided half. Upon the death of a joint tenant, his interest by operation of law automatically passes to the surviving joint tenants. Upon the death of a tenant in common, his interest passes to his heirs. 5.40

When persons hold property as joint tenants or as tenants in common, state law determines who is taxed on income from the property. In most cases, the income is divided equally among the tenants. If the property is sold, the sale price is allocated in equal amounts to the tenants.[31] 5.41

Community Property Income. A husband and wife domiciled in a state that has the community property system of ownership of marital property (Arizona, California, Idaho, Louisiana, Nevada, New Mexico, Texas, and Washington) may each report one-half of the community income in separate returns.[32] Each state has its own rules for determining whether income is community income or separate income. Generally, however, income earned by the spouses through their efforts or investments after their marriage is community income. 5.42

30. Bessemer Invest. Co. v. Com., 31 F.2d 248 (2nd Cir. 1929), 7 AFTR 8551, reversing 8 BTA 1011.
31. Treas. Dept. booklet *Your Federal Income Tax*, 1968 ed., p. 58.
32. Mim. 3853, X–1, C.B. 139.

Likewise, income from property acquired after marriage by the husband, the wife, or both (except property acquired by gift, bequest, devise, or inheritance) is generally community income. Property acquired by either spouse before marriage is separate property and so continues through all changes as long as it can be traced.[33]

5.43 For income tax purposes, the rules for community income are important only when separate returns are filed by a husband and wife in a community property state. If they file a joint return, they get the benefit of income splitting.

5.44 **Gifts to Minors.** Under model acts adopted by all the states and the District of Columbia, title to securities can be transferred to minors without the formalities of a special guardianship or trust. Income from property so transferred is taxed to the minor. But if the income is used to discharge a personal obligation to support the minor, it is taxed to that person, regardless of who made the gift.[34]

Corporation v. Shareholders

5.45 The general rule is that a corporation is an entity separate and apart from its shareholders, even if all of its stock is owned by one person.

Moline Properties, Inc. v. *Com.*
Supreme Court of the United States, 1943[35]

Mr. Justice REED delivered the opinion of the Court.

Petitioner seeks to have the gain on sales of its real property treated as the gain of its sole stockholder and its corporate existence ignored as merely fictitious. Certiorari was granted because of the volume of similar litigation in the lower courts and because of alleged conflict of the decision below with other circuit court decisions. ...

Petitioner was organized by Uly O. Thompson in 1928 to be used as a security device in connection with certain Florida realty owned by him. The mortgagee of the property suggested the arrangement, under which Mr. Thompson conveyed the property to petitioner, which assumed the outstanding mortgages on the property, receiving in return all but the qualifying shares of stock, which he in turn transferred to a voting trustee appointed by the creditor. The stock was to be held as security for an additional loan to Mr. Thompson to be used to pay back taxes on the property. Thompson owned

33. Robert M. Drysdale v. Com., 232 F.2d 633 (6th Cir. 1956), 56–1 USTC ¶9508, 49 AFTR 964. Income, rents, and profits from separate property constitute separate income in Arizona, California, Nevada, New Mexico, and Washington; whereas income accruing to separate property in Idaho, Louisiana, Oklahoma, and Texas constitutes community income. In Idaho, income accruing to a wife's separate property constitutes separate income to her if the deed of conveyance provides that the income is to be for her separate use and benefit. Separate property earnings not attributable to community efforts remain separate income in Louisiana and Texas. See discussion at paragraphs 19.10–19.16 of Mertens, *The Law of Federal Income Taxation.*

34. Rev. Rul. 56–484, 1956–2 C.B. 23.

35. 319 U.S. 436 (1943), 43–1 USTC ¶9464, 30 AFTR 1291, affirming 131 F.2d 388 (5th Cir. 1942), 30 AFTR 289.

other real property, title to which he held individually. In 1933 the loan which occasioned the creation of petitioner was repaid and the mortgages were refinanced with a different mortgagee; control of petitioner reverted to Mr. Thompson. The new mortgage debt was paid in 1936 by means of a sale of a portion of the property held by petitioner. The remaining holdings of the petitioner were sold in three parcels, one each in 1934, 1935, and 1936, the proceeds being received by Mr. Thompson and deposited in his bank account.

Until 1933 the business done by the corporation consisted of the assumption of a certain obligation of Thompson to the original creditor, the defense of certain condemnation proceedings and the institution of a suit to remove restrictions imposed on the property by a prior deed. The expenses of this suit were paid by Thompson. In 1934 a portion of the property was leased for use as a parking lot for a rental of $1,000. Petitioner has transacted no business since the sale of its last holdings in 1936 but has not been dissolved. It kept no books and maintained no bank account during its existence and owned no other assets than as described. The sales made in 1934 and 1935 were reported in petitioner's income tax returns, a small loss being reported for the earlier year and a gain of over $5,000 being reported for 1935. Subsequently, on advice of his auditor, Thompson filed a claim for refund on petitioner's behalf for 1935 and sought to report the 1935 gain as his individual return. He reported the gain on the 1936 sale.

The question is whether the gain realized on the 1935 and 1936 sales shall be treated as income taxable to petitioner, as the Government urges, or as Thompson's income. The Board of Tax Appeals held for petitioner on the ground that because of its limited purpose, the corporation "was a mere figmentary agent which should be disregarded in the assessment of taxes." *Moline Properties, Inc.* v. *Commissioner,* 45 B.T.A. 647. The Circuit Court of Appeals reversed on the ground that the corporate entity, chosen by Thompson for reasons sufficient to him, must now be recognized in the taxation of the income of the corporation. *Commissioner* v. *Moline Properties, Inc.,* 5 Cir., 131 F.2d 388.

The doctrine of corporate entity fills a useful purpose in business life. Whether the purpose be to gain an advantage under the law of the state of incorporation or to avoid or to comply with the demands of creditors or to serve the creator's personal or undisclosed convenience, so long as that purpose is the equivalent of business activity or is followed by the carrying on of business by the corporation, the corporation remains a separate taxable entity. In *Burnet* v. *Commonwealth Imp. Co.,* 287 U.S. 415, 53 S. Ct. 198, 77 L. Ed. 399, this Court appraised the relation between a corporation and its sole stockholder and held taxable to the corporation a profit on a sale to its stockholder. This was because the taxpayer had adopted the corporate form for purposes of his own. The choice of the advantages of incorporation to do business, it was held, required the acceptance of the tax disadvantages.

To this rule there are recognized exceptions. ... A particular legislative purpose, such as the development of the merchant marine whatever the corporate device for ownership, may call for the disregarding of the separate entity, ... as may the necessity of striking down frauds on the tax statute. ... In general, in matters relating to the revenue, the corporate form may be disregarded where it is a sham or unreal. In such situations the form is a bald and mischievous fiction. ... The petitioner corporation was created by Thompson for his advantage and had a special function from its inception. At that time it was clearly not Thompson's alter ego and his exercise of control over it was negligible. It was then as much a separate entity as if its stock had been transferred outright to third persons. The argument is made by petitioner that the force of the rule requiring its separate treatment is avoided by the fact that Thompson was coerced into creating petitioner and was completely subservient to the creditors. But this merely serves to emphasize petitioner's separate existence. ... Business necessity, i.e., pressure from creditors, made petitioner's creation advantageous to Thompson.

When petitioner discharged its mortgages held by the initial creditor and Thompson came into control in 1933, it was not dissolved, but continued its existence, ready again to serve his business interests. It again mortgaged its property, discharged that new mortgage, sold portions of its property in 1934 and 1935 and filed income tax returns showing these transactions. In 1934 petitioner engaged in an unambiguous business venture of its own—it leased a part of its property as a parking lot, receiving a substantial rental. The facts, it seems to us, compel the conclusion that the taxpayer had a tax identity distinct from its stockholder.

Petitioner advances what we think is basically the same argument of identity in a different form. It urges that it is a mere agent for its sole stockholder and "therefore the same tax consequences follow as in the case of any corporate agent or fiduciary." There was no actual contract of agency, nor the usual incidents of an agency relationship. Surely the mere fact of the existence of a corporation with one or several stockholders, regardless of the corporation's business activities, does not make the corporation the agent of its stockholders. Therefore, the question of agency or not depends upon the same legal issues as does the question of identity previously discussed. ...
Affirmed.

5.46   In *National Investors Corp.* v. *Hoey*,[36] the Second Circuit Court of Appeals said: "... to be a separate jural person for purposes of taxation, a corporation must engage in some industrial, commercial, or other activity besides avoiding taxation; in other words, ... the term 'corporation' will be interpreted to mean a corporation which does some 'business' in the ordinary meaning; and ... escaping taxation is not 'business' in the ordinary meaning."

5.47   When the Commissioner seeks to have the separate corporate entity ignored on the ground that it is a sham or has as its only purpose the avoidance of federal income taxes, he meets with a measure of success. When the taxpayer seeks such result, however, he seldom prevails.

5.48   **Dummy Real Estate Corporations.** A line of cases has developed involving dummy real estate corporations. In these cases, the record title to real property was in the corporation, but written agreements provided that the beneficial ownership was in the individuals. The decisions in favor of the taxpayers were based not on ignoring the separate corporate entity but on the finding that the ownership in fact was in the individuals.

36. 144 F.2d 466 (2nd Cir. 1944), 44–2 USTC ¶9407, 32 AFTR 1219 reversing 52 F.2d 556 (D.C., N.Y., 1943), 31 AFTR 934; similarly, Howard A. Jackson v. Com., 223 F.2d 389 (2d Cir. 1956), 56–1 USTC ¶9506, 49 AFTR 1208, affirming 24 T.C. 1 (1955).

The first such case was *Stewart Forshay*.[37] A building in New York   5.49
City was conveyed by three individuals to a corporation organized
by them under an agreement that the corporation was to hold the title
for their benefit. In 1924 the building was sold at a gain. The Board of
Tax Appeals held that under New York law, although record title
was in the corporation, legal and equitable title was in the individuals. Accordingly, gain on the sale was taxable to them and not to
the corporation. The board held that the corporation was a mere
dummy, that it did not engage in business, hold directors' meetings,
declare dividends, or perform acts other than executing the deed of
conveyance as the record title holder after the sale had been made
by the persons having the beneficial interest.

On a similar set of facts again involving New York City real estate,   5.50
the board also found in favor of the taxpayers that the title holding
corporation *Moro Realty Holding Corporation*[38] was a mere dummy.

In a case[39] involving Texas oil properties, the Tax Court distin-   5.51
guished the dummy real estate corporation cases from the *Moline
Properties* decision:

> Undoubtedly, the rule laid down in the *Moline* case is thoroughly sound,
> but in our judgment it has no application under the facts of the case before
> us. Here it was specifically provided by appropriate resolution of the cor-
> porate Board of Directors that all properties standing in the name of the
> corporation or to which it will have legal title should not belong to the
> corporation but would be held by it as agent or trustee for Miller and would
> transfer the legal title to such property at such time as Miller may direct.
>
> .   .   .
>
> The petitioner does not contend that it was not a distinct corporate entity
> nor does it seek to have its corporate entity disregarded. It stands on the
> perfectly simple proposition that the property involved was in fact the prop-
> erty of Miller and the income therefrom taxable to him.
>
> We think it is fundamentally correct to assume that where income is de-
> rived from property, the basic test for determining who is to bear the tax is
> that of ownership. Cf. *Pollack* v. *Farmers Loan & Trust Co.*, 158 U.S. 601;
> *Eisner* v. *Macomber*, 252 U.S. 189 [33 AFTR 3020]. In the instant case it
> is obvious that the oil leases standing in the name of the corporation were
> in fact the property of Miller and that the corporation acted for Miller in
> collecting the royalties and paying them over to him. Whether the rela-
> tionship was one of agency or of trust is immaterial. *Stewart Forshay*, 20
> B.T.A. 537.

In order to establish actual ownership in individuals when a title-   5.52
holding corporation acts as nominee or agent, written documents
should be sufficient in form and substance to satisfy local property
law. To rely upon being able to disregard the separate corporate
entity of the title-holding corporation is quite risky.

---

37. 20 BTA 537 (1930) (NA).

38. 25 BTA 1135 (1932) (NA, 1939–2 C.B. 59; nonacquiescence withdrawn and
acquiescence substituted 1947–1 C.B.–3).

39. Industrial Union Oil Co., 5 TCM 879 (1946), ¶46,251 P–H Memo T.C.

The Fruit and the Tree

5.53   The poetic sounding words "the fruit and the tree" stand for the principle that an assignment of earned income will not be recognized for tax purposes. If income is severed from the security or the person who earned it, such as by an assignment, it remains taxable to the owner of the security or the person who earned it, even though the cash is actually paid to the assignee. If a man tells his employer to pay a portion of his salary to his son, the father remains taxable on it. If the amount is large enough, he could also become liable for gift tax. If a man clips an unmatured interest coupon from a bond and gives it to his daughter, the father will have taxable interest income on the maturity date of the coupon, even though the daughter actually receives the cash when she turns in the coupon.

5.54   The famous case of *Lucas* v. *Earl* [40] held that a husband was taxable on his entire earnings, despite an agreement made with his wife (before the Sixteenth Amendment was adopted) that each would have one-half interest in the other's earnings. Mr. Justice Holmes delivered the opinion of the Court and said:

There is no doubt that the statute could tax salaries to those who earned them and provide that the tax could not be escaped by anticipatory arrangements and contracts however skillfully devised to prevent the salary when paid from vesting even for a second in the man who earned it. ... We think that no distinction can be taken according to the motives leading to the arrangement by which the fruits are attributed to a different tree from that on which they grew.

5.55   The same principle was applied to an assignment of investment income in another famous case. Extracts from it follow:

Helvering v. *Horst*
Supreme Court of the United States, 1940 [41]

[FACTS:] In 1934 and 1935 respondent, the owner of negotiable bonds, detached from them negotiable interest coupons shortly before their due date and delivered them as a gift to his son who in the same year collected them at maturity.

[ISSUE:] The sole question for decision is whether the gift, during the donor's taxable year, of interest coupons detached from the bonds, delivered to the donee and later in the year paid at maturity, is the realization of income taxable to the donor.

[DECISION:] Donor is taxable.

[REASONING:] The holder of a coupon bond is the owner of two independent and separable kinds of right. ... Together they are an obligation to pay principal and interest given in exchange for money or property which was presumably the consideration for the obligation of the bond. Here respondent, as owner of the bonds, had acquired the legal right to demand

40. 281 U.S. 111 (1930), 2 USTC ¶496, 8 AFTR 10287.
41. 311 U.S. 112, 24 AFTR 1058, 40–2 USTC ¶9787.

payment at maturity of the interest specified by the coupons and the power to command its payment to others which constituted an economic gain to him.

... Where the taxpayer does not receive payment of income in money or property realization may occur when the last step is taken by which he obtains the fruition of the economic gain which has already accrued to him. ...

... The question here is, whether because one who in fact receives payment for services or interest payments is taxable only on his receipt of the payments, he can escape all tax by giving away his right to income in advance of payment. ...

... Income is "realized" by the assignor because he, who owns or controls the source of the income, also controls the disposition of that which he could have received himself and diverts the payment from himself to others as the means of procuring the satisfaction of his wants. The taxpayer has equally enjoyed the fruits of his labor or investment and obtained the satisfaction of his desires whether he collects and uses the income to procure those satisfactions, or whether he disposes of his right to collect it as the means of procuring them.

. . .

... To say that one who has made a gift thus derived from interest or earnings paid to his donee has never enjoyed or realized the fruits of his investment or labor because he has assigned them instead of collecting them himself and then paying them over to the donee, is to affront common understanding and to deny the facts of common experience. Common understanding and experience are the touchstones for the interpretation of the revenue laws.

. . .

The dominant purpose of the revenue laws is the taxation of income to those who earn or otherwise create the right to receive it and enjoy the benefits of it when paid. ...

. . .

... The owner of a negotiable bond and of the investment which it represents, if not the lender, stands in the place of the lender. When, by the gift of the coupons, he has separated his right to interest payments from his investment and procured the payment of the interest to his donee, he has enjoyed the economic benefits of the income in the same manner and to the same extent as though the transfer were of earnings and in both cases the import of the statute is that the fruit is not to be attributed to a different tree from that on which it grew. ...

5.56 An anticipatory assignment of income by gift does not accelerate the year of taxability. For example, a gift in 1969 of interest coupons maturing in 1970 does not result in taxable income to the donor in 1969 (although he may be liable for gift tax for that year); but rather the donor will have taxable income in 1970 when the coupons mature.[42]

42. Rev. Rul. 69–102; S. M. Friedman v. Com., 41 T.C. 428, affirmed 346 F.2d 506 (6th Cir. 1965), 15 AFTR2d 1174, 65–2 USTC ¶9473.

5.57   To summarize, the concept of the "fruit and the tree" doctrine then is simply this: the income (*fruit*) is taxable to the person who earns it, by reason of his control over the source of the income (*tree*), whether that source is securities or earnings.

EXAMPLE   A gives his son the right to all the dividends (*fruit*) from X Company stock (*tree*) owned by A. These dividends are taxable to A. A must give his son the stock to avoid being taxed on the dividends.

5.58   Now change the above example. Assume that A gave his son the stock but retained all rights to receive the dividends himself. Who is taxed on the dividends, A who receives them or his son who now owns the stock? A, not his son, realizes the income. Here the dividend rights were not contracted *away;* they were *retained.* There is no anticipatory assignment of future income, since it is the tree, not the fruit, being sold.[43]

Allocation of Income between Controlled Taxpayers

5.59   Code Section 482 empowers the Commissioner to allocate gross income, deductions, credits, and allowances among two or more organizations, trades, or businesses (whether or not incorporated) when (1) they are owned or controlled directly or indirectly by the same interests and (2) he determines that such allocation is necessary in order to prevent evasion of taxes or clearly to reflect income.

5.60   Regulation 1.482–1(a)(3) defines control as follows:

The term "controlled" includes any kind of control, direct or indirect, whether legally enforceable, and however exercisable or exercised. It is the reality of the control which is decisive, not its form or the mode of its exercise. A presumption of control arises if income or deductions have been arbitrarily shifted.

The goal of the statutory allocation procedure is to insure that controlled taxpayers are placed on a parity with uncontrolled taxpayers. Transactions between controlled taxable entities must be such as would have been consummated in an arm's-length negotiation between strangers.

5.61   With respect to the allocation of gross income, Reg. 1.482–1(d)(4) adopted April 15, 1968, provides:

(4) If the members of a group of controlled taxpayers engage in transactions with one another, the District Director may distribute, apportion, or allocate income, deductions, credits, or allowances to reflect the true taxable income of the individual members under the standards set forth in this section and in § 1.482–2 notwithstanding the fact that the ultimate income anticipated from a series of transactions may not be realized or is realized during a later period. For example, if one member of a controlled group

43. W. S. Heminway, 44 T.C. 96 (1965) (Acq.).

sells a product at less than an arm's-length price to a second member of the group in one taxable year and the second member resells the product to an unrelated party in the next taxable year, the district director may make an appropriate allocation to reflect an arm's-length price for the sale of the product in the first taxable year, notwithstanding that the second member of the group had not realized any gross income from the resale of the product in the first year. Similarly, if one member of a group lends money to a second member of the group in a taxable year, the district director may make an appropriate allocation to reflect an arm's-length charge for interest during such taxable year even if the second member does not realize income during such year. The provisions of this subparagraph apply even if the gross income contemplated from a series of transactions is never, in fact, realized by the other members.

The Tax Court has repeatedly[43A] held that the second part of the example in the regulation is invalid to the extent that it authorizes the creation of income where none exists. In *Smith-Bridgman & Co.*[44] a wholly owned subsidiary loaned money to its parent corporation for which the latter delivered its non-interest-bearing demand note. The Tax Court found for the taxpayer and held that the Commissioner was arbitrary and capricious in imputing fictitious interest income to the subsidiary.

To the contrary, the Second Circuit Court of Appeals in 1972[45] upheld the regulation and imputed interest income at 5 percent on a non-interest-bearing loan.

5.62

Dividends

Three dates are pertinent to taxes on dividends from stock: the date on which the board of directors declares a dividend, the record date, and the payment date. A resolution adopted on March 1, 1973 might read: "There is hereby declared a dividend of $1 per share on the outstanding shares of common stock of this corporation, payable March 15, 1973, to shareholders of record on March 10, 1973." March 1, 1973 is the declaration date; March 10, 1973 is the record date, and March 15, 1973 is the payment date. If shares of stock are sold before the record date, the purchaser is entitled to receive the dividend, and he is taxed on it. If the shares of stock are sold after the record date, but before the payment date, the seller will receive the dividend and will be taxed on it. When shares are sold between

5.63

43A. Smith-Bridgman & Co., 16 T.C. 287 (1951) (Acq. and explanation of it in T.I.R. 838 of August 2, 1966); Huber Homes, Inc., 55 T.C. 598 (1971); Kerry Investment Co., 58 T.C. 479 (1972) (NA) (on appeal to 9th Cir.); Kahler Corp., 58 T.C. 496 (NA) (1972) (on appeal to 8th Cir.); to same effect Tennessee-Arkansas Gravel Co. v. Com., 112 F.2d 508 (6th Cir., 1940), 25 AFTR 97.
44. Ibid.
45. B. Forman Co., Inc. v. Com., 453 F.2d 1144 (2nd Cir., 1972), 29 AFTR2d 72–403.

the declaration date and the record date, ordinarily the selling price will increase by the amount of the dividend that will become payable to the purchaser. Such increase, so far as the seller is concerned, is merely part of the selling price of the shares and part of his capital gain or loss. So far as the purchaser is concerned, such additional amount paid by him becomes part of the purchase price of the stock and is not separately deductible. Going back to the example, let us assume that $50 was the price per share on February 28, 1973. If no other factors influenced the price of the stock on March 1, 1973, it would ordinarily sell for $51 at the close of business of the stock exchange on March 1. If 100 shares of stock are sold on March 3, 1973, the seller would receive $5,100. From that total he would then subtract his cost, to determine the amount of his capital gain or loss. The purchaser's basis for the shares he acquired would similarly be $5,100, and the $100 includible therein would not be separately deductible. On March 15, 1973, the purchaser would receive a dividend of $100, and all of that sum would be taxable to him as ordinary income. If the sale were to occur on March 11, 1973, the selling price of the shares ordinarily would have declined by the amount of the dividend, so that the seller would receive $5,000. On March 15, the seller would then receive a dividend in the amount of $100, and all of it would be taxable to him as ordinary income.

5.64   The applicable regulation in Reg. 1.61–9(c) reads:

When stock is sold, and a dividend is both declared and paid after the sale, such dividend is not gross income to the seller. When stock is sold after the declaration of a dividend and after the date as of which the seller becomes entitled to the dividend, the dividend ordinarily is income to the seller. When stock is sold between the time of declaration and the time of payment of the dividend, and the sale takes place at such time that the purchaser becomes entitled to the dividend, the dividend ordinarily is income to him. The fact that the purchaser may have included the amount of the dividend in his purchase price in contemplation of receiving the dividend does not exempt him from tax. Nor can the purchaser deduct the added amount he advanced to the seller in anticipation of the dividend. That added amount is merely part of the purchase price of the stock. In some cases, however, the purchaser may be considered to be the recipient of the dividend even though he has not received the legal title to the stock itself and does not himself receive the dividend. For example, *if the seller retains the legal title to the stock as trustee solely for the purpose of securing the payment of the purchase price, with the understanding that he is to apply the dividends received from time to time in reduction of the purchase price, the dividends are considered to be income to the purchaser.* [Emphasis supplied.]

5.65   A dividend declared before a decedent's death is not includible as income in his final return when the record date is after the date of death;[46] instead, it is income to the estate.

5.66   Where shares of stock are the subject matter of a gift and the gift is made after the record date but before the payment date, the IRS holds

46. Estate of Putnam v. Com., 324 U.S. 393 (1945), 45–1 USTC ¶9234, 33 AFTR 599.

that the donor is taxable on the dividend.[47] If the gift is made after the date of the declaration, but before the record date, the Third Circuit Court of Appeals has held[48] that the donor is taxable on the dividend income. The court relied upon the "fruit and the tree" doctrine. It held that under corporate law the declaration of a dividend gives rise to a debt, and it disregarded the fact that the owner of that debt is not ascertainable until the record date. It distinguished (at least it thought it did) a U.S. Supreme Court case in which it was held that dividend income cannot even accrue until the owners of the debt become ascertainable on the record date.[49] This Third Circuit decision seems wrong, but as yet there are no cases to the contrary.

Interest on Bonds Sold between Payment Dates

Interest income to the seller on bonds sold between payment dates is covered by Reg. 1.61–7(d):   5.67

When bonds are sold between interest dates, part of the sales price represents interest accrued to the date of the sale and must be reported as interest income [by the seller].

Interest accruing after the date of sale is taxable to the buyer. Both seller and buyer disregard the accrued interest in determining selling price and cost.[50]

Some years ago, Harold Wells purchased at face value a $1,000 bond of   EXAMPLE 1
the Standard Co. Interest at 6 percent is due Jan. 1 and July 1 (each interest payment, therefore, is $30). On June 1, Wells sold the bond to Edward Frey for $1,025 (of which $25 represented accrued interest to be collected July 1). Wells reports $25 interest; Frey reports $5 interest. Since the accrued interest is disregarded in determining both selling price and cost, Wells has no gain or loss (cost $1,000; selling price $1,000). The basis of the bond to Frey is $1,000.

Assume the same facts as in Example 1, except that the bond was an   EXAMPLE 2
exempt municipal bond. Neither Wells nor Frey will report any interest; Wells has no gain or loss (cost $1,000; selling price $1,000), and the basis of the bond to Frey is $1,000.

A taxpayer must show how much of the money received or paid by   5.68
him on the sale or purchase between interest dates is allocated to capital investment and how much to accrued interest. Otherwise, the construction most favorable to the government will be adopted.

47. I.T. 4007, 1950–1 C.B. 11; contra: F. J. Matchette v. Helvering, 81 F.2d 73 (2nd Cir. 1936), 36–1 USTC ¶9068, 17 AFTR 186.
48. Estate of T. E. G. Smith v. Com., 292 F.2d 478 (3rd Cir. 1961), 61–2 USTC ¶9543, 8 AFTR2d 5040, affirming 34 T.C. 842.
49. Fn. 46 *supra*.
50. Sol. Op. 46, 3 C.B. 90; I.T. 1337, I–1 C.B. 29; I.T. 2050, III–2 C.B. 16.

SPECIFIC TREATMENT OF CERTAIN ITEMS

Gains from Illegal Activity

5.69   Earlier in this chapter we discussed the meaning of income in general and learned that it includes "all income from whatever source derived." Including gains from illegal activity? Yes. In Reg. 1.61-14(a), the statement is made that "illegal gains constitute gross income."

5.70   Although an unqualified "yes" to the above question can now be given, there was a period of time between the Supreme Court cases of *Com.* v. *Wilcox*[51] decided in 1946 and *James* v. *U.S.*[52] decided in 1961 when doubt existed concerning treatment of certain illegal gains, especially embezzlement gains. In *Wilcox* the Court held that embezzled funds were not taxable because they were not received under a claim of right and because an unconditional obligation to repay existed at all times. In *James*, the Court reversed itself and applied the claim of right doctrine (discussed in chapter 14) to embezzled funds, because the embezzler does not have "a consensual recognition, express or implied, of an obligation to repay."

5.71   The courts have included in income the gains from carrying on illegal trades or businesses, whether the business involved racetrack bookmaking,[53] card playing,[54] selling unlawful insurance policies,[55] showing prizefight pictures illegally,[56] conducting lotteries,[57] or providing "protection" by racketeers.[58] The same is true for gains from isolated or casual illegal acts; for example, graft,[59] bribes,[60] fraudulently misapplied moneys of a client by an attorney,[61] and ransom moneys obtained by a kidnapper.[62]

Prizes and Awards

5.72   Prior to the year 1954, confusion existed as to whether prizes and awards constituted taxable gross income or nontaxable gifts within the specific statutory exclusion of 1939 Code Section 22(b)(3), now Section 102(a). As part of the 1954 Code, Section 74 was enacted. The

51. 327 U.S. 404 (1946), 46–1 USTC ¶9188, 34 AFTR 811.
52. 366 U.S. 313 (1961), 61–1 USTC ¶9449, 7 AFTR2d 1361.
53. James P. McKenna, 1 BTA 326 (1925) (Acq.).
54. L. Weiner, 10 BTA 905 (1928).
55. Patterson v. Anderson, 20 F. Supp. 799 (D.C., N.Y., 1937), 20 AFTR 164, 37–2 USTC ¶9461.
56. George L. Rickard, 15 BTA 316 (1929) (Acq.).
57. Christian H. Droge, 35 BTA 829 (1937) (Acq.).
58. Humphreys v. Com., 125 F.2d 340 (7th Cir. 1942), 28 AFTR 1030, 42–1 USTC ¶9237, affirming 42 BTA 857 (1940).
59. Chadick v. U.S., 77 F.2d 961 (5th Cir. 1935), 16 AFTR 218, 35–2 USTC ¶9416.
60. U.S. v. Commerford, 64 F.2d 28 (2nd Cir. 1933), 12 AFTR 364.
61. U.S. v. Wampler, 5 F. Supp. 796 (D.C., Md., 1934), 13 AFTR 195.
62. Humphreys v. Com., *supra* fn. 58.

then new 1954 Code section provides a general rule that money, goods, or services received as a prize or award are taxable. Regulation 1.74–1(a) provides that:

(1) ... Prizes and awards which are includible in gross income include (but are not limited to) amounts received from radio and television giveaway shows, door prizes, and awards in contests of all types, as well as any prizes and awards from an employer to an employee in recognition of some achievement in connection with his employment.

(2) If the prize or award is not made in money but is made in goods or services, the fair market value of the goods or services is the amount to be included in income.

Fair market value depends on the facts in each individual case. A marketable prize is generally included at its resale value less selling expenses.[63] What if the prize is not marketable or transferable—what value is included in the winner's income? The Tax Court indicates that its value is the price of similar goods or similar services that the winner, in his financial situation, could and would otherwise pay.[64]

5.73

In partial recognition of the fact that the courts in 1953 and prior years had held some prizes and awards to be nontaxable gifts, Section 74 also contains exceptions to the general rule. It excludes from gross income certain scholarships and fellowship grants (discussed in the subsequent paragraphs) and also prizes and awards:

5.74

1. made in recognition of some religious, scientific, charitable, educational, artistic, literary, or civic achievement, when
2. the recipient was selected without any action or entry on his part, and
3. is not bound to render any future services as a condition to receiving the prize.

The Nobel prize and Pulitzer prize are examples of awards excluded from income.

In 1969 the Ninth Circuit Court of Appeals reluctantly concluded that awards or trophies given to sports figures for outstanding performance or popularity are not made in recognition of religious, charitable, scientific, educational, artistic, literary, or civic achievement and, accordingly, are taxable under the general rule of Section 74.[65]

5.75

Scholarship and Fellowship Grants

Section 117 was enacted in 1954 to end the confusion existing in determining whether a scholarship or fellowship grant constituted income or a gift. The exclusion from gross income of an amount which is a scholarship or fellowship grant is now controlled solely

5.76

63. L. W. McCoy, 38 T.C. 841 (1962) (Acq.).
64. Reginald Turner, ¶54,142 P–H Memo T.C. 13 TCM 462.
65. Maurice M. Wills v. Com., 411 F.2d 537 (9th Cir. 1969), 23 AFTR2d 69–1515.

by Section 117, and the provisions of Section 102 relating to gifts have no application [Reg. 1.117–1(a)].

5.77 The full amount received as a scholarship or a fellowship by a candidate for a degree at an educational institution is excludable from gross income. However, any portion received that represents payment for teaching or other services in the nature of part-time employment is taxable unless services of that type are required of all students as a condition to receiving such a degree. Further, if a scholarship is awarded by a past, present, or future employer, Reg. 1.117–4(c)(1) and (2) state that the grant is not a tax-free scholarship if it is "compensation for past, present, or future employment services" or if it is for study undertaken "primarily for the benefit of the grantor."

5.78 With respect to a scholarship at an educational institution received by an individual who is not a candidate for a degree and also with respect to a fellowship, whether or not at an educational institution, received by an individual who is not a candidate for a degree, there are limitations. The grantor must be an exempt organization or a governmental body, and the amount of the exclusion is restricted to $300 per month for not more than thirty-six months.

5.79 Regulation 1.117–3 defines scholarship, fellowship grant, and educational institution as follows:

A *scholarship* generally means an amount paid or allowed to, or for the benefit of a student ... to aid such individual in pursuing his studies.

... *educational institution* means only an educational institution which normally maintains a regular faculty and curriculum and normally has a regularly organized body of students in attendance at the place where its educational activities are carried on.

A *fellowship grant* generally means an amount paid or allowed to, or for the benefit of an individual to aid him in the pursuit of study or research.

5.80 Amounts received can cover a wide range of expenses and still be excludable. Excludable amounts include amounts received for:

Tuition, matriculation, and other fees [Reg. 1.117–3(a) and (c)].

Family allowance [Reg. 1.117–3(a) and (c)].

Expenses for travel (including meals and lodging while traveling and allowance for travel of the individual's family), research, clerical help, or equipment incurred to effectuate the purpose for which the scholarship or the fellowship grant was awarded [Reg. 1.117–1(b)] and provided that the amount is specifically designated to cover such expenses [Reg. 1.117–1(b)(2)(i)]. The excess of any amount received over the amount actually used for such expenses will be income to the recipient if not returned to the grantor [Reg. 1.117–1(b)(3)].

Contributed services and accommodations, which means services and accommodations such as room, board, laundry service, and similar services [Reg. 1.117–3(d)].

5.81 Certain amounts do not come under Section 117. These amounts may be taxable as compensation under Section 61 or excludable from gross income as a gift under Section 102 or may be covered by some other section of the Code. For example, a scholarship or fellowship grant "does not include any amount provided by an individual to aid a relative, friend, or other individual in pursuing his studies where the grantor is motivated by family or philanthropic considerations" [Reg. 1.117–3(a) and (c)]. In addition, Reg. 1.117–4 lists the following items as not considered to be scholarships or fellowship grants:

1. Educational and training allowances to veterans.
2. Allowances to members of the Armed Forces of the United States. For example, students at the United States Naval Academy cannot exclude the amounts received under Section 117.
3. Amounts paid as compensation for services or primarily for the benefit of the grantor.

Treasure Finders

The finder of buried treasure must include its value, as measured in United States currency, in income.[66]   5.82

Receipts in Kind

Earlier in this chapter we said that the form of a benefit did not interfere with the benefit being included in gross income. As previously recited, this doctrine is set forth in Reg. 1.61–1(a):   5.83

Gross income includes income realized in any form, whether in money, property, or services. Income may be realized, therefore, in the form of services, meals, accommodations, stocks, or other property, as well as in cash.

The problem is generally one of determining the amount to be included. In connection with the amount included in income when compensation is paid other than in cash, Reg. 1.61–2(d) states: 5.84

If services are paid for other than in money, the fair market value of the property or services taken in payment must be included in income. If the services were rendered at a stipulated price, such price will be presumed to be the fair market value of the compensation received in the absence of evidence to the contrary.

Fair market value is determined after consideration of all the facts and circumstances. "The value sought will be the selling price, assuming a transfer between a willing seller and a willing buyer. ..." [Reg. 1.631–1(d)(2).]   5.85

66. Rev. Rul. 53–61, 1953–1 C.B. 17; Cesarini v. U.S., 296 F. Supp. 3 (D.C., Ohio, 1969), 23 AFTR2d 69–997, affirmed per curiam 428 F.2d 812 (6th Cir., 1970), 26 AFTR 2d 70–5107.

Gain on Cancellation of Indebtedness

5.86   If a debt is settled or discharged for less than the amount due, an economic benefit is realized because the assets have been relieved of a liability to which they were previously subject. The general rule as developed by the courts and partially codified in the statute is that such a gain on cancellation of indebtedness constitutes taxable income. However, there must be a true cancellation, not a satisfaction in exchange for services or property. For example, if an individual performs services for a creditor who in consideration thereof cancels the debt, the debtor realizes income in the amount of the debt as compensation for his services. Similarly, if a debtor settles with his creditor by giving him property, the transaction is treated as a sale or exchange of the property just as if the debtor had first sold the asset for cash equivalent to the amount of the debt and had applied the cash to the payment of the debt.[67]

5.87   To the general rule that the amount of the gain from cancellation of indebtedness is income there are the following exceptions:

1. If the cancellation was motivated by a donative intent and accordingly was gratuitous, a gift results, and gifts are specifically excluded from taxable gross income by Section 102.
2. If a shareholder in a corporation that is indebted to him gratuitously forgives the debt, the transaction amounts to a contribution to the capital of the corporation.
3. If immediately after the cancellation the taxpayer is still insolvent because his liabilities exceed the *fair market value* of his assets, the cancellation is without tax consequences.
4. Somewhat in accord with exception 3, income is not realized from the discharge of indebtedness as the result of an adjudication in bankruptcy by a federal district court if immediately thereafter the taxpayer's other liabilities exceed the value of his assets. Further, the cancellation or reduction of indebtedness resulting from the approval in a bankruptcy proceeding of a corporate reorganization, an "arrangement" or "real property arrangement," or a "wage earner's plan" does not result in taxable income.
5. If the substance of a transaction is a reduction in purchase price, gain on cancellation of indebtedness does not arise.
6. If property is subject to a mortgage but the taxpayer is not personally liable on the mortgage, a cancellation of part or all of the mortgage liability does not result in taxable income.

When income does result from the cancellation of indebtedness, the taxpayer has an election available to avoid reporting the amount as income, provided the debt was incurred (a) by a corporation, or (b) by an individual in connection with property used in his trade or business. The election is found in sections 108 and 1017 and provides for the taxpayer consenting to have the basis of his property reduced by the amount of the gain excluded from gross income.

67. Peninsula Properties Co., Ltd., 47 BTA 84 (1942) (Acq.).

Purchase by the Issuer of His Own Obligations. Gain from cancella-   5.88
tion of indebtedness arises not only from agreements with creditors
reducing or eliminating accounts payable such as for rent or interest,
but also from the purchase by the taxpayer of his own bonds, notes,
or other obligations at a price less than the issuing price. Regulation
1.61–12(c) reads as follows:

(c) **Issuance and repurchase of corporate bonds.**—(1) If bonds are issued
by a corporation at their face value, the corporation realizes no gain or loss.

(2) If, subsequent to February 28,1913, bonds are issued by a corporation
at a premium (as defined in subparagraph (4) of this paragraph), the net
amount of such premium, excluding any portion thereof which is attributable
to a conversion feature of the bond under paragraph (c) of § 1.171–2, is income
which should be prorated or amortized over the life of the bonds. If bonds
were issued by a corporation prior to March 1, 1913, at a premium, the net
amount of such premium was income for the year in which the bonds were
issued and should not be prorated or amortized over the life of the bonds.

(3) If bonds are issued by a corporation and are subsequently repurchased
by the corporation at a price which is exceeded by the issue price plus any
amount of discount already deducted, or (in the case of bonds issued subsequent to February 28, 1913) minus any amount of premium already returned
as income, the amount of such excess is income for the taxable year.

(4) For purposes of this paragraph, bond premium equals the excess of
the issue price of the bond (as defined in paragraph (b)(2) of § 1.1232–3)
over the amount payable at maturity (or in the case of a callable bond, at
the earlier call date).

(5) The provisions of this paragraph are illustrated by the following
example:

Example (i) M Corporation, on January 1, 1946, the beginning of its
taxable year, issued for $115,000, 3 percent bonds, maturing 10 years from
the date of issue, with a stated redemption price at maturity of $100,000.
The bonds were convertible into common stock at the option of the holder.
The value of the conversion feature of the bonds, as determined under paragraph (c) of § 1.171–2, is $11,500. The net amount, or amortizable portion,
of bond premium which is included in income over the 10-year life of the
bonds is $3,500, computed as follows:

Issue price	$ 115,000
Less: Redemption price	100,000
Premium	$ 15,000
Value of conversion feature	11,500
Amortizable amount	$ 3,500

(ii) On January 1, 1950, M Corporation repurchased all of the bonds for
a total price of $110,000. M Corporation thereby realized income for the
taxable year 1950 in the amount of $3,600, computed as follows:

Issue price	$115,000
Less: Portion of original premium previously amortized, 1946-1949 (4/10 × $3500)	1,400
	$113,600
Repurchase price	110,000
Income	$ 3,600

(6) For purposes of this paragraph, a debenture, note, or certificate or other evidence of indebtedness, issued by a corporation and bearing interest shall be given the same treatment as a bond.

(7) For rules relating to amortization of bond discount and the deduction upon repurchase of bonds at an amount in excess of their issue price, see § 1.163–3. [For amortization of bond premium, see para. 8.154–8.156 of this text.]

5.89   In line with this regulation the Supreme Court had held that when a corporation purchases its own bonds, or bonds on which it is primarily liable, at less than their issue price, assets are released from the obligations, a clear gain is realized, and the amount of the gain is ordinary income.[68] However, if a sister corporation is utilized to purchase the bonds at a discount, no gain is realized because the issuing corporation is still liable.[69]

5.90   **Gifts.** In business, the cancellation of indebtedness by a creditor will almost never be a gift. Back in 1943, the United States Supreme Court startled ordinary people by holding in *Helvering* v. *American Dental Company*[70] that a corporation, solvent both before and after the transactions, received a gift, not taxable income, from the cancellation in one instance—and the reduction in another—of its liabilities to unrelated creditors for rent and accrued interest that it had deducted in prior years. In 1949 the Court had second thoughts in *Com.* v. *Jacobson;*[71] and although it did not expressly overrule *American Dental*, it made it quite clear that in normal circumstances businessmen (including investors in corporations) should not be treated as ever making gratuitous gifts to one another.

5.91   The Court of Claims discussed the problem of finding a gift in a business situation in *Marshall Drug Co.* v. *U.S.*[72] The court said that the gift concept

> ... does not apply if the transaction is in fact a transfer of the obligation for the best price available. It does not apply, it seems to us, to the case at bar. The cancellations here were not intended to be gifts. Gifts as a rule are on a personal basis. Plaintiff's creditors were in business. ... The cancelling creditors accounted for the amounts cancelled not as charitable contributions or gifts but as bad debts. These were business dealings. Each cancellation was the result of a creditor's individual business judgment. It was not a gift. The result to plaintiff was an increase in his net worth. The cancellations clearly constituted income.

5.92   **Insolvency.** The rule that taxable income is not realized by a taxpayer from cancellation of indebtedness when he is insolvent (using market values of assets) both before and after the cancellation is based on

68. U.S. v. Kirby Lumber Co., 284 U.S. 1 (1931), 10 AFTR 458, 2 USTC ¶814; Helvering v. American Chicle Co., 291 U.S. 426 (1934), 13 AFTR 876, 4 USTC ¶1240.
69. Peter Pan Seafoods, Inc. v. U.S. (9th Cir. 10–15–69).
70. 318 U.S. 322 (1943), 30 AFTR 397, 43–1 USTC ¶9318.
71. 336 U.S. 28 (1949), 37 AFTR 516, 49–1 USTC ¶9133.
72. 95 F. Supp. 820 (Ct. Cl. 1951), 40 AFTR 380, 51–1 USTC ¶9192.

judge-made law.[73] If the cancellation results in the taxpayer becoming solvent, income results in the amount of the lower of (a) the amount of the cancellation or (b) the amount by which the market value of assets exceeds the then existing liabilities.[74]

Reduction of Purchase Price. When the essence of a transaction is a   5.93
reduction in purchase price, the courts have found that gain on cancellation of indebtedness did not arise.[75] The basis of the asset is then reduced by the adjustment. In order that the cancellation of debt may be treated as a reduction in purchase price, these facts must exist:

1. The debt must have arisen in connection with the purchase (i.e., be a purchase money obligation) and be secured by the property.[76]
2. The negotiations must be direct with the vendor and must be in connection with the purchase price and not the result of an arm's-length transaction relating solely to the debt itself or to a purchase of the obligations at less than par in the market.[77]
3. The taxpayer must still have the asset.[78]
4. The value of the asset must have depreciated below the unpaid balance of the obligation by at least the amount of the cancellation.[79]

The foregoing principles are exemplified in the case of *Hirsch* v.   5.94
Com.,[80] decided by the Seventh Circuit Court of Appeals in 1940. In 1928 the taxpayer purchased certain real estate for $29,000, paying $10,000 in cash and assuming a mortgage indebtedness of $19,000. Partial payments were made until on April 5, 1936, the balance remaining due was $15,000. At that time the property had depreciated in value to $8,000. The taxpayer began negotiations with the mortgagee for settlement, with the result that the mortgagee accepted $8,000 in payment of the balance of $15,000 remaining due. Upon receipt of the $8,000, the mortgagee released the mortgage. The $7,000 reduction was held not to be income.

Gain from cancellation of indebtedness was found to exist, how-   5.95
ever, in the following circumstances. The taxpayer sold a farm in 1946 for $15,000. He received $5,000 in cash and a purchase money mortgage in the amount of $10,000. The adjusted basis of the farm was in excess of the selling price, and the taxpayer deducted the full amount of the loss in computing net income for 1946. In 1947 the taxpayer,

73. Astoria Marine Construction Co., 12 T.C. 798 (1949).
74. Lakeland Grocery Co., 36 BTA 289 (1937); Haden Co., ¶39,465 P–H Memo BTA, affirmed 118 F.2d 285 (5th Cir. 1941), 26 AFTR 679, 41–1 USTC ¶9331.
75. Hirsch v. Com., 115 F.2d 656 (7th Cir. 1940), 40–2 USTC ¶9791, 25 AFTR 1038; Helvering v. A. L. Killiam Co., 128 F.2d 433 (8th Cir. 1942), 29 AFTR 528, 42–2 USTC ¶9487, affirming 44 BTA 1697.
76. E. W. Edwards, 19 T.C. 275 (1952) (Acq.).
77. Fifth Ave.–14th St. Corp. v. Com., 147 F.2d 453 (2d Cir. 1944), 33 AFTR 692, 45–1 USTC ¶9115.
78. B. F. Avery & Sons, Inc., 26 BTA 1393 (1932).
79. *Supra fn.* 77; cf. I.T. 4018, 1950–2 C.B. 20.
80. *Supra fn.* 75.

being in need of funds, offered to accept $9,000 from the buyer in satisfaction of the mortgage indebtedness, and such offer was accepted. The buyer was fully able to pay the entire amount of such indebtedness, and there had been no decrease in the value of the mortgaged property. The Internal Revenue Service ruled[81] that the discount of $1,000 allowed to the buyer upon settlement represented ordinary income to him. It further held that the taxpayer sustained an ordinary loss, fully deductible, and that the transaction did not constitute a sale or exchange.

5.96 **No Personal Liability.** When a taxpayer purchases property on which there exists a mortgage at the time of acquisition, he can either assume the mortgage or take title subject to the mortgage. If he assumes the mortgage, he becomes personally liable; in other words, not only that particular piece of property, but all of his assets can be reached by the mortgagee to satisfy the mortgage liability. If he merely takes title subject to the mortgage, however, he does not become personally liable, and the mortgagee can look only to the property securing the mortgage for its satisfaction. If a taxpayer takes title to property subject to a mortgage but does not assume it, and later obtains a satisfaction and release of the mortgage by paying an amount less than the amount due on it, he does not realize taxable income[82] because he had no personal liability on the mortgage. The basis of the property is reduced by the amount saved. However, there would be taxable income, unless Section 108 applied, if he had assumed the mortgage and thereby had become personally liable.

5.97 **Election to Exclude from Gross Income.** As mentioned earlier, if taxable gain results from cancellation of indebtedness which was incurred or assumed by either (a) a corporation or (b) an individual in connection with property used in his trade or business, an election can be made to exclude the amount of the gain from gross income by the taxpayer consenting to have that amount applied in reduction of the basis of property. The determination as to whether an indebtedness was incurred or assumed by an individual in connection with property used in his trade or business depends upon the facts of each particular case. Regulation 1.108(a)–1(a)(2) offers a guide by allowing the exclusion to proceeds of a debt used to purchase, improve, or repair property used in a trade or business. It is not enough, however, to show merely that the debt was secured by business property.

5.98 If the debt cancelled was represented by bonds or other obligations, paragraphs (1) and (2) of Reg. 1.108(a)–1(b) prescribe the treatment of any unamortized premium or discount entering into the calculation of the amount of gain to be both excluded from gross income and used to reduce the basis of property:

81. I.T. 4018, 1950–2 C.B. 20.
82. Hiatt, 35 BTA 292 (1937) (Acq.); Fulton Gold Corp., 31 BTA 519 (1934).

(b)(1) If, as of the first day of the taxable year in which a discharge of indebtedness occurs, there is unamortized premium, the amount of the income attributable to such premium shall be excluded from gross income. For example: On January 1, 1955, the M Corporation (which files its return on a calendar year basis) had outstanding an issue of A bonds of the face value of $10,000, and as of that day there was $100 unamortized premium on this bond issue. On September 1, 1955, the M Corporation purchased these bonds for $9,000. The total amount to be excluded from gross income under this section is $1,100.

(2) If, as of the first day of the taxable year in which a discharge of indebtedness occurs, there is unamortized discount, the amount of the deduction attributable to such discount shall be disallowed as a deduction. For example: On January 1, 1955, the N Corporation (which files its return on a calendar year basis) had outstanding an issue of B bonds of the face value of $10,000, and as of that day there was $50 unamortized discount on this bond issue. On September 1, 1955, the N Corporation purchased these bonds for $9,000. The total amount to be excluded from gross income under this section is $950.

The consent should be filed in duplicate on Form 982 at the time of filing the original return. In filing this form, the taxpayer consents to have the basis of his property adjusted in accordance with the regulations prescribed under Section 1017 which are in effect at the time of filing such return. The regulations also provide that the consent may be filed with an amended return or claim for credit or refund, if the taxpayer establishes to the satisfaction of the Commissioner reasonable cause for failure to file the necessary consent with his original return, but this procedure is risky.   5.99

Alimony and Separate Maintenance Payments

Code Sec. 71 provides that gross income includes periodic payments of alimony if the payments received from a husband are made under any of the following: 5.100

Decree of divorce or separate maintenance
Written instrument incident to a divorce or separate maintenance status
Written separation agreement
Any kind of decree requiring payments for support or maintenance

If the payments are taxable to the wife, they are deductible by the husband under Section 215. In the unusual circumstance where the wife pays alimony to the husband, she obtains a deduction for such payments, and the husband is taxable on them [Section 7701(a)(17)].

Prior to 1942, the Code contained no provisions taxing alimony payments to the wife, with a corresponding deduction for the husband; but in 1942, the forerunners of sections 71 and 215 were enacted. At that time, however, the provisions taxing alimony payments to the wife and allowing the husband a deduction for them were limited to   5.101

payments pursuant to a decree of divorce or a decree of separate maintenance. The House Ways and Means Committee Report in 1942 explained the new amendment as follows: [83]

> The existing law does not tax alimony payments to the wife who receives them, nor does it allow the husband to take any deduction on account of alimony payments made by him. He is fully taxable on his entire net income even though a large portion of his income goes to his wife as alimony or as separate maintenance payments. The increased surtax rates would intensify this hardship and in many cases the husband would not have sufficient income left after paying alimony to meet his income tax obligations.
>
> The bill would correct this situation by taxing alimony and separate maintenance payments to the wife receiving them, and by relieving the husband from tax upon that portion of such payments which constitutes income to him under the present law.

5.102 The provisions were expanded in 1954, upon enactment of the Internal Revenue Code of 1954. The Senate Finance Committee Report [84] said:

> ... Attention has been called to the fact that the present treatment discriminates against husbands and wives who have separated although not under a court decree.
>
> For this reason both the House bill and your committee's bill extend the tax treatment described above to periodic payments made by a husband to his wife under a written separation agreement even though they are not separated under a court decree, if they are living apart and have not filed a joint return for the taxable year.

This Committee's proposal was incorporated in Section 71(a)(2). The provisions of Section 71(a)(2) are limited to those cases where the separation agreement was executed after August 16, 1954 or was materially altered after that date.

5.103 Paragraphs (1) and (2) of Section 71(a) pertain respectively to decrees of divorce or separate maintenance, and to written separation agreements. A result similar to that flowing from these two paragraphs is obtained under paragraph (3) thereof pertaining to decrees for support. The same Senate Finance Committee Report explains the reasons for the adoption of this paragraph in the following language:

> ... It also provides that this treatment is to be applicable where a wife is separated from her husband if she receives periodic payments from him under *any type* of decree (entered after the date of enactment of this bill) requiring the husband to make payments for her support and maintenance.
>
> ... Amendment was made by your committee to cover cases where amounts made under a court decree for support have not been called separate maintenance payments. So long as the husband and wife are separated, and not filing a joint return, it would appear that the tax effect in such cases should be the same as in the case of a decree of separate maintenance.

83. H.Rep. 2333, 77th Cong., 2nd sess., 1942, p. 46.
84. S.Rep. 1622, 83rd Cong., 2nd sess., 1954, p. 10.

Paragraph (3) of Section 71(a) was made applicable to the decrees of support entered after March 1, 1954. The types of decrees contemplated are those for: (1) temporary alimony entered during the pendency of a suit for divorce or separate maintenance,[85] (2) interlocutory divorce decrees which do not become final under state law until after a stipulated period of time,[86] and (3) decrees for support of an abandoned wife.[87]

5.104

The only payments that are deductible by the husband and taxable to the wife are "periodic payments." Congress intended to draw a line between outright property settlements, which really represent a division of a husband's capital, and periodic payments resembling a division of his income. An example of a periodic payment is one in which the divorce decree provides for the payment of $500 per month to the wife for the balance of her life. A principal sum paid in one installment is a property settlement and does not qualify as alimony. In many divorce decrees, however, the principal sum is specified to be paid in installments. If the installment period extends for more than ten years, Section 71(c)(2) provides that such installment payments are to be considered as periodic payments. Further, if the installment period is ten years or less, the payments will nevertheless be treated as periodic payments if the decree or contract or local law provides that such payments will cease or be adjusted upon any one of the following contingencies: death of either spouse, remarriage of the wife, change of economic status of either spouse.

5.105

A decree or separation agreement providing that the husband is to pay the wife $1,000 per month for nine years is a property settlement, and none of the payments qualify as periodic payments. If that decree or separation agreement provides that the payments of $1,000 per month are to cease upon the remarriage of the wife (or upon her death), a contingency is present, preventing the mathematical calculation of the liability (although one presumably could be made actuarily), and each of the payments qualifies as a periodic payment.

5.106

If a divorce decree provides for a payment to the wife of $10,000 two years after entry of the decree, plus $300 per month until her remarriage or death, the $10,000 is a nondeductible property settlement and the $300 per month is a periodic payment.[88]

5.107

Installment payments extending over a period of more than ten years are treated as periodic payments, but the maximum amount taxable to the wife and deductible by the husband in any one year is limited to 10 percent of the principal sum. This provision was put into Section 71(c)(2) to prevent avoidance of the spirit of the ten-year rule.

EXAMPLE

The qualifying instrument specifies a principal sum of $110,000 to be paid at the rate of $10,000 per year. The husband makes a payment of $20,000

85. Reg. 1.71–1(b)(3)(i).
86. *Ibid.*
87. Rev. Rul. 58–321, 1958–1 C.B. 35.
88. Alton F. Lounsbury, 37 T.C. 163.

Gross
Income
in a year, $10,000 for the current year and $10,000 paid in advance; the gross income of the wife and the deduction to the husband will be limited by the 10 percent rule to $11,000.

The 10 percent rule applies to advance payments but not to payments that cover default in payments for a prior year. Thus, the 10 percent limitation would not apply in the example if $20,000 was paid for the current year plus a prior year.

5.108   The ten-year-10-percent rule does not apply to an outright property settlement coupled with a separate periodic payment plan. Thus, if the husband pays $50,000 plus $500 a month in alimony, none of the $50,000 outright property settlement is taxable to the wife or deductible by the husband.

5.109   **Payments to Support Minor Children.** Code Sec. 71(b) provides that alimony does not include that part of any payment which "the terms of the decree, instrument, or agreement, fix, in terms of an amount of money or a part of the payment, as a sum which is payable for the support of minor children of the husband." The Supreme Court has strictly construed this language.[89] The amount of the payments allocable to child support must be specifically designated in the decree or written instrument. If it is not, the entire sum paid for the support of the wife and minor children of the husband is includible in the wife's gross income as alimony. In *Ida Mae Gilbert*[90] a Family Court ordered the separated husband "to pay $80 biweekly for petitioner and one child." Even though the wife testified that half was intended for her and half for the child, the Tax Court held that the full amount was taxable to her as alimony. The failure of the order to specify the portion applicable to the child was fatal "even though the lack of specificity may be attributable to the lack of artistry of the drafter."

5.110   **Property Settlements.** In most common law states real property owned by the husband is subject to dower rights of his wife, and such rights can only be nullified by her joining in a deed of sale of such property, dying before her husband, or validly releasing such rights. In addition, most common law states provide that she is entitled to a stipulated percentage of any personal property owned by him at his death if she survives him. Further, all states have laws empowering a judge in a divorce action to award some of the husband's property to the wife.

5.111   As mentioned earlier, a property settlement in reality represents a division of a husband's separate capital. It is a taxable event—an exchange giving rise to either gain or loss.[91] The husband transfers property to his wife, and she surrenders her marital rights in the property. Such rights are deemed to be equal to the value of the property received. The transferor husband will have a taxable gain to the extent

89. Com. v. Lester, 366 U.S. 299 (1961), 7 AFTR 2d 1445.
90. ¶69,101 P–H Memo TC.
91. U.S. v. T. C. Davis, 370 U.S. 65 (1962), 62–2 USTC ¶9509, 9 AFTR2d 1625.

that the value of the property on the date of the transfer exceeds his adjusted basis, usually his original cost. If such value is less than his cost, the loss will not be deductible unless the transfer is made after the effective date of the divorce decree.[92] As to the wife, she will have neither gain nor loss, since the rights she relinquishes are deemed to have a value equal to the property received.[93]

5.112

In community property states, if a property settlement merely results in an equal division of the community property, no gain or loss is realized.[94]

Indirect Payments of Alimony. Sometimes the husband makes certain payments for the wife's benefit instead of making the payments directly to her. These are considered payments of alimony made to the wife. Life insurance premiums will be considered alimony if the policies are irrevocably assigned and there is no chance for the husband to recapture any benefit under the policy.[95] Alimony will also include payments by the husband for the support of a wife's relative, such as her mother. **5.113**

In some instances, however, benefits received by the wife are not considered alimony. For example, the wife's legal fees paid by the husband are not considered includible alimony, because they do not have a "periodic quality."[96] If the wife uses the husband's home, there is no includible alimony because presumably the use of the home does not meet the requirement of a "payment."[97] **5.114**

Annuities

Every annuity payment received consists partly of a return of capital (the premium paid) and partly of income. Section 72 pertains to the taxation of annuities, and subsection (b) thereof describes the manner in which the nontaxable return of capital portion is to be determined. A Senate Finance Committee report[98] explains the method as follows: **5.115**

> In the case of amounts received as an annuity (other than certain employee annuities), the proportionate part of each payment which is to be considered a return of investment (and thus excludable from gross income) is to be determined by the ratio which the investment in the contract bears to the expected return under the contract. ... Once determined for a particular contract the excludable portion of the payment remains fixed despite the fact that the individual may die before or after his life expectancy.

· · · · ·

92. Sec. 267; also see ¶9.12.
93. Rev. Rul. 67–221, 1967–2, C.B. 63.
94. F. R. Walz, 32 BTA 718 (1935); A. Y. Oliver, 8 TCM 403 (1949).
95. I.T. 4001, 1950–1 C.B. 27.
96. I.T. 3856, 1947–1 C.B. 23; see also ¶7.00.
97. Pappenheimer v. Allen, 164 F.2d 428 (5th Cir. 1947), 36 AFTR 406, 47–2 USTC ¶9384.
98. S. Rep. 1622, 83rd Cong., 2d sess. 1954, pp. 11, 171.

... In the usual case the exclusion will equal the amount the annuitant paid for the annuity, divided by his life expectancy at the time the payments begin. This exclusion is to remain the same even though he outlives this life expectancy. Under this rule, the company providing the annuity will be able to supply the annuitant with a statement indicating that for the rest of his life a stated amount of his annuity income will be excluded annually from his income subject to tax.

Regulation 1.72–4(a)(2) illustrates the above by the following example:

EXAMPLE
FROM REG.

Taxpayer A purchased an annuity contract providing for payments of $100 per month for a consideration of $12,650. Assuming that the expected return under this contract is $16,000, the exclusion ratio to be used by A is $12,650/$16,000 or 79.1 percent (79.06 rounded to the nearest tenth). If 12 such monthly payments are received by A during his taxable year, the total amount he may exclude from his gross income in such year is $949.20 ($1,200 × 79.1%). The balance of $250.08 ($1,200 less $949.20) is the amount to be included in gross income. If A instead received only five such payments during the year, he should exclude $395.50 ($500 × 79.1%) of the total amount received.

5.116 **Exclusion Ratio.** The computation of the excluded portion of each annuity payment is generally determined by the computation first of an exclusion ratio. That ratio, computed as of the "annuity starting date," is determined by dividing the investment in the contract by the expected return under the contract. Such nontaxable portion of each annuity payment can be expressed by this formula:

$$X = \frac{\text{Investment in the contract}}{\substack{\text{Expected return under the} \\ \text{contract}}} \times \substack{\text{Amount received as an} \\ \text{annuity}}$$

5.117 **Annuity Starting Date.** The "annuity starting date" is important because it fixes, among other things, the occasion for a determination of the investment in the contract as well as the life expectancy of the annuitant. Regulation 1.72–4(b) provides:

(b) Annuity starting date.—(1) Except as provided in subparagraph (2) of this paragraph, the annuity starting date is the first day of the first period for which an amount is received as an annuity, except that if such date was before January 1, 1954, then the annuity starting date is January 1, 1954. The first day of the first period for which an amount is received as an annuity shall be whichever of the following is the later:

(i) The date upon which the obligation under the contract became fixed, or

(ii) The first day of the period (year, half-year, quarter, month, or otherwise, depending on whether payments are to be made annually, semiannually, quarterly, monthly, or otherwise) which ends on the date of the first annuity payment.

(2) Notwithstanding the provisions of subparagraph (1) of this paragraph,

the annuity starting date shall be determined in accordance with whichever of the following provisions is appropriate:

(i) In the case of a joint and survivor annuity contract described in Section 72(1) and paragraph (b)(3) of § 1.72–5, the annuity starting date is January 1, 1954, or the first day of the first period for which an amount is received as an annuity by the surviving annuitant, whichever is the later;

(ii) In the case of the transfer of an annuity contract for a valuable consideration, as described in Section 72(g) and paragraph (a) of § 1.72–10, the annuity starting date shall be January 1, 1954, or the first day of the first period for which the transferee received an amount as an annuity, whichever is the later; and

(iii) If the provisions of paragraph (e) of § 1.72–11 apply to an exchange of one contract for another, or to a transaction deemed to be such an exchange, the annuity starting date of the contract received (or deemed received) in exchange shall be January 1, 1954, or the first day of the first period for which an amount is received as an annuity under such contract, whichever is the later.

Amount Received as an Annuity. An "amount received as an annuity" is defined in Reg. 1.72–2(b)(2) as follows: 5.118

Amounts subject to section 72 ... are considered "amounts received as an annuity" only in the event that all of the following tests are met:

(i) They must be received on or after the "annuity starting date" as that term is defined in § 1.72–4(b);

(ii) They must be payable in periodic installments at regular intervals (whether annually, semiannually, quarterly, monthly, weekly, or otherwise) over a period of more than one full year from the annuity starting date; and

(iii) Except as indicated in subparagraph (3), the total of the amounts payable must be determinable at the annuity starting date either directly from the terms of the contract or indirectly by the use of either mortality tables or compound interest computations, or both, in conjunction with such terms and in accordance with sound actuarial theory.

The regulations cover other refinements, such as amounts to be received for a definitely determinable time (including those geared to life expectancy) in contracts providing periodic payments that vary in accordance with investment expense (as in some profit-sharing plans), cost-of-living indices, and other fluctuations.

Investment in Contract. In determining the "investment in the contract," the question is what is the "net" cost of the contract. To determine this, nontaxable benefits from the company and other amounts excluded from income are subtracted from the aggregate amount of premiums. Regulation 1.72–6(a) provides: 5.119

(a) General rule.—(1) For the purpose of computing the "investment in the contract," it is first necessary to determine the "aggregate amount of premiums or other consideration paid" for such contract. See Section 72(c)(1). This determination is made as of the later of the annuity starting date of the contract or the date on which an amount is first received thereunder as an annuity. The amount so found is then reduced by the sum of the following amounts in order to find the investment in the contract:

(i) The total amount of any return of premiums or dividends received (including unrepaid loans or dividends applied against the principal or interest on such loans) on or before the date on which the foregoing determination is made, and

(ii) The total of any other amounts received with respect to the contract on or before such date which were excludable from the gross income of the recipient under the income tax law applicable at the time of receipt.

Amounts to which subdivision (ii) of this subparagraph applies shall include, for example, amounts considered to be return of premiums or other consideration paid under Section 22(b)(2) of the Internal Revenue Code of 1939 and amounts considered to be an employer-provided death benefit under Section 22(b)(1)(B) of such Code. For rules relating to the extent to which an employee or his beneficiary may include employer contributions in the aggregate amount of premiums or other consideration paid, see § 1.72–8. If the aggregate amount of premiums or other consideration paid for the contract includes amounts for which deductions were allowed under Section 404 as contributions on behalf of a self-employed individual, such amounts shall not be included in the investment in the contract.

(2) For the purpose of subparagraph (1) of this paragraph, amounts received subsequent to the receipt of an amount as an annuity or subsequent to the annuity starting date, whichever is the later, shall be disregarded. See, however, § 1.72–11.

(3) The application of this paragraph may be illustrated by the following examples:

EXAMPLES
FROM REG.

Ex. 1

In 1950, B purchased an annuity contract for $10,000 which was to provide him with an annuity of $1,000 per year for life. He received $1,000 in each of the years 1950, 1951, 1952, and 1953, prior to the annuity starting date (January 1, 1954). Under the Internal Revenue Code of 1939, $300 of each of these payments (3% of $10,000) was includible in his gross income, and the remaining $700 was excludable therefrom during each of the taxable years mentioned. In computing B's investment in the contract as of January 1, 1954, the total amount excludable from his gross income during the years 1950 through 1953 ($2,800) must be subtracted from the consideration paid ($10,000). Accordingly, B's investment in the contract as of January 1, 1954, is $7,200 ($10,000 less $2,800).

Ex. 2

In 1945, C contracted for an annuity to be paid to him beginning December 31, 1960. In 1945 and in each successive year until 1960, he paid a premium of $5,000. Assuming he receives no payments of any kind under the contract until the date on which he receives the first annual payment as an annuity (December 31, 1960), his investment in the contract as of the annuity starting date (December 31, 1959) will be $75,000 ($5,000 paid each year for the 15 years from 1945 to 1959, inclusive).

Ex. 3

Assume the same facts as in example (2), except that prior to the annuity starting date C has already received from the insurer dividends of $1,000 each in 1949, 1954, and 1959, such dividends not being includible in his gross income in any of those years. C's investment in the contract, as of the annuity starting date, will then be $72,000 ($75,000 − $3,000).

Note that Reg. 1.72–6 provides that the investment in the contract shall generally be determined "as of the *later* of the annuity starting date of the contract or the date on which an *amount* is *first* received thereunder as an annuity."

Adjustment for Refund Feature. The investment in the contract is reduced by the value of a refund feature. The definition of that term is in Section 72(c)(2). The rule is illustrated by the Senate Finance Committee report,[99] which said:

Any refund paid to a beneficiary at the death of an annuitant is to be exempt from tax. However, to avoid granting a double exclusion, the annuitant's cost (to be spread tax-free over his expected life) is to be reduced by the refund anticipated computed in accordance with his life expectancy.

Code Sec. 72(c)(2) also requires the reduction by the actuarial value of the prospective refund to be "computed without discount for interest."

... The effect of this computation is to include in the gross income of the annuitant the interest which it is anticipated will accrue from the reserve for the death benefit.[100]

Regulation 1.72–7(b)(4) illustrates the adjustment of investment for the refund feature in the case of a single life annuity by the following example:

On January 1, 1954, a husband, age sixty-five, purchased for $21,053, an immediate installment refund annuity payable $100 per month for life. The contract provided that in the event the husband did not live long enough to recover the full purchase price, payments were to be made to his wife until the total payments under the contract equaled the purchase price. The investment in the contract adjusted for the purpose of determining the exclusion ratio is computed in the following manner:

Cost of the annuity contract (investment in the contract, unadjusted)		$21,053
Amount to be received annually	$1,200	
Number of years for which payment guaranteed ($21,053 divided by $1,200)	17.5	
Rounded to nearest whole number of years	18	
Percentage located in Table III for age 65 (age of the annuitant as of the annuity starting date) and 18 (the number of whole years) (percent)	30	
Subtract value of the refund feature to the nearest dollar (30% of $21,053)		$ 6,316
Investment in the contract adjusted for the present value of the refund feature without discount for interest		$14,737

99. *Ibid.* p. 11.
100. *Ibid.* p. 174.

If, in the above example, the guaranteed amount had exceeded the invest- ment in the contract, the percentage found in Table III should have been applied to the lesser of these amounts since any excess of the guaranteed amount over the investment in the contract (as found under § 1.72–6) would not have constituted a refund of premiums or other consideration paid. In such a case, however, a different multiple might have been obtained from Table III since the number of years for which payments were guaranteed would have been greater.

The Table III referred to in the example is set forth in Reg. 1.72–9. The pertinent portion is given below.

TABLE III. PERCENT VALUE OF REFUND FEATURE

AGES OF MALES AND FEMALES

YRS. DURATION OF GUARANTEED AMT.	M 61	F 66	M 62	F 67	M 63	F 68	M 64	F 69	M 65	F 70
14		17%		18%		20%		21%		22%
15		19		20		21		23		24
16		20		22		23		24		26
17		22		23		25		26		28
18		23		25		26		28		30
19		25		27		28		30		32
20		27		28		30		32		33
21		28		30		32		33		35
22		30		32		33		35		37
23		32		33		35		37		39
24		33		35		37		39		41
25		35		37		39		41		42
26		37		38		40		42		44

5.122 **Expected Return.** The amount of the "expected return" [Code Sec. 72(c)(3)] is relatively easy to determine if the contract provides for specific periodic payments to be paid over a fixed number of months or years, without regard to life expectancy. Regulation 1.72–5(c) states that in this case "the expected return is determined by multiply- ing the fixed number of years or months for which payments are to be made on or after the annuity starting date by the amount of the pay- ment provided in the contract for each such period." However, the expected return on contract payments governed by life expectancies is complex because of the various combinations of provisions in such contracts. The regulations go into great detail. The general principle is illustrated by using an example from Reg. 1.72–5 involving a single life annuity. The portion of Table I reproduced at the bottom of p. 149 is taken from Reg. 1.72–9.

1.72–5(a) Expected return for but one life.—(1) If a contract to which Section 72 applies provides that one annuitant is to receive a fixed monthly income for life, the expected return is determined by multiplying the total of the annuity payments to be received annually by the multiple shown in

Table I of § 1.72–9 under the age (as of annuity starting date) and sex of the measuring life (usually the annuitant's). Thus, where a male purchases a contract providing for an immediate annuity of $100 per month for his life and, as of the annuity starting date (in this case the date of purchase), the annuitant's age at his nearest birthday is sixty-six, the expected return is computed as follows:

> Monthly payment of $100 × 12 months
>   equals annual payment of $ 1,200
> Multiple shown in Table I, male, age 66   14.4
> Expected return ($1,200 × 14.4) $17,280

(2)(i) If payments are to be made quarterly, semiannually, or annually an adjustment of the applicable multiple shown in Table I may be required. A further adjustment may be required where the interval between the an-nuity starting date and the date of the first payment is less than the interval between future payments. Neither adjustment shall be made, however, if the payments are to be made more frequently than quarterly. The amount of the adjustment, if any, is to be found in accordance with the following table:

if the number of whole months from the annuity starting date to the first payment date is	0-1	2	3	4	5	6	7	8	9	10	11	12
And Payments under the contract are to be made:												
Annually	+.5	+.4	+.3	+.2	+.1	0	0	−.1	−.2	−.3	−.4	−.5
Semiannually	+.2	+.1	0	0	−.1	−.2						
Quarterly	+.1	0	−.1									

Thus, for a male, age sixty-six, the multiple found in Table I adjusted for quarterly payments the first of which is to be made one full month after the annuity starting date, is 14.5 (14.4 + 0.1); for semiannual payments the

TABLE I. ORDINARY LIFE ANNUITIES—ONE LIFE—EXPECTED RETURN MULTIPLES

MALE	FEMALE	MULTIPLES
61	66	17.5
62	67	16.9
63	68	16.2
64	69	15.6
65	70	15.0
66	71	14.4
67	72	13.8
68	73	13.2
69	74	12.6
70	75	12.1

Gross
Income

first of which is to be made six full months from the annuity starting date, the adjusted multiple is 14.2 (14.4 − 0.2); for annual payments the first of which is one full month from the annuity starting date, the adjusted multiple is 14.9 (14.4 + 0.5). If the annuitant in the example shown in subparagraph (1) of this paragraph were to receive an annual payment of $1,200 commencing 12 full months after his annuity starting date, the amount of the expected return would be $16,680 ($1,200 × 13.9 [14.4 − 0.5]).

5.123   The determination of expected return becomes more complex in the case of joint and survivor annuities. In the two basic types, the contract pays an annuity to:

1. One person during his lifetime and to another thereafter if he outlives the first.
2. Two persons jointly until one dies, and thereafter to the survivor during his lifetime.

When any of the many variations of these types of contracts are encountered, the regulations should be consulted.

5.124   **Employee Annuities.** Code Sec. 72(d) concerning employee annuities provides for a special cost recovery exclusion formula to be applied in certain cases as a substitute for the regular exclusion ratio. A congressional committee report [101] explains the reasoning and treatment as follows:

So employees will not have to make computations where small amounts of exclusions are involved, an individual receiving a pension financed in part by contributions from his employer will not be taxed under the life expectancy method if the amounts payable under the annuity in the first 3 years equal, or exceed, his cost for the annuity. Such individuals are to exclude all annuity payments until they have recovered their capital tax-free; thereafter, all annuity payments will be taxable in full except, of course, for the retirement income credit. ...

5.125   The employee's cost includes his direct contributions and amounts paid by the employers where (1) the amount was taxed to the employee or (2) the amount would have been tax-free to the employee if paid directly. There is an exception if it is tax-free by reason of the income having been earned outside the United States [Code Sec. 72(f)].

5.126   **Refunds and Lump Sum Payments.** Code Sec. 72(e)(2) provides for the treatment of refunds and certain lump sum payments. Amounts (in the nature of a refund of consideration paid) received in full discharge of the obligation under the contract, and any amounts received under an annuity contract on its surrender, redemption, or maturity are taxed only to the extent that they exceed the aggregate premiums or other consideration paid.

101. *Ibid.* p. 11.

Dividends on Life Insurance and Endowment Policies

Dividends paid by an insurance company on unmatured life in- 5.127
surance or endowment policies generally are not taxable, because in
substance they are partial refunds of premium payments. Should the
total dividends received exceed the total premiums paid, the excess
would be taxable. Dividends on endowment policies are fully taxable
if received after payment of the proceeds has started [Code Sec. 72(e);
Reg. 1.72–11].

Interest credited annually on dividends left with the insurance 5.128
company is income to the insured if he is entitled to withdraw it.

Services of a Child

The amount a child receives is included in his gross income and 5.129
not the gross income of the parent. This is true regardless of any provision of the state law relating to who is entitled to the earnings of
the child and regardless of whether the income is in fact received by
the child [Reg. 1.73–1(a)]. A "parent" includes any individual who is
entitled to the services of the child by reason of having parental
rights and duties in respect to the child [Reg. 1.73–1(c)].

Social Security Benefits

Benefits received under the Social Security and Railroad Retire- 5.130
ment programs [102] are not subject to tax. Social Security benefits that
are exempt include primary insurance benefits, benefit payments to
wife, child, widow, parent, and lump-sum death payments.[103]

Damages

Earlier in the chapter, we said that gross income includes items 5.131
substituting for profits and excludes items substituting for capital.
Damages are included or excluded from income in accordance with
this concept. But personal rights are considered to be capital in nature, so that damages awarded for injury to them are treated as nontaxable capital receipts. In *Edward H. Clark* [104] the issue concerned
the inclusion in gross income of an amount received from taxpayer's tax counsel to compensate the taxpayer for a loss suffered from
wrong tax advice. The court held that the amounts were excludable
from gross income. The court said:

It has been held that payments in settlement of an action for breach of
promise to marry are not income. ... Compromise payments in settlement of
an action for damages against a bank on account of conduct impairing the

102. I.T. 3662, 1944–1 C.B. 72.
103. I.T. 3447, 1941–1 C.B. 191.
104. 40 BTA 333 (1939) (Acq. 1957–1 C.B. 4; N.A. 1939–2 C.B. 45 withdrawn).

taxpayer's good will by injuring its reputation are also not taxable. ... The same result follows in the case of payments in settlement for injuries caused by libel and slander. ... Damages for personal injury are likewise not income. ...

The theory of those cases is that recoupment on account of such losses is not income since it is not "derived from capital, from labor or from both combined." ... And the fact that the payment of the compensation for such loss was voluntary, as here, does not change its exempt status. ... It was, in fact, compensation for a loss which impaired petitioner's capital.

Moreover, so long as petitioner neither could nor did take a deduction in a prior year of this loss in such a way as to offset income for the prior year, the amount received by him in the taxable year, by way of recompense, is not then includable in his gross income. ...

Taxable Damages

5.132   COMPENSATION FOR LOSS OF PROFITS. Substitutes for profits are taxable. Thus, damages received because of a breach of employment contract are taxable.[105] Proceeds received from use and occupancy insurance are taxable because they replace lost profits.[106] Also included in income are compensatory damages for patent infringment[107] and breach of contract or fiduciary duty, but reduced by any loss sustained in a prior year which did not result in a tax benefit. Damages are includible in income if they represent compensation for loss of profits that would have been included in income if received in the regular course of affairs.[108]

5.133   ANTITRUST AND SIMILAR ACTIONS. The Clayton Act (15 U.S.C. 15) forbids monopolistic practices including any criminal conspiracy to fix and maintain prices, terms, and conditions for the sale of manufactured goods. Any private party who has been injured by such practices or conspiracy may sue for treble damages—one-third compensatory and two-thirds punitive. The punitive portion of any recovery must be fully included in gross income on the authority of *Com. v. Glenshaw Glass Co.*, [109] but the compensatory portion is taxable only to the extent of losses sustained in the current and prior years which resulted in a tax benefit.[109A] Further, recoveries under the S.E.C. Act of 1934 or the Investment Company Act of 1940 are taxable.[110]

Nontaxable Damages

5.134   LOSS OF PERSONAL RIGHTS. Damages for alienation of affection,[111] or breach of promise to marry,[112] an amount received in

---

105. Elmer John La Pointe, ¶43,278 P–H Memo T.C.
106. Massillon–Cleveland–Akron Sign Company, 15 T.C. 79 (1950) (Acq.).
107. Mathey v. Com., 177 F.2d 259 (1st Cir. 1949), 38 AFTR 770, 49–2 USTC ¶9428.
108. Swastika Oil & Gas Co. v. Com., 123 F.2d 382 (6th Cir. 1941), 28 AFTR 322, 41–2 USTC ¶9727, cert. denied 317 U.S. 639.
109. *Supra* fn. 11. See extract of court opinion, para. 5.20.
109A. Sec. 186 and Reg. 1.186–1. See also paragraphs 7.31–7.33.
110. General American Investors Co., Inc. v. Com., *supra* fn. 7.
111. Sol. Op. 132, I–1 C.B. 92 (1922).
112. L. McDonald, 9 BTA 1340 (1928) (Acq.). Rev. Rul. 58–418, 1958–2 C.B. 18.

compromise of a suit for annulment of marriage,[113] and other payments received for the loss of personal rights are excluded from gross income. Damages for personal slander and libel are excluded from gross income,[114] but not when the slander or libel pertains to the individual's business or profession. For example, damages received by a lawyer for libel to his professional reputation constitute income. Business libel is distinguished from ordinary defamation of character.[115]

5.135 Payments received as damages for invasion of the right of privacy arising from the production of a motion picture about the life of an individual are nontaxable,[116] but amounts received in advance for granting permission to make the picture are taxable.[117]

5.136 Damages for personal injury and sickness are excluded by Section 104. The tax treatment will be covered in the next chapter.

5.137 DAMAGE TO GOODWILL. To the extent that the goodwill of a business has a cost, damages for injury to it are excluded,[118] but damages received in excess of such cost constitute gross income.[119]

5.138 RETURN OF CAPITAL. Damages for injury to, or destruction of, property are excluded from gross income unless they exceed the tax basis of the property. The amount up to the basis is considered a return of capital.[120] This follows the basic concept: substitutes for capital are not income.

QUESTIONS AND PROBLEMS

1. Neal owned 100 shares of B corporation stock, which he purchased on January 1, 1973, for $10 per share. On January 31, he sold 50 shares for $30 per share. What was Neal's economic, financial, and gross income from B corporation stock?
2. Does the "realization" doctrine mean that no income is recognized unless the taxpayer receives cash? Explain.
3. (a) What is the difference between gross receipts and gross income?
   (b) Are the following items deductible in determining gross income: (1) statutory depletion allowances based on a percentage of gross income; (2) selling expenses; (3) casualty losses; (4) supplies consumed in manufacture?

113. I.T. 1852, II–2 C.B. 66.
114. C. A. Hawkins, 6 BTA 1023 (1927) (Acq.); Rev. Rul. 58–418, 1958–2 C.B. 18.
115. Sol. Op. 132, I–1 C.B. 92 (1922).
116. Madelon W. Meyer v. U.S., 173 F. Supp. 920 (D.C., Tenn., 1959), 3 AFTR2d 1314, 59–1 USTC ¶9409.
117. Runyon, Jr. v. U.S., 281 F.2d 590 (5th Cir. 1960), 60–2 USTC ¶9648, 6 AFTR2d 5345, affirming 4 AFTR2d 5354 (D.C., Fla., 1959); Meyer v. U.S. supra fn. 116.
118. Farmers' and Merchants' Bank of Cattletsburg v. Com., 59 F.2d 912 (6th Cir. 1932), 3 USTC ¶972, 11 AFTR 619.
119. Raytheon Production Corp. v. Com., 144 F.2d 110 (1st Cir. 1944), 44–2 USTC ¶9424, 32 AFTR 1155.
120. Strother v. Com., 55 F.2d 626 (4th Cir. 1932), 10 AFTR 1139, affirmed 287 U.S., 308 (1932), 3 USTC ¶999, 11 AFTR 1091.

4. A lessee occupied a building under a lease with ten years yet to run. The landlord had an opportunity to sell the property at a substantial profit, but the prospective purchaser required that he be given free and clear title unencumbered by any existing leases. Owing to real estate market conditions, the leasehold has a value of $100,000. The landlord pays this sum to the lessee in return for cancellation of the lease. Is the $100,000 received by the lessee a return of capital or taxable income?

5. Upon the expiration of a lease, the landlord receives the land back with a building on it having a market value of $65,000. The tenant had voluntarily and with his own funds constructed the building some years before at a cost of $200,000. As a result of the termination of the lease, does the landlord have includible gross income? If so, how much? Why?

6. Jack Brown negotiates an employment contract with a domestic corporation under which he is to be paid $50,000 per year for five years, and the corporation, in addition, is to pay all of his federal and state income taxes on that salary. Are the payments of such taxes additional income to Brown? Why? If taxable to him, is the amount of the tax on the $50,000 also subject to tax?

7. In preparing the tax return of an individual, you note the following items:
   (a) Interest of $100 on a savings account on which he is listed as a joint tenant. All the money in the account was put in by his uncle. Withdrawals during the year were made only by the uncle and for his benefit.
   (b) Dividends of $500 on stock of his minor son. This stock was given to the son by his grandmother, and $300 of the dividends was used for support of the son. The other $200 was placed in a savings account in the son's name.
   (c) An estate of which the taxpayer was sole legatee received $2,500 in dividends and interest. No distribution was made to the taxpayer. There was no provision in the will one way or the other about distributions of income during administration of the estate.
   (d) A trust of which the taxpayer was sole beneficiary received dividends and interest of $1,000. The trust instrument provided that income should be distributed currently, but no distributions were made.
   (e) Taxpayer received a check in the amount of $300 for interest on a corporate bond purchased September 30. The interest was received on December 31 and covered the period from July 1 to December 31.
   (f) Taxpayer purchased stock from his brother. His brother retained all rights to the dividends thereon. The taxpayer received $600 dividends on the stock and immediately endorsed the dividend checks over to his brother.
   Which of these items should be included in gross income?

8. Which of the following statements are true?
   (a) A taxpayer will be taxed on the gain from sale of securities purchased and sold in his name, though he can prove that the securities were purchased and sold for someone else.
   (b) Some income from illegal activities is not taxable because the Fifth Amendment provides that an individual does not have to incriminate himself.

9. Glass Jaw, a professional fighter, in order to avoid income taxes, incorporated himself and fought opponents as president of the K.O. Corporation. All proceeds from his fights were paid to the K.O. Corporation. Glass Jaw used the earnings of the K.O. Corporation to pay himself an annual salary that would extend well beyond his boxing career. On his individual return, Glass Jaw reported only the salary that he earned from the K.O. Corporation, while all proceeds of his fights were reported on the return of the K.O. Corporation.
   (a) Under what theory presented in this chapter could Glass Jaw be taxed on the earnings of the K.O. Corporation?
   (b) What changes in the K. O. Corporation would you suggest to overcome the above theory?

10. A sells shares of stock in X Corporation to B for $1,000. The contract of sale provides that A is to retain record title until the shares are paid for, B is to pay $400 down, and all dividends received are to be applied on the purchase price. To whom are the dividends taxable?

11. David Smith files his returns on the cash basis. On July 2, 1966, at the "flat" price of $6,900 he purchased 10 bonds of the W Corporation, each in the principal amount of $1,000—bearing interest at 5 percent per annum, payable each January 1 and July 1—and each having attached to it defaulted interest coupons, due each January 1 and July 1 in the years 1964, 1965, and 1966. The bonds had been issued on July 1, 1961, at par and were due on January 1, 1973. No interest was paid on the bonds after July 1, 1963; but on January 1, 1973, they were redeemed at par plus accrued interest.
   (a) What is the amount of the gain in 1973?
   (b) What is the amount of the interest income in 1973?
   (c) If Smith had purchased the bonds at par on the issuance date, what is the amount of the interest income in 1973?

12. A son owns a building that he has leased to a tenant under a net lease for $20,000 per year. He draws up a written document assigning one-half of the future rents to his elderly mother and directs the tenant to pay such half to her.
   (a) What are the tax consequences?
   (b) Do you know of another way in which the desired result could be accomplished?

13. A father gave his son bonds of a listed corporation in the principal amount of $10,000; however, before doing so he clipped and retained the coupons falling due over the next five years. Who will be taxable on such interest?

14. Indicate whether each of the following statements is true or false:
   (a) A prize from an employer for a suggestion on how to increase production is taxable.
   (b) A fellowship grant awarded by the ABC Manufacturing Company to an individual not a candidate for a degree is taxable.
   (c) The taxpayer found a valuable ruby. It was appraised at $5,000. The taxpayer need not report any income until he sells the ruby.

15. A, an employee of Z Corporation received on July 1, 1973, as compensation for services, 100 shares of Z Corporation common stock, par value $10 a share, which has a market value on July 1, 1973, of $15 per share. On December 31, 1973, the stock has a market value of $11 a share. What amount should A report as income for the year 1973 with respect to the stock received?

16. On December 31, 1962, a corporation issued $100,000 of 5 percent

20-year, debenture bonds ($100 face value) which were sold at $95. At the end of the 10th year it purchased for retirement $10,000 of such bonds at $75. What are the tax consequences of the bond retirement?

17. As a general rule, what are several exceptions, both judicial and statutory, that provide for no income on cancellation of indebtedness?

18. H and W were married in 1946. In February, 1969 they were divorced. A 15-year-old son (S) has been since that date, and will continue to be, in the custody of his mother (W). During 1972, H had ordinary gross income of $50,000 and he made timely payments under the divorce decree. Neither H nor W nor S had any relevant financial transactions during 1972 other than those expressly stated in this question.

Assume the alternative terms of the decree set forth below, and that all payments were timely made. What would H's income be in 1972 in each situation:

(a) Under terms of the divorce decree, H was to pay $300 per month to W for the support of W and S until her death or remarriage. W used $100 per month from these payments for the full support of S.

(b) Under terms of the divorce decree, H was to pay $200 per month for W's support plus $100 per month for the support of S. W used the $100 per month for the full support of S.

(c) Under the terms of the divorce decree, H was to pay W $96,000 at the rate of $1,000 per month. H's obligation was unaffected by W's death or remarriage, or by his own death, or by any other contingency. W used $100 per month for the full support of S.

(d) Under the terms of the decree H was to pay W $96,000 at the rate of $8,000 per year. W used $100 per month for the support of S.

(e) Under the terms of the decree H is to take out a life insurance policy on his life in the principal amount of $500,000. It is to be irrevocably assigned by him to W. In addition he is to pay the annual premium of $7,000 per year.

19. Taxpayer, age fifty, paid $30,000 for a nonrefund annuity payable $200 per month for his life only, commencing at age sixty-five. What amount, if any, of the annuity payments will taxpayer be required to report as gross income each year?

20. Sometimes damages are taxable and in other circumstances are nontaxable. Below is a list of common situations. Indicate whether or not the damages are taxable or nontaxable, giving your reason.

(a) Payment to a politician in settlement of a suit for damages for failure to obtain his permission to make a movie on the story of his life.

(b) Payment to a wife for alienation of the affections of her husband.

(c) Payment to a public accountant for slanderous statements that ruined his business.

(d) Payments from a use and occupancy insurance policy to a retail store owner because of a fire.

EXCLUSIONS

FROM

GROSS INCOME

DEATH BENEFITS . . . 159

    Life Insurance Proceeds . . . 159

        TRANSFERS OF LIFE INSURANCE POLICIES . . . 162

    Employee Death Benefits . . . 163

        PAYMENTS TO WIDOWS . . . 163

GIFTS AND INHERITANCES . . . 164

    Gift versus Compensation . . . 164

        TIPS AND HONORARIA . . . 168

    Bequests . . . 169

INTEREST ON GOVERNMENT OBLIGATIONS . . . 170

    Interest on Local Government Securities . . . 170

        RESTRICTIONS . . . 172

            INDUSTRIAL DEVELOPMENT BONDS . . . 172
            ARBITRAGE BONDS . . . 173

    Interest on Federal Securities . . . 173

        U.S. SAVINGS BONDS . . . 173

COMPENSATION FOR INJURIES OR SICKNESS . . . 175

    Limitations on Exclusion . . . 175
    Workmen's Compensation . . . 176
    Damages Received on Account of Personal Injuries or Sickness . . . 176
    Accident or Health Insurance . . . 176

Allowances to the Uniformed Forces for Personal Injury or
Sickness . . . 177
Employee Accident and Health Benefits . . . 177

UNINSURED PLANS . . . 178
WAGE CONTINUATION PLANS . . . 179

DETERMINING THE AMOUNT TO BE EXCLUDED . . . 181

RECOVERY OF BAD DEBTS, PRIOR TAXES, AND DELINQUENCY
AMOUNTS . . . 182

Tax Benefit Doctrine . . . 182
Recovery of Bad Debts . . . 183
Recovery of Prior Taxes and Delinquency Amounts . . . 184
Computation of Recovery Exclusion . . . 184

DIVIDEND EXCLUSION . . . 185
CONTRIBUTION TO CAPITAL . . . 186

Contributions by Shareholders . . . 186
Contributions by Nonshareholders . . . 186

MEALS OR LODGING FURNISHED FOR THE CONVENIENCE
OF THE EMPLOYER . . . 187

Convenience of Employer . . . 187
Condition of Employment . . . 188
Business Premises of Employer . . . 189
Furnished in Kind . . . 190
Cash Allowances . . . 190
Partners and Sole Proprietors . . . 190

REIMBURSEMENTS FOR LIVING EXPENSES ARISING FROM
CASUALTIES . . . 191

DEATH BENEFITS

Life Insurance Proceeds

A provision in one form or another excluding life insurance pro- 6.1
ceeds from gross income has been in all Revenue acts since 1913.
The present provisions are contained in subsections (a), (c), (d),
and (e) of Section 101. Read all of these subsections. Regulation
1.101–1(a)(1) provides:

> Section 101(a)(1) states the general rule that the proceeds of life insurance
> policies, if paid by reason of the death of the insured, are excluded from the
> gross income of the recipient. Death benefit payments having the char-
> acteristics of life insurance proceeds payable by reason of death under con-
> tracts, such as workmen's compensation insurance contracts, endowment
> contracts, or accident and health insurance contracts, are covered by this
> provision. ... The exclusion from gross income allowed by section 101(a)
> applies whether payment is made to the estate of the insured or to any bene-
> ficiary (individual, corporation, or partnership) and whether it is made di-
> rectly or in trust.

To be able to exclude amounts received under a life insurance con- 6.2
tract by reason of the death of the insured, the courts have super-
imposed these other requirements:

1. The amount must not be a substitute for income that would have
   been taxable had the insured lived.
2. There must be an element of insurance risk on the part of the insurer.
3. The purchaser of the policy must have an insurable interest.

The first of these principles is exemplified by the case of Landfield 6.3
Finance Co. v. U.S.[1] There a creditor received proceeds from an
insurance company in an amount sufficient to cover both his loan and
the ordinary interest income that the debtor would have paid had he
lived. The Seventh Circuit Court of Appeals held that the amount of
the proceeds equal to the accrued interest was taxable.

Underlying the policy or contract of insurance there must be an 6.4
element of insurance risk on the part of the insurance company or
other insurer. As stated in Rev. Rul. 65–57[2] the risk must be an
actuarial one under which the premium cost is based upon the likelihood that the insured will live for a certain period and the insurer
stands to suffer a loss if the insured does not in fact live for the expected period.

Where there is a simultaneous purchase of a life insurance policy 6.5
and a nonrefund life annuity contract for a single premium equal to

---

1. 24 AFTR2d 69–5744 (7th Cir. 1969), affirming 296 F.2d 1118 (D.C., Ill., 1969),
69–1 USTC ¶9175, 23 AFTR2d 69–601.
2. 1965–1 C.B. 56; similarly, Rev. Rul. 55–313, 1955–1 C.B. 219.

at least the face value of the life insurance contract, and one could not have been purchased without the other, it has been held that the requisite element of insurance risk is lacking, so that the excess of proceeds received over net premiums paid is taxable gross income.[3] In *Helvering* v. *Le Gierse*[4] involving federal estate tax, a woman simultaneously purchased a nonrefund life annuity policy and a life insurance policy for an aggregate single premium of $27,125. Upon her death one month later at age eighty, the life insurance proceeds of $25,000 were paid to the beneficiary, her daughter. The United States Supreme Court held that the only risk present in the transaction was that the amount of the single premium might earn less than the amounts payable as an annuity but that this was an investment risk. There was no insurance risk because at the time the transaction was executed, the company could not lose even if the insured died the following day. Accordingly, the $25,000 was not received under a life insurance contract.

6.6 A further requirement for the exclusion under Section 101 is that the person taking out the policy must have an insurable interest.[5] Insurance possesses some of the elements of a wagering contract. To prevent persons from gambling on the lives of others, general law requires that the insured have an insurable interest in the person insured by him. An individual always has an insurable interest in his own life, and can purchase a policy naming anyone he wishes as the beneficiary. If the death of a person insured may result in a financial loss to the person purchasing the insurance, an insurable interest exists. Accordingly, an employer, partner, creditor, spouse, or dependent relative has an insurable interest. It is sufficient that the insurable interest exist at the time the policy is purchased; a subsequent change in relationship does not make the contract illegal.

6.7 Lump sum payments received on the death of the insured clearly are excludable from gross income. However, many beneficiaries elect not to take the proceeds in a lump sum immediately after death of the insured, but instead to receive the proceeds at a later date or ratably over a period of time under one of the options customarily found in life insurance policies. One option usually available is to leave the proceeds on deposit with the insurance company and receive interest. Such interest income is not "paid by reason of the death of the insured," and accordingly is taxable income [Section 101(c)].

6.8 Under another option the beneficiary can elect installment payments of designated amounts. The aggregate of such amounts will be more than the proceeds payable in a lump sum. That portion of each installment payment received which diminishes the principal is

---

3. Rev. Rul. 65–57, 1965–1 C.B. 56.
4. 312 U.S. 531 (1941), 41–1 USTC ¶10,029; 25 AFTR 1181.
5. Atlantic Oil Co. v. Patterson, 63–1 USTC ¶9445, 11 AFTR2d 1506 (D.C., Ala., 1963), affirmed per curiam 331 F.2d 516 (5th Cir. 1964), 64–1 USTC ¶9425, 13 AFTR2d 1267; Ducros v. Com., 272 F.2d 49 (6th Cir. 1959), 59–2 USTC ¶9785, 4 AFTR2d 5856, reversing 30 T.C. 1337; but see Rev. Rul. 61–134, 1961–2 C.B. 250.

excludable from gross income. The word *principal* means the amount payable in a lump sum on death. The additional portion of each installment payment is treated as interest and taxed. However, if the beneficiary involved is the surviving spouse of the insured, an aggregate of not more than $1,000 of such interest under all policies on the insured payable to her is excludable annually. Regulation 1.101–4(a)(2) gives the following:

A surviving spouse elects to receive all of the life insurance proceeds with respect to one insured, amounting to $150,000, in ten annual installments of $16,500 each, based on a certain guaranteed interest rate. The prorated amount is $15,000 ($150,000 ÷ 10). As the second payment, the insurer pays $17,850, which exceeds the guaranteed payment by $1,350 as the result of earnings of the insurer in excess of those required to pay the guaranteed installments. The surviving spouse shall include $1,850 in gross income and exclude $16,000—determined in the following manner:

Fixed payment (including guaranteed interest)	$16,500
Excess interest	1,350
Total payment	$17,850
Prorated amount	15,000
Excess over prorated amount	$ 2,850
Annual excess over prorated amount excludable under section 101(d)(1)(B)	1,000
Amount includible in gross income	$ 1,850

Assume the same facts as in example (1), except that the surviving spouse dies before receiving all ten annual installments and the remaining installments are paid to her estate or beneficiary. In such a case, $15,000 of each installment would continue to be excludable from the gross income of the recipient, but any amounts received in excess thereof would be fully includible.

The provisions of Sections 101(c) and 101(d) are mutually exclusive. In order for Section 101(d) to apply, there must be a series of payments. If the surviving spouse is the beneficiary of a life insurance policy in the amount of $20,000, but elects under the policy not to take the proceeds until five years after death and then to obtain $24,000, the $4,000 is taxable interest income under Section 101(c), and the exclusion of $1,000 per year under Section 101(d) does not apply [Reg. 1.101–4(g), Example (1)].

Another option usually available to the beneficiary is to take the proceeds in the form of an annuity for her life. In such an instance a portion of each annuity payment is includible in gross income under Section 101(d). The excludable portion of the lump sum death benefit is determined by dividing such amount by the life expectancy of the beneficiary. In turn, the years of life expectancy are determined from the mortality table used by the insurer in determining the benefits to be paid.

EXAMPLE   If the lump sum death benefit payable under the policy is $60,000 and the beneficiary elects in lieu thereof to take $5,000 per year for life, then, if such beneficiary's life expectancy is 20 years, $3,000 ($60,000 ÷ 20) of each $5,000 payment is excludable. Further, if the beneficiary is the surviving spouse, an additional $1,000 is excludable each year [Reg. 1.101–4(c) and (g), Example (3)].

6.10   **Transfers of Life Insurance Policies.** If a life insurance policy is transferred for a valuable consideration, only a portion of the proceeds received on death of the insured can be excluded from gross income. The amount paid to the transferor plus any premium subsequently paid by the transferee is excludable, but any additional proceeds are taxable. This limitation on the amount excludable from gross income applies only to transfers for a valuable consideration. In other types of transfers, such as gifts, the proceeds are fully nontaxable. Regulation 1.101–1(b) provides:

(1) In the case of a transfer, by assignment, or otherwise, of a life insurance policy or any interest therein for a valuable consideration, the amount of the proceeds attributable to such policy or interest which is excludable from the transferee's gross income is generally limited to the sum of (i) the actual value of the consideration for such transfer, and (ii) the premiums and other amounts subsequently paid by the transferee. ...

(4) ... a "transfer for a valuable consideration" is any absolute transfer for value of a right to receive all or a part of the proceeds of a life insurance policy. Thus, the creation, for value, of an enforceable contractual right to receive all or a part of the proceeds of a policy may constitute a transfer for a valuable consideration of the policy or an interest therein. On the other hand, the pledging or assignment of a policy as collateral security is not a transfer for a valuable consideration of such policy or an interest therein, and section 101 is inapplicable to any amounts received by the pledgee or assignee.

EXAMPLE
FROM REG.   (5) ... Example (1) A pays premiums of $500 for an insurance policy in the face amount of $1,000 upon the life of B, and subsequently transfers the policy to C for $600. C receives the proceeds of $1,000 upon the death of B. The amount which C can exclude from his gross income is limited to $600 plus any premiums paid by C subsequent to the transfer.

6.11   This limitation does not apply and the full amount payable at death is nontaxable if (1) the basis of the transferor in the contract carries over to the transferee and becomes his basis, which will occur in certain tax-free incorporations of proprietorships and partnerships and in certain tax-free corporate mergers discussed in a later chapter, or (2) the transfer of the contract was to the insured, a partner of the insured, a partnership that includes the insured, or a corporation of which the insured is a shareholder or officer [Section 101(a)(2)]. The following example of the second exception is based upon Example (7) of Reg. 1.101–1(b)(5):

EXAMPLE

Jack pays premiums of $500 for an insurance policy in the face amount of $1,000 upon his own life and subsequently transfers the policy to his wife, Jane, for $600. Jane later transfers the policy without consideration to their son. Prior to the death of Jack, the son transfers the policy without consideration to Jack, the insured. Jack's estate receives the proceeds of $1,000 upon the death of Jack. The entire $1,000 is to be excluded from the gross income of Jack's estate. Had the son retained the policy, his exclusion would be that of Jane, namely $600, plus premiums paid by him (the son) subsequent to the transfer.

6.12

The second exception pertaining to transfers to partners, partnerships, and corporations in which the insured is a shareholder or officer was new with the 1954 Code. It is of material benefit to small businesses. For example, assume that two individuals, Black and Brown, own equal portions of all the stock of a small manufacturing corporation. Upon the death of either, the corporation would not have sufficient liquid assets to buy the stock, nor would the surviving shareholder. If Black is no longer insurable, he could transfer a policy on his life—owned by him and taken out many years ago when he was insurable—to the corporation for an amount of money equal to its then market value. Upon his subsequent death, the corporation would exclude all of the proceeds from gross income. The cash could then be used to buy the decedent's stock. There would be no income to the estate, because upon his death, the basis of the stock to the estate would be its fair market value.

Employee Death Benefits

6.13

Section 101(b) provides that there is to be excluded from gross income amounts received (whether in a single sum or otherwise) by the beneficiaries or the estate of an employee up to $5,000 in the aggregate, if such amounts are paid by or on behalf of an employer and are paid by reason of the death of the employee. This exclusion does not apply to accrued wages paid after death to the estate nor to similar items, such as accrued vacation pay.

6.14

Payments to Widows. It has become rather common for corporations, after the death of executives, to pay a death benefit to the widow. Such death benefit may consist of a continuation of the deceased executive's salary for a period of several years, or it can be in the form of a lump sum payment. To the extent that such benefits do not exceed $5,000, they are clearly exempt. Further, the Service and the courts will usually regard such benefits as deductible, ordinary and necessary business expenses paid for past services or to boost the morale of surviving employees. Any aggregate amount paid to the widow in excess of $5,000 may be a gift to her and, therefore, not taxable under Section 102(a) as discussed starting at paragraph 6.17. As to the employer, any excess over $5,000 paid in 1963 or later years, if treated as a gift to the widow, is deductible only to the extent of $25 because of the limitation imposed on deductions of business gifts by Section 274(b) and Reg. 1.274–3(b)(1). Accordingly, the maximum deduction of an employer for payments made to an employee's widow is $5,025, if the amount paid to her in excess of $5,000 is considered a gift.

6.15   To the contrary, if payments in excess of $5,000 received by a widow are taxable gross income to her, then the full amount paid is deductible by the employer but only in the years when actually paid whether the employer is on the cash or accrual basis.[6]

6.16   The limitation of $25 for a deduction of a business gift was added to the Code by the Revenue Act of 1963. One of the purposes was to put a stop to the Service being whipsawed in cases involving payments to widows. In one hundred or so cases, widows sought to have the payments treated as nontaxable gifts, and the employers sought to deduct the amounts as ordinary and necessary business expenses. First, the courts agreed that Section 101(b) means only that the first $5,000 of death benefits paid to a widow are exempt from tax and that no inferences can be drawn from that section as to the treatment to her of amounts above that ceiling. In 1962 the Service agreed that the $5,000 limitation does not apply where the payment is a gift under Section 102(a).[7] Second, in *Com. v. Duberstein*[7A] the U.S. Supreme Court held that, even if a payment in excess of $5,000 was a gift in the hands of the widow, under appropriate circumstances it could be treated as a deductible, ordinary and necessary business expense by the employer.

GIFTS AND INHERITANCES

6.17   The value of property received by gift, bequest, devise, or inheritance is expressly excluded from gross income by Section 102(a). The exclusion does not apply to: (1) the *income* from property received by gift or bequest, or (2) the gift or bequest consisting of *income* from property rather than the property itself.

Gift versus Compensation

6.18   A provision excluding gifts and inheritances from gross income has been in the law since the Revenue Act of 1913. Ever since, the courts have been required in numerous instances to determine whether a

6. Rev. Rul. 54–625, 1954–2 C.B. 85; Rev. Rul. 55–212, 1955–1 C.B. 299; Reg. 1.404(a)–12.

7. Rev. Rul. 62–102, 1962–2 C.B. 37.

7A. 363 U.S. 278 (1960), 60–2 USTC ¶9515, 5 AFTR 2d 1626.

particular payment was a nontaxable gift or taxable compensation. In fact, the very first decision of the Board of Tax Appeals issued back in 1924 involved the question whether a particular individual who was the director and general superintendent of a corporation had received a gift or compensation from it.[8] For purposes of general law, a gift has been defined as "a voluntary transfer of property by one to another, without any consideration or compensation therefor."[9] Such a definition is not controlling for income tax purposes. Further, the decisions in court cases involving federal estate and gift taxes may be analogous, but again do not control in deciding whether a particular payment received is a gift or compensation. It is the intent of the parties that controls. Even if the amount is called a bonus or honorarium, if the parties intended to make a gift, that fact will control. Similarly, if the parties call a particular payment a gift, but it is in fact compensation for past or future services, it will be treated as compensation.

6.19 A landmark case, which is as authoritative today as when decided back in 1937 by the United States Supreme Court, is *Bogardus* v. *Com.*[10] The Universal Oil Products Company began business in 1914, its only asset being an application for a patent for a process to refine petroleum and manufacture gasoline. Its business prospered, and in 1931 the shareholders sold all of their stock in it to an unrelated corporation for $25 million. Prior to the sale, and in contemplation of it, the old shareholders of Universal Oil Products created another corporation called Unopco Corporation. It acquired a portion of the assets of Universal, and its shareholders were the same persons as the old shareholders of Universal. Upon the sale of the stock of Universal, some of its employees continued in the employ of the new owners, but others did not. A few days after the sale of the stock in Universal, meetings of the board of directors and of the shareholders of Unopco were held. At these meetings, resolutions were adopted that the sum of $607,000 be paid as a bonus to sixty-four former and present employees, attorneys, and experts of Universal Oil Products Company, in recognition of their valuable and loyal services to Universal Oil Products Company. Payments ranged in amount from $500 to $100,000. Some of the recipients had been out of the employ of Universal for many years, and one of them was the sister of an employee killed in an explosion about the year 1919.

6.20 In a speech at the meeting of the stockholders of Unopco, its president said they had reason to congratulate themselves on their great good fortune in the Universal Company, that they had profited largely, and that during the years when they were struggling and moving forward they had had the loyal support of a number of employees. He said he thought it would be a nice and generous thing to show their appreciation by remembering them in the form of a gift or honorarium.

8. John H. Parrott, 1 BTA 1.
9. 38 Corpus Juris Secundum 779.
10. 302 U.S. 34, 37-2 USTC ¶9534, 19 AFTR 1195.

The resolution to that effect was unanimously approved. None of the recipients had ever been employed by Unopco or by any of the former stockholders, as such, of Universal. The attorneys for the government and the taxpayers stipulated that "said payments were not made or intended to be made by said Unopco Corporation or any of the stockholders as payment or compensation for any services rendered or to be rendered or for any consideration given or to be given by any of said employees, attorneys, or experts to said Unopco Corporation or to any of its stockholders." Unopco charged the disbursement to surplus on its books of account and did not claim a deduction in its return. The Supreme Court held that the amount of $10,000 received by the taxpayer here was a gift and not compensation. Extracts from the opinion of the Court follow:

... The statute definitely distinguishes between compensation on the one hand and gifts on the other, the former being taxable and the latter free from taxation. The two terms are, and were meant to be, mutually exclusive; and a bestowal of money cannot, under the statute, be both a gift and a payment of compensation ...

If the sum of money under consideration was a gift and not compensation, it is exempt from taxation and cannot be made taxable by resort to any form of subclassification. If it be in fact a gift, that is an end of the matter; and inquiry whether it is a gift of one sort or another is irrelevant. This is necessarily true, for since all gifts are made nontaxable, there can be no such thing under the statute as a taxable gift. A *claim* that it is a gift presents the sole and simple question of whether its designation as such is genuine or fictitious—that is to say, whether, though *called* a gift it is in *reality* compensation. ...

6.21   In the year 1960, in the case of *Com.* v. *Duberstein et al.*,[11] the government asked the United States Supreme Court to promulgate a new test in this area to serve as a standard to be applied by the lower courts and by the Tax Court in dealing with the numerous cases that arise. Its proposed test was stated to be: "Gifts should be defined as transfers of property made for personal as distinguished from business reasons." The Court declined to adopt that test.

6.22   Duberstein was president of the Duberstein Iron & Metal Company, a corporation in Dayton, Ohio. For some years this company had done business with Mohawk Metal Corporation whose headquarters were in New York City, and whose president was named Berman. From time to time, Berman would ask Duberstein whether he knew of potential customers for some of Mohawk's products in which Duberstein's company itself was not interested. Duberstein provided the names of potential customers for these items. One day in 1951, Berman telephoned Duberstein and said that the information Duberstein had given him had proved so helpful that he wanted to give the latter a Cadillac as a present. Duberstein stated that Berman owed him nothing, but Berman insisted, and Duberstein

11. 363 U.S. 278, 60–2 USTC ¶9515, 5 AFTR2d 1626.

agreed to accept the Cadillac. Mohawk deducted the value of the Cadillac as a business expense in its tax return, but Duberstein did not include it in his gross income for 1951, deeming it a gift. Primarily because the Tax Court, as the trier of fact, found that the automobile was intended by the payor to be remuneration for services rendered to it by Duberstein, the United States Supreme Court held that this alleged gift was in fact compensation for services rendered. Extracts from the Court's opinion follow:

... the Government suggests that we promulgate a new "test" in this area to serve as a standard to be applied by the lower courts and by the Tax Court in dealing with the numerous cases that arise. We reject this invitation. We are of opinion that the governing principles·are necessarily general and have already been spelled out in the opinions of this Court, and that the problem is one which, under the present statutory framework, does not lend itself to any more definitive statement that would produce a talisman for the solution of concrete cases.

The cases at bar are fair examples of the settings in which the problem usually arises. They present situations in which payments have been made in a context with business overtones ... an employer making a payment to a retiring employee; a businessman giving something of value to another businessman who has been of advantage to him in his business. In this context, we review the law as established by the prior cases here.

The course of decision here makes it plain that the statute does not use the term "gift" in the common law sense, but in a more colloquial sense. This Court has indicated that a voluntary executed transfer of his property by one to another, without any consideration or compensation therefor, though a common law gift, is not necessarily a "gift" within the meaning of the statute. For the Court has shown that the mere absence of a legal or moral obligation to make such a payment does not establish that it is a gift ... and, importantly, if the payment proceeds primarily from "the constraining force of any moral or legal duty," or from "the incentive of anticipated benefit" of an economic nature, ... it is not a gift. And, conversely, "where the payment is in return for services rendered, it is irrelevant that the donor derives no economic benefit from it." ... a gift in the statutory sense, on the other hand, proceeds from a "detached and disinterested generosity," ... "out of affection, respect, admiration, charity or like impulses." And in this regard, the most critical consideration, as the court was agreed in the leading case here is the transferor's "intention". ... "What controls is the intention with which payment, however voluntary, has been made". ...

The government says that this "intention" of the transferor cannot mean what the cases on the common law concept of gift called "donative intent." With that we are in agreement, for our decisions fully support this. Moreover, the *Bogardus* case itself makes it plain that the donor's characterization of his action is not determinative—that there must be an objective inquiry as to whether what be called a gift, amounts to it in reality. ... It scarcely needs adding that the parties' expectations or hopes as to the tax treatment of the conduct in themselves have nothing to do with the matter.

.   .   .   .   .

... the government's proposed "test" while apparently simple and precise in its formulation, depends frankly on a set of "principles" or "presumptions" derived from the decided cases, and concededly subject to various exceptions. ... The government derives its test from such propositions as the following: that payments by an employer to an employee, even though voluntary, ought, by and large, to be taxable; that the concept of a gift is inconsistent with a payment's being a deductible business expense; that a gift involves "personal" elements; that a business corporation cannot properly make a gift of its assets. The government admits that there are exceptions and qualifications to these propositions. We think, to the extent they are correct, that these propositions are not principles of law but rather maxims of experience that the tribunals which have tried the facts of cases in this area have enunciated in explaining the factual determinations. Some of them simply represent truisms: it doubtless is, statistically speaking, the exceptional payment by an employer to an employee that amounts to a gift. ... The taxing statute does not make nondeductibility by the transferor a condition on the "gift" exclusion; nor does it draw any distinction, in terms, between transfers by corporations and individuals, as to the availability of the "gift" exclusion to the transferee. The conclusion whether a transfer amounts to a "gift" is one that must be made on consideration of all the factors.

. . . . .

... We are in agreement, on the evidence we have set forth, that it cannot be said that the conclusion of the Tax Court was "clearly erroneous." It seems to us plain that as trier of the facts it was warranted in concluding that despite the characterization of the transfer of the Cadillac by the parties and the absence of any obligation, even of a moral nature, to make it, it was at bottom a recompense for Duberstein's past services or an inducement for him to be of further service in the future. ...

6.23   In Rev. Rul. 69–140 [12] the Service ruled that, if a majority stockholder makes gifts of shares of stock to employees of a corporation basing the number of shares allotted to each on the number of years of service, the employees receive ordinary compensation income. The ruling referred to both the *Bogardus* and *Duberstein* cases. The same result was reached in Rev. Rul. 69–369 where as part of a preconceived plan the majority stockholder gave the shares to the corporation and it distributed them to the employees. Further, the corporation was not entitled to a deduction for compensation paid. However, in Rev. Rul. 69–368 the stockholder when contributing his shares to the corporation stipulated that it could use them as it saw fit. Later the corporation decided to distribute the shares to its employees. The employees were held to have realized compensation income in the amount of the fair market value of the shares, and the corporation was entitled to a deduction of the same amount.

6.24   **Tips and Honoraria.** Regulation 1.61–2(a)(1) provides:

... tips, bonuses (including Christmas bonuses), termination or severance pay, rewards, jury fees, marriage fees and other contributions received by a clergyman for services ... are income to the recipients unless excluded by law.

12. 1969–1 C.B. 46.

The regulation is supported by the courts, which hold that tips and similar amounts are "conferred on the basis of a consideration which is related to service. This makes it clearly income. ..."[13] "A payment may be compensation for services rendered although made voluntarily and without legal obligation. ..."[14]

6.25 Effective January 1, 1966, the Social Security Amendments of 1965 subjected tips to Social Security tax and withholding of income tax where the amount of tips received during one calendar month during employment for one employer amounts to $20 or more. The employee is required to file one or more statements with his employer during the month and up to the tenth day after the month showing the amounts of tips received. To the extent that wages paid by the employer are sufficient, the employer then must withhold the employee's share of Social Security tax and also income tax. If the amount of wages payable is not sufficiently large to permit withholding of the entire amount, the employer then is required to give the employee, with a copy to Internal Revenue Service, a written statement showing the amount of withholding tax and Social Security tax that could not be withheld.

Bequests

6.26 A bequest is a gift (a legacy) of personal property to a legatee pursuant to the provisions of a will. A devise is a gift of real property to a devisee pursuant to the provisions of a will. Both a bequest and a devise are within the scope of the word *inheritance,* but inheritance also includes real and personal property received from an estate where the decedent did not leave a valid will; that is, where he died intestate. For the sake of convenience in this discussion and also because most of the points relate to persons who die testate (i.e., leaving a valid will), the term *bequest* has been used to embrace devises and inheritances, also.

6.27 A bequest from the principal (i.e., corpus) of an estate, when received as such, is always tax-free under Section 102. The following types of bequests are taxable and do not come within the exclusion provisions of this section:

1. The bequest of income from property.
2. The portion of each distribution that is actually out of income in those cases where the bequest is to be distributed at intervals out of either corpus or income.
3. The amount includible in income of the beneficiaries under the provisions in Subchapter J pertaining to the taxation of estates, trusts, and their beneficiaries.

6.28 There is an exception to the second item in the tabulation. Section 663(a)(1) provides that if *under the terms of the will* (1) the bequest

13. Roberts v. Com., 176 F.2d 221 (9th Cir. 1949), 49–2 USTC ¶9330, 38 AFTR 296.
14. Hubert, 20 T.C. 201 (1953), affirmed 212 F.2d 516 (5th Cir. 1954) 54–1 USTC ¶9378, 45 AFTR 1465.

is of a specific sum of money or of specific property, (2) is payable all at once or in not more than three installments, and (3) is payable out of either corpus or income, then the amount of such bequest is excludable from gross income, and is tax-free. Regulation 1.663(a)–1(b)(2) states that the following amounts are not considered as gifts or bequests of a sum of money or of specific property within the meaning of Section 663(a)(1) and, therefore, are taxable to the extent paid from income:

(i) An amount which can be paid or credited only from the income of an estate or trust, whether from the income for the year of payment or crediting, or from the income accumulated from a prior year;

(ii) An annuity, or periodic gifts of specific property in lieu of or having the effect of an annuity;

(iii) A residuary estate or the corpus of a trust; or

(iv) A gift or bequest paid in a lump sum or in not more than three installments, if the gift or bequest is required to be paid in more than three installments under the terms of the governing instrument.

Paragraph (3) of the same section of the Regulations gives the following example:

Under the terms of a will, a legacy of $5,000 was left to A, 1,000 shares of X company stock was left to W, and the balance of the estate was to be divided equally between W and X. No provision was made in the will for the disposition of income of the estate during the period of administration. The estate had income of $25,000 during the taxable year 1954, which was accumulated and added to corpus for estate accounting purposes. During the taxable year, the executor paid the legacy of $5,000 in a lump sum to A and transferred the X company stock to W. No other distributions to beneficiaries were made during the taxable year. The distributions to A and W qualify as exclusions within the meaning of Section 633(a)(1).

6.29 Amounts received from the estate of a decedent by an heir in settlement of a will contest are treated as bequests.[15]

INTEREST ON GOVERNMENT OBLIGATIONS

Interest on Local Government Securities

6.30 Section 103(a)(1) provides for the exclusion from gross income of *interest* on the *obligations* of a state, a territory, or a possession of the United States, or any *political subdivision* of any of the foregoing, or the District of Columbia. A similar exclusion has been provided since the Revenue Act of 1913. Notice that the words *interest, obligations,* and *political subdivision* have been emphasized. The interpretation of these terms will be reviewed in the next several paragraphs.

15. Lyeth v. Hoey, 305 U.S. 188 (1938), 38–2 USTC ¶9602, 21 AFTR 986; Charlotte Keller, 41 BTA 478 (1940).

Interest has been defined as the compensation allowed by law or   6.31
fixed by the parties for the use, forbearance, or detention of money.[16]
According to this concept, gain from the sale of state or municipal
bonds [17] does not constitute interest, but gain from the sale of certificates of indebtedness for past-due municipal bond interest coupons
has been considered tax-free interest and not taxable gain.[18] A premium that a state pays pursuant to the bonds' terms, in order to redeem them prior to the regular maturity date,[19] does not meet the
definition of interest because the premium is not paid for the use,
forbearance, or detention of money. In 1957, and again in 1960, the
Internal Revenue Service issued rulings concerning the treatment of
discount on municipal bonds purchased by investors.[20] If a series
of municipal bonds maturing in varying years is purchased by a
dealer at an amount slightly above the aggregate par value, then
resold by him to the public—some issues at a premium and some
issues at a discount—the discount element is not interest. If the bonds
purchased at a discount by investors are held until maturity, they
will then realize recognized gain in the amount of the redemption
price received over the purchase price paid. In the event the investors sell the bonds before maturity, the discounted amount that
they paid for the bonds will represent their tax basis for the measurement of gain or loss.

The term *obligation* has been interpreted by the courts as referring   6.32
only to obligations issued in the exercise of the state's or political
subdivision's borrowing power. Thus interest on a condemnation
award is not excluded, because the award can in no way affect the
borrowing power of a state. There is no borrowing. Instead, there is
a purchase by the state under its right of eminent domain.[21] This
same reasoning has been applied to deny the exclusion to interest
paid on a refund of taxes [22] or paid in addition to the principal sum
awarded as damages for personal injury.[23]

Regulation 1.103–1 provides: 6.33

... Certificates issued by a political subdivision for public improvements
(such as sewers, sidewalks, streets, etc.) which are evidence of special
assessments against specific property, which assessments become a lien
against such property and which the political subdivision is required to enforce, are, for purposes of this section, obligations of the political subdivision
even though the obligations are to be satisfied out of special funds and not
out of general funds of taxes.

16. Fall River Electric Co., 23 BTA 168 (1931).
17. Willicuts v. Bunn, 282 U.S. 216 (1931), 2 USTC ¶640, 9 AFTR 584.
18. Palm Beach Tr. Co., 9 T.C. 1060, affirmed 174 F.2d 527 (C.A., D.C., 1949),
49–1 USTC ¶9246, 37 AFTR 1478.
19. G.C.M. 21890, 1940–1 C.B. 85.
20. Rev. Rul. 57–49, 1957–1 C.B. 62; Rev. Rul. 60–210, 1960–1 C.B. 38.
21. U.S. Trust Co. of N.Y. v. Anderson, 65 F.2d 575 (2d Cir. 1933), 3 USTC ¶1125,
12 AFTR 836, Rev. Rul. 72–77; Holley v. U.S., 124 F.2d 909 (6th Cir. 1942), 42–1 USTC
¶9205, 28 AFTR 863.
22. I.T. 1748, II–2 C.B. 92 (1923).
23. Theodate Pope Riddle, 27 BTA 1339 (1933).

Accordingly, interest is exempt on special assessment bonds issued by a municipality under a general statute for the purpose of providing funds for the installation of a municipal water system, the bonds and interest being payable only out of a special fund created through the setting aside of a certain proportion of the revenue of the municipally owned utility.[24]

6.34   Interest payable by a municipality or state under written agreements or notes issued as part of the purchase price of materials or construction work is tax-exempt.[25]

6.35   The third term, *political subdivision*, is defined by Reg. 1.103–1:

> ... The term "political subdivision," for purposes of this section, denotes any division of the State, Territory, or possession of the United States which is a municipal corporation, or to which has been delegated the right to exercise part of the sovereign power of the State, Territory, or possession of the United States. As thus defined, a political subdivision of a State, Territory, or possession of the United States may or may not, for purposes of this section, include special assessment districts so created, such as road, water, sewer, gas, light, reclamation, drainage, irrigation, levee, school, harbor, port improvement, and similar districts and divisions of a State, Territory, or possession of the United States.

The following are examples of political subdivisions and obligations thereof which have qualified for the exclusion of interest: Mackinac Bridge Authority;[26] Maine Turnpike Authority;[27] State University;[28] Port of New York Authority Bonds;[29] Triborough Bridge Authority (N.Y.);[30] N.Y. State Housing Finance Agency;[31] federally backed bonds of local housing authorities.[32]

Restrictions

6.36   INDUSTRIAL DEVELOPMENT BONDS. In recent years municipalities have used industrial development bonds to attract industry. A city wishing to persuade a particular corporation to establish and operate a factory would issue industrial development bonds of say $5,000,000 and use the proceeds to purchase land and erect the building. The corporation then would lease the factory from the city for a rental equal to the amount necessary to pay the interest and amortize the principal on the bonds. The city would use the rental proceeds

24. Rev. Rul. 58–452, 1958–2 C.B. 37.

25. Newlin Machinery Corp., 28 T.C. 837 (Acq.); Rev. Rul. 60–179, 1960–1 C.B. 37; Com. v. Henry Von L. Meyer, 104 F.2d 155 (2nd Cir. 1939), 39–1 USTC ¶9518, 23 AFTR 31.

26. Rev. Rul. 55–75, 1955–1 C.B. 238.

27. Rev. Rul. 55–76, 1955–1 C.B. 239; see also Rev. Rul. 54–496, 1954–2 C.B. 60.

28. G.C.M. 10557, XI–1 C.B. 21 (1932).

29. Shamberg, 3 T.C. 131, affirmed 144 F.2d 998 (2nd Cir. 1944), 44–2 USTC ¶9446, 32 AFTR 1295, cert. denied.

30. White, 3 T.C. 156, affirmed 144 F.2d 1019 (2nd Cir. 1944), 44–2 USTC ¶9447, 32 AFTR 1316, cert. denied.

31. Rev. Rul. 60–248, 1960–2 C.B. 35.

32. Sec. 5(d), U.S. Housing Act of 1937, as amended.

to service the outstanding bonds. The lease and the plant would be pledged as security for payment of the bonds. In March, 1968, the Internal Revenue Service acted to revoke Rev. Rul. 54–106, holding that interest on industrial development bonds is tax-exempt, by publishing proposed Reg. 1.103–7 to terminate the tax-exempt status. Prompted by that occurrence, Congress inserted in the Revenue and Expenditure Control Act of 1968 an amendment to Section 103 that limits the types and amounts of new industrial development bonds from which the interest will qualify for tax exemption. Interest on industrial development bonds issued before May 1, 1968, remains tax-free. Further, where a commitment to issue such bonds existed before May 1, 1968, and the bonds were actually issued before January 1, 1969, the interest will not be taxed. Finally, if the issue of new bonds is $1,000,000 or less (under certain circumstances up to $5,000,000), the interest will be tax-exempt. There are also exemptions for bonds, no matter how large the issue, whose proceeds are used to acquire or provide certain specified facilities.

ARBITRAGE BONDS. With exceptions to be found in Section 103 added to the Code by the Tax Reform Act of 1969, interest on arbitrage bonds issued by state and local governments after October 9, 1969, is taxable. An arbitrage bond is one the proceeds of which are invested in other bonds, taxable government or corporate, providing a higher return. **6.37**

Interest on Federal Securities

Interest on federal securities may be entirely exempt, partially exempt, or entirely taxable. It is mostly a matter of memory as to which is which; but today the income from such types of securities is usually taxable, because the exemption provisions pertain only to securities issued many years ago. For the applicable provisions see Section 103 and the regulations thereunder. **6.38**

U.S. Savings Bonds. There are two types of U.S. Savings Bonds currently outstanding—those issued at par and paying interest semiannually, and those issued at a discount, for example, having a principal amount of $100 and purchased for $75. Those issued at par and paying interest currently include Series G, H, and K, as well as Investment Series A–1965 and B–1975–1980 bonds. Those issued at a discount include Series E, F, and J. Interest received on the current income bonds is of course taxable when received. Interest on discount bonds is represented by the amount of the discount and accrues ratably until the maturity date according to the table of redemption values printed on each bond. A cash basis taxpayer owning any of these discount bonds (1) may defer reporting the interest until the year he cashes the bonds or the year they mature, whichever is earlier, or (2) may elect to report the accrued interest each year.[33] **6.39**

33. T.D. Circular No. 653, 8th Revision, Dec. 1, 1969, 34 F.R. 19402.

Once a person elects to report the interest each year, he must continue to do so for all discount bonds owned and those subsequently acquired. He may not change to the deferral method unless he first receives permission to do so. If he is deferring the reporting of interest and wishes to change to reporting the interest each year, he can do so without obtaining permission; however, in the year of change he must report all interest not previously reported on all such bonds.

6.40   Series E bonds can be held beyond maturity. These bonds, held beyond maturity, will continue to earn interest through increases in redemption values. If a taxpayer has chosen the deferral method of reporting the increase in redemption values but continues to hold the bonds beyond maturity date, no interest need be included in income for the year of maturity, but instead will be reported in the year of actual redemption or the year in which the period of extension ends, whichever is earlier.[34]

Series E bonds are issued in three approved forms of registration: (1) one person as sole owner, (2) two persons as owner and beneficiary, such as "John Smith, but on his death John Smith, Jr.," or (3) two persons as co-owners, either as owners in common, or as owners in the alternative with right of survivorship.[35] If John Brown
6.41   buys a bond in the name of himself and Jane Brown as co-owners, whether or not in the alternative with right of survivorship, the interest is the income of John Brown because he is the one who contributed the purchase price. If John Brown and Jane Brown buy bonds in co-ownership, each contributing part of the purchase price, the interest is income to each of them in proportion to their respective contributions to the purchase price. If John Brown and Jane Brown receive the bonds in co-ownership as a gift from Grandfather Brown, the interest is income to John and Jane—50 percent to each co-owner. If a father with his own funds purchases a Series E bond and has it registered in the names of himself and his son in the alternative as co-owners, he will realize interest income in the amount of the increment in value on that later date upon which he may cause the bond to be reissued in the name of his son.[36] If a bond is purchased in the name of an individual as the owner with another person named as beneficiary upon death, and the owner dies before maturity, there is no taxable income realized by the estate of the owner, but instead the beneficiary, upon cashing the bond or upon the happening of the maturity date, will realize interest income in the full amount of the increment in value since date of purchase of the bond by the owner.[37]

34. *Ibid.*
35. *Some Legal Aspects of United States Savings Bonds* (Washington, D.C.: Govt. Printing Office), p. 4.
36. Rev. Rul. 55–278, 1955–1 C.B. 471.
37. Rev. Rul. 64–104, 1964–1 C.B. 223.

COMPENSATION FOR INJURIES OR SICKNESS

To alleviate the hardships arising from injuries or sickness, Con- 6.42
gress has granted full or partial exclusion of benefits and other payments received by individuals attributable to injuries and illness.
The subject is covered by Code Sections 104, 105, and 106; and
amounts received are categorized by their source:

1. Workmen's compensation
2. Damages
3. Accident or health insurance policies purchased by the individual
   or anyone else other than an employer
4. A national government in the case of members of the armed forces
   and the U.S. government in the case of certain Public Health and
   Foreign Service officers
5. Employers or insurance policies purchased by employers

Limitations on Exclusion

In chapter 10, we shall see that an individual is allowed a deduc- 6.43
tion under Section 213 for medical expenses, subject to a floor on the
amount deductible. In addition to payments to hospitals, physicians,
dentists, and drugstores, premiums for accident or health insurance
are also deductible, one-half of such premiums up to $150 being de-
ductible in full without any floor. In the first four categories listed
in the preceding paragraph, any portion of a payment received that
is a reimbursement of medical expenses deducted in the same or a
prior year is taxable, but all of the balance is nontaxable. If no deduction was allowed for medical expenses—for example, because
the amount was not large enough to be deductible—then the full
amount of the benefit payment is excludable from gross income.
The fifth source listed above will be discussed later. Only amounts
that specifically reimburse an individual for medical expenses and
do not exceed the amount deducted are includible in gross income
[Reg. 1.105–2].

Assume that in a prior year an individual was involved in an automobile EXAMPLE 1
accident. In that prior year he spent the sum of $5,000 for hospital and
medical bills, and after applying the limiting factors of Section 213, deducted
$4,000. In the current year he recovers $20,000 from the offender's insurance
company. Of that sum, $5,000 is stated to be reimbursement for hospital and
medical expenditures, and $15,000 is stated to be damages. The sum of
$16,000 can be excluded from the current year's income, but the amount of
$4,000 must be included.

The facts are the same as in Example 1, except that no part of the $20,000 EXAMPLE 2 award is described as being reimbursement for hospital and medical expenditures. The full $20,000 is excludable from income.

Workmen's Compensation

6.44   Every state has a workmen's compensation law imposing liability on employers to make payments to their employees for work-connected injuries or illness. Most employers purchase insurance against this risk. Amounts received because of occupational sickness or injury are fully exempt from tax. If the employee turns over his workmen's compensation payments to his employer, and the employer continues to pay the employee all or a part of his regular salary, not only the amount of the workmen's compensation is exempt, but also the excess of the salary payments received over the amount of workmen's compensation may be fully or partly exempt from tax (as explained in paragraph 6.54) because it is received under a sick-pay plan.

EXAMPLE   Jones is hurt on the job and out of work for six weeks. His employer continues to pay him his salary of $200 a week, or $1,200 for the time he is absent. He received $30 a week, or a total of $180, as workmen's compensation because of the injury, and turns it all over to his employer under his employment contract. The $30 is fully excludable from his income, and the balance of $170 a week is received under a sick-pay plan.[38]

Damages Received on Account of Personal Injuries or Sickness

6.45   Regulation 1.104–1(c) provides:

Section 104(a)(2) excludes from gross income the amount of any damages received (whether by suit or agreement) on account of personal injuries or sickness. The term "damages received (whether by suit or agreement)" means an amount received (other than workmen's compensation) through prosecution of a legal suit or action based upon tort or tort type rights, or through a settlement agreement entered into in lieu of such prosecution.

Accident or Health Insurance

6.46   Section 104(a)(3) excludes amounts received through accident or health insurance for personal injuries or sickness except to the extent of any reimbursement for medical expenses deducted under Section 213. If an individual with his own funds purchases an accident or health insurance policy, any recovery is clearly tax-exempt. Similarly, if the policy is a group policy purchased by an employer, but all of the premiums are paid by the employee, any recovery is tax-exempt. However, if the employer pays a part or all of the premiums under that group policy, Section 104 does not apply to exempt the

38. *Your Federal Income Tax*, 1973 ed., pp. 61, 64.

proceeds, but Section 105 may. In the case of a sole proprietor, Rev. Rul. 58–90[39] holds that if such a person purchases an individual insurance policy providing income replacement payments in the event of his sickness or disability, benefits received are tax-exempt under Section 104, but the premium payments are nondeductible personal expenditures.

Allowances to the Uniformed Forces for Personal Injury or Sickness

Regulation 1.104–1(e) provides:

6.47

Section 104(a)(4) excludes from gross income amounts which are received as a pension, annuity, or similar allowance for personal injuries or sickness resulting from active service in the armed forces of any country, or in the Coast and Geodetic Survey, or the Public Health Service. Section 104(a)(4) is applicable to a pension, annuity, or similar allowance received by the beneficiaries of an individual by reason of the death of such individual due to a personal injury or sickness resulting from service in the armed forces of any country, or the Coast and Geodetic Survey, or the Public Health Service. For purposes of this section, that part of the retired pay of a member of an armed force, computed under 10 U.S.C. 1402(d), on the basis of years of service, which exceeds the retired pay that he would receive if it were computed on the basis of percentage of disability is not considered as a pension, annuity, or similar allowance for personal injury or sickness, resulting from active service in the armed forces, or in the Coast and Geodetic Survey, or the Public Health Service. ...

Employee Accident and Health Benefits

Among the more common fringe benefits provided for employees are accident and sickness benefits. Some employers finance their liabilities under these plans by buying insurance; others do not. In insured plans, sometimes the employer will pay the full amount of the premiums, sometimes an employer and his employees will share the cost. Whether or not a plan is insured, Section 105 applies to the benefits received by employees.

6.48

Under all plans, regardless of whether the employee pays any part of the cost, the following amounts are excludable from gross income:

6.49

1. Reimbursements for medical expenses of the employee, his wife, or dependents to the extent that the reimbursement (a) does *not* exceed the actual expenses incurred and (b) *does* exceed any amount deducted under Section 213 as medical expenses.[40]

Medical expenses incurred last year were $2,000; amount deducted on the return for that year was $500. Reimbursement received this year is $2,000. The sum of $500 is taxable and $1,500 is excludable.

EXAMPLE 1

39. 1958–1 C.B. 88.
40. Rev. Rul. 69–154.

EXAMPLE 2   Same facts as Example 1 except that reimbursement is $2,200. Again the sum of $500 is taxable and $1,500 is excludable. As to the remaining $200 of recovery, some or all of it will be taxable if the employer paid part or all of the cost of providing that benefit, as discussed in the next paragraph.

2. Benefits paid for the permanent loss or loss of use of a member or function of the body, or the permanent disfigurement of the employee, his wife, or dependents, if the amounts payable are based on the nature of the injury and not on the time the employee is absent from work. (The employee need not report in gross income the amounts of medical expense deductions he took under Section 213.)

EXAMPLE 3   An employee lost the sight of one eye as the result of an automobile accident. His medical expenses totaled $4,000; and of that amount, $1,500 was deducted. A benefit payment of $10,000 is received. The full $10,000 is excludable from gross income.

3. Amounts of sick pay called a "wage continuation plan" in Section 105(d), constituting wages or payments in lieu of wages for a period during which the employee is absent from work on account of personal injuries or sickness, beginning after a waiting period and subject to a maximum exclusion of $100 per week.

6.50   If benefits received exceed the limits described above (for example, in the case of reimbursement for medical expenses) or do not exactly fit within the exclusion provisions of Section 105 (for example, where a benefit for loss of a limb is measured by the period of absence from work), then such benefits are taxable to the extent that the employer bears their cost.[41] If the employee also pays part of the cost, the proportionate part of the benefit attributable to his ratio of the cost may be excludable under Section 104(a)(3); detailed allocation rules for this are provided in Reg. 1.105–1(c), (d), and (e).

6.51   Section 106 of the Code provides that the gross income of an employee does not include contributions by his employer to accident or health plans for his employees.

6.52   **Uninsured Plans.** As mentioned previously, an employer's accident and health plan can be insured or not insured. Either way, the provisions of Section 105 apply. Frequently, there is a question whether direct benefit payments by an employer were made pursuant to a plan. If they were not, then quite probably such payments would represent additional taxable compensation. Regulation 1.105–5(a) defines a plan as follows:

... In general, an accident or health plan is an arrangement for the payment of amounts to employees in the event of personal injuries or sickness. A plan may cover one or more employees, and there may be different plans for different employees or classes of employees. An accident or health plan may be either insured or noninsured, and it is not necessary that the plan be in writing or that the employees' rights to benefits under the plan be enforceable.

41. *Ibid.*

However, if the employees' rights are not enforceable, an amount will be deemed to be received under a plan only if, on the date the employee became sick or injured, the employee was covered by a plan (or a program, policy, or custom having the effect of a plan) providing for the payment of amounts to the employee in the event of personal injuries or sickness, and notice or knowledge of such plans was reasonably available to the employee. It is immaterial who makes payment of the benefits provided by the plan. For example, payment may be made by the employer, a welfare fund, a state sickness or disability benefits fund, an association of employers or employees, or by an insurance company.

Exclusions from Gross Income

A plan can be discriminatory.[42] In a closely held corporation, it is advisable that any plan cover not only the stockholder-officers but also one or more nonshareholder employees. Further, the plan (or a program, policy, or custom having the effect of a plan) must contain these features:

6.53

1. It must have been in existence prior to the occurrence of the illness;[43]
2. Payments must not be discretionary on the part of the employer;[44] and
3. If shareholder-employees are involved, payments to them must be primarily related to their employee status.[45]

Wage Continuation Plans. An employee who receives benefits under a wage continuation plan to compensate for loss of wages during a temporary absence due to illness or injury can exclude a limited amount of the payments from gross income. Benefits paid for the first thirty days of absence cannot be excluded unless the rate of payment is 75 percent or less of the employee's weekly wage rate. The weekly exclusion is limited to $75 a week. If the employee is not hospitalized at least one day during his absence, he cannot exclude any benefits for the first seven days of absence [Sec. 105(d); Reg. 1.105–4]. After the first thirty days of absence, up to $100 a week may be excluded, even if the benefits are more than 75 percent of the weekly wage rate.

6.54

Yost is injured on the job in January. He spends two days in the hospital and is absent from work thirty days. His normal salary is $120 a week. If he receives sick-pay benefits at a rate of more than $90 a week (75% × $120 = $90), he cannot exclude any amount. If the benefit is between $75 and $90 a week, he can exclude $75 a week. If the benefit is less than $75, he can exclude the full benefit.

Example 1

Assume the same facts in Example 1, except that Yost is not hospitalized. He can exclude nothing for the first seven days of absence, whether the benefits are paid at a rate that is more or less than $90 a week.

Example 2

42. Bogene, ¶68–147 P–H Memo T.C.; S. Rep. 1622, 83d Cong., 2d sess., 1954, pp. 15–16; Conf. Rep. 2543, 83d Cong., 2d sess., 1954, pp. 24–25.
43. Reg. 1.105–5(a).
44. Estate of Leo P. Kaufman, 35 T.C. 663 (1961), affirmed 300 F.2d 128 (6th Cir. 1962), 62–1 USTC ¶9299, 9 AFTR2d 900; Larkin, 48 T.C. 629 (1967), affirmed 394 F.2d 494 (1st Cir. 1968), 68–1 USTC ¶9362, 21 AFTR2d 1307.
45. Smithback, ¶69,136, P–H Memo T.C.; Larkin, *supra* fn. 44.

EXAMPLE 3   Johnson is absent from work thirty-five consecutive days because of illness. He receives his full weekly wage of $135 as sick-pay benefits for the time he is absent. He cannot exclude the benefits received for the first thirty days of absence. For the last five days he can exclude the benefits at the rate of $100 a week.

6.55   The exclusion applies to:

1. All employees who meet the tests, including for example, civilian employees of government,[46] nonresident aliens.[47]
2. The part of a decedent's salary that would have been excludable sick pay had it been paid to him and that is received by his estate or beneficiary.[48]
3. Wages received for paid holidays during illness or injury, unless the holiday is the first or last day of absence.[49]

6.56   The exclusion does not apply to:

1. Self-employed persons[50] or salaried partners,[51] including benefits to self-employed individuals paid under a self-employed retirement plan [Reg. 1.105–5(b)].
2. Absence due to pregnancy, since pregnancy is not a sickness,[52] but exclusion applies from time labor commences to end of period taxpayer is physically incapacitated as a result of childbirth or miscarriage. Exclusion generally applies also if absence was advised by physician, to prevent miscarriage, and physician's supporting statement is presented.[53]
3. Commissions received by salesman for sales he made before his sickness or injury (but he can exclude commissions on sales by a substitute).[54]
4. Absence due to illness in the family or quarantine, even though the absence is charged to sick leave.[55]
5. Any portion of a year-end bonus determined by the profits of the company for the entire year.[56]
6. Lump sum or terminal leave payments on separation from employment because of illness or injury.[57]

6.57   Whether an employee is absent from work depends upon the circumstances. A farm worker who lives on the premises of his employer is absent from work if he is unable to work because of illness or in-

46. Rev. Rul. 55–85, 1955–1 C.B. 15.
47. Rev. Rul. 56–514, 1956–2 C.B. 499.
48. Rev. Rul. 59–64, 1959–1 C.B. 31.
49. Rev. Rul. 63–219, 1963–2 C.B. 76.
50. *Your Federal Income Tax*, 1973 ed., p. 61.
51. Rev. Rul. 56–326, 1956–2 C.B. 100.
52. Rev. Rul. 55–263, 1955–1 C.B. 16.
53. Rev. Rul. 59–170, 1959–1 C.B. 36.
54. Rev. Rul. 58–462.
55. Rev. Rul. 55–283, 1955–1 C.B. 17.
56. Rev. Rul. 60–203, 1960–1 C.B. 41.
57. Rev. Rul. 58–178, 1958–1 C.B. 51.

jury, even though he remains on the employer's premises. A person is not absent from work if he performs any service for his employer at his regular place of employment or substantial service at any other place, even though the work he does is not his regularly assigned job. Thus, if he performs substantial services for his employer while confined to his home, he is not absent from work. A period of absence will end when the individual begins performing substantial services for his employer;[58] however, a period of absence does not end if the employee merely holds an occasional short conference with other employees or with clients while confined to the hospital or his home [Reg. 1.105–4(a)(5)].

6.58 The exclusion applies only to amounts received for periods the employee would be at work except for a personal injury or illness. Thus, if an employer's plan provides for the payment of a disability pension for the time an employee is disabled because of an injury or illness, he can exclude sick pay until he reaches retirement age. He may not exclude the pension he receives after reaching regular retirement age [Reg. 1.105–4(a)(3)]. A taxpayer receiving a disability pension did not lose the exclusion at age sixty when the regular retirement age was sixty-five and voluntary retirement with less benefits was permitted at age sixty.[59] Pension plans that allow early retirement at the employee's option, without regard to disability, are not sick-pay plans.[60]

6.59 If an employee is injured or becomes ill during his paid vacation, he may not exclude any of his vacation pay as sick pay. If a person is absent because of illness or injury, then, having recovered, continues his absence by taking a vacation, the pay he receives for the vacation may not be excluded. Teachers who become ill or are injured during the summer or other vacation period when they are not expected to teach may not claim an exclusion for the vacation period [Reg. 1.105–4(a)(3)], but they may claim the exclusion for amounts received while on a sabbatical leave to restore their health.[61]

6.60 DETERMINING THE AMOUNT TO BE EXCLUDED. Regulation 1.105–4 gives these rules for finding the excludable amount for daily absences, weekly benefit rates, and for determining a waiting period before benefits can be excluded:

1. Wage continuation plan benefits are presumed to be paid only for normal working days unless the plan or terms of employment provide otherwise [Reg. 1.105–4(b)].

EXAMPLE FROM REG. Crane normally works 5 days a week (Monday through Friday) at a weekly wage of $70. The employer's wage continuation plan allows payment of full salary during absence for illness. After thirty-two days of ab-

58. *Your Federal Income Tax*, 1970 ed., p. 38.
59. Com. v. Winter, 303 F.2d 150 (3rd Cir. 1962), 62–1 USTC ¶9473, 9 AFTR2d 1482.
60. Rev. Rul. 59–158, 1959–1 C.B. 34.
61. Rev. Rul. 58–91, 1958–1 C.B. 49.

sence, Crane returns to work on a Wednesday. The benefit Crane received for days he did not work in the week he returned is $28 ($70 ÷ 5 = $14 a day × 2 = $28).

2. The regular weekly rate of benefits used to determine the exclusion generally will be the average weekly wages paid for the last four normal work weeks immediately before the absence began. If wages are paid for pay periods, other than weekly pay periods, the weekly rate of wages is found by determining the annual rate and dividing by 52 [Reg. 1.105–4(e)].

3. After the weekly rate of benefits is found, the daily rate of exclusion is determined. This is figured by dividing the lower of the weekly rate of benefits, or $75 ($100 for periods after the first thirty days of absence), by the number of workdays in the normal workweek. The exclusion is figured by multiplying the applicable daily rate by the number of workdays that the taxpayer was absent in the period for which an exclusion is allowable [Reg. 1.105–4(f)].

4. In counting the days of a waiting period, absence starts the moment an employee is absent from work and ends the moment he returns. If he is ill and leaves work during normal working hours, the partial day counts as the first day absent [Reg. 1.105–4(e)(2)]. Once counting starts, non-work days, such as Sunday, are counted as days absent.

6.61   Nontaxable amounts received under wage continuation plans for sickness or injury must be included in gross wages on return Form 1040 and must then be subtracted. A statement must be attached to return Form 1040, showing the nature of the illness or injury, the dates of absence from work, and how the exclusion was computed. If the taxpayer was hospitalized, the dates of admission and discharge should be shown. A separate statement must be submitted for each period of absence.[62] Form 2440 for this purpose may be obtained from the Revenue Service. Under certain conditions, a statement prepared by the employer may be substituted for the employee's statement.[63] Sick pay is an exclusion in the year received, not in the year the absence occurred.

6.62   Sick pay is not a reimbursement of expenses paid for medical care. Hence, an employee receiving sick pay not only can exclude it from gross income, but also can claim a medical expense deduction under Section 213 for his medical expenses [Code Sec. 105(e)(1); also see chapter 10 for deduction of medical expenses].

RECOVERY OF BAD DEBTS, PRIOR TAXES, AND DELINQUENCY AMOUNTS

Tax Benefit Doctrine

6.63   Section 111 excludes from gross income amounts of recoveries of bad debts, prior taxes, or delinquency amounts to the extent that

62. *Your Federal Income Tax,* 1970 ed., p. 41.
63. Rev. Proc. 57–1, 1957–1 C.B. 721.

such items, when deducted in a prior year, did not result in a reduction of income tax. To the extent that a tax benefit was secured in a prior year, the amount of the recovery is taxable. However, it has been held that the tax-benefit theory applies only when the original deduction was proper, and that the recovery of an amount improperly expensed in a closed year is not taxable.[64] This section is substantially the same as Section 22(b)(12) of the 1939 Code added by Section 112 of the Revenue Act of 1942. It was enacted to standardize the tax-benefit rule developed by the courts and rulings of the Internal Revenue Service.

6.64   Section 111(a) applies the tax-benefit doctrine only to the recovery of a "bad debt, prior tax, or delinquency amount." The Supreme Court[65] in the year following the adoption of the predecessor of Section 111 upheld the Tax Court's theory that the tax-benefit doctrine applies to many items other than those specified in Section 111. Accordingly, the regulations were expanded to coincide with the Supreme Court's opinion. Regulation 1.111–1(a) now provides:

... The rule of exclusion so prescribed by statute applies equally with respect to all other losses, expenditures, and accruals made the basis of deductions from gross income for prior taxable years, including war losses referred to in section 127 of the Internal Revenue Code of 1939, but not including deductions with respect to depreciation, depletion, amortization, or amortizable bond premiums.

Depreciation, etc., are treated in a similar manner by other parts of the Code. Regulation 1.111–1(a)(1) also provides:

An example of the other items not expressly referred to in section 111, but nevertheless subject to the rule of exclusion, is a loss sustained upon the sale of stock and later recovered, in whole or in part, through an action against the party from whom such stock had been purchased.

6.65   The gross income exclusion under Section 111 is referred to as the "recovery exclusion." It is defined in Section 111(b)(4) as:

... the amount ... of the deductions or credits allowed, on account of such bad debt, [etc.,] which did not result in a reduction of the taxpayer's tax under this subtitle ... reduced by the amount excludable in previous taxable years with respect to such bad debt, [etc.,]. ...

Recovery of Bad Dabts

6.66   As we shall learn in chapter 9, there are two methods available for deducting bad debts: the specific charge-off and the reserve. Section 111 applies only to recoveries on specific receivables charged off

---

64. Adolph B. Canelo III, 53 T.C. 217 (1969).
65. Dobson v. Com., 320 U.S. 489 (1943), 44–1 USTC ¶9108, 31 AFTR 773.

and deducted as bad debts in a prior year. With respect to recovery of bad debts where the taxpayer uses the reserve method, Reg. 1.111–1(a)(1) provides:

> If a bad debt was previously charged against a reserve by a taxpayer on the reserve method of treating bad debts, it was not deducted, and it is, therefore, not considered a section 111 item.

Under the reserve method, recoveries are credited to the reserve.

Recovery of Prior Taxes and Delinquency Amounts

6.67   These items may be illustrated as follows:

EXAMPLE   Suppose that a taxpayer failed to pay a local franchise tax on time but later, in 1966, paid the tax *with interest* and took a deduction in that year for the two amounts. Assume further that in 1967 it was determined that the franchise tax did not apply to this business, and both interest and tax were refunded. *Both* of these amounts are Section 111 items, the refunded *interest* being an example of a recovered "delinquency amount" as defined in Section 111(b)(3). The tax itself is a "prior tax" as defined in Section 111(b)(2).

Computation of Recovery Exclusion

6.68   In connection with the amount of a recovery exclusion allowable for the year of recovery, Reg. 1.111–1(b)(1) and (2)(i) provide:

> (1) *Amount of recovery exclusion allowable for year of recovery.* For the year of any recovery, the section 111 items which were deducted or credited for one prior year are considered as a group and the recovery thereon is considered separately from recoveries of any items which were deducted or credited for other years. This recovery is excluded from gross income to the extent of the recovery exclusion with respect to this group of items as (i) determined for the original year for which such items were deducted or credited (see subparagraph (2) of this paragraph) and (ii) reduced by the excludable recoveries in intervening years on account of all section 111 items for such original year. A taxpayer claiming a recovery exclusion shall submit, at the time the exclusion is claimed, the computation of the recovery exclusion claimed for the original year for which the items were deducted or credited, and computations showing the amount recovered in intervening years on account of the section 111 items deducted or credited for the original year.
>
> (2) *Determination of recovery exclusion for original year for which items were deducted or credited.* (i) The recovery exclusion for the taxable year for which section 111 items were deducted or credited (that is, the "original taxable year") is the portion of the aggregate amount of such deductions and credits which could be disallowed without causing an increase in any tax of the taxpayer imposed under subtitle A (other than the accumulated earnings tax imposed by section 531 or the personal holding company tax imposed by section 541) of the Internal Revenue Code of 1954 or corresponding provisions of prior income tax laws (other than the World War II excess profits tax imposed under subchapter E of chapter 2 of the Internal Revenue Code of

1939). For the purpose of such recovery exclusion, consideration must be given to the effect of net operating loss carryovers and carrybacks or capital loss carryovers.

DIVIDEND EXCLUSION

An individual may exclude from his gross income the first $100 of dividends received from qualified domestic corporations [Code Sec. 116(a); Reg. 1.116–1]. In a joint return, husband and wife each are entitled to exclude up to $100 in dividends received by each spouse [Reg. 1.116–1(b)].

6.69

Mr. Vickers received $300 and Mrs. Vickers received $75 in dividends during their taxable year. Mr. Vickers may exclude $100 and Mrs. Vickers $75, a total of $175 in their joint return.

EXAMPLE

Stock owned jointly is provided for in Reg. 1.116–1(c):

6.70

Where two or more persons hold stock as tenants in common, as joint tenants, or as tenants by the entirety, the dividends received with respect to such stock shall be considered as being received by each tenant to the extent that he is entitled under local law to a share of such dividends. Where dividends constitute community property under local law, each spouse shall be considered as receiving one-half of such dividends.

The exclusion applies only to distributions of cash and property defined as dividends by Section 316 [Reg. 1.116–1]. Thus the following do not qualify for the exclusion:

6.71

1. Patronage dividends paid by either exempt or taxable farm cooperatives.
2. Dividends on life insurance policies.
3. Interest (commonly referred to as dividends) on deposits or withdrawable accounts paid by mutual savings banks, cooperative banks, domestic building and loan associations, and federal savings and loan associations. However, dividends on the permanent nonwithdrawable stock of savings and loan associations do qualify for the exclusion.
4. Corporate distributions such as nontaxable stock dividends; certain liquidating distributions; certain stock redemptions; distributions that are a return of capital.
5. Amounts equal to cash dividends received by an individual to compensate him for dividends on stock that he has loaned to another to cover a short sale.[66]

Dividends from regulated investment companies (Mutual Funds) are subject to a special rule [Reg. 1.116–1(d)(2)(iii)]. The part that is a capital gain dividend does not qualify; the part representing divi-

6.72

---

66. Rev. Rul. 60–177, 1960–1 C.B. 9.

dends from income qualifies with certain limits. Regulated investment companies notify shareholders of the qualified and nonqualified
portions.

CONTRIBUTION TO CAPITAL

6.73   Gross income of a corporation does not include *any* contribution
to its capital [Section 118]. See also paragraphs 19.14–19.17.

Contributions by Shareholders

6.74   Regulation 1.118–1 provides:

> ... if a corporation requires additional funds for conducting its business
> and obtains such funds through voluntary pro rata payments by its share-
> holders, the amounts so received being credited to its surplus account or to
> a special account, such amounts do not constitute income, although there
> is no increase in the outstanding shares of stock of the corporation. In such a
> case the payments are in the nature of assessments upon, and represent an
> additional price paid for, the shares of stock held by the individual share-
> holders, and will be treated as an addition to and as a part of the operating
> capital of the company.

Contributions by Nonshareholders

6.75   Contributions to the capital of a corporation by persons other than
shareholders are provided for in the same Reg. 1.118–1:

> Section 118 also applies to contributions to capital made by persons other
> than shareholders. For example, the exclusion applies to the value of land
> or other property contributed to a corporation by a governmental unit or by
> a civic group for the purpose of inducing the corporation to locate its busi-
> ness in a particular community, or for the purpose of enabling the corpora-
> tion to expand its operating facilities.[67] However, the exclusion does not
> apply to any money or property transferred to the corporation in considera-
> tion for goods or services rendered,[68] or to subsidies paid for the purpose of
> inducing the taxpayer to limit production.[69] [Footnote references supplied.]

6.76   The corporation takes over the shareholders' basis of property contributed by them, but special rules govern the basis of contributions
to the corporation by persons not shareholders. When property other
than money is contributed to capital, and the property is not contributed by a shareholder as such, the basis of the property becomes
zero [Section 362(c)(1)].

67. Edwards v. Cuba R.R. Co., 268 U.S. 628 (1925), 1 USTC ¶139, 5 AFTR 5398,
affirming 298 F. 664 (D.C., N.Y., 1921), 4 AFTR 3967.
68. Teleservice Company of Wyoming v. Com., 254 F.2d 105, (3rd Cir. 1958), 58–1
USTC ¶9383, 1 AFTR2d 1249, cert. denied.
69. I.T. 2767, XIII–1 C.B. 35 (1934).

If a capital contribution of money is made by someone not a share- 6.77
holder, the basis of any property bought with the money during the
twelve-month period beginning on the day the contribution is received is reduced by the contribution.[70] Any money left over reduces
the basis of other property held by the corporation at the end of the
twelve-month period in the following order: (1) depreciable property,
(2) property subject to amortization, (3) property subject to depletion
(except percentage depletion), (4) other property. The basis of property in each category is reduced in proportion to the relative basis of
the properties. But the basis of the various units of property within a
category may be adjusted differently if the Revenue Service consents.
Request for the change should be filed with the return for the tax
year the property was transferred to the corporation [Code Sec.
362(c)(2); Reg. 1.362–2].

MEALS OR LODGING FURNISHED FOR THE CONVENIENCE OF THE EMPLOYER

The value of any meals or lodging furnished to an employee by his 6.78
employer may be excluded from gross income if certain tests are met
[Section 119]. Meals are excludable only if furnished (1) for the
convenience of the employer and (2) *on* the employer's "business
premises." Lodging is excludable if these requirements are met, but
then only if the employee was also "required to accept such lodging ...
as a condition of his employment."

Convenience of Employer

Meals furnished without a charge "will be regarded as furnished for 6.79
the convenience of the employer if such meals are furnished for a
substantial noncompensatory business reason of the employer" [Reg.
1.119-1(a)(2)]. The regulation gives several examples of substantial
noncompensatory business reasons, such as meals being furnished
during the employee's working hours because:

1. Employee must be available for emergency call during his meal period.
2. Employer's business is such that the employee must be restricted to a
   short meal period, perhaps 30 or 45 minutes, and the employee could
   not be expected to eat elsewhere in this short time, but not so that the
   employee can be let off earlier in the day.
3. Employee could not otherwise eat proper meals within a reasonable
   meal period, insufficient eating facilities being available in the vicinity
   of the employer's premises.

70. Before the 1954 Code, the basis of property contributed by a government or
community group was the basis of the property in the hands of the transferor. Brown
Shoe Co. v. Com., 339 U.S. 583 (1950), 39 AFTR 327, 50–1 USTC ¶5958. The basis was
zero with respect to contributions by present and prospective customers for the extension of utility services. Detroit Edison Co. v. Com., 319 U.S. 98 (1943), 43–1 USTC
¶9418, 30 AFTR 1096.

4. Employee works in a restaurant or other food service during meal period, whether the meal is furnished during, immediately before, or immediately after the working hours of the employee.

There is also a *de minimus* rule. If as to a few employees, such as executives, a compensatory element does exist, the value of their meals is not taxable, provided that a greater number of other employees are furnished meals for a substantial noncompensatory business reason.

6.80   Meals will be regarded as furnished for a compensatory business reason of the employer when the meals are furnished to the employee to promote the morale or good will of the employee or to attract prospective employees [Reg. 1.119–1(a)(2)(iii)]. Meals furnished on nonworking days do not qualify for the exclusion under Section 119. If the employee is required to occupy living quarters on the business premises of his employer as a condition of his employment, the exclusion applies to the value of any meal furnished without charge to the employee and the employee's family on such premises.

6.81   If an employer provides meals that an employee may or may not purchase, the meals will not be regarded as furnished for the convenience of the employer. If the employee is charged a flat amount, the value may be excluded if the tests of Section 119 are met; "... in the absence of evidence to the contrary, the value of the meals may be deemed to be equal to the amount charged for them" [Reg. 1.119–1(a)(3)(ii)].

Condition of Employment

6.82   The value of lodging is excludable if furnished (1) for the convenience of the employer, (2) on the employer's business premises, and (3) as a condition of employment (see paragraph 6.77). The meaning of lodging required "as a condition of employment" is explained in Reg. 1.119–1(b):

... The requirement ... that the employee is required to accept such lodging as a condition of his employment means that he be required to accept the lodging in order to enable him properly to perform the duties of his employment. Lodging will be regarded as furnished to enable the employee properly to perform the duties of his employment when, for example, the lodging is furnished because the employee is required to be available for duty at all times or because the employee could not perform the services required of him unless he is furnished such lodging. If the tests described in subparagraphs (1), (2), and (3) of this paragraph are met [referring to tests mentioned in the introductory clause of this paragraph] the exclusion shall apply irrespective of whether a charge is made, or whether, under an employment contract or statute fixing the terms of employment, such lodging is furnished as compensation. If the employer furnishes the employee lodging for which the employee is charged an unvarying amount irrespective of whether he accepts the lodging, the amount of the charge made by the employer for such lodging is not, as such, part of the compensation includible in the gross income of the employee; whether the value of the lodging is excludable from gross income under section 119 is determined by applying the other rules of this paragraph. If the tests described in subparagraphs (1), (2), and (3) of this paragraph are not met, the employee shall include in gross income the value of the lodging regardless of whether it exceeds or is less than the amount charged. In the absence of evidence to the contrary, the value of the lodging may be deemed to be equal to the amount charged.

Business Premises of Employer

Regulation 1.119–1(c)(1) gives this definition: 6.83

For purposes of this section, the term "business premises of the employer" generally means the place of employment of the employee. For example, meals and lodging furnished in the employer's home to a domestic servant would constitute meals and lodging furnished on the business premises of the employer. Similarly, meals furnished to cowhands while herding their employer's cattle on leased land would be regarded as furnished on the business premises of the employer.

In the case of *Com. v. Charles N. Anderson* [71] the taxpayer was the   6.84
manager of a motel. When he first began managing the motel, he and his family occupied two rooms in it. Subsequently, because of its being less costly, the taxpayer's employer bought a small house two short blocks from the motel to use as a manager's house, and the taxpayer and his family moved into the house. The employer furnished the laundry, cleaning, and utilities for the house and furnished milk and some groceries to the taxpayer. The remaining groceries were purchased by the taxpayer's wife at supermarkets or grocery stores, and the taxpayer was reimbursed by his employer for the amounts so expended. The Tax Court held that the amounts received by the taxpayer as reimbursement for groceries purchased by his wife were includible in his income, as such amounts were not furnished in kind, and the taxpayer failed to show that these payments were not compensation. This issue was not appealed. The Tax Court also held that the house owned by the employer was "generally" a part of the business premises of the employer. However, on appeal the Sixth Circuit Court of Appeals reversed that portion of the decision and held that the phrase "on the business premises" means either the place where the employee performs a significant portion of his duties or the place where the employer conducts a significant portion of his business. Accordingly, the rental value of the house, the value of the laundry and cleaning services, utilities, milk, and groceries from the motel kitchen furnished to the taxpayer were taxable to him as compensation.

71. 371 F.2d 59 (6th Cir. 1966), 67–1 USTC ¶9136, 19 AFTR 318, reversing 42 T.C. 410.

Furnished in Kind

6.85   Meals and lodging must be furnished in kind by the employer. Regulation 1.119–1(c)(2) explains:

The exclusion provided by section 119 applies only to meals and lodging furnished in kind by an employer to his employee. If the employee has an option to receive additional compensation in lieu of meals or lodging in kind, the value of such meals and lodging is not excluded from gross income. However, the mere fact that an employee, at his option, may decline to accept meals tendered in kind will not of itself require inclusion of the value thereof in gross income. Cash allowances for meals or lodging received by an employee are includible in gross income to the extent that such allowances constitute compensation.

Cash Allowances

6.86   Notice that the regulation does not say that all cash allowances are includible in gross income—only those that constitute compensation. This is an important difference. Supper money is a nontaxable cash allowance for meals.[72] Another example is the basic cash allowance for subsistence and quarters given members of certain federal uniformed services. The value of quarters furnished to officers and enlisted personnel of the Armed Forces, Coast and Geodetic Survey, and Public Health Service, or amounts received by them as commutation of quarters are not taxable [Reg. 1.61–2], since they are required to be available for service twenty-four hours a day.

6.87   The exclusion applies to the value of meals and lodging furnished in kind, even though the value thereof is deducted from the employee's salary.[73]

Partners and Sole Proprietors

6.88   Section 262 prohibits the deduction of personal, living, or family expenses. Therefore, a sole proprietor cannot deduct the food he eats or the depreciation on, and utilities pertaining to, his lodging. Nothing comparable to Section 119 exists in the parts of the Code pertaining to deductions. For that reason taxpayers have tried to induce courts to carry the concept of Section 119 over into the deduction provisions as a matter of judicial gloss. They have argued that the expenses are deductible because they are for the convenience of a business. However, Section 119 relates literally to convenience of the "employer," *not* to convenience of the "business." The Third, Fourth, Eighth, and Tenth Circuit Courts of Appeal have refused to import the philosophy of Section 119 into the deduction provisions, noting that in any case such persons are not considered "employees"

72. O.D. 514, 2 C.B. 90 (1920).
73. J. Melvin Boykin v. Com., 260 F.2d 249 (8th Cir. 1958), 2 AFTR2d 6028, 58–2 USTC ¶9900.

working for "employers."[74] The decisions in those cases pertain to partners and involve 1939 Code years; but their holdings are applicable to sole proprietors for both 1939 and 1954 Code years.

If a partner in a 1954 Code year in circumstances giving rise to the receipt of meals and lodging furnished by the partnership is in substance the same as an outsider employee, then the value of the meals and lodging is not taxable to him.[75] Section 707(a) was new in the 1954 Code and provides that if a partner engages in a transaction with a partnership other than in his capacity as a partner, he shall be treated as a stranger.

6.89

REIMBURSEMENT FOR LIVING EXPENSES ARISING FROM CASUALTIES

If the principal residence of an individual is damaged or destroyed by fire, storm, or other casualty in 1969 or later so that he temporarily must rent other quarters, an amount received from an insurance company to reimburse him for the extra living expenses incurred for himself and members of his household is not taxable (Section 123). Prior to enactment of this amendment in 1969 the weight of authority was to the contrary.[76]

6.90

QUESTIONS AND PROBLEMS

1. Frederick George took out a policy of life insurance on his own life on September 2, 1933, naming his wife, Lydia, as beneficiary. The annual premium was $750. Frederick died on September 15, 1972, at the age of sixty-four, after paying total premiums of $29,250. Lydia had the option under the policy to take the face value of $50,000 in a lump sum or to receive $600 a month payable on the first day of each month for 100 months. If the wife elected to take the installments and died before the end of 100 months, the commuted value of the remaining installments was to be paid to the beneficiary she named. The wife elected to take the installments and named her daughter as secondary beneficiary. The first installment payment of $600 was made on October 1, 1972, to the wife, Lydia, who reports her income on the cash basis.
   (a) What part of the installments, if any, must be included in the income of the wife for the calendar year 1972?
   (b) What part of the installments, if any, would be includible in the income of the wife for the calendar year 1973?

74. T. Robinson v. Com., 273 F.2d 503 (3rd Cir. 1960), 60–1 USTC ¶9152, 5 AFTR2d 315; Com. v. Doak, 234 F.2d 704 (4th Cir. 1956), 56–2 USTC ¶9708, 49 AFTR 1491, Com. v. Moran, F.2d 595 (8th Cir. 1956), 56–2 USTC ¶9879, 50 AFTR 64; Briggs v. U.S., 238 F.2d 53 (10th Cir. 1956), 56–2 USTC ¶10,020, 50 AFTR 667; also Rev. Rul. 53–80, 1953–1 C.B. 62; *contra:* Papineau, 16 T.C. 130 (1951)(NA).

75. Armstrong v. Phinney, 394 F.2d 661 (5th Cir. 1968), 68–1 USTC ¶9355, 21 AFTR2d 1260.

76. Cases holding the insurance taxable and the living expenses nondeductible personal expenditures: Millsap, Jr. v. Com., 387 F.2d 420 (8th Cir. 1968), 68–1 USTC ¶9141, 21 AFTR2d 376; Arnold v. U.S., 289 F. Supp. 206 (D.C., N.Y., 1968), 22 AFTR2d 5661; *contra:* Conner, 24 AFTR2d 69–5638 (D.C., Texas, 1969).

(c) If Lydia died on July 10, 1973, when the commuted value of the remaining installments was $45,350, what amount, if any, would be included in the gross income of her daughter Mary for the calendar year 1973 on a cash basis? Explain.

(d) If the face value of the policy was to be paid to Lydia in a lump sum on the death of the insured, what amount, if any, constitutes income to her for the calendar year 1972? Explain.

2. Mrs. Murray elected to receive the proceeds of her deceased husband's $50,000 life insurance policy as a $4,000 per annum lifetime annuity. Mrs. Murray's remaining life expectancy by the insurance company's mortality tables is seventeen years. Her husband had paid forty-three annual premiums of $1,000 when he died. What amount, if any, does Mrs. Murray include in her gross income?

3. Pete Estes pays premiums on a $20,000 life insurance policy on his own life. Pete purchases a car from Ed for $3,500 and in payment gives $900 in cash and assigns the policy at a stipulated value of $2,600. At that time the cash surrender value of the policy was $2,500. Subsequently, Pete dies and the proceeds of the policy are remitted to Ed. Ed paid $750 in premiums after he acquired ownership of the policy. Answer the following:

(a) Must Ed include any portion of the proceeds in his gross income for the year? If so, how much?

(b) If Pete had repurchased the policy from Ed, what portion of the proceeds would have to be included in the gross income of Pete's wife, assuming that she becomes the beneficiary?

4. When James Robinson died in December, his employer, Pacific, Inc., voted the next year to pay his daughter $1,800, his son $3,000, and his widow $7,200. The payments to the children were made at once, but the payments to the widow were to be made in three equal annual installments. Pacific deducts the payments as a business expense. Pacific paid no other amounts to Robinson's estate or to his beneficiaries. How will the payments be taxed?

5. Donald Kane organized the Kane Manufacturing Company and served as president for thirty years. He resigned on December 31, because of his poor health. The old employees who knew how much the company's growth was the result of Kane's individual efforts took up a collection to show their appreciation. The board of directors heard about this and voted a $10,000 payment to Kane. The chairman of the board declared he would not be responsible for the payment and insisted that the payment be approved at a shareholder's meeting. This was done.

At the employees' annual dinner held the following June, the employees gave Kane an oil painting worth $3,500, and the new president gave him a company check for $10,000. An Internal Revenue agent claims Kane received taxable income of $13,500. Can you defend Kane against this claim?

6. William McKenzie received interest from the following sources:

City of Portland bonds	$100.00
State of Oregon bonds	$ 50.00
State of Oregon — interest on income tax refund	$ 45.00
U.S. Treasury 3 ½ % bonds, issued in June, 1955	$350.00
City of Portland — interest on judgment	$400.00

How much interest must be included in income?

7. Joe Doaks owns U.S. Series E bonds in the face amount of $1,000 that he purchased on issuance for $750. The maturity date of the Series E bonds was extended some years ago, but the period of extension expires in December of this year.
   (a) Could he have had any interest income from those bonds in prior years? Explain.
   (b) Assuming he had no interest income in prior years and he turns the bonds in for redemption this December, what will be the amount of income and what will be its nature?
   (c) Suppose he fails to turn the bonds in until the following July. What is the amount of income this year? Next year?

8. Skyline, Inc. pays the premium on an accident and health policy covering its office staff. While working on the reproduction machine, Helen Jensen loses part of her little finger and receives $2,500 award under the plan. She incurred $600 in medical expenses and deducted $500. How much of the $2,500 is taxable income?

9. Maple, Inc., a growing company in the forest products industry, needed a financial vice-president. Mr. Tom Johnson accepted the position with the provision that in addition to his annual salary of $50,000, Maple would pay all of the medical and dental expenses of Mr. Johnson and his dependents. Maple agreed, even though Johnson would be the only employee so covered. Several months later, Mrs. Johnson's auto slid off the road while she was on a ski trip. She and her two daughters were injured. Maple paid $25,000 to Mr. Johnson during 1966 for medical expenses, including $300 to cover his travel expenses in going to the scene of the accident. Such travel expenses are not medical expenses within the meaning of Section 213. On his return he deducted medical expenses of $20,000. How much, if any, of the $25,000 is taxable?

10. William Wilson is employed by Golf, Inc., at a weekly salary of $200. He normally works five days a week (Monday through Friday). Golf has a plan under which it pays regular wages to employees absent because of sickness or injury. On Monday, March 19, Wilson became ill at work and left at noon. He recovered and returned to work on Thursday, April 29, in the sixth week after becoming ill. He was treated at home for the entire period. Under its wage continuation plan, Golf paid Wilson his full salary during his absence.
    (a) For what period of his absence will Wilson be able to exclude any amount of what Golf paid him?
    (b) What amount will Wilson be able to exclude?
    (c) Would the exclusion be greater if Wilson's absence were due to injury or his illness had required hospitalization?

11. Buddy Benson was ill for a forty-two-day period during the year. His employer has a wage continuation plan whereby the employee receives $80 per week during his illness. Buddy's regular pay is $120 per week. Determine the applicable sick-pay exclusion rate under the following conditions:
    (a) Buddy was hospitalized for a five-day period beginning on the fourth day of his absence.
    (b) Buddy was ill at home during his absence.

12. A corporation claimed and was allowed a bad debt deduction in the amount of $8,000 on its return for last year, which showed a net loss of $450. This year the corporation unexpectedly received payment of $800 on the debts charged off last year.

Assuming that there is no carry-back or carry-over of the net loss of $450 to any other year, what effect, if any, does the recovery have in the computation of taxable income for this year if in both years (a) the corporation was on the specific charge-off method for bad debts; (b) the corporation was on the reserve method?

13. Mr. and Mrs. Holder received the following distribution from companies in which they held common stock:

Mr. Holder:
General Motors	$ 25
Investors Trust (a regulated investment company, 25% considered capital gain)	200

Mrs. Holder:
Xerox	$ 30
Mexican Foods (a Mexican corp.)	100
Continental National Bank (paid on common stock)	20

The Holders file a joint return. What amount of the above income is subject to tax as ordinary income?

14. Joe Stover received the following dividends during the year:

American Telephone & Telegraph	$ 25
Mid-Western Farm Cooperative for patronage	325
Homebody Mutual Savings & Loan	15
General Dynamics	22
Manhattan Fund ($35 is attributable to a return of capital)	62

Determine the amount of dividend income which may be excluded from taxable income.

15. (a) Robert Becknal, a chef at the Royal Restaurant, is required to be on the job from 4:00 P.M. to 11:00 P.M. six nights a week. Besides meals, Becknal receives an annual salary of $10,000. The Royal places a fair market value of $1,000 on the meals eaten by Becknal. What amount should Becknal report as taxable compensation?

(b) James Johnson, a salesman for the Northwest Garden Supply, worked overtime forty separate occasions during the year. Each time Johnson received $5 as supper money. On the average, Johnson estimates that his cost was $3 per supper. What part, if any, of the $200 (40 × $5) is taxable?

7

DEDUCTIONS IN GENERAL

INTRODUCTION . . . 197
DEDUCTIONS A MATTER OF LEGISLATIVE GRACE . . . 197
NONDEDUCTIBLE ITEMS . . . 197
ORDINARY AND NECESSARY BUSINESS EXPENSES . . . 198

In General . . . 198

DISTINGUISHED FROM CAPITAL EXPENDITURES . . . 199

REPAIRS . . . 199

DEFINITION OF "ORDINARY AND NECESSARY" . . . 201
REASONABLE AMOUNTS . . . 202
CARRYING ON A TRADE OR BUSINESS . . . 203

PROFIT VERSUS PLEASURE . . . 204

VIOLATION OF PUBLIC POLICY . . . 206

FINES AND PENALTIES . . . 208
ANTITRUST DAMAGE PAYMENTS . . . 208
BRIBES OR KICKBACKS TO PUBLIC OFFICIALS . . . 208
OTHER BRIBES OR KICKBACKS . . . 208
ILLEGALITY OF BUSINESS . . . 209

LEGAL EXPENSES . . . 209

EXPENSE OR CAPITAL EXPENDITURE . . . 209
CRIMINAL DEFENSE . . . 210

ANTITRUST PROCEEDINGS . . . 211
EDUCATIONAL EXPENSES . . . 211
ASSOCIATION DUES . . . 213
TRAVEL AND ENTERTAINMENT EXPENSES . . . 213
COMPENSATION FOR PERSONAL SERVICES OF EMPLOYEES . . . 216

COMPENSATION ELEMENT . . . 216
SERVICES RENDERED . . . 217

REASONABLE AMOUNT . . . 217
BONUSES . . . 218

DEATH BENEFITS . . . 219
OTHER EMPLOYEE BENEFITS . . . 219
RENTALS AND ROYALTIES . . . 219

LEASE WITH OPTION TO PURCHASE . . . 220
TRANSACTIONS WITH RELATED PARTIES . . . 221
ROYALTIES . . . 222

ADVERTISING . . . 222
LEGISLATIVE APPEARANCES (LOBBYING EXPENSES) . . . 223
EXPENSES RELATING TO TAX-EXEMPT INCOME . . . 223

Employees . . . 225

DEDUCTIBLE IN DETERMINING ADJUSTED GROSS INCOME . . . 225

REIMBURSED EXPENSES . . . 225
TRAVEL AWAY FROM HOME . . . 226

Definition of "Home" . . . 226
Necessity of Overnight Trip . . . 227

TRANSPORTATION COSTS . . . 227
OUTSIDE SALESMEN'S EXPENSES . . . 228
MOVING EXPENSES . . . 228

DEDUCTIBLE FROM ADJUSTED GROSS INCOME WHEN STANDARD
DEDUCTION NOT USED . . . 229

**NONBUSINESS EXPENSES FOR PRODUCTION OF INCOME OR
IN CONNECTION WITH TAX LIABILITIES . . . 230**

Introduction . . . 230
Expenses for Production of Income . . . 231

INVESTORS' EXPENSES . . . 232
BUSINESS INVESTIGATION EXPENDITURES . . . 233
PROXY CONTEST . . . 234
LEGAL EXPENSES . . . 235
REAL ESTATE INVESTMENT EXPENSES . . . 236
RESIDENTIAL PROPERTY . . . 237

Tax Determinations . . . 238

INTRODUCTION

7.1
Section 63 provides that for all taxable entities except those individuals who elect to use the standard deduction, the term "taxable income" means gross income "... minus the deductions allowed by this chapter ..." (i.e., Chapter 1 of the Code). If an individual elects to use the standard deduction, then to him the term "taxable income" means adjusted gross income minus the standard deduction and the deductions for personal exemptions. Such an individual forgoes the right to claim itemized deductions. Almost all of the deductions available are provided for in Sections 141 through 145 (standard deduction for individuals), Sections 151 through 154 (deductions for personal exemptions), Sections 161 through 187 (itemized deductions for individuals and corporations), Sections 211 through 218 (additional itemized deductions for individuals), and Sections 241 through 249 (special deductions for corporations).

DEDUCTIONS A MATTER OF LEGISLATIVE GRACE

7.2
Although the definition of gross income contained in Section 61 is, in general, all inclusive, this is not true of deductions. Only items specifically provided for in some Section of the Code can be deducted. In *Helvering* v. *Independent Life Insurance Company*[1] the United States Supreme Court said: "Unquestionably Congress has power to condition, limit, or deny deductions from gross income in order to arrive at the net that it chooses to tax." This approach was expanded by that Court in *New Colonial Ice Company, Inc.* v. *Helvering*[2] where it said: "Whether and to what extent deductions should be allowed depends upon legislative grace; and only as there is clear provision therefor can any particular deduction be allowed."

NONDEDUCTIBLE ITEMS

7.3
To clarify doubt about whether a particular item comes within one of the deduction categories, in other instances to prevent a double deduction, and in still others to put limitations on one or more deductible categories, Sections 261 through 277 set forth certain items that are not deductible. Among the items most commonly encountered are:

Personal, living, and family expenses (except as otherwise provided in the Code).
Capital expenditures (except enumerated expenditures).

1. 292 U.S. 371 (1934), 4 USTC ¶1290, 13 AFTR 1175.
2. 292 U.S. 435 (1934), 4 USTC ¶1292, 13 AFTR 1180.

Premiums and certain other amounts paid in connection with certain life insurance, endowment, and annuity contracts.

Expenses and interest incurred that relate to tax-exempt income.

Taxes and other carrying charges that the taxpayer has elected to treat as chargeable to capital account.

Losses, expenses, and interest with respect to transactions between related taxpayers.

Deductions, credits, and other allowances provided under the Code, which were made available to a taxpayer as a result of certain types of acquisitions where the principal purpose of the acquisitions was to evade or avoid federal income tax by securing the benefit of the deductions, credits, or other allowances.

Worthless debts owed by political parties.

Unsubstantiated or excessive entertainment, business gifts, and travel expenses.

Federal income taxes (including social security and railroad retirement taxes paid by employees); federal war profits and excess profits taxes; estate, inheritance, legacy, succession, and gift taxes; income, war profits, and excess profits taxes imposed by a foreign country or a possession of the United States if the taxpayer elects to take a foreign tax credit for these taxes; and taxes on real property that must be treated as imposed on another taxpayer because of apportionment between buyer and seller.

Most of these nondeductible items will be encountered in this and the next three chapters in the discussion of the related deductions.

ORDINARY AND NECESSARY BUSINESS EXPENSES

In General

7.4 Section 162(a) in its opening clause states: "There shall be allowed as a deduction all the ordinary and necessary expenses paid or incurred during the taxable year in carrying on any trade or business." There then follow in paragraphs (1), (2), and (3) of Section 162(a) and in succeeding subsections of Section 162 provisions pertaining to particular types of business expenses.

7.5 Regulation 1.162–1 bears the heading "Business Expenses" and states in Subsection (a):

In general. Business expenses deductible from gross income include the ordinary and necessary expenditures directly connected with or pertaining to the taxpayer's trade or business, except items which are used as the basis for a deduction or a credit under provisions of law other than section 162. The cost of goods purchased for resale, with proper adjustment for opening and closing inventories, is deducted from gross sales in computing gross income. ... Among the items included in business expenses are management expenses, commissions ..., labor, supplies, incidental repairs, operating expenses of automobiles used in the trade or business, traveling expenses while away from home solely in the pursuit of a trade or business ..., advertising and other selling expenses, together with insurance premiums against fire, storm, theft, accident, or other similar losses in the case of a business, and rental for the use of business property. No such items shall be included in business expenses, however, to the extent that it is used by the taxpayer in computing the cost of property included in its inventory or used in determining the gain or loss basis of its plant, equipment, or other property. ... Penalty payments with respect to Federal taxes, whether on account of negligence, delinquency, or fraud, are not deductible from gross income. The full amount of the allowable deduction for ordinary and necessary expenses in carrying on a business is nevertheless deductible, even though such expenses exceed the gross income derived during the taxable year from such business. ...

Section 212 (pertaining to expenses incurred by individuals in the 7.6 production of income or the determination, collection, or refund of any tax and discussed later in this chapter) and Section 162(a) are broad in scope, whereas all of the other deduction sections are specific and rigid. Section 162(a) applies to all business enterprises, no matter in what form conducted, and authorizes the deduction of all operating expenses. However, to be deductible under Section 162(a), an expenditure must not only be "ordinary and necessary" and incurred in connection with "carrying on any trade or business," but it must be *reasonable in amount* and *not violate public policy,* further limitations that have been created by the courts.

Before examining the four factors—ordinary and necessary, carry- 7.7 ing on a trade or business, reasonable amount, and public policy—we must distinguish between business expenses and capital expenditures.

Distinguished from Capital Expenditures. Even though a business 7.8 expenditure may be ordinary and necessary, it is not deductible if capital in nature. A repair to depreciable property is a deductible ordinary and necessary business expense, but an amount spent to restore the depreciable property to its original condition is a nondeductible capital expenditure. If a sea wall protecting a plant is destroyed by a hurricane, the cost of building a new wall is a capital expenditure; if the sea wall instead develops a crack, the cost of fixing the crack is a deductible repair expenditure. Other examples of capital expenditures are amounts spent to acquire property or amounts spent preliminary to the construction of a building, such as architects' plans, maps, abstracts, and surveys; costs of protecting or defending title to property; commissions paid upon the purchase of property; the cost of securing a television franchise, a patent, or a copyright; and the incorporation expenses of a corporation. See paragraph 8.157 for types of incorporation expenditures that can be amortized after being capitalized.

REPAIRS. Regulation 1.162–4 attempts to distinguish between 7.9 incidental repairs (expense items) and replacements (capital items) as follows:

The cost of incidental repairs which neither materially add to the value of the property nor appreciably prolong its life, but keep it in an ordinarily efficient operating condition, may be deducted as an expense, provided the cost of acquisition or production or the gain or loss basis of the taxpayer's plant, equipment, or other property, as the case may be, is not increased by the amount of such expenditures. Repairs in the nature of replacements, to the extent that they arrest deterioration and appreciably prolong the life of the property, shall either be capitalized and depreciated in accordance with section 167 or charged against the depreciation reserve if such an account is kept.

A multitude of cases in this area prove the difficulty of distinguishing between expenditures for incidental repairs and those that constitute capital additions. The major stumbling block usually is the question whether such amounts have appreciably prolonged the life of the property.

7.10 In *Oberman Mfg. Co.*[3] the company moved into a 200- by 300-foot plant that it leased at $30,000 a year for fifteen years, plus renewal options. Two or three years later the roof began to leak. After spot repairs failed to stop the leaks, a new roof was installed at a cost of $21,000. Oberman deducted the amount as a repair, but the Service held that it had to be capitalized. The Tax Court agreed with Oberman. The sole reason for the repair was to prevent leaks. It was not in any way intended to prolong the life of the property, increase its value or make it adaptable to a different use. The proper test is "... whether the expenditure materially enhances the value, use, life expectancy, strength, or capacity as compared with the status of the asset prior to the condition necessitating the expenditure." A "no" answer points to a fully deductible expense, a "yes" answer to a capital expenditure. Here the property was originally leak-free and the repair merely restored it to that condition.

7.11 Expenditures for the replacement or substantial repair of a major unit or structural part of a building may not normally be deducted as repairs. Thus, the cost of replacing heating-pipe systems, constructing a new roof, or extensively overhauling boilers must be capitalized if the work extends the life of the property beyond the original estimate.[4] A Tax Court case,[5] however, allowed as a deduction a $12,000 expenditure for the complete resurfacing of a defective roof of a building. Because of special defects inherent in the original roof, the resurfacing did not materially add to the life of the property, but merely restored it to its previous efficient operating condition.

7.12 It has been held that expenditures for repairs to a building must be capitalized when such repairs are incurred at the same time the build-

3. 47 T.C. 471 (1967).

4. Camilla Cotton Oil Co., 31 T.C. 560 (1958) (Acq.); Wood Preserving Corp. of Baltimore, Inc. v. U.S., 233 F.Supp. 600 (D.C., Md., 1964), 14 AFTR2d 6088, affirmed 347 F.2d 117 (4th Cir. 1965), 16 AFTR2d 5040.

5. Munroe Land Co., ¶66, 002 P-H Memo T.C. (1966).

ing is being generally renovated; the fact that the repairs considered alone would otherwise be deductible is immaterial.[6]

Definition of "Ordinary and Necessary." The words *ordinary and necessary* are not defined in the Regulations, but they have been the subject of many court decisions. In the case of *Deputy* v. *du Pont*[7] the United States Supreme Court explained what is meant by "ordinary."

7.13

... Ordinary has the connotation of normal, usual, or customary. To be sure, an expense may be ordinary though it happens but once in the taxpayer's lifetime. ... Yet the transaction which gives rise to it must be of common or frequent occurrence in the type of business involved. ...

This case in turn relied upon a previous United States Supreme Court decision, *Welch* v. *Helvering*.[8] There a former officer of a bankrupt corporation wished to strengthen his own credit standing and to reestablish his relationship with the bankrupt company's former customers upon entering a similar grain commission business of his own. After the discharge in bankruptcy of the corporation, he voluntarily made substantial payments to its creditors. In denying a deduction for these amounts the Court found the payments were "necessary" in the sense that they were appropriate and helpful but that they were not "ordinary":

7.14

We may assume that the payments to creditors of the Welch Company were necessary for the development of the petitioner's business, at least in the sense that they were appropriate and helpful. ... He certainly thought they were, and we should be slow to override his judgment. But the problem is not solved when the payments are characterized as necessary. Many necessary payments are charges upon capital. There is need to determine whether they are both necessary and ordinary. Now, what is ordinary, though there must always be a strain of constancy within it, is none the less a variable affected by time and place and circumstance. Ordinary in this context does not mean that the payments must be habitual or normal in the sense that the same taxpayer will have to make them often. A lawsuit affecting the safety of a business may happen once in a lifetime. The counsel fees may be so heavy that repetition is unlikely. None the less, the expense is an ordinary one because we know from experience that payments for such a purpose, whether the amount is large or small, are the common and accepted means of defense against attack. ...

... Here, indeed, as so often in other branches of the law, the decisive distinctions are those of degree and not of kind. One struggles in vain for any verbal formula that will supply a ready touchstone. The standard set up by the statute is not a rule of law; it is rather a way of life. Life in all its fullness must supply the answer to the riddle.

6. I. M. Cowell, 18 BTA 997 (1931) (Acq.); Herman Barron ¶63,315 P–H Memo T.C. (1963).
7. 308 U.S. 488 (1940), 40–1 USTC ¶9161, 23 AFTR 808.
8. 290 U.S. 111 (1933), 3 USTC ¶1164, 12 AFTR 1456.

The Court then held that these payments were capital expenditures to build a reputation, and that reputation, like learning, is akin to a capital asset.

7.15   In *Dunn & McCarthy, Inc.* v. *Com.*,[9] decided by the Second Circuit Court of Appeals, the president of a corporation borrowed money from several of the corporation's top salesmen, who worked directly under him, to cover personal debts. He committed suicide and died hopelessly insolvent. The corporation repaid the loans in order to keep the good will of its customers and preserve the salesmen's morale. The Court distinguished the *Welch* holding and found the expenditures to be ordinary on the ground that they were made to retain existing good will rather than to aid in the acquisition of a new business as involved in the *Welch* case. The Court stated, "It was the kind of outlay which we believe many corporations would make, and have made, under similar circumstances." This case stands for the proposition that *an expenditure need not be recurring in order to be deductible as an ordinary expense.*

7.16   **Reasonable Amounts.** In only one place does Section 162 use the word *reasonable*. This is in Section 162(a)(1) where it is said that there shall be allowed as a deduction "a reasonable allowance for salaries or other compensation for personal services actually rendered." However, the courts have held that in order for a business expense to be ordinary and necessary, it also must be reasonable in amount. In the case of *Com.* v. *The Lincoln Electric Co.*,[10] the Sixth Circuit Court of Appeals said:

> The deduction authorized by our prior ruling was plainly based on the broader ground of ordinary and necessary expenses, which would include items not of a compensatory nature, such as rent, advertising, transportation and communication charges, repairs and other such operating charges. Such payments are made proper deductions by the statute, but with respect to them there is no express statutory provision limiting them to a reasonable amount, as is the case in payments of compensation for personal services. However, the element of reasonableness is inherent in the phrase "ordinary and necessary." Clearly it was not the intention of Congress to automatically allow as deductions operating expenses incurred or paid by the taxpayer in an unlimited amount. ...

Reasonableness is always a question of fact. Payments arising out of dealings at arm's length are seldom questioned. The subject of reasonableness of compensation is discussed later in this chapter.

7.17   Rentals or other payments for the use of property paid to related persons or entities and found to be excessive in amount have been reduced or disallowed. The fact that a rental payment of a certain amount is legally required by a binding agreement is immaterial. In the case of *Utter McKinley Mortuaries*,[11] the controlling stockholder

9. 139 F.2d 242 (2nd Cir. 1943), 43–2 USTC ¶9688, 31 AFTR 1043.

10. 176 F.2d 815 (6th Cir. 1949), 49–2 USTC ¶9388, 38 AFTR 411.

11. ¶53,253 P–H Memo T.C., affirmed 225 F.2d 870 (9th Cir. 1955), 55–1 USTC ¶9338, 47 AFTR 1938.

of a corporation leased a mortuary from an unrelated person for $200 a month plus 5 percent of the annual gross receipts in excess of $55,200. He then immediately subleased the property to the corporation for $1,000 per month. The Tax Court found that for the years 1944, 1945, and 1946 the rental paid by the controlling stockholder to the unrelated person was $2,100, $2,400, and $2,907, whereas for those same years the rental paid by the corporation to the controlling stockholder was $10,500, $12,000, and $12,000. The Commissioner allowed as deductions to the corporation only the amounts of rents that were paid by the controlling stockholder to the unrelated person, and the court upheld this action of the Commissioner. Extracts from its opinion follow:

The rule controlling this issue is whether the amounts claimed as rent were, in fact, rent or something else paid under the guise of rents. The inquiry is whether the petitioner was required to pay these amounts as rent. Where the relationship between the lessor and lessee is close with no arm's-length dealing between them, the question of whether the amount paid is reasonable or excessive depends upon what the lessee would have been required to pay a stranger in an arm's-length transaction. ...

Petitioner's contention that the $1,000 per month rental was reasonable under the existing facts and circumstances is not well founded. The close relationship between the sublessor and the petitioner and the obvious effect of reducing taxes which grew out of the lease agreement justify our careful scrutiny of the transaction. ... In the foregoing discussion we have subjected the transactions between Maytor H. McKinley and his wholly controlled corporation to such a scrutiny. In view thereof we cannot agree that the arrangement between them created a legitimate business expense which was deductible in toto under the statute. No event occurred between the execution of the lease by the Colemans [the stranger] to Maytor and his sublease to petitioner which would enhance the value of the property leased and justify such a rental. It is unnecessary in our view of the matter to determine whether the excess payment over the rent required was a gift, a distribution of profits, excessive compensation, unreasonable rentals, or otherwise. It is sufficient for present purposes to hold, as we do, that the amounts disallowed by the respondent in the respective taxable years were not required to be made as a condition to the continued use or possession of the Coleman mortuary. ...

Carrying on a Trade or Business. In addition to being ordinary and necessary and reasonable in amount, to be deductible as a business expense under Section 162(a) the amount must have been paid or incurred "in carrying on any trade or business."   7.18

Neither the Code nor the Regulations define the phrase "trade or business." Ordinarily, this phrase is understood to mean an activity in which the taxpayer engages on a more or less full-time basis for the purpose of earning a profit or gaining a livelihood. This would include the activities of manufacturers, wholesalers, retailers, service organizations, employees, professional artists or athletes, architects, attorneys, certified public accountants, and other professional persons. In *International Trading Co.* v. *Com.*,[12] the Seventh Circuit   7.19

12. 275 F.2d 578 (7th Cir. 1960), 60–1 USTC ¶9335, 5 AFTR2d 970.

Court of Appeals said: "Whether activities of a taxpayer amount to 'carrying on a trade or business' within the statute is largely a matter of degree, and for a determination requires an examination of the facts in each case. ..." To carry on a trade or business involves holding one's self out to others as engaged in the selling of goods or services.[13]

7.20   Some investors have offices and employees to carry on their activities in trading in securities. No matter how large the investments, whether speculative or conservative in character, or how continuous, the activity does not constitute a trade or business.[14] Accordingly, the expenses are not deductible as business expenses under Section 162 and for that reason are not deductible from gross income in determining adjusted gross income; however, they are deductible from adjusted gross income in determining taxable income under Section 212 pertaining to expenses incurred for the production of income.

7.21   If an individual is an investor in, and a promoter of, many corporations, he has sometimes been held to be in the business of promoting corporations.[15]

7.22   PROFIT VERSUS PLEASURE. Section 162 allows deductions for ordinary and necessary expenses incurred in carrying on a trade or business. Sections 212(1) and (2) allow deductions for all ordinary and necessary expenses incurred in the production or collection of income or the management, conservation, or maintenance of property held for the production of income. On the other hand, Section 262 denies a deduction for personal, living, or family expenses.

7.23   Accordingly, under the law it has always been necessary for a taxpayer seeking to deduct losses from an alleged trade or business to prove that the enterprise was entered into for the purpose of making a profit, either now or ultimately. And, as to property held for the production of income, the taxpayer has always had the burden of proving that his dominant motive in holding the property was to make a profit, even if only through appreciation, and not to satisfy a personal desire, such as to have a recreational facility. If a taxpayer could not establish such a profit motive, the losses from operations were considered personal in nature and not deductible. As can be imagined, many hundreds of cases have been litigated through the years as to what was the real nature of an activity. The types of activities questioned were those primarily of gentlemen farmers — farming, ranching, cattle breeding, horse breeding, and horse racing. In recent years, the question also arose as to whether losses arising primarily from depreciation and maintenance of a winter or summer home could be deducted where the owner used the premises for part of the year and

13. Deputy v. du Pont, 308 U.S. 488 (1940), 40–1 USTC ¶9161, 23 AFTR 808; Helvering v. Wilmington Trust Co., 124 F.2d 156 (3rd Cir. 1941), 41–2 USTC ¶9666, 28 AFTR 624, reversing 42 BTA 173 (1940) (124 F.2d 156 was reversed on another point in 316 U.S. 164 (1942), 42–1 USTC ¶9441, 28 AFTR 1467).

14. Deputy v. du Pont, *ibid.*; Higgins v. Com., 312 U.S. 212 (1941), 1941–1 USTC ¶9233, 25 AFTR 1160.

15. Whipple v. Com., 373 U.S. 193 (1963), 63–1 USTC ¶9466, 11 AFTR2d 1454.

either rented it out or attempted to do so for the balance of the year.[16]

Starting with the year 1970, Section 183, added by the Tax Reform Act of 1969, is determinative as to the nature of the activity. If it is a business or validly profit motivated, all expenses are deductible even though they result in a net loss from operations. On the other hand, if the activity (which can be active or passive in character) has predominant overtones of being a hobby (active character) or consists of renting out on a non-commercial basis a resort home (passive character), Section 183, as interpreted by Regs. 1.183–1 and 2, permits a deduction of only:

7.24

1. expenditures, such as real estate taxes and interest on a mortgage, which would be deductible in any event even if they pertained to a personal residence [Reg. 1.183–1(b)(1)(i)];
2. other expenses, such as maintenance and utility charges, which do not also involve an adjustment to the basis of property, but only to the extent of the gross income from the activity after reduction by the amounts allowable under subparagraph (1) above [Reg. 1.183–1(b)(1)(ii)]; and
3. other expenses, such as depreciation, which result in (or if otherwise allowed would have resulted in) an adjustment to the basis of property, but only to the extent of the gross income from the activity after reducing such gross income by the amounts allowable under both subparagraphs (1) and (2) above [Reg. 1.183–1(b)(1)(iii)].

The basis of depreciable property is adjusted only by the amount of depreciation allowed as a deduction [Reg. 1.183–1(b)(2)(ii)].

(i) A, an individual, owns a small house located near the beach in a resort community. Visitors come to the area for recreational purposes during only three months of the year. During the remaining 9 months of the year houses such as A's are not rented. Customarily, A arranges that the house will be leased for 2 months of 3-month recreational season to vacationers and reserves the house for his own vacation during the remaining month of the recreational season. In 1971, A leases the house for 2 months for $1,000 per month and actually uses the house for his own vacation during the other month of the recreational season. For 1971, the expenses attributable to the house are $1,200 interest, $600 real estate taxes, $600 maintenance, $300 utilities, and $1,200 which would have been allowed as depreciation had the activity been engaged in for profit. Under these facts and circumstances, A is engaged in a single activity, holding the beach house primarily for personal purposes, which is an "activity not engaged in for profit" within the meaning of section 183(c). See paragraph (b)(9) of § 1.183–2.

EXAMPLE FROM REG.

(ii) Since the $1,200 of interest and the $600 of real estate taxes are specifically allowable as deductions under sections 163 and 164(a) without regard to whether the beach house activity is engaged in for profit, no allocation of these expenses between the uses of the beach house is necessary. However, since section 262 specifically disallows personal, living, and family expenses as deductions, the maintenance and utilities expenses and the depreciation from the activity must be allocated between the rental use and

16. John R. Carkhuff, 1969 P–H T.C. Memo ¶69,066, affirmed 425 F.2d 1400 (6th Cir., 1970), 25 AFTR2d 70–1119.

the personal use of the beach house. Under the particular facts and circumstances, 2/3 (2 months of rental use over 3 months of total use) of each of these expenses are allocated to the rental use, and 1/3 (1 month of personal use over 3 months of total use) of each of these expenses are allocated to the personal use as follows:

	RENTAL USE 2/3 — EXPENSES ALLOCABLE TO SECTION 183(B) (2)	PERSONAL USE 1/3 — EXPENSES ALLOCABLE TO SECTION 262
Maintenance expense $600	$ 400	$200
Utilities expense $300	200	100
Depreciation $1,200	800	400
Total	$1,400	$700

The $700 of expenses and depreciation allocated to the personal use of the beach house are disallowed as a deduction under section 262. In addition, the allowability of each of the expenses and the depreciation allocated to section 183(b)(2) is determined under paragraph (b)(1)(ii) and (iii) of this section. Thus, the maximum amount allowable as a deduction under section 183(b)(2) is $200 ($2,000 gross income from activity, less $1,800 deductions under section 183(b)(1)). Since the amounts described in section 183(b)(2) ($1,400) exceed the maximum amount allowable ($200), and since the amounts described in paragraph (b)(1)(ii) of this section ($600) exceed such maximum amount allowable ($200), none of the depreciation (an amount described in paragraph (b)(1)(iii) of this section) is allowable as a deduction.

7.25   The limitations of Section 183 apply to each separate activity engaged in by an individual or Subchapter S corporation where the activity is not engaged in for profit. Based upon the Senate Finance Committee Report,[17] an activity will be treated as engaged in for profit and outside the scope of Section 183 if the taxpayer has a good faith expectation of profit whether or not that expectation is a reasonable one. The report gives as examples of individuals outside the scope of Section 183: a bona fide inventor, an investor in a wildcat oil well, and a poor person engaged in what appears to be an inefficient farming operation. It seems obvious that the section is directed against "gentlemen farmers" with country estates who do not have a bona fide expectation of making a profit. This same Senate Finance Committee Report states that in determining whether an activity is engaged in for profit, an objective rather than a subjective test is to be employed. The regulations follow this same approach.

7.26   Subsection (d) sets up rebuttable presumptions. Please read it.

7.27   **Violation of Public Policy.** Prior to 1970 the courts and the Internal Revenue Service developed a principle that, even if a payment is "ordinary," it is not "necessary" and not deductible if in direct or severe violation of public policy. The underlying reason for this hold-

17. S. Rept. No. 91–552, p. 103.

ing was that, if a deduction could be taken for the expenditure, the Federal government in substance would be paying a part of the cost of the taxpayer's wrongdoing.

7.28 This problem was considered by the United States Supreme Court in *Tank Truck Rentals, Inc.* v. *Commissioner.*[18] There, the taxpayer paid hundreds of fines imposed on it and its drivers for violating state maximum weight laws. The taxpayer faced the problem of differing state weight restrictions on routes through numerous states, originating or terminating at points in Pennsylvania. In order to be competitive, the taxpayer could not operate partial loads and decided deliberately to operate in violation of the weight laws. The Court stated:

> ... [D]eductibility under § 23(a)(1)(A) [now Section 162(a)] is limited to expenses that are both ordinary and necessary to carrying on the taxpayer's business. ... A finding of "necessity" cannot be made, however, if allowance of the deduction would frustrate sharply defined national or state policies proscribing particular types of conduct, evidenced by some governmental declaration thereof. ...
>
> .   .   .   .   .
>
> Here we are concerned with the policy of several States "evidenced" by penal statutes enacted to protect their highways from damage and to insure the safety of all persons using them. ... It is clear that assessment of the fines was punitive action and not a mere toll for use of the highways. ... Petitioner's failure to comply with the state laws obviously was based on a balancing of the cost of compliance against the chance of detection. Such a course cannot be sanctioned, for judicial deference to state action requires, whenever possible, that a State not be thwarted in its policy. We will not presume that the Congress, in allowing deductions for income tax purposes, intended to encourage a business enterprise to violate the declared policy of a State. To allow the deduction sought here would but encourage continued violation of state law by increasing the odds in favor of noncompliance. This could only tend to destroy the effectiveness of the State's maximum weight laws.

7.29 Prior to the time of enactment of the Tax Reform Act of 1969 there was no statutory provision (other than a limited one pertaining to payments to foreign officials) setting forth "public policy" standards for denying deduction of business expenses. The judge-made law had developed rather well, but there were still grey areas. The 1969 Act eliminated most areas of uncertainty by denying deductions under specified circumstances for four types of expenditures:

1. Fines or penalties for violation of law—Section 162(f);
2. Two-thirds of treble damage payments to private party claimants under antitrust laws—Section 162(g) [see paragraph 7.33];
3. Bribes or kickbacks paid to public officials—Section 162(c)(1);
4. Other unlawful business-type bribes or kickbacks—Section 162(c)(2).

18. 356 U.S. 30 (1958), 1 AFTR2d 1154.

7.30   FINES AND PENALTIES. The principle of *Tank Truck Rentals, Inc.* has been codified in Section 162(f): "No deduction shall be allowed under subsection (a) [pertaining to ordinary and necessary business expenses] for any fine or similar penalty paid to a government for the violation of any law."

7.31   ANTITRUST DAMAGE PAYMENTS. Under the antitrust laws (Clayton Act and Sherman Act) the United States can institute criminal prosecutions. In addition, under Section 4A of the Clayton Act it may sue for actual damages and under the False Claims Act for specific penalties and double damages. Suits for treble damages, three times the amount of actual damage, can also be insti'ited under Section 4 of the Clayton Act by private parties who have been compelled to pay higher prices by reason of any criminal conspiracy to fix and maintain prices, terms, and conditions for the sale of manufactured items.

7.32   The full amount of damages, both actual and punitive, paid to the Federal government is not deductible.[19]

7.33   As for payments to private parties, their deductibility depends upon whether there was first a criminal prosecution in which the government was successful. If a taxpayer is convicted in a criminal proceeding for the violation of the Federal antitrust laws (or pleads guilty or *nolo contendere*), no deduction is allowable for the punitive two-thirds of any amount thereafter paid on any judgment for damages entered in a civil suit or in settlement of any such suit.[20] The remaining one-third is deductible because it represents restoration of actual damages sustained by the claimant. If there was no prior criminal prosecution in which the government was successful, the full amount paid in satisfaction of any judgment entered in a civil suit or in settlement thereof is deductible.[21]

7.34   BRIBES OR KICKBACKS TO PUBLIC OFFICIALS. Any illegal payment to a public official or employee is not deductible, whether or not there is a criminal prosecution.[22]

7.35   OTHER BRIBES OR KICKBACKS. A kickback and a discount or allowance of the same amount result in identical amounts of financial net income, but differ in nature. A kickback is a payment to a third person who is neither the purchaser nor the seller in a sales transaction. On the other hand, a discount or allowance is a reduction of the sales price granted to the purchaser by the seller. It is deductible in determining gross income and not from gross income. Accordingly, it need not be an ordinary and necessary business expense and is taken into account even if the granting of the allowance violates some law, such as a minimum-price law imposed by a state on sales of milk,[23]

19. Rev. Rul. 64–224, 1964–2 C.B. 52.
20. Section 162(g) added by the Tax Reform Act of 1969 overrules the contrary portion of Rev. Rul. 64–224.
21. S. Rept. No. 91–552, p. 274.; Reg. 1.162–22.
22. Section 162(c)(1).
23. Pittsburgh Milk Co., 26 T.C. 707 (1956) (Acq.); Atzingen-Whitehouse Dairy

or the granting of a discount by an insurance agent to a customer.[24]

The deductibility of bribes and kickbacks to other than government 7.36 officials and employees depends upon whether they are illegal under any law of the United States or under any law of a state (but only if such state law is generally enforced). Further, the Federal or state law must subject the payor to a criminal penalty or the loss of a license or privilege to engage in a trade or business. If there is such a law, the illegal bribe, kickback, or other payment is not deductible whether or not any criminal or civil court action ensues. Under Section 162(c)(2) the term "kickback" is broadened to include a payment made in consideration of the referral of a client, patient, or customer.

ILLEGALITY OF BUSINESS. A number of cases involve deduc- 7.37 tions where the activity itself is illegal, such as gambling contrary to state law and the prohibited operation of a liquor business. It is generally considered that expenses of an illegal business are deductible if they are of an operating nature, such as rent and wages,[25] but are not deductible if they are inherently of an illegal nature, such as bribes and protection payments.[26]

Legal Expenses. Like any other expenditure, to be deductible under 7.38 Section 162(a) a legal expense must be an ordinary and necessary one incurred in connection with a business activity. For example, a taxpayer is entitled to deduct legal expenses incurred in defending against a claim brought against him for personal injuries allegedly inflicted by him in the course of his trade or business. However, if the injury to the other person happened while the taxpayer was engaged in personal pursuits, such as when driving a car when commuting to work, the fees and expenses are not deductible.[27]

EXPENSE OR CAPITAL EXPENDITURE. The nature of the legal 7.39 services rendered determines whether or not the fee for such services is deductible and if so, how. Fees paid for the following types of services have been held deductible as business expenses: collection of a business debt,[28] recovery of business insurance premiums,[29] recovery of damages,[30] action for accounting against agent,[31] and defense against an action by a former partner for an accounting of partnership income.[32] Legal expenses in federal civil tax matters are deductible

Co., 36 T.C. 173 (1961) (Acq.).

24. Allen Schiffman, 47 T.C. No. 52 (1967).

25. G. A. Comeaux, 10 T.C. 201 (1948), affirmed 176 F.2d 394 (10th Cir. 1949), 49–2 USTC §9358, 38 AFTR 343.

26. Frank A. Maddas, 40 BTA 572 (1939), affirmed 114 F.2d 548 (3rd Cir. 1940), 40–2 USTC §9596, 25 AFTR 672.

27. Henke v. Jarecki (D.C., Ill., 1956), 56–1 USTC §9511, 51 AFTR 1159; W. S. Dickason, 20 BTA 496 (1930); Samuel E. Mulholland, 16 BTA 1331 (1929).

28 Ernest Koerner, ¶51,275 P–H Memo T.C.

29. Alexander Sprunt & Son, Inc. v. Com., 64 F.2d 424 (4th Cir. 1933), 12 AFTR 411, reversing 24 BTA 599.

30. J. D. Wineland et al., ¶51,294 P–H Memo T.C.

31. Bula Croker, 27 BTA 588.

32. Kornhauser v. U.S., 276 U.S. 145 (1928), 1 USTC ¶284, 6 AFTR 7358.

as business expenses if related to a business. Accordingly, in the case of an individual engaged in business, they are deductible in determining adjusted gross income even though they are alternatively deductible under Section 212(3).

7.40   Legal fees paid by a nondealer on the casual sale of real property must be deducted from the sales proceeds in calculating the capital gain or loss.[33]

7.41   If the services pertain to the cost of defending or perfecting title to an asset[34] or pertain to the acquisition of an asset, the fee must be capitalized as a part of the cost of the related asset. If a recovery of money is a recovery of capital and therefore nontaxable, the legal expenses are also capital in nature and not deductible.[35]

7.42   Sometimes part of the services are business expenses, and the other part capital in nature. In that event the fee must be allocated. In *Morgan's Est. v. Com.*,[36] decided by the Fifth Circuit Court of Appeals, the taxpayer had acquired oil property. Thereupon a former business partner challenged the taxpayer's title and demanded an accounting for one-half interest. The taxpayer was allowed a deduction for a portion of the legal costs in unsuccessfully defending himself. The court noted the difficulty of an apportionment where both property and income are the objectives of a suit, and said:

> The exact line of demarcation between expenses incurred in litigation in the defense of income (deductible) and those incurred in the defense of title (nondeductible) is not always clear. ... Nevertheless, the basic principles underlying a determination of the nature of the expenditures involved are well settled. We do not look only to the subjective motives of the taxpayer in defending such litigation or those of the party who initiated the suit. Rather, we must look to the issues involved, the nature and objectives of the suit in which the expenditures were made, the defenses asserted, the purpose for which the claimed deductions were expended, the background of the litigation, and all facts pertaining to the entire controversy out of which the disputed expenses arose.

7.43   CRIMINAL DEFENSE. Legal fees expended in a criminal defense, whether successful[37] or not,[38] are deductible when the alleged crime directly relates to a business or an income-producing activity. Further, it does not matter whether the business or activity is legal or illegal.

33. S. C. Chapin, 12 T.C. 235, affirmed 180 F.2d 140 (8th Cir. 1950), 50–1 USTC ¶9171, 38 AFTR 1489.

34. Reg. 1.212–1(k)

35. Pennroad Corp., 21 T.C. 1087, affirmed on another issue in 228 F.2d 329 (3rd Cir. 1955), 56–1 USTC ¶9124, 48 AFTR 746; Iowa Southern Utilities Co., 21 TCM 1427 (1962), affirmed 333 F.2d 382 (8th Cir. 1964), 64–2 USTC ¶9580, 14 AFTR2d 5061, cert. den. 379 U.S. 946.

36. 332 F.2d 144 (5th Cir. 1964), 64–2 USTC ¶9507, 13 AFTR2d 1548.

37. Peoples-Pittsburgh Trust Co., Exr. v. Com., 60 F.2d 187 (3rd Cir. 1932), 11 AFTR 730, affirming 21 BTA 588; Union Investment Co., 21 T.C. 659 (1954) (Acq.); Rev. Rul. 68–662.

38. Com. v. Tellier, 383 U.S. 687 (1966), 66–1 USTC ¶9319, 17 AFTR2d 633; Mitchell v. U.S., 23 AFTR2d 69–918 (Ct. Cls., 1969).

A criminal charge against a corporate executive alleging fraud in making out a corporation's tax return was held directly related to his business of being an employee.[39] However, a dentist in *Richard F. Smith*[40] was denied a deduction for attorney fees paid in connection with a partially successful defense of a criminal indictment for tax fraud where the income omitted from tax returns consisted primarily of dividends; the court held the fraudulent returns did not bear any direct relationship to his dental practice.

ANTITRUST PROCEEDINGS. Legal fees and related expenses incurred in defending a criminal prosecution for violation of the antitrust laws and also in defending against civil suits for damages under those laws are deductible.[41] It is immaterial that a portion or all of any damages paid may not be deductible.

7.44

Educational Expenses. A large number of court cases have involved contentions by individuals that they are entitled to deduct educational expenditures as ordinary and necessary business expenses. Reg. 1.162–5 lays down these basic rules:

7.45

(a) A taxpayer can deduct expenses for education undertaken for the purpose of
   (i) maintaining or improving skills required in his employment or business,
   (ii) retaining a salary or job status, or
   (iii) qualifying him (even if the courses lead to a degree) for advancement or for a specialty within his field.
(b) Educational expenditures which are personal or capital in nature are not deductible even though the education maintains or improves skills required in the individual's employment, trade, or business or meets the express requirements of his employer or applicable law or regulations. There are two categories:
   (i) expenditures made to meet the minimum educational requirements for qualification in an individual's employment, trade, or business;
   (ii) expenditures made to qualify the individual for a new trade or business.

Where an individual travels away from home primarily to obtain education, the expenses of which are deductible, his expenses for travel, meals, and lodging while away from home are also deductible. However, if the individual engages in personal activity on such trip, the portion of the expenses attributable to such activity is not deductible. If the individual's travel away from home is primarily personal, his traveling expenses are not deductible.

7.46

39. Peoples-Pittsburgh Trust Co., Exr. v. Com., *supra* fn. 40.
40. 31 T.C. (1958) (Acq.).
41. Rev. Rul. 66–330.

7.47   The following examples are from the regulations:

EXAMPLES   D, who holds a bachelor's degree, obtains temporary employment as an
FROM REG.   instructor at University Y and undertakes graduate courses as a candidate for
            a graduate degree. D may become a faculty member only if he obtains a
Ex. 1   graduate degree and may continue to hold a position as instructor only so
            long as he shows satisfactory progress towards obtaining this graduate de-
            gree. The graduate courses taken by D constitute education required to meet
            the minimum educational requirements for qualification in D's trade or busi-
            ness and, thus, the expenditures for such courses are not deductible.

Ex. 2   E, who has completed two years of a normal three-year law school course
            leading to a bachelor of laws degree (LL.B.), is hired by a law firm to do legal
            research and perform other functions on a full-time basis. As a condition to
            continued employment, E is required to obtain an LL.B. and pass the State
            bar examination. E completes his law school education by attending night
            law school, and he takes a bar review course in order to prepare for the State
            bar examination. The law courses and bar review course constitute education
            required to meet the minimum educational requirements for qualification in
            E's trade or business and, thus, the expenditures for such courses are not
            deductible.

Ex. 3   A, a self-employed individual practicing a profession other than law, for
            example, engineering, accounting, etc., attends law school at night and after
            completing his law school studies, receives a bachelor of laws degree. The
            expenditures made by A in attending law school are nondeductible because
            this course of study qualifies him for a new trade or business.

Ex. 4   B, a general practitioner of medicine, takes a two-week course reviewing
            developments in several specialized fields of medicine. B's expenses for the
            course are deductible because the course maintains or improves skills re-
            quired by him in his trade or business and does not qualify him for a new
            trade or business.

Ex. 5   A, a self-employed tax practitioner, decides to take a one-week course in
            new developments in taxation, which is offered in City X, 500 miles away
            from his home. His primary purpose in going to X is to take the course, but
            he also takes a side trip to City Y (50 miles from X) for one day, takes a sight-
            seeing trip while in X, and entertains some personal friends. A's transpor-
            tation expenses to City X and return to his home are deductible but his
            transportation expenses to City Y are not deductible. A's expenses for meals
            and lodging while away from home will be allocated between his educa-
            tional pursuits and his personal activities. Those expenses which are entirely
            personal, such as sightseeing and entertaining friends, are not deductible to
            any extent.

7.48   Deductions have usually (but not always) been denied to revenue
            agents for the cost of obtaining a law degree on the ground that the
            degree is not required by the employer as a condition of continued
            employment and qualifies the individual for a new profession.[42] A

42. James J. Engel, ¶62,244 P-H Memo T.C.; J. L. Weiler, 54 T.C. 398 (1970).

policeman cannot deduct the cost of a general college education.[43]
Costs incurred in taking a C.P.A. review course are nondeductible
personal expenditures;[44] but if an individual is already a C.P.A., the
expenditures for additional tax courses taken to improve his tax
knowledge would be deductible.

Association Dues. Generally, Reg. 1.162–15(c) provides that dues 7.49
paid to organizations directly related to the taxpayer's trade or business are deductible as ordinary and necessary business expenses
under Section 162(a). Thus, dues paid by businesses to trade associations, such as the American Mining Congress and the National
Retail Merchants Association, and to specific bodies, such as a Chamber of Commerce and other civic improvement associations, are deductible.

If a substantial part of the activities of an association are political, 7.50
then the portion of the dues applicable to such activities is not deductible [Reg. 1.162–20(c)(3)].

Travel and Entertainment Expenses. Traveling expenses incurred 7.51
while away from home (such as travel fares, meals, and lodging) are
deductible. A discussion of the phrase "away from home" appears
later in this chapter in paragraphs 7.89–7.95. Regulation 1.162–2
describes the nature of the deduction for traveling expense and the
limitations and restrictions thereon as follows:

(a) Traveling expenses include travel fares, meals and lodging, and expenses incident to travel such as expenses for sample rooms, telephone and
telegraph, public stenographers, etc. Only such traveling expenses as are
reasonable and necessary in the conduct of the taxpayer's business and directly attributable to it may be deducted. ...

(b)(1) If a taxpayer travels to a destination and while at such destination
engages in both business and personal activities, traveling expenses ... are
deductible only if the trip is related primarily to the taxpayer's trade or business. If the trip is primarily personal in nature, the traveling expenses ...
are not deductible even though the taxpayer engages in business activities
while at such destination. However, expenses while at the destination which
are properly allocable to the taxpayer's trade or business are deductible even
though the traveling expenses ... are not deductible.

(2) Whether a trip is related primarily to the taxpayer's trade or business or
is primarily personal in nature depends on the facts and circumstances in each
case. The amount of time during the period of the trip which is spent on personal activity compared to the amount of time spent on activities directly
relating to the taxpayer's trade or business is an important factor in determining whether the trip is primarily personal. ...

(c) Where a taxpayer's wife accompanies him on a business trip, expenses
attributable to her travel are not deductible unless it can be adequately shown
that the wife's presence on the trip has a bona fide business purpose. ...

(d) Expenses paid or incurred by a taxpayer in attending a convention or

43. Cato Noonan Estate, ¶69,070 P–H Memo T.C.; James A. Carroll, 51 T.C. 213
(1968), affirmed 24 AFTR2d 69–5766 (7th Cir. 1969).
44. Rev. Rul. 69–292.

other meeting may constitute an ordinary and necessary business expense under Section 162 depending upon the facts and circumstances of each case. ... The allowance of deductions for such expenses will depend upon whether there is a sufficient relationship between the taxpayer's trade or business and his attendance at the convention or other meeting so that he is benefiting or advancing the interests of his trade or business by such attendance. ...

(e) Commuters' fares are not considered as business expenses and are not deductible.

7.52   In 1962, Section 274 was added to the Code to provide restrictions on the deductibility of travel, entertainment, and gift expenses otherwise allowable under other sections of the Code (especially Sections 162(a) and 212) because of what was thought to be excessive expense account abuses by stockholders, officers, and employees of businesses. In general, Section 274 limits the types of entertainment expenses that can be deducted, limits the dollar amount of gifts that can be deducted, and provides that all entertainment, gift, and travel expenses must be substantiated by the taxpayer before a deduction can be taken.

7.53   Regulations 1.274–2(a)(1) and (2) set forth the general rules with respect to the deductibility of entertainment expenses as follows:

... (1) *Entertainment activity.* Except as provided in this section, no deduction otherwise allowable under chapter 1 of the Code shall be allowed for any expenditure with respect to entertainment unless the taxpayer establishes—

(i) That the expenditure was directly related to the active conduct of the taxpayer's trade or business, or

(ii) In the case of an expenditure directly preceding or following a substantial and bona fide business discussion (including business meetings at a convention or otherwise), that the expenditure was associated with the active conduct of the taxpayer's trade or business.

Such deduction shall not exceed the portion of the expenditure directly related to (or in the case of an expenditure described in subdivision (ii) above, the portion of the expenditure associated with) the active conduct of the taxpayer's trade or business.

(2) *Entertainment facilities.* Except as provided in this section, no deduction otherwise allowable under chapter 1 of Code shall be allowed for any expenditure with respect to a facility used in connection with entertainment unless the taxpayer establishes—

(i) That the facility was used primarily for the furtherance of the taxpayer's trade or business, and

(ii) That the expenditure was directly related to the active conduct of such trade or business.

Such deduction shall not exceed the portion of the expenditure directly related to the active conduct of the taxpayer's trade or business.

7.54   With certain limited exceptions, Section 274(b) provides that no deduction will be allowed for gifts made by a taxpayer (in connection with his trade or business) to an individual to the extent that the cost of the gifts to the individual exceeds $25 during the taxpayer's taxable year. For example, assume that a taxpayer gave to each of two individual customers a matched set of golf clubs during a particular year. If each set had a cost of $300, the taxpayer could take only a $50 deduction for the gifts.

The gist of the substantiation rules is reflected in Reg. 1.274–5(a): 7.55

In general. No deduction shall be allowed for any expenditure with respect to—

(1) Traveling away from home (including meals and lodging) deductible under section 162 or 212,

(2) Any activity which is of a type generally considered to constitute entertainment, amusement, or recreation, or with respect to a facility used in connection with such an activity, including the items specified in section 274(e), or

(3) Gifts defined in section 274,

unless the taxpayer substantiates such expenditure as provided in paragraph (c) of this section. This limitation supersedes with respect to any such expenditure the doctrine of *Cohan* v. *Commissioner* (C.C.A.2d, 1930) 39 F.2d 540. The decision held that, where the evidence indicated a taxpayer incurred deductible travel or entertainment expenses but the exact amount could not be determined, the court should make a close approximation and not disallow the deduction entirely. Section 274(d) contemplates that no deduction shall be allowed a taxpayer for such expenditure on the basis of such approximations or unsupported testimony of the taxpayer. For purposes of this section, the term "entertainment" means entertainment, amusement, or recreation, and use of a facility therefor; and the term "expenditure" includes expenses and items (including items such as losses and depreciation).

Accordingly, as provided in Reg. 1.274–5, for each expenditure 7.56
the taxpayer must maintain data or a diary substantiating the:

1. Amount;
2. Time and place of travel or entertainment (or use of a facility with respect to entertainment), or date and description of a gift;
3. Business purpose; and
4. Business relationship to the taxpayer of each person entertained, using an entertainment facility, or receiving a gift.

In addition, a receipt must be obtained where practicable for any expenditure for lodging while away from home and for any other expenditure of $25 or more. In lieu of accounting for the actual amount spent, certain reasonable per diem allowances for travel away from home and mileage allowances may be deducted if all the other substantiation requirements are met (e.g., time and place of travel). If the documentation and business purposes are not within the prescribed requirements of Section 274 and the regulations thereunder, it is possible under certain circumstances not only that the business will be denied a deduction, but also that the recipient, even if only in an employee's status, will be deemed to have taxable income in the amount of the reimbursement he receives.

7.57   Subsection (e) provides the only exceptions to the stringent requirements of the other subsections of Section 274. Each exception has technical requirements and space limits a full discussion of these here. The exceptions pertain to business meals, food and beverage for employees, expenses treated as compensation, reimbursed expenses, recreational expenses for employees, employee and stockholder business meetings, meetings of business leagues, items available to the public, and entertainment sold to customers.

7.58 **Compensation for Personal Services of Employees.** Pursuant to Reg. 1.162–7(a):

> There may be ... [included] among the ordinary and necessary expenses paid or incurred in carrying on any trade or business a reasonable allowance for salaries or other compensation for personal services actually rendered. The test of deductibility in the case of compensation payments is whether they are reasonable and are in fact payments purely for services.

Thus, the right to take a deduction for compensation for personal services depends upon:

1. The payment being, in fact, compensation;
2. Personal services having actually been rendered by the payee; and
3. Reasonableness of the amount paid.

7.59   COMPENSATION ELEMENT. Regulation 1.162–7(b)(1) requires that to be deductible as compensation, a payment must in fact be made for services and not be in substance a dividend or part of the purchase price of assets:

> Any amount paid in the form of compensation, but not in fact as the purchase price of services, is not deductible. An ostensible salary paid by a corporation may be a distribution of a dividend on stock. This is likely to occur in the case of a corporation having few shareholders, practically all of whom draw salaries. If in such a case the salaries are in excess of those ordinarily paid for similar services and the excessive payments correspond or bear a close relationship to the stockholdings of the officers or employees, it would seem likely that the salaries are not paid wholly for services rendered, but that the excessive payments are a distribution of earnings upon the stock. An ostensible salary may be in part payment for property. This may occur, for example, where a partnership sells out to a corporation, the former partners agreeing to continue in the service of the corporation. In such a case it may be found that the salaries of the former partners are not merely for services, but in part constitute payment for the transfer of their business.

It has been held that bookkeeping entries, descriptions, or labels affixed to a payment do not fix conclusively its nature or character. Thus, calling a payment "salary" when it is not such in fact will not assure deductibility,[45] just as failure to describe a payment properly will not preclude its deductibility if the amount actually represents compensation.[46]

SERVICES RENDERED. A bona fide employment relationship 7.60 must exist if payments are to be deductible. Thus, reasonable wages a father pays to his minor child for services actually rendered as a bona fide employee of his trade or business are deductible.[47] A deduction for compensation can be taken in a particular year even though the services were not rendered in that year; it is sufficient if the services were rendered previously and the liability for the compensation is incurred or the compensation is paid during the taxable year.[48] Payments to widows or other family members of a deceased employee generally have been held to be deductible when made in recognition of past services rendered by the employee and not as a subterfuge for dividend distributions to widows of deceased officer-shareholders.[49]

REASONABLE AMOUNT. The Internal Revenue Service will 7.61 scrutinize carefully any large payment of compensation to an officer of a corporation who is also the controlling stockholder, particularly where the corporation has a history of paying small dividends. The Service will suspect that a portion of the compensation is in substance a disguised dividend. From an overall standpoint it does result in lower taxes if a corporation disburses a deductible payment, rather than a nondeductible dividend, to its stockholders.

Bob Smith owns 90 percent of the stock of a corporation and is its chief EXAMPLE executive officer. His wife owns the other 10 percent. If the top corporate rate is 50 percent and his rate is less than 50 percent, an overall saving will result to the extent that an increase in compensation of say $1,000 does not put him over the 50 percent individual rate. On the other hand, a dividend of $1,000 out of pretax corporate earnings of $2,000 will, at an individual top bracket rate of 50 percent, result in a total tax of $1,500 ($1,000 corporate and $500 individual) on pretax corporate earnings of $2,000. The effective overall tax rate is 75 percent ($1,500 ÷ $2,000).

---

45. Brush-Moore Newspapers v. Com., 95 F.2d 900 (6th Cir. 1938), 38–1 USTC ¶9247, 21 AFTR 37, cert. den. 305 U.S. 615.
46. R. J. Reynolds Tobacco Co., ¶56,161 P–H Memo T.C. (1956), affirmed 260 F.2d 9 (4th Cir. 1958), 58–2 USTC ¶9867, 2 AFTR2d 5892.
47. I.T. 3767, 1945 C.B. 101; cf. The Home Sales Co., ¶57,078 P–H Memo T.C. and Logan Lumber Co., ¶64,126 P–H Memo T.C.
48. Lucas v. Ox Fibre Brush Co., 281 U.S. 115 (1930), 2 USTC ¶522, 8 AFTR 10901; Jewell Ridge Coal Sales Co., Inc., ¶57,030 P–H Memo T.C.
49. Weyenberg Shoe Mfg. Co., ¶64,322 P–H Memo T.C.; Oppenheimer Casting Co., ¶63,216 P–H Memo T.C. The deduction was denied in Interstate Drop Forge Co. v. Com., 326 F.2d 743 (7th Cir. 1964), 64–1 USTC ¶9182, 13 AFTR2d 363, and Nickerson Lumber Co. v. U.S., 214 F.Supp. 87 (D.C., Mass., 1963), 63–1 USTC ¶9316, 11 AFTR2d 1094.

7.62   Regulation 1.162–7(b)(3) provides that reasonable compensation is "... such amount as would ordinarily be paid for like services by like enterprises under like circumstances." In determining reasonableness of compensation, a variety of factors must be considered. Primary among them are comparisons of compensation paid to comparable employees in the same or comparable businesses, contribution to the business, extent and scope of the work, ratio of compensation to gross income, qualifications of the employee, relationship between salaries and stockholdings, and the pattern of determination of compensation.[50] These circumstances are taken into consideration as of the date when the employment contract is entered into, not when the compensation is questioned. Thus, Reg. 1.162–7(b)(2) provides that if contingent compensation is paid pursuant to a free bargain between the employer and the individual made before the services are rendered and under good faith to secure services without advantage to either party, the deduction will be allowed even though the amount would appear to be greater than that which ordinarily would have been paid. In one situation, the basic salaries of $8,000 and $14,000 ballooned to $115,000 and $176,984, respectively, based on an employment agreement utilizing a percentage of profits. The Court of Claims found that the full amount was deductible because the contract was reasonable when entered into and the parties did not expect such a tremendous increase in business.[51] However, the courts still have the tendency to utilize hindsight in comparing the efforts and abilities of the individuals involved to compensation received.

7.63   When the Service disallows a closely held corporation's deduction for compensation paid to its stockholder-executives, the result will be, in effect, a double tax. The amount disallowed is taxed to both the corporation and the shareholder. However, if before the compensation is received the corporation and the stockholder-executive enter into a binding contract that he will repay to the corporation any amount that is disallowed as a deduction by the Service, the repayment will be deductible by the executive.[52] As to the corporation, the amount of the recovery ought not to be taxable income, because the original payment did not give rise to a tax benefit.

7.64   BONUSES. The regulations do not distinguish between wage or salary payments and bonuses. All such payments and bonuses are deductible if, in total, they meet the overall test of being reasonable and constituting payment for services rendered as provided by Reg. 1.162–9. Bonuses are often based on the preceding year's operating results. Even though the amounts cannot be computed until the next year, they are deductible on the accrual basis in the prior year if a communicated formula for their computation then existed.[53]

---

50. Mayson Manufacturing Co. v. Com., 178 F.2d 115 (6th Cir. 1949), 49–2 USTC ¶9467, 38 AFTR 1028.

51. Robert Rogers, Inc. v. U.S., 93 F.Supp. 1014 (Ct. Cls., 1950), 50–2 USTC ¶9510, 39 AFTR 1366.

52. Vincent E. Oswald, 49 T.C. 645 (1968) (Acq.); Rev. Rul. 69–115.

53. Josiah Wedgwood & Sons, Ltd., 3 BTA 355 (Acq.); See also ¶15.87–15.90.

Death Benefits. Death benefits paid to the family of a deceased em- 7.65
ployee generally are deductible. Though the payments are in some
respects a voluntary donation, they are made in most cases because
of the services rendered by the employee to the business. The courts
have generally ignored the humanitarian aspects of the payments and
have considered the entire amount as a payment for past services
rendered by the deceased employee; consequently, the amount is a
proper, ordinary, and reasonable business expense to the employer.[54]
If it can be shown that the death benefit was not intended to represent
additional compensation and was made without intending to gain any
benefit for the employer (e.g., by increasing the morale of the remaining employees), probably no deduction will be allowed; this is especially true where the payment is made to the widow of a deceased
stockholder-employee.[55]

Other Employee Benefits. Various other employee benefits are de- 7.66
ductible even though they may not constitute taxable income to the
employee. These include the ordinary fringe benefits, such as annual
company picnics; cost of turkeys, hams, and similar merchandise of a
nominal value distributed generally at Thanksgiving and Christmas
time; and amounts paid by the employer on account of injuries received by employees. Included in the employee benefit category, as
described in Reg. 1.162–10, are dismissal wages, unemployment
benefits, guaranteed annual wages, vacations, sickness benefits, and
payments under similar welfare benefit plans. In addition, contributions to supplemental unemployment benefit plans, such as those
existing in the automobile industry, are deductible as compensation.[56]
Pension payments made directly to retired employees and contributions to qualified pension or profit-sharing plans are also deductible. Pensions are discussed in chapter 17.

Rentals and Royalties. Section 162(a)(3) provides that a deduction 7.67
can be taken for "rentals or other payments required to be made as a
condition to the continued use or possession, for purposes of the trade
or business, of property to which the taxpayer has not taken or is not
taking title or in which he has no equity."

  "Property" includes personal property, such as machinery, equip- 7.68
ment, and vehicles, as well as land and buildings. The rental deduction is conditioned upon the fact that the deduction must be for rent
and not for a payment that is labeled "rent" but that actually is some-

54. Weyenberg Shoe Mfg. Co., ¶64,322 P–H Memo T.C.; Com. v. Champion Spark
Plug Company, 266 F.2d 347 (6th Cir. 1959), 59–1 USTC ¶9438, 3 AFTR2d 1385: Fifth
Avenue Coach Lines, Inc., 31 T.C. 1080 (1959) (Acq.), affirmed in part and reversed
in part without discussion of this point 281 F.2d 556 (2nd Cir. 1960), 60–2 USTC
¶9628, 6 AFTR2d 5265, cert. den. 366 U.S. 964.
    55. Loewy Drug Company of Baltimore City v. U.S., 356 F.2d 928 (4th Cir. 1966),
66–1 USTC ¶9254, 17 AFTR2d 380, Interstate Drop Forge Co. v. Com., 326 F.2d 743
(7th Cir. 1964), 64–1 USTC ¶9182, 13 AFTR2d 363; Nickerson Lumber Company v.
U.S., 214 F.Supp. 87 (D.C., Mass., 1963), 63–1 USTC ¶9316, 11 AFTR2d 1094.
    56. Rev. Rul. 60–330, 1960–2 C.B. 46.

thing else. If a payment actually represents a distribution of profits or payment for capital items, a designation of the payment as "rent" will not give rise to a deduction for rent.[57]

7.69   LEASE WITH OPTION TO PURCHASE. Frequently a lease will contain a provision giving the lessee an option to purchase. There are many variations of the manner in which the purchase price is stated in the event of exercise of the option. It can be a price as of the date of the lease but to be reduced by all or a part of the rental payments. Also it can be a stipulated amount as of the end of the term of the lease, or a series of reducing amounts as of designated dates. Depending upon the amount of the purchase price in relation to the value of the article as of the option date, such a lease can in substance be an installment purchase agreement.

7.70   If a lease containing an option to purchase is a true lease, the amounts paid as rent are deductible as such, and the additional amount paid to purchase the item then becomes the taxpayer's basis for the property. On the other hand, if the contract is in substance an installment sales contract, the payments are not deductible as rent, but instead merely reduce the capitalized liability for the purchase price. The interest element in the installment payments will be deductible as such.

7.71   In order to determine whether payments under a contract are truly rent or in substance installments on a purchase price, a number of tests are in use. The Tax Court has applied an economic test. If the amounts of the payments exceed a fair rental for the use of the property and the so-called lessee by reason of the payments is building up an equity in the property, no part of the payments is deductible as rent. In *Chicago Stoker Corp.*,[58] it said:

If payments are large enough to exceed the depreciation and value of the property and thus give the payor an equity in the property, it is less of a distortion of income to regard the payments as purchase price and allow depreciation on the property than to offset the entire payment against the income of one year.

7.72   To the contrary, some of the circuit courts of appeal have held that the economic test is only one of many factors to be considered.

7.73   In an attempt to establish criteria for distinguishing between a rental and a purchase, the Internal Revenue Service has established a multi-factor test in Section 4.01 of Rev. Rul. 55–540,[59] as follows:

Whatever interest is obtained by a lessee is acquired under the terms of the agreement itself. Whether an agreement, which in form is a lease, is in

57. Elliot v. Robinson, 262 F.2d 383 (9th Cir. 1958), 59–1 USTC ¶9129, 3 AFTR2d 301; Hightower v. Com., 187 F.2d 535 (5th Cir. 1951), 51–1 USTC ¶9199, 40 AFTR 306; Ratterman, ¶48,130 P-H Memo T.C., affirmed 177 F.2d 204 (6th Cir. 1949), 38 AFTR 762.

58. 14 T.C. 441 (1950).

59. 1955–2 C.B. 39.

substance a conditional sales contract depends upon the intent of the parties as evidenced by the provisions of the agreement, read in the light of the facts and circumstances existing at the time the agreement was executed. In ascertaining such intent no single test, or any special combination of tests, is absolutely determinative. No general rule, applicable to all cases, can be laid down. Each case must be decided in the light of its particular facts. However, ... it would appear that in the absence of compelling persuasive factors of contrary implication an intent warranting treatment of a transaction for tax purposes as a purchase and sale rather than as a lease or rental agreement may in general be said to exist, if for example, one or more of the following conditions are present:

(a) Portions of the periodic payments are made specifically applicable to an equity to be acquired by the lessee. ...

(b) The lessee will acquire title upon the payment of a stated amount of "rentals" which under the contract he is required to make. ...

(c) The total amount which the lessee is required to pay for a relatively short period of use constitutes an inordinately large portion of the total sum required to be paid to secure the transfer of the title. ...

(d) The agreed "rental" payments materially exceed the current fair rental value. This may be indicative that the payments include an element other than compensation for the use of property. ...

(e) The property may be acquired under a purchase option at a price which is nominal in relation to the value of the property at the time when the option may be exercised, as determined at the time of entering into the original agreement, or which is a relatively small amount when compared with the total payments which are required to be made. ...

(f) Some portion of the periodic payments is specifically designated as interest or is otherwise readily recognizable as the equivalent of interest. ...

The following examples illustrate the problem: 7.74

EXAMPLE 1

A manufacturer offers to sell a machine for $100,000 payable in full within thirty days or to lease it for a term of five years. At the end of the term of the lease the lessee will have the option to purchase the machine for $10,000. At the end of that five-year term it is estimated that the machine will have a value of $50,000. The anticipated normal useful life of the machine is ten years, and the salvage value at that future date is presently estimated to be $10,000. The amount of the rent for the five-year term will aggregate $100,000 plus 7 percent interest on declining balances of the $100,000. In substance, such a lease is an installment sale contract. The lessee is not entitled to deduct his payments as rent, but instead is entitled to a deduction for depreciation of $100,000 over the estimated ten-year life. Salvage is disregarded because of Section 167(f). He will also be entitled to deduct the interest element.

EXAMPLE 2

The facts are the same as in Example 1, but the term of the lease is ten years, there is no option to purchase until the expiration of the ten-year term, and the option price is $10,000. This is a true lease.

TRANSACTIONS WITH RELATED PARTIES. The Internal Revenue 7.75 Service gives close attention to a sale-and-leaseback or gift-and-lease-back transaction involving closely related parties if deduction of the rental payment is attempted. The Fifth Circuit Court of Appeals denied a rental deduction to an individual who had donated property to a trust and then leased the donated property from the trust. The trust had been created for the benefit of his children, and he was the trustee. The theory was that the donor was actually doing no more than making periodic gifts under the guise of rental payments to the trust.[60]

7.76   In a somewhat similar set of circumstances, the Seventh Circuit Court of Appeals allowed[61] a rental deduction. A physician created an irrevocable trust for the benefit of his wife and children and conveyed to a bank, as trustee, a building in part of which he conducted a clinic. Simultaneously, a ten-year lease was entered into by him with the trustee. Because the instrument contained provisions for the determination of the amounts of a fair rental and because he retained no significant control over the trust, the Court allowed the rental payments to be deducted as a business expense. However, if the same factual situation were to arise today and concern property transferred in trust after October 9, 1969, the portion of the income distributable to the wife would be taxed to the husband-grantor [Section 677 as amended by the Tax Reform Act of 1969].

7.77   ROYALTIES. Royalties are exactions made for the sale or use of copyrighted books, poems, musical scores, or other literary efforts; for the use of patents and secret formulae; and for the extraction of minerals or the cutting of timber. To the extent that the royalty payments are solely for these purposes, they are deductible. Any such payment is not deductible, however, to the extent that it is a disguised distribution of dividends or in substance the purchase price of property.

7.78   **Advertising.** Advertising expenditures, whether directed toward immediate sales or the future long-range benefit of the business, are deductible. There is a need only to show that the purpose of the payment had a reasonable relationship to the business activities. Regulation 1.162–20(a)(2) provides:

> Expenditures for institutional or "goodwill" advertising that keeps the taxpayer's name before the public are generally deductible as ordinary and necessary business expenses, provided the expenditures are related to the patronage the taxpayer might reasonably expect in the future. For example, a deduction will ordinarily be allowed for the cost of advertising that keeps the taxpayer's name before the public in connection with encouraging contributions to such organizations as the Red Cross, the purchase of United States Savings Bonds, or participation in similar causes. ...

Also deductible are advertising expenditures made for the purpose of presenting views on social, economic, financial, and other condi-

60. Van Zandt v. Com., 341 F.2d 440 (5th Cir. 1965), 65–1 USTC ¶9236, 15 AFTR2d 372, cert. den. 382 U.S. 814.
61. Skemp v. Com., 168 F.2d 598 (7th Cir. 1948), 48–1 USTC ¶9300, 36 AFTR 1089.

tions of a general nature.[62] Deduction has been denied to private electric companies for advertising expenditures that attempted to prevent encroachment by public or government supported power projects,[63] however, since this was held not to be within the normal concept of advertising (i.e., promoting the sale of goods). Payments made to intermediate organizations, such as a trade association that promotes the taxpayer's industry, type of product, or even the community in which the taxpayer is located, are deductible.[64]

7.79

Advertising encouraging individuals to vote for specific legislation or to vote in a partisan manner on political issues or for a particular candidate is nondeductible under Section 162(e)(2) and Reg. 1.162–20(c)(4). Expenditures for advertising space in the program of a political convention are not deductible unless the convention is one held for the purpose of nominating candidates for the offices of president and vice-president of the United States and the proceeds are used solely to defray the costs of such convention or a subsequent one [Section 276(c)].

Legislative Appearances (Lobbying Expenses). In 1962, Section 162(e) was added to the Code, providing for the deductibility of certain types of expenses with respect to legislative matters if the legislative proposals will (or may reasonably be expected to) affect the taxpayer's trade or business. Regulation 1.162–20(c)(2) defines these deductible expenses as those in direct connection with:

7.80

(a) appearances before, submission of statements to, or sending communications to, the committees, or individual members of Congress or of any legislative body of a State, a possession of the United States, or a political subdivision of any of the foregoing with respect to legislation or proposed legislation of direct interest to the taxpayer, or

(b) communication of information between the taxpayer and an organization of which he is a member with respect to legislation or proposed legislation of direct interest to the taxpayer and to such organization.

However, no deduction is allowed for expenditures in connection with legislation in which a taxpayer has a personal as distinguished from a business interest. Furthermore, no deduction is allowed for the cost of participating in a political campaign, or for the cost of attempts to influence the general public as to legislative matters, elections, or referendums.[65] For political contributions, refer back to paragraph 3.108.

Expenses Relating to Tax-Exempt Income. Section 265 disallows the following types of deductions.

7.81

62. Reg. 1.162–20(a)(2); I.T. 3564, 1942–2 C.B. 87; I.T. 3581, 1942–2 C.B. 88.
63. Special Ruling, February 13, 1958, 586 CCH Standard Federal Tax Reporter ¶6352; South Western Electric Power Co. v. U.S., 312 F.2d 437 (Ct. Cls., 1963), 63–1 USTC ¶9101, 11 AFTR2d 455.
64. Rev. Rul. 58–209, 1958–1 C.B. 19.
65. Rev. Rul. 62–156.

Deductions
in General

1. Expenses of all types allocable to tax-exempt income other than interest.

2. Nonbusiness expenses of the type described in Section 212, allocable to tax-exempt interest and incurred by individuals, estates, and trusts for the production of income.

3. Interest on indebtedness incurred or continued to purchase or carry obligations on which the interest is wholly tax-exempt.

This is the principle behind the disallowance: since the gross income is not taxable, the expense of earning it should not be used to reduce other income that is taxable.

7.82   If an expense, whether business or nonbusiness, pertains both to exempt and taxable income, Reg. 1.265–1(c) requires that a reasonable proportion of the expense be allocated to each class of income.

7.83   With respect to item 3 above, only that interest expense is not deductible that is incurred on indebtedness directly related to the purchase or carrying of tax-exempt obligations.[66] In *Wisconsin Cheeseman, Inc.* v. *U.S.*[67] a corporation engaged in a seasonal business owned municipal bonds and each year pledged them as collateral for bank loans needed to supply working capital for the peak period. The court held the bank loans were directly related to the carrying of the tax-exempt obligations and denied a deduction for interest expense. Because the need for short-term working capital recurred each year, the court believed the bonds should have been sold to provide such funds and eliminate the need for borrowing. However, in the same case the court allowed a deduction for interest on a mortgage loan incurred to finance construction of a new plant. It held that the loan was not directly related to carrying the municipal bonds because it would have been imprudent for the company to reduce its liquid assets by selling the municipal bonds in order to avoid obtaining a mortgage loan.

7.84   The *Bernard H. Jacobson*[68] case is an example of interest on indebtedness incurred to purchase obligations with wholly tax-exempt interest (paragraph 7.81). A husband and wife had obtained bank loans on the security of common stock and deposited the proceeds in their separate bank accounts. On the same day or a few days later, they purchased tax-exempt securities in amounts that were for the most part the same as the amount of the indebtedness incurred. The Tax Court held that the bank loans were incurred to purchase or carry tax-exempt obligations and, accordingly, the interest was not deductible.

66. Wisconsin Cheeseman, Inc. v. U.S., 388 F.2d 420 (7th Cir. 1968), 68–1 USTC ¶9145, 21 AFTR2d 383; Illinois Terminal Railroad Co. v. U.S., 375 F.2d 1016 (Ct. Cls., 1967), 67–1 USTC ¶9374, 19 AFTR2d 1219. See also J. E. Leslie v. Com., 413 F.2d 636 (2nd Cir., 1969), 69–2 USTC ¶9540, 24 AFTR2d 5219, cert. denied; Edmund F. Ball, 54 T.C. 1200 (1970) (NA); Batten v. U.S., 322 F. Supp. 629 (D.C., Va., 1971), 71–1 USTC ¶9163, 27 AFTR2d 71–513; Rev. Proc. 72–18.
67. *Ibid.*
68. 28 T.C. 579 (1957).

Deductible in Determining Adjusted Gross Income. The concept of 7.85
adjusted gross income was explained in chapter 3, where we also
pointed out (paragraph 3.10) that the following categories of expenses of employees are deductible in determining adjusted gross
income:

> Expenses for which an employee is reimbursed by his employer, or for
> which he receives an expense allowance
> His travel expenses (including meals and lodging) while he is away from
> home in connection with his employment
> His transportation expenses while he is on his employer's business
> *Any* of his trade or business expenses if he is an outside salesman
> His moving expenses, to the extent they are deductible under Section 217

REIMBURSED EXPENSES. If an employee incurs expenses on be- 7.86
half of his employer and is reimbursed for such expenses, the reimbursement constitutes an item of gross income; and the expenses may
be deducted to the extent of the reimbursement in arriving at adjusted
gross income. The reimbursed expenses that may be deducted in
arriving at adjusted gross income include not only those that would
otherwise be deductible in arriving at adjusted gross income (e.g.,
transportation expenses) but also those that would be deductible only
from adjusted gross income if no reimbursement had been received
(e.g., special work clothing). To the extent that the expenses exceed
the reimbursement, such excess expenses are deductible in arriving
at adjusted gross income or deductible from adjusted gross income
depending on the nature of the expenses. To the extent that the excess represents travel expenses while away from home, transportation
expenses, outside salesman's expenses, and Section 217 moving expenses, the amount is deductible in determining adjusted gross income. Any excess represented by other types of deductible expenses
can be deducted only from adjusted gross income. See the example
in paragraph 3.18.

Regulation 1.162–17(b)(1) provides that if an employee receives a 7.87
reimbursement exactly equal to the expenses and makes a sufficient
accounting to the employer of the expenses, then he need not report
the reimbursement as income and he is not allowed a deduction for
the expenses. In rulings[69] the Commissioner announced that an accounting will be deemed to have been made if an employee's per
diem allowance to cover food, lodging, and incidentals is not more
than the greater of (1) $36 per day or (2) the maximum per diem rate
authorized to be paid by the Federal government in the locality in
which the travel is performed, and if the mileage allowance on his
automobile is not more than fifteen cents per mile.

If an employee is entitled to receive reimbursements from his em- 7.88

69. Rev. Rul. 71–412, as modified by Rev. Rul. 72–508.

ployer for expenses incurred, but fails to ask for reimbursement, he will not be allowed a deduction for such expenses. He is treated as a volunteer. A person who voluntarily pays the expenses of another is not allowed to deduct them.

7.89   TRAVEL AWAY FROM HOME. Traveling expenses, including all or part of the amounts spent for lodging and meals, are deductible under Sec. 162(a)(2) as ordinary and necessary expenses provided they are reasonable in amount and are incurred in *travel away from home* in pursuit of business.

7.90   *Definition of "home."* Probably no other aspect of this highly litigated area, the travel expense deduction, has received more attention over the years than the requirement that the expense be incurred "while away from home." Through the years, many government victories have stemmed from the interpretation that "home" is a term of art, with a meaning different from its normal usage as residence, domicile, or dwelling place. The Tax Court rather consistently has held that a person's "home" for tax purposes is his "place of employment, or post or station at which he is employed," with the exception that, if a new place of employment is only temporary, as distinguished from indefinite or indeterminate, his "home" remains at his original and principal place of employment.[70]

7.91   That also is the position of the Internal Revenue Service[71] and of the Second, Third, Fourth, Seventh, and Eighth Circuit Courts of Appeal.[72] However, the Fifth, Sixth, and Ninth Circuit Courts of Appeal,[73] have held that a man's home is his place of residence and that the test to apply is whether it is reasonable to expect him to move closer to his place of employment. The United States Supreme Court has held that the home of a man in the armed forces is his permanent place of duty,[74] but has not yet ruled on civilian employees.

7.92   In *Com.* v. *Flowers*[75] the United States Supreme Court approved the disallowance of a deduction for travel expenses claimed by the vice-president and general counsel of a railroad. He lived in Jackson, Mississippi, but the railroad had its main office in Mobile, Alabama. In order that travel expenses away from home might be deducted, the Court held that three tests had to be met:

(1) The expense must be a reasonable and necessary traveling expense, as that term is generally understood. This includes such items as transportation fares and food and lodging expenses incurred while traveling.

70. Emil J. Michaels, 53 T.C. No. 28 (1969); Bixler, 5 BTA 1181, 1184; Priddy, 43 BTA 18, 31; F. Garlock, 34 T.C. 611 (1960); Sand, T.C. Memo 1969–155.
71. Rev. Rul. 60–189, 1960–1 C.B. 60.
72. See citations in Com. v. Stidger, 386 U.S. 287 (1967), 67–1 USTC ¶9309, 19 AFTR2d 939, fn. 11.
73. U.S. v. LeBlanc, 278 F.2d 571 (5th Cir. 1960), 60–1 USTC ¶9472, 5 AFTR2d 1460; Burns v. Gray, 287 F.2d 698 (6th Cir. 1961), 61–1 USTC ¶9294, 7 AFTR2d 847; John J. Harvey v. Com., 283 F.2d 491 (9th Cir. 1960), 60–2 USTC ¶9771, 6 AFTR2d 5780.
74. Com. v. Stidger, *supra* fn. 75.
75. 326 U.S. 465 (1946), 46–1 USTC ¶9127, 34 AFTR 301.

(2) The expense must be incurred "while away from home."

(3) The expense must be incurred in pursuit of business. ...

Deductions for the cost of meals, lodging, and transportation expenses incurred on his frequent trips between the two cities were disallowed. The exigencies of the business did not require maintenance of a residence in Jackson; that was his personal choice. Accordingly, the travel expenses were nondeductible personal expenses. This case is sometimes erroneously cited as authority for the proposition that a man's post of duty is his "home." Actually, however, the basis of the Court's holding was that there was no business necessity for the employee to maintain his residence in another city.

7.93 Twelve years later in *Peurifoy v. Com.*,[76] the United States Supreme Court held that three construction workers were entitled to deduct their board and lodging at a construction site some distance from their homes because their employment was temporary, contrasted with indefinite or indeterminate. As a result, the Internal Revenue Service issued a ruling[77] that if an individual accepts employment in a city distant from that in which he maintains his residence, and the duration of his assignment there is one year or more, his "tax home" is in the area of his employment. If the assignment to the other location is temporary and involves a stay of less than one year, his "tax home" remains in the place of his usual employment.

7.94 If an individual has no permanent residence, no business post of duty, and travels constantly, his "home" is wherever he happens to be. As a result, his travel expenses are not deductible. In *Moses Mitnick*,[78] the manager of theatrical road shows who had no fixed headquarters and no permanent residence was held to have had his "home" wherever a particular show happened to be.

7.95 *Necessity of overnight trip.* There is no dispute about the deductibility of transportation costs on one-day trips, because Section 62(2)(C) specifically allows them. However, the cost of meals en route is not deductible unless the trips are overnight or sufficiently long in duration so that time for sleep is desirable and taken.[79]

7.96 TRANSPORTATION COSTS. Section 62(2)(C) allows a deduction for transportation expenses paid in connection with services performed as an employee. As indicated earlier, this provision was new in the 1954 Code. Regulation 1.62–1(g) provides:

... "Transportation," as used in Section 62(2)(C), is a narrower concept than "travel," as used in Section 62(2)(B), and does not include meals and lodging. The term "transportation expense" includes only the cost of transporting the employee from one place to another in the course of his employment, while he is not away from home in a travel status. Thus, transportation costs may include cab fares, bus fares, and the like, and also a pro rata share

76. 358 U.S. 59 (1958), 58–2 USTC ¶9925, 2 AFTR2d 6055.

77. *Supra*, fn. 71.

78. 13 T.C. 1 (1949).

79. Correll v. U.S., 389 U.S. 299 (1967), 68–1 USTC ¶9101, 20 AFTR2d 5845; Rev. Rul. 63–239, 1963–2 C.B. 87.

of the employee's expenses of operating his automobile, including gas, oil, and depreciation. ... Transportation expenses do not include the cost of commuting to and from work; this cost constitutes a personal, living, or family expense and is not deductible. ...

Each year an employee or self-employed person has an option to deduct, in lieu of actual expenses, local or overnight travel at twelve cents per mile for the first 15,000 miles of business use of his automobile and nine cents thereafter. If, as an employee, any reimbursement is less, he can deduct the excess of these permitted ceilings over the reimbursement received.[79A]

7.97   OUTSIDE SALESMEN'S EXPENSES. Under Section 62(2)(D) an outside salesman may deduct, in arriving at adjusted gross income, all expenses incurred on behalf of his employer in his capacity as an outside salesman (e.g., transportation and entertainment expenses), even though such expenses would otherwise be deductible only from adjusted gross income. Regulation 1.62–1(h) gives us a definition:

> ... An outside salesman is an individual who solicits business as a full-time salesman for his employer away from his employer's place of business. The term "outside salesman" does not include a taxpayer whose principal activities consist of service and delivery. For example, a bread driver-salesman or a milk driver-salesman would not be included within the definition. However, an outside salesman may perform incidental inside activities at his employer's place of business, such as writing up and transmitting orders and spending short periods at the employer's place of business to make and receive telephone calls, without losing his classification as an outside salesman.

7.98   MOVING EXPENSES. Through the years there was much conflict between employees and the Service on the deductibility of moving expenses and the includibility of reimbursements in income. Some of the disagreement was resolved by the enactment of Section 217 in 1964; hopefully all remaining areas of contention are eliminated for 1970 and subsequent years by the amendments made to Section 217 by the Tax Reform Act of 1969.

7.99   The principles of Section 217 are simple. All reimbursements received by a new or old employee from an employer to cover expenses incurred in moving from one place of residence to another caused by a change in the place of employment are includible in gross income. Then the expenses, whether or not reimbursed, are deductible in determining adjusted gross income. The same principles apply to proprietors and partners. As with too many sections of the Code, these basic principles are then applied through arbitrary rules.

7.100   Only the following types of moving expenses are deductible:

1. The cost of moving household goods and personal effects.
2. The expense of the employee and his household members of traveling (including meals and lodging) from the old to the new residence. If a personal automobile is used, a standard six cents a mile rate can be used.[80]
3. The cost of house-hunting trips incurred after obtaining employment

79A. Rev. Proc. 70–25; Rev. Rul. 70–559.
80. Rev. Proc. 71–2.

at the new location.
4. The cost of meals and lodging in temporary quarters at the new location for a period up to thirty days.
5. The expenses incurred in selling the old residence and in purchasing the new; also expenses of settling an old lease or the acquisition of a new lease. These include such items as brokers' commissions, closing costs, attorneys' fees, and loan placement fees (to the extent that these are not deductible as interest). The deduction does not reduce selling price of the old residence or increase basis of the new. No deduction is given for loss on sale of the old residence, and no part of the purchase price of the new residence can be deducted.

No dollar limits are placed on expenses in categories 1 and 2. But for the other categories, the deduction is limited to $2,500, of which not more than $1,000 can be for house-hunting trips and temporary living costs. The figures are halved on the separate return of a married person. 7.101

In order for these moving expenses to be deductible, two conditions must be met. First, the change in job location would have required at least fifty miles additional commuting if taxpayer had not changed his residence. Second, the taxpayer must be employed full time (by any employer) in the general vicinity of the new job location for thirty-nine weeks during the twelve months following the move. However, this condition is waived if taxpayer is unable to satisfy it because of death, disability, or discharge (other than for willful misconduct) if otherwise it was reasonable to expect that taxpayer would have fulfilled the condition. The self-employed must continue work in the new location (as a self-employed person or as an employee) for at least seventy-eight weeks during the twenty-four months following the move, of which at least thirty-nine must be in the first twelve months. 7.102

Suppose an employee pays his moving expenses in 1970, but has not met the thirty-nine-week test by the time his 1970 return is due. He can take a 1970 deduction if it is still possible to meet the test. However, if he later fails the test, he must report an equal amount as 1971 income. Or he may omit the deduction from his 1970 return and file for a refund when the test is met. 7.103

Deductible from Adjusted Gross Income When Standard Deduction Not Used. All expenses of an employee incurred in connection with his employment, other than those described in the preceding paragraphs 7.85 through 7.103, are deductible only from adjusted gross income, and then only if he does not elect to take the standard deduction. 7.104

Dues and assessments paid to labor unions are deductible if used to meet the expenses of strictly labor union activities, for the support of old-age pension funds, or for "out-of-work" benefit payments to the extent they are applied to unemployed members who are capable of working.[81] 7.105

81. I.T. 3634, 1944 C.B. 90; Rev. Rul. 54–190, 1954–1 C.B. 46; I.T. 2888, XIV–1 C.B. 54 (1935).

7.106   When the taxpayer is employed in a mechanical trade that requires small tools of a consumable nature, he is entitled to deduct the cost of tools he purchases, provided that a condition of his employment is that he must furnish his own tools.[82]

7.107   The position of the Internal Revenue Service is that the cost and expense of maintenance of uniforms are generally allowable where "... (1) The uniforms are specifically required as a condition of employment and (2) are not of a type adaptable to general or continued usage to the extent that they take the place of ordinary clothing."[83] If the cost of clothing is deductible, it is generally held that the expenses of laundering or cleaning also are deductible.

7.108   No clothing deduction is allowed merely because the employee's occupation is such that the clothing he wears at work becomes soiled quickly, is subject to unusual wear and tear, or must be extra heavy because of the climate. This covers such employees as auto mechanics, building contractor superintendents, railroad switchmen, painters, and builders.[84] Highly stylized clothing, shoes unsuitable for personal wear by a fashion coordinator, and dress clothes purchased by a musician have been held to be deductible.[85]

NONBUSINESS EXPENSES FOR PRODUCTION OF INCOME OR IN CONNECTION WITH TAX LIABILITIES

Introduction

7.109   Section 212 allows as a deduction ordinary and necessary expenses paid or incurred:

1. For the production or collection of income
2. For the management, conservation, or maintenance of property held for the production of income
3. In connection with the determination, collection, or refund of any tax

Section 212 applies only to individuals, trusts, and estates, not to corporations or partnerships. Such expenses are deductible only *from* adjusted gross income and only when itemized deductions are claimed.

7.110   The origin of the deductibility of the first two types of expenses was the Revenue Act of 1942. Until that year there had been no provision in any Revenue Act specifically providing for the deductibility of expenses relating to the production of income. In seeking deductions for such expenses, taxpayers relied, sometimes successfully and

---

82. *Your Federal Income Tax* (1973 ed.) p. 103.
83. Rev. Rul. 70–474.
84. Louis M. Roth, 17 T.C. 1450 (1952); A.D. Crews, ¶52,153 P–H Memo T.C.; Rev. Rul. 57–143, 1957–1 C.B. 89; William Auerbacher, ¶56,218 P–H Memo T.C.
85. B. L. Yeomans, 30 T.C. 757; Wilson J. Fisher, 23 T.C. 218 (Acq.), affirmed on another issue in 230 F.2d 79 (7th Cir. 1956), 56–1 USTC ¶9258, 49 AFTR 203.

other times not, upon the provision in prior revenue acts allowing a deduction for business expenses. The court decision that triggered action by Congress was *Higgins* v. *Com.*,[86] decided by the United States Supreme Court in 1941. It held that the expenses of an office maintained by a wealthy taxpayer for the purpose of managing his securities and real estate were personal expenses, not those of a trade or business, and therefore not deductible. As a result of the Revenue Act of 1942 and present Section 212, that decision no longer states the law.

7.111 The third type of expense pertaining to expenses paid or incurred in connection with the determination, collection, or refund of any tax was new in the Revenue Act of 1954.

Expenses for Production of Income

7.112 In concluding this chapter, we shall use the phrase *expenses for the production of income* to mean nonbusiness expenses of that type, including expenses for the collection of income and for the management, conservation, or maintenance of property held for the collection of income.

7.113 To be deductible under Section 212, an expense must be ordinary and necessary. Regulation 1.212–1(d) provides:

> Expenses, to be deductible under Section 212, must be "ordinary and necessary." Thus, such expenses must be reasonable in amount and must bear a reasonable and proximate relation to the production or collection of taxable income or to the management, conservation, or maintenance of property held for the production of income.

Further, it cannot relate to a hobby. The provisions of Section 183 apply; see paragraphs 7.22 to 7.26. Finally, it must not be personal in nature, constitute a capital item, violate public policy, be allocable to tax-exempt income such as municipal bond interest, or otherwise run afoul of any of the other prohibitions of the Code. In other words, all of the restrictions applicable to the deductibility of business expenses are also applicable to the deductibility of expenses for the production of income.

7.114 To be deductible as an expense relating to the production of income, the income need not be realized in the same year or in fact ever be realized. Regulation 1.212–1(b) is explanatory of this statement:

> (b) The term "income" for the purpose of Section 212 includes not merely income of the taxable year but also income which the taxpayer has realized in a prior taxable year or may realize in subsequent taxable years; and is not confined to recurring income but applies as well to gains from the disposition of property. For example, if defaulted bonds, the interest from which if received would be includible in income, are purchased with the expectation of realizing capital gain on their resale, even though no current yield thereon is anticipated, ordinary and necessary expenses thereafter

86. 312 U.S. 212 (1941), 41–1 USTC ¶ 9233, 25 AFTR 1160.

paid or incurred in connection with such bonds are deductible. Similarly, ordinary and necessary expenses paid or incurred in the management, conservation, or maintenance of a building devoted to rental property purposes
are deductible notwithstanding that there is actually no income therefrom
in the taxable year, and regardless of the manner in which or the purpose for
which the property in question was acquired. Expenses paid or incurred in
managing, conserving, or maintaining property held for investment may be
deductible under Section 212 even though the property is not currently productive and there is no likelihood that the property will be sold at a profit
or will otherwise be productive of income and even though the property is
held merely to minimize a loss with respect thereto.

7.115 **Investors' Expenses.** *Investor* at this point is an individual who is a
casual or passive investor in stocks, bonds, and other securities. Traders and dealers are not involved, because they are in the business of
buying and selling securities, and all of their expenses are business
expenses deductible under Section 162 rather than Section 212. A
trader is an individual who *actively* buys and sells stocks and securities for his own account; he does not sell to the public, nor act as a
broker for the public. Further, a person is not a trader even if his investments are large and many, as in *Higgins* v. *Com.*, mentioned
earlier: he must actively and regularly turn them over. If an individual's principal occupation is to trade in securities for his own account,
he quite probably is a trader. A dealer is an individual (or other entity)
whose stock in trade consists of stocks and securities that are sold to
the public.[87] A dealer may or may not also be a broker. The expenses of
an investor are deductible only *from* adjusted gross income; whereas
the expenses of a trader or dealer are deductible *in determining* adjusted gross income.

7.116 Deductible expenses incurred by an individual in connection with
securities and other investments include those paid for: custodian
services for the collection of income, safekeeping, and the delivery
and receipt of securities acquired or disposed of; investment advice,
including financial publications and books; compensation for secre-
taries, bookkeepers, and other office employees; office rent; safe-
deposit box rentals; accounting and auditing services; short-sale
dividends (i.e., those amounts paid by investors or traders for ordinary cash dividends on stock borrowed to cover short sales); and legal
services. However, the expenses of an investor in attending stockholders' meetings of corporations in which he owns stock ordinarily
are nondeductible personal expenditures because they are not ordinary and necessary expenses incurred for the production of income.[88]

7.117 An individual can also be a passive investor in real estate, oil and
gas, and other property. However, all of such a person's deductions
attributable to income from rents and royalties are deductible *in
determining* adjusted gross income, as provided in Section 62(5).

87. Reg. 1.471–5.
88. Rev. Rul. 56–511, 1956–2 C.B. 170.

State stock transfer taxes are not to be treated as a reduction of the 7.118 selling price but are deductible as taxes under Section 164 by investors, traders, and dealers [Reg. 1.164–1(a)].

Because commissions paid in purchasing or selling securities are 7.119 capital in nature and must be added to the cost of the security or deducted from the selling price as provided by Reg. 1.263(a)–2(e), such commissions are not allowed as deductions under Section 212.

Business Investigation Expenditures. Prior to reaching a decision to 7.120 establish a business, expenditures are frequently incurred in exploring the possibilities. Such an investigation does not constitute carrying on a business, and the expenses are not deductible under Section 162 as ordinary and necessary business expenses whether or not the business later is actually entered into.[89] Similarly, the courts have held that they are not deductible by an individual under Section 212 as nonbusiness expenses incurred in the production of income. The Tax Court pointed out in *Morton Frank:*[90]

There is a basic distinction between allowing deduction for the expense of producing or collecting income, in which one has an existent interest or right, and expenses incurred in an attempt to obtain income by the creation of some new interest.

In that case the Tax Court held that travel expenses and legal fees spent in looking for a newspaper business to buy were not deductible as business expenses nor as nonbusiness expenses incurred in the production or collection of income. Business investigation expenses must be capitalized.

If the business is eventually entered into, the expenditures be- 7.121 come part of the basis of what is acquired.[91] If then later that business is abandoned, a loss deduction under Section 165(c)(2) is allowable.[92] That section provides that there shall be allowed as a deduction any loss sustained by an individual, which is not compensated for by insurance or otherwise, if the loss is "incurred in any transaction entered into for profit, though not connected with a trade or business." The subject is discussed more fully in paragraphs 9.21 through 9.23.

If the business is never entered into, it is the position of the Service 7.122 that no deduction is ever allowable whether as a loss or otherwise.[93] However, if the activities are specific in nature, and involve more than a general investigation, the Tax Court has found that the activities constitute "a transaction" and has allowed a loss deduction under Section 165(c)(2). The case was *Harris W. Seed.*[94] There the taxpayer and several other individuals sought to form a savings and loan asso-

89. George C. Westervelt, 8 T.C. 1248 (1947); Frank B. Polacheck, 22 T.C. 858 (1954); Morton Frank, 20 T.C. 511 (1953); Eugene H. Walet, Jr., 31 T.C. 461, 471 (1958).
90. *Supra,* fn. 90.
91. Dwight A. Ward, 20 T.C. 332 (1953).
92. Rev. Rul. 57–418, 1957–2 C.B. 143; C. T. Parker, 1 T.C. 709 (1943).
93. Rev. Rul. 57–418, *supra,* fn. 93; *contra,* Duryea, 6 TCM 926 (1947).
94. 52 T.C. No. 93 (1969).

ciation in Goleta, California. They (a) employed a law firm to handle the incorporation and the charter application, (b) agreed between themselves to pay, and did pay, the preincorporation expenses, (c) hired a firm to make a regional economic survey, (d) employed a C.P.A. to prepare financial statements to accompany the application, (e) solicited the general public to subscribe for shares, and (f) subscribed to shares of stock to be paid for upon issuance of the charter. However, the savings and loan commissioner of the State of California denied this group's application and approved that of another, so that the sought-for charter was never issued and the business never began. The court held these activities created a "transaction"; and, because the transaction was abandoned, the taxpayer's expenditures were deductible.

7.123 **Proxy Contests.** If proximately related to either the production or collection of income or to the management, conservation, or maintenance of property held for the production of income, the Fourth Circuit Court of Appeals has held[95] that proxy fight expenditures are deductible by a stockholder under Section 212, and the Service has announced[96] that it will follow that decision. In the case involved, *R. Walter Graham v. Com.*, the taxpayer was a substantial stockholder in the New York Central Railroad and was a member of a stockholders' committee that successfully sought through a proxy solicitation to obtain dominant representation on the board of directors. The aim of the committee was to change business policies of the railroad and thereby to enhance the value of the outstanding shares and also to increase the dividends. The court held that amounts paid resulting from his being a member of that committee were ordinary and necessary expenses incurred in the production or collection of income or for the management, conservation, or maintenance of property held for the production of income.

7.124 In reaching its conclusion in the *Graham* case, the Fourth Circuit distinguished the facts involved from the instance in which a small stockholder in a large corporation takes it upon himself to crusade for a particular point of view. It pointed in particular to the case of *J. Raymond Dyer*.[97] In that case the taxpayer was a practicing lawyer in St. Louis. In January, 1957, he purchased 250 shares of the common stock of Union Electric Company, which at that time had outstanding 10.3 million shares of such stock. In that same year he waged a fight to persuade other shareholders not to grant proxies to Union Electric management for a shareholders' meeting. The Tax Court held that (probably because of the ratio of the expenses to the investment involved) the proxy fight expenses were not deductible under Section 212 because they were not sufficiently related to an expense for the production of income.

95. R. Walter Graham v. Com., 326 F.2d 878 (4th Cir. 1964), 64–1 USTC ¶9192, 13 AFTR2d 423.
96. Rev. Rul. 64–236, 1964–2 C.B. 64.
97. 36 T.C. 456 (1961) (Acq.).

Although Section 212 does not apply to a corporation, expenses in- 7.125
curred by one in connection with a proxy fight or a stockholder's
derivative suit have usually been allowed as a deductible Section 162
business expense.[98]

Legal Expenses. The deductibility of legal expenses depends upon 7.126
their nature. Earlier in this chapter legal expenses pertaining to a
trade or business were discussed. At this point the subject is the deductibility of nonbusiness legal expenses relating to income-producing property or activities. As is true of all other types of nonbusiness
expenses, the expenditure must not be personal or pertain to a capital
transaction.

In *Lykes* v. *U.S.*,[99] the United States Supreme Court pointed out 7.127
that the immediate purpose for incurring the legal fees controls their
deductibility rather than the remote contribution they may make to
the conservation of a taxpayer's income-producing assets by reducing
his general liabilities:

Legal expenses do not become deductible merely because they are paid
for services which relieve a taxpayer of liability. That argument would carry
us too far. It would mean that the expense of defending almost any claim
would be deductible by a taxpayer on the ground that such defense was made
to help him keep clear of liens whatever income-producing property he might
have. For example, it suggests that the expense of defending an action based
upon personal injuries caused by a taxpayer's negligence while driving an
automobile for pleasure should be deductible. Section 23(a)(2) [now Section
212] never has been so interpreted by us. ...

Legal fees incurred because of a divorce action — whether pertain- 7.128
ing to the divorce litigation itself, a property settlement, division of
community property, or provisions for alimony — arise out of a personal
or family relationship. They are not deductible under Section 212(2)
as expenses incurred "for the management, conservation, or maintenance of property held for the production of income."[100] In *U.S.* v.
Gilmore et al.,[101] the wife sued for divorce, alleging infidelity, and the
husband filed a counterclaim for divorce. The husband prevailed and
was granted an absolute divorce; the wife's community property
claims were denied in their entirety, and she was held entitled to no
alimony. If she had prevailed, the husband would have lost control
of three corporations from which he derived substantially all of his
income. In reaching its conclusion the United States Supreme Court
said:

98. Locke Manufacturing Companies v. U.S., 237 F.Supp. 80 (D.C., Conn., 1964),
65–1 USTC ¶9115, 14 AFTR2d 6104; Central Foundry Co., 49 T.C. 234 (1967) (Acq.);
Rev. Rul. 67–1, C.B. 28.

99. 343 U.S. 118 (1952), 52–1 USTC ¶9259, 41 AFTR 606.

100. U.S. v. Patrick, 372 U.S. 53 (1963), 63–1 USTC ¶9286, 11 AFTR2d 764, reversing 288 F.2d 292 (4th Cir. 1961), 61–1 USTC ¶9364, 7 AFTR2d 1067; U.S. v. Gilmore,
372 U.S. 39 (1963), 63–1 USTC ¶9285, 11 AFTR2d 758, reversing 290 F.2d 942 (Ct.
Cls., 1961), 61–2 USTC ¶9499, 7 AFTR2d 1576.

101. *Supra,* fn. 121.

... the origin and character of the claim with respect to which an expense was incurred, rather than its potential consequences upon the fortunes of the taxpayer, is the controlling basic test of whether the expense was business [i.e., pertaining to profit-seeking activities] or "personal" and hence whether it is deductible or not under § 23(a)(2) [now Section 212(1) and (2)].

Since the origin of the wife's claim was the marital relationship, the Court held the legal fees were nondeductible personal expenditures.

7.129   The Tax Court, however, distinguished the *Gilmore* case in *Ruth K. Wild*[102] and allowed a wife to deduct the portion of attorney fees paid by her that were allocable to negotiations for taxable alimony during the pendency of a divorce suit filed by her. It allowed the deduction under Section 212(1) and pointed out that the *Gilmore* case concerned Section 212(2). It also relied upon Reg. 1.262–1(b)(7), which was issued prior to the promulgation of the *Gilmore* decision in 1963 but was not thereafter revoked or changed. The regulation reads:

(7) Generally, attorney's fees and other costs paid in connection with a divorce, separation, or decree for support are not deductible by either the husband or the wife. However, the part of an attorney's fee and the part of the other costs paid in connection with a divorce, legal separation, written separation agreement, or a decree for support, which are properly attributable to the production or collection of amounts includable in gross income under Section 71 are deductible by the wife under Section 212.

7.130   Further, both the United States Supreme Court and the Court of Claims have allowed deductions under Section 212(3) for attorney fees paid for tax advice concerning alimony and property settlements.[103]

7.131   Regulation 1.212–1(k) is concerned primarily with expenditures that must be capitalized:

(k) Expenses paid or incurred in defending or perfecting title to property, in recovering property (other than investment property and amounts of income which, if and when recovered, must be included in gross income), or in developing or improving property, constitute a part of the cost of the property and are not deductible expenses. Attorneys' fees paid in a suit to quiet title to lands are not deductible, but if the suit is also to collect accrued rents thereon, that portion of such fees is deductible which is properly allocable to the services rendered in collecting such rents. Expenses paid or incurred in protecting or asserting one's rights to property of a decedent as heir or legatee, or as beneficiary under a testamentary trust, are not deductible.

7.132   **Real Estate Investment Expenses.** Whether or not real estate held for investment is considered a trade or business, expenses incurred in connection with it, if not deductible as business expenses under

102. 42 T.C. 706 (1964).
103. U.S. v. Davis, 370 U.S. 65 (1962), 62–2 USTC ¶9509, 9 AFTR2d 1625; W. K. Carpenter v. U.S., 338 F.2d 366 (Ct. Cls., 1964), 64–2 USTC ¶9842, 14 AFTR2d 5897.

Section 162, are deductible under Section 212. As provided by
Reg. 1.212–1(b):

... [O]rdinary and necessary expenses paid or incurred in the management, conservation, or maintenance of a building devoted to rental purposes are deductible notwithstanding that there is actually no income therefrom in the taxable year, and regardless of the manner in which or the purpose for which the property in question was acquired. Expenses paid or incurred in managing, conserving, or maintaining property held for investment may be deductible under Section 212 even though the property is not currently productive and there is no likelihood that the property will be sold at a profit or will otherwise be productive of income and even though the property is held merely to minimize a loss with respect thereto.

The deductions include such items as repair costs, management expenses, compensation paid to clerical help, accounting fees, maintenance costs, depreciation, interest, and taxes. Expenses related to rental property such as those described in the preceding sentence are allowed as deductions from gross income in computing the amount of adjusted gross income.

Residential Property. Regulation 1.212–1(h) provides: 7.133

Ordinary and necessary expenses paid or incurred in connection with the management, conservation, or maintenance of property held for use as a residence by the taxpayer are not deductible. However, ordinary and necessary expenses paid or incurred in connection with the management, conservation, or maintenance of property held by the taxpayer as rental property are deductible even though such property was formerly held by the taxpayer for use as a home.

Conversion of a personal residence to rental property takes place   7.134
when efforts are made to rent the property, even though no income in fact is received and even though, concurrently with the offer to rent, the property also is listed for sale.[104] Mere abandonment of property as a personal residence by itself will not convert the property to a status of being held for the production of income.[105] When the property has been converted, the tax basis for depreciation becomes the lesser of the cost or the fair market value at the date it is offered for rent.

If a personal residence is inherited by a taxpayer but never occu-   7.135
pied by him, maintenance expenses are allowed if it is immediately listed for rent or sale.[106]

The deductibility of losses on sales of residential property is dis-   7.136
cussed in paragraph 9.22.

104. William C. Horrmann, 17 T.C. 903 (1951) (Acq.).
105. Warren Leslie, Sr., 6 T.C. 488 (1946) (Acq.); John M. Coulter, ¶50,077 P–H Memo T.C.
106. Anna C. Newberry, ¶45,077 P–H Memo T.C.

Tax Determinations

7.137   Section 212(3) also provides for the deductibility of all the ordinary and necessary expenses paid or incurred during the taxable year "in connection with the determination, collection, or refund of any tax." Regulation 1.212–1(1) defines the scope of deductibility:

> Expenses paid or incurred by an individual in connection with the determination, collection or refund of any tax, whether the taxing authority be Federal, State or municipal, and whether the tax be income, estate, gift, property, or any other tax, are deductible. Thus, expenses paid or incurred by the taxpayer for tax counsel or expenses paid or incurred in connection with the preparation of his tax returns or in connection with any proceedings involved in determining the extent of tax liability or in contesting his tax liability are deductible.

Accordingly, fees paid to accountants and attorneys for preparing returns, giving advice, assisting in revenue agent's examinations, and preparing protests, claims for refunds, and requests for rulings are deductible. The tax services need not concern a trade or business or income-producing property.

QUESTIONS AND PROBLEMS

1. (a) Marlon Coil Co. moved its heavy production equipment to a new plant in the same city. The sum of $75,000 was paid to an outside trucking firm that specialized in this type of moving, and $25,000 in wage costs of its own employees were directly attributable to the move. Is all or any part of the $100,000 deductible? Discuss. [The answer cannot specifically be found in the textbook, but can be deduced from the principles given in the first part of chapter 7. The reasons for your answer are the important thing.]
   (b) The new plant was equipped with an electrical distribution system, the cost of which had been capitalized. In connection with the movement of the equipment, it was necessary to wire the machinery in such a way as to facilitate its connection to the electrical distribution system that had been installed in the new plant. In the year in issue there was expended for such wiring $15,000. Is the amount deductible or must it be capitalized? Why?
2. *Research Problem.* Paragraph 7.8 of the text mentions several types of capital expenditures. Consult either P–H *Federal Taxes* or CCH *Standard Federal Tax Reporter* and prepare a list of other capitalizable expenditures.
3. The maintenance foreman of Blake Corporation submitted, for approval, vouchers for the items listed below. How should the various items be treated by the corporation for tax purposes?
   (a) $3,600 for cost of material and labor used in winterizing a building formerly used only during the summer. The value of the building increased as a result of the expenditure.
   (b) $2.50 for a starter spring to be used on the power lawnmower. The

mower had been expected to last an additional three years, but would not run without the spring.

(c) $2,500 for materials and labor needed to renovate and place in service a piece of heavy duty machinery that had previously been retired. After the renovation, the machine had a useful life of about three years.

(d) $10.42 for additional insulation needed for the building being winterized.

4. Roy Merck, who had been raised on a cattle ranch in Nebraska, decided to move to Alaska where his older brother had moved several years earlier. Before moving, Roy purchased six Angus-Highland cattle, which he thought would survive well in Alaska, and shipped them to his brother's ranch there. After failing in several attempts to obtain a homestead allotment, he made arrangements to use his brother's ranch for his cattle operation and hoped to expand his "herd." To make a living he took a job as a laborer, but was able to spend two months each year on his brother's ranch. In Year One he had a gross income of $6,500 and paid $5,500 to maintain his cattle. In Year Two, the amounts were $6,800 and $3,500. In the light of Section 183, do you believe these expenditures are deductible? Why?

5. In each of the following instances, how many "activities" do you believe there are under Section 183 in the case of a corporate executive with substantial independent wealth?

(a) A 640-acre farm in Kentucky on which purebred cattle and racing horses are raised. Separate books are kept for the gross receipts, and overall expenses are allocated on the basis of acreage and barns utilized.

(b) An 80-acre plantation in Louisiana on which he lives. He has three sources of receipts—eggs from a small chicken hatchery, sales of produce, and sales of culled calves from a breeding herd. Separate books on the gross receipts and direct expenses are kept.

(c) Three separate farms within a radius of fifteen miles, operated by tenant farmers. He kept no formal books, but did receive twice a year financial statements from the respective tenant farmers.

6. In the current year Abbott paid the following amounts in connection with his manufacturing business operated as a proprietorship. What amounts, if any, constitute a deductible expense?

(a) $300 in traffic fines levied against his truck drivers.

(b) $30,000 in treble damages in settlement of a judgment entered against him last year in a civil suit by a customer under the Clayton Act. Although the government once had threatened criminal proceedings, he was never indicted.

(c) $50,000 in treble damages paid to the U.S. government in settlement of a civil suit under the False Claims Act for products sold to an instrumentality of the government; no criminal action was ever instigated.

(d) $1,000 at Christmas time to the purchasing agent of one of his customers.

(e) $3,000 to his attorney to be paid by him to the chief of the State Highway Commission, which was a customer.

(f) $2,100 to the Excel Corporation after its purchasing agent threatened to return merchandise that had been delivered to it, on the ground that it was overpriced.

7. Mr. S. Touch agreed to assign his title to a housing development and to pay $10,000 in cash to Hard Rock Realty Corporation if the corporation would assist him in obtaining certain valuable lands. The corporation assisted Mr. Touch in the property acquisition, but he refused to deliver the title to the development or to pay the cash to the corporation. The corporation successfully sued Mr. Touch for the title and the cash and incurred legal fees of $2,500 in connection with the suit. The legal fees were deducted by the corporation on its tax return as an ordinary and necessary business expense. Discuss the propriety of the deduction.

8. *Research Problem.* Brief *Com.* v. *Tellier,* 383 U.S. 687 (1966), 66–1 USTC § 9319, 17 AFTR2d 633.

9. A revenue agent took several courses in the M.B.A. program of a graduate school of business. He contended that his tuition was deductible on the ground that the courses improved his skills as a field agent. Was he right?

10. The Norton Food Processing Corporation has a policy of rewarding its employees at the end of the year. Each employee receives a large gift box of samples of the company's products, nonexecutive employees receive cash bonuses, and executives receive unrestricted shares of the corporation's capital stock. In addition, out of gratitude for the work of an employee who retires, is severely disabled, or dies, a cash payment is made to the employee or to an individual previously selected by the employee. How should the corporation handle the above items for tax purposes?

11. All of the capital stock of Hoot Feather Corporation is owned by Mr. B. Little. Mr. Little has been leasing a large building, which he owns, to the corporation for $250,000 per year. Recently a bona fide offer of $150,000 per year was made by a stranger to rent the building.

    Mr. Little's brother, John, is in the office furnishings business. During 1973 John rented certain furniture and equipment to the corporation at an annual rental of $2,000 per year for the first three years and $1 per year thereafter, with an option to purchase for $2,100 at any time. The life of this type of furniture and equipment is four years.

    On its return for 1973, the corporation deducted the $252,000 rental expenditures. Under what theory or theories could all or a part of the deduction be denied?

12. The Moore Egg Corporation raises chickens and sells both chickens and eggs throughout a wide territory. Recently legislation has been proposed to put chickens and eggs under federal price controls. In an effort to prevent the legislation from passing, the following statement has been added during the current year to the corporation's billboard advertisements:

    KEEP THE GOVERNMENT OUT OF YOUR HEN
    HOUSE. PROTEST PRICE CONTROLS.

    Previous to this year, the corporation has deducted the entire cost of billboard advertising. What result this year?

13. State whether or not each of the expenditures listed below is deductible under current tax principles and give your reasons.

    (a) Mr. J. Smith, president of ABC Corporation, took Mr. Z. Jones, the corporation's most important customer, to lunch at a local businessmen's restaurant and paid the check for $15.00. There was no discussion of business at the meal.

(b) Mr. Smith took Mr. and Mrs. E. C. North to the All-Star football game. The tickets cost $30 ($10 apiece). Mr. Smith had spent the afternoon preceding the game with Mr. North discussing a contract for the purchase of supplies that the ABC Corporation wished to buy from Mr. North.

(c) On behalf of the ABC Corporation, Mr. Smith presented to Miss A. Wadhams a diamond wrist watch in honor of her thirty-fifth anniversary of service with the corporation. The watch cost $350.

(d) Mr. Smith, on behalf of ABC Corporation, took a three-day trip to Washington, D.C., to testify against pending legislation before the Senate Finance Committee. The three days were spent solely on business. The expenses of the trip were $400. The testimony related to legislation of direct interest to the business of ABC Corporation.

14. *Research Problem.* An individual borrowed $10,000 at 5 percent per annum on his life insurance policies and used the proceeds to pay off the mortgage on his home. Two years later, with money saved in the intervening period, he purchased municipal bonds in the principal amount of $15,000 bearing interest at the rate of $4\frac{1}{2}$ percent per annum.

First brief the cases cited in fn. 66 and digest the ruling there cited. Then submit your opinion as to how much, if any, of the interest on the life insurance loans is deductible after the municipal bonds are purchased.

15. Jim Cox and Tom Nox are both piano repairmen, and each earns $15,000 per year salary. Jim's employer pays for all of Jim's professional dues, tools, and uniforms, whereas Tom has to pay $700 out of his own pocket for the same items. Tom was complaining to Jim that Jim actually earned $700 a year more than Tom because of the difference in the source of payment of their employment-related expenses. Jim pointed out that Tom could deduct the cost of the above items on his tax return and thus pay a lesser amount of tax than Jim; consequently, the difference in their earnings was actually less than $700. Assuming that all of their other items of income and expense are equal, is Jim correct?

16. Listed below are expenses paid by Mr. F. Teal. How should the expenses be handled for tax purposes?

(a) Rental of safe-deposit box for securities

(b) Accountant's fee for preparing personal income tax return

(c) Taxes, repairs, and advertising with respect to vacant factory building held for prospective sale

(d) Plane fare, cost of meals, entertainment expenses, telephone bills, hotel bills, and other expenses relating to a proposed establishment of a tourist camp in Minnesota (Mr. Teal decided he did not wish to be involved.)

(e) Attorney's fees in connection with obtaining title to land to be used for a new housing development

17. (a) An outside salesman incurred the expenses listed below in the city in which he is employed. The expenses were required but were not reimbursed by his employer. Which of the expenses are deductible in arriving at adjusted gross income and which of the expenses are deductible from adjusted gross income on the salesman's tax return?

(1) Automobile expenses incurred in soliciting business
(2) Contributions to a church to which he regularly sells office supplies
(3) Cost of entertaining customers at his luncheon club
(4) Cost of his meals while entertaining customers

(b) Mr. A. Barnett moved from New York to California for the purpose of commencing employment with a new employer. Assuming that he qualifies for the moving expense deduction, which of the expenses listed below incurred in connection with the move will be allowed as a deduction without question by the Internal Revenue Service?
(1) Penalty for breaking a lease
(2) Loss on disposition of personal furniture
(3) Cost of meals while en route to California
(4) Cost of new furniture
(5) None of these

(c) If you regularly worked in two or more separate areas, the position of the Internal Revenue Service would be that your home for tax purposes would be which one of the places listed below?
(1) The place where your family resides
(2) The place where you vote
(3) Your primary place of employment
(4) At your election, either the place where you reside or the place where you vote
(5) None of these

18. The Moving Specialty Corporation has prepared its tax return for the calendar year 1972 and has submitted it to you for your review. Which of the following items shown on the return do you feel may be questioned by the Internal Revenue Service? Why do you feel these items are questionable?

Gross receipts from moving	$270,000
Amounts received from repair shops for referring customers with broken furniture	2,000
Total receipts	$272,000

Expenses
   Salaries:

Truck drivers	$ 40,000	
Office help	8,000	
Joe Morgan, President	32,000	
Jerry Morgan, Vice-President	24,000	
Joe Morgan, Jr., Treasurer	16,000	
Jerry Morgan, Jr., Secretary	8,000	
Total salaries		$128,000
Gas, oil, and insurance		30,000
Supplies		1,000
Depreciation (trucks and building)		17,000
Commission paid to city officials for recommending Moving Specialty Corporation when moving municipal equipment		5,000
Country club membership for Joe Morgan		2,300
Overloading fines		2,000

Attorney's fees to unsuccessfully defend over-loading charges	500	
New cab and van	7,200	193,000
Taxable income		$ 79,000

Dividends paid

Joe Morgan	$2,000
Jerry Morgan	1,500
Joe Morgan, Jr.	1,000
Jerry Morgan, Jr.	500
	$5,000

19. Rotr Corporation, whose capital stock is listed on the New York Stock Exchange, has outstanding over 5 million shares of capital stock. Mrs. C. Sunstrand, a holder of ten shares worth about $250, closely followed the activities of the corporation and became unhappy with the way the management was handling the corporate affairs. As part of a plan to organize a stockholder's revolt, Mrs. Sunstrand took a number of speech improvement courses in order to present her ideas as forcefully as possible. She attempted to present her views at the annual stockholders' meeting but was ejected for using slanderous language. Subsequently she unsuccessfully brought a suit against the corporation and its officers, to obtain an order that the minutes of the annual stockholders' meeting should include the remarks she would have made had she not been ejected from the meeting. A copy of the minutes is sent to each stockholder. On her tax return, Mrs. Sunstrand deducted the cost of the speech lessons and attorney fees. When challenged on the deductions by the Internal Revenue Service, she stated that all expenditures were incurred to protect the value of her stock in the corporation and thus were deductible under Section 212. What result?

20. Mr. P. Sims purchased residential property on July 1, 1957, for use as a personal residence at a cost of $26,000. He allocated $20,000 of the cost to the building and $6,000 of the cost to the land. Mr. Sims occupied the residence until January 1, 1972, when he converted it into rental property. The fair market value of the property at the date of conversion was $24,000, of which $18,000 was allocated to the building and $6,000 was allocated to the land.
    (a) What is the depreciation allowable for the calendar year 1972 at a 4 percent annual rate computed on the straight-line basis? Assume the building has no salvage value.
    (b) Assuming the property was sold on January 1, 1973, for $23,000, compute the allowable gain or loss. Show your computation.

21. The Internal Revenue Service has disallowed a portion of the compensation paid to stockholder-officers of a closely-held corporation. The excessive amounts were not in proportion to stockholdings. The corporation loses deduction of the excess payment in the current year and
    (a) Must regard the excess payments as a return of capital and so report them to the recipients.
    (b) May capitalize the excess payments as goodwill and amortize this amount over five years.

(c) May carry the excess payments forward five years until used up.

(d) May apply this excess against capital gains in current and future years.

(e) None of the above answers is correct.

8

DEPRECIABLE
AND DEPLETABLE
PROPERTY

DEPRECIATION . . . 248

Nature and Definition . . . 248
Types of Depreciable Property . . . 249

TANGIBLE PROPERTY . . . 249
INTANGIBLES . . . 249
MASS ASSETS . . . 251

Allowed or Allowable . . . 252
Salvage Value . . . 252
Methods of Computing Depreciation . . . 253

STRAIGHT-LINE . . . 255
150 PERCENT DECLINING-BALANCE . . . 255
200 PERCENT DECLINING-BALANCE . . . 255
SUM-OF-THE-YEARS DIGITS . . . 256
OTHER METHODS . . . 257
COMPARISON OF DEPRECIATION METHODS . . . 258

Restrictions on Accelerated Depreciation of Buildings . . . 258
Rehabilitation of Housing Property . . . 261
Additional First-Year Depreciation . . . 261
Depreciation Accounting . . . 262

TYPES OF ASSET ACCOUNTS . . . 262
RESERVE FOR DEPRECIATION . . . 263
COMPOSITE RATES FOR MULTIPLE-ASSET ACCOUNTS . . . 263
RETIREMENTS UNDER THE FACTS AND CIRCUMSTANCES AND
    GUIDELINE LIFE SYSTEMS . . . 264

ITEM ACCOUNTS . . . 264
MULTIPLE-ASSET ACCOUNTS . . . 265

Normal Retirements . . . 265
Abnormal Retirements . . . 266

AVERAGING CONVENTIONS . . . 267

245

Useful Life Systems . . . 267

FACTS AND CIRCUMSTANCES . . . 267
GUIDELINE LIFE SYSTEM FOR PRE-1971 ASSETS . . . 268

TAXABLE YEARS 1962 THROUGH 1970 . . . 268

Reserve Ratio Test . . . 271

TAXABLE YEARS ENDING IN 1971 OR LATER . . . 272
CLASS LIFE ASSET DEPRECIATION RANGE SYSTEM . . . 273

HISTORY . . . 273
ENACTMENT OF THE CLADR SYSTEM . . . 274
SUMMARY OF THE CLADR SYSTEM . . . 275
DEFINITIONS . . . 276
ELIGIBLE PROPERTY . . . 276

Mandatory Exclusions . . . 276
Optional Exclusions . . . 277

ELECTION . . . 278
RECORD-KEEPING REQUIREMENTS . . . 278
COMPUTATION OF ALLOWABLE DEPRECIATION . . . 279

Methods of Depreciation . . . 279
Changes in Methods of Depreciation . . . 279
Selection of Asset Depreciation Period . . . 279
Leased Property . . . 280

DEPRECIABLE BASES . . . 280
AVERAGING CONVENTIONS . . . 280

Half-Year Convention . . . 280
Modified Half-Year Convention . . . 280

SALVAGE AND REMOVAL COSTS . . . 281

Binding Nature of Taxpayer's Estimate . . . 281
Adjustment of Salvage for Retirements . . . 281
Reusable Material . . . 281
Deduction for Dismantling Costs . . . 281

REPAIRS AND IMPROVEMENTS . . . 281

Repair Allowance and Election . . . 282

ACCOUNTING FOR RETIREMENTS . . . 284

Ordinary Retirements . . . 284
Extraordinary Retirements . . . 284
Special Rule for Nontaxable Transactions . . . 285
*Election to Allocate Special Basis Vintage
  Accounts to Abnormal Retirements* . . . 285
*Recognition of Gain When the Depreciation
  Reserve Exceeds the Asset Account* . . . 285
Recognition of Losses on Termination . . . 285

APPLICATION OF CLADR TO OTHER PROVISIONS . . . 285
REVENUE PROCEDURE 72-10 AND EXAMPLES . . . 285

Comparison of Facts and Circumstances Life System with the
   CLADR Life System for Post-1970 Assets . . . 289

Normal and Extraordinary Obsolescence under the
   Facts and Circumstances Life System . . . 290

AMORTIZATION . . . 292

Trademarks and Trade Names . . . 292
Leased Property . . . 292
Amortizable Bond Premium . . . 293
Corporate Organizational Expenditures . . . 294

INVESTMENT CREDIT . . . 294

Recapture . . . 299
Presentation in Financial Statements . . . 301

DEPLETION . . . 303

Economic Interest . . . 304
Methods . . . 305

COST DEPLETION . . . 305
PERCENTAGE DEPLETION . . . 305

GROSS INCOME FROM THE PROPERTY . . . 306
NET INCOME LIMITATION . . . 307

ILLUSTRATION . . . 307

The Property . . . 309

DEPRECIATION

Nature and Definition

8.1   The purpose of an allowance for depreciation is to provide a deduction for the consumption of the cost, i.e., the original investment in property that is consumed by use in a trade or business or held for the production of income. This deduction for the exhaustion, wear and tear, and obsolescence is allowed when the property is devoted to these uses, even if it is idle or not in full use during the taxable year involved. Congress has stated its views as follows: "Depreciation allowances are the method by which the capital invested in an asset is recovered tax free over the years it is used in a business. The annual deduction is computed by spreading the cost over its estimated useful life."[1]

8.2   As defined by Reg. 1.167(a)–1, depreciation is "that amount which should be set aside for the taxable year in accordance with a reasonably consistent plan, not necessarily at a uniform rate, whereby the aggregate of the amounts so set aside, plus the salvage value, will equal, at the end of the useful life of the depreciable property, the cost or other basis of the property." As there stated, the sum total of the depreciation deduction over the period of years may not exceed the cost of the property as reduced by salvage value.

8.3   Assets are recorded in accounts—item or multiple asset. To each account, a method of calculating depreciation is applied—the most common ones being straight-line, declining balance, and sum-of-the-years-digits. The rate of depreciation under any method of calculating depreciation is based on the estimated average useful life of the assets in the particular account; and in making the estimate of average useful life, there are three life systems in current use. The general rule, or "Facts and Circumstances" system, has been available for all years from 1913 to date unless the Guideline life or the Class Life Asset Depreciation Range system was in force and also was elected. The Guideline life system of Rev. Proc. 62–21 was available for the years from 1962 through 1970 as to all assets in use in those years no matter when acquired. Further, that same Guideline life system, with some modifications, is optionally available under Reg. 1.167(a)–12, issued April 22, 1972, for 1971 and subsequent taxable years but only as to assets acquired in 1970 and prior years.

8.4   The Class Life Asset Depreciation Range (CLADR) system started with 1971 acquisitions of assets; unlike the Guideline life system, it does not apply to earlier years' acquisitions. There was also an Asset Depreciation Range system adopted by regulations in 1971. However, it never became effective, as the Congress, in enacting the Revenue Act of 1971, replaced it with the CLADR system.

1. H.R. Rep. 1337, 83rd Cong., 2d sess., 1954, p. 22.

Types of Depreciable Property

Both property used in a trade or business and property held for the 8.5
production of income are depreciable [Section 167(a)]. Such property
can be both tangible and, in a number of instances, intangible.

Tangible Property. Regulation 1.167(a)–2 pertaining to tangible prop- 8.6
erty provides:

The depreciation allowance in the case of tangible property applies only
to that part of the property which is subject to wear and tear, to decay or
decline from natural causes, to exhaustion, and to obsolescence. The allowance does not apply to inventories or stock in trade, or to land apart from
the improvements or physical development added to it. The allowance does
not apply to natural resources which are subject to the allowance for depletion provided in Section 611. No deduction for depreciation shall be allowed
on automobiles or other vehicles used solely for pleasure, on a building used
by the taxpayer solely as his residence, or on furniture or furnishings therein,
personal effects, or clothing; but properties and costumes used exclusively
in a business, such as a theatrical business, may be depreciated.

Land is not depreciable; land improvements are. They include paved
surfaces, sidewalks, canals, waterways, drainage facilities and sewers,
wharves, bridges, fences, landscaping, and shrubbery.[2] General costs
incurred during construction of a building are subject to depreciation
to the extent that they can be allocated to depreciable property. Such
general costs would include engineering and architect fees, insurance, depreciation on equipment, legal fees, and interest on construction loans[3] if an election was made to capitalize such interest
as a carrying charge under Section 266. A corporation building a rental
housing project cannot depreciate sidewalks, curbs, paved streets,
sewers, and watermains on land that is then deeded over to a municipality, because it does not continue to have a depreciable interest
therein.[4] Similarly, special assessments paid by a corporation to
cover the cost of improvements made by a city, such as streets and
sidewalks on the adjacent publicly owned property, are not depreciable.[5] The cost incurred by a subdivider to construct roads and
install curbs, gutters, waterlines, and storm sewers is not depreciable,
but instead is allocable to the bases of the lots that such expenditures
benefit.[6]

Intangibles. If intangible property has a determinable useful life, it 8.7
can be depreciated, otherwise not. Regulation 1.167(a)–3 provides:

2. Depreciation Guidelines, Rev. Proc. 62–21, 1962–2 C.B. 418, as supplemented
by Rev. Proc. 65–13, Group One; Rev. Proc. 72–10.
3. Algernon Blair, Inc., 29 T.C. 1205.
4. Algernon Blair, *ibid.*
5. F. M. Hubbell Son & Co. v. Burnet, 51 F.2d 644 (8th Cir. 1931), 10 AFTR 298,
affirming 19 BTA 612 (1930).
6. Frank B. Cooper, 31 T.C. 1155 (1959); Wood v. Com., 245 F.2d 888 (5th Cir.
1957), 51 AFTR 811.

If an intangible asset is known from experience or other factors to be of use in the business or in the production of income for only a limited period, the length of which can be estimated with reasonable accuracy, such an intangible asset may be the subject of a depreciation allowance. Examples are patents and copyrights. An intangible asset, the useful life of which is not limited, is not subject to the allowance for depreciation. No allowance will be permitted merely because, in the unsupported opinion of the taxpayer, the intangible asset has a limited useful life. No deduction for depreciation is allowable with respect to goodwill. For rules with respect to organizational expenditures, see Section 248 and the regulations thereunder. For rules with respect to trademark and trade name expenditures, see Section 177 and the regulations thereunder.

8.8   On the sale of a business, the seller will frequently give the buyer a covenant not to compete for a stated term of years. A payment by a buyer for such a covenant can be depreciated over the period specified in the covenant.[7] However, if a lump sum is paid for both goodwill and a covenant not to compete, generally the courts have held that the covenant is not severable from the goodwill and that no part of the sum can be allocated to that covenant and then be depreciated.[8]

8.9   The purchase price of contracts has been allowed to be depreciated in some cases, in others not, depending upon whether the contracts had a determinable life. Some contracts on which depreciation has been allowed are: an exclusive franchise for the sale of equipment for a definite term of years,[9] a franchise to represent food producers,[10] an insurance renewal commission contract,[11] and a contract to print a newspaper for a period of thirty years.[12]

8.10   In Rev. Rul. 56–520,[13] the Internal Revenue Service ruled that expenditures incurred by a taxpayer to obtain permission from the Federal Communications Commission to operate a television broadcasting station on a certain channel constitute capital expenditures that may not be depreciated. In Rev. Rul. 57–377,[14] the Service held that a network affiliation contract acquired in a purchase of an entire broadcasting station is not depreciable, because it has an indefinite life and is similar to goodwill. Such a contract under regulations of the Federal Communications Commission cannot be for a term in excess of two years, but then it is renewable indefinitely for succeeding two-year terms. The Seventh Circuit Court of Appeals[15] and the Third Circuit Court of Appeals[16] both have similarly held that net-

7. Carboloy Company, Inc., ¶43,325 P-H Memo T.C.
8. Toledo Blade Co., 11 T.C. 1079 (1948).
9. Automatic Heating & Cooling Co., ¶42,561 P-H Memo BTA.
10. A. H. Morse Co. v. Com., 208 F.2d 751 (1st Cir. 1953), 45 AFTR 18.
11. H. B. Hill, 3 BTA 761; Hugh H. Hodges, 50 T.C. 428 (1968)(Acq.).
12. Birmingham News Co. v. Patterson, Jr., 224 F. Supp. 670 (D.C., Ala., 1963) 13 AFTR2d 539, affirmed 345 F.2d 531 (5th Cir. 1965), 15 AFTR2d 1079.
13. 1956–2 C.B. 170.
14. 1957–2 C.B. 146.
15. Com. v. Indiana Broadcasting Corp., 350 F.2d 580 (7th Cir. 1965), 65–2 USTC ¶9620, 16 AFTR2d 5465, reversing 41 T.C. 793, cert. denied.
16. Westinghouse Broadcasting Co., 309 F.2d 279 (3rd Cir. 1962), 62–2 USTC ¶0776, 10 AFTR2d 5800, affirming 36 T.C. 912, cert. denied.

251

Depreciable
and
Depletable
Property
8.11

work affiliation contracts do not have an ascertainable life and, accordingly, cannot be depreciated.

Mass Assets. A doctrine has been developed by the courts that a "mass asset" is indivisible, has no determinable life, and is nondepreciable; however, in 1968 the Tax Court, in a case mentioned below, found that a mass asset had a determinable life and allowed depreciation. The term has been applied to group purchases of customer lists,[17] customer routes,[18] location leases for vending machines,[19] subscription lists of publishers of newspapers,[20] and other types of contracts.[21] In *Metropolitan Laundry Co.* v. *U.S.,*[22] the court said:

> [An] asset in the form of a list of customers regularly subscribing for goods or services is not to be regarded as an aggregation of disconnected individual subscribers. Such lists have been treated as unitary structures irrespective of incidental fluctuations and alterations. . . . The gradual replacement of old patrons with new ones is not to be regarded as the exchange of old capital assets for new and different ones, but rather as the process of keeping a continually existing capital asset intact. And, expenditures incurred in replacing patrons are ordinary business expenses in the nature of upkeep costs, *not* new capital investments. . . .

However, if, at the time of negotiating the purchase, the individual contracts are separately valued and paid for, the mass-asset doctrine has not been applied and depreciation on the contracts has been allowed.[23] Further, in 1968 the doctrine was attacked in an article in a leading law review,[24] and the Tax Court, in an apparent reversal of its long-standing position, allowed depreciation on customer lists that had been purchased separate and apart from the business of the seller.[25]

17. Metropolitan Laundry Co. v. U.S., 100 F. Supp. 803 (D.C., Calif., 1951), 52–1 USTC ¶9129, 41 AFTR 297; similarly, Golden State Towel and Linen Service, Ltd. v. U.S., 373 F.2d 938 (Ct. Cls., 1967), 19 AFTR2d 950; [both cases concerned deductions for losses].

18. *Ibid.*

19. Sam Scalish, 21 T.C.M. 260 (1962).

20. National Weeklies, Inc. v. Reynolds, 43 F. Supp. 554 (D.C., Minn., 1941), 28 AFTR 1440, 42–1 USTC ¶9304.

21. Boe v. Com., 35 T.C. 720 (1961), affirmed 307 F.2d 339 (9th Cir. 1962), 10 AFTR2d 5458 (medical service contracts); Thrifticheck Service Corp. v. Com., 33 T.C. 1038 (1960), affirmed 287 F.2d 1 (2nd Cir. 1961), 7 AFTR2d 723 (bank customer accounts).

22. *Supra,* fn. 17.

23. Com. v. Seaboard Finance Co., 367 F.2d 646 (9th Cir. 1966), 18 AFTR2d 5803; Super Food Services, Inc. v. U.S., 69–2 USTC ¶9557 (7th Cir. 1969), 24 AFTR2d 69–5309.

24. Note, "Amortization of Intangibles: An Examination of the Tax Treatment of Purchased Goodwill," Harvard Law Review, 81: 859 (1968), note 7.

25. Manhattan Co. of Virginia, Inc., 50 T.C. 78 (1968).

Allowed or Allowable

8.12   Depreciation allowable in a prior year but not deducted cannot be claimed in any subsequent year. Further, such allowable depreciation must be deducted in determining the adjusted basis of the asset under Section 1016(a)(2). In addition, if the depreciation claimed and allowed was more than the amount properly allowable, then the amount allowed shall also reduce basis to the extent that the excessive amount resulted in a tax benefit for a prior year. Regulation 1.167(a)–10(a) reads:

A taxpayer should deduct the proper depreciation allowance each year and may not increase his depreciation allowances in later years by reason of his failure to deduct any depreciation allowance or of his action in deducting an allowance plainly inadequate under the known facts in prior years. The inadequacy of the depreciation allowance for property in prior years shall be determined on the basis of the allowable method of depreciation used by the taxpayer for such property or under the straight-line method if no allowance has ever been claimed for such property. The preceding sentence shall not be construed as precluding application of any method provided in Section 167(b) if taxpayer's failure to claim any allowance for depreciation was due solely to erroneously treating as a deductible expense an item properly chargeable to capital account. For rules relating to adjustments to basis, see Section 1016 and the regulations thereunder.

Salvage Value

8.13   Regulation 1.167(a)–1(c) provides:

Salvage value is the amount (determined at the time of acquisition) which is estimated will be realizable upon sale or other disposition of an asset when it is no longer useful in the taxpayer's trade or business or in the production of his income and is to be retired from service by the taxpayer. *Salvage value shall not be changed at any time after the determination made at the time of acquisition merely because of changes in price levels. However, if there is a redetermination of useful life . . . , salvage value may be redetermined based upon facts known at the time of such redetermination of useful life.* Salvage, when reduced by the cost of removal, is referred to as net salvage. The time at which an asset is retired from service may vary according to the policy of the taxpayer. If the taxpayer's policy is to dispose of assets which are still in good operating condition, the salvage value may represent a relatively large proportion of the original basis of the asset. However, if the taxpayer customarily uses an asset until its inherent useful life has been substantially exhausted, salvage value may represent no more than junk value. . . . [Emphasis supplied]

8.14   Under all life systems, the aggregate of the depreciation deductions for all years of use of each item of property plus salvage value cannot exceed its cost or other basis. If the life system is Facts and Circumstances and the method is straight-line or sum-of-the-years-digits, the salvage value is taken into account either by a reduction of the amount subject to depreciation or by a reduction in the rate of depreciation. If the method is a declining-balance one, salvage is ignored, but the asset cannot be depreciated below salvage value. Under the Guideline life system and the Class Life Asset Depreciation Range system, salvage value also is ignored, but again the asset cannot be depreciated below salvage value. However, under all systems, if the asset is personal property, was acquired after October 16, 1962, and has an estimated useful life of at least three years, Section 167(f) and Reg. 1.167(f)–1 permit a taxpayer to elect for all purposes to ignore the first 10 percent of the adjusted basis of the property.

EXAMPLE

A truck is purchased at a cost of $5,000. The first $500 of salvage value can be ignored, so that, if estimated salvage is $1,500, the truck can be depreciated down to $1,000. If estimated salvage were to be $400, the full cost of $5,000 could be depreciated.

8.15 Salvage value is affected by the estimated amount of the cost of removal and disposition, which may equal or exceed the gross salvage value. In one situation, proof based on past experience made it reasonable to believe that the cost of removal would exceed gross salvage; the taxpayer was allowed to reflect a negative salvage value. This in substance increased the amount of the annual allowance for depreciation.[26]

8.16 Revenue Ruling 67–272 states that the Commissioner may require redetermination of useful life or salvage value whenever it becomes apparent that either of these factors has been miscalculated. Such adjustment, it goes on to hold, will ordinarily be made starting with the earliest year then open for assessment under the limitations provisions of the Code, but will be made in the light of the relevant facts known or fairly ascertainable as of the end of such open year. To the extent that this ruling holds that the Service can adjust salvage value without at the same time adjusting the useful life, it may be invalid as contrary to the third sentence of the regulation quoted above.[27]

8.17 The mere fact that an asset is sold for more than its depreciated cost does not necessarily prove that the depreciable life used was too short or that the amount of estimated salvage originally taken into account was too low.[28] Inflation or a sudden change in market value may be the reason for the gain.

Methods of Computing Depreciation

8.18 Three methods are specifically provided by Code Sec. 167: straight-line, declining-balance, and sum-of-the-years-digits, although the

26. Portland General Electric Co. v. U.S., 223 F. Supp. 111 (D.C., Ore., 1963), 13 AFTR2d 400, on rehearing 14 AFTR2d 5009.

27. See also Macabe Co., 42 T.C. 1105, 1108, fn. 8.

28. Fribourg Navigation Company, Inc. v. Com., 383 U.S. 272 (1966), 17 AFTR2d 470, 66–1 USTC ¶9280; Motorlease Corp. v. U.S., 383 U.S. 573 (1966), 17 AFTR2d 617; U.S. v. S. & A. Company, 338 F.2d 629 (8th Cir. 1964), 14 AFTR2d 5964, cert. denied.

200 percent declining-balance and years-digits methods cannot be used on certain buildings and there are other restrictions on property acquired used. Other reasonable methods, discussed in later paragraphs, are also allowable under Reg. 1.167(b)–4. Depreciable assets are recorded in accounts—item or multiple-asset. As to each account a different method can be used. Further, if a particular method was chosen in a prior year for a type of property, a different method can be elected without permission for similar property acquired in a later year, provided that such property is recorded in a new account. If an individual investor owns rental property and does not keep formal books, each piece of property will constitute an item account unless perhaps he groups them on his tax return in computing depreciation.

8.19   Under the Facts and Circumstances and the Guideline life systems, but with one exception, once a method has been adopted for a particular account, it must be followed in future years unless permission to change is secured from the Internal Revenue Service. Such permission is sought by filing Form 3115, Application for Change in Accounting Method, with the Commissioner in Washington, D.C. within the first ninety days of the year in which the change is to become effective. However, automatic permission to change from most methods can be obtained by filing that form with the District Director within the same ninety-day period and attaching to it the data called for in Rev. Proc. 67–40. The one exception to the rule that permission must be obtained to change from one method to another is that a taxpayer who uses any percent declining-balance method on property acquired new by him may elect to change to the straight-line method at any time. Ordinarily, a change from the 200 percent declining-balance method is beneficial when the asset has reached a point slightly over 60 percent of the estimated total useful life.

8.20   As pointed out in paragraph 8.109, the regulations pertaining to the CLADR system permit certain changes to be made without permission. Other changes require it.

8.21   If a taxpayer erroneously expenses a capital addition in the year of acquisition and later, upon examination of the return for that year, is required to capitalize it, he is entitled to use any method of depreciation which would have been available to him had he originally capitalized the asset in his return.[29] Suppose, however, that the taxpayer either claimed no depreciation in the first year for which it was allowable or used the straight-line method in a year while the property was still under construction and not depreciable, and then in both instances in the next year used the straight-line method. Can he now elect to use the declining-balance method starting with the first year for which it was depreciable? The courts have held "No" on the ground that the taxpayer properly made a choice of method and the error in choice of year must be disregarded.[30]

29. Reg. 1.167(a)–10(a) quoted in paragraph 8.12.
30. Henry M. Rodney, ¶53 T.C. 287 (11–25–69); Missouri Public Service Co. v. U.S., 370 F.2d 971 (8th Cir. 1967), 19 AFTR2d 395.

Straight-Line. The tax basis—ordinarily cost (less estimated salvage value)—is spread evenly over the estimated remaining useful life of the property. For example, if an asset has a ten-year life, $\frac{1}{10}$ the cost (less salvage) may be deducted each year.

8.22

150 Percent Declining-Balance. Except as to certain types of buildings, the declining-balance method using a rate not in excess of 150 percent of the straight-line rate is available for new and used tangible property whether acquired before or after 1954. Thus, for an asset with a ten-year life, the annual declining-balance rate would be 15 percent; i.e., 150 percent of 10 percent. The 150 percent method leaves a substantial residuum (approximately 20 percent) undepreciated at the end of the normal life.

8.23

200 Percent Declining-Balance. In order to provide incentives for expansion and to allow capital equipment benefits for expansion comparable to that in other major manufacturing countries, the 200 percent declining-balance method was made available by the Revenue Act of 1954. It is applicable only to property which (a) is not intangible, (b) has a useful life of three years or more, and (c) is new in use and acquired after December 31, 1953, or construction of which was completed after that critical date. Again, restrictions have been imposed on its application to certain types of buildings. It has been held by the Supreme Court that in determining whether property, in that instance automobiles, had a useful life of at least three years, the intrinsic life of the property itself as shown by the experience of others is not determinative, but rather the particular taxpayer's own experience.[31] The rate used is 200 percent of the straight-line rate. Since the annual allowance is computed by applying this uniform rate to the adjusted basis (which constantly declines as basis is reduced by prior depreciation), the result is a fast write-off in the early years. Salvage value is not considered in the computation, but depreciation is not allowable beyond the salvage value point. Under this method, approximately 11 percent of the cost remains at the end of a ten-year useful life and ranges up to 12.7 percent at the end of useful life for assets having a life of forty years.

8.24

On January 1, 1973, taxpayer bought a new machine with a useful life of 10 years, for $5,000. Salvage value was $800, but under Sec. 167(f) (paragraph 8.14 above) the first 10 percent of cost can be disregarded, so that the amount becomes $300. Under the 200 percent declining-balance method, the rate is 20 percent (twice the 10 percent straight-line rate, unadjusted for salvage, for this asset). The allowance for the first year is $1,000 (20 percent of $5,000). The allowance for the second year will be 20 percent of $4,000 ($5,000 − $1,000) or $800, and so on; but the machine cannot be depreciated after the adjusted basis (cost less depreciation reserve) reaches $300.

EXAMPLE

31. Hertz Corp. v. U.S., 364 U.S. 122 (1960), 5 AFTR2d 1792.

8.25 **Sum-of-the-Years-Digits.** The Revenue Act of 1954 also provided an alternative method of rapid depreciation for new as opposed to used property, which is more complicated to use than the declining-balance method but possibly more beneficial, since it does not result in an un-realistic amount of unrecovered cost remaining at the end of the esti-mated useful life. Under this method, the rate is applied to a constant original cost (reduced by estimated salvage value under the Facts and Circumstances life system unless the amount is less than 10 percent of basis) in a manner similar to the straight-line method, but the rate varies and is reduced as the taxpayer moves from the initial use of the property toward the end of the useful life. The rate for any year is a fraction, of which the denominator is the sum of the digits represent-ing the total years of estimated life and the numerator is the remaining years of useful life at the beginning of the year. For example, if the useful life is five years, the denominator for each year remains a con-stant 15 (1 + 2 + 3 + 4 + 5); the numerator for the first year would be 5, the remaining life at the beginning of the year; the second year's numerator would be 4, and so on. In the first year, the ratio to be ap-plied to the original cost, as reduced by salvage, would be $\frac{5}{15}$, in the second year $\frac{4}{15}$, and so on. This method results in slightly less depre-ciation deductions in the early years of the life of an asset than does the 200 percent double declining-balance method, but then gradually it begins to provide more.

EXAMPLE   G acquires new property on January 1, 1973, at a cost of $1,500. It has an estimated useful life of five years. Its estimated salvage value is $150 [which can be disregarded because of Sec. 167(f)]. The depreciation deduction for each year is computed as follows:

YEAR	FRACTION OF COST	DEPRECIATION DEDUCTION
1	$\frac{5}{15}$	$ 500
2	$\frac{4}{15}$	400
3	$\frac{3}{15}$	300
4	$\frac{2}{15}$	200
5	$\frac{1}{15}$	100
	Total cost	$1,500

8.26   Under the sum-of-the-years-digits method, depreciation may also be computed by applying changing fractions to the unrecovered cost less any salvage value taken. The numerator changes each year to correspond with remaining useful life of the asset (including the year for which the allowance is computed), and the denominator changes each year to correspond with the sum of the numbers representing the remaining useful life.

Assume the facts in the example in paragraph 8.25. Under the remaining life plan, the fraction used for the first year would be $\frac{5}{15}$, 5 being the remain-ing years of life, and 15 the sum of 5 + 4 + 3 + 2 + 1. For the second year, the fraction would change to $\frac{4}{10}$, 4 being the remaining years of life and 10 being the sum of $4 + 3 + 2 + 1$. For the third year, the fraction would change to $\frac{3}{6}$, and so on. These fractions are applied to the unrecovered cost.

As an aid to computing the depreciation under the sum-of-the-years-digits methods, a decimal rate table from 1 to 100 years has been set up in Reg. 1.167(b)–3(a)(2) on the basis of the remaining useful life of an asset. The decimal, however, is applied against the unrecovered basis of the asset rather than the original cost. As we would expect, the answer is the same regardless of which approach is utilized.

8.27

Other Methods. There are other methods available under the Facts and Circumstances life system, but not under the Guideline and generally not under the CLADR life systems.

8.28

In some situations, the useful life of a tangible asset can better be related to physical use, such as *machine-hours,* than to a period of time, since the exhaustion from wear and tear and obsolescence is sometimes more a function of use than of time, especially in industries where two and three shifts are common. The useful life is computed by machine-hours, and an hourly rate of depreciation is derived by dividing the depreciable cost (net of salvage) by the number of hours of useful life estimated. The annual depreciation deduction is then the number of hours the machine has actually been utilized during the year multiplied by the amount determined.

8.29

A similar result is obtained for equipment used in mines, oil wells, and timber operations by prorating depreciation on the basis of units produced—the *unit-of-production* method. The depreciable cost (net of salvage) is divided by the estimated units of production, and the annual deduction is determined by multiplying actual production for that period of time by the amounts so determined.

8.30

An anachronistic method is the *retirement* method of accounting, still partially used by some railroads and, until about 1938, in common use by gas and electric distribution companies. The cost of property retired each year is credited to the capital asset account, and this amount, less salvage value, is considered the depreciation expense. As one would expect, there is much more fluctuation in the depreciation charge-off resulting from this type of method than from any other.

8.31

Another specialized method applicable to single-purpose and special-purpose equipment required for a single job, such as a bridge or dam, is the *job-basis* method in which the charge for depreciation is the difference between the cost of the equipment at the beginning of a job and its salable value at the end.

8.32

The *income-forecast* method[32] generally is used to depreciate television tapes, movie films, and taped shows. Since the useful life does not depend upon passage of time or wear and tear, it is estimated in terms of the anticipated dollar earnings (gross income less expenses

8.33

32. Described and approved in Rev. Rul. 60–358, 1960–2 C.B. 68.

of distribution). Annual depreciation is determined by the dollars earned within the taxable year. An adjustment of the income forecast may be made if the original estimate proves to be substantially over- or understated.[33]

8.34 **Comparison of Depreciation Methods.** The following example compares the straight-line, the 150 percent declining-balance, the 200 percent declining-balance, and the sum-of-the-years-digits methods as applied to a $100 asset with a ten-year useful life. The amounts are rounded to the nearest dollar.

EXAMPLE

| | STRAIGHT-LINE | | DECLINING-BALANCE | | | | SUM-OF-THE-YEARS-DIGITS | |
| | | | ANNUAL DEDUCTION | | CUMULATIVE COST RECOVERED | | | |
YEAR	ANNUAL DEDUC-TION	CUMULA-TIVE COST RECOV-ERED	150%	200%	150%	200%	ANNUAL DEDUC-TION	CUMULA-TIVE COST RECOV-ERED
1	$10	$ 10	$15	$20	$15	$20	$18	$ 18
2	10	20	13	16	28	36	16	34
3	10	30	11	13	39	49	15	49
4	10	40	9	10	48	59	13	62
5	10	50	8	8	56	67	11	73
6	10	60	6	7	62	74	9	82
7	10	70	6	5	68	79	7	89
8	10	80	5	4	73	83	5	94
9	10	90	4	3	77	86	4	98
10	10	100	3	3	80	89	2	100

Restrictions on Accelerated Depreciation of Buildings

8.35 Since the enactment in 1954 of the provisions permitting the 200 percent declining-balance method and the sum-of-the-years-digits methods, a number of attempts were made in Congress to restrict their applicability to buildings. Two of these legislative efforts were successful.

8.36 Under the Investment Credit and Accelerated Depreciation Suspension Act of 1966, the provisions of which were terminated by the Investment Credit and Accelerated Depreciation Restoration Act of 1967, Section 167(i) was added to the Code so that these two methods of accelerated depreciation were suspended as to any buildings, their structural components, and land improvements, that cost more than $50,000. However, the terms "buildings" and "structural compo-

33. Another method for depreciating television films is described and was approved in Kiro, Inc., 51 T.C. 155 (1968).

nents" were defined so as to exclude special-purpose buildings hous- ing machinery, storage facilities such as grain bins and oil tanks, machinery permanently affixed to a building required principally for a manufacturing process,[34] and new elevators and escalators. The period of suspension was from October 10, 1966, through March 9, 1967. If the physical construction, reconstruction, or erection of a building (a) began during the suspension period, or (b) was ordered during that time, and none of the exceptions listed in Code sections 167(i) and 48(h) applied, the 200 percent declining-balance and the sum-of-the-years-digits methods were not available during the suspension period or at any time thereafter. Only the 150 percent declining-balance or the straight-line method of depreciation could be used.

Depreciable and Depletable Property

The suspension of the 200 percent declining-balance and the sum-of-the-years-digits methods did not affect machinery, equipment, and the types of property excluded from the terms "buildings" and "structural components" whether acquired before, during, or after the suspension period. They remained eligible for these accelerated depreciation methods.

8.37

The Tax Reform Act of 1969 was the second law to put restrictions on the applicability of accelerated depreciation methods to buildings. It added Section 167(j) to the Code. The reason for the amendment is set forth in the Senate Finance Committee Report: [35]

8.38

General reasons for change. Accelerated depreciation will frequently allow deductions in excess of the amount required to service the mortgage during the early life of the property, thus producing in many cases a tax loss deductible against other income even though there is a positive cash flow. In addition, accelerated depreciation usually produces a deduction far in excess of the actual decline in the usefulness of the property. In addition, by holding the property for 10 years, the taxpayer can arrange to have all the gain resulting from excess depreciation (which was offset against ordinary income) taxed as a Section 1231 gain, at capital gain rates. The tax advantage increases as the taxpayer's income moves into higher tax brackets.

As a result of the fast depreciation and the ability to deduct amounts in excess of the taxpayer's equity, economically profitable real estate operations normally produce substantial tax losses, sheltering from income tax the economic profit of the operation and permitting avoidance of income tax on the owner's other ordinary income, such as salary and dividends. Later, the property can be sold and the excess of the sale price over the remaining basis is treated as capital gain except for the limitations in Section 1250.

Because of the present tax situation, when investment is solicited in a real estate venture it has become the practice to promise a prospective investor substantial tax losses which can be used to diminish the tax on his income from other sources. Thus, there is, in effect, substantial dealing in "tax losses" produced by depreciable real property. The committee, agreeing with the House, believes the desired solution is the elimination of these losses in those cases where there is no true economic loss.

34. Reg. 1.48–1(e) made applicable by Code Section 167(i).
35. S. Rep. 91–552, 91st Cong., 1st sess., 1969, p. 212.

8.39   Broadly speaking, there are three types of depreciable buildings— commercial (stores), industrial (factories), and residential (apartment buildings, town houses, and single-family homes held for rental purposes). The restrictions of Section 167(j) apply principally to commercial and industrial properties; to a major extent, residential buildings are exempted from restrictions. Just as in the case of the Investment Credit and Accelerated Depreciation Suspension Act of 1966, the term "building" includes structural components, but excluded are special-purpose buildings housing machinery, storage facilities such as grain bins and oil tanks, machinery permanently affixed to a building and required principally for a manufacturing process, and new elevators and escalators. These excluded items, together with machinery and equipment, continue to be eligible for all of the methods of depreciation described in Section 167(b).

8.40   In summary, Section 167(j) provides that:

(1) New commercial and industrial buildings can be depreciated only under the straight-line, 150 percent declining-balance, or other method which during the first two-thirds of the useful life does not exceed an amount available under the 150 percent declining-balance method. The 200 percent declining-balance and sum-of-the-years-digits methods cannot be used.

(2) Used commercial and industrial buildings acquired by a taxpayer can be depreciated only under the straight-line method, unless the Commissioner permits the use of another type.

(3) New residential buildings continue to be eligible for the 200 percent declining-balance and the sum-of-the-years-digits methods.

(4) Used residential buildings having a remaining life of at least twenty years when acquired by a taxpayer may be depreciated under the 125 percent declining-balance method; but, if the remaining life when acquired is less than twenty years, only the straight-line method can be used unless the Commissioner permits otherwise.[36]

8.41   For a building to qualify as a residential building, at least 80 percent of the gross rental income must be rental income from dwelling units. Hotels and motels are not eligible.

EXAMPLE 1   In 1970, a taxpayer placed a newly constructed building in service. The rental income for that year totaled $100,000, consisting of $25,000 from stores and $75,000 from apartments. In 1971, the stores again produced $25,000, but the apartments increased to $100,000. In 1972 a restaurant was opened on the top floor, so that the rental mix became $25,000 from stores, $15,000 from the restaurant, and $100,000 from the apartments. The 80 percent test was met in 1971, but not in 1970 or 1972. Accordingly, the 150 percent declining-balance method can be elected for 1970, and for 1971 a change can be made to the 200 percent declining-balance or sum-of-the-years-digits methods. Then for 1972, the taxpayer must revert to the 150 percent declining-balance method. None of these changes in method is treated as a change in method of accounting.

36. H.R. Rep. 91–782, 91st Cong., 1st sess., 1969, pp. 320–22 (Statement of the Managers on the Part of the House after the Conference Committee agreement).

Assume the same facts as in the preceding example, except that in 1970 EXAMPLE 2 when the building was purchased, it was fifteen years old and had a remaining life of twenty-five years. The taxpayer would be restricted to the straight-line method for 1970 and 1972 but could use the 125 percent declining-balance method for 1971.

Where the taxpayer is the first user, the restrictions of Section 117(j) 8.42 do not apply to new property of which construction was begun before July 25, 1969, or for which a written binding contract was entered into before that date for the construction or permanent financing of any part of it. In other words, property constructed, for example, in 1968 can continue to be depreciated in later years under the 200 percent declining-balance or sum-of-the-years-digits methods. Similarly, the new rules on used property only apply to used buildings acquired on or after July 25, 1969.

Rehabilitation of Housing Property

Capitalizable expenditures made on or after July 25, 1969, and be- 8.43 fore January 1, 1975, to rehabilitate low- and moderate-income rental housing can be depreciated over a period of sixty months using the straight-line method and no salvage value [Section 167(k)]. There is a ceiling and a floor on the amounts that qualify. The aggregate expenditures during this span of years cannot exceed $15,000 for each house or apartment, and more than $3,000 must be spent on the house or apartment in two consecutive years. Hotels and motels are not eligible.

Additional First-Year Depreciation

All taxpayers, except trusts, may elect under Section 179 to write off 8.44 in the year of acquisition 20 percent of the cost of *tangible personal* property that has a useful life of at least six years. The maximum qualifying cost of property (new or used) is limited to $10,000 annually ($20,000 on a joint return). This additional first year "bonus" depreciation is allowed to the taxpayer in the year in which he first places the assets in use and is allowed in addition to regular depreciation computed by any of the methods set forth above. The amount of "bonus depreciation" is a reduction of the basis upon which depreciation is computed under any of the ordinary methods. Salvage value is not considered in applying the 20 percent. But in figuring normal depreciation, the basis must be reduced by both the additional allowance and salvage value (if salvage value is a factor).

On December 1, 1972, G, who uses straight-line depreciation, paid $10,000 EXAMPLE for a machine with a useful life of ten years, and he installed it on that day. Salvage value is estimated to be $1,500. The initial first-year allowance is $2,000 (20 percent of $10,000), despite the fact that the machine was acquired almost at the end of the taxable year. This reduces the basis for normal depreciation to $8,000. Normal straight-line depreciation for a year of twelve months would be $750 [10 percent × $7,500 ($8,000 less $500 salvage value in excess of 10 percent of cost)]. Because only one month remained in the year after installation, the regular straight-line allowable deduction is $\frac{1}{12}$ of $750, or $62.50. The total first-year depreciation is $2,062.50.

Depreciation Accounting

8.45 **Types of Asset Accounts.** A taxpayer can establish as many accounts as he desires to record the cost of depreciable property, and for each account he can use any depreciation method permitted under Section 167. If he sets up a separate account for each asset, these are item accounts. If he combines a number of assets into one account, these are multiple-asset accounts. There are three varieties of the latter. A "group account" is used for assets that are alike, e.g., automobiles. A "classified account" contains assets having a similar use or function, such as machinery and equipment or furniture and fixtures. A "composite account" contains dissimilar assets, such as the entire generating and transmission plant of an electric utility company.

8.46 From the aspect of recording additions and retirements of assets, multiple-asset accounts are of two types: open-end and years-of-acquisition. In an open-end account, all assets—no matter when acquired—are added into one aggregate asset account, and all retirements are cleared out of that aggregate at their unadjusted bases. Under the years-of-acquisition (also called "vintage") method, a subaccount is set up for each year's additions; and, when an asset is retired, its unadjusted basis is credited to the subaccount for the year in which the asset was acquired.

8.47 There is no requirement of consistency between the books and tax returns. The groupings of assets entering into multiple-asset accounts per books frequently differ from the groupings used for tax purposes. This will almost always be true if either the Guideline or the CLADR life system discussed later herein is adopted for tax purposes. Among large taxpayers it is common to keep separate depreciable-property records for tax purposes. One reason is that there will usually be some differences between the cost for financial accounting use and the unadjusted basis for tax purposes. The principal tax requirement applicable to grouping of assets is that there must be at least one separate account for each different depreciation method.[37] For example, an asset depreciated under the straight-line method cannot be combined in the same account with an asset depreciated under a declining-balance method. Further, the grouping principles applied for tax purposes in one year do not bind the taxpayer for assets acquired in subsequent years. In each year, a taxpayer can set up new accounts for new additions, and as to each account elect any depreciation method permitted by Section 167.

37. Reg. 1.167(b)–0(c).

Reserve for Depreciation. The amount of the provision for deprecia- 8.48
tion each year is a debit and a deduction in determining taxable income. The credit can be made directly to the affected asset account,
but now, almost universally the practice is to record the credit in a
reserve-for-depreciation account, sometimes also called "accrued
depreciation" on financial statements. There are no restrictions on
the number of reserve accounts, but the best practice is to have a
separate reserve account for each asset account and subaccount used
for tax purposes.

A reserve for depreciation applicable to a multiple-asset account 8.49
will consist of the accumulated amounts of depreciation claimed over
the years, minus adjustments for retirements and plus adjustments
for salvage.

Composite Rates for Multiple-Asset Accounts. When item accounts 8.50
are used, there will be a separate reserve for depreciation on each
asset. Accordingly, on a sale, exchange, destruction, abandonment,
or scrapping of the asset, it is easy to determine the amount of the
gain or loss. From the money or fair-market value of property received
is subtracted the adjusted basis. And the adjusted basis is the unadjusted basis, usually cost, less the reserve for depreciation.

However, in the case of multiple-asset accounts, the calculation is 8.51
not that simple. In a classified or composite multiple-asset account,
the rate of depreciation applied to the account is derived from the
weighted average of all of the rates applicable to the varying types of
assets in the account.

Assume that a classified account consists of the following: EXAMPLE

ASSET	UNADJUSTED BASIS	STRAIGHT-LINE DEPRECIATION RATE	ANNUAL DEPRECIATION
Lathes	$40,000	8%	$3,200
Milling machines	15,000	20	3,000
Widgets	30,000	5	1,500
Total	$85,000		$7,700

The composite rate of depreciation will be 9 percent ($7,700 ÷ $85,000),
and this rate will be applied to the balance in the account each year until
the mix becomes substantially different and warrants a change in rate. This
composite rate envisages that the average life of the lathes is $12\frac{1}{2}$ years,
milling machines 5 years, and widgets 20 years. The adjusted basis of
any asset in the account is determined by subtracting the accumulated depreciation applicable to it from its unadjusted cost. Such accumulated
depreciation is calculated, not by using the composite rate, but by using the
average rate applicable to the subgroup of which the asset is a part.[38]

38. Reg. 1.167(a)–8(c)(3).

Reverting to the example, suppose that a milling machine that cost $3,000 is sold at the end of 2 years. The accumulated depreciation applicable to it would be $1,200 ($3,000 × 20% × 2), so that the adjusted basis would be $1,800 ($3,000 − $1,200). This is so even though the individual lives of the milling machines ranged from 4 to 6 years, with an average of 5, and this particular machine when acquired had an estimated life of 4 years.[39]

8.52 **Retirements under the Facts and Circumstances and Guideline Life Systems.** The discussion in the following paragraphs 8.53 through 8.64 applies only to the Facts and Circumstances and Guideline life systems. Regulation 1.167(a)–11, concerning the CLADR life system, contains its own definitions of normal and abnormal retirements, together with the tax treatment to be accorded them.

8.53 The opening paragraph of Reg. 1.167(a)–8(a) gives the definition of *retirement* as applied to depreciable property and also an introduction to the tax consequences:

(a) Gains and losses on retirements. For the purposes of this section the term "retirement" means the permanent withdrawal of depreciable property from use in the trade or business or in the production of income. The withdrawal may be made in one of several ways. For example, the withdrawal may be made by selling or exchanging the asset, or by actual abandonment. In addition, the asset may be withdrawn from such productive use without disposition as, for example, by being placed in a supplies or scrap account. The tax consequences of a retirement depend upon the form of the transaction, the reason therefor, the timing of the retirement, the estimated useful life used in computing depreciation, and whether the asset is accounted for in a separate or multiple-asset account. Upon the retirement of assets, the rules in this section apply in determining whether gain or loss will be recognized, the amount of such gain or loss, and the basis for determining gain or loss.

8.54 A retirement means that a depreciable asset has been permanently withdrawn from use in the business. This can happen by reason of a sale, exchange, abandonment, casualty, or scrapping.

8.55 ITEM ACCOUNTS. If an item account is involved, gain or loss will be realized. Ordinarily, it will also be recognized.[40] The account will be closed out, and gain or loss will be reflected in taxable income.

8.56 If there is a disposition of the asset, the gain or loss will be recognized unless one of the nonrecognition sections applies, such as Section 1031, pertaining to the exchange of property held for productive use or investment, or Section 1033, pertaining to involuntary conversions. For details of the various types of nontaxable exchanges, see Chapter 11. Any gain from a taxable sale or exchange of property held for more than six months will be treated as a Section 1231

39. *Ibid.*
40. Reg. 1.167(a)–8(a) and (d).

long-term capital gain, except that the portion of the gain equal to "recaptured depreciation" will be taxed as ordinary income under Sections 1245 and 1250. If a loss results, there is no "recaptured depreciation," and it is an ordinary one to the extent that the aggregate of the gains and losses from the sales or exchanges of depreciable property held for more than six months results in a net loss [Section 1231]. These subjects were touched upon in chapter 2 and are covered more fully in chapter 12.

8.57   If the asset is transferred to a supplies or scrap account and is not physically disposed of, the credit for salvage value, and therefore the basis of that asset in the supplies or scrap account, will be the estimated salvage value or the fair-market value at time of retirement, whichever is greater.[41] The loss will always be an ordinary one and outside the scope of Section 1231, because there is no sale or exchange. If the asset is abandoned, the loss is an ordinary one under the provisions of Section 165 (see chapter 9).

8.58   MULTIPLE-ASSET ACCOUNTS. The rules are different for multiple-asset accounts, and the recognition of gain or loss in taxable income depends first upon whether the retirement is normal or abnormal. Gains and losses on normal retirements are not reflected in taxable income, but instead are recorded in the depreciation reserve. But gains and losses on abnormal retirements do enter into taxable income unless one of the nonrecognition sections of the Code applies.

8.59   *Normal Retirements.* Is there any logic to the rule that losses on normal retirements do not reduce taxable income? To find out, examine the mechanics of a homogeneous group account. In such a group, the rate applied is based upon the average of the estimated lives in the group. When an asset is retired in less than the average number of years but within the span of years used in setting the average, it will not have been fully depreciated. On the other hand, another asset in the group that is retired one or more years after the expiration of the average life will seemingly have been over-depreciated. The deficiency in depreciation allowed on the first asset is made up by the extra depreciation allowed on the second asset. The same results will occur in a heterogeneous classified or composite multiple-asset account. This is the reason that losses on normal retirements are not allowable as deductions in determining taxable income; instead, they are recorded in the depreciation reserve.

EXAMPLE   Assume that four similar machines are all acquired on the same day and that each costs $1,000. Their respective lives are estimated to range from fifteen to twenty-five years, with an average of twenty years. The straight-line rate would then be five percent. One machine is retired at the end of fifteen years, two at the end of twenty years, and the last at the end of twenty-five years. At the end of twenty-five years, the accumulated depreciation for the group will be represented by:

41. Reg. 1.167(a)–8(a)(3).

Machine #1	$ 750
Machine #2 and #3	2,000
Machine #4	1,250
	$4,000

The seeming loss of $250 on the retirement of machine #1 is made up by machine #4 that lasted for twenty-five years.

8.60   If a normal retirement results from a sale, there can be a gain. Unless salvage was disregarded under Section 167(f) because it amounted to less than 10 percent of the unadjusted basis, such a gain ordinarily is caused by a change in price levels, so that the amount realized exceeds the originally estimated salvage. In practice such gains are seldom recognized but instead are credited to the depreciation reserve. Reg. 1.167(a)–8(e)(2) reads as follows:

(2) Where multiple-asset accounts are used and acquisitions and retirements are numerous, if a taxpayer, in order to avoid unnecessarily detailed accounting for individual retirements, consistently follows the practice of charging the reserve with the full cost or other basis of assets retired and of crediting it with all receipts from salvage, the practice may be continued so long as, in the opinion of the Commissioner, it clearly reflects income. Conversely, where the taxpayer customarily follows a practice of reporting all receipts from salvage as ordinary taxable income, such practice may be continued so long as, in the opinion of the Commissioner, it clearly reflects income.

8.61   To reflect a normal retirement, the asset account is credited for the amount of the unadjusted basis of the asset, and the reserve for depreciation is debited in the same amount. Any salvage value, including cash on a sale or other value received on an exchange, is credited to the reserve. The effect, of course, is to reflect gain or loss in the reserve for depreciation.

8.62   *Abnormal Retirements.* All retirements other than normal retirements are abnormal. Regulations 1.167(a)–8(b) defines the concepts as follows:

(b) Definition of normal and abnormal retirements. For the purpose of this section the determination of whether a retirement is normal or abnormal shall be made in the light of all the facts and circumstances. In general, a retirement shall be considered a normal retirement unless the taxpayer can show that the withdrawal of the asset was due to a cause not contemplated in setting the applicable depreciation rate. For example, a retirement is considered normal if made within the range of years taken into consideration in fixing the depreciation rate and if the asset has reached a condition at which, in the normal course of events, the taxpayer customarily retires similar assets from use in his business. On the other hand, a retirement may be abnormal if the asset is withdrawn at an earlier time or under other circumstances, as, for example, when the asset has been damaged by casualty or has lost its usefulness suddenly as the result of extraordinary obsolescence.

Any gain or loss realized on an abnormal retirement is recognized just as and to the same extent as in the case of an item account. See paragraph 8.56 for the recognition of gain or loss and paragraph 8.51 for the manner in which to determine adjusted basis of the asset abnormally retired. 8.63

Averaging Conventions. Under the Facts and Circumstances and Guideline life systems, the period for depreciation of an asset begins when it is placed in service and ends when it is retired. A proportionate part of one year's depreciation is allowable for the part of the first and last years during which the asset was in service. In the case of multiple-asset accounts, it is customary to use an averaging convention. The one most commonly used is described in Reg. 1.167(a)–10(b). As there stated, an assumption is made that all additions and retirements to the asset account occur uniformly throughout the taxable year. Then depreciation is computed on the average of the beginning and ending balances of the asset account for the taxable year. An example of the application of this convention to a years-of-acquisition multiple-asset account, using the straight-line method of depreciation and a rate of 20 percent, follows: 8.64

EXAMPLE

YEARS OF ACQUISI- TION	ASSET BALANCE 1-1-70	1970 ADDITIONS	1970 RETIRE- MENTS	ASSET BALANCE 12-31-70	AVERAGE BALANCE	1970 DEPRECIA- TION
1968	$50,000	$ —	$4,000	$46,000	$48,000	$ 9,600
1969	14,000	—	2,000	12,000	13,000	2,600
1970	—	12,000	1,000	11,000	5,500	1,100
Totals	$64,000	$12,000	$7,000	$69,000	$66,500	$13,300

Use of an averaging convention is not appropriate when there is an unusual and major addition or retirement early or late in the year. In such event, depreciation should be separately calculated on the unusual item for the part of the year during which it was in service.[41A]

Useful Life Systems

Facts and Circumstances. The following definition of useful life appears in Reg. 1.167(a)–1(b) and applies primarily to the Facts and Circumstances life system: 8.65

> For the purpose of section 167 the estimated useful life of an asset is not necessarily the useful life inherent in the asset but is the period over which the asset may reasonably be expected to be useful to the taxpayer in his

41A. Rev. Rul. 73–202.

trade or business or in the production of his income. This period shall be determined by reference to his experience with similar property taking into account present conditions and probable future developments. Some of the factors to be considered in determining this period are (1) wear and tear and decay or decline from natural causes, (2) the normal progress of the art, economic changes, inventions, and current developments within the industry and the taxpayer's trade or business, (3) the climatic and other local conditions peculiar to the taxpayer's trade or business, and (4) the taxpayer's policy as to repairs, renewals, and replacements. Salvage value is not a factor for the purpose of determining useful life. If the taxpayer's experience is inadequate, the general experience in the industry may be used until such time as the taxpayer's own experience forms an adequate basis for making the determination. The estimated remaining useful life may be subject to modification by reason of conditions known to exist at the end of the taxable year and shall be redetermined when necessary regardless of the method of computing depreciation. *However, estimated remaining useful life shall be redetermined only when the change in the useful life is significant and there is a clear and convincing basis for the redetermination.* . . . [Emphasis supplied.]

8.66   Under the Facts and Circumstances life system, the taxpayer selects a life for an account and then upon examination of the return has the burden of proving that the estimated life is correct. Today there is a tendency on the part of revenue agents, when examining accounts containing pre-1971 assets, to assert that the shortest proper life is the life set forth in Rev. Proc. 62–21. That ruling established the Guideline life system.

8.67   It is possible for the taxpayer and the Commissioner to agree, in writing, upon the useful life and the correlative rates of depreciation of property [Sec. 167(d)]. The rate agreed upon is binding in the absence of factors that arise later to indicate need of modification. Entering into such agreements is a rarity.

8.68   **Guideline Life System for Pre-1971 Assets – TAXABLE YEARS 1962 THROUGH 1970.** In 1920, the Service issued Bulletin F, setting forth lives of categories of depreciable property based on statistical studies made by it. This bulletin was updated a few times; but long before 1962, it had become obsolete. In 1962, Revenue Procedure 62–21[42] was issued, setting forth guideline lives for approximately seventy-five broad classes of multiple-asset accounts, in place of the method in the old Bulletin F that assigned lives to depreciable assets on an item-by-item basis (over 5,000 in total). In many cases, a taxpayer may use only three or four classes to compute depreciation for all of his assets.

8.69   In 1962, the Treasury Department, in a number of press and information releases, announced that the guideline lives were materially shorter than those in use by most companies. That statement was true; but a few companies, even after rigorous examinations by

42. 1962–2 C.B. 418.

revenue agents, were (and still are) using shorter ones. The use of the procedure and lives is purely elective. In fact, a taxpayer can adopt the mechanical procedures, including the *grouping* of assets into the specified classes of multiple-asset accounts, and yet claim shorter or longer lives than those set forth in the procedure.

Revenue Proc. 62–21 was issued July 11, 1962, and could be used in tax returns due on or after July 12, 1962, including extensions of time. Treasury Release No. I.R.–517 of July 11, 1962, contained the statement: "Any taxpayer who wishes to use the new guideline lives—or a life longer than the guidelines—may do so initially as a matter of right and without question by the Internal Revenue Service for a period of three years." Because so many calendar-year corporations secure extensions of time for filing, the procedure could have been used by quite a number in their 1961 returns. Actually it was not. By far the greatest proportion of corporations that elected to change to the new guideline procedures and lives did so for the first time in their 1962 returns due in 1963—some switched later. In fact, upon examination of any return for the years 1962 through 1970, the taxpayer has a right to elect for the first time to change from the Facts and Circumstances life system to the Guideline Procedure of Rev. Proc. 62–21.

8.70

The Guideline life system applies only to assets acquired in 1970 and all prior taxable years. For taxable years starting no earlier than 1961 and continuing through 1970, the system is embodied in Rev. Proc. 62–21. For taxable years starting with 1971, Rev. Proc. 62–21 is not applicable; however, the Guideline life system is optionally available or can be continued under Reg. 1.167(a)–12, but only as to assets acquired in 1970 and prior years.

8.71

An election is made by guideline classes. A taxpayer may choose to apply the Guideline life system to one or more guideline classes and to have the rest of his assets examined under the Facts and Circumstances life system. But he may *not* have the guidelines apply to only part of the assets in a guideline class.

8.72

Under the procedure, all assets in item or multiple-asset accounts must be grouped into the applicable guideline classes. This can be done by means of tax working papers or permanent records. The financial accounting records and groupings can be and usually are different.

8.73

The classes are contained within four categories called groups. Group One contains the assets common to all types of industries. Group Two contains the classes of assets pertaining to nonmanufacturing activities, excluding transportation, communications, and public utilities. Group Three pertains to manufacturing. Group Four contains the guideline lives for the transportation, communication, and public utility industries.

8.74

The description of the classes in Group One and their respective guideline lives are:

8.75

CLASS		YEARS
1. Office furniture, fixtures, machines, and equipment		10
2. Transportation equipment		
(a) Aircraft (air frames and engines, except aircraft of air transport companies)		6
(b) Automobiles, including taxis		3
(c) Buses		9
(d) General-purpose trucks —		
Light		4
Heavy		6
(e) Railroad cars (except cars of railroad companies)		15
(f) Tractor units (over the road)		4
(g) Trailers and trailer-mounted containers		6
(h) Vessels, barges, and tugs		18
3. Land improvements		20
4. Buildings (13 subclasses of types of buildings)		40 to 60
5. Subsidiary assets (includes jigs, dies, molds, patterns, returnable containers, pallets, crockery, glassware, and linens) — lives determined by facts and circumstances		

8.76   In Group Three, pertaining to manufacturing, there is a single guideline class and life for each type of industry. All depreciable property of a company in that industry, unless it is covered by another guideline class, such as office furniture and fixtures, is included. For example, the class life for the lumber, wood products, and furniture manufacturing industry is ten years. Assume that the classified accounts per books for production machinery of a company in that industry show the following amounts:

ACCOUNTS	ORIGINAL COST	LIFE USED IN YEARS	DEPRECIATION RATE	ANNUAL STRAIGHT-LINE DEPRECIATION
A machines	$120,000	12	8-1/3%	$10,000
B machines	100,000	8	12-1/2	12,500
C machines	200,000	20	5	10,000
	$420,000			$32,500

The weighted-average depreciable life per books for the three accounts is 12.8 years ($420,000 ÷ $32,500). However, the composite guideline life for this class is only 10 years. To adopt that life for tax purposes (it need not also be used on the books), the company has two choices: It can use a 10-year life for each account, or it can change the lives of the respective accounts in order to achieve a weighted-average life of 10 years. One such shift might be:

ACCOUNTS	ORIGINAL COST	LIFE USED IN YEARS	DEPRECIATION RATE	ANNUAL STRAIGHT-LINE DEPRECIATION
A machines	$120,000	8	12-1/2%	$15,000
B machines	100,000	8	12-1/2	12,500
C machines	200,000	14	7-7/10	14,280
	$420,000			$41,780

If, at the time of the adoption of the guideline lives, the company was using the 200 percent declining-balance method on the A machines, it would continue to use that method and apply a rate of 25 percent to the depreciated balance at the beginning of the year.

The Guideline Procedure speaks of "lives"—useful lives, guideline lives, and class lives. The lives given allow for salvage. Consequently, in depreciation computations, the lives may be directly converted into rates, and no adjustment for salvage is necessary.

The Revenue Procedure applies only to taxpayers using orthodox methods of depreciation measured by estimated useful lives—straight-line, declining-balance, and sum-of-the-years-digits. It has no application to any of the unusual methods, such as machine-hour or unit of production.

Upon adopting the Guideline Procedure in 1962, many taxpayers set up an open-end multiple-asset account and added to it fully depreciated assets that were still in use. As a result and because of the mathematics involved, extraordinarily large deductions for depreciation were obtained under the straight-line and sum-of-the-years-digits methods. Accordingly, Rev. Proc. 65–13 was issued in 1965. Under that Procedure, starting in that year, the Guideline Procedure cannot be used for any open-end multiple-asset account to which current additions are added if the account is being depreciated under either the straight-line or sum-of-the-years-digits method. It can be used if 1965 and subsequent years' additions are recorded in years-of-acquisition accounts or are depreciated as item accounts. Open-end multiple-asset accounts can continue to be used under the double declining-balance method.

Reserve Ratio Test. Revenue Procedure 62–21, which is applicable to taxable years ending no later than December 31, 1970, provides for a reserve ratio test. This is a device used to determine whether a taxpayer's retirement and replacement practices justify his continued use of the guideline lives. Generally speaking and subject to certain transitional and "trending" rules, if the test is not met, the lives will be lengthened. The "reserve ratio" is the ratio of the total of the depreciation reserves for the assets in any guideline class to the aggregate bases of those assets. For example, if the original cost of assets in a guideline class is $200,000 and the total of the reserves for depreciation is $100,000, the reserve ratio is 50 percent ($100,000 ÷ $200,000).

The reserve ratio will vary depending upon the rate of growth in dollars of assets in an account and the method of depreciation used. In a mature and stabilized account of large size, new assets will be added only to replace old ones retired. Under the straight-line method of depreciation, the proper ratio will approximate 50 percent. Under the 200 percent declining-balance method, the theoretically appropriate ratio will be about 67 percent; and, under the sum-of-the-years-digits method, the ratio will be around 70 percent.

In a growing account, a majority of the assets will be newer and not yet half-depreciated. The reserve ratio, therefore, will be less than for

Depreciable and Depletable Property

8.77

8.78

8.79

8.80

8.81

8.82

a mature account. The converse will be true of a shrinking account, so that there the ratio will be higher.

8.83   There are two optional variations of the reserve ratio test. One is called the tabular form and is set forth in Rev. Proc. 62–21. The other is called the guideline form and is described in Rev. Proc. 65–13. In each ruling there are tables showing appropriate ranges in reserve ratios based upon the method of depreciation used, length of lives, and rate of growth of assets. The reserve ratio test is met if the taxpayer's actual reserve ratio is not higher than the applicable reserve ratio upper limit.

8.84   TAXABLE YEARS ENDING IN 1971 OR LATER. It was announced by the Treasury Department on January 11, 1971, that the reserve ratio test prescribed in Rev. Proc. 62–21 (as amended and supplemented), pertaining to depreciation guidelines and rates, would be eliminated for taxable years ended after December 31, 1970:

Thus, a taxpayer who has elected to be examined under Rev. Proc. 62–21 and has satisfied the reserve ratio test for taxable years ending before January 1, 1971, may continue to use the prescribed guideline lives for all subsequent years without application of the reserve ratio test. Where such guideline lives test is satisfied, the taxpayer's depreciation deduction for the assets in that guideline class will not be disturbed. Where a taxpayer has so elected but has not satisfied the reserve ratio test for all such years, adjustments may be made to asset lives as provided in Rev. Proc. 62–21 for taxable years up to and including the taxpayer's last taxable year ending before January 1, 1971. The life as so adjusted for the last taxable year ending before January 1, 1971, will be used for subsequent years, but no further adjustments may be made by application of the reserve ratio test for any subsequent taxable year.

The elimination of the reserve ratio test for years ending after December 31, 1970, was accomplished by Reg. 1.167(a)–12.

8.85   This new regulation, applicable only to assets placed in service before January 1, 1971, and only to taxable years ending after December 31, 1970, also:

1. Permits taxpayers who have adopted the Guideline Procedure of Rev. Proc. 62–21 in a prior taxable year to continue that system without the necessity of changing or regrouping their depreciation accounts; and
2. Permits taxpayers to adopt for the first time the Guideline life system for one or more classes of assets.[43]

The election is an annual one for each designated guideline class and is made in the income tax return for the taxable year. In other words,

43. Rev. Proc. 62–21, Part II, Sec. 1, and Reg. 1.167(a)–12(f) as proposed April 22, 1972.

with respect to the multiple-asset accounts in a guideline class containing only pre-1971 assets, the election for the class can be made for 1971; the Facts and Circumstances system can be used for 1972, and then the Guideline system again used in 1973.

8.86   The guideline classes are the same as those in Rev. Proc. 72–10, issued February 22, 1972, to implement the CLADR system. Further, the classes listed in Rev. Proc. 72–10 are substantially the same as the classes described in Rev. Proc. 62–21 as amended and supplemented. The lives to be used for each class are those set forth in Rev. Proc. 72–10, but without any 20 percent range above or below. However, if for the last taxable year ending before January 1, 1971, the taxpayer was able to justify a shorter life under the reserve ratio test of Rev. Proc. 62–21, then such shorter life may be used in 1971 and subsequent years.

Class Life Asset Depreciation Range System

8.87   HISTORY. Because of dissatisfaction with the Guideline life system of Rev. Proc. 62–21, and particularly its reserve ratio test, a new system of useful life depreciation was designed in 1971 to cover assets placed in service in 1971 or later, but not earlier. It was called the Asset Depreciation Range (ADR) System and did not require a reserve ratio test. The outlines of the new system were announced by President Nixon and the Treasury Department on January 11, 1971,[44] and proposed regulations were published on March 13, 1971. The regulations became final on June 23, 1971, and were numbered Section 1.167(a)–11. About the same time, they were amplified by Rev. Proc. 71–25.

8.88   Once the ADR system became official on June 23, 1971, a taxpayer had his choice of three systems of useful lives with respect to assets placed in service on or after January 1, 1971: the ADR system of Reg. 1.167(a)–11 and Rev. Proc. 71–25, the guideline lives of Rev. Proc. 62–21, and the actual life of property to the taxpayer as determined on the basis of his own facts and circumstances. Once he selected the life system, then the taxpayer, subject to any applicable limitation, could choose the desired method—declining-balance, sum-of-the-years-digits, or straight-line, and the desired types of accounts—item or multiple-asset.

8.89   The Asset Depreciation Range System represented a modification of the Guideline system. Under ADR, only machinery and equipment were eligible; buildings were not. Otherwise the industry groupings and classes within industries were substantially the same. Also, the "asset guideline period" for each class under ADR was identical with the life in years assigned by Rev. Proc. 62–21; but in Rev. Proc. 71–25 pertaining to ADR, there was assigned to each class of assets

---

44. Reproduced as part of Extra Edition No. 4, dated January 12, 1971, of the CCH Standard Federal Tax Reporter.

not only the asset guideline period but also a range from 20 percent below to 20 percent above such period. Within that range, the taxpayer could select for each vintage account within each class any desired life in years. There would never be a reserve ratio test that could cause a lengthening of life, but no account could be depreciated below salvage value (after ignoring the first 10 percent of basis as permitted by Section 167[f]).

8.90   Another principal feature of ADR was a provision allowing a mathematically determined amount of maintenance, repairs, and alterations to be deducted currently as repairs. There were also other provisions, designed to minimize disputes between the Service and taxpayers on salvage value and the mechanics of calculations.

8.91   As stated in Paragraph 8.69, the guideline lives of Rev. Proc. 62–21 were materially shorter than those in use in 1962 by most companies. A Senate Finance Committee Report stated:

> The lives selected for use under the guidelines were determined by reference to the useful lives claimed by the taxpayers surveyed and generally the lives selected were the useful lives equal to the lives being claimed by the taxpayers at the 30th percentile—that is, 29 percent of the assets had shorter lives and 70 percent had longer lives.[45]

With the advent of ADR, these lives were permitted to be shortened by another 20 percent. Such magnanimity on the part of the Treasury Department proved to be too much for some people.

8.92   At the time of the public hearings on the ADR regulations, then in proposed form, a number of attorneys questioned the authority of the Treasury Department by administrative action to prescribe such short useful lives. As soon as the regulations became final, a number of lawsuits were filed to have them declared invalid. The Internal Revenue Service responded in part in August, 1971, by publishing its position paper as Announcement 71–76.[46] It reviewed the history of the depreciation provisions of the taxing statutes and their regulations, explained the reasons for adoption of the ADR system, and argued that legal authorities supported its adoption.

8.93   Congress also took note of the legal controversy. As a result, when considering the bill which became the Revenue Act of 1971, it inquired into the merits of the new system and with only minor changes approved it in Section 109 of that Revenue Act. However, in the process, the Congress did give the system a new name: Class Life Asset Depreciation Range System. This new system for determining lives replaces both the original ADR system and the guideline lives procedure as to assets placed in service in 1971 or later.

8.94   ENACTMENT OF THE CLADR SYSTEM. As previously mentioned, Reg. 1.167(a)–11 adopted June 23, 1971, set forth all of the rules per-

45. S. Rep. 92–437, 92nd Cong., 1st sess., 1971, p. 46.
46. 1971–34 I.R.B. (8–23–71) p. 29; 1971 CCH Standard Federal Tax Reporter, P6738;; 1971 P-H Federal Taxes, ¶55,456.

taining to the Asset Depreciation Range System. The enactment of Section 109 of the Revenue Act of 1971 made changes necessary, although, for the most part, they were not major ones. The amendments to this section of the regulations were adopted by T.D. 7272 on April 20, 1973. The amended regulation applies to all eligible assets placed in service on or after January 1, 1971, and the original form of Regulation 1.167(a)–11, adopted by T.D. 7128 on June 23, 1971, has been superseded *ab initio*. As also previously mentioned, the original form of Reg. 1.167(a)–11 was supplemented by Rev. Proc. 71–25. That Revenue Procedure was superseded by Rev. Proc. 72–10, and, in turn, was supplemented by Rev. Proc. 73–2 and 73–8.

8.95 The first step in the implementation of the CLADR system was the publication on January 28, 1972, of T.D. 7159. This Treasury Decision contained temporary regulations on elections to use the Class Life ADR System. Generally speaking, elections filed before February 1, 1972, to use the superseded ADR system were to be treated as elections to use the Class Life ADR System. And elections filed after January 31, 1972, but before the amendments to Reg. 1.167(a)–11 became final, are to be made in accordance with such proposed amendments.

8.96 SUMMARY OF THE CLADR SYSTEM. A summary of the Class Life Asset Depreciation Range System appears in amended Reg. 1.167(a)–11(a)–(1):

This section provides an asset depreciation range and class life system for determining the reasonable allowance for depreciation of designated classes of assets placed in service after December 31, 1970. The system is designed to minimize disputes between taxpayers and the Internal Revenue Service as to the useful life of property, and as to salvage value, repairs, and other matters. The system is optional with the taxpayer. The taxpayer has an annual election. Generally, an election for a taxable year must apply to all additions of eligible property during the taxable year of election, but does not apply to additions of eligible property in any other taxable year. The taxpayer's election, made with the return for the taxable year, may not be revoked or modified for any property included in the election. Generally, the taxpayer must establish vintage accounts for all eligible property included in the election, must determine the allowance for depreciation of such property in the taxable year of election, and in subsequent taxable years, on the basis of the asset depreciation period specified in the election, and must apply the first-year convention specified in the election to determine the allowance for depreciation of such property. This section also contains special provisions for the treatment of salvage value, retirements, and the costs of the repair, maintenance, rehabilitation or improvement of property. In general, a taxpayer may not apply any provision of this section unless he makes an election and thereby consents to, and agrees to apply, all the provisions of this section. A taxpayer who elects to apply this section does, however, have certain options as to the application of specified provisions of this section. A taxpayer may elect to apply this section for a taxable year only if for such taxable year he complies with the reporting requirements of paragraph (f) (4) of this section.

8.97   For assets placed in service in 1971 or later, a taxpayer has his choice of two options in determining useful life—the Class Life ADR System or the general rules using estimated life based on facts and circumstances (the Facts and Circumstances life system).

8.98   DEFINITIONS. Some new terms are coined in amended Reg. 1.167(a)–11(b)(4):

> *Asset guideline class*—A category of assets for which a separate asset guideline period is set forth in Rev. Proc. 72–10 or a supplement to it.
> *Asset guideline period*—The class life in years designated in Rev. Proc. 72–10 for each asset guideline class. Initially, these periods were the same as those specified in the guideline life Rev. Proc. 62–21.
> *Asset depreciation range*—A period of years which extends from 80 percent of the asset guideline period to 120 percent of such period, determined in each case by rounding any fractional part of a year to the nearer of the nearest whole or half year.
> *Asset depreciation period*—The period selected by the taxpayer from the asset depreciation range or, if no asset depreciation range is in effect for the class, the asset guideline period.
> *Vintage account*—An item or closed-end multiple-asset account containing only property first placed in service during the same taxable year.

8.99   ELIGIBLE PROPERTY. With but few exceptions, all depreciable tangible property, both new and used, is eligible for the Class Life Asset Depreciation Range System.[47] The exceptions are for mandatory exclusions and optional exclusions.

8.100   *Mandatory Exclusions.* The following types of property are are not eligible for the CLADR System:

1. Intangibles, including patents, copyrights, and franchises.
2. Property amortized under special sections. If the taxpayer has elected to depreciate or amortize property in accordance with certain special sections of the Internal Revenue Code, then such property is not included in the CLADR election. These Sections are 167(k), rehabilitation of low-income housing; 169, pollution-control facilities; 184, railroad rolling stock; 185, railway grading and tunnels; 187, coal-mining safety equipment; 188, on-the-job training and child care facilities; and Reg. 1.162–11(b), leasehold improvements.[48]
3. Property depreciated under special methods. If any otherwise eligible property is depreciated under the unit-of-production, retirement, machine-hour, or sinking-fund method, then such property must be excluded from the CLADR System unless such unusual method is applied to at least 75% of the unadjusted basis of all eligible property in all vintage accounts of the same asset guideline class.[49]
4. Pre-1971 property involved in a mere change of form of conducting business. Property placed in service after December 31, 1970, by a

47. Reg. 1.167(a)–11(b)(2).
48. Amended Reg. 1.167(a)–11(b)(5)(v)(b).
49. This is an interpretation of ambiguous language contained in amended Reg. 1.167(a)–11(b)(5)(v)(a) and Reg. 1.167(a)–11(b)(4)(iii)(d).

transferee is not eligible for CLADR if the transferor placed the property in service prior to January 1, 1971, and the transfer is considered a mere change in the form of conducting a trade or business. The transfer is a mere change in form if (a) the basis of the transferred property carries over in whole or in part from the transferor to the transferee, *or* (b) the transferor retains a substantial interest in such trade or business. This includes the retention of a substantial interest by the partners, beneficiaries, or shareholders if the transferor is a partnership, estate, trust or corporation. It also includes transfers between corporations in an affiliated group. The interest retained by the transferor is considered substantial if it is substantial in relation to the total interest of all persons in the trade or business.[50]

Depreciable
and
Depletable
Property

Optional Exclusions. At his option, a taxpayer may exclude certain other types of property:

8.101

1. Special 10% used-property rule. The CLADR election includes all eligible property, whether new or used. Further, all such property also fits within the definitions of Section 1245 property and Section 1250 property.

   The term "Section 1245 property" is defined in Section 1245(a)(3) and consists of (a) depreciable personal property, (b) depreciable tangible real property which is used as an integral part of manufacturing, production, or extraction, or of furnishing transportation, communications, electrical energy, gas, water, or sewage disposal services, or which constitutes a research or storage facility used in connection with any of these activities, (c) an elevator or escalator, or (d) so much of any other real property which is a pollution control facility, railroad grading, railroad tunnel bore, on-the-job training facility, or a child-care facility and which has been amortized under Sections 169, 185, or 188. "Section 1250 property" consists of all other depreciable real property. A simple way to remember what these two broad categories of property cover is to think of Section 1245 property as meaning machinery and grain storage bins and to think of Section 1250 property as meaning factory and apartment buildings. The two sections were originally inserted in the Code so as to treat at least a portion of a gain on the sale of depreciable property as a recapture of depreciation and, accordingly, ordinary income. That subject is covered starting with paragraph 12.113.

   At present, under Rev. Proc. 72–10 there is no specific used-property asset guideline class. So long as that condition continues, then as to all used Section 1245 property additions, there is an option to exclude all of them provided that the unadjusted basis of used Section 1245 property additions exceeds 10 percent of the unadjusted basis of both new and used Section 1245 property additions.[51] A similar option is granted with respect to used Section 1250 property.[52]

   Used property may not be placed in the same vintage account as new property; and Section 1245 property may not be combined with Section 1250 property in the same vintage account.[53]

50. Amended Reg. 1.167(a)–11(b)(7).
51. Amended Reg. 1.167(a)–11(b)(5)(iii).
52. *Ibid.*
53. Amended Reg. 1.167(a)–11(b)(3)(ii).

2. Property subject to investment credit. The taxpayer may elect to exclude from the CLADR election any pre-termination property (defined in paragraph 8.165 which qualifies for the investment tax credit under the transitional or replacement rules of the Tax Reform Act of 1969,[54] discussed in paragraphs 8.165–8.167. However, a taxpayer has no such election as to investment credit property qualifying under Section 50 and, in general, acquired after August 15, 1971. Such property must be included in an election to use CLADR.

3. Public utility property. Public utility property that would otherwise be eligible property may not be included within the CLADR election unless the taxpayer meets certain requirements relating to normalization of the tax deferral for both rate making and financial reporting.[55]

4. Buildings and other Section 1250 property. Buildings and other Section 1250 property were excluded from the original ADR system, but are included in the Class Life ADR System and also were included in the guideline procedure. In Rev. Proc. 72–10, asset guideline periods are assigned to buildings, and the periods vary by the type of building. However, no 20 percent range above or below the period is provided for. The periods assigned in Rev. Proc. 72–10 are the same as in the Guideline Procedure and have generally been considered by taxpayers to be too long. The Treasury Department has been asked by the Congress to restudy the lives before December 31, 1973, to see if they can be shortened. In the interim, there is a transitional rule. The taxpayer can elect to exclude one or more buildings or other items of Section 1250 property placed in service between January 1, 1971, and December 31, 1973, provided that he can justify a life shorter than the guideline period assigned.[56]

5. Subsidiary assets. The term "subsidiary assets" includes jigs, dies, molds, returnable containers, glassware, silverware, and textile-mill cam assemblies. Such assets placed in service between January 1, 1971, and December 31, 1973 (or such earlier date on which a class life for subsidiary assets is prescribed), may be excluded from an asset guideline class provided these assets constitute a significant portion (3 percent or more) of the class.

8.102   ELECTION. The Class Life ADR System is elective. The election is an annual one and is made by filling in and attaching Form 4832 to the return for the year. Once made for a particular year, it cannot be changed, but there is a new and separate election for assets acquired in a later year even though such assets may be in the same guideline class.

8.103   If an election is made, it applies to all eligible assets placed in service during the year. The system cannot be elected only for some classes of assets and not others.

8.104   RECORD-KEEPING REQUIREMENTS. The records required to be maintained by the taxpayer as a part of the CLADR system are extensive and complex. In most cases, the election will require a

54. Amended Reg. 1.167(a)–11(b)(5)(iv).
55. Amended Reg. 1.167(a)–11(b)(6).
56. Amended Reg. 1.167(a)–11(b)(5)(vi).

review and possible revision of the taxpayer's accounting system for depreciable assets.

For each year or "vintage" for which the election is made, separate vintage accounts must be established for each different asset guideline class. Separate vintage accounts must also be established to segregate (1) different methods of depreciation, (2) different depreciable lives, (3) new assets, (4) used assets, (5) real property, (6) personal property, (7) livestock, and (8) property for which the taxpayer has elected the special 20 percent bonus depreciation in the year of acquisition. The taxpayer may establish any number of additional accounts within each classification. *These vintage accounts must maintain their identity until the last asset in the account is retired.*   8.105

After the accounts have been established, all calculations and records pertaining to assets subject to the CLADR system must be reflected on a vintage account basis. The items which must be maintained on a vintage account basis include the following: 8.106

1. Retirements
2. Depreciation expense
3. Reserve for depreciation
4. Salvage (original estimate and adjustments)

In addition, the taxpayer must establish the accounts necessary to accumulate the costs which qualify for the repair allowance by asset guideline class.   8.107

COMPUTATION OF ALLOWABLE DEPRECIATION

Methods of Depreciation. The straight-line method (SL), a declining-balance method (DB), or the sum-of-the-years-digits method (SYD) may be elected for those accounts containing qualified assets. The SYD method of depreciation will be less complicated and more beneficial under the Class Life ADR System. The assets will be depreciated under the SYD method by simply applying the appropriate SYD fraction to the unadjusted cost of assets in the vintage account (which is not reduced by normal retirements or salvage).   8.108

Changes in Methods of Depreciation. Any vintage account may be changed from the sum-of-the-years-digits or declining-balance method to the straight-line method. Also, any vintage account may be changed from a declining-balance method to the sum-of-the-years-digits method. These changes may be accomplished as of the beginning of any year without permission of the Internal Revenue Service.   8.109

Selection of Asset Depreciation Period. An asset depreciation period must be chosen for each vintage account from a range of 20 percent below to 20 percent above the current asset guideline period. Any fractions are rounded to the nearest whole or half year. Property must be classified in the asset guideline class for the activity in which the property is primarily used, even though that activity may be insubstantial in relation to all the taxpayer's activities. A subsequent change in primary purpose will not require the reclassification of the asset or a revision in depreciation period.   8.110

8.111   The asset guideline classes, periods, and depreciation ranges which are in effect on the last day of the taxable year of each year of election apply for all vintage accounts established during the taxable year. However, if the asset guideline period is changed during a year, by the IRS issuing an amendment to Rev. Proc. 72–10, the lower limit of the asset depreciation range for the class of assets cannot be longer than that which was in effect on the first day of the taxable year. Thus, for planning purposes, taxpayers may rely on asset guideline periods in effect at the beginning of the year. Once a depreciation period is selected, it is binding on both the taxpayer and the Internal Revenue Service.

8.112   *Leased Property.* The asset depreciation range and asset depreciation period for eligible property subject to a lease is to be determined without regard to the lease period. The appropriate asset guideline class will be determined by the primary use of the property by the lessee unless there is an asset guideline class in effect for the lessors of such property.

8.113   DEPRECIABLE BASES. The depreciation rate based on the useful life chosen for each account is applied to the original cost of the assets included in the vintage account (unadjusted basis) for straight-line and sum-of-the-years-digits accounts. The rate is applied to the adjusted basis of the account (original cost less accumulated reserve) for declining-balance accounts. While estimated salvage does not reduce the basis for depreciation under SL, SYD, or DB, no vintage account can be depreciated below estimated salvage. *Normal retirements will not reduce basis for the determination of SL and SYD depreciation.* The DB basis for depreciation will be reduced only to the extent of salvage realized on normal retirements.

8.114   AVERAGING CONVENTIONS. If the Class Life ADR System is elected, the taxpayer must choose between two averaging conventions for the determination of allowable depreciation of additions and extraordinary retirements. The taxpayer may choose only one of these conventions for all eligible property for which the Class Life ADR is elected in any vintage year. The convention elected will apply to extraordinary retirements from the particular vintage account. A different convention may be elected for each vintage year.

8.115   *Half-Year Convention.* Under the half-year convention, all property placed in service during the year is treated for depreciation purposes as being placed in service on the first day of the second half of the taxable year. Within certain limitations, this convention existed under previous regulations.

8.116   *Modified Half-Year Convention.* Under the modified half-year convention:

All property which is placed in service during the first half of the taxable year is treated as being placed in service on the first day of the taxable year, and

All property which is placed in service during the second half of the taxable year is treated as being placed in service on the first day of the succeeding taxable year.

This allows a full year's depreciation for assets placed in service during the first half of the year but no depreciation for assets placed in service during the last half of the year.

SALVAGE AND REMOVAL COSTS. The taxpayer must estimate 8.117 the salvage value for each vintage account based on facts and circumstances existing at the close of the year in which the account is established. This estimate is made at the time of the election of CLADR and is included as a part thereof. A vintage account cannot be depreciated below estimated salvage value. For this purpose, "salvage value" is defined as gross salvage value less any reduction elected under Sec. 167(f). Section 167(f) provides that the estimated gross salvage may be reduced by an amount not in excess of 10 percent of the cost of the assets if the assets are personal property (other than livestock) with a life of three years or more. Salvage value is not reduced for either removal or dismantling costs.

Binding Nature of Taxpayer's Estimate. The Internal Reve- 8.118 nue Service is bound to accept the taxpayer's estimated salvage value unless there is a "determination of salvage" for an account which exceeds the original estimate by more than 10 percent of the original cost of the assets in the account. The salvage value may not be redetermined merely because of fluctuations in price levels or as a result of facts and circumstances occurring after the close of the taxable year of election. The taxpayer's estimate of salvage must give adequate consideration to the customary timing of retirements and the condition of the assets at that time.

The regulations also state that if the taxpayer follows a practice of 8.119 consistently understating estimated salvage value to take advantage of the CLADR system, an adjustment will be made to the taxpayer's estimate of salvage even if such adjustment is less than 10 percent.

Adjustment of Salvage for Retirements. Salvage originally 8.120 estimated for a vintage account may be reduced to reflect the effect of retirements under various acceptable methods detailed in the regulations.

Reusable Material. Reusable materials resulting from nor- 8.121 mal retirements may be priced based on any reasonable method consistently applied. However, the value so determined may not exceed the original cost of the asset. The amount determined is credited to the depreciation reserve account and becomes the tax basis of the reusable material. Alternatively, reusable material can be consistently valued at zero. No entry would be made to the reserve account and no basis would be allocated to the reusable materials.

Deduction for Dismantling Costs. The costs of dismantling, 8.122 removing, or demolishing an asset are deductible from gross income in the year paid or incurred and are not charged to the reserve for depreciation.

REPAIRS AND IMPROVEMENTS. In general, expenditures that 8.123 substantially prolong the life of an asset, or increase its value, or adapt it to a different use are capital expenditures. Since many expenditures have characteristics common to both capital expenditures and current expenses, it is often difficult to determine to which category a particular expenditure should be charged. The CLADR system includes an election to use an objective procedure for determining whether these expenditures should be treated as deductible expenses or capital expenditures.

8.124   The new election is available only for expenditures which contain elements of both capitalizable improvements and repairs. It is not available for expenditures which are predominantly capital in nature. These expenditures are called "excluded additions." An "excluded addition" is defined as:

1. An expenditure for an additional identifiable unit of property,
2. An expenditure increasing the productivity or capacity of an existing identifiable unit of property by more than 25 percent of its productivity or capacity when first acquired by the taxpayer, or
3. An expenditure which modifies an existing identifiable unit of property for a substantially different use.

Excluded additions are added to the appropriate vintage account and recovered through depreciation.

8.125   *Repair Allowance and Election.* Expenditures that are clearly repairs and expenditures that have characteristics of both repairs and improvements are lumped together in figuring the repair allowance.

8.126   The repair allowance under CLADR is called the "asset guideline class repair allowance." The annual repair allowance is determined independently for each asset guideline class. The repair allowance is equal to the average unadjusted basis of "repair allowance property" multiplied by the "repair allowance percentage" for the particular asset guideline class.

8.127   "Repair allowance property" generally includes all assets in a guideline class whether placed in service before or after 1970, and whether or not in 1971 and each of the subsequent years CLADR was elected. In other words, to use this election of asset guideline class repair allowance, it is necessary to go back to the inception of the business and to categorize all of the assets still in existence into one of the guideline classes. All retirements are excluded from "repair allowance property" even though normal retirements do not reduce CLADR vintage accounts for purposes of computing depreciation.

8.128   The "repair allowance percentages" are set out in Rev. Proc. 72–10 in tabular form for each asset guideline class. For example, for companies engaged in the manufacture of lumber, wood products, and furniture, the asset guideline class is No. 24.4, the asset guideline period is 10 years, the asset depreciation range is from 8 to 12 years, and the "annual asset guideline repair allowance percentage" is 6.5 percent. The percentage of 6.5 percent is applied to the average of the cost (unadjusted basis) of all the property in the guideline class at the beginning and the end of the year. If the average cost of assets in the class is $100,000, the repair allowance is $6,500. That is the maximum deduction. If the expenditures totaled $4,000, only $4,000 could be deducted.

If the taxpayer elects the repair allowance, all eligible expenditures applicable to a particular asset guideline class, not in excess of the repair allowance for that particular class, may be deducted currently. Any expenditures in excess of the amount of the repair allowance are considered a "property improvement" and added to a "special basis vintage account," the cost of which is recovered through depreciation.   8.129

In a year for which the CLADR system is elected, the taxpayer may elect to apply the repair allowance rules to expenses incurred in that year. Each guideline class for which the repair allowance is elected must be specified in the tax return. The taxpayer may treat expenditures relating to one asset guideline class under the repair allowance and elect not to use the repair allowance for other asset guideline classes. Likewise, the taxpayer can treat expenditures for any asset guideline class differently in a succeeding year.   8.130

Before starting a calculation of the repair allowance, it is well to group by guideline classes all depreciable tangible asset accounts containing assets in service at the beginning of the year and then again at the end of the year. If an attempt is made to pick only those accounts which fit within the elected class, some assets may be missed. The fact that CLADR did not become effective until 1971, or that the Facts and Circumstances life system may have been used in all prior years, is immaterial. In determining the aggregate "repair allowance property" in a class: 8.131

1. Include all property mandatorily or optionally excluded in computing CLADR depreciation.
2. Include pure capital expenditures and other "excluded additions."
3. Deduct ordinary retirements which were not removed from CLADR vintage accounts for 1971 and later years.
4. Do not include in the year-end total the current year "property improvements"; i.e., the excess of pure and mixed repair expenditures over the maximum amount allowable under the CLADR life system. This becomes depreciable property at the start of the next year.

Having determined the amount of the "repair allowance property" at the beginning and again at the end of the year for the elected guideline class, the steps to calculate the repair allowance for the year are: 8.132

1. Add the amounts of the repair allowance property at the beginning and end of the year, and determine the average for the year by dividing by 2.
2. Multiply the average by the "annual asset repair allowance percentage" as given in Rev. Proc. 72–10. The result is the maximum allowance.
3. Determine the amount of pure and mixed repair expenditures for the year. In other words, from all expenditures during the year for both

(a) pure and mixed repair expenditures, and (b) capitalized "excluded additions," subtract the amount of "excluded additions." The result is the amount of the pure and mixed repair expenditures.

4.   The deduction is the amount of the pure and mixed repair expenditures not in excess of the maximum allowable under step 2 above.
5.   Any excess of pure and mixed repair expense over the maximum allowable is a "property improvement," to be placed in a "special basis vintage account" and depreciated commencing the following year.

An example of the calculation of the repair allowance is on page 288–89.

8.133   ACCOUNTING FOR RETIREMENTS. An asset in a vintage account is retired when the asset is permanently withdrawn from use in the business. This may occur as a result of a sale or exchange, physical abandonment, transfer to supplies or scrap, or any other act which amounts to a permanent disposition of the asset. In order to determine the tax treatment to be accorded a retirement, the taxpayer must first determine whether the retirement is ordinary or extraordinary.

8.134   By definition, the term "ordinary retirement" means any retirement from a vintage account that is not an "extraordinary retirement."

8.135   An extraordinary retirement occurs:

1.   When an item of property is permanently retired as a direct result of fire, storm, shipwreck, or other casualty, or
2.   When an asset is retired as a direct result of the termination or disposition of a business or other income-producing process, operation, facility, or unit and the unadjusted basis of the assets retired as a result of the disposition exceeds 20 percent of the unadjusted basis of the vintage account immediately before the disposition. For this purpose only, all of the accounts (other than a special basis vintage account) of the same vintage which have the same asset depreciation period are treated as a single vintage account.

8.136   *Ordinary Retirements.* Generally, neither gains nor losses are recognized upon ordinary retirements. Any proceeds realized are added to the reserve for depreciation of the particular vintage account. The unadjusted basis of the asset retired in an ordinary retirement is not removed from the vintage account, nor is the depreciation reserve reduced by either the cost of the retired asset or the accumulated depreciation of the retired asset.

8.137   *Extraordinary Retirements.* Unless one of the special non-recognition sections of the Code applies, gain or loss is recognized upon an extraordinary retirement in the year in which the retirement occurs. The basis of the retired asset and related depreciation reserve are removed from the accounts. The depreciation reserve retired is determined by computing the depreciation applicable to the retired asset, using the depreciation method and life selected for the vintage account.

Special Rule for Nontaxable Transactions. In the case of **8.138** an ordinary or an extraordinary retirement where the gain or loss is not recognized because of a special nonrecognition section of the Code, such as like-kind exchanges, the unadjusted basis of the asset and related depreciation reserve are removed from the accounts. The related depreciation reserve is computed in the same way as for extraordinary retirements.

Election to Allocate Special Basis Vintage Accounts to **8.139** *Abnormal Retirements.* Under the repair allowance provision, eligible expenditures incurred during the taxable year in excess of the asset guideline repair allowance are recorded in a "special basis vintage account." The unadjusted basis of this account is then recovered through depreciation over the asset depreciation period selected for the account. Generally, the unadjusted basis, adjusted basis, and depreciation reserve accounts of "special basis vintage accounts" are not allocated to any specific asset in the related asset guideline class. However, in the event of an extraordinary retirement, the taxpayer may elect to allocate portions of related "special basis vintage accounts" to the assets retired. The net amount allocated is treated as additional basis for determining gain or loss on the retirement.

Recognition of Gain When the Depreciation Reserve Ex- **8.140** *ceeds the Asset Account.* Gain is recognized to the extent salvage realized causes the depreciation reserve of a vintage account to exceed the unadjusted basis of the account at the end of the taxable year. The entire gain, to the extent of depreciation allowances previously claimed, will be taxed as ordinary income pursuant to the recapture provisions. If the gain exceeds the total of depreciation allowances previously claimed, the excess gain will be taxed as a Section 1231 gain. The depreciation reserve is reduced by the amount of any gain recognized; therefore, the depreciation reserve will never exceed the unadjusted basis of the vintage account.

Recognition of Losses on Termination. A loss is recognized **8.141** if, after the last asset has been retired from a particular vintage account, the unadjusted basis of the account exceeds the depreciation reserve. This amount is normally deductible either as an ordinary loss or as depreciation. However, if the last asset is retired in a taxable sale or exchange, the loss is accorded Section 1231 treatment.

APPLICATION OF CLADR TO OTHER PROVISIONS. The CLADR **8.142** period elected by the taxpayer is expressly controlling for all purposes of the Internal Revenue Code. This rule applies to all assets in a vintage account even though actual lives of individual assets may be substantially longer or shorter than the CLADR period elected.

REVENUE PROCEDURE 72–10 AND EXAMPLES. A copy of portions **8.143** of this procedure appears on page 286. It is followed by an example of the calculation of depreciation under the CLADR life system and then an example of the CLADR repair allowance.

| Asset Guideline Class | Description of Assets Included | Asset Depreciation Range (in years) | | | Annual Asset Guideline Repair Allowance Percentage |
		Lower Limit	Asset Guideline Period	Upper Limit	
00.2	Transportation Equipment:				
00.21	Aircraft (airframes and engines) except aircraft of air transportation companies	5	6	7	14.0
00.22	Automobiles, taxis	2.5	3	3.5	16.5
00.23	Buses	7	9	11.0	11.5
00.24	General purpose trucks, including concrete ready-mix trucks and ore trucks for use over-the-road:				
00.241	Light (actual unloaded weight less than 13,000 pounds)	3	4	5	16.5
00.242	Heavy (actual unloaded weight 13,000 pounds or more)	5	6	7	10.0
70.11	Office furniture, fixtures, and equipment: Includes furniture and fixtures which are not a structural component of a building. Includes such assets as desks, files, safes, and communications equipment (not to include communications equipment which is included in other ADR classes)	8.0	10.0	12.0	2.0
70.13	Data Handling Equipment, except Computers: Includes typewriters, calculators, adding and accounting machines, copiers and duplicating equipment	5.0	6.0	7.0	15.0

EXAMPLE 1

Depreciation Deduction
CLADR Asset Guideline Class 70.11

		1972 DEPRECIATION	
		FACTS AND CIRCUMSTANCES AND GUIDELINE LIFE SYSTEMS	CLADR
Unadjusted basis of assets placed in service prior to 1971—			
Balance 1-1-72	$500,000		
Balance 12-31-72	450,000		
Total	$950,000		
Average (÷ 2)	$475,000		
Guideline life method for assets from 1962 through 1970		$27,500	$ —
Facts and Circumstances life method for assets acquired prior to 1962		15,000	—
1971 CLADR vintage account—			
Acquisitions in class in 1971	$ 60,000		
Less-			
Mandatory and optional exclusions in 1971	20,000	2,000	—
Balance 12-31-71	$ 40,000		
Ordinary retirement in 1972 was $1,000 but not credited to account	—	—	—
Extraordinary retirement 5-31-72	8,000[1]		
Balance 12-31-72	$ 32,000		
Life (lower limit)—8 years ($32,000 ÷ 8)		—	4,000
1972 CLADR vintage account—			
Acquisitions in class	$ 80,000		
Less—Mandatory and optional exclusions	8,000	400	—
Balance 12-31-72	$ 72,000		
Average under half-year convention	$ 36,000	—	4,500
Totals		$44,900	$ 8,500
			44,900
Depreciation deduction for 1972			$53,400

(1) Modified half-year convention was used in 1971.

EXAMPLE 2

CLADR Repair Allowance (Based on Facts of Example 1)
Reconciliation of Depreciable Basis
to Repair Allowance Property

	1-1-72	12-31-72
Unadjusted basis of assets placed in service in years prior to 1971	$500,000	$ 450,000
1971 CLADR vintage account—		
Depreciable balances	40,000	32,000
Add—Mandatory and optional exclusions in 1971	20,000	20,000
(Less)—Ordinary retirement in 1972	–	(1,000)
1972 CLADR vintage account—		
Depreciable balance	–	72,000
Add—Mandatory and optional exclusions	–	8,000
Repair allowance property	$560,000	$ 581,000

Stated Another Way

	1-1-72	12-31-72
Unadjusted basis of all property in asset guideline class as determined for tax depreciation purposes, no matter what life system is used	$560,000	$ 582,000
(Less)—Ordinary retirements which were not removed from CLADR vintage accounts in 1971 and later years	–	(1,000)
	$560,000	$ 581,000

Calculation of Repair Allowance

Repair allowance property—	
1-1-72	$ 560,000
12-31-72	581,000
Total	$1,141,000
Average (÷2)	$ 570,500
Repair allowance % for class	2%
Maximum repair allowance	$ 11,410

Total expenditures in 1972 for repairs, improvements, and rehabilitation of property originally acquired in the current or any prior year [note that this is the full amount of $80,000 acquisitions in 1972 shown in Example 1, plus $9,000 of pure and mixed repair expenditures]	$ 89,000
(Less)—Excluded additions capitalized	(80,000)
Pure and mixed repair expenditures	$ 9,000
Repair allowance (lower of $9,000 or $11,410)	$ 9,000

Comparison of Facts and Circumstances Life System with the CLADR Life System for Post-1970 Assets

Some salient points concerning the two systems are:　　　　8.144

Choice of Systems. Each year starting in 1971, there is a new election for assets placed in service in that year to depreciate them under either the Facts and Circumstances or the CLADR system. If the CLADR system is elected for a year, all additions of eligible property in all classes must be included. However, there are mandatory and optional exclusions. If a shorter life is justifiable for an optionally excludable addition during the year, the maximum deduction for depreciation can be obtained by depreciating that asset under the Facts and Circumstances life system and depreciating the remainder of the class under the CLADR system.

Period of Life. Under the Facts and Circumstances system, the taxpayer must select the life and then be prepared to prove its accuracy—usually a difficult feat. Under the CLADR system, the taxpayer selects a life within the 20 percent range specified in Rev. Proc. 72–10, and no proof is necessary.

Accounts. Both item and multiple-asset accounts can be used under both systems. However, under the CLADR system, every multiple-asset account must be of the vintage type; it cannot be open-end.

Methods by Accounts. The straight-line, declining-balance, and sum-of-the-years-digits methods are available for each account under both systems.

Salvage. The 10 percent of cost exclusion permitted by Section 167(f) is available under both systems, but no account can be depreciated below salvage value after applying Section 167(f). Under the CLADR system, removal and dismantling costs do not reduce gross salvage and thereby end up as debits to the reserve for depreciation. Instead, such expenses are deductible in determining taxable income. However, under the Facts and Circumstances system, such expenditures usually reduce the amount of gross salvage credited to the reserve for depreciation.

Averaging Conventions. Under the CLADR system, there are only two averaging conventions available for current-year additions and retirements in multiple-asset accounts—the half-year and modified half-year. Both are also available under the Facts and Circumstances system, as is the availability of using actual dates of installation or removal for unusually large amounts.

8.145 **Normal and Extraordinary Obsolescence Under the Facts and Circumstances Life System.** In setting a rate of depreciation based upon the useful life of an asset, normal obsolescence is taken into account. If, later, an event occurs or becomes definitely foreseeable, extraordinary obsolescence may result, and the remaining useful life of the asset will be shortened. The provision for extraordinary obsolescence thereupon becomes a part of the depreciation deduction. Regulation 1.167(a)–9 reads as follows:

The depreciation allowance includes an allowance for normal obsolescence which should be taken into account to the extent that the expected useful life of property will be shortened by reason thereof. Obsolescence may render an asset economically useless to the taxpayer regardless of its physical condition. Obsolescence is attributable to many causes, including technological improvements and reasonably foreseeable economic changes. Among these causes are normal progress of the arts and sciences, supersession or inadequacy brought about by developments in the industry, products, methods, markets, sources of supply, and other like changes, and legislative or regulatory action. In any case in which the taxpayer shows that the estimated useful life previously used should be shortened by reason of obsolescence greater than had been assumed in computing such estimated useful life, a change to a new and shorter estimated useful life computed in accordance with such showing will be permitted. No such change will be permitted merely because in the unsupported opinion of the taxpayer the property may become obsolete at some later date. ...

8.146 The United States Supreme Court has defined *obsolescence:*

This Court, without undertaking a comprehensive definition, has held that obsolescence for purposes of the revenue acts may arise from changes in the art, shifting of business centers, loss of trade, inadequacy, supersession, prohibitory laws and other things which, apart from physical deterioration, operate to cause plant elements or the plant as a whole to suffer diminution in value. ... In general, obsolescence under the act connotes functional depreciation, as it does in accounting and engineering terminology. More than nonuse or disuse is necessary to establish it. But not every decision of management to abandon facilities or to discontinue their use gives rise to a claim for obsolescence. For obsolescence under the act requires that the operative causes of the present or growing uselessness arise from external forces which make it desirable or imperative that the property be replaced. What those operative causes may be will be dependent on a wide variety of factual situations.[57]

Extraordinary obsolescence means an acceleration of *functional* depreciation. The remaining cost of the property is then deducted over the shortened period, at the end of which it is estimated that the property will no longer have any useful value. If the change in the art, science, or business were to occur suddenly, almost overnight rendering property obsolete, a deduction for extraordinary obsolescence could be taken in that one year; but it is more likely that the property would be abandoned and an abandonment loss claimed. A deduction for extraordinary obsolescence should be claimed as soon as the conditions that require its reflection become operative; otherwise, the Commission in a later year may claim that extraordinary obsolescence was allowable in that earlier year and, not having been claimed then, is lost forever.

8.147

Under the Guideline life system for pre-1971 assets, it does not seem that the onset of extraordinary obsolescence can be used to shorten the life of a guideline class. However, when that event occurs, a taxpayer can switch to the Facts and Circumstances system and then shorten the life of the asset. In the alternative, he can remain on the Guideline system and then, when the asset is abandoned, he can claim an abnormal retirement together with an abandonment loss under Section 165.

8.148

As to the CLADR system, proposed Reg. 1.167(a)–11(g)(1)(i) provides in part:

8.149

. . . an election to apply this section [of the regulations] to eligible property constitutes an agreement under Section 167(d) and this section to treat the asset depreciation period for each vintage account as the useful life of the property in such account for all purposes of the Code, including Sections 46 [investment credit], 47 [dispositions of investment credit property], 48 [definition of investment credit property], 57 [tax preference items], 163(d) [limitation on deduction of interest on investment indebtedness], 167(c) [3-year life required for property to be eligible for accelerated depreciation], 167(f)(2) [3-year life required for disregarding 10% of cost of personal property when estimating salvage value], 179 [additional first-year allowance for depreciation], 312(m) [effect of depreciation on corporate earnings and profits], 514(a) [unrelated debt-financed income of exempt organizations], and 4940(c) [excise tax based on investment income of exempt private foundations]. For example, since Section 167(c) requires a useful life of at least 3 years and the asset depreciation range period selected is treated as the useful life for purposes of Section 167(c), the taxpayer may adopt a method of depreciation described in Section 167(b)(2) or (3) for an account only if the asset depreciation period selected for the account is at least 3 years.

57. Real estate—Land Title & Trust Co. v. U.S., 309 U.S. 13 (1940), 23 AFTR 816, 40–1 USTC ¶9184.

Accordingly, because an election to use CLADR is treated as the making of an agreement under Section 167(d), the commencement of extraordinary obsolescence may not permit a shortening of the life of the class below the guideline period prescribed in Rev. Proc. 72–10. Nevertheless, in the year when the asset is scrapped, a taxpayer can claim an abnormal retirement and an abandonment loss.

AMORTIZATION

8.150   There is no definition of this term in the Internal Revenue Code. As used therein, however, it means that the cost of a tangible or intangible asset is spread over a term of years on a straight-line depreciation basis with no salvage taken into account. Frequently the term of years is an arbitrarily specified one having nothing to do with estimated life. The terms "amortization" and "depreciation" are not mutually exclusive.

8.151   There are many types of assets or expenditures subject to amortization, including: pollution-control facilities, railroad rolling stock and right-of-way investments, coal-mine safety equipment, research and experimental expenditures, bond discount, trademarks and trade names, leasehold improvements, leasehold costs, bond premium, and corporate organizational expenditures. Only the last five will be discussed here.

Trademarks and Trade Names

8.152   The courts early held[58] that trademarks and trade names were not depreciable; but Section 177 was added to the Code effective January 1, 1956, allowing an elective amortization period of not less than sixty months.

Leased Property

8.153   If a lessee erects a building or makes other improvements on leased property, the lessee is entitled to deduct either depreciation or amortization.[59] If the useful life of the improvements is less than the remaining term of the lease, he deducts depreciation over such useful life. If the life of the improvements is longer than the remaining term of the lease, he deducts amortization over the remaining period of the lease. If the lessee has an option to renew the lease, Section 178 should be consulted to determine the depreciation or amortization period.

8.154   If a leasehold is acquired for business purposes for a specified sum, the purchaser may take as an ordinary deduction in his return an

58. Norwich Pharmacal Co., 30 BTA 326 (1934), concerning trademarks; Paul Jones & Co. v. Lucas, 15 AFTR 681 (1931), concerning trade names.
59. Reg. 1.167(a)–4.

aliquot part of such sum each year, based upon the number of remaining years of the lease.[60] If the lease contains an option to renew, the renewal period must also be taken into account in determining the annual amount of amortization. However, under Section 178, it need not be if 75 percent or more of the cost of the lease is attributable to the unexpired initial period.

Amortizable Bond Premium

Section 171 pertains to the amortization of bond premium. For the purposes of that section, a bond is defined in Subsection (d) as any bond, debenture, note, or certificate or other evidence of indebtedness, issued by any corporation and bearing interest (including any like obligation issued by a government or political subdivision). Such an instrument need not be issued in registered form nor have interest coupons attached to it. The section does not apply to dealers. As to the necessity to amortize premium, the rules are these: — 8.155

Fully taxable bonds. Every type of taxpayer has an *election* to amortize the premium. The amount of the amortization is deductible (but in the case of an individual, only if the standard deduction is not used) and there is a corresponding reduction in basis.

Fully tax-exempt bonds. If the interest on the bonds, such as those of states and municipalities, is wholly tax-exempt, every taxpayer is *required* to amortize the premium. The amount of the amortization is not deductible, but does reduce basis.

Partially taxable bonds. If the owner of the bond is a corporation, it *must* amortize the premium and correspondingly reduce basis. The amount of the amortization is deductible. If the owner is any other type of taxpayer, there is an *election* to amortize and there will be no reduction of basis unless amortization is elected. If amortization is elected, its amount is deductible.

Ordinarily the amount of the premium is the excess of the taxpayer's basis over the amount payable at maturity. However, if the bond is convertible into stock, the portion of the premium attributable to the conversion feature cannot be amortized;[61] in substance, such portion represents the purchase price of an option to acquire stock. — 8.156

Many bonds are callable before maturity, and usually an amount in excess of the principal amount payable on maturity must be paid if called for redemption before that date. A premium on a taxable callable bond is amortizable to maturity or earlier call date. However, for taxable bonds acquired after 1957, regardless of when issued, the earlier call date may be substituted for the maturity date only if a smaller deduction results from amortizing the premium to the earlier call date [Section 171(b)]. — 8.157

60. Reg. 1.162–11(a).
61. Reg. 1.171–2(c).

Corporate Organizational Expenditures

8.158   Section 248 permits a corporation to elect to amortize capital-type expenditures made incident to its creation. The period of amortization may not be for less than sixty months and must commence with the month in which the corporation begins business. Regulation 1.248–1(b)(2) states:

> The following are examples of organizational expenditures within the meaning of Section 248 and this section: legal services incident to the organization of the corporation, such as drafting the corporate charter, bylaws, minutes of organizational meetings, terms of original stock certificates, and the like; necessary accounting services; expenses of temporary directors and of organizational meetings of directors or stockholders; and fees paid to state of incorporation.

Stock issue expenses are not included and also cannot be deducted as business expenses. The regulations and a majority of the courts also hold that reorganization and recapitalization expenditures cannot be amortized or otherwise deducted.

INVESTMENT CREDIT

8.159   This credit is a direct credit against the tax otherwise computed and is allowed by Section 38 and Sections 46 through 50. The amount is normally at the rate of 7 percent of the cost of qualifying property purchased or constructed during the year. There are ceilings imposed on the amount of credit which can be claimed in a particular year, but there are provisions for the carry-back and carry-over of unused credits.

8.160   The history of the investment credit has been "go and stop." It was first enacted in 1962 to spur modernization of machinery and equipment. In 1966, President Johnson asked Congress to suspend its provisions because of its inflationary effect on the economy. The result was the Investment Credit and Accelerated Depreciation Suspension Act of 1966. Not many months later, he had second thoughts and asked that the suspension period be ended. This was accomplished by the Investment Credit and Accelerated Depreciation Restoration Act of 1967. The provisions of these two acts pertaining to the accelerated depreciation of buildings were discussed in paragraphs 8.56 and 8.57. Then in 1969, President Nixon became convinced that the investment credit was too inflationary in effect; but one economist in a public speech at the time took issue with that premise and said, "To blame capital investment for the inflationary pressures in 1969 is like blaming the thermometer for the temperature."[62] The inflation argument prevailed, and the credit commenced being phased out

62. Leif H. Olsen, Senior Vice President and Economist of the First National City Bank, before the twenty-first National Tax Conference of the Tax Foundation, Inc., in New York City on December 2, 1969.

starting with 1969. The credit was again restored by the Revenue Act of 1971. As the bill progressed through the House and Senate, the revitalized credit was called the "job development credit," but that term is not used in the Code. Sections 101 through 108 of the Act added Section 50 to the Code and amended Sections 46, 47, 48, 49, 169, and 1245 of the Code. The result was another suspension period, beginning roughly April 19, 1969, and ending August 15, 1971.[63]

The first year for which the credit was available was 1962. Through the years, changes have been made in the definitions of the types of property which qualify. For all years for which the credit was or is available, the property must be tangible and can be either new or used. For 1971 and later years, the qualifying categories are called "Section 38 property" and are described in Section 48(a) as:

1. Tangible personal property;
2. Other tangible property if used as an integral part of manufacturing, production, or extraction, or of furnishing transportation or certain public utility services;
3. New elevators or escalators;
4. Coin-operated vending machines and coin-operated washing machines and dryers;
5. Livestock, other than horses, to the extent set forth in Section 48(a)(6).

Included within the second category are special-purpose buildings housing machinery, storage facilities for the bulk storage of fungible commodities (including commodities in a liquid or gaseous state), and machinery permanently affixed to a building and required principally for a manufacturing process. Excluded are:

1. All other buildings and their structural components;
2. Property (other than coin-operated vending machines, washers, and dryers) used in connection with furnishing lodging which is predominantly nontransient;
3. Property used by a tax-exempt organization;
4. Property leased to, or by, governmental bodies;
5. Property used predominantly outside the United States, with ten exceptions listed in Section 48(a)(2);
6. Property written off under a statutory five-year amortization provision such as is available for rehabilitation expenditures, pollution-control facilities, railroad rolling stock, coal-mine safety equipment, job-training facilities, and child-care centers.

There are limitations imposed by Section 46(d)(3) on the availability of the credit to certain lessors. Prior to the 1969 repeal of the investment credit, a lessor of qualifying property was entitled either to use the credit himself or to pass it through to the lessee. He can still pass the credit through, subject to the rules of Section 48(d); but in only two situations can an individual, partnership, or Subchapter S corporation as a lessor retain the credit. The new restriction was imposed to prevent an individual from unduly sheltering otherwise taxable

63. Sec. 49(a) and 50(c).

Depreciable and Depletable Property

8.161

8.162

income. The two instances in which a taxpayer that is not taxed as a corporation can utilize the credit when leasing the property to another taxpayer are set forth in Section 46(d)(3) and are described by the Senate Finance Committee in its report[64] as follows:

> The bill provides that the credit is to be available to an individual (or other noncorporate) lessor in only two situations. First, if the property which is the subject matter of the lease has been manufactured or produced by the lessor, the lessor is not to be denied the credit. The terms "manufacture" and "production" in this case include the construction or reconstruction of property. Thus, if two individuals are in the business of manufacturing a product and then lease instead of sell the product, they are not to be denied the credit with respect to the product assuming it otherwise qualifies as investment credit property. In these situations, the lease arrangement is an integral part of the taxpayer's business and is not likely to have been entered into for the purpose of reducing tax liabilities.
>
> Second, the bill provides, in general, for the allowance of the credit in the case of short-term leases, since in these cases the leasing activity constitutes a business activity of the taxpayer, rather than a mere investment, i.e., a financing arrangement. The bill provides that two conditions must be satisfied for the credit to be available to a noncorporate lessor under this alternative. First, the term of the lease (taking into account options to renew or extend) must be less than 50 percent of the useful life of the property subject to the lease. The useful life of the property for this purpose is the life used in determining the amount of allowable credit and for depreciation purposes. Second, for the first 12 months after the transfer of the property to the lessee, the sum of the deductions allowable to the lessor with respect to the leased property solely by reason of section 162 (other than rental payments and reimbursed expenses with respect to the property) must exceed 15 percent of the rental income produced by the property during the 12-month period.

8.163   Section 38 property can be either new or used. Property is new if (1) it was constructed, reconstructed, or erected by the taxpayer, or (2) it was acquired by and its original use began with the taxpayer [Section 48(b)]. The purchaser of a rebuilt machine is not the original user, and the property is not new. However, Reg. 1.48–2(b)(7) states: "Property will not be treated as reconditioned or rebuilt merely because it contains some used parts." For example, Rev. Rul. 68–111 held that a diesel-electric locomotive, constructed with not more than 20 percent used materials and parts, was new. However, where the transactions consisted first of a purchase of used freight cars and then their reconstruction, Rev. Rul. 70–135 held the cost of reconstruction was "new" property, but the purchase price of the cars qualified only as used property.

8.164   If used property of the Section 38 type is *purchased* by the taxpayer, it can qualify, but the maximum amount of cost is limited to $50,000 in any one year [Section 48(c)]. If the aggregate purchase price exceeds this ceiling, the taxpayer can select the particular items of used

64. No. 92–437, p. 44.

property, up to the ceiling amount, with respect to which he wishes to claim the investment credit.

8.165 The first suspension period began October 10, 1966, and ended March 9, 1967. With the exceptions stated in Section 48(h), property acquired or constructed in that period was not eligible for the credit. Then by reason of the Investment Credit and Accelerated Depreciation Restoration Act of 1967, property constructed or acquired on or after March 10, 1967, again qualified. That period terminated April 18, 1969, because of the enactment of Section 49 added to the Code by the Tax Reform Act of 1969. As provided in the first sentence of Section 49(a), property became ineligible for the credit if (1) the physical construction, reconstruction, or erection began after April 18, 1969, or (2) it was acquired after April 18, 1969. However, in neither circumstance did the prohibition apply if the item was "pre-termination" property. In other words, pre-termination property continued to be eligible for the investment credit even though construction was completed or the acquisition occurred after April 18, 1969.

8.166 Subsection (b) of Section 49 defines what is meant by pre-termination property. It consists of property essentially committed for at April 18, 1969. Property obtained or completed after that date is eligible if (1) a "binding contract" to acquire or construct it was in effect on, and at all times after, April 18, 1969; (2) under the "equipped building" and "plant facility" rules, more than 50 percent of a planned plant or plant facility was acquired or contracted for before April 19, 1969; or (3) under the "machinery or equipment rule," parts and components comprising more than 50 percent of the cost of such items in a piece of machinery were on hand before April 19, 1969. Under Section 49(a), there are other types of qualifying pre-termination property where the property was involved in certain leasing transactions, tax-free exchanges, exchanges of barges for ocean-going vessels, or production of new-design products. There was also a requirement in Section 49(d) that any property otherwise qualifying as pre-termination property had to be placed in service by December 31, 1975; but that restriction was repealed by the Revenue Act of 1971.

8.167 The Revenue Act of 1971 again restored the investment credit. To be eligible, the property must first be "Section 38 property." If it is, then, under Code Section 50 added by this latest act, the property qualifies for the investment credit if (1) in the case of construction, reconstruction, or erection of property, such work is completed by the taxpayer after [August 15, 1971, or is begun by the taxpayer after] March 31, 1971; or (2) in the case of the acquisition of property, such acquisition occurs either (a) after August 15, 1971, or (b) after March 31, 1971, and before August 16, 1971, pursuant to an order which was placed after March 31, 1971.

8.168 The period from April 19, 1969, through August 15, 1971, is not called a second suspension period in the Code or Committee reports, but it is helpful to think of it as such. Property acquired or constructed during that period can qualify for the credit only if it is pre-termination property. However, property acquired or constructed after August 15, 1971, can qualify either as pre-termination property or under Section 50. Sometimes both provisions will be applicable.

8.169   The credit is 7 percent (except for public utility companies) of the "qualified investment" each year in the cost or basis of all new Section 38 property and up to $50,000 of used Section 38 property [Section 46(c)]. The amount of the qualified investment is determined by the estimated depreciable life of the property when placed in service. Under the law applicable to the periods from 1962 through 1970 during which the investment credit was available, the property had to have a life of at least eight years in order to be taken into account at 100 percent of cost or basis, and there were reductions if the estimated life was less. The Revenue Act of 1971 shortened these lives by one year.

OLD LAW		1971 LAW	
DEPRECIABLE LIFE	% OF COST OR BASIS	DEPRECIABLE LIFE	% OF COST OR BASIS
8 years or more	100%	7 years or more	100%
6 to under 8	66-2/3%	5 to under 7	66-2/3%
4 to under 6	33-1/3%	3 to under 5	33-1/3%

EXAMPLE   A calendar-year corporation purchases the following units of property after August 15, 1971, and places them in service, one each month, starting with September 1971:

PROPERTY	YEARS OF LIFE	COST	QUALIFIED INVESTMENT %	QUALIFIED INVESTMENT AMOUNT
A	10	$ 80,000	100%	$ 80,000
B	6	90,000	66-2/3%	60,000
C	4	30,000	33-1/3%	10,000
D	2	100,000	–	–
Total qualified investment				$150,000
Credit at 7%				$ 10,500

Note that the full percentage of the credit is available no matter how early or late in the year property is placed in service. Also, there is no credit available if the property has an estimated depreciable life of less than three years.

8.170   The maximum rate of credit is less for property acquired or constructed by public utility companies—i.e., property used in supplying electricity, water, sewage disposal, gas through a local distribution system, telephone, or telegraphic service. However, property attributable to gas transmission lines, as opposed to a local distribution system, does qualify for the full 7 percent credit, assuming that the useful life is long enough. For 1970 and prior years, the maximum credit was 3 percent; starting in 1971, it is 4 percent.

Stated another way, the credit rates under the 1971 law based on the *full* cost or basis of property, instead of on the qualified investment, are as follows for property qualifying under the acquisition dates of Section 50: 8.171

	PUBLIC UTILITY PROPERTY	OTHER PROPERTY
7 years or more	4%	7%
5 to under 7	2-2/3%	4-2/3%
3 to under 5	1-1/3%	2-1/3%

As to pre-termination property, the years of life required by the old law govern. If property placed in service in 1971 or later qualifies as both pre-termination and Section 50 property, it would seem that the shorter lives of Section 50 would prevail. 8.172

Once a tentative investment credit has been determined by applying the rate to the amount of qualified investment for the year, a further limitation applies. The investment credit allowable in any taxable year may not exceed an amount equal to the first $25,000 of tax liability plus 50 percent (25 percent for years ending on or before March 9, 1967) of any tax liability in excess of $25,000. For this purpose, tax liability means the tax computed in the regular manner after reduction for credits for foreign taxes, partially tax-exempt interest, and retirement income. The amount of $25,000 is reduced to $12,500 each for married persons filing separate returns, unless one of the spouses is not entitled to an investment credit for that year. If the amount of the investment credit exceeds the limitation, it may be carried back three years and forward seven years, in each case to be used in the earliest of the ten years. An additional three years is added to the seven-year carry-over period for carry-overs from 1970 and prior years. The limitation based upon the amount of tax liability always applies to the year to which the credit is sought to be carried. 8.173

Recapture

To discourage taxpayers from securing a higher investment credit by assigning an unrealistically long life to the particular assets, there is a "recapture" provision that, in effect, reimburses the United States Treasury if subsequent events do not justify the life originally assigned. If, before the end of the useful life originally assigned, investment property is disposed of (other than by inheritance or certain tax-free corporate acquisitions) or ceases to be qualified investment property, the aggregate of the investment credits previously allowed 8.174

8.175 in all prior taxable years is reduced to an amount that would have been allowed had the original useful life been forecast accurately.

8.175 If the recomputed credit is less than the credit previously allowed as a reduction of income tax, the reduction in the credit becomes a tax liability for the year the property is disposed of—the recapture year [Section 47(a)]. The investment credit recapture is payable as tax for the recapture year, whether or not income tax is otherwise payable for that year and irrespective of any net operating loss the taxpayer may have for that year. Furthermore, the tax payable as investment credit recapture is not reduced by other tax credits, such as for foreign taxes, dividends received, retirement income, or other investment credits [Reg. 1.47–1(b)(2)].

8.176 The investment credit also becomes subject to recapture if property on which a credit was allowed ceases to be property qualifying for such credit before the expiration of its life used for such credit calculation, or if nonpublic utility property becomes public utility property before the expiration of such period.

8.177 If the investment credit allowable when the property was placed in service has not been used as a tax reduction, but is reflected in an unused credit carry-over, an early disposition of the property will result in an adjustment of the carry-over. If the credit has been used in part as a tax reduction and in part as an increase in an unused credit carry-over, the recapture will both adjust the carry-over and result in a tax liability for the recapture year [Reg. 1.47–1(a)(1)].

8.178 The principles discussed above are illustrated in Reg. 1.47–1(d) by the following examples:

EXAMPLE 1 (i) X Corporation, which makes its returns on the basis of the calendar year, acquired and placed in service on January 1, 1962, three items of Section 38 property, each with a basis of $12,000 and an estimated useful life of fifteen years. The amount of qualified investment with respect to each such asset was $12,000. For the taxable year 1962, X Corporation's credit earned of $2,520 was allowed under Section 38 as a credit against its liability for tax of $4,000. On December 2, 1965, one of the items of Section 38 property is sold to Y Corporation.

(ii) The actual useful life of the item of property which is sold on December 2, 1965, is three years and eleven months. The recomputed qualified investment with respect to such item of property is zero ($12,000 basis multiplied by zero applicable percentage) and X Corporation's recomputed credit earned for the taxable year 1962 is $1,680 (7 percent of $24,000). The income tax imposed by chapter 1 of the Code on X Corporation for the taxable year 1965 is increased by the $840 decrease in its credit earned for the taxable year 1962 (that is, $2,520 original credit earned minus $1,680 recomputed credit earned).

EXAMPLE 2 (i) The facts are the same as in Example 1, except that for the taxable year 1962, X Corporation's liability for tax under Section 46(a)(3) is only $1,520. Therefore, for such taxable year, X Corporation's credit allowed under Section 38 is limited to $1,520, and the excess of $1,000 ($2,520 credit earned minus $1,520 limitation based on amount of tax) is an unused credit. Of such $1,000 unused credit, $100 is allowed as a credit under Section 38 for the taxable year 1963, $100 is allowed for 1964, and $800 is carried to the taxable year 1965.

(ii) The actual useful life of the item of property which is sold on December 2, 1965, is three years and eleven months. The recomputed qualified investment with respect to such item of property is zero ($12,000 basis multiplied by zero applicable percentage), and X Corporation's recomputed credit earned for the taxable year 1962 is $1,680 (7 percent of $24,000). If such $1,680 recomputed credit earned had been taken into account in place of the $2,520 original credit earned, X's credit allowed for 1962 would have been $1,520, and of the $160 unused credit from 1962, $100 would have been allowed as a credit under Section 38 for 1963, and $60 would have been allowed for 1964. X Corporation's $800 investment credit carry-over to the taxable year 1965 is reduced by $800 to zero. The income tax imposed by chapter 1 of the Code on X Corporation for the taxable year 1965 is increased by $40 (that is, the aggregate reduction in the credits allowed by Section 38 for 1962, 1963, and 1964).

Under Code Sec. 47(b) recapture is not required on the disposition of property by reason of death. On the death of a taxpayer, property on which an investment credit was allowed is presumed to have been held for a period equal to the period estimated in calculating the credit [Reg. 1.47–3(b)]. If property is transferred in a transaction described in Section 381(a), dealing with tax-free transfers by corporations pursuant to reorganizations and to liquidations of controlled subsidiaries, recapture does not occur. These transactions represent transfers of property in which the basis of property carries through to the transferee, and certain accounting methods and other tax attributes also carry over to the transferee. 8.179

Recapture does not occur when property is transferred in connection with a mere change in form of carrying on a trade or business, provided the taxpayer maintains a substantial interest in the business, and the property transferred remains in the same trade or business. This exception will prevent recapture of investment credit on transfers of property pursuant to the change of a proprietorship into a partnership, the change of a proprietorship into a corporation, or a change of a partnership into a corporation. 8.180

Investment credit is subject to recapture on transfers of property by gift, sale, or exchange (including exchanges of like-kind property subject to Section 1031). 8.181

When property is transferred in a transaction exempt from recapture of investment credit (other than transfers by death), the possibility of recapture remains with the property. Recapture will still occur if an early disposition occurs in a subsequent transaction that is not exempt. For this purpose, the useful life of the property is measured from the date the property was placed in service during the year the investment credit was earned [Reg. 1.47–3(e)]. 8.182

Presentation in Financial Statements

In the Revenue Act of 1971, Congress did something unusual. In Section 101(c) of that Act, it provided that in financial statements sub- 8.183

ject to the jurisdiction of any Federal agency, a corporation must be allowed to "flow through" into net income the full amount of the reduction in tax arising from an investment credit.[65] On the other hand, a corporation, if it wishes, can defer the amount of the credit and amortize it into financial net income over a period of time such as the depreciable life of the property involved.

8.184   Extracts from the Senate Finance Committee Report and the Conference Committee Report follow:

> *Accounting for the investment tax credit.* The procedures employed in accounting for the investment credit in financial reports to shareholders, creditors, etc., can have a significant effect on reported net income and thus on economic recovery. The committee, as was the House, is concerned that the investment credit provided by the bill have as great a stimulative effect on the economy as possible. Therefore, from this standpoint it would appear undesirable to preclude the use of "flow through" in the financial reporting of net income.
>
> If the investment credit is thought of as decreasing the price of the equipment purchased, it can be argued that reflecting the benefit of the credit in income over the life of the asset is appropriate. However, the investment credit may also be thought of as a selective tax rate reduction applicable in those cases where the desired investments are being made. In this latter event, it is difficult to see why the current "flow through" should be prevented in the financial reporting of income.
>
> In view of these considerations, the committee believes that it is unwise to require either type of financial reporting but believes that it is desirable that the companies generally indicate in their reports the method they follow in treating the investment credit for financial reporting purposes. Nothing in this discussion is intended to have any effect on the treatment of the credit for rate-making purposes in the case of regulated industries.
>
> [Conference Report]
> . . . The conference agreement clarifies the application of the Senate amendment by providing that taxpayers for purposes of reporting to Federal agencies and for purposes of making financial reports subject to regulation by Federal agencies are to be permitted to account for the tax benefit of the investment credit either currently in the year in which the investment credit is taken as a tax reduction, or ratably over the life of the asset. This includes not only reports made to the Federal Government, but also reporting to stockholders to the extent any Federal agency has the authority to specify the method of such reporting. This treatment is to be available notwithstanding any other law or regulation under law. The method used after the date of the bill must be consistently followed unless permission to make a change in the method of reporting is obtained from the Secretary or his delegate. The requirements set forth in this provision are not to apply to reports of public utilities for which other rules are provided under Section 105 of the bill.

65. Sec. 101(c) of the bill was added by Senate floor amendment to codify Finance Committee's language on accounting for the credit in financial reports. See Cong. Record—Senate (11–15–71), p. 18626; see also Sec. 105(e) of the bill.

DEPLETION

Natural resources, such as oil and gas, iron ore, coal, uranium, sulphur, other minerals and natural deposits, and timber, are wasting assets. As they are consumed in production, capital is being consumed. For that reason, ever since 1913, Congress has provided for some type of deduction for the depletion of such natural resources. The present provisions are contained in Sections 611 to 614.   8.185

The law on depletion allowances has been evolutionary. The 1913 and 1916 Acts provided an unsatisfactory allowance on extraction in the tax year, based on in-mine value. This was followed by "cost" depletion (1918 Act) and the now-obsolete "discovery" depletion (1921 Act). Cost depletion is an allowance based on the cost of a property, and discovery depletion was based on the value of a mineral deposit when discovered. The 1926 Act introduced "percentage" depletion for oil and gas, and it limited discovery depletion to mines. Percentage depletion is an allowance based on a stipulated percent of gross income from a mineral property. Because of its simplicity, percentage depletion gradually replaced discovery depletion as to mines, wells, and natural deposits. Under the 1954 Code, the higher of cost or percentage depletion is allowed as a deduction on all minerals, including oil and gas, except those extracted from inexhaustible sources such as air or the sea. Percentage depletion can be taken even if the taxpayer has no cost or other basis for his mineral interest. Only cost depletion (which requires a basis) is available for timber.   8.186

Depletion is allowable when the taxpayer realizes ordinary income attributable to the production and sale of minerals from a mineral deposit in which he has an economic interest. This income can represent proceeds from minerals produced and sold currently, or it can be a bonus received in a leasing transaction representing advance payment for minerals to be produced and sold in the future. The important thing is that the income must be attributable to production and sale of minerals produced or to be produced.   8.187

Depletion is not allowable on the proceeds from sale of a mineral interest. Instead, the seller deducts the cost of the interest sold, and the resulting gain or loss is treated as a capital gain or loss or a Section 1231 gain or loss. (See chapters 11 and 12.) The purchaser must capitalize the purchase payment as cost of the interest acquired.   8.188

The basis of the taxpayer's interest in a property is reduced by the amount of depletion allowed or allowable.[66] In the case of percentage depletion, the aggregate allowances over the years can exceed basis, but the adjusted basis for determining gain or loss on a sale or ex-   8.189

---

66. James Petroleum Corp., 24 T.C. 509 (Acq.), affirmed 238 F.2d 678 (2nd Cir.), 50 AFTR 771, holding that the basis of oil properties sold had to be reduced by allowable cost depletion where such amount exceeded percentage depletion allowed in prior years. See also paragraph 11.39.

change of the property will not be less than zero.[67] The Service holds that after the adjusted basis of a property has been reduced to zero, any subsequent percentage depletion allowance should be applied against the basis of subsequent capital additions to that property.[68]

Economic Interest

8.190   To be entitled to a deduction for depletion, the taxpayer must have an "economic interest" in the mineral deposit or standing timber which gives rise to the income received. This concept was developed by the United States Supreme Court in *Palmer* v. *Bender*.[69] In that case, the Court held that an economic interest requires two factors to have existed: (1) an acquisition by investment of an interest in the mineral in place or in the standing timber, and (2) the receipt of income, based upon a legal relationship, derived from the extraction of the mineral or the cutting of the timber to which extraction or cutting the taxpayer must look for a return of his capital. Later, this same Court interpreted the second factor to mean that the taxpayer must look *solely* to the extraction of the mineral or the cutting of timber for a return of his capital. Depletion was denied to a seller on proceeds that were not solely dependent upon production, but which also were payable out of proceeds from a subsequent sale of any part of the fee interest.[70]

8.191   Subsequently, these concepts were incorporated in the regulations, the latest version of which is in Reg. 1.611–1(b)(1):

(b) Economic interest.—(1) Annual depletion deductions are allowed only to the owner of an economic interest in mineral deposits or standing timber. An economic interest is possessed in every case in which the taxpayer has acquired by investment any interest in mineral in place or standing timber and secures, by any form of legal relationship, income derived from the extraction of the mineral or severance of the timber, to which he must look for a return of his capital. But a person who has no capital investment in the mineral deposit or standing timber does not possess an economic interest merely because through a contractual relation he possesses a mere economic or pecuniary advantage derived from production. For example, an agreement between the owner of an economic interest and another entitling the latter to purchase or process the product upon production or entitling the latter to compensation for extraction or cutting does not convey a depletable economic interest. Further, depletion deductions with respect to an economic interest of a corporation are allowed to the corporation and not to its shareholders.

8.192   The required investment in the property may be acquired by purchase or exchange, gift or inheritance, for services or as a liquidating distribution. The holder of the interest need not incur any cost

67. Rev. Rul. 54–421, 1954–2 C.B. 162.
68. *Ibid.*
69. 287 U.S. 551 (1933), 11 AFTR 1106.
70. Anderson v. Helvering, 310 U.S. 404 (1940), 24 AFTR 967.

measured in dollars or have a basis. Usually the holder will have once had at least a fee or leasehold in the producing properties, but not necessarily. In *Com.* v. *Southwest Exploration Co.*,[71] the United States Supreme Court held that the owners of uplands on the coast of California had an economic interest in an off-shore oil lease granted to a drilling company by the State of California. An indispensable easement had been granted by the upland owners to the drilling company so that the latter could erect its derricks and other equipment on the land to do the required slant drilling. For the easement the drilling company agreed to pay $24\frac{1}{2}$ percent of the net profits to be realized from production. These amounts received by the upland owners were held subject to depletion by them.

Methods

Under present law, the depletion allowance is the greater of cost depletion or percentage depletion.[72] The allowance is determined separately for each *property;* thus, in the same year, cost depletion can be claimed on one depletable property and percentage depletion on another.   **8.193**

Cost Depletion. Cost depletion is similar to unit-of-production depreciation in that it represents the amortization of the cost of a property over its productive life on the basis of units produced. Only the cost of the natural resource itself is depletable—not the cost of the surface of the land under which a mineral deposit is located or on which timber is growing. If both the surface and mineral or timber rights are acquired for a single price, such lump-sum price must be allocated between the surface and the underlying minerals or timber based upon fair-market values on the date of acquisition. If it was not known at that time that any minerals existed, nothing can be allocated to cost of the minerals.[73]   **8.194**

The amount of cost depletion in any one year is determined by following these steps. First, ascertain the adjusted basis of the property (cost minus prior-year depletion allowances, cost or percentage). Second, determine the number of units of the product (tons of ore, barrels of oil, or cubic feet of gas) remaining as of the beginning of the year. This number should be based upon a survey or appraisal by a qualified geologist or engineer. Third, calculate the cost per unit by dividing the adjusted basis by the units remaining at the start of the year. Finally, calculate cost depletion by multiplying the cost per unit by the units sold, not the units produced, during the year.   **8.195**

Percentage Depletion. In the case of those mines, wells, and other natural deposits listed in Section 613(b), percentage depletion is allowable when it is greater than cost depletion. Percentage depletion   **8.196**

71. 350 U.S. 308 (1956), 48 AFTR 683.
72. Reg. 1.611–1(a)(1).
73. Mertens, *Law of Federal Income Taxation*, Section 21.32, p. 99.

is calculated by multiplying the "gross income from the property" by the depletion percentage appropriate for the mineral as provided by Section 613(b). The result is then compared to 50 percent of the taxable income from the property before depletion, and the lesser amount is the percentage depletion allowance. The depletion percentages in Section 613(b) vary from 5 percent for gravel and certain clays to 22 percent for sulphur, uranium, oil and gas, and certain other minerals.

8.197   GROSS INCOME FROM THE PROPERTY. "Gross income from the property," in the case of an oil and gas well, refers to the value of the oil and gas sold during the taxable year in the immediate vicinity of the well. Thus if the oil or gas is sold after being hauled to a pipeline terminal, the actual sales proceeds are reduced by the hauling charges to arrive at the gross income from the property to which the percentage depletion rate is applied. If the oil or gas is processed into a refined product before it is sold, the gross income from the property is based on a representative market or field price of the oil or gas before such processing.[74] In the case of properties other than oil and gas wells, gross income from the property refers to the gross income from mining. This includes any sales value attributable to treatment processes that are considered as part of mining and those necessary or incidental thereto. These processes are described for various minerals in Section 613(c)(4) and include such processes as (1) for coal—cleaning, sizing, and loading for shipment; (2) for sulphur recovered by the Frasch process—cleaning, pumping to vats, cooling, and loading for shipment; and (3) for lead, zinc, copper, uranium, and other ores that are not customarily sold in crude form—crushing, grinding, and other processes used in the separation or extraction of the product from the ore.

8.198   A lease owner's gross income from the property does not include any royalties *paid* to a lessor, sublessor, or other owner of an economic interest in the property. A royalty for this purpose is a payment resulting solely from sales of minerals produced. Such payments are depletable by the owners of the royalty interests and not by the operator of the mine or well.[75]

8.199   If, in a leasing transaction, the lessor retains a continuing interest in the mineral such as a royalty, overriding royalty, or similar interest, the bonus paid to the lessor as consideration for the lease is generally treated for tax purposes as an advance royalty. As such, the bonus constitutes gross income from the property to the lessor and is depletable by him. The lessee includes it in his cost of the lease recoverable through his depletion allowance.[76] If the lease expires without any production of minerals, the lessor is required to return to income the depletion previously allowed on the bonus. Since the

74. Reg. 1.613–3(a).
75. Reg. 1.613–2(c)(5); Helvering v. Twin Bell Oil Syndicate, 293 U.S. 312 (1934), 14 AFTR 712.
76. Reg. 1.612–3(a) and (d).

bonus is depletable to the lessor, the lessee is required to reduce his depletable income from the property by a like amount to prevent such amount from being depleted twice. This reduction is effected by pro-rating the bonus over the lessee's gross income from the property on the basis of the ratio of each year's production to total estimated production from the lease.[77] This reduction in gross income is made only for purposes of the percentage depletion calculation. The lessee is not allowed a tax deduction for the bonus except to the extent the depletion allowance itself represents such a deduction.

NET INCOME LIMITATION. As indicated earlier, percentage depletion for any year can never exceed 50 percent of the taxable income from the property for that year.[78] This taxable income is the excess of the gross income over all tax deductions attributable to developing, producing, and selling the production from that property. Such costs and expenses include depreciation of equipment and an appropriate share of overhead applicable to the property, but they do not include the depletion being calculated.[79]

8.200

Illustration. The application of the principles discussed above are illustrated by the following example:

8.201

EXAMPLE

Operator A, a cash-basis taxpayer, owns an oil and gas lease on which the first productive wells were drilled by him and completed in 1971. In 1972, production began, and 22,857 barrels were produced and sold at $3 per barrel. The purchaser directly paid the owner of the $\frac{1}{8}$ royalty interest the amount due him, calculated as follows:

Sales price ($3 × 2,857 barrels)	$8,571
Less —	
Hauling charge @ 20¢ per barrel	$ 571
State severance taxes @ 10¢ per barrel	286
	$ 857
Net remittance	$7,714

The amount of $7,714 is ordinary income to the royalty interest owner; from this amount, $1,760 of percentage depletion can be deducted ($7,714 + $286 = $8,000 × 22%), so that $5,954 ($7,714 − $1,760) is includible in his adjusted gross income.

At the end of 1972, an engineering study indicated recoverable reserves were 262,857 barrels, of which 230,000 barrels were applicable to the $\frac{7}{8}$ working interest owned by operator A. A's cost in the lease was $10,000, consisting of an $8,000 lease bonus to the landowner (which was depletable ordinary income to him) and $2,000 for title work.

From the $60,000 due A for his 20,000 barrels of oil, the purchaser deducted hauling charges of $4,000, and $2,000 for state severance taxes cover-

77. Reg. 1.613–2(c)(5)(ii).
78. Sec. 613(a); Reg. 1.613–1.
79. Reg. 1.613–4(a).

ing the 20,000 barrels sold for the account of A, and remitted $54,000 to A in 1972. Expenses paid in 1972 in producing the 22,857 barrels were $8,000 for operating expenses, $5,000 for depreciation, and $2,000 for general overhead applicable to the producing lease. Also paid in 1972 was $20,000 of intangible drilling costs incurred in 1971, and pursuant to Section 263(c) and Reg. 1.612–4, operator A elects to expense rather than to capitalize such amount. Operator A's allowable depletion for 1972 is calculated as follows:

Cost depletion —

Adjusted basis of property		$ 10,000
Barrels of oil at beginning of year —		
Reserves estimated at end of year	$230,000	
Production during year	20,000	
Reserves at beginning of year		250,000
Cost per barrel $\left(\dfrac{\$\ 10,000}{250,000}\right)$		$.04
Cost depletion (20,000 × $.04)		$ 800

Percentage depletion —

Gross income from the property—			
Sales (20,000 × $3)		$ 60,000	
Less: Hauling charges	$4,000		
Aliquot part of lease bonus			
$\left(\dfrac{20,000}{250,000} \times \$8,000\right)$	640	4,640	
Gross income from the property		$ 55,360	

Expenses —

Severance taxes	$ 2,000	
Operating expenses	8,000	
Depreciation	5,000	
Overhead	2,000	
Intangible drilling costs	20,000	
Total expenses		37,000
		$ 18,360
Add: Aliquot part of lease bonus excluded above		640
Net income from the property before depletion		$ 19,000
50% of net income		$ 9,500
22% of gross income from the property		12,179
Percentage depletion (lesser of above two amounts)		9,500

Allowable depletion —

Cost depletion	$	800
Percentage depletion		9,500
Allowable depletion (greater of cost or percentage)		9,500

In the above calculation of cost depletion, the best estimate of barrels of oil under the lease was an estimate at the end of the year. Thus it was necessary to add to that figure the number of barrels produced during the year. This gave the number of barrels at the beginning of the year, based on the best information available at the end of the year.

In calculating percentage depletion it was necessary to reduce gross sales of oil to *gross income from the property* by deducting hauling charges and an aliquot part of the lease bonus. The bonus was allocated to the current year on the ratio of current production to total estimated reserves. Note that the bonus so excluded was added back in determining the taxable income before depletion.

The Property

In the preceding paragraphs, the term *the property* is used quite prominently. The concept of *property* for depletion purposes is technical and complex; nevertheless, an understanding of the term and the proper identification of each *property* is extremely important in the calculation of depletion. The term *property* is defined in Section 614(a) as "each separate interest owned by the taxpayer in each mineral deposit in each separate tract or parcel of land." This definition is deceptively simple, and its application often requires extensive reference to the regulations, Treasury rulings, and court decisions. In the case of operating interests in oil and gas wells, Section 614(b) grants an exception to this definition. It provides that where several interests are owned in a single tract of land, all such interests shall be treated as a single property unless the taxpayer elects to treat one or more of them as separate properties. This exception relates only to operating interests which are those, usually leaseholds, that are burdened with the costs of developing and operating the property.[80] These are in contrast to nonoperating interests, such as royalties and overriding royalties, which entitle their owners to shares of production without regard to expenses thereof. Two or more nonoperating interests in the same tract may be treated as a single property only when so permitted by the Treasury after a showing that a principal purpose for such treatment is not the avoidance of tax.[81]

8.202

80. Sec. 614(d).
81. Sec. 614(e).

QUESTIONS AND PROBLEMS

1. Brown, a member of a law partnership, (a) owns a condominium apartment in Miami Beach that he bought upon completion of construction of the building; each year he occupies it during the month of February and rents it to strangers for the balance of the year; (b) owns a six-apartment building that he bought when it was ten years old; (c) uses one room in his residence as a study in which to do research and writing; he purchased the house in 1968 when it was five years old and immediately commenced using this room as a study; and (d) has a small law library in that study consisting of books bought secondhand. Is each of these assets depreciable, and if so, what methods are available?

2. A machine was purchased January 1 of this year for $20,000 by a calendar-year and accrual-basis corporation. It has an estimated useful life of ten years and a salvage value of $1,500. Under the Facts and Circumstances life system:

   (a) What is the maximum amount of depreciation available for this year, assuming no other depreciable property is purchased? Show all computations under all methods available, based on the facts given.

   (b) Assuming the machine was purchased October 1, what would your answer be?

   (c) Would your answer be any different if this were a cash-basis proprietorship?

3. Throughout the year 1970, an accrual-basis corporation purchased a total of forty machines, which it recorded in a multiple-asset account that throughout the history of the account had reflected additions and retirements not segregated by years of acquisition. For that year, the entries in the account were:

BALANCE JANUARY 1	NEW PROPERTY ADDITIONS	RETIREMENTS	BALANCE DECEMBER 31
$1,000,000	$200,000	$(50,000)	$1,150,000

   The guideline life was twelve years for assets of this type, but an engineering study made by the company in the preceding year shows that its experience has been that assets of this type have a life of fifteen years.

   (a) Disregarding any limit that might be imposed by a reserve ratio test, what depreciable life is the shortest allowable?

   (b) What depreciation methods are available?

4. In October, 1969, a corporation entered into a contract for the construction of a sixty-story combination office and apartment building in Chicago. It was completed on January 1, 1972, at an aggregate cost of $10,000,000. The portion of the cost allocable to the first forty floors, containing offices and stores, is $6,000,000, and the cost allocable to the top twenty floors, containing apartments, is $4,000,000. In 1972, the sources and amounts of the rental income were as follows:

Offices	$100,000	
Apartments	600,000	
Total	$700,000	

In addition, the corporation itself occupied offices in the building for which it could have received rental income of $500,000 had it rented the space to others. The estimate life of the building is fifty years.

What was the maximum allowable amount of depreciation on the building for 1972?

5. Under the Facts and Circumstances life system, will there be any effect on subsequent years' depreciation applicable to the remaining assets in a multiple-asset account arising from crediting gains from normal retirements to the reserve for depreciation? Restrict your answer to straight-line, 200 percent declining-balance, and sum-of-the-years-digits methods.

6. John Jones rents office space in a large building. In February 1973, he ordered window air-conditioning units, and they were installed on July 1 of that year at an aggregate cost of $10,000. For the calendar year 1973, he files a joint individual income tax return with his wife and uses the Facts and Circumstances life system.

   (a) What is the maximum amount of depreciation he can claim for 1973, assuming that the equipment has an estimated useful life of ten years and a salvage value of $1,200?

   (b) Is he entitled to any investment credit for 1973? If so, how much?

7. On January 4, 1972, Tyme Motor Freight, Inc., an accrual-basis and calendar-year corporation, purchased ten truck tractors at a cost of $12,100 each and recorded them in item accounts. Salvage value was estimated at $900 each at the end of a seven-year useful life. The straight-line method and the Facts and Circumstances life system were used in the 1972 return, and the corporation also elected the additional 20 percent first-year depreciation allowance and to reduce salvage value to the minimum allowable for assets acquired in 1972. Depreciation per books was computed without regard to these elections.

   (a) What amount of depreciation was claimed in the 1972 return?

   (b) Assume that tractor A in 1973 was idle for three months awaiting a replacement part. What would be the amount of depreciation applicable to it for 1973?

   (c) What was the adjusted basis of tractor A on December 31, 1973?

   (d) What amount of investment credit, if any, was allowable for 1972 on all of the tractors?

   (e) What tax effects would there be for 1974 if on December 28, 1974, tractors A, B, and C were sold for an aggregate price of $24,000?

8. Under the Class Life Asset Depreciation Range System:

   (a) Can open-end multiple-asset accounts be used?

   (b) Can a taxpayer calculate the current year's depreciation by using the actual dates of additions and retirements in a multiple-asset account? Why?

   (c) Can the CLADR system be used in calculating depreciation on current-year additions of eligible property in one class, and the Facts and Circumstances system for current-year additions of eligible property in another class?

9. A corporation is contemplating whether or not to elect the CLADR system of depreciation in its calendar-year 1972 return. Its dilemma is occasioned by these facts:

	1972 DEPRECIATION	
	FACTS AND CIRCUMSTANCES SYSTEM	CLADR
New factory building completed and put into service early in 1972	$100,000	$ 80,000
Other current-year capital expenditures for new assets	52,000·	60,000
Total	$152,000	$140,000

The taxpayer would like to have the maximum amount of depreciation available for 1972. What would you advise the corporation to do?

10. *Research Problem* [To answer some parts of this problem, it would be well to consult either the CCH *Standard Federal Tax Reporter* or P-H *Federal Taxes.*]

A partnership, engaged in the practice of law, has four equal partners. It reports taxable income on the basis of calendar years and uses the cash method of accounting. On the following dates, it purchased the following described equipment from an office-supply store pursuant to orders which in each instance were placed five days earlier:

DATE	DESCRIPTION	COST
1/10/72	1 desk (new)	$350.00
1/10/72	1 chair (new)	75.00
1/10/72	1 credenza (new)	300.00
9/15/72	1 reconditioned copying machine	250.00
		$975.00

The firm has a multiple-asset account as of the beginning of the year for furniture and fixtures purchased sporadically over the years from 1962 through 1970. There were no purchases in 1971.

(a) If the Facts and Circumstances life system was used through 1971, can these assets be added to it and that system be continued in 1972? If so, what methods of depreciation are available?

(b) If the Guideline life system was used through 1970, could it also have been used in 1971?

(c) Can these 1972 acquisitions be added into the same multiple-asset account and then the Guideline life system be continued in 1972? If so, what methods of depreciation are available?

(d) Under the CLADR system, can these 1972 acquisitions be added into the old multiple-asset account?

(e) Under the CLADR system, can all of these 1972 acquisitions be placed in a new single multiple-asset account?

(f) Under Rev. Proc. 72–10, what is the shortest life available for the 1972 acquisitions?

(g) Using that shortest life determined under part (f), what is the maximum amount of depreciation allowable on the 1972 acquisitions for the year 1972 under the CLADR system?

11. Assume the same facts as in Problem 10.

    (a) What is the maximum amount of investment credit available for 1972?

    (b) To whom is it available?

    (c) If all of the assets are transferred by the partnership to a professional corporation on May 1, 1973, in a nontaxable transaction, and if the four former partners continue as equal shareholders in the new corporation, will there be any recapture of the investment credit? How much?

    (d) If the professional corporation thereafter sells the credenza on September 15, 1973, will there be any recapture of the investment credit? If so, how much?

12. On September 1, 1971, a manufacturing corporation commenced business and installed machinery in its plant that it purchased for $980,000. For the indicated calendar years, its Federal income tax liability, before deducting any investment credit, was:

1971	$30,000
1972	50,000
1973	70,000

What amount of investment credit, if any, is allowable in those years?

13. In 1972, operator A acquires an oil and gas leasehold interest in a 640-acre tract from landowner X. Under the lease agreement, operator A pays landowner X a lease bonus of $10,000, and X reserves a royalty interest of $\frac{1}{8}$ of all minerals produced and sold from the tract covered by the leasehold. In 1973, after a producing well is drilled by another operator on some nearby acreage, Operator A assigns a $\frac{1}{2}$ interest in the leasehold to operator B. In this assignment, A reserves an overriding royalty out of the $\frac{1}{2}$ interest assigned that entitles him to receive $\frac{1}{16}$ of the minerals produced from the $\frac{1}{2}$ interest assigned to B. B pays A $25,000 for this assignment. Later that year, B sells $\frac{1}{2}$ of his interest to C for $15,000 and reserves no interest out of the interest he assigns. No oil is produced during 1972 and 1973. How much percentage depletion is allowable in 1972 and 1973 to each of the parties—X, A, and B? At the end of 1973, what is the adjusted basis (cost minus allowable depletion) of A, B, and C in their respective interests in the leasehold?

14. An oil operator owns an oil and gas leasehold for which he paid a landowner $15,000 and incurred other costs of $1,000. The landowner reserved a $\frac{1}{8}$ royalty. In 1972, the operator drilled two producing oil wells, from which in 1972 and 1973 he sold oil and incurred expenses as follows:

	1972	1973
Total sales of oil from wells	$ 24,000	$72,000
Intangible drilling costs deductible as expense	100,000	—
Lease operating expenses	4,000	10,000
Depreciation	1,000	5,000

Hauling charges	$ 1,600	$ 4,800
State production taxes	2,000	6,000
State ad valorem taxes	1,000	1,000

When the wells were completed, a petroleum engineer estimated the reserves attributable to each well were 100,000 barrels. In 1972, there were 8,000 barrels sold at $3 per barrel, and in 1973, there were 24,000 barrels sold at the same price. The landowner's share of the sales proceeds shown above were paid directly to him by the purchaser of the oil. Show the calculation of the maximum depletion allowable to the operator for 1972 and 1973.

9

LOSSES

AND

BAD DEBTS

LOSSES . . . 317

    Basic Concepts . . . 317

        DEFINITION . . . 317
        NECESSITY OF EXISTENCE OF BASIS . . . 318
        REALIZATION AND RECOGNITION . . . 318

    Restrictions on Deductible Losses . . . 319

        PUBLIC POLICY . . . 319
        LOSSES BETWEEN RELATED TAXPAYERS . . . 320

    Year of Deductibility . . . 322
    Business or Profit-Motivated Transactions of Individuals . . . 324
    Abandonment and Loss of Useful Value . . . 327

        DEPRECIABLE PROPERTY . . . 327

            ABANDONMENT . . . 327
            LOSS OF USEFUL VALUE . . . 328

        NONDEPRECIABLE PROPERTY . . . 328

    Demolition of Buildings . . . 330
    Worthless Securities . . . 330
    Casualty Losses . . . 331

        DEFINITION OF CASUALTY . . . 332
        MEASURE OF LOSS . . . 334
        YEAR OF DEDUCTIBILITY . . . 335
        DISASTER LOSSES . . . 336

    Theft Losses . . . 336
    Wagering Losses . . . 337

NET OPERATING LOSS CARRY-OVERS AND CARRY-BACKS . . . 337
BAD DEBTS . . . 339

Distinguished from Section 165 Losses . . . 339
Types and Methods of Deduction . . . 339
Definition of Debt . . . 340
Basis . . . 342
Worthlessness . . . 342
Nonbusiness Debts . . . 344
Sureties, Guarantors, and Indemnitors . . . 346
Reserves for Certain Guaranteed Debt Obligations . . . 350
Statute of Limitations . . . 352
Change in Method . . . 352

LOSSES

Section 165 states, with respect to corporations, that "there shall 9.1
be allowed as a deduction any loss sustained during the taxable year
and not compensated for by insurance or otherwise." A similar deduction is allowed to individuals, but only if (1) the losses are incurred
in a trade or business, (2) the losses are incurred in any transaction
entered into for profit though not connected with a trade or business,
or (3) the losses are of property not connected with a trade or business, and are caused by a casualty or theft.

Basic Concepts

Definition. The word *loss* is a comprehensive one:[1] "... failure to 9.2
keep that which one has is a loss ... there are many kinds of loss:
money out-of-pocket, a judgment, changing the status from solvency
to insolvency."[2] A loss differs from an expense. An expense is an
expenditure for which no asset, tangible or intangible, is acquired.
A loss can, but usually does not, result from an expenditure. It most
frequently is caused by a sale, exchange, destruction, worthlessness,
or a taking away, such as by theft. A loss can be either voluntary or
involuntary. It arises out of the occurrence of an event. A decrease
in market value but not to zero while the asset is still owned is not
a loss.

The mere fact that cost exceeds appraised value does not give rise 9.3
to a loss. In *M. J. Hellmers*[3] the Board of Tax Appeals held that the
excess of the contract price of a home over its value when completed
is not a deductible loss. Similarly, it held[4] that the purchase of the
goods of a competitor at more than their actual value in order to
eliminate his competition does not give rise to a deductible loss.
Again, in the late 1930s the Federal Power Commission adopted a
rule requiring that the properties of a public utility company be stated
at original cost when first devoted to public use. To comply with that
order, Gulf Power Company wrote down its plant accounts to their
original cost when owned by a predecessor utility company. The
Tax Court held[5] that such write-off did not result in a deductible loss.

In order to be allowable as a deduction, "a loss must be evidenced 9.4
by closed and completed transactions, fixed by identifiable events"
[Reg. 1.165–1(b)]. In determining the amount of a loss, inflation and
deflation are ignored. The dollar used is a constant dollar.

---

1. Ernest E. Lloyd, 8 BTA 1029 (1927).
2. Electric Reduction Co. v. Lewellyn, 11 F.2d 493 (3rd Cir. 1926), 5 AFTR 5897,
reversed 275 U.S. 243, 1 USTC ¶260, 6 AFTR 7074.
3. 5 BTA 198 (1926).
4. Schuman Piano Co., 10 BTA 118 (1928).
5. Gulf Power Co., 10 T.C. 852 (1948).

EXAMPLE   Assume that a man bought a personal residence in 1954 for $20,000. At the end of 1970 it is appraised as being worth $45,000. The increase was partly due to the fact that he had made a bargain purchase in 1954, but it was primarily a result of inflation through the years. In February, 1971, over vigorous objections from him and his neighbors, the district in which his home is located was rezoned. As a result, the value of the home decreased to $27,500. But the decrease is not a loss, because he still owns the house: no "event" has occurred. If he should sell the house in March or April, 1971, for $27,500, he still would not have sustained a loss, but instead would have had a profit of $7,500, measured by the excess of the dollars he received on the sale over the dollar price he paid in 1954.

9.5   **Necessity of Existence of Basis.** To be deductible, the loss must relate to capital, and the asset must have a basis. A right to earn profits is not a property right and is not an asset for tax purposes.[6] A loss of future profits is not deductible. The United States Supreme Court has said:[7] "Nothing in Section 23(e) [now Section 165(c)] indicates that Congress intended to allow petitioner to reduce ordinary income actually received and reported by the amount of income he failed to realize." In the case of *Palmer Hutcheson*[8] the taxpayer voluntarily withdrew from membership in a partnership engaged in the practice of law. The partnership agreement provided that, in the case of any such withdrawal, the partner would forfeit the amount paid in by him for his interest in the capital of the firm and would also forfeit any right to earned but uncollected fees. The Tax Court allowed a deduction for the loss of his capital interest in the amount he had paid for it, but refused to allow a deduction for his share in the earned but uncollected fees. In doing so it said:

This amount was never reported as income, and petitioners show no other way of having obtained a basis for this claimed loss ... to allow petitioners this amount as a loss would be akin to allowing a deduction for a bad debt arising from unpaid wages, salaries, rents, and other similar items of taxable income which were never reported as income by the taxpayer.

9.6   **Realization and Recognition.** A loss or gain can be realized but not recognized: an event can result in economic loss or a gain, but a provision in the Internal Revenue Code may say that the particular loss or gain, because of the nature of the transaction, shall not be recognized for income tax purposes. The transaction is treated, so far as giving rise to taxable income or deductible loss, as if it never happened. Usually the basis of the old property carries over and becomes the basis of the new property.

9.7   Section 1001(a) pertains to the determination of the amount of a realized gain or loss and provides:

The gain from the sale or other disposition of property shall be the excess of the amount realized therefrom over the adjusted basis provided in Sec-

6. International Boiler Works, 3 BTA 283, 290 (1926).
7. Hort v. Com., 313 U.S. 28 (1941), 25 AFTR 1207, 41–1 USTC ¶9354.
8. 17 T.C. 14 (1951).

tion 1011 for determining gain, and the loss shall be the excess of the adjusted basis provided in such section for determining loss over the amount realized.

Under Section 1001(b), in general, the amount realized from the sale or other disposition of property is the sum of any money received plus the fair-market value of property (other than money) received. Sections 1001(c) and 1002 then say that even though a gain or loss may be realized, it shall not be recognized if there is a provision in the Code so stating. There are a number of such provisions. Among them are exchanges pursuant to a nontaxable corporate reorganization within the scope of Section 368, exchanges of property held for productive use or investment pursuant to Section 1031, certain exchanges of insurance policies under Section 1035, and an exchange of common stock for common stock in the same corporation or of preferred stock for preferred stock in the same corporation pursuant to Section 1036. The subject of nontaxable, and accordingly nonrecognized, gains and losses is discussed elsewhere in this book, particularly in chapter 11.

Restrictions on Deductible Losses

Section 165 is a catchall section allowing deductions for losses. It applies to losses arising from sale, exchange, retirement, obsolescence or abandonment of property, demolition of buildings, worthlessness of securities, casualties, wagering, theft, disasters, and confiscation of property by the government of Cuba before January 1, 1964. However, there are restrictions. As mentioned in paragraph 2.7 and discussed more fully in chapter 12, corporations can use capital losses only to offset capital gains; individuals also can do the same, but in addition are allowed a small annual deduction from ordinary income. Further, a loss is not deductible if its allowance would be against public policy, and losses from certain transactions between related taxpayers are not deductible.

Public Policy. An illustration of the statement that a loss is not deductible if its allowance would be against public policy is found in the case of *Hopka* v. *United States*.[9] The taxpayer had been the owner and operator of slot machines in Waterloo, Iowa. The police of that city confiscated the machines, and later, under proper judicial proceedings, they were forfeited to the State of Iowa and destroyed. In his 1948 return the taxpayer claimed a loss deduction in the amount of the adjusted basis of these machines. The United States District Court for Iowa upheld the Commissioner's disallowance of the deduction as being against public policy. A pertinent extract from its opinion follows:

It was heretofore noted that in the present case the taxpayers make the claim for deduction under the "loss" sections of the Internal Revenue Code

9. 125 F. Supp. 474 (D.C. Iowa, 1961), 61–2 USTC ¶9546, 8 AFTR2d 5047.

of 1939 rather than under the provision relating to "ordinary and necessary
expenses". It would seem that, if the allowance of the deduction would
frustrate state policy, the matter of what section of the Internal Revenue
Code the deduction is claimed under would not be material. The particular
line or page of the tax return on which the deduction is claimed would appear
to be wholly irrelevant. The test to be applied is the same whether a claim
for deduction is claimed as a matter of "ordinary and necessary expenses"
or as a loss. The test is whether the deduction would frustrate a sharply defined state policy.

9.11   Under Section 165 there is no requirement that any loss sustained
in a business be "ordinary and necessary" as is true in the case of
business expenses.[10]

9.12   **Losses between Related Taxpayers.** In chapter 15, attention is directed to the fact that Section 267(a)(2) disallows the deduction of
expenses and interest when the payor is on the accrual method of
accounting and the payee uses the cash method and is also a "related"
person, unless such amounts are paid within two and one-half months
after the close of the taxable year of the accrual-basis payor. Section
267(a)(1) prohibits the deduction of losses from sales or exchanges
of property (other than arising from distributions in corporate liquidations), directly or indirectly, between these same "related" persons.
This paragraph (1) of Section 267(a) was originally enacted in 1934
as Section 24(a)(6) of the Revenue Act of 1934. The background of the
enactment is spelled out in the United States Supreme Court opinion
in *John P. McWilliams et al. v. Com.:* [11]

... Section 24(b) [of the 1939 Code, now Section 267(a)(1) of the 1954
Code] states an absolute prohibition—not a presumption—against the allowance of losses on any sales between the members of certain designated
groups. The one common characteristic of these groups is that their members,
although distinct legal entities, generally have a near identity of economic
interest. It is a fair inference that even legally genuine intragroup transfers
were not thought to result, usually, in economically genuine realizations of
loss, and accordingly that Congress did not deem them to be appropriate
occasions for the allowance of deductions.

The pertinent legislative history lends support to this inference. The congressional committees, in reporting the provisions enacted in 1934 merely
stated that "the practice of creating losses through transactions between
members of a family and close corporations has been frequently utilized for
avoiding the income tax," and that these provisions were proposed to "deny
losses to be taken in the case of [such] sales" and "to close this loophole of
tax avoidance." Similar language was used in reporting the 1937 provisions.
Chairman Doughton of the Ways and Means Committee, in explaining the
1937 provisions to the House, spoke of "the artificial taking and establishment
of losses where property was shuffled back and forth between various legal
entities owned by the same person or persons," and stated that "these trans-

10. W. R. Hervey, 25 BTA 1282, 1291 (1932).
11. 331 U.S. 694 (1947), 35 AFTR 1184, 47–1 USTC ¶9289.

actions seem to occur at moments remarkably opportune to the real party in interest in reducing his tax liability but, at the same time, allowing him to keep substantial control of the assets being traded or exchanged."

We conclude that the purpose of Section 24(b) [now Section 267(a)(1)] was to put an end to the right of taxpayers to choose by intrafamily transfers and other designated devices, their own time for realizing tax losses on investments which, for most practical purposes, are continued uninterrupted.

The related persons to which Section 267 applies are:

9.13

1. Members of a family, that is, brothers and sisters (whether by the whole or half blood), spouse, ancestors, and lineal descendants.
2. An individual and a corporation of which *more* than 50 percent in value of the outstanding stock is owned, directly or indirectly, by or for such individual.
3. Two corporations, in each of which *more* than 50 percent in value of the outstanding stock is owned, directly or indirectly, by or for the same individual, if either one of the corporations for its taxable year immediately preceding the taxable year in which the sale or exchange occurs was a personal holding company or a foreign personal holding company.
4. Certain parties to a trust as detailed in Section 267(b).
5. A person and an organization which is tax-exempt under Section 501, provided that such organization is controlled directly or indirectly by such person or members of his family.

Section 267(c) sets out the rules pertaining to constructive ownership of stock. Sometimes these are called rules of attribution. A taxpayer is deemed to own stock actually owned by another taxpayer
if certain relationships exist. These rules are applied to determine
whether an individual owns, directly or indirectly, more than 50 percent of the outstanding stock of a corporation.

9.14

A husband owns 75 percent and his wife 25 percent of the outstanding stock of a corporation. Neither the husband's brother nor the wife's father own any. After applying the rules of constructive ownership, the husband is deemed to be the owner of 100 percent of the outstanding stock; similarly, the wife is deemed to be the owner of 100 percent; the husband's brother is deemed to be the owner of 75 percent; and the wife's father is deemed to be the owner of 25 percent.

EXAMPLE 1

PERSON	ACTUAL	STOCK OWNERSHIP CONSTRUCTIVE	TOTAL UNDER SECTION 267
Husband	75%	25%	100%
Wife	25%	75%	100%
Husband's brother	None	75%	75%
Wife's father	None	25%	25%

Black and Brown are law partners and each owns exactly 50 percent of the outstanding stock of a corporation (note that Section 267(b)(2) applies only

EXAMPLE 2

where an individual owns *more* than 50 percent of the outstanding stock). By application of Section 267(c)(3), since Black and Brown each own some stock in the corporation, each is considered to own the stock owned by his partner. As a result, Black and Brown, for purposes of Section 267, each own 100 percent of the stock of the corporation.

9.15   Not only direct, but also indirect, sales or exchanges between related persons come within the scope of Section 267. One example of an indirect sale would be a sale by a husband through a dummy or straw man to his wife. The United States Supreme Court has also extended the meaning of the word *indirectly* in the case of *John P. McWilliams et al.* v. *Com., supra,* to apply to sales of stock through a broker of securities listed on the New York Stock Exchange by a member of a family, where purchases of like securities at similar prices are made on the same day by another member of the family.

9.16   Section 267 applies only to losses, not to gains. Accordingly, it can happen that if a number of separate items are sold to a related person for a lump sum, there may be a taxable gain on the transfer of some of the items and a nondeductible loss on the others.

9.17   Any disallowed loss has no effect on either the transferor or the transferee so far as the basis of the property or any other property is concerned. If the transferee later sells the property with respect to which the transferor had an unallowable loss, then any gain to the transferee is taxed only to the extent that it exceeds the loss that was disallowed to the transferor. However, if the transferee sells at a loss, he uses his original cost as his basis in determining his own loss. The transferor's loss that was disallowed is lost forever.

Year of Deductibility

9.18   As stated previously, in order that a loss can occur, it must have resulted from an event such as a sale, exchange, disposition, abandonment, or worthlessness. Regulation 1.165–1(b) provides:

> To be allowable as a deduction under Section 165(a), a loss must be evidenced by closed and completed transactions, fixed by identifiable events, and, except as otherwise provided in section 165(h) and section 1.165–11, relating to disaster losses, actually sustained during the taxable year. Only a bona fide loss is allowable. Substance and not mere form shall govern in determining a deductible loss.

9.19   The general rule applicable to the year of deductibility is that a loss is deductible in the year in which it occurs, but not earlier than the year in which claims of the taxpayer for insurance or other recompense are settled or the amounts become ascertainable with reasonable certainty. There are two exceptions. In the case of a "disaster" —provided the president of the United States declares the location to be a disaster area qualifying for federal aid—the taxpayer has an election under Section 165(h) and Reg. 1.165–11 to claim his casualty loss, not in the year in which it occurred, but instead in the preceding year. Losses arising from theft (including embezzlement) are treated as sustained in the taxable year in which the taxpayer discovers the loss. If in the year of discovery there exists a claim for reimbursement with respect to which there is a reasonable prospect of recovery, no portion of the loss can be deducted until it can be ascertained with reasonable certainty whether or not such reimbursement will be received [Reg. 1.165–8 and 1.165–1(d)(2)(i)].

Regulations 1.165–1(d)(1) and (2) set forth the rule for the year of deductibility of losses other than disaster and theft losses:

9.20

(d) Year of deduction. (1) A loss shall be allowed as a deduction under section 165(a) only for the taxable year in which the loss is sustained. For this purpose, a loss shall be treated as sustained during the taxable year in which the loss occurs as evidenced by closed and completed transactions and as fixed by identifiable events occurring in such taxable year. For provisions relating to situations where a loss attributable to a disaster will be treated as sustained in the taxable year immediately preceding the taxable year in which the disaster actually occurred, see section 165(h) and section 1.165–11.

(2) (i) If a casualty or other event occurs which may result in a loss, and in the year of such casualty or event, there exists a claim for reimbursement with respect to which there is a reasonable prospect of recovery, no portion of the loss with respect to which reimbursement may be received is sustained, for purposes of section 165, until it can be ascertained with reasonable certainty whether or not such reimbursement will be received. Whether a reasonable prospect of recovery exists with respect to a claim for reimbursement of a loss is a question of fact to be determined upon an examination of all facts and circumstances. Whether or not such reimbursement will be received may be ascertained with reasonable certainty, for example, by a settlement of the claim, by an adjudication of the claim or by an abandonment of the claim. When a taxpayer claims that the taxable year in which a loss is sustained is fixed by his abandonment of the claim for reimbursement, he must be able to produce objective evidence of his having abandoned the claim, such as the execution of a release.

(ii) If in the year of the casualty or other event a portion of the loss is not covered by a claim for reimbursement with respect to which there is a reasonable prospect of recovery, then such portion of the loss is sustained during the taxable year in which the casualty or other event occurs. For example, if property having an adjusted basis of $10,000 is completely destroyed by fire in 1961, and if the taxpayer's only claim for reimbursement consists of an insurance claim for $8,000 which is settled in 1962, the taxpayer sustains a loss of $2,000 in 1961. However, if the taxpayer's automobile is completely destroyed in 1961 as a result of the negligence of another person and there exists a reasonable prospect of recovery on a claim for the full value of the automobile against such person, the taxpayer does not sustain any loss until the taxable year in which the claim is adjudicated or otherwise settled. If the automobile has an adjusted basis of $5,000 and the taxpayer secured a judgment of $4,000 in 1962, $1,000 is deductible for the taxable year 1962. If in 1963 it becomes reasonably certain that only $3,500 can ever be collected on such judgment, $500 is deductible for the taxable year 1963.

(iii) If the taxpayer deducted a loss in accordance with the provisions of this paragraph and in a subsequent taxable year receives reimbursement for such loss, he does not recompute the tax for the taxable year in which the deduction was taken but includes the amount of such reimbursement in his gross income for the taxable year in which received, subject to the provisions of section 111, relating to recovery of amounts previously deducted.

There does not exist a "reasonable prospect of recovery" if there is only a remote hope of recovery in the indefinite future. As stated by the United States Supreme Court, "One does not need to be an incorrigible optimist." [12]

Business or Profit-Motivated Transactions of Individuals

9.21

Except in the case of casualty and theft losses, Section 165(c) requires that in order for an individual to deduct a loss it must have been incurred in a trade or business or must have been incurred in a transaction entered into for profit. An interesting case that well illustrates the problems involved in determining whether a particular transaction was entered into for profit follows:

E. T. Weir v. Com.

U.S. Circuit Court of Appeals for the Third Circuit, 1940 [13]

[Facts: In 1925 the taxpayer became a tenant in the Schenely Apartments (not a cooperative apartment building or a condominium), which building was owned by the Bellefield Co. In order to become a stockholder in that company, and thereby have some influence in maintaining standards in the apartment building, the taxpayer in 1925 and 1926 bought 250 shares of the preferred stock of that company at a cost of $25,000. In 1932 the taxpayer sought to have his rent reduced but was unsuccessful. Accordingly, he decided to move out of the apartment and sold his stock on December 16, 1932, at a loss in the amount of $21,296.25. Early in 1933 his rent was reduced from $18,600 to $10,000 per year; thereupon he changed his mind and renewed his lease on February 28, 1933. Then he once more purchased 250 shares of the preferred stock of the Bellefield Co. The Commissioner denied a deduction for the loss sustained on the sale and alleged that the purchase of the stock in 1925 and 1926 was not motivated by a desire to make a profit. Extracts from the court's opinion holding against the Commissioner follow:]

The limitation of deductible losses, outside the sphere of the taxpayer's trade or business, to those incurred in "transactions entered into for profit," first appeared on the statute books as § 5 (a) (5th) of the Revenue Act of 1916. It has been construed ever since in terms of the taxpayer's state of mind. ...

·   ·   ·   ·   ·

12. U.S. v. S. S. White Dental Mfg. Co., 274 U.S. 398 (1927), 6 AFTR 6750, 1 USTC ¶235.

13. 109 F.2d 996 (3rd Cir. 1940), 24 AFTR 453, 40-1 USTC ¶9200, reversing 39 BTA 400 on point discussed in text, cert. denied 60 S. Ct. 1080.

When stock is the subject matter of the transaction, the taxpayer's optimism stands on a much firmer footing. More than twenty years ago a terse Office Decision ruled that the "profit" which must be intended on the purchase of property might relate to income flowing from the tenure of that property, as well as gains realized from its resale. ... This construction is of course an eminently reasonable, indeed necessary, one—otherwise it would be virtually impossible to buy bonds at a premium "for profit"—and it has been consistently followed. By hypothesis, the purchase of stock carries with it in the form of dividends a share in the earnings and profits of the corporation. Again, by hypothesis, although profits are not always forthcoming, the corporation, at least, is trying to earn them, and generally does. Of course if the corporation cannot earn them, and the taxpayer knows that its stock is worthless, his acquisition of that stock is surely not for profit. ... The simpler case is where the corporation is not even trying to earn profits, and the taxpayer has been instrumental in its organization. ... So, the intention to purchase stock must from the very nature of the thing purchased include the intention to receive profits (dividends or accretion in value) unless the purchaser knows at the time of purchase that such profits are an impossibility.

Before proceeding further, it is appropriate to notice a timeworn but salient distinction and corresponding difference in terminology. We quote:

> "... 'Intent' may be used in at least three distinct legal meanings. It may designate simply the exercise of willpower necessary to cause muscular or physical movement. This concept is, of course, irrelevant in the field of tax law. Secondly, it may denote the immediate result desired by the actor. Thirdly, it may signify the ultimate reason for aiming at that immediate objective. At this point, however, intent shades into motive, which is really the ulterior intent or the cause of the intent. Intent, in other words, is the object of the act; motive, in turn, is the object or spring of the intent. Using the terms in these senses, intent is frequently material to tax questions; whereas motive—properly enough—is of importance only in comparatively rare instances."

—Paul, *Motive and Intent in Federal Tax Law, Selected Studies in Federal Taxation,* Second Series, pp. 257–58.

Petitioner's profit intention must, we think, be taken for granted. His purchase of preferred stock is of course conceded, and that is sufficient to establish prima facie his intent to profit. The deduction has been allowed on similar showings. ... Nothing in the record tends to disprove the intention so established. It is not suggested that petitioner knew, or had any cause to know, that his purchase would be profitless. Furthermore, petitioner's intention and motive of influencing the "standards" of the corporation through his stock ownership presents no repugnancy. One does not exhibit an intention to bid farewell to profits by signing a proxy. This last, it will be noted, serves to distinguish the decisions dealing with nonincome producing property. If, for instance, the taxpayer has purchased a yacht, his cruising about in it presupposes a state of mind inconsistent with making a profit out of it by chartering. Hence that inconsistency must be resolved by ascertaining whether the intention or motive of pleasure or that of profit is the "prime thing". ... In the instant case, on the other hand, no such resolution is necessary. We have a profit intention, side by side with a non-profit motive.

We are brought, then, to the final question: is the requirement "for profit" satisfied by the petitioner's intention or by his motive? ...

The benefit of increased revenue is certainly not assured when there is no intention to profit. But the profit intention and the profit motive each assure that benefit with equal force. The public coffers are weighted with the same amount from taxes on Bellefield Company dividends, whether the stock is held with the motive of voting or with the motive of profit. That portion of petitioner's capital was "used to produce taxable income." That being so, petitioner is entitled to his deduction. We need hardly add that a contrary position would only serve to embroil the administrators of the taxing statute in a hectic and ridiculous search for nonprofit motives.

9.22   A loss sustained on the sale of residential property used as such up to the time of the sale is not deductible, because the acquisition of the property was not profit-motivated [Reg. 1.165–9(a)]. If property used as a personal residence is rented out and then sold, any loss sustained will be deductible. The amount of the deductible loss is measured by the lower of: (1) fair market value of the property at the time of conversion to rental use less depreciation allowed or allowable since that date or (2) adjusted basis for loss at the time of conversion, determined without regard to fair market value, less depreciation allowed or allowable since that date. Regulation 1.165–9(c) gives the following example:

EXAMPLE
FROM REG.

(1). Residential property is purchased by the taxpayer in 1943 for use as his personal residence at a cost of $25,000, of which $15,000 is allocable to the building. The taxpayer uses the property as his personal residence until January 1, 1952, at which time its fair market value is $22,000, of which $12,000 is allocable to the building. The taxpayer rents the property from January 1, 1952, until January 1, 1955, at which time it is sold for $16,000. On January 1, 1952, the building has an estimated useful life of twenty years. It is assumed that the building has no estimated salvage value and that there are no adjustments in respect of basis other than depreciation, which is computed on the straight-line method. The loss to be taken into account for purposes of section 165(a) for the taxable year 1955 is $4,200, computed as follows:

Basis of property at time of conversion for purposes of this section (that is, the lesser of $25,000 cost or $22,000 fair market value)	$22,000
Less: Depreciation allowable from January 1, 1952, to January 1, 1955 (3 years at 5% based on $12,000, the value of the building at time of conversion, as prescribed by § 1.167(g)-1)	1,800
Adjusted basis prescribed in § 1.1011-1 for determining loss on sale of property	$20,200
Less: Amount realized on sale	16,000
Loss to be taken into account for purposes of section 165(a)	$ 4,200

In this example the value of the building at the time of conversion is used as the basis for computing depreciation. See example (2) of this paragraph wherein the adjusted basis of the building is required to be used for such purpose. [In example (2) referred to, the original cost of the house was $10,000 and its fair market value on date of conversion to rental use was $12,000. Depreciation was allowable only on the cost of $10,000. The loss was determined by subtracting the sales proceeds from the original cost of the land and building less depreciation allowed on the cost of the building.]

If stock is purchased in a club as a condition of membership and a loss is sustained upon disposition of it at a later date, the loss is not deductible.[14] If a taxpayer could prove that his acquisition of the stock in a club and his actual use of the club were primarily to further his trade or business and directly related to active conduct of that trade or business, he ought to be allowed a deduction.[15]   **9.23**

Abandonment and Loss of Useful Value

A loss can result from the abandonment or loss of useful value of property, tangible or intangible, depreciable or nondepreciable. The amount of the loss will be the adjusted basis reduced by any salvage value.   **9.24**

DEPRECIABLE PROPERTY. The term "depreciable property" includes not only property as to which depreciation deductions are claimed under Section 167 but also property that is depreciable in nature but that is amortized.   **9.25**

ABANDONMENT. Regulation 1.167(a)(8), part of which was discussed in paragraphs 8.46, 8.54, and 8.55, makes the following statement about abandonment of depreciable property: **9.26**

(a) ... Upon the retirement of assets, the rules in this section apply in determining whether gain or loss will be recognized, the amount of such gain or loss, and the basis for determining gain or loss: ...
(4) Where an asset is retired by actual physical abandonment (as, for example, in the case of a building condemned as unfit for further occupancy or other use), loss will be recognized measured by the amount of the adjusted basis of the asset abandoned at the time of such abandonment. In order to qualify for the recognition of loss from physical abandonment, the intent of the taxpayer must be irrevocably to discard the asset so that it will neither be used again by him nor retrieved by him for sale, exchange, or other disposition.

There must be a complete and permanent abandonment of the property. If the use of equipment ceases, but the taxpayer continues to hold it for stand-by use, there has been no abandonment.[16] For   **9.27**

14. Samuel Riker, Jr., 6 BTA 890 (1927); James F. Curtis, 39 BTA 366 (1939), affirmed on other points 110 F.2d 1014 (2nd Cir.), 24 AFTR 836; John S. Martin, ¶44,198 P–H Memo T.C.
15. This is the authors' opinion, taking into account Section 274.
16. Boston Elevated Railway Co., 16 T.C. 1084, affirmed without discussion of this point 196 F.2d 923 (1st Cir. 1952), 41 AFTR 1353.

example, if a gas distribution company, after converting to natural gas, retains a building and equipment for the manufacture of gas for possible emergency use in the future, there has been no abandonment. Again, if a factory building is closed down, but the equipment inside is maintained and protected against corrosion because of the possibility that it may become necessary or desirable to reopen the factory, there has been no abandonment. However, if machinery is dismantled and put into a scrap heap awaiting sale to a buyer of scrap metal, there has been an abandonment of the machinery. In *Realty Operators, Inc.*,[17] the owner of the equity in an office building, after a foreclosure action was started, gave up peaceful possession to the mortgagee and in the year 1936 adopted a resolution abandoning "any and all rights, title and interests which it has or might have in and to the said property." A certified copy of the resolution was immediately forwarded to the mortgagee. The foreclosure action proceeded and in 1937, pursuant to an order of the court, the taxpayer signed a master's deed for the purpose of "placing of record that it has no right, title and interest therein." The Board of Tax Appeals held that an abandonment occurred in 1936 upon adoption of the resolution, surrender of possession, and notification of the abandonment to the mortgagee. It held further that thereupon the taxpayer ceased to have any equitable interest in the property, even though it continued to have legal title until conclusion of the foreclosure action in 1937.

9.28   LOSS OF USEFUL VALUE. As applied to depreciable property, the term "loss of useful value" means sudden extraordinary obsolescence; that subject was discussed in paragraphs 8.73 to 8.75. There would then be a loss resulting from an abnormal retirement.

9.29   **Nondepreciable Property.** Regulation 1.165–2 applies to land and other types of nondepreciable property, both tangible and intangible. It reads in part as follows:

Obsolescence of nondepreciable property.
(a) Allowance of deduction—A loss incurred in a business or in a transaction entered into for profit and arising from the sudden termination of the usefulness in such business or transaction of any nondepreciable property, in a case where such business or transaction is discontinued or where such property is permanently discarded from use therein, shall be allowed as a deduction under section 165(a) for the taxable year in which the loss is actually sustained. For this purpose, the taxable year in which the loss is sustained is not necessarily the taxable year in which the overt act of abandonment, or the loss of title to the property, occurs.
(b) Exceptions—This section does not apply to losses sustained upon the sale or exchange of property, losses sustained upon the obsolescence or worthlessness of depreciable property, casualty losses, or losses reflected in inventories required to be taken under section 471. The limitations con-

17. 40 BTA 1051 (1939).

tained in sections 1211 and 1212 upon losses from the sale or exchange of capital assets do not apply to losses allowable under this section.

The heading "Obsolescence of Nondepreciable Property" appearing as the description of the subject matter of this section of the regulations is quite misleading. More properly, it should read: "Abandonment or Sudden Loss of Useful Value of Nondepreciable Property."

9.30

Note that there are two principal requirements with respect to the abandonment or loss of useful value of nondepreciable property; it must (1) arise in a business or in a transaction entered into for profit, and (2) result from the *sudden* termination of the usefulness of such property in such business or transaction. The suddenness requirement will usually be fulfilled by an actual abandonment. However, the courts have held and the Service agrees that a deduction for loss of useful value is allowable only in the year in which property, whether real or personal, first becomes worthless, even if the overt act of abandonment or the loss of title occurs in a later year.[18]

9.31

Nonuse of property is not the equivalent of abandonment, especially where the property is not disposed of and might become productive or profitable in the future. In *Hazeltine Corp.* v. *U.S.*[19] the Court of Claims held that mere nonuse of three trademarks since 1930 did not indicate an abandonment in 1930, but instead the trademarks were abandoned in 1944 when the board of directors adopted a resolution directing such abandonment and instructing that the cost of the trademarks be written off the books of account. Extracts from the trial commissioner's opinion follow:

... It has been held by the Courts, however, that mere nonuse of a trademark is not enough to establish abandonment. ... Although the public demand for a particular product previously associated with a trade-mark disappears, the owner of the trade-mark can still retain it with the possibility of using it again upon another product of the same class. ...

The abandonment of an asset involves an actual intent on the part of the owner to abandon it, plus an act or acts by the owner designed to carry out such intention. ... The element of intent is especially important in considering whether there has been an abandonment. ... Whether there was an intention to abandon and an act or acts of abandonment in a particular case must be ascertained from all the pertinent facts. ...

It is my opinion that the facts of the present case do not show either an intention to abandon or an act of abandonment of the trade-marks ... prior to 1943. On the contrary, the conduct of the plaintiff in consistently showing these trade-marks as assets on its books and records prior to 1943 tends to establish the lack of any intention by the plaintiff to abandon the trade-marks during the pre-1943 period. ...

---

18. Alice V. Gordon, 46 BTA 1201 (Acq., 1951–1 C.B. 2), affirmed 134 F.2d 685 (7th Cir. 1943), 43–1 USTC ¶9376, 30 AFTR 1178; Rev. Rul. 54–581, 1954–2 C.B. 112.

19. 170 F. Supp. 615 (Ct. Cls., 1959), 59–1 USTC ¶9242, 3 AFTR2d 640; also in support: Lewis Corp., 22 TCM 35 (1963), Jones Beach Theatre Corp., 25 TCM 527 (1966).

The trial commissioner then went on to say that the adoption of the resolution by the board of directors in 1943, declaring the three trademarks would not be reregistered, but would be abandoned, evidenced only an intent to abandon. The act of abandonment, he held, occurred in 1944 when the directors adopted a resolution abandoning the trademarks and directed the officers to write their cost off the books of account.

Demolition of Buildings

9.32   If at the time improved real property is purchased there is an intention on the part of the purchaser to demolish the buildings situated thereon, no part of the purchase price is allocable to the buildings; and the cost of the demolition, reduced by any proceeds from the sale of materials or scrap, is added to the cost of the land. If the intention to demolish the buildings is formed sometime after acquisition of the real property, an abandonment loss is allowable under Section 165 in the amount of adjusted basis of the building plus the cost of demolition, reduced by any proceeds from the sale of materials or scrap [Reg. 1.165–3].

Worthless Securities

9.33   Portfolio investments held by any taxpayer are capital assets. Any loss due to worthlessness of any such security is treated under Section 165(g)(1) as a capital loss as of the last day of the taxable year. If a security becomes worthless within six months after its acquisition, this rule can result in such a capital loss becoming a long-term one. For purposes of all of Section 165(g), securities are defined as (1) shares of stock, (2) stock rights, and (3) bonds, debentures, notes, certificates, or other written evidence of indebtedness issued by a corporation or by a government or political subdivision, with interest coupons or in registered form. If a bond, note, or debenture is not issued in registered form and does not have attached interest coupons, it is not a security for purposes of Section 165.

9.34   Securities, as defined in the preceding paragraph, owned as stock in trade by a dealer in securities (as contrasted to a trader, investor, or speculator) are not capital assets, and any loss from worthlessness is an ordinary loss.

9.35   A special rule applies to a domestic corporation that owns securities of an affiliated corporation, either domestic or foreign. A subsidiary corporation is affiliated with its domestic parent if (1) at least 80 percent of the voting power of all classes of stock and at least 80 percent of each class of nonvoting stock is owned directly by the parent, and (2) more than 90 percent of the aggregate of its gross receipts for all taxable years has been from other than passive income. For the detailed requirements of the types of income, see Section 165(g)(3)(B). If the two tests are met, the loss from worthlessness of any security is an ordinary one.

The Board of Tax Appeals in *Sterling Morton*[20] held that shares of   9.36
stock or other securities must pass two tests in order to be deemed
worthless:

The ultimate value of stock, and conversely its worthlessless, will depend
not only on its current liquidating value, but also on what value it may acquire in the future through the foreseeable operations of the corporation. Both
factors of value must be wiped out before we can definitely fix the loss. If
the assets of the corporation exceed its liabilities, the stock has a liquidating
value. If its assets are less than its liabilities, but there is a reasonable hope
and expectation that the assets will exceed the liabilities of the corporation
in the future, its stock, while having no liquidating value, has a potential
value and cannot be said to be worthless. The loss of potential value, if it
exists, can be established ordinarily with satisfaction only by some "identifiable event" in the corporation's life which puts an end to such hope and
expectation.

In determining the assets of the corporation for this purpose, market
values, not book amounts, are used. If a corporation has an excess of
liabilities over the market value of its assets but is still engaged in
business, it will be extremely difficult to obtain a deduction for worthlessness of its stock or securities. The burden of proof is always on
the taxpayer. Because it is so difficult to prove the year in which a
security becomes worthless, a special statutory period of limitations
on refund claims was enacted some years ago. In lieu of the ordinary
rule of three years from the date the return was filed, or two years
from the date upon which a deficiency in tax was paid, Section 6511(d)
prescribes a period of seven years within which a claim for refund
can be filed in the case of a loss due to the worthlessness of a security.

Casualty Losses

When an individual suffers a loss arising from damage to or destruc-   9.37
tion of *property* from "fires, storms, shipwrecks, or other casualty, or
from theft," a deduction is allowed whether or not the property was
strictly of a personal type or was connected with a trade or business
or a transaction entered into for profit. Although a corporation is entitled to deduct all types of losses, including casualty losses, under
Section 165(a) to the extent not compensated for by insurance or
otherwise, nevertheless the rules in the regulations under Section
165 pertaining to casualty losses govern the amount of the deduction
for that type of a loss. The subject of theft losses is discussed herein
a few paragraphs later.

In the case of an individual's property that is not used in a trade or   9.38
business or in a transaction entered into for profit—used or owned by
him for pleasure, living, or other personal reasons—a loss in whole
or in part of his property is deductible only if it arises from a casualty.

20. 38 BTA 1270 (1938).

The loss must be of the property itself. If a storm causes a power failure and damage to a house, resulting in expenses for temporary housing, damage to the douse is deductible, but not the expense of the temporary housing.[21] However, if insurance proceeds are received as reimbursement of the cost of the temporary housing, such amount is excluded from gross income by Section 123. When a well on residential property became contaminated, the cost of buying drinking water at a store and the cost of drilling a new well were held not to be deductible.[22] Also, amounts paid to others in settlement of judgments for personal injuries resulting from an automobile collision are not deductible as a casualty loss.[23] Because the loss must pertain to the taxpayer's own property, a payment to another for damage to his property arising from a casualty is not deductible.[24]

9.39   The casualty must damage the property itself. If it merely reduces the resale value of property, no loss can be deducted. In *Pulvers* v. *Com.*[25] a landslide ruined three nearby homes, but did no physical damage to the residence of the taxpayer. The Ninth Circuit Court of Appeals held he was not entitled to a casualty loss deduction because the diminution in value was due to buyer resistance caused by fears of further landslides.

9.40   **Definition of Casualty.** Court decisions and IRS rulings hold that *other casualty* means a casualty of the same general nature as "fires, storms, shipwreck." *Casualty* as used in Section 165(c)(3) means an identifiable event of a sudden, unexpected, and unusual nature;[26] and damage or loss resulting from progressive deterioration of property through a steadily operating cause does not constitute a casualty loss.[27]

9.41   The courts have found a steadily operating cause rather than a sudden and unexpected casualty in a number of instances. A loss caused by Dutch elm disease was held not to be deductible because damage caused by disease is not sudden but progressive.[28] In a particular locality where Dutch elm disease was prevalent, a loss of trees was not a sudden and unexpected casualty.[29] Rusting and corrosion of reinforcing steel used in cement sill and floor beams of

21. Rev. Rul. 59–398, 1959–2 C.B. 76.

22. Richard A. Dow, 16 T.C. 1230 (1951).

23. Karl Stern v. Carey, 119 F. Supp. 488 (D.C. Ohio, 1953), 54–1 USTC ¶9190, 45 AFTR 741; similarly Dickinson, 20 BTA 496.

24. C. W. Stoll, 5 TCM 731 (1946).

25. 407 F.2d 838 (9th Cir. 1969), 23 AFTR 69–678, affirming 48 T.C. 245.

26. Bercaw, 6 TCM 27 (1947), affirmed 165 F.2d 521 (4th Cir. 1948), 48–1 USTC ¶9153, 36 AFTR 659.

27. Rev. Rul. 79, 1953–1 C.B. 41.

28. Burno v. U.S., 174 F. Supp. 203 (D.C. Ohio, 1959), 59–2 USTC ¶9514, 3 AFTR2d 1520, affirmed per curiam 284 F.2d 436 (6th Cir. 1960), 61–1 USTC ¶9127, 6 AFTR2d 6036. The District Court opinion is well reasoned and reviews a great many court decisions pertaining to all types of casualties.

29. Appelman v. U.S., 338 F.2d 729 (7th Cir. 1964), 14 AFTR2d 5957, reversing 12 AFTR2d 5551 (D.C. Ill.).

a house built on an island was not a sudden casualty.[30] Nor was suddenness found in losses caused by infestation of rats,[31] erosion,[32] and
moth damage to a fur coat.[33]

9.42 Cases involving termite damage have turned upon facts and testimony concerning suddenness. The Ninth[34] and Second[35] Circuit
Courts of Appeal and the Internal Revenue Service[36] have held that
termite damage results from progressive deterioration rather than a
sudden invasion by a hostile force. The Eighth Circuit[37] and the
District Courts of Missouri and South Carolina[38] have held to the contrary.

9.43 The element of suddenness was found to be present where a loss
was occasioned by an earthquake or a flood,[39] by a sudden freeze,[40] a
relatively rapid and severe sinking of land,[41] and blasting in a quarry
near a taxpayer's residence.[42]

9.44 Losses from automobile accidents today are probably the most
prevalent casualty loss. Regulation 1.165–7(a)(3) reads as follows:

> An automobile owned by the taxpayer, whether used for business purposes
> or maintained for recreation or pleasure, may be the subject of a casualty
> loss. ... In addition, a casualty loss occurs when an automobile owned by the
> taxpayer is damaged and when:
> (i) The damage results from the faulty driving of the taxpayer operating
> the automobile but is not due to the willful act or willful negligence of the
> taxpayer or of one acting in his behalf, or
> (ii) The damage results from the faulty driving of the operator of the
> vehicle with which the automobile of the taxpayer collides.

9.45 In a very early case, and still a landmark one, *Shearer v. Anderson*,[43]
the taxpayer's automobile overturned, primarily because of an icy
road, while the car was "in the unlawful and unauthorized possession
of plaintiff's chauffeur." The Second Circuit Court of Appeals held
this was a deductible casualty loss and pointed out that it was "not
caused by the willful act or neglect of the owner or of one acting in
his behalf."

30. Matheson et al. v. Com., 54 F.2d 537 (2nd Cir. 1931), 2 USTC ¶830, 10 AFTR
945, affirming 18 BTA 674.
31. Banigan, 10 TCM 561 (1951).
32. Texas & Pacific Ry. Co., 1 TCM 863 (1943).
33. Rev. Rul. 55–327, 1955–1 C.B. 25.
34. U.S. v. Rogers, 120 F.2d 244 (9th Cir. 1941), 41–1 USTC ¶9442, 27 AFTR 423.
35. Fay v. Helvering, 120 F.2d 253 (2nd Cir. 1941), 41–2 USTC ¶9494, 27 AFTR 432.
36. Rev. Rul. 63–232.
37. Rosenberg, 198 F.2d 46 (8th Cir. 1952), 52–2 USTC ¶9377, 42 AFTR 303.
38. Shopmaker v. U.S., 119 F. Supp. 705 (D.C. Mo., 1953), 54–1 USTC ¶9195,
45 AFTR 758; Buist v. U.S., 164 F. Supp. 218 (D.C. S.C., 1958), 58–2 USTC ¶9806,
2 AFTR2d 5584.
39. Lyman v. Com., 83 F.2d 811 (1st Cir. 1936), 36–2 USTC ¶9307, 17 AFTR 1197.
40. U.S. v. Barrett, 202 F.2d 804 (5th Cir. 1953), 53–1 USTC ¶9284.
41. Grant v. Com., 30 BTA 1028 (1934).
42. Durden, 3 T.C. 1 (1944).
43. 16 F.2d 995 (2nd Cir. 1927), 1 USTC ¶210, 6 AFTR 6483.

9.46   A mysterious disappearance of property is not a casualty loss; neither is an accidental loss of property. In this area the courts have created a further requirement that there must be intervention of a sudden or destructive force in order to have a deductible casualty loss. Damage or a loss caused by carelessness does not result from the intervention of a sudden or destructive force and is not a casualty. In *Stevens v. Com.*,[44] while the taxpayer was hunting ducks and in the act of retrieving a decoy, his ring slipped from his finger and was lost in muddy water. The court held this occurrence was not a casualty. Deductions have also been disallowed for the accidental breakage of eyeglasses,[45] a watch,[46] and glassware.[47]

9.47   **Measure of Loss.** Regulation 1.165–7(b)(1) provides:

> (b) Amount deductible.—(1) General rule.—In the case of any casualty loss whether or not incurred in a trade or business or in any transaction entered into for profit, the amount of loss to be taken into account for purposes of section 165(a) shall be the lesser of either–
> (i) The amount which is equal to the fair market value of the property immediately before the casualty reduced by the fair market value of the property immediately after the casualty; or
> (ii) The amount of the adjusted basis prescribed in ¶ 1.1011–1 for determining the loss from the sale or other disposition of the property involved
>
> However, if property used in a trade or business or held for the production of income is totally destroyed by casualty, and if the fair market value of such property immediately before the casualty is less than the adjusted basis of such property, the amount of the adjusted basis of such property shall be treated as the amount of the loss for purposes of section 165(a).

9.48   In computing a loss on nonbusiness property, it is treated as a unit. Thus, although a specific item may be damaged, such as shade trees around a home, the measure of the damage is the decline in value of the property as a whole, but not more than the adjusted basis. A different rule applies to business or income-producing property. It must be separated into its component parts—land, building, trees, shrubs; and a separate deduction is figured for each item [Reg. 1.165–7(b)(2)].

9.49   Since 1964, a further adjustment must be made by individuals who sustain a loss of property not connected with a trade or business. The first $100 of loss from each casualty during a year is not deductible, and for this purpose a husband and wife filing a joint return are treated as one individual [Section 165(c)(3)].

44. 6 TCM 805 (1947), ¶47,191 P–H Memo T.C.
45. Samuel Poorman, Jr., 45 BTA 73, affirmed on another point 131 F.2d 946 (9th Cir. 1942), 30 AFTR 507.
46. Willard J. Thompson, 15 T.C. 609, affirmed on another point 193 F.2d 586 (10th Cir. 1951), 41 AFTR 619.
47. Robert M. Diggs, 18 TCM 443 (1959), ¶59,099 P–H Memo T.C. affirmed 281 F.2d 326 (2nd Cir. 1960), 6 AFTR2d 5095.

During the year a storm damages the taxpayer's residence to the extent of $500 and on another occasion a collision damages his automobile fenders in the amount of $90. The total casualty loss deduction is $400 ($500 − $100), and the $90 fender damage is not deductible. **EXAMPLE 1**

The facts are the same as in Example 1, except that the damage to the automobile occurred while it was parked in the driveway of his home and was caused by the same storm. The amount deductible is $490 ($500 + $90 − $100). **EXAMPLE 2**

If damage is sustained by property used partially for business and partially for nonbusiness purposes, Reg. 1.165–7(c)(iv) provides: **9.50**

... the $100 limitation applies only to that portion of the loss properly attributable to the nonbusiness use. For example, if a taxpayer sustains a $1,000 loss in respect of an automobile which he uses 60 percent for business and 40 percent for nonbusiness, the loss is allocated 60 percent to business and 40 percent to nonbusiness use. The $100 limitation applies to the portion of the loss allocable to the nonbusiness use.

In applying the $100 floor, it makes no difference whether the car was being used for business or pleasure when it was damaged. The allocation is made in accordance with the actual percentage of total usage.[48]

Regulation 1.165–7(a)(2)(ii) provides that the cost of repairs to the property is acceptable as evidence of the loss of value if the taxpayer shows all four of the following: **9.51**

(a) the repairs are necessary to restore the property to its condition immediately before the casualty
(b) the amount spent for such repairs is not excessive
(c) the repairs do not care for more than the damage suffered
(d) the value of the property after the repairs does not, as a result of the repairs, exceed the value of the property immediately before the casualty

Year of Deductibility. A casualty loss must be deducted in the year sustained, even though the amount of loss could be better established in a subsequent year when the property is sold or when the loss is discovered.[49] When the taxpayer has a claim against a third party for reimbursement, the deduction is not allowed, however, "... until it can be ascertained with reasonable certainty whether or not such reimbursement will be received" [Reg. 1.165–1(d)(2)(i)]; for example, when litigation over a claim for reimbursement is resolved.[50] De- **9.52**

---

48. Imeson, ¶69,180 P–H Memo T.C.
49. Reg. 1.165–1(d); Alfred M. Cox, ¶65,005 P–H Memo T.C., affirmed 354 F.2d 659 (3rd Cir. 1966), 17 AFTR2d 228.
50. Callan v. Westover, 116 F. Supp. 191 (S.D. Cal., 1953), 44 AFTR 731, affirmed *sub nom,* Riddell v. Callan, 235 F.2d 190 (9th Cir. 1956), 49 AFTR 1721; The Wellston Company, 24 TCM 306 (1965), ¶65,055 P–H Memo T.C. (taxpayer need not be "an incorrigible optimist" re prospect of recovery).

ductibility is deferred for only that portion of the loss which is subject to a reasonable likelihood of reinbursement; the balance is deductible immediately [Reg. 1.165–1(d)(2)(ii)].

9.53 **Disaster Losses.** There is another exception, and a beneficial one, to the general rule that a casualty loss must be deducted in the year in which sustained. If (1) a disaster occurs during a year and (2) the president of the United States declares the area to be a disaster area warranting federal assistance, the taxpayer can elect to treat such disaster as having been incurred in the prior year and can deduct its amount in that prior year. The election is made by claiming the deduction in the return, an amended return, or a claim for refund. The deadline for so electing is the later of (1) the date prescribed for the filing of the income tax return (disregarding extensions of time) for the taxable year in which the disaster actually occurred, or (2) the due date of the return for the preceding year, taking into account any extensions of time for filing.

Theft Losses

9.54

Section 165(c)(3) also allows a deduction for any loss "arising from theft" of property not connected with a trade or business. Because a theft may not be discovered for a matter of years, the deduction is allowed in the year in which the theft is discovered [Section 165(e)]. As with casualty losses, only the excess of the loss over $100 is deductible, and the amount of the loss is measured by the lower of the value of the stolen property or the taxpayer's adjusted basis in the property at the time of the theft [Reg. 1.165–8(c)]. A stolen art object may be worth much more than its tax basis, but no relief for this lost
9.55 appreciation is available in the form of a tax deduction.

The regulations define *theft* as including, but not necessarily limited to, larceny, embezzlement, and robbery [Reg. 1.165–8(d)]. The taxpayer must show that the property actually was stolen: a "mysterious disappearance" or "loss by some mischance or inadvertence" is not considered a theft loss.[51] Usually, making a police report and showing that there was breaking and entry will assist in proving that
9.56 the property was stolen rather than mislaid.

Generally, if someone has misappropriated the taxpayer's property, a deduction for a theft loss will be allowed.[52] This includes wrongful appropriation by the members of a taxpayer's family.[53] Amounts ap-

51. Mary Frances Allen, 16 T.C. 163 (1951); Jane U. Elliott, 40 T.C. 304 (1963) (Acq.).

52. Thomas Miller, 19 T.C. 1946 (1953); Norton v. Com., 333 F.2d 1005 (9th Cir. 1964), 13 AFTR2d 1775.

53. Saul M. Weingarten, 38 T.C. 75 (1962) (Acq., 1963–1 C.B. 1).

propriated by a husband or wife from the other spouse ordinarily are not deductible because most states consider that embezzlement cannot occur within the marriage relationship.[54] One jilted suitor who found that his ex-fiancée had appropriated a joint savings account was unable to prove a theft. He did obtain a deduction for a nonbusiness bad debt, to the extent that the conversion of funds created a creditor-debtor relationship.[55]

Wagering Losses

Under Section 165(d), gambling losses are deductible only to the extent of offsetting gambling gains. Gambling losses in excess of gambling gains are not deductible.   9.57

Gambling gains and losses may be offset, regardless of source. For example, losses incurred in horse-race betting and in card games can be commingled and offset against gains from one or both activities.[56] A partner's individual gambling losses can be offset by his share of the partnership gambling gains or vice versa. The burden is on the taxpayer to prove that gambling losses were incurred in the amount claimed. There is no carry-back or carry-forward of net gambling losses from one year to offset gambling gains in another. These gambling limitations apply whether the taxpayer is a professional gambler or not.[57]   9.58

A nonprofessional gambler must include gross gambling gains in gross income and adjusted gross income. He can deduct his gambling losses only *from* adjusted gross income and then only if he itemizes deductions, but a professional gambler deducts his gambling losses in determining adjusted gross income.   9.59

NET OPERATING LOSS CARRY–OVERS AND CARRY–BACKS

At least intermittently since 1918 there has been a provision in the revenue laws allowing a carry-over, and sometimes a carry-back, for varying periods of time of net operating losses arising in businesses. The amount of the net operating loss is allowed as a deduction in the year to which carried. The purpose of the provision, of course, is to even out, over a span of years, periods of profits and losses from operations.   9.60

54. Grover Tyler, 13 T.C. 186 (1949).
55. Kliks v. U.S. (D.C. Ore., 1966), 17 AFTR2d 213.
56. Scott-Nickels Bus Co., ¶56,120 P–H Memo T.C.
57. Skeeles v. U.S., 95 F. Supp. 242 (Ct. Cl., 1951), 40 AFTR 197, cert. denied 341 U.S. 948.

9.61   A net operating loss consists of the excess of business deductions over business gross income, and for this purpose casualty losses, whether of individuals or of corporations, are treated as business losses. The year in which such a minus amount of taxable income results is called the *loss year*. The net operating loss sustained in that year is carried back for three years, and then forward for five years. In other words, there is a total of eight other years in which that net operating loss can be utilized. The loss is carried back to the earliest of the eight years, and then forward one by one to the most distant year. For example, a net operating loss sustained in 1970 is carried back first to 1967. Any portion not utilized in 1967 is then carried into 1968; any portion not utilized in 1968 is carried into 1969; any balance is carried into 1971; and so on through the year 1975.

9.62   In the case of individuals, estates, and trusts the purpose of the law is to allow the carry-back and then carry-over of an economic loss determined after excluding the excess of nonbusiness deductions over nonbusiness income. A nonbusiness deduction can never give rise to a net operating loss. Such a taxpayer can have a net operating loss, accordingly, only by experiencing a net loss from the operation of a business as a proprietor or through a partnership, or by sustaining a somewhat major casualty loss (as mentioned previously, a casualty loss is always treated as a business loss).

9.63   The deficit in taxable income shown by a taxpayer on his return for a loss year is not the amount of the net operating loss for that year that may be carried backward or forward. It must first be modified by the adjustments set forth in Section 172(d). Similarly, when a net operating loss is carried forward through an intervening year, modifications must be made in the amount of the taxable income of that intervening year. For example, if there is a net operating loss of $50,000, determined as provided in Sections 172(c) and (d), for the year 1970, that loss must first be carried back to the year 1967. If the tax return for the year 1967 shows a plus amount of taxable income in the amount of $10,000, only $10,000 of the operating loss will be utilized in the year 1967. The remaining amount of $40,000 is then available to be carried into 1968. However, seldom will the amount of $40,000, as used in this example, be the amount available for carry-over into 1968. It must first be adjusted by certain elements of income and deductions applicable to the intervening year 1967. Such modifications as to this intervening year are required by Section 172(b)(2), which incorporates many of the modifications required under Section 172(d) pertaining to the manner in which to compute the net operating loss of the loss year. On the other hand, if in this example the taxable income shown in the 1967 return was $50,000 or more, no modification would be required to be made to the taxable income of that year and the full carry-back from 1970 to 1967 would be utilized.

9.64   An example of the calculation of a net operating loss for an individual follows:

	BUSINESS	NON-BUSINESS	TOTAL
Gross income:			
Salary	$ 10,000	$ —	$ 10,000
Interest on savings	—	500	500
Excess of net long-term capital gain over net short-term capital loss from sale of securities	—	2,000	2,000
Deduction under Sec. 1202 of 50% of net gain	—	(1,000)	(1,000)
	$ 10,000	$ 1,500	$ 11,500
Deductions:			
Flood loss on residence not covered by insurance	$ 20,000	$ —	$ 20,000
Interest on mortgage	—	800	800
Medical expenses	—	300	300
Personal exemptions	—	3,000	3,000
	$ 20,000	$ 4,100	$ 24,100
Net (loss) per return	$(10,000)	$(2,600)	$(12,600)

Modifications:	
Add back deduction under Sec. 1202	1,000
Add back personal exemptions	3,000
Add back excess of nonbusiness deductions totaling $1,100 ($800 + $300) over nonbusiness income of $500	600
Net operating (loss)	$ (8,000)

The amount of $8,000 is the net economic loss sustained after excluding the excess of nonbusiness deductions over nonbusiness income. Note that the effect in this example is to reduce the amount of the casualty loss by both salary income and the full net long-term capital gain.

BAD DEBTS

Distinguished from Section 165 Losses

9.65 A bad debt is a loss of a capital item, a debt receivable, arising from inability to collect the amount due. Nevertheless, Section 165 pertaining to losses does not apply—only Section 166. The courts have held[58] that the provisions of sections 165 and 166 are mutually exclusive.

Types and Methods of Deduction

9.66 The two types of bad debts, business and nonbusiness, are self-explanatory. The only purpose of a corporation is to engage in business, so that if one of its receivables becomes worthless or uncollectible

58. Spring City Foundry Co. v. Com., 292 U.S. 182, 13 AFTR 1164; Edmund Thomas Gulledge, Sr., ¶57,029 P-H Memo T.C., affirmed without discussion of this point 249 F.2d 225 (4th Cir. 1957), 52 AFTR 731.

in whole or in part, the debt is a business bad debt. Individuals, trusts, and estates, unless they are engaged in a trade or business, can have only nonbusiness bad debts. A business bad debt is fully deductible in determining taxable income; a nonbusiness bad debt is treated as a short-term capital loss.

9.67   Business bad debts may be deducted by the specific charge-off or the reserve method. *Specific charge-off*, to a major extent, is a misnomer. Originally, this was the only method available to taxpayers, and in order to be deductible, the debt had to be charged off the books of account, proven to be completely worthless, and so ascertained. For many years now the rule has been that if a debt is completely worthless, a deduction is allowable, even though the receivable is not charged off the books of account. However, for a business bad debt that is only partially worthless there must be a charge-off of that amount accompanied by proof of its worthlessness. Under the reserve method, a deduction is allowable each year in the amount of the provision of a reasonable addition to the reserve for bad debts. Any recoveries are credited to the reserve, and charges are debited to the reserve.

9.68   The reserve method is not available to nonbusiness bad debts, and a deduction becomes available as a short-term capital loss in the year when worthlessness occurs.

9.69   If a bond, debenture, note, certificate, or other evidence of indebtedness issued by a corporation or by a government or political subdivision has attached interest coupons or was issued in registered form, then any loss from the worthlessness of such an obligation is governed by the provisions of Section 165(g) and is a capital loss (except where such security was issued by an "affiliated" corporation as explained previously in paragraph 9.35). If written evidence of indebtedness has been issued without interest coupons attached, and not in registered form—ordinarily true of promissory notes— the bad debt provisions of Section 166 apply.

Definition of Debt

9.70   Regulation 1.166–1(c) reads in part:

Only a bona fide debt qualifies for purposes of Section 166. A bona fide debt is a debt which arises from a debtor-creditor relationship based upon a valid and enforceable obligation to pay a fixed or determinable sum of money.

Back in 1933 the Court of Claims said: [59] "The relationship of debtor and creditor arises where one person, by contract or law, is liable or bound to pay another an amount of money, certain or uncertain, and

59. Birdsboro Steel Foundry & Machine Co. v. U.S., 3 F. Supp. 640 (Ct. Cls., 1933), 12 AFTR 1048.

it is not necessary that the debt shall be due in the sense that it is then collectible; it must be an outstanding obligation, which, if not due at the time, will certainly become due at some future date." Loans to relatives or friends may actually be gifts; the facts will determine which. In the case of *Robert L. Bradford* [60] a middle-aged man of relatively modest income loaned $3,500 to a young woman employed in his office and obtained an unsecured promissory note from her. He testified that the girl was only a casual acquaintance and that the money was loaned to help her start a business. Actually, the court found that she spent the money for hospital and doctor bills. The court held that in substance this was a gift and not a loan. In doing so it said:

It is not necessary that a loan be made strictly as a matter of business as a condition precedent to its deduction when it is found to be uncollectible. It must be shown, however, that there was a loan in fact. The unusualness of this transaction required more satisfactory evidence than that produced by petitioner.

If a note is given to evidence a loan, but there is a distinct understanding that payment will never be demanded, a debt does not arise. [61]

9.71   If an advance by a stockholder to his corporation is in fact a contribution to capital, a true debt does not exist. In the case of *Sam Schnietzer*, [62] the Tax Court said:

Whether a stockholder's advance of funds to his corporation is to be deemed a capital contribution or a loan is not a new question. It has arisen tax-wise in issues involving, as here, the proper treatment of unrecovered advances as a bad debt or as a capital loss deduction ... and in issues involving a corporation's right to deduct amounts paid on such advances under the guise of interest. ...

This question is one of fact ... and in deciding whether or not a debtor–creditor relation resulted from advances, the parties' true intent is relevant ... bookkeeping, form, and the parties' expressions of intent or character, the expectation of repayment, the relation of advances to stock holdings, and the adequacy of the corporate capital previously invested are among circumstances properly to be considered, for the parties' formal designations of the advances are not conclusive, ... but must yield to "facts which even indirectly may give rise to inferences contradicting" them. ... As the Supreme Court said, however, in *Talbot Mills* v. *Com.* [326 U.S. 521]:

"... There is no one characteristic, ... which can be said to be decisive in the determination of whether the obligations are risk investments in the corporations or debts. So-called stock certificates may be authorized by corporations which are really debts and promises to pay may be executed which have incidents of stock. ..."

60. 4 TCM 87, ¶45,040 P–H Memo T.C. (1945).
61. Farmers & Merchants National Bank of Nacona, Tex., 10 BTA 709 (1928).
62. 13 T.C. 43 (1949), affirmed 183 F.2d 70 (9th Cir. 1950), 39 AFTR 636, cert. denied 1-2-51.

9.72   At the time the debt is created, there must exist a reasonable belief that it will be repaid. The Supreme Court has held[63] that no debt exists if it is worthless when acquired.

Basis

9.73   To be deductible, a debt must have a basis. Claims for unpaid wages, rent, interest, and similar items are not deductible unless the taxpayer in some prior year reported them as income because of being on the accrual basis. If a note receivable is inherited by an individual, its basis to him is not the principal amount, but rather fair market value at the date of death or the optional valuation date (six months later). The amount is usually the one used in the final determination of the federal estate tax liability.

Worthlessness

9.74   As pointed out previously, if a taxpayer prior to the year 1942 was not using the reserve method for business bad debts, he had to use the specific charge-off method. If a specific debt became wholly worthless, the amount became deductible in the year when the taxpayer ascertained that the debt was worthless and also charged it off his books of account. In 1942 those requirements were changed. Ever since, a specific debt has been deductible under Section 166(a)(1) only in the year that it actually became worthless. Although the term *specific charge-off method* is still used today referring to debts that become wholly worthless, it is a misnomer. Only in the case of a partially worthless debt need there be a charge-off. Regulation 1.166–3 reads as follows:

(a) Partial worthlessness—(1) Applicable to specific debts only. A deduction under section 166(a)(2) on account of partially worthless debts shall be allowed with respect to specific debts only.

(2) Charge-off required. (i) If, from all the surrounding and attending circumstances, the district director is satisfied that a debt is partially worthless, the amount which has become worthless shall be allowed as a deduction under section 166(a)(2) but only to the extent charged off during the taxable year.

(ii) If a taxpayer claims a deduction for a part of a debt for the taxable year within which that part of the debt is charged off and the deduction is disallowed for that taxable year, then, in a case where the debt becomes partially worthless after the close of that taxable year, a deduction under section 166(a)(2) shall be allowed for a subsequent taxable year but not in excess of the amount charged off in the prior taxable year plus any amount charged off in the subsequent taxable year. In such instance, the charge-off in the prior taxable year shall, if consistently maintained as such, be sufficient to that extent to meet the charge-off requirement of section 166(a)(2) with respect to the subsequent taxable year.

63. Eckert v. Burnet, 283 U.S. 140 (1931), 9 AFTR 1413.

(iii) Before a taxpayer may deduct a debt in part, he must be able to demonstrate to the satisfaction of the district director the amount thereof which is worthless and the part thereof which has been charged off.

(b) Total worthlessness. If a debt becomes wholly worthless during the taxable year, the amount thereof which has not been allowed as a deduction from gross income for any prior taxable year shall be allowed as a deduction for the current taxable year.

With respect to evidence of worthlessness, paragraphs (a), (b), and 9.75 (c) of Reg. 1.166–2 provide:

(a) General rule. In determining whether a debt is worthless in whole or in part, the district director will consider all pertinent evidence, including the value of the collateral, if any, securing the debt and the financial condition of the debtor.

(b) Legal action not required. Where the surrounding circumstances indicate that a debt is worthless and uncollectible and that legal action to enforce payment would in all probability not result in the satisfaction of execution on a judgment, a showing of these facts will be sufficient evidence of the worthlessness of the debt for purposes of the deduction under section 166.

(c) Bankruptcy.—(1) General rule. Bankruptcy is generally an indication of the worthlessness of at least part of an unsecured and unpreferred debt.

(2) Year of deduction. In bankruptcy cases a debt may become worthless before settlement in some instances; and in others, only when a settlement in bankruptcy has been reached. In either case, the mere fact that bankruptcy proceedings instituted against the debtor are terminated in a later year, thereby confirming the conclusion that the debt is worthless, shall not authorize the shifting of the deduction under section 166 to such later year.

Special rules apply to banks or other regulated corporations. If a debt is charged off in whole or in part in obedience to the specific orders of a regulatory authority, then the debt to the extent charged off during the taxable year will be conclusively presumed to have become worthless or worthless only in part, as the case may be, during such taxable year, provided that a deduction for such amount so charged off is then claimed.

Prior to 1942 the test of worthlessness was a subjective rather than 9.76 an objective one. The taxpayer could properly claim the deduction in the year in which there was a bona fide ascertainment by him of the worthlessness of the debt, irrespective of whether its worthlessness could have been ascertained prior to the year when it was discovered, so long as the taxpayer exercised reasonable judgment.[64] For the years since 1942, the law requires that the loss, to be deductible, "must have been sustained *in fact* during the taxable year."[65] The Court of Claims has said:[66]

64. Minneapolis, St. Paul & Sault Ste. Marie Railroad Company v. U.S., 64–1 USTC ¶9213 (Ct. Cls., 1964), 13 AFTR2d 472.
65. Boehm v. Com., 326 U.S. 287, 292 (1945), 45–2 USTC ¶9448.
66. *Supra*, fn. 64.

... The taxpayer now not only has the burden of proving that the debt had some intrinsic value at the beginning of the year it allegedly became worthless and that it became worthless in the taxable year in question, but also ... the taxpayer must show that throughout the entire life of the debt, the evidence reasonably available to him pointed out that it was possessed of some value and had not become wholly worthless.

Nonbusiness Debts

9.77 The provisions pertaining to nonbusiness debts also came into the law with the Revenue Act of 1942. Prior to that time there was no distinction made between business and nonbusiness bad debts. Both were deductible in full.

9.78 An individual, a trust, or an estate may also deduct a nonbusiness debt only in the year that in fact total worthlessness occurs. The deduction then is not an ordinary one, but instead a short-term capital loss. Regulation 1.166–5(b) defines nonbusiness debts:

(b) Nonbusiness debt defined. For purposes of section 166 and this section, a nonbusiness debt is any debt other than—

(1) A debt which is created, or acquired, in the course of a trade or business of the taxpayer, determined without regard to the relationship of the debt to a trade or business of the taxpayer at the time when the debt becomes worthless; or

(2) A debt the loss from the worthlessness of which is incurred in the taxpayer's trade or business.

The question whether a debt is a nonbusiness debt is a question of fact in each particular case. The determination of whether the loss on a debt's becoming worthless has been incurred in a trade or business of the taxpayer shall, for this purpose, be made in substantially the same manner for determining whether a loss has been incurred in a trade or business for purposes of section 165(c)(1). For purposes of subparagraph (2) of this paragraph, the character of the debt is to be determined by the relation which the loss resulting from the debt's becoming worthless bears to the trade or business of the taxpayer. If that relation is a proximate one in the conduct of the trade or business in which the taxpayer is engaged at the time the debt becomes worthless, the debt comes within the exception provided by that subparagraph. The use to which the borrowed funds are put by the debtor is of no consequence in making a determination under this paragraph. For purposes of section 166 and this section, a nonbusiness debt does not include a debt described in section 165(g)(2)(C). See § 1.165–5, relating to losses on worthless securities.

9.79 Paragraph (d) of this same section of the Regulations then gives these five examples:

The application of this section may be illustrated by the following examples involving a case where A, an individual who is engaged in the grocery business and who makes his return on the basis of the calendar year, extends credit to B in 1955 on an open account:

(1) In 1956 A sells the business but retains the claim against B. The claim

becomes worthless in A's hands in 1957. A's loss is not controlled by the non-business debt provisions, since the original consideration has been advanced by A in his trade or business.

(2) In 1956 A sells the business to C but sells the claim against B to the taxpayer, D. The claim becomes worthless in D's hands in 1957. During 1956 and 1957, D is not engaged in any trade or business. D's loss is controlled by the nonbusiness debt provisions even though the original consideration has been advanced by A in his trade or business, since the debt has not been created or acquired in connection with a trade or business of D and since in 1957 D is not engaged in a trade or business incident to the conduct of which a loss from the worthlessness of such claim is a proximate result.

Ex. 2

(3) In 1956 A dies, leaving the business, including the accounts receivable, to his son, C, the taxpayer. The claim against B becomes worthless in C's hands in 1957. C's loss is not controlled by the nonbusiness debt provisions. While C does not advance any consideration for the claim, or create or acquire it in connection with his trade or business, the loss is sustained as a proximate incident to the conduct of the trade or business in which he is engaged at the time the debt becomes worthless.

Ex. 3

(4) In 1956 A dies, leaving the business to his son, C, but leaving the claim against B to his son, D, the taxpayer. The claim against B becomes worthless in D's hands in 1957. During 1956 and 1957, D is not engaged in any trade or business. D's loss is controlled by the nonbusiness debt provisions even though the original consideration has been advanced by A in his trade or business, since the debt has not been created or acquired in connection with a trade or business of D and since in 1957 D is not engaged in a trade or business incident to the conduct of which a loss from the worthlessness of such claim is a proximate result.

Ex. 4

(5) In 1956 A dies; and, while his executor, C, is carrying on the business, the claim against B becomes worthless in 1957. The loss sustained by A's estate is not controlled by the nonbusiness debt provisions. While C does not advance any consideration for the claim on behalf of the estate, or create or acquire it in connection with a trade or business in which the estate is engaged, the loss is sustained as a proximate incident to the conduct of the trade or business in which the estate is engaged at the time the debt becomes worthless.

Ex. 5

If an individual makes a bona fide loan to a corporation in which he is a stockholder, subsequent worthlessness of the debt ordinarily will be treated as a nonbusiness bad debt because the individual was not engaged in the business of making loans to corporations. Further, if an individual is a "wheeler-dealer" investor in a number of corporate enterprises, the Supreme Court has held in *Whipple* v. *Com.*[67] that if his only income resulting therefrom is received in his capacity as an investor, his activities do not constitute a trade or business. Accordingly, if a loan made by him to one of his corporate enterprises becomes worthless, he sustains a nonbusiness bad debt. If a taxpayer is engaged in a regular course of promoting corporations for a fee or commission or for a profit on their sale, he may be engaged in the

9.80

67. 374 U.S. 858 (1963), 11 AFTR2d 1454, reversing and remanding 301 F.2d 108 (5th Cir. 1961) and affirming on this point T.C. Memo 1960–36.

business of promoting corporations, so that a loss on a loan to one of them would be an ordinary bad debt.[68]

9.81 The *Whipple* case was followed by the Tax Court in *Estate of Ira A. Campbell*.[69] A prominent New York lawyer, during his fifty years or so of law practice, made loans to, or investments in, a great number of projects ranging from patents, new products, oil well drilling, manufacture of automobile accessories, and mineral properties in foreign countries, to a corporation engaged in preparing income tax returns for its customers. In holding that certain worthless loans were nonbusiness bad debts, the Tax Court said:

> ... There is no convincing evidence to show that Ira provided any appreciable services to the various corporations. His field was admiralty law, which occupied his full time, and he had no special training in the various fields covered by the various enterprises in which he was interested ... Ira drew no salaries from the corporations and received few dividends from them. There is nothing in the record to indicate that Ira promoted these various corporations and enterprises for a fee or a commission, or for a profit on their sale. ... Ira's role was that of an investor whose profit would come from the enhancement in value of his investment due to the successful operations of a venture.

9.82 In 1965, however, a practicing attorney was allowed to deduct as a business bad debt amounts he had loaned to a corporate client, in which he was a minority stockholder, to assist the client to stay in business, since the loan was proximately related to his law practice. In the past, a substantial portion of his total fees had been received from this client and also from two similar corporations; and he expected that if the corporation could stay in business, he would derive more fees in the future.[70] Further, it has been held that working as a corporate executive for a salary is a trade or business. Accordingly, when an officer and minority stockholder made loans to a corporation to enable it to stay in business and to be able to continue to pay him a salary, he was allowed a business bad debt deduction when the loans became uncollectible.[71]

Sureties, Guarantors, and Indemnitors

9.83 In lieu of making a loan directly to a corporation an individual frequently can accomplish the same economic effect by becoming a surety on, or a guarantor of, a loan obtained by the corporation from a stranger, or sometimes by becoming an indemnitor on an obligation of the corporation.

68. *Ibid.* and Giblin v. Com., 227 F.2d 692 (5th Cir. 1956), 56–1 USTC ¶9103, 48 AFTR 478.
69. 23 TCM 398 (1964), affirmed per curiam 343 F.2d 462 (2nd Cir. 1965), 65–1 USTC ¶9325, 15 AFTR2d 652.
70. Frank A. Garlove, 24 TCM 1049 (1965), ¶65,201 P–H Memo T.C.
71. Trent v. Com., 291 F.2d 669 (2nd Cir. 1961), 7 AFTR2d 1599.

There are historic, theoretical differences between contracts of   9.84
suretyship and guaranty, but the trend of modern law is to treat the
two as synonymous. In fact, the Restatement of the Law of Security,
Section 82, p. 231, says "the term 'guaranty' as used in this Restatement is a synonym for suretyship." Further, in tax matters the courts
have now started to treat losses arising from indemnity contracts in the
same manner as those arising from suretyship and guaranty contracts.
In the next few paragraphs we will point out the original, and still in
some states, meanings of suretyship, guaranty, and indemnity. The
reason is that the tax law has developed from those concepts.

A surety is one who is primarily liable on an obligation to the   9.85
creditor to the same extent as the principal debtor for whom he is a
surety. The surety can become such for a consideration, such as receipt of payment of a premium for a performance or fidelity bond. Or,
purely out of friendship, an individual as an accommodation maker
can sign a note on the face of it along with the signature of the principal
debtor.

A guarantor has secondary liability. The creditor must first take   9.86
steps to enforce the liability against the principal debtor before he
can sue the guarantor. In the case of a promissory note, this status
would arise from an individual indorsing a note with qualifying words
that he was doing so only as a guarantor. If the words are "payment
guaranteed," this is an "absolute guaranty" and is treated as creating
a suretyship. If the words are "collection guaranteed," the relationship is a true guaranty one; the creditor must first proceed against the
principal debtor before he can sue the guarantor.

Under a contract of indemnity, the indemnitor for a consideration   9.87
enters into an agreement to provide security or protection against loss
or damage which may be sustained in the future by the indemnified
party from the default of another or from a casualty. A fire insurance
policy is a typical example of an indemnity contract.

Both a surety and a guarantor are answerable for the debt, default,   9.88
or miscarriage of another—namely, the primary debtor. In the event
of his default, a surety or guarantor can be called upon by the creditor
to pay the amount which is in default. Upon his doing so, he becomes
subrogated to the rights of the creditor. In other words, upon the payment by the surety or the guarantor of the debt, the debtor's obligation
to the creditor becomes an obligation to the surety or guarantor under
the general legal doctrine of subrogation. A new debt is not created,
but the old debt is shifted from the creditor to the surety or guarantor.
If the surety or guarantor then is unable to recover from the debtor,
he has a loss from the worthlessness of a debt—a bad debt loss. Under
the laws of many states, the doctrine of subrogation does not apply if
the guarantor pays only a part of the debt rather than all of it.

Under general law, the doctrine of subrogation does not apply to a   9.89
contract of indemnity.

As stated, the payment by a guarantor of the obligation of the   9.90

debtor gives rise to a bad debt by reason of the application of the legal doctrine of subrogation. In *Max Putnam v. Com.*,[72] the Supreme Court said:

> ... Under the doctrine of subrogation, payment by the guarantor, as we have seen, is treated not as creating a new debt and extinguishing the original debt, but as preserving the original debt and merely substituting the guarantor for the creditor. The reality of the situation is that the debt is an asset of full value in the creditor's hands because backed by the guaranty. The debtor usually is not able to reimburse the guarantor and in such cases that value is lost at the instant that the guarantor pays the creditor. But that this instant is also the instant when the guarantor acquires the debt cannot obscure the fact that the debt "becomes" [as that word is used in Section 166(a)(1)] worthless in his hands.

In that case a lawyer participated in the organization of a corporation and as an accommodation comaker signed promissory notes of the corporation payable to a bank for money borrowed by it. When the corporation became insolvent, he paid the notes. The court held that the payment was as a guarantor and gave rise to a bad debt. Further, because he was not in the business of guaranteeing loans, it was a nonbusiness bad debt. The court also held that the provisions of Section 165 pertaining to losses and of Section 166 pertaining to bad debts are mutually exclusive; if Section 166 applies, Section 165 cannot.

9.91   Because the doctrine of subrogation does not apply in many states to partial payments by guarantors and in any state to a payment by an indemnitor, there was substantial agreement until the year 1970 that such payments were not deductible as bad debts but rather, if at all, as losses under Section 165(c)(2) incurred in transactions entered into for profit. The Eighth Circuit Court of Appeals in the year 1934 so held in the case of an indemnity payment.[73] Then in the first few months of 1970 the Third and Ninth Circuit Courts of Appeal decided to disregard the legal niceties of the presence or absence of subrogation.

9.92   The first case was *Stratmore v. U.S.*[74] decided by the Third Circuit Court of Appeals. There, a husband and wife, who were officers and shareholders of a corporation, guaranteed promissory notes of that corporation. The corporation went into bankruptcy, and the taxpayers, in settlement of their guaranty obligation, paid a portion of the debt. Under applicable state law, the doctrine of subrogation did not apply. The Court held that the guaranty loss resulted in a nonbusiness bad debt and said:

72. 352 U.S. 8 (1956), 50 AFTR 502, 57–1 USTC ¶9200.
73. Howell v. Com., 69 F.2d 447 (8th Cir. 1934), 4 USTC ¶1236; 13 AFTR 716.
74. 25 AFTR2d 70–371 (3rd Cir. 1970), reversing 292 F. Supp. 59 (D.C., N.J., 1968), 23 AFTR2d 69–630.

It is not meaningful to emphasize unduly the common law principle of subrogation in analyzing the substantial realities upon which federal taxation is based. When the creditor turns to the guarantor for payment, the debt is already uncollectible. In both *Putnam* and the present case the claims against the debtors were at all relevant times no more collectible in the hands of the guarantors than in those of the original lender. To allow the tax result to turn on the presence or absence of this technical right of subrogation under state law would be to undermine the *Putnam* doctrine: taxpayers could change capital losses to ordinary losses almost at will. For example, every guarantor could obtain an ordinary loss simply by reaching an agreement with the creditor for payment of less than the full amount of the guarantor's liability, and thus avoiding any subrogation. We hold that taxpayers' payment pursuant to the guarantees was not a loss under section 165(c)(2) but rather a non-business bad debt under section 166(d).

The next case was *U.S. v. Hoffman*.[75] The taxpayers made payments to a bonding company under a prior agreement by which the taxpayers had agreed to indemnify the company for losses it sustained as guarantor of performance of construction contracts made by the taxpayers' family corporation. The Ninth Circuit Court of Appeals held that the indemnity payments were not deductible as ordinary losses incurred in a transaction entered into for profit within the scope of Section 165(c)(2), but in line with the rationale of the *Stratmore* case held that, by reason of economic reality and Congressional purpose, there must be a common tax treatment of all losses suffered by a corporate shareholder in providing his corporation with financing, so that the loss was a nonbusiness bad debt under Section 166.   9.93

In summary, the weight of authority now is that payments by individuals as sureties, guarantors, and indemnitors are deductible as bad debts, business or nonbusiness, depending upon the facts. In the case of a corporation, such payments are always business bad debts.   9.94

There is one statutory exception to these rules, which is contained in Section 166(f), and another special provision pertaining to reserves for bad debts arising from certain guaranteed debt obligations of dealers in property. The latter provision will be discussed later. At this point, Section 166(f) will be explained.   9.95

If an individual guarantees the debt of another and makes good on his guaranty, his payment under the general rules explained above will be treated as a nonbusiness bad debt unless it arose out of his trade or business. In 1954, Congress granted partial relief from this restriction on the type of deduction by inserting Section 166(f) in the Code. It provides that a payment by a noncorporate taxpayer in discharge of part or all of his liability as a guarantor, endorser, or indemnitor of an obligation on which the principal debtor was another *noncorporate* taxpayer will be an ordinary business bad debt deduction provided that (1) the proceeds of the obligation were used in the   9.96

75. 25 AFTR2d 70–921 (9th Cir. 1970), reversing 266 F. Supp. 884 (D.C., Ore.), 19 AFTR2d 997.

trade or business of the borrower, and (2) the obligation of the borrower was worthless at the time of such payment by the guarantor.

9.97   If an individual wishes to help a friend or relative to start a business as a proprietor or member of a partnership, he should not directly loan money to him but instead should guarantee a loan made to him by someone else, such as a bank. Then if the business fails, the taxpayer will have an ordinary deduction in the amount of his guaranty payment rather than a nonbusiness bad debt deductible only as a short-term capital loss.

Reserves for Certain Guaranteed Debt Obligations

9.98   Business enterprises have the choice of deducting bad debts when incurred under the charge-off method of Section 166(a) or of deducting a provision to a reserve for anticipated bad debts under Section 166(c). As noted before, the United States Supreme Court held in *Max Putnam* v. *Com.* that a payment in satisfaction of a guaranty results in the shifting of the same debt obligation from the creditor to the guarantor. For that reason by early 1966, the Eighth, Ninth, and Tenth Circuit Courts of Appeal had held [76] that the reserve for bad debts method could be used by dealers in real property and tangible personal property currently to deduct anticipated guaranty losses on obligations arising from their sale of such property. The Tax Court [77] and the Commissioner, [78] however, persisted in their view that the reserve method could not be used.

9.99   Late in 1966, Congress resolved the controversy by inserting Section 166(g) in the Code, effective as to taxable years ending after October 21, 1965, the date the bill was introduced. This subsection is explained in the Senate Finance Committee report: [79]

Reserve for guaranteed obligations.—The bill adds a new provision to the Internal Revenue Code (a new subsection (g) in section 166) under which a deduction can be taken for additions to a reserve for bad debts arising out of the taxpayer's liability as a guarantor, endorser, or indemnitor on debt obligations attributable to his sale of property in the ordinary course of his business. This bad debt reserve may be attributable to the sale by the taxpayer of either real property or tangible personal property and services related to these properties. The debt need not initially be the debt owing to the taxpayer as long as it arises from the sale by him of the property and he is guaranteeing payment. Thus, this includes cases both where the purchaser borrows from a bank or other financial institution to make partial payment for the property and the dealer guarantees the payment of the debt, as well as where the debt is initially owing to the dealer and he discounts the paper

76. Bolling et al. v. Com., 357 F.2d 3 (8th Cir. 1966), 17 AFTR2d 451, reversing ¶64,143 P-H Memo T.C.; Wilkins Pontiac v. Com., 298 F.2d 893 (9th Cir. 1962), 9 AFTR 330, reversing 34 T.C. 1065; Foster Frosty Foods v. Com., 332 F.2d 230 (10th Cir. 1964), 13 AFTR2d 1566, reversing 30 T.C. 772.

77. Mike Persia Chevrolet, Inc., 41 T.C. 198 (1963).

78. Rev. Rul. 62–214, 1962–2 C.B. 72.

79. S. Rep. 1710, 89th Cong., 2d sess., 1966, pp. 3–4, accompanying H.R. 11782.

with the financial institution which has recourse to him for payment of the debt should the purchaser fail to make the payments.

If a dealer establishes one of these new reserves for guaranteed debt obligations and also maintains a reserve for bad debts (under provisions of existing law) for accounts receivable from customers which he does not sell, the dealer is to maintain two separate reserves for income tax purposes. The amount of reasonable additions to the reserves are [sic] to be determined separately for each reserve and not on an aggregate basis.

.   .   .

New reserve only way of taking guaranteed bad debt deductions for future. —The bill provides that the new reserve previously described is to be the only reserve through which a deduction is to be allowed for any addition to a reserve for bad debts which arise out of the taxpayer's liability as guarantor, endorser, or indemnitor of debt obligations. For example, if the taxpayer has an account receivable from a customer simply for services rendered (not in connection with a sale of a property) the bill provides that no deduction is to be allowed for an addition to a reserve for liabilities arising out of the sale with recourse of such a debt obligation.

To prevent the deduction of provisions to the reserve to cover guar- **9.100** anty obligations incurred in years prior to the institution of this reserve, it is required that in the first year of the establishment of the reserve an initial balance be set up to cover guaranty obligations incurred in prior years. It is called a suspense account, and no current deduction is permitted. The same Senate Finance Committee report explains its function:

The function of the suspense account is to give the dealer a deduction in subsequent years for the opening balance in his reserve for guaranteed bad debts (for which he has not up to that time received a deduction) if he goes out of the business for which the reserve is maintained, or if he no longer needs the reserve—for example, because he finances the customer paper himself rather than discounting it to others, or because his volume of credit sales declines.

Section 166(g) is now the sole authority for a guarantor to set up **9.101** a bad debt reserve. If its requirements are not met, the guarantor cannot use a reserve; he can only deduct as he makes good on his guaranty. For example, only those who are dealers in real property or tangible personal property can qualify. In *Budget Credits, Inc.* v. *Com.*,[80] a retailer, in order to insulate itself from goodwill problems associated with collections, set up a subsidiary and sold its receivables to it. The subsidiary in turn sold them to a bank with recourse. The subsidiary purchased defaulted accounts and tried to collect them. The Sixth Circuit Court of Appeals held that the subsidiary could not deduct additions to a bad debt reserve to cover its potential liability as a guarantor. The court held that a guarantor can use a bad debt reserve only if the receivables it has guaranteed arose through sales

80. 24 AFTR2d 69–5697 (6th Cir. 1969), affirming 50 T.C. 52.

by *it* of real property or tangible personal property. Here, the receivables did not arise from sales by the subsidiary of such property. On the other hand, if the parent had sold the receivables to the bank with recourse, it could have set up a reserve for bad debts and deducted additions to it.

Statute of Limitations

9.102   In lieu of the ordinary three-year period of limitations within which a claim for refund can be filed, Section 6511(d) allows a period of seven years from the date prescribed by law for filing the return with respect to which the claim is made in the case of a debt deductible under Section 166 as wholly worthless. The seven-year period does not apply to deductions under the reserve method nor to partially worthless debts. This longer period of time for claiming a refund has been allowed by Congress because of the great difficulty in proving the exact year in which a debt becomes wholly worthless.

Change in Method

9.103   Regulation 1.166–1(b) states that a taxpayer filing a return of income for the first taxable year for which he is entitled to a bad debt deduction may select either the so-called specific charge-off method or the reserve method for treating bad debts. Once the elected method is approved by the District Director, the taxpayer must continue to use that method for all subsequent years unless he obtains permission to change to the other method. Application for such permission must be made by filing Form 3115 with the Commissioner within ninety days after the beginning of the taxable year in which it is desired to make the change.

9.104   The change ordinarily sought is from the so-called specific charge-off method to the reserve method. Upon such a change a reasonable reserve must be set up for the receivables at the end of that year which, based upon experience, may become worthless in the future. Revenue Procedure 64–51 inaugurated a simplified procedure for obtaining consent to change from the specific charge-off method to the reserve method. As required by the regulations pertaining to changes in methods of accounting, the same Form 3115 is used and must be filed within ninety days after the beginning of the year in which the change is to be effected. In that form the taxpayer must make reference to this Revenue Procedure. If the form is timely filed, consent is automatically granted without notification from the Commissioner. Then, for the year of the change a deduction is allowed for bad debts actually charged off in the year plus 10 percent of the initial reserve for bad debts to be set up at the end of the year. The remaining 90 percent of the initial reserve is then deducted ratably over each of the succeeding nine years. The initial reserve is computed by determining the ratio of the preceding five years' actual loss experience and applying this average rate to the trade receivables at the end of the year of change. In the subsequent nine years the taxpayer, in addition to deducting $\frac{1}{10}$ the initial reserve, will also be entitled to a deduction for a reasonable addition to the reserve for bad debts. There are special rules and procedures for commercial banks, mutual savings banks, and domestic building and loan associations.

QUESTIONS AND PROBLEMS

1. An individual owned slot machines in several private clubs located in a state where gambling was illegal. He regularly reported his gross income from these machines and deducted depreciation on them at the rate of 20 percent a year under the straight-line method. At a time when the machines that originally cost $20,000 were depreciated to $5,000 and had a market value of at least that amount, the state police confiscated and destroyed the machines. (a) What amount was deductible in the year of such confiscation? (b) Under what section of the Code was the amount deductible?

2. The majority owner of the stock of a corporation sells property to it for $50,000. (a) If the adjusted basis of that property is $60,000, what is the amount of the deductible loss? (b) If the adjusted basis is $45,000, what, if any, is the amount of the taxable gain?

3. Jones joins a country club so that he and his family can play golf and swim. As a condition of membership he is required to buy a share of stock for $1,000 and pay an initiation fee of $2,000. Five years later his firm transfers him to another city. He resigns from the club and receives $800 for his share of stock. (a) In that year what amount, if any, is the deductible capital loss on the sale of the stock? (b) To what amount and in what year is the initiation fee deductible? (c) Suppose the stock were sold for $1,100, is there a taxable capital gain?

4. In 1965 an individual purchases a forty-year-old walk-up apartment building. The cost of the building was $20,000 and the land $5,000. In 1971 the city condemns the building as unfit for human occupancy. In that same year the owner decides to raze the building rather than spend $75,000 to rebuild it, and notifies the tenants to move. In 1972 upon termination of a suit for eviction against one of the tenants, the building is demolished. In what year is the abandonment loss deductible? Is it an ordinary loss or a capital one?

5. A rather old lathe is removed from the manufacturing line and is placed in a storage room, so that, if necessary, it can be used again. If the lathe was separately depreciated in an item account, is its adjusted basis deductible as an abandonment loss?

6. A parent corporation owns 100 percent of the capital stock of a subsidiary corporation for which it paid $100,000, and it also has an open account receivable from it in the amount of $300,000 by the end of 1968. The subsidiary is engaged in manufacturing and meets the gross receipts test of Section 165(g)(3)(B). In 1968, owing to recurring losses, the liabilities exceed the book value of the assets. In 1969 the liabilities exceed the market value of the assets. The company continues to operate until 1972. In that year the subsidiary is liquidated, and on its then aggregate receivable of $500,000 the parent corporation receives assets having a market value of $10,000 and a book value of $1,000.

Nothing is recovered on the stock investment. (a) What amounts, if any, are deductible; in what year or years are they deductible; and are they fully deductible or capital losses? (b) Suppose that upon liquidation in 1972, the parent corporation receives assets having a market value of $550,000 and an adjusted basis of $400,000, what are the tax consequences to the parent corporation?

7. A landslide damaged Skid Walter's house on February 22, 1972. To restore the destroyed property, Skid paid the following amounts:

(a) $3,000 to a building contractor to repair damage to the house. The house originally cost $30,000 and was worth approximately $40,000 at the time of the slide.

(b) $1,000 to replace personal effects, including furniture, which were destroyed. At the time of the loss, the items were worth about $700, although they had cost Skid $900 a few years earlier.

(c) $300 to replace luggage lost by a house guest at the time of the landslide. The luggage originally cost $500 but was probably worth only about $300 at the time of the loss.

Skid filed a claim with his insurance company for $4,300, but the company informed Skid that he had a $2,000 deductible policy. They also refused to pay for the $300 luggage loss or more than $200 for the personal effects. Skid demanded at least $500 for the personal effects, and after eighteen months collected $400.

On February 25, 1972, the president of the United States declared the area hit by the landslide a disaster area qualifying for federal assistance. (a) What amount is deductible as a casualty loss by Skid Walter in 1972? (b) What alternative is available to Skid?

8. The Reed Corporation had a fire in its main office on July 2, 1972, which destroyed some of its office equipment completely. The equipment destroyed had a fair market value of $3,000 before the fire and an adjusted basis to the corporation of $5,000. The property was not covered by insurance.

(a) State the amount of the casualty loss the corporation was entitled to deduct on its 1972 return.

(b) If the fair market value of the equipment before the fire had been $7,000, what would be the amount of the casualty loss deduction?

(c) Assume the above property was a private residence. What amount would be allowable as a casualty deduction under a and b?

9. A corporate taxpayer has a frozen food warehouse full of meat and other frozen foods on February 1, 1973. That evening, a bad storm with sleet and freezing rain shuts down electric power for many hours. As a result, food in the warehouse thawed and spoiled. There was no insurance recovery. (a) Is this a casualty loss for tax purposes? (b) What are the criteria for a casualty loss?

10. (a) The taxpayer while driving his own automobile—which he uses solely for pleasure and commuting—through his own negligence, but not willful negligence, hits another car. As a result the taxpayer pays:

(1) Repairs to own car	$1,400
(2) Payment for repairs to other car	1,000
(3) Payment for injuries to driver of other car	5,000
(4) Payment for injuries to neighbor who was riding as passenger in the taxpayer's car	1,500

(5)	Police court fine for negligent driving	$ 100
	Attorney fees:	
(6)	For police court hearing	50
(7)	For negotiating settlements with injured persons	1,000

The taxpayer's insurance company reimbursed him for 80 percent of the items described in 2 and 3, a total of $4,800 (80 percent of $6,000). The original cost and values of the two cars are:

	TAXPAYER'S CAR	OTHER CAR
Original cost and adjusted basis	$3,800	$3,400
Value immediately before accident	2,500	2,800
Value immediately after accident	1,200	1,500

Tabulate and total the amounts, if any, that are deductible (1) as a casualty loss and (2) otherwise.

(b) Suppose the taxpayer in *a* is engaged in business as a sole proprietor and was driving his business car on a business trip. All of the facts are the same except that the adjusted basis of his car immediately before the accident was $1,200. How much is deductible (1) as a casualty loss and (2) otherwise?

11. Richard Wagner in the taxable year 1972 sustains the losses listed below. Indicate the amount of the loss and the year in which the loss, if any, may be deducted.

(a) Loss by embezzlement during 1972 of $1,500 by a clerk in Wagner's business, but not discovered until 1973.

(b) Loss of a wallet worth $50 containing $200 in cash left by Wagner in a taxi while commuting to his home from his office.

(c) Destruction of wife's fur coat by moths. The coat cost $3,000, had a value of $2,000 when put in her closet the preceding summer, and had a value of $200 when taken out of storage.

12. Early in March a corporation obtains an extension of time from March 15 to June 15 within which to file its accrual method calendar year return. On March 14 a nearby river overflows its banks and floods the area including the corporation's manufacturing plant. On March 16 the president of the United States declares the district to be a disaster area qualifying for federal assistance under Title 42 of the U.S. Code. The corporation in April determines that the flood damage was $50,000. (a) What is the earliest year in which that amount is deductible? (b) The home of the corporation's president is also within the flooded area, and the damage to it is $5,000. The president filed his return for the preceding year on January 31. Can he deduct that amount in the preceding year by filing an amended return or a claim for refund? (c) Must he deduct the loss in that preceding year?

13. Jerry Dice, a calendar-year taxpayer on the cash method of accounting, won $10,000 in the Irish Sweepstakes. The money was paid to him in November. On December 24, Mr. Dice bet the entire amount on the College of Hard Knocks to beat Electoral College that day in the Soup Bowl. Hard Knocks took it on the chin, and Mr. Dice lost the entire $10,000. On his tax return, Jerry offset his Irish Sweepstakes'

win with his football loss and claimed the standard deduction. Was this correct? Explain.

14. During the absence of a bank teller who was recuperating from an emergency operation, a bank examiner in 1972 discovered that the teller embezzled a total of $100,000 ratably over the ten years ending in 1969. Subsequent investigation in 1972 disclosed that the teller lost it in gambling, and the most the bank could recover from him was $10,000. This amount of recovery was ascertained in 1972 but was not actually received until 1973. How much, if anything, was deductible in 1972 by this cash-method bank?

15. Assume that a corporation is not using the reserve method for deducting bad debts. Must it charge a worthless receivable off its books in order to obtain a bad debt deduction?

16. A son loans $1,000 to his elderly mother who has no assets and whose only income is a monthly social security check of $60. He requests and obtains a promissory note payable on demand. One year later, she dies destitute without having made any payment on the note. When is the $1,000 deductible?

17. An individual worked for an employer who became a bankrupt. The employer owed him $500 in wages but never paid the amount. Is the individual entitled to a bad debt deduction of $500?

18. An individual who owned stock of a corporation personally guaranteed a bank loan of $100,000 to his corporation. The corporation ceased business, was liquidated, and was unable to pay the bank loan. Upon payment of the $100,000 pursuant to his guarantee obligation, is the individual entitled to a deduction under the following circumstances:
    (a) He owned 90 percent of the stock, was the president, and received a salary of $80,000 per year
    (b) He owned 45 percent of the stock but was not an officer or employee
    (c) He owned 1 percent of the stock, was executive vice-president, and was told by the board of directors that if he did not participate with other officers in guaranteeing the bank loan, he would be fired

19. An individual in 1968 invested $1,000 in the common stock of a new corporation being organized by his brother to manufacture plastic shower stalls. On April 1, 1969, he loaned the corporation $2,000 and received its promissory note for that amount due April 1, 1973, and bearing interest at 5 percent per annum. No interest was ever paid. In 1972 the corporation was adjudicated a bankrupt; and on December 31, 1972, it was ascertained that ten cents on the dollar would be payable to all unsecured creditors. The individual bought the stock in the corporation only to help his brother get started in a business and never had any real hope that he would realize a profit on that stock. What amount, if any, was deductible in 1972 attributable to (a) the stock, (b) the note, and (c) the unpaid interest? For each amount, cite the authority and state whether the deduction was an ordinary one or a capital loss.

10

OTHER DEDUCTIONS ALLOWED WHETHER BUSINESS OR PERSONAL

INTRODUCTION . . . 359
INTEREST . . . 359

> **Definition . . . 360**
> **Indebtedness . . . 361**
> **Economic Substance and Sham Transactions . . . 362**
> **Interest on Debt versus Dividend on Stock . . . 364**
>
>> RISK CAPITAL . . . 365
>> THIN CAPITALIZATION . . . 365
>> HYBRID SECURITIES . . . 366
>
> **Interest Deductions Specifically Prohibited . . . 368**
> **Installment Purchases . . . 369**

PREMIUM ON REDEMPTION OF BONDS . . . 370
TAXES . . . 371

> **Allocation of Real Property Taxes on Sales . . . 373**
> **Nondeductible Taxes . . . 374**

CHARITABLE CONTRIBUTIONS . . . 374

> **Introduction . . . 374**
> **Qualifying Beneficiaries . . . 376**
>
>> PRIVATE OPERATING FOUNDATIONS . . . 377
>
> **Calculation of Limitations on Deductions . . . 377**
> **Pledges . . . 379**
> **Accrual Basis Corporations . . . 380**
> **Methods of Making Gifts . . . 380**
>
>> CASH . . . 380

PROPERTY . . . 380

SPECIFIC ITEM LIMITATIONS . . . 381

Ordinary Income Appreciated Property . . . 381
Appreciated Tangible Personal Property with Unrelated Use . . . 382
Appreciated Capital Gain Property Given to Certain Private Foundations . . . 382

AGGREGATE 30 PERCENT LIMITATION . . . 383
RENTAL VALUE AND OTHER FREE USE . . . 384

PERSONAL SERVICES . . . 384

MEDICAL EXPENSES . . . 384

Qualifying Expenditures . . . 385

MEDICAL v. PERSONAL EXPENDITURES . . . 385

Limitations . . . 386
Reimbursements Received in Later Years . . . 387

EXPENSES FOR HOUSEHOLD AND DEPENDENT CARE SERVICES . . . 387
TENANT-STOCKHOLDERS OF COOPERATIVE HOUSING CORPORATIONS . . . 387

INTRODUCTION

In chapters 7, 8, and 9 we discussed deductions allowable to indi-   10.1
viduals and corporations arising from a business and to individuals
arising from transactions entered into for profit. We also covered
casualty losses incurred in both personal and business type circumstances, and before that, in chapter 5, the deductibility of alimony.
Here we are concerned with other deductions allowed, whether
business or personal in nature—interest, taxes, charitable contributions, medical expenses, child care expenses, and expenditures of
tenant–stockholders of cooperative housing corporations. Naturally,
only the deductions for interest, taxes, and charitable contributions
are applicable to both individuals and corporations; the balance
pertain to individuals.

Deductions for interest, taxes, and casualty losses have been part   10.2
of the modern income tax law from its inception in 1913.[1] The first
two of these are even older, dating back to the taxing statutes of the
last century. The apparent reason for the deductibility of taxes and
interest is the difficulty of distinguishing between expenditures of
this type made for business reasons and those incurred for personal
reasons. Also, the deduction for state taxes serves to alleviate a double-
taxation problem. Deductions for casualty losses and medical expenses
simply result from congressional sympathy for personal misfortune.
The same sympathy is reflected in the allowance of the charitable contribution deduction, which tends to encourage philanthropic activities.

Generally, it is unnecessary for a corporation to rely specifically on   10.3
the provisions allowing these special deductions, since most corporate expenditures are deductible as ordinary and necessary business expenses (as discussed in chapter 7). Yet, some of these sections
do apply to corporations, primarily in the form of limitations affecting
deductibility.

INTEREST

Section 163(a) expressly provides "there shall be allowed as a   10.4
deduction all interest paid or accrued within the taxable year on
indebtedness." Interest is deductible whether incurred for personal
or business reasons, although the Code denies a deduction in five
specific situations, discussed in paragraph 10.29. The determination
of what exactly is "interest on indebtedness" is extremely difficult,
and this problem is discussed below. Chapters 14 and 15 consider the
proper time to deduct interest.

1. Tariff Act of October 3, 1913.

Definition

10.5   Interest "... is the amount which one has contracted to pay for the use of borrowed money ... 'interest' means what is usually called interest by those who pay and those who receive the amount so denominated ... and ... the words of the statute permit the deduction of that sum, and do not refer to some esoteric concept derived from subtle and theoretical analysis."[2] "Interest" includes discount on a financial obligation[3] and the premium or penalty paid for the privilege of prepaying a debt.[4] (Also see paragraph 10.34.) The facts, not the terms employed, control in every case. There is no requirement that deductible interest be ordinary and necessary, or even that it be reasonable.[5] Moreover, it is not essential that interest be computed at a fixed stated rate. All that is required is that a sum definitely ascertainable be paid for the use of borrowed money pursuant to the agreement of the lender and borrower.[6] Accordingly, in *Dorzback* v. *Collison*,[7] the taxpayer was allowed to deduct as much as $10,346.32 annual interest on a debt of $8,500 where interest was calculated at 25 percent of the net profit of the business. Other courts have also held that payments of unusual amounts of interest are deductible.[8]

10.6   Some lending institutions require the advance payment of "points" or a loan-processing fee, particularly on mortgage loans. If this fee is in addition to interest and other fees for title reports and drafting documents, the Service held in Rev. Rul. 69–188 that these "points" are interest and deductible as such when paid by the borrower. If the borrower does not obtain the funds to pay the fee from the lender, the amount is deductible in the year paid.[9] However, if the "points" are subtracted from the gross proceeds of the loan, the amount of such discount must be amortized and deducted pro rata over the term of the loan.[10] When the "points" are paid for services in processing the loan documents, the amount does not constitute interest, is not deductible, and does not become an additional cost of any property acquired.[11] If the seller of a house pays the "points" to the lending institution to enable the buyer to obtain a mortgage loan, the amount is not deductible as interest by the seller because it is paid on the

2. Old Colony R.R. Co. v. Com., 284 U.S. 552, 10 AFTR 786 (1932), 3 USTC ¶880.
3. U.S. v. Collier, 104 F.2d 420 (5th Cir. 1939), 39–2 USTC ¶9557, 23 AFTR 60; I.T. 3298, 1939–2 C.B. 164.
4. Rev. Rul. 57–198, 1957–1 C.B. 94.
5. Dorzback v. Collison, 195 F.2d 69 (3rd Cir. 1952), 41 AFTR 878, 52–1 USTC ¶9263.
6. Utility Trailer Mfg. Co. v. U.S., 212 F. Supp. 773 (S.D. Cal., 1962), 11 AFTR2d 1114, 63–1 USTC ¶9394.
7. Dorzback, *supra*, fn. 5.
8. A. R. Jones Syndicate v. Com., 23 F.2d 833 (7th Cir. 1927), 1 USTC ¶266, 6 AFTR 7223; Wiggin Terminals, Inc. v. U.S., 36 F.2d 893 (1st Cir. 1929), 8 AFTR 9925, 1930 CCH ¶9077.
9. Rev. Rul. 69–582.
10. J. R. Hopkins, 15 T.C. 160 (1950) (Acq.); I.T. 3298, 1939–2 C.B. 164.
11. Rev. Rul. 67–297, 1967–2 C.B. 87.

indebtedness of another. However, the payment does reduce the amount realized on the sale.[12]

Other
Deductions
Allowed
Whether
Business or
Personal

10.7

Indebtedness

For interest on indebtedness to be deductible, the indebtedness must constitute an "unconditional and legally enforceable obligation to pay."[13] Consequently, indebtedness does not exist where there is a lack of consideration (as in the case of a gift of a promissory note, resulting in an unenforceable obligation),[14] or when the debt or claim is created only upon a contingency to happen in the future.[15] However, even though a corporate obligation was created by an *ultra vires* act, the Commissioner must treat it as enforceable.[16] The fact that an obligation is legally enforceable under local law does not determine whether there is "indebtedness" within the meaning of the Code.[17]

> ... The statutory deduction for interest is confined to amounts chargeable against the taxpayer on his own indebtedness, and he may not deduct interest on the indebtedness of another, even though he has by legal contract agreed to pay such interest.[18]

Thus, amounts paid by guarantors and endorsers will not be allowed as interest deductions,[19] although they may fall within other categories of deductions such as bad debts or losses,[20] or ordinary and necessary expenses.[21] However, because a taxpayer has a property interest to protect:

> ... Interest paid by the taxpayer on a mortgage upon real estate of which he is the legal or equitable owner, even though the taxpayer is not directly liable upon the bond or note secured by such mortgage, may be deducted as interest on his indebtedness ... [Reg. 1.163–1(b)].[22]

12. Rev. Rul. 68–650.
13. Jewel Tea Co. v. U.S., 90 F.2d 451 (2nd Cir. 1937), 37–2 USTC ¶9331, 19 AFTR 852; First National Co., 32 T.C. 798 (1959), reversed and remanded on other grounds 289 F.2d 861 (6th Cir. 1961), 7 AFTR2d 1948; see also Farley Realty Corp. v. Com., 279 F.2d 701 (2nd Cir. 1960), 5 AFTR2d 1946; Utility Trailer Mfg. Co. v. U.S., *supra* fn. 6.
14. Johnson v. Com., 86 F.2d 710 (2nd Cir. 1936), 18 AFTR 650; see also Estate Planning Corp., 101 F.2d 15 (2nd Cir. 1939), 22 AFTR 403, 39–1 USTC ¶9235.
15. Superior Garment Co., 1965 P–H T.C. Memo Dec. ¶65,283, 24 TCM 1571.
16. Oxford Development Corp., 23 TCM 1085, ¶64,182 P–H Memo TC.
17. Weller v. Com., 270 F.2d 294 (3rd Cir. 1959), 4 AFTR2d 5453, 59–2 USTC ¶9667.
18. Eskimo Pie Corporation, 4 T.C. 669 (1945), affirmed 153 F.2d 301 (3rd Cir. 1946), 34 AFTR 853, 46–1 USTC ¶9152.
19. William H. Simon, 36 BTA 184 (1937).
20. See chapter 9.
21. S.M. 1298, 2 C.B. 113 (1920).
22. Also note that Code Sec. 216, *infra* para. 10.93, specifically allows tenant-stockholders to deduct interest on indebtedness for which the cooperative corporate entity is the obligor.

Other
Deductions
Allowed
Whether
Business or
Personal

Indebtedness need not arise from a voluntary act by the taxpayer, since a judgment may constitute an indebtedness[23] as well as federal income tax liabilities.[24]

Economic Substance and Sham Transactions

10.8   Even though all courts recognize the principle that every taxpayer has the legal right to decrease the amount of what otherwise would be his taxes or altogether to avoid them by means that the law permits, they also hold that there must be economic substance to a transaction in order that alleged indebtedness arising from the transaction can result in a deduction for interest. A transaction without economic substance is said to be a sham.

10.9   In *Knetsch* v. *United States*[25] the taxpayer in 1953 purchased a single-premium deferred annuity in the principal amount of $4 million that would increase in value at the rate of $2\frac{1}{2}$ percent compounded annually. The purchase price was $4,004,000, and in payment thereof he gave the insurance company his check for $4,000 and signed a nonrecourse note for the balance. The note bore interest at $3\frac{1}{2}$ percent and was payable annually in advance. He paid the first year's interest in the amount of $140,000. By the end of the first contract year, the loan value of the policy was to be $4,100,000; however, the excess of this amount over any existing indebtedness could be borrowed at any time prior to the end of the contract year. Accordingly, five days after he purchased the policy and prepaid the interest of $140,000, he borrowed $99,000 of the increase in loan value, executed a $3\frac{1}{2}$ percent note for that amount, and prepaid the first year's interest thereon of $3,465. At this point the taxpayer was out of pocket $48,465 ($4,000 cash purchase price plus $143,465 interest paid minus $99,000 loan value borrowed), and he owned a policy having a net equity of $1,000. In 1954 the procedure was repeated. He paid $147,105 as interest and borrowed the full increase of $104,000 in the loan value of the policy. The respective amounts of $143,465 and $147,105 were deducted as interest in his 1953 and 1954 returns.

10.10   The United States Supreme Court affirmed the holding of the trial court that there was no commercial economic substance to the transaction and it was a sham. Deductions were denied for the interest payments. The Supreme Court also pointed out that without regard to tax consequences no economic gain was possible. The taxpayer's total out-of-pocket cost of $91,570 for the two years was a nondeductible fee paid to the insurance company for providing the facade of loans whereby the taxpayer sought to reduce his taxes.

10.11   Section 264, discussed later in this chapter, now specifically denies a deduction for interest on systematic borrowings on annuity policies.

23. Estate of Daniel Buckley, 37 T.C. 664 (1962).
24. Rev. Rul. 57–481, 57–2 C.B. 48.
25. 364 U.S. 361 (1960), 60–2 USTC ¶9785, 6 AFTR2d 5851, 1961–1 C.B. 34.

Accounting entries, the execution of purchase and sale orders, and the signing of notes all constitute form. If in substance there is not a borrowing of money, there can be no deduction for interest paid for the use or forbearance of money. **10.12**

Another case involving a sham indebtedness is *Bridges* v. *Com.*[26] Through a broker, the taxpayer arranged to purchase United States Treasury bonds. The full amount of the purchase price was borrowed from banks, and the taxpayer prepaid the interest on his notes. The bonds were retained by the banks as collateral for the notes and were never in his possession. Later the banks purchased the bonds or caused them to be redeemed at maturity and extinguished the liability of the taxpayer on the notes. Deductions were claimed for the prepaid interest; and for the years in which the banks purchased the bonds or caused them to be redeemed, small long-term capital gains were reported. Without regard to tax consequences, there was an economic loss. In denying deductions for the interest the Tax Court said: **10.13**

... The term "interest" as used in the statute has a commercial connotation, that is, regardless of the purpose for which the money is borrowed or the use to which it is put, and regardless of any tax consequences resulting therefrom, the amounts paid as interest must have commercial reality, there must be some valid commercial reason for paying interest, the borrower must in fact receive something in the transaction itself which would warrant the payment of interest. To be deductible, the amounts must, in fact, constitute interest—that is, compensation for the use or forbearance of money, ... paid with respect to genuine indebtedness. ...

In affirming the Tax Court, the Fourth Circuit Court of Appeals pointed out the criteria to examine when determining whether a particular transaction is a sham: **10.14**

... Although the [Supreme] Court speaks in terms of what Knetsch, the taxpayer [in *Knetsch* v. *U.S.* discussed above in paragraphs 10.9 and 10.10], actually got "for his out-of-pocket difference," it is clear from the opinion as a whole that, as the result might apply to situations generally, what the Court meant was not so much what the taxpayer ultimately gets for his outlay, but rather what are the *possibilities* in that regard under the terms of the specific transaction under consideration. We do not construe the Court to mean, nor do we intend to hold, that the transaction is a sham simply because it proves to be unprofitable and even though it results in a loss and a reduction of income tax liability. If there is, under the realities of the terms of the transaction, some reasonable hope of the transaction appreciably affecting the taxpayer's beneficial interest other than by tax reduction, the transaction would not be a sham for tax purposes. ... Furthermore, if there is, under the realities of the terms of the transaction, some real risk of loss to the taxpayer, other than whatever loss might be actually "built-in" (as it was in the instant case), the transaction would not be a sham for tax purposes. ...

---

26. 39 T.C. 1064, affirmed 326 F.2d 180 (4th Cir. 1963), 64–1 USTC ¶9103, 12 AFTR2d 6037.

Other
Deductions
Allowed
Whether
Business or
Personal

In the instance case Bridges entered into two transactions, as to each of which he agreed to and did pay out substantially more money than he could even hope to recover from any increase in value of the securities he purchased. In other words, it is clear that there was no prospect whatever of any financial profit from the transactions alone. In neither case did he stand to gain on the over-all transaction due to a rise in the market price or value of the securities, nor did he risk any loss from a fall in the market price or value of the securities. In neither case did Bridges, *at any time,* have the uncontrolled use of additional money, of the securities he had purchased or of the interest on the securities. As was stated by the Tax Court, "we have been shown no way in which petitioner could have benefited economically from the transaction(s) except through a tax deduction." In fact, it was candidly admitted by Bridges under cross-examination that the only objective consideration involved in the transactions was the tax consideration. Since the maturity dates of the promissory notes and the securities were the same, the total amount of the "loans" was the same as the face amount of the securities at their maturity and Bridges had prepaid all the interest charged by the banks, there was never any benefit extended by the banks to Bridges and never any risk assumed by the banks. Assuredly, taxpayer did not receive money or equivalent economic benefits in the amount of the bank loans. Actually, no real indebtedness was created and the Tax Court was fully justified in finding that, as payments of interest "on indebtedness," the transactions were shams. Paraphrasing the language of the Supreme Court in *Knetsch,* it is patent that there was nothing of substance to be realized by Bridges from either transaction beyond a tax deduction; and plainly the transactions did not in any wise affect his beneficial interest except to reduce his tax.

Interest on Debt versus Dividend on Stock

10.15   Since interest is deductible and dividends are not, the distinction between debt instruments and stock certificates is quite important. If in view of all facts and circumstances surrounding the transaction, so-called loans are deemed to be additional investments of equity capital, interest paid on the loans is not deductible by the corporation. Furthermore, the interest payments along with any principal payments are treated as distributions to the stockholders and as dividends to the extent of the corporation's earnings and profits.

10.16   Through the years there has been much litigation in this area. Even if an instrument very clearly read like one creating debt, courts have held it to be in substance an equity investment, and therefore stock, usually on the ground that the corporation was too thinly capitalized and the money was accordingly invested as risk capital. Or the instrument may have recited some of the elements of debt and others of an equity type, with the latter prevailing. Such an instrument is called a "hybrid security."

10.17   To decrease the future amount of litigation, the Tax Reform Act of 1969 inserted Section 385 in the Code delegating to the Commissioner authority to promulgate regulatory guidelines for determining whether a corporate obligation constitutes stock or indebtedness.

Read that section. The Senate Finance Committee Report[27] pertaining to Code Section 385 reads in part as follows:

The provision also specifies certain factors which may be taken into account in these guidelines. It is not intended that only these factors be included in the guidelines or that, with respect to a particular situation, any of these factors must be included in the guidelines, or that any of the factors which are included by statute must necessarily be given any more weight than other factors added by regulations.

It is apparent that, even after the regulations are issued, there will be room for argument, but the regulations undoubtedly will spell out the minimum requirements for "safe harbors."

10.18

To facilitate an understanding of the five factors listed in Section 385 that are to be taken into account in determining whether a corporate obligation constitutes stock or indebtedness, we will now discuss some landmark court decisions and one ruling.

10.19

Risk Capital. As the Seventh Circuit Court of Appeals stated[28] in 1942:

10.20

It is often said that the essential difference between a creditor and a stockholder is that the latter intends to make an investment and take the risks of the venture, while the former seeks a definite obligation, payable in any event.

Thin Capitalization. Treating debt as stock will occur frequently where a closely held corporation upon organization was too thinly capitalized—the ratio of debt to equity investment was too high. The theory is that no corporation following sound business practices would issue such a high percentage of debt unless it had assurances that the holders of the debt instruments would not press for payment and would treat them as stock. The Tax Court has allowed an interest deduction and recognized the debt as bona fide in two cases[29] where the ratio of debt to equity investment was nine to one, but it looked only at the instrument itself and the surrounding circumstances. It did not even comment about thin capitalization. Most tax practitioners have recommended a debt to equity ratio of no more than four or five to one, but the reasonableness of the ratio alone is not controlling. Other important factors were pointed out by a District Court of Florida in *Daytona Marine Supply Co. et al.* v. *U.S.*,[30] in which it in turn relied upon decisions of the Fifth and Ninth Circuit Courts of Appeal.[31] There the ratio of bonds to stock was four to one.

10.21

27. S. Rep. No. 91–552, 91st Cong., 1st Sess., 1969, p. 138.

28. Com. v. Meridian & Thirteenth Realty Co., 132 F.2d 182 (7th Cir. 1942), 42–2 USTC ¶9725, 30 AFTR 559.

29. Bacon, Inc., 4 T.C. 1107 (1945) (Acq.); Idaho Lumber & Hardware Co., 4 TCM 290.

30. 61–2 USTC ¶9523, 7 AFTR2d 1650.

31. Rowan v. U.S., 219 F.2d 51 (5th Cir. 1955), 55–1 USTC ¶9188, 46 AFTR 1636; Wilshire and Western Sandwiches, Inc. v. Com., 175 F.2d 718 (9th Cir. 1949), 49–2 USTC ¶9331, 38 AFTR 116.

Other
Deductions
Allowed
Whether
Business or
Personal

In holding that the bonds constituted bona fide debt and that interest on them was deductible, the court noted with approval that the following factors were present:

1. The intent at time of issuance was to create a debtor–creditor relationship.
2. The bonds were recorded as liabilities on the balance sheet.
3. There was a fixed maturity date.
4. The bonds gave a preferred position as to payment of interest and principal at maturity and were not subordinated to any other creditors.
5. The bonds granted no voting power.
6. There was a fixed rate of interest not dependent upon earnings.
7. The bonds contained a schedule for redemption or retirement before maturity.
8. The obligation to pay was unconditional.
9. Adequate consideration was paid to the corporation for the bonds.

Not all of these factors need be present to have a true indebtedness. The most important are: a fixed maturity date, unconditional obligation to pay, and a fixed rate of interest. Subordination to claims of general creditors should be avoided,[32] but in one ruling[33] the Service permitted such subordination because the debentures had priority over the shareholders.

10.22   There is no mathematical magic in the ratio of debt to equity, although it probably is true that the higher the ratio of debt the more vulnerable the parties become.

10.23   Many courts are critical of the "thin capitalization" rule when the creditors' percentage of the outstanding debt of a corporation is disproportionate to their ownership of the stock of the corporation.[34] In *Leach Corporation*,[35] the Tax Court stated:

> ... The sharply disproportionate ratio between ownership of stock and bonds goes far to overcome the high debt-to-equity ratio here. The bondholders owned only some 48 percent of the stock. The situation would have been quite different had all the stock and bonds been owned by the same interests in substantially the same proportion ... but where the disproportion is so substantial and the parties ... so ... unrelated ... such disproportion tends strongly to neutralize the inferences that might otherwise be drawn from the high debt-to-equity ratio.

10.24   **Hybrid Securities.** Hybrid securities are instruments with some of the characteristics both of debentures and stock certificates. The nine characteristics of debt listed in paragraph 10.21 in the discussion of thin capitalization are all valid factors to be taken into account in

32. I.T. 3555, 1942–1 C.B. 223; Swoby Corp., 9 T.C. 887; Green Bay and Western R.R. Co. v. Com., 147 F.2d 585 (7th Cir. 1945), 45–1 USTC ¶9189, 33 AFTR 715.
33. Rev. Rul. 68–54, 1968–1 C.B. 69.
34. Earle v. W. J. Jones & Son, 200 F.2d 846 (9th Cir. 1952), 42 AFTR 1033; Rowan v. U.S., 219 F.2d 51 (5th Cir. 1955), 46 AFTR 1636.
35. 30 T.C. 563 (1956) (Acq.).

determining whether a hybrid security is debt or stock, for it cannot be both. In *John Kelley Company*,[36] a landmark case involving hybrid securities, the determining factors were recited to be:

1. Name given to the certificate
2. Presence or absence of maturity date
3. Source of the payments on the certificates
4. Right to enforce the payment of principal and interest
5. Participation in management
6. Status equal to or inferior to that of regular corporate creditors
7. Intent of the parties

Preferred stock, although possessing a few debt characteristics, ordinarily is not a hybrid security and is stock.[37] Preferred stock may or may not have a maturity date, may or may not be callable, is entitled to dividends before dividends are paid on common stock, is entitled to preference in liquidation over common stockholders, but can receive dividends only out of earnings and to the extent thereof. The holder of preferred stock is not entitled to payment of the amount of the certificate in any event and is not entitled to his dividend unless it is first declared. A creditor is entitled to interest whether or not there are earnings and is entitled to be paid the principal amount of the indebtedness before any amounts are paid to common or preferred stockholders. In the event of default, he can sue and enforce payment.

10.25

In the *John Kelley Company* case a corporation, all of whose common and preferred stock was owned directly or as trustee by members of a family group, was recapitalized by the issuance of $150,000 income debenture bearer bonds, issued under a trust indenture, calling for 8 percent interest, noncumulative. They were offered only to shareholders of the taxpayer but were assignable. The greater part, $114,648, was issued in exchange for the original preferred, at the call price of such preferred, and the balance was sold to two shareholders at par. The debentures were payable in twenty years, December 31, 1956, with payment of interest conditioned upon the sufficiency of the net income to meet the obligation. The holders had priority of payment over stockholders but were subordinated to all other creditors. The debentures were redeemable at the taxpayer's option and carried the usual acceleration provisions for specific defaults. The holders had no right to participate in management. Common stock was owned in the same proportion by the same stockholders both before and after the reorganization, but the debentures were not held in the same proportion as the stock.

10.26

In affirming the holding of the Tax Court that these debentures constituted indebtedness and the annual payments thereon were interest, the United States Supreme Court said:

10.27

36. 1 T.C. 457 (1943), affirmed 326 U.S. 521 (1946), 46–1 USTC ¶9133, 34 AFTR 314.
37. Com. v. Meridian & Thirteenth Realty Co., *supra* fn. 28.

Other
Deductions
Allowed
Whether
Business or
Personal
In the *Kelley* case, there were sales of the debentures as well as exchanges of preferred stock for debentures, a promise to pay a certain annual amount, if earned, a priority for the debentures over common stock, the debentures were assignable without regard to any transfer of stock, and a definite maturity date in the reasonable future. These indicia of indebtedness support the Tax Court conclusion that the annual payments were interest on indebtedness.

10.28   Where four-fifths of the outstanding stock of a corporation was canceled by a closely held corporation, and in exchange it issued pro rata to the shareholders restricted, registered, and subordinated notes with a fixed maturity date, a minimum interest rate of two percent, and a maximum rate of ten percent depending upon earnings, the United States Supreme Court held that the notes were not indebtedness.[38] It found that tax avoidance was the dominating motive of the taxpayers and that the only purpose of the recapitalization was to attempt to convert nondeductible dividends into deductible interest. Note here, as elsewhere in other tax-saving attempts, that there must be a corporate or shareholder business or economic reason for the transaction other than the saving of income taxes.

Interest Deductions Specifically Prohibited

10.29   The Code specifies five situations in which interest is nondeductible or the amount is limited:

1. INTEREST ON DEFERRED INCOME. Interest payments are generally not deductible on life insurance, endowment, or annuity contracts if the individual is following a plan of systematically borrowing amounts equal to the increase in the cash value of the insurance contract to pay all or part of the premiums, or if all the premiums are paid within four years (Code Section 264). This prevents taxpayers from deducting interest expense when they are not paying tax on the corresponding interest buildup in the reserve in the policy.[39]

2. INTEREST RELATING TO TAX–EXEMPT INVESTMENTS. Code Sec. 265(2) prevents the taxpayer from borrowing funds to purchase tax-exempt securities in order to obtain an interest deduction while not reporting interest income. An interest deduction is denied for indebtedness incurred or continued to purchase or carry *wholly* tax-exempt obligations. The deduction is denied even if the funds were borrowed without intent later to carry or purchase tax-exempt securities, and the taxpayer had other funds that could have been used to pay for them,[40] but see paragraph 7.83. Deductions allowed on later loan: Edmund F. Ball, 54 T.C. 1200 (1970)(NA).

38. Talbot Mills v. Com., 326 U.S. 521 (1946), 46–1 USTC ¶9133, 34 AFTR 314, affirming 3 T.C. 95.

39. H.R. Rep. 749, 88th Cong., 1st sess., 1969, p. 60, 1964–1 C.B. (Part 2) 125, and S. Rep. 830, 88th Cong., 1st sess., p. 77, 1964–1 C.B. (Part 2) 505 (discussion of reasons for provision).

40. Bishop v. Com., 342 F.2d 757 (6th Cir. 1965), 65–1 USTC ¶9304, 15 AFTR2d 620.

Other
Deductions
Allowed
Whether
Business or
Personal

3. CARRYING CHARGES. Under Section 266, carrying charges, such as mortgage and loan interest, and taxes relating to real or personal property, may be capitalized at the taxpayer's election even though otherwise deductible. Charges so capitalized are, of course, not deductible as current expenses (Reg. 1.266–1).

4. INTEREST ON DEBTS BETWEEN RELATED TAXPAYERS. Interest accrued at the end of the year by an accrual basis obligor and payable to a cash basis obligee is not deductible by the obligor unless paid within $2\frac{1}{2}$ months after the close of his taxable year if certain relationships exist between the obligor and obligee [Code Sec. 267(a)(2); Reg. 1.267(a)(1)(b)]. This is discussed more fully in chapter 15.

5. INTEREST ON INVESTMENT INDEBTEDNESS. For 1972 and later years, Section 163(d) imposes limits on a deduction for interest paid or incurred by an individual, estate, or trust to purchase or carry investments. These limitations do not apply to interest incurred on funds borrowed for other purposes, such as a home mortgage, installment purchases, consumer goods, and personal or student loans. In addition, interest on funds borrowed in connection with a trade or business are not affected.[41] The first $25,000 of annual interest to purchase or carry investments continues to be fully deductible by individuals. Any excess is deductible only to the extent of net investment income; any further excess is offset against long-term capital gain. One-half of any remaining excess is deductible; the other half disallowed. Any amount disallowed can be carried forward ad infinitum to future years. This monstrously technical addition to the Code made by the Tax Reform Act of 1969 probably has no application other than to perhaps 1,000 individuals out of the millions of taxpayers.

Installment Purchases

Because carrying charges on installment sales normally contain an interest element, Section 163(b) of the Code allows an interest deduction on installment contracts. When personal property or educational services are purchased under a contract providing that all or part of the price is to be paid in installments, in which a carrying charge is separately stated but the interest charge cannot be determined, Section 163 provides a formula for the interest deduction.

The interest deduction is "... 6 percent of the average unpaid balance under the contract during the taxable year [limited to the amount of the carrying charge or actual payment]. For purposes of this computation, the average unpaid balance under the contract is the sum of the unpaid balance outstanding on the first day of each month beginning during the taxable year, divided by 12" [Reg. 1.163–2(b)]. The following example is copied from the regulation:

On January 20, 1955, A purchased a television set for $400, including a stated carrying charge of $25. The down payment was $50, and the balance was paid in 14 monthly installments of $25 each, on the 20th day of each month commencing with February. Assuming that A is a cash method,

41. H.R. Rep. 91–413 (Part 1), 91st Cong., 1st sess., 1969, General Explanation, p. 73. Also see p. 72 thereof for background of provision.

Other
Deductions
Allowed
Whether
Business or
Personal

calendar year taxpayer and that no other installment purchases were made, the amount to be treated as interest in 1955 is $12.38, computed as follows:

YEAR 1955

FIRST DAY OF:	UNPAID BALANCE OUTSTANDING
January	$ 0
February	350
March	325
April	300
May	275
June	250
July	225
August	200
September	175
October	150
November	125
December	100
	2,475

Sum of unpaid balances $2,475 ÷ 12 = $206.25;
6 percent thereof = $12.38.

10.32   In applying the formula exemplified above, Reg. 1.163–2(2)(1) states that the due dates specified in the contract are to be used and the actual dates of payments are to be ignored.

10.33   Since 1964, a taxpayer is entitled to a deduction for imputed interest under Section 483 if he purchases or exchanges any properties in a taxable transaction in which no interest is stated on unpaid balances, some or all of the payments are due more than one year after the date of such transaction, and the sales price is more than $3,000. If the purchaser is entitled to a deduction for interest on an installment obligation under Section 163(b) as explained in the above paragraphs, Section 483 does not apply to him. Section 483 was enacted primarily to preclude capital gain treatment to the seller of property for a lump sum price to be collected over a number of taxable years. Since the lump sum price probably includes a charge for interest even though unstated, this provision takes the interest factor into account for tax purposes. See paragraph 11.27 for a discussion of Section 483.

PREMIUM ON REDEMPTION OF BONDS

10.34   When a corporation calls its bonds in advance of maturity pursuant to a provision in the bond indenture, a premium is usually payable. This premium partakes of the nature of interest, but for tax purposes is deductible by the corporation as an ordinary and necessary business expense under Section 162(a).[42]

If the bond is convertible into stock and was issued on or after September 5, 1968, any premium paid to repurchase it is deductible only to the extent of one year's interest at the rate specified in the bond, unless the corporation can demonstrate to the satisfaction of the Commissioner "that an amount in excess of one year's interest does not include any amount attributable to the conversion feature."[43] If the convertible bond was issued prior to September 5, 1968, and recites an amount of premium that will be paid upon its call before maturity, the amount of such premium is deductible, but nothing more. Any excess paid over the recited call premium the Service holds does not relate to the cost of borrowing money, but represents an expenditure to preclude conversion of the bonds into stock.[44]   **10.35**

If an individual pays a penalty to his mortgagee in connection with an early payment of a portion or all of the balance due on the mortgage, the penalty is deductible as interest.[45]   **10.36**

TAXES

Section 164 specifically provides that certain types of taxes are deductible as taxes, whether incurred in a business, an income-producing activity, or a personal transaction. This is true only if the tax is imposed upon the person paying or incurring the liability for the tax. Then the amount is deductible as a tax in the year in which it is paid or the liability is incurred, depending upon the method of accounting used, even though the tax pertains to a capital item or inventory.   **10.37**

Under Section 164 and the regulations, the following types of taxes imposed upon the taxpayer are deductible as taxes: **10.38**

1. State and local, and foreign, real property taxes
2. State and local personal property taxes
3. State and local, and foreign, income, war profits, and excess profits taxes
4. State and local general retail sales taxes and compensating use taxes
5. State and local taxes on the sale of gasoline, diesel fuel, and other motor fuels
6. All other state and local, and foreign, taxes incurred in a trade or business or in the production of income
7. Special assessments to the extent imposed for maintenance, repair, or the meeting of interest charges

42. American Chicle Co., 23 B.T.A. 221 (1931), affirmed without discussion of this point 65 F.2d 454 (2nd Cir. 1933), 12 AFTR 806, which was reversed without discussion of this point 291 U.S. 426 (1934), 13 AFTR 876; Reg. 1.163–3(c).
43. Reg. 1.163–3(c)(2).
44. Rev. Rul. 69–243; *contra* Roberts & Porter, Inc. v. Com., 307 F.2d 745 (7th Cir. 1962), 62–2 USTC ¶9738, 10 AFTR2d 5686.
45. Rev. Rul. 57–198, 1957–1 C.B. 94.

10.39   As mentioned briefly in chapter 3, any such taxes incurred by an individual in a trade or business or in obtaining rental or royalty income should be deducted in determining adjusted gross income. Other taxes, such as a real property tax on a personal residence, can be deducted only as itemized deductions.

10.40   With respect to transfer taxes imposed by states on the sale or other transfer of securities and real estate, Reg. 1.164–1(a) provides:

> ... Dealers or investors in securities and dealers or investors in real estate may deduct State stock transfer and real estate transfer taxes, respectively, under Section 164 to the extent they are expenses incurred in carrying on a trade or business or an activity for the production of income.

Such transfer taxes are separately deductible and should not be treated as a reduction of the sales price in computing the gain or loss on the sale.

10.41   If a tax, such as a sales or use tax, is imposed on the vendor or some other person and is passed along as part of the purchase price, it remains a part of the purchase price. If the item acquired is capital in nature, or inventory, the expenditure must be capitalized as part of the cost. If the goods or services were purchased in connection with a trade or business or the production of income and properly may be expensed, so also may the amount of the tax be expensed. If the transaction or expenditure was personal in nature, the amount paid for the tax is not deductible.

10.42   In determining upon whom a tax is imposed, the general rule is that local law governs. There are three exceptions:

1. In every sale of real property, whether business, income producing, or personal in nature, the seller and the purchaser split the deduction for state and local property taxes, and the amount allocated to each is treated as imposed upon him and paid by him to the governmental body levying the tax.
2. If, under local law, a general retail sales tax or a retail sales tax on gasoline, diesel fuel, and other motor fuels is imposed upon the vendor, but the amount of the tax is separately stated, the tax will be treated for federal income tax purposes as having been imposed upon the purchasing consumer, but only if the transaction was not in connection with the purchaser's trade or business.
3. If a corporation pays a tax imposed on a shareholder on his interest as a shareholder and the corporation is not reimbursed, the tax is deductible by the corporation.

10.43   Contributions required from employers under the Social Security program, that is, contributions under the Federal Insurance Contributions Act (old-age and survivors' insurance), the Federal Unemployment Tax Act, and the Railroad Retirement Act, are excise taxes and are deductible *only* as business expenses or as expenses incurred in the production of income. If the contribution pertains to wages paid a domestic servant, both it and the wages are nondeductible personal expenditures.

If a tax paid by an individual is attributable to a trade or business,   10.44
business property, rental property, or royalty-producing property, it is
deductible in determining adjusted gross income. All other taxes are
deductible as itemized deductions.

Allocation of Real Property Taxes on Sales

State and local governments levy real property taxes on the value   10.45
of land and buildings or other improvements on it. The taxes are
levied for a property tax year, which may or may not coincide with the
fiscal year of the particular governmental body. In each year there is
an assessment date as of which the value of the property is determined
and the taxes are assessed. There is also a lien date, usually a little
later, upon which the taxes assessed become a lien on the property.
Upon a sale of real estate, it has been customary for many years to
apportion the real estate taxes between the buyer and the seller upon
the basis of the number of months that have elapsed from the beginning of the property tax year in which the sale occurs to the date
of sale. This custom was recognized for the first time by the drafters of
the 1954 Code. Section 164(d) provides that if real property is sold
during any real property tax year, then the seller is treated as having
paid real property tax apportioned to date of sale, and the balance of
the tax is treated as having been imposed on the buyer. The assessment date and the lien date are disregarded. Regulation 1.164–6(b)(3)
gives the following example:

The real property tax year in County R is April 1 to March 31. A, the owner   EXAMPLE
on April 1, 1954, of real property located in County R sells the real property   FROM REG.
to B on June 30, 1954. B owns the real property from June 30, 1954, through
March 31, 1955. The real property tax for the real property tax year April 1,
1954–March 31, 1955, is $365.

For purposes of Section 164(a), $90 (90/365 × $365, April 1, 1954–June 29,
1954) of the real property tax is treated as imposed on A, the seller, and $275
(275/365 × $365, June 30, 1954–March 31, 1955) of such real property tax is
treated as imposed on B, the purchaser.

There are various special rules set forth in Reg. 1.164–6 applying to
sellers and purchasers, depending upon the accounting method used
and whether or not the taxes for the real property tax year were paid
prior to or after the date of sale; but the general rule is as set forth
above.

A purchaser who pays delinquent taxes on property, which accrued   10.46
prior to his purchase, may not deduct the amount paid. The amounts
were never his obligation or chargeable to the current year. Consequently, the amount when paid by him is treated as part of the purchase price of the property.

Nondeductible Taxes

10.47   By reason of Sections 164(c), 266, and 275, the following types of taxes are not deductible:

1. Federal income, war profits, and excess profits taxes
2. Federal social security taxes imposed on employers of household help
3. Federal self-employment tax
4. Federal social security and railroad retirement taxes imposed on employees
5. Federal and state estate, inheritance, legacy, succession, and gift taxes
6. Income, war profits, and excess profits taxes imposed by any foreign country or possession of the United States, if the taxpayer claims to any extent a foreign tax credit
7. Taxes on real property to the extent that Section 164(d) requires such taxes to be treated as imposed on another taxpayer in the case of a sale of such property
8. Taxes assessed against local benefits (special assessments, for example, to install a new sidewalk) of a kind tending to increase the value of the property assessed
9. Otherwise deductible taxes pertaining to real or personal property which a taxpayer elects to capitalize as a part of the basis of such property pursuant to Section 266 pertaining to carrying charges

CHARITABLE CONTRIBUTIONS

Introduction

10.48   Section 170 grants a deduction to every taxpayer for contributions to charitable and educational *organizations*—the term used is generic and refers to the types of organizations specified in Section 170(c). A House Ways and Means Committee report explains:

> ... The exemption from taxation of money or property devoted to charitable and other purposes is based upon the theory that the Government is compensated for the loss of revenue by its relief from financial burden which would otherwise have to be met by appropriations from public funds, and by the benefits resulting from the promotion of the general welfare.[46]

10.49   Through the years, many charitable and educational organizations have applied for, and obtained, rulings that they are tax-exempt under Section 501 and that contributions to them are deductible for income tax purposes under Section 170, for estate tax purposes under Section 2055, and for gift tax purposes under Section 2522. Periodically, the Internal Revenue Service publishes a cumulative list of such organizations;[47] however, many exempt organizations, such as churches, are not shown in that list because they have never sought a ruling.

46. H.R. Rep. 1860, 75th Cong., 3d sess., p. 19.
47. U.S. Treas. Dept. Publ. No. 78 (Rev. 12–68) with bimonthly cumulative supplements.

A contribution made directly to a beggar or impoverished person **10.50**
is not deductible, no matter how praiseworthy the act may be. If the
donation is made to a qualified charitable organization and it in turn
contributes all or part of the funds to needy individuals, the donation
is deductible. For example, if an individual gives $25 to a needy
family, to buy a Christmas dinner, the amount is not deductible. If
he gives $25 to the Salvation Army or a church to enable it to buy
Christmas dinners for the needy people it chooses, the amount is
deductible. To be deductible, the contribution must be made to an
organized charitable or educational entity of the type specified in
Section 170(c).

Even if a contribution is made to such an organized charitable or **10.51**
educational entity, it is not deductible if the amount is earmarked to
benefit a specified individual. The Tax Court has said: [48]

Charity begins where certainty in beneficiaries ends, for it is the uncertainty of the objects and not the mode of relieving them which forms the
essential element of charity. ... Whenever the beneficiary is designated by
name and his merit alone is to be considered, the bequest is private and
not public and ceases to have the peculiar merit of charity.

Sums contributed to finance a musical education for a specific tal-
ented individual,[49] and payments to a parochial school for the education of particular children[50] have been held not to be deductible.

There are limitations on the maximum amounts deductible. The **10.52**
limits for individuals are percentages of the taxpayer's "contribution base." This term is defined in Section 170(b)(1)(F) as adjusted
gross income computed without regard to any net operating loss
carry-back to the taxable year under Section 172. Tersely stated, the
rules for an individual are the following:

1. To the extent contributions are paid "to or for the use of" the broad category of organizations specified in Code Sec. 170(c), the amounts are
deductible up to a maximum of 20 percent of his contribution base;
2. To the extent contributions are paid "to" a narrower group of "public"
organizations, the amounts are deductible up to a maximum of 50%
of his contribution base, but with a five-year carry-forward of unused
charitable contributions;
3. Subject to stringent limitations, until 1975 there is a larger (formerly
unlimited) deduction under Section 170(b)(1)(C) for charitable contributions.

However, as discussed in paragraphs 10.69 to 10.77, if the contribution is in the form of property, the amount of its value taken into
account may have to be reduced.

48. S. E. Thomason, 2 T.C. 441 (1943).
49. Cap Andrew Tilles, 38 BTA 545 (1938), affirmed 113 F.2d 907 (8th Cir. 1940),
25 AFTR 560, cert. den. 311 U.S. 703.
50. Rev. Rul. 54–580, 1954–2 C.B. 97.

10.53   In the case of corporations, the maximum amount deductible is 5 percent of taxable income with a few special provisions about the manner in which the taxable income is computed and also with a five-year carry-forward of contributions in excess of the limit.

Qualifying Beneficiaries

10.54   The types of beneficiaries that qualify for the 20 percent limit for individuals and the 5 percent limit for corporations and some of which also qualify for the 50 percent limitation and the larger (formerly unlimited) deduction are listed in Section 170(c).

10.55   The majority of charitable contributions are to the organizations described in Section 170(c)(2). Included in the category are nonprofit hospitals, universities, the American Red Cross, community funds, and private foundations.

10.56   In 1954, Congress carved out of the organizations specified in Section 170(c) "public" types of entities and provided in Section 170(b)(1)(A) that contributions "to" (not "for the use of") these shall be deductible to the extent of an additional 10 percent of adjusted gross income for a total of 30 percent. The Tax Reform Act of 1969 increased the deductible limit to 50 percent of the taxpayer's contribution base, except that for some gifts of appreciated property only 30 percent of the aggregate value can be taken into account. See paragraphs 10.75 to 10.77.

10.57   In broad terms, there are nine principal types of such "public" organizations:

1. Churches
2. Tax-exempt educational organizations, such as universities
3. Hospitals
4. Active medical research organizations working with hospitals
5. Organizations publicly supported to a substantial extent, such as the American Red Cross and community chests
6. Federal, state, or local governmental units if the contribution is made for exclusively public purposes
7. Private *operating* foundations as defined in Section 4942(j)(3) and discussed in paragraph 10.60
8. Private foundations (as defined in Section 509(a) and described in paragraph 2.19) that are nonoperating and that distribute contributions received within a particular year either within that year or within $2\frac{1}{2}$ months after the end of the year, provided that the distribution is treated as a distribution of corpus under Sections 170(b)(1)(E)(ii) and 4942(h)
9. Private foundations that are pooled community funds as defined in Section 170(b)(1)(E)(iii)

The limit on the amount of an individual's contributions to these nine types of organizations is 50 percent (30 percent in the case of certain appreciated property) of the taxpayer's contribution base, but only if the gift is made "to" them. If it is made "for the use of" such organizations, then the limitation of 20 percent of the contribution base applies.

In I.T. 1867[51] the Internal Revenue Service many years ago held   10.58
that the phrase "for the use of" has a meaning similar to "in trust for" and that the phrase is expressive of the "right of exclusive appropriation or enjoyment of the thing donated." Accordingly, if an individual makes a contribution to a trust, which in turn is directed to pay such amount to one of the 50 percent types of entities specified in Section 170(b)(1)(A), the contribution is "for the use of" such organization and is deductible only to the extent of 20 percent of adjusted gross income. In addition to a contribution through a trust, a payment by an individual of a liability of a charitable organization made directly to its creditor would be a payment "for the use of" the charity.[52]

Private Operating Foundations. Private foundations are of two types   10.59
—operating and nonoperating. Every private foundation that is not an operating one is nonoperating.

A private operating foundation is defined in Section 4942(j)(3).   10.60
One of the principal requirements is that substantially all (at least 85 percent according to the Senate Finance Committee Report[53]) of its income must be spent directly for the active conduct of its activities representing the purpose or function for which it is organized and operated. In order that potential contributors will be able to identify private operating foundations, late in 1972 the Service published a "Tentative Cumulative List of Organizations Described in Section 170(c)" (Pub. 78 (Tentative) 10–72), which identifies by a code number such types of foundations.

Calculation of Limitations on Deductions

If the total contributions made by an individual during a particular   10.61
taxable year are in excess of 20 percent of his contribution base, and if some, but not all, of the contributions are paid "to" the "public" types of organizations eligible for the 50 percent limit, the 50 percent-type contributions are first deducted. Then, by reason of Section 170(b)(1)(B), the 20 percent type contributions are deductible, if at all, to the extent of the *lesser* of (1) 20 percent of his contribution base or (2) the excess of 50 percent of the contribution base over the 50 percent-type contributions. Any unused 50 percent-type contributions can be carried forward to the five succeeding taxable years, but there is no carry-over available for unused 20 percent-type contributions.

51. II–2 C.B. 155; similarly, Rev. Rul. 57–562, 1957–2 C.B. 159.
52. *Supra* fn. 48 at p. 444.
53. S. Rep. 91–552, 91st Cong., 1st sess., 1969, p. 60.

10.62   The following example illustrates the fact that there can never be a carry-over of 20 percent-type contributions. It also serves to point out that contributions to "public" type organizations are always utilized first up to a total of 50 percent of the contribution base, before any portion of the 20 percent-type is taken into consideration.

EXAMPLE

LINE		TAXPAYERS		
		A	B	C
(1)	Contribution base	$50,000	$50,000	$50,000
(2)	Limit at 50%	$25,000	$25,000	$25,000
(3)	Limit at 20%	$10,000	$10,000	$10,000
	Contributions paid:			
(4)	50%-type	$ 5,000	$25,000	$30,000
(5)	20%-type	20,000	5,000	4,000
(6)	Total	$25,000	$30,000	$34,000
	Deductible amounts:			
(7)	50%-type to extent of 50% of contribution base	$ 5,000	$25,000	$25,000
(8)	20%-type to the extent of the lesser of:			
(9)	20% of contribution base	$10,000	$10,000	$10,000
	or			
(10)	50% of contribution base	$25,000	$25,000	$25,000
(11)	Less 50%-type contributions up to that limit	5,000	25,000	25,000
(12)	Balance	$20,000	$ —	$ —
(13)	Deductible 20%-type	$10,000	$ —	$ —
(14)	Total deduction [line (7) plus line (13)]	$15,000	$25,000	$25,000
(15)	Nondeductible portion	$10,000	$ 5,000	$ 9,000
(16)	Carry-over	—	—	5,000
(17)	Lost	$10,000	$ 5,000	$ 4,000

10.63   A carry-over is available in each of the succeeding five taxable years to the extent that contributions in each such year to "public" type organizations are less than 50 percent of adjusted gross income in such years. The following schedule exemplifies the rules contained in Section 170(d)(1):

	CONTRIBU-TION YEAR	SUCCEED-ING YEAR	SECOND SUCCEED-ING YEAR	THIRD SUCCEED-ING YEAR
Contribution base	$50,000	$30,000	$60,000	$80,000
50% thereof	25,000	15,000	30,000	40,000
20% thereof	10,000	6,000	12,000	16,000
Contributions made during the year:				
50%-type	$35,000	$13,000	$35,000	$30,000
20%-type	3,000	1,000	—	—
Total	$38,000	$14,000	$35,000	$30,000
Deduction:				
50%-type	$25,000	$13,000	$30,000	$30,000
20%-type	—	—	—	—
Carry-over from prior year	—	2,000	—	10,000
Total	$25,000	$15,000	$30,000	$40,000
Nondeductible portion of current year contributions	$13,000	$ 1,000	$ 5,000	$ —
Carry-over to 5 succeeding years	10,000	—	5,000	—
Lost	$ 3,000	$ 1,000	$ —	$ —

Note that in the first succeeding year $2,000 of the $10,000 carry-over had to be used even though the effect was to disallow $1,000 of 20 percent-type contributions made in that year. The $10,000 carry-over deducted in the third succeeding year consists of the $8,000 balance from the contribution year and $2,000 from the second succeeding year.

Pledges

A pledge to a charitable organization is not a contribution, even   10.64
though stated so firmly that it can be enforced against an estate. No
income tax deduction is allowable until payment or other satisfaction
of the pledge is made.[54] Section 170(a)(1) requires "payment."

The Internal Revenue Service has ruled that the satisfaction of a   10.65
pledge of a specific dollar amount to a charitable organization by the
donation of appreciated properties does not result in taxable gain to
the donor, since the transfer cannot be regarded both as a contribution and as the satisfaction of a debt.[55] In effect, the Revenue Service
holds that for federal income tax purposes, a charitable pledge does
not create a debt.

From the aspect of tax planning it may be preferable to give, or

54. Rev. Rul. 55–410, 1955–1 C.B. 297.
55. Ibid.

Other
Deductions
Allowed
Whether
Business or
Personal

satisfy a pledge with, appreciated securities rather than cash, for the appreciation is not taxed to the donor (but see paragraphs 10.69 to 10.77). However, depreciated securities should never be the subject matter of a charitable contribution. The securities should first be sold to establish a loss, and the resulting cash should be given.

Accrual Basis Corporations

10.67　　Cash basis corporations must make payments of their charitable donations before the end of their taxable years. However, under Section 170(a)(2) an accrual basis corporation can elect to deduct contributions authorized by its board of directors during the taxable year (but not paid), if they are paid by the fifteenth day of the third month after the close of the taxable year. The election is made by reporting the contribution on the return and attaching a copy of the directors' resolution and a written declaration that it was adopted during the taxable year. Under the penalties of perjury, this must be verified by a statement signed by an authorized officer. If less than the amount authorized is paid within two and one-half months after the close of the taxable year, only the amount actually paid is deductible in the return for the year during which the resolution was adopted. The balance will be deductible when, as, and if actually paid.

Methods of Making Gifts

10.68　　**Cash.** The simplest type of contribution is a payment of cash to a charitable organization. No question of the value of the contribution is involved; and assuming proof of payment can be made by means of a canceled check or a receipt from the charitable organization, the contribution will be deductible within the percentage limits previously noted. When cash is paid for a ticket to a benefit performance, only any excess of the amount paid over the normal purchase price of a ticket is deductible,[56] because only to that extent is there a gift of something for nothing. Similarly, in one Tax Court case,[57] the taxpayer was denied a deduction for the amount paid for lottery tickets sold by a charitable organization, because in the opinion of the court the entire amount was paid as consideration for a chance to win much more than the actual cost.

10.69　　**Property.** Prior to 1970, a contribution in the form of property was deductible to the extent of its fair market value on the date of the gift, and generally no gain or loss was recognized for the amount of the difference between value and adjusted basis.[58] That principle still

---

56. TIR 747, 1965 P–H Federal Taxes ¶54,935.
57. Douglas Goldman, 46 T.C. 136 (1966).
58. Rev. Rul. 55–138, 1955–1 C.B. 223; Rev. Rul. 55–275, 1955–1 C.B. 295; Rev. Rul. 55–531, 1955–2 C.B. 520; David C. White v. Brodrick, 104 F. Supp. 213 (D.C., Kans., 1952), 41 AFTR 1253; Campbell v. Charles N. Prothro, et ux, 209 F.2d 331 (5th Cir. 1954), 45 AFTR 131.

Other
Deductions
Allowed
Whether
Business or
Personal

applies for property having a value less than adjusted basis. However, for appreciated property, even as little appreciation as one percent over adjusted basis, there are two types of limitations on the amounts of value that can be deducted:

1. Specific item limitations, and
2. an aggregate 30 percent limitation.

The two types of limitations are mutually exclusive; if one applies, the other does not. The specific item limitations apply to both individuals and corporations. After they are so applied, the ceilings of 5 percent of the contribution base for corporations and 20 percent or 50 percent for individuals come into operation. The aggregate 30 percent limitation applies only to individuals and, as pointed out in paragraph 10.75, evidently also only in instances of 50 percent type deductions.

SPECIFIC ITEM LIMITATIONS. Section 170(e), added by the Tax 10.70
Reform Act of 1969, imposes limitations on the value which can be deducted for contributions of specific items of appreciated property falling within certain categories. The classes of property and affected donees are these:

1. "Ordinary income" property regardless of the kind of charitable donee;
2. Tangible personal property if the donee's use is unrelated to its charitable function.
3. "Capital gain" property given to certain private foundations;

Land and other Section 1231 assets used in a trade or business and held for more than six months are includible in these three categories if their value is more than adjusted basis.

Ordinary income appreciated property. The term "ordinary 10.71
income" property is not adequately defined in Section 170(e)(1)(A), but is property which, if sold, would result in some portion of the gain being taxed as ordinary income or as a short-term capital gain. According to the House Ways and Means Committee Report,[59] it includes inventory, Section 306 stock (stock acquired in a nontaxable reorganization or recapitalization which is taxed as a dividend when sold, as discussed in Chapter 19), stock rights held for six months or less, depreciable property subject to recapture of depreciation, and other types of property subject to ordinary income recapture, such as mining exploration, farm loss, and farm development expenditures.

If inventory items or short-term capital assets are contributed, the 10.72
deduction allowable is only the amount of the taxpayer's adjusted basis. If the property contributed would result in recapture if sold, the result depends upon the holding period of the property. If it was held for six months or less, the deduction is the amount of the adjusted

59. H.R. No. 91–413 (Part 1), p. 55.

Other
Deductions
Allowed
Whether
Business or
Personal
basis. If it was held for more than six months, the value of the property must be reduced by the amount of the recapturable element. This is the amount deductible. However, there are two circumstances which require a further reduction: (1) the contribution is of tangible personal property and its use by the donee is unrelated to the purpose or function constituting the basis for its tax exemption (paragraph 10.73), or (2) the contribution is of any kind of property to a "nonpublic" private foundation as discussed in paragraph 10.74.

EXAMPLE 1   An individual bought stock for $3,000 and contributed it to charity four months later when it was worth $5,000. Because the $2,000 of appreciation is short-term capital gain, the charitable deduction is only $3,000.

EXAMPLE 2   A machine was held for more than six months by a donor and was contributed by him to the college of engineering of a university for use in its educational program. At the time of the contribution, its fair market value was $10,000 and its adjusted basis was $5,000. Further, there was $3,000 of recapturable depreciation. The deduction available is $7,000 ($10,000 minus $3,000).

10.73   *Appreciated tangible personal property with unrelated use.* The amount of the deductible value of appreciated tangible personal property held for more than six months is also limited if the use by the donee is unrelated to the purpose or function constituting the basis for its exemption. As an illustration, if, in Example 2 of paragraph 10.72, the machine had been donated to the college of liberal arts for the purpose of having the college resell it, such use, namely, sale, by the college would be unrelated to the purpose or function constituting the basis for its exemption. The fair market value is first reduced by any recapturable element but not below adjusted basis. From the remaining amount is deducted the adjusted basis. The resulting amount of appreciation is then reduced by 50 percent in the case of an individual and by $62\frac{1}{2}$ percent for corporations. The adjusted basis plus the balance of appreciation so calculated is the amount of the deduction.

10.74   *Appreciated capital gain property given to certain private foundations.* Paragraph 10.57 listed nine principal types of "public" charitable organizations, the last three pertaining to three variations of private foundations. If the gift is to a "nonpublic" private foundation and consists of a capital asset as defined in Section 1221 or of Section 1231 property, so that a long-term capital gain would have been realized had the property been sold, the value of the property must be reduced in the same manner as recited in paragraph 10.73.

EXAMPLE   An individual gives a Section 1231 asset to a private foundation that is not of the "public" type. His adjusted basis is $4,000, fair market value is $7,000, and recapturable depreciation under Section 1245 is $2,000. The deduction is $4,500, computed as follows: $7,000 − $2,000 = $5,000 − 50% of $1,000 ($5,000 − $4,000) = $4,500. The deductible $500 ($4,500 − $4,000) of appreciation does not trigger any capital gains tax, and, of course, the nondeductible recapturable depreciation of $2,000 does not cause any reportable ordinary income.

AGGREGATE 30 PERCENT LIMITATION. If an appreciated capital 10.75
asset as defined in Section 1221 or appreciated Section 1231 property
is contributed by an individual to a "public" type charity as defined
in paragraph 10.57, and if none of the limitations on deductible value
provided for in Section 170(e) and discussed in the preceding paragraphs 10.70 to 10.74 applies, then the full fair market value is deductible and there is no tax payable on the appreciation in value;
however, in any one year the maximum amount for such property
which can be deducted in the aggregate is 30 percent of the contribution base. Based on the Committee Reports it seems that this 30 percent limitation only applies if the contribution is "to" a public type
charity so that the 50 percent ceiling discussed in paragraph 10.52
applies. In that event, contributions of cash and of property whose
deductible value is limited are first applied in determining the
50 percent ceiling; only then is this 30 percent type property taken
into account.

An individual has adjusted gross income, his contribution base, of $100,000. EXAMPLE
During the year he makes a cash gift of $40,000 to a hospital and a gift of
securities held for more than six months having a value of $35,000 to a uni-
versity. The ceiling on his aggregate deduction is $50,000 (50% of $100,000)
and the maximum amount that can be deducted for the securities is $30,000
(30% of $100,000). The deduction will consist of the full $40,000 of cash and
$10,000 out of the $30,000 deductible value of the securities. The remaining
$25,000 ($35,000 − $10,000) in value of the securities is available as a carry-
over in succeeding years [Section 170(b)(1)(D)(ii)].

As indicated in the preceding example, if appreciated securities 10.76
are donated in a particular year up to an amount not in excess of 30%
of the contribution base for that year, but then some portion of such
amount is not deductible because of the 50% limitation on total gifts,
the nondeductible amount can be carried over to each of the five succeeding years as a 30% type contribution in those years.

Assume the same facts as in the preceding example. In the first succeeding EXAMPLE
year, his adjusted gross income is $50,000. He makes another cash contribu-
tion of $10,000 to a hospital, and that is the only contribution he makes during
that year. The ceiling on deductions is $25,000 (50% of $50,000) so that, in
addition to the $10,000 contributed in that year, he may also deduct as a
carryover from the preceding year the amount of $15,000 ($25,000 minus
$10,000). The remaining $10,000 of carryover from the preceding year is
then available as a deduction in the next succeeding year.

The 30% ceiling can be avoided if the taxpayer elects under Section 10.77
170(b)(1)(D)(iii) to reduce the amount of the appreciation taken into
account by 50%, just as if the property had been given to a charity
whose use of it is not related to the basis of its exempt status or had
been given to a "nonpublic" type charitable foundation. In that event
the 50% ceiling applies. Circumstances would have to be quite un-

usual, such as death of the donor in the year of the gift (because no carry-over would be available to the estate), to make this election worthwhile.

10.78   RENTAL VALUE AND OTHER FREE USE. The granting of the free use and occupancy of a portion or all of a building or other property does not result in a deductible charitable contribution in the amount of the value of such use and occupancy [Section 170(f)(3)].

10.79 **Personal Services.** No deduction is allowable for the value of contributions of personal services to charitable organizations.[60] The Service has also held that the donation of blood by individuals is similar to rendering services and therefore the value of the blood is not deductible.[61] This ruling is of doubtful validity because clearly it seems that blood is property.

10.80   Unreimbursed expenditures by individuals for charitable organizations may generally be treated as deductible contributions.[62] The Revenue Service has held that expenses incurred for operation, repair, and maintenance of an automobile directly attributable to its use in rendering gratuitous service to charitable organizations are deductible as a charitable contribution. No deduction, however, is allowed for the rental value of the use of the automobile or for depreciation attributable to such use.[63] The Service has adopted a standard mileage rate of six cents per mile for computing the allowable deduction for such use of an automobile. Since this allowance does not cover depreciation, no adjustment to the basis of the automobile is required, owing to the use of the standard rate.[64]

MEDICAL EXPENSES

10.81   Section 213 allows a deduction for expenses, including medical insurance premiums, paid for medical care of the taxpayer, his spouse, and dependents, to the extent such amounts paid exceed insurance or similar recoveries. This is another exception to the general rule that personal expenses are not deductible; however, net medical expenses are deductible only to the extent they exceed a certain percentage of income—the higher a taxpayer's income, the higher the nondeductible base will be. The intent is to provide deductibility for substantial and unexpected medical costs that are difficult for the ordinary taxpayer to bear.[65]

60. Reg. 1.170–2(a); Rev. Rul. 57–135, 1957–1 C.B. 307; O.D. 712, 3 C.B. 188 1920).
61. Rev. Rul. 162, 1953–2 C.B. 127.
62. Reg. 1.170–2(a)(2); Rev. Rul. 58–240, 1958–1 C.B. 141.
63. Rev. Rul. 58–279, 1958–1, C.B. 145; I.T. 3918, 1948–2, C.B. 33; Clinton H. Mitchell, 42 T.C. 953 (1964) (Acq.).
64. Rev. Proc. 64–15, 1964–9, I.R.B. 34, as amended by Rev. Proc. 70–24.
65. S. Rep. 1631, 77th Cong., 2d sess., p. 6, pertaining to Section 127 of the Revenue Act of 1942, the original source of 1954 Code Sec. 213.

Qualifying Expenditures

Section 213(e) states that the term "medical care" means amounts 10.82
paid for:

1. Diagnosis, cure, mitigation, treatment, or prevention of disease, or for
   the purpose of affecting any structure or function of the body
2. Transportation primarily for, and essential to, medical care
3. Insurance (including Medicare insurance premiums under the Social
   Security Act) covering medical care

The regulations define "medical care" as including the 10.83

... diagnosis, cure, mitigation, treatment, or prevention of disease. Expenses paid for "medical care" shall include those paid for the purpose of
affecting any structure or function of the body, or for transportation primarily
for and essential to medical care. ...
... Amounts paid for operations or treatments affecting any portion of the
body, including obstetrical expenses and expenses of therapy or X-ray treatments, are deemed to be for the purpose of affecting any structure or function
of the body and are therefore paid for medical care. Amounts expended for
illegal operations or treatments are not deductible. Deductions for expenditures for medical care allowable under section 213 will be confined strictly
to expenses incurred primarily for the prevention or alleviation of a physical
or mental defect or illness. Thus, payments for the following are payments for
medical care: Hospital services, nursing services (including nurses' board
where paid by the taxpayer), medical laboratory, surgical, dental and other
diagnostic and healing services, X-rays, medicine and drugs, ... artificial
teeth or limbs, and ambulance hire. However, an expenditure which is
merely beneficial to the general health of an individual, such as an expenditure for a vacation, is not an expenditure for medical care. [Regs.
1.213–1(e)(1)(i), (ii).]

Medical v. Personal Expenditures. Expenses normally incurred for 10.84
personal pleasures that also have therapeutic benefits are generally
not deductible. The attitude of the courts and the Internal Revenue
Service seems to deny a deduction unless the specific expense is the
only one that could bring about the desired therapeutic result. Consequently, where dance lessons, even though recommended by a
doctor, were only one of many activities suggested to help strengthen
the taxpayer's legs, the deduction was denied on the grounds that the
taxpayer was primarily satisfying social desires.[66] Similarly, when a
taxpayer went to a resort that specialized in restoring health, his expenditures for the trip were considered personal, since it was not
absolutely necessary for him to restore his health in that particular
manner.[67] Where clarinet lessons were the best method of correcting
malocclusion of a child's teeth, however, the benefits of this one particular treatment were held to be sufficiently unique to support a

66. John J. Thoene, 33 T.C. 62 (1959).
67. Rev. Rul. 57–130, 1957–1 C.B. 108.

Other
Deductions
Allowed
Whether
Business or
Personal
medical expense deduction.[68] Expenditures for food, rent, and other living expenses incurred while away from home for medical purposes are not deductible as medical expenses unless paid as part of a hospital bill or as a necessary incident to medical care in an approved institution.[69]

Limitations

10.85   Medical insurance premiums for policies covering the taxpayer, his spouse, and dependents are separately deductible as medical expense in the amount of one-half of the premiums up to a maximum of $150, and the amount of the taxpayer's adjusted gross income is immaterial. Any balance of such premiums is then added to all other medical expenses.

10.86   Also, there is a uniform rule for all taxpayers that, excluding the first $150 of medical insurance premiums, only those medical expenditures in excess of 3 percent of adjusted gross income are deductible. In determining the amount over 3 percent of adjusted gross income, drugs and medicines are included only to the extent that they exceed 1 percent of adjusted gross income. Thus, when drugs and medicine expenses in excess of 1 percent of adjusted gross income are added to all other qualifying expenses and 3 percent of adjusted gross income is subtracted from the total, the balance is the allowable medical expense deduction [Code Sec. 213(a), (b)].

EXAMPLE   Taxpayer incurs gross medical expenses of $800 (exclusive of medical care insurance premium), drugs and medicines $125, and receives $150 insurance reimbursement. He spends $400 for medical care insurance. Adjusted gross income is $10,000. The deduction is computed as follows:

Medicine and drugs		$125
Less 1% of adjusted gross income		(100)
Allowable medicine and drugs		$ 25
Medical care cost net of insurance recovery		
($800-$150 reimbursement)		650
Medical care insurance premiums	$400	
Less portion deductible under Section 213(a)(2)	(150)	250
Total		$925
Less 3% of adjusted gross income		(300)
Medical expense deduction under Section 213(a)(1)		$625
Special medical care insurance premium deduction		150
Total Section 213 medical care deduction		$775

10.87   There are no ceilings on medical expense deductions, and deductibility is allowed to the full extent of the excess of such expenses over the percentage base [Code Sec. 213(c)].

68. Rev. Rul. 62–210, 1962–2 C.B. 89.
69. Robert M. Rose, 52 T.C. No. 56 (1969).

Reimbursements Received in Later Years

If a medical expense reimbursement is received in a year subsequent to that in which the expenses were paid, the reimbursement is included in income if it is not more than the amount of the previous deduction. If it is more than the previous deduction, an amount equal to the prior deduction is includible in income and the remainder is not taxable because of Section 104(a)(3) discussed in paragraph 6.43. Reverting to the example above, if a reimbursement of $600 is received in a subsequent year, all of it would be includible in gross income. If $700 were received, $625 would be taxable and $75 would be exempt. **10.88**

EXPENSES FOR HOUSEHOLD AND DEPENDENT CARE SERVICES

The popular label of Section 214 is "child care expenses," but the deduction in fact is not limited to expenses for the care of a taxpayer's children. Rather, the deduction is available up to a maximum of $4,800 per year for expenditures for household services and for the care of the following classes of individuals: **10.89**

(1) A dependent under the age of 15 who may be claimed as an exemption;
(2) A disabled dependent of any age; and
(3) A disabled husband or wife.

The expenses must be incurred for the purpose of enabling the taxpayer to be gainfully employed. Under the regulations applicable to 1971 and prior years and presumably under amendments yet to be issued for 1972 and subsequent years, the deduction is available for a period during which the taxpayer looks for employment, and the term "employment" includes self-employment. Pursuing educational courses or studies has been ruled not to qualify as an active search for gainful employment.[70] **10.90**

There are a number of limits on the amount of a deduction which can be claimed; and, if the adjusted gross income of a taxpayer and his spouse is $27,600 or more, no deduction is available. **10.91**

TENANT–STOCKHOLDERS OF COOPERATIVE HOUSING CORPORATIONS

The owner of a house or a condominium is directly assessed for state and local real estate taxes; and for that reason, he can deduct them. If there is a mortgage on his property, he can deduct the interest. The tenant of an apartment or other type of residence cannot **10.92**

---

70. Rev. Rul. 56–169, 1956–1 C.B. 135.

deduct any portion of his rent, even though a portion of it is designed to cover real estate taxes and mortgage interest.

10.93   A cooperative housing corporation is one that owns both the apartment building and the land upon which it is built. Occasionally, such a corporation will also be used to own a town house or row house development. It is similar to a regular corporation in that it has officers, directors, and stockholders; but no person can occupy an apartment in the building unless he is a stockholder or a tenant of a stockholder. The ownership of a share of stock carries with it the right to occupy an apartment; and in the Code, such a person is called a tenant–stock-holder. The corporation itself, not the stockholder, is assessed for state and local real estate taxes and obtains its own mortgage covering the entire building. Each month each tenant–stockholder is assessed an amount of money to cover real estate taxes, interest and principal payments on the mortgage, and maintenance costs. Because the portion of each month's payments allocable to real estate taxes and mortgage interest is not a payment of the shareholder's own liability, but rather that of the separate juridical entity of the corporation, such payments are not deductible under the general rules applying to deductions of real estate taxes and interest.

10.94   Under Section 216 of the Code, a tenant–stockholder of a cooperative housing corporation is entitled to deduct amounts paid or accrued—depending upon his method of accounting—to the corporation, to the extent that these amounts represent his proportionate share of the corporation's real estate taxes and interest.

10.95   Since 1961, Section 216(c) has allowed tenant–stockholders to deduct depreciation to the extent that the apartment is used in a trade or business or for the production of income. Accordingly, if the apartment is subleased or a portion of it is used as an office, depreciation is deductible.

QUESTIONS AND PROBLEMS

1. Mr. Dunne files his return on the cash receipts and disbursements method of accounting. His records pertaining to money borrowed during the year ended December 31, 1972, indicate the following: (1) interest payment of $60 on July 1, 1972, representing a full year's interest on a $1,000 loan made that day (2) discount of $160 deducted by the lender on October 1, 1972, when Mr. Dunne signed a note for $1,000 due October 1, 1974, and received $840 in cash; no repayments were made in 1972. (a) What is Mr. Dunne's interest deductio, for the calendar year 1972? (b) Assuming Mr. Dunne was an accrual basis taxpayer, what would be his 1972 interest deduction?

2. (a) Early in 1972, A purchases, on contract, B's home, on which there is a $10,000 mortgage. B continues as mortgagor. B fails to make the November and December mortgage payments, and A, to protect his interests as equitable owner of the house, makes the two mortgage payments including an amount designated as interest. Is A entitled to an interest deduction on his 1972 tax return?

Other
Deductions
Allowed
Whether
Business or
Personal

(b) F's son, S, purchases a home and assumes a mortgage which F signs as guarantor. S has difficulty in making the payments, and F makes several payments for his son. Is F entitled to an interest deduction for the interest element of the mortgage payments?

3. On January 1, 1972, Tip gave Tap a gift of $10,000. Tap then loaned Tip $10,000 at 8 percent interest. At the end of the year, Tip paid Tap the $800 interest due. On January 1, 1973, Tap gave Tip a gift of $800 and gratuitously forgave the loan of $10,000. Tip deducted $800 in interest expense on his 1972 return. Under what theory could the deduction best be denied?

4. The Quixotic Corporation deducted $50,000 for interest on a debenture containing the following pertinent provisions:
   (a) The face amount of the debenture is due August 15, 2067.
   (b) The interest is 6 percent per annum.
   (c) Interest payments may be reduced or suspended if the board of directors decides earnings are insufficient to warrant payment.
   (d) When dividends on common stock exceed $6 per share, the debenture holders are to receive increased interest payments to match the dividends over $5 per share received by the common stockholders.
   (e) In the event of liquidation, the debenture holders are to share equally with the holders of the common stock.
   (f) On all matters submitted to the common-stock shareholders for a vote, the debenture holder will have one vote for every $1,000 face value debenture.

   Under what theory could an interest deduction best be denied?

5. Richard Roe was engaged in the wholesale grocery business, as an individual proprietor, and kept his business books on the accrual basis but reported his investment income and personal expenses on a cash basis. On December 31, 1971, his business net worth was $100,000. The Star Corporation was organized by Roe on that day. The corporation issued ten shares of $100 par value capital stock and a 5 percent interest-bearing note for $99,000 due in thirty years to Roe in exchange for his net business assets.

   The corporation keeps its books on the accrual basis and in 1972 no part of the note or interest was paid. On December 31, 1972, an accrual was made on the corporation's books as follows:

Interest expense	$4,950	
Richard Roe		$4,950

   The corporation reported a net profit of $6,000 for 1972. On March 31, 1973, the corporation paid Roe $4,950 in discharge of the interest accrued.
   (a) May the corporation properly deduct the $4,950 as interest expense on its 1972 return? Explain.
   (b) Under what theory could an interest deduction be denied even if payment was made in 1972?

6. In May of 1972, Frank Beals borrowed $200,000 from Fast National Bank and purchased 1,000 shares of stock in the Zorro Corporation at $200 per share. The stock appreciated in value and in June, 1973, Frank sold the stock for $350,000 and invested the proceeds in City of Denver Bridge and Highway bonds, interest on which was tax-

Other
Deductions
Allowed
Whether
Business or
Personal

exempt. On his 1973 tax return, Frank deducted the interest expense relating to the 1972 loan, which is still outstanding. Under what Code section could the interest deduction be challenged?

7. Wally Frank owns 35 percent of the outstanding stock of Piping Hot Co., Inc., Wally's wife owns 20 percent, and good friends own 45 percent. Wally has loaned the corporation $5,000 at 6 percent interest in a bona fide, arm's-length transaction. Piping Hot accrued and deducted the interest due to Wally on its 1972 tax return, but because of tight money position the company did not pay Wally until March 28, 1973. Wally properly included the interest income on his 1973 return. May the corporation properly deduct the interest expense in 1972?

8. On November 2, 1972, Mr. Walter Kay purchased furniture for his home for $650, which included carrying charges of $24. The down payment was $50, and the balance was payable in twelve monthly installments of $50 each, on the first day of each month starting with December, 1972. (a) Mr. Kay made the payments when due and is a calendar-year cash-basis taxpayer. How much may Mr. Kay treat as interest for 1972? (b) How much would Mr. Kay treat as interest in 1973? The final payment was made on November 1, 1973, and the sum of the unpaid monthly balances during 1973 amounts to $3,300.

9. (a) Mr. Paul, a cash-basis taxpayer, owns a two-family house and files his return on a calendar-year basis. Both apartments are of equal size and one is rented, while he lives in the other. Each of the twelve monthly mortgage payments that Mr. Paul made during the taxable year to a bank included an escrow amount of $50 for taxes. On July 31 of the same year, the bank paid the local school tax of $400 and a special assessment for sidewalks of $50 for Mr. Paul. What amount may Mr. Paul deduct as taxes *from* adjusted gross income?

(b) An individual sells his personal residence on February 1, 1972. The real estate taxes for the calendar year 1972 become due and payable on July 1, 1972. The real property tax year begins January 1, and the unpaid taxes become a lien on October 1. The purchaser pays the taxes when they become due. Both parties are on the cash and calendar-year basis. (1) Who may deduct the real estate taxes and in what proportion? (2) If the seller were on the accrual basis, would your answer be different?

(c) XYZ Corporation is a calendar-year accrual-basis corporation. The reserve for real estate taxes at year-end was $13,000. Taxes paid during the year were $20,000 and a monthly provision of $1,500 is made. The corporation is liable for real estate taxes as of December 31 and must pay them prior to March 1. The accrual is reasonable. What amount is deductible in the current year's tax return? What amount would be deductible if XYZ Corporation were a cash-basis corporation?

10. Paul Shotgun was released in 1972 after serving twenty years in prison. Unaware that the tax laws had changed since 1952, Paul deducted all of the taxes that he was accustomed to deducting and a few others that he thought should be allowed.

What of the following expenditures should Paul have deducted?
(a) Driver's license
(b) Sales tax on new car purchased in state
(c) Compensating use tax imposed by state Y on car to make up dif-

Other
Deductions
Allowed
Whether
Business or
Personal

ference in uniform rates between states

(d) Personal property tax on car imposed by state Y, based on the value of the car

(e) Real estate transfer tax imposed by state Y on new home purchase

(f) Sales tax on gambling equipment purchased

(g) State income tax

(h) Federal cigarette and alcohol taxes

(i) State tax on alcoholic beverages (the state has no general sales tax)

(j) Federal gasoline tax

(k) State gasoline tax

(l) Sales tax charged tailor for material for custom-made suit. The tax was not separately stated

(m) Federal income tax

(n) State inheritance tax on legacy left by executed friend

11. Recently a police officer who was the father of a family of eight children was killed in the line of duty. The public, through news reports, learned that the family of the police officer was left in financial difficulties. A number of individuals sent contributions directly to the family of the policeman, to help them through financial hardships. Other individuals merely made unrestricted contributions to the Policemen's Benevolent Fund, a nonprofit organization operated by the police department for the benefit of the families of policemen who are killed or seriously wounded in the line of duty. The fund is supported solely by contributions from the public. Some of the funds contributed to the fund were used to provide a cash award to the widow of the deceased officer. How do the donors treat the contributions on their income tax returns?

12. Mr. Bill Spears made the following charitable donations during 1972:

(a) An organ from his home which cost $800 in 1960 and had a current value of $500 was contributed to a church.

(b) $100 in cash was given to an organization created in England and operated exclusively for medical research.

(c) A parcel of land worth $6,000 was given to the city of Philadelphia, to be used as a public park. (Mr. Spear's adjusted basis was $1,000.)

(d) $400 in cash was given to a Philadelphia political committee.

Ignoring maximum limitations, how much may Bill deduct as charitable contributions?

13. Which of the following is correct?

(a) An individual's deduction for charitable contributions is limited basically to 20 percent of adjusted gross income, but the limit becomes 50 percent to the extent that the excess contributions are paid to or for the use of churches, educational organizations, hospitals, or private foundations.

(b) An individual may carry over all unused contributions for five years.

(c) A corporation may carry over unused contributions until exhausted.

(d) A taxpayer contributed to a charitable organization depreciable business property that had been held and depreciated for five years. Subject to maximum limitations, the taxpayer may deduct the fair market value of the property at the time of the contribution.

14. During the taxable year, an individual had the following transactions:

(a) He contributed stock in the Widget Corporation held by him for

Other
Deductions
Allowed
Whether
Business or
Personal

ten years, adjusted basis $1,000 and fair market value $20,000, in satisfaction of the balance of $20,000 due on a pledge to a university that he had made a year earlier.

(b) He contributed to a hospital stock in Conservative Corporation held by him for five months, adjusted basis $2,500 and fair market value $3,000.

(c) He gave away two oil paintings he had owned for several years— one to the Salvation Army and the other to the Art Museum. The first had an adjusted basis of $750 and a value of $1,000. The second had an adjusted basis of $1,000 and a value of $1,500.

(d) He gave another $3,000 in cash to a university with the stipulation that it be used to defray the cost of room, board, and tuition of a talented young man who had worked for him the preceding summer.

(e) He donated his own blood to a blood bank, and the value of his blood was $50.

(f) As an alumnus, member of the class of 1950, he organized a class reunion on campus and spent $200 of his own funds in setting it up and attending it.

(g) A store in a building that he owned became vacant, and on January 1 he leased it to the athletic department of the university for use as a ticket office, at a rent of $1.00 per pear. The true rental value was $2,400 per year.

What is the aggregate amount of the charitable contributions? Does he have any taxable income from any of these transactions?

15. Art Moline, a lumberjack, was severely injured in a logging operation. He carried no hospitalization insurance and was forced to bear all expenses resulting from the accident. Among his expenditures were the items below. Which are allowable in computing his medical expense deduction?

(a) Chartering plane to fly Mr. Moline to the nearest hospital.

(b) Hospital room charges (includes meals served during hospital stay).

(c) Drugs and X-ray treatments prescribed by doctor specifically for Mr. Moline's illness.

(d) Doctor bills.

(e) Eyeglasses to correct permanent eye damage caused by the accident.

(f) Power steering and power brakes ordered by Mr. Moline's doctor to reduce strain. The value of the car was increased by approximately half the cost of the items.

(g) Cost of trip to Florida where Mr. Moline decided to go to recuperate.

16. On January 1, 1972, Mr. Laird, age 66, purchased a one-year hospitalization insurance policy for $250. On June 15, 1972, Mr. Laird was injured in an accident and incurred $5,000 in medical expenditures of which the insurance policy paid $2,000. For the year ending 1972, Mr. Laird had adjusted gross income of $20,000. What amount may be deducted for medical expenditures?

17. Theodore Teft has an adjusted gross income of $15,000. On December 1, 1972, his wife became ill and Teft was forced to place his 3-year-old child in a special home, since his job prevented him from caring for the child while his wife was incapacitated.

On January 15, 1973, Teft's wife was transferred to a hospital where

393

Other
Deductions
Allowed
Whether
Business or
Personal

she spent four months recovering from her illness. During the entire period from December 1, 1972, the child remained in the home, until his mother returned from the hospital. The cost of maintaining the child was $130 in 1972 and $620 in 1973. What amount may Teft deduct for child care expenses in 1972 and 1973? (Assume Teft is on the calendar year for tax purposes.)

18. Dave Oconer occupies an apartment in a building owned by a cooperative housing corporation. Each tenant owns stock in the corporation proportionate to the value of his apartment, and all pay monthly amounts to the corporation for the purpose of meeting the expenses pertaining to the building. For the year just ended, the total paid by him was earmarked for the following items:

Real estate taxes	$1,200
Interest on mortgage	1,000
Salaries of maintenance employees	500
Auditor's fee	50
Decorating of common halls	100
Repairs to elevator	300
Storm damage to roof	150
	$3,300

How much is deductible by him?

19. *Cumulative Problem.* In 1972 an individual had the following items of income, expenses, and losses:

	EXPENDITURES OR LOSSES	RECEIPTS
(1) Salary		$45,000
(2) Alimony payments to first wife	$10,000	
(3) Separate payments for support of one child living with first wife, being more than 50 percent of total support	2,400	
(4) Annual payment of fare for private bus taken from home to depot, where train is taken into city	300	
(5) Dividends on stock held in joint names of taxpayer and his second wife		1,000
(6) Interest on State of Georgia general obligation bonds		1,200
(7) Net rental income on a residence formerly occupied as such by the taxpayer until December 31, 1969:		

Gross rent		$ 3,600
Less —		
Real estate taxes	$ 1,200	
Decorating	300	
		$ 1,500

Other
Deductions
Allowed
Whether
Business or
Personal

	EXPENDI-TURES OR LOSSES	RECEIPTS
Net rental income		$ 2,100

The house was purchased new, had an adjusted basis of $35,000 (excluding land), a fair market value of $50,000 (excluding land), and an estimated remaining life of 25 years on January 1, 1970.

(8) Removal of large ornamental tree in front of home destroyed by lightning — value of land and house:

		EXPENDI-TURES OR LOSSES	RECEIPTS
Before casualty	$52,000		
After casualty	51,000		
Difference		$1,000	
Cost of removing tree	600		
Cost of new, smaller trees	200	800	

(9) Charitable contributions:

	EXPENDI-TURES OR LOSSES	RECEIPTS
Cash to Community Fund	50	
Inherited painting to church for resale by it (adjusted basis $200) — value	600	

(10) Taxes paid —

	EXPENDI-TURES OR LOSSES	RECEIPTS
State income tax	800	
Personal property tax	100	
Real estate taxes on present home	2,000	
Social security taxes on part-time domestic help	50	
Automobile license fees	40	
State sales taxes	400	

(11) Interest on mortgage on present home — 1,000

(12) Payment to nursing home for the balance of amount due for board, room, and care for aged mother in excess of $1,000 per year (her only income) received by her as Social Security benefits and assigned by her to the nursing home — 2,600

(13) Medical expenses for mother — 800

(14) Medical and hospital bills paid account second wife's illness (claim for reimbursement of $2,400 filed with insurance company but not received until January, 1973) — 3,000

(15) Medical insurance premiums — 240

(16) Payment made to airline company for charges made by a thief who stole taxpayer's wallet containing an airline credit card — 700

There are no children of the second marriage; his second wife has no income or deductions other than as indicated; and both are under 65.

Prepare a schedule showing the computation of gross income, adjusted gross income, deductions, exemptions, and taxable income. Also compute the amount of income tax liability for the year.

Other Deductions Allowed Whether Business or Personal

SALES AND OTHER DISPOSITIONS OF PROPERTY

INTRODUCTION . . . 399
DETERMINATION OF GAIN OR LOSS . . . 400
AMOUNT REALIZED . . . 400

Mortgages of Seller . . . 401
Deferred Payments and Notes . . . 401

CASH METHOD TAXPAYERS . . . 401

CONTRACTUAL RIGHTS TO RECEIVE MONEY . . . 401
NEGOTIABLE NOTES . . . 402
NONNEGOTIABLE NOTES . . . 402

ACCRUAL METHOD TAXPAYERS . . . 403
INCOME FROM COLLECTION . . . 404

Imputed Interest in Certain Deferred Payments . . . 405

BASIS AND ADJUSTMENTS TO BASIS . . . 408

Cost . . . 409

MORTGAGES . . . 409
ALLOCATED REAL ESTATE TAXES . . . 410
COST OF SHARES OF STOCK SOLD . . . 410

Inventory Items . . . 410
Property Acquired from a Decedent . . . 410

PROPERTY AFFECTED . . . 411
PROPERTY RECEIVED AS A GIFT IN CONTEMPLATION OF DEATH . . . 412
JOINT OWNERSHIP OF PROPERTY . . . 412
INCOME IN RESPECT OF A DECEDENT . . . 413

Property Acquired by Gift . . . 414
Life Estates and Remainders . . . 415
Property Acquired Before March 1, 1913 . . . 416
Substituted Basis . . . 417

NONTAXABLE EXCHANGES . . . 417

Exchange of Property Held for Productive Use or Investment . . . 418

EFFECT OF BOOT . . . 419
EFFECT OF LIABILITIES . . . 420
PARTIAL BUSINESS USE . . . 421
BASIS OF PROPERTY RECEIVED IN NONTAXABLE EXCHANGES . . . 421
REQUIREMENT THAT AN EXCHANGE TAKE PLACE . . . 422

Certain Exchanges of Insurance Policies . . . 423
Stock for Stock of Same Corporation . . . 424
Exchange of Stock for Property . . . 424
Involuntary Conversions . . . 425

TRANSACTIONS CONSTITUTING INVOLUNTARY CONVERSIONS . . . 425
RECOGNITION OF GAIN OR LOSS . . . 428
PERIOD FOR REPLACEMENT . . . 428
REPLACEMENT BY SIMILAR PROPERTY . . . 428
METHODS OF REPLACEMENT . . . 430
REPORTING ON INVOLUNTARY CONVERSION . . . 431
BASIS OF REPLACEMENT PROPERTY . . . 431

Sale of Residence . . . 432

REPLACEMENT PERIOD . . . 433
EXCHANGES TREATED AS SALES AND PURCHASES . . . 434
SPECIAL RULE FOR HUSBAND AND WIFE . . . 434
INVOLUNTARY CONVERSION OF RESIDENCES . . . 434
INFORMATION TO BE REPORTED ON RETURN . . . 434
SALE OR EXCHANGE OF RESIDENCE BY PERSON AGED
   SIXTY-FIVE OR OVER . . . 435

Certain Sales of Low-income Housing Projects . . . 436
Certain Repossessions of Real Property . . . 436

WHEN GAIN OR LOSS IS REPORTED . . . 438

When Sale Occurs . . . 438

REAL PROPERTY . . . 438
CASUAL SALES OF PERSONAL PROPERTY . . . 439

When Gain or Loss Is Realized . . . 439

    CASUAL SALES OF PROPERTY . . . 439
    SALES OF GOODS . . . 441
    ESCROWS . . . 441

Stock Exchange Transactions . . . 442

    PUTS AND CALLS . . . 442

INTRODUCTION

Gain from the sale or other disposition of property is includible in gross income as defined in Section 61. Loss from any such sale or other disposition is made deductible by Section 165. Individuals, however, must limit loss deductions to losses incurred in a trade or business, in transactions entered into for profit, or arising from casualty or theft. Gain from the sale of personal assets such as paintings or jewelry is taxable, but a loss is not deductible. The rules for determining the amount of any gain or loss are in Section 1001. Regulation 1.61–6(a) provides:

11.2

§ 1.61–6. Gains derived from dealings in property.—(a) *In general.* Gain realized on the sale or exchange of property is included in gross income, unless excluded by law. For this purpose property includes tangible items, such as a building, and intangible items, such as goodwill. Generally, the gain is the excess of the amount realized over the unrecovered cost or other basis for the property sold or exchanged. The specific rules for computing the amount of gain or loss are contained in section 1001 and the regulations thereunder. When a part of a larger property is sold, the cost or other basis of the entire property shall be equitably apportioned among the several parts, and the gain realized or loss sustained on the part of the entire property sold is the difference between the selling price and the cost or other basis allocated to such part. The sale of each part is treated as a separate transaction and gain or loss shall be computed separately on each part. Thus, gain or loss shall be determined at the time of sale of each part and not deferred until the entire property has been disposed of. This rule may be illustrated by the following examples:

A, a dealer in real estate, acquires a ten-acre tract for $10,000, which he divides into twenty lots. The $10,000 cost must be equitably apportioned among the lots so that on the sale of each A can determine his taxable gain or deductible loss.

B purchases for $25,000 property consisting of a used car lot and adjoining filling station. At the time, the fair market value of the filling station is $15,000 and the fair market value of the used car lot is $10,000. Five years later B sells the filling station for $20,000 at a time when $2,000 has been properly allowed as depreciation thereon. B's gain on this sale is $7,000, since $7,000 is the amount by which the selling price of the filling station exceeds the portion of the cost equitably allocable to the filling station at the time of purchase reduced by the depreciation properly allowed.

The tax consequences flowing from sales and other dispositions of property involve four determinations: first, the amount of the gain or loss; second, the portion of such amount that is recognized for tax purposes; third, the reporting time of the gain or loss; and fourth, the applicability of the special treatment of capital gains and losses. The first three topics are discussed in this chapter, and capital gains and losses in chapter 12.

DETERMINATION OF GAIN OR LOSS

11.4   Under Section 1001(a), gain from the sale or other disposition of property is equal to the excess of the amount realized over the adjusted basis of the property for determining gain. Loss from the sale or other disposition of property is equal to the excess of the adjusted basis for determining loss over the amount realized. Ordinarily, the adjusted basis for determining gain is the same as the adjusted basis for determining loss; however, in a few instances such amounts are different.

AMOUNT REALIZED

11.5   The first step in determining gain or loss from the sale or other disposition of property is to determine the amount realized. Under Section 1001(b), the amount realized is equal to any money plus the fair market value of any property other than money received from the sale or other disposition. In casual sales of property by one other than a dealer, the amount realized must also be reduced by selling expenses such as commissions, advertising expenditures, legal fees, and other expenses directly related and attributable to the disposition of the property.

11.6   The fair market value of property received is often not easy to determine. Fair market value has been defined as "the price at which property would change hands in a transaction between a willing buyer and a willing seller, neither being under compulsion to buy or sell, and both being reasonably informed as to all relevant facts."[1] Although this definition sounds simple enough, its application is seldom simple. The determination of fair market value requires consideration of all the facts and circumstances surrounding each particular transaction; for example: prices at which similar properties are currently being bought and sold; recent bona fide offers to buy or sell the same or similar property; the replacement cost of the property; the property's original cost, its age, condition, state of repair and obsolescence; availability of substitute property; the earning power of the property. Qualified appraisers are often needed to evaluate many of these factors.

11.7   Sometimes the value of property received is impossible to determine, but the value of the property given up is readily ascertainable. In such an instance, where transactions are made at arm's length, the value of the property received is presumed to be equal to the value of the property surrendered.[2] Refer back to paragraph 5.111 pertaining to property settlements during divorce proceedings.

1. O'Malley v. Ames, 197 F.2d 256 (8th Cir. 1952), 52–1 USTC ¶9361, 42 AFTR 19.
2. U.S. v. Davis, 370 U.S. 65 (1962), 62–2 USTC ¶9509, 9 AFTR2d 1625.

Many times the values finally used for tax purposes are the result 11.8
of negotiations and compromise between taxpayers and the Internal
Revenue Service. In spite of the difficulties of determining fair market
values, it has been held that only in rare and unusual circumstances
will property be considered not subject to valuation.[3] However, in
the case of deferred payment obligations, fairly often the obligation
does not have a present market value.

Mortgages of Seller

If property is sold subject to an outstanding mortgage, or if the 11.9
buyer assumes such a mortgage on the property, the amount of the
mortgage is treated as part of the amount realized by the seller
whether or not the seller was personally liable on the mortgage.[4]

Deferred Payments and Notes

Both cash and accrual basis taxpayers who sell property for obliga- 11.10
tions of the purchaser instead of, or in addition to, cash may elect
the installment method of reporting income if the sale qualifies
under Section 453(b). The installment method is discussed starting at
paragraph 16.5. Here we are concerned only with sales that do not
qualify for, or for which the taxpayer has elected not to use, that
method. Such sales are called deferred payment sales not on the
installment plan.

Cash Method Taxpayers. The deferred payments may be evidenced 11.11
by a promise in a contract, negotiable promissory notes, or nonnegotiable promissory notes. In order for a cash basis taxpayer to have
a taxable event at the time of receipt of any such instrument, the latter
must have a fair market value and the instrument must have been
accepted as payment of the obligation and not as mere evidence
of it.[5]

CONTRACTUAL RIGHTS TO RECEIVE MONEY. A contractual prom- 11.12
ise to pay money in the future ordinarily has no market value when received, and no income is realized from the contract until payments
are received.[6] This is so no matter what may be the financial strength
of the promissor. As Judge Learned Hand said in *Bedell* v. *Com.:*[7]

3. Reg. 1.1001–1(a); Rev. Rul. 58–402, 1958–2 C.B. 15; Boudreau v. Com., 134 F.2d
360 (5th Cir. 1943) 43–1 USTC ¶9327, 30 AFTR 1132.
4. Crane v. Com., 331 U.S. 1 (1941), 47–1 USTC ¶9217, 35 AFTR 776.
5. Dudley T. Humphrey, 32 BTA 280 (1935) as to nonnegotiable notes; Robert J.
Dial, 24 T.C. 117 (1955) (Acq.) as to negotiable notes.
6. Curtis B. Andrews, 23 T.C. 1026 (1955); Alfred M. Bedell v. Com., 30 F.2d
622 (2nd Cir. 1929), 1 USTC ¶359, 7 AFTR 8469; Nina J. Ennis, 17 T.C. 465 (1951).
Alice G. K. Kleberg, 43 BTA 277 (1941).
7. *Ibid.*

It is absurd to speak of a promise to pay a sum in the future [under the terms of a contract with no separate notes] as having a "market value," fair or unfair. Such rights are sold, if at all, only by seeking out a purchaser and higgling with him on the basis of the particular transaction.

11.13   However, if a particular type of contract is freely assignable and is "bankable," it may have a taxable value when received. This was the case in *Frank Cowden, Sr. v. Com.*[8] There the taxpayer granted an oil-and-gas lease to Stanolind Oil and Gas Company and, separate from the instrument of lease, received a contract by which Stanolind unconditionally obligated itself to pay a lease bonus of $500,969 in two equal installments, one-half nine months later and the balance in the following year. Upon receipt of the separate contract, the taxpayer assigned it to a bank and received the face amount less a nominal discount.

11.14   Testimony was offered that the banks in the locality quite frequently purchased paper of this type. The Fifth Circuit Court of Appeals remanded the case to the Tax Court to decide whether under the facts the paper had a market value when received. The Tax Court then held that it did.

11.15   NEGOTIABLE NOTES. For notes to have a fair market value upon receipt, in addition to the requirement that they be received in payment, and not as evidence, of an obligation; they must also be *negotiable* or *freely transferable,* have been made by a *responsible and solvent* individual or entity, not be subject to setoffs or contingencies, and be of a kind that is frequently sold to lenders or investors.[9]

11.16   If a negotiable note states a fair rate of interest and is adequately secured, its fair market value is probably the face amount. On the other hand, if the interest rate is less than the going rate, the note has a value less than the face amount, whether or not the note is secured. This could also be true in the case of unsecured notes subordinated to the claim of general creditors, even though the interest rate is the prevailing one.

11.17   NONNEGOTIABLE NOTES. The form of a note determines whether it is negotiable or not.[10] The status of negotiability gives "holders in due course" of commercial paper a preferred standing by protecting them from certain defenses, particularly any claims by the payor against the bearer or payee named in the note.[11] The primary requirements to make a note a negotiable one are that it be in writing and be made payable to "bearer" or "to the order of" a

8. 289 F.2d 20 (5th Cir. 1961), 61–1 USTC ¶9382, 7 AFTR2d 1160, reversing and remanding 20 T.C.M. 1134; on remand ¶61,229 Memo T.C.; also Rev. Rul. 68–606, 1968–2 C.B. 42.

9. Frank Cowden, Sr. v. Com., *ibid.*

10. Anderson and Kumpf, *Business Law—Uniform Commercial Code,* 7th ed., Comprehensive vol., p. 272.

11. *Ibid.*, p. 326.

named person. If these magic words are not used, the note is non-negotiable. However, like any piece of property it is assignable, unless the instrument prohibits such assignment or restricts it, such as by requiring first the permission of the payor.

11.18 For the receipt of a nonnegotiable note to give rise to a taxable event, a closed transaction, the note must be the "equivalent of cash." In addition, again, it must have been received in payment of an obligation and not as mere evidence of an obligation to make payments in the future.

11.19 A number of cases blithely make the statement that the courts have repeatedly held that a nonnegotiable note does not have a market value when received.[12] However, when the authors read those cases it was found that the statement was dictum and that the true holding of the particular court was that the note was not accepted in payment of an obligation but only as evidence of it. This much is certain: a nonnegotiable note that is subject to agreements and conditions does not have a market value.[13] But, if a nonnegotiable note is freely assignable and is frequently bought by banks, it does have a market value.[14]

Accrual Method Taxpayers. On sales of property by accrual basis 11.20 taxpayers, the rules may be different depending upon whether the property is real or personal.

11.21 Regulation 1.453–6(a)(1) pertains to deferred payment sales of real property not under the installment method. It provides that "the obligations of the purchaser received by the vendor are to be considered as an amount realized to the extent of their fair market value in ascertaining the profit or loss from the transaction." Seemingly, this means that all of the principles discussed in the preceding paragraphs also apply to accrual basis taxpayers where the sale is of real property, because the regulation does not restrict its application to cash method taxpayers. However, in 1963 the Tax Court held in *First Savings & Loan Association*[15] that this accrual basis seller of homes had to recognize the full face value of notes received from the individual purchasers. Its holding was based on two grounds: (1) in applying Section 1001(b) an accrual basis taxpayer does not treat an unconditional right to receive money as property received, but rather as money received to the full extent of the face value of the right, and (2) in any event the taxpayer did not prove that the notes received had a fair market value less than their face amounts.

11.22 The principle pertaining to sales of personal property seems settled. An unconditional promise to pay a sum certain must be in-

---

12. See, for example, Nina J. Ennis, *supra* fn. 6, and Sam F. McIntosh, ¶67,230 P-H Memo T.C. (1967).

13. E. J. Hudson, 11 T.C. 1042 (Acq.), affirmed on other issues in 183 F.2d 180 (5th Cir. 1950), 50–2 USTC ¶9371, 39 AFTR 646.

14. Frank Cowden, Sr. v. Com., *supra* fn. 8.

15. 40 T.C. 474 (1963).

cluded in gross proceeds in its face amount whether embodied in a contract, negotiable note, or nonnegotiable note.[16]

11.23 **Income from Collection.** Where an obligation is worth its face value, everything is reported at the time of sale and subsequent collections are merely a recovery of capital except to the extent that imputed interest may be present under Section 483 (see paragraph 11.27 et seq.).

11.24 Where the obligation has a zero value, the taxpayer reports no part of such obligation as income at the time of sale. His basis in the property sold, reduced by any cash or other property having a fair market value that he receives on the sale, becomes his basis in the obligation without fair market value. If at the time of sale the cash and other property having a fair market value exceed the adjusted basis of the property surrendered, there is gain to that extent, and the basis of the obligation is zero. Each subsequent collection on the obligation is all income. However, if there is no gain, the taxpayer is entitled to first completely recover his basis in the obligation out of initial payments received on it. Only thereafter are payments with respect to it taxable. This treatment, known as the "return-of-capital rule," originated with the United States Supreme Court's decision in *Burnet v. Logan.*[17]

11.25 If a note has a fair market value but one that is less than the principal amount, such lesser value and not the principal amount represents proceeds realized at the time of sale and also becomes the unadjusted basis of the note in the hands of the holder. A closed transaction occurs at the moment of sale giving rise to gain or loss. A portion of each payment thereafter received on the note will constitute a nontaxable return of capital in the ratio of the fair market value of the note to its principal amount, and the balance of each payment will be taxable income.

EXAMPLE An individual investor sold his stock in a corporation to another individual. His adjusted basis was $90,000 and he received in exchange $50,000 in cash and the purchaser's unsecured negotiable promissory note for $100,000 payable in ten equal annual installments with interest at 5 percent per annum on the unpaid balances of principal outstanding from time to time. On the date of issuance of the note the prevailing interest rate was 8 percent; accordingly the value of the unsecured 5 percent note was only $80,000. In the year of sale the seller reported a capital gain of $40,000

$$[(\$50,000 + \$80,000 = \$130,000) - \$90,000]$$

so that $80,000 became his unadjusted basis for the $100,000 note.

At the end of the first year the purchaser pays $10,000 in principal and $5,000 in interest. Of the $10,000 principal payment, $8,000 is a return of capital and $2,000 is ordinary income. The $5,000 for interest is also ordinary

16. George L. Castner Co., Inc., 30 T.C. 1061 (1958); Jones Lumber Co., Inc. v. Com., 404 F.2d 764 (6th Cir. 1968), 22 AFTR2d 5927.
17. 283 U.S. 404 (1931), 9 AFTR 1453.

income. At this point the seller's adjusted basis of the note is $72,000 ($80,000 − $8,000).

If the purchaser (perhaps due to overextending himself in acquiring control of corporations) then becomes bankrupt and his trustee in bankruptcy pays $9,000 in full satisfaction of the remaining $90,000 due on the note, the seller has a nonbusiness bad debt of $63,000 ($72,000 − $9,000). As discussed in paragraph 9.78, such nonbusiness bad debt is deductible only as a short-term capital loss.

As mentioned previously, when an obligation with no fair market value is received upon a sale, the tax consequences of the transaction remain open. This means that if the property sold was a capital asset, the collections on the obligation are capital gain [18] (unless there is imputed interest under Section 483 as discussed starting in paragraph 11.27); otherwise they are ordinary income. However, when the obligation has a fair market value, even though less than the face amount, the transaction is closed. Despite the fact that the property sold may have been a capital asset, the income portion of each payment received is ordinary income [19] unless the issuer of the obligation was a corporation and the other provisions of Section 1232 apply (see paragraph 12.92).

Imputed Interest in Certain Deferred Payments

If a capital or Section 1231 asset is sold under a deferred payment plan, the amount of interest stated to be payable on the deferred payments is ordinary income, and only the balance is accorded capital gain treatment. In 1963 the Treasury Department made representations to Congress that many taxpayers when selling capital assets under an installment plan were not mentioning interest in the contract or notes, but instead were incorporating the computed amount thereof in the amounts of the installment payments. The result was that under the law as it then existed, the seller obtained capital gain treatment of that portion of the price that was in substance interest. As a consequence, Section 483 was added to the Code by Section 224 of the Revenue Act of 1964. The opening paragraph of the House Ways and Means Committee Report pertaining to its technical explanation of this section of the bill contains the sentence: "In general, in the case of a contract for the sale or exchange of property which provides for little or no interest on deferred payments under the contract, the new section treats a portion of such payments as interest."

Under Section 483 and the regulations pertaining thereto, interest at the rate of 5 percent per annum will be imputed to exist in any installment payment if:

11.26

11.27

11.28

18. Westover v. Smith, 173 F.2d 90 (9th Cir. 1949), 49–1 USTC ¶9189, 37 AFTR 1001; Susan J. Carter, 9 T.C. 364 (1947), affirmed 170 F.2d 911 (2nd Cir. 1948), 48–2 USTC ¶9415, 37 AFTR 573.
19. Pat O'Brien, 25 T.C. 376 (1955).

1. The sales price of the property is more than $3,000.
2. At least one payment is due more than one year after the date of the sale or exchange.
3. The particular installment payment is due more than six months after the date of the sale or exchange.
4. The contract provides for interest of less than 4 percent per annum on each installment due more than six months after the date of the sale or exchange.

Only that part of the deferred payments not so treated as interest is considered in determining the amount realized from the sale of the property. The portion of the deferred payments that is treated as interest but is not stated in the contract as interest is called "unstated interest."

11.29   To ascertain the existence and amount of unstated interest, two determinations are necessary. The first ascertains only whether or not unstated interest exists. If the contract calls for interest to be payable with the deferred payments in an amount at least equal to 4 percent simple interest, no unstated interest is deemed to be included in the deferred payments.[20] If the interest called for by the contract does not meet this 4 percent test, a calculation is made using tables provided by the regulations.[21] The present value of all deferred payments, including interest, is computed under such tables based on a 4 percent discount rate. This present value is compared to the total amount of the deferred payments exclusive of interest. If the deferred payments exclusive of interest exceed the present value of all deferred payments including interest, unstated interest is deemed to exist, and the second determination is called for.

11.30   The second determination calculates the portion of each deferred payment that must be treated as interest. This determination requires a present-value calculation similar to the one described above, except that the table provided in the regulations for this calculation is based on a discount rate of 5 percent instead of 4 percent. The total amount of unstated interest required to be treated as interest income by the seller of the property is the excess of the total deferred payments, exclusive of interest, over the present value of such payments, including interest, as determined by this second calculation.

11.31   The amount of this unstated interest is allocated ratably to all payments due more than six months after the sale, to determine the portion of each that is treated as interest.

11.32   In both the 4 percent and 5 percent calculations described above, the present value of any payment due within six months of the date of sale is considered to be equal to the amount of such payment.

11.33   The effect of these rules is that if property is sold for deferred payments bearing simple interest of at least 4 percent, no additional interest is imputed to the deferred payments. On the other hand, if the interest stated in the contract is less than 4 percent, interest is

20. Reg. 1.483–1(d)(2).
21. Reg. 1.483–1(g).

imputed in an amount sufficient to bring the total interest up to 5 percent per annum.

If the liability for any particular payment, its amount, or its due date is not determinable at the time of sale, the unstated interest, if any, included in such payment is determined with respect to that payment alone at the time it actually is received.[22]

The foregoing rules are illustrated in these examples taken for the most part from the regulations:

11.35

On December 31 A sells a capital asset having an adjusted basis of $4,000 for the sum of $7,000 payable $500 immediately, $500 within sixty days, and $2,000 at the end of each year for the next three years. No interest is provided for in the contract. There is no interest element in the first two $500 payments because they are within six months of the sale. The interest element in the remaining $6,000 of payments is computed as follows:

EXAMPLES
FROM REG.

Ex. 1

Sum of payments to which Section 483 applies	$6,000.00
Less present value of $2,000 due every 12 months for 3 years discounted at 5% per annum compounded semiannually: $2,000 $\times$ 2.72006 [factor for 3 years, column (b), Table III, Reg. 1.483-1 (g)]	5,440.12
Total unstated interest	$ 559.88

The seller's capital gain is $2,440.12 ($7,000 − $559.88 − $4,000) reportable in the year of sale or on the installment basis. On the cash basis he has interest income of $186.63 ($559.88 ÷ 3) as each $2,000 installment is received. The buyer's unadjusted basis is $6,440.12 ($7,000 − $559.88) and on the cash basis he deducts $186.63 interest as each installment is paid.

On December 31, A sells property to B under a contract providing that B make payments of $2,040 ($2,000 sales price plus $40 interest), $2,080 ($2,000 sales price plus $80 interest), and $2,120 ($2,000 sales price plus $120 interest), such payments being due, respectively, one, two, and three years from the date of sale. The determination of whether there is total unstated interest under the contract is made in the following manner:

Ex. 2

(i) Sum of payments to which Section 483 applies:		$6,000.00
(ii) Sum of:		
Present value of $2,040 due 1 year from date of sale: $2,040 $\times$ .96154 [factor for 9 to 15 mos., col. (a), Table 1]	$1,961,54	
Present value of $2,080 due 2 years from date of sale: $2,080 $\times$ .92593 [factor for 21 to 27 mos., col. (a), Table 1]	1,925.93	
Present value of $2,120 due 3 years from date of sale: $2,120 $\times$ .89286 [factor for 33 to 39 mos., col. (a), Table 1]	1,892.86	$5,780.33

Table I appears in Reg. 1.483–1(g) and the factors used in column (a) thereof are based upon 4 percent per annum simple interest. In the foregoing

22. Code Sec. 483(d).

computation the sum of the payments to which Section 483 applies ($6,000) exceeds the sum of the present values of such payments and the present values of the stated interest payments ($5,780.33). Accordingly, there is total unstated interest under the contract.

The computation of the amount of such total unstated interest based on 5 percent per annum compounded semiannually is as follows:

Sum of payments to which Section 483 applies		$6,000.00
Less:		
Present value of $2,040 due 1 year from date of sale: $2,040 × .95181 [factor for 9 to 15 mos., col. (b), Table 1]	$1,941.69	
Present value of $2,080 due 2 years from date of sale: $2,080 × .90595 [factor for 21 to 27 mos., col. (b), Table 1]	1,884.38	
Present value of $2,120 due 3 years from date of sale: $2,120 × .86230 [factor for 33 to 39 mos., col. (b), Table 1]	1,828.08	5,654.15
Total unstated interest		$ 345.85

11.36   These rules concerning interest on certain deferred payments apply both to the seller and the buyer of property. However, the rules do not apply at all to the extent set forth in the following circumstances described in Section 483(f):

1. If the amounts payable under the contract are treated under Code Sec. 163(b), relating to carrying charges, as if they included interest, no unstated interest will be imputed to, and deductible by, the purchaser of the property, but will be imputed to the seller.
2. If the property sold is neither a capital asset nor real property or depreciable property held for more than six months and used in a trade or business (which under Section 1231 can qualify for capital gain treatment), no unstated interest will be imputed to the seller; however, the purchaser will treat such unstated interest as a deduction and not as part of his cost of the property.
3. Unstated interest will not be imputed to either the buyer or seller in connection with any transfer of patents described in Code Sec. 1235(a).
4. The rule of imputed interest will not apply to amounts received or paid as annuities to which Code Sec. 72 applies.

BASIS AND ADJUSTMENTS TO BASIS

11.37   The second step in determining gain or loss on disposition of property is to determine the adjusted basis of the property. Basis is the amount treated for tax purposes as a taxpayer's capital investment in property. It is not necessarily the same as his investment in the financial sense; consequently, his gain or loss on disposition of property for tax purposes is not always the same as his gain or loss in the financial or accounting sense.

During the period property is held by a taxpayer, its basis is in- **11.38** creased to reflect additional capital investments. It is reduced for depreciation, amortization, depletion, and other recoveries of capital by the taxpayer. The resulting amount is called the adjusted basis. The amount of the basis before making these adjustments is called the unadjusted basis.

As just stated, in determining adjusted basis a taxpayer ordinarily **11.39** is required to reduce basis by the amount of depreciation, depletion, or amortization properly allowable in calculating taxable net income but not less than the amount actually allowed. This is known as the "allowed-or-allowable rule." It prevents a taxpayer from maintaining a high adjusted basis in property by failing to claim an adequate provision for depreciation, depletion, or amortization in a year such taxpayer might be subject to an unusually low rate of tax. However, for years after 1951, basis is not reduced by the excess of amounts actually allowed over that properly allowable if such excess did not result in a reduction of tax (Section 1016). (Also see paragraph 8.13.)

The most common rule is that the unadjusted basis of property is its **11.40** original cost to the taxpayer. The code provides a number of exceptions to this rule, notably in the case of property acquired from a decedent, property acquired by gift, and property acquired in nontaxable exchanges for other property.

Cost

Unless otherwise provided by the code, the basis of property is its **11.41** cost. Cost is defined in Reg. 1.1012–1 as "the amount paid for such property in cash or other property." If property is acquired in a taxable exchange for other property, the cost of the property acquired is the amount of its fair market value and not the fair market value of the property given up. However, if the value of the property received cannot be determined with reasonable accuracy and if the exchange of properties constituted an arm's-length transaction, then the value of the property surrendered can be used as the value and, therefore, the cost of the property acquired.[23] In the rare and unusual circumstance that the value of neither can be ascertained, the depreciated cost of the property surrendered can be used as the cost of the property acquired.[24]

Mortgages. When property is acquired that has a mortgage on it, the **11.42** amount of that mortgage is included in the cost of the property, whether or not it is assumed by the taxpayer.[25] Also, when property

23. U.S. v. Davis, *supra* fn. 2; Philadelphia Park Amusement Co. v. U.S., *infra* fn. 24.

24. Helvering v. Tex-Penn Oil Co., 300 U.S. 481, 499, 37–1 USTC ¶9194, 18 AFTR 1174; Gould Securities Co. v. U.S., 96 F.2d 780, 38–1 USTC ¶9301, 21 AFTR 266; both cases are cited in support of the statement in the text in Philadelphia Park Amusement Co. v. U.S., 126 F. Supp. 184 (Ct. Cl. 1954), 46 AFTR 1293.

25. Crane v. Com., *supra* fn. 4.

is acquired on credit, cost includes the amount of the taxpayer's obligations. This is true whether the taxpayer uses the cash or accrual method of accounting. However, in the case of deferred payments, the portion of such deferred payments treated as interest under Section 483 is not included in cost of the property.

11.43   **Allocated Real Estate Taxes.** The cost of real property includes any real estate taxes paid by the buyer or reimbursed by the buyer to the seller which under Section 164(d) are treated as imposed upon the seller. Cost does not include any real estate taxes paid by the buyer or reimbursed to the seller by the buyer that under Section 164(d) are treated as imposed upon the buyer [Reg. 1.1012–1(b)].

11.44   **Cost of Shares of Stock Sold.** When shares of stock in a corporation are sold out of lots acquired at different times or at different prices, particularly when all of such shares are represented by one certificate, the shares sold will be deemed to come out of the earliest acquisitions unless the shares sold and their cost can be specifically identified. Specific identification can be made by maintaining records of costs by certificate numbers. When securities are held in the custody of a broker or other agent, the taxpayer may specifically identify the securities sold by notifying the broker or agent which shares are to be transferred and having him confirm the instructions in writing to the taxpayer within a reasonable period of time. If this procedure is followed, the shares sold will be considered to be the shares specified in such instructions regardless of which certificates are actually delivered [Reg. 1.1012–1(c)].

Inventory Items

11.45   The basis of property included in inventory of the taxpayer is the last inventory value of that property (Section 1013). (See chapter 15 concerning valuation of property in inventory.)

Property Acquired from a Decedent

11.46   Unless the Code specifically provides otherwise, the basis of property acquired from a decedent is the fair market value of that property at the date of decedent's death. If the executor or administrator of the decedent's estate elects to value the estate property for estate tax purposes at a date six months after the decedent's death or, if earlier, the date of disposition of the property, the property's basis will be its value at that alternate valuation date [Section 1014(a)]. If the estate is not subject to federal estate tax, as in the case of a small estate, the basis of property is its value at date of decedent's death. The optional valuation date cannot be used to determine basis in this event.[26]

26. Rev. Rul. 56–60, 1956–1 C.B. 443.

When inherited property is encumbered by debt, the basis of that property is its fair market value at date of decedent's death without reduction by the amount of the debt and whether or not such debt is assumed by the person taking the property from the decedent. 11.47

According to the regulations, the purpose of the rules governing basis of property acquired from a decedent is to establish a basis for such property equal to the value used for federal estate tax purposes. Accordingly, Reg. 1.1014–1(a) provides that the value used for federal estate tax purposes—or in the absence of a federal estate tax return, the value used for state inheritance tax purposes—will be deemed to be the fair market value of the property at date of decedent's death or the optional valuation date if appropriate. This presumption has been held to be rebuttable; therefore, if the taxpayer can establish that the fair market value of the property at the appropriate valuation date was actually greater than that used for estate tax purposes, the basis of the property will be such greater value.[27] 11.48

Property received from an estate in settlement of a cash legacy is not considered to have been acquired from a decedent. The basis of property so acquired is its value at the date received by the taxpayer rather than its value at the date of decedent's death. The settlement of a cash legacy by the transfer of property other than cash is a taxable transaction for the estate. Therefore, gain or loss on the transfer of the property is recognized to the estate, and the basis of such property in the hands of the transferee is its fair market value at the date transferred [Reg. 1.1014–4(a)(3)]. 11.49

Property Affected. "Property acquired from a decedent" includes all property acquired by bequest, devise, or inheritance, or by the decedent's estate from a decedent. Upon the death of an individual, his estate immediately comes into existence, even though the executor or administrator may not be appointed until sometime later. Under some state laws real property passes immediately upon death to the heirs or devisees. In other states it passes first to the estate and then from the estate to the heirs or devisees. In all states, personal property passes first to the estate and after debts are paid, from the estate to the heirs or legatees. Whether or not property first passes to an estate and then from it to the heirs, devisees, and legatees, it is "property acquired from a decedent." Further, of course, in the hands of the estate, the property is "property acquired from a decedent." Property purchased by the estate is not "property acquired from a decedent," and the adjusted basis of the estate becomes the adjusted basis of any person to whom it may be distributed. For tax purposes, property acquired from a decedent also includes the following general types of property described in detail in Section 1014(b): 11.50

27. Rev. Rul. 54–97, 1951–1 C.B. 113; Estate of Devereux, ¶48,208 P–H Memo T.C. (1948).

1. The surviving spouse's own one-half share of community property, provided the decedent's share was at least one-half of the property and such share was includible in his estate for estate tax purposes.
2. Property transferred by a decedent during his lifetime to a trust in which he reserves the right to receive or to direct the disposition of the income and to revoke, alter, amend, or terminate the trust.
3. Property passing without full and adequate consideration under a general power of appointment exercised by the decedent's will. (For example, assume that a husband died some years ago. Under his will he set up a trust, and a portion of his estate was bequeathed to that trust. Under the trust provisions, income from the property is payable to his wife for her life; on her death the trust terminates, and the property passes to their children. In addition, in the provisions of the will creating the trust, she was given a general power of appointment exercisable in her will to appoint or bequeath the property to anyone she wishes rather than to all of their children. If she does so, then the basis of that property will be the fair market value as of the date of *her* death or the alternate valuation date.)
4. In the case of decedents dying after December 31, 1953, any property included in the gross estate of the decedent for estate tax purposes, except annuities and stock of a foreign corporation having a limited number of individuals as shareholders and which for United States tax purposes is specially treated as a foreign personal holding company, and except property described elsewhere in section 1014(b).

11.51 **Property Received as Gift in Contemplation of Death.** The value of property transferred by gift in contemplation of death is included in the decedent's estate for estate tax purposes. Such property is considered acquired from the decedent; thus, its basis to the taxpayer is fair market value on date of death or the alternate valuation date, reduced by the amount of any depreciation, depletion, or amortization allowed or allowable to the taxpayer before the decedent's death [Section 1014(b)(9)].

EXAMPLE   Taxpayer A received from his father as a gift on January 1, 1969, a piece of rental real estate. Under the rules concerning property received by gift, A's basis in this property was $12,000. During 1969 and 1970 A was allowed depreciation of $500 per year on certain improvements on the property. A's father died on January 1, 1971, and the property was included in his estate as a gift in contemplation of death. The value of the property on January 1, 1971, was $18,000. A's adjusted basis in the property at January 1, 1971, is $17,000 ($18,000 fair market value at decedent's death less $1,000 of depreciation allowed to A during his holding period prior to decedent's death).

If the property is sold by the taxpayer before the decedent's death, this rule does not apply, and the basis of the property is determined in the manner provided for gift property [Section 1014(a)]. (See paragraph 11.56 et seq.)

11.52 **Joint Ownership of Property.** If two persons own property together with the right of survivorship, they are called joint tenants. Under the laws of some states, if the owners are husband and wife, they are called tenants by the entirety. When one such owner dies, his interest passes to the survivor. For estate tax purposes, the total value of property held in joint tenancy or in tenancy by the entirety is included in the estate of the first tenant to die, unless it can be proved that the survivor contributed to the cost of acquiring the property. In that event, the portion of the property acquired by the survivor's contribution is not included in the estate of the decedent. That portion of the property which is included in the decedent's estate is considered to be property acquired from a decedent by the survivor. The survivor's basis of the portion included in the decedent's estate is its fair market value at date of the decedent's death or the alternate valuation date. The basis of that part of the property not included in the decedent's estate is the survivor's cost or other basis.

11.53   The survivor's total basis in the property is reduced by the amount of depreciation, depletion, and amortization allowed to him before the decedent's death. If the decedent and survivor filed joint income tax returns, the survivor's share of such allowances is determined by allocating the total allowances between the decedent and survivor, on the basis of income from the property allocable to each under local law. Regulation 1.1014–6(a)(3) illustrates this calculation with the following example:

EXAMPLE FROM REG.   On July 1, 1952, H purchased for $30,000 income-producing property which he conveyed to himself and W, his wife, as tenants by the entirety. Under local law each spouse was entitled to one-half of the income therefrom. H died on January 1, 1955, at which time the fair market value of the property was $40,000. The entire value of the property was included in H's gross estate. H and W filed joint income tax returns for the years 1952, 1953 and 1954. The total depreciation allowance for the year 1952 was $500 and for each of the other years 1953 and 1954 was $1,000. One-half of the $2,500 depreciation will be allocated to W. The adjusted basis of the property in W's hands as of January 1, 1955, was $38,750 ($40,000 value on the date of H's death, less $1,250, depreciation allocated to W for periods before H's death). However, if, under local law, all of the income from the property was allocable to H, no adjustment under this paragraph would be required and W's basis for the property as of the date of H's death would be $40,000.

Income in Respect of a Decedent. The basis of property representing rights to receive income in respect of a decedent is not determined by reference to fair market value at date of decedent's death [Section 1014(c)]. In effect, the basis of such rights is the same as their adjusted basis to the decedent—usually zero.   11.54

A taxpayer receiving income in respect of a decedent is required to include it in gross income to the same extent it would have been included in gross income by the decedent if received prior to his death. The character of the gross income is the same as it would have been to the decedent. Taxpayers required to report the income in this manner include the estate of the decedent and any other persons who acquire the right to receive the income by reason of the decedent's death. If the estate of the decedent transfers the right to receive such   11.55

income to an heir, devisee, or legatee, the income should be reported by such transferee when received regardless of the method of accounting used by the transferee [Reg. 1.691(a)–2]. The term "income in respect of a decedent" refers to an amount that a decedent was entitled to receive as gross income, but that, because of his method of accounting, was not includible in his gross income for any period prior to his death. Thus, the term includes income accrued at death of a decedent who used the cash receipts and disbursements method of accounting, income that accrued to a decedent solely by reason of his death where the decedent used the accrual method of accounting, and income to which the decedent had a contingent right at the time of his death. Such term also includes installment obligations held by a decedent on which he had elected to report income by the installment method [Reg. 1.691(a)–1].

Property Acquired by Gift

11.56   The basis of property acquired by gift depends upon the date of the gift and whether the basis is being used to determine gain or to determine loss on disposition of the property.

11.57   The basis of property received by gift before 1921 is the fair market value of the property at date of the gift [Section 1015(c) and Reg. 1.1015–3].

11.58   When property is acquired by gift after 1920, its basis for determining gain on disposition is equal to its adjusted basis in the hands of the donor or the last preceding owner by whom it was not acquired by gift. For purposes of determining loss on disposition of such property, its basis is the lesser of the adjusted basis in the hands of the donor or the last preceding owner by whom it was not acquired by gift or its fair market value at the time of the gift [Section 1015(a) and Reg. 1.1015–1(a)]. This rule may be illustrated by the following:

EXAMPLE   A is given income-producing property that, in the hands of the donor at the date of gift, has an adjusted basis of $20,000. The fair market value of the property at the date of gift is $15,000. Assume no gift tax is paid on this gift. If A should sell the property for $25,000, his basis for determining gain would be $20,000, the adjusted basis of the property in the hands of the donor at the date of gift. If A should sell the property for $10,000, his basis for determining loss would be $15,000, the fair market value of the property at the date of gift. If A should sell the property for $18,000, no gain or loss would be recognized to A because for purposes of determining gain the basis of the property would be $20,000, whereas for purposes of determining loss the basis would be $15,000.

11.59   The above rules do not apply to property acquired by gift if it is treated as a gift in contemplation of death by the donor and is held by the donee until after the death of the donor. Property so acquired and held is treated as property acquired from a decedent, and basis is determined by reference to fair market value of the property at date of death of the decedent.

When property is acquired by gift on or after September 2, 1958, the basis as determined by the above rules is increased by the amount of any gift tax paid on the gift. However, the basis may not be increased to an amount greater than the property's fair market value at the date of the gift [Section 1015(d)(1)]. If property is acquired by gift before September 2, 1958, and is not disposed of by the donee before that date, the basis is increased as of September 2, 1958, by the amount of any gift tax paid with respect to the gift. In this case, however, the increase cannot be more than the excess of fair market value at the date of the gift over the adjusted basis of the property in the hands of the donor at that date. When several taxable gifts are made in the same year, this increase in basis is determined for each by allocating the gift tax to all gift properties in proportion to their respective taxable-gift values. **11.60**

If property is purchased at less than fair market value under circumstances that make the acquisition in part a purchase and in part a gift, basis of the property is the sum of (1) the greater of the amount paid by the transferee for the property or the transferor's adjusted basis at the time of the transfer, and (2) the appropriate increase in the basis by reason of gift tax paid with respect to the gift. The effect of this rule can be illustrated by the following table in which it is assumed that (1) in 1970 a father sells property to a son for less than fair market value, (2) the transaction represents in part a sale and in part a gift, and (3) no gift tax is paid on the gift. **11.61**

			BASIS TO DONEE		EXAMPLE
			FOR DETERMINING		
SALES PRICE	FAIR MARKET VALUE	ADJUSTED BASIS TO DONOR	GAIN	LOSS	
$30,000	$60,000	$30,000	$30,000	$30,000	
60,000	90,000	30,000	60,000	60,000	
30,000	90,000	60,000	60,000	60,000	
30,000	60,000	90,000	90,000	60,000	

If any gift tax had been paid on the gift, the basis indicated above would be increased by the amount of such gift tax but not to an amount in excess of fair market value of the property.

Life Estates and Remainders

Where several taxpayers acquire interests in one property from a decedent or by gift, the basis of all taxpayers ordinarily is determined by reference to the uniform basis of the property. This basis is the value of the property at date of death of the decedent or the adjusted basis of the donor as further adjusted, where appropriate, for the gift tax paid. (See discussion beginning at paragraph 11.60.) **11.62**

Frequently, such multiple interests consist of a life estate, or an interest for a term of years, and a remainder interest. The owner of a life estate is called a life tenant, and the owner of the remainder interest is called a remainderman. The life tenant owns the property **11.63** and is entitled to its income during his life. He also is entitled to deduct the depreciation and depletion attributable to the property during his life. On his death, the property and its future income vests in the remainderman. The adjusted basis of a life estate, other term interest, or a remainder interest at any given date is determined by allocating the adjusted basis of the total property among the various interests by use of mortality tables found in Reg. 1.1014. This rule may be illustrated as follows:

EXAMPLE   Improved realty having a fair market value of $20,000 at death of a decedent on January 1, 1966, was devised to A for life with remainder over to B. On January 1, 1970 A and B both sell their interests to C for $22,500, of which A receives $12,500 and B receives $10,000. During each of the years 1966 to 1969, inclusive, A was allowed a deduction of $300 for depreciation. Thus, the adjusted uniform basis of the property is $18,800 ($20,000 minus $1,200 depreciation). At the time of the sale, A was thirty-nine years of age. Reg. 1.1014 provides that the basis of A is determined by applying a life factor of 0.63898 to the total basis of the property; thus A's portion of the uniform basis adjusted to the date of sale is $12,013 (0.63898 × $18,800). A's gain on the sale is $487 ($12,500 − $12,013). B's basis will be that portion of the uniform adjusted basis not applicable to A ($18,800 − $12,013 = $6,787); accordingly, B's gain on the sale is $3,213 ($10,000 − $6,787).

11.64   Under Section 1001(e), enacted in 1969, a taxpayer who disposes of a life or term interest after October 9, 1969, is not allowed to deduct any basis in determining his gain or loss unless his disposition is part of a transaction in which the entire interest relating to the uniform basis in the property is transferred. For this purpose, an income interest in a trust is considered a term interest. The effect of this 1969 provision is that all proceeds received on the disposition of a life or term interest after October 9, 1969, are treated as gain on the disposition without diminution for the transferor's basis, unless the entire interest in the property is transferred in the same disposition. Thus in the foregoing illustration, if C had purchased only A's life interest in the property, A's gain would have been $12,500, the amount of his proceeds.

11.65   It should be noted that the rules discussed in the foregoing paragraphs apply only where several taxpayers acquire interests in property from a single decedent or donor and determine their bases by reference to the uniform basis of the property. A taxpayer who purchases a life estate, term interest, or remainder interest in property determines his basis in the property and gain or loss on disposition in accordance with the general rules discussed elsewhere in this chapter.

Property Acquired Before March 1, 1913

11.66   The basis of property acquired before March 1, 1913, also depends in part upon whether the basis is being determined for purposes of measuring gain or loss from disposition of the property. For purposes of determining gain, the basis of property acquired before March 1, 1913, is the greater of the fair market value of the property as of March 1, 1913, or its cost or other basis adjusted to that date. For purposes of computing loss, the basis is the taxpayer's cost or other basis adjusted to March 1, 1913, without regard to fair market value (Section 1053).

Substituted Basis

In discussing the basis of property acquired by gift, we noted that under certain circumstances the basis is determined by reference to the basis of the property in the hands of the donor or other previous owner. Basis determined in this manner is referred to as "substituted basis." Substituted basis is also determined in some instances by reference to the basis of property previously held by the taxpayer [Section 1016(b)]. In determining the adjusted basis of property having a substituted basis, adjustment must be made for all appropriate items occurring not only during the holding period of the taxpayer but also during the holding period of the prior owner, with respect to whom the basis is determined, and during the holding period of any other property with respect to which such basis is determined [Section 1016(b)].

11.67

The Code stipulates a variety of situations in which the basis of property is a substituted basis. They involve acquisitions of property not only by gift but also in nontaxable transactions, such as certain exchanges of property of like kind, exchanges or replacements of property in connection with certain involuntary conversions, transfers of property to controlled corporations solely in exchange for stock, transfers of property in connection with tax-free reorganizations of corporations, and various other situations. Substituted basis of property will be discussed further in connection with these types of nontaxable transactions.

11.68

NONTAXABLE EXCHANGES

As a general rule, all gains realized on sales and other dispositions of property are recognized for tax purposes; however, the Code provides a number of exceptions. For the most part, these exceptions involve situations in which property is exchanged or otherwise disposed of and other property is acquired that is considered to be substantially a continuation of the taxpayer's investment in the first property. Examples of property dispositions upon which gain or loss is not recognized are: exchanges of certain property for property of like kind; involuntary conversions of property into other property similar or related in service or use; the sale of a residence followed by the reinvestment of the proceeds in another residence; certain exchanges of insurance policies, and exchanges of stock for stock of the same corporation. There are also nontaxable exchanges of property for stock and of stock in one corporation for stock in another in connec-

11.69

tion with the organization and reorganization of corporations as discussed briefly in chapter 19.

11.70   When gain or loss is not recognized on these transactions, it does not mean that the gain is entirely tax-exempt or that the loss will never be utilized for tax purposes. The nonrecognition of gain or loss on the property transferred is usually accompanied by a correlative determination or adjustment of basis in the property received that postpones the recognition of gain or loss until the new property is depreciated, sold, or otherwise disposed of in a taxable transaction. The following paragraphs will discuss the nature of these nontaxable transactions and the determination of the basis of new property acquired in them.

Exchange of Property Held for Productive Use or Investment

11.71   Under Section 1031, no gain or loss is recognized when property held for productive use in a trade or business or for investment is exchanged for property of a like kind to be held for either purpose. Thus, property held for productive use in a trade or business may be exchanged for property of like kind to be held for investment, and property held for investment may be exchanged for property of like kind to be held for productive use in a trade or business. For this purpose, stock in trade or other property held primarily for sale, shares of stock, bonds, notes, and other securities are not treated as property held for productive use in a trade or business or as property held for investment.

11.72   Paragraphs (b), (c), and (d) of Reg. 1.1031(a)–1 provide:

(b) As used in section 1031(a), the words "like kind" have reference to the nature or character of the property and not to its grade or quality. One kind or class of property may not, under that section, be exchanged for property of a different kind or class. The fact that any real estate involved is improved or unimproved is not material for that fact relates only to the grade or quality of the property and not to its kind or class. Unproductive real estate held by one other than a dealer for future use or future realization of the increment in value is held for investment and not primarily for sale.

(c) No gain or loss is recognized if (1) a taxpayer exchanges property held for productive use in his trade or business, together with cash, for other property of like kind for the same use, such as a truck for a new truck or a passenger automobile for a new passenger automobile to be used for a like purpose; or (2) a taxpayer who is not a dealer in real estate exchanges city real estate for a ranch or farm, or exchanges a leasehold of a fee with 30 years or more to run for real estate, or exchanges improved real estate for unimproved real estate; or (3) a taxpayer exchanges investment property and cash for investment property of a like kind.

(d) Gain or loss is recognized if, for instance, a taxpayer exchanges (1) Treasury bonds maturing March 15, 1958, for Treasury bonds maturing December 15, 1968, unless section 1037(a) [or so much of section 1031 as relates to section 1037(a)] applied to such exchange, or (2) a real estate mortgage for consolidated farm loan bonds.

11.73   As pointed out in the regulations above, a leasehold interest of thirty years or more is considered the equivalent of a fee interest. Accordingly, an exchange of a thirty-year leasehold for fee simple title to another piece of real estate is one of like-kind properties. An exchange of real property for personal property is not one of like-kind properties. For example, the transfer of a vacant lot for a new Cadillac and money would be fully taxable. It has been held that an exchange of a partnership interest in a tavern for a partnership interest in an auto supply firm is a nontaxable exchange of like-kind properties.[28] Under Section 1031(e), added in 1969, livestock of different sexes are not property of like kind.

Effect of Boot. No gain or loss is recognized if property qualifying under Section 1031 is exchanged solely for other qualifying property of like kind. If, in addition to receiving the property of like kind, the taxpayer receives money or other property that is not of like kind, any gain realized on the transaction is recognized but only to the extent of the money or the fair market value of other property received [Section 1031(b)]. The money and the other property received are generally referred to as "boot." Losses are not recognized on exchanges of property for property of like kind plus boot [Section 1031(c)]. The effect of the rules concerning the receipt of boot is illustrated in Reg. 1.1031(b)–1(b):

11.74

A, who is not a dealer in real estate, in 1954 exchanges real estate held for investment, which he purchased in 1940 for $5,000 for other real estate (to be held for productive use in trade or business) which has a fair market value of $6,000, and $2,000 cash. The gain from the transaction is $3,000, but is recognized only to the extent of the cash received of $2,000.

EXAMPLE
FROM REG.

If the taxpayer transfers money in addition to property qualified for nonrecognition of gain or loss in exchange for qualified property of like kind, no gain or loss is recognized to him. [See Reg. 1.1031(a)–1(c) quoted in paragraph 11.72.]

11.75

If the boot transferred by the taxpayer is in the form of *other property*, no gain or loss will be recognized on the like-kind property exchanged; however, gain or loss will be recognized on the boot property transferred. Presumably, this gain or loss should be determined by allocating the fair market value of the property received between the like-kind property and the boot property given up on the basis of their relative fair market values. Under the presumption that in an arm's-length transaction the value of property received is equal to the value of property given up, this procedure would allocate to the boot property an amount equal to its fair market value. Thus the gain or loss recognized on the boot property would be equal to the difference between its adjusted basis to the taxpayer and its fair market value [Reg. 1.1031(d)–1(e)]. No loss will be recognized, however, unless the fair market value of the total property received is less than the total basis of the properties given up.

11.76

28. Miller v. U.S., 63–2 USTC ¶9606, 12 AFTR2d 5244 (D.C. Ind., 1963). But Est. of Rollin E. Meyer, Sr., 58 T.C. No. 32 (1972), contains dictum that same type of business may be required.

11.77 **Effect of Liabilities.** The amount of any mortgage or other liability against the property transferred by the taxpayer is treated as money received by him whether the other party assumes the mortgage or merely takes the property subject to such mortgage [Reg. 1.1031(d)–2]. Any gain realized by a taxpayer on such an exchange of property of like kind is therefore recognized to the extent of such liabilities plus any other boot received by the taxpayer.

11.78   For determining the amount of liabilities treated as boot received by a taxpayer on an exchange, the amount of boot given by the taxpayer is offset against any liabilities assumed by the other party or subject to which the other party takes property. For this purpose, boot given by the taxpayer includes money, property, liabilities assumed by him, and liabilities subject to which he receives property. If liabilities assumed or taken over by the taxpayer exceed the liabilities assumed or taken over by the other party, such excess is not offset against money or other property received by the taxpayer. Example (2) in Reg. 1.1031(d)–2 illustrates this point:

EXAMPLE FROM REG.

(a) D, an individual, owns an apartment house. On December 1, 1955, the apartment house owned by D has an adjusted basis in his hands of $100,000, a fair market value of $220,000 but is subject to a mortgage of $80,000. E, an individual, also owns an apartment house. On December 1, 1955, the apartment house owned by E has an adjusted basis of $175,000, a fair market value of $250,000, but is subject to a mortgage of $150,000. On December 1, 1955, D transfers his apartment house to E, receiving in exchange therefor $40,000 in cash and the apartment house owned by E. Each apartment house is transferred subject to the mortgage on it.

(b) D realizes a gain of $120,000 on the exchange, computed as follows:

Value of property received		$250,000
Cash		40,000
Liabilities subject to which old property was transferred		80,000
Total consideration received		$370,000
Less —		
Adjusted basis of property transferred	$100,000	
Liabilities to which new property is subject	150,000	250,000
Gain realized		$120,000

For purposes of section 1031(b), the amount of "other property or money" received by D is $40,000. [Consideration received by D in the form of a transfer subject to a liability of $80,000 is offset by consideration in the form of a receipt of property subject to a $150,000 liability. Thus, only the consideration received in the form of cash, $40,000, is treated as "other property or money" for purposes of section 1031(b).] Accordingly, under section 1031(b), $40,000 of the $120,000 gain is recognized. ...

(c) E realizes a gain of $75,000 on the exchange, computed as follows:

Value of property received	$220,000
Liabilities subject to which old property was transferred	150,000
Total consideration received	$370,000

Less —		
Adjusted basis of property transferred	$175,000	
Cash	40,000	
Liabilities to which new property is subject	80,000	295,000
Gain realized		$ 75,000

For purposes of section 1031(b), the amount of "other property or money" received by E is $30,000. (Consideration received by E in the form of a transfer subject to a liability of $150,000 is offset by consideration given in the form of a receipt of property subject to an $80,000 liability and by the $40,000 cash paid by E. Although consideration received in the form of cash or other property is not offset by consideration given in the form of an assumption of liabilities or a receipt of property subject to a liability, consideration given in the form of cash or other property is offset against consideration received in the form of an assumption of liabilities or a transfer of property subject to a liability.) Accordingly, under section 1031(b), $30,000 of the $75,000 gain is recognized. ...

Partial Business Use. Where property is used in part for business or investment purposes and in part for personal purposes, the rules concerning nonrecognition of gain on exchanges of property of like kind apply only to the business or investment portion of the property. With respect to the personal use part of the property, gain on a sale or exchange is recognized, whereas any loss on sale or exchange is not recognized. A common example of an asset used partly for business and partly for personal purposes is a salesman's automobile.   11.79

Basis of Property Received in Nontaxable Exchanges. In nontaxable exchanges of property held for productive use or investment, the new basis of property received is determined by reference to basis of the property exchanged, using the following formula: 11.80

Basis of property acquired = basis of property transferred + any boot given and any gain recognized − any boot received and any loss recognized on boot property transferred.

This formula may be illustrated by the following:

A taxpayer exchanged an apartment house having an adjusted basis of $75,000 for a farm. No boot was involved. No gain or loss is recognized, and the basis of the farm becomes $75,000. Fair market values of the properties are not significant in determinations of this type.   EXAMPLE 1

A taxpayer traded an old machine used in his business for a new machine and $1,000 cash. The adjusted basis of his old machine was $5,500, but its fair market value was $6,000. The fair market value of the new machine was $5,000.   EXAMPLE 2

Gain realized on the exchange is $500, and the gain recognized is $500. Basis of the new machine is $5,000 computed as follows:

Adjusted basis of old machine	$5,500
Plus gain recognized on exchange	500
	$6,000
Minus amount of money received	1,000
Basis of new machine	$5,000

EXAMPLE 3   A taxpayer acquired a new machine having a fair market value of $5,000 for a cash payment of $3,000 plus a trade-in allowance on an old machine of $2,000. The adjusted basis of the old machine was $1,000.

No gain or loss is recognized, and the adjusted basis of the new machine to the taxpayer is $4,000.

EXAMPLE 4   A taxpayer transferred investment real estate having an adjusted basis of $5,000 but a fair market value of only $4,000, and he received investment real estate having a fair market value of $3,500 plus cash of $500.

The $1,000 loss on the exchange is not recognized for tax purposes. The basis of the real estate received is $4,500 (adjusted basis of property transferred minus cash received).

11.81   The correlation between the rules for determining basis and the rules governing gains and losses on exchanges of like-kind property can be illustrated by an extension of example 4. Assume that the taxpayer eventually sells the new investment real estate for $3,500. At that time, a loss of $1,000 will be recognized for tax purposes. That loss represents the difference between the taxpayer's original investment of $5,000 and the $4,000 cash ultimately realized from the old and new property.

11.82   When the taxpayer receives not only like-kind property but also other property, the total basis of the properties transferred in the exchange increased by any gain and decreased by any loss recognized must be allocated to the individual properties acquired. For this purpose, an amount of basis equal to the fair market value of the other property is allocated to such other property [Reg. 1.1031(d)–1(e)]. Paragraph (c) of Reg. 1.1031(d)–1 contains the following example:

EXAMPLE
FROM REG.   A, who is not a dealer in real estate, in 1954 transfers real estate held for investment which he purchased in 1940 for $10,000 in exchange for other real estate (to be held for investment) which has a fair market value of $9,000, an automobile which has a fair market value of $2,000, and $1,500 in cash. A realizes a gain of $2,500, all of which is recognized under section 1031(b). The basis of the property received in exchange is the basis of the real estate A transfers ($10,000) decreased by the amount of money received ($1,500) and increased in the amount of gain that was recognized ($2,500), which results in a basis for the property received of $11,000. This basis of $11,000 is allocated between the automobile and the real estate received by A, the basis of the automobile being its fair market value at the date of the exchange, $2,000, and the basis of the real estate received being the remainder, $9,000.

11.83   **Requirement That an Exchange Take Place.** In order for gain or loss not to be recognized under Section 1031, the transaction must constitute an exchange of property. An exchange is a transfer of property in return for other property. Whether a transaction is an exchange is not always apparent. It has been held that a three-cornered exchange of properties that constitutes a unified transaction can qualify as a nontaxable exchange under Section 1031.[29] It is the position of the Internal Revenue Service that a sale of real property for cash accompanied by a leaseback for a term of thirty years or more is an exchange of like-kind properties accompanied by boot in the amount of the cash, and no loss is recognized.[30] A sale of real property for cash accompanied by a leaseback for a term of less than thirty years has uniformly been held to constitute a sale and not an exchange.[31] As far as the customer is concerned, a trade-in of a used automobile or truck for a new one accompanied by a payment of cash is an exchange.[32]

11.84

It is not necessary that the other party to the exchange own the like-kind property at the time of the agreement. In *J. H. Baird Publishing Co.*,[33] the taxpayer in 1956 deeded business real property to a real estate agent but retained the use of the property rent-free until the real estate agent should acquire a lot, construct a new building thereon, and transfer it to the taxpayer. The real estate agent then sold the property to a stranger subject to the rent-free use by the taxpayer. With a part of the proceeds, the agent bought a lot, constructed a building on it, and in 1957 transferred it to the taxpayer together with an amount of cash. The Tax Court held that the taxpayer made a like-kind exchange in 1957 and was taxable only on the recognized gain to the extent of the money received.

Certain Exchanges of Insurance Policies

Under Section 1035, gain or loss is not recognized on certain exchanges of life insurance or endowment contracts on the same insured person or annuity contracts with the same obligee. Gain or loss is not recognized on transfer of:

11.85

1. A life insurance contract for (a) another life insurance contract, (b) an endowment insurance contract, or (c) an annuity contract.
2. An endowment insurance contract for (a) another endowment insurance contract that provides for regular payments beginning at a date not later than the date payments would have begun under the contract transferred, or (b) an annuity contract.
3. An annuity contract for another annuity contract.

29. Rev. Rul. 57–244, 1957–1 C.B. 247.
30. Rev. Rul. 60–43, 1960–1 C.B. 687; to the contrary, Jordan Marsh Co. v. Com., 269 F.2d 453 (2nd Cir. 1959), 59–2 USTC ¶9641, 4 AFTR2d 5341.
31. Standard Envelope Mfg. Co., 15 T.C. 41; May Department Stores Co., 16 T.C. 547.
32. W. H. Hartman Co., 20 BTA 302 (Acq.).
33. 39 T.C. 608 (1962); similarly: Coastal Terminals, Inc. v. U.S., 320 F.2d 333 (4th Cir. 1963), 63–2 USTC ¶9623, 12 AFTR2d 5247; Alderson v. Com., 317 F.2d 790 (9th Cir. 1963), 63–2 USTC ¶9499, 11 AFTR2d 1529.

11.86   In each of the transactions described above, the nonrecognition of gain applies only to the transfer of the first contract mentioned. Gain is *not* recognized on the transfer of a life insurance contract in exchange for an annuity contract or on the transfer of an endowment insurance contract for an annuity. Gain *is* recognized on the transfer of an annuity contract in exchange for a life insurance contract or on the exchange of an endowment insurance contract for a life insurance contract.[34]

11.87   If boot is given or received in an exchange of insurance policies on which gain otherwise would not be recognized under Section 1035(a), it has the same effect on recognition of gain that it has in the case of exchanges of property of like kind under Section 1031. Furthermore, the basis of insurance policies acquired in exchange for other insurance policies, where gain is not recognized under Section 1035, is determined under the same rules as those applicable to property acquired in like-kind exchanges [Section 1035(c)].

Stock for Stock of Same Corporation

11.88   Under Section 1036(a) no gain or loss is recognized on the exchange of common stock in a corporation solely for common stock in the *same* corporation, or on an exchange of preferred stock in a corporation solely for preferred stock in the *same* corporation. This section applies even though voting common is exchanged for nonvoting common, or voting preferred is exchanged for nonvoting preferred. The exchanges can be between individuals or between the issuing corporation and shareholders. Section 1036(a) does not apply to an exchange of stock in one corporation for stock in another. The rules concerning boot and the determination of basis of the stock received are the same as those applicable to like-kind exchanges under Section 1031.

Exchange of Stock for Property

11.89   No gain or loss is recognized to a corporation on the receipt of money or property in exchange for its own stock regardless of whether the stock is being originally issued or is treasury stock (Section 1032). Such gain is not recognized even though the corporation deals in its own stock in the same manner that it may deal in stock of other corporations. Accordingly, no gain is recognized on a corporation's transfer of treasury stock in exchange for money or property with a value substantially in excess of the corporation's cost of its treasury stock (Reg. 1.1032–1).

11.90   In a transaction that is taxable to the person transferring property to a corporation in exchange for its stock, the basis of the property received by the corporation is the fair market value of the property. If the property is received from a controlling stockholder, or if the trans-

34. Reg. 1.1035–1; W. Stanley Barrett, 42 T.C. 993 (1964).

fer is in connection with a tax-free corporate organization or reorganization, the corporation will have a substituted basis for the
property equal to the transferor's basis plus any gain recognized[35]
(see chapter 19).

Involuntary Conversions

If property is destroyed or otherwise involuntarily taken and the   11.91
taxpayer receives compensation for such destruction or taking, the
original property is said to have been involuntarily converted into
the money or other property received as compensation. Because
the adjusted basis of the property destroyed or taken away will frequently be less than the amount of the compensation received, Congress thought it would be unjust to tax the resulting gain under all
circumstances, and it inserted Section 1033 in the Code as a relief
measure.

Regulation 1.1033(a)–1(a) reads in part: 11.92

... An "involuntary conversion" may be the result of the destruction of
property in whole or in part, the theft of property, the seizure of property,
the requisition or condemnation of property, or the threat or imminence of
requisition or condemnation of property. An "involuntary conversion" may
be a conversion into similar property or into money or into dissimilar property. Section 1033 provides that, under certain specified circumstances, any
gain which is realized from an involuntary conversion shall not be recognized. In cases where property is converted into other property similar or
related in service or use to the converted property, no gain shall be recognized regardless of when the disposition of the converted property occurred
and regardless of whether or not the taxpayer elects to have the gain not
recognized. In other types of involuntary conversion cases, however, the
proceeds arising from the disposition of the converted property must (within
the time limits specified) be reinvested in similar property in order to avoid
recognition of any gain realized. ... Section 1033 applies only with respect to
gains; losses from involuntary conversions are recognized or not recognized
without regard to this section.

Transactions Constituting Involuntary Conversions. An involuntary   11.93
conversion occurs when property is destroyed in whole or in part, is
stolen, is seized for public use in condemnation proceedings,[36] or
is sold or exchanged because of the threat or imminence of condemnation proceedings, and the taxpayer receives insurance proceeds, a
condemnation award, or other property in exchange for the original
property. If livestock are destroyed, sold, or exchanged because of
disease, such destruction, sale, or exchange is treated as an involuntary conversion [Section 1033(e)]. If livestock (other than poultry)
held for draft, dairy, or breeding purposes are sold or exchanged in
numbers exceeding the number the taxpayer would ordinarily sell in
accordance with his usual business practices, such sales or exchanges

35. Code Sec. 362(a) and Reg. 1.362–1.
36. Rev. Rul. 57–314, 1957–2 C.B. 523.

will be treated as involuntary conversions when made solely on account of drought [Section 1033(f)]. A sale of property lying within an irrigation project may also qualify as an involuntary conversion if the sale is made in order to conform to the acreage limitation provisions of federal reclamation laws [Section 1033(d)]. Finally, if elected by a taxpayer, certain sales or exchanges of radio and television broadcasting stations and stock in corporations owning such stations may be treated as involuntary conversions where the Federal Communications Commission certifies that such sales or exchanges are necessary or appropriate to effectuate a change in policy or the adoption of a new policy by the Commission [Section 1071(a)].

11.94   Not all involuntary conversions qualify for the nonrecognition of gain; only those specified in Section 1033. In Rev. Rul. 57–314 the Internal Revenue Service gave its definition of *condemnation:*

> It is the position of the Internal Revenue Service that the term "condemnation," as used in Section 1033 of the Code, refers to the process by which private property is taken for public use without the consent of the property owner but upon the award and payment of just compensation.

It then went on to hold that a condemnation of rental property by a public authority on the ground that structural defects and sanitary deficiencies make the property unfit for human habitation is not a condemnation within the meaning of Section 1033 because it is not a taking for public use.

11.95   A condemnation award must be distinguished from severance damages. A condemnation award constitutes a payment for property condemned or seized. An award of severance damages represents compensation for the diminution in value of the remaining portion of the property. Any severance damages received are applied against the adjusted basis of that portion of the retained property that is damaged, and only to the extent that the amount of such damages exceeds such adjusted basis is there any taxable gain.[37] If, in a condemnation proceeding, there is an award for the value of the property seized, severance damages for the diminution in value of the remaining property, and a special assessment against the remaining property to cover the cost of improvements to be made which will benefit the remaining property, G.C.M. 23698 [38] states that the two awards and the one assessment are to be handled in the following manner. First, the amount of the special assessment is used to reduce the amount of the award for severance damages. If the assessment is less than the award, only the net amount reduces the basis of the retained property. If the assessment is more than the amount of the award for severance damages, such excess is applied to reduce the amount of the condemnation award. Such reduced amount of the condemnation award then becomes the measure of any gain arising from involuntary conversion.

37. Rev. Rul. 68–37, 1968–1 C.B. 359.
38. 1943 C.B. 340, as amplified by Rev. Rul. 68–37 *ibid.*

A condemnation proceeding of this type frequently happens when only a portion of a tract of land is condemned for the purpose of building a highway or a street.

The case of *Harry G. Masser* [39] concerned two pieces of property **11.96** operated as an economic unit. One piece was sold under threat of condemnation and then the other was sold. The taxpayer operated an interstate truck line and had a terminal serving the New York metropolitan area. This terminal consisted of a terminal building plus eight lots directly across the street. The lots were used for the parking of trucks and equipment operating in and out of the terminal building, and the Tax Court found that in the trucking business it is accepted practice to have adequate parking space adjacent to the terminal building. The property was located in Union City, New Jersey. The Housing Authority of that city threatened to start condemnation proceedings for the seizure of the parking lots. Upon the advice of an attorney the taxpayer sold the parking lots to the Housing Authority, and shortly thereafter sold the terminal building to another industrial corporation. With the proceeds from the sales of the two pieces of property the taxpayer purchased new terminal facilities, including adequate parking space, in Weehawken, New Jersey. The court found that the only adequate lots available for parking facilities in the Union City area were one and one-half miles away from the Union City terminal building, and that it would not have been economical for the taxpayer to use those lots for parking purposes because of the distance from the terminal. In holding that Section 1033 applied to both the sale of the parking lots and the sale of the terminal building, the court said:

> Bearing in mind two basic principles, that "taxation ... is eminently practical," *Tyler* v. *U.S.*, 281 U.S. 497, 503, and that a relief provision "should be liberally construed to effectuate its purpose," *Massillon–Cleveland–Akron Sign Co.*, 15 T.C. 79, 83, we are of the opinion that when two pieces of property, practically adjacent to each other, were acquired for the purpose of being used and were used in a taxpayer's business as an economic unit, when one of the pieces of property was involuntarily sold as a result of the threat of condemnation, when it was apparent that the continuation of the business on the remaining piece of property was impractical, and as a result of the involuntary sale of the one piece of property the taxpayer in the exercise of good business judgment sold the other piece of property, and when the proceeds of both sales were expended in the acquisition of property similar to the economic unit consisting of the two properties sold, the transaction, considered as a whole, constitutes an involuntary conversion of one economic property unit within the meaning of Section 112(f) [now Section 1033].

In Rev. Rul. 59–361 [40] the Internal Revenue Service announced that it would follow the holding in the *Masser* case and said:

> Accordingly, where all the facts and circumstances show a substantial economic relationship between the condemned property and the other

---

39. 30 T.C. 741 (1958) (Acq.).
40. 1959–2 C.B. 183. Also see Rev. Rul. 73–35.

property sold by the taxpayer, so that together they constituted one economic property unit, such as existed in the *Masser* case, involuntary conversion treatment for the proceeds of the involuntary sale will be permitted. The taxpayer must show the unavailability of suitable nearby property of a like kind to that converted, and the proceeds of the voluntary sale must be expended in acquiring property of a like kind.

11.97 **Recognition of Gain or Loss.** Section 1033 applies only to gains and not losses arising from involuntary conversions of property. Such losses are recognized or not recognized according to the usual rules of taxation.

11.98 If property is converted directly into other property similar or related in service or use to the original property, gain is not recognized. This nonrecognition of gain is mandatory.[41] If property is involuntarily converted into money or other property not similar or related in service or use to the converted property (as through receipt of insurance proceeds, condemnation proceeds, or proceeds from a sale or exchange of the property under a threat of condemnation), the taxpayer may replace the converted property under certain circumstances and avoid the recognition of gain. Provided (1) the property is replaced within the designated period, (2) the replacement property is similar or related in service or use to the property converted, and (3) the taxpayer makes a proper election, gain will be recognized only to the extent the amount realized from the involuntary conversion exceeds the cost of the replacement property [Section 1033(a)(3)(A)].

11.99 **Period for Replacement.** The period during which the property must be replaced with other property similar or related in service or use to the converted property begins with the earlier of (1) the date of destruction, seizure, and so on, of the converted property, or (2) the earliest date of the threat or imminence of condemnation. The period ends (1) two years after the close of the first taxable year in which any part of the gain on conversion is realized, or (2) at the end of an extended period requested by the taxpayer prior to the expiration of the first period and approved by the District Director of Internal Revenue. The replacement period may be extended by the District Director even though such extension was not requested by the taxpayer within the replacement period otherwise designated, provided the taxpayer can show reasonable cause for failing to request the extension [Reg. 1.1033(a)–2(c)(3)].

11.100 **Replacement by Similar Property.** The meaning of the term "property similar or related in service or use" has led to much litigation. There are now two tests to determine whether replacement property falls within the meaning of this term. These tests are the "like-kind" test and the "functional-use" test.

11.101 The "like-kind" test is described in Section 1033(g) and applies only to real property held for productive use in a trade or business or

41. Reg. 1.1033(a)–2(b).

investment, which is condemned, seized, requisitioned, or sold, or exchanged owing to threat or imminence thereof after December 31, 1957. Such property may be replaced with property of like kind to be held either in a trade or business or for investment, and such property will be treated as property similar or related in service or use to the property converted [Section 1033(g)]. For this purpose, the term *like kind* has the same meaning it has under Section 1031. That is, it refers to the nature or character of the property and not to its grade or quality (see paragraphs 11.71 et seq.). The "like-kind" test does not apply to involuntary conversions involving personal property, or to thefts, or destruction of property.

11.102

The "functional-use" test is applicable to any property, real or personal, that has been the subject of any type of involuntary conversion. In the case of real property held for productive use in a trade or business or for investment and that is involuntarily converted under the circumstances described in the preceding paragraph, the "functional-use" test is available in lieu of the "like-kind" test. The "functional-use" test generally is more difficult to meet than the "like-kind" test. To meet the "functional-use" test, the replacement property need not be a physical duplication of the converted property; however, it must have the same general characteristics. Further, if the taxpayer is the owner–user, it must have the same end use.

11.103

Regulation 1.1033(a)–2(c)(9) provides:

There is no investment in property similar in character and devoted to a similar use if—

(i) The proceeds of unimproved real estate, taken upon condemnation proceedings, are invested in improved real estate.

(ii) The proceeds of conversion of real property are applied in reduction of indebtedness previously incurred in the purchase of a leasehold.

(iii) The owner of a requisitioned tug uses the proceeds to buy barges.

Paragraph (i) of this regulation is applicable only when the condemned unimproved real estate was stock in trade of a dealer in real estate or was otherwise not held for productive use in a trade or business or for investment. If it is so held, the "like-kind" test of Section 1033(g) applies, so that the replacement with improved real estate is a qualified one.

11.104

If the taxpayer is a lessor of the properties, the properties must be similar or related in their relationships to the taxpayer. The Internal Revenue Service expressed its position on this matter in Rev. Rul. 64–237: [42]

In previous litigation, the Service has taken the position that the statutory phrase, "similar or related in service or use," means that the property acquired must have a close "functional" similarity to the property converted. Under this test, property was not considered similar or related in service or use to the converted property unless the physical characteristics and end uses of the

42. 1964–2 C.B. 319.

converted and replacement properties were closely similar. Although this "functional-use" test has been upheld in the lower courts, it has not been sustained in the appellate courts with respect to investors in property, such as lessors.

In conformity with the appellate court decisions, in considering whether replacement property acquired by an investor is similar in service or use to the converted property, attention will be directed primarily to the similarity in the relationship of the services or uses which the original and replacement properties have to the taxpayer-owner. In applying this test, a determination will be made as to whether the properties are of a similar service to the taxpayer, the nature of the business risks connected with the properties, and what such properties demand of the taxpayer in the way of management, services and relations to its tenants.

For example, where the taxpayer is a lessor, who rented out the converted property for a light manufacturing plant and then rents out the replacement property for a wholesale grocery warehouse, the nature of the taxpayer–owner's service or use of the properties may be similar although that of the end users change. The two properties will be considered as similar or related in service or use where, for example, both are rented and where there is a similarity in the extent and type of the taxpayer's management activities, the amount and kind of services rendered by him to his tenants, and the nature of his business risks connected with the properties.

In modifying its position with respect to the involuntary conversion of property held for investment, the Service will continue to adhere to the functional test in the case of owner–users of property. Thus, if the taxpayer–owner operates a light manufacturing plant on the converted property and then operates a wholesale grocery warehouse on the replacement property, by changing his end use he has so changed the nature of his relationship to the property as to be outside the nonrecognition of gain provisions.

11.105   Although this revenue ruling indicates that the Internal Revenue Service is taking a more liberal interpretation of "property similar or related in service or use," the meaning of the term continues to be more restrictive than the meaning of "like-kind" applicable to exchanges of property under Section 1031.

11.106   **Methods of Replacement.** Involuntarily converted property may be replaced by two methods. First, similar or related property may be directly purchased, or second, control of a corporation owning property qualifying as similar or related under the functional-use test may be acquired through purchase of its stock. For this purpose, control of a corporation means the ownership of stock possessing at least 80 percent of the total combined voting power of all classes of stock entitled to vote and at least 80 percent of the total number of shares of all the other classes of stock of the corporation [Reg. 1.1033(a)–2(c)(1)]. In determining the amount of gain to be recognized, the cost of the stock is treated as if it were the direct cost of the replacement property.

11.107   Replacement property or stock is considered to have been purchased if it is acquired in such a manner that its unadjusted basis to the taxpayer, before adjustment for the involuntary conversion, is its cost. Stock acquired by gift, for example, does not qualify.

Reporting on Involuntary Conversion. Any gain on involuntary conversion of property should be reported in the taxpayer's return for the year or years in which realized. If part or all of the gain is elected not to be recognized, that part of the gain should be excluded from gross income, and a statement should be included in each return giving details of the involuntary conversion and the replacement or intention to replace the property. If the replacement is not completed within the prescribed period, then an amended return should be filed and the appropriate amount of gain reported. A failure to include the gain in gross income in the return for the year realized will be deemed to be an election to have such gain recognized only to the extent the proceeds are not properly reinvested. After a return is filed in which gain on an involuntary conversion is included in gross income, the election not to recognize gain can still be made, providing that decision is made before the end of the period prescribed for replacement of the property and, of course, the replacement property is acquired before the end of that period. When this occurs, a claim for refund should be filed.[43]

11.108

Basis of Replacement Property. Where property is involuntarily converted directly into other property similar or related in service or use to the taxpayer, the basis of the replacement property is the same as the adjusted basis of the converted property. Where property or stock in a corporation is purchased as a replacement of property involuntarily converted into cash, the basis of the replacement property and/or stock is equal to its cost to the taxpayer minus any gain not recognized on the involuntary conversion [Section 1033(c); Reg. 1.1033(c)–1]. If the cash invested in the replacement property is more than the proceeds of the involuntary conversion, such excess is a capital expenditure and not a loss.

11.109

The following example illustrates the recognition of gain or loss on involuntary conversions and the determination of basis of replacement property.

11.110

EXAMPLE

Taxpayer's factory building was destroyed by a hurricane. The adjusted basis of the building to taxpayer immediately before its destruction was $60,000. The old building was replaced with a new building at a cost of $75,000. The following table illustrates the gain or loss recognized and the basis of the replacement building if various amounts of insurance proceeds are received. Taxpayer elects under Section 1033(a)(3) for gain not to be recognized.

ADJUSTED BASIS OF OLD BUILDING	INSURANCE PROCEEDS	COST OF REPLACEMENT BUILDING	GAIN OR (LOSS) RECOGNIZED	BASIS OF NEW BUILDING
$60,000	$90,000	$75,000	$15,000	$60,000
60,000	50,000	75,000	(10,000)	75,000
60,000	70,000	75,000	—	65,000

43. Reg. 1.1033(a)–2(c)(2); Rev. Rul. 63–127, 1963–2 C.B. 333.

Sale of Residence

11.111   Ordinarily, gain is recognized on the sale or exchange of a personal residence (loss is not, because it is deemed personal in nature); however, Section 1034 provides a special rule whereby all or part of a gain on sale or exchange of a principal residence is not recognized under the following conditions:

1. The taxpayer buys other property and uses it as his principal residence within one year before or after the sale of his previous principal residence, or
2. Taxpayer begins construction of a new residence within one year before or after the sale of his previous principal residence and uses the new property as his principal residence within eighteen months after the sale of the old residence.

11.112   Under these conditions gain is recognized only to the extent that the "adjusted sales price" of the old residence exceeds the cost of the new residence. The basis of the new residence is its cost reduced by the amount of gain on the sale of the old residence which was not recognized under Section 1034. The provisions of this section are mandatory and not elective.

11.113   The term "new residence" refers to property purchased by the taxpayer and used as his principal residence and the cost of which is considered in determining the gain to be recognized on sale of the old residence. The term "new" does not imply that the taxpayer must be the original user of the property [Section 1034(a) and Reg. 1.1034–1(b)(2)].

11.114   The "adjusted sales price" of the old residence is the "amount realized" reduced by the "fixing-up" expenses. The "amount realized" is the sales price less the expenses of sale, such as real estate commissions, advertising expenses, and legal expenses [Reg. 1.1034–1(b)(4)]. "Fixing-up" expenses are expenses incurred in connection with the old property to assist in its sale, which are: (1) for work performed during a ninety-day period before the date of the sales contract, (2) paid before thirty days after the sale date, (3) are not otherwise deductible in determining taxable income, and (4) are not properly includible in basis of the property sold [Section 1034(b); Reg. 1.1034–1(b)(6)]. Although fixing-up expenses are deductible in determining the amount of the sales price that must be reinvested to avoid recognition of gain on the old residence, they are not deductible in determining the amount of gain realized on the old residence.

11.115   The above rules may be illustrated as follows:

EXAMPLE   Taxpayer sold his principal residence on June 15, for $18,000. The adjusted basis of the residence was $12,000. In February of the same year Taxpayer had spent $300 on interior repainting. In May of that year Taxpayer had the exterior repainted at a cost of $200. All repainting costs were paid before the house was sold. In order to facilitate its sale, Taxpayer added a garage to the property in April, at a cost of $2,500. Taxpayer's costs for advertising, real estate commission, and closing of his sale amounted to $1,200. The following table illustrates the calculation of Taxpayer's recognized gain on the sale of his old property assuming that in November of the same year he acquires another property that he uses as his principal residence.

	ASSUMING COST OF NEW PROPERTY IS		
	$12,500	$15,000	$18,000
Sales price	$18,000	$18,000	$18,000
Less selling expenses	1,200	1,200	1,200
Amount realized	$16,800	$16,800	$16,800
Deduct adjusted basis of old residence (includes cost of new garage)	14,500	14,500	14,500
Gain realized	$ 2,300	$ 2,300	$ 2,300
Amount realized	$16,800	$16,800	$16,800
Less fixing-up expenses (cost of painting performed within 90 days prior to sale of house)	200	200	200
Adjusted sales price	$16,600	$16,600	$16,600
Cost of new residence	12,500	15,000	18,000
Excess of adjusted sales price over cost of new residence	$ 4,100	$ 1,600	$ —
Gain recognized (lesser of gain realized or excess of adjusted sales price over cost of new residence)	$ 2,300	$ 1,600	$ —
Gain not recognized	$ —	$ 700	$ 2,300
Basis of new house (cost less gain not recognized)	$12,500	$14,300	$15,700

Replacement Period. In order to avoid recognition of gain on sale of an old residence, other property must be *purchased* and used as a principal residence within a period beginning one year prior to the date of sale of the old residence and ending one year after sale date [Section 1034(a)]. If the new residence is *constructed* by the taxpayer, construction must be commenced within a period beginning one year before the sale of the old residence and ending one year after sale; but the taxpayer will have until eighteen months after the sale within which to complete construction of the new residence and to occupy it as his principal residence [Section 1034(c)(5)]. If the taxpayer buys a partially built new residence from a builder, the transaction is not treated as the commencement of a new residence by him; accordingly the eighteen-month rule will not apply.   11.116

The replacement period is suspended while the taxpayer or his spouse is on extended active duty with the United States Armed   11.117

Forces, but replacement of the residence must still be completed within four years from the date the old residence is sold [Section 1034(h)].

11.118 **Exchanges Treated as Sales and Purchases.** For purposes of Section 1034, the exchange of an old residence for other property is treated as a sale, and the acquisition of a new residence by the exchange of other property is treated as a purchase [Section 1034(c)(1)].

11.119 **Special Rule for Husband and Wife.** The special rule on nonrecognition of gain applies to husband and wife regardless of which spouse owned and sold the old residence and regardless of which spouse purchased the new residence, provided that both spouses consent and provided that both spouses used each residence, in turn, as their principal residence. Any reduction in basis of the new residence resulting from nonrecognition of gain on the old residence is allocated between the spouses in the ratio of their ownership of the new residence. Thus, if the old residence was owned and sold by the husband, and the new residence was purchased by the wife, the special rule could prevent the recognition of gain on the old residence; however, the gain not recognized would reduce the basis of the new residence to the wife. If the new residence was owned equally by the husband and wife, the reduction in basis would be divided equally between them.

11.120 **Involuntary Conversions of Residences.** The involuntary conversion of a residence after December 31, 1953, is not, as a general rule, treated as a sale of a residence for purpose of Section 1034. However, a taxpayer may elect such treatment with respect to a seizure, requisition, or condemnation of his principal residence, or its sale or exchange under threat or imminence thereof after December 31, 1957. This election does not apply to involuntary conversions resulting from destruction or theft of property [Section 1034(i); Reg. 1.1034–1(b)]; to these, the rules of Section 1033 are applicable. If the replacement rules applying to residences under Code Sec. 1034 should be easier to meet than the replacement rules applying to involuntary conversions under Section 1033, a taxpayer may wish to elect treatment under Section 1034.

11.121 **Information to Be Reported on Return.** If a residence is sold or exchanged at a gain, all pertinent details of the transaction should be reported in the taxpayer's return for the year of sale, even though part or all of the gain is not recognized. If the old residence has been replaced, the information reported in the return should show the cost of the new residence and the calculation of the gain recognized, if any.

11.122 If the new residence has not been acquired and used by the filing date of the return, but if replacement is intended, a statement should be attached to the return showing the calculation of gain realized on the old residence. The statement should indicate that purchase of a new residence is contemplated, and no gain should be included in gross income. When the new residence is purchased and occupied, complete details should be supplied to the District Director in writing. If the new residence is not purchased and occupied within the required period, that fact also should be reported to the District Director, and the additional tax applicable to the gain then recognized on the old residence should be paid. Information concerning replacement of the residence or failure to replace it should be supplied to the Internal Revenue Service as soon as practicable. The time period within which tax may be assessed on the gain on the old residence does not expire until three years after the date the Service receives notice of the replacement or the failure to replace [Section 1034(j); Reg. 1.1034–1(i)].

Sale or Exchange of Residence by Person Aged Sixty-five or Over. 11.123
Under Section 121, if a person aged sixty-five years or over sells his residence, part or all of the gain may not be recognized, provided the taxpayer has owned and used the property as his principal residence for periods aggregating five out of the eight years preceding the sale. Replacement of the residence is not required.

If the adjusted sales price of the property is $20,000 or less, no gain 11.124
is recognized. If the adjusted sales price exceeds $20,000, the gain is recognized only in the ratio of such excess to the total adjusted sales price [Section 121(b)]. Thus the gain not recognized can be expressed by the formula:

$$\text{Gain not recognized} = \frac{\$20,000}{\text{Adjusted sales price}} \times \text{Total gain realized.}$$

This special rule for nonrecognition of gain to persons aged sixty- 11.125
five or over applies to only one sale by a taxpayer or his spouse. Furthermore, the treatment is elective. The election may be made or revoked at any time before the expiration of the period for filing a claim for refund of tax for the year of sale. If a taxpayer is married, his spouse also must join in the making or revocation of the election [Section 121(c)].

If a taxpayer over sixty-five buys a replacement residence, the rules 11.126
for nonrecognition of gain of both Section 1034 and 121 apply. Thus, if the taxpayer's adjusted sales price is in excess of $20,000, he may elect that a part of the gain not be recognized because of his age. The gain thus not recognized is deducted from the adjusted sales price of the property to determine the amount that must be reinvested in a replacement residence to avoid recognition of the remaining gain [Section 121(d)(7)]. Regulation 1.121–5(g) gives the following example:

Taxpayer A sells his residence for $32,000, incurs $2,000 in fixing-up EXAMPLE
expenses described in section 1034(b)(2), and has a basis of $23,000 for such FROM REG.
residence. Accordingly, $6,000 ($20,000/$30,000 × $9,000) of gain is excluded from his gross income under this section. If he purchases a new resi-

dence within one year for $23,000, only $1,000 of his gain is taxable since his adjusted sales price for purposes of section 1034 is $24,000 ($32,000 − $2,000 − $6,000).

In no event can the recognized gain after applying Section 1034 exceed the amount of the gain realized reduced by any amount elected not to be recognized under Section 121.

Certain Sales of Low-income Housing Projects

11.127   In order to encourage investment in low-income housing projects, the 1969 Tax Reform Act extended to the investors in such projects elective tax benefits similar to those enjoyed by taxpayers who sell and replace their residences (Section 1039). That is, gain on the "approved disposition" of a qualified housing project may not be recognized to the extent the net amount realized is reinvested in another qualified housing project. For this purpose, a "qualified housing project" is a project to provide rental or cooperative housing for low-income families on which (1) a mortgage is insured under the National Housing Act, and (2) the owner's rate of return on his investment and the occupancy charges to tenants are limited by the National Housing Act.

11.128   An "approved disposition" is one made to tenants or occupants of the project, or to a nonprofit organization formed solely for their benefit, that is approved by the Secretary of Housing and Urban Development under the National Housing Act.

11.129   If the taxpayer so elects, gain on such an approved disposition will not be recognized if the net amount realized is reinvested in another qualified project within the reinvestment period. This is the period beginning one year before such disposition and ending one year after the close of the first taxable year in which any part of the gain is realized. The period may be extended if approved by the Treasury after application by the taxpayer. If the net amount realized exceeds the cost of the reinvestment project, then gain is recognized to the extent of such excess. The calculation of the gain that a taxpayer may elect not to recognize under these provisions is quite technical, and close adherence to the requirements of the code and regulations is very important.

11.130   If gain is not recognized by reason of these provisions, the taxpayer's basis in the replacement project is equal to its cost minus the gain not recognized.

Certain Repossessions of Real Property

11.131   Before Section 1038 was added to the Code, the repossession of real property by a secured creditor who had sold the property was ordinarily treated as a taxable transaction. Recognized gain or loss was measured by the difference between the fair market value of the repossessed property and the taxpayer's adjusted basis in the secured obligations. For taxable years beginning after September 2, 1964, Section 1038 provides a different treatment for all taxpayers other than domestic building and loan associations. Under that section, if a taxpayer sells real property, takes in payment secured obligations of the buyer, and subsequently repossesses the real property, no loss is recognized on the repossession. Furthermore, gain is recognized only to the extent that cash or other property the seller has received from the buyer exceeds the amount of gain on the original sale which the seller has included in gross income. This recognized gain is further limited to the amount of gain realized on the original sale reduced by any gain previously reported and further reduced by the taxpayer's repossession costs.

The basis of the repossessed property is equal to the sum of (1) the taxpayer's basis in the secured obligations, (2) the gain recognized on the repossession, and (3) the taxpayer's repossession costs [Section 1038(c)].

11.132

EXAMPLE

In 1968, Taxpayer sold a piece of real estate for $100,000. The adjusted basis of the real estate plus selling expenses was $70,000, leaving a profit of $30,000. Taxpayer received a down payment of $20,000 plus a $5\frac{1}{2}$ percent mortgage, payable $20,000 annually beginning in 1969. Taxpayer collected the mortgage payment due in 1969. In 1970 the buyer defaulted and Taxpayer foreclosed, incurring foreclosure costs of $2,000. Taxpayer reported gain on sale of the property of $6,000 in 1968 and $6,000 in 1969, using the installment method. Taxpayer's gain on foreclosure in 1970 was $16,000 computed as follows:

Total amount received before foreclosure		$40,000
Less gain previously reported		12,000
Tentative gain on foreclosure		$28,000
Limitation on recognized gain —		
Gain on original sale		$30,000
Less gain previously reported	$12,000	
Repossession costs	2,000	14,000
Gain to be recognized		$16,000
Gain recognized on repossession		$16,000

Basis of the repossessed real estate is $60,000 calculated as follows:

Basis of obligation prior to repossession | face value of $60,000 less gain to be reported on collection thereof (30%) of $18,000|	$42,000
Gain recognized on repossession	16,000
Costs of repossession	2,000
Basis of property repossessed	$60,000

The reasonableness of the above results can be understood if it is assumed that Taxpayer then sells the property for $60,000. No further gain would be recognized on such sale. The total amount realized by Taxpayer would be $100,000 ($20,000 in 1968; $20,000 in 1969; $60,000 on final sale). His total gain would be $28,000, representing the excess of the total amount realized over his original basis of $70,000 and his repossession costs of $2,000. The total gain reported by Taxpayer has also been $28,000, representing $12,000 reported on the installment basis and $16,000 reported on the repossession.

11.133   If any part of the secured obligations remain unsatisfied after the repossession, their basis becomes zero. If the taxpayer realizes any further collections from the original purchaser, all of such collections will be included in gross income.

11.134   If, prior to the repossession, taxpayer claimed any deductions for bad debts or worthlessness of the secured obligations, the repossession will be treated as a recovery of such charge-offs; accordingly, their amounts will be included in gross income to the extent they resulted in tax benefit to the taxpayer [Section 1038(d)].

11.135   If the repossessed property was a residence of the taxpayer and gain was not recognized on the original sale under Section 1034 because of a replacement with a new residence, or under Section 121 because of the taxpayer's age, no repossession gain will be recognized if the reacquired residence is resold within one year. The resale is then treated as part of the original sale of the residence on which gain or loss was not recognized [Section 1038(e)].

11.136   Section 1038 makes no provision concerning the character of the gain recognized on repossession of real property. Presumably, such gain will have the same character as the gain on the original sale of the property.

WHEN GAIN OR LOSS IS REPORTED

11.137   The amount of a gain or loss realized on the sale or exchange of property and the treatment of nontaxable exchanges are discussed earlier in this chapter. The inquiry at this point is the time for reporting that gain or loss. A gain or loss from the sale or exchange of property is not realized and should not be reported until the sale or exchange is a closed and completed transaction and thus deemed to be effective for federal income tax purposes. Once the transaction is so completed, the time for reporting the resulting gain or loss is determined by the accounting method used by the taxpayer [Section 451(a) and Reg. 1.451–1(a)].

When Sale Occurs

11.138   **Real Property.** A sale of real property is deemed completed and effective on the earliest of (1) the date of delivery of the deed or (2) the date upon which possession together with the benefits and burdens of ownership are transferred to the buyer.[44] Legal title may be re-

44. Rev. Rul. 69–93, IRB 1969–9 p. 40, superseding L.O. 988, 2 C.B. 84 (1920).

served by the seller or placed in escrow as security for the payment of the purchase price, but this will not preclude completion of a sale when the buyer has obtained possession and becomes the equitable owner.

In the sale of businesses or rental properties, the contract of sale frequently provides that the net income from the property from a specified date prior to the closing date (that is, the date upon which the deed is delivered) is to be treated as belonging to the purchaser. Such income is nevertheless taxable to the seller if possession and the incidents of ownership are not transferred to the purchaser prior to the closing date.[45]

11.139

A contract to sell real estate is an executory contract and does not in and of itself constitute a closed transaction giving rise to gain or loss. Until a seller has performed all of the conditions precedent set forth in the contract, the buyer has not become unconditionally liable to pay the purchase price. Conditions *subsequent* to the transfer of title or possession, such as the right of the buyer to reject title after he is in possession, the retention by the seller of an option to repurchase, or a collateral agreement to perform other services, will not necessarily prevent completion of sale.

11.140

Casual Sales of Personal Property. Sales of personal property are governed by the rules that are applicable to real property. Personal property can be either tangible or intangible. In practice, most sales of personal property occur when title passes. The local law of sales governs the determination of the date of sale.

11.141

In sales of shares of stock, sometimes it is provided in the contract of sale that dividends after a certain date are to be applied against the purchase price. If at the time of the payment of a dividend the purchaser is the beneficial owner of the stock, he and not the seller is taxable on the dividend.[46]

11.142

When Gain or Loss Is Realized

Casual Sales of Property. The time when a sale is completed and the time for reporting income or loss do not necessarily coincide. Under the cash method of accounting, gain is realized on that date when the aggregate of money and other property having a market value is actually or constructively received and such aggregate exceeds the adjusted basis. Under the accrual method, gain is realized when the taxpayer acquires an unqualified right to receive payment of a reasonably ascertainable amount in excess of adjusted basis. In both instances, conditions subsequent that may require adjustment of the price are disregarded. However, under either method of accounting a necessary condition precedent is that the sale or exchange must be a completed transaction as discussed in paragraph 11.138.

11.143

45. 2 Lexington Avenue Corp., 26 T.C. 816 (1956).
46. Fay Harvey Moore v. Com., 124 F.2d 991 (7th Cir. 1941), 28 AFTR 884, 41-2 USTC ¶9766, reversing, on the issue discussed in the text, 42 BTA 949.

11.144   A loss from the sale or exchange of property is deductible, whether the taxpayer is on the accrual or the cash basis, when (1) the sale is completed, (2) the buyer becomes unconditionally liable to pay the purchase price, and (3) the purchase price is readily determinable. Thus, a loss is deductible by an accrual basis taxpayer in accordance with the same rules used in determining when a gain is accruable, and a cash basis taxpayer may deduct a loss in accordance with rules applied to accrual basis taxpayers.

11.145   Payments for an option to buy property are not income in the hands of the recipient until the option lapses or is exercised. In *Hunter* v. *Com.*,[47] this was held to be true even where the payments received for the option exceeded the basis of the property that was the subject of the option. If the option is exercised, the payments represent proceeds from the sale of the property.[48] If the option is not exercised, the payments represent ordinary income rather than proceeds from the sale of property, in accordance with the provisions of Reg. 1.1234–1(b).

11.146   Even though a contract of sale provides that the buyer may require the seller to return a portion or all of the consideration upon the happening of some future event, the gain on the sale cannot be deferred until it is determined that such event will or will not occur. Rather, as soon as the contract is completed, the gain is reportable in accordance with the method of accounting used by the seller.[49] If the subsequent event results in a reduction of the sales price, a loss occurs at that time.[50]

11.147   If in form a sale occurs and title passes, but the agreement between the parties is that the sale is conditional upon the happening of a future event, no sale occurs unless and until that event happens. In *Alphonse L. Babin, Sr.*,[51] land was sold by the taxpayer to a subdivision developer. There was an oral agreement that if the developer could not resell the land, the deal would be canceled and the parties restored to their original position. When the developer became unable to resell the lots, the taxpayer refunded the consideration he had received, and the developer reconveyed the land. The Tax Court held that the original sale was never consummated and no gain or loss was recognized.

11.148   If the property sold is reacquired by the seller by means of repurchase or repossession because of the buyer's default in payment, the taxability of the original sale will generally not be affected. The tax consequences of certain repossessions of real property were discussed earlier in this chapter.

11.149   The entry of a court order in a condemnation proceeding vesting

---

47. 140 F.2d 954 (5th Cir. 1944), 44–1 USTC ¶9207, 32 AFTR 213 affirming ¶43,288 P–H Memo T.C.
48. Virginia Iron, Coal & Coke Co. v. Com., 99 F.2d 919 (4th Cir. 1938), 38–2 USTC ¶9572, 21 AFTR 1221 cert. den. 5–15–39.
49. Boston American League Baseball Club, 3 BTA 149 (1925).
50. W. M. Davey, 30 BTA 837 (1934); Jacob Carp, 31 B.T.A. 541 (1934).
51. ¶62,177 P–H Memo T.C. (1962), 21 TCM 979.

title and possession of property in a city or other public body constitutes a sale or exchange, but of itself does not give rise to gain or loss. There must be an award or a payment. The courts have held that gain to an accrual basis taxpayer arises when the litigation is settled, not at the time when the property is taken.[52] In *Koppers Co.*,[53] the Tax Court held that a condemnation award became income on the accrual basis in the year in which a decree was entered awarding damages, even though by the end of that year the time for appeal had not expired. Before the close of that year, however, the city had decided not to appeal. This is the opinion of only one court; in similar circumstances other courts might hold that gain does not result until the decision becomes final by expiration of the time for appeal (see chapter 15).

11.150   A cash basis taxpayer does not realize gain or loss until the amount of the proceeds of a condemnation award are made unconditionally available to him.[54] If the amount of a condemnation award is paid without restriction to the former owner of condemned property and such amount exceeds his adjusted basis, he realizes taxable gain at that point even though he litigates to recover a larger amount and ultimately prevails.[55] The treatment of a gain from a condemnation award as an involuntary conversion was discussed earlier in this chapter.

Sales of Goods. Acceptable accounting methods reflected on the books govern the time for reporting gain or loss on sales of inventory. Regulation 1.446–1(c)(1)(ii) provides in part as follows: 11.151

> … a taxpayer engaged in a manufacturing business may account for sales of his product when the goods are shipped, when the product is delivered or accepted, or when title to the goods passes to the customer, whether or not billed, depending upon the method regularly employed in keeping his books.

Escrows. If the purchase price under the contract of sale is placed in escrow, such consideration is deemed not to have been received by the seller until the conditions for which the escrow was created are satisfied, such as the buyer's approval of the title or performance by the seller of conditions set forth in the contract of sale. However, an escrow account may not be used to defer income artificially until a later year where the buyer is willing to pay the proceeds directly to the seller[56] or where the seller instructs the escrow agent to retain   11.152

52. Patrick McGuirl. Inc., 74 F.2d 729 (2nd Cir. 1935), 35–1 USTC ¶9055, 14 AFTR 910 cert. den. 5–6–35, affirming ¶35,023 P–H Memo BTA.

53. 3 T.C. 62 (1944), affirmed on other points 151 F.2d 267 (3rd Cir. 1945), 45–2 USTC ¶9398, 34 AFTR 151.

54. Nitterhouse v. U.S. 207 F.2d 618 (3rd Cir. 1953), 44 AFTR 527, 53–2 USTC ¶9573, cert. den. 4–12–54, affirming 111 F. Supp. 339 (D.C. Penn.), 53–1 USTC ¶9254, 43 AFTR 794.

55. Estate of Jacob Nesler, 17 T.C. 1085 (1951).

56. Williams v. U.S., 219 F.2d 523 (5th Cir. 1955), 55–1 USTC ¶9220, 46 AFTR 1725, affirming District Court for Southern District of Mississippi.

the purchase price until a year after the year in which the conditions for which the escrow was created are satisfied.[57]

11.153   In *Solomon Silberblatt*,[58] the Board of Tax Appeals held that where stock certificates were placed in escrow under a contract for their sale and could be reclaimed by the seller if any one of the installment payments was not made when due, title to the stock certificates did not pass to the buyer until completion of the escrow conditions; namely, payment of all of the installments agreed upon. The sale was not completed until the last installment was paid, and the loss occurred then. One year later, in the similar case of *Jacob Carp*,[59] because the escrow agreement did not provide for recall of the certificates in the event of default, the board held that title passed to the purchaser when they were placed in escrow and that, accordingly, gain was realized at that time.

Stock Exchange Transactions

11.154   In general, stock exchange transactions are governed by the above rules pertaining to the time when sale occurs in casual sales of property and when gain or loss is realized. Primarily because of the methods of settlement of transactions made through stock exchanges, such transactions deserve special comment.

11.155   When a sale of securities is made through a stock exchange, delivery of the property by the seller and payment by the buyer do not take place until a specified number of days after the sale is made. Settlement for sales made through the New York Stock Exchange does not take place until the fifth business day after the sale is made. Gain or loss on sales made through a stock exchange are realized by accrual and cash basis taxpayers as follows:

Gain:
Accrual basis — sale date
Cash basis — settlement date

Loss:[60]
Accrual basis — sale date
Cash basis — sale date

Thus, it is possible for a cash-basis taxpayer to make a sale close to the end of one year and not to be taxed on the gain until the following year.

11.156   **Puts and Calls.** A "put" is an option to sell designated property at a stipulated price within an agreed period of time. A "call" is an option to buy designated property at a stipulated price within an agreed period of time. As puts and calls are options, the general rules contained in Section 1234 of reporting income from options apply. The headnote of Rev. Rul. 58–234[61] reads:

57. William Holden, 6 BTA 605 (1927).
58. 28 BTA 73 (1933).
59. 31 BTA 541 (1934).
60. G.C.M. 21503, 1939–2 C.B. 205.
61. 1958–1 C.B. 279 modifying I.T. 3835, I.T. 2266, and O.D. 1028.

The amount (premium) received by the writer (issuer or optionor) for granting a "put" or "call" option, which is not exercised, constitutes ordinary income, for Federal income tax purposes, under Section 61 of the Internal Revenue Code of 1954, to be included in his gross income only for the taxable year in which the failure to exercise the option becomes final.

Where a "put" option is exercised, the amount (premium) received by the writer (issuer or optionor) for granting it constitutes an offset against the option price, which he paid for the securities involved upon its exercise, in determining the (net) cost basis to him of the securities that he purchased pursuant thereto, for subsequent gain or loss purposes.

Where a "call" option is exercised, the amount (premium) received by the writer (issuer or optionor) for granting it is includible by him, with the option price which he received for the securities involved upon its exercise, in the (total) amount realized by him for the securities that he sold pursuant thereto, for the purpose of determining his gain or loss on their sale. For such purpose, if the amount (premium) received for granting a "call" option is, under its terms, applicable, upon its exercise, on, to, or against the option price specified therein, such price thus adjusted (reduced) is considered the real option price.

On the sale by the option holder (optionee) of the stock involved in a "put" option, upon its exercise, the cost (premium) of the option to him should be offset against the option price, thereupon received or accrued, in computing the (net) amount realized by him for the stock that he sold pursuant thereto, for the purpose of determining his gain or loss on its sale.

The above holdings do not apply to amounts (sales proceeds) received by an option dealer from sales of "put" and "call" options which were written (issued or granted) by others and held by him for sale to his customers in the ordinary course of his business as such dealer, nor to amounts (commissions or fees) received by an option broker for selling "put" and "call" options for his principals as such broker.

QUESTIONS AND PROBLEMS

1. Give the general rule for determining if losses are deductible for tax purposes by individuals.
2. A subdivider buys a rectangular five-acre tract of vacant land for $10,000, puts in streets, sidewalks, and sewers surrounding the tract at a cost of another $10,000, and then subdivides the tract into ten lots of equal frontage and depth. Is the basis of each lot $2,000? Give reasons for your answer.
3. Give the formula for determining each of the following items for tax purposes.
   (a) Gain on the sale or exchange of property.
   (b) Loss on the sale or exchange of property.
4. Explain the concepts of the following terms used for tax purposes: (a) *basis, adjusted basis,* and *substituted basis;* (b) *realized* gains and losses and *recognized* gains and losses.
5. Explain the effect of a mortgage on (a) the amount realized from sale of property and (b) the cost of the property purchased. Does it make any difference in either case whether or not the mortgage is assumed by the buyer?
6. Taxpayer A sells a tract of undeveloped land to B on June 30, 1972. A's adjusted basis in the land is $50,000, and his sale commission and

other selling expenses are $3,500. The land is subject to a mortgage that had an unpaid balance at date of sale of $30,000. A receives $20,000 in cash and takes a negotiable promissory note from B for $25,000 payable on or before July 1, 1974. B's note bears interest at 6 percent and is secured by a vendor's lien and deed of trust on the land, both of which are subordinate to the mortgage. B has an excellent credit rating and A's credit risk on B's note is minimal. Real estate taxes on the property for the year April 1, 1972 through March 31, 1973 are $1,200. B agrees to, and does, bear and pay all current year taxes when they become due on October 1, 1972. B refuses to assume the mortgage but agrees to take the property subject to such mortgage. During 1972 he pays $5,000 on such mortgage. (a) What is A's gain on sale of his land? (b) What is B's basis in the land?

7. On September 15, 1972, Taxpayer A purchased twenty-five shares of XYZ Corporation's common stock for $100 per share or $2,500. On February 2, A bought another twenty-five shares of XYZ Corporation common stock at $110 per share or $2,750. On March 4, 1973, A sold forty shares of XYZ Corporation common for $85 per share or $3,400. All of this stock was held for A by his broker. Because of his preoccupation over the market decline, A did not think to tell the broker which stock to sell. How much gain or loss is recognized to A on sale of his XYZ Corporation stock?

8. On December 31, 1972, Taxpayer A sold a small office building for $25,000 cash. He acquired this building on September 30, 1967, from his father as a gift. His father's adjusted basis in the building at the date of gift was $15,000. Fair market value of the property at date of gift was $17,500. A's father paid $4,000 gift tax on the gift. Depreciation of $500 per annum was allowable with respect to the property after its acquisition by A. He claimed this amount in the years 1969 through 1972. A did not claim any depreciation in 1967 because he was in a substantial loss position for tax purposes, but in 1968 he claimed $625. His return for 1968 was never examined; therefore, A received full tax benefit for the depreciation claimed in 1968. A's selling expenses were $2,000 and all real property taxes were allocated between the parties on a monthly basis. What was A's gain on sale of his property in 1972?

9. Give the formula for determining each of the following items for tax purposes.

   (a) Basis of property received on an exchange of property held for investment or for use in a trade or business for other property of like kind to be so held. Make the formula broad enough to reflect the possibility of boot received and gain or loss recognized in part.

   (b) Basis of property purchased as replacement for property involuntarily converted where gain is either not recognized or recognized only in part under Section 1033(a)(3).

10. On July 1, 1971, the XYZ Corporation bought a new truck for $8,000. Depreciation allowed and allowable on the truck during 1971 and 1972 was $3,500. On January 1, 1973, the corporation acquired a new truck that had a list price of $11,000. The XYZ Corporation traded in its old truck and received a trade-in allowance of $6,000. In addition to the trade-in allowance, XYZ paid $5,000 in cash for the new truck.

    (a) How much gain is recognized on the disposition of the old truck?
    (b) What is the basis of the new truck?

11. In 1965, Taxpayer A constructed an apartment house at a total cost of $350,000 for land, buildings, and furnishings. Depreciation allowed and allowable prior to June 30, 1972, was $50,000. On June 30, 1972, A exchanged this apartment house and $50,000 for a tract of unimproved ranch land that he hoped to lease out as grazing land. At the date of exchange, A's apartment building had a mortgage outstanding against it of $200,000 and a fair market value of $275,000. Fair market value of the unimproved land acquired was $125,000, and it had no mortgage debt. (a) How much gain or loss is recognized on this exchange? (b) What is A's basis in the land acquired?

12. Assume the same facts as in problem 11, but change the fair market value of the apartment house to $500,000 and the ranch land to $350,000. Assume further that the transferee of the apartment house accepts it subject to the mortgage but does not assume the mortgage. (a) How much gain or loss was recognized to A? (b) What is A's basis in his land received?

13. A taxpayer owned a golf course having an adjusted basis of $200,000. In order to acquire land for a highway, the state instituted condemnation proceedings against a strip of land 100 yards wide, running through the sixteenth fairway. The court awarded $50,000 as a condemnation award for the strip and $20,000 severance damages. There was no vacant land adjacent to the remaining golf course acreage. Six months later, the taxpayer sold the remaining tract of land for $150,000 and purchased another tract that he developed into a golf course for a total outlay of $250,000. (a) What amount of gain or loss was realized on the condemnation, and (b) what is the basis of the new golf course? Explain your answer.

14. The taxpayer upon reaching age sixty-five retired and sold the home he had lived in for the past twenty years. The sales price was $44,000, and he paid the real estate broker a commission of $2,600 and an attorney $400. Within sixty days prior to selling the house he had the outside painted at a cost of $1,000 and paid that bill a week after selling the house. His adjusted basis for the house was $30,000. Two months after the sale he bought a smaller home for $29,500. (a) What amount of gain was realized on the sale? (b) What amount is recognized? (c) What is the basis of the new home? Assume the taxpayer wants to pay the minimum tax possible.

15. Explain the philosophy behind the provision that gains and losses on some exchanges of property are not recognized for tax purposes.

16. On June 20, 1970, Smith entered into a contract with Jones whereby Smith agreed to rent his personal residence to Jones on a month-to-month basis for $150 a month effective July 1, 1970, and Jones was to take possession of the property on July 1, 1970. The contract further provided that Jones, if he so desired, could purchase the residence at any time for $30,000 less two-thirds of any rent paid to the date of purchase. On February 1, 1972, Jones exercised his option to purchase the property and paid $28,100 to Smith. Because of unforeseen title difficulties, Smith did not transfer title to Jones until January 3, 1973. For Smith, when did a sale occur for income tax purposes? In answering this problem, assume that the Internal Revenue Service would not contend that the contract was a conditional sales contract.

17. Assume the same facts as in Problem 16 except that the contract dated June 20, 1970, stated Smith would sell and Jones would buy the property on February 1, 1972, for $30,000 less any rent paid to date of purchase. Would this change your answer to Problem 16?

18. On December 1, 1971, Able, a cash-basis and calendar-year taxpayer, advertised his personal 1929 automobile for sale at a price of $1,000. On the same day, Baker paid $400 to Able with the understanding that Baker would have the right to purchase the automobile at any time before February 1, 1972, for an additional consideration of $600. Able and Baker further had an understanding that if Baker did not purchase the automobile by February 1, 1972, Able was to return $300 to Baker. Baker did not purchase the automobile by February 1, 1972. On February 2, 1972, Baker told Able to keep the $300 and paid an additional $100 to Able with the understanding that if Baker did not purchase the automobile by February 1, 1973, for an additional consideration of $500, Able was to return $300 to Baker. On January 10, 1973, Baker paid $500 to Able and took possession of the automobile.

    (a) When did the sale take place?

    (b) Assume the basis of the automobile to Able was $950, what amount of income or loss should be reported by Able for each of the years 1971, 1972, and 1973?

19. Arthur, a cash-basis and calendar-year taxpayer, sold 1,000 shares of capital stock of a corporation to Bates on July 1, 1972, for a consideration of $100,000. The basis of the stock to Arthur was $40,000. Before Bates could pay the $100,000 to Arthur, Collins obtained a court order directing Bates to place $50,000 of the purchase price in escrow because of a possible claim Collins had against Arthur. Bates, on July 31, 1972, placed $50,000 in escrow and paid $50,000 to Arthur. The stock was transferred to Bates on July 31, 1972. On January 31, 1973, a court order directed that $30,000 of the amount in escrow be paid to Collins in settlement of his claim against Arthur. The $30,000 was paid to Collins on February 1, 1973, and the remaining $20,000 in the escrow account was paid to Arthur on February 1, 1973. How much income from the sale of the stock should be reported by Arthur in each of the years 1972 and 1973?

12

CAPITAL GAINS
AND LOSSES

INTRODUCTION . . . 449
DEFINITION OF CAPITAL ASSET . . . 449

    Bulk Sales . . . 450
    Stock in Trade . . . 450
    Goodwill . . . 453
    Covenant Not to Compete . . . 453
    Assignment of Anticipated Ordinary Income . . . 454
    Commodity Futures and Hedging . . . 455

**DEFINITIONS OF SHORT- AND LONG-TERM CAPITAL GAINS
   AND LOSSES . . . 458**
TREATMENT OF NET CAPITAL GAINS . . . 458

    Individuals . . . 459
    Corporations . . . 460
    Example of Alternative Tax . . . 462

TREATMENT OF CAPITAL LOSSES . . . 464

    Individuals . . . 464
    Corporations . . . 469

**MINIMUM TAX ON TAX PREFERENCES AND EXCESS INVEST-
   MENT INTEREST . . . 470**

    Minimum Tax . . . 470
    Excess Investment Interest . . . 470

HOLDING PERIOD . . . 471
SALE OR EXCHANGE . . . 473

    Patents . . . 476

        GENERAL RULES . . . 477
        SPECIAL RULES OF SECTION 1235 . . . 478

Transfers of Franchises, Trademarks, and Trade Names . . . 479

Dispositions Treated as Sales or Exchanges . . . 480

RETIREMENT OF BONDS . . . 481
FAILURE TO EXERCISE OPTION . . . 482
CANCELLATIONS OF LEASES AND DISTRIBUTOR AGREEMENTS . . . 483

SHORT SALES OF STOCK . . . 483
WASH SALES . . . 484
SALES OF PROPERTY USED IN A TRADE OR BUSINESS . . . 485

Section 1231 . . . 485
Types of Gains and Losses Taken into Account . . . 485

RECAPTURE OF DEPRECIATION AND OF OTHER DEDUC-
TIONS . . . 487

Section 1245 Recapture of Depreciation on Properties Other Than
Buildings . . . 488

SECTION 1245 PROPERTY . . . 489
EXCEPTIONS TO SECTION 1245 RECAPTURE . . . 490
RECOMPUTED BASIS . . . 492

Section 1250 Recapture of Depreciation on Buildings and Certain
Other Real Property . . . 492

ADDITIONAL DEPRECIATION . . . 493
APPLICABLE PERCENTAGE . . . 494

FOR ADDITIONAL DEPRECIATION ALLOWED BEFORE 1970 . . . 494
FOR ADDITIONAL DEPRECIATION ALLOWED AFTER 1969 . . . 494

ILLUSTRATION . . . 495
MAJOR IMPROVEMENTS . . . 495
EXCEPTIONS TO SECTION 1250 RECAPTURE . . . 496

Section 1251 Recapture of Farm Losses . . . 496

FARM RECAPTURE PROPERTY . . . 497
THE EXCESS-DEDUCTIONS ACCOUNT . . . 497
EXCEPTIONS TO RECAPTURE . . . 498
POSSIBLE CONFLICT WITH SECTION 1245 . . . 499

Section 1252—Recapture of Soil- and Water-Conservation
Expenditures and Land-Clearing Expenses . . . 499

GAIN FROM SALE OF DEPRECIABLE PROPERTY BETWEEN
RELATED TAXPAYERS . . . 500

INTRODUCTION

Gains and losses from sales or other dispositions of property fall $\quad$ 12.1
into two classes: (1) capital gains and losses, and (2) ordinary gains and
losses. In the first case there must be a *sale or exchange,* and in both
cases the gain or loss must not only be realized but also recognized.
Nontaxable exchanges, although they may result in *realized* gain or
loss, do not give rise to any *recognized* gain or loss (unless boot is
received).

Ordinary gains generally are included in income in full. Ordinary $\quad$ 12.2
losses, provided they are incurred in a trade or business or in other
transactions entered into for profit, generally are deductible in full.
Capital gains and losses receive special treatment for tax purposes.
This special treatment is favorable with respect to long-term gains
(generally involving lower than usual tax rates) but unfavorable with
respect to both short-term and long-term capital losses.

The treatment of capital gains and losses was briefly discussed in $\quad$ 12.3
paragraphs 2.5 to 2.7 and again in paragraphs 3.21 to 3.23. At this
point, read that material again.

For purposes of the capital-gain and -loss provisions, all property is $\quad$ 12.4
divided into three classes: capital assets, Section 1231 assets, and
ordinary assets. Very roughly, capital assets consist of investment
property and nonbusiness property; Section 1231 property consists
of business real property and business depreciable property held
for more than six months; and ordinary assets consist of inventories,
stock in trade, and other noninvestment assets. A net gain on the
sale or exchange of Section 1231 property is treated as a long-term
capital gain except to the extent of ordinary income resulting from
recapture of depreciation and other deductions subject to recapture.
A net loss on the sale or exchange of Section 1231 property is an
ordinary loss.

The first part of this chapter will discuss the definition of a capital $\quad$ 12.5
asset, the special tax treatment accorded capital gains and losses, and
the various elements entering into the determination of capital gains
and losses. The latter part of the chapter is devoted to Section 1231
assets and to recapture of depreciation and other prior deductions
upon a sale or exchange. The tax rates cited in this chapter are those
applicable after the Tax Reform Act of 1969 was enacted, exclusive
of the surtax then scheduled to expire on June 30, 1970.

DEFINITION OF CAPITAL ASSET

The term "capital asset" is defined in Section 1221 as all property $\quad$ 12.6
except the following:

1. Stock in trade, inventory, and other property held primarily for sale
   to customers in the ordinary course of business.

2. Depreciable property used in a trade or business and real property used in a trade or business.
3. Accounts and notes receivable acquired in the ordinary course of a trade or business for services rendered or from the sale of stock in trade, inventory, or other property held for sale to customers.
4. A copyright, a literary, musical, or artistic composition held by a person whose personal efforts created it or held by a taxpayer whose basis is determined by reference to such person's basis.
5. A letter or memorandum or similar property held by a person for whom such property was prepared or produced or held by a taxpayer whose basis is determined by reference to such person's basis.
6. Obligations of the federal or a state government or one of their political subdivisions that are issued on a discount basis and payable without interest at a fixed maturity date not exceeding one year from the date of issue.

12.7   Real property and depreciable property used in a trade or business are not capital assets; however, Section 1231 provides that under certain circumstances a net gain on their sale or exchange may be treated as a capital gain (see paragraph 12.109 et seq.).

12.8   The principal capital assets are investment property, such as stocks, bonds, and real estate not used in a trade or business, and other non-business property. Since the favorable tax treatment accorded capital gains is an exception to normal income tax treatment, the definition of capital assets is narrowly applied and its exclusions are broadly interpreted.[1]

Bulk Sales

12.9   In *Williams* v. *McGowan*[2] the Second Circuit Court of Appeals held that, upon a bulk sale of a going business, each type of asset sold must be examined to determine whether or not it is a capital asset. The business as a whole cannot be treated as a single asset or entity. Similarly, the Ninth Circuit Court of Appeals in *Grace Bros., Inc.* v. *Com.*[3] held that the bulk sale of inventory to one company did not change its character of stock in trade and convert it into a capital asset.

Stock in Trade

12.10   As provided in Section 1221(1), property held primarily for sale to customers in the ordinary course of trade or business is not a capital asset. Even if the stock in trade is customarily sold to a restricted num-

---

1. Paul K. Ashby, 37 T.C. 92; Corn Products Refining Co. v. Com., 350 U.S. 46, 52, 55–2 USTC ¶9746, 47 AFTR 1789.
2. 152 F.2d 570 (2nd Cir. 1945), 46–1 USTC ¶9120, 34 AFTR 615.
3. 173 F.2d 170 (9th Cir. 1949), 49–1 USTC ¶9181, 37 AFTR 1006, affirming 10 T.C. 158.

ber of customers[4] or only to a single vendee,[5] it is still stock in trade and not a capital asset. It has been held however by the Tax Court and the Sixth Circuit Court of Appeals, in *Acro Mfg. Co. v. Com.,*[6] that, in order to be an ordinary asset, an inventory must not only be owned by the taxpayer, but must also be used in carrying on *its* trade or business. Further, under the plain requirements of Section 1221, accounts receivable are capital assets unless acquired by the taxpayer in carrying on *its* business; and real estate and depreciable property are capital assets unless used by the taxpayer in *its* trade or business.

Acro Mfg. Co.

39 T.C. 377 (1962)

[Facts: The principal business of the taxpayer was the manufacture and sale of precision switches and thermostatic controls. On December 9, 1954, in a nontaxable reorganization under Section 368(a)(1)(B), it acquired all of the outstanding capital stock of Universal Button Company solely in exchange for 55,000 shares of its own voting common stock. Button was engaged in the business of manufacturing metal buttons for work clothes. In May 1955 the taxpayer entered into an agreement with Talon, Incorporated, under which the taxpayer agreed first to cause a complete liquidation to be made of Button, and immediately thereafter to sell to Talon all of its net assets. The complete liquidation occurred on June 30, 1955, and later on that same date all of the assets were sold to Talon. The property sold consisted of accounts receivable, inventories, land, buildings, and other fixed and depreciable assets. The basis of the distributed property in the hands of the taxpayer was the same as it was in the hands of Button pursuant to Section 334(b)(1). In its return the taxpayer claimed an ordinary loss on the sale of these assets. The Commissioner contended that the loss was a capital loss. An extract from the court's opinion follows.]

Respondent [the Commissioner] argues that the term "capital asset" includes all classes of property not specifically excluded by section 1221, citing Regulations 1.1221–1(a). He admits that the assets in question were accounts receivable, inventories, real estate, and depreciable property used or acquired by Button in carrying on its business and were, therefore, not capital assets in Button's hands. However, respondent contends that in order to qualify as other than capital assets *in the hands of petitioner,* these assets must be: (1) Accounts receivable, acquired by petitioner in carrying on its business; (2) inventories of petitioner used in carrying on its business; and (3) real estate and depreciable property used by petitioner in its business. It is the respondent's position that the assets in question, in addition to falling within particular categories of property enumerated, must have been acquired or used by petitioner in carrying on its business in order to fall within the exceptions provided by section 1221, and since this element of acquisition or use in connection with a business of the petitioner is completely lacking in the instant case, the assets in question, in the hands of petitioner, are capital assets.

4. Patterson v. Belcher *et al.*, 302 F.2d 289 (5th Cir. 1962), 62–1 USTC ¶9426, 9 AFTR2d 1316.

5. Jantzer v. Com., 284 F.2d 348 (9th Cir. 1960), 60–2 USTC ¶9802, 6 AFTR2d 5882.

6. 39 T.C. 377, affirmed 334 F.2d 40 (6th Cir. 1964), 14 AFTR2d 5106.

We agree with respondent. It is the petitioner who is before us. Regardless of what nature the assets in question had in the hands of its predecessor in title, our concern is with their tax nature in petitioner's hands. Were the assets acquired or used in connection with a business of petitioner? The principal business activity of petitioner was the manufacture and sale of precision switches and thermostatic controls. No evidence has been introduced showing that petitioner was in, or ever intended entering, the button business. Petitioner has argued that it in fact owned, operated, and used in its business the assets for a short time on June 30, 1955, between the time when those assets were distributed to it upon the liquidation of Button and the time when the transaction with Talon was closed. We find that ownership for such a minimal, transitory period is insufficient to establish "use" of the distributed assets in petitioner's business or to place petitioner in the button business.

Petitioner has also argued that where one of the essential purposes of acquiring property is to sell it, the property does not qualify as a capital asset ... Section 1221, of course, provides that the term "capital asset" does not include property held by the taxpayer primarily for sale to customers in the ordinary course of his trade or business. The critical language here is—*in the ordinary course of the taxpayer's trade or business.* In ascertaining whether the assets acquired for sale were so acquired in the ordinary course of the taxpayer's trade or business, "the test normally applied ... is the frequency and continuity of the transactions claimed to result in a trade or business," ... . We find no evidence in the instant case showing petitioner to have been in the business of selling assets such as those involved herein, much less that such assets were sold with any degree of "frequency and continuity." ...

. . .

It is our opinion that petitioner neither acquired nor used the Button assets in *its* business, neither did petitioner enter into the button business. Petitioner held the assets in question as capital assets. The sale of such assets resulted in a capital loss to petitioner.

12.11 Section 1221(1) denies capital gain treatment to profits reaped from the sale of "property held by the taxpayer *primarily* for sale to customers in the ordinary course of his trade or business." (Emphasis supplied.) In 1966 the United States Supreme Court in *Malat et ux.* v. *Riddell*[7] held that the word *primarily* as used in this section means "of first importance" or "principally"; it does not mean a "substantial" purpose. In that case several individuals who were in the real estate business organized a joint venture and acquired 44.901 acres of raw land. The inner portion consisting of 24.646 acres was subdivided into 105 lots. Gain on the sale of such lots was reported by them as ordinary income. The remaining 20.255 acres were sold in two parcels to two separate buyers and the gain on these two sales was reported as long-term capital gain. In its original opinion the United States District Court for the Southern District of California held[8] that the two parcels were held primarily for sale to customers in the ordinary course of trade or business. It reached this conclusion because it found that the taxpayers in acquiring the entire 44.901

7. 383 U.S. 569 (1966), 66–1 USTC ¶9317, 17 AFTR2d 604.
8. 64–1 USTC ¶9432, 13 AFTR2d 1348.

acres had an alternative purpose. First, if they could obtain acceptable construction financing or rezoning from multiple residential to commercial, they would develop it for rental; or second, if either or both failed to develop, they would sell the property in bulk. Neither rezoning nor acceptable financing could be obtained for the 20.255 acres sold in bulk, but on the original hearing the District Court evidently felt that this outer portion was held primarily for sale because the inner portion had been subdivided. Upon remand by the United States Supreme Court the District Court held[9] that the 20.255 acres were not held primarily for sale to customers in the ordinary course of their trade or business.

Goodwill

Goodwill is a capital asset, and a gain realized on its sale is a capital gain. The purchaser cannot amortize goodwill, however, because the Service and the courts have taken the position that its life is indefinite and not measurable. Goodwill is well defined in the following extract from the opinion of the Ninth Circuit Court of Appeals in *Grace Bros., Inc.* v. *Com.:* [10]

12.12

What is goodwill?
It is the sum total of those imponderable qualities which attract the customer of a business—what brings patronage to the business. Mr. Justice Cardozo, in a famous case, has called it "a reasonable expectance of preference ... (which) may come from succession in place or name or otherwise to a business that has won the favor of its customers." ...
The Supreme Court has held it to mean every positive advantage that has been acquired by the old firm in the progress of its business, whether connected with the premises in which the business was previously carried on, or with the name of the late firm, or with any other matter carrying with it the benefit of the business. ...
So, the goodwill may attach to (1) the business as an entity, (2) the physical plant in which it is conducted, (3) the trade-name under which it is carried on and the right to conduct it at the particular place or within a particular area, under a trade name or trademark; (4) the special knowledge or the "know-how" of its staff; (5) the number and quality of its customers. (5 Paul and Mertens, Law of Federal Income Taxation, 1934, Section 52.34, n. 96; Paul, Federal Estate and Gift Taxation, 1942, Sections 18.04, 18.16.). ...

Covenant Not to Compete

If the seller of a going business agrees not to compete with the purchaser for a term of years, such agreement is called a covenant not to compete. It is not a capital asset, but merely an agreement to refrain from doing something in the future. Accordingly, amounts received for a covenant not to compete are ordinary income to the seller and deductible by the payor. If the parties do not treat the covenant as

12.13

9. 66–2 USTC ¶9564, 18 AFTR2d 5015.
10. *Supra* fn. 3.

a separate and distinct item, and where the primary function of the covenant is to assure the purchaser the beneficial enjoyment of the goodwill, the covenant is regarded as nonseverable and ancillary to the goodwill. In such an instance, no part of the consideration received will be allocable to the covenant not to compete, so that the full amount received will constitute capital gain.[11]

Assignments of Anticipated Ordinary Income

12.14   Even though a property interest may not fall within one of the five categories of exclusions from capital assets, if in substance its sale constitutes an *assignment of anticipated ordinary income*, the courts will treat the sale as resulting in ordinary income. The basis for this treatment was discussed by the United States Supreme Court in *Com. v. P. G. Lake, Inc., et al.*[12] This case involved sales of mineral production payments which under present law (Section 636) are treated as mortgage loans; nevertheless the Court's discussion of their treatment under the law as it then existed provides an excellent commentary on the principles which still apply to capital gains and to assignments of anticipated income.

12.15   The *Lake* case involved sales of (1) a carved-out oil payment of $600,000, payable out of 25 percent of the oil attributable to the taxpayer's working interests in two leases, (2) oil payments carved out of the taxpayer's royalty interests, and (3) a $50,000 sulphur payment carved out of an overriding royalty held by the taxpayer in a sulphur deposit. Sales of carved-out mineral production payments are sales of rights to receive a certain share of production from a mineral property retained by the seller, or the right to receive the proceeds from sale of that share of production until a certain amount of mineral or a certain sum of money has been received. The United States Supreme Court held that even though the oil payments constituted interests in land, and the transfers constituted sales, the gain still should be treated as ordinary income for tax purposes. The reasoning of the Court is set forth in the following excerpts from its opinion:

(1) First, as to whether the proceeds were taxable as long term taxable gains under § 117 [now Sections 1201, 1221, and 1222] or as ordinary income subject to depletion. The Court of Appeals started from the premise, laid down in Texas decisions, ... that oil payments are interests in land. We too proceed on that basis; and yet we conclude that the consideration received for these oil payment rights (and the sulphur payment right) was taxable as ordinary income, subject to depletion.

The purpose of § 117 [now Sections 1201, 1221, and 1222] was "to relieve the taxpayer from ... excessive tax burdens on gains resulting from a conversion of capital investments, and to remove the deterrent effect of those

11. Lee Ruwitch, 22 T.C. 1053; Aaron Michaels, 12 T.C. 17; Toledo Newspaper Co., 2 T.C. 794; Rodney B. Horton, 13 T.C. 143.
12. 356 U.S. 260 (1958), 58–1 USTC ¶9428, 1 AFTR2d 1394.

burdens on such conversions." ... And this exception has always been narrowly construed so as to protect the revenue against artful devices ...

We do not see here any conversion of a capital investment. The lump sum consideration seems essentially a substitute for what would otherwise be received at a future time as ordinary income. The pay-out of these particular assigned oil payment rights could be ascertained with considerable accuracy. ...

... The substance of what was assigned was the right to receive future income. The substance of what was received was the present value of income which the recipient would otherwise obtain in the future. In short, consideration was paid for the right to receive future income, not for an increase in the value of the income-producing property.

... We have held that if one, entitled to receive at a future date interest on a bond or compensation for services, makes a grant of it by anticipatory assignment, he realizes taxable income as if he had collected the interest or received the salary and then paid it over. That is the teaching of *Helvering* v. *Horst*, 311 U.S. 112 [24 AFTR 1058], ... and it is applicable here. As we stated in *Helvering* v. *Horst*, sup., 117, "The taxpayer has equally enjoyed the fruits of his labor or investment and obtained the satisfaction of his desires whether he collects and uses the income to procure those satisfactions, or whether he disposes of his right to collect it as the means of procuring them." There the taxpayer detached interest coupons from negotiable bonds and presented them as a gift to his son. The interest when paid was held taxable to the father. Here, even more clearly than there, the taxpayer is converting future income into present income.

The *Lake* decision emphasizes the distinction between a "conversion of a capital investment" and the assignment of the "right to receive future income." The *Lake* case also emphasizes that the basic purpose of the capital-gain treatment is to relieve a taxpayer from an excessive tax burden on a gain resulting from a conversion of capital investment. Such a gain normally is the result of property's appreciation in value over a considerable period of time, and taxing such a gain at ordinary rates would work an obvious hardship on a taxpayer. By its conclusion in the *Lake* decision, the Supreme Court demonstrated that the capital gain provisions are to be narrowly construed.

12.16

Commodity Futures and Hedging

Staple commodities are traded on the various commodity exchanges, such as the Chicago Board of Trade, the Chicago Mercantile Exchange, the New York Mercantile Exchange, and the New York Produce Exchange. The principal commodities are wheat, soybeans, corn, coffee, sugar, tobacco, butter, and eggs. There are two types of trading: cash and futures. In cash trades, the commodity itself is actually purchased either for immediate or later actual delivery. If the delivery is to be immediate, it is called a spot deal, although many dealers use the terms *cash* and *spot* interchangeably.[13] In a futures

12.17

13. C. F. Phillips and D. J. Duncan, *Marketing Principles and Methods,* 5th ed. (Homewood, Ill.: Richard D. Irwin, Inc., 1964), p. 480.

transaction, a contract for future delivery in a designated month of a specified quantity of a commodity is bought or sold. The holder of a futures contract in the month specified for delivery can insist upon such delivery, but in practice this seldom occurs. Instead, prior to the stipulated month, the holder of a contract calling for delivery of a commodity will enter into another contract selling an equivalent amount. Then through the clearinghouse of the exchange, one contract will be set off against the other and a money adjustment will be made.

12.18   In *Com. v. George W. Covington et al.,*[14] the following statement appears in the separate concurring opinion of one of the judges of the Fifth Circuit Court of Appeals:

> Transactions in commodity futures are commonly spoken of as purchases and sales of a specific commodity such as corn, wheat, or cotton, but the traders really acquire rights to the specific commodity rather than the commodity itself. These rights are intangible property which may appreciate or depreciate in value. They are capital assets held by the taxpayer (whether or not connected with his trade or business), but, unless they are hedges (which are in a class by themselves), they cannot be regarded as stock in trade or other property of a kind which would properly be included in the inventories of the taxpayer if on hand at the close of the taxable year. Neither are they property held by the taxpayer primarily for sale to customers in the ordinary course of his trade or business.

This same case also held that setting off one contract against another has the legal effect of making or taking delivery; accordingly, a setoff results in a sale or exchange.

12.19   In *Fulton Bag & Cotton Mills*[15] the Tax Court said: "The term 'hedge' is elusive and incapable of being defined with exactness and precision. ..." The Sixth Circuit Court of Appeals in 1941 gave the following broad definition:[16]

> A hedge is a form of price insurance; it is resorted to by business men to avoid the risk of changes in the market price of a commodity. The basic principle of hedging is the maintenance of an even or balanced position. ...

In 1955 the United States Supreme Court in *Corn Products Refining Co. v. Com.*[17] broadened the definition of hedging and held that dealing in futures as a part of a manufacturing activity is a hedging operation.

14. 120 F.2d 768 (5th Cir. 1941), 41–2 USTC ¶9522, 27 AFTR 502, affirming 42 BTA 601.
15. 22 T.C. 1044 (1954).
16. Com. v. Farmers & Ginners Cotton Oil Co., 120 F.2d 772 (6th Cir. 1941), 41–2 USTC ¶9523, 27 AFTR 506, reversing 41 BTA 1083, cert. den.
17. 350 U.S. 46 (1955), 55–2 USTC ¶9746, 47 AFTR 1789.

Corn Products Refining Company v. Com.

Supreme Court of the United States, 1955

[Facts: The taxpayer is a manufacturer of products made from grain corn. Most of its products in the years at issue, 1940 and 1942, were sold under contracts requiring shipment in thirty days at a set price or at market price on the date of delivery, whichever was lower. The storage facilities of the company could hold only a three-week supply of corn. To avoid being adversely affected by increases in the price of spot corn and to make sure of having an adequate supply of raw corn, it began in 1937 to establish a long position in corn futures. At harvest time each year it would buy futures when the price appeared favorable. It would take delivery on such contracts as it found necessary to its manufacturing operations and sell the remainder in early summer if no shortage was imminent. If shortages appeared, however, it sold futures only as it bought spot corn for grinding. In this manner it reached a balanced position with reference to any increase in spot corn prices. It made no effort to protect itself against a decline in prices. In 1940 the company experienced a profit in corn futures, but in 1942 it suffered a loss. It contended that its futures were capital assets and that its transactions were not hedges. Extracts from the Court's opinion follow:]

We find nothing in this record to support the contention that Corn Products' futures activity was separate and apart from its manufacturing operation. On the contrary, it appears that the transactions were vitally important to the company's business as a form of insurance against increases in the price of raw corn. Not only were the purchases initiated for just this reason but the petitioner's sales policy, selling in the future at a fixed price or less, continued to leave it exceedingly vulnerable to rises in the price of corn. Further, the purchase of corn futures assured the company a source of supply which was admittedly cheaper than constructing additional storage facilities for raw corn. Under these facts it is difficult to imagine a program more closely geared to a company's manufacturing enterprises or more important to its successful operation.

.   .   .

Nor can we find support for petitioner's contention that hedging is not within the exclusions of Section 117(a) [now Section 1221]. Admittedly, petitioner's corn futures do not come within the literal language of the exclusions set out in that section. They were not stock in trade, actual inventory, property held for sale to customers, or depreciable property used in a trade or business. But the capital asset provision of Section 117 [now Section 1221] must not be so broadly applied as to defeat rather than further the purpose of Congress ... Congress intended that profits and losses arising from the everyday operation of a business be considered as ordinary income or loss rather than capital gain or loss. The preferential treatment provided by Section 117 [Section 1221] applies to transactions in property which are not the normal source of business income. It was intended "to relieve the taxpayer from ... excessive tax burdens on gains resulting from a conversion of capital investments, and to remove the deterrent effect of those burdens on such conversions" ... since this section is an exception from the normal tax requirements of the Internal Revenue Code, the definition of a capital asset must be narrowly applied and its exclusions interpreted broadly. This is necessary to effectuate the basic Congressional purpose. This Court has always construed narrowly the term "capital assets" in Section 117 [now Section 1221]. ...

.   .   .

We believe that the statute clearly refutes the contention of Corn Products. Moreover, it is significant to note that practical considerations lead to the same conclusion. To hold otherwise would permit those engaged in hedging transactions to transmute ordinary income into capital gain at will. The hedger may either sell the future and purchase in the spot market or take delivery under the future contract itself. But if a sale of the future created a capital transaction while delivery of the commodity under the same future did not, a loophole in the statute would be created and the purpose of Congress frustrated.

As indicated by the *Covington, Fulton,* and *Corn Products* cases, if a speculator or trader buys and sells commodity futures as he would shares of stock, he has capital gain or loss; but if he deals in commodity futures as a form of price insurance, and such futures are related to his business of production and sales of goods, he is hedging, and his gains and losses are ordinary ones.

DEFINITIONS OF SHORT– AND LONG–TERM CAPITAL GAINS AND LOSSES

12.20   To determine the proper tax treatment of capital gains and losses, such gains and losses must first be separated into short-term and long-term. Short-term gains and losses result from sales or exchanges of capital assets that have been held for six months or less. Long-term capital gains and losses result from sales or exchanges of capital assets that have been held for *more* than six months. All short-term gains and short-term losses are combined to determine the net short-term capital gain or loss. Likewise, all long-term gains and losses are combined to determine the net long-term capital gain or loss. The net short-term capital gain or loss and the net long-term capital gain or loss are then combined to determine the net capital gain or loss for the year. This procedure must be followed to determine whether special treatment is available for any excess of a net long-term capital gain over a net short-term capital loss and also to determine whether the overall result is a net capital loss.

TREATMENT OF NET CAPITAL GAINS

12.21   If a taxpayer's net capital gain consists of an excess of net long-term gain over net short-term loss, such excess is taxed under preferential rules.

12.22   The preferential treatment granted net long-term capital gains dates back to 1921. At that time Congress thought it inequitable to telescope into one year and tax at the top of graduated tax brackets an appreciation in value that had built up over a period of years. From 1921 through 1941 the holding period to obtain this benefit varied from one to two or more years. In 1942 the minimum holding period was reduced to six months and one day because Congress thought such a relatively short holding period would benefit overall tax revenues by encouraging taxpayers to realize capital gains.[18]

If the net capital gain consists of both a net short-term gain and a net 12.23 long-term gain, the short-term gain is included in ordinary income in full, and the net long-term gain is given the preferential treatment. If a taxpayer's net capital gain represents an excess of net short-term gain over net long-term loss, the net capital gain is included in ordinary income in full, and no special tax calculations are applied. The mechanics of the preferential tax treatment given the excess of net long-term capital gain over net short-term capital loss depend upon whether the taxpayer is an individual or a corporation.

Individuals

Under Section 1202, an individual taxpayer is granted a special 12.24 deduction equal to 50 percent of the excess of net long-term capital gain over net short-term capital loss. Also, disregarding this deduction under Section 1202, the individual's effective tax rate is limited to 25 percent on the first full $50,000 of such excess [Section 1201(b)]. Finally, if the excess of net long-term capital gain over net short-term capital loss is more than $50,000, the individual's effective tax rate on the full amount over such $50,000 is limited to $29\frac{1}{2}$ percent for taxable years beginning in 1970, and to $32\frac{1}{2}$ percent for taxable years beginning in 1971. After 1971 this amount over $50,000 less the applicable 50 percent deduction is subject to the regular tax rates applicable to income in excess of the sum of ordinary income plus one-half of the $50,000 of net long-term capital gains. Because of the special 50 percent deduction, the effective rates on this income may still be less than the tax on an equal amount of ordinary income.

In case of a married taxpayer filing a separate return, the $50,000 12.25 referred to in the preceding paragraph should be read as $25,000.

Before enactment of the Tax Reform Act of 1969 the maximum tax 12.26 rate of 25 percent was applicable to all of an individual's excess of net long-term capital gain over net short-term capital loss. That act limited the 25 percent effective rate to the $50,000 of such excess discussed in the preceding paragraphs; however, during a transitional period the 25 percent rate continues to apply, regardless of the $50,000 limitation, to long-term capital gains attributable to:

1. Amounts received before 1975 from sales or other dispositions pursuant to binding contracts entered into on or before October 9, 1969. (These will include amounts being reported on the installment method of accounting, but not gains described in Section 1235 relating to patents and in Section 631 relating to timber, coal, and iron ore), and
2. Taxable distributions from a corporation made before October 10, 1970, pursuant to a plan of complete liquidation adopted on or before October 9, 1969.

18. Report of Senate Finance Committee on Revenue Bill of 1943, 1942–2 C.B. 545.

12.27   These transitional gains are counted first in arriving at the $50,000 to which the 25 percent maximum effective rate applies. If they are less than $50,000, other gains may be included until the $50,000 limit is reached; however, if the transitional gains exceed $50,000 in one year, they are the only gains subject to the 25 percent maximum effective rate in that year [Section 1201(d)]. Of course, in no event will the amount subject to the 25 percent maximum rate be more than the excess of net long-term capital gain over net short-term capital loss.

12.28   The applicable Sections 1201 and 1202 that produce these results are difficult to interpret, and careful study of these sections as well as of the definitions in Section 1222 is necessary for a clear understanding of capital gains. First of all, it must be remembered that gross income as defined in Section 61(a) includes 100 percent of a net capital gain. Sections 1202 and 62(3) then provide that there shall be allowed as a deduction in determining adjusted gross income, and accordingly taxable income, 50 percent of the excess of net long-term capital gain over any net short-term capital loss. After this point, only 50 percent of the excess of net long-term capital gain over net short-term capital loss is included in taxable income. If the individual's top tax bracket is 40 percent, he would pay a tax at an effective rate of no more than 20 percent (40 percent of 50 percent) on the full amount of such excess. Because individual tax brackets exceed 50 percent, and Congress wished to impose a maximum rate of 50 percent on part of this includible excess, Section 1201 comes into operation when the individual's taxable income reaches a top regular tax bracket of more than 50 percent.

12.29   Under the mechanics of Section 1201, the 50 percent of the excess of net long-term capital gain over net short-term capital loss that remains in taxable income is removed and put to one side so that the graduated rates will apply only to that portion of taxable income that consists of ordinary net income. The full amount of the excess of net long-term capital gain over net short-term capital loss is then separately taxed at the appropriate rates. The sum of the tax on ordinary taxable income and the separate tax on the excess of net long-term capital gain over net short-term capital loss is then called the "alternative tax" by Section 1201. An individual's tax will be the lesser of this alternative tax or his tax calculated in the regular manner. In no event can an individual's tax on his first full $50,000 of net long-term capital gain ever exceed 25 percent, and it can be less if enough of his total taxable income including capital gains is taxed in rate brackets of less than 50 percent. See illustration in paragraph 3.23.

Corporations

12.30   A corporation is not allowed the special deduction for 50 percent of the excess of net long-term capital gain over net short-term capital loss (Section 1202). However, a corporation does get the benefit of an alternative tax by which its effective tax rate on the excess of net long-term capital gain over net short-term capital loss is limited (Section 1201). Generally, these limited rates are 28 percent in taxable years beginning in 1970 and 30 percent thereafter. However, like. individuals, corporations are also subject to transitional rules under which a 25 percent maximum rate will continue to apply to net long-term capital gains attributable to (1) amounts received before 1975 pursuant to contracts entered into on or before October 9, 1969, and (2) taxable corporate distributions made before October 10, 1970, pursuant to plans of complete liquidation adopted on or before October 9, 1969. These gains may include amounts reported on the installment method of accounting, but not gains described in Sections 1235 and 631 [Section 1201(d)].

12.31 Under the alternative tax calculation of Section 1201(a), the full amount of the excess of net long-term capital gain over net short-term capital loss is first removed from taxable income. The regular corporate rates are then applied to the balance to determine a partial tax. The capital-gains tax is then calculated by applying the appropriate preferential rates to the excess of net long-term capital gain over net short-term capital loss. The sum of the partial tax and the capital-gains tax is the alternative tax. The tax liability is the lesser of such alternative tax or the tax computed in the regular manner under Section 11 on taxable income including the full amount of the excess of net long-term capital gain over net short-term capital loss. The tax computed in the regular manner will always be less than the alternative tax if total taxable income is no more than $25,000, because the rate on such amount is only 22 percent. The alternative tax will always be the lesser if the ordinary income exceeds $25,000, because in the regular tax calculation the net long-term capital gain would then be subject to a 48 percent tax rate. In those cases where ordinary income is less than $25,000 but total taxable income exceeds $25,000, both the regular and alternative tax calculations may be necessary to determine the lesser tax.

12.32 If a corporation's excess of net long-term capital gain over net short-term capital loss contains both transitional gains taxable at 25 percent and other gains taxable at 28 percent or 30 percent, the determination of the capital-gain tax in the alternative calculation requires two steps. First the 25 percent rate is applied to the transitional gains. Then the 28 or 30 percent rate is applied to the remaining excess of net long-term capital gain over net short-term capital loss. These two results are then added to the partial tax to arrive at the alternative tax.

12.33 If a corporation has a net loss from operations and realizes a net long-term capital gain, the operating loss must be offset against the net long-term capital gain for the purpose of determining taxable income. In such an instance it can happen that the tax computed in the regular manner under Section 11 will be less than the alternative tax under Section 1201(a). An important point here is that a net operating loss available otherwise as a carry-back or carry-over at a potential tax benefit of 48 percent (using 1970 rates and disregarding the surtax) is used to generate only a 25, 28, or 30 percent tax benefit when it offsets a net long-term capital gain. Ordinarily such a result should be avoided.

Example of Alternative Tax

12.34   The alternative tax calculations for both individuals and corporations under various circumstances can be illustrated by the following example. For purposes of this example the following terms as defined in Section 1201 and Section 1222 are used in order to simplify the nomenclature. "Net Section 1201 gain" is the full excess of net long-term capital gain over net short-term capital loss. "Subsection (d) gain" is the net long-term capital gain described heretofore (transitional items in full plus an additional amount, if any, up to a total of $50,000), which is subject to the 25 percent maximum tax rate.

EXAMPLE   Individuals A and B, who each file joint income tax returns, and corporations X and Y each have taxable income, before any capital-gain deductions, of $84,000 for the calendar year 1971. This taxable income is composed of ordinary income and capital gains and losses as indicated. The tax liability of each taxpayer is as calculated below.

	INDIVIDUALS		CORPORATIONS	
	A	B	X	Y
Ordinary taxable income	$ 30,000	$ 30,000	$ 30,000	$ 30,000
Short-term capital gain	$ 4,000	$ 26,000	$ 4,000	$ 24,000
Short-term capital (loss)	(10,000)	(10,000)	(10,000)	(2,000)
Net short-term capital gain (loss)	$ (6,000)	$ 16,000	$ (6,000)	$ 22,000
Long-term capital gain —				
Attributable to 1968 contract	$ 40,000	$ 40,000	$ 40,000	$ —
Attributable to 1971 sales	22,000	2,000	22,000	62,000
Long-term capital (loss)	(2,000)	(4,000)	(2,000)	(30,000)
Net long-term capital gain (loss)	$ 60,000	$ 38,000	$ 60,000	$ 32,000
Net capital gain (loss)	$ 54,000	$ 54,000	$ 54,000	$ 54,000
Taxable income before any capital gain deductions	$ 84,000	$ 84,000	$ 84,000	$ 84,000
Net Section 1201 gain — Excess of net long-term capital gain over net short-term capital loss	$ 54,000	$ 38,000	$ 54,000	$ 32,000

	INDIVIDUALS		CORPORATIONS	
	A	B	X	Y
Subsection (d) gain — 1968 contract gain	$ 40,000	$ 40,000	$ 40,000	$ —
Additional amount from other net long-term capital gains to reach ceiling of $50,000 (individuals only)	10,000	—	—	—
Total	$ 50,000	$ 40,000	$ 40,000	$ —
Excess of net Section 1201 gain over Subsection (d) gain	$ 4,000	$ —	$ 14,000	$ 32,000

TAX CALCULATIONS

Regular tax —				
Taxable income before capital gain deduction	$84,000	$84,000	$84,000	$84,000
Deduct — 50% of Section 1201 gain (individuals only)	27,000	19,000	—	—
Taxable income	$57,000	$65,000	$84,000	$84,000
Regular tax	$20,710	$24,970	$33,820	$33,820
Alternative tax —				
Taxable income	$57,000	$65,000	$84,000	$84,000
Deduct — Section 1201 gains included in taxable income	27,000	19,000	54,000	32,000
Taxable income for partial tax (ordinary income)	$30,000	$46,000	$30,000	$52,000
Partial tax	$ 7,880	$15,060	$ 7,900	$18,460
Capital gains tax on —				
Lesser of full net Section 1201 gain or full Subsection (d) gain at 25 percent	12,500	9,500	10,000	—
Balance of Section 1201 gain (see below for Individual A)	1,060	—	4,200	9,600
Alternative tax	$21,440	$24,560	$22,100	$28,060
Tax payable (lesser of regular or alternative tax)	$20,710	$24,560	$22,100	$28,060

CAPITAL GAINS TAX ON BALANCE OF
NET SECTION 1201 GAIN FOR INDIVIDUAL A

Regular tax on total taxable income (see above)		$20,710
Ordinary income	$30,000	
50 percent of Subsection (d) gain	25,000	
Ordinary income and Subsection (d) gain subject to regular tax	$55,000	
Regular tax on ordinary income and Subsection (d) gain		19,650
Tax on excess ($4,000) of Section 1201 gain over Subsection (d) gain at regular rates		$ 1,060
Tax on excess of Section 1201 gain over Subsection (d) gain at 32 ½ percent maximum rate ($4,000 × 32 ½ %)		$ 1,300
Tax — smaller of above two taxes		$ 1,060

TREATMENT OF CAPITAL LOSSES

12.35   The special tax treatment given to capital gains is favorable to tax-payers, but the special treatment given to capital losses is unfavorable.

12.36   Short-term capital losses are applied first against short-term capital gains. Any excess loss is then subtracted from long-term capital gains. Any balance of the loss is a net short-term capital loss. Similarly, any long-term capital loss is first applied against long-term capital gains. Any excess loss is then subtracted from net short-term capital gain. Any balance of the loss is a net long-term capital loss. In these computations, 100 percent of the gains and losses are taken into account.

Individuals

12.37   In years beginning after 1969, if an unmarried individual's capital losses exceed his capital gains, so that he has either a net short-term or long-term capital loss or both, the aggregate net capital loss is deductible to the extent of the smallest of:

1. $1,000
2. his taxable income from other sources before his deduction for personal exemptions, or
3. the sum of
   (a) the excess of his net short-term capital loss over his net long-term capital gain and
   (b) 50 percent of the excess of his net long-term capital loss over his net short-term capital gain.

If an individual computes his tax by use of the optional tax table, his deduction for a net capital loss is determined in the same manner except that his adjusted gross income before such net capital loss is used in lieu of his taxable income. If married taxpayers file a joint return, the same limitations are computed, and the capital-loss deduction is determined with respect to the combined taxable income and the combined gains and losses of the spouses [Reg. 1.1211–1(d)]. If married taxpayers file separate returns, the limitations apply to the net capital losses of each spouse, and further the deduction is limited to $500 in lieu of the $1,000 allowed an unmarried taxpayer and married taxpayers filing a joint return [Section 1211(b)].

Under limitation (3) discussed in the preceding paragraph, only 50 percent of an individual's excess of net long-term capital loss over net short-term capital gain can be deducted against ordinary income. This treatment is consistent with the effective inclusion in taxable income of only 50 percent of net long-term capital gains. It was placed in the law for the first time by the Tax Reform Act of 1969 and is effective for years beginning in 1970 and later.

Married taxpayers who file a joint return have taxable ordinary income of $20,000 before deducting personal exemptions. Their capital transactions show a long-term loss of $1,800. For years beginning before 1970 their deduction against ordinary income would be $1,000. For years beginning in 1970 and later the deduction is only $900.

The facts are the same as in Example 1 except the long-term loss is $2,400. For years beginning both before 1970 and in 1970 and later the deduction would be $1,000, that is, $2,400 limited to $1,000 (before 1970) and 50 percent of $2,400 limited to $1,000 (1970 and later).

The facts are the same except taxpayers have a net short-term loss of $500 and a net long-term loss of $600. For years beginning before 1970 the ordinary deduction was $1,000. For years beginning in 1970 and later the ordinary deduction is $800, that is, the $500 short-term loss taken at 100 percent plus 50 percent of the $600 long-term loss.

For years beginning before 1970, net capital losses, whether short-term or long-term, were deductible against ordinary income to the extent of the lesser of $1,000 or taxable income from other sources before deductions for personal exemptions (or adjusted gross income in case the optional tax table is used). Furthermore, in years beginning before 1970 the $1,000 limitation applied to separate returns of married taxpayers in lieu of the $500 in later years.

With certain limitations, an unused capital loss of an individual can be carried over indefinitely to subsequent years until it is used either as a deduction against capital gains or as a deduction against ordinary income [Section 1212(b)]. The tax treatment of capital-loss carry-overs was changed in 1964 and again in 1969. Both changes involved some transitional rules. In an attempt to simplify the discussion of capital-loss carry-overs the rules applicable to years beginning in 1970 and later will be discussed and illustrated first; thereafter the transitional rules of 1964 and 1969 will be discussed.

Capital
Gains
and Losses

12.38

EXAMPLE 1

EXAMPLE 2

EXAMPLE 3

12.39

12.40

12.41   With respect to loss carry-overs arising in years beginning in 1970 or later; (1) any excess of net short-term capital loss over net long-term capital gain is treated as a short-term capital loss in succeeding years; (2) any excess of net long-term capital loss over net short-term capital gain is treated as a long-term capital loss for succeeding years; and (3) if there is both a net short-term capital loss and net long-term capital loss, each is treated as a like capital loss for succeeding years. In other words, the amount of capital-loss carry-over retains its original character, short-term or long-term as the case may be, and is combined with like gains and losses in the year to which carried.

12.42   In determining the amount of a capital-loss carry-over to subsequent years the total of the net capital losses for the current year must be reduced by an amount relating to the capital-loss deduction allowed against ordinary income [Section 1212(b)]. This reduction is the sum of (1) the deduction allowed against ordinary income plus (2) an amount equal to the excess of such deduction over the net short-term capital loss of the year. This formula accomplishes these results. If a net short-term capital loss exists, it is used as a deduction from ordinary income before any net long-term capital loss is used. Any such net short-term capital loss so deducted reduces the remaining amount of the net short-term capital loss available as a carry-over dollar-for-dollar. To the extent any net long-term capital loss is used as a deduction, twice the amount so deducted reduces the remaining amount of the net long-term capital loss available as a carry-over.

12.43   It should be remembered that, although only one-half of any net long-term capital loss can be used as a deduction from ordinary income up to a maximum of $1,000 in any one year, the full amount carried over can be used first to offset a net long-term capital gain and then any net short-term capital gain realized in a subsequent year.

EXAMPLE   In 1970 an individual incurred a net long-term capital loss of $11,000. After deducting $1,000 of that amount in computing taxable income for 1970 (a joint return) there remained an unused long-term capital loss of $10,000. This loss was then reduced by $1,000, representing the excess of the $1,000 deduction over the net short-term loss, which that year was zero, leaving a long-term capital-loss carry-over of $9,000. In 1971, he has a net long-term capital gain of $5,000. The net long-term capital-loss carry-over to that year of $9,000 is combined with this net long-term capital gain, and the result is a net long-term capital loss of $4,000; $1,000 is then deducted from ordinary income. The $4,000 loss is then reduced by the $1,000 deduction and another $1,000 representing the excess of the deduction over the net short-term capital loss of zero, leaving the balance of $2,000 as a long-term capital-loss carry-over to 1972.

In 1972 he has a net short-term capital loss of $200 and a net long-term capital loss of $500. The $2,000 net long-term capital-loss carry-over is combined with the current $500, so that the net long-term capital loss is $2,500. There is then deducted $1,000 from ordinary income. The carry-over to 1973 and subsequent years is $900, computed as follows:

Net short-term capital loss	$ 200	Capital
Net long-term capital loss	2,500	Gains
		and Losses
Total	$2,700	
Less:		
Deduction from ordinary income	$1,000	
The amount of that same deduction ($1,000) reduced by the net short-term capital loss of $200	800	
	$1,800	
Net long-term carry-over	$ 900	

As indicated previously, if an individual sustains both a net short-term capital loss and a net long-term capital loss, the amount deductible against ordinary income up to a maximum of $1,000 comes first out of the net short-term capital loss of that year. In subsequent years, if the capital-loss carry-overs are deducted from ordinary income, the amount of the net short-term capital-loss carry-over must be exhausted before using up any of the net long-term capital-loss carry-over.

12.44

In 1970, 1971, and 1972 an individual and his wife have capital gains and losses and other taxable income as indicated below. Assuming they file a joint return, their capital losses carried forward are as indicated:

EXAMPLE

	1970	1971	1972
Taxable income (ordinary) before exemptions	$ 20,000	$ 800	$ 12,000
Short-term capital gains and (losses) —			
Carry-over from prior years	$ —	$ (4,000)	$ —
Incurred during current year:			
Gains	10,000	15,500	—
(Losses)	(15,000)	(12,000)	(400)
Net short-term gain or (loss) including carry-over	$ (5,000)	$ (500)	$ (400)
Long-term capital gains and (losses) —			
Carry-over from prior years	$ —	$ (2,000)	$ (2,400)
Incurred during current year:			
Gains	20,000	5,000	1,800
(Losses)	(22,000)	(6,000)	—
Net long-term gain (loss) including carry-over	$ (2,000)	$ (3,000)	$ (600)

Capital
Gains
and Losses

	1970	1971	1972
Net capital gain or (loss) including carry-overs	$ (7,000)	$ (3,500)	$ (1,000)
Less:			
Amount of loss deductible	1,000	800	700
Excess of amount deductible over net short-term capital loss	—	300	300
Total capital loss carry-over	$ (6,000)	$ (2,400)	$ —

In 1970, the amount deductible is limited to $1,000, the smallest of the three possible allowances. This deduction comes first out of the $5,000 net short-term capital loss for the year. Since no part of the deduction comes out of long-term losses, the total loss for the year is reduced by only $1,000 to arrive at the loss carry-over of $6,000 ($4,000 short-term and $2,000 long-term). In 1971, the amount deductible from ordinary income is limited to the amount of ordinary income, $800. This deduction exceeds the net short-term capital loss for the year by $300; therefore $300 of the deduction represents the use of net long-term capital loss. Accordingly, the net capital loss for the year is reduced by the deduction of $800 plus an amount equal to this excess of $300, to leave a carry-over to 1972 of $2,400. In 1972, all of the loss carry-over is a net long-term capital loss, and accordingly it eliminates the net long-term capital gain of $1,800 incurred that year, leaving a net long-term capital loss for the year of $600. The short-term loss in 1972 is $400, giving a net capital loss of $1,000. The amount deductible against ordinary income is $700, the sum of the short-term capital loss of $400 and 50 percent of the net long-term capital loss of $600. This deduction of $700 exceeds the short-term capital loss by $300; therefore, the net capital loss is reduced by the sum of these two items or $1,000, leaving no carry-over to 1973. In other words, the net capital loss of $1,000 is reduced first by $300, being the short-term loss deducted, and then by $600, being twice the long-term loss deducted, leaving no carry-over to 1973.

12.45   Prior to 1964 all capital-loss carry-overs of individuals were treated as short-term capital losses in the years to which carried. The Revenue Act of 1964 provided for the short-term or long-term character to continue in the carry-over; however, it provided a transitional rule that all capital-loss carry-overs arising prior to 1964 would continue to be treated as short-term capital losses in the years to which carried. Accordingly, any capital-loss carry-over arising prior to 1964 is applied first against net short-term capital gain for the year to which carried, then against net long-term capital gain, and then against ordinary income to the extent allowable.

12.46   In years beginning before 1970, 100 percent of net long-term capital loss could be deducted against ordinary income (to a limit of $1,000 per year) in lieu of only 50 percent thereof as is the case in years beginning in 1970 and later. As a transitional rule, the Tax Reform Act of 1969 provided that any long-term loss carry-overs originating before 1970 would not be subject to the 50 percent limitation; accordingly, long-term capital-loss carry-overs originating in years beginning in 1969 or earlier may be deducted dollar-for-dollar against ordinary income—subject, of course, to the $1,000 per year limit.

In 1969 a taxpayer has a net capital-loss carry-over to 1970, all long-term, of $5,000. In 1970 this is a long-term loss carry-over, which can be deducted against capital gain. Any amount not used to offset capital gain can be deducted against ordinary income to the extent of $1,000. Any portion of the capital-loss carry-over not used in 1970 can be carried forward in full and deducted in 1971, subject only to the limitation of $1,000 on any part used as a deduction against ordinary income.

Corporations

Capital losses of corporations are treated differently from those of individuals. A corporation's capital losses are deductible only to the extent of its capital gains [Section 1211(a)]. If a corporation's capital losses exceed its capital gains, such excess (net capital loss) is carried back to the three preceding taxable years and forward to the five succeeding taxable years (Section 1212) as a short-term capital loss. During those eight years, the capital loss carried back or forward is deducted to the extent of any net capital gain recognized in those years in the order of their occurrence. When capital losses carried back or forward from several years become deductible, the amount deductible is considered to consist of the amount carried from the earliest year or years (Section 1212).

12.47

Net capital losses carried back can be deducted against net capital gains only to the extent such deductions do not create or increase net operating losses. Any carry-back not deductible because of this rule can be carried to the next succeeding year in the eight-year period [Section 1212(a)(1)]. Thus a corporation's capital-loss carry-back is not used up against prior-year capital gains that already have been offset by ordinary losses. Furthermore a net capital loss may not be carried from or to a taxable year for which the corporation is an electing Subchapter S corporation [Section 1212(a)(3)].

12.48

Net capital losses attributable to foreign-expropriation capital losses may not be carried back, but they may be carried forward ten years. Where foreign-expropriation capital losses and other capital losses are incurred in the same year and both are carried forward, the foreign-expropriation capital loss is deductible in a subsequent year only after the other capital loss is deducted [Section 1212(a)(2); Reg. 1.1212–1(a)(2)].

12.49

For years beginning before 1970, capital losses could be carried only forward; accordingly, net capital losses incurred in taxable years beginning in 1970 and later years are carried back before being carried forward, but losses incurred in taxable years beginning before 1970 are carried only forward.

12.50

MINIMUM TAX ON TAX PREFERENCES AND EXCESS INVESTMENT INTEREST

Minimum Tax

12.51   The Tax Reform Act of 1969 made a number of changes that limited or restricted the tax benefits of capital gains. One of the most significant of these restrictions involves the minimum tax on tax preferences (see paragraph 3.80 et seq.). For taxable years beginning in 1970 this minimum tax is 10 percent of an amount based on nine items defined in Section 57 as "tax preferences."

12.52   For individuals, one of these tax preferences is the 50 percent deduction allowed with respect to net long-term capital gains. That is to say, 50 percent of an individual's excess of net long-term capital gain over net short-term capital loss is included in the tax preferences for individuals, and under certain circumstances a minimum tax of 10 percent thereof must be paid in addition to income tax otherwise payable.

12.53   For corporations, the tax preference is the excess of net long-term capital gain over net short-term capital loss multiplied by a fraction. The numerator of the fraction is the normal and surtax rate for the year reduced by the alternative tax rate for the year, and the denominator is the normal and surtax rate for the year. Accordingly, for 1971 and later years 37.5 percent of the excess of a corporation's net long-term capital gain over net short-term capital loss is a tax preference $\left[\dfrac{(48-30)}{48} = .375\right]$.

Excess Investment Interest

12.54   For taxable years beginning in 1972 and later, Section 163, as enacted by the Tax Reform Act of 1969, provides that interest incurred on indebtedness to carry investments is deductible by individuals only to the extent of the aggregate of the following in the order listed:

1. $25,000
2. Net investment income
3. The excess of net long-term capital gain over net short-term capital loss
4. One-half of the remainder of investment interest. See also paragraph 10.29.

12.55   To the extent investment interest is deductible because of an excess of net long-term capital gain over net short-term capital loss, the third item above, that much of the net long-term capital gain is treated as ordinary income. Thus, with respect to that portion of the net long-term capital gain, the 50 percent deduction is not allowed, the alternative tax does not apply, and the gain is not a tax preference. Corporations are subject to this provision only if they are Subchapter S corporations.

HOLDING PERIOD

The classification of capital gains and losses as either short-term or long-term is extremely important. This classification is determined by the holding period of the assets sold or exchanged. If an asset sold was held for *more* than six months, the gain or loss on sale or exchange is long-term. If the holding period was *six months or less,* the gain is short-term. The difference of one day in the holding period of an asset can make a substantial difference in the tax consequences of the sale or exchange; consequently, it is quite important that a taxpayer's records show the exact dates property was acquired and disposed of.

12.56

In figuring the holding period of property, the day the property was acquired is *excluded* and the day it was disposed of is *included.*[19] If property was bought April 8, 1966, and sold October 8, 1966, it was held for exactly six months; therefore, gain or loss on its sale is a short-term gain or loss.

12.57

The computation of the holding period of an asset is based upon calendar months without regard to the number of days contained in a particular calendar month. As stated in I.T. 3985:[20]

12.58

... a "month" is a period of time terminating with the day of the succeeding month (of the calendar) numerically corresponding to the day (date) of the month of its beginning, less one, except if there be no corresponding day of the succeeding month the period terminates with the last day of the succeeding month.

In amplifying I.T. 3985, Rev. Rul. 66–7[21] held:

... the determination of the holding period of "capital assets" ... must be made with reference to calendar months and fractions thereof, rather than with reference to days ...

... the holding period of a capital asset begins to run on the day following the date of acquisition of the asset involved. Accordingly, a capital asset acquired on the last day of any calendar month, regardless of whether the month has 31 days or less, must not be disposed of until on or after the first day of the seventh succeeding month of the calendar year in order to have been "held for more than 6 months" within the meaning of Sections 1222(3) and (4) of the Code.

In *E. T. Weir* v. *Com.,*[22] the Tax Court held that the holding period of shares of stock acquired on May 1, 1944, and sold on November 1,

19. E. T. Weir v. Com., 10 T.C. 996 (1948), affirmed per curiam, 173 F.2d 222 (3rd Cir. 1949), 49–1 USTC ¶9190, 37 AFTR 1022.
20. 1949–2 C.B. 51, amplified by Rev. Rul. 65–5, 1966–1 C.B. 92, Rev. Rul. 66–6, 1966–1 C.B. 161, and Rev. Rul. 66–7, 1966–1 C.B. 189.
21. *Supra* fn. 20.
22. *Supra* fn. 19.

1944, was not more than six months, even though such period consisted of at least 184 days, which was more than one-half of the days in that year. Accordingly, the taxpayer was held to have realized a short-term capital gain.

12.59   The holding period of a capital asset ordinarily is measured from the time the property was acquired by the taxpayer.[23] Section 1223 provides a number of exceptions to this rule. These exceptions relate primarily to property that has a substituted basis, that is, a basis determined with respect to property previously held by the taxpayer or property held by a previous owner. When property has a substituted basis, the holding period generally is measured from the transaction that established the basis of the property. Thus, where the basis of property is determined by reference to the basis in the hands of a previous owner, the holding period of the property includes the holding period of that previous owner.

12.60   The holding period of property acquired by gift after 1920 normally includes the holding period of the donor. However, if the property had a value lower than cost at the date of gift, and the sale results in a loss, the basis will be determined by the fair market value at date of gift and not basis in the hands of the donor; therefore, the holding period will begin with the date of the gift and will not include the holding period of the donor.[24] If the gift was included in the donor's estate as a gift in contemplation of death, and the donee held the property until after the donor's death, the holding period begins with the date of the gift, because that is the date upon which he acquired possession, and the fact that the basis is fixed as of the later date of death of the donor is immaterial.[25]

12.61   When property is acquired from a decedent, the holding period begins with the date of death, not from any later date of distribution from the estate to an heir.[26]

12.62   When a capital asset or property described in Section 1231 (real or depreciable property used in a trade or business, etc.) is acquired in a nontaxable exchange in which the basis of the property exchanged carries over to the property acquired, its holding period will include the holding period of the property exchanged [Section 1223(1)]. Likewise, the holding period of a new residence will include the holding period of an old residence if the acquisition of the new one resulted in gain or loss not being recognized on the sale of the old residence [Section 1223(7)].

12.63   The holding period of a partnership interest begins on the date the interest is acquired. The holding period of property, other than inventory, received as a distribution from a partnership includes the period the property was held by the partnership [Section 735(b)].

12.64   If stock in a corporation is received as a nontaxable distribution on

23. Nancy K. McFeely v. Com., 296 U.S. 102 (1935), 36–1 USTC ¶9008, 16 AFTR 965; Rev. Rul. 59–86, 1959–1 C.B. 209.
24. Rev. Rul. 59–416, 1959–2 C.B. 160.
25. Rev. Rul. 59–86, 1959–1 C.B. 209; see ¶11.51.
26. Nancy K. McFeely v. Com., *supra* fn. 23.

other stock of such corporation, the holding period of the stock distributed will include the holding period of such other stock. The same rule applies to the holding period of stock rights acquired in a nontaxable distribution on stock [Section 1223(5)]. However, when stock is acquired by the exercise of stock rights, the holding period of the stock begins on the date the rights were exercised. The holding period of the rights is not added to the actual holding period of the stock acquired by their exercise [Section 1223(6)].

12.65 If the acquisition of stock or securities resulted in loss not being recognized on the sale or exchange of substantially identical stock or securities under the "wash sales" provisions of Section 1091 (paragraph 12.105), the holding period of the stock or securities acquired will include the holding period of such substantially identical stock or securities sold or exchanged [Section 1223(4)].

12.66 In summary, if property is acquired in any manner other than by purchase, taxable exchange, or from a decedent, reference should be made to Section 1223 to see if the holding period includes any part of the holding period of a previous owner or of previously owned property.

SALE OR EXCHANGE

12.67 The special tax treatment accorded capital gains and losses does not apply to every disposition of a capital asset. The special treatment applies only to gains and losses resulting from sales or exchanges of capital assets or from other transactions that are treated under the Code as sales or exchanges (see paragraph 12.91 et seq.). The collection of a debt is not a sale or exchange but rather a termination of the debt. Similarly, the leasing of property is not a sale or exchange. Further, even if a bona fide sale occurs, if the effect of the sale is to convert what would otherwise be ordinary income into capital gain, the courts are likely to treat the gain as resulting in ordinary income. These points are illustrated by the next two cases. The first one concerns collection of a debt.

Calvin Hudson et al.

20 T.C. 734 (1953)

[Facts: The taxpayers had purchased a judgment from the legatees of an estate. The taxpayers later settled the judgment with the judgment debtor for an amount in excess of what they had paid for the judgment. The question in the case was whether the gain realized on settlement of the judgment was capital gain or ordinary income. The Tax Court held the gain was ordinary income because the settlement of the judgment was not a *sale or exchange*. The following excerpts from the decision explain this principle.]

... There is no question about the bona fides of the transaction, nor is there any disagreement about the fact that the judgment, when entered and transferred, was property and a capital asset. The parties differ, however, on the question of whether there was a "sale or exchange of a capital asset." Section 117(a)(4) [now Section 1222(3)]. Petitioners and respondent both adhere to the principle that the words "sale or exchange" should be given their ordinary meaning. Petitioners, citing authority, define the word "sale" as follows:

"A sale is a contract whereby one acquires a property in the thing sold and the other parts with it for a valuable consideration ... or a sale is generally understood to mean the transfer of property for money. ...."

Also, "Sell in its ordinary sense means a transfer of property for a fixed price in money or its equivalent."

We cannot see how there was a transfer of property, or how the judgment debtor acquired property as the result of the transaction wherein the judgment was settled. The most that can be said is that the judgment debtor paid a debt or extinguished a claim so as to preclude execution on the judgment outstanding against him. In a hypothetical case, if the judgment had been transferred to someone other than the judgment debtor, the property transferred would still be in existence after the transaction was completed. However, as it actually happened, when the judgment debtor settled the judgment, the claim arising from the judgment was extinguished without the transfer of any property or property right to the judgment debtor. In their day-to-day transactions, neither businessmen nor lawyers would call the settlement of a judgment a sale; we can see no reason to apply a strained interpretation to the transaction before us. When petitioners received the $21,150 in full settlement of the judgment, they did not recover the money as the result of any sale or exchange but only as a collection or settlement of the judgment.

It is well established that where the gain realized did not result from a sale or exchange of a capital asset, the gain is not within the provisions of section 117(a)(4) [now Section 1222(3)]. ...

... In another situation, a redemption of bonds before maturity by the issuing corporation was not a sale or exchange of capital assets ... In a similar situation in *Bingham* v. *Commissioner,* 105 F.2d 971, 972, the court said:

"What may have been property in the hands of the holder of the notes simply vanished when the surrender took place and the maker received them. He then had, at most, only his own obligations to pay himself. Any theoretical concept of a sale of the notes to the maker in return for what he gave up to get them back must yield before the hard fact that he received nothing which was property in his hands but had merely succeeded in extinguishing his liabilities by the amounts which were due on the notes. There was, therefore, no sale of the notes to him in the ordinary meaning of the word and no exchange of assets for assets since the notes could not, as assets, survive the transaction. That being so, such a settlement as the one this petitioner made involved neither a sale nor an exchange of capital assets within the meaning of the statute. ...."

12.68   The remarks in the *Hudson* case that the retirement of bonds, notes, and other evidences of debt does not constitute a sale or exchange are true today only with respect to debt obligations issued by individuals, partnerships, trusts, and estates. Under Section 1232, retirements of debt obligations issued by any corporation or governmental body now are *treated as* sales or exchanges under certain circumstances (paragraph 12.92).

Occasionally the conflict between capital gain and ordinary income for tax purposes is resolved on the basis of the overall effect of the transaction rather than by reference to the existence of a sale or exchange or to the property's qualification as a capital asset. The next case involves the sale of an endowment policy for more than its net premium cost but slightly less than what its redemption value would be a few days later. An endowment policy is a capital asset, but any gain upon its surrender for redemption is ordinary income because there is no sale or exchange.

12.69

In *Com.* v. *Percy W. Phillips* [27] the taxpayer transferred an endowment policy on his own life to his two law partners twelve days before its maturity. Premiums on the policy had been prepaid for twenty-one years. The taxpayer contended that the endowment policy constituted property, he had made a sale of such property, and therefore he was entitled to capital gain treatment. The Fourth Circuit Court of Appeals held that a sale may not be used as a device to convert ordinary income into capital gain where that is the sole purpose of the sale. Accordingly, it held the taxpayer's gain on the sale of the endowment policy was ordinary income. The broad principle upon which this decision is based is indicated by the following excerpts from the decision:

12.70

... The Tax Court held that there had been full compliance with the requirements of a real and bona fide sale, and the fact that the purchase by the transferees may have been one of accommodation does not affect the nature of the transaction as a sale. ... Disregarding the motive and accommodation factors, as we must for this purpose, it necessarily follows that the Tax Court was correct in concluding that the transaction represented an unequivocal and bona fide sale.

Taxpayer urges that the endowment policy constituted "property" and, as such, was only subject to capital gains treatment. This argument does not necessarily follow. That it was "property" in the broad sense of the word does not satisfy the requirements of the law for capital gain purposes. In *Hort* v. *Commissioner,* 313 U.S. 28 [41–1 USTC ¶9394, 25 AFTR 1207], a fifteen-year lease was held to be "property," but when cancelled by the lessor and lessee under an agreement wherein the lessor received a lump sum payment, the consideration received was not, for the purposes of internal revenue laws, deemed to be a return of capital, the court noting (313 U.S. 31):

"Where, as in this case, the disputed amount was essentially a substitute for rental payments which §22(a) [now Section 61(a)] expressly characterizes as gross income, it must be regarded as ordinary income, and it is immaterial that for some purposes the contract creating the right to such payments may be treated as 'property' or 'capital.'"

This brings us to a consideration of the principal argument advanced in this court by the Commissioner. Reliance is placed upon the recent decisions in *Commissioner* v. *P. G. Lake, Inc.,* 356 U.S. 260 [58–1 USTC ¶9428, 1 AFTR2d 1394], and *Arnfeld* v. *U.S., supra,* [163 F.Supp. 865 (Ct. Cls., 1958), 58–2 USTC ¶9692, 2 AFTR2d 5336, cert. den.], the latter being an opinion of the Court of Claims decided subsequent to the [decision by the Tax Court in the] present case.

27. 275 F.2d 33 (4th Cir. 1960), 60–1 USTC ¶9294, 5 AFTR2d 855.

In accepting the theory advanced by the Commissioner we recognize that the line of demarcation is not clear. There are, of course, factual differences in *Lake* and *Arnfeld* which the taxpayer insists afford an opportunity to distinguish the principles there invoked. We believe, however, that we are required to adopt the view that since the amounts receivable upon maturity or surrender of the endowment policy unquestionably would have been taxable as ordinary income, the taxpayer may not convert such income into capital gain by a bona fide sale of the contract which is the means of producing such ordinary income. The cash value of the policy was equivalent to the reserve value which, in turn, was computed on the basis of three percent compound interest. The sale of the policy was, as said by Mr. Justice Douglas in *Lake*, "essentially a substitute for what would otherwise be received at a future time as ordinary income." Manifestly the consideration paid by taxpayer's partners was "not for an increase in the value of income-producing property." The policy had a face value of $27,000, and its cash surrender value as of March 7, 1952 (the date of the assignment), was $26,973.78. The increased value had already accrued, and we cannot accept the suggestion that the assignees would pay out $26,750 merely to receive an increase in value of $26.22. While the tax-saving motive is not to be considered in ascertaining the bona fides of the sale or assignment, we think that it may play some part in determining whether or not the consideration was paid for an increase in the value of income-producing property, and whether the amount so received was essentially a substitute for what would have otherwise been received as ordinary income in a matter of twelve days.

. . .

... It is illogical to assume that Congress intended to permit, even through the medium of a bona fide sale, the conversion of what is the equivalent of ordinary income into a capital gain in light of the language of § 22(b)(2)(A) [now Section 72]. The teachings of *Lake* and *Arnfeld* preclude us from so holding.

12.71   It probably is significant that in both the *Lake* and the *Phillips* cases, the amount of the ordinary income which otherwise would have been received could be ascertained with considerable accuracy. The *Phillips* case illustrates again the narrow construction of the capital-gains provisions.

12.72   Based on the *Lake, Phillips,* and other recent decisions, it appears taxpayers seeking capital-gain benefits should keep in mind the original purpose of such benefits. That purpose was to avoid the application of ordinary tax rates to gains that accrue over a lengthy period of time. Furthermore, the necessity that there be both a bona fide conversion of capital investment and the absence of a conversion of ordinary income into capital gain is quite important in obtaining the benefit of capital-gain treatment.

Patents

12.73   A patent is an exclusive franchise or privilege granted by the United States government to a patentee, his heirs or assigns, for a term of seventeen years "to exclude others from making, using, or selling" an invention throughout the United States.[28] It is an intangible asset, and its cost is depreciable over its life of seventeen years.

There are general rules and the special rules of Section 1235 applicable to sales and exchanges of patents and interests therein.   12.74

General Rules. If a patent is held as an investment, it is a capital   12.75
asset under Section 1221. A taxpayer who finances the efforts of an inventor would ordinarily fit into this category. The inventor himself will qualify for this treatment if inventions and patents sold by him are not numerous and he is not a professional, as distinguished from an amateur, inventor.[29]

If a patent is owned by a business, the invention is used in that   12.76
business, the patent was held for more than six months, and the taxpayer did not hold the patent for sale to customers in the ordinary course of his trade or business, it is a Section 1231 asset. Any gain on a sale or exchange of it will be treated as a long-term capital gain if the sum of all gains and losses on Section 1231 assets in that year is a net gain. The holding period of a patent owned by an inventor commences not when the patent is issued, but on the earlier date when the invention was reduced to practice.[30]

If a taxpayer is in the business of selling patents either because he   12.77
is a professional inventor or because of financial dealings, any gain or loss on a sale or exchange is an ordinary one, unless the provisions of Section 1235 apply (see paragraph 12.82).

Where patents are capital assets or Section 1231 assets, much con-   12.78
troversy has arisen over whether a particular transaction was a sale or a license. The three attributes of a patent are the rights "to make, use, and sell" the underlying invention. If all three of these rights are exclusively conveyed by the assignment either throughout the United States or within and throughout a specified part of the United States for a lump-sum consideration, a sale has occurred.[31] Similarly, if the conveyance is an exclusive one of an undivided portion of these three rights for a lump-sum price, a sale has occurred.[32] In *Kimble Glass Co.*,[33] the Tax Court held that a conveyance of the rights only to manufacture and sell resulted in a license and not a sale. In other cases, the courts have held that a sale did occur where the right to "use" the invention was not conveyed, but such right under the particular circumstances was not a substantial one.

The statements in an instrument that it is a license and that the con-   12.79
sideration to be received is a royalty are not decisive as to the nature

28. Title 35, United States Code, Section 154.
29. See Casey, "Sale of Patents, Copyrights and Royalty Interests," Proceedings of N.Y.U. 7th Annual Institute on Federal Taxation 383 (1949); Woodward, "Sales of Patents and Copyrights," Proceedings of N.Y.U. 9th Annual Institute on Federal Taxation 987 (1951).
30. Carl G. Dreymann, 11 T.C. 153 (1948).
31. Waterman v. Mackenzie, 138 U.S. 252 (1891) (a patent law case).
32. Orla E. Watson et al. v. U.S., 222 F. 2d 689 (10th Cir. 1955), 55–1 USTC ¶9455, 48 AFTR 1256.
33. 9 T.C. 183 (1947).

of the transaction. If in fact all of the patentee's "right, title, and interest" in the patent property are transferred through the grant of an exclusive license to manufacture, use, and sell for the life of the patent, a sale has occurred.

12.80   If part or all of the consideration paid for the patent is based upon quantity produced or sales proceeds realized, the Commissioner through the years has wavered in his treatment of the transaction. In *Edward C. Meyers*,[34] an inventor in 1932 granted to B. F. Goodrich Rubber Company an exclusive license to manufacture, use, and sell an invention in consideration of certain annual payments based upon the sales proceeds to be realized from the manufacture and sale of rubber-covered flexible steel track. The agreement was called a license, and the payments were called royalties. The court held that the conveyance in 1932 constituted not a license but a sale of a capital asset, and that the so-called royalties received in 1941, the year at issue, constituted long-term capital-gain income. In 1946 the Commissioner announced his acquiescence in that decision, but in 1950 withdrew it and announced nonacquiescence. In 1958 he reversed himself again and announced acquiescence. With very few exceptions, the courts both before and after 1950 have held that if a sale of a patent has occurred, and it was a capital asset in the hands of the taxpayer, then the mere fact that part or all of the consideration received is based upon subsequent sales or production does not convert the sale into a license. The annual payments constitute capital-gain proceeds and not ordinary royalty income.[35]

12.81   **Special Rules of Section 1235.** The Commissioner's announcement in 1950 of his nonacquiescence in *Edward C. Meyers* accompanied by the simultaneous publication of Mim. 6490 announcing that he would not follow the *Meyers* case prompted Congress when enacting the 1954 Code to insert Section 1235. There was no similar section in the 1939 Code.

12.82   Under Section 1235, if an individual "holder of a patent" transfers substantially all of the rights under the patent, the transfer will be treated as a sale or exchange of a capital asset held for more than six months. This treatment is applied regardless of the actual holding period of the patent, and regardless of whether the consideration for the transfer is payable periodically over the life of the patent or is contingent upon the productivity, use, or disposition of the patent. A transfer to members of the holder's family other than brothers or

34. 6 T.C. 258 (1946) (Acq., 1946–1 C.B. 3; NA 1950–1 C.B. 7; Acq. Rev. Rul. 58–353, 1958–2 C.B. 408); see also Mim. 6490, 1950–1 C.B. 9 (revoked by Rev. Rul. 58–353).

35. Kimble Glass Co., 9 T.C. 188; Carroll Pressure Roller Corporation, 28 T.C. 1288 (1957) (Acq., 1958–2 C.B. 6) pertaining to the years 1952 and 1953, Com. v. Hopkinson, 126 F.2d 406 (2nd Cir. 1942), 28 AFTR 1349, affirming 42 BTA 580; Briggs v. Hofferbert, 85 F.Supp. 941 (D.C. Md., 1949), 38 AFTR 569, affirmed 178 F.2d 743 (4th Cir. 1949), 38 AFTR 1218.

sisters, a corporation controlled by him at least to the extent of 25 percent, and certain trusts are outside the scope of Section 1235.

The term "holder of a patent" has a fairly restricted meaning. It includes only an individual whose efforts created the patent rights (whether he be an amateur or a professional inventor) or any other individual who acquired his interest in the patent from the creator in exchange for money or money's worth before the patented invention is reduced to practice. The term "holder" does not include the employer of the creator nor a person related to the creator such as his spouse, ancestors, lineal descendents, or any other person described in Section 267(b) as modified by Section 1235(d). It should be noted also that Section 1235 does not apply to a transfer of a patent by a corporation, trust, or estate.

12.83

A transfer can be outside the scope of Section 1235 for any number of reasons. If that occurs, the transaction is subject to the general rules discussed above.[36]

12.84

Transfers of Franchises, Trademarks, and Trade Names

For a number of years the courts have struggled with the question as to whether proceeds from the grant or transfer of franchise rights should be treated as capital gain when the transferor reserves significant powers or rights in connection with the franchise. A number of these cases involved franchises for distribution of Dairy Queen products.[37] The proceeds in question usually involved both payments of fixed amounts and additional payments contingent on the volume of sales or production or some other measure of the use or disposition of the rights transferred. Transferors of the franchises usually reserved various rights and imposed various restrictions, which led the courts to a variety of conflicting decisions. As observed by Judge Brown of the Fifth Circuit in one concurring opinion, these issues occupied "the attention of no less than 18 Circuit Judges, one District Judge whose 'extremely able decision' was last found to be both wrong and right, and an undisclosed number of Tax Court Judges."[38] Most of these decisions held that the fixed payments were entitled to capital-gain treatment while the contingent payments were treated as ordinary income. One case implied that both types of payments could be capital gain if they represented proceeds from the sales of property, and in some decisions both types of payments were treated as ordinary income.

12.85

36. Rev. Rul. 69–482.
37. Dairy Queen of Oklahoma, Inc. v. Com., 250 F.2d 503 (10th Cir. 1957), 52 AFTR 1092, 58–1 USTC ¶9155; Gowdey's Estate v. Com., 307 F.2d 816 (4th Cir. 1962), 10 AFTR2d 5106, 62–2 USTC ¶9722; V. H. Moberg v. Com., 305 F.2d 800 (5th Cir. 1962), 10 AFTR2d 5348; T. E. Moberg v. Com., 305 F.2d 800 (9th Cir. 1962), 10 AFTR2d 5974; U.S. v. Wernentin, 354 F.2d 757 (8th Cir. 1965), 17 AFTR2d 011, 66–1 USTC ¶9140.
38. V. E. Moberg, 365 F.2d 337 (5th Cir. 1966), 18 AFTR2d 5470, 66 USTC ¶9602.

12.86 The Tax Reform Act of 1969 sought to put an end to this controversy. It added Section 1253 to the code which provides that "a transfer of a franchise, trademark, or trade name shall not be treated as a sale or exchange of a capital asset if the transferor retains any significant power, right, or continuing interest with respect to the subject matter of the franchise, trademark, or trade name." This section provides that the renewal of a franchise, trademark, or trade name will be treated as a transfer thereof; but it excepts from its application the transfer of a franchise to engage in professional football, basketball, baseball, or other professional sport.

12.87 Section 1253(b)(2) lists six types of rights as being included within the term "significant power or right or continuing interest," so that the presence of any one or more of them will result in proceeds received on a transfer being treated as ordinary income. Read that paragraph. In addition, the report[39] of the Senate Finance Committee indicates that if the transferor's conduct constitutes participation in the commercial or economic activities of the transferee's business, this will be regarded as a retention of a significant power, right, or continuing interest.

12.88 If the right to receive payments contingent on the productivity or use of the rights transferred is "a substantial element under the transfer agreement" all payments received under the transfer, contingent or fixed, will be treated as ordinary income [Section 1253(b)(2)(F)]. If contingent payments are required but do not constitute a substantial element under the agreement, and if no other significant power, right, or continuing interest is reserved by the transferor, fixed (noncontingent) payments may be treated as proceeds from sale of capital assets; however, contingent payments will always be ordinary income [Section 1253(c)]. Generally speaking, these provisions make it rather difficult for most transferors of franchises to treat the proceeds from the transfers as capital gains.

12.89 The payor's tax treatment of payments is consistent with the treatment accorded the payee. If the latter has ordinary income, the payor has an ordinary deduction. Read Section 1253(d).

12.90 If a transfer qualifies as a sale or exchange of a capital asset, noncontingent payments made for such transfer will be treated by the payor as the cost of the assets acquired. If the assets have definitely determinable useful lives, these costs may be depreciated or amortized over such lives; however, if the useful lives are not definitely determinable, no depreciation or amortization will be allowable (see paragraph 8.8).

Dispositions Treated as Sales or Exchanges

12.91 A number of transactions that actually are not sales or exchanges are brought within the capital-gains treatment by specific provisions of

39. Report of Senate Finance Committee on Section 516 of Tax Reform Act of 1969.

the code. These provisions are exceptions to the general rule governing capital gains. Unless a transaction is covered by one of these specific provisions, there must be a sale or exchange in order that a gain on disposition of a capital asset can qualify for capital-gains treatment.

Retirement of Bonds. As indicated by the *Hudson* case above, the retirement of a bond or other evidence of debt is not a sale or exchange. Nevertheless, Section 1232 extends capital-gain treatment to holders of certain bonds, notes, debentures, certificates, or other evidences of indebtedness that are capital assets in the hands of the taxpayer, and that *are issued by any corporation, or government, or political subdivision thereof.* Section 1232 provides that amounts received on retirement of these bonds and other debt instruments, *shall be considered* as amounts received in exchange therefor. 12.92

With respect to bonds and other evidences of indebtedness issued before 1955, this rule applies only to those originally issued with interest coupons or in registered form and to those that were in such form on March 1, 1954. 12.93

Regardless of the above rules, any long-term gain on sale or exchange of bonds and other evidences of indebtedness issued by a government or political subdivision thereof after 1954 is treated as ordinary income to the extent of that portion of any original-issue discount that is applicable to the period the bond is held by the taxpayer [Section 1232(a)(2)]. Long-term gains on sale or exchange of bonds or other evidences of indebtedness issued by corporations on or before May 27, 1969, receive the same treatment. However, if at the time of original issue there was an intent to call the bond before maturity, the gain is treated as ordinary income to the extent of the full original-issue discount. 12.94

With respect to bonds and other evidences of indebtedness issued by corporations after May 27, 1969, any original-issue discount applicable to the holder is required to be amortized into income on a monthly basis by the holder. The amount so amortized is added to the holder's basis of the evidence of indebtedness. Any gain on sale, exchange, or retirement of these evidences of indebtedness held for more than six months is treated in full as long-term capital gain. Again, however, if at the time of issuance there was an intent to call the indebtedness before maturity, any such gain is treated as ordinary income to the extent of the unamortized original-issue discount. These rules on original-issue discount do not apply to the holder of an evidence of indebtedness purchased at a premium; and original-issue discount is decreased by any amount a purchaser pays in excess of the original-issue price plus the original-issue discount applicable to the period prior to the purchase. 12.95

Original-issue discount is the excess of the stated redemption price of the bond at maturity over the price for which the bond is issued. If this discount is less than one-fourth of 1 percent of the redemption price multiplied by the number of years to maturity, the original-issue discount is ignored [Section 1232(b)]. The discount applicable 12.96

to the period the bond is held by the taxpayer is the ratio of the number of full months he holds the bond to the number of full months between the original-issue date and the stated maturity date [Reg. 1.1232(3)(c)].

12.97   Bonds convertible into stock usually yield less interest than pure debt bonds. For example, a corporation that might get only $800 for a $1,000 five percent nonconvertible bond may be able to sell the same bond for $1,000 if it is made convertible into stock of the corporation. In December, 1968, the American Institute of Certified Public Accountants took the position that the value of the conversion right should be disregarded so that it would not cause an original-issue discount on the sale of such a bond. Section 1232(b)(2) agrees with this view. It requires an allocation of the issue price between the evidence of indebtedness and any separate warrant or other security issued with the evidence of indebtedness as an investment unit. If the issue price allocated to the evidence of indebtedness is less than the maturity amount, the difference is original-issue discount. The Code does not require any such allocation to the value of a convertibility feature in the evidence of indebtedness; and the issuer has no deduction for amortization of such value.[40]

12.98   The issue price of an evidence of indebtedness issued for property ordinarily is the stated redemption price at maturity. This general rule also applies to bonds issued pursuant to certain reorganizations of corporations. An exception to this rule is made, however, in the case of bonds issued (other than in connection with certain reorganizations) that are traded on an established securities market or bonds issued for stock or securities that are traded on an established securities market. In these cases, the issue price of the bonds is the fair market value of the property received [Section 1232(b)(2)].

12.99   Original-issue discount is deductible by the issuing corporation on an amortization basis from the date of issuance to the date of maturity (or in the case of a callable bond, to the earlier call date). It is in reality interest (Reg. 1.163–3).

12.100   **Failure to Exercise Option.** Under Section 1234(a), gain or loss attributable to the sale or exchange of a privilege or option to buy or sell property is considered gain or loss from the sale or exchange of property that has the same character as the property to which the option relates has in the hands of the taxpayer or would have in his hands if acquired by him. For example, loss from failure to exercise an option purchased in a hedging transaction is treated as ordinary loss. Section 1234(b) also provides that a loss incurred in connection with a taxpayer's failure to exercise an option shall be treated as a loss from the sale or exchange of the option on the date it expires. Thus, although the failure to exercise is not technically a sale or exchange, it is treated as a sale or exchange for tax purposes.

12.101   This rule does not apply to options held by a dealer in options, compensatory stock options of employees, or any other options if the gain attributable to them would be treated as ordinary income without

40. Chock Full O' Nuts Corp. v. U.S., 453 F.2d 300 (2nd Cir., 1971), 29 AFTR2d 72–305.

regard to Section 1234. Likewise, this rule does not apply to a loss incurred on failure to exercise an option to sell property where property intended to be used in exercising such option is acquired on the same day the option is acquired. Such a loss is not recognized but is added to the cost of the property with which the option was identified [Section 1233(c)].

Cancellations of Leases and Distributor Agreements. The cancellation of a lease or the cancellation of a distributor's agreement does not constitute a sale or exchange. However, Section 1241 provides that "amounts received by a lessee for the cancellation of a lease or by a distributor of goods for the cancellation of a distributor's agreement (if the distributor has a substantial capital investment in the distributorship), shall be considered as amounts received in exchange for such lease or agreement." 12.102

SHORT SALES OF STOCK

A short sale of stock occurs when a person sells shares that he does not own or, if he does own them, without actually selling those particular shares at that time. His broker borrows or buys the shares to cover the short sale, but eventually the customer must buy and deliver the shares he sold short in order to cover his obligation. A person sells short when he anticipates that the market will drop; if he guesses wrong, he can sustain a sizable loss. Regulation 1.1233–1(a) sets forth the general rules pertaining to gains and losses from short sales as follows: 12.103

(1) For income tax purposes a short sale is not deemed to be consummated until delivery of property to close the short sale. Whether the recognized gain or loss from a short sale is capital gain or loss or ordinary gain or loss depends upon whether the property so delivered constitutes a capital asset in the hands of the taxpayer.

(2) Thus, if a dealer in securities makes a short sale of X Corporation stock, ordinary gain or loss results on closing of the short sale if the stock used to close the short sale was stock which he held primarily for sale to customers in the ordinary course of his trade or business. If the stock used to close the short sale was a capital asset in his hands, or if the taxpayer in this example was not a dealer, a capital gain or loss would result.

(3) Generally, the period for which a taxpayer holds property delivered to close a short sale determines whether long-term or short-term capital gain or loss results.

(4) Thus, if a taxpayer makes a short sale of shares of stock and covers the short sale by purchasing and delivering shares which he held for not more than six months, the recognized gain or loss would be considered short-term capital gain or loss. If the short sale is made through a broker and the broker borrows property to make a delivery, the short sale is not deemed to be consummated until the obligation of the seller created by the short sale is finally discharged by delivery of property to the broker to replace the property borrowed by the broker.

Even though a taxpayer owns securities at the time he makes a short sale of such securities, no gain or loss is realized until he covers his short position with the securities owned at the time of the sale or with securities purchased after the sale was made.

12.104 If a taxpayer at the time of a short sale holds securities substantially identical to that sold short or if he acquires such substantially identical securities after the short sale and continues to own them after he closes the short sale, technical rules in Section 1233 and Reg. 1.1233–1(c) govern whether the gain or loss on the short sale is long-term or short-term and also govern the holding period of the substantially identical securities. The purpose of these rather complex rules is to prevent the use of short sales for the artificial conversion of short-term gains into long-term gains and long-term losses into short-term losses.

WASH SALES

12.105 A wash sale is a sale or other disposition of stock or securities at a loss accompanied by a purchase of substantially identical stock or securities during a period beginning thirty days before the date of sale or other disposition and ending thirty days after that date—a total of sixty-one days. Section 1091 denies a deduction in such circumstances. In addition to an acquisition by purchase within the sixty-one-day period, the rule also applies to an acquisition (a) by an exchange upon which the entire amount of gain or loss is recognized and (b) by a contract entered into or an option obtained during the sixty-one-day period to acquire substantially identical stock or securities. If the disposition during the sixty-one-day period is at a gain it is not a wash sale, and the gain will be taxable. The rule does not apply to individuals who are traders or dealers in securities and to corporations that are dealers in securities if the sale or other disposition is made in the ordinary course of their businesses.

12.106 When a loss is disallowed because of its being a wash sale, the basis of the substantially identical stock or securities acquired during the sixty-one-day period is the cost thereof plus the amount of the loss disallowed.

EXAMPLE On March 8, a taxpayer buys 100 shares of stock for $6,000 and then sells them on December 10 of the same year for $4,000. At that point he has sustained a long-term capital loss in the amount of $2,000. If he purchases 100 shares of the same stock at any time between the preceding November 10 and the following January 9 at a cost of $3,500, the long-term capital loss of $2,000 is not allowable, and the basis of the shares purchased becomes $5,500 ($3,500 + $2,000).

12.107 The date used for the wash-sale rule is the contract date upon which the broker contracts to buy or sell, not the settlement date, which is usually five business days later under the rules of the stock exchanges.

SALES OF PROPERTY USED IN A
TRADE OR BUSINESS

Real property used in a trade or business and depreciable property   12.108
used in a trade or business are excluded from the definition of capital
assets [Section 1221(2)]. However, Section 1231 provides special
treatment for gains and losses from sales or exchanges of such property
held for more than six months. At one time this special treatment
could be even more favorable than that accorded capital assets, but
the trend toward requiring recapture of depreciation on dispositions
of Section 1231 property is rapidly diminishing the benefit of Section 1231.

Section 1231

Gains and losses subject to the provisions of Section 1231 and the   12.109
assets involved in dispositions giving rise to such treatment are generally referred to as "Section 1231 gains and losses" and "Section 1231
assets." In determining the tax treatment of Section 1231 gains and
losses, it is first necessary to aggregate all such gains and losses. If
the aggregate gains exceed the aggregate losses, all gains and losses
are treated as net long-term capital gains and losses. If the aggregate
losses exceed the aggregate gains, all the gains and losses are treated
as ordinary gains and losses. In this connection, however, if any part
of the gain on any asset included in the aggregation represents the
recapture of depreciation or other prior-year ordinary deduction (see
paragraph 12.113 et seq.) that part of the gain is not subject to Section 1231; therefore, in determining whether Section 1231 gains
exceed losses, it is necessary to exclude from consideration that part
of any gain that represents such recapture income.

Types of Gains and Losses Taken into Account

Taken into account under Section 1231 are gains and losses arising   12.110
from the following transactions:

1. Sales or exchanges of real property used in the taxpayer's trade or
   business and held for more than six months.
2. Sales or exchanges of depreciable property used in the taxpayer's trade
   or business and held for more than six months.
3. Sales or exchanges of livestock (other than poultry) held for draft, breeding, dairy, or sporting purposes and held by the taxpayer for twelve
   months or more. For cattle and horses acquired after 1969 the required
   holding period is twenty-four months; further the permissible "sporting" purpose applies only to acquisitions after 1969.

4. Sales or exchanges of unharvested crops on land used in the trade or business and held for more than six months, if sold, exchanged, or involuntarily converted at the same time and to the same person as such land.

5. Cutting or other disposal of timber, and the receipt of coal and domestic iron-ore royalties, which are treated as sales or exchanges under Section 631.

6. Involuntary conversions (other than those arising from a casualty or theft and other than those gains that the taxpayer elected under Section 1033 not to have recognized) of the above types of properties and of capital assets held for more than six months regardless of whether personal or held for the production of income and regardless of whether insured.

7. Involuntary conversions (other than those gains that the taxpayer elected under Section 1033 not to have recognized) arising from casualty or theft of the properties described above in 1 through 5 and of capital assets held for more than six months regardless of whether personal or held for the production of income and regardless of whether insured, but only if the gains from the casualties or thefts exceed the losses.

12.111   Number 7 above states the rule for 1970 and later years. All gains and losses from casualties and thefts must be netted regardless of whether the property is insured or not. If there is a net gain, such amount is combined with the regular Section 1231 items listed in 1 through 6 to determine whether there is a net gain on Section 1231 transactions, and therefore, a net long-term capital gain (except for any recapture), or a fully deductible net loss. On the other hand, if there is a net loss, such amount is not combined with the regular Section 1231 gains and losses. Instead, each recognized gain is taxed as a capital gain—if the asset involved was a capital asset—or as ordinary income, and each loss is deductible as a casualty or theft loss subject to the $100 exclusion applicable to each personal loss. This $100 exclusion is not taken into account if there is an overall net gain from these casualty or theft losses.

LINES		INDIVIDUALS		
		A	B	C
	During 1971 three individuals who all own their separate proprietorship businesses have the following transactions involving assets held for more than six months and realize the indicated gains and (losses):			
1	Gain on sale of machine used in business	$ 3,000	$ 3,000	$ 3,000
2	(Loss) on sale of land and building used in business	(5,000)	(5,000)	(8,000)
3	Gain on involuntary conversion arising from condemnation of land held as an investment	10,000	10,000	10,000
4	Subtotal — regular Section 1231 transactions	$ 8,000	$ 8,000	$ 5,000

		INDIVIDUALS			
		A	B	C
	Net casualty and theft occurrences:			
5	Gain from fire insurance recovery on warehouse that burned down and was not replaced	$ 6,000	$ —	$ 6,000
6	Uninsured theft of negotiable 3% bearer bond (cost $5,000 and value $4,000)	(4,000)	(4,000)	(4,000)
7	Net	$ 2,000	$ (4,000)	$ 2,000
8	Amount of line 7 taken into account for Section 1231	$ 2,000	$ —	$ 2,000
9	Total net long-term gain under Section 1231 (line 4 plus line 8)	$ 10,000	$ 8,000	$ 7,000
	Ordinary income portion attributable to recapture of depreciation:			
10	Machine	$ 3,000	$ 3,000	$ 3,000
11	Warehouse	5,000	—	5,000
12	Total	$ 8,000	$ 3,000	$ 8,000
13	Aggregate net gains and (losses) subject to Section 1231 (line 9 less line 12)	$ 2,000	$ 5,000	$ (1,000)

Note that B has a net loss of $4,000 from casualty and theft occurrences. Accordingly, that amount does not enter into the Section 1231 calculations, but is separately deductible to the extent of $3,900 ($4,000 less $100 exclusion) as a theft loss. Both A and B have aggregate net gains from transactions that are subject to Section 1231; therefore all of such gains and losses are treated as long-term capital gains and losses. C has an aggregate net loss of $1,000; therefore all of his gains and losses subject to Section 1231 are treated as ordinary gains and losses.

12.112 Section 1231 gains and losses do not include gains and losses from sales or exchanges of property includible in inventory or held for sale to customers in the ordinary course of business. Likewise, they do not include gains and losses from copyrights, literary, musical, or artistic compositions or from letters or memoranda-type property held by a taxpayer described in Section 1221(3).

RECAPTURE OF DEPRECIATION AND OF OTHER DEDUCTIONS

12.113 The recapture provisions were enacted in the 1960s. Their purpose is to reduce or eliminate the net long-term capital gain benefit available under Section 1231 so that at least a part of such gain will be treated as ordinary income. The part so treated is based on deprecia- tion and certain other deductions allowed in prior years and is called a recapture of those amounts. The proponents of recapture believed it was inequitable to allow taxpayers to deduct depreciation, amortiza- tion, and certain other amounts from ordinary income and then re- coup these deductions by a sale or other disposition of the related properties at long-term capital gain rates.

12.114   Under the recapture rules the effect of inflation is completely ig- nored. If the value of tools and machinery increases in terms of dol- lars because of inflation, and if such tools and machinery are sold for an amount greater than their depreciated original cost, the govern- ment under Section 1245 will take back or "recapture" the deprecia- tion allowed in previous years by taxing as ordinary income that portion of the gain equal to depreciation allowed after 1961. To the extent that any such gain is attributable to inflation, this recapture treatment seems unfair.

12.115   The recapture rules were enacted at various times, and accordingly they provide for the recapture of deductions incurred after various dates. For example, Section 1245 provides for recapture of deprecia- tion allowed after 1961 on some properties (mostly personal property), after June 30, 1963 on elevators and escalators, and after 1969 on live- stock. It also provides for recapture of amortization allowed after 1967 on pollution control facilities, and after 1969 on railroad grading and railroad tunnel bores. Section 1250 provides for recapture of depreciation on depreciable real property, principally buildings, allowed after 1963. Section 1251 calls for the recapture of certain amounts of farm losses incurred by cash-basis farmers after 1969 upon the sale of designated types of farm property. Finally, Section 1252 requires recapture of varying percentages of deductions allowed to farmers after 1969 for soil and water conservation expenditures under Section 175 and for land clearing expenditures under Section 182.

12.116   These recapture sections take precedence over all other sections of the Code. This means that if some other section provides for non- recognition of gain on a particular exchange or disposition, neverthe- less gain will be recognized to the extent of the recapture element unless the applicable recapture section provides otherwise.

Section 1245 Recapture of Depreciation on Properties Other Than Buildings

12.117   Under Section 1245, any gain realized on the sale, exchange, or in- voluntary conversion of certain depreciable property other than buildings is recognized as ordinary income to the extent of certain depreciation and amortization allowed in 1962 and later years. If such property is disposed of in a transaction other than a sale, ex- change, or involuntary conversion, ordinary income is recognized to the extent that the property's fair market value exceeds its adjusted basis. Except where other periods are specified, the ordinary income so recognized cannot exceed the depreciation allowed after 1961.

In the case of elevators and escalators, the ordinary income is limited to the depreciation allowed after June 30, 1963. In the case of livestock, it is limited to depreciation allowed after December 31, 1969.

With respect to properties on which amortization has been allowed under Sections 169 and 185 (pollution control facilities, railroad grading, and railroad tunnel bores) Section 1245 income includes depreciation and amortization for all periods beginning with the month in which such amortization is first allowed. If the property disposed of was subject to amortization allowances under Section 168, relating to emergency facilities (no longer in effect), or to amortization in lieu of depreciation, such amortization allowances are subject to recapture the same as depreciation [Reg. 1.1245–2(a)(3)]. 12.118

Depreciation recapture is calculated separately with respect to each item of property [Reg. 1.1245–1(a)(1) and (d)]. Losses incurred on one item may not be offset against Section 1245 income applicable to another item, even though both are disposed of in the same transaction. 12.119

Section 1245 Property. Depreciation is recaptured under Section 1245 on the disposition of only "Section 1245 property." This property is defined in Section 1245(a)(3): 12.120

(3) Section 1245 Property.—For purposes of this section, the term "section 1245 property" means any property which is or has been property of a character subject to the allowance for depreciation provided in Section 167 (or subject to the allowance of amortization provided in Section 185) and is either—

(A) personal property,

(B) other property (not including a building or its structural components) but only if such other property is tangible and has an adjusted basis in which there are reflected adjustments described in paragraph (2) for a period in which such property (or other property)—

(i) was used as an integral part of manufacturing, production, or extraction or of furnishing transportation, communications, electrical energy, gas, water, or sewage disposal services, or

(ii) constituted research or storage facilities used in connection with any of the activities referred to in clause (i),

(C) an elevator or an escalator, or

(D) so much of any real property [other than any property described in subparagraph (B)] which has an adjusted basis in which there are reflected adjustments for amortization under Section 169 or 185.

This definition is deceptively simple, and it must be analyzed very carefully to determine its application. In practice, it will probably apply to most depreciable property other than buildings. 12.121

Personal property can be Section 1245 property whether it be tangible or intangible. Thus, patents and copyrights are included. Further, local law will govern in determining what types of tangible property are personal property. All movable tangible property, such as trucks, automobiles, furniture, and filing cabinets, are personal property. Usually, if a machine when installed becomes permanently attached to a building, so that concrete would have to be broken to 12.122

remove it, it is real property. If it can be removed merely by unscrewing bolts and screws, it is personal property.

12.123 Some real property improvements are specifically included in Section 1245 property. These are (1) escalators and elevators, and (2) pollution control facilities and railroad grading and railroad tunnel bores on which amortization under Sections 169 and 185 has been allowed. Other real property is Section 1245 property if (1) it is tangible, (2) it is not a building or a structural component of a building, and (3) depreciation was allowed with respect to the property for some period during which it was used as an integral part of manufacturing, production or mining, or the furnishing of transportation and public utility services, or constituted research or storage facilities for the aforenamed types of business activities. A leasehold of any Section 1245 property is also Section 1245 property.

12.124 **Exceptions to Section 1245 Recapture.** Section 1245 income is recognized on any disposition of Section 1245 property unless Subsection (b) thereof provides an exception or limitation. Thus Section 1245 income will be recognized when a corporation distributes property as a dividend in kind or in partial or complete liquidation even though gain or loss might not otherwise be recognized to the distributing corporation on such a transfer.

12.125 Transactions to which Section 1245 does not apply, or applies only to a limited extent, are described in Section 1245(b) and include the following situations:

1. *Gifts:* Depreciation is not recaptured on dispositions of property by gift. However, if the donee's basis on disposition of the property is determined by reference to the donor's basis, the depreciation allowed the donor after the appropriate date will be subject to recapture on the donee's disposition of the property. Thus the "Section 1245 potential" of the property will carry through to the donee.

2. *Transfers at death:* Section 1245 does not apply to transfers by reason of death. However, if income in respect of a decedent would have represented Section 1245 income if received by the decedent, it is also Section 1245 income to the person receiving it by reason of the decedent's death.

3. *Certain tax-free transactions:* Depreciation is recaptured only to a limited extent in certain tax-free transactions in which the transferor's basis in the property carries through and becomes the basis of the transferee. These transactions are (a) a parent corporation's liquidation of a controlled subsidiary where its basis in the subsidiary's stock does *not* become its basis for the assets received (Section 332); (b) transfers of property to corporations controlled by the transferors (Section 351); (c) transfers of property pursuant to certain corporate reorganizations under sections 361, 371(a), and 374(a); (d) contributions of property to partnerships by partners (Section 721); and (e) distributions of property by partnerships to partners (Section 731). In these transactions, Section 1245 applies only to the extent that gain is recognized to the transferor under some other section of the Code. That is, depreciation is not recaptured if the transaction is otherwise tax-free.

4. *Like-kind exchanges, involuntary conversions, etc.:* Depreciation is recaptured on exchanges of like-kind property and involuntary conversions only to the extent of the sum of (a) gain which is otherwise recognized thereon under Sections 1031 and 1033 and (b) the fair market value of any property received by the taxpayer that is not Section 1245 property but is property of a kind that will not give rise to recognized gain under sections 1031 and 1033 (property of like-kind or property similar or related to the property transferred or converted).
5. *Transfers pursuant to order of FCC or SEC:* Rules similar to those described at 3 and 4 above also apply to depreciation recapture in connection with sales or exchanges made to effectuate policies of the Federal Communications Commission or in obedience to orders of the Securities and Exchange Commission and described in Sections 1071 and 1081.

Except for transfers at death, all the exceptions noted above involve transactions in which the basis of the property carries through, in whole or in part, either from the transferor to the transferee or from the property transferred to the property received. Whenever this basis carries through, the Section 1245 potential in that basis also carries through. Thus, when Section 1245 property is disposed of in a transaction to which recapture rules apply, the amount subject to recapture includes not only the appropriate deductions allowed to the taxpayer, but also those allowed to a previous owner or on previously owned property with respect to which the property's basis in the hands of the taxpayer is determined [Reg. 1.1245–2(a)(4)]. However, depreciation and amortization are recaptured only once. If Section 1245 gain was recognized in part on a transaction listed in Section 1245(b), those deductions recaptured will not again be subject to recapture on subsequent disposition of the property [Reg. 1.1245–2(c)(4)].

Taxpayer acquired a race horse for use in his horse-racing and breeding operations on January 1, 1969, for $12,000. Depreciation allowed in 1969 was $2,400 and $1,920 in 1970, a total of $4,320. On January 1, 1971, taxpayer exchanged that horse for another and received cash boot of $500. The value of the new horse was $10,500. Depreciation allowed on the new horse in 1971 was $750. On December 31, 1971, this horse was sold for $10,000. Taxpayer has no farm losses under Section 1251.

Adjusted basis of the horse sold on December 31, 1971, was $6,930 computed as follows:

Cost of horse purchased January 1, 1969	$12,000
Less depreciation allowed in 1969 and 1970	4,320
Adjusted basis at date of trade	$ 7,680
Add gain recognized on trade (boot received), all subject to Section 1245	500
	$ 8,180
Less boot received	500
Basis of new horse	$ 7,680
Less depreciation allowed in 1971	750
Adjusted basis at December 31, 1971	$ 6,930

The gain on sale of the horse on December 31, 1971 for $10,000 was $3,070, of which $2,170 was ordinary income under Section 1245. The $2,170 represents the total Section 1245 potential of the horse calculated as follows:

Depreciation allowed on old horse in 1970	$1,920
Less Section 1245 gain on trade	500
Section 1245 potential carried over to new horse	$1,420
Depreciation allowed on new horse in 1971	750
Total Section 1245 potential	$2,170

The remainder of the gain, $900 ($3,070 − $2,170), is subject to the provisions of Section 1231 and, depending upon other Section 1231 transactions in the same year, can be a long-term capital gain.

12.127 **Recomputed Basis.** To provide for the tax consequences described in the preceding paragraphs, Section 1245 introduces a new concept called "recomputed basis." Although its results are the same as those described above, the mechanics of the income calculation are somewhat different. "Recomputed basis" means the adjusted basis of the Section 1245 property at the date disposed of plus the adjustments to basis for depreciation and amortization allowed since 1962 or such other date prescribed for the particular type of property involved. Section 1245 then provides that ordinary income will be recognized in an amount as follows:

1. In the case of a sale or exchange, the *lesser* of the following:
   (a) Excess of amount received over the adjusted basis (that is, in the ordinary case, cost less accumulated depreciation) of the property disposed of, or
   (b) Excess of the recomputed basis of the property disposed of over its adjusted basis.
2. In the case of a disposition that is not a sale or exchange, the lesser of the following:
   (a) Excess of the fair market value of the property disposed of over its adjusted basis (ordinarily the depreciated cost), or
   (b) Excess of the recomputed basis of the property disposed of over its adjusted basis.

Section 1250 Recapture of Depreciation on Buildings and Certain Other Real Property

12.128 Under Section 1250, depreciation is recaptured by treating as ordinary income some part of the gain on disposition of Section 1250 property that otherwise would be treated as long-term capital gain. Section 1250 property is any depreciable real property that is not Section 1245 property [Section 1250(c)]. This generally will include buildings and leaseholds of buildings. Like Section 1245, Section 1250 recognizes income on any disposition of Section 1250 property regardless of other Code sections, unless Section 1250(d) provides an exception or limitation. If the disposition of property is not a sale or exchange, Section 1250 income is based on the excess of the property's fair market value over its adjusted basis.

Section 1250 does not apply to a gain on the sale of land; therefore, it is important that the sales price of improved real estate be properly allocated between the land and any building or other improvements thereon. 12.129

The holding period of property acquired begins the day after acquisition. The holding period of property constructed by the taxpayer begins on the first day of the month during which the property is placed in service [Section 1250(e)]. 12.130

Section 1250 was first enacted in 1964, and it recaptures only depreciation allowed after 1963. In the Tax Reform Act of 1969 the application of Section 1250 was strengthened and extended, particularly as it applies to nonresidential property. Its rules are now quite complex in that the recapture of depreciation allowed in 1970 and later years is calculated first under rules applicable to those years. Then, if the gain is large enough, additional recapture is calculated under somewhat different rules with respect to depreciation allowed during the period 1964–1969 inclusive. 12.131

The amount of ordinary income recognized under Section 1250 with respect to depreciation allowed in each period is calculated by using two new terms, "additional depreciation" and "applicable percentage." Their meanings are explained below. The calculations are made by multiplying the lower of (a) the additional depreciation, or (b) the gain realized on sale or exchange of the property (or in the absence of a sale or exchange, the excess of the property's fair market value over its adjusted basis) by the applicable percentage for the period. 12.132

Additional Depreciation. If Section 1250 property (other than "rehabilitation expenditure" property) is held one year or less, the term "additional depreciation" means all depreciation allowed after 1963. If the property is held longer than one year, additional depreciation is the excess of depreciation allowed after 1963 under an accelerated method (such as declining-balance or sum-of-the-years-digits) over the depreciation that would have been allowable under the straight-line method. Thus, if property is held for more than one year, Section 1250 will apply only if accelerated depreciation has been allowed [Section 1250(b)]. 12.133

For purposes of Section 1250, rehabilitation expenditures for which depreciation is allowed over a sixty-month period under Section 167(k) (discussed in paragraph 8.37) are treated separately from the remainder of the property to which those expenditures apply. With respect to the expenditures, "additional depreciation" means all of the portion allowed of this five-year depreciation if the property is disposed of within one year from the time such expenditures are incurred. If the property is held for more than one year after the rehabilitation expenditures were incurred, the additional depreciation is, like other Section 1250 property, the excess of the depreciation 12.134

allowed over depreciation calculated on the straight-line method using the regular useful life of the property [Section 1250(b)(4)].

12.135 **Applicable Percentage.** The applicable percentage depends upon the nature of the property and the period during which the additional depreciation was allowed.

12.136   FOR ADDITIONAL DEPRECIATION ALLOWED BEFORE 1970. The applicable percentage for additional depreciation allowed before 1970 is 100 percent if the disposition of the property occurs during the first 20 months after its acquisition. If the property is held over 20 full months, the applicable percentage is 100 percent less 1 percent for each month the property is held over the 20 months' period. Thus, if property is held ten years (120 months), the applicable percentage to be applied to additional depreciation allowed before 1970 is zero, and none of that depreciation is recaptured [Section 1250(a)(2)(B)].

12.137   FOR ADDITIONAL DEPRECIATION ALLOWED AFTER 1969. The general rule under Section 1250(a)(1)(C) for depreciation allowed after 1969 is that the "applicable percentage" is 100 percent. But there are special rules pertaining to four types of circumstances or properties:

1. With respect to property sold pursuant to a binding written contract in effect on July 24, 1969, the applicable percentage for post-1969 depreciation will be the same as that for depreciation allowed before 1970, namely 100 percent less 1 percent for each full month the property is held for more than twenty full months.

2. With respect to low-income housing projects constructed, reconstructed, or acquired before January 1, 1975, as to which a mortgage is insured under Section 221(d)(3) or 236 of the National Housing Act— or which housing is financed or assisted by direct loan or tax abatement under similar provisions of state or local law—and as to which the owner is limited as to rentals and rate of return on his investment [described in Section 1039(b)(1)(B)], the applicable percentage is 100 percent minus 1 percent for each full month the property was held after the date the property was held for twenty full months.

3. With respect to residential rental property that is eligible for depreciation under the 200 percent declining-balance and the sum-of-the-years-digits methods and that is defined in Section 167(j)(2) and discussed in paragraph 8.40—other than that covered by 1 or 2 above—the applicable percentage is 100 percent minus 1 percent for each full month the property was held after the date the property was held for 100 full months. This means there will be no recapture after the property is held for sixteen years and 8 months.

4. With respect to low-income rental housing as to which rehabilitation expenditures are allowed to be depreciated over a sixty-month period under Section 167(k), the applicable percentage is 100 percent minus 1 percent for each full month in excess of 100 full months after the date on which such property was placed in service. This applicable percentage applies both to the "additional depreciation" attributable to

the cost of acquisition of the building and to the "additional depreciation" under Section 1250(b)(4) applicable to the capitalized rehabilitation expenditures.

Illustration. Recapture under Section 1250 can be illustrated as follows:

A commercial building purchased in 1963 for $100,000 was sold in 1971
for $70,000, after being held ninety-six months. Depreciation allowed on the
property was $39,000, being $3,000 in 1963, $30,000 during the years 1964
through 1969, and $6,000 during 1970 and 1971. Depreciation on a straight-
line method would have been $24,000, being $1,500 in 1963, $18,000 during
the years 1964 through 1969, and $4,500 during 1970 and 1971. The gain
realized on the sale was $9,000 [$70,000 − ($100,000 − $39,000)]. Section
1250 income (that is, depreciation recaptured) is $3,300, calculated in the
following manner.

The applicable percentage for the depreciation allowed during 1970 and
1971 is 100 percent under the general rule. The applicable percentage for
depreciation allowed during 1964 through 1969 is 24 percent (100 percent
minus 1 percent for each of the seventy-six months the property was held
over the 20 months). The additional depreciation for the years 1970 and 1971
is $1,500 ($6,000 depreciation allowed minus $4,500 depreciation under
the straight-line method). The additional depreciation for the years 1964
through 1969 is $12,000 ($30,000 − $18,000).

Under Section 1250, the first depreciation to be recaptured is the additional depreciation allowed after 1969. Since this additional depreciation
($1,500) is less than the gain on disposition of the property ($9,000), the
depreciation recaptured is 100 percent (the applicable percentage) of such
additional depreciation, or $1,500.

Since the gain on disposition of the property exceeded the post-1969
additional depreciation by $7,500, this much of the additional depreciation
for the years 1964 through 1969 is also subject to recapture. The applicable
percentage for those years is applied to the lower of this remaining gain
($7,500) or the additional depreciation for the period ($18,000); thus, 24
percent of $7,500 (or $1,800) of depreciation for 1964 to 1969 is recaptured as
ordinary income. The total depreciation to be recaptured is $3,300 ($1,500
for 1970 and 1971 plus $1,800 for 1964 through 1969). The remainder of the
gain realized, namely $5,700 ($9,000 − $3,300) is subject to Section 1231.
Note that none of the depreciation before 1964 would be subject to recapture in any event [Section 1250(b)(3)].

Major Improvements. Section 1250 involves one complication that
was not involved in Section 1245. Depreciation recapture with respect
to any major improvements of real property is calculated separately
from the rest of the property, because the holding period and the resulting applicable percentage of such major improvements will be
different from that of the rest of the property. Major improvements
are treated separately only if they are substantial. The test of whether
or not improvements are substantial is quite complex, and any calculation will require specific reference to Section 1250(f). Similar
complications arise when proceeds from sales of low-income housing

projects are reinvested *along with additional sums of money* in other qualified low-income housing and gain is not recognized under Section 1039. Careful reference to Section 1250(d)(8) and regulations to be issued thereunder will be required in these circumstances.

12.140 **Exceptions to Section 1250 Recapture.** Similar to Section 1245, Section 1250 applies to any dispositions of property except those specifically excepted by Section 1250(d). These exceptions and limitations are substantially the same as those excepted from Section 1245. Thus depreciation of real property is not recaptured in the case of a gift, but the recapture potential carries through to the donee, and the donee takes the donor's holding period. Recapture occurs on transfers by reason of death only in connection with income in respect of a decedent. In the case of like-kind exchanges, involuntary conversions, and reinvestment of sale proceeds in low-income housing projects under Section 1039, the gain treated as ordinary income under Section 1250 is limited to the greater of (1) the gain otherwise recognized on the transaction or (2) the excess of the amount of Section 1250 gain that would be recognized if the transaction were fully taxable over the value of Section 1250 property acquired. In the case of an involuntary conversion, Section 1250(d)(4) includes in the first limitation any proceeds reinvested in stock of a controlled corporation. In these transactions in which Section 1250 gain is not recognized, the Section 1250 potential and holding period carries through to the Section 1250 property received in the transaction. In these transactions, other than involuntary conversions and like-kind exchanges, the holding period of the property also carries through to the new owner.

12.141 In the case of tax-free transfers involving corporations and partnerships in which the transferor's basis carries over to the transferee, the Section 1250 gain recognized is limited to the gain otherwise recognized in the transaction. Further, to the extent the Section 1250 gain is not recognized, the Section 1250 potential and holding period carries through to the transferee corporation.

Section 1251—Recapture of Farm Losses

12.142 Section 1251 provides for the recapture of certain farm losses in a manner similar to the recapture of depreciation under Sections 1245 and 1250. The purpose of Section 1251 is to minimize the use of farming operations by high-bracket taxpayers as tax shelters. In 1969 and earlier years this tax shelter was available because of two tax aspects of farming. First, cash-basis taxpayers, engaged in farming, often incurred significant losses because of expenditures incurred in raising breeding animals, in clearing land, in soil and water conservation activities, and in raising crops that were later sold with the land. These expenditures invariably added substantial value to the breeding herd and the land involved. Second, these losses could often be recouped from the sale of the breeding animals after holding them more than twelve months and from the sale of the land after holding it more than six months. Although the expenditures that added value to these assets were deductible against the taxpayer's ordinary income from other sources, the recoupment of these expenditures through sale of the breeding animals or land was treated as long-term capital gain under Section 1231. This combination of ordinary deductions and recoupment through long-term capital gains was a very advantageous tax shelter. The Tax Reform Act of 1969 substantially limits this tax shelter through the application of Section 1251.

Farm Recapture Property. Under Section 1251 the farm losses are "recaptured" by treating as ordinary income the gain from sale of farm "recapture property" that otherwise would be treated as long-term capital gain under Section 1231. For this purpose, "farm recapture property" includes real property (other than buildings qualifying as Section 1250 property), livestock held for breeding purposes, and unharvested crops sold with land that is or has been used in the taxpayer's farming business. Farm recapture property also includes such assets received by the taxpayer from previous owners with respect to whom the taxpayer's basis in such property is determined. The gain on the sale or exchange of this farm recapture property, or—in dispositions other than sales or exchanges—the excess of its fair market value over adjusted basis, is treated as ordinary income to the extent of certain farm losses previously incurred by the taxpayer. 12.143

The Excess-Deductions Account. The taxpayer's net farm losses that are subject to recapture are only those accounted for in a record maintained for tax purposes that is referred to as an "excess-deductions account" or "EDA." 12.144

In the case of corporations and trusts, an amount equal to the total farm net loss is added each year to the excess-deductions account. 12.145

In the case of individuals and estates, each year only the taxpayer's farm net loss in excess of $25,000 is added to the excess-deductions account, and that is added only if the taxpayer has nonfarm adjusted gross income for that year of more than $50,000. The same limitations apply to an electing Subchapter S corporation for any taxable year, provided that no shareholder of the corporation has a farm net loss. If a married individual files a separate return and if his spouse has any nonfarm adjusted gross income for the taxable year, these amounts of $25,000 and $50,000 should be read as $12,500 and $25,000 respectively. 12.146

Each year, if there is any amount in the excess-deductions account at the close of the taxpayer's taxable year before any deductions therefrom, there will be deducted from the account an amount equal to the farm net income for the year. There also will be deducted any amount necessary to adjust the account for losses added in prior years that did not result in any tax benefit to the taxpayer. Finally, there must be deducted an amount equal to the gain on sale or other disposition of farm recapture property that is treated as ordinary 12.147

income under Section 1251. Farm recapture income of any year is always limited to the balance in this EDA account at the end of that year before deducting any current-year recapture income.

12.148   **Exceptions to Recapture.** If a taxpayer so desires, he may be exempt from the application of Section 1251 by electing to use the accrual method of accounting for his farm operations and electing to capitalize all expenditures properly chargeable to capital accounts even though he may have available elections under other sections of the Code to deduct such expenditures.

12.149   Like Sections 1245 and 1250, unless Section 1251(d) provides an exception, Section 1251 will apply to the transfer of any farm recapture property irrespective of other provisions of the Code. Transactions on which gain will not be recognized pursuant to exceptions in Section 1251(d) are gifts, transfers at death, certain corporate transactions on which no gain or loss is recognized pursuant to Sections 332, 351, 361, 371(a), and 374(a), and certain like-kind exchanges and involuntary conversions.

12.150   In the case of exchanges of like-kind properties and involuntary conversions, Section 1251 gain will be recognized only to the extent of gain recognized under Sections 1031 and 1033 plus the fair market value of other property acquired that is not farm recapture property but with respect to which no gain is otherwise recognized.

12.151   If farm recapture property is transferred between corporations in transactions in which no gain or loss is recognized under the exceptions of Section 1251(d), the acquiring corporation succeeds to and takes into account the excess-deductions account of the transferor corporation.

12.152   A special rule applies if the farm recapture property is transferred by gift. If the potential gain (excess of fair market value over adjusted basis) of the farm recapture property transferred by gift during any one year is more than 25 percent of the potential gain of all farm recapture property of the taxpayer, the donee of the property succeeds to and takes into account a share of the donor's excess-deductions account equal to the ratio thereof that the potential gain on the property he receives bears to the potential gain of all farm recapture property of the donor immediately before the gift.

12.153   Partnerships also have special treatment under Section 1251. Each partner takes into account separately his distributive share of farm net losses and gains on disposition of farm recapture property. Such items are then treated as the taxpayer's own items in his return. If farm recapture property is contributed to a partnership and gain is not recognized under other partnership tax rules, the transferring partner recognizes gain on the transfer under Section 1251(d)(5) but only to the extent that the fair market value of the farm recapture property exceeds the value of the taxpayer's partnership interest attributable to such property. In this connection, it appears that the partnership interest attributable to such property will be measured by the extent to which gain with respect to the farm recapture property is allocated to the distributing partner by the partnership agreement.

If farm recapture property is transferred to a controlled corporation solely in exchange for stock or securities and gain is not recognized to the transferor, then the stock or securities received by the transferor are treated as farm recapture property. 12.154

Finally, if the farm recapture property consists of land, the potential gain in such land—and the Section 1251 income recognized on the disposition of that land—will be limited to the deductions allowed with respect to such land for soil- and water-conservation expenditures (Section 175) and expenditures for land clearing (Section 182) for the taxable year and the preceding four taxable years. 12.155

Possible Conflict with Section 1245. Section 1251 is silent concerning the effect of Section 1245. This gives rise to an apparent conflict in that the disposition of some farm recapture property might involve the recapture of depreciation under Section 1245 and the recapture of farm losses under Section 1251. If the recapture is recognized under Section 1245, the EDA would not be reduced unless the recapture income is included in farm net income. This inclusion is far from clear under the provisions of the Code [see definition at Section 1251(e)(2)]. If the income is recognized under Section 1251, such recapture income would reduce the excess-deductions account [Section 1251(b)(3)]. Presumably, regulations will be issued to clarify this conflict. 12.156

Section 1252—Recapture of Soil and Water Conservation Expenditures and Land Clearing Expenses

The Tax Reform Act of 1969 also extended the recapture concept to deductions attributable to soil- and water-conservation expenditures and land-clearing expenditures that a taxpayer has elected to treat as expenses under Sections 175 and 182. These recapture rules apply on the disposition of farm land on which such expenditures were made, and recapture occurs under the appropriate circumstances without regard to the excess-deductions account (EDA) of the taxpayer. 12.157

Under Section 1252 the amount of ordinary income recognized depends upon the holding period of the farm land. The ordinary income recognized is the lower of (a) the *applicable percentage* of the total deductions allowed under Sections 175 (soil and water conservation expenditures) and 182 (land clearing expenditures) to the taxpayer after December 31, 1969 with respect to the farm land disposed of or (b) the gain on sale or exchange of the land (or the excess of the fair market value of the land over its adjusted basis in case of a disposition other than a sale or exchange). These recapture rules do not apply if the recapture rules of Section 1251 apply to the disposition. 12.158

For purposes of Section 1252 the *applicable percentage* applied to the deduction is determined as follows: 12.159

If the farm land is disposed of:	The applicable percentage is:
within five years after the date it was acquired	100 percent
within the sixth year after it was acquired	80 percent
within the seventh year after it was acquired	60 percent
within the eighth year after it was acquired	40 percent
within the ninth year after it was acquired	20 percent
10 years or more after it was acquired	0 percent

12.160   Section 1252(b) provides that regulations shall be prescribed by the Treasury to apply rules for purposes of Section 1252 similar to those of Section 1245.

GAIN FROM SALE OF DEPRECIABLE PROPERTY BETWEEN RELATED TAXPAYERS

12.161   Section 1239 provides another exception to capital-gain benefits on the sale or exchange of property subject to depreciation. Under Section 1239, gain recognized on the transfer of depreciable property is considered ordinary income and not capital gain where the sale is between either (a) an individual and his spouse, or (b) an individual and a corporation controlled by the transferor and/or his spouse, minor children, and minor grandchildren. Control for this purpose means the ownership of more than 80 percent in value of the outstanding stock of the corporation.

12.162   Recognized gains are treated as ordinary income under this section, whether the sale is from husband to wife, from wife to husband, from an individual to the controlled corporation, or from the controlled corporation to the individual.

12.163   This rule applies only when the property sold is subject to depreciation in the hands of the transferee. The purpose of the provision is rather obvious. Without such a rule, one of the related parties could sell property to the other at a gain; and under appropriate circumstances, that gain could be taxed at a preferential rate as a long-term capital gain. The purchaser would get a stepped-up basis in the property; that is, the basis to the purchaser would be greater than the basis to the seller by an amount equal to the seller's gain. This step-up in basis would then be subject to depreciation in the hands of the buyer. The depreciation would be deductible against ordinary income taxable at rates that might be substantially greater than the preferential rate paid by the seller on the capital gain. This possibility would encourage related taxpayers to sell depreciable property to each other solely for tax avoidance purposes.

Although the purpose of Section 1239 is to prevent such tax avoidance possibilities, the section applies to any transaction described therein, whether or not tax avoidance is a motive of the parties for making the transaction. 12.164

In chapter 9 it was pointed out that Section 267(a)(1) disallows any loss on the sale of property between related taxpayers. The persons and entities deemed related are more extensive in Section 267 but include the relationships covered in Section 1239. If a husband sells depreciable property at a gain to his wife, he realizes ordinary income. If he sells it at a loss, the loss is not deductible. 12.165

QUESTIONS AND PROBLEMS

1. Indicate whether each of the following statements is true or false. Statements partially false or obviously incomplete are "false."
   (a) Gain on sale of stock bought January 18 and sold July 18 of the same year will be long-term.
   (b) Gain on sale of an automobile used in a trade or business is not treated as capital gain.
   (c) An unmarried individual's effective tax rate on long-term capital gains of $50,000 in one year is 25 percent of such gain.
   (d) A corporation's maximum effective tax rate on long-term capital gains for taxable years beginning after 1970 is 30 percent.
   (e) Net capital gains and net capital losses receive more favorable tax treatment than ordinary gains and ordinary losses.
   (f) All capital-loss carry-overs of corporations are treated as short-term capital losses.
   (g) Capital-loss carry-overs must be utilized as deductions within the five years succeeding the year incurred or such losses will not be deductible at all. This is true for (1) corporations, (2) taxpayers other than corporations.
   (h) The holding period of a capital asset sometimes includes the holding period of a previous owner if the asset is acquired by: (1) gift; (2) inheritance; (3) exchange of like-kind property; (4) one corporation on transfer from another corporation pursuant to a tax-free reorganization.
   (i) A sale or exchange (or a transaction treated as such by the Code) is a requisite for capital-gain treatment.
   (j) If all sales of real and depreciable property used in a trade or business result in gains, such gains will be treated as capital gains.
   (k) The amount of an owner's depreciation on a building determined under the straight-line method is not subject to recapture.
2. What is the definition of a capital asset?
3. Explain the general rules concerning the determination of holding period of an asset that has a substituted basis.
4. Explain why it is advisable for taxpayers to time their sales of depreciable property used in a trade or business so that gains are realized in years different from those in which losses are realized.
5. In years beginning after 1969, to what extent are capital losses deductible by (a) individuals, (b) corporations?

6. Calculate the 1972 tax liability of individuals A and B, both filing separate returns, and of corporations X and Y under circumstances set forth below. Assume all transactions originate in 1972.

	INDIVIDUALS		CORPORATIONS	
	A	B	X	Y
Taxable income before capital gains and (losses)	$ 60,000	$26,000	$20,000	$ 8,000
Long-term capital gains	40,000	70,000	20,000	25,000
Long-term capital (losses)	(5,000)	(5,000)	—	(5,000)
Short-term capital gains	8,000	—	10,000	5,000
Short-term capital (losses)	(11,000)	(5,000)	(5,000)	(3,000)

7. *Cumulative Problem.* Calculate the tax liability of Taxpayer M, a married man filing a joint return, for the calendar year 1972. M and his wife have two children and income and expenses as follows:

Salary	$25,000
Interest on corporate bonds	$ 500
Gain on sale of stock in XYZ Corporation bought on January 10, 1960, for $1,500	$ 900
Loss on loan to C, a former college classmate. Loan was $500, C gave M a 6 percent, 3-year note falling due in 1969. C took bankruptcy in 1971, and M received $100 in 1972 in final settlement of his note. Loan had no business connection	$ (400)
Gain on sale of breeding herd on farm. Animals had been held from three to four years	$ 1,200
Loss on worthless stock of ABC Corporation, which went bankrupt in 1972. Stock was acquired in 1965	$ (1,800)
Loss on farming operations	$ (5,000)
Contributions, taxes, and other allowable deductions, exclusive of personal exemptions	$ 3,000
Loss on sale of farm equipment, all long-term	$ (1,500)

8. Taxpayer operates a machine shop. In 1969 he purchased a heavy-duty machine for $20,000. Using the double declining-balance method of depreciation, taxpayer depreciated the machine as follows (all numbers rounded):

1969	$4,000
1970	3,200
1971	2,600
1972	2,000

(a) On January 1, 1973, taxpayer exchanged the machine for a smaller machine worth $11,000 and also received $3,000 in cash. How much gain or loss is recognized on the exchange? Is it ordinary income or capital gain? What is taxpayer's basis in the new machine?

(b) Assume taxpayer claims and is allowed depreciation of $1,000 on the new machine in 1973 and then sells it on January 1, 1974, for $10,000. How much gain or loss is recognized on the sale? Is the gain or loss ordinary or capital?

9. Taxpayer bought a tract of land in 1960 for $20,000. In December, 1968, he constructed a warehouse on the tract at a cost of $200,000, which he leased to a tenant for ten years beginning January 1, 1969. Depreciation allowed and allowable on the building for the years 1969 through June 30, 1973, was as follows:

1969	$10,000
1970	9,500
1971	9,025
1972	8,574
1973	4,073

On a straight-line basis, depreciation on this building would have been $4,500 per annum, based on a forty-year life and a 10 percent salvage factor.

On July 1, 1973, the land and building were exchanged for a large tract of unimproved land valued at $210,000. At the time of exchange, the land given up had appreciated in value to $30,000. This figure was based on other sales of unimproved land in the area. How much gain or loss is recognized? Is the amount recognized ordinary or capital?

10. Landlord leased business land to R Corporation. Several years later, which was ten years before the lease termination, S Corporation offered the landlord a substantially higher rental. S Corporation got a lease, but only after landlord paid R Corporation $8,000 for cancellation of the original lease. How does R Corporation treat the $8,000? Explain.

11. ABC, a manufacturing corporation, on March 15 paid $10,000 for an eight-month option to purchase land for a new plant. The option subsequently expired. Explain the tax treatment of the $10,000 expenditure.

12. A corporation bought 360-day noninterest-bearing United States Treasury bills at a discount having a maturity date ten months later and sold them two months before maturity at a gain of $20,000. Is this gain ordinary or capital? Why?

13. Sam Shane recently invented a device that improves the present process of converting salt water into fresh water. He has had a number of offers for the patent rights to the device. Because he needs funds immediately, he must accept one of the offers before six months has expired.

(a) Comment briefly on the tax consequences of each:

J Company is willing to pay Sam $500,000 for all of Sam's rights to the device.

K Company offers Sam $50,000 immediately plus 5 percent of the net proceeds from the sales of each device during the next ten years, in exchange for all of Sam's rights.

L Company is not interested in obtaining exclusive rights to the patent, but wishes to pay $100,000 for the right to manufacture the devices under a licensing agreement.

M Company desires to purchase only the foreign rights to the patent for $80,000.

(b) If the Q. T. Corporation owned the patent, (1) how would Section 1235 affect the tax consequences of the company's sale of the patent rights and (2) what would be the tax consequences of each of the four offers in (a)?

14. For six years, X owned a building that he had been leasing to his wholly owned corporation. The building had a fair market value of $100,000, and the land on which it stood had a fair market value of $25,000. X's adjusted basis for the building was $50,000, and his adjusted basis for the land was $12,500. X sold the land and the building to the corporation on December 31, 1973, for $125,000. This was his only transaction within the year. Discuss how much and what type of income is reportable. Explain.

15. A taxpayer, filing his return on a calendar-year basis, bought personal property on January 1, 1964, for $10,000. He used the property in his business and claimed depreciation deductions of $600 for each of the years 1964 through 1971. He sold the property on October 31, 1972, for $7,000. His depreciation for that part of 1972 during which he held the property was $500.

(a) What is the amount of the taxpayer's gain on the sale?

(b) How much is Section 1231 capital gain and how much is Section 1245 ordinary income?

(c) Does it make any difference whether the taxpayer is an individual or a corporation? If so, what is the difference?

16. The taxpayer (T) is on a calendar-year accounting period. Established depreciation policy is to claim no depreciation in the year of purchase and a full year's depreciation in the year of sale. T is a corporation and has $500,000 of taxable ordinary income and no capital gains or losses without considering the following transactions:

ASSET	DATE OF PURCHASE	COST	ACCUMULATED DEPRECIATION AS OF DEC. 31, 1973	DEPRECIATION METHOD	LIFE	SELLING PRICE	DATE OF SALE
(1) Warehouse	12/31/58	$100,000	$50,000	S/L	30 Yrs.	$110,000	12/31/73
(2) Machinery	12/31/70	20,000	6,000	S/L	10 Yrs.	25,000	12/31/73

(a) What is the amount of gain or loss, and the tax thereon, resulting from the sale of the warehouse?

(b) What is the amount of gain or loss, and the tax thereon, resulting from the sale of machinery?

17. On January 1, 1973, a calendar-year taxpayer sells a commercial building for $9,000. He had bought the property on January 1, 1969, for $10,000. He had computed depreciation under the declining-balance method using 200 percent of the straight-line rate and a thirty-year useful life, so that on the date of sale the accumulated depreciation allowed was $2,412 ($667 in 1969, $622 in 1970, $581 in 1971, and $542 in 1972). If he had used a straight-line method he would have used a $1,000 salvage value. (Ignore the value of land.)

(a) What is the amount of "additional depreciation" as defined in Section 1250 for the period during which the taxpayer held the property?

(b) How much of the gain is ordinary income?

18. Mr. James purchased an auto on January 1, 1973, for $3,500. At the date of acquisition the estimated life of the auto was three years and estimated salvage value was $500.

During 1973 the auto was used as follows:

Business use	12,000 miles
Nonbusiness use	4,000 miles

On Form 1040 for 1973 Mr. James deducted business auto expenses of $1,440 (12,000 miles @ 12¢ per mile).

Mr. James sold the auto on January 1, 1974, for $2,400.

(a) How much gain or loss from this transaction should Mr. James report on his 1974 income tax return?

(b) Will such gain or loss be treated as a capital or ordinary gain or loss on Form 1040? Why?

19. The XYZ Corporation is a calendar-year taxpayer. On December 31, 1971, it sold a commercial building and the underlying land it had used in its business. Gain realized and recognized was $250,000 on the building and $20,000 on the land. Depreciation claimed on the building to the date of sale was $300,000. Explain how the gain will be treated for income-tax purposes under each of the following situations:

DEPRECIATION

	HOLDING PERIOD	AFTER 1969		BEFORE 1964	
		ACTUAL	STRAIGHT-LINE	ACTUAL	STRAIGHT LINE
1.	12 months	$300,000	$300,000	—	—
2.	13 months	300,000	300,000	—	—
3.	12 months	300,000	150,000	—	—
4.	24 months	300,000	300,000	—	—
5.	18 months	300,000	150,000	—	—
6.	24 months	300,000	180,000	—	—
7.	5 years	120,000	120,000	—	—
8.	5 years	100,000	80,000	—	—
9.	11 years	50,000	40,000	$95,000	$60,000

13

ACCOUNTING
PERIODS

TAXABLE YEAR . . . 507

  Definitions and General Data . . . 507
  Change of Taxable Year . . . 509

ANNUALIZED INCOME FOR SHORT PERIODS . . . 512

  General Rule . . . 512
  Election . . . 512

TAXABLE YEAR

Definitions and General Data

The period for which a return is made is called a *taxable year*. Usually it is a period of twelve months. Never can it be more than twelve months, except when a fifty-two–fifty-three week year has been properly adopted. It will be a period of less than twelve months when a change in the taxable year occurs; and it also can be a period of less than twelve months for a new or terminated corporation and sometimes for a new or terminated partnership, trust, or estate. 13.1

If a taxpayer keeps no books or does not have a proper annual accounting period, he must use the calendar year as his taxable year. Because most individuals do not keep books, almost all report their taxable income on the basis of the calendar year. 13.2

A fiscal year is either (1) a period of twelve months ending on the last day of any month other than December or (2) a period varying between fifty-two and fifty-three weeks, ending always on the same day of the week. 13.3

EXAMPLE

If a corporation regularly uses a twelve-month period ending January 31 in computing its net income per books, it is using a fiscal year and (except when there has been an unauthorized change to such fiscal year for tax purposes) must report its taxable income on the basis of that same fiscal year. Similarly, if a corporation computes its book net income on the basis of a fifty-two or fifty-three-week period ending always on the last Saturday in March, it is using a fiscal year.

Regulation 1.441–2(a) describes the date on which a fifty-two–fifty three-week fiscal year must end: 13.4

Section 441(f) provides, in general, that a taxpayer may elect to compute his taxable income on the basis of a fiscal year which—
(1) Varies from 52 to 53 weeks,
(2) Ends always on the same day of the week, and
(3) Ends always on—
(i) Whatever date this same day of the week last occurs in a calendar month, or
(ii) Whatever date this same day of the week falls which is nearest to the last day of the calendar month.

EXAMPLE FROM REG.

For example, if the taxpayer elects a taxable year ending always on the last Saturday in November, then for the year 1956, the taxable year would end on November 24, 1956. On the other hand, if the taxpayer had elected a taxable year ending always on the Saturday nearest to the end of November, then for the year 1956, the taxable year would end on December 1, 1956. Thus, in the case of a taxable year described in subparagraph (3)(i) of this paragraph, the year will always end within the month and may end on the last day of the month, or as many as six days before the end of the month.

In the case of a taxable year described in subparagraph (3)(ii) of this paragraph, the year may end on the last day of the month, or as many as three days before or three days after the last day of the month.

13.5   A newly organized corporation can adopt either the calendar year or any fiscal year as its taxable year. This is done by filing the first return and keeping the books on the basis of the chosen year. Usually a corporation does not commence business until sometime after the date of incorporation. As the first return cannot cover a period of more than twelve months and the Service may take the position that the period of inactivity should be reflected in a return, it is advisable to file a return covering the period from the date of incorporation to the date of the chosen year-end. For example, assume the date of a certificate of incorporation is October 10, 1967, business does not start until December 20, 1967, and a fiscal year ending November 30 is desired. A short period return for the taxable year ending November 30, 1967, should be timely filed.

13.6   Regulation 1.441–1(b) pertains to the adoption of a taxable year. Although it speaks in terms of all new taxpayers, in practice a fiscal year can be adopted without permission only by new corporations, trusts, and estates. It reads in part as follows:

(3) A new taxpayer in his first return may adopt any taxable year which meets the requirements of section 441 and this section without obtaining prior approval. The first taxable year of a new taxpayer must be adopted on or before the time prescribed by law (not including extensions) for the filing of the return for such taxable year. ...

(4) After a taxpayer has adopted a calendar or a fiscal year, he must use it in computing his taxable income and making his returns for all subsequent years unless prior approval is obtained from the Commissioner to make a change or unless a change is otherwise permitted under the Internal Revenue laws or regulations. ...

13.7   A newly organized corporation should usually adopt the natural year of its industry as its fiscal year. The natural year ordinarily is one ending when inventories and receivables are at a low point. It should also be kept in mind that if the fiscal year adopted results in a short period (that is, a period of less than twelve months), it may be possible to keep taxable net income for that initial period below $25,000 and thus have that income taxed at only 22 percent.

13.8   In the case of a partnership, any partner who has an interest of 5 percent or more in profits or capital is called a "principal partner" by Section 706(b)(3). The taxable year used by principal partners restricts the freedom of a new partnership in choosing its taxable year. Regulation 1.442–1(b)(2)(i) reads in part:

A newly formed partnership may adopt a taxable year which is the same as the taxable year of all its principal partners (or is the same taxable year to which its principal partners who do not have such taxable year concurrently change) without securing prior approval from the Commissioner. If all its principal partners are not on the same taxable year, a newly formed partnership may adopt a calendar year without securing prior approval from the Commissioner. If a newly formed partnership wishes to adopt a taxable year that does not qualify under the preceding two sentences, the adoption of such year requires the prior approval of the Commissioner in accordance with section 706(b)(1) and paragraph (b) of § 1.706–1. ...

13.9 The distributive shares of partnership net income are taxed to the partners whether distributed or not. Such share of income for the entire taxable year of the partnership is included in the taxable year of the partner during which the partnership's year ends.

EXAMPLE If an individual is a member of a partnership having a fiscal year ending June 30, 1970, and if that individual uses the calendar year as his taxable year, he would include in his taxable income for the calendar year 1970 the full twelve months' income of the partnership for its taxable year ending June 30, 1970. Six months of partnership income earned in calendar year 1969 would be taxed to the individual for calendar year 1970, but the partnership income for the last six months of 1970 would not be includible in his income until 1971.

13.10 An individual operating a business as a sole proprietor and also having other income cannot use one taxable year for his business and another for his other income. He must use the same taxable year for the reporting of all of his income. Revenue Ruling 57–389 [1] provides:

For Federal income tax purposes, a business which is conducted as a sole proprietorship must use the same accounting period as the proprietor since the income and deductions for the business must be included in his individual return. ... Accordingly, where an individual on a calendar year basis has income as an employee for a portion of the calendar year, but for the remainder of the year operates as a sole proprietorship, he must include in his income, for the calendar year, not only his earnings as an employee during such year but also the income and deductions from his business operations for the remainder of such year. If he desires to change his accounting period, he must first obtain the prior approval of the Commissioner. ...

Change of Taxable Year

13.11 The general rule is that no taxpayer can change his taxable year unless he first obtains approval from the Commissioner (Section 442). The necessary approval is obtained in one of two ways: (1) by specifically asking for permission, or (2) automatically by meeting conditions laid down in the Regulations.

13.12 Specific application for permission to change from one taxable year to another is made by filing Form 1128 with the Commissioner of Internal Revenue, Washington, D.C., on or before the last day of the calendar month following the close of the short period that will result from changing to another taxable year. For example, if a corporation

1. 1957–2 C.B. 298.

is using the calendar year as its taxable year and wishes to change to a June 30 fiscal year starting with the period ending June 30, 1973, a return for the full calendar year 1972 is required and then another return covering the short period from January 1, 1972, to June 30, 1973. Accordingly, in such an instance, Form 1128 must be filed on or before July 31, 1973.

13.13   Regulation 1.442–1(b)(1) states that approval of a change in taxable years will be granted if the taxpayer establishes a substantial business purpose for making the change and a substantial distortion of income will not result. This paragraph of the regulations gives the following examples of distortions of income:

... The following are examples of effects of the change which would substantially distort income: (i) deferral of a substantial portion of the taxpayer's income, or shifting of a substantial portion of deductions, from one year to another so as to substantially reduce the taxpayer's tax liability; (ii) causing a similar deferral or shifting in the case of any other person, such as a partner, a beneficiary, ...; or (iii) creating a short period in which there is ... (a) a substantial net operating loss, ...

Approval will not be granted unless the taxpayer agrees to any terms, conditions, and adjustments imposed by the Commissioner.[1A]

13.14   Until early in 1966 the policy of the Internal Revenue Service had been strict application of the quoted portion of the Regulations whenever a net operating loss would occur in the short period. In January of that year, the Service relented somewhat and published Revenue Procedure 66–6,[2] reading in part as follows:

Sec. 3 Procedure.—The Service will ordinarily approve a request for a change in accounting period under the following circumstances, provided the taxpayer otherwise qualifies for such change:

(i) The change results in a short period of nine months or longer and the net operating loss for the full 12-month period beginning with the first day of the short period equals or exceeds the net operating loss for the short period, or

(ii) The net operating loss for the short period cannot be carried back to prior taxable years, or

(iii) The net operating loss for the short period is not substantial in amount. For such purposes a net operating loss is considered not substantial if it does not exceed the greater of (1) $5,000.00, or (2) one percent of the taxpayer's average annual taxable income for the three years preceding the short period or $25,000.00, whichever is smaller.

In other cases involving a net operating loss in the short period the Commissioner may, under the authority of section 1.442–1(b)(1) of the regulations, approve a request for change in accounting period if the taxpayer agrees, in lieu of a net operating loss carry-back, to deduct the amount of the net operating loss ratably over the 10-year period following the short period.

1A. Most calendar year partnerships can secure permission to change to a year ending September 30 — —. See Rev. Proc. 72–51.

2. I.R.B. 1966–4, 24.

Once approval has been granted by the Commissioner, it is bind-   13.15
ing on the taxpayer [Reg. 601.204(a)]. He cannot change his mind and
continue using his former taxable year.

Automatic approval without filing Form 1128 can be obtained in   13.16
three instances and then only by meeting the conditions described
in paragraphs (c), (d), and (e) of Reg. 1.442–1:

1. Corporations that meet five specified tests.
2. Subsidiary corporations that join with the common parent corporation
   in filing a consolidated return but whose accounting periods differ
   from that of the common parent.
3. Newly married couples whose accounting periods differ and who
   desire to have the same accounting period in order to be eligible to
   file a joint return.

The five tests that a corporation must meet in order to change its   13.17
taxable year automatically and without permission are set forth in
Reg. 1.442–1(c)(2) as amended December 27, 1972:

(i) The corporation has not changed its annual accounting period at
any time within the ten calendar years ending with the calendar year which
includes the beginning of the short period required to effect the change of
annual accounting period;

(ii) The short period required to effect the change of annual accounting
period is not a taxable year in which the corporation has a net operating
loss as defined in section 172;

(iii) The taxable income of the corporation for the short period required
to effect the change of annual accounting period is, if placed on an annual
basis ... [the method of annualizing is described later in this chapter], 80
percent or more of the taxable income of the corporation for the taxable year
immediately preceding such short period;

(iv) If a corporation had a special status either for the short period or for
the taxable year immediately preceding such short period, it must have the
same special status for both the short period and such taxable year (for the
purpose of this subdivision, special status includes only: a personal holding
company, a foreign personal holding company, a corporation which is an
exempt organization, a foreign corporation not engaged in trade or business
within the United States, a Western Hemisphere trade corporation, and a
China Trade Act corporation); and

(v) The corporation does not attempt to make an election under section
1372(a) that purports to initially become effective with respect to a taxable
year which (*a*) would immediately follow the short period required to effect
the change of annual accounting period, and (*b*) would begin after August
23, 1972.

A corporation taking advantage of these provisions must also file a
statement with the District Director at, or before, the time (including
extensions) for filing the return for the short period required by the
change. This statement must contain information indicating that all
five conditions have been met.

If a revenue agent's subsequent examination results in changes in   13.18
taxable income, so that in fact all five conditions were not met, then
the statement just described is treated as a timely application for
approval to change the annual accounting period.

ANNUALIZED INCOME FOR SHORT PERIODS

General Rule

13.19   When a taxpayer with the approval of the Commissioner (either automatically or through consent following application on Form 1128) changes his annual accounting period, a short-period return is required and the taxable income for such short period must be annualized. This is accomplished by multiplying the taxable income by twelve and dividing the result by the number of months in the short period. A calculation of the tax on such annualized income is then made, but the tax actually payable is only a portion of the amount so computed. Such portion is determined by applying a fraction to the calculated tax. The numerator of the fraction is the number of months in the short period, and the denominator is twelve.

EXAMPLE   The X Corporation makes a return for a six-month period ending June 30, 1973, because of a change in annual accounting period permitted under Code Sec. 442. Income for the short period is as follows:

Gross income	$75,000
Business expenses and deduction	55,000
Taxable income	$20,000
Taxable income annualized (20,000 x 12/6)	$40,000
Tax on annual basis —	
First $25,000 @ 22%	$ 5,500
Next $15,000 @ 48%	7,200
Total	$12,700
Tax payable (6/12 of $12,700)	$ 6,350

13.20   The deduction for personal dependents' exemptions must be prorated when an individual changes his annual accounting period, and he cannot use the standard deduction for the short period (Section 142).

13.21   Only when a short period results from a *change* in accounting period is annualization of the taxable income required. It is not required when the short period results from (1) death of an individual, (2) termination of a partnership, (3) a new corporation not being in existence for the first part of a twelve-month period ending on the last day of the fiscal year adopted by that corporation, (4) liquidation or dissolution of a corporation, or (5) the first return of a decedent's estate.

Election

13.22   In some cases, the requirement to place the income for a short period on an annual basis may result in hardship. If an individual or corporate taxpayer changes from a calendar year to a June 30 year and has taxable income of $20,000 in the short period but only $5,000 in the next six months, annualization of the $20,000 results in applying the effective tax rate applicable to $40,000 to the $20,000 earned in the short period. If he had not changed his period, such $20,000 of income would have been taxed at only the effective rate applicable to $20,000. In requiring annualization, Congress did not want to penalize taxpayers but only to reap the amount of tax on the short-period income that would be due if the accounting period had not been voluntarily changed. Accordingly, the relief provision of paragraph (2) of Section 443(b) was put into the law. In general, the relief granted is to use the actual net income of a twelve-month period instead of annualized net income, compute a tax on such actual net income, and then prorate the computed amount of tax.

For (1) a taxpayer not in existence twelve months after the beginning of the short period and (2) a corporation that has distributed substantially all of its assets after the end of the short period and before the expiration of twelve months after the beginning of the short period, the period used consists of the twelve months ending with the close of the short period. In these two cases, the return for the short period should reflect the income for the short period, and in addition there should be attached to it another return showing the income for the twelve months ending with the close of the short period. **13.23**

In all other instances, the twelve-month period starts with the beginning of the short period. The taxpayer must first file his return for the short period using annualized income. Thereafter he files claim for refund form 843 with the District Director. This claim must set forth the computation of the taxable income for the twelve-month period and the tax thereon. It must be filed "not later than the time (including extensions) prescribed for filing the return for the taxpayer's first taxable year which ends on or after the day which is 12 months after the beginning of the short period."[3] **13.24**

A taxpayer changes his annual accounting period from the calendar year to a fiscal year ending September 30 and files a return for the short period from January 1, 1972, to September 30, 1972. His claim for refund form 843 seeking the benefits of Code Sec. 443(b)(2) must be filed not later than the time prescribed (including extensions obtained) for filing his return for the fiscal year ending September 30, 1973. **EXAMPLE**

The tax payable under the relief provisions of Code Sec. 443(b)(2) is the greater of: **13.25**

(a) An amount which bears the same ratio to the tax computed on the taxable income which the taxpayer has established for the twelve-month period as the taxable income computed on the basis of the short period bears to the taxable income for such twelve-month period; or

(b) The tax computed on the taxable income for the short period without placing the taxable income on an annual basis.

3. Reg. 1.443–1(b)(2)(c)(v)(a).

However, the tax payable can never exceed the amount based on an-nualized income computed under Code Sec. 443(b)(1).

EXAMPLE   A corporation changes its annual accounting period from the calendar year to a fiscal year ending June 30. For the six months ended June 30, 1972, its taxable income is $20,000; for the twelve months ending December 31, 1972, it is $30,000. The resulting amounts of tax under Code Sec. 443(b)(1) and 443(b)(2) are:

Sec. 443(b)(1):	
Annualized income (12/6 × $20,000)	$40,000
Tax on annualized income	$12,700
Tax liability (6/12ths)	$ 6,350
Sec. 443(b)(2), method *a*:	
Actual income for 12 months	$30,000
Tax on $30,000 @ 48% less $6,500	$ 7,900
Tax prorated 20,000/30,000 × $7,900	$ 5,267
Sec. 443(b)(2), method *b*:	
Actual income for short period	$20,000
Tax @ 22%	$ 4,400
Tax liability under Sec. 443(b)(2), greater of $5,267 or $4,400	$ 5,267

After the return for the short period is filed and the tax of $6,350 is paid, a claim for refund of $1,083 ($6,350 − $5,267) would be filed.

QUESTIONS AND PROBLEMS

1. An individual has been working as a pharmacist for a drug chain. On July 1, 1972, he resigns and as a sole proprietor opens his own drug-store. He would like to use a January 31 fiscal year.
   (a) What taxable year has he probably been using?
   (b) Can he file two returns — one for the calendar year 1972 reporting his salary income during the first six months plus all investment income and another for the drugstore for the seven months ending January 31, 1973?
2. An individual dies on September 3, 1972, leaving an estate. His will is admitted to probate on September 15, 1972, and his widow qualifies as executrix on September 20, 1972. During his lifetime the individual had been using the calendar year as his taxable year.
   (a) Must the decedent's income for the period from January 1 to September 3, 1972, be annualized?
   (b) When will the first taxable year of the estate start?
   (c) When will the first taxable year of the estate end?
   (d) Must the income of the estate for its first taxable year be annualized?

3. Three individuals form a partnership on March 1, 1972, to engage in the practice of law. Can the partnership adopt a fiscal year ending February 28, 1973? Explain.

4. A corporation organized in 1922 has been reporting its income on a calendar year basis for the last five years. Before then it used a January 31 fiscal year. It wishes to change to a fiscal year ending September 30, commencing with the period ending September 30, 1973.

   (a) Must it obtain permission?
   (b) If so, what form is used; when and where is it filed?
   (c) Suppose that the short period from January 1, 1973, to September 30, 1973, results in a loss, is it likely that the Commissioner will grant permission? Explain.

14

CASH METHOD
OF ACCOUNTING

METHODS AVAILABLE . . . 517

    Restrictions . . . 517
    "Books" . . . 518

ADOPTION OF METHOD . . . 519
CASH METHOD . . . 519

    Receipt of Gross Income . . . 519

        CONSTRUCTIVE RECEIPT . . . 519

            YEAR-END INTEREST . . . 521
            YEAR-END DIVIDENDS . . . 521

        PROPERTY AND ITS VALUE . . . 523

            CHECKS . . . 524
            CONTRACTUAL RIGHTS TO RECEIVE COMPENSATION . . . 524
            NOTES . . . 525

    Deductions . . . 525

            WHEN IS PAYMENT MADE? . . . 525
            CONSTRUCTIVE PAYMENT . . . 526
            CHECKS . . . 527
            NOTES . . . 529

ADVANCE PAYMENTS . . . 530

    Insurance Premiums . . . 530
    Rents . . . 531
    Interest . . . 531

METHODS AVAILABLE

The Code permits three overall methods of accounting: cash, ac- 14.1
crual, and hybrid. In addition there are specific methods applicable
to designated items, accounts, or transactions. Examples of the latter
are: the installment method as to sales (Sec. 453), amortization of
organization expense of a corporation (Sec. 248), expensing soil and
water conservation expenditures (Sec. 175), expensing or amortizing
research and experimental expenditures (Sec. 174). This chapter and
the next one are concerned only with overall methods.

If a taxpayer is engaged in more than one trade or business, he 14.2
may use a different method of accounting for each trade or business.
If he conducts a business as a sole proprietor or through a partnership,
he may use the accrual or a hybrid method of accounting for the business and the cash method for his personal income (such as interest
and dividends) and deductions.

Restrictions

The restrictions imposed by the Code and Regulations on the adop- 14.3
tion or use of an overall method are these:

1. Taxable income must be computed under the method of accounting on
   the basis of which the taxpayer regularly computes his income in keeping his books [Sec. 446(a)].
2. If no method of accounting has been regularly used by the taxpayer, or
   if the method used does not clearly reflect income, the computation of
   taxable income is to be made under a method that does, in the opinion
   of the Commissioner, clearly reflect income [Sec. 446(b)].
3. In every instance in which the production, purchase, or sale of merchandise is an income-producing factor, inventories must be reflected
   in taxable income as of the beginning and end of each taxable year; and
   the accrual method must be used for the inventory accounts, purchases,
   and sales (Sec. 471 and Reg. 1.471–1).
4. All items of gross profit and deductions must be treated with consistency from year to year [Reg. 1.446–1(c)(2)(ii)

Difficulties arise in the application of these rules. Frequently the requirement of consistency will conflict with Rule No. 1.

These rules of the Code and Regulations have been the subject of 14.4
much litigation. Mertens' *Law of Federal Income Taxation*, Section
12.05, digests these court opinions as follows:

If the taxpayer is on some consistent basis of accounting such as the cash or
accrual basis, that method will bind him and will also bind the Commissioner
if the Commissioner or the courts believe that the method employed by the
taxpayer does "clearly reflect the income." But if the method of accounting

is held not to clearly reflect the income, it will be disapproved even though it has been consistently followed by the taxpayer for many years. The primary emphasis in all Revenue Acts from 1918 to date has been upon the two points, that the method of accounting must be one regularly employed by the taxpayer, and that it must clearly reflect income. If, in the opinion of the Commissioner, the taxpayer's method does not clearly reflect his income, the remedy is to require a computation on a basis which will correctly reflect the annual income. A provision in the Code, however, may merit a different treatment of certain items from that recorded in the taxpayer's records under the method of accounting regularly employed.

The requirement that the method of accounting must clearly reflect income has been interpreted by the Second Circuit to mean that the income must be reflected with as much accuracy as standard methods of accounting permit. In the eventuality that no "method" has been employed by the taxpayer, the Commissioner may compute the income according to a method which in his opinion does "clearly reflect the income." The impossibility of defining this phrase in general language has made it necessary to apply it in the light of the particular case, the particular business involved, the particular method employed, and with reference to the specific item of income or deduction involved. Divergent interpretations are possible and two taxpayers using, in general, the same method of accounting might properly treat similar items differently so long as there is consistency of treatment by each taxpayer. (Reprinted by permission of Callaghan & Company, the copyright owner.)

"Books"

14.5   Neither the Code nor the Regulations adequately define the word "books." Regulation 1.446–1(a)(1) provides that taxable income shall be computed under the method of accounting on the basis of which "a taxpayer regularly computes his income in keeping his books." In the third subsequent paragraph of that section, it is stated that each taxpayer is required to make a return of his taxable income for each taxable year, and must maintain accounting records that will enable him to file a correct return:

> Accounting records include the taxpayer's regular books of account and such other records and data as may be necessary to support the entries on his books of account and on his return, as for example, a reconciliation of any differences between such books and his return.

14.6   Referring to individuals, Reg. 1.446–1(b)(2) states:

> A taxpayer whose sole source of income is wages need not keep formal books in order to have an accounting method. Tax returns, copies thereof, or other records may be sufficient to establish the use of the method of accounting used in the preparation of the taxpayer's income tax returns.

In practice, however, an individual who is not engaged in business as a proprietor and who does not keep formal books and records will be required by the Commissioner to use the cash receipts and disbursements method of accounting.

ADOPTION OF METHOD

Regulation 1.446–1(e)(1) provides: 14.7

A taxpayer filing his first return may adopt any permissible method of accounting in computing taxable income for the taxable year covered by such return. ... Moreover, a taxpayer may adopt any permissible method of accounting in connection with each separate and distinct trade or business, the income from which is reported for the first time. ...

CASH METHOD

Regulation 1.446–1(c)(1)(i) describes this method: 14.8

Cash receipts and disbursements method. Generally, under the cash receipts and disbursements method in the computation of taxable income, all items which constitute gross income (whether in the form of cash, property, or services) are to be included for the taxable year in which actually or constructively received. Expenditures are to be deducted for the taxable year in which actually made. ...

There is an obvious advantage for federal income tax purposes in 14.9 reporting taxable income under the cash receipts and disbursements method of accounting. In a growing, profitable enterprise, the excess of accounts receivable over accrued expenses does not become included in taxable income until the end of the life of the enterprise. Further, the cash basis method affords a great deal of flexibility in accelerating or deferring the receipt of income and the hastening or postponing of the deductibility of expenses through the timing of payments.

The ensuing paragraphs will discuss the problems pertaining first 14.10 to the receipt of items of gross income and then to payments. Under the cash method *timing* of transactions is the important factor.

Receipt of Gross Income

Constructive Receipt. The doctrine of constructive receipt was 14.11 created many years ago by the Internal Revenue Service to prevent taxpayers from having unfettered control over the timing of the receipt of income and thereby the year in which it would be taxable. The doctrine is described in Reg. 1.451–2(a):

Income although not actually reduced to a taxpayer's possession is constructively received by him in the taxable year during which it is credited to his account, set apart for him, or otherwise made available so that he may draw upon it at any time, or so that he could have drawn upon it during the taxable year if notice of intention to withdraw had been given. However, income is not constructively received if the taxpayer's control of its receipt is subject to substantial limitations or restrictions. ...

If an item of gross income is constructively received by a taxpayer in a particular year, it is taxable to him in that year and not in a later year when he actually takes possession of it.

EXAMPLE   A corporation uses a biweekly payroll period. On December 28, a clerk from the treasurer's office distributes the paychecks to employees, one of whom is away from his desk and does not go to the treasurer's office to pick up his check until the next week, which is in the month of January. This employee will have had constructive receipt in December of his salary for that two-week period.

14.12   The doctrine of constructive receipt is not a one-way street. A taxpayer can also invoke it. In the case of *Lewis H. Ross* v. *Com.*[1] (1st Cir. 1948), the taxpayer was contending that salaries paid to him by a closely held corporation did not constitute income to him in the years in which he received the money, but rather in an earlier year, then barred by the statute of limitations, because of the doctrine of constructive receipt. Extracts from the court's opinion follow:

> ... Nevertheless, we should now pass on the respondent's suggestion that, even if such findings are made in the petitioner's favor, he may not invoke the doctrine of constructive receipt because the doctrine was designed only to protect the revenue and is not available for a taxpayer's defense, or, in the alternative, because the petitioner is now precluded from taking a position inconsistent with his theory in the years when the salary was credited to him.
>
> The doctrine of constructive receipt was, no doubt, conceived by the Treasury in order to prevent a taxpayer from choosing the year in which to return income merely by choosing the year in which to reduce it to possession. Thereby the Treasury may subject income to taxation when the only thing preventing its reduction to possession is the volition of the taxpayer. But is the doctrine to be deemed merely an available tool of the Commissioner, or is it a test of *realization* of income within the meaning of Section 42 of the Code providing that income shall be taxed in the year it is received? ...
>
> However, in this Circuit at least, it seems settled that the doctrine of constructive receipt can be asserted by a taxpayer to defeat an attempt to assert a tax in a later year ... the doctrine does not merely afford a special choice which the Commissioner may, if he sees fit, exercise retroactively against a taxpayer, but a rule of law, determining what constitutes taxable income, and as such presumably binding on all parties. To allow the Commissioner to refrain, at his own option, from asserting his claim until years later is against the important policy underlying the statute of limitations. If this view means avoidance of taxation in some cases, it must be remembered that if such avoidance is fraudulent the tax may be assessed or collected at any time. Internal Revenue Code Section 276(a). If every opportunity for escaping taxation is to be barred, even in the absence of fraud, such complete safeguards are for Congress to devise.

1. 169 F.2d 483, 48–2 USTC ¶9341, 37 AFTR 193; followed: F. D. Bissett & Son, Inc., 56 T.C. 453 (1971), and Lacy Contracting Co., 56 T.C. No. 34 (1971).

YEAR-END INTEREST. Turning to interest, Reg. 1.451–2(b), as 14.13
amended December 27, 1971, provides:

Examples of constructive receipt. Amounts payable with respect to interest
coupons which have matured and are payable but which have not been
cashed are constructively received in the taxable year during which the
coupons mature, unless it can be shown that there are no funds available for
payment of the interest during such year. Dividends on corporate stock are
constructively received when unqualifiedly made subject to the demand of
the shareholder. However, if a dividend is declared payable on December 31
and the corporation followed its usual practice of paying the dividends by
checks mailed so that the shareholders would not receive them until January
of the following year, such dividends are not considered to have been constructively received in December. Generally, the amount of dividends or interest credited on savings bank deposits or to shareholders of organizations
such as building and loan associations or cooperative banks is income to the
depositors or shareholders for the taxable year when credited. However,
if any portion of such dividends or interest is not subject to withdrawal at
the time credited, such portion is not constructively received and does not
constitute income to the depositor or shareholder until the taxable year in
which the portion first may be withdrawn. Accordingly, if, under a bonus or
forfeiture plan, a portion of the dividends or interest is accumulated and may
not be withdrawn until the maturity of the plan, the crediting of such portion
to the account of the shareholder or depositor does not constitute constructive
receipt. In this case, such credited portion is income to the depositor or
shareholder in the year in which the plan matures. However, in the case of
certain deposits made after December 31, 1970, in banks, domestic building
and loan associations, and similar financial institutions, the ratable inclusion
rules of section 1232(a)(3) apply. See § 1.1232-3A. Accrued interest on un-
withdrawn insurance policy dividends is gross income to the taxpayer for
the first taxable year during which such interest may be withdrawn by him.

YEAR-END DIVIDENDS. If a corporation as a matter of regular 14.14
business policy mails year-end dividend checks on December 31, so
that they cannot be received by the shareholders until January, they
are not taxable to the shareholders until January.

Sewell L. Avery v. Com.

U. S. Supreme Court, 1934[2]

Mr. Justice McREYNOLDS delivered the opinion of the Court.

The petitioner was a large stockholder, and president, of the United States
Gypsum Company. In November, 1924, the Company declared a dividend
payable on or before the 31st day of December following. Its check, dated
December 31st, for the amount attributable to his stock, payable to him, was
received by petitioner January 2, 1925. In November, 1929, another dividend
was declared, payable on or before the following December 31st, and the
Company's check for petitioner's portion was received by him January 2,
1930.

Annually, dividend checks, signed by the proper corporate officers and
dated December 31st, were on that day mailed out to all stockholders except

2. 292 U.S. 210 (1934) 4 USTC ¶1277, 13 AFTR 1168, reversing 67 F.2d 310 (7th
Cir. 1933), which affirmed BTA memo decision.

those who were officers and employees, including the petitioner. Checks for the latter were held in the treasurer's office until the first business day of the next month and then distributed through the office mail.

The Company declared dividends quarterly; and in every instance they were made payable on or before the last day of some month. The dividend checks never left the treasurer's office or went to the mailing department until the afternoon of the last day of the month. They were mailed on the last day of the month so as to be in the stockholders' hands on the first business day of the following month. The practice was without exception that no stockholder, whether employee or officer, should receive his check before the first business day of the month following the month in which the dividend was made payable.

Petitioner kept his accounts on the cash receipts and disbursements and calendar-year basis.

The Commissioner assessed the dividends above described as part of the petitioner's income for the years 1924 and 1929. The Board of Tax Appeals approved; and the Court below affirmed this action. The facts are not in dispute. The only question for our determination is when, within intendment of the statutes, the dividends were "received" by petitioner.

He maintains that under the plain language of the Revenue Acts of 1924 and 1928 the dividends—like other assessable items—should be treated as income for the taxable years during which they were actually received—1925 and 1930. The Commissioner claims that under Treasury Regulations promulgated in 1921 and in effect ever since, the dividends constituted income for the years in which they were declared and made payable. The regulation specially important here (No. 65, Art. 1541) follows:

> "Dividends. ... A taxable distribution made by a corporation to its shareholders shall be included in the gross income of the distributees when the cash or other property is unqualifiedly made subject to their demands."

The Revenue Act of 1924, c. 234, 43 Stat. 253, provides:

> "Sec. 212. (b) The net income shall be computed upon the basis of the taxpayer's annual accounting period (fiscal year or calendar year as the case may be) in accordance with the method of accounting regularly employed in keeping the books of such taxpayer; but if no such method of accounting has been so employed, or if the method employed does not clearly reflect the income, the computation shall be made in accordance with such method as in the opinion of the Commissioner does clearly reflect the income.
>
> If the taxpayer's annual accounting period is other than a fiscal year as defined in section 200 or if the taxpayer has no annual accounting period or does not keep books, the net income shall be computed on the basis of the calendar year.
>
> "Sec. 213. For the purposes of this title, ... (a) The term "gross income" includes gains, profits, and income. ... The amount of all such items shall be included in the gross income for the taxable year in which received by the taxpayer, unless, under methods of accounting permitted under subdivision (b) of section 212, any such amounts are to be properly accounted for as of a different period.
>
> "Sec. 1001. The Commissioner with the approval of the Secretary, is authorized to prescribe all needful rules and regulations for the enforcement of this Act."

. . .

... When a dividend unqualifiedly becomes subject to a taxpayer's demand is essentially a question of fact. Here, the Board of Tax Appeals and the Circuit Court of Appeals agree that the dividends were subject to the taxpayer's demand on December 31st.

It is unnecessary for us to determine how far the quoted Treasury Regulation was incorporated into the Acts of 1924 and 1928. If we assume that the Regulations, in effect, became part of those enactments, nevertheless we think the Commissioner's action was erroneous. In the disclosed circumstances the dividends cannot properly be considered as cash or other property unqualifiedly subject to the petitioner's demand on December 31st. It was the practice of the Company to pay all dividends by checks not intended to reach stockholders until the first business day of January; there is nothing to show that petitioner could have obtained payment on December 31st, he did not expect this and the practice shows the company had no intention to make actual payment on that day. Nothing indicates that it recognized an unrestricted right of stockholders to demand payment except through checks sent out in the usual way. The checks did not constitute payments prior to their actual receipt. The mere promise or obligation of the corporation to pay on a given date was not enough to subject to petitioner's unqualified demand "cash or other property"; and none of the parties understood that it was.

As a result of this Supreme Court decision the regulations of the Internal Revenue Service were changed shortly afterwards. Regulation 1.451–2(b) provides: **14.15**

... Dividends on corporate stock are constructively received when unqualifiedly made subject to the demand of the shareholder. However, if a dividend is declared payable on December 31 and the corporation followed its usual practice of paying the dividends by checks mailed so that the shareholders would not receive them until January of the following year, such dividends are not considered to have been constructively received in December. ...

These present Regulations recognize the practical problem described by the Third Circuit Court of Appeals in a 1954 case:[3]

Surely we may take judicial notice of the fact that it is common corporate practice, at least among large corporations, to mail dividend checks to the stockholders. Orderly business administration requires such a course. Confusion would result if the stockholders of any large corporation descended in a body on the treasurer's office and demanded forthwith payment of their dividends.

The converse of this rule applied to year-end dividends is also true. In determining the amount of a corporation's accumulated earnings, dividends are deductible on the date on which they are received by the shareholders (Reg. 1.561–2).   **14.16**

Property and Its Value. As explained in chapter 5, income can be received in the form of property. Such property is includible in taxable income of the year when received in the amount of its fair market   **14.17**

3. Maurice Fox v. Com., 218 F.2d 347, 55–1 USTC ¶9130, 46 AFTR 1459, affirming 20 T.C. 1094.

value. If it has no value when received, then generally income is not realized until the property is converted into cash or exchanged for other property having a market value. The pertinent questions at this point are (1) what types of property ordinarily are deemed to have a fair market value when received and (2) in the case of other types of property, what factors should be taken into account to determine value?

14.18   CHECKS. A check is a conditional payment; when it is honored by the drawee bank, payment relates back to the date of receipt of the check.[4] A check constitutes taxable income in the year in which received by a cash-basis taxpayer even if received after banking hours on the last day of the year.[5] The taxpayer does not realize income in the year in which he receives the check if he agreed not to cash the check until the next year[6] or not to cash it until authorized to do so by the payor.[7] If the payee knows that the payor does not have sufficient money on deposit to cover the check, he does not realize income until the following year when he presents the check for payment.[8] If a check were to be received on December 31, presented for payment on January 3, and then returned by the bank because of insufficient funds, income would not have been realized on December 31. Failure of the bank to honor the check relates back to the date of receipt of the check.

14.19   CONTRACTUAL RIGHTS TO RECEIVE COMPENSATION. As noted in paragraphs 11.12 to 11.14 pertaining to contractual obligations received on sales of property, a contractual promise to make payments of money in the future ordinarily does not constitute income when received. There are two reasons: (1) the contract almost always is not accepted as payment of the obligation but only as evidence of it and (2) the contract usually does not have a fair market value. These same principles are also applicable to agreements to pay compensation or a pension in the future.

14.20   However, if an employer sets up a nonqualified pension plan or other nonqualified plan of deferred compensation and externally funds it by setting up a trust or entering into an annuity contract with an insurance company, the contractual promise to pay may constitute income when received by the employee (see chapter 17). Further, annuity contracts purchased from an insurance company do have a present value and are taxable when assigned to the employee. In *Renton K. Brodie,*[9] an executive received a bonus in the form of a deferred annuity contract purchased from an insurance company. He was taxed on its cost although it was nonassignable and had no cash

4. Estate of M. J. Spiegel et al., 12 T.C. 524 (1949) (Acq.)—see ¶14.27 for extracts from opinion.

5. C. F. Kahler, 18 T.C. 31; O. E. Stephens, 15 TCM 1471.

6. L. M. Fischer, 14 T.C. 792.

7. G. M. Johnson, 25 T.C. 499 (Acq.).

8. C. Goodman, 5 TCM 1126, 1198, affirmed on other grounds 176 F.2d 389, 49–2 USTC ¶9362 (2nd Cir.).

9. 1 T.C. 275.

surrender value. This case has been followed by a great many other courts.

NOTES. In paragraphs 11.15 to 11.19 the consequences of the receipt of notes upon the sale of property were discussed. All of those principles are also applicable to the receipt of notes as compensation.   14.21

To constitute present income, not only must a note have a fair market value, but it must have been received in payment of an obligation and not as mere evidence of it. In the case of *Robert J. Dial*,[10] two doctors incorporated a nonprofit medical clinic from which they drew compensation for services rendered to it. From 1936 to 1945 the clinic had financial difficulties, was unable to pay portions of the salaries due the doctors, and also borrowed money from them. At a time when the clinic owed the doctors $120,000, it issued to them its negotiable mortgage bonds and notes in that amount. Extracts from the court's opinion holding that these bonds and notes did not constitute income when received follow: 14.22

> ... the whole record here before us demonstrates beyond question that the essential fact necessary to support his determination is absent, namely, that the negotiable instruments were received in payment of the prior debt. ...
>
> We are convinced that the only intent which prompted the issuance of the notes to Robert and Dwight in 1945 was that a plan be adopted providing for a funding of the debts owed to them. The notes were never meant to be anything more than additional security for the principal debts, for nobody intended them to be payment thereof. We are satisfied that this is true even though Robert and Dwight were two of the Clinic's trustees, *Schlemmer* v. *U. S., supra*, and even though the notes or bonds received by them were secured obligations. *Mellinger* v. *U. S., supra*.
>
> Since we conclude that such notes or bonds were not received by Robert and Dwight in payment of the principal debts owed to them by the Clinic, such transation cannot result in taxable income to them in 1945.

Deductions

When Is Payment Made? Code Sec. 461 contains the general rules for determining the proper taxable year in which deductions are to be taken; it is an important section to be studied. Reg. 1.461–1(a)(1) explains the year of deduction under the cash method as follows: 14.23

> Under the cash receipts and disbursements method of accounting, amounts representing allowable deductions shall, as a general rule, be taken into account for the taxable year in which paid. Further, a taxpayer using this method may also be entitled to certain deductions in the computation of taxable income which do not involve cash disbursements during the taxable year, such as the deductions for depreciation, depletion, and losses under sections 167, 611, and 165, respectively. If an expenditure results in the creation of an asset having a useful life which extends substantially beyond the close of the taxable year, such an expenditure may not be deductible, or may be deductible only in part, for the taxable year in which made. ...

10. 24 T.C. 117 (1955) (Acq.).

14.24   To obtain a deduction, a cash basis taxpayer must make a payment, so it is important to ascertain what constitutes a "payment."

14.25   **Constructive Payment.** In determining when income is taxed, a taxpayer using the cash receipts and disbursements method of accounting is taxable on cash or property constructively received. The corollary is not true, even though logical. The weight of authority holds that in determining when payment is made, there is no such thing as constructive payment. Actual payment is required.

Vander Poel, Francis & Company, Inc.

8 T.C. 407 (1947)

[Facts: Vander Poel and Francis were the controlling stockholders and officers of this corporation. During 1942 the board of directors established the amounts of their salaries. The amounts so voted were credited on the books to the respective accounts of these two officers, and the amounts at all times during 1942 were available to them and could have been drawn down, although the two men drew only part of their salaries. They were authorized jointly to sign checks on all bank accounts and were authorized to draw checks to the order of each other. At the end of the year, the corporation was solvent and had a substantial bank balance. The individuals in their 1942 returns reported the full amounts of their salaries under the doctrine of constructive receipt. The corporation was on the cash receipts and disbursements method of accounting and deducted the full amounts of the salaries voted to the officers.]

BLACK, Judge: ... The Commissioner in his determination of the deficiencies has allowed as a deduction for petitioner all the cash which these two officers drew in 1942, but has disallowed the $11,781.51 which they did not draw but which was unconditionally credited to their respective accounts. The contention of petitioner is that it unconditionally credited the full amount of these salaries to the two officers in 1942; that they could have drawn the entire amounts due them at any time they wished; that their failure to do so was the voluntary act of their own; that unquestionably each was taxable on his entire 1942 salary under the doctrine of constructive receipt; and that each did actually return his full salary for taxation and pay income tax thereon. "Therefore," says petitioner, "the doctrine of constructive payment should be applied under the above facts and petitioner should be allowed to deduct the full amount of these salaries instead of the portions which the Commissioner has allowed."

The Commissioner, on his part, makes no contention that the salaries voted to these two officers were not reasonable in amount and bona fide in every respect, but he takes the position that petitioner was on the cash basis and is entitled to deduct only the amounts which it acutally paid in 1942 on these salaries in cash or other property and that it can not deduct, under the doctrine of "constructive payment," the amounts which were not paid in 1942 but were credited to the two officers' accounts. Respondent concedes that the doctrine of "constructive receipt" has had frequent application, but not so the doctrine of "constructive payment," and that the "constructive receipt" cases are not controlling. We think the weight of authority supports respondent.

.   .   .   .

... It is perfectly clear from the facts in the instant case that there was "constructive receipt" by Vander Poel and Francis of the salaries voted to them by petitioner in 1942. They properly returned these salaries for taxation on their 1942 returns under the doctrine of "constructive receipt." But the weight of authority as we interpret the authorities is against the doctrine that "constructive payment" is a necessary corollary of "constructive receipt." Mertens, in his Law of Federal Income Taxation, vol. 2, sec. 10.18, says:

"Constructive Payments as Deductions. Under the doctrine of constructive receipt a taxpayer on the cash basis is taxed upon income which he has not as yet actually received. Logically it would seem that where the payee is held to have constructively received an item as income, the payor should be entitled to deduct the same item as constructively paid, but the statute rather than logic is the controlling force in tax cases and so it is not surprising to find such reasoning often rejected. The difference is that the statute is presumed to reach and tax all income, and the doctrine of constructive receipt is an aid to that end. It must be remembered that the doctrine of constructive receipt is designed to effect a realistic concept of realization of income and to prevent abuses. Deductions, on the other hand, are a matter of legislative grace, and the terms of the statute permitting the particular deduction must be fully met without the aid of assumptions. "What may be income to the one may not be a deductible payment by the other." A review of the cases indicates that the courts will seldom support a doctrine of constructive payment in the sense in which it is used in this chapter, i.e., to determine when an item has been paid rather than who has paid it."

       .   .   .

If in any of our decisions, memorandum opinions or otherwise, we have said anything to the contrary of the above holdings, we think it is against the weight of authority and should not be followed. Therefore, ... we sustain the Commissioner. ...

14.26 Although there is no doctrine of constructive payment, as opposed to constructive receipt, a theory that sounds like constructive payment has been supplied to determine who really made a payment. This is not constructive payment; it is a question of identifying the true taxpayer. In *Royal Oaks Apartments, Inc.*[11] a cash-basis corporation sold all of its assets and adopted a plan of complete liquidation. It made a liquidating distribution to its shareholders, but retained insufficient cash to pay a subsequently assessed state income tax. Upon demand being made, the shareholders sent the corporation their checks payable directly to the state. The corporation with its own transmittal letter then mailed the checks to the state. Under state law, the excessive liquidating distribution was recoverable by the corporation. The Tax Court concluded that in form and substance the corporation paid the tax and was entitled to deduct it in determining federal taxable net income.

14.27 **Checks.** In paragraph 14.18 it was pointed out that the receipt of a check is a conditional payment and that, when it is honored by the bank, the payment relates back to the date of receipt of the check so

11. 43 T.C. 243 (1964) (Acq.).

that income is realized on that date. All of the principles set forth there pertaining to income are also true with respect to the issuance of checks as giving rise to a deduction for payment. However, there is one important difference. To have income a check must be received,[12] but to have a deduction the check need only be mailed.

Estate of M. J. Spiegel et al.

12 T.C. 524(1949) (Acq.)

[Facts: M. J. Spiegel died January 8, 1943, and his cash-basis return for 1942 was thereafter filed by his executors. On December 30, 1942, decedent drew two checks payable to two charities. The checks were delivered to, and received by, the charities on December 31, 1942, one of them after banking hours. One check was deposited by the payee in its bank account on January 8, 1943, and was presented to, and paid by, the decedent's bank on January 11, 1943. The other check was deposited by the payee in its bank on January 4, 1943, and was presented to, and paid by, the drawee bank on January 4, 1943.]

OPPER, Judge: The first question, and the only one on the merits, is whether respondent erred in disallowing as charitable deductions for 1942 two contributions, one of $5,000, and another of $2,800, made by decedent by checks dated December 30, 1942, and delivered on December 31, 1942, but not cashed until in January 1943. ...

. . .

... We may assume that decedent's delivery of checks to the charities in question was at the time no more than a conditional payment of the charitable contribution for which the deduction is here sought. If the subsequent honoring of the checks by fulfilling the condition subsequent related the payment back to the date of delivery, the fact of the contribution and the time it was paid would become fixed.

. . .

It would seem to us unfortunate for the Tax Court to fail to recognize what has so frequently been suggested, that as a practical matter, in everyday personal and commercial usage, the transfer of funds by check is an accepted procedure. The parties almost without exception think and deal in terms of payment except in the unusual circumstance, not involved here, that the check is dishonored upon presentation, or that it was delivered in the first place subject to some condition or infirmity which intervenes between delivery and presentation.

. . .

With knowledge of the prevalence of this practice, and of the necessity of treating tax questions from a practical rather than a theoretical viewpoint, it would be astonishing indeed if by the use of the word "payment," in section 23(o), Congress did not intend to include a check given absolutely and in due course subsequently presented and paid. ... We conclude that decedent, upon the issuance and delivery of the checks in question, made a conditional payment of charitable contributions which, upon the presentation and payment of the checks, became absolute and related back to the time when the checks were delivered.

. . .

12. Louis Titus, 2 B.T.A. 754; J. D. Gillis, 19 TCM 383 (1960), ¶60, 071 P–H Memo T.C.

... we conclude that here the contributions were made by the decedent in his lifetime in the year in issue, and that they are hence deductible in full as claimed by petitioners.

14.28   In *Estelle Broussard*[13] the Tax Court held that delivery to, and receipt by, an agent of a religious order on December 31 of a check made payable to that order constituted payment of the charitable contribution on December 31. Again involving deductibility of a charitable contribution, in *Eli B. Witt Est.* v. *Fahs*[14] the United States District Court of Florida held that by both legal theory and business usage the United States mail is the transmitting agent of the sender.

14.29   Regulation 1.170–1(b) pertaining to charitable contributions follows these court cases:

> (b) *Time of making contribution.* Ordinarily, a contribution is made at the time delivery is effected. In the case of a check, the unconditional delivery (or mailing) of a check which subsequently clears in due course will constitute an effective contribution on the date of delivery (or mailing). If a taxpayer unconditionally delivers (or mails) a properly endorsed stock certificate to a charitable donee or the donee's agent, the gift is completed on the date of delivery (or mailing, provided that such certificate is received in the ordinary course of the mails). If the donor delivers the certificate to his bank or broker as the donor's agent, or to the issuing corporation or its agent, for transfer into the name of the donee, the gift is completed on the date the stock is transferred on the books of the corporation.

For purposes of the deductibility of charitable contributions and of other types[15] of expenditures, it seems settled that the United States mail is the agent of the sender, so that payment is made when a check is mailed. However, the United States mail is not the agent of the recipient in determining the date of the receipt of income in the form of a check issued in payment for services rendered[16] or in payment of a dividend.[17]

Notes. The giving of a note does not constitute payment, except in the rare instance that the note is accepted as the payment of cash or equivalent.[18]

14.30

     In *Helvering* v. *Julian Price*[19] the taxpayer executed a guaranty agreement in 1929 as to the collectibility of certain assets of a corporation of which he was a large stockholder. In 1931 he gave his

14.31

---

13. 16 T.C. 23 (1951).

14. 160 F. Supp. 521, 56–1 USTC ¶9534, 51 AFTR 1320.

15. W. W. Flint, 237 F. Supp. 551 (D.C., Idaho, 1964), 65–1 USTC ¶9169, 15 AFTR2d 014 (state income taxes); Amoroso, 10 TCM 186 (1951) ¶51, 058 P–H Memo T.C., affirmed on other grounds 193 F.2d 583 (1st Cir. 1951), 52–1 USTC ¶9135, 41 AFTR 616 (commissions paid).

16. *Supra* fn. 12.

17. Sewell L. Avery v. Com., *supra* fn. 2; dictum to the contrary for a charitable contribution is in Eli B. Witt Est. v. Fahs, *supra* fn. 14.

18. Mertens, *Law of Federal Income Taxation,* Sec. 12.54 (1961 revision).

19. 309 U.S. 409, 40–1 USTC ¶9336, 24 AFTR 657.

note secured by collateral in support of his guaranty. In 1932 he gave another note in exchange for his 1931 note and claimed a guaranty loss in his 1932 return in the amount of the 1932 note. The Supreme Court denied the deduction of any loss and held that the giving of the 1932 note did not constitute the payment of cash or its equivalent.

14.32   In S. E. Thomason [20] a cash-basis taxpayer was indebted for principal and interest on his promissory note. He borrowed additional funds from the same bank and gave a new note for the aggregate principal and the accrued interest. The Board of Tax Appeals held that there had been no payment of interest.

14.33   In cases arising under Code Sec. 267(a)(2) pertaining to unpaid expenses and interest between related taxpayers using different accounting methods, however, the courts and the Internal Revenue Service have held that if a solvent corporation on the accrual basis delivers its note to a cash-basis payee within two and one-half months after the end of the year of accrual of the expense and if the payee accepts the note as payment (which usually is the case), then the note does constitute payment of the obligation to the extent of its fair market value.[21]

ADVANCE PAYMENTS

14.34   Prepaid income is taxable when received, but prepaid expenses, whether of a cash or an accrual basis taxpayer, are usually required to be prorated over the periods to which they relate.

Insurance Premiums

14.35   Prepaid insurance premiums that constitute business expenses have been the subject of much litigation and changing rules over the years.

14.36   The Tax Court,[22] the First Circuit Court of Appeals,[23] and the Internal Revenue Service [24] hold that amounts paid in advance for insurance premiums should be prorated over the years to which they apply. The Eighth Circuit, however, holds [25] that a taxpayer on the cash basis may deduct the full amount of the prepaid premiums in the year of payment. It was pointed out in two later Tax Court cases [26] that the Eighth Circuit was greatly influenced by the taxpayer's consistent practice over a long period of years.

20. 33 BTA 576.

21. Musselman Hub-Brake Co. v. Com., 139 F.2d 65 (3rd Cir. 1944), 43–2 USTC ¶9666, 31 AFTR 1001; Celina Mfg. Co. v. Com., 142 F.2d 449 (6th Cir. 1944), 44–1 USTC ¶9236, 32 AFTR 672; Rev. Rul. 55–608, 1955–2 C.B. 546.

22. Martha R. Peters, 4 T.C. 1236.

23. Com. v. Boylston Market Assn., 131 F.2d 966, 42–2 USTC ¶9820, 30 AFTR 512.

24. G.C.M. 23,587, 1945 C.B. 213.

25. Waldheim Realty & Investment Co. v. Com., 245 F.2d 823, 57–2 USTC ¶9717, 51 AFTR 801.

26. Louise K. Herter, T.C. Memo, 1961–19; Harry W. Williamson, 37 T.C. 941 (1962).

Rents

Prepaid rent is taxable when received but deductible by the payor   14.37
only over the years to which it applies.[27]

Interest

It is the position of the Service that a prepayment of interest by a   14.38
cash-basis taxpayer may distort income.[28] If it does, then the amount
must be prorated over the period to which it applies. A prepayment
for a period of more than twelve months beyond the end of the taxable year, in the view of the Service, must always be prorated; and a
prepayment for not more than such a twelve-month period sometimes
may be required to be prorated.

QUESTIONS AND PROBLEMS

1. In preparing the calendar-year 1972 return of an individual, you note
   that he had the following income relating to the year 1972:

Interest from a savings and loan association credited on its books December 31, 1972, available for withdrawal on that date, but notice of it not received until 1973 and not posted on passbook until 1973	$ 300
Interest coupons dated and due December 31, 1972, but not detached from debentures and presented for payment until January 1973	$ 200
Dividend check dated December 31, 1972, received January 2, 1973, from a large listed corporation in an envelope postmarked December 31, 1972	$ 1,000
Dividend from a closely held corporation of which this individual was the president, and whose board of directors declared the dividend December 15, 1972, to stockholders of record December 31, 1972, payable January 10, 1973, check received January 10, 1973	$ 5,000
Check from a publishing company covering royalties for the month of November, 1972, on sales of a book written by this individual; check dated December 31, 1972, mailed that day, and received January 3, 1973	$ 500
Bonus from his corporate employer voted by the board of directors in November, 1972, based on a percentage of profits before taxes of the year 1972, received in February, 1973	$20,000
Salary check for the last half of the month of December, 1972, dated December 31, 1972, but not picked up by him from the treasurer until January 3, 1973, because he was on vacation in the Bahamas from December 14, 1972, until January 2, 1973	$ 1,250
Check for interest on a mortgage loan to an individual; check received at his home on December 30, 1972, deposited for payment on January 2, 1973, returned by the bank on January 4, 1973, because of insufficient funds, but subsequently redeposited and honored on January 10, 1973	$ 75

What is the taxable gross income from these items for 1972?

27. *Main & McKinney Bldg. Co. of Houston, Texas* v. *Com.,* 113 F.2d 81, 25 AFTR
338 (5th Cir. 1940), cert. den. 311 U.S. 688.
28. Rev. Rul. 68–643, 1968–2 C.B. 76; contrary: J. D. Fackler, 39 B.T.A. 395 (Nonacq.).

2. Your client and his two brothers own all stock of a corporation and constitute the majority of its board of directors. On December 24, 1972, the board declares a dividend payable December 31, 1972, to stockholders of record that date. Your client as president signs the dividend checks and the nonrelated controller also countersigns them on that date.

   (a) By the time the checks are countersigned, banking hours had ended, so on December 31, your client hands his check to his secretary and causes her to deposit it on January 2, 1973. Is this 1972 or 1973 income?

   (b) Instead, suppose that for the past five years similar dividend declarations had been made, and it was the consistent practice of the controller, after he countersigned the checks on December 31, to mail them on that date to the homes of the shareholders. He follows this same practice on December 31, 1972. Is the amount of the dividend to your client 1972 or 1973 income?

3. In February, 1972, an individual received from his corporate employer unrestricted ownership of a fully paid annuity contract issued by an insurance company under which monthly annuity payments are to start at age sixty-five in 1977. The annuity is nonassignable, has no cash surrender value, and was given in recognition of services rendered in 1971. Does this annuity contract constitute taxable income? If so, when? In what amount?

4. In payment of a bonus for 1972, a solvent corporation on March 1, 1973, gave its vice-president its negotiable note in the amount of $5,000 payable March 1, 1974, bearing no interest until maturity but 6 percent thereafter. Does that note constitute income in 1972, 1973 or 1974? In what amount?

5. An individual mailed checks to charities on December 31, 1972, in the sum of $1,000. The checks were received by the charities in 1973 and then cashed. When are these charitable contributions deductible?

6. An individual was indebted to a bank for $3,000. When his note matured on May 1, 1972, he needed additional funds and borrowed another $1,000 by giving a note in the amount of not only the $4,000 principal but also the accrued interest of $180 — a total of $4,180. On May 1, 1973, he paid the note in full, plus interest thereon of $250.80. What amounts of interest are deductible in 1972 and 1973?

7. An individual was required on April 15, 1972, to file a declaration of estimated New York State income tax, and in 1972 paid three quarterly installments totaling $750. In addition, when filing his 1971 New York State income tax return on April 15, 1972, he paid $1,000 in tax for 1971 over and above the amount of $600 he had paid during 1971 on his 1971 declaration of estimated tax.

   (a) For 1972, what is the amount of the deduction for New York State income taxes paid?

   (b) Suppose that on April 15, 1973, he finds that he has overpaid his estimated 1970 state income tax and obtains a refund in 1973 of $250 of the $750 he had previously paid in 1972. What then is the amount of the deduction for 1972?

8. Jim Scrooge, a calendar-year and cash-basis taxpayer, owns a small printing plant. He has established a policy of paying salaries only on every second Friday. Consequently, if an employee fails to collect his salary on the Friday it is made available to him, he must wait two weeks before he can collect the amount due him.

When an employee does not pick up his salary, Mr. Scrooge puts the amount due into short-term notes and collects interest on the funds due his employees.

Recently Mr. Scrooge remarked to a friend of his that on Friday, December 31, he really takes advantage of his employees with his payroll system. As Mr. Scrooge sees it, his employees have to report the amount due on a constructive receipt basis, even though they do not pick up their salary. All interest earned on these funds goes to Mr. Scrooge and not the employees, and the interest is reported the following year. Finally, because he has set aside the funds for his employees, he is allowed to deduct the salaries which were not collected and are deductible as if they actually were paid on December 31.

Is Mr. Scrooge correct as to the tax consequences of his system?

15

ACCRUAL METHOD
OF ACCOUNTING

UNCOLLECTED INCOME . . . 537

    Unconditional Right to Receive . . . 537

        CONSTRUCTION CONTRACTS . . . 539
        FINANCE CHARGES . . . 540
        DEALERS' RESERVES . . . 541

    Determinable Amount . . . 542
    Collectible Amount . . . 543

PREPAID INCOME . . . 545

    Advance Rentals and Royalties . . . 546
    Receipts and Receivables for Future Services . . . 547
    Advance Payments for Merchandise . . . 552

DEDUCTIONS . . . 554

    Liability and Determinable Amount . . . 554
    Correction of Estimated Amounts . . . 557
    Subsequent Events and Refunds . . . 557
    Contested Amounts . . . 559
    Probable Inability to Pay . . . 559
    Reserves for Estimated Future Expenses . . . 561
    Vacation Pay . . . 565
    Expenses and Interest Owed to Related Persons . . . 567
    Year-End Bonuses . . . 569

INVENTORIES . . . 571

Valuation . . . 572
Cost . . . 573
Goods Unsalable at Normal Prices . . . 575
Market . . . 576
Identification . . . 576

15.1   Under the accrual method of accounting as it is used for financial reporting purposes, the goal is to reflect revenues when earned, gains when realized, losses as soon as they become evident, and to match costs and expenses with the revenues to which they relate. Revenues received but not yet earned are deferred to future periods. Costs and expenses not represented by cash disbursements or specific amounts payable are accrued on an estimated basis and reflected as liabilities. Expenses paid in advance are set up as assets to be charged to future periods. Items first recognized in the current period that apply to prior periods, or adjustments in the current period of estimates made in providing for costs, expenses, or losses in prior periods, when material in amount, are usually charged or credited directly to retained earnings (earned surplus).

15.2   From the first to the most recent revenue act, the starting point in determining taxable net income of a business enterprise has been its book net income. The goal of the tax law is the same as that of the accounting profession—to determine net income for the period. The federal government, however, is interested in collecting taxes as soon as possible on revenue realized though not yet earned and is prone to require that deductions for expenses and losses be accurate and provable. For this reason, differences have arisen between financial and tax law concepts of the proper periods in which transactions should be reflected. These variations first developed in case law, but many have been incorporated in the regulations. In addition, there are differences based upon specific requirements of the Internal Revenue Code.

15.3   Regulation 1.446–1(c)(1)(ii) describes the accrual method as follows:

> Generally under an accrual method, income is to be included for the taxable year when all the events have occurred which fix the right to receive such income and the amount thereof can be determined with reasonable accuracy. Under such a method, deductions are allowable for the taxable year in which all the events have occurred which establish the fact of the liability giving rise to such deduction and the amount thereof can be determined with reasonable accuracy. The method used by the taxpayer in determining when income is to be accounted for will be acceptable if it accords with generally recognized and accepted income tax accounting principles and is consistently used by the taxpayer from year to year. For example, a taxpayer engaged in a manufacturing business may account for sales of his product when the goods are shipped, when the product is delivered or accepted, or when title to the goods passes to the customer, whether or not billed, depending upon the method regularly employed in keeping his books. Likewise, the extent to which indirect costs shall be included in computing cost of goods sold depends upon the method used by the taxpayer in treating such items in keeping his books.

536

The Board of Tax Appeals in *H. H. Brown Company* [1] explained the theory of the accrual method in the following words:

The basic idea under the accrual system of accounting is that the books shall immediately reflect obligations and expenses definitely incurred and income definitely earned without regard to whether payment has been made or whether payment is due. Expenses incurred in the operations for a particular year are properly accrued in the accounts for that year, although payment may not be due until the following year. Under the accrual system, the word "accrued" does not signify that the item is due in the sense of being then payable. On the contrary, the accrual system wholly disregards due dates.

UNCOLLECTED INCOME

Income collected or constructively received is taxed to an accrual basis taxpayer in the year when it is collected or constructively received just as in the case of cash basis taxpayers, unless it is accruable in a different year. If the income has not yet been reduced to possession or constructively received, it becomes taxable under the accrual method of tax accounting when these three circumstances are present: (1) there is an unconditional right to receive, (2) the amount is determinable with reasonable accuracy, and (3) the amount is collectible.

15.5

Regulation 1.451–1(a) pertaining to the general rule for the taxable year of inclusion reads in part as follows:

15.6

... Under an accrual method of accounting, income is includible in gross income when all the events have occurred which fix the right to receive such income and the amount thereof can be determined with reasonable accuracy. Therefore, under such a method of accounting if, in the case of compensation for services, no determination can be made as to the right to such compensation or the amount thereof until the services are completed, the amount of compensation is ordinarily income for the taxable year in which the determination can be made. ... Where an amount of income is properly accrued on the basis of a reasonable estimate and the exact amount is subsequently determined, the difference, if any, shall be taken into account for the taxable year in which such determination is made.

Unconditional Right to Receive

Income is not accruable until there arises an unconditional right to receive it. If a taxpayer's right to receive income is dependent upon future events, there is no accrual until those contingencies occur or lapse.

15.7

In *H. Liebes & Co.* v. *Com.*,[2] the Ninth Circuit Court of Appeals said:

15.8

1. 8 BTA 112 (1927) (Acq.).
2. 90 F.2d 932 (9th Cir. 1937), 37–2 USTC ¶9361, 19 AFTR 965, affirming 34 BTA 677.

Income accrues to a taxpayer, when there arises to him a fixed or unconditional right to receive it, if there is a reasonable expectancy that the
right will be converted into money or its equivalent.

The issue was the time of accrual of a claim for damages against the
United States. Judgment was rendered by a United States District
Court in favor of the claimant in 1928, the time for appeal expired in
1929, and payment was received in 1929. The income was held to
accrue in 1929 when the time for filing an appeal expired.

15.9   In *Webb Recess Co., Ltd.,*[3] the taxpayer on June 28, 1919, entered
into a contract for the sale and installation of a machine. Payments
totaling $15,000 were received between June 28, 1919, and October,
1919, when installation was completed. The total price was $32,000
and notes were to be executed for the balance of $17,000. The con-
tract provided that after installation the machine was to be tested,
if found to meet the guaranty set forth in the contract was to be forthwith accepted, and the notes for $17,000 were to be delivered. The
testing and acceptance occurred in January, 1920, and the notes were
signed and delivered on January 26, 1920. The Board of Tax Appeals
held that the test and acceptance constituted conditions precedent to
the consummation of the sale, and that accordingly the gross profit
accrued in 1920. In another case for a later year involving the same
taxpayer and similar facts, the same result was reached.[4]

15.10   In the case of *John Graf Company*[5] the taxpayer, an accrual basis
beer distributor, had sued a brewing company alleging poor quality of
beer. The suit was settled out of court in 1934 by the brewing company
contracting to allow discounts totaling $2,450 on future purchases. If
sufficient beer was not purchased to use up the total allowable discount of $2,450, any balance would be forfeited and no cash payment
in lieu thereof would be made. In holding that the taxpayer beer
distributor did not realize, in 1934, the full amount of the discount
available on beer not ordered in that year, the Tax Court said:

It is plain from the contract that it was the intent that the discounts might
materialize in years other than the taxable year, or might not be realized at
all, depending upon the measure of fulfillment of a contract, optional in
that respect with the petitioner. ... We can not think the fact that the option
was in the petitioner removes the element of uncertainty or contingency
which ordinarily prohibits application of ideas of accrued income, for the
contingencies of business, that is as to whether petitioner's business would,
or would not, justify it in ordering additional beer from the Starr Canning
Co. [the brewing company], is a contingency as real as that of condition in
liability for payment by an obligor, which is commonly held to prevent
accrual of income. Taxation is practical, ...

Although the Starr Canning Co. was under liability to pay the discounts,
this was subject to a condition—the requirements of the petitioner in its business of selling beer. Realistic approach to this question compels the con-

3. 3 BTA 247 (1925) (Acq.).
4. 9 BTA 238 (1927) (Acq.).
5. 39 BTA 379 (1939).

clusion that petitioner's income would not be accurately reflected by the inclusion therein of discounts, the receipt of which was not certain. Although the payment thereof could be compelled by the petitioner, it was conjoined with and dependent upon further business expenditures by it. We do not think such a contingent element should enter into the computation of income. ... We hold that the inclusion of any amount above $727.50 [representing discounts earned in 1934 on beer purchased in that year] in the petitioner's income for the year 1934 was error.

In *Standard Lumber Co.*,[6] the taxpayer on January 1, 1952, purchased 5 percent debentures of and from a 62 percent owned subsidiary. In order to induce the Reconstruction Finance Corporation to make a loan to the subsidiary, the taxpayer on December 31, 1953, executed a "consent" and "standby agreement" by which it agreed that no principal and interest on the debentures would become payable until the R.F.C. loan had been fully paid. The taxpayer also agreed that in the interim it would "take no action to assert, collect or enforce all or any part of the Debenture." On its books and in its return for 1954, the taxpayer accrued and reported the interest as income but, of course, did not receive any. If the R.F.C. loan were never repaid in full, the taxpayer would never recover any principal or interest on the debentures. The court held that this contingency so qualified the taxpayer's right to receipt of the interest that it was not properly includible in income for the year 1954.

15.11

Construction Contracts. Construction contracts frequently present knotty problems as to the year in which income should be reported. Long-term construction contracts can be accounted for under any of three methods: accrual, percentage of completion, or completed contract. The percentage of completion and completed contract methods are discussed in chapter 16. At this point, the subject is the accrual method. It is available for use not only for long-term but also for short-term construction contracts.

15.12

As pointed out above in paragraph 15.5, the first requirement for the accruability of income is that there must be an unconditional right to receive. This means that all events must have occurred, other than minor ministerial or clerical acts, which entitle the taxpayer to receive the money. In construction contracts it is customary for progress billings to be made by the contractor as the work proceeds and also for an amount equal to 10 percent or more of the full contract price to be retained by the hiring governmental body or other entity until completion of the entire job and acceptance. The question has been litigated as to when the retained amount becomes accruable.

15.13

In *S. J. Harry Co.*,[7] a subcontractor kept its books and reported its taxable income from long-term construction contracts under the

15.14

6. 35 T.C. 192 (1960) (Acq.). A similar result was reached in a case involving management fees: Commercial Solvents Corporation, 42 T.C. 455 (1964).

7. 4 BTA 211 (1926) (Acq.); also: Charles F. Dally v. Com., 227 F.2d 724 (9th Cir. 1956), 56–1 USTC ¶9109, 48 AFTR 495, cert. den.; L. O. Layton, 11 TCM 1115, ¶52,330 P-H Memo T.C.

accrual method. It entered into a subcontract with a prime contractor for the performance of some of the work under the latter's prime contract with a city. The prime contract provided that the city would withhold payment of 10 percent of the contract price until final completion of all work and acceptance by the city. The subcontract similarly provided that 10 percent of the amount payable under it should not become payable by the prime contractor until after completion of the entire contract and acceptance by the city. The Board of Tax Appeals held that the 10 percent did not accrue as income as the work progressed and would not become taxable unless and until there occurred completion of the entire construction work and acceptance by the city. Until that time, all events would not have occurred which would entitle the subcontractor to receive the 10 percent retained.

15.15   In determining when all events have occurred that are conditions precedent to the right to receive money, the performance of minor ministerial or clerical acts is disregarded. This is particularly true if the performance of such acts is within the control of the taxpayer. If a contract requires that after completion of a portion of a job the contractor shall become entitled to payment upon his certifying such completion and submitting an invoice, the delay by him in doing so does not postpone accrual of the income. The acts are ministerial in nature and within his control.[8] On the other hand, a required audit of reimbursable costs was held not to be a mere ministerial or clerical act. In *U.S. v. D. Allan Harmon*[9] the amount retained by the Federal Public Housing Authority under a cost-plus-fixed-fee contract for the construction of three housing projects was 30 percent of the fixed fee. Such retained amount was not to become payable until after, first, formal acceptance of the completed work by designated government officials, and then audit by the Housing Authority of the reimbursable costs. To the extent that any costs were not reimbursable, they were deductible from the fixed fee. The court held that an unconditional liability on the part of the government to pay a fixed and definite sum did not arise until after completion of the audit, and until that time no portion of the retained amount could become income.

15.16   **Finance Charges.** Retail dealers in automobiles, trucks, appliances, and furniture sell many items under installment sales contracts that add finance charges to the selling price. The courts have been presented with the question of when such dealers using the accrual method (not the installment method) should include the finance charges in income.

15.17   In *Gunderson Bros. Engineering Corp.*,[10] the taxpayer sold trucks and trailers on a deferred-payment basis. Customers were required to pay a finance charge in addition to the cash selling price, and they

8. Charles F. Dally v. Com., *supra* fn. 7.

9. 205 F.2d 919 (10th Cir. 1953), 53–2 USTC ¶9479, 44 AFTR 232, affirming 44 AFTR 1334 (D.C. Okla.).

10. 42 T.C. 419 (1964).

signed installment contracts plus nonnegotiable promissory notes for the unpaid balance. A portion of the finance charge was refundable to the customer in the event of early payment. The taxpayer's consistent accounting practice was to accrue the sales price in the year of sale, but to accrue the finance charge only as earned each month through use of the sum-of-the-months-digits method. The Commissioner sought to require accrual of the entire finance charge in the year of sale, but the court held that the taxpayer's method was proper. It stated that the amount to be received as a finance charge was not fixed and reasonably ascertainable at the time of sale, because early payment would result in a reduction of the charge. Accrual arose only as each monthly installment became due. The Service now agrees that if a finance charge is subject to abatement upon prepayment, such charge accrues ratably only as each monthly installment becomes due.[11]

15.18

If a dealer pledges his receivables, including the service charges, the finance charges continue to accrue each month as earned. However, if the dealer sells his receivables, he must accrue all the unreported deferred income from the service charges. This is so even though he continues to bear the risk of loss and the bank or finance company withholds in a reserve account an amount greater than the total deferred charges.[12]

15.19

Dealer's Reserves. Many retail dealers selling goods on the installment plan sell to finance companies or banks the installment paper received from customers. The finance company may or may not buy the paper at a discount below face value; however, it is customary for the finance company to retain a percentage of the sales price agreed upon for the paper and to credit this amount on its books to a dealer's reserve account. This reserve is then charged with any uncollected installment loans. When the balance in the reserve exceeds an agreed upon percentage of the balance due on the installment paper, the excess is refunded to the dealer by the finance company. When all the accounts are collected, the remaining balance in the reserve is paid to the dealer. Until 1959, much litigation occurred over whether the amounts retained by banks and finance companies were accruable by the dealers when credited to the reserve or when actually paid to them. The controversy was resolved in 1959 by the United States Supreme Court in *Com.* v. *Hansen, et al.*,[13] and it there held that the amounts retained were accruable by dealers when credited to the reserve. Extracts from the opinion follow:

It is therefore clear that the retained percentages of the purchase price of the installment paper, from the time they were entered on the books

11. Rev. Rul. 67–316, 1967–2 C.B. 171; similarly Luhring Motor Company, Inc., 42 T.C. 732 (1964), and *Smith Motors, Inc.* v. *U.S.*, 61–2 USTC ¶9627, 8 AFTR2d 5336 (D.C., Vt., 1961).

12. Federated Department Stores, Inc., 51 T.C. No. 51 (1968), affirmed 25 AFTR2d 70–1269 (6th Cir. 1970).

13. 360 U.S. 446, 59–2 USTC ¶9533, 3 AFTR2d 1690.

of the finance companies as liabilities to the respective dealers, were vested in and belonged to the respective dealers, subject only to their several pledges thereof to the respective finance companies as collateral security for the payment of their then contingent liabilities to the finance companies.

. . .

It is true that the amounts retained by any one of the finance companies, and entered on its books as a liability to a particular dealer, are subject to such liabilities as the dealer may have contractually assumed to the finance company, but only the obligations of the dealer to the finance company arising from those liabilities may be offset against a like amount in the dealer's reserve account. Hence, those liabilities and obligations provide the only conditions that can affect full cash payment to the dealer of his reserve account. No amount may be charged by the finance company against the dealer's reserve account which he has not thus authorized.

It follows that only one or the other of two things can happen to the dealer's reserve account: (1) the finance company is bound to pay the full amount to the dealer in cash, or (2) if the dealer has incurred obligations to the finance company under his guaranty, endorsement, or contract of sale, of the installment paper, the finance company may apply so much of the reserve as is necessary to discharge those obligations, and is bound to pay the remainder to the dealer in cash.

. . .

In any realistic view we think that the dealer has "received" his reserve account whether it is applied, as he authorized, to the payment of his obligations to the finance company, or is paid to him in cash.

It follows that the amounts [of purchase price of the installment paper] that were withheld by the finance companies constituted accrued income to these accrual basis dealers at the time the withheld amounts were entered on the books of the finance companies as liabilities to the dealers, for at the time the dealers acquired a fixed right to receive the amounts so retained by the finance companies.

Determinable Amount

15.20   In order that an item of income may be accruable, its amount must be determinable with reasonable accuracy. In *Globe Corporation* [14] the taxpayer had government contracts in the year 1945 for the performance of certain packaging and preservation services. Prices were not stipulated in the contracts, but instead they provided that the amounts to be paid would be fixed on a fair and equitable basis through negotiation after delivery. The services were completed and the goods delivered in 1945. In late 1945 and continuing until the middle of 1946, there were offers and counteroffers of amounts due. Final agreement was reached in the middle of 1946 and payment was then made. The Commissioner contended that because the services were performed in 1945, the amounts payable accrued in that year. The Tax Court held to the contrary, that the amounts accrued in 1946, for it was not until that year that the amount payable was determinable with reasonable accuracy.

14. 20 T.C. 299 (Acq.).

Collectible Amount

As pointed out in paragraph 15.5, the third and final condition to be met in order that uncollected income may be accrued is that the amount must be collectible. Even though notes or other receivables may not be marketable, they may still be collectible.[15] **15.21**

Uncollected income can be in the form of an open account receivable or a note receivable. In either case it is a right to receive money. As pointed out in paragraphs 11.20 to 11.22, if the right received arises from a sale of real property, it would seem that under Reg. 1.453–6(a)(1) an accrual basis seller should report such right at its fair market value. However, if the sale is of personal property, the full face value of the right must be reported as income. This is also true with respect to accruals for interest, rental income, and compensation due for services rendered. Any failure in the future to receive the full face amount is provided for in the bad debt and loss provisions of the Code. **15.22**

The possibility that a purchaser or other debtor may default on his obligation is not sufficient to defer accruing income that has been earned. Only if there is clear and convincing proof that real doubt and uncertainty exists as to whether an amount due will ever be collected, can there be postponement of reporting income.[16] The question then arises as to the point of time as of which collectibility must be tested. **15.23**

In *Spring City Foundry Co.* v. *Com.,*[17] merchandise was sold during the year 1920 on open account. Late in 1920 the vendee encountered financial straits and a receiver was appointed in December. In 1922 and 1923 the taxpayer received payments totaling $27\frac{1}{2}$ per cent. Under the revenue act applicable to 1920, a bad debt deduction was available only for debts that were completely worthless, not merely partially worthless. In holding that the gross income on the sales had to be accrued and taxed in 1920, the Supreme Court, in effect, held that in the sale of merchandise, collectibility of the unpaid account is to be determined as of the date of sale, not at year-end. **15.24**

The courts have held, to the contrary, that year-end is the time to test collectibility for interest, rental income, and such categories. In *Suffolk & Berks,*[18] an estate kept its books on the accrual basis and the issue was whether or not unpaid rent for 1934 should be accrued and taxed that year. The court held that the rent was not accruable in 1934 because of the financial condition of the lessee. In *Corn Exchange Bank* v. *U.S.,*[19] the taxpayer bank in 1918 had made loans to the Brooklyn Rapid Transit Corporation. Interest on the loans **15.25**

15. Jones Lumber Co., Inc., v. Com., 404 F.2d 764 (6th Cir. 1968), 69–1 USTC ¶9113, 22 AFTR2d 5927.

16. Cuba R. Co., 9 T.C. 211 (1947); Jones Lumber Co., Inc. v. Com., *ibid.* Mertens, Law of Federal Income Taxation, §12.60.

17. 292 U.S. 182 (1934), 13 AFTR 1164.

18. 40 BTA 1121 (1939).

19. 37 F.2d 34 (2nd Cir. 1930), 8 AFTR 9954.

was accrued on its books, which were kept on an accrual basis. The Brooklyn Rapid Transit Corporation went into receivership on December 31, 1918, before the close of the business day. The bank received knowledge of its receivership the same day. The court held that the accrued interest did not constitute taxable income for the year 1918.

15.26   Even though funds are not available when evidence of a debt is received, income must be accrued if it is likely that money will be available, particularly if the taxpayer has it within his power to compel the funds to be made available. In *Consoer, Older & Quinlan, Inc. v. Com.*,[20] the taxpayer was engaged in performing engineering services for villages near Chicago, and its income was reported on the accrual basis. The projects that it supervised were carried out under the special assessment provisions of the Local Improvement Act of Illinois. Its compensation was fixed at 5 percent of the cost of construction, payable solely in special assessment vouchers out of the first installment (there were generally ten installments to the assessment), when collected. It received these vouchers immediately after the award of the contract, although its work was perhaps at that time only 40 percent completed. The vouchers were not due until January 2 of the succeeding year. The court held that the amounts of the vouchers became taxable income on the accrual basis in the year when received. The opinion pointed out that the taxpayer's right was absolute and unqualified. The taxpayer could compel by mandamus the levy of an assessment and thus force the funds to be made available to him.

15.27   If an item is properly accruable in a particular year, an event occurring subsequent to that year has no effect on the accruability. The taxpayer's only remedy is a bad-debt deduction in that later year. In *Automobile Ins. Co. of Hartford, Conn. v. Com.*,[21] the taxpayer in 1928 accrued on its books and reported as taxable income the full amount of an award allowed to it by the Mixed Claims Commission of the United States and Germany. A partial payment was received in 1928 and additional payments were received in 1929 and 1930. The Commissioner sought to tax the payments received in 1929 and 1930 as income in those years, on the grounds that those portions of the award should not have been accrued in 1928. The Second Circuit held against the Commissioner and said:

Whether the petitioner was entitled to accrue this income in 1928 depends upon whether it then had and was justified in having a reasonable expectation that payment would be made in due course. Events of later years rendering doubtful collection of an obligation are not relevant to the propriety of accruing the obligation as income of an earlier year.

. . .

... it is true that payment of such awards was not absolutely certain in 1928, for that depended upon the continued willingness and ability of the

20. 85 F.2d 461 (7th Cir. 1936), 18 AFTR 450.
21. 72 F.2d 265 (2nd Cir. 1934), 14 AFTR 424.

German government to perform its engagements with the United States and upon the latter's continued cooperation in aiding award claimants to obtain payment; they had no means of enforcing collection for themselves. ... The petitioner's right to receive the amount of its award became fixed in 1928, and there then existed reasonable ground to believe that it would ultimately be paid. ...

PREPAID INCOME

Under the accrual method of accounting used in preparing financial statements, revenues received but not yet earned are deferred and are not taken into income until they are earned. The inquiry at this point is whether or not this rule of deferment is also applicable to an accrual basis taxpayer for federal income tax purposes.

15.28

When the 1954 Code was enacted, it contained Section 452. This section gave statutory recognition to the well-established accounting principle of matching income and expenses. It permitted certain types of advance payments received to be spread over the years to which they related and in which the expenses incident to the earning of such income would be incurred. This section of the Code was repealed in June, 1955, retroactive to the date of enactment. A companion Section 462 contained in the original 1954 Code, which allowed deductions for provisions to certain reserves for estimated expenses, was also repealed retroactively in June, 1955.

15.29

The repeal of these two sections was prompted by fears of possible serious effect on tax revenues. The original estimate made during the hearings on the bill, which later became the 1954 Code, was that Sections 452 and 462 would result in the government's loss of $45 million in taxable revenue during its fiscal year ending June 30, 1955. In early spring of 1955, however, revised estimates indicated that the revenue loss might be as great as $1 billion. The repeal was accomplished by P.L. 74 enacted June 15, 1955. In the Senate Finance Committee report accompanying the bill, the following statement was made: [22]

15.30

Your Committee desires to make its position clear that it expects to report out legislation dealing with prepaid income and reserves for estimated expenses at an early date. As indicated above, the existing rulings of the Treasury Department and the court decisions dealing with estimated expenses and prepaid income are now in such a state of confusion and uncertainty that in the opinion of your Committee legislative action is required on these subjects. In addition, your Committee believes that it is essential that the income tax laws be brought into harmony with generally accepted accounting principles. Moreover your Committee believes that the present status, where some taxpayers are able to defer prepaid income while others are not, is inequitable and should not be allowed to continue. In order to eliminate this uncertainty and discrimination, definite rules must be written into the income tax law. For these reasons your Committee plans

22. Sen. Rep. No. 372, 84th Cong., 1st Sess.

to begin studies in the near future to devise proper substitutes for the sections now being repealed.

In the intervening years since 1955 there has been no general legislation in this area. Congress did add Code Sec. 455 pertaining to prepaid subscription income as part of the Technical Amendments Act of 1958 and also, in 1961, added Code Sec. 456 pertaining to prepaid dues income of certain membership organizations such as automobile clubs.

15.31   The problems concerning the time of taxability of prepaid income relate primarily to advance rentals and royalties, receipts for future services, and advance payments on sales of merchandise.

Advance Rentals and Royalties

15.32   Regardless of the method of accounting used by a taxpayer, advance rentals and royalties must be included in income for the year of receipt, regardless of the period to which such rentals or royalties are applicable. Regulation 1.61–8(b) reads as follows:

> Gross income includes advance rentals, which must be included in income for the year of receipt regardless of the period covered or the method of accounting employed by the taxpayer. An amount received by a lessor from a lessee for canceling a lease constitutes gross income for the year in which it is received, since it is essentially a substitute for rental payments. ...

15.33   Payments received by a lessor without restriction on disposition—such as a bonus for executing the lease, or as rentals or royalties applicable to future periods—have been held by the courts to be taxable when received, whether in cash or in the form of a note of a solvent lessee.[23] For example, advance rentals applicable to the last month of the tenancy are reportable in the year of receipt.[24] Further, the Tax Court has held that advance payments for chartering yachts are taxable on receipt rather than when the charter services are subsequently performed, even though the amounts are refundable if the yachts cannot be furnished within a stated time.[25]

15.34   Although the rule is that advance payments of rent are taxable for the year of receipt rather than during any later year to which they pertain, the courts have held that a security deposit does not become taxable in the year when received. In an opinion handed down in 1952,[26] the Tax Court, in holding that certain payments were security deposits, discussed the tax principles involved:

> The issue before us is whether the sum of $33,320 received on the execution of the lease in 1946 should be included in petitioner's gross income for that year. The legal principles by which the issue is to be resolved are not

23. See cases cited in 1970 *P–H Federal Taxes* ¶20,309(5) and (10).
24. Neils Schultz, 44 BTA 146.
25. Lee Johns, ¶59,119 P–H Memo T.C., 15 TCM 603 (1956).
26. John Mantell, 17 T.C. 1143.

in dispute. If the sum is received under a present claim of full ownership, subject to the lessor's unfettered control, and is to be applied to the rent for the last year of the term, it is income in the year of receipt even though under certain circumstances a refund may be required. ...

If, on the other hand, the sum was deposited to secure the lessee's performance under the lease, it is not taxable income even though the fund is deposited with the lessor instead of in escrow and the lessor has temporary use of the money. ...

In some instances the deposit serves as security for the lessee's performance and, in addition, if any or all of it remains during the final period of the lease, it is to be applied to rent. It then becomes necessary to determine whether the deposit was primarily a security payment or a prepayment of rent. ... This question of fact is resolved by reference to the intention and acts of the parties ascertained from the lease agreement and the circumstances incident thereto. ...

Receipts and Receivables for Future Services

For more than ten years and continuing until August, 1970, the Internal Revenue Service vigorously pressed a contention that all payments actually or constructively received by a taxpayer for future services to be rendered were taxable in the year of receipt, without regard to the taxpayer's accounting system, and regardless of whether such receipts would be offset by expenses in future years. 15.35

In *Your Health Club, Inc.*,[27] the taxpayer was engaged in the business of operating a health club. It entered into contracts with its members under which it agreed to perform certain services over the course of a year. In most instances, full payment was received in cash at the time the contract was entered into, but in some instances there were accounts receivable accrued. The amounts paid in cash were deposited in the taxpayer's general bank account and were subject to no restrictions on use or application. However, it was the policy of the taxpayer that if a member requested cancellation of his contract prior to the expiration of its term, the taxpayer would make a refund based upon the number of months yet to run under the contract. The Tax Court held in favor of the Commissioner that all fees became taxable income in the year received or accrued, regardless of whether all of the services required under such contracts had been performed by year-end. 15.36

In *Prichard Funeral Home, Inc.*,[28] the taxpayer was engaged in the business of providing funeral services. During the years at issue, a number of individuals made advance payments to the taxpayer for their own anticipated funeral services. In holding for the Commissioner that these prepaid funeral expenses were includible in taxpayer's income in the year of receipt, the Tax Court stated: 15.37

This court, as well as numerous other courts, has consistently taken the position that the respondent has authority to require that prepaid income

27. 4 T.C. 385 (1944).
28. 21 TCM 1399 (1962); ¶62,259 P-H Memo T.C.

be reported no later than the year in which it is received provided such income is subject to unrestricted use by the taxpayer. ... The salient facts ... demonstrate clearly that the amounts received by petitioner as prepaid funeral expenses were subject to no limitation, contractual or otherwise as to the disposition, use, or enjoyment by the petitioner. The payors did not request or require petitioner to segregate the amounts paid in separate bank accounts or in any other manner. Furthermore, there is no evidence in the record to indicate that the payors intended petitioner to act merely as either their agent, conduit, trustee or depository with respect to the funds. ...

. . . . .

The petitioner in order to sustain its position places considerable reliance upon the fact that the payors had the right at any time to demand a refund of the prepayments. The identical argument was proffered by the taxpayers in Brown vs. Helvering [291 U.S. 193 (1934)]. The Supreme Court in rejecting this argument said, "but the mere fact that some portion of it might have to be refunded in some future year in the event of cancellation ... did not affect its quality as income." ...

15.38   *Schlude* v. *Com.*,[29] a landmark case, was decided by the U.S. Supreme Court in 1963. It held that accrual basis taxpayers must include in their taxable income all advance payments in the form of cash and negotiable notes, plus contract installments due but remaining unpaid at year-end. The taxpayers were husband and wife and formed a partnership to operate dancing studios under franchise agreements with Arthur Murray, Inc. The partnership reported its taxable income under the accrual method of accounting. There were two types of contracts with the students. Under a so-called cash plan contract, the student was required to pay the entire down payment in cash at the time the contract was executed, with the balance due in later installments. Under the deferred payment contract, only a portion of the down payment was paid in cash at the time of signing the agreement; the balance of the down payment was to be paid in deferred installments. In addition, the remaining balance of the contract price was to be paid in the manner set forth in a negotiable note that accompanied the contract. Contracts of both types were noncancellable and provided for no refunds to students. The negotiable notes were discounted at a local bank with full recourse, and 50 percent was held by the bank in a reserve account, unavailable to the studio, until the note was fully paid.

15.39   In a five-to-four decision, with a vigorous dissenting opinion,[30] the U.S. Supreme Court held in the *Schlude* case that the Commissioner

29. 372 U.S. 128 (1963), 11 AFTR2d 751, affirming, reversing, and remanding 296 F.2d 721 (8th Cir.), 8 AFTR2d 5966.

30. It is interesting to note that the High Court of Australia in a 1966 case involving facts similar to those in the *Schlude* case reached a contrary result: Arthur Murray (N.S.W.) Pty. Ltd. v. The Commissioner of Taxation. It allowed advance payments for dance lessons to be given in a subsequent year to be deferred and be taxed in that year.

properly exercised his discretion under Code Sec. 446(b) to reject the studio's accounting system as not clearly reflecting income, and properly included as income in each particular year advance payments by way of cash, negotiable notes, and contract installments falling due but remaining unpaid during the year. From the repeal of Sections 452 and 462 a legislative purpose was found that taxpayers in general should not be permitted to defer the receipt of income. The Court took note of the step-by-step approach of Congress in granting the deferral privilege to only limited groups of taxpayers while continuing to study the entire problem.

15.40

However, the courts and the government agree that income is not accruable for *future payments due in later years* on a contract for the performance of services if the services have not yet been rendered and no notes have been given in advance.[31] Such a contract is executory as to both parties, and no account receivable arises until each due date for a payment.

15.41

A final, significant court case was *Artnell* v. *Com.*[32] There, all of the net assets of the White Sox Corporation, which reported its income under the accrual method and was on an October 31 fiscal year, were acquired by Artnell in May, 1962. The White Sox Corporation was liquidated on May 31, 1962 and filed a short period income tax return for the period from November 1, 1961 to May 31, 1962. During this period the corporation had collected $954,024 in advance ticket sales, advance radio and television revenues, and sales of season parking passes. Of this amount, $762,777 was for games to be played after May 31, 1962. Out of these receipts the corporation would be required to pay the Federal Admissions Tax, City Admission Tax, and visiting team shares.

15.42

The Seventh Circuit Court of Appeals in 1968 held that the portion of the receipts representing Federal Admissions Tax was not income to Artnell because, when collected, it became a trust fund under Code Sec. 7501. As to all other amounts, the Court pointed to the fact that here, unlike the facts present in *Schlude,* the deferred income was allocable to games that were to be played on a fixed schedule and, except for rain dates, there was certainty. In *Schlude,* there were no fixed dates in the future on which the services had to be rendered. The Seventh Circuit then remanded the case to the Tax Court to determine whether the system of tax accounting used by Artnell involving deferral of prepaid income clearly reflected income. In response to the remand, the Tax Court then held[33] that Artnell's tax accounting method did clearly reflect income because it was in accord with financial accounting principles.

15.43

On August 6, 1970, the Internal Revenue Service issued a press

31. Dissenting opinion of Judge Pierce, 32 T.C. 1271 (1959), conceded as being valid principle in brief of the United States before U.S. Supreme Court in Schlude; also see Shuster v. Helvering, 121 F.2d 643 (2nd Cir. 1941), 41–2 USTC ¶9601, 27 AFTR 714, affirming 42 BTA 255 (cash-basis taxpayer).

32. 400 F.2d 981 (7th Cir. 1968), 68–2 USTC ¶9593, 22 AFTR2d 5590, reversing and remanding 48 T.C. 414.

33. 70,085 P–H Memo TC (1970).

release stating that it was abandoning its prior position that advance payments are, with limited exceptions, includible in an accrual basis taxpayer's income in the year of receipt. Thereupon, Revenue Procedure 70–21 was issued. The first part of the ruling gave as authority for the change in posture the discretion granted to the Commissioner by Section 446(b) to determine whether or not a method of accounting clearly reflects income. On July 12, 1971, this ruling was superseded by Rev. Proc. 71–21; the new ruling continued the principles set forth in the earlier one and amplified them. Revenue Procedure 71–21 applies not only to payments received but also to amounts due and payable. It reads in part as follows:

Section 3. Permissible Methods

.01 An accrual method taxpayer who receives a payment for services to be performed by him in the future and who includes such payment in gross income in the year of receipt is using a proper method of accounting.

.02 An accrual method taxpayer who, pursuant to an agreement (written or otherwise), receives a payment in one taxable year for services, where all of the services under such agreement are required by the agreement as it exists at the end of the taxable year of receipt to be performed by him before the end of the next succeeding taxable year, may include such payment in gross income as earned through the performance of the services, except as provided in sections 3.07, 3.08, and 3.11. However, if the inclusion in gross income of payments received is properly deferred under the preceding sentence and for any reason a portion of such services is not performed by the end of the next succeeding taxable year, the amount allocable to the services not so performed must be included in gross income in such next succeeding year, regardless of when (if ever) such services are performed.

.03 Except as provided in sections 3.04 and 3.05, a payment received by an accrual method taxpayer pursuant to an agreement for the performance by him of services must be included in his gross income in the taxable year of receipt if under the terms of the agreement as it exists at the end of such year:

(a) Any portion of the services is to be performed by him after the end of the taxable year immediately succeeding the year of receipt; or

(b) Any portion of the services is to be performed by him at an unspecified future date which may be after the end of the taxable year immediately succeeding the year of receipt.

• • •

.06 In any case in which an advance payment is received pursuant to an agreement which requires the taxpayer to perform contingent services, the amount of an advance payment which is earned in a taxable year through the performance of such services may be determined (a) on a statistical basis if adequate data are available to the taxpayer; (b) on a straight-line ratable basis over the time period of the agreement if it is not unreasonable to anticipate at the end of the taxable year of receipt that a substantially ratable portion of the services will be performed in the next succeeding taxable year; or (c) by the use of any other basis that, in the opinion of the Commissioner, results in a clear reflection of income.

.07 Where an agreement requires that a taxpayer perform contingent services (including for this purpose the replacement of parts or materials where the obligation to replace is incidental to an agreement providing for the performance of personal services) with respect to property which is sold, leased, built, installed, or constructed by such taxpayer (or a related person as defined in section 3.10), advance payments received with respect to such agreement may be included in gross income under the method prescribed in section 3.02 only if in the normal course of his business the taxpayer offers to sell, lease, build, install, or construct the property without such a contingent service agreement.

.08 This Revenue Procedure has no application to amounts received under guaranty or warranty contracts or to a prepaid rent or prepaid interest. However, for purposes of this Revenue Procedure and section 1.61–8(b) of the Income Tax Regulations (requiring "advance rentals" to be included in income in the year of receipt), the term "rent" does not include payments for the use or occupancy of rooms or other space where significant services are also rendered to the occupant, such as for the use or occupancy of rooms or other quarters in hotels, boarding houses, or apartment houses furnishing hotel services, or in tourist homes, motor courts, or motels. See section 1.1372–4(b)(5)(vi) of the regulations.

• • •

.11 The amount of any advance payment includible as gross receipts in gross income in the taxable year of receipt by a taxpayer under the foregoing rules shall be no less than the amount of such payment included as gross receipts in gross income for purposes of his books and records and all reports (including consolidated financial statements) to shareholders, partners, other proprietors or beneficiaries and for credit purposes.

.12 The above rules may be illustrated in part as follows:

On November 1, 1970, A, a calendar year accrual method taxpayer in the business of giving dancing lessons, receives a payment for a one year contract commencing on that date which provides for 48 individual, one hour lessons. Eight lessons are provided in 1970. Under the method prescribed in Section 3.02, A must include $\frac{1}{6}$ of the payment in income for 1970, and $\frac{5}{6}$ of such payment in 1971, regardless of whether A is for any reason unable to give all the lessons under the contract by the end of 1971.

EXAMPLE 1 FROM REV. PROC.

Assume the same facts as in Example 1 except that the payment is received for a two year contract commencing on November 1, 1970, under which 96 lessons are provided. The taxpayer must include the entire payment in his gross income in 1970 since a portion of the services may be performed in 1972.

EXAMPLE 2 FROM REV. PROC.

On June 1, 1970, A, a calendar year accrual method taxpayer who is a landscape architect, receives a payment for services which, under the terms of the agreement, must be completed by December, 1971. On December 31, 1970, B estimates that $\frac{3}{4}$ of the work under the agreement has been completed. Under the method prescribed in Section 3.02, B must include $\frac{3}{4}$ of the payment in 1970. The remaining $\frac{1}{4}$ of such payment must be included in 1971, regardless of whether B is for any reason unable to complete the job in 1971.

EXAMPLE 3 FROM REV. PROC.

In 1970, C, a calendar year accrual method taxpayer in the television repair business, receives payments for one-year contracts under which C agrees to repair (or, incidental to providing such repair service, to replace)

EXAMPLE 4 FROM REV. PROC.

certain parts in the customer's television set if such parts fail to function properly. The television sets to be serviced under C's contracts were not sold, leased, built, installed, or constructed by C or by a person related to C within the meaning of section 3.10. Therefore, section 3.07 does not apply, and C may adopt the method prescribed in section 3.02. Under such method C must include such payments in income over the period earned in accordance with one of the bases prescribed in section 3.06, provided that any portion of the payments not included in income in 1970 must be included in income in 1971.

EXAMPLE 5
FROM
REV.
PROC.

In 1971, D, a calendar year accrual method taxpayer in the business of manufacturing, selling and servicing television sets, receives payments for one-year contingent service contracts with respect to television sets sold by D in 1971. D offers television sets for sale without contingent service contracts. Under these circumstances, the requirement of section 3.07 is satisfied, and D may adopt the method prescribed in section 3.02. Under such method D must include such payments in income over the period earned in accordance with one of the bases prescribed in section 3.06, provided that any portion of the payments not included in income in 1971 must be included in income in 1972.

Advance Payments for Merchandise

15.44   In the late 1960s, the Internal Revenue Service also started a drive to tax in the year of receipt amounts received as nonrefundable advances for merchandise to be sold and delivered in a subsequent year. The courts upheld the Commissioner in *Hagen Advertising Displays, Inc.*,[34] *Modernaire Interiors, Inc.*,[35] and *S. Garber, Inc.*[36] But then again, in the same press release referred to above and issued on August 6, 1970, the Commissioner modified his position. Regulation 1.451–5 now holds that, at the taxpayer's election, advance payments received for the sale of goods to be delivered in a future year may be included in income in either the year of receipt or the year in which the payments are ordinarily accruable under the taxpayer's method of accounting. However, if deferral is elected, that same method must be used in all financial statements and reports. Thus, if for financial accounting purposes, sales are recorded as of the date of shipment and advance payments are not taken into income until that time, the same treatment can be used for tax purposes.

15.45   There is an exception to the deferral method for "substantial advance payments" received with respect to inventoriable goods. A taxpayer is treated as having received substantial advance payments if, on the last day of a taxable year, he has received advance payments in that and prior years which equals or exceeds the estimated cost of the goods to be sold under the agreement. If such an aggregate amount is received and if on the same last day of the year there are on

34. 47 T.C. 139 (1966), affirmed 407 F.2d 1105 (6th Cir., 1969), 69–1 USTC ¶9254, 23 AFTR2d 69–768.
35. 27 TCM 1334, ¶68,252 P–H Memo T.C.
36. 51 T.C. 733 (1969).

hand (or available through the normal source of supply) goods of substantially similar kind and in sufficient quantity to satisfy the sale agreement, the taxpayer must include in income all advances received or receivable by the end of the second year following the year in which substantial advance payments are received to the extent not already included in income.

If advance payments are included in income in the second following year under this exception, the estimated cost of the goods to be sold must be eliminated from the closing inventory of that year if they (or substantially similar goods) are in the inventory. If the goods are not on hand on the last day of that second following year, the estimated cost of goods necessary to satisfy the agreement must be deducted.

The following illustration of this exception is from Reg. 1.451(c)(4) and, in fact, can occur under a lay-away plan of a retailer, but, of course, the dollar amounts would be larger:

In 1971, X, a calendar year accrual method taxpayer, enters into a contract for the sale of goods (properly includible in X's inventory) with a total contract price of $100. X estimates that his total inventoriable costs and expenditures for the goods will be $50. X receives the following advance payments with respect to the contract:

1971	$35
1972	20
1973	15
1974	10
1975	10
1976	10

The goods are delivered pursuant to the customer's request in 1977. X's closing inventory for 1972 of the type of goods involved in the contract is sufficient to satisfy the contract. Since advance payments received by the end of 1972 exceed the inventoriable costs X estimates that he will incur, such payments constitute "substantial advance payments". Accordingly, all payments received by the end of 1974, the end of the second taxable year following the taxable year during which "substantial advance payments" are received, are includible in gross income for 1974. Therefore, for taxable year 1974 X must include $80 in his gross income. X must include in his cost of goods sold for 1974 the cost of such goods (or similar goods) on hand or, if no such goods are on hand, the estimated inventoriable costs necessary to satisfy the contract. Since no further deferral is allowable for such contract, X must include in his gross income for the remaining years of the contract, the advance payment received each year. Any variance between estimated costs and the costs actually incurred in fulfilling the contract is to be taken into account in 1977, when the goods are delivered. . . .

If advance payments are received for a gift certificate under which the goods to be sold in the future are not identifiable in the year the certificate is sold, the advance payment may be deferred for no longer than the second year following the year of receipt. If the goods to be sold are still not identifiable at that time, no deduction for their estimated cost is available.

DEDUCTIONS

15.49   The general rule setting forth the year in which deductions are allowable is stated in Section 461(a):

> The amount of any deduction or credit allowed by this subtitle shall be taken for the taxable year which is the proper taxable year under the method of accounting used in computing taxable income.

If an amount is not claimed until several years after the year in which it should have been claimed, the period of limitations within which a claim for refund may be filed may have expired. In that event, a deduction will never be allowed—unless the peculiar circumstances of the inconsistency sections (1311–1314) permit it.

Liability and Determinable Amount

15.50   Paragraphs (2) and (3)(i) of Reg. 1.461–1(a) set forth the general rule governing the taxable year in which accrual basis taxpayers are entitled to deductions:

> (2) *Taxpayer using an accrual method.* Under an accrual method of accounting, an expense is deductible for the taxable year in which all the events have occurred which determine the fact of the liability and the amount thereof can be determined with reasonable accuracy. However, any expenditure which results in the creation of an asset having a useful life which extends substantially beyond the close of the taxable year may not be deductible, or may be deductible only in part, for the taxable year in which incurred. While no accrual shall be made in any case in which all of the events have not occurred which fix the liability, the fact that the exact amount of the liability which has been incurred cannot be determined will not prevent the accrual within the taxable year of such part thereof as can be computed with reasonable accuracy. For example, A renders services to B during the taxable year for which A claims $10,000. B admits the liability to A for $5,000 but contests the remainder. B may accrue only $5,000 as an expense for the taxable year in which the services were rendered. In the case of certain contested liabilities in respect of which a taxpayer transfers money or other property to provide for the satisfaction of the contested liability, see § 1.461–2. ...
>
> (3) *Other factors which determine when deductions may be taken.* (i) Each year's return should be complete in itself, and taxpayers shall ascertain the facts necessary to make a correct return. The expenses, liabilities, or loss of one year cannot be used to reduce the income of a subsequent year. ... However, in a going business there are certain overlapping deductions. If these overlapping items do not materially distort income, they may be included in the years in which the taxpayer consistently takes them into account.

15.51   The first sentence of Paragraph (2) of Reg. 1.461–1(a) is based upon the United States Supreme Court decision in *U.S. v. P. Chauncey*

Anderson et al.[37] and is sometimes called the "all-events test." The Revenue Act of 1916 enacted in September, 1916, imposed an excise tax on the manufacture of munitions. The taxpayers used the accrual method of accounting and on their books deducted a provision to a reserve for munitions taxes in determining that income. However, such reserve was not deducted in their 1916 tax returns; instead, the taxpayers sought to deduct the munitions taxes in 1917. In holding that this excise tax was deductible in 1916, the Court said:

In a technical legal sense it may be argued that a tax does not accrue until it has been assessed and becomes due; but it is also true that in advance of the assessment of a tax, all the events may occur which fix the amount of the tax and determine the liability of the taxpayer to pay it. In this respect, for purposes of accounting and of ascertaining true income for a given account-ing period, the munitions tax here in question did not stand on any different footing than any other accrued expenses appearing on appellee's books. In the economic and bookkeeping sense with which the statute and Treasury decision were concerned, the taxes had accrued.

The Court respected accounting practice and disregarded the fact that the munitions tax was not assessed or paid until 1917 and that no re-turn of that tax was filed until 1917.

As required by the Regulations, the fact of liability must exist in a particular year in order that an amount may be deductible. In *Com.* v. *The H. B. Ives Company*[38] in November, 1953, the board of directors of this accrual basis corporation adopted a resolution appropriating money for the purchase of annuity contracts for four employees, and the amount of liability was set up on the books. Owing to difficulties in obtaining the correct ages of the employees, the annuity contracts with insurance companies were not executed until January 15, 1954. The Second Circuit Court of Appeals held that all events had not occurred in 1953 to fix the fact of liability. It held that the liability to pay did not become certain until 1954. Citing *American Automobile Association* v. *U.S.,*[39] it held that although accruing the liability at the end of 1953 may have been in accord with business standards and generally accepted accounting principles, nevertheless the principles of tax law must prevail.

15.52

The fact of liability also was found not to be present in *Peoples Bank & Trust Co.* v. *Com.*[40] In its returns for calendar years 1962, 1963, and 1964 this accrual basis bank claimed a deduction for esti-mated interest payable on its passbook savings accounts for the months of November and December of each year. Under its bylaws it paid interest on May 1 and November 1, but only on sums not with-drawn prior to those respective dates. The Court held that on Decem-ber 31, "all events" had not occurred to determine liability, because it would not be known until the following May 1 whether any interest

15.53

37. 269 U.S. (1926), 1 USTC ¶155, 5 AFTR 5674.
38. 297 F.2d 229 (2nd Cir. 1961), 62–1 USTC ¶9165, 9 AFTR2d 323, reversing and remaining 18 TCM 845.
39. 367 U.S. 687 (1961), 61–2 USTC ¶9517, 7 AFTR2d 1618.
40. 415 F.2d 1341 (7th Cir. 1969), 24 AFTR2d 69–5330, affirming 50 T.C. 750.

would be payable on the balances in the accounts in the preceding November and December.

15.54   Contrary to his own Regulations, the Commissioner has sometimes contended that an expense should be accrued in a particular year if the fact of liability arose in that year, even though the amount was not determinable then, but did become known before the due date of the return. In *Sico Foundation* v. *U.S.*,[41] professional services were rendered to the foundation in 1950, the bills were received in January, 1951, and paid in 1951. The Court of Claims held that on December 31, 1950, the amount of the liability for these fees was not determinable and that, accordingly, the expense accrued in 1951. This same court, in *Canton Cotton Mills* v. *U.S.*,[42] had previously held similarly that legal fees accrue in the year in which the bills are received. In that case, the services were rendered in 1934, 1935, and 1936, but no bills were received until February, 1936. It pointed out that no fee arrangements had been made by the end of 1935, and stated:

> The mere fact that some services had been performed would not establish an accrual. ... The general rule, as deduced from *U.S.* v. *Anderson*, is that an expense accrues in the year in which all the events occur which determine the liability *and fix its amount*. If the liability is contingent *or its amount unsettled*, the expense does not accrue.

The Tax Court and many other courts have similarly held that legal fees are deductible not in the year in which the services are rendered by the attorneys, but only in the year in which the bills are received and the amounts thereby become determinable.

15.55   Bookkeeping entries do not control. If the fact of liability, and the amount thereof, can be determined with reasonable accuracy in a particular year, the item is deductible in that year even though no entry is made on the books. In *Aluminum Castings Co.* v. *Routzahn*[43] the United States Supreme Court held that the munitions tax levied by the Revenue Act of 1916 accrued in that year even though the liability was not recorded on the books until 1917. In *Wolf Manufacturing Co.*,[44] an accrual basis manufacturing corporation was allowed a deduction for expenses incurred in 1919, even though the entries pertaining to those expenses were recorded in the books of account for the year 1920. In *Armstrong Cork Co.*,[45] the head office of this company in Pittsburgh did not learn until 1923 that its French branch had paid certain French taxes in 1922 which were attributable to the years 1918, 1919, and 1920, and in the year 1923 recorded those taxes as an expense in its books of account. The Court held that these taxes were deductible in the years 1918, 1919, and 1920, but not in 1923 when

41. 61–2 USTC ¶9732 (Ct. Cls., 1961), 8 AFTR2d 5683, rehearing denied 9 AFTR2d 405.
42. 119 Ct. Cls. 24, 51–1 USTC ¶9131, 39 AFTR 1399.
43. 282 U.S. 92 (1930); 2 USTC ¶615, 9 AFTR 567.
44. 10 BTA 1161 (1928).
45. 24 BTA 1 (1931).

the corporation entered them on its books of account. A similar result was reached in *The Texas Company (South America) Ltd.*[46]

Correction of Estimated Amounts

What should be done when it is discovered that an estimated deduction claimed in a prior year was either overstated or understated? The last sentence of Reg. 1.461–1(a)(2) states:

15.56

> Where a deduction is properly accrued on the basis of a computation made with reasonable accuracy and the exact amount is subsequently determined in a later taxable year, the difference, if any, between such amounts shall be taken into account for the later taxable year in which such determination is made.

This sentence was added by T.D. 6282 approved December 19, 1957, filed with the Federal Register December 24, 1957. No similar sentence appeared in the Regulations under the 1939 Code. Accordingly, old cases[47] under the 1939 Code holding that the correction should be related back to the year of the event, even when admittedly the estimate was reasonably accurate, are obsolete.

A similar rule exists with respect to estimated amounts of properly accruable *income* items. Regulation 1.451–1 provides:

15.57

> Where an amount of income is properly accrued on the basis of a reasonable estimate and the exact amount is subsequently determined, the difference, if any, shall be taken into account for the taxable year in which such determination is made.

An old case[48] and a ruling[49] requiring a relation-back approach are now obsolete.

Subsequent Events and Refunds

The tax benefit doctrine was discussed in paragraphs 6.63 to 6.68 pertaining to recovery of bad debts, prior taxes, and delinquency amounts. It was there mentioned that Section 111 excludes from gross income amounts of recoveries of such items to the extent that when deducted in a prior year they did not result in a reduction of income tax. To the extent a tax benefit was secured in a prior year, the amount of the recovery is taxable. Here we are concerned with the proper year in which to report recoveries of items properly deducted with full tax benefit in a prior year.

15.58

Deductibility of properly accrued expenses is unaffected by events

15.59

46. 9 T.C. 78 (1947).
47. Fraser Brick Co., 10 BTA 1252 (Acq.); Beacon Coal Co., 9 BTA 280; Leamington Hotel Co., 26 BTA 1004.
48. Continental Tie and Lumber Co. v. U.S., 286 U.S. 290 (1931), 3 USTC ¶937, 11 AFTR 4.
49. Mim. 5897, 1945 C.B. 131.

of a subsequent year that result in a credit or refund of part of the deducted expense. In *Jamaica Water Supply Co.*,[50] the corporation received refunds in its fiscal years ended June 30, 1934, and June 30, 1935, from an insurance company representing adjustment of compensation insurance premiums paid during the respective preceding years. The full amount of the premiums paid was properly deductible from income in the years in which paid, and the refunds accordingly became income in the years in which received. There are a number of other cases similarly holding that if a refund of an expense properly accrued and deducted in a prior year is received in a later year, the amount of that refund does not relate back to the prior year.

15.60   The force of the annual accounting concept, and the impropriety of relating back to an earlier year transactions of a later year, are well illustrated in the case of *Security Flour Mills Co.* v. *Com.*[51] The taxpayer conducted a flour mill and reported its income on the accrual basis. As a first domestic processor of wheat, it was subject to the processing tax levied under the Agricultural Adjustment Act of 1933. During the year 1935, the taxpayer collected this tax from its customers as a part of the sales price but did not separately identify any part of that sales price as representing the tax. In that year it also instituted a suit against the United States to enjoin the collection of these processing taxes and obtained a temporary injunction enjoining collection on the condition that meanwhile it file information returns and pay the amount of the tax to a depository. It accrued the amount of the processing taxes so contested, and deducted this contested amount in its 1935 income tax return. Early in 1936, the taxpayer won its lawsuit concerning the processing taxes, when the United States Supreme Court held that the taxing provisions of the Agricultural Adjustment Act were unconstitutional. As a result, the impounded processing taxes were paid over to the taxpayer in 1936. In the years 1936, 1937, and 1938, it repaid to its customers the amounts of processing tax included in the sales price of flour sold to them in 1935 which had not been paid to the Collector of Internal Revenue as processing taxes, but instead had been paid to, and then returned by, the depository.

15.61   The Supreme Court held that the taxpayer could not accrue as a deduction in 1935 the amount of any liability for processing taxes, because it was contesting that liability in 1935 and the contest was not resolved until 1936. It further held that the amounts of the payments made to customers in 1936, 1937, and 1938 as refunds of processing taxes collected from them, which were never paid over to the government, could not be related back to 1935. To do so would amount to approval of a transactional method of accounting. The Court held that the 1939 Code authorized the use of only a cash or an accrual method of accounting, and not a "transactional" method.

15.62   Even though the 1954 Code does authorize a hybrid method of accounting, it is believed that this United States Supreme Court decision

---

50. 42 BTA 359.
51. 321 U.S. 281 (1944), 44–1 USTC ¶9219, 31 AFTR 1214.

is applicable today. As a result, deductions arising in a later year can generally be claimed only in that year even though they are related transactionally to an earlier year.

Contested Amounts

15.63

The general principle is that a contested liability is not accruable until the contest is settled or a final decision of a court is entered.[52] What is a contest? Litigation in the courts is a contest,[53] but not as to a taxpayer who is not a party to the suit and who sits idly by awaiting final outcome.[54] So also a protest formally lodged with the tax authorities is a contest.[55] However, the mere filing of a state tax return showing a stated liability pursuant to the mandate of a self-assessment statute does not entail a denial by the taxpayer that it owes an amount of tax greater than that specified on the return;[56] as a result any later deficiency assessed and paid will relate back to and be deductible in the year for which assessed.[57]

15.64

In 1961 the United States Supreme Court held in *U.S.v. Consolidated Edison Company of New York, Inc.*,[58] that real property taxes paid under protest, and thereafter immediately contested, did not accrue in the year in which the amounts were paid, but rather in the later year in which the contest was finally determined. To overturn that holding, Section 461(f) was inserted in the 1954 Code by the Revenue Act of 1964. By its terms the subsection applies to all types of liabilities for expenses, but has its most frequent application to real property taxes. Now, if such a tax is paid under protest and litigation is started to obtain a refund, the payment is deductible on the accrual basis in the year in which paid. If in a later year a refund is obtained of the real property tax, such refund will constitute income in that later year to the extent a federal income tax benefit was obtained in the prior year.

Probable Inability to Pay

15.65

It was noted in paragraph 15.21 that uncollected income should not be accrued where the amount is not collectible. The converse is not true, at least so far as interest is concerned. The Eighth and Fifth Circuit Courts of Appeal have held that interest accrues as a deduction

52. Dixie Pine Products Co. v. Com., 320 U.S. 516 (1944), 44–1 USTC ¶9127, 31 AFTR 956.
53. Ibid.
54. Lutz v. Com., 396 F.2d 412 (9th Cir. 1968), 21 AFTR2d 1425, reversing 45 T.C. 615.
55. G.C.M. 25298, 1947–2 C.B. 39; Great Island Holding Corp., 5 T.C. 150 (1945).
56. Dravo Corp. v. U.S., 348 F.2d 542 (Ct. Cl., 1965), 16 AFTR 5179.
57. Dravo Corp. v. U.S., *ibid.*; Rev. Rul. 68–631. However, if a taxpayer has consistently deducted additional state taxes in the year when finally determined, he must continue to do so unless he receives permission to change (Rev. Rul. 69–336).
58. 366 U.S. 380 (1961), 61–1 USTC ¶9462, 7 AFTR2d 1451.

even though there is no reasonable probability that the debtor will ever be able to pay it.

Zimmerman Steel Co. v. Com.

Eighth Circuit Court of Appeals, 1942 [59]

[Facts: At the end of 1935, Zimmerman Steel Company owed a related company a substantial sum of money evidenced by notes payable representing advances made to it from 1921 to 1933 plus accrued interest. The last payment on the indebtedness was made in 1929. At the end of 1935, 1936, and 1937, the taxpayer's liabilities exceeded its assets by substantial amounts, and its operations for 1923 to 1937 inclusive except 1928, 1929, and 1930 resulted in net losses. For the years 1936 and 1937 the taxpayer accrued on its books the interest payable on the notes and deducted such interest in its returns. However, the creditor company did not accrue such interest as income on its books or in its returns for the years 1936 and 1937 on the ground that it was uncollectible. On December 17, 1941, the Board of Tax Appeals held in favor of the Commissioner that the accrued interest payable was not deductible "since there was no reasonable expectation of such obligation being discharged in the normal course of business." Shortly thereafter the taxpayer corporation went into bankruptcy. Extracts from the opinion of the Court of Appeals follow.]

Though it is earnestly insisted for the government that the conclusion of the Board was without error, it is admitted in brief that "there are no court decisions directly holding that an accrued item of expense may not be deducted when there is no reasonable expectancy that it will be paid." Our own search has confirmed the admission. The law is that if a method of bookkeeping employed by a taxpayer "does not clearly reflect the income, the computation shall be made in accordance with such method as in the opinion of the Commissioner does clearly reflect the income" (Section 41) [now Sec. 446] and the real facts, not forms of entry, must measure the tax. But where interest actually accrues on a debt of a taxpayer in a tax year the statute plainly says he may deduct it. That he has no intention or expectation of paying it, but must go into bankruptcy as this taxpayer was obliged to do, can not of itself justify denial of deduction in computing the taxpayer's net income. It is true that if a man's gains at the end of the year consist of bad debts he can have no net income to tax. But neither does he have such net income if the interest on what he owes amounts to more than his gains.

. . .

We conclude that the decision of the Board on the facts which were found by it was erroneous. It is therefore reversed and the cause is remanded for further proceedings.

Reversed and remanded.

15.66   The Fifth Circuit Court of Appeals followed the *Zimmerman Steel Co.* case in *Fahs v. John W. Martin et al.*,[60] and extended the holding to allow the deductibility of interest on interest on defaulted bonds. The debtor company was in Bankruptcy Court in a Section 77 reor-

59. 130 F.2d 1011 (8th Cir. 1942), 42–2 USTC ¶9697, 30 AFTR 41, reversing 45 BTA 1041.

60. 224 F.2d 387 (5th Cir. 1955), 55–2 USTC ¶9546, 47 AFTR 1430, affirming 123 F. Supp. 404, 46 AFTR 354 (D.C., Fla., 1954).

ganization, and the interest on the bonds had been in default since 1931. But in 1972 the Fifth Circuit in *Tampa & Gulf Coast R.R.* v. *Com.*[61] refused to follow its prior decision in *Fahs*. The indebtedness involved was that of a wholly owned subsidiary and was owed to the parent corporation. The sole income of the subsidiary was from rent paid by the parent; and the court found that tax avoidance was the principal purpose of the rent being so low as to prevent the payment of interest to the parent.

15.67

The Tax Court is unwilling to go quite as far as the Eighth and Fifth Circuit Courts of Appeal. In *Edward L. Cohen*[62] the Tax Court stated its position:

> The rule which emerges from the decisions of this court is that deductions for accrued interest are proper where it cannot be "categorically said that at the time these deductions were claimed that the interest would not be paid, even though the course of conduct of the parties indicated that the likelihood of payment of any part of the disallowed portion was extremely doubtful."

In that case the court allowed the deduction of accrued interest to a stockbroker who used the accrual method of accounting on his books, and in doing so the court said: "There may have been doubt as to the ultimate ability of the petitioner to pay the accrued interest in full, but there was no certainty that he would be unable to do so."

15.68

The Internal Revenue Service has also ruled on this problem in Rev. Rul. 70–367[63] A railroad company filed a petition under Section 77 of the Bankruptcy Act pertaining to railroads. The petition was approved and the company was authorized to continue in possession and control of its properties and assets. A plan of reorganization was approved by the courts, but not yet accepted by the creditors, under which old bonds, together with interest to January 1, 1969, were to be exchanged for new securities aggregating the same face value, but composed of first mortgage bonds, general mortgage bonds, and stock. The interest rate on the new bonds was to be different from the interest rate on the old bonds. The Service held that the interest on the old bonds outstanding of the railroad company would continue to accrue as a deduction until the date of the consummation of the proposed reorganization and stated specifically: "The doubt as to payment of such interest is not a contingency of a kind that postpones the accrual of the liability until the contingency is resolved."

Reserves for Estimated Future Expenses

15.69

Subject to a few exceptions carved out by some Circuit Courts of Appeal, it is the general rule that no deduction is allowed for provisions to reserves for anticipated future expenses prior to the time when all the events fixing the fact of liability have occurred. The

61. 72–2 USTC ¶9746 (5th Cir., 1972), affirming 56 T.C. 1393.
62. 21 T.C. 855 (1954).
63. 1970–2 C.B. 37.

Code authorizes deduction of provisions for estimated expenses in only a very limited number of cases—bad debts, certain guaranteed debt obligations, depreciation, depletion, and amortization. Special rules pertaining to vacation pay will be discussed later.

15.70   Deductions have been denied for provisions to the following types of reserves relating to currently earned income:

Cash discounts (estimates of amounts expected to be allowed on accounts receivable outstanding at the close of the taxable year because of early payment by customers)[64]

Price adjustments expected to be made on shipments in transit at the close of the taxable year owing to anticipated shortage in weight or shrinkage during passage, such amounts to be determined upon unloading of the cargo[65]

Anticipated renegotiation refunds on government contracts where no legally enforceable claim against the taxpayer existed during the year[66]

Self-insurance reserves[67]

Injuries and damages reserve to cover probable settlement costs for damage claims arising out of accidents of a transportation company[68]

Guarantees under sales contracts[69]

15.71   Although provisions to reserves for estimated expenses generally are not deductible, some Circuit Courts of Appeal have made a few exceptions. The Third, Fourth, Ninth, and Fifth Circuit Courts of Appeal have allowed deductions of reasonably accurate estimates of expenses to render future services required by law or contract. In *Denise Coal Co. v. Com.*[70] and *Harrold v. Com.*,[71] the Third and Fourth Circuit Courts of Appeal allowed deductions to coal operators engaged in stripping operations to deduct the estimated cost of back filling required by law and contract based on the tonnage of coal

64. Shapleigh Hardware Co. v. U.S., 81 F.2d 697 (8th Cir. 1936), 17 AFTR 428; G.C.M. 1342, VI–1 C.B. 177 (1927); and other cases cited in *P–H 1970 Federal Taxes* ¶20,580(5).

65. David J. Joseph, Inc. v. Com., 136 F.2d 410 (5th Cir. 1943), 31 AFTR 171 affirming ¶42,519 P–H Memo BTA; and other cases cited in *P–H 1970 Federal Taxes* ¶20,580(20).

66. The Overlakes Corp., 41 T.C. 503 (1964).

67. Spring Canyon Coal Co. v. Com., 43 F.2d 78 (10th Cir. 1930), 9 AFTR 30, cert. den. 10–26–31, affirming 13 BTA 189; and other cases cited in *P–H 1970 Federal Taxes* ¶20,584.

68. Com. v. Milwaukee & Suburban Transport Corp., 367 U.S. 906 (1961), 7 AFTR2d 1649, *per curiam,* vacating and remanding 283 F.2d 279 (7th Cir.), 6 AFTR2d 5719 60–2 USTC ¶9741, which had reversed on this issue ¶59, 216 P–H Memo T.C. 18 TCM 1039; on remand 293 F.2d 628 (7th Cir), 8 AFTR2d 5455, 61–2 USTC ¶9653 affirming ¶59,216 P–H Memo T.C., 18 TCM 1039, rehearing denied 10–9–61, cert. den. 1–22–62.

69. Amounts paid as credits or refunds under guarantees upon goods sold, are deductible in the year when taxpayer admits his liability and the amount is determinable. See cases and rulings cited in *P–H 1970 Federal Taxes* ¶20,581.

70. 271 F.2d 930 (3rd Cir. 1959), 4 AFTR 2d 5815, reversing on this issue 29 T.C. 528.

71. 192 F.2d 1002 (4th Cir. 1951), 41 AFTR 442, reversing 16 T.C. 134.

stripped during the taxable year. In both instances neither the fact nor the amount of the liability was contested by the taxpayer, and the estimate was reasonably accurate and based upon adequate experience.

The Ninth Circuit Court of Appeals, in *Pacific Grape Products* 15.72 *Co. v. Com.*,[72] held that the estimated cost of labeling, packaging, and shipping goods could be accrued on the date of billing.

Pacific Grape Products Co. v. Com.

U.S. Circuit Court of Appeals for the Ninth Circuit, 1955

POPE, Circuit Judge: Petitioner is a canner of fruit and fruit products. It regularly billed its customers for all goods ordered by them, but not yet shipped and remaining in petitioner's warehouse, on December 31 in each year. It accrued upon its books the income from the sales of such unshipped goods in the taxable years ending on the days of such billing. On the same date it also credited to the accounts of brokers the brokerage due on account of sales of such unshipped goods, and accrued the cost of such unshipped goods including therein the anticipated cost of labeling, packaging and preparing the same for shipment. For many years the petitioner reported its income accordingly. (It filed its returns on the calendar year, accrual basis.)

The Commissioner, in determining deficiencies for the years 1940 to 1944, held petitioner's method of accounting did not clearly reflect its income and made adjustments by excluding from the computation of income for the years 1939, 1940 and 1941, the sales prices of unshipped goods billed on December 31 of those years, and included such amounts in the computations of income for the years 1940, 1941 and 1942 respectively. He likewise transferred to these later years the brokerage fees and the estimated costs mentioned which related to these goods. The result was a deficiency in income tax for the years 1940 and 1943, and in excess profits tax for the years 1940, 1941, 1942 and 1944, and in declared value excess profits tax for the year 1944. The determinations mentioned were upheld by the Tax Court on petition for redetermination.

.   .   .

Since title had ... passed to the buyers, it is plain that petitioner's method of accounting and accruing in such years its gross income from sales of such merchandise clearly reflected its income. Consistently, and to make reflection of income complete, it properly accrued its shipping expenses relating to this merchandise as part of its cost of goods sold in the respective years billed. The record shows that the items making up these expenses were either precisely known or determinable with extreme accuracy. Labels and cases for packing were on hand. The expenses of labor in labeling and casing were determinable on the basis of petitioner's past experience. Freight costs were available from published rate schedules. ...

.   .   .

72. 219 F.2d 862 (9th Cir. 1955), 55–1 USTC ¶9247, 47 AFTR 214, reversing 17 T.C. 1097.

Finally, we are of the view that the petitioner's method of accounting clearly and accurately reflected its income wholly apart from the question whether title to the goods did or did not pass to the buyers on the dates of billing. Upon this aspect we are agreed with what the six dissenting judges said in this case.

Not only do we have here a system of accounting which for years has been adopted and carried into effect by substantially all members of a large industry, but the system is one which appeals to us as so much in line with plain common sense that we are at a loss to understand what could have prompted the Commissioner to disapprove it. Contrary to his suggestion that petitioner's method did not reflect its true income it seems to us that the alterations demanded by the Commissioner would wholly distort that income. It is reasonable that both the taxpayer and the Government should be able accurately to ascertain the income accruing to the taxpayer on account of each annual pack. The Commissioner would break up the petitioner's product for the year 1940 and throw the receipts from the portion shipped before December 31 into gross income for that year and the receipts from the unshipped portion into the following year. If in a succeeding year there arose a market shortage which led to a demand which brought about almost complete shipment of the pack before December 31, the Commissioner's accounts for that succeeding year would cover one nearly complete pack and portions of the income and deductions relating to the preceding pack. We see no reason for any such requirement on the part of the Commissioner.

The judgment of the Tax Court is reversed and the cause is remanded with directions to modify the judgment in accordance with this opinion.

15.73   Specifically following *Pacific Grape Products Co.*, the Fifth Circuit Court of Appeals, in *E. W. Schuessler v. Com.*,[73] allowed a deduction to a retailer of gas furnaces for the year 1946 of a provision to a reserve for the estimated cost of turning furnaces on and off each year for five years. It was established that such service would cost $2 per call and that the taxpayer sold the furnaces for $20 to $25 more than his competitors because of his guarantee to the purchasers that he would turn the furnaces off and on each spring and fall for five years. The court held that in the year of sale a legal liability arose to render such services and that allowing a deduction for the provision to this reserve results in an accounting method that most accurately reflects the taxpayer's income on an annual accounting basis.

15.74   The Tax Court has consistently denied the deduction of a reserve for estimated expenses even though the cost of such future expense is determined with reasonable accuracy.[74]

15.75   In summary, the decisions pertaining to the deductibility of reserves for estimated expenses are in conflict. Undoubtedly, the United

73. 230 F.2d 772 (5th Cir. 1956), 56–1 USTC ¶9368, 49 AFTR 322, reversing 24 T.C. 247.

74. National Bread Wrapping Machine Co., 30 T.C. 550 (1958); Streight Radio & Television, Inc., 33 T.C. 127 (1959) affirmed without discussion of this point in 280 F.2d 883 (7th Cir. 1960), 6 AFTR2d 5247; Curtis R. Andrews, 23 T.C. 1026 (1955); Bell Electric Co. 45 T.C. 14 (1965).

States Supreme Court will be called upon within the next few years to decide the issue. In *Milwaukee and Suburban Transport Co.* v. *Com.*,[75] the United States Supreme Court reversed and remanded the decision of the Seventh Circuit Court of Appeals allowing the deduction of an estimated amount of liability for claims filed against the company due to accidents, and in effect commanded the Seventh Circuit to affirm the decision of the Tax Court disallowing the deduction of such estimated amount. This action of the Supreme Court did not dispose of the issue as to whether all reserves for estimated future expenses are deductible.

15.76

Before leaving the subject of reserves for estimated future expenses, the point should be made that bookkeeping terminology does not control. An account labeled a reserve may nevertheless be a true liability account. This is frequently the case in connection with *reserves for quantity discounts*. In I.T. 3633[76] the Service ruled on the deductibility of quantity discounts. In 1942 a corporation had advised several of its customers that if, during 1943, their orders were large enough to enable it to reduce costs, refunds would be made to them on a quantity discount basis. The Service ruled as follows:

If the taxpayer keeps its books and files its returns on the accrual basis and pursuant to binding agreements in writing between the taxpayer and its customers, the taxpayer has definitely obligated itself to make refunds in specified amounts, such amounts are deductible for the taxable year within which the liability to make the refunds accrues and the amounts thereof are determined and become fixed.

15.77

A similar result was reached in *Albert C. Becken, Jr.*[77] A wholesale jeweler entered into an agreement to give one of its customers a 10 percent trade discount provided that its purchases totaled a certain number of dollars. As of December 31, 1941, that customer had made the required minimum amount of purchases and, accordingly, became entitled to a 10 percent discount on all purchases. The taxpayer credited the amount to a reserve for discounts but was allowed the deduction because it constituted a true accrued liability.

Vacation Pay

15.78

For a number of years, a hotly contested issue has involved the right of an employer, following the accrual method of accounting, to deduct for tax purposes in the current year the cost of vacations not to be taken by the employees until the following year. There are two

75. *Supra*, fn. 70.
76. 1944 C.B. 89; declared obsolete in Rev. Rul. 68–100, but principle still valid.
77. 5 T.C. 498 (1945).

rules presently in force pertaining to the accrual of vacation pay: the liberal rule of I.T. 3956[78] and the strict rule of Rev. Rul. 54–608.[79]

15.79 In I.T. 3956, issued in 1949, several railroad corporations had entered into union contracts under which an employee who worked no less than 160 days during the calendar year was to be granted a specified number of days of vacation in the subsequent calendar year, or pay in lieu thereof. If his employment terminated prior to the scheduled vacation period, then no payment in lieu of vacation was to be made to him unless the termination was caused by furlough due to force reduction, leave of absence, or illness. If a man retired, he became entitled to pay in lieu of vacation.

15.80 The ruling held that toward employees as a group, a liability arose at the end of each year for vacation pay to be granted in the subsequent year. Accordingly, in the year the union contract was entered into, granting for the first time this right to a vacation or pay in lieu thereof in the subsequent year, a double deduction was allowed—a deduction for the amount of the vacation pay actually paid during that year and also a deduction at the year-end for the accrued vacation pay to be granted in the subsequent year. Corporations were granted the right, if they wished, to continue to deduct vacation pay under the so-called cash method, provided a substantial contingency existed as stated in this concluding sentence of the ruling:

> However, such taxpayers may accrue and deduct vacation pay for the year in which it is paid if that has been the consistent practice of the taxpayer and if there is a substantial condition to actual payment, such as being in the employ of the employer at the time of the scheduled vacation.

In practice, this ruling was applied to all vacation pay plans that were communicated to employees, even orally, whether or not the liability arose from a union contract.

15.81 In the year 1954 the Commissioner had second thoughts about vacation pay and I.T. 3956, because of certain court decisions since 1949. The Tax Court in 1950[80] and again in 1952[81] held that no deduction for accrued vacation pay was allowable at the end of a particular taxable year for vacations or payment in lieu thereof to be granted during the subsequent year, if each particular employee had to be on the payroll at the time of the vacation period. The Tax Court also held that the amount of the liability at any year-end was not determinable with reasonable accuracy. Even if the liability allegedly arising at year-end could be computed with accuracy, based upon the payroll as of that date, the amount of the liability would not be payable in all events to particular individuals.

78. 1949–1 C.B. 78.
79. 1954–2 C.B. 8.
80. Tennessee Consolidated Coal Co., 15 T.C. 424 (1950).
81. E. H. Sheldon & Co., 19 T.C. 481 (1952), affirmed on this point 214 F.2d 655 (6th Cir. 1954), 45 AFTR 1791; similarly Morrisdale Coal Mining Co., 19 T.C. 208 (1952).

The strict rule of Rev. Rul. 54–608 [82] was published in 1954. The 15.82
pertinent portions read as follows:

> ... it is held that no accrual of vacation pay can take place until the fact of
> liability to a specific person has been clearly established and the amount
> of the liability to each individual is capable of computation with reasonable
> accuracy. It is further held that no distinction should be made between vaca-
> tion plans under written contracts and vacation plans under oral agreements
> providing the vacation plan or policy was communicated to the employee
> prior to the beginning of the vacation year and that under such plan the em-
> ployees' rights to a vacation with pay (or payment in lieu thereof) are vested at
> the time that the employer seeks to accrue the deduction.
>   I.T. 3956, *supra,* is hereby revoked, ... However, under the authority of
> sections 3791(b) of the 1939 Code and 7805(b) of the 1954 Code, such revo-
> cation and modification will not be applicable with respect to taxable years to
> which the provisions of the 1939 Code are applicable. This Revenue Ruling
> will be applied only to taxable years ending on or after June 30, 1955.

Revenue Rul. 54–608 states that it supersedes the liberal rule only 15.83
for taxable years ending on or after June 30, 1955; however, a series of
rulings and laws have deferred its applicability until taxable years
ending on or after January 1, 1973. In the meantime, employers who
have consistently accrued vacation pay from years earlier than 1959,
in reliance upon I.T. 3956, can continue to do so. Employers who
came into existence in 1959 or later must use the so-called cash
method of deducting vacation pay unless they meet the strict per employee requirements of Rev. Rul. 54–608.

Expenses and Interest Owed to Related Persons

In 1937 the House Ways and Means Committee reported as fol- 15.84
lows: [83]

> ... Under existing law, some individuals have attempted to take advantage
> of the difference in operation between different accounting methods of re-
> porting income to obtain artificial deductions for interest and business ex-
> penses. For example, it was found that an individual on the accrual basis
> became indebted either to an individual with whom he enjoyed a special
> relationship, such as a member of his family, or to a corporation which he
> controlled, and his creditor reported income on the cash basis. Thereafter as
> interest became due on the indebtedness, the debtor on the accrual basis
> reported the interest as a deduction for income-tax purposes, but he did not
> make any actual payment to his creditor. Since the creditor was on a cash
> basis, he reported no income and thus the sum involved escaped income tax
> altogether, for usually in these cases if the payment were finally made it was
> done at a time when the creditor had offsetting losses. The use of this device
> as a practical matter is restricted to situations where the parties occupy special
> relationships to each other because an ordinary bona fide creditor would not
> permit his debtor to engage in such a practice.

82. 1954–2 C.B. 8.
83. H.R. Rep. No. 1546, 75th Cong., 1st sess., 1937, p. 29.

Your committee recommends that section 24 of the Revenue Act of 1936 be amended by adding a new subsection [now § 267(a)(2)] under which it is provided that where the creditor, by reason of his method of accounting, is not required to include in his gross income the amount of the expenses or the interest until it is paid, no deduction shall be allowed to the debtor under section ... [now § 162 and § 212] (for expenses) or section ... [now § 163] (for interest) for sums not paid by the debtor during his taxable year or within $2\frac{1}{2}$ months after the close of such year. This provision is limited in its application to cases in which both the taxpayer and the person to whom the payment is to be made are, at the close of the year of the taxpayer or at any time within $2\frac{1}{2}$ months thereafter, persons between whom losses would not be allowed under section ... [now § 267(a)(1)].

15.85 The bill that this report accompanied became the Revenue Act of 1937, and the amendment became Section 24(c) of the 1939 Code. As later amended, it is now Section 267(a)(2) of the 1954 Code.

The applicable Regulations are in Reg. 1.267(a)–1(b) and read as follows:

(1) No deduction shall be allowed a taxpayer for trade or business expenses otherwise deductible under section 162, for expenses for production of income otherwise deductible under section 212, or for interest otherwise deductible under section 163—

(i) If, at the close of the taxpayer's taxable year within which such items are accrued by the taxpayer or at any time within $2\frac{1}{2}$ months thereafter, both the taxpayer and the payee are persons within any one of the relationships specified in section 267(b) (see § 1.267(b)–1); and

(ii) If the payee is on the cash receipts and disbursements method of accounting with respect to such items of gross income for his taxable year in which or with which the taxable year of accrual by the debtor–taxpayer ends; and

(iii) If, within the taxpayer's taxable year within which such items are accrued by the taxpayer and $2\frac{1}{2}$ months after the close thereof, the amount of such items is not paid and the amount of such items is not otherwise (under the rules of constructive receipt) includible in the gross income of the payee.

(2) The provisions of section 267(a)(2) and this paragraph do not otherwise affect the general rules governing the allowance of deductions under an accrual method of accounting. For example, if the accrued expenses or interest are paid after the deduction has become disallowed under section 267(a)(2), no deduction would be allowable for the taxable year in which payment is made, since an accrual item is deductible only in the taxable year in which it is properly accruable.

(3) The expenses and interest specified in section 267(a)(2) and this paragraph shall be considered as paid for purposes of that section to the extent of the fair market value on the date of issue of notes or other instruments of similar effect received in payment of such expenses or interest if such notes or other instruments were issued in such payment by the taxpayer within his taxable year or within $2\frac{1}{2}$ months after the close thereof. The fair market value on the date of issue of such notes or other instruments of similar effect is includible in the gross income of the payee for the taxable year in which he receives the notes or other instruments.

(4) The provisions of this paragraph may be illustrated by the following example:

A, an individual, is the holder and owner of an interest-bearing note of the M Corporation, all the stock of which was owned by him on December 31, 1956. A and the M Corporation make their income tax returns for a calendar year. The M Corporation uses an accrual method of accounting. A uses a combination of accounting methods permitted under section 446(c)(4) in which he uses the cash receipts and disbursements method in respect of items of gross income. The M Corporation does not pay any interest on the note to A during the calendar year 1956 or within 2½ months after the close of that year, nor does it credit any interest to A's account in such a manner that it is subject to his unqualified demand and thus is constructively received by him. M Corporation claims a deduction for the year 1956 for the interest accruing on the note in that year. Since A is on the cash receipts and disbursements method in respect of items of gross income, the interest is not includible in his return for the year 1956. Under the provisions of section 267(a)(2) and this paragraph, no deduction for such interest is allowable in computing the taxable income of the M Corporation for the taxable year 1956 or for any other taxable year. However, if the interest had actually been paid to A on or before March 15, 1957, or if it had been made available to A before that time (and thus had been constructively received by him), the M Corporation would be allowed to deduct the amount of the payment in computing its taxable income for 1956.

Section 267 applies only when a debtor and creditor are closely related, as set forth in Section 267(b). Section 267(c) states that, in the case of closely held corporations, an individual will be deemed to constructively own stock held by other members of his family or by other corporations that he controls. These rules of attribution in a number of respects differ from other rules of attribution to be found elsewhere in the Code.

15.86

Year-End Bonuses

Bonus payments to employees are deductible as compensation and accordingly are subject to the following rules governing the deductibility of compensation generally:

15.87

1. The bonus payment when added to other compensation paid must be reasonable in relationship to the value of the services rendered.
2. The payment must be purely for services rendered—not based on stock holdings without regard to the value of services rendered.
3. If payable by an accrual basis employer to a "related" cash-basis individual, the amount must be paid during the year in which it accrued or within 2½ months thereafter.

Our inquiry at this point is the time for deducting year-end bonuses accrued but not paid during the year. Compensation is deductible by an accrual basis employer only in the year in which a fixed liability or obligation to pay is created to pay a definite or ascertainable amount. The obligation to pay must be an absolute one. If it is

15.88

conditioned upon a future event or a contingency, a definite obligation does not arise during the year, and the compensation is not deductible prior to the happening of the contingency upon which it is dependent. The authorization should usually be in the form of a resolution by the board of directors in the case of a corporation. Informal authorizations have been upheld by the courts, but clear-cut proof of the finality of that informal authorization has been required. Book entries serve as evidence but are not determinative. When an accrual basis taxpayer was unequivocally obligated to pay an officer's salary but did not accrue the liability on its books during the year in which the obligation arose, deduction was denied in the subsequent year of payment.[84]

15.89   A published ruling[85] concerned a bonus based upon a percentage of profits:

> ... it is held that bonuses payable under an incentive compensation plan, the exact amounts of which cannot be determined and paid by an accrual basis taxpayer until early in the year immediately following the close of the taxable year of accrual, would properly be accruable and deductible for Federal income tax purposes, subject to the test of "reasonableness" under section 23(a) [now § 162(a)] of the Code, for the year to which they relate, provided the total bonuses are definitely determinable through a formula in effect prior to the end of the taxable year and the employer has definitely obligated itself, prior to the close of such taxable year to make payment thereof by delivering to each employee concerned either a written or oral notice of the percentage of such total to be awarded to him and that payment of such bonuses is made as soon after the close of the taxable year as is administratively feasible. ...

By Rev. Rul. 61–127 the foregoing ruling was modified so as to eliminate the requirement of separate notices to each employee; notice to the affected employees as a group is sufficient.

15.90   Courts have held that if a definite amount is authorized to be paid as a bonus to a *group* of employees, that amount is deductible in the year of authorization even though the amounts payable out of that fund to *each* individual employee are not determined until the subsequent year.[86] The reason for this result was pointed out by the Second Circuit Court of Appeals in one[87] of these cases:

> That obligation [to pay the bonus authorized and accrued] could have been enforced by the employees as a class, and we do not think that a court would be unable to devise some equitable method for apportioning the sum among them.

84. Bear Film Co., 18 T.C. 354 (1952), affirmed without discussion of this point 219 F.2d 231 (9th Cir. 1955), 46 AFTR 1692.

85. Rev. Rul. 55–446, 1955–2 C.B. 531.

86. Odell Hardware Co., 8 BTA 485 (1927); Willoughby Camera Stores, Inc. v. Com., 125 F.2d 607 (2nd Cir. 1942), 42–1 USTC ¶9242, 28 AFTR 1108, reversing 44 BTA 520.

87. Willoughby Camera Stores, *supra* fn. 89.

In 1969 the deductibility of accrued liabilities to groups of individuals for other types of payments was upheld.[88] Based upon these court cases the principle today is this: If the fact of liability is present and the amount is determinable, the accrued liability is allowable as a deduction even though the liability is to a group of individuals, the time of payment is not certain, and the members of the group are subject to change.

INVENTORIES

Inventories must be used in determining taxable income by every manufacturing and merchandising business. They cannot be used by a real estate dealer,[89] persons engaged in the business of the culture of oysters,[90] fish hatcheries,[91] and flower growers. Personal service businesses, such as those of architects, consulting engineers, lawyers, and public accountants do not have inventories. Their work in process represented by charts, papers, and salary costs is considered prepaid expense—deductible on the cash basis as incurred and deductible on the accrual basis in the taxable period to which it relates.

Regulation 1.471–1 reads as follows:

15.91

15.92

In order to reflect taxable income correctly, inventories at the beginning and end of each taxable year are necessary in every case in which the production, purchase, or sale of merchandise is an income-producing factor. The inventory should include all finished or partly finished goods and, in the case of raw materials and supplies, only those which have been acquired for sale or which will physically become a part of merchandise intended for sale, in which class fall containers, such as kegs, bottles, and cases, whether returnable or not, if title thereto will pass to the purchaser of the product to be sold therein. Merchandise should be included in the inventory only if title thereto is vested in the taxpayer. Accordingly, the seller should include in his inventory goods under contract for sale but not yet segregated and applied to the contract and goods out upon consignment, but should exclude from inventory goods sold (including containers) title to which has passed to the purchaser. A purchaser should include in inventory merchandise purchased (including containers), title to which has passed to him, although such merchandise is in transit or for other reasons has not been reduced to physical possession, but should not include goods ordered for future delivery, transfer of title to which has not yet been effected. ...

88. Washington Post Co. v. U.S., 23 AFTR2d 69–515 (Ct. Cl., 1969) (bonus payments to independent distributors); Lukens Steel Co., 442 F.2d 1131 (3rd Cir., 1971), 27 AFTR2d 71–1286, 71–1 USTC ¶9374, affirming 52 T.C. 764 (supplemental unemployment benefits plan), but I.R.S. will not follow—Rev. Rul. 72–34.

89. Atlantic Coast Realty Co., 11 BTA 416 (1928); Albert F. Keeney, 17 BTA 560 (1929).

90. O.D. 684, 1920 C.B. 80, amended by I.T. 2704, 1933 C.B. 169.

91. L. M. Bryan, 44 BTA 141 (1941).

15.93   The general principles imposed in valuing inventories are set forth in Reg. 1.471–2(a) and (b):

> (a) Section 471 provides two tests to which each inventory must conform:
>   (1) It must conform as nearly as may be to the best accounting practice in the trade or business, and
>   (2) It must clearly reflect the income.
> (b) It follows, therefore, that inventory rules cannot be uniform but must give effect to trade customs which come within the scope of the best accounting practice in the particular trade or business. In order clearly to reflect income, the inventory practice of a taxpayer should be consistent from year to year, and greater weight is to be given to consistency than to any particular method of inventorying or basis of valuation so long as the method or basis used is substantially in accord with §§ 1.471–1 through 1.471–9. An inventory that can be used under the best accounting practice in a balance sheet showing the financial position of the taxpayer can, as a general rule, be regarded as clearly reflecting his income.

15.94   There are methods of valuation, determining cost, determining market, and identification. There is also a regulation permitting the write-down of goods unsalable at normal prices.

Valuation

15.95   The two methods of valuation optionally available in the alternative to all types of businesses are (a) cost or (b) cost or market, whichever is lower. If the latter method is elected, each item in the inventory must be priced at the lower of cost or market. A taxpayer cannot value the entire inventory first at cost and then at market and use the lower of the two results.

15.96   Special methods are also available in special businesses. Dealers in securities may use either of the standard methods or the alternative method of valuing their inventories strictly at market, irrespective of cost. Miners and manufacturers who produce different kinds, sizes, or grades of products may allocate their production costs among the various products in accordance with their respective selling values. Retail merchants may use the retail method in determining valuation based on either (a) cost or (b) cost or market, whichever is lower. Under this device the selling price of the closing inventory is reduced by the mark-on percentage that was added to cost to cover selling expenses, overhead, and profit.[92] Farmers can use the cash method of accounting, but, if they elect to keep inventory records, there are special methods available.[93]

92. The retail method is described in Reg. 1.471–8 and examples of it are to be found in 703 CCH Standard Federal Tax Reporter ¶2950.01 and 1970 P–H Federal Taxes, vol. 3, ¶20,761.
93. See Reg. 1.471–6 and explanations in 734 CCH Standard Federal Tax Reporter ¶2946.01–2946.022 and 1970 P–H Federal Taxes, vol. 3, ¶20,736.

Cost

Wholesalers and retailers encounter few problems in determining the cost of opening and ending inventories. Regulation 1.471–3(a) and (b) provides the rules for them as follows:

Cost means:
(a) in the case of merchandise on hand at the beginning of the taxable year, the inventory price of such goods.
(b) In the case of merchandise purchased since the beginning of the taxable year, the invoice price less trade or other discounts, except strictly cash discounts approximating a fair interest rate, which may be deducted or not at the option of the taxpayer, provided a consistent course is followed. To this net invoice price should be added transportation or other necessary charges incurred in acquiring possession of the goods.

Manufacturers, however, do have problems. Sound accounting practices used for financial statement purposes should govern in determining what is "cost" for tax purposes. Consistency is also a cardinal principle. But it should also be recognized that the goal of financial accounting is to "fairly present" the results of operations; while the requirement of Section 446(b) is that the method of accounting used for tax purposes "clearly reflect" income. The two concepts are not identical.

In determining the cost of manufactured goods, the following methods are the principal ones which are or have been in use, but no comment should be inferred as to whether the first two of these alternative methods reflect sound accounting principles: (a) prime cost, (b) direct cost, and (c) full absorption cost. The latter method is the only one specifically approved by the Internal Revenue Service in its regulations and is described in Reg. 1.471–3(c) quoted in paragraph 15.102. On September 14, 1973, the Service finalized Reg. 1.471–11 requiring the use of the full absorption or a modified full absorption method.

Under the prime-cost method of valuing inventories, indirect manufacturing expenses (overhead) are charged off currently to profit and loss. Accordingly, under this method the value of inventories includes only the costs of direct labor and direct materials and excludes overhead costs. This method is contrary to Reg. 1.471–3(c) and was held improper in *Photo-Sonics, Inc. v. Com.*,[94] *Dearborn Gage Co.*,[95] and *All-Steel Equipment, Inc., infra.*

Under the direct-cost method, items of indirect manufacturing expenses (overhead) are segregated between those that are fixed and those that vary directly with the volume of production. The items of fixed overhead expense are charged off currently to profit and loss, while appropriate portions of the variable overhead expenses are allocated to and included in the valuation of the inventories. Thus, the valuation of inventories under the direct-cost method includes the costs of direct labor, direct materials, and variable over-

94. 357 F.2d 656 (9th Cir. 1966), 66–1 USTC ¶9282, 17 AFTR2d 482.
95. 48 T.C. 190 (1967).

head, but excludes all fixed overhead costs. The use of this method, where it had been consistently used for many prior years, was approved in *McNeil Machine & Engineering Co.* v. *U.S.* (Ct. Cl. Commissioner's Report, 3–29–67),[96] and *Geometric Stamping Co.*[97]

15.102   The full-absorption-cost method is the one preferred by the Service. Under it *all* elements of factory overhead, fixed and variable, are treated as product costs and allocated to inventory. Regulation 1.471–3(c) states that cost means:

> In the case of merchandise produced by the taxpayer since the beginning of the taxable year, (1) the cost of raw materials and supplies entering into or consumed in connection with the product, (2) expenditures for direct labor, (3) indirect expenses incident to and necessary for the production of the particular article, including in such indirect expenses a reasonable proportion of management expenses, but not including any cost of selling or return on capital, whether by way of interest or profit.

At first blush it would seem that this regulation makes the full-absorption method mandatory in all cases; but, as pointed out by the Court of Claims' Commissioner in *McNeil Machine & Engineering Co.* v. *U.S., supra,* the regulation does not indicate whether *all* indirect costs must be included in inventory or whether it is sufficient if only those costs identifiable with production are included. Note also Reg. 1.471–2, quoted in paragraph 15.90 to the effect that inventory rules cannot be uniform and great weight is to be given to consistency. The full-absorption method was approved in *Frank G. Wikstrom & Sons, Inc.,*[98] *Photo-Sonics, Inc.* v. *Com.,*[99] *Dearborn Gage Co.,*[100] and *All-Steel Equipment, Inc.*[101]

15.103   In *All-Steel Equipment, Inc.,* the corporation was engaged in the manufacture and sale of metal office furniture, and used the accrual method of accounting and the calendar year. It commenced business in 1912 and since at least 1928 had valued its inventories under the prime cost method. Its returns for all years since 1916, except for the years 1928 and 1951, were audited by the Service, and its use of the prime cost method was not challenged until the issuance of a notice of deficiency with respect to 1962 and 1963, the years involved in the case. The Commissioner determined that the full absorption method had to be used and increased the closing inventory for 1962 by $494,367.99 and the closing inventory for 1963 by $604,450.78. As he left the opening inventory on the prime cost method, the effect was to telescope into the year 1962 all additional net income attributable to prior years arising from capitalizing manufacturing overheads. However, he did agree that for the year 1962

96. 677 CCH Standard Federal Tax Reporter ¶8173; 1967 P–H Federal Taxes ¶58.636.

97. 26 T.C. 301 (1956).

98. 20 T.C. 359 (1953).

99. *Supra,* fn. 93.

100. *Supra,* fn. 94.

101. 54 T.C. No. 176 (9–30–70), reversed in part as to repairs in 72–2 USTC ¶9660 (7th Cir., 1972).

the taxpayer was entitled to a deduction in the amount of the excess of the value of inventories existing at January 1, 1954, computed under the full absorption method over the value of such inventories as of that date computed under the prime cost method. This he was required to do by the provisions of Section 481 pertaining to changes in accounting methods and discussed in paragraphs 16.57 through 16.60.

The Tax Court held:

1. The prime cost method of valuing inventories is an erroneous one for federal income tax purposes because it is contrary to Reg. 1.471–3(c) and is not a method approved by the American Institute of Certified Public Accountants (Accounting Research Bulletin No. 43 (1961)).
2. There is no such thing as immateriality in the determination of federal taxable net income.
3. The consistent use of an erroneous method does not justify its continued use.
4. Under the full absorption method, those items of overhead need not be capitalized as a part of inventory costs which (a) are specifically made deductible by the Code or (b) would be incurred by a company engaged in strictly a merchandising operation.
5. Expenditures for taxes, losses, research and experiment, and repairs are deductible in full under Sections 164, 165, and 174 and Reg. 1.162–4; but on appeal the 7th Circuit held repairs had to be capitalized.

The Commissioner for the purposes of this case asked the Court not to consider the includibility in inventory costs of profit-sharing contributions made by the corporation on behalf of factory employees. Further, it is interesting to note that nowhere in the opinion is there any mention of depreciation. The reason is that the 90-day letter did not assert that any portion of depreciation on manufacturing equipment should be capitalized.

Many companies claim accelerated depreciation for tax purposes but book only straight-line depreciation. At this writing it is the position of the Service that only the book amount of depreciation need be reflected in the cost of inventories.[102] Further, Rev. Rul. 141[103] permits (unless a change in accounting method is involved), but does not require, taxpayers to treat depreciation and depletion as elements of cost of goods sold, and thus in valuing inventories.

Overtime costs incurred for direct and indirect labor in excess of the manufacturer's average anticipated costs are a part of the cost of production and must be taken into account in valuing inventories.[104]

Goods Unsalable at Normal Prices

Whether merchandise is valued at cost or the lower of cost or market, Reg. 1.472–1(c) permits their value to be written down

---

102. Rev. Rul. 70–346.
103. 1953–2 C.B. 101.
104. Rev. Rul. 69–373.

when such merchandise is unsalable at normal prices or unusable in the normal way:

> ... Any goods in an inventory which are unsalable at normal prices or unusable in the normal way because of damage, imperfections, shop wear, changes of style, odd or broken lots, or other similar causes, including second-hand goods taken in exchange, should be valued at bona fide selling prices less direct cost of disposition, whether subparagraph (1) or (2) of this paragraph is used, or if such goods consist of raw materials or partly finished goods held for use or consumption, they shall be valued upon a reasonable basis, taking into consideration the usability and the condition of the goods, but in no case shall such value be less than the scrap value. Bona fide selling price means actual offering of goods during a period ending not later than 30 days after inventory date. The burden of proof will rest upon the taxpayer to show that such exceptional goods as are valued upon such selling basis come within the classifications indicated above, and he shall maintain such records of the disposition of the goods as will enable a verification of the inventory to be made.

Market

15.108 Regulation 1.471–4 provides that, under ordinary circumstances and for normal goods in an inventory, the market value of purchased goods is the current bid price prevailing at the date of inventory for the particular merchandise in the volume in which usually purchased by the taxpayer. If it is impossible to obtain a current bid price, the best available evidence must be used.

15.109 If the taxpayer is a manufacturer, the market value of work in process and finished goods is the reproduction cost—the amount that would have to be spent at current prices for materials, labor, and overhead to bring the article to a comparable state of completion.

15.110 Goods on hand or in process of manufacture for delivery upon firm sales contracts, that is, those not legally subject to cancellation by either party, must be valued at cost where the contracts were entered into before the date of the inventory, the contracts specify fixed prices, and the taxpayer is protected against actual loss. The goods can be specific or fungible. In *Bibb Mfg. Co.* v. *Rose* [105] the court held that to the extent that cotton on hand used to manufacture cotton fabrics was necessary to fulfill legally enforceable contracts that were in force at the end of the year, the ending inventory was required to be valued at cost. This was so even though the taxpayer acceded to the wishes of its customers and later modified and canceled contracts.

Identification

15.111 In a business of any size, goods on hand at the end of the year will have been so intermingled that it will be impossible to identify specific items with specific invoices. As set forth in Reg. 1.471–2(d), the

105. 81 F.2d 228 (5th Cir. 1936), 36–1 USTC ¶9081, 17 AFTR 208.

normal practice is to apply the rule of "first in, first out" (FIFO). In lieu thereof, all taxpayers have the right to adopt the LIFO method, based on the assumption that goods on hand at the end of a year were those first acquired and that the sales during the year were were of the goods last acquired. The Regulations pertaining to this method are quite detailed and are to be found in Reg. 1.472–1 to Reg. 1.472–8(h)(2).

In general, the LIFO method is adopted simply by using it in the tax return and filing with it Form 960 in triplicate. Only the cost method of valuation can be used in conjunction with the LIFO identification method. There cannot be any write-downs to market value. In the year of adoption, both the opening and the closing inventories must be determined by use of the cost method; but for that first year the opening inventory will have been determined by use of the first-in, first-out identification rule. If the closing inventory for the year preceding such first year was valued at other than cost, the value must be readjusted to the cost basis. Increases in the closing inventory occurring from year to year may be valued consistently on the basis of (1) most recent costs, (2) costs in the order of acquisition of goods in the taxable year, (3) average costs in the taxable year, or (4) any proper method which in the opinion of the Commissioner clearly reflects income. Manufacturers may value raw material purchased or initially produced under one of the foregoing methods and value goods in process and finished goods under any other proper method.

15.112

LIFO may not be used if the taxpayer uses any different inventory method for credit purposes or for reports to shareholders, partners or other proprietors. This provision does not apply to interim reports or to any other reports for periods shorter than the taxpayer's whole taxable year. Taxpayers using LIFO may not change to another method except with the approval of the Commissioner under the general rules for a change in accounting methods (discussed towards the end of chapter 16) or unless the Commissioner (at his option alone) requires a change because the taxpayer has issued financial statements using a different method.

15.113

QUESTIONS AND PROBLEMS

1. An accrual basis individual sued a corporation for patent infringement. The case was settled before trial and the settlement agreement provided for payment in two installments. The agreement further provided that if the second payment was not made when due, the entire agreement would be voided, the amount of the first payment would be retained, and the suit would be reinstituted. The agreement was entered into in 1971 and the first installment was received then. The second installment was due in 1973. When did the amount of the second installment accrue as income?

2. A corporation manufactured prefabricated housing units and used the accrual method. In January it entered into a fixed price contract with

the Federal Public Housing Authority for the manufacture and delivery of 1,000 units. The contract provided:

> The contractor shall be paid, upon the submission of properly certified invoices or vouchers semimonthly, 90 percent of the prices stipulated herein for articles delivered or services rendered, less deductions, if any, as herein provided. The remaining 10 percent of the prices stipulated herein shall not be paid until all of the construction and erection work of all of the dwelling units has been finished and finally accepted by the contracting officer.

An invoice in the amount of 90 percent of the stipulated price covering houses delivered from December 16 to December 31 was presented by the taxpayer to the Housing Authority on January 6 of the following calendar year. (a) When did the amount equal to 90 percent of the stipulated price covering houses delivered in December accrue? Why? (b) When did the remaining 10 percent of the stipulated price accrue? Why?

3. The Federal Development Company, owner of an office building, sold it for $500,000. The contract provided that $50,000 should be withheld and not become payable until a certain tenant moved out. At the closing in 1972, the purchaser withheld the $50,000. If the tenant moved out by March 1, 1973, the full amount of the $50,000 then became payable. For each day that the tenant occupied the premises after March 1, the amount payable was to be reduced by $500. The agreement also provided that for the period from the closing date to March 1, 1973, interest was to be paid on the $50,000 by the purchaser to the seller and the $50,000 was to be treated as if it had first been paid by the purchaser to the seller and then repaid by the seller to the purchaser as a guarantee fund. When did the $50,000 accrue as income to the Federal Development Company, the seller?

4. In *Gunderson Bros. Engineering Corp.* (paragraph 15.17) the taxpayer also did not accrue that portion of a finance charge applicable to a skipped or late payment until paid. Was this correct?

5. During 1973 an accrual basis automobile dealer sold to a finance company $100,000 in installment notes received from customers. The finance company paid the dealer $95,000 in total for these notes as they were sold to it. The balance of $5,000 was credited by the finance company on its books to a dealer reserve account. At the beginning of 1973 the balance in this account was $4,000, and at the end of 1973 the balance was $8,000. How much of the amount in the dealer's reserve account accrued as income to the automobile dealer in 1973?

6. In 1973 an accrual basis merchandising corporation encountered financial difficulties, and a receiver was appointed for it. As of December 31, 1973, its books showed the following unpaid liabilities:

For goods purchased from January through November, 1973	$150,000
Interest on bank loan due November 15, 1973	$ 20,000
Rent payable for the months of October and November, 1973	$ 10,000

The financial condition of this company at December 31, 1973, was such that it was highly improbable that any of these debts will be paid. What amount, if any, accrued as income to each of these creditors in 1973?

7. A lease was entered into on February 1, 1973, for a ten-year period ending January 31, 1983. As it required, $1,000 rent for January, 1983, was paid to the lessor on February 1, 1973, in addition to the rent for the month of February, 1973. To the accrual basis landlord, when does the $1,000 rent for January, 1983, become taxable? For the accrual basis tenant, when is it deductible?

8. A secretarial school reporting income on the calendar year and accrual basis collected tuition in December, 1972, applicable to the succeeding six months and deferred it on its books of account. In 1973 as the months expired, the amounts were transferred to income. When is the tuition taxable?

9. Can the merchandising corporation in question 6 deduct the three debts listed?

10. On December 31, 1972, and January 1, 1973, an accrual basis and calendar-year corporation credited amounts to certain reserve accounts as follows:

December 31, 1972 —
    Reserve for Salesmen's Bonuses: one percent of 1972 net sales to be paid to salesmen on the payroll at June 30, 1973. The amount to be received by each salesman shall be that portion of the total bonus which his net sales for 1972 bears to the net sales for 1972 of all salesmen on the payroll at June 30, 1973.

    Reserve for Warranty Claims: one percent of 1972 net sales for warranty costs to be incurred in 1973 with respect to 1972 sales.

January 1, 1973 —
    Reserve for Rebates: one percent of 1972 net sales to be paid to customers who place $100,000 or more in orders during the first six months of 1973. The amount to be paid to each customer shall be one percent of the net sales made to that customer during 1972.

The corporation has a contractual obligation to pay the bonuses, rebates, and warranty costs. Indicate the deductibility or nondeductibility for 1972 of the amounts credited to each reserve account.

11. The Ball Corporation and the Cat Corporation, accrual basis and calendar-year taxpayers, each have a vacation plan that provides that an employee with two or more years of service as of December 31 of each year shall be entitled to a three-week vacation with pay, provided such employee is on the payroll on the subsequent June 30. The Ball Corporation was incorporated in 1943, and the Cat Corporation was incorporated in 1964. The Internal Revenue Service allows the Ball corporation to accrue and deduct as of December 31 of each year the estimated vacation payroll for the subsequent year. However, the Internal Revenue Service allows the Cat Corporation to deduct its vacation payroll only when paid. What is a possible explanation for the difference in treatment of the two corporations in the deductibility of vacation pay?

12. An individual owns 45 percent of the outstanding capital stock of the Smith Manufacturing Corporation. If the remaining 55 percent of the outstanding stock is owned as indicated below, how much of the outstanding stock is considered as being owned by the individual in applying Section 267?
    (a) 15 percent by his mother-in-law; 40 percent by a trust of which his wife is the sole beneficiary.
    (b) 35 percent by his only son; 20 percent by his daughter-in-law.

(c) 15 percent by his wife; 40 percent by his partner in the Dolt Company (a partnership).

13. On January 15, 1973, the board of directors of an accrual basis and calendar-year corporation passed a resolution to pay to each officer of the corporation 10 percent of his gross salary for 1972 in recognition of his contribution to the substantially increased profits for 1972. The resolution stated that the additional compensation was to be a charge against 1972 profits. No such bonus was ever paid in the past, and the officers had not been expecting the bonus. In what year is the bonus deductible?

14. A corporation had the following items of inventory on hand at the end of a particular year:

ITEM	COST	MARKET VALUE
A	$10,000	$15,000
B	10,000	9,000
	$20,000	$24,000

Assuming the "cost or market, whichever is lower" method of valuing inventory is used by the corporation, what was the value of the inventory?

15. A corporation adopted the LIFO method of inventory, both for statement and income tax purposes, effective with its year ended December 31, 1962. In connection with obtaining a loan from a bank, the corporation issued to the bank a balance sheet as of December 31, 1972, on which inventories were valued at current cost rather than LIFO cost. The corporation has requested you to prepare its 1972 income tax return. Should the inventories be valued at LIFO cost or current cost on the return?

Multiple Choice Questions

16. The Mart, a retail clothing store, was organized as a sole proprietorship on January 1, 1972. Its records for 1972 reflect the following:

Cash sales	$15,000
Total sales on account	45,000
Cash purchases	8,000
Purchases on account in 1972 paid for in 1972	20,000
Sales returns and allowances	500
Accounts Payable 12/31/72 (all for merchandise)	2,500
Trade accounts receivable 12/31/72	10,000

The Inventory of merchandise on hand at December 31, 1972, was valued at its cost, $6,500.

(a) Indicate which of the following represents the store's net cost of goods sold.
  (1) $24,000
  (2) $24,500
  (3) $21,500

(4) $30,500
(5) $22,000

(b) Which of the amounts shown below is the correct gross profit earned by The Mart in 1972?
(1) $46,000
(2) $36,000
(3) $35,500
(4) $45,500
(5) $38,000

17. The records of Red Mfg. Co., at the end of its first quarter of operation, disclose the following:

Costs:

Factory expenses	$32,000
Direct labor	12,000
Administrative and sales expense	4,000
Raw materials used	10,000
Land purchased	6,000
Work in process	6,000

Sold — 10,000 units

Produced — 16,000 units

What is the unit cost of finished goods on hand at the close of the period?
(a) $3.00
(b) $3.375
(c) $4.00
(d) $4.80
(e) $5.40
(f) None of the above

16

OTHER ACCOUNTING METHODS, CHANGES, AND CLAIM OF RIGHT

HYBRID METHOD . . . 584
INSTALLMENT METHOD . . . 584

In General . . . 584
Dealers in Personal Property . . . 585

ELIGIBLE DEALERS . . . 585
ELIGIBLE SALES . . . 585
COMPUTATION OF INCOME . . . 586
INITIAL ADOPTION OF METHOD . . . 588
CHANGE FROM ACCRUAL TO INSTALLMENT METHOD . . . 588
DEFAULTS AND REPOSSESSIONS . . . 590

Sales of Real Estate and Casual Sales of Personal Property . . . 590

ELIGIBLE SALES . . . 591

EVIDENCES OF INDEBTEDNESS . . . 591
NUMBER OF PAYMENTS . . . 592

ELIGIBLE SALES . . . 585
COMPUTATION OF INCOME . . . 586
REDUCTION OF SELLING PRICE IN SUBSEQUENT YEAR . . . 595
DEFAULTS AND REPOSSESSIONS . . . 596

PERSONAL PROPERTY . . . 596
REAL PROPERTY . . . 596

Disposition of Installment Obligations . . . 596

LONG-TERM CONSTRUCTION CONTRACTS . . . 598

Percentage of Completion Method . . . 599
Completed Contract Method . . . 600

CHANGES IN ACCOUNTING METHODS . . . 601

Consent of Commissioner . . . 601
Right of Commissioner to Require a Change . . . 603
Adjustments Under Section 481 . . . 603
What Is a Method? . . . 604
Revenue Procedure 70–27 . . . 608
Change in Billing Practice . . . 609

CLAIM OF RIGHT DOCTRINE . . . 609

HYBRID METHOD

16.1   A hybrid method of accounting is an overall method—partly cash and partly accrual. It has nothing to do with the treatment of specific items or accounts, such as the installment method, amortization of corporate organization expenses, or the treatment of research and development expenses. Prior to enactment of the 1954 Code, there was a somewhat widely held belief that taxable income had to be computed on either a cash or an accrual basis and no other—there could not be a hybrid method.

16.2   The 1954 Code for the first time gave legislative approval to the use of a hybrid method. The Senate Finance Committee Report[1] explained this new provision as follows:

> ... All methods of accounting recognized under existing law are continued. In addition one or more hybrid methods may be authorized in the regulations issued under paragraph (4). One such method, in the case of a small retail store, will be an accrual of items affecting gross income such as purchases, sales of goods, accounts payable, and accounts receivable. In such a case items of deduction such as rent, interest, clerks' salaries, insurance and similar items may be accounted for on a cash basis. Any such hybrid method is, of course, subject to the requirements of subsection (b) that there be a clear reflection of income under the method.

16.3   The concept of a "hybrid method" applies to a single business. If there are two or more separate businesses, a different accounting method can be used for each. Similarly, if an individual is a proprietor or a member of a partnership, one method of accounting—such as the accrual method—can be used for his business and another method—such as the cash method—for his separate personal items of income and expense.

16.4   Whenever production, purchase, or sale of merchandise is an income-producing factor (see paragraph 15.92), inventories must be reflected in taxable income as of the beginning and end of each taxable year, and the accrual method must be used for the inventory accounts, purchases, and sales. A cash method for income, however, may not be combined with accruals of expenses. Similarly, a taxpayer who uses an accrual method of accounting in computing business expenses must use an accrual method in computing items affecting gross income from his trade or business.[2]

INSTALLMENT METHOD

In General

16.5   In the installment method of accounting, the *gross* profit from a sale is reported ratably as collections are received. Under Section 453 it

1. S. Rep. No. 1622, 83rd Cong., 2d sess. 1954, p. 300.
2. Reg. 1.446–1(c)(1)(iv)(a).

585

Other
Accounting
Methods,
Changes,
and Claim
of Right

is available to dealers in personal property who regularly sell or otherwise dispose of personal property on the installment plan, to dealers in real property, and to persons who make a casual sale of real or of personal property other than inventory items. The installment method applies only to sales at a profit. If a loss is incurred it must be deducted in full in the year of sale and cannot be spread over the period of the payments. The use of this method is elective, not mandatory. Once a dealer in personal property adopts the installment method, he must continue to use it unless and until he receives permission from the Commissioner to change to another acceptable method. Dealers in real property and taxpayers making casual sales of real property or of personal property other than inventory items can make or not make an election to use the installment method on each sale.

Dealers in Personal Property

Eligible Dealers. Regulation 1.453–1 does not specifically define which types of dealers in personal property are eligible to adopt the installment method, but merely states that "persons who regularly sell or otherwise dispose of personal property on the installment plan ... [may] elect to return the income from the sale or other disposition thereof on the installment method." The important part of this definition consists of the words "regularly sell." The courts have considered as factors (1) the number and frequency of installment sales, (2) the dollar volume of installment sales as compared to total sales, and (3) whether the dealer has held himself out to the public as willing to sell on the installment plan.[3] In G.C.M. 1162[4] the Service held that a single sale of an inventory item of personal property on installment terms cannot be reported on the installment method by a dealer not regularly selling on the installment plan. Of course, he is not eligible to claim this as a casual sale eligible for the installment method, because eligible casual sales can be of only non-inventory items.

16.6

Eligible Sales. The traditional sale qualifying for installment sales treatment is defined in Reg. 1.453–2(b)(1) as: "A sale of personal property by the taxpayer under any plan for the sale or other disposition of personal property which plan, by its terms and conditions, contemplates that each sale under the plan will be paid for in two or more payments." The installment method applies only to *installment* sales; it has no application to sales on open account or sales for cash.[5] There is no requirement that there be any minimum amount of down payment or that the dealer retain any form of title to the merchandise until the account is paid. Also, there is no minimum period of time

16.7

3. Louis Greenspon, 23 T.C. 138, modified without discussion of this point in 229 F.2d 947 (8th Cir. 1956), 56–1 USTC ¶9249, 48 AFTR 979.
4. VI–1 C.B. 22, declared obsolete in Rev. Rul. 68–674 but still sound in principle.
5. Rev. Rul. 54–111, 1954–1 C.B. 76.

over which the installment payments must be made. In one case,[6] the court approved the use of the installment method on sales of ready-to-wear clothing where credit terms required payment in periods as short as three months.

16.8 If a sale is made under a revolving credit plan under which it is contemplated that such sale will be paid for in two or more payments and if in fact two or more payments are made, then at the election of the dealer such revolving credit plan sales can be treated as installment sales [Reg. 1.453–2(b)(2)]. Regulation 1.453–1(a)(1) has this to say about such an election:

> ... A dealer who makes sales of personal property under both a revolving credit plan and a traditional installment plan may elect to report only sales under the traditional installment plan on the installment method; or he may elect to report only sales under the revolving credit plan on the installment method; or he may elect to report both sales under the revolving credit plan and the traditional installment plan on the installment method. ...

16.9 The term "revolving credit plan" includes cycle budget accounts, flexible budget accounts, continuous budget accounts, and other similar plans or arrangements for the sale of personal property under which the customer agrees to pay each month a part of the outstanding balance of his account. The percentage of charges under a revolving credit plan that will be treated as sales on the installment plan is computed by making an actual segregation of charges in a statistical sample of the revolving credit accounts [Reg. 1.453–2(d)(2)].

16.10 **Computation of Income.** The income to be reported from installment sales in any taxable year is that proportion of the installment payments actually received in that year which the gross profit realized or to be realized bears to the total contract price. Gross profit means sales less cost of goods sold [Reg. 1.453–1(b)(1)].

16.11 The first step in the calculation of income from installment sales is to segregate payments received by the years of sales to which they relate. This determination is necessary because payments received in a particular year will be received not only for sales made in that year, but also on sales made in prior years when the gross profit ratio probably would have been different. The second step is to determine the gross profit percentage applicable to sales made on the installment plan each year. Such gross profit percentage for a particular year is determined by dividing the gross profit realized or to be realized on the total sales on the installment plan by the total sales price of all such sales made during that year.

16.12 Gross profit, not net income from installment sales, is deferred and reported ratably as payments are received. This means that only items entering into the cost of goods sold are taken into account in determining the deferred gross profit. Stated another way, expenses

6. Lenox Clothes Shops, Inc., 45 BTA 1122, affirmed in part without discussion of this point in 139 F.2d 56 (6th Cir. 1943), 43–2 USTC ¶9665, 31 AFTR 996.

properly chargeable to the cost of goods sold are, in effect, deductible ratably over the period in which payments of the sales price are received, but all other expenses are deductible when incurred.

Cost of goods sold for tax purposes frequently does not include all items ordinarily included in cost of goods sold for financial accounting purposes.[7] Note the set-up of corporation return form 1120. The form seems to require that each statutory deduction for depreciation, interest, state and local taxes, losses, and bad debts be deducted from gross income in determining net taxable income. To the extent that any of these items are part of selling expenses, the form and financial accounting practices agree. For example, depreciation on the building, fixtures, and furniture pertaining to the selling facilities are certainly part of selling expenses and not deductible in determining gross income. However, if the merchandiser also first manufactures the products, as pointed out in paragraph 15.105, the Service permits under Rev. Rul. 141, but does not require (however, generally accepted accounting principles do so require), that depreciation on the manufacturing facilities be treated as a part of the cost of inventories and of cost of goods sold. In a merchandising business, Reg. 1.61–3(a) states, percentage depletion, selling expenses, and losses are "not ordinarily used in computing cost of goods sold." The Board of Tax Appeals[8] and the Tax Court[9] have held that promotional expenses, general expenses, losses, depreciation on selling facilities, interest, and taxes do not enter into the cost of goods sold and are deductible when paid or accrued.

16.13

A dealer must maintain his records so that he can compute separately for each year the amount of gross profit applicable to cash sales, open account sales, and installment sales.[10] Regulation 1.453–2(c)(2) requires that any carrying charges be included in the total selling price. For this reason, the gross profit margin on installment sales including carrying charges will be more than that on cash or open account sales. Accordingly, if the gross profit percentage applied to installment sales to determine the amount to be reported as income were to be based upon the aggregate of all types of sales, that percentage ordinarily would be lower than the correct amount. Then in order to report accurately the total gross profit that will eventually be earned from all types of sales, it would be necessary to increase the amount of gross profit actually earned on the cash and open account sales.

16.14

For dealers in personal property, and for them only, the terms "total contract price" and "total selling price" are synonymous. The contract price must include the amount of carrying charges or interest

16.15

7. It is true that Reg. 1.61–3 pertaining to the determination of gross income from business states: "The cost of goods sold should be determined in accordance with the method of accounting consistently used by the taxpayer." In many areas, however, a taxpayer can be correctly consistent in his financial treatment and differently consistent in his tax treatment of the same items.

8. Franc Furniture Co., 1 BTA 420.

9. A. Finkenberg's Sons, Inc., 17 T.C. 973.

10. Rev. Rul. 54–111, 1954–1 C.B. 76; *contra:* Blum's, Inc., 7 B.T.A. 737 (Nonacq.).

Other
Accounting
Methods,
Changes,
and Claim
of Right

that is added to the cash selling price and is treated as part of the selling price when billing the customer. If, by chance, such carrying charge or interest is not treated as part of the selling price when billing the customer, but instead is treated as a service charge and added contemporaneously with the sale on the books of account of the seller, it must nevertheless be included in the total contract price [Reg. 1.453–2(c)(2)]. If a state sales tax is imposed upon the vendor, its amount also is includible in the contract price.[11] If, under state law, sales tax is imposed upon the purchaser, and the vendor merely acts as a collection agent, its amount is not part of the total contract price and does not enter into the calculation of gross profit. If the sales tax is collected in installments, each proportionate part of it should not be treated as part of the installment payments received for the sale of the merchandise. If a dealer has elected to treat revolving credit plans as installment sales, carrying charges are not included in the total contract price [Reg. 1.453–2(c)(3)].

16.16 **Initial Adoption of Method.** A new enterprise can adopt the installment method, without permission, simply by using it in the tax return filed for the first taxable year. Similarly, when a taxpayer has been in business for some time, but first begins to make installment sales, he may without permission use the installment method in the return for the year in which such installment sales are made for the first time. Regulation 1.453–8(a)(2) states that the return should contain a statement that the installment method of accounting is being adopted, and it should specify the type or types of sales included within such election.

16.17 **Change from Accrual to Installment Method.** Without permission, any taxpayer can change from the accrual to the installment method of reporting installment sales. Almost always, however, there will be additional tax. Payments received in installment-method years applicable to sales made in prior accrual method years are again taxed to the extent of the gross profit included in them. The fact that the entire gross profit on such accrual method sales has already been fully taxed is immaterial [Reg. 1.453–2(e) and Reg. 1.453–7]. The tax imposed for the year of change or any subsequent taxable year— Reg. 1.453–7(a)(1) calls them "adjustment years"—is reduced by a tax credit, called an "adjustment" in the Regulations, which theoretically may eliminate, but more frequently merely reduces, the double taxation of payments received and already taxed in prior accrual method years.

16.18 Regulation 1.453–7(b) sets forth the rules for determining the amount of this tax credit. Assume, for example, that a corporation is a dealer in personal property and wishes to change from the accrual to the installment method of accounting. Assume that the corporate income tax rate is a flat 50 percent (and remains so for a few years),

11. Rev. Rul. 60–53, 1960–1 C.B. 185.

589

Other
Accounting
Methods,
Changes,
and Claim
of Right

that the taxpayer realizes a 40 percent gross profit on its merchandise sales, and a 10 percent net profit before income taxes. Its operations in the year prior to adoption of the installment method might look something like this:

Sales	$100,000
Cost of goods sold	60,000
Gross profit	$ 40,000
Other deductible expenses	30,000
Taxable income	$ 10,000
Corporate income tax	$ 5,000

If $10,000 of installments is collected in the next year, resulting from sales made in the year shown above, 40 percent or $4,000, equal to the gross profit, is fully includible in taxable income in the year received despite the fact that it was also fully includible in the prior year, the year of sale, under the accrual method then used. A credit will be allowed against the tax in the year of second inclusion, but the credit will be limited to 50 percent of the *net* profit of $1,000 (10 percent of the $10,000 collected) rather than equal to 50 percent of the gross profit of $4,000 taxed twice.

Until the adoption of the 1954 Code there was no provision in the law for a tax credit or adjustment. Payments received in the year of change or later that were fully taxed in prior accrual method years were again subjected to tax on the gross profit element without any relief. The reason for this apparent inequity was the fact that despite a change from the accrual to the installment method, the ordinary and necessary business expenses and other itemized deductions continue to be deductible when accrued. Accordingly, in the first one or two years of a changeover to the installment method, the result will be a decrease in the tax revenues of the government. This point and the legislative history of the enactment of the installment provisions are explained in *Blum's, Incorporated.*[12] In the process of enacting the 1954 Code, Congress became persuaded that the inequity should be at least partially alleviated, perhaps because taxpayers found ways to circumvent the double taxation.

16.19

The tax penalty of a changeover from the accrual to the installment method of accounting can be avoided if the taxpayer on the last day of the year preceding the year in which the installment method is elected sells all of its installment accounts receivable.[13] It must be a bona fide sale, not in substance a loan with the accounts pledged as collateral.

16.20

An election to change the reporting of installment sales from the accrual method to the installment method pursuant to Section 453(c)(1)

16.21

12. 7 BTA 737 (1927) (NA).
13. City Stores Co. v. Smith, 154 F.Supp. 348 (DC), 57–2 USTC ¶9960, 1 AFTR2d 418; Rev. Rul. 59–343, 1959–2 C.B. 136, in which the Service announced it would follow the City Stores' decision.

Other
Accounting
Methods,
Changes,
and Claim
of Right

can be revoked at any time before the expiration of three years following the date of the filing of the tax return for the year of change [Section 453(c)(4)]. In such event the unreported profit must be accrued in the prior years affected by the revocation.

16.22 **Defaults and Repossessions.** Upon default by a purchaser and if the seller does not repossess the goods he originally sold, the seller is entitled to a bad-debt deduction in an amount equal to the unrecovered cost of the goods.[14] The unpaid face amount of the obligations is not the measure of the bad-debt deduction, because that is not its basis to the taxpayer. As explained in paragraph 16.41, the original basis of an installment obligation is "the excess of the face value of the obligation over an amount equal to the income which would be returnable were the obligation satisfied in full" [Reg. 1.453–9(b)(2)]. Stated in reverse, the basis of an obligation is an amount equal to the unrecovered cost of the goods. If the taxpayer is using a reserve for bad debts method with respect to installment sales, such reserve must be a separate one, and the charge will be against such separate reserve.[15]

EXAMPLE   In year one, a dealer sells an article for $100. It cost him $70. He receives $20 down, two installments each of $10 in year one and two in year two. The purchaser then defaults and the article cannot be found to be repossessed. The gross income realized was $18 (30 percent of $60), and his return of capital was $42 ($60 − $18). The bad-debt loss is $28 ($70 − $42).

16.23   If, upon default, the dealer repossesses the goods, he has gain or loss equal to the difference between the fair market value of the goods sold and the unpaid amount of the outstanding obligations that are satisfied by the repossession, but reduced by the amount that would be returnable as income if the notes were paid in full. In other words, that amount of the contract price that represents the cost of the goods sold, as reduced by that portion of installments received that represents recovery of capital, becomes the basis of the installment obligation, and that basis is measured against the fair market value of the repossessed property. Any gain will constitute ordinary income for a dealer in personal property. Any loss will be an ordinary loss. The repossessed goods are then included in inventory at their fair market value.

Sales of Real Estate and Casual Sales of Personal Property

16.24   Section 453(b) applies to sales of real estate by dealers and other persons and also to the sales of personal property by persons who are not dealers or merchants in personal property.

14. Blum's, Inc., 7 BTA 737 (1927) (NA); Lenox Clothes Shops, Inc., *supra*, fn. 6.
15. I.T. 3957, 1949–1 C.B. 65.

Eligible Sales. Paragraphs (1) and (2) of Reg. 1.453–1(c) read as follows: 16.25

(1) Income from the sale or other disposition of real property or from casual sales or other casual dispositions of personal property may be reported on the installment method for taxable years beginning after December 31, 1953, only if, in the taxable year of the sale or other disposition, (i) there are no payments or (ii) the payments (exclusive of evidences of indebtedness of the purchaser) do not exceed 30 per cent of the selling price.

(2) The income from a casual sale or other casual disposition of personal property may be reported on the installment method only if (i) the property is not of a kind which would properly be included in the inventory of the taxpayer if on hand at the close of the taxable year, and (ii) its sale price exceeds $1,000.

EVIDENCES OF INDEBTEDNESS. A prime requisite for availability   16.26
of the installment method is that in the year of sale there be either (1) no payments or (2) payments not in excess of 30 percent of the selling price. In both instances "evidences of indebtedness" of the purchaser are disregarded in determining what is a payment. An evidence of indebtedness can consist of a promise to pay contained in a contract or any form of note, secured or unsecured.

Prompted by a desire to put a stop to the increasing use of bonds   16.27
and debentures in corporate take-overs and the subsequent election of the installment method by selling shareholders, Congress in the Tax Reform Act of 1969 drastically limited the types of evidences of indebtedness that can be disregarded in determining the amount of payments in the year of sale. These limitations apply not only to debt obligations issued in a corporate acquisition but also to all other types of sales. The new subsection (b)(3) of Section 453 applies to sales occurring after May 27, 1969. Under this subsection the following types of bonds, debentures, notes, and other debt obligations must be treated as year-of-sale payments and the equivalent of cash:

(1) those issued by an individual, corporation, governmental body, or other entity which are payable on demand;
(2) those issued by a corporation or governmental body either (a) with coupons attached, or (b) in registered form (other than those that the taxpayer establishes will not be readily tradable in an established securities market), or (c) in any form designed to render them readily tradable in an established securities market.

With respect to category (2) the Senate Finance Committee Report[16] states:

The Committee does not intend that ordinary promissory notes are to be included within the category of indebtedness which is treated as payments received in the year of sale, even though it is possible for these notes to be assigned by one party to another party.

16. S. Rep. 91–552, 91st Cong., 1st sess., 1969, p. 146.

Other
Accounting
Methods,
Changes,
and Claim
of Right
Regulation 1.453–3 confirms the Committee Report and holds that ordinary promissory notes, even if negotiable, which are payable other than on demand, are not to be treated as the equivalent of cash unless there are many similar types of notes outstanding and they are traded at least in an over-the-counter market.

16.28   NUMBER OF PAYMENTS. To have an installment sale, there must be at least two payments including the down payment, if any.[17]

EXAMPLE 1   On October 1 Brown, at a gain, sells sixty acres of land for $12,000, payable $2,000 on closing of title November 15 and $10,000 the following January 2. The $10,000 obligation is evidenced by a negotiable promissory note in that amount due January 2. This is an installment sale.

EXAMPLE 2   Assume the same facts as in Example 1 except that no down payment is received in the year of sale and the note is in the principal amount of $12,000. This is not an installment sale because there is only one payment.

16.29   **Election of Method.** Unlike a dealer in personal property who regularly sells on the installment plan, a dealer in real estate, such as a subdivider, has an option on each separate sale under an installment plan to report it under the installment method. He can use the installment method on the sale of one or more parcels and his regular method of accounting, cash or accrual, on others.[18] On casual sales of real estate or of personal property other than inventory items, the installment method can be elected for one casual sale and not for another.

16.30   As to the manner of electing the installment method Reg. 1.453–8(b)(1) provides:

A taxpayer who sells or otherwise disposes of real property, or who makes a casual sale or other casual disposition of personal property, and who elects to report the income therefrom on the installment method must set forth in his income tax return (or in a statement attached thereto) for the year of the sale or other disposition the computation of the gross profit on the sale or other disposition under the installment method. In any taxable year in which the taxpayer receives payments attributable to such sale or other disposition, he must also show in his income tax return the computation of the amount of income which is being reported in that year on such sale or other disposition.

For many years, the Commissioner contended that a taxpayer, in order to report a sale of property on the installment basis, had to make an express election in an original and timely return for the year of sale. However, in keeping with court decisions holding that neither the Internal Revenue Code nor the regulations supported his contention, the Commissioner ruled in Technical Information Release 756[19] on August 24, 1965, that he would recognize valid elections made in

17. Rev. Rul. 69–462.
18. Reg. 1.453–5(a).
19. *P-H 1970 Federal Taxes* ¶20,421(5), revoking Rev. Rul. 93 and modifying Rev. Rul. 56–396; Rev. Rul. 65–297, 1965–2 C.B. 152.

593

Other
Accounting
Methods,
Changes,
and Claim
of Right

certain amended or delinquent returns. Among other situations, the Commissioner will permit an election to be made in an amended return for a year still open under the Statute of Limitations if the sale occurred in that year but the first payment was not received until a subsequent year. As pointed out in the ruling, however, which is in accordance with a United States Supreme Court decision,[20] if a taxpayer adopts one appropriate method of reporting the sale in his original return, such as reporting the full amount of the gain, he cannot later change his mind and elect the installment method.

Computation of Income. In the calculation of "gross profit," "selling price," "contract price," and "payments in the year of sale," there are a few differences between dealers in personal property and persons selling real property (whether or not as a dealer) or making casual sales of personal property.   16.31

For financial accounting purposes, selling expenses are not deducted in determining gross profit. This rule is followed for tax purposes in sales of real property by dealers, but not in casual sales of real or personal property by nondealers [Reg. 1.453–1(b)(1)]. The reason is apparent. A dealer derives ordinary income from his sale of real estate, whereas an investor has capital gain income. The effect of requiring the investor to deduct commissions and other selling expenses in determining gross profit from sales of real or personal property is to reduce the tax benefit of such expenses to the same rate applicable to the net capital gain.   16.32

Selling expenses include the cost of advertising property, sales commissions,[21] title expenses,[22] legal fees,[23] and revenue stamps.[24] All of these are currently deductible by dealers when paid or accrued, depending upon the method of accounting used,[25] but all of them are deductible only as offsets against the selling price in determining the gross profit on casual sales of real or personal property by nondealers.   16.33

If the purchaser assumes an existing mortgage or takes title subject to it, there may be an effect on the "selling price," "contract price," and "payments in the year of sale." Regulation 1.453–4(c) provides: 16.34

In the sale of mortgaged property the amount of the mortgage, whether the property is merely taken subject to the mortgage or whether the mortgage is assumed by the purchaser, shall, for the purpose of determining whether a sale is on the installment plan, be included as part of the "selling price"; and for the purpose of determining the payments and the total contract price as those terms are used in section 453, and §§ 1.453–1 through 1.453–7,

---

20. Pacific National Co. v. Welch, 304 U.S. 191 (1938), 38–1 USTC ¶9286, 20 AFTR 1248.

21. I.T. 2305, V–2 C.B. 108; I.T. 2340, VI–1 C.B. 43; E. A. Giffin, 19 BTA 1243; H. M. N. Muhle, 19 BTA 1247.

22. E. A. Giffin, *ibid.*

23. W. O. Garrett, 19 BTA 1256.

24. E. A. Giffin, *supra,* fn. 21; Rev. Rul. 65–313.

25. Highlands, Evanston-Lincolnwood Subdivision, 32 BTA 760; I.T. 2305, V–2 C.B.108; T. M. Divine, Jr., 62–2 USTC ¶9632 (D.C. Tenn., 1962), 10 AFTR2d 5403.

Other
Accounting
Methods,
Changes,
and Claim
of Right
the amount of such mortgage shall be included only to the extent that it exceeds the basis of the property. The term "payments" does not include amounts received by the vendor in the year of sale from the disposition to a third person of notes given by the vendee as part of the purchase price which are due and payable in subsequent years. Commissions and other selling expenses paid or incurred by the vendor shall not reduce the amount of the payments, the total contract price, or the selling price.

16.35   "Payments in the year of sale" also include option payments received in or prior to the year of sale and installment payments received in the year of sale. "Contract price" and "selling price" also include liens and accrued expenses of the seller assumed by the buyer, and such liens and expenses are considered "payments" when discharged by the buyer.

16.36   The following example compares a sale of real property by (1) a dealer and (2) a nondealer. It is assumed that real property with an adjusted basis of $40,000, and subject to a mortgage of $49,000, is sold for $100,000 payable as follows: cash in the year of sale, $20,000; assumption of mortgage, $49,000; new second mortgage taken back by the seller, $29,000, with the first payment due in the next year; and assumption by the buyer of interest accrued at date of sale on existing mortgage in the amount of $2,000 not due and not paid until the next year. Advertising expenses and commissions of $6,000 plus title expenses and attorney fees in the amount of $2,000 are incurred by the seller.

EXAMPLE

	DEALER	NONDEALER
Selling price		
Cash	$ 20,000	$ 20,000
Assumption of mortgage by buyer	49,000	49,000
New second mortgage	29,000	29,000
Accrued interest assumed by buyer	2,000	2,000
Total	$100,000	$100,000
Deductions		
Selling expenses:		
Advertising and sales commission	$ —	$ 6,000
Title expenses and attorney fee	—	2,000
Adjusted basis of property	40,000	40,000
Total	$ 40,000	$ 48,000
Gross profit	$ 60,000	$ 52,000
Contract price		
Cash	$ 20,000	$ 20,000
Excess of mortgage assumed by buyer over adjusted basis of property	9,000	9,000
New second mortgage	29,000	29,000
Accrued interest assumed by buyer	2,000	2,000
Total	$ 60,000	$ 60,000

Payments received in year of sale		
Cash	$ 20,000	$ 20,000
Excess of mortgage assumed by buyer over adjusted basis of property	9,000	9,000
	$ 29,000	$ 29,000
Ratio of payments received in year of sale to selling price ($29,000/$100,000)	29%	29%
Ratio of gross profit to contract price:		
($60,000/$60,000)	100%	—
($52,000/$60,000)	—	86.67%

Because the payments received in the year of sale by both the dealer and the nondealer are less than 30 percent of the selling price, the installment method for reporting the profit may be elected. For the year of sale, the dealer will report 100 percent of the payments received in the amount of $29,000 and the nondealer will report 86.67 percent of $29,000. By the time the second mortgage is paid off and the accrued interest on the first mortgage is paid, each will have reported and paid tax on the respective amounts of gross profit of $60,000 and $52,000.

If the buyer were to prepay the accrued interest of $2,000 in the year of sale, this amount would be included in the "payments" received in the year of sale, the total of such payments would be $31,000 or 31 percent of the selling price, and the installment method would not be available.

The dealer will separately deduct in full the amounts of the selling expenses when paid or accrued, depending upon his method of accounting. Under the installment method, the nondealer, in effect, is required to prorate these deductions.

Reduction of Selling Price in Subsequent Year. If the selling price is   16.37
reduced in a subsequent year before all of the installments are paid, the reportable remaining gross profit is correspondingly reduced.[26] No loss deduction is allowable in that year unless the reduction in price results in a revised gross profit less than the amount already reported. After a reduction in selling price, the new gross profit percentage to be applied to each subsequent installment payment is determined by (1) subtracting from the original amount of the gross profit the amount of profit already reported and also the amount of the reduction in price, (2) determining the balance of the payments due after the reduction in price, and (3) dividing the amount determined in step 1 by the amount determined in step 2.

A seller sold property to a buyer for $100,000 which had an adjusted basis   EXAMPLE 1
of $60,000. The down payment was $20,000 and the balance was represented by eight promissory notes, each in the amount of $10,000, due at one year intervals. After a total of $30,000 had been paid, the two notes due in the seventh and eighth years totaling $20,000 were canceled, to settle a dispute involving a latent defect in the property sold.

26. J. P. Jerpe, 45 BTA 199 (1941).

Other
Accounting
Methods,
Changes,
and Claim
of Right

The originally expected gross profit was $40,000 ($100,000 − $60,000). Of this amount $12,000 (40/100 × $30,000) was reported as taxable income prior to the reduction in price. After such reduction, the revised total gross profit became $20,000 ($40,000 − $20,000). Of this amount $12,000 had already been reported, so that only $8,000 ($20,000 − $12,000) remained. The remaining installment payments totaled $50,000 ($100,000 − $30,000 − $20,000). Accordingly, 16 percent ($8,000/$50,000) of each installment payment will constitute income when received.

EXAMPLE 2   Assume the facts in Example 1, except that the seller's basis was $80,000, so that the originally expected gross profit was $20,000. Of the $30,000 in payments received before the reduction in price, $6,000 (20/100 × $30,000) was reported as realized gross profit. The reduction in price of $20,000 results in a revised gross profit of zero. Accordingly, a loss of $6,000 is deductible in the year in which the price was reduced.

16.38   A reduction in the selling price that occurs in a year later than the year of sale is disregarded in determining whether payments received in the year of sale were less than 30 percent of the selling price.[27] Assume that the original selling price is $50,000, and in the year of sale $14,000 is received. The following year, the price is reduced by $10,000 to $40,000. Although the first year payments of $14,000 are more than 30 percent of $40,000, the right to use the installment method is not lost. The facts as they existed in the year of sale control.

16.39   **Defaults and Repossessions.** PERSONAL PROPERTY. The same rules apply to a casual seller of, or a dealer in, personal property. A default without recovery of the goods results in a bad-debt deduction measured by the unrecovered cost of the goods sold (paragraphs 16.22, 16.23). A repossession results in gain or loss measured by the difference between the fair market value of the repossessed goods and the unpaid amount of the installment obligations satisfied by the repossession but reduced by the amount that would be returnable as income if the notes were paid in full [Reg. 1.453–1(d)].

16.40   REAL PROPERTY. If real property is sold and an indebtedness secured by the property is accepted by the seller, then upon repossession of the property no loss is allowable, but gain to a limited extent may be realized. This result is caused by Section 1038 enacted in 1964 and is discussed starting with paragraph 11.131.

Disposition of Installment Obligations

16.41   Section 453(d) provides that gain or loss is realized upon the sale, exchange, distribution (for example, as a dividend by a corporation to its shareholders), or transfer (such as by a gift directly or in trust) except where such transfer occurs by reason of death or a nontaxable exchange. Subsections (a) and (b) of Reg. 1.453–9 provide:

27. Vincent P. Vigilante, P–H T.C. Memo ¶66,161 (7–7–66); Dalriada Realty Co., Inc., 5 BTA 905 (1926) (Acq.).

(a) *In general.* Subject to the exceptions contained in section 453(d)(4) and paragraph (c) of this section, the entire amount of gain or loss resulting from any disposition or satisfaction of installment obligations, computed in accordance with section 453(d), is recognized in the taxable year of such disposition or satisfaction and shall be considered as resulting from the sale or exchange of the property in respect of which the installment obligation was received by the taxpayer.

Other
Accounting
Methods,
Changes,
and Claim
of Right

(b) *Computation of gain or loss.* (1) The amount of gain or loss resulting under paragraph (a) of this section is the difference between the basis of the obligation and (i) the amount realized, in the case of satisfaction at other than face value or in the case of a sale or exchange, or (ii) the fair market value of the obligation at the time of disposition, if such disposition is other than by sale or exchange.

(2) The basis of an installment obligation shall be the excess of the face value of the obligation over an amount equal to the income which would have been returnable had the obligation been satisfied in full.

(3) The application of subparagraphs (1) and (2) of this paragraph may be illustrated by the following examples:

(1) In 1960 the M Corporation sold a piece of unimproved real estate to B for $20,000. The company acquired the property in 1948 at a cost of $10,000. During 1960 the company received $5,000 cash and vendee's notes for the remainder of the selling price, or $15,000, payable in subsequent years. In 1962, before the vendee made any further payments, the company sold the notes for $13,000 in cash. The corporation makes its returns on the calendar year basis. The income to be reported for 1962 is $5,500, computed as follows:

EXAMPLES
FROM
REG.

Ex. 1

		$13,000
Proceeds of sale of notes		
Selling price of property	$20,000	
Cost of property	10,000	
Total profit	10,000	
Total contract price	20,000	
Percent of profit, or proportion of each payment returnable as income, $10,000 divided by $20,000, 50 percent		
Face value of notes	15,000	
Amount of income returnable were the notes satisfied in full, 50 percent of $15,000	7,500	
Basis of obligation — excess of face value of notes over amount of income returnable were the notes satisfied in full		$ 7,500
Taxable income to be reported for 1962		$ 5,500

(2) Suppose in example (1) the M Corporation, instead of selling the notes, distributed them in 1962 to its shareholders as a dividend, and at the time of such distribution, the fair market value of the notes was $14,000. The income to be reported for 1962 is $6,500, computed as follows:

Ex. 2

Fair market value of notes	$14,000
Basis of obligation — excess of face value of notes over amount of income returnable were the notes satisfied in full (computed as in example (1)	7,500
Taxable income to be reported for 1962	$ 6,500

Other
Accounting
Methods,
Changes,
and Claim
of Right

When installment obligations are transmitted on the death of the holder, no gain or loss is recognized to the decedent's estate; rather, the transferee reports income on the receipt of payments, his basis being the face value less the amount the decedent would have included in income if the notes were paid in full as provided in Section 453(d)(3) and Section 691(a)(4).

LONG–TERM CONSTRUCTION CONTRACTS

16.42   If a construction contract is "long-term," the net income can be reported by an accrual basis taxpayer under any one of three methods: accrual, percentage of completion, or completed contract. If a taxpayer uses the cash method of accounting, ordinarily he can use that method on long-term contracts,[28] but he has an option to adopt the percentage of completion or completed contract method. Chapter 15 explained the accrual method; here, after a discussion of some preliminary data, the percentage of completion method and then the completed contract method are covered.

16.43   *Long-term contract* is defined in Reg. 1.451–3(a):

> The term "long-term contracts" means building, installation, or construction contracts covering a period in excess of one year from the date of execution of the contract to the date on which the contract is finally completed and accepted.

According to this regulation, a construction job contracted for in October and finished in January of the following year is not a long-term contract job; but if the work is not completed until at least twelve months later, it is. The courts have held that a construction contract is long-term even if it spans less than twelve months, provided that it covers at least parts of two taxable years and provided such types of contracts have consistently been treated as long-term.[29] A construction contract for work completed in a few weeks or months is not long-term merely because of a covenant by the taxpayer to maintain it in good condition for a period of years.[30]

16.44   In order to use a long-term contract method, books must be kept.[31] If, in the books, all accounts are kept under either the cash[32] or ac-

28. C. A. Hunt Engineering Co., Inc., 15 TCM 1269 (1956), P–H Memo T.C. ¶56,248; G.C.M. 22,682, 1941–1 C.B. 307.

29. L. A. Wells Construction Co., 46 BTA 302, affirmed 134 F.2d 623 (6th Cir. 1943), 30 AFTR 1177; Fort Pitt Bridge Works, 24 BTA 626, reversed on another point in 92 F.2d 825 (3rd Cir., 1957), 20 AFTR 310; Daley v. U.S., 243 F.2d 466 (9th Cir. 1957), 51 AFTR 117, cert. den.

30. Uvalde Co., 1 BTA 932; Quality Roofing Co., 16 BTA 1370; Scholl Co., 30 BTA 993.

31. J. B. Clover, P–H Memo T.C. ¶42,648, affirmed on another issue in 143 F.2d 570 (9th Cir. 1944), 32 AFTR 1023.

32. There is no case squarely holding that where the books are kept on a cash basis, a long-term contract method can be adopted for tax purposes; but inferences to that effect can be drawn from C. A. Hunt Engineering Co., Inc., and G.C.M. 22682, *supra*, fn. 28, and also from Robert M. Robinson, P–H Memo BTA ¶41,406.

599

Other
Accounting
Methods,
Changes,
and Claim
of Right

crual[33] method, a taxpayer can single out long-term construction contracts and as to them elect either the completed contract or percentage
of completion method. It is true that Section 446(a) provides that taxable income shall be computed under the method of accounting used
in keeping the books; however, Reg. 1.446–1(a) states that where
special tax treatment is provided for certain items, the tax treatment of
those items can differ from the book treatment. The long-term contract method seems to be one of these special items. Nevertheless, if a
taxpayer uses the completed contract method on his books, he must
use that method in his returns, because there is no special provision in
the Code granting the right to use the cash or accrual method on long-
term construction contracts when the books reflect the completed
contract method.[34]

16.45

Once a method of accounting for long-term contracts is adopted, it
must continue to be used in future years unless and until permission
is obtained to change to another method [Reg. 1.451–3(c)]. The courts
have held that filing a return on the accrual basis constitutes an election and precludes filing an amended return on the completed contract method.[35] Further, an election to report on the completed
contract method bars an amended return on the percentage of completion method.[36]

Percentage of Completion Method

Regulation 1.451–3(b)(1) describes the percentage of completion
method:

16.46

> Gross income derived from long-term contracts may be reported according
> to the percentage of completion method. Under this method, the portion of
> the gross contract price which corresponds to the percentage of the entire
> contract which has been completed during the taxable year shall be included
> in gross income for such taxable year. There shall then be deducted all ex-
> penditures made during the taxable year in connection with the contract,
> account being taken of the material and supplies on hand at the beginning and
> end of the taxable year for use in such contract. Certificates of architects or
> engineers showing the percentage of completion of each contract during the
> taxable year shall be available at the principal place of business of the tax-
> payer for inspection in connection with an examination of the income tax
> return.

Actual payments in a particular year, whether more or less than the
includible amount of the contract price, are disregarded. All expenses
during the year are deducted in accordance with the general method
of accounting used by the taxpayer. Further, the gross contract price
used in computing accrued income is the amount stipulated in the

33. R. G. Bent Co., 26 BTA 1369 (1932) (Acq.).
34. Badgley v. Com., 59 F.2d 203 (2nd Cir. 1932), 11 AFTR 415, affirming 21
BTA 1055; Russell G. Finn, 22 BTA 799 (1931).
35. Daley v. U.S., 243 F.2d 466 (9th Cir. 1957), 57–1 USTC ¶9602, 51 AFTR 117,
cert. den., affirming 139 F.Supp. 376 (D.C. Calif.), 56–1 USTC ¶9392, 49 AFTR 706.
36. James C. Ellis, 16 BTA 1225.

contract. It is not reduced by any amount to be retained until final completion and acceptance.

16.47   The quoted regulation provides that architects' or engineers' certificates should be available to show the percentage of completion, but this statement probably applies only when the certificates offer that type of information. In Office Decision 933,[37] the Commissioner ruled that estimates of completion could be based on the ratio of actual costs incurred each year to the estimate of total costs that will be incurred.

Completed Contract Method

16.48   The completed contract method is a modification of the accrual method insofar as the time of reporting accrued income and expense is concerned. Expenses are accumulated until the construction work specified in the contract is physically completed and accepted. The income or loss accrues and is reported in the year of completion and acceptance and is measured by the difference between the contract price and the accumulated expense. General expenses not directly attributable to the long-term contract—such as office salaries, rent, and taxes—should be deducted currently in accordance with the general method of accounting used by the taxpayer.

16.49   Regulation 1.451–3(b)(2) describes this method:

> Gross income derived from long-term contracts may be reported for the taxable year in which the contract is finally completed and accepted. Under this method, there shall be deducted from gross income for such year all expenses which are properly allocable to the contract, taking into account any material and supplies charged to the contract but remaining on hand at the time of completion.

16.50   Frequent controversies arise between the Commissioner and taxpayers concerning the time when a contract is completed for the purpose of accruing income under the completed contract method. Regulation 1.451–3(b)(2), quoted above, provides: "Gross income derived from long-term contracts may be reported for the taxable year in which the contract is *finally completed and accepted*." [Emphasis added.] The Tax Court has usually held that, "finally completed" means "substantially completed" and that "substantially completed" means about 99 percent completed.[38] The First,[39] Ninth,[40] and Sixth[41] Circuit Courts of Appeal have held that "finally completed and accepted"

37. 4 C.B. 86 (1921), declared obsolete in Rev. Rul. 68–575, but the principle still seems valid.

38. Ehret-Day Co., 2 T.C. 25 (1943).

39. Rice, Barton & Fales, Inc. v. Com., 41 F.2d 339 (1st Cir. 1930), 2 USTC ¶545, 8 AFTR 10866.

40. E. E. Black, Limited v. J. M. Alsup, 211 F.2d 879 (9th Cir. 1954), 45 AFTR 1345.

41. Thompson-King-Tate, Inc. v. U.S., 296 F.2d 290 (6th Cir. 1961), 62–1 USTC ¶9116, 8 AFTR2d 5920, reversing 185 F.Supp. 748 (D.C. Ky.), 60–2 USTC ¶9640, 6 AFTR2d 5455.

601

Other
Accounting
Methods,
Changes,
and Claim
of Right

means total completion and acceptance. Further, the Sixth and Ninth Circuit Courts of Appeal expressly rejected the doctrine of "substantially completed." Finally, according to the Tax Court, if a contract is completed and accepted, income or loss must be reported on the date such event occurs even though there then exist disputed or contingent claims. These additional amounts accrue when the disputes and contingencies are resolved.[42]

CHANGES IN ACCOUNTING METHODS

If a taxpayer wishes to change his method of tax accounting, he first must obtain permission from the Commissioner. If it is the Commissioner who properly finds that the method in use does not clearly reflect taxable income, he can unilaterally impose a change. If the taxpayer initiates the change, he must take into account all adjustments necessary solely because of the change, in order to prevent amounts from being duplicated or omitted. When the Commissioner initiates the change for a taxpayer who has been in business at least since 1953, there is another facet. Usually the change will involve an acceleration in reporting income from credit accounts. If those same or similar accounts existed at the beginning of the first 1954 Code year, there can be deducted from income in the year of the change any balances which existed at the beginning of that first 1954 Code year [Section 481(a)(2)].

16.51

Consent of Commissioner

With certain exceptions (such as a change from the accrual to the installment method by a dealer in personal property, or a change from the FIFO to the LIFO inventory method, but not vice versa, as to the latter), a taxpayer must obtain the approval of the Commissioner when he desires to change either his overall method of accounting for income tax purposes or the treatment of material items of income or deductions [Section 446(e)]. The purpose of this requirement is to insure that changes will not distort income to the point where tax revenues will be adversely affected. If an additional deduction will result from the change in method, it is the Commissioner's current practice to require such deduction to be spread over a ten-year period extending into the future.

16.52

The Commissioner's regulations concerning changes in accounting methods and the procedures to be followed in obtaining his approval are contained in Reg. 1.446-1(e) (as amended November 17, 1970) from which the following excerpts are taken:

16.53

(2) (ii) (*a*) A change in the method of accounting includes a change in the overall plan of accounting for gross income or deductions or a change in the treatment of any material item used in such overall plan. Although a method

42. A. S. Wikstrom, Inc., ¶69,032 P–H Memo T.C.; C. H. Leavell & Co., 53 T.C. No. 42 (1969).

Other
Accounting
Methods,
Changes,
and Claim
of Right

of accounting may exist under this definition without the necessity of a pattern of consistent treatment of an item, in most instances a method of accounting is not established for an item without such consistent treatment. A material item is any item which involves the proper time for the inclusion of the item in income or the taking of a deduction. Changes in method of accounting include a change from the cash receipts and disbursements method to an accrual method, or vice versa, a change involving the method or basis used in the valuation of inventories (see sections 471 and 472 and the regulations thereunder), a change from the cash or accrual method to a long-term contract method, or vice versa (see § 1.451–3), a change involving the adoption, use or discontinuance of any other specialized method of computing taxable income, such as the crop method, and a change where the Internal Revenue Code and regulations thereunder specifically require that the consent of the Commissioner must be obtained before adopting such a change.

(3) (i) Except as otherwise provided under the authority of subdivision (ii) of this subparagraph, in order to secure the Commissioner's consent to a change of a taxpayer's method of accounting, the taxpayer must file an application on Form 3115 with the Commissioner of Internal Revenue, Washington, D. C. 20224, within 180 days after the beginning of the taxable year in which it is desired to make the change. The taxpayer shall, to the extent applicable, furnish (a) all information requested on such form, disclosing in detail all classes of items which would be treated differently under the new method of accounting and showing all amounts which would be duplicated or omitted as a result of the proposed change and (b) the taxpayer's computation of the adjustments to take into account such duplications or omissions. The Commissioner may require such other information as may be necessary in order to determine whether the proposed change will be permitted. Permission to change a taxpayer's method of accounting will not be granted unless the taxpayer and the Commissioner agree to the terms, conditions, and adjustments under which the change will be effected. See section 481 and the regulations thereunder, relating to certain adjustments required by such changes, section 472 and the regulations thereunder, relating to changes to and from the last-in, first-out method of inventorying goods, and section 453 and the regulation thereunder, relating to certain adjustments required by a change from an accrual method to the installment method.

(ii) Notwithstanding the provisions of subdivision (i) of this subparagraph, the Commissioner may prescribe administrative procedures, subject to such limitations, terms, and conditions as he deems necessary to obtain his consent, to permit taxpayers to change their accounting practices or methods to an acceptable treatment consistent with applicable regulations. Limitations, terms, and conditions, as may be prescribed in such administrative procedures by the Commissioner, shall include those necessary to prevent the omission or duplication of items includible in gross income or deductions.

16.54 Under the Class Life Asset Depreciation Range System, no permission is needed to make certain changes in depreciation methods, as discussed in paragraph 8.109. Automatic permission is also available in two instances—a change in the method of computing depreciation under the Facts and Circumstances and Guideline life systems (Rev. Proc. 67–40), and a change from the charge-off to the reserve method for bad debts (Rev. Proc. 64.51). These two types of automatic changes were discussed in paragraphs 8.19 and 9.104.

Even though a taxpayer changes his tax accounting method without 16.55 first obtaining permission, the Commissioner's acceptance of returns on the new basis for a number of years—particularly if the returns were examined—has frequently been held implied consent. In that event, the taxpayer cannot revert to the old method; further, if the new method correctly reflects income, the Commissioner cannot compel a change to the old method. In *Tampa Tribune Publishing Co.* v. *Tomlinson* [43] the taxpayer in 1932 changed without permission from the accrual to the cash method both on its books and tax returns. Twenty-two years later, the Commissioner objected to the change in method and asserted a deficiency for 1947 by computing income under the accrual method. He admitted that the cash method also clearly reflected income. The District Court held that acceptance by the Commissioner on the changed basis was tantamount to approval and resulted in implied consent to the change.

Right of Commissioner to Require a Change

If the taxpayer's method of tax accounting does not clearly reflect income, the Commissioner can require it to be changed. It is immaterial that the method was followed for a number of prior years. Even though a taxpayer whose business requires the use of inventories has for many years used the cash method of accounting, the Commissioner can require the use of the accrual method.[44] He cannot impose the use of one improper method for another improper method, however, or otherwise abuse his power to require a change.[45]

Adjustments Under Section 481

Section 481 requires that adjustments be taken into account for the 16.57 year of change to prevent items from being duplicated or omitted. If the Commissioner is the one who initiates the change and if the taxpayer was in existence prior to 1954, the amount of the ending balance of any account being increased or added to taxable income in the year of change must be reduced by the amount in the same or a similar predecessor account as of the beginning of the first year subject to the 1954 Code.

Prior to 1954, the courts had developed two principles. If a tax- 16.58 payer-initiated change in tax accounting was accepted by the Commissioner, whether or not the taxpayer first asked for permission, all items pertaining to the change were required to be taken into account in the year of change except those previously taxed. For example, if

43. 57-1 USTC ¶9,421 (D.C. Fla., 1957), 52 AFTR 1799.
44. Caldwell v. Com., 202 F.2d 112 (2nd Cir. 1953), 53-1 USTC ¶9218, 43 AFTR 271, affirming on this point P-H Memo T.C. ¶51,119; Charles D. Mifflin, 24 T.C. 973 (1955).
45. Russell v. Com., 45 F.2d 100 (1st Cir. 1930), 9 AFTR 519, reversing 12 BTA 56; Harden v. Com., 223 F.2d 418 (10th Cir. 1955), 47 AFTR 1284, affirming 48 AFTR 1268 (D.C.Okla.) and reversing 21 T.C. 781.

Other
Accounting
Methods,
Changes,
and Claim
of Right

the taxpayer of his own volition switched from the cash to the accrual method, for the year of the change the beginning amounts of inventory, accounts receivable, and accounts payable would be zero. If the Commissioner required the change, the courts allowed beginning amounts to be set up for any accounts affected by the change. On a change from the cash to the accrual method, for example: amounts as of the beginning of the year could be set up for inventory despite the fact that the cost of the inventory had been deducted in prior years; a beginning amount could be set up for accounts receivable even though such amount was not reflected in prior years' sales income; and a beginning amount could be set up for accounts payable even though the expenses were not deducted in prior years.

16.59   The Internal Revenue Code of 1954 inserted Section 481 into the tax law. It had no counterpart in the 1939 Code. As originally enacted, it provided that all adjustments pertaining to the change in method, except the amounts in similar accounts existing at the beginning of the first 1954 Code year, should be taken into account in the year of change, whether or not the change was initiated by the Commissioner. The Technical Amendments Act of 1958 amended Section 481 to restore the principles developed by the courts under the 1939 Code, and this section as so amended is the law today.

16.60   An example of the present rules follows:

A taxpayer makes a change from the cash to the accrual method of accounting effective in 1972. Unaccrued items are as follows:

EXAMPLE

	JANUARY 1	
	1972	1954
Accounts receivable	$32,000	$22,000
Accounts payable	19,000	14,000
Unrecorded income	$13,000	$ 8,000

If the taxpayer initiates the change, he must take into account $13,000 additional income. If the Commissioner initiates the change, the taxpayer must take into account only $5,000 additional income ($13,000 less $8,000).

What Is a Method?

16.61   Regulation 1.446–1(a)(1) provides: "The term 'method of accounting' includes not only the over-all method of accounting of the taxpayer but also the accounting treatment of any item." Over the years, in an attempt to avoid the necessity of applying for consent to a different treatment of an item, taxpayers have contended that they have a right to correct the erroneous treatment of an account or an item and that the correction of an error is not a change in accounting method. In order to avoid the provisions of Section 481 permitting tax-free adjustments in accounts existing at the beginning of the 1954 Code, the Commissioner has similarly contended that the correction of an error is not a change in accounting method initiated by him.

Under the latest court decisions, discussed in the following paragraphs, an erroneous method of accounting or erroneous treatment of a significant item is a method of accounting. There is no such thing as a right to correct an error and thus avoid either Section 446 or 481.

The next two cases to be discussed concern taxpayers who sought to correct the erroneous treatment of material items.   16.62

Commissioner v. O. Liquidating Corporation

U.S. Circuit Court of Appeals for the Third Circuit, 1961 [46]

[Facts: Taxpayer used the accrual method of accounting as its overall method for reporting income and expense. However, for years prior to 1953, it followed the practice of accruing as income, at the end of each year, dividends on insurance policies—even though such dividends were not declared by the insurance company until the following year. Effective in 1953, the taxpayer changed its treatment of the dividends and began to report the dividends only when received. The Commissioner contended that the taxpayer could not make the change without first securing his consent.]

EXCERPTS FROM OPINION

On review of the record we agree with the Commissioner's contention that while taxpayer did not change its overall method of accounting it did change its treatment of a significant item ... and that its action constituted a change in the method of accounting with in the meaning of the Treasury Regulations. ...

.   .   .

It is not dispositive that taxpayer's former consistent method of reporting the insurance dividends in the instant case was not correct under the accrual accounting system since it could not be changed without the Commissioner's prior consent.

.   .   .

On consideration of the record we certainly cannot say that the Commissioner abused his statutory discretion in refusing to grant retroactive consent in the instant case to taxpayer's unilateral change in its method of accounting of the very sizeable dividend income involved.

In *American Can Co.* v. *Com.*,[47] the taxpayer had been deducting   16.63 vacation pay and state property taxes in the years when paid rather than in the years in which they accrued. In its return for the year 1953, without first obtaining permission, the taxpayer changed procedures and deducted these amounts on an accrual basis. The Commissioner admitted that both items accrued in 1953 but contended they could be deducted only on a paid basis in that year, because the change was a change in an accounting method, and his consent to the change had not been secured. The Tax Court held that the taxpayer had a right to correct the error in the treatment of these two items, but the Second Circuit Court of Appeals reversed. An extract from the latter's opinion follows:

46. 292 F.2d 225 (3rd Cir. 1961), 7 AFTR2d 1633, cert. den., reversing P–H Memo TC ¶61,029.
47. 317 F.2d 604 (2nd Cir. 1963), 63–2 USTC ¶9514, 11 AFTR2d 1555, reversing on this point 37 T.C. 198.

Other
Accounting
Methods,
Changes,
and Claim
of Right

The Commissioner petitions for review of the Tax Court's holding that a taxpayer need not obtain his prior permission to change the method of accounting of a significant item when the change is to correct a previous, but erroneous, method. Ordinarily, of course, the taxpayer must obtain the Commissioner's consent to a change in accounting methods ... [§ 446 and Reg. 1.446–1(e)(2)]. Here the taxpayer, without consulting the Commissioner, changed its accounting of local taxes and vacation pay from the cash basis to the accrual method so as to bring the manner of accounting these items into accord with its general method. The Tax Court, four judges dissenting, approved the change and allowed the deductions claimed. Its ruling is contrary to the holding of the Third Circuit in C.I.R. v. O. Liquidating Corp. ... and of the Fifth Circuit, ... The courts of appeals have the better view: A change in accounting method will almost certainly result in some distortion of taxable income, and the Commissioner must insure that such distortion is not overly detrimental to the government. ... Here the Commissioner is not necessarily opposed to the change in accounting method which the taxpayer wants to make; rather, he demands merely that taxpayer consult with the Internal Revenue Service before making the change so that a distortion of taxable income overly detrimental to the government will not result from the change. ...

16.64   In *Fruehauf Trailer Co.*,[48] the Commissioner was the one who argued that the correction of an error was not a change in an accounting method and that accordingly Section 481 did not apply.

Beginning of the problem. During the 1920s, Fruehauf adopted the practice of valuing used trailers in its inventory at $1 each. Used trailers were acquired as trade-ins (sometimes repossession). In the early years the value of these was actually inconsiderable; typically, such trailers were not roadworthy or required substantial modifications to make them salable. The $1 valuation at the time apparently was not unreasonable. As the industry grew and trailers were upgraded in size and quality, the $1 valuation became ridiculously low. As of December 31, 1957, Fruehauf had 9,257 trailers on hand, valued at $9,257 for tax purposes. On the basis of lower of cost or market, the valuation would have exceeded $17 million!

The Service first proposed to correct this erroneous inventory practice for the years 1942 through 1945. The inventory valuation amounts for those years are shown in the following tabulation:

AS OF DECEMBER 31	NUMBER OF TRAILERS	VALUE AT LOWER OF COST OR MARKET	VALUED FOR TAX PURPOSES	UNDER-STATEMENT
1941	879	$568,108.76	$879	$567,229.76
1942	153	206,768.94	153	206,615.94
1943	37	53,785.54	37	53,748.59
1944	144	160,933.59	144	160,789.59
1945	759	678,448.94	759	677,689.94

Fruehauf maintained to the Service that it would agree to the correction from the $1 per unit valuation to the lower-of-cost-or-market method provided that the beginning inventory for the first year, 1942, was also restated on the proper basis. This would have had the effect of eliminating forever from taxable income approximately $567,000. The Service, under this proposal,

48. 42 T.C. 83, affirmed on the issue that the Commissioner was not estopped to require a change in the inventory valuation in 356 F.2d 975 (6th Cir. 1966), 66–1 USTC ¶9299, 17 AFTR2d 560, cert. den.

607

Other
Accounting
Methods,
Changes,
and Claim
of Right

would collect tax initially on only about $110,000, but with the promise of more in the future, because the inventory was building up. The Appellate Division accepted Fruehauf's proposal for the computation of the adjustment, waiver forms were executed, and the taxpayer considered the matter settled. In subsequent tax returns, and for financial statement purposes, Fruehauf commenced to reflect the higher inventory values.

The case was subject to review by the Congressional Joint Committee on Internal Revenue Taxation; and after considerable delay within the Service, the Chief Counsel's office finally concluded that it would not submit to the Joint Committee a proposal that permitted about a half million dollars to escape tax. Fruehauf, accordingly, was required to continue as before, using $1 per trailer as its method of valuation.

Second round. The subject was raised again by the Service in connection with its examination of the returns for the years 1954, 1955, and 1956. For these years the pertinent inventory values for used trailers are shown in the table.

AS OF DECEMBER 31	NUMBER OF TRAILERS	VALUE AT LOWER OF COST OR MARKET	VALUED FOR TAX PURPOSES	UNDER-STATEMENT
1953	2,411	$ 2,512,057.97	$2,411	$ 2,509,646.97
1954	3,600	5,696,885.84	3,600	5,693,285.84
1955	5,514	9,917,136.55	5,514	9,911,622.55
1956	9,226	16,259,583.81	9,226	16,250,357.81

The Internal Revenue Service contended that it was merely correcting an error and accordingly was entitled to correct the ending inventory for the year 1954 without making a corresponding adjustment for the beginning inventory. Understandably, Fruehauf chose to litigate, contending alternatively: (1) that IRS should be estopped from insisting upon any change at all in light of its previous actions on the same matter; (2) that, under a long line of cases commencing with *The Thomas Shoe Company*,[49] a corresponding correction must be made as of the beginning of the year of change to avoid distorting the income; and (3) that the inventories in question were being valued in accordance with a "method of accounting," so that by operation of Section 481 of the Internal Revenue Code of 1954, omission from income of the amount of understatement as of January 1, 1954, was mandatory because the change was initiated by the Service. The Service denied that the use of $1 per unit constituted a method of accounting, and in the course of the court proceedings sought to avoid the application of the principle of consistency with respect to beginning and ending inventories by limiting the adjustment of trailer valuations at the close of the year 1954 to units that appeared in the ending inventory for the first time. Under this approach, any trailers on hand January 1, 1954, and still on hand December 31, 1954, were permitted to remain valued at $1. This was alleged to conform with Section 1013 of the Code, which provides that if the property should have been included in the last inventory, the basis should be the last inventory value. This was no real concession, since the turnover of trailers was rapid, and the tax on uncorrected items would merely have been postponed one year.

Tax Court's decision. The Tax Court held that the Service was not estopped from demanding a change in the method of valuing the trailers; however, it held that Fruehauf's $1 valuation practice constituted a method of accounting for purposes of Section 481. It also held that the taxpayer was other-

49. 1 BTA 124 (1924).

Other
Accounting
Methods,
Changes,
and Claim
of Right

wise entitled to have its beginning inventory for the year 1954 restated on the correct basis in accordance with the *Thomas Shoe* decision and following cases. The correct value was applied to *all* the trailers on hand January 1, 1954, including those unsold during 1954 and still on hand December 31, 1954, and the Service's attempt to limit a correction to the ending inventory was defeated. About $2.5 million (the January 1, 1954, understatement) escaped taxation altogether. Had the change been made in 1942, approximately $500,000 untaxed income would have gone untaxed.

16.65   Subsequently, the Service announced its acquiescence to this decision. It now agrees that the correction of a consistently followed method of inventory valuation is a change in a method of accounting.

Revenue Procedure 70–27

16.66   Because of continuing uncertainty about what constituted a method of accounting, and to facilitate obtaining permission to make changes, the Service issued Revenue Procedure 64–16[50] in 1964. Six years later that ruling was superseded and slightly changed by Rev. Proc. 70–27. It applies to changes in "accounting practice" and most changes in accounting methods. Section 3.01 of Rev. Proc. 70–27 reads:

A taxpayer's request to change his accounting practice or method for Federal income tax purposes to an acceptable practice or method consistent with the Regulations will ordinarily receive favorable consideration, provided he proposes and agrees as a condition to the change to take the necessary resulting adjustment into account ratably over an appropriate period, prescribed by the Commissioner, generally ten years.

Under the ruling, the application for permission to make a change also is made on Form 3115. Normally it should be filed within 180 days from the beginning of the taxable year for which the change is requested, but, upon a showing of good cause, the Commissioner may accept the application if it is filed within nine months after the beginning of such taxable year. Further, if a taxpayer's return for a prior year is under examination by the Service and there is an issue involving a change in accounting practice or method, the taxpayer may request application of the new procedure. The filing of the application will suspend audit action, and, if the application is granted, the permission will generally be applicable to the most recent taxable year for which a return has been filed.

16.67   Revenue Procedure 70–27 deals with a change from an unacceptable to an acceptable practice, rather than from one acceptable practice to another. Further, the procedure does not apply when the year in which an erroneous practice or method was initiated by the taxpayer is under examination by the Service.

50. 1964–1 (Part 1) C.B. 677; Rev. Proc. 65–32 [quoted in full at 734 CCH Standard Federal Tax Reporter ¶2771.30] amplified Rev. Proc. 64–16 by giving an example of the application of the latter procedure to a change in the method of valuing inventory.

In effect, taxpayers using this procedure will be waiving their right 16.68
to have pre-1954 adjustments excluded from taxable income under the
"escape hatch" of Section 481(a)(2). In the usual case, therefore, it will
be disadvantageous to use the procedure if the adjustment required is
adverse to the taxpayer and if the adjustment affects a recurring item
in existence as of the beginning of the first taxable year starting after
December 31, 1953. This will be the case, for example, where inventory has been consistently undervalued (in the Service's view) in
conflict with the very strict Treasury Regulations.

Change in Billing Practice

It is the position of the Service that a change in billing practice by 16.69
an accrual basis taxpayer is a change in accounting method if the result
is to defer to a later year the reporting of gross revenues.

Many electric and gas distribution companies some years ago 16.70
changed from monthly to bimonthly cycle billing of customers, principally to save manpower in reading meters. In 1965 the Service
ruled[51] that such a change is a change in accounting method. It
stated that it would permit the change provided that the utility company would agree to adjustments that would avoid distortions of
income or expense in the year of change. The adjustment usually required is that estimated unbilled revenue existing at the end of the
year of change be included in income in that year and then be deducted ratably over the ensuing ten years. No utility company has yet
litigated the validity of this ruling.

In *Decision, Inc.*[52] the Commissioner lost in his contention that a 16.71
change in billing practice for advertising space by this publisher was
a change in accounting method requiring advance approval.

CLAIM OF RIGHT DOCTRINE

Income received by the taxpayer under a claim of right and without 16.72
restriction on its disposition is includible in his taxable income at
the time of receipt, although his right to retain it is disputed at the
time of receipt, or later, and although repayment of part or all of the
income may be required in a later year. This *claim of right* doctrine
applies to both cash and accrual basis taxpayers. Its origin is the 1932
decision of the United States Supreme Court in *North American Oil
Consolidated* v. *Burnet*.[53] The issue was the year of taxability of
certain income. Extracts from the Court's opinion follow:

The money was paid to the company under the following circumstances:
Among many properties operated by it in 1916 was a section of oil land, the
legal title to which stood in the name of the United States. Prior to that year,
the government, claiming also the beneficial ownership, had instituted a suit

51. Rev. Rul. 65–287, 1965–2 C.B. 150.
52. 47 T.C. 58 (1966).
53. 286 U.S. 417 (1932), 3 USTC ¶943, 11 AFTR 16.

Other
Accounting
Methods,
Changes,
and Claim
of Right

to oust the company from possession; and on February 2, 1916, it secured the appointment of a receiver to operate the property, or supervise its operations, and to hold the net income thereof. The money paid to the company in 1917 represented the net profits which had been earned from that property in 1916 during the receivership. The money was paid to the receiver as earned. After entry by the District Court in 1917 of the final decree dismissing the bill, *the money was paid, in that year, by the receiver to the company.* ... The government took an appeal (without supersedeas) to the Circuit Court of Appeals. In 1920, that court affirmed the decree. ... In 1922, a further appeal to this Court was dismissed by stipulation. ... [Emphasis supplied.]

It is conceded that the net profits earned by the property during the receivership constituted income. The company contends that they should have been reported by the receiver for taxation in 1916; that, if not returnable by him, they should have been returned by the company for 1916, because they constitute income of the company accrued in that year; and that, if not taxable as income of the company for 1916, they were taxable to it as income for 1922, since the litigation was not finally terminated in its favor until 1922.

First. The income earned in 1916 and impounded by the receiver in that year was not taxable to him, because he was the receiver of only a part of the properties operated by the company. ...

Second. The net profits were not taxable to the company as income of 1916. For the company was not required in 1916 to report as income an amount which it might never receive. ... There was no constructive receipt of the profits by the company in that year, because at no time during the year was there a right in the company to demand that the receiver pay over the money. Throughout 1916 it was uncertain who would be declared entitled to the profits. It was not until 1917, when the District Court entered a final decree vacating the receivership and dismissing the bill, that the company became entitled to receive the money. Nor is it material, for the purposes of this case, whether the company's return was filed on the cash receipts and disbursements basis, or on the accrual basis. In neither event was it taxable in 1916 on account of income which it had not yet received and which it might never receive.

Third. The net profits earned by the property in 1916 were not income of the year 1922—the year in which the litigation with the government was finally terminated. They became income of the company in 1917, when it first became entitled to them and when it actually received them. If a taxpayer receives earnings under a claim of right and without restriction as to its disposition, he has received income which he is required to return, even though it may still be claimed that he is not entitled to retain the money, and even though he may still be adjudged liable to restore its equivalent. ... If in 1922 the government had prevailed, and the company had been obliged to refund the profits received in 1917, it would have been entitled to a deduction from the profits of 1922, not from those of any earlier year. ...

16.73   If in the same year that funds are mistakenly received, the taxpayer discovers and admits the mistake, renounces his claim to the funds and recognizes his obligation to repay them, the claim of right doctrine does not apply.[54]

16.74   Amounts taxable under a claim of right in the year of receipt become deductible in a later year when the amounts are repaid (under the cash basis) or when the liability for repayment is recognized (un-

---

54. U.S. v. Merrill, 211 F.2d 297 (9th Cir. 1954); Charles Kay Bishop, 25 T.C. 969 (1956).

611

Other
Accounting
Methods,
Changes,
and Claim
of Right

der the accrual basis). To be deductible, any such repayment must not be voluntary. It should arise out of compromise of the controversy or be caused by some compelling circumstance such as a court judgment. Because of the graduated tax brackets in the federal income tax system, it will frequently happen that a deduction for a later repayment will give rise to much less tax benefit than the additional tax imposed for the year of receipt of the income. To ameliorate this hardship, Congress, when enacting the 1954 Code, inserted new Code Section 1341. This section is somewhat technical, provides only a limited amount of relief, and can be applicable only when the amount repaid in a later taxable year is more than $3,000.

16.75 The case of *George L. Blanton v. Com.*[55] is an example of a voluntary repayment. There the Commissioner disallowed the deduction of a portion of an executive's compensation as unreasonable and excessive. The executive then entered into an agreement with the corporation to repay the excessive amount, and did so in a later year. The Fifth Circuit held that repayment by the executive was not deductible as a business expense, nor was it deductible under Section 1341 as the restoration of an amount received under a claim of right. There was no dispute over his right to receive the salary, and the repayment was voluntary.

16.76 The correct way to handle such situations is exemplified by *Vincent E. Oswald.*[56] There a corporation adopted a bylaw in 1952 requiring every officer to repay to the corporation any compensation which the Service might disallow as excessive. Upon examination of the corporation's return for 1960, a $5,000 bonus paid to Mr. Oswald was disallowed as a deduction. In 1964 he repaid the $5,000 to the corporation. The Tax Court allowed him a deduction of that amount for 1964 as an ordinary and necessary business expense of his business of being a corporate officer. Section 1341 is not applicable to instances of this type.[57]

QUESTIONS AND PROBLEMS

1. An individual uses various methods of accounting for items shown on his income tax returns as follows:

> Business items:
> Sales — Cash
> Inventories — Accrual
> Other business income — Cash
> Operating expenses — Accrual
>
> Personal items:
> Income (dividends, interest, etc.) — Cash
> Deductions (medical, contributions, etc.) — Cash

Discuss the propriety of the method used for each item.

55. 379 F.2d 558 (5th Cir. 1967), 67–2 USTC ¶9561, 20 AFTR2d 5062.
56. 49 T.C. 645 (Acq.) (1968).
57. Rev. Rul. 69–115.

Other
Accounting
Methods,
Changes,
and Claim
of Right

2. For the purpose of installment method calculations and eligibility, prepare a descriptive list of the types of evidences of indebtedness that can be disregarded in determining payments made in the year of a sale occurring in 1972.

3. A dealer in real estate, a calendar-year taxpayer, sold four parcels of land in 1972 to individuals. The details of the transactions are as follows:

	PARCEL				
	A	B	C	D	TOTAL
Selling price	$900	$10,600	$7,500	$6,000	$25,000
Basis to seller	200	3,600	2,500	3,700	10,000
Expenses of sale (commissions, etc.)	—	1,800	1,500	1,700	5,000
Payments received in 1972	—	3,500	500	2,000	6,000
Installment obligations received maturing in 1973 and later years. (The obligations had a fair market-value equal to par when received and provided for 9% interest per annum.)	900	7,100	7,000	4,000	19,000

What is the amount of income to be reported for 1972 under the installment method?

4. Assume the same facts as in Problem 3 with the exception that the sales were casual sales of personal property made by a cash-basis individual. What is the amount of income to be reported for 1972 assuming the individual elects the installment method for casual sales of personal property?

5. *Cumulative Problem.* A calendar-year corporation purchased and placed in service a new printing press on January 2, 1966. The press had a depreciable basis of $100,000 and a useful life of ten years to the corporation when acquired. The corporation uses the straight-line method in computing depreciation, and estimated salvage was 10% of the unadjusted basis. On January 2, 1973, the press was sold for $80,000, payable as follows under the contract of sale (no notes received):

$20,000 on January 2, 1973,

$20,000 on January 2 of each of the years 1974, 1975, and 1976 together with interest thereon at $8\frac{1}{2}$% per annum.

(a) If the installment method is used, how much gain from the sale is reportable for each of the years 1973 through 1976? (b) Assuming there are no other gains or losses, what kind of gain is reportable in those years?

6. On April 1, 1972, Jones, a calendar-year taxpayer, sold capital stock of a corporation he held as an investment for $100,000. The purchaser paid $20,000 on April 1, 1972, and agreed to pay $20,000 on April 1, 1973, and $60,000 on April 1, 1974, with each installment payment to bear 9 percent per annum interest. No notes were received. The basis of the stock to Jones was $50,000. An election was made on the 1972 income tax return of Jones to report the gain from the sale on the installment method. On February 1, 1973, Jones died and his entire estate passed to his son.

613

Other
Accounting
Methods,
Changes,
and Claim
of Right

(a) How much of the gain should be reported on the 1972 and 1973 income tax returns of Jones?

(b) What is the value of the installment obligations for Federal estate tax purposes?

(c) How much of the gain should be reported by Jones's son on his 1973 and 1974 income tax returns?

7. A calendar-year taxpayer made a casual sale of personal property in 1972 for a price in excess of $1,000 with payments to be received only in 1974 and 1975. Will the Internal Revenue Service allow him to report the gain from the sale on the installment method under the circumstances listed below?

(a) An election to use the installment method is made on his 1974 income tax return.

(b) The entire gain is reported on his 1972 income tax return, the gain is eliminated on his 1972 amended income tax return, and the installment method is elected on his 1972 amended income tax return.

8. In 1971, a calendar-year corporation entered into a contract to construct a building for $500,000. The building was completed and the customer accepted and took possession of the building in 1973. In connection with the contract, the corporation's books show the following information:

YEAR	PAYMENTS RECEIVED	COSTS INCURRED	PERCENTAGE OF COMPLETION AT END OF YEAR
1971	$ 50,000	$200,000	35%
1972	50,000	100,000	80
1973	400,000	100,000	100

(a) Assuming the corporation uses the "percentage-of-completion" method of accounting, how much income or loss from the contract should be reported for each of the years 1971, 1972, and 1973?

(b) Assuming the corporation uses the "completed-contract" method of accounting, how much income or loss from the contracts should be reported for each of the years 1971, 1972, and 1973?

9. *Refresher Question.* Jones operated a building construction firm as a proprietorship. For income tax purposes, he reported income and losses from building contracts under the "completed-contract" method. On December 31, 1972, he incorporated his firm. On the date of incorporation, his books showed the following information with respect to one of the building contracts transferred to the corporation:

YEAR	PAYMENTS	COSTS INCURRED	PERCENTAGE OF COMPLETION AT END OF YEAR
1971	$100,000	$ 75,000	20%
1972	200,000	150,000	60

The payments received were based on the percentage of completion. What is likely to be the income tax consequence to Jones as a result of transferring the contract to the corporation?

10. On September 1, 1972, Freeway Builders, Inc., was incorporated and went into the business of building highways. On December 1, 1972, Freeway's president and its controller came to you for tax advice. They tell you that they wish to use the percentage-of-completion method

614

Other
Accounting
Methods,
Changes,
and Claim
of Right

of accounting for financial statement purposes, but that the corporation will be extremely short of cash and they wish to defer the payment of income taxes as long as possible. Following is their estimate of income from jobs which the corporation has contracted to do:

JOB NUMBER	STARTING DATE	PROJECTED COMPLETION DATE	ESTIMATED TOTAL PROFIT	INTERIM DATA
1	9-1-72	2-28-73	$ 40,000	12-31-72 — 10% complete 1-31-73 — 50% complete
2	1-1-73	6-30-73	180,000	Will be completed ratably over 6 months
3	2-1-73	7-31-74	360,000	Will be completed ratably over 18 months

Assume that the total of general expenses not directly attributable to the long-term contracts are exactly offset by other income.

(a) Make recommendations for an accounting period and method of accounting to be used for tax purposes.

(b) By which method should the corporation keep its books?

(c) Prepare a schedule showing by fiscal years a comparison of income under the percentage-of-completion method with income under the tax method you recommend.

(d) How should the corporation proceed in order to assure that your tax recommendation is available?

(e) What documents must be filed by the corporation?

11. You have been approached by a physician who is unhappy with his method of accounting. Since 1960, when the doctor first opened his practice, his accountant kept the books and filed tax returns using the accrual method for his business income from his professional practice. The doctor would like to change to the cash method for tax purposes, but continue to maintain his professional books on the accrual basis. His reason is that substantially all professional men use the cash receipts and disbursements method of accounting to report their taxable income, and he believes that it is unfair for him to be required to pay taxes on income before he receives it. You ascertain that at the beginning of the year of change the only accrual basis accounts that would be eliminated under the cash method are:

Accounts receivable for fees not then collected	$10,000
Accrued expenses not then paid	2,000
	$ 8,000

(a) Would this change constitute a change in accounting method, change in accounting practice, or a correction of an error?

(b) Must the consent of the Commissioner be obtained for this change?

(c) What adjustments might the Commissioner require if his permission is sought?

(d) If the change is made without consent, what alternatives are open to the Commissioner?

(e) What relief is provided by Revenue Procedure 70–27?

(f) If the books are kept on the accrual method, and the tax returns are prepared on the cash method, is there a conflict under Section 446(a)?

Other
Accounting
Methods,
Changes,
and Claim
of Right

12. The Mack Corporation, an accrual basis and calendar-year taxpayer, entered into a twenty-year lease agreement with the Nann Corporation whereby a building was leased to the Nann Corporation effective January 1, 1972. The terms of the lease provided that rent with respect to each semiannual period would be paid to the Mack Corporation one month after the end of the semiannual period. The rent for the period July 1, 1972, to December 31, 1972, was paid on January 31, 1973, and was included on the 1973 income tax return of the Mack Corporation. Upon examination of the 1972 income tax return of the Mack Corporation, the Internal Revenue Service insisted that the rent for the period July 1, 1972 to December 31, 1972, be included on the 1972 return.

(a) Did the Internal Revenue Service have the right to insist that the rent be reported on the accrual method?

(b) Assume the Internal Revenue Service accepted the cash method of reporting the rent for the years through 1972 but then insisted that the rent be reported on the accrual method for 1973. Did the Internal Revenue Service have the right to insist on the change for 1973?

13. For many years, a calendar-year corporation used the FIFO method of valuing inventories. Then, on June 1, 1972, it filed a Form 3115 with the Commissioner of Internal Revenue requesting permission to change to the LIFO method of valuing inventories effective with the calendar year 1972. On September 1, 1972, the Commissioner informed the corporation that permission was denied because the Form 3115 had not been filed by the required date. Is it possible for the corporation to use the LIFO method on its 1972 income tax return even though the Commissioner has denied permission to make the change?

14. In the case of *North American Oil Consolidated* v. *Burnet,* extracts from which are quoted in paragraph 16.72, for what year would the corporation have been entitled to a deduction if in 1922 the government had prevailed in its suit to oust the corporation from possession of the properties, and in that same year the corporation refunded the profits received in 1917 from the receiver?

15. Mr. Lewis in 1970 received a bonus of $22,000. A state court in 1972 decided that the amount of the bonus had been improperly computed and was excessive to the extent of $11,000. The amount of $11,000 was repaid by Mr. Lewis to the corporation in 1972. Assume that the amount of the tax payable on the 1970 return of Mr. Lewis, including the full $22,000 bonus, amounted to $17,000. If the $11,000 repayment made in 1972 could be related back and deducted in 1970, the tax liability for the year would be only $11,475. For 1972, his tax liability before deducting the repayment of $11,000 in excessive bonus is $16,000; and if the $11,000 repayment is deducted, the tax liability decreases to $10,790. Does Code Sec. 1341 apply? What will the final amounts of tax liability be for the years 1970 and 1972?

17

DEFERRED

COMPENSATION

QUALIFIED PENSION, PROFIT-SHARING, AND STOCK BONUS
PLANS . . . 618

   The Fund Holder . . . 618
   The Plan . . . 619
   Nondiscrimination and Coverage . . . 620
   Distinctions Between Qualified Plans . . . 621
   Forfeitures and Vesting . . . 623
   Benefits . . . 623

      PENSION PLANS . . . 623
      PROFIT-SHARING PLANS . . . 625
      STOCK BONUS PLANS . . . 625

   Deductions . . . 625

      PENSION PLANS . . . 626
      PROFIT-SHARING AND STOCK BONUS PLANS . . . 626
      TWO OR MORE PLANS . . . 627

   Taxation of Benefits . . . 627

      TRUSTEED PLANS . . . 627
      ANNUITY PLANS . . . 627
      LUMP-SUM PAYMENTS . . . 628

   Tax Advantages . . . 628

NONQUALIFIED FUNDED PLANS . . . 629
NONQUALIFIED NONFUNDED PLANS . . . 631
RETIREMENT PLANS FOR THE SELF-EMPLOYED . . . 632

STOCK OPTIONS . . . 634

Statutory Stock Options . . . 635

RESTRICTED STOCK OPTIONS AND EMPLOYEE STOCK-PURCHASE
PLANS . . . 635
QUALIFIED STOCK OPTIONS . . . 635

Nonstatutory Stock Options . . . 636

17.1   In Chapter 5 it was stated that compensation received in kind is taxable and must be included in gross income in the amount of its fair market value. And in paragraph 14.19 we pointed out that a contract containing a promise to make payments of money in the future ordinarily does not have a taxable present value when received by a cash basis taxpayer.

17.2   These two premises affect methods of granting deferred compensation to employees and of allowing them to purchase stock in the employer corporation, at a bargain price, it is hoped. However, the Code also contains specific provisions in these areas.

17.3   The first part of this chapter is concerned with deferred compensation and the latter part with stock options. Code Sections 401 through 405 deal with various types of plans of deferred compensation, and Sections 421 through 425 concern statutory stock options.

17.4   A plan of deferred compensation can be either funded or nonfunded. Section 401 pertains to funded pension, profit-sharing, and stock bonus plans—that is, those plans in which contributions by employers or by both employers and employees are set aside in a separate fund held by a third party and invested. If the tests as to nondiscrimination and coverage imposed by Section 401 are met, the plan is called a "qualified" one; otherwise the plan is nonqualified. Qualification results in special tax benefits including tax-free accumulation of earnings on the fund's investments, current deduction of an employer's contributions, and postponement of taxation to employees until their respective portions of the fund are distributed or are made available to them.

17.5   A nonfunded plan is always a nonqualified one. Accordingly, a contractual plan of deferred compensation, because it is either not funded at all or not externally funded by deposit with a third party, is always nonqualified.

QUALIFIED PENSION, PROFIT–SHARING, AND STOCK BONUS PLANS

The Fund Holder

17.6   Prior to 1963 Section 401 contemplated only two types of third-party fund holders—a trust and an insurance company. Now contributions can also be paid to a bank provided that (1) the funds are held in a separate custodial account and (2) the funds are invested solely in regulated investment company stock (mutual funds) or solely in annuity, endowment, or life insurance contracts. In that event the account is treated as a trust [Section 401(f)]. Contributions can also be paid to an investment company operating as a "face-amount certificate company" for the purchase of nontransferable "face-amount certificates." These are similar to annuity contracts and are defined in the Investment Company Act of 1940 in the following manner:

"Face-amount certificate" means any certificate, investment contract, or other security which represents an obligation on the part of the issuer to pay a stated or determinable sum or sums at a fixed or determinable date or dates more than twenty-four months after the date of issuance, in consideration of the payment of periodic installments of a stated or determinable amount (which security shall be known as a face-amount certificate of the "installment type"); or any security which represents a similar obligation on the part of a face-amount certificate company, the consideration for which is the payment of a single lump sum (which security shall be known as a "fully paid" face-amount certificate).

Finally, the United States government can be the third party fund-holder provided that the contributions are used to purchase special United States government retirement bonds pursuant to Section 405; but these bonds pay modest interest yields based upon today's norm.

Although the earnings of a trust are ordinarily taxable, Section 501(a) exempts a trust from taxation if it is part of a qualified pension, profit-sharing, or stock bonus plan. The trust can invest in whatever it wishes (subject to the rules of Sections 503 and 511 through 515 pertaining to prohibited transactions and business income), or it can use its funds in whole or in part to purchase annuity contracts.

17.7

If an insurance company is the third-party fund holder, a trust need not be a conduit. In such an instance the contributions are paid directly to the insurance company by the employer for premiums on annuity contracts. The insurance company invests the money and is then given favorable tax treatment on income derived from such investments.

17.8

The Plan

17.9

A "plan" must meet these requirements:

1. There must be a definite, written program;
2. It must be communicated to the employees;
3. It must be designed and applied solely to benefit the employees (including the self-employed) and their beneficiaries with no possibility of reverter of any portion of the fund or its income to the employer prior to satisfaction of all liabilities with respect to employees and their beneficiaries.
4. It must be a permanent and continuing program; abandonment requires a valid business reason.

The typical plan is so entitled, is adopted by the board of directors, and is usually approved by the shareholders. The document itself is quite formal and detailed, but then a description of it in summary form is prepared and distributed to all existing and new employees. If the plan encompasses a trust, there is a separate trust instrument between the employer and the trustee. Internal Revenue Service Publication 778 (2–72) supplements the regulations pertaining to Section 401 and contains the qualification guides established by the Service. It should be studied by every serious student of the subject.

Nondiscrimination and Coverage

17.10   Section 401(a) requires that a qualified plan not discriminate in favor of employees who are "officers, shareholders, persons whose principal duties consist in supervising the work of other employees, or highly compensated employees." To meet that test, Section 401(a)(3) in subparagraph (A) gives certain percentages of the total employees that can be covered to have a qualified plan and in subparagraph (b) permits the Internal Revenue Service alternatively to approve classifications of employees that an employer proposes to set up for purposes of coverage. A qualified plan can cover all employees with certain years of service (for example, five years), or all employees earning over a stated amount of compensation (for example, $6,000 per year.[1] However, a plan that excludes employees earning less than a stated amount must "integrate" with Social Security, that is, the Social Security benefits that will be available plus the benefits under the plan cannot be a higher percentage of pay for higher-bracket employees than for lower-bracket employees.[2] Finally, even if the class of employees covered is nondiscriminatory, the benefits or contributions provided for the employees within the class cannot be discriminatory.

17.11   The percentage requirements of Section 401(a)(3)(A) are illustrated in the following example from Reg. 1.401–3(a)(3) as amended July 21, 1971:

EXAMPLE FROM REG.   A corporation adopts a plan at a time when it has 1,000 employees. The plan provides that all full-time employees who have been employed for a period of two years and have reached the age of 30 shall be eligible to participate. The plan also requires participating employees to contribute 3 percent of their monthly pay. At the time the plan is made effective 100 of the 1,000 employees had not been employed for a period of two years. Fifty of the employees were seasonal employees whose customary employment did not exceed five months in any calendar year. Twenty-five of the employees were part-time employees whose customary employment did not exceed 20 hours in any one week. One hundred and fifty of the full-time employees who had been employed for two years or more had not yet reached age 30. The requirements of section 401(a)(3)(A) will be met if 540 employees are covered by the plan, as shown by the following computation:

(i)   Total employees with respect to whom the percentage requirements are applicable (1,000 minus 175 (100 plus 50 plus 25)) 825

(ii)   Employees not eligible to participate because of age requirements 150

(iii)   Total employees eligible to participate 675

(iv)   Percentage of employees in item (i) eligible to participate 81 + %

(v)   Minimum number of participating employees to qualify the plan (80 percent of 675) 540

---

1. Reg. 1.401–3(e); Rev. Rul. 71–446.
2. Reg. 1.401–3; Rev. Rul. 71–446, 1971–2 C.B. 187.

If only 70 percent, or 578, of the 825 employees satisfied the age and service requirements, then 462 (80 percent of 578) participating employees would satisfy the percentage requirements.

If there is a plan for salaried personnel comprised primarily of top executives and another plan for union employees, the benefits going to each group must be comparable. If the contribution rate into the plan for the hourly workers is, for example, 4 percent of their wages and the contribution rate to the plan for salaried personnel comprised primarily of executives is 15 percent of their compensation, the salaried plan will not qualify.[3] Separate plans for salaried and hourly workers can provide different benefits, but only if the members of the salaried plan consist primarily of employees who are not officers, shareholders, or supervisors.

17.12

Distinctions Between Qualified Plans

There are three broad categories of qualified plans—pension, profit sharing, and stock bonus. The first two are the most common.

17.13

The ordinary type of pension plan is one under which the amount of retirement benefits is first determined and then the required amount of annual contributions is actuarially computed. Regulation 1.401–1(b)(i) states:

17.14

A pension plan within the meaning of section 401(a) is a plan established and maintained by an employer primarily to provide systematically for the payment of definitely determinable benefits to his employees over a period of years, usually for life, after retirement. Retirement benefits generally are measured by, and based on, such factors as years of service and compensation received by the employees. *The determination of the amount of retirement benefits and the contributions to provide such benefits are not dependent upon profits.* Benefits are not definitely determinable if funds arising from forfeitures on termination of service, or other reason, may be used to provide increased benefits for the remaining participants... .

A plan designed to provide benefits for employees or their beneficiaries to be paid upon retirement or over a period of years after retirement will, for the purposes of section 401(a), be considered a pension plan if the employer contributions under the plan can be determined actuarially on the basis of definitely determinable benefits, or, as in the case of money purchase pension plans, such contributions are fixed without being geared to profits. A pension plan may provide for the payment of a pension due to disability and may also provide for the payment of incidental death benefits through insurance or otherwise. However, a plan is not a pension plan if it provides for the payment of benefits not customarily included in a pension plan such as layoff benefits or benefits for sickness, accident, hospitalization, or medical expenses (except medical benefits described in section 401(h)... . [Emphasis supplied.]

Note that this regulation also classifies a money purchase plan as a pension plan. Under such a plan a fixed amount for the benefit of

17.15

3. Rev. Rul. 66–15, 1966–1 C.B. 83, as amplified by Rev. Rul. 70–183, 1970–1 C.B. 103; I.R.S. Publication 778(2–72), Part 4(m).

Deferred
Compensa-
tion

each employee participant, usually a percentage of compensation, is paid annually by the employer, without regard to the existence of profits. The benefits will be whatever amount can be provided by the contributions so that, unlike the usual type of pension plan, the benefits do not determine the amount of required contribution.

17.16   A profit-sharing plan is not designed to provide a stipulated amount of monthly retirement income but rather to provide a fund built up out of contributions from annual profits or accumulated profits of an employer that will be available to the employee later, usually on retirement. Regulation 1.401–1(b)(1)(ii) reads:

> A profit-sharing plan is a plan established and maintained by an employer to provide for the participation in his profits by his employees or their beneficiaries. The plan must provide a definite predetermined formula for allocating the contributions made to the plan among the participants and for distributing the funds accumulated under the plan after a fixed number of years, the attainment of a stated age, or upon the prior occurrence of some event such as layoff, illness, disability, retirement, death, or severance of employment. A formula for allocating the contributions among the participants is definite if, for example, it provides for an allocation in proportion to the basic compensation of each participant. A plan (whether or not it contains a definite predetermined formula for determining the profits to be shared with the employees) does not qualify under section 401(a) if the contributions to the plan are made at such times or in such amounts that the plan in operation discriminates in favor of officers, shareholders, persons whose principal duties consist in supervising the work of other employees, or highly compensated employees. ... A profit-sharing plan within the meaning of section 401 is primarily a plan of deferred compensation, but the amounts allocated to the account of a participant may be used to provide for him or his family incidental life or accident or health insurance.

The second sentence of this regulation permits distribution of the fund after a "fixed number of years." The Service held in Rev. Rul. 71–295[4] that this number can be as few as two.

17.17   Although a profit-sharing plan must contain a predetermined formula for allocating contributions among participants and for distributing the accumulated funds, there is no requirement that there be a predetermined formula setting the amount or percentage of the annual profits that must be paid into the plan. Regulation 1.401–1(b)(2) reads in part as follows:

> ... In the case of a profit-sharing plan, ... it is not necessary that the employer contribute every year or that he contribute the same amount or contribute in accordance with the same ratio every year. However, merely making a single or occasional contribution out of profits for employees does not establish a plan of profit-sharing. To be a profit-sharing plan, there must be recurring and substantial contributions out of profits for the employees. In the event a plan is abandoned, the employer should promptly notify the district director, stating the circumstances which led to the discontinuance of the plan.

17.18   Some companies have a thrift plan, sometimes called a savings

4. See also I.R.S. Pub. 778(2–72), Part 2(c).

plan, and it too can be a qualified plan. Such a plan calls for contributions by employees that are matched in some proportion by the company. If the company contribution is payable irrespective of profits, the plan is classified as a pension plan; but, if the contribution is payable only out of profits, it is a profit-sharing plan.[5]

Stock bonus plans are somewhat rare. They are defined in Reg. 1.401–1(b)(1)(iii) as follows: **17.19**

A stock bonus plan is a plan established and maintained by an employer to provide benefits similar to those of a profit-sharing plan, except that the contributions by the employer are not necessarily dependent upon profits and the benefits are distributable in stock of the employer company. For the purpose of allocating and distributing the stock of the employer which is to be shared among his employees or their beneficiaries, such a plan is subject to the same requirements as a profit-sharing plan.

Forfeitures and Vesting

As noted previously, it is permissible to have a uniform waiting period before new employees become eligible for coverage under the plan. When that period expires and the employee becomes covered, the plan can provide that his rights under the plan are not to vest until after the expiration of a designated period of time or the occurrence of a certain event or are to vest in increasing percentages over a period of years. For example, a plan could provide that an employee shall have no vested rights to any benefits under the plan during his first three years of coverage, but then for each year of service thereafter his rights shall vest at the rate of 10 percent per year. At the end of thirteen years of coverage under the plan he would be fully vested. If he were to resign or be discharged during the first three years of coverage he would forfeit all benefits allocated to him. If the resignation or discharge were to occur between the fifth and thirteenth year of coverage, he would forfeit a portion of his benefits. Most plans provide that payment of vested benefits will not be made prior to normal retirement date or earlier death or disability. **17.20**

In the instance of a profit-sharing plan, forfeitures may be used to reduce future contributions of the employer, but it is more usual to allocate them to the other participants. In the case of a pension plan, forfeitures must be used to reduce future contributions of the employer and they cannot be allocated to other participants. **17.21**

If for a valid business reason a plan is terminated or contributions are discontinued, the plan must provide that each participant will have an immediate vested right to benefits then accrued and funded. Section 401(a)(7). **17.22**

Benefits

Pension Plans. There are many formulas used in determining the **17.23**

5. George Thomas Washington and V. Henry Rothschild, 2nd, *Compensating the Corporate Executive*, 3rd ed. (New York, The Ronald Press Company, 1962), II, 658, fn. 9.

Deferred Compensation

benefits to be paid upon retirement. The principal ones are money purchase, flat percentage, flat benefit, and percentage of compensation times years of service. In turn these formulas determine the amount of the annual contributions required. As indicated in paragraphs 17.6 and 17.7, the contributions can be paid to a noninsured trust for investment in securities and other assets, to a trust for investment in annuity contracts, directly to an insurance company for payment of premiums usually on annuity contracts, to a bank as custodian for investment in mutual funds or in annuity, endowment, or life insurance contracts, to a face-amount certificate company for the purchase of nontransferable face amount certificates, or to the United States government for purchase of special United States government retirement bonds. Before retirement each employee may then select one of whatever optional methods of payment are provided for in the plan. The types of options will be influenced by the type of plan. Some of the options usually found are: payment in cash or in kind in a lump sum, nonrefund annuity with payments for life but ceasing immediately upon death after retirement, refund life annuities with payment of an additional amount if the annuitant should die before having received a predetermined benefit amount, joint and survivor annuities.

17.24   The money purchase plan was discussed in paragraph 17.15, but it is not in common use.

17.25   Under a flat percentage type of pension plan, the employee receives a retirement benefit equal to a fixed percentage of compensation regardless of years of employment.

EXAMPLE   A plan provides that all employees will receive a retirement income of 50 percent of their average compensation since date of employment. John Smith has been a member of the plan for thirty years; his average salary for all those years was $7,500, but his average salary for the last five years was $20,000. On retirement he will receive an annual pension of $3,750. However, if the average compensation designated in the plan were the average for his last five years before retirement, the pension would be $10,000.

Under this type of plan no credit is given for length of service, so that a relatively new employee can receive the same or a greater pension than another employee with a lifetime of service and approximately the same terminal salary.

17.26   Under flat benefit plans the pension is an arbitrary amount unrelated to earnings or service. Some union negotiated plans are of the flat benefit type.

17.27   The percentage of compensation times years of service benefit plan is also known as the unit benefit method. A specified small percentage of each year's compensation is allowed as that year's pension credit, or a small percentage of average annual compensation may be allowed per year of participation. When past-service credit is given, that is, for years of employment before adoption of the plan or for years of employment with another company before becoming a member of the plan, the percentage for that benefit is usually smaller than for future service.

A pension plan uses a formula of 1½ percent of annual compensation for   EXAMPLE
each year of service subsequent to the plan's adoption, and 1 percent for each
year of past service for a maximum of ten years. Retirement age under the
plan is sixty-five. Paul Jones, an employee, is forty years of age at the time
the plan becomes effective and is immediately covered. At this time he has
been employed by the firm for fifteen years. His salary is $10,000 per year
and does not change. His retirement income will be computed as follows:

1 1/2 percent of $10,000 x 25 (years of service from age 40 to age 65)	$3,750
1 percent of $10,000 x 10 (maximum years of service prior to adoption of plan)	1,000
Total annual pension	$4,750

When a pension plan is first adopted, it is common to give some   17.28
credit for prior years of service; for that reason variations of the
foregoing example are in common use. In the foregoing example, a
past-service pension benefit of $1,000 per year is provided. This
amount multiplied by the average life expectancy of a man age sixty-
five, reduced by a mortality factor for a man age forty, discounted
by an assumed forfeiture percentage and taking into account an assumed rate of interest on a fund to provide such a benefit, results in
an amount required to pay such an amount at the rate of $1,000 per
year starting at age sixty-five. Such amount is called past-service
cost. The amount can change from year to year during existence of
the plan to reflect changes in assumptions and whether or not any
part of it was funded in a prior year.

Profit-Sharing Plans. In paragraphs 17.6, 17.7, and 17.23 mention was   17.29
made of the types of third-party holders for contributions and investments. Further, in paragraph 17.23 mention was made of optional methods of payments of benefits usually made available to
employees. Those same third-party holders, investments, and options will also be found in profit-sharing plans.

Stock Bonus Plans. The holder in a stock bonus plan will always be   17.30
a trust, investments will always be in stock of the employer corporation, and benefits are distributed in the form of company stock.

Deductions

Only employers, and not employees, receive deductions for con-   17.31
tributions to qualified plans. The provisions are in Section 404. Even
though a contribution is deductible only under Section 404, the
amount must still be an ordinary and necessary business expense
under Sections 162 or 212 and not result in the payment of unreasonable compensation. For example, in *Bardahl Manufacturing Corp.*[6]
this closely held corporation paid a salary of $3,000 to the wife of the

6. 19 T.C.M. 1245 (1960).

president and made contributions to qualified pension and profit-sharing plans for her. The Tax Court held that reasonable compensation per year for her services did not exceed $600, disallowed the deduction of the remaining $2,400, and disallowed the contributions made on her behalf to the qualified plans.

17.32   In general, contributions are deductible only in the year in which paid. Section 404(a)(1), (2), (3). But an accrual-method employer is given a grace period for payment. Under Section 404(a)(6) it can deduct an amount paid before the due date (as extended) of its return for the accrual year provided that the liability accrued in that year. There are also limitations on the amounts that can be deducted in any one year and in some instances provisions for the carry-over of amounts not currently deductible.

17.33   **Pension Plans.** Paragraphs (A), (B), and (C) of Section 404(a)(1) provide the following alternative limits on the amount of a deduction in any one year for contributions paid to a pension plan:

(A) an amount not in excess of 5 percent of the compensation otherwise paid or accrued during the taxable year to all participating employees;
(B) to the extent necessary to fund the remaining unfunded cost of current and past-service credits on a level basis over the remaining future service; or
(C) to fund benefits on the basis of "normal cost" plus 10 percent of past-service or supplemental costs.

17.34   Regulation 1.404(a)–6(a)(2) defines normal cost and past-service or supplemental cost as follows:

... "Normal cost" for any year is the amount actuarially determined which would be required as a contribution by the employer in such year to maintain the plan if the plan had been in effect from the beginning of service of each then included employee and if such cost for prior years had been paid and all assumptions as to interest, mortality, time of payment, etc., had been fulfilled. Past service or supplementary cost at any time is the amount actuarially determined which would be required at such time to meet all the future benefits provided under the plan which would not be met by future normal costs and employee contributions with respect to the employees covered under the plan at such time.

17.35   If an amount that is in excess of the applicable limitation is paid into a pension plan in a year, the excess can be carried over indefinitely to succeeding years, but in any such succeeding year the aggregate deduction cannot exceed the applicable limitation.

17.36   **Profit-Sharing and Stock Bonus Plans.** In the case of a profit-sharing or stock bonus plan, Section 404(a)(3) imposes a limitation of 15 percent of the compensation otherwise paid or accrued during the taxable year to all employees under the plan. If a contribution of more than this amount is paid in any one year, the excess can be carried forward indefinitely to succeeding years, but in no such succeeding year can the aggregate deduction exceed 15 percent of the compensation otherwise paid or accrued during such year to covered employees.

Two or More Plans. If one or more employees are beneficiaries under   17.37
(1) a pension plan and a profit-sharing or stock bonus plan, (2) an
annuity type of pension plan and a profit-sharing or stock bonus plan,
or (3) a noninsured pension plan, an annuity type of pension plan,
and a profit-sharing or stock bonus plan, in connection with two or
more trusts, or one or more trusts and an annuity plan, the aggregate
amount deductible cannot exceed 25 percent of the compensation
otherwise paid or accrued to all of the persons who are beneficiaries
of the plans. If an excessive amount is paid in any year, such excess
can be carried forward indefinitely to future years. In any such
succeeding year, the aggregate deduction cannot exceed 30 percent
of the compensation otherwise paid or accrued in such year to the
beneficiaries under the plans. Section 404(a)(7).

Taxation of Benefits

Trusteed Plans. Under Section 402(a)(1) amounts distributed or made   17.38
available (other than in one lump sum as discussed below in paragraphs 17.41 and 17.42) to the beneficiary of a tax-exempt trust which
is part of a qualified pension, profit-sharing, or stock bonus plan, are
taxable to him in the year distributed or made available to him after
retirement under the annuity rules of Section 72. If the plan was
noncontributory, all amounts are ordinary income. If the plan was
contributory, the discussion in paragraph 17.40 applies.

Partial distributions from a qualified plan to an employee during   17.39
employment, and not as an annuity, are taxable to the employee as
ordinary income to the extent they exceed the employee's total contributions to the plan. Section 72(e)(1)(B).

In previous years an employee contributed a total of $1,500 to his com-   EXAMPLE 1
pany's profit-sharing plan. Pursuant to an election exercised before the due
date of availability and before retirement, he withdraws $1,000 (representing
a mix of his own and company contributions, earnings thereon, and forfeitures). On that date the total amount to his credit in the profit-sharing plan
and fully vested is $10,000. In the year of withdrawal he has no taxable in-
come. He merely reduces his aggregate unrecovered contributions to the
plan from $1,500 to $500.

Assume the same facts as in Example 1, but the withdrawal is $2,300.   EXAMPLE 2
He has $800 ($2,300 − $1,500) of ordinary income.

Annuity Plans. Under a noncontributory annuity plan, whether or not   17.40
through a trust as a conduit, all annual amounts (not lump sum)
received also are ordinary income. However, if the employee contributed toward the plan, the aggregate amount of his contributions
becomes his "investment in the contract," so that under the rules of
Section 72 discussed in paragraphs 5.115 to 5.123 he is entitled to
recover such investment tax-free over his life expectancy. Nevertheless, as pointed out in paragraph 5.124 pertaining to Section 72(d),
if the retired employee will receive during the first three years an
amount equal to or less than his prior contributions, he may exclude all of his annuity receipts until he has recovered his capital tax-

free. Thereafter, all annuity receipts will be taxable in full as ordinary income.

Robinson is an employee of Conglomerate Corporation. During the years of his service he contributed $6,000 into a qualified annuity plan and the corporation contributed $24,000. Robinson, of course, paid no tax on the $24,000 that his employer contributed. Robinson retired on January 1, 1970, and became entitled to a life annuity of $275 per month ($3,300 per year). He was sixty-five years old on his birthday nearest January 1, 1970. He is entitled to exclude the first $6,000 of annuity receipts so that not until late in 1971 will he commence having ordinary annuity income, and then it will be in the full amount received.

17.41 **Lump-Sum Payments.** If an employee or his beneficiary receives his entire fund in one taxable year because of separation from service whether before or after reaching retirement age, death, or death after retirement, at least a portion of it will be taxed as a long-term capital gain. That part which will be so treated consists of employer contributions made before 1970, earnings of the fund for all years whether derived from employer contributions made before 1970 or later, unrealized appreciation of securities no matter what was the source of the funds used to purchase the investments, and forfeitures allocated to his account from unvested portions of the accounts of other employees who resigned or were discharged but only if so allocated before 1970. The balance of the lump-sum distribution will be taxed as ordinary income.

At the close of the last plan year beginning before 1970, an employee's account on the books of the trustee showed accrued benefits of $10,000. This consisted of employer's contributions of $7,000, income of $1,000, unrealized appreciation in investment portfolio of $1,500, and forfeitures of $500. In plan years beginning in 1970 and later the employer contributes $8,000, the fund earns $1,200, there is unrealized depreciation in the portfolio of $800, and there are forfeitures of $1,000. The employee retires in 1976 and receives a lump-sum distribution of $19,400. Of that amount $10,400 is a long-term capital gain and $9,000 is ordinary income. The $9,000 consists of the $8,000 of employer contributions and the $1,000 of forfeitures occurring in 1970 and later.

17.42 If a lump-sum distribution includes appreciated securities of the employer, the employee is taxed at the time of the distribution only to the extent of the basis of the securities to the trust. Part of that basis will be taxed as capital gain and the balance as ordinary income, depending upon whether the employer's contributions of the securities or of money to purchase them were made before 1970 or later. The unrealized appreciation is not taxed to the employee until he sells the securities, and then as a capital gain.

Tax Advantages

17.43 The chief tax advantages of qualified pension and profit-sharing plans are these:

1. contributions by the employer to the plan are currently deductible;
2. the income of the fund is exempt from Federal income taxation;
3. each beneficiary is taxed upon distributions only when he receives them or when they are made available to him;
4. under some circumstances the employee can obtain his share at capital-gain rates;
5. the value of death benefits payable under the plan to any beneficiary of a deceased employee (other than his executor) is, to the extent attributable to employer contributions, excluded from his gross estate for estate-tax purposes. [Sec. 2039(c)]

NONQUALIFIED FUNDED PLANS

A nonqualified funded plan of deferred compensation includes both a trusteed plan and an annuity plan which do not comply with the nondiscrimination and coverage provisions of Section 401. It also includes a funded trust that is not exempt from taxation under Section 501(a); this ordinarily will occur only when the trust has engaged in one or more of the prohibited transactions described in Section 503.

17.44

The Tax Reform Act of 1969 changed the law governing the taxation of employee beneficiaries of such plans and the deductibility of contributions by employers but only with respect to the time of deductibility by employers and taxability to employees of contributions made and premiums paid after August 1, 1969. The old rules still apply to the deductibility of contributions and premiums paid on or before August 1, 1969, and to the time of taxability to employee beneficiaries of distributions from such contributions and premiums.

17.45

As to contributions made and premiums paid to a nonqualified trust or under a nonqualified annuity plan on or before August 1, 1969, the rules are these:

17.46

1. If the employee's rights under the plan are nonforfeitable at the time of the employer's contribution, the employer obtains a current deduction and the employee has current income; but the employee will have no cash with which to pay the tax unless the benefits are simultaneously or shortly thereafter paid to him.
2. If the employee's rights are then forfeitable, the employer (according to Reg. 1.404(a)–12) never obtains a deduction, not even when benefits are paid by the plan to the employee, and the employee does not realize income unless and until cash is paid to him.
3. If a trusteed plan is used, the income from the funds is currently taxable to the trust.

The pertinent part of Reg. 1.404(a)–12 referred to in 2 above reads:

17.47

If an amount is paid during the taxable year to a trust or under a plan and the employee's rights to such amounts are forfeitable at the time the amount is paid, no deduction is allowable for such amount for any taxable year.

17.48   In 1959, the Court of Claims in *Russell Manufacturing Co. v. U.S.*[7] held Reg. 1.404(a)–12 invalid and allowed an employer corporation a deduction, in the year of payment, for benefits paid by a nonexempt trust to employees whose rights theretofore had been forfeitable. Later that year, the Internal Revenue Service announced[8] that it would not follow *Russell Manufacturing Co.* In 1963 and in 1967 the Court of Claims nevertheless again allowed deductions to corporations when funds were paid by nonqualified trusts in *Mississippi River Fuel Corp.*[9] and in *Buttrey Stores, Inc. v. U.S.*[10]

17.49   As to contributions and premium payments made after August 1, 1969, the time of taxability to employee beneficiaries dictates the year of deductibility by the employer. The provisions as to taxability are in Sections 402(b) and 403(c) and as to deductibility in Section 404(a)(5). As of the date of this writing, there are no regulations.

17.50   In determining the time of taxability to employees' beneficiaries under the new rules, there are two important terms incorporated by reference to Section 83 pertaining to restricted stock—"substantial risk of forfeiture" and "transferability."

17.51   Section 83(c)(1) states:

> The rights of a person in property are subject to a substantial risk of forfeiture if such person's rights to full enjoyment of such property are conditioned upon the future performance of substantial services by any individual.

In other words, if an employee's interest in a nonqualified trust or nonqualified annuity plan is forfeitable until he completes a designated period of future employment, his interest in the trust or plan remains forfeitable until that date.

17.52   Ordinarily the rights of an employee in a nonqualified trust or nonqualified annuity plan are not transferable until retirement, sometimes earlier termination of employment, or death; and, when they do become transferable, there is no requirement on the part of the employee to perform future services. Section 83(c)(2) states:

> The rights of a person in property are transferable only if the rights in such property of any transferee are not subject to a substantial risk of forfeiture.

This language would seem to have little application to nonqualified trusts and plans.

17.53   Contributions to nonqualified trusts and payments of premiums made after August 1, 1969, become taxable to the extent of the employee's interest in the plan on that date when his interest first becomes nonforfeitable ("not subject to a substantial risk of forfeiture")

---

7. 175 F.Supp. 159, 59–2 USTC Par. 9582, 4 AFTR 2nd 5167.
8. Rev. Rul. 59–383, 1959–2 C.B. 456.
9. 314 F.2d 953, 63–1 USTC ¶9392, 11 AFTR 2d 1244.
10. 375 F.2d 799 (Ct. Cl., 1967), 67–1 USTC ¶9371, 19 AFTR 2d 1207.

or transferable. This means, for example, that if an employer makes contributions to a nonqualified trust between August 2, 1969, and December 31, 1972, and on the latter date an employee's rights first become nonforfeitable or transferable, he would be taxed in 1972 on his share of the contributions made in that period. Thereafter, he would be currently taxable on future contributions. Income of a nonqualified trust is not taxable to a beneficiary until distributed.

When distributions begin from the nonqualified trust or nonqualified annuity plan, the annuity rules of Section 72 apply, and for that purpose the employee's previously taxed portion of the contributions and payments becomes his investment in the contract.

17.54

Under Section 404(a)(5) as amended by the Tax Reform Act of 1969, the employer becomes entitled to a deduction for his contributions in the taxable year in which an amount attributable to the contribution is includible in the gross income of employee beneficiaries. Whatever amount is taxable to the employees in that year is deductible by the employer. There is a further requirement that, to have a deduction, separate accounts under the plan must be maintained for each employee.

17.55

Nonqualified funded plans never were too attractive and they are less so now.

17.56

NONQUALIFIED NONFUNDED PLANS

In recent years there has been keen competition among employers to acquire and retain top executives. Retirement benefits under qualified plans often are not sufficiently attractive to these key employees. Accordingly, many corporations use nonqualified and nonfunded contractual plans of deferred compensation. These usually cover only a few top executives and thus are discriminatory by design.

17.57

A nonqualified nonfunded plan of deferred compensation represents only the unsecured contractual promise of the employer to pay. The term "nonfunded" means that the employer's obligation is not externally funded with an irrevocable trust or insurance company for the benefit of the employees. It also means that the employer does not fund his bookkeeping reserve for the deferred compensation liability through the purchase of insurance or investments in such a way that the cash surrender value of the insurance and the investments are held in trust for the employees, either constructively or expressly, and thus beyond reach of general creditors of the corporation. If an employer purchases an endowment or life insurance policy to provide cash with which to pay his ultimate liability and if the employer retains all rights of ownership of the policy and is also the beneficiary, then the nonqualified plan is not funded, provided that there was no intent to impress a trust on such insurance policy for the benefit of employees.

17.58

Prior to 1960 most tax practitioners were extremely careful when setting up nonqualified plans to insert provisions creating substantial

17.59

forfeitability features and also frequently making the amount of the benefits not presently determinable, in gearing them to future profits or the future cost of living index. They were fearful of the doctrine of constructive receipt and also of some possible application of the doctrine of economic benefit. However, Rev. Rul. 60–31, published by the Internal Revenue Service in 1960,[11] seems to suggest that it may no longer be necessary to insert forfeitability provisions in a deferred-compensation contract in order to guard against constructive receipt and current taxability of the employees. In one example of a typical deferred-compensation contract of employment, Rev. Rul. 60–31 held that the employee was not taxable until he actually received cash benefits in his retirement years despite the fact that there was no specific provision in the contract for possible forfeiture by the employee of his right to future distribution.

RETIREMENT PLANS FOR THE SELF–EMPLOYED

17.60   Starting in the late 1950s, Congressman Keogh, at the behest of groups of self-employed professional men, introduced a bill in each session of Congress seeking to amend the Internal Revenue Code to provide retirement plans for the self-employed that would be similar to qualified pension plans available for employees of corporations. In each session of Congress he was able to have assigned to the bill the number H.R. 10. Finally in 1962, Congress approved his bill. For that reason, today self-employed retirement plans are frequently referred to as "Keogh Plans" or "H.R. 10 Plans."

17.61   Effective with respect to taxable years beginning in 1963 and later, all self-employed individuals, including partners, are permitted to set up a qualified retirement plan. Within limits they obtain a current deduction from taxable income in the amount of the annual contribution to such a plan and then have ordinary income after retirement in the amount of money received from the fund. Contributions that are nondeductible—because they are in excess of the permitted limit—may also be made. This can be advantageous because the earnings of the fund are not currently taxable.

17.62   A sole proprietor is treated as both an employee and his own employer; a partnership is considered the employer of each of the partners. In this way most of the rules that apply to plans for employees are brought into operation. In addition, however, plans for the self-employed are subject to some special provisions.

17.63   Section 401(c)(3) introduces a new term, "owner-employee." He is an individual who owns all of an unincorporated business or who is a partner owning more than a 10 percent capital or profits' interest in the firm. All other self-employed individuals are merely called "self-employed." In reading the Code it must always be kept in mind

11. 1960–1 C.B. 174 as modified by Rev. Rul. 64–279 and Rev. Rul. 70–435, 1970–2 C.B. 100; similarly, Rev. Rul. 69–649, 1969–2 C.B. 106, and Rev. Rul. 69–650, 1969–2 C.B. 106.

that all "owner-employees" are also "self-employed" but not all persons who are "self-employed" are "owner-employees."

Employees of the self-employed are individuals who are em- 17.64 ployed by the self-employed but who do not own any part of the business. They are frequently referred to as "common-law employees."

If the trade or business is owned by a partnership, an individual 17.65 partner may not set up his own plan. The partnership is the employing entity and it must establish the plan. The partners themselves are considered partnership employees. However, a partner who is an owner-employee does have an election as to his own coverage by the plan.

An owner-employee, or a partnership one of whose partners is 17.66 an owner-employee, must include in the plan all full-time nonseasonal employees with three or more years of service. Further, contributions for such employees must be nonforfeitable at the time they are made. In other words, these common-law employees must have fully vested rights in their respective shares of the annual contributions at the time they are made.

Every self-employed individual can contribute for himself each 17.67 year a total of up to 10 percent of his "earned income" for that year or $2,500, whichever is less. To the extent of this limit, the contribution is deductible by him in determining adjusted gross income. His contribution to a plan must be out of his earned income derived from the business with respect to which the plan is established.

"Earned income" is the measuring rod for permissible contribu- 17.68 tions. For all practical purposes, earned income, even in the case of a business in which capital is a material income-producing factor, means taxable net income from the business after deducting contributions made to the plan on behalf of common-law employees. Income derived from rents, investments, and capital gains cannot be counted as part of earned income. For example, an attorney whose entire income is derived from fees for professional services has only earned income. But an attorney whose income comes from fees, plus dividends and other return on investment, may count only income derived from fees as earned income.

Johnson, a pharmacist on a calendar-year basis, is the sole owner of a EXAMPLE drugstore that nets him $22,000 per year. Both his personal services and his capital are material income-producing factors. He sets up a self-employed plan for himself, two pharmacists he employs, and a messenger boy. His "self-employment earned income" is $22,000 per year less contributions made by him to the plan for the benefit of those of these three employees who have been full-time nonseasonal employees with three or more years of service. Assuming that amount is $2,000, his earned income for the purpose of computing the limitation on a contribution for his own benefit will be $20,000. This means that he will be able to contribute to the plan on his own behalf $2,000 (because less than $2,500) and deduct that same amount in the year of payment.

STOCK OPTIONS

17.69   In *G. S. Carter*,[12] the Tax Court defined an option as "a contract to keep an offer open for a certain period of time" and cited *Restatement, Contracts*, Sec. 24. There, one day in 1953, the chief executive officer of City Products Corporation offered to sell the taxpayer 300 shares of treasury stock for $8,400. The stock on that day had a market value of $9,487.50. The taxpayer accepted the offer immediately and bought the stock that day. There were no restrictions on the shares. The court held this was a mere purchase-and-sale transaction, not a stock option. As this was a bargain purchase from an employer, the court upheld the Commissioner in taxing $1,087.50 ($9,487.50 − $8,400) as compensation received in the year of purchase of the stock under the authority of Sec. 39.22(a)–1(c) of Reg. 118 now embodied in Reg. 1.61–2(d)(2).

17.70   *Option* is defined in Reg. 1.421–1(a)(1):

> For the purpose of section 421, the term "option" includes the right or privilege of an individual to purchase stock from a corporation by virtue of an offer of the corporation continuing for a stated period of time, whether or not irrevocable, to sell such stock at a price ... such individual being under no obligation to purchase. ...

17.71   An employee stock-option plan is a contractual arrangement between a corporation and one or more of its employees, whereby the employee is given the right to purchase stock of the employer. The employee may benefit from such a plan by being given an opportunity to buy stock at a price below market or by being given the opportunity to participate in the increase in market value of the employer's stock without being required to make an investment until he exercises his option. Stock-option plans may be used to allow key personnel to participate in the growth of the company and to provide additional compensation, which, under certain circumstances, may be taxed to them at capital-gains rates. Such plans have little attraction for an executive in a closely held company. There is no market for the stock, and possession will carry little incentive value unless the corporation or other stockholders are somehow committed to retire the stock. In addition, the value of the stock may not be ascertainable with any degree of accuracy. Some relief is now given, but it results in ordinary income to the employee involved in the year the stock option is exercised.

17.72   There are two categories of stock-option plans: statutory and non-statutory. Statutory stock options consist of *qualified* stock options as defined in Code Sec. 422, employee stock-purchase plans as defined in Code Sec. 423, and *restricted* stock options as defined in Code Sec. 424. All other stock options are nonstatutory.

12. 36 T.C. 128 (1961).

Statutory Stock Options

Restricted Stock Options and Employee Stock-Purchase Plans. Re-   17.73
stricted stock options came into existence in 1950 when Congress
inserted Sec. 130A in the 1939 Code. Upon enactment of the 1954
Code it became Sec. 421. In 1964 Congress thought it had been too
liberal back in 1950, and it created the *qualified* stock option. No
new restricted stock-option plans for key employees can be adopted
after January 1, 1964, but restricted stock options can be granted in
1964 and later years if granted pursuant to certain written contracts
entered into before 1964 [Code Sec. 424(c)(3)]. Between 1950 and
1963 a number of corporations utilized the restricted stock-option
provisions to set up *employee stock-purchase plans* for broad groups
of employees of all employees. The Revenue Act of 1964 set up
special rules for such plans in Code Sec. 423, such rules being concerned principally with nondiscrimination and broad distribution
of the benefits.

Under the expiring class of restricted stock options, it was possible   17.74
for an executive to purchase stock at 85 percent of its market value on
the date the option was granted and to sell for long-term capital gain
income (except for a small amount) after holding the stock for as little
as six months, provided he purchased the stock no less than one and
one-half years after the grant date [Code Sec. 424(a)(1)].

Qualified Stock Options. The provisions pertaining to qualified stock   17.75
options continue many of the restrictions applicable to restricted stock
options but are more stringent concerning price and holding period:

1. The option price must be at least equal to the fair market value of
   the stock at the time the option is granted.
2. If an option is exercised and there was a failure in good faith of the
   option price to have equaled 100 percent of fair market value at the
   time of granting it, the individual must report as ordinary income in
   the taxable year of exercise of the option, the lesser of:
   (a) 150 percent of the difference between cost and fair market value
       at the time of option grant, or
   (b) the difference between cost and fair market value at time of exer-
       cise of the option.
   This provision was added to the 1964 Revenue Act in an attempt to
   make the benefits of stock options applicable to the employees of
   closely held corporations. While the provision adds some relief to
   employees of corporations whose stock is not listed, the problem of
   valuation of nontraded stock has not been solved.
3. The option must be granted in connection with employment by a
   corporation and such employment must be continuous. The option
   must be granted by the employer corporation or its parent or a subsidiary to purchase stock in any such corporation. Exceptions are
   provided under certain conditions in connection with certain corporate reorganizations, acquisitions, and liquidations.
4. An individual, immediately after the option is granted, may not own
   stock representing more than 5 percent of the combined voting stock

or value of all classes of stock of the employer corporation or its parent or subsidiary corporation.

5. The option by its terms must not be exercisable by an individual while there is outstanding a *qualified* stock option or *restricted* stock option previously granted to him by the employer corporation or predecessor corporation or certain other related corporations. There are certain exceptions to this general rule.

6. The option must be granted within ten years of the date on which the plan is adopted, or the date of approval by the stockholders, whichever is earlier.

7. The option by its terms must be exercised not later than five years from the date it was granted.

8. The option by its terms must not be transferable by the optionee otherwise than by will or the laws of descent and distribution, and must be exercised during his lifetime only by him.

9. The option stock must not be disposed of by the employee within three years after the day of transfer of the stock.

10. At the time the employee exercises the option, he must be an employee of either the corporation granting the option or its parent or subsidiary, and such employment must have been continuous. (Exception is made under certain conditions in connection with certain corporate reorganizations, acquisitions, and liquidations.) A grace period of three months after termination of employment is permitted.

Nonstatutory Stock Options

17.76   As indicated above, a nonstatutory stock option is any compensatory option given to an employee or independent contractor if the option does not meet the requirements of Code Sec. 422, 423, and 424 pertaining to qualified stock options, employee stock-purchase plans, and restricted stock options.

17.77   There is an element of compensation in every employee stock option, nonstatutory as well as statutory. In the case of the nonstatutory option, however, the employer is allowed a deduction for the element of compensation. Corresponding taxability to the employee has not been so well accepted, and taxpayers have fought it on the theories that a nontaxable gift is really involved or that no tax should attach to a transaction that is basically nothing more than the transfer for worthwhile business motives of a proprietary interest in an employer corporation. In *Com.* v. *LoBue* [13] the taxpayer had been granted a series of options to buy stock in his employer. In the corporation's return, the difference between cost of the shares and their market value when delivered was deducted as compensation paid. The Commissioner was seeking to tax this same amount to the employee-taxpayer as compensation received. The U.S. Supreme Court said:

We have repeatedly held that in defining "gross income" as broadly as it did in § 22(a) [now Sec. 61(a)], Congress intended to "tax all gains except those specifically exempted." ... The only exemption Congress provided

13. 351 U.. 243 (1956), 49 AFTR 832, 56–2 USTC ¶9607.

from this very comprehensive definition of taxable income that could possibly have application here is the gift exemption of § 22(b)(3). But there was not the slightest indication of the kind of detached and disinterested generosity which might evidence a "gift" in the statutory sense. These transfers of stock bore none of the earmarks of a gift. They were made by a company engaged in operating a business for profit, and the Tax Court found that the stock option plan was designed to achieve more profitable operations by providing the employees "with an incentive to promote the growth of the Company by permitting them to participate in its success." 22 T.C. at 445. ... Under these circumstances the Tax Court and the Court of Appeals properly refrained from treating this transfer as a gift. The Company was not giving something away for nothing.

. . .

... When assets are transferred by an employer to an employee to secure better services they are plainly compensation. It makes no difference that the compensation is paid in stock rather than in money. Section 22(a) taxes income derived from compensation "in whatever form paid." And in another stock option case we said that § 22(a) "is broad enough to include in taxable income any economic or financial benefit conferred on the employee as compensation, whatever the form or mode by which it is effected." *Commissioner* v. *Smith*, 324 U.S. 177, 181. ... LoBue received a very substantial economic and financial benefit from his employer prompted by the employer's desire to get better work from him. This is "compensation for personal service" within the meaning of § 22(a). LoBue nonetheless argues that we should treat this transaction as a mere purchase of a proprietary interest on which no taxable gain was "realized" in the year of purchase. It is true that our taxing system has ordinarily treated an arm's-length purchase of property even at a bargain price as giving rise to no taxable gain in the year of purchase. See *Palmer* v. *Commissioner*, 302 U.S. 63, 69 [37–2 USTC para. 9532]. But that is not to say that when a transfer which is in reality compensation is given the form of a purchase the Government cannot tax the gain under § 22(a). The transaction here was unlike a mere purchase. It was not an arm's-length transaction between strangers. Instead, it was an arrangement by which an employer transferred valuable property to his employees in recognition of their services. We hold that LoBue realized taxable gain when he purchased the stock.

LoBue gave his employer promissory notes for the option price of the shares, but the shares were not delivered until the notes were paid in cash. The market value of the shares was lower when the notes were given than when the cash was paid. The Supreme Court held that because the options were not transferable, the gain should be measured not as of the grant date but as of the time the options were exercised. It then remanded the case to the Court of Appeals with directions to remand it to the Tax Court to determine whether the delivery of the promissory notes marked the completion of the stock purchase and thereby determined the exercise date. On remand, the Tax Court held[14] that LoBue exercised his option when he gave his unconditional notes for the shares.   **17.78**

Under Reg. 1.421–6, there are a number of dates upon which an employee who receives an option to purchase stock may realize ordinary   **17.79**

14. 28 T.C. 1317 (1957), affirmed *per curiam* 256 F.2d 735 (3rd Cir., 1958).

taxable income. The particular date applicable depends upon the circumstances.

17.80   If the option itself has a readily ascertainable fair market value when granted, the employee receiving that option is treated as realizing compensation on the date of the grant in an amount equal to the excess, if any, of the fair market value of the option over any amount paid for such option. Detailed provisions are set forth defining what will constitute a readily ascertainable fair market value. These provisions are so strict that an employee of a closely held corporation will almost never be able to show that an option received by him had a readily ascertainable fair market value on the date he received it. An employee of a corporation whose shares of stock are listed on an exchange or actively traded over-the-counter, will also have much difficulty in proving a value for the option unless the option is freely transferable and similar options are actively traded on an established market, as might be the case for stock warrants or stock rights. If the unusual happens and the employee can prove that an option has a readily ascertainable fair market value when granted, he realizes compensation income only on the date of the receipt of the option, and he is not deemed to realize any additional ordinary income upon exercise of the option. Any gain realized by such a person upon a sale or exchange of the stock acquired would be capital gain, long- or short-term as the case may be.

17.81   Section 83 of the Code was inserted by the Tax Reform Act of 1969. It applies to restricted stock and restricted property conveyed in exchange for services. The restrictions pertain to value, transferability, or forfeiture. An option is property, but Section 83(e) provides that the section shall not apply to "the transfer of property pursuant to the exercise of an option with a readily ascertainable market value at the date of grant." Accordingly, if the option is in the form of stock warrants which are traded on an exchange or over the counter on the date of grant, the exercise of the warrant will not bring Section 83 into operation, and it probably will never apply because it is unlikely that the stock received would have any restrictions on it.

17.82   Section 83(e) also states the section shall not apply to "the transfer of an option without a readily ascertainable fair market value." The "transfer of an option" means a sale or other disposition of the option contract itself. The term does not include the exercise of the option. Accordingly, if an option without a readily ascertainable fair market value is exercised, and the stock or other property received contains restrictions affecting value, transferability, or forfeiture, Section 83 does apply starting with the date of exercise.

17.83   Regulation 1.421–6(d) provides that the grant of an option without an ascertainable fair market value does not result in compensation income on the date of grant. Then Reg. 1.83–1 and 1.83–7, as proposed June 3, 1971, point out the dates and measures of taxability.

17.84   On date of exercise of the option, if the stock or other property received has no restrictions affecting value, disposition, or required holding period, compensation income is realized in the amount of the difference between the fair market value of the stock or other property received and the price paid.

If an option does not have an ascertainable fair market value before exercise and the stock or other property received does have restrictions, compensation income will be realized on either one of two dates:

1. When the stock to be received is freely transferable and not subject to any condition requiring future performance of substantial services, the employee realizes income on the date he exercises the option, provided that on such date of exercise he obtains an unconditional right to receive the stock subject only to the performance by him of an act, such as making payment, which he can do at any time.
2. When the stock to be received is not freely transferable and is subject to a condition requiring future performance of substantial services, income is realized only on the date the first of these restrictions lapses.

The amount of the compensation income is the excess of the fair market value of the stock (determined without regard to any restriction other than a restriction which by its terms will never lapse) on the respective dates mentioned above over the amount (if any) paid for the stock.

EXAMPLE

On October 1, 1970, a corporation grants to Jones, its executive vice-president, an option to purchase 1,000 shares of its stock at a price of $10 per share. The option is for a period of five years and is not transferable. Further, upon exercise of the option the certificate for the shares will be indorsed with a statement that the shares cannot be sold to anyone other than the corporation for a period less than three years from the date of the certificate and then only at book value as of the latest fiscal year-end of the corporation. There is no requirement in the option agreement that Jones perform future services. Jones exercises his option on October 1, 1972, and purchases the 1,000 shares on that date. The respective fair market values of each share were as follows: $11 on date of grant, $15 on date of exercise, and $14 on October 15, 1972, the date of the stock certificate, and $16 on October 16, 1975. The book value per share on date of the certificate was $9 and on October 16, 1975, was $12. The amount of compensation income is measured by the fair market value on date of exercise because the book value restriction will lapse at the end of three years. Accordingly, he has compensation income of $5,000 ($15 fair market value less $10 price = $5 × 1,000 shares = $5,000).

17.86

The employer is entitled to a deduction for compensation paid in the amount of whatever the compensation element is which is taxable to the recipient of a nonstatutory stock option, and the time of deduction is the taxable year of the employer in which or with which ends the taxable year of the recipient in which the amount was taxed. Section 83(h).

QUESTIONS AND PROBLEMS

1. The Black Corporation establishes a contributory pension trust plan in which all full-time employees with three years of service are eligible

to participate. Each employee who elects to participate must contribute 5 percent of his basic annual wages not including any payments for overtime or bonuses. There are 420 eligible employees of whom 300 earn less than $10,800 per year. Of these 300 only fifty elect to join the plan. Of the remaining 120 employees making $10,800 or more per year, all twenty supervisors and officers join plus eighty of the others. Can the plan be a qualified one?

2. An accrual and calendar-year basis corporation had created a qualified pension plan for its employees. It secured an extension to June 15, 1973, within which to file its corporation income tax return for the calendar year 1972. On June 2, 1973, it filed the return and in it claimed a deduction for a correctly computed accrued liability to the plan of $75,000. That amount was then paid to the trustee under the plan on June 10, 1973. Was the amount properly deductible in the 1972 return?

3. In 1971 a corporation set up a trusteed profit-sharing plan covering all employees and secured a determination letter from the local District Director of Internal Revenue that it qualified under Section 401. For that year the payroll was $200,000 and the contribution was $24,-000. For 1972 the payroll was $240,000 and the contribution was $50,000. For 1973 the payroll was $300,000 and the contribution was $25,000. What amount is deductible each year?

4. Mr. Easter retired from the employ of a corporation on January 1, 1972, following his sixty-fifth birthday. He was a participant in a qualified contributory pension trust and commencing with January, 1972, started receiving a monthly pension of $300. His life expectancy on date of retirement was fifteen years. During his years of employment he contributed a total of $6,000 into the plan. What is the amount of his taxable pension income for each of the years 1972, 1973, 1974, and 1975?

5. In 1967, the taxpayer's employer granted him an option to purchase ten shares of its stock for $100 per share. The fair market value of the stock was then $100 per share. The option, which could not be transferred, had to be exercised within five years and while the taxpayer was still employed by the corporation.

In January, 1970, the taxpayer purchased ten shares of stock under the option. Previously he had not owned any of his employer's stock. The fair market value of the stock at that time was $110 per share.

In February, 1973, the taxpayer sold the stock for $130 per share.

a. What income, if any, did the taxpayer have to report in 1967?

b. What income, if any, was recognized in 1970?

c. Determine the gain from the sale of the stock in 1973. Specify what part, if any, is reportable as ordinary income.

d. Suppose that he sold all of the shares in December, 1972, instead of in February, 1973. Would your answers to (a), (b), and (c) be any different?

6. What are the differences between a qualified employee stock purchase plan and a qualified stock option plan? (a) qualified stock options, (b) restricted stock options, (c) qualified employee stock purchase plans, (d) nonstatutory stock options, (e) purchase from a corporation by an employee of treasury shares for more than their cost to the corporation but less than their market value on the date of purchase? The answer is not in the textbook, but it can be ascertained from the Code.

7. Are the following stock options—(a) a convertible bond, (b) shares of preferred stock convertible into common, (c) stock warrants, (d) a

stock subscription agreement at the time of organization of a corporation, (e) a duly authorized letter from a corporation addressed to ten
of its executives granting them the right to purchase shares of another
company which are owned by the corporation issuing the letter?

8. If a freely transferable and nonforfeitable option is issued by a closely
   held corporation to a new executive, ordinarily when will compensation income result? Why? How should its amount be determined?

9. Assume the same facts as in the example in paragraph 17.85, with the
   respective separate exceptions noted below, and in each instance give
   the amount of the compensation element and the year of taxability:
   (a) The book value restriction is to be binding forever on Jones, his
       executor, administrator, heirs, and assigns.
   (b) There is no book value restriction.
   (c) There is no book value restriction but a requirement that the
       shares cannot be transferred to anyone (other than to the corpora-
       tion for $10 per share) until after October 15, 1975, and then only
       if Jones remains in full-time employment until that date.

10. Do tax preference items for the calculation of the minimum tax on
    tax preferences result and in what amount, from (a) qualified stock
    options, (b) restricted stock options, (c) qualified employee stock
    purchase plans, (d) nonstatutory stock options, (e) purchase from a
    corporation by an employee of treasury shares for more than their cost
    to the corporation but less than their market value on the date of
    purchase? The answer is not in the textbook, but can be ascertained
    from the Code.

18

PARTNERSHIPS

TAX CONCEPT . . . 643
DEFINITION . . . 644
FORMATION . . . 645

No Recognition of Gain or Loss on Contribution of Property to a
  Partnership . . . 645
Carry-Over Basis of Property . . . 646
Basis of Partner's Interest in Partnership . . . 646

OPERATIONS . . . 647

Determination of Taxable Income . . . 647

PARTNERSHIP TAXABLE YEAR . . . 647

TERMINATION . . . 648

ELECTIONS . . . 649
PASS-THROUGH OF SPECIAL ITEMS . . . 649

Partner's Distributive Share . . . 650

EFFECT OF PARTNERSHIP AGREEMENT . . . 650
EFFECT OF TAX-AVOIDANCE MOTIVE . . . 650
LIMITATION ON PARTNER'S SHARE OF LOSS . . . 651

Transactions between Partner and Partnership . . . 651

PARTNERS' SALARIES AND OTHER GUARANTEED PAYMENTS . . . 651
GAINS AND LOSSES ON SALES OF PROPERTY . . . 651

SALE OR EXCHANGE OF PARTNERSHIP INTEREST . . . 652

Unrealized Receivables and Inventory . . . 652

DISTRIBUTIONS FROM PARTNERSHIPS . . . 653

Recognition of Gain or Loss . . . 653
Partner's Basis in Property Received . . . 654

FAMILY PARTNERSHIPS . . . 655
SPREAD SHEET FOR PARTNERSHIP INCOME TAX RETURN . . . 655

Assumed Facts . . . 656
Reconciling Items between Book and Tax Income . . . 656
Income and Expense Groupings for Tax Return Presentation . . . 657
Allocations to Partners . . . 657

TAX CONCEPT

In chapter 4, paragraphs 4.21 through 4.28, the tax concepts of partnerships are introduced, and those paragraphs should be read again at this time. As indicated there, a partnership is a unique entity for tax purposes. Although it does not pay tax as such, it is an important vehicle for determining the taxable income or loss of its partners. A partnership is required to calculate its taxable income or loss and file an information return on Form 1065. For this purpose, a partnership must establish its own taxable year and its own accounting method. Items of income and expense that do not require separate consideration in the returns of the partners are combined in the partnership return to determine the partnership's taxable income or loss. This taxable income or loss is then allocated to the partners. All items that have separate tax significance or require separate tax treatment at the partner level are segregated in the partnership return and allocated individually to partners.

Each partner reports in his own return his share of the partnership's taxable income or loss and his share of each partnership item that is separately allocated. These amounts are reported by each partner in his taxable year with which or within which the partnership year ends without regard to when or if the partnership income is actually paid out to him.

Prior to 1954 much confusion existed about whether partnerships should be treated as separate entities for tax purposes or as mere aggregations of taxpayers. Under the "entity" concept transactions between a partnership and one of its partners would be treated the same as transactions between the partnership and outsiders. Under the "aggregate" concept, such transactions would be looked through and considered for tax purposes as transactions between only the dealing partner and the other partners. Accordingly, if a partner sold property to a partnership in which he owned a one-third interest, he would be considered for tax purposes as selling only two-thirds of his interest (the portion going to his partners). Subchapter K of the 1954 Code sets forth many specific tax rules that attempt to clarify the tax effect of partnership transactions. In some cases these rules apply the entity concept and in others the aggregate concept. The complexities of these applications make the understanding of partnership taxation very interesting and sometimes quite difficult. A wise professor once advised his students that accounting problems of partnerships should be approached with great caution, because they often appear to be so simple, when in reality they are so extremely complex.[1] This advice is particularly relevant today to tax problems of partnerships.

1. John H. Newlove, in lecture to accounting class at The University of Texas at Austin in 1948.

DEFINITION

18.4   The definition of a partnership for income tax purposes is considerably broader than the common-law definition. Section 761(a) defines a partnership as follows:

> For purposes of this subtitle, the term "partnership" includes a syndicate, group, pool, joint venture, or other unincorporated organization through or by means of which any business, financial operation, or venture is carried on, and which is not, within the meaning of this title, a corporation or a trust or estate.

Because associations are taxed as corporations, they are not partnerships for tax purposes, even though they may be under local law.

18.5   Not all joint undertakings are partnerships. Regulation 1.761–1(a)(1) provides in part:

> ... A joint undertaking merely to share expenses is not a partnership. For example, if two or more persons jointly construct a ditch merely to drain surface water from their properties, they are not partners. Mere coownership of property which is maintained, kept in repair, and rented or leased does not constitute a partnership. For example, if an individual owner, or tenants in common, of farm property lease it to a farmer for a cash rental or a share of the crops, they do not necessarily create a partnership thereby. Tenants in common, however, may be partners if they actively carry on a trade, business, financial operation, or venture and divide the profits thereof. For example, a partnership exists if coowners of an apartment building lease space and in addition provide services to the occupants either directly or through an agent.

18.6   Section 761 grants an elective exclusion to certain partnerships availed of (1) solely for investment purposes, or (2) solely for the joint production, extraction, or use of property, but not for the purpose of jointly selling services or property so produced or extracted. The regulations call the first type of organization an investing partnership and the second type an operating agreement. The pertinent provisions of Reg. 1.761–1(a)(2) are:

> (ii) *Investing partnership.* Where the participants in the joint purchase, retention, sale, or exchange of investment property—
>   (a) Own the property as coowners,
>   (b) Reserve the right separately to take or dispose of their shares of any property acquired or retained, and
>   (c) Do not actively conduct business or irrevocably authorize some person or persons acting in a representative capacity to purchase, sell, or exchange such investment property, although each separate participant may delegate authority to purchase, sell, or exchange his share of any such investment property for the time being for his account, but not for a period of more than a year, then
> such group may be excluded from the application of the provisions of subchapter K. ...

(iii) *Operating agreements*. Where the participants in the joint production, extraction, or use of property—

(a) Own the property as coowners, either in fee or under lease or other form of contract granting exclusive operating rights, and

(b) Reserve the right separately to take in kind or dispose of their shares of any property produced, extracted, or used, and

(c) Do not jointly sell services or the property produced or extracted, although each separate participant may delegate authority to sell his share of the property produced or extracted for the time being for his account, but not for a period of time in excess of the minimum needs of the industry, and in no event for more than one year, then

such group may be excluded from the application of the provisions of subchapter K. ...

However, the preceding sentence does not apply to any unincorporated organization one of whose principal purposes is cycling, manufacturing, or processing for persons who are not members of the organization.

These elective exclusions are used extensively by investment groups and groups engaged in the joint development of natural resources.

FORMATION

For tax purposes, the formation of a partnership does not require the execution of a formal partnership agreement. Although some partnerships are formed in this manner, many are not. Any substantive arrangement between two or more taxpayers which results in a relationship between the parties that qualifies as a partnership under the definition of Section 761(a) will be treated for tax purposes as the formation of a partnership. The act of forming a partnership ordinarily does not have any tax consequences. These ordinarily arise when property is transferred to the partnership. **18.7**

No Recognition of Gain or Loss on Contribution of Property to a Partnership

No gain or loss is recognized for tax purposes when a partner contributes property to the capital of a partnership. This is true whether the contribution occurs at the inception of the partnership or at a later time (Section 721). **18.8**

If a partner renders services to a partnership in exchange for an interest in the partnership capital, the regulations indicate that income will be recognized to that partner in an amount equal to the fair market value of the capital interest received [Reg. 1.721–1(b)(1)]. The income will be recognized to the partner at such time as the interest in the capital is transferred to him, provided that there then exists no substantial restriction on his right to withdraw or dispose of such capital interest. **18.9**

The cited regulation states that a partner will be deemed to have received an interest in partnership capital in exchange for services **18.10** whenever any other partner gives up any part of his right to be repaid his contributions in favor of the partner rendering the services.

Carry-Over Basis of Property

18.11   Since no gain or loss is recognized to a partner on the contribution of property to the capital of a partnership, the partnership's tax basis of the property for calculation of gain, loss, depreciation, or depletion is the same as the partner's adjusted basis in the property immediately before the transfer (Section 723). The partnership's holding period of a contributed asset includes the period the asset was held by a partner prior to the time he contributed it to the partnership (Reg. 1.723–1).

Basis of Partner's Interest in Partnership

18.12   For tax purposes, a partner's interest in a partnership is considered to be an asset that can be sold, exchanged, or otherwise disposed of by the partner (Section 741). Accordingly, such partnership interest has a basis for purposes of determining gain or loss that is separate and apart from the partnership's basis in its assets. Further, the basis of a partner's interest in a partnership is determined without regard to any amount shown in the partnership books as the partner's "capital," "equity," or similar account. The basis of a partner's interest in a partnership is equal to the sum of the consideration paid for his interest, any cash contributed to the partnership, and his basis in any property contributed (Sections 722 and 742).

EXAMPLE   A contributes property with an adjusted basis to him of $400 and a value of $1,000. B contributes $1,000 cash. Although the partnership's books may show that each has a capital account of $1,000, the basis of A's interest is only $400 and B's interest, $1,000.

18.13   By reason of Section 705(a) the partner's basis must be adjusted for certain items and transactions occurring during the holding period of the partnership interest, as follows:

1. Increased by the sum of his distributive share of
   (a) Taxable income of the partnership
   (b) Exempt income of the partnership
   (c) The excess of the deductions for depletion over the partnership's basis of property subject to the depletion
2. Increased by any additional capital contributions
3. Decreased (but not below zero) by
   (a) Distributions received from the partnership
   (b) His distributive share of losses of the partnership
   (c) His distributive share of expenditures of the partnership which are not deductible for tax purposes and are not capital expenditures

Further, under Section 752 for all purposes except sale or exchange of a partnership interest, a partner's share of increases and decreases in partnership liabilities is treated as an adjustment of the basis of his partnership interest.

If it is not practicable to determine the adjusted basis of a partnership interest under the above method, an alternative method may be used under which the adjusted basis is determined by reference to the partner's share of the partnership's adjusted basis in its assets [Section 705(b); Reg. 1.705–1(b)].

OPERATIONS

After a partnership is formed and begins operations, its more significant tax considerations relate to the determination of its taxable income (or loss), the determination of the partners' distributive shares of such income, and the determination of any particular tax consequences from transactions between the partners and the partnership.

Determination of Taxable Income

Partnership taxable income or loss generally is determined according to tax rules applicable to individuals [Section 703(a)]. However, no deduction is allowed for items of a personal nature, such as the standard deduction, medical and dental expenses, alimony, personal moving expenses, personal exemptions, foreign taxes, and expenses for care of certain dependents. Furthermore, because charitable contributions and net operating losses must be calculated at the level of the individual taxpayer, they are not deductible in calculating partnership net income. A partner's share of any of these items paid by the partnership should be allocated separately to the partners and each partner then considers them in his own tax return. Before being allocated to partners, however, the amounts of these items, plus items of income and expense entering into the taxable-income calculation, must be determined at the partnership level in accordance with the partnership's taxable year, method of accounting, and other elective procedures.

Partnership Taxable Year. As an entity for computing taxable income, a partnership is required to establish its own taxable year. The taxable year of the partnership is quite significant to the partners because each partner reports his distributive share of partnership income (whether or not distributed to him) in his own taxable year with, or within, which the taxable year of the partnership closes [Section 706(a)]. Unless a partnership had established its taxable year prior to 1954, or unless it obtains permission from the Commissioner of Internal Revenue to use some other taxable year, it is required to use the same taxable year as that of *all* its "principal" partners. For this purpose, a principal partner is one having an interest of 5 percent or more in partnership profits or capital. If all the principal partners of a partnership do not use the same taxable year, the partnership must either adopt a calendar year or obtain permission from the Commissioner of Internal Revenue to use some other year. See also paragraph 13.8. A partnership may change its taxable year, provided that permission to make such a change is obtained from the Commissioner of Internal Revenue.[2] If a partner disposes of his entire interest in a partnership by sale or exchange, the taxable year of the partnership closes with respect to that partner, but only as to him, on the date of such disposition [Section 706(c)]. That partner reports his distributive share of the partnership's taxable income for the period ending with the date of such disposition in his taxable year that includes that date. If the partnership uses a taxable year different from that of the partner, this can result in a bunching of income in one calendar year.

EXAMPLE   A partnership reports its income on the basis of a fiscal year ending January 31. In a particular calendar year, one member of the firm who owns a 30 percent interest sells or exchanges his entire interest on November 30. For that calendar year the individual will report his share of the firm's income for the twelve months ended January 31 and also his share of its income for the ten months ended November 30. As a result, in one calendar year he will be taxed on twenty-two months of income. However, the partnership itself will continue to use a January 31 fiscal year, so that the persons continuing as members of the firm will not be affected by the withdrawal of the one partner.

18.18   If a partner retires from his firm under a liquidation arrangement, although under local law he may cease to be a partner on the date of his retirement, for tax purposes he will be treated as remaining a partner until his interest in the partnership has been completely liquidated [Reg. 1.736–1(a)(1)(ii)]. Not until the date of the final liquidating payment will the partnership year close as to him. Reverting to the preceding example, one sees that if the partner, instead of selling or exchanging his interest, transferred it to the firm for liquidation on November 30, but then did not receive his last liquidating distribution until the following January, the partnership year as to him would not close until that January and there would be no bunching of income.

18.19   TERMINATION. The foregoing discussion points up the fact that ordinarily nothing should be done to cause two profitable taxable periods to end in the same calendar year. If a partnership is terminated, its taxable year ends on the date of termination. The Internal Revenue Code and not local law governs whether or not a partnership has terminated. As recited in Section 706(c)(1), unless a partnership is terminated, its taxable year does not close as the result of the death of a partner, the admission of a new partner, the retirement of a partner, or the sale or exchange of a partner's interest. Under Section 708(b) a partnership is terminated if (1) it ceases to carry on any business or (2) 50 percent or more of the total interest in partnership capital is sold or exchanged within a period of twelve consecutive months. There are special provisions for consolidations and divisions of partnerships.

2. Most calendar year partnerships can secure permission to use a year ending no earlier than September 30. See Rev. Proc. 72–51.

Upon the death of one partner in a two-member partnership, the   18.20
partnership is not considered terminated if the estate or other suc-
cessor-in-interest continues to share in the profits or losses of the partnership business [Reg. 1.708–1(b)(1)(i)(a)].

Elections. All elections affecting the computation of partnership taxa-   18.21
ble income must be made by the partnership except for the election
to treat foreign income taxes as a credit or as a deduction and for the
elections under Sections 615 and 617 relating to mining exploration
expenditures [Section 703(b)]. In this connection, Reg. 1.703–1(b)
provides:

(1) General rule. Any elections (other than those described in subparagraph (2) of this paragraph) affecting the computation of income derived from
a partnership shall be made by the partnership. For example, elections of
methods of accounting, of computing depreciation, of treating soil- and water-
conservation expenditures, of treating exploration expenditures, and the option to deduct as expenses intangible drilling and development costs, shall be
made by the partnership and not by the partners separately. All partnership
elections are applicable to all partners equally, but any election made by a
partnership shall not apply to any partner's nonpartnership interests.

(2) *Exceptions.* (i) Each partner shall add his distributive share of taxes
described in Section 901 paid or accrued by the partnership to foreign countries or possessions of the United States (according to its method of treating
such taxes) to any such taxes paid or accrued by him (according to his method
of treating such taxes) and may elect to use the total amount either as a credit
against tax or as a deduction from income.

(ii) Each partner shall add his distributive share of expenses described in
Section 615 [pre-1970 mining exploration expenditures] or Section 617 [de-
duction and recapture of certain mining exploration expenditures] paid or
accrued by the partnership to any such expenses paid or accrued by him and
shall treat the total amount according to his method of treating such expenses,
notwithstanding the treatment of the expenses by the partnership.

Pass-Through of Special Items. After being calculated at the partner-   18.22
ship level, all items that are subject to limitation or special treatment
dependent on other items in a partner's return are excluded from
partnership taxable income and allocated separately to partners.
Some of these items are specified in Sections 702 and 703, and are
listed in paragraph 18.16; however, Reg. 1.702–1(a)(8)(ii) expands this
list as follows:

(ii) Each partner must also take into account separately his distributive
share of any partnership item which if separately taken into account by any
partner would result in an income tax liability for that partner different from
that which would result if that partner did not take the item into account
separately. Thus, if any partner would qualify for the retirement income
credit under Section 37 if the partnership pensions and annuities, interest,
rents, dividends, and earned income were separately stated, such items must
be separately stated for all partners. Under Section 911(a), if any partner is
a bona fide resident of a foreign country who may exclude from his gross
income the part of his distributive share which qualifies as earned income as
defined in Section 911(b), the earned income of the partnership for all
partners must be separately stated. Similarly, all relevant items of income or

deduction for the partnership must be separately stated for all partners in determining the applicability of Section 270 (relating to "hobby losses") and the recomputation of tax thereunder for any partner.

18.23   Pursuant to these rules, separate classification and allocation to partners is required for deductions subject to special elections, limitations, or recapture, such as foreign income taxes, medical expenses, charitable contributions, moving expenses, and farm losses. Similar treatment is required for income items such as capital gains and losses, gains and losses subject to Section 1231, and gains and losses on farm recapture property. Items of tax preference on which the minimum tax of 10 percent is imposed must also be calculated for each partner.

18.24   As the tax laws grow more complex, and the multitude of special applications increase, it appears the number of partnership items that require separate allocation will continue to increase.

Partner's Distributive Share

18.25   The share of the partnership's taxable income, loss, deduction, or credit that is reportable for tax purposes by any given partner is referred to as that partner's distributive share.

18.26   **Effect of Partnership Agreement.** Each partner's distributive share of any item of the partnership is determined in accordance with the partnership agreement [Section 704(a)]. The partnership agreement may be in writing or it may be oral, and the arrangement may be formal or informal. Furthermore, if the partnership agreement is amended for any taxable year, the amendment will be recognized for that year provided it is made prior to the due date (without extensions) of the partnership return [Reg. 1.761–1(c)]. The partnership agreement may provide a single ratio for the sharing of all items of income, deduction, gain, loss, or credit of the partnership; or it may provide different ratios for different items. The ratio for sharing profits need not necessarily be the same as the ratio for sharing losses. If the partnership agreement does not provide specifically for the sharing of any item, that item will be shared in accordance with the ratio provided for taxable income generally. Unless a tax-avoidance motive is involved, as discussed in the following paragraphs, any bona fide agreement among the partners on the sharing of items will be effective for tax purposes.

18.27   **Effect of Tax-Avoidance Motive.** If avoidance or evasion of tax is the principal purpose of any provision of a partnership agreement providing for the allocation between partners of a particular item of partnership income, deduction, or credit, such provision will be ignored for tax purposes. In that event, the particular item will be allocated to the partners in accordance with the ratio applicable to taxable income in general [Section 704(b); Reg. 1.704–1(b)(2)].

Limitation on Partner's Share of Loss. A partner's deduction for his   18.28
share of a partnership taxable loss is limited to the adjusted basis of
his partnership interest at the end of the partnership year in which the
loss is incurred [Section 704(d) and Reg. 1.704–1(d)], and his share of
the loss correspondingly reduces his basis. In this connection, the
partner's basis of his partnership interest includes his share of any
liabilities of the partnership [Section 752]. A partner's share of any
loss that is not deductible because of this limitation may be deducted
by the partner in succeeding years to the extent of the partner's adjusted basis in his partnership interest at the end of those years
[Section 704(d)].

Transactions between Partner and Partnership

When a partner enters into a transaction with a partnership other   18.29
than in his capacity as a partner, the transaction ordinarily is treated
the same as a transaction between the partnership and one who is not
a partner [Section 707(a)]; however, certain special rules have been
provided to prevent tax avoidance.

Partners' Salaries and Other Guaranteed Payments. Payments to   18.30
partners determined without regard to partnership income, such as
salaries and other payments for services rendered to the partnership
and interest payments for the use of partners' capital, are referred to
in the Code as "guaranteed payments." They are treated as income to
the partners and deductions in determining taxable income of the
partnership [Section 707(c)]. A partner is required to report his guaranteed payments in the same taxable year in which he reports his
share of the related partnership income, that is, his taxable year with
or within which ends the partnership taxable year in which such guaranteed payments are deductible [Reg. 1.707–1(c)].

A partner's receipt of a salary or other guaranteed payment does   18.31
not entitle him to treatment as an employee for purposes such as the
sick pay exclusion of Section 105(d), participation in a qualified
profit-sharing plan or pension plan, or withholding taxes [Reg.
1.707–1(c)].

Gains and Losses on Sales of Property. As a general rule, gains and   18.32
losses on sales of property between a partnership and a partner are
recognized for tax purposes in the same way as those between unrelated parties. Two exceptions to this general rule are discussed
below.

First, losses are not deductible when incurred on sales or ex-   18.33
changes of property between a partnership and partner who owns directly or indirectly more than 50 percent of the capital or profits
interest of the partnership or between two partnerships if the same
partners own directly or indirectly more than 50 percent of the capital
or profits interest of both. If the property is subsequently sold at a
gain by the transferee, his or its gain will be recognized for tax pur-

poses only to the extent that it exceeds the loss previously disallowed under this rule [Section 707(b)(1)].

18.34   Second, gain on the sale of property between a partnership and a partner or between two partnerships will be treated as ordinary income rather than capital gain if the property will not be a capital asset in the hands of the transferee and if one of the following circumstances exists:

1. The partner owns directly or indirectly 80 percent or more of the capital interest or profits interest in the partnership.
2. The two partnerships have more than 80 percent of the capital or profits interest of each owned by the same persons [Section 707(b)(2)].

For this purpose and following the technical definition of capital assets, real or depreciable property used in a trade or business is not considered to be a capital asset [Reg. 1.707–1(b)(2)].

18.35   In determining the ownership of a capital or profits interest in a partnership, a partner's ownership is determined in accordance with the constructive ownership rules set forth in Section 267 [Section 707(b)(3)]. Under these rules, a partner is deemed the owner of a partnership interest owned by certain members of his family. He also can be deemed the owner of a proportionate part of a partnership interest owned by a corporation, another partnership, or an estate or trust in which he has an interest. These indirect ownership rules are quite complex; any situation involving their possible application should be studied with extreme care.

SALE OR EXCHANGE OF PARTNERSHIP INTEREST

18.36   A partner's interest in a partnership is a capital asset, and any gain or loss recognized on the sale, exchange, or liquidation of the partnership interest is treated as a capital gain or loss in most instances (Section 741). To the extent the gain or loss recognized on the sale, exchange, or liquidation of the interest is attributable to the partnership's "unrealized receivables" and/or "substantially appreciated inventory," such gain is treated as ordinary income (Section 751).

Unrealized Receivables and Inventory

18.37   To understand the tax consequences of sales or exchanges of partnership interests and of distributions from partnerships, it is necessary first to have a basic understanding of the partnership tax concepts of unrealized receivables and inventories. Unrealized receivables and inventories generally can be thought of as "ordinary income assets": if they are sold or collected, they would bring ordinary income to the partnership.

18.38   Unrealized receivables include (1) any rights to receive amounts (not previously included in income of a partnership) in payment for services rendered *or to be rendered* and for goods delivered *or to be delivered,* to the extent that such amounts would be treated as ordinary income when received, and (2) any real or depreciable property to the extent that recapture income would be recognized under Sections 617 (mining property), 1245, 1250, 1251, or 1252 if such property were sold by the partnership at its fair market value [Section 751(c)].

The definition of inventory items is very broad and includes (1) property that in the hands of either the partnership or a selling or distributee partner would be inventory, stock in trade, or property held primarily for sale to customers in the ordinary course of the trade or business, and (2) any other property of the partnership that on sale or exchange would not be treated as a capital asset or property described in Section 1231 [Section 751(d)(2)]. **18.39**

From the preceding definitions, it is obvious that almost any property of a partnership that would produce ordinary income if sold by the partnership can be considered as either unrealized receivables or inventory. Special rules relating to unrealized receivables and inventory are found throughout the sections of the code and regulations dealing with sales or exchanges of partnership interests and with distributions from partnerships. Invariably, the purposes and effects of these special rules are (1) to prevent income attributable to these items from being treated as capital gain, and (2) to prevent any increase or "step-up" in tax basis of any of these items on their distribution from a partnership. **18.40**

DISTRIBUTIONS FROM PARTNERSHIPS

The tax consequences of distributions from partnerships involve (1) the recognition of gain or loss to the partnership and to the distributee partner, and (2) the determination of basis of the property distributed to the partners. Sometimes, determination of the partner's basis in property distributed by the partnership is dependent upon whether the distribution is in liquidation of the partner's interest in the partnership. **18.41**

Recognition of Gain or Loss

In the more common cases, gain or loss is not recognized by either the partnership or the partner on the distribution of money or property by a partnership. However, gain is recognized to the partner when he receives money from the partnership in excess of the adjusted basis of his partnership interest. Also, loss is recognized to a partner when a distribution liquidates his partnership interest, the property received consists exclusively of money, unrealized receivables, or inventory, and the partner's basis in his partnership interest exceeds the sum of the money received plus the basis to the partnership of the unrealized receivables and inventory (Section 731). **18.42**

If a partner receives a distribution from his partnership consisting of a disproportionate share of his interest in unrealized receivables or substantially appreciated inventory items and gives up an interest in other property, both the partner and the partnership may be required to recognize gain or loss for tax purposes [Section 751(b)]. Also, gain or loss may be recognized to both if the converse occurs and a **18.43** partner gives up an interest in unrealized receivables or substantially appreciated inventory and receives a disproportionate interest in other property. With certain exceptions such transactions are treated as taxable exchanges between the partner and the partnership. Tax consequences of such transactions are extremely complex and discussion of them is not practicable in this chapter. All students of taxation should be aware that such problems exist, and they should be prepared to research them thoroughly when encountered.

Partner's Basis in Property Received

18.44   If a distribution does not liquidate the partner's interest in the partnership, he treats the distribution as a reduction in the basis of his partnership interest. The amount of such reduction is equal to the amount of any money received plus the partnership's basis in property distributed. As a general rule, a partner's basis in property received from a partnership is the same as the partnership's adjusted basis in that property, but there are two exceptions to this general rule.

18.45   The first exception is that a partner's basis in property received on a distribution from a partnership cannot exceed the amount of his adjusted basis in his partnership interest before the distribution [Section 732(a)(2)]. Accordingly, when the partnership's adjusted basis in distributed property exceeds the partner's adjusted basis in his partnership interest, then the partner's adjusted basis must be allocated over the property received. That allocation is made in the following manner:

1. Basis is first allocated to any money received.
2. Basis is then allocated to unrealized receivables and inventory in amounts equal to the partnership's adjusted basis therein.
3. Any basis remaining is then allocated to other properties received in proportion to the partnership's adjusted basis in such properties.
4. If the partner's adjusted basis in his partnership interest after being reduced by the amount of money received is less than the adjusted basis of the partnership in the unrealized receivables and inventory items, the remaining basis is allocated to the unrealized receivables and inventory items in proportion to their relative adjusted bases to the partnership [Section 732(c)(1)].

18.46   The second exception to the above general rule applies only where a distribution liquidates a partner's interest in the partnership. In such a liquidating distribution, if the partner receives property other than money, unrealized receivables, and inventory the amount of his adjusted basis in his partnership interest must be allocated over the property received, even though such basis is greater than the partnership's adjusted basis in the property distributed. The allocation is made in the same manner as the allocation described in the preceding paragraph. The result is that the partner takes a basis in property other than money, unrealized receivables, or inventory that is greater than the partnership's adjusted basis in such property. It should be noted, however, that his basis in unrealized receivables and inventory is never any more than the adjusted basis of the partnership in such property [Reg. 1.732–1(c)].

At this point it should be noted again that partnership tax rules involving unrealized receivables and inventory effectively prevent any proceeds from sale of such assets from being treated as capital gain. These rules also prevent any step-up in basis of such assets on their distribution from a partnership.

18.47

FAMILY PARTNERSHIPS

Many controversies have developed over the tax consequences of so-called family partnerships. These are partnerships composed of several members of the same immediate family that are used to spread taxable income from a family business among various members of the family, minimizing the effect of the graduated individual tax rates. Because of this obvious tax advantage, family partnerships generally are scrutinized closely by the Internal Revenue Service to make certain that in substance they constitute true partnership arrangements.

18.48

Extensive regulations govern family partnerships [Reg. 1.704–1(e)]. These regulations make it clear that where capital is a material income-producing factor in a family partnership the income of the partnership attributable to such capital is taxable to the true owners of the capital interest in the partnership. Similarly, to the extent partnership income is attributable to services rendered by the partners, the income is taxable to the partners rendering the services. Thus, if the provisions of the family-partnership agreement provide for the sharing of income in a manner that does not properly recognize the value of partners' capital and services, such provisions will be ignored for tax purposes; and the income will be allocated to partners so that it properly reflects such values. Such allocation for tax purposes will also reflect the true ownership of the capital interests of the partnership.

18.49

SPREAD SHEET FOR PARTNERSHIP INCOME TAX RETURN

The partnership federal income tax return (Form 1065) is an information return. If properly prepared, it will give each partner the information he needs to reflect his share of partnership operations in his own income tax return.

18.50

The preparation of a partnership return will invariably involve a number of reclassifications of data shown on the books of the partnership. Ordinarily it also will involve a number of adjustments to convert the book income and expenses to the amounts reportable for federal income tax purposes. Working papers supporting the partnership return should show and explain these reclassifications and adjustments so that the partnership return can be reconciled to the partnership books. To achieve these objectives the use of a tax spread sheet is an invaluable tool.

18.51

18.52   On pages 658–659 is shown an illustration of a typical partnership tax spread sheet. The following paragraphs explain its use.

Assumed Facts

18.53   The spread sheet was prepared in connection with the 1972 federal income tax return of the Jones and Smith Partnership. Jones and Smith are equal partners except for the following items:

1. In 1966 Jones and Smith invested equal amounts of surplus cash in municipal securities and oil and gas royalties. Because of the investment objectives of each, it was agreed that Jones would take all the interest income and any gain or loss on disposition of the municipal securities, and Smith would take all income, depletion, and gains or losses on disposition of the royalties.
2. Part of the partnership's machinery was contributed by partner Smith. This machinery had an adjusted basis to Smith of $15,000, but Smith and Jones agreed that the value thereof for purposes of partnership capital was $20,000. Accordingly, Jones and Smith agreed that 66⅔ percent of the annual depreciation allowable for tax purposes would be allocated to Jones and 33⅓ percent would be allocated to Smith. For book purposes, depreciation is calculated on the $20,000 value and allocated equally to the partners.

18.54   Insurance expense recorded on the books includes $12,000 of premiums on lives of the partners. These premiums are not deductible for income tax purposes. Depletion on the oil royalties is recorded on the books on the basis of cost of the royalties. For tax purposes, depletion is allowable at the rate of 22 percent of gross income. All of the interest income except $100 is attributable to the municipal securities.

Reconciling Items between Book and Tax Income

18.55   The first objective of a tax spread sheet is to provide a reconciliation between beginning and ending balances in partners' capital accounts, and between net income for book purposes and net income for tax purposes. This is done by means of the "tax adjustments" column. This column is also labeled "Schedule M" at the top because each partner's share of these reconciling items should be entered in Schedule M of the partnership return. The first column, which is the starting point of the spread sheet, reflects the income and expenses and summary of partners' capital accounts as reflected on the books. Appropriate entries are made in the adjustments column to increase or decrease the various items of book income and expense to amounts appropriate for tax purposes. These adjustments are totaled on the net-profit line of the spread sheet, and the total represents the net difference between book and tax net income of the partnership.

Each tax adjustment is explained by footnotes at the bottom of the 18.56
work sheet. At the lower part of the spread sheet each tax adjustment
is allocated between the two partners. Each partner's share of the
adjustments is brought down to the line on which his share of the
book income appears in the first column. Each partner's distributive
share of the taxable net income of the partnership can then be determined by applying his share of the adjustments to his share of the
partnership's book income.

Income and Expense Groupings for Tax Return Presentation

The second function of the tax spread sheet is to group the various 18.57
items of taxable income and expense for proper presentation on
the income tax form. The spread sheet facilitates this grouping by
providing appropriate columns to the right of the tax-adjustment
column corresponding to the appropriate lines and schedules on the
tax return form. For example, columns 3 through 8 on the spread sheet
represent lines on page 1 of the return. These columns contain the
items of income and expense that enter into the determination of
taxable income. Columns 9 through 13 are provided for those items
of taxable income and expense that are required by the Code and
regulations to be allocated separately to partners. Since all items
required to be separately allocated are also required to be presented
in Schedule K of the return form, these latter columns are appropri-
ately headed "Schedule K."

Each item of book income and expense is adjusted by the appro- 18.58
priate amount shown in the tax-adjustment column, if any, and the
amount as adjusted is then extended into the appropriate column on
the spread sheet. The spread sheet is footed and crossfooted. The
total of each column is then either posted to the appropriate line on
page 1 of the return form or it is included in the appropriate column
of Schedule K.

Allocations to Partners

The spread sheet also facilitates the allocation to partners of all 18.59
items entering into the determination of partnership taxable income. Just as the tax adjustments were allocated to partners at the
lower part of the tax spread sheet, each total of columns 9 through
13 is allocated to partners in accordance with the partnership agreement. The amount allocated to each partner is brought down to the
appropriate line at the lower part of the spread sheet on which the
partner's share of book income appears in the first column. For
example, all of the income from oil royalties and all of the depletion
thereon are shown on the line for partner Smith, because by agreement Smith is entitled to them. In the tax-adjustment column, the
entry eliminating the tax-exempt interest from further consideration
is extended down to the lower part of the schedule on the Jones
line. Accordingly, pursuant to the agreement the depreciation sepa-

Jones and Smith Partnership
Federal Income Tax Spread Sheet
1972

Description	1 Per Books	2 Schedule M Tax Adjustments (dr) cr	3 Page 1 -- Line 26	4 Ordinary Income Gross Profit	5 Other Income (line number)
Income -					
Sales	332,188			332,188	
Returns & allowances	(11,005)			(11,005)	
Gain on sale of assets	66,750				
Interest income	1,510	① (1,410)			(6) 100
Oil & gas royalties	5,356				
	394,799				
Expenses -					
Purchases	217,504			(217,504)	
Inventory variation	15,250			(15,250)	
Salaries	80,310				
Insurance	3,636	② 1,200			
Rent	12,000				
Depreciation - machinery	10,468	③ (1,500) ④ 2,000			
Depreciation - fixtures	850				
Taxes	3,035				
Depletion	765	⑤ (413)			
Donations	2,560				
Legal & auditing	1,560				
Dues & subscriptions	158				
Sundry expenses	843				
	348,939				
Net profit	45,860	(123)	(21,131)	88,429	100
Partners' Capital					
Beginning balance		SCH M, COL a			
Jones	165,350				
Smith	200,250				
Total	365,600				
Additions (withdrawals)		SCH M, COL b			
Jones	(20,100)				
Smith	(35,200)				
Total	(55,300)				
Distributive income (loss)		① (1,470) ② 600 ③ (1,000)			
Jones	21,340		(10,565)	SCH M COL 3 SCH K COL 4	
Smith	24,520	② 600 ⑤ (413) ④ 1,000 ⑥ (500)	(10,566)		
Total	45,860	(123)	(21,131)		
Ending balance					
Jones	166,590				
Smith	189,570				
Total	356,160				

SCH M Col 7
SCH M. COL 1 & 3 **Explanation of Tax Adjustments:**

① Eliminate tax exempt interest, allocable to Jones per partnership agreement.

② Eliminate nondeductible premiums on partner life insurance; shared equally.

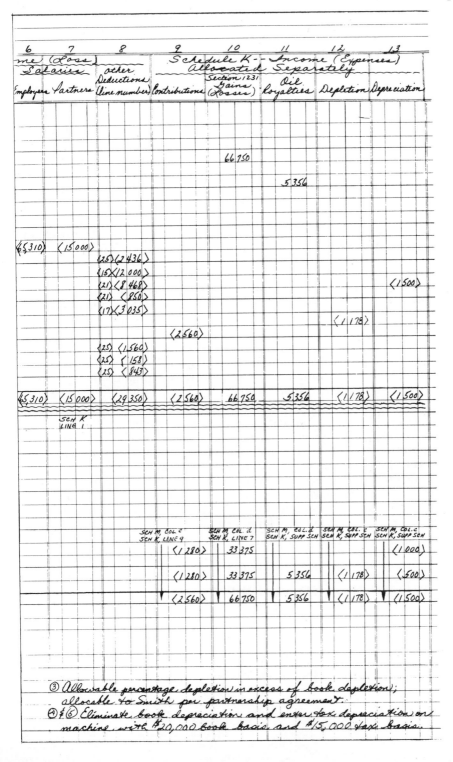

6	7	8	9	10	11	12	13
me (Loss) Salaries		other	Schedule K — Income (Expenses) Allocated Separately				
Employees	Partners	Deductions (line number)	Contributions	Section 1231 Gains (Losses)	Oil Royalties	Depletion	Depreciation
				66 750			
					5 356		
⟨5 310⟩	⟨15 000⟩						
		⟨25⟩⟨2 436⟩					
		⟨15⟩⟨12 000⟩					⟨1 500⟩
		⟨21⟩⟨8 468⟩					
		⟨21⟩ ⟨850⟩				⟨1 178⟩	
		⟨17⟩⟨3 035⟩					
			⟨2 560⟩				
		⟨25⟩ ⟨1 560⟩					
		⟨25⟩ ⟨158⟩					
		⟨25⟩ ⟨843⟩					
⟨5 310⟩	⟨15 000⟩	⟨29 350⟩	⟨2 560⟩	66 750	5 356	⟨1 178⟩	⟨1 500⟩
	SCH K LINE 1						

			SCH M, COL e SCH K, LINE 9	SCH M, COL d SCH K, LINE 7	SCH M, COL. d SCH K, SUPP SCH	SCH M, COL. e SCH K, SUPP SCH	SCH M, COL. e SCH K, SUPP SCH
			⟨1 280⟩	33 375			⟨1 000⟩
			⟨1 280⟩	33 375	5 356	⟨1 178⟩	⟨500⟩
			⟨2 560⟩	66 750	5 356	⟨1 178⟩	⟨1 500⟩

③ Allowable percentage depletion in excess of book depletion; allocable to Smith per partnership agreement.

④ & ⑥ Eliminate book depreciation and enter tax depreciation on machine with $20,000 book basis and $15,000 tax basis.

rately allocated for tax purposes is shown two-thirds ($1,000) on the Jones line, and one-third ($500) on the Smith line. Finally, charitable contributions, Section 1231 gains, and the balance of the ordinary income of the partnership (to be shown on line 27 of page 1) is allocated equally to the partners in accordance with the general profit-sharing ratio of the partnership.

18.60   When the spread sheet is completed to this point, all amounts should be footed and crossfooted. The footings of the ordinary income or loss columns (4 through 8) should be crossfooted and the total entered in column 3 on the net-profit line. The cross footing of columns 1 and 2 should then agree with the cross footing of column 3 (ordinary income or loss) and columns 9 through 13 (the schedule K items). This provides a mathematical proof that all items of book income and tax adjustments have been properly extended. The spread sheet now contains all amounts necessary for completion of the ordinary income section of the return on page 1. It also identifies the information to be included in Schedule M and Schedule K, analyses of the partners' capital accounts, and the income and expense items separately allocated to partners.

18.61   Appropriate cross-reference should be entered on the spread sheet to indicate when and where the various columnar totals are posted to the tax return form. For example, the items in the per books column in the Schedule M section of column 1 should be posted to columns a, f, and g of Schedule M. These items show the beginning and ending balances in the partners' capital accounts and the capital additions or withdrawals of capital. The items at the lower part of the schedule in column 2 represent tax adjustments that should be entered on the appropriate partner's line in columns d and e of Schedule M. The information shown in columns 3 and 7 and in columns 9 through 13 of the spread sheet are also entered in Schedule K of the return form because these are the items allocated to partners. If appropriate columns are not provided in Schedule K of the return form, a supplementary schedule should be attached.

18.62   Of course the size of the spread sheet and the number of columns required for proper classification and grouping of the various items will vary with the complexity of the partnership's business. Although exact makeup of the spread sheet might vary, the basic principles illustrated here have been of substantial help in the preparation of partnership returns.

QUESTIONS AND PROBLEMS

1. Which of the following is a partnership for purposes of the Internal Revenue Code:
   (a) A and B own adjoining farms. Because of frequent flooding, they enter into a written agreement to share equally the costs of constructing and maintaining a ditch to drain the surface waters from their properties.
   (b) C and D are brothers and coowners of a small office building left

to them by their father. They hire a real estate management firm to supply protective, janitorial, telephone, answering, and other services to the tenants.

(c) S's father, P, has operated a successful manufacturing business for many years. In order to lower his personal income taxes, P gives $50,000 to S, S then indorses the check for $50,000 back to his father in payment of that portion of an interest in the business, and S and P enter into a partnership agreement whereby S receives a $5,000 annual salary and receives 30 percent of the profits. S, a minor, is prohibited from transferring or liquidating his partnership interest unless P offers to buy it. S is in college for most of the year but does attend a partner's meeting held each year on December 24.

2. Individual B, as a proprietor, directly owns the assets listed below. Adjusted basis and fair market values are as listed. B proposes to contribute these assets to a business of which Individual C will be a part owner and will act as general manager. C will also contribute $100,000 to be used as working capital. B is to own 85 percent of the business and C is to own 15 percent. C is also to draw a salary of $25,000 per year for his services as general manager. B and C form their new business as a partnership.

	ADJUSTED TAX BASIS	FAIR MARKET VALUE
Cash	$ 25,000	$ 25,000
Inventory (first in, first out)	75,000	100,000
Machinery and equipment	300,000	300,000
Land	50,000	200,000
Total	$450,000	$625,000

(a) How much gain, if any, is recognized to B on the transfer of his property to the partnership? Is it capital gain or ordinary income?

(b) What is the basis of the partnership in the assets received from B?

3. The AB Partnership uses a calendar year for tax purposes. Partner A uses a fiscal year ending June 30, and Partner B uses a calendar year. Partner A draws an annual salary of $15,000, and profits after that salary are divided equally. Taxable net income after the partner's salary is $40,000 for 1972 and $50,000 for 1973. How much gross income does A report (salary plus distributive share) with respect to the partnership for his fiscal year ended June 30, 1973, under the following circumstances?

(a) Neither A nor B changes his partnership interest during 1972 and 1973.

(b) On March 31, 1973, A sells his entire interest in the partnership and does not draw any salary after that date. For the three months ended March 31, 1973, A's salary is $3,750 and partnership taxable net income is $12,500.

(c) On October 31, 1972, A sells two-thirds of his interest to an unrelated party. He continues to draw his salary after the sale. Net income for the years 1972 and 1973 is earned by the partnership ratably each month during the years.

4. M and N form a partnership. M contributes property valued at $50,000 with an adjusted basis to him of $30,000. N contributes his services.

M and N are to share profits and capital equally, and there are no "restrictions" on N's capital interest. Does N recognize taxable income under the present arrangement? Why? How much? When?

5. On January 1, A, B, and C, organize a partnership. A's capital contribution consists of land—with an adjusted basis of $5,000 and a fair market value of $12,000—plus $25,000 cash. In March, A contributes another $5,000 in cash and in November he receives a partnership distribution of $8,000. At the end of the year it is determined that A's share of partnership taxable income before deducting contributions is $7,000 and his share of charitable contributions is $250. A is considering selling his interest in the partnership and asks you to calculate his basis as of December 31. (Do not use the "alternative" method.)

6. Partnership CD is liquidated, and the following assets are distributed equally to Partners C and D:

	PARTNERSHIP'S ADJUSTED BASIS	FAIR MARKET VALUE
Cash	$200,000	$200,000
Inventory	100,000	135,000
Machinery and equipment	50,000	50,000
Land	25,000	35,000
Total	$375,000	$420,000

C's basis for his partnership interest is $140,000 and D's is $200,000. How much gain or loss does each recognize for tax purposes on the liquidation, and what is the basis of each partner in the assets received on the liquidation?

7. Carl, Frank, and Frank's father have equal interests in a partnership. In 1972 Frank sells property to the partnership for $8,000. Frank's adjusted basis in the property is $6,000. In 1973 the partnership sells the property for $11,000. What is the taxable gain or loss allowed to Frank? To the partnership?

19

CORPORATIONS

INTRODUCTION . . . 666

WHAT IS A CORPORATION? . . . 666

    Characteristics of an Association . . . 667

    Professional Corporations . . . 668

TRANSFERS OF PROPERTY TO A CORPORATION . . . 669

    Contributions to Capital . . . 670

    Sales of Treasury Stock . . . 670

    Organization of a Corporation—Section 351 . . . 671

        TRANSFER OF PROPERTY . . . 671

        CONTROL . . . 671

        STOCK OR SECURITIES . . . 671

        OTHER PROPERTY OR MONEY (BOOT) . . . 672

        BASIS . . . 673

        INVESTMENT COMPANIES . . . 673

    Losses on Small Business Stock—Section 1244 . . . 673

        BENEFITS AVAILABLE . . . 673

        SECTION 1244 STOCK . . . 674

        "SMALL BUSINESS CORPORATION" . . . 674

        IMPORTANCE OF PLAN . . . 674

DISTRIBUTIONS TO SHAREHOLDERS . . . 675

    General Rule—Treatment as Dividend . . . 675

    Earnings and Profits . . . 675

    Property Dividends . . . 676

        EFFECT ON PAYEE . . . 676

        EFFECT ON DISTRIBUTING CORPORATION . . . 677

        EFFECT ON EARNINGS AND PROFITS OF DISTRIBUTING
          CORPORATION . . . 677

Stock Dividends . . . 678

GENERAL RULE—NONTAXABLE . . . 678
EXCEPTIONS—TAXABLE . . . 678
BASIS AND HOLDING PERIOD OF NONTAXABLE DIVIDEND
STOCK . . . 679

Redemptions of Stock . . . 680

TAXATION OF SHAREHOLDER . . . 680
ATTRIBUTION RULES FOR STOCK OWNERSHIP . . . 682
TAXATION OF DISTRIBUTING CORPORATION . . . 682

Section 306 Stock . . . 683

PARTIAL LIQUIDATIONS—SECTION 346 . . . 684
COMPLETE LIQUIDATIONS . . . 686

General Rules . . . 686
One-Month Liquidations—Section 333 . . . 687
Twelve-Month Liquidations—Section 337 . . . 688
Intercorporate Liquidations of Subsidiaries—Section 332 . . . 689

CARRY-OVER OF BASIS . . . 690
STEP-UP IN BASIS—SECTION 334(b)(2) . . . 690

REORGANIZATIONS . . . 690

The Six Types of Reorganizations . . . 692
Asset Acquisitions . . . 692

STATUTORY MERGERS AND CONSOLIDATIONS—A-TYPE . . . 693
STOCK FOR ASSETS—C-TYPE . . . 694

Stock Acquisitions—B-Type . . . 696
Corporate Divisions—D-Type . . . 697
Recapitalizations—E-Type . . . 698
Changes in Form—F-Type . . . 698
Further Requirements of Reorganizations . . . 698

PARTY TO A REORGANIZATION . . . 699
PLAN OF REORGANIZATION . . . 699
NONSTATUTORY REQUIREMENTS . . . 699

Exchanges Pursuant to Corporate Reorganizations . . . 700

EXCHANGES BY SHAREHOLDERS . . . 700
EXCHANGES BY CORPORATIONS . . . 700

Distributions Under Section 355 . . . 701
Carry-over of Corporate Attributes . . . 702

BASIS . . . 702
OTHER TAX ATTRIBUTES—SECTION 381 . . . 703

**SPECIAL LIMITATIONS ON NET OPERATING LOSS
CARRY-OVERS . . . 704**

PENALTY SURTAXES ON CERTAIN CORPORATIONS . . . 705

    Personal Holding Companies . . . 705
    Unreasonable Accumulation of Earnings . . . 706

SUBCHAPTER S CORPORATIONS . . . 706

    Stock and Shareholder Requirements . . . 707
    Income Requirements . . . 707
    Election and Shareholder Consents . . . 708
    How Income Is Taxed to Shareholders . . . 708
    Treatment of Net Operating Losses . . . 709
    Qualified Pension and Profit Sharing Plans for
        Shareholder-Employees . . . 709
    Pros and Cons of Electing Subchapter S . . . 710

WESTERN HEMISPHERE TRADE CORPORATIONS . . . 710
INSURANCE COMPANIES AND CERTAIN OTHER
   FINANCIAL INSTITUTIONS . . . 711
MULTIPLE CORPORATIONS . . . 711

    Limitation on Multiple Surtax Exemptions and Accumulated
      Earnings Credits . . . 711
    Disallowance of Multiple Surtax Exemptions and Accumulated
      Earnings Credits . . . 713
    Consolidated Returns . . . 713
    100 Percent Dividends Received Deduction . . . 714

OTHER TRANSACTIONS BETWEEN CORPORATIONS AND
   SHAREHOLDERS . . . 714

INTRODUCTION

19.1   The purpose of this chapter is to discuss in a rather general way some of the more important tax concepts and special provisions applicable to corporations. Paragraphs 4.1 through 4.2 discussing the elements of the corporation income tax return should be read again at this time.

19.2   Most special provisions applicable to corporations have been enacted in order to levy a reasonable tax on corporate income without discouraging the use of the corporate form of business organization. The corporation as a legal entity is very important to our business system. It is recognized for both business and tax purposes as an entity separate and apart from its shareholders; yet it is an organization whose primary purpose is to benefit its shareholders. Because of this purpose, a corporation's activities invariably involve a number of transactions with its shareholders. Some of these transactions require special treatment to prevent prohibitive tax burdens, and others require special treatment to prevent undue tax advantages. Preserving a reasonable middle ground between these two extremes provides a constant challenge to the architects of tax policy, to tax administrators, and to tax practitioners.

WHAT IS A CORPORATION?

19.3   For tax purposes, business organizations are classified as corporations, partnerships, or trusts, in accordance with standards set forth in the Code and the regulations. These are not necessarily the same classifications used for legal and general business purposes. This principle has been recognized by the Supreme Court and is explained in Reg. 301.7701–1(b) and (c):

(b) *Standards*   The Internal Revenue Code prescribes certain categories, or classes, into which various organizations fall for purposes of taxation. These categories, or classes, include associations (which are taxable as corporations), partnerships and trusts. The tests, or standards, which are to be applied in determining the classification in which an organization belongs (whether it is an association, a partnership, a trust, or other taxable entity) are determined under the Internal Revenue Code. ...

(c) *Effect of Local Law*   As indicated in paragraph (b) of this section, the classes into which organizations are to be placed for purposes of taxation are determined under the Internal Revenue Code. Thus, a particular organization might be classified as a trust under the law of one state and a corporation under the law of another state. However, for purposes of the Internal Revenue Code, this organization would be uniformly classed as a trust, an association (and, therefore, taxable as a corporation), or some other entity, depending upon its nature under the classification standards of the Internal Revenue Code. Similarly, the term "partnership" is not limited to the common-law meaning of partnership, but is broader in its scope and includes groups not commonly called partnerships. See Sec. 1.761–1 of this chapter (Income Tax Regulations) and Sec. 301.7701–2. The term "corporation" is not limited to the artificial entity usually known as a corporation, but includes also an association, a trust classified as an association because of its nature or its activities, a joint-stock company and an insurance company. Although it is the Internal Revenue Code rather than local law which establishes the tests or standards which will be applied in determining the classification in which an organization belongs, local law governs in determining whether the legal relationships which have been established in the formation of an organization are such that the standards are met. Thus, it is local law which must be applied in determining such matters as the legal relationships of the members of the organization among themselves and with the public at large, and with the interests of the members of the organization in its assets. Nevertheless, the labels applied by local law to organizations which may now or hereafter be authorized by local law, are in and by themselves of no importance in the classification of such organizations for the purpose of taxation under the Internal Revenue Code. ...

This quotation makes it clear that corporations for tax purposes are not limited to organizations formed as corporations under local law. Although local law determines the legal relationships resulting from various types of organizations, the effect of those relationships upon the classification of an organization for tax purposes is determined by rules set forth in the Code and regulations.

Characteristics of an Association

19.4 Unincorporated organizations that are classified for tax purposes as corporations are referred to as "associations" (Reg. 301.7701–2); for purposes of general law they are frequently partnerships. An association or partnership is brought into being by an agreement of the members. No sovereign body, such as a state, grants to it a certificate evidencing that it is a separate juridical entity. The tax distinctions between associations, partnerships, and trusts are not always readily apparent, but the effect of these distinctions on the tax positions of organizations and their members can be drastic. For example, a double tax on income of a partnership or trust that is classified unexpectedly as an association can be very burdensome to the partners or beneficiaries if they have based their financial and tax planning on a single tax applicable to a partnership or trust. Likewise, the tax and financial planning of members of a partnership would be disrupted considerably if anticipated losses of the partnership were not deductible by the partners because the partnership is classified unexpectedly as an association. Obviously, adequate tax and financial planning for any organization requires advance knowledge of the correct classification of the organization for tax purposes.

19.5 The Treasury Department has devoted extensive regulations to the distinctions between associations, partnerships, and trusts (Reg. 301.7701–1 through 301.7701–4). For the most part, these regulations are based on guidelines discussed by the Supreme Court in its landmark decision of *Morrissey* v. *Com.*[1]

19.6   Based on the *Morrissey* decision, the regulations set forth six corporate characteristics to be used as tests to distinguish between unincorporated organizations treated for tax purposes as corporations (associations) and those treated as partnerships or trusts. These characteristics are as follows:

1. Associates
2. An objective to carry on business and divide the gains therefrom
3. Continuity of life
4. Centralization of management
5. Liability for corporate debts limited to corporate property
6. Free transferability of interests

Although other factors may be significant in determining whether an organization will be taxed as a corporation, partnership, or trust, ordinarily these six characteristics are the major determining factors. The existence or absence of these characteristics must be determined in the light of all facts and circumstances in each situation. The regulations provide that in order for an organization to be classified as an association for tax purposes it must have *more* corporate characteristics than noncorporate characteristics [Reg. 301.7701–2(a)(3)].

19.7   Associates and an objective to carry on business and divide the gains therefrom (characteristics 1 and 2 above) are common to both corporations and partnerships; therefore, the regulations recognize that ordinarily these characteristics are not pertinent to classification of an organization as either an association or partnership. Thus, such classification depends upon the presence or absence of the other characteristics: continuity of life, centralization of management, limited liability, and free transferability of interests. If more than two of these are present, the organization is an association taxable as a corporation; if two or less are present, it is a partnership.

19.8   Similarly, since characteristics 3, 4, 5, and 6 are all common to corporations and trusts, the presence or absence of these characteristics is not pertinent generally to the classification of an organization as either a corporation or trust. Generally, such classification depends upon the presence or absence of characteristics 1 and 2 [Reg. 301.7701–2(a)(3)].

Professional Corporations

19.9   For almost a decade a controversy raged between the Internal Revenue Service and professional men over the use of associations taxable as corporations and professional corporations for the conduct of professional practices. The successful use of these associations and corporations enables professional men to obtain the tax benefits of qualified pension and profit-sharing plans and other employee benefits. Until August 8, 1969, the Internal Revenue Service vig-

1. 296 U.S. 344 (1935), 36–1 USTC ¶9020, 16 AFTR 1274.

orously resisted all moves in this direction. Beginning with the case of *U.S.* v. *Kintner*,[2] taxpayers won numerous victories in the courts. After losing the *Kintner* decision the Internal Revenue Service announced it would not follow the case. It contended that an association of professional men formed to obtain the benefits of corporate status and to set up a qualified pension plan was in substance a partnership for tax purposes.[3]

In November, 1960, the Treasury Department amended its regula- 19.10 tions in an attempt to bar corporate treatment for unincorporated professional associations. The professionals fought back by getting many of their states to enact laws permitting the formation of special professional corporations. On February 2, 1965, the Treasury added Subsection (h) to Reg. 301.7701–2 to provide that even if a professional organization is a corporation under state law, it is a partnership for federal income tax purposes. Taxpayers continued the battle, and time after time their position was upheld by the courts. Reg. 301.7701–2 (h) was declared invalid in several cases.[4]

On August 8, 1969, the Internal Revenue Service finally issued 19.11 Technical Information Release No. 1019[5] and announced it was conceding that "organizations of doctors, lawyers, and other professional people organized under state professional association acts will, generally, be treated as corporations for tax purposes." This announcement was not a complete concession on the part of the Internal Revenue Service, however, because it reserved the right to "conclude differently in any case that reflects special circumstances not present in the *O'Neill*[6] or *Kurzner*[7] cases."

TIR 1019 represents a significant victory for taxpayers; however, 19.12 such victory may be short-lived. While considering the Tax Reform Act of 1969, Congress rejected a proposal to limit the tax benefits of qualified pension and profit-sharing plans of professional corporations the way it already had limited them for self-employed individuals. However, Congress did so limit such plans of Subchapter S corporations. Whether Congress will continue to allow professional corporations to enjoy the full benefits of qualified pension and profit-sharing plans remains to be seen.

TRANSFERS OF PROPERTY TO A CORPORATION

As indicated earlier, many transactions between corporations and 19.13 their shareholders require special treatment to prevent undue tax burdens or undue tax advantages. Many of these transactions involve transfers of property to the corporation by shareholders and others.

2. 216 F.2d 418 (9th Cir. 1954), 54–2 USTC ¶9626, 46 AFTR 995.
3. Rev. Rul. 56–23, 1956–1 C.B. 598.
4. See for example, U.S. v. Empey, 406 F.2d 157 (10th Cir. 1969), 69–1 USTC ¶9158, 23 AFTR2d 425; O'Neill v. U.S., 410 F.2d 888 (6th Cir. 1969), 69–1 USTC ¶9372, 23 AFTR2d 1247; and Kurzner v. U.S., 413 F.2d 97 (5th Cir. 1969), 69–1 USTC ¶9428, 23 AFTR2d 1481.
5. *P–H 1969 Federal Taxes* ¶55,334.
6. *Supra* fn. 4.
7. *Supra* fn. 4.

Some of these transactions are not taxable because they are deemed not to result in sufficient change in the overall economic position of the shareholders to justify the imposition of a tax. Others are taxable because a sufficient change is deemed to occur. A basic rule to keep in mind is that transactions between corporations and their shareholders are taxable to the same extent as transactions between unrelated parties unless the Code contains a specific provision to the contrary.

Contributions to Capital

19.14   Receipt of a capital contribution is not treated as gross income by a corporation whether the contribution is in the form of money or property and whether it is received from a shareholder or nonshareholder (Section 118). Refer back to paragraphs 6.73–6.77.

19.15   If property is received as a capital contribution from shareholders as such, the corporation's basis in the property received is equal to the adjusted basis of the property to the contributing shareholders [Section 362(a)].

19.16   There is no exchange involved in a contribution to capital by a shareholder. If the corporation issues stock or securities for the money or property received, Section 351 concerning transfers to new or existing corporations or Section 368 pertaining to reorganizations may apply so as to bring about nonrecognition of any gain; but Section 118 is not applicable.[8]

19.17   Occasionally corporations receive capital contributions in property or money from nonshareholders. Section 362(c) provides that where property is received as a capital contribution from one who is not a shareholder, the basis of the property received shall be zero. If money is received as a capital contribution from one who is not a shareholder, then the corporation is required to reduce its basis in property by an amount equal to the money received [Section 362(c); Reg. 1.362–2]. An example of a contribution to capital by a nonshareholder is a contribution in aid of construction paid to a utility company to extend its distribution main or electric transmission line. The money received does not constitute taxable income, but the utility must correspondingly reduce first the basis of depreciable property constructed with the money, and then the basis of other property to the extent of any excess money.

Sales of Treasury Stock

19.18   Gains and losses realized by a corporation on transactions in its own stock are not recognized for income tax purposes (Section 1032). When a corporation issues its stock for money or property, it realizes neither gain nor loss. Even without the benefit of Section 1032, this is a capital transaction. Similarly, if it later purchases some outstanding shares for more or less than the amount originally paid in on original issuance, no gain or loss results. If it does not cancel the stock certificate purchased, thereby retiring the shares represented by it, the shares become treasury shares and have a basis equal to the

8. Werner Abegg, 50 T.C. 145 (1968).

amount paid for them. If later these treasury shares are sold by the corporation for more or less than their cost, Section 1032 states that no gain or loss on such sale shall be recognized.

Sales of treasury stock for cash should not be confused with transfers of property in acquisition of treasury stock. Section 311(d)(2) provides, with certain exceptions, that if appreciated property is transferred in redemption of stock, gain will be recognized equal to the excess of the property's fair market value over its adjusted basis.

19.19

Organization of a Corporation—Section 351

When a corporation is organized, the shareholders usually transfer money or property or both to the corporation in exchange for its stock. Sometimes securities such as bonds, debentures, or long-term notes and sometimes even short-term notes and open accounts receivable are received in addition to stock. Further, it is not uncommon for similar transfers of property to be made later in the lives of corporations after they are established and operating. As a general rule, transfers of property to corporations in exchange for stock are taxable to the transferors. However, when these transfers of property are made by a shareholder or group of shareholders who are in control of the corporation, the change in relationship of the shareholders to the transferred property is more one of form than of substance. For this reason and in order not to inhibit such transactions, it has long been recognized in our tax law that, under certain circumstances, such transfers should not be taxed.

19.20

Transfer of Property. Under Section 351, no gain or loss is recognized on the transfer of property to a corporation if (1) the transfer is in exchange solely for stock or securities of the corporation, and (2) immediately after the transfer the transferors are in control of the corporation. This exemption applies only to transfers of property, including cash. The receipt of stock in exchange for services rendered to a corporation constitutes a taxable receipt.

19.21

Control. Under Section 351, "control" means the ownership of stock possessing at least 80 percent of the total combined voting power of all voting stock and at least 80 percent of the total number of shares of all other classes of stock of the corporation [Section 368(c)].

19.22

Section 351 is intended to apply only when the transfers do not alter the underlying control of the property. Thus, a primary requirement of such tax-exempt transfer is control of the corporation by the transferor or transferors immediately after the transfer.

19.23

Stock or Securities. Not only must the transferors be in control of the corporation but also the consideration they receive must be stock or securities that represent a continuing interest in the corporation and thus in the property transferred to it. In this connection, the definition of "securities" has been the subject of considerable litigation. No clear-cut definition is available, and determination of whether an evidence of indebtedness qualifies as a security depends upon all the facts of each situation. Clearly, open accounts receivable do not qualify. Ordinarily, short-term notes (less than five years) will not be

19.24

672

considered securities.[9] On the other hand, long-term bonds in registered form most probably will qualify. In between these extremes, there is much room for question. The following comment by the Fifth Circuit Court of Appeals summarizes the criteria to be considered:

> The test as to whether notes are securities is not a mechanical determination of the time period of the note. Though time is an important factor, the controlling consideration is an overall evaluation of the nature of the debt, degree of participation and continuing interest in the business, the extent of proprietary interest compared with the similarity of the note to a cash payment, the purpose of the advances, etc. It is not necessary for the debt obligation to be the equivalent of stock since Sec. 112(b)(5) [now Section 351] specifically includes both "stock" and "securities."[10]

Although the definition is far from exact, securities can be thought of as evidences of indebtedness that are of sufficient formality and duration so as to represent a continuing interest in the property transferred; they are in contrast to other debt instruments that are treated as the equivalent of cash.

19.25 **Other Property or Money (Boot).** If the stockholder receives money or property, other than stock or securities, in a transaction otherwise qualifying under Section 351, the nonrecognition of gain does not apply to that other property or money (sometimes called "boot"). When boot is received, any gain realized on the transfer is recognized, but only to the extent of the fair market value of the boot received. To determine this gain recognized, it first is necessary to determine the total gain realized on the transfer. This gain is the excess of the total fair market value of the stock, securities, and other property or money (boot) received over the adjusted basis of the property transferred. This gain then is recognized only to the extent of the boot received [Section 351(b)].

19.26 When the property transferred to the corporation is subject to a liability, or when other liabilities of the shareholder are assumed by the corporation, such liabilities ordinarily are not considered boot, and normally they do not cause a transfer otherwise subject to Section 351 to be taxable. However, if the principal purpose of the transfer of property or the assumption of debt is to avoid federal income tax or if it is not a bona fide business purpose, then the "subject to" debt or the assumed debt is treated as other property or money, and gain is recognized accordingly [Section 357(b)]. Ordinarily, if the indebtedness was incurred in connection with the acquisition or operation of the property transferred, such transfer is not considered to involve a tax-avoidance purpose.

19.27 If indebtedness to which the property transferred is subject, along with indebtedness assumed by the corporation, exceeds the transferor's adjusted basis in the property, gain is recognized to the extent of such excess [Section 357(c)].

19.28 Section 351 applies to the transfer of property to a corporation not only on its original organization but also on later transfers to it.

9. *P-H 1970 Federal Taxes* ¶18,022 (cases cited therein).
10. Camp Wolters Enterprises, Inc. v. Com., 230 F.2d 555 (5th Cir. 1956), 56-1 USTC ¶9314, 49 AFTR 283, affirming 22 T.C. 737.

Basis. A corporation's basis in property received from a controlling 19.29
shareholder or group of shareholders is the same as the adjusted basis
of the shareholder increased by any gain recognized to the shareholder [Section 362(a)].

The shareholder's basis in stock and securities received for the 19.30
property is the same as his adjusted basis in the property increased
by any gain recognized on the transfer and decreased by any liabilities assumed by the corporation and any liabilities to which the
property is subject and decreased further by any money and fair
market value of other property received [Section 358].

Investment Companies. In 1967 Congress acted to prohibit what it 19.31
considered to be unintended tax benefits from Section 351. It provided
that Section 351 would not apply to transfers of property to so-called
"swap" funds after June 30, 1967. This prohibition applies to transfers
of property to investment companies that result in diversification of
the transferor's interest. An investment company is either a regulated
investment company, a real-estate investment trust, or a corporation
more than 80 percent of value of whose assets are held for investment
and are either readily marketable stocks or securities, or interests in
regulated investment companies or real-estate investment trusts
[Reg. 1.351–1(c)(1)].

Losses on Small Business Stock—Section 1244

If individuals conduct their businesses as proprietorships or 19.32
partnerships, losses incurred are deductible as ordinary losses. If
those individuals incorporate their businesses, the losses incurred
are deductible only by the corporations (except where Subchapter S
is both available and elected). The individuals incur the economic
burden of the operating losses in the form of losses in value of their
corporate stocks. However, as indicated in chapters 7 and 12, when
such losses are realized from sale, exchange, or worthlessness of the
corporate stocks, they are capital losses, and they receive generally
less favorable tax treatment than ordinary losses. To prevent the fear
of this undesirable tax treatment from inhibiting the use of corporations by small businessmen, Section 1244 was added to the Code in
1958.

Benefits Available. The benefits of Section 1244 are available only to 19.33
individuals or to partnerships to whom the Section 1244 stock is
issued. Thus, the benefits are not available to corporations, estates,
or trusts, or to individuals who receive the stock from previous shareholders either by purchase, gift, devise, or otherwise.

Under Section 1244, a qualifying individual may treat the loss in- 19.34
curred on disposition or worthlessness of Section 1244 stock as an
ordinary loss, to the extent of $25,000 in any one taxable year for a
single individual, or to $50,000 in any one taxable year in the case of a
married couple filing a joint return. However, Section 1244 does not
permit operating losses of a corporation to be deducted by its shareholders.

19.35 **Section 1244 Stock.** Section 1244 stock can be only common stock in a domestic corporation, and then only if:

    (A) the corporation adopted a plan after June 30, 1958, to offer such stock for a specified period ending not later than two years after the plan was adopted,

    (B) the corporation was a "small business corporation" at the time the plan was adopted,

    (C) no portion of a prior stock offering was outstanding at the time the plan was adopted,

    (D) the stock was issued by the corporation pursuant to such plan for money or property other than stock and securities, and

    (E) during the corporation's most recent five taxable years preceding the date the loss was sustained (or such shorter period of the corporation's life), the corporation derived more than 50 percent of its aggregate gross receipts from sources other than royalties, rents, dividends, interest, annuities, and sales or exchanges of stock or securities. However, this limitation does not apply if during this period the corporation incurs aggregate net losses.

19.36 **"Small Business Corporation."** To be a "small business corporation," the corporation must have equity capital, including the stock to be offered under the plan, of less than $1,000,000. Further, the stock being offered under the plan plus the aggregate amount of other equity capital received between June 30, 1958, and the adoption of the plan must not exceed $500,000.

19.37 **Importance of Plan.** The above definitions of Section 1244 stock and "small business corporations" indicate the detailed rules that must be observed if an individual is to obtain the ordinary-loss treatment of Section 1244. Such meticulous requirements are typical of many relief provisions involving corporations and their shareholders. Probably the most troublesome rules of Section 1244 are those dealing with the plan for issuance of the Section 1244 stock. Regulation 1.1244(c)–1(c) refers to this required plan as follows:

    (c) *Written plan.* (1) The common stock must be issued pursuant to a written plan adopted by the corporation after June 30, 1958, to offer only such stock during a period specified in the plan ... The plan must specifically state, in terms of dollars, the maximum amount to be received by the corporation in consideration for the stock to be issued pursuant thereto ...

Regulation 1.1244(c)–1(h) makes it clear that in order for stock to qualify as Section 1244 stock, it must be the only stock issued by the corporation between the date the plan is adopted and the date the last Section 1244 stock is issued. In this connection, if another offering of stock is made by the corporation subsequent to *or simultaneously with* the adoption of the plan for issuance of Section 1244 stock, stock issued pursuant to the plan after such other offering will not qualify as Section 1244 stock.

Obviously considerable care must be exercised in issuing Section 1244 stock; however, that care can be quite valuable if the corporate venture is not successful. Qualifying under Section 1244 should be considered by every corporation issuing stock if it has any chance of meeting the requirements.

19.38

DISTRIBUTIONS TO SHAREHOLDERS

Some of the more troublesome tax problems involving corporations relate to distributions to shareholders. Corporations are not allowed deductions for distributions to shareholders in their capacity as shareholders; however, the tax consequences to the shareholders are not so easily determined.

19.39

General Rule—Treatment as Dividend

As a general rule, any distribution to a shareholder by a corporation out of its earnings and profits for the taxable year or out of its earnings and profits accumulated after February 28, 1913, is treated as a dividend and is ordinary income to the shareholder [Sections 301(a), 301(c)(1), and 316]. Any part of a distribution that exceeds the earnings and profits of the corporation is treated by the shareholder as a return of his capital and is applied to reduce his basis in the stock with respect to which the distribution is received. Any such distribution in excess of both the earnings and profits of the corporation and the shareholder's basis in his stock is treated by Section 301(c) as a capital gain to the shareholder. These general rules apply to distributions paid in cash. Distributions paid in other property or stock are subject to these general rules plus several special rules discussed later in this chapter.

19.40

Earnings and Profits

The term "earnings and profits" is not specifically defined in the code, although Section 312 pertains to the subject. Neither can an all-inclusive definition be found in the regulations or published court decisions, although court decisions and rulings have established certain guidelines. These indicate that earnings and profits of any taxable year generally can be determined by (1) starting with taxable income; (2) adding back (a) any tax-exempt income and (b) the excess of depreciation allowed under an accelerated method over the amount allowable under the straight-line method for taxable years beginning after June 30, 1972; (3) deducting federal income taxes; and (4) deducting realized expenditures and losses not deducted for income tax purposes, but which also are not chargeable to a capital account (for example, expenditures contrary to public policy). Losses and expenditures actually sustained, but which are expressly made non-deductible in determining taxable income by some provision of the

19.41

Code, are deductible for determining earnings and profits. However, the law providing for *nonrecognition* of gains and losses prevails in determining both taxable income and earnings and profits. Thus, gains and losses that are not recognized, such as in like-kind exchanges, and which result in carry-overs of basis to other property, are disregarded for purposes of earnings and profits. Tax-accounting principles governing the accrual of items of income and expense in determining taxable income also apply in determining earnings and profits. Finally, deductions allowed in determining taxable income that ignore economic reality and have been granted for various social or economic purposes are not taken into account in determining earnings and profits. For example (1) the excess of percentage depletion over cost depletion and (2) the 85 percent or 100 percent dividends-received deduction, are disregarded in determining earnings and profits. The amount of the earnings and profits or deficit of any year is determined under the provisions of the law as it existed in that year unless a provision of Section 312 requires otherwise.

19.42   A distribution comes first out of earnings and profits of the year in which paid and then out of earnings, if any, accumulated after February 28, 1913, and existing at the beginning of the corporation's taxable year [Section 316(a)].

EXAMPLE   If a corporation had a deficit of $100,000 at the beginning of the year, earned $50,000 of earnings and profits during the year, and paid a dividend of any amount up to $50,000 during that year, the distribution would be a dividend. If it paid $60,000, the first $50,000 would be a dividend and the balance of $10,000 a distribution out of capital. If it paid only $30,000, the balance of $20,000 would be added to any accumulated earnings and profits or, as in this case, reduce any accumulated deficit.

Property Dividends

19.43   **Effect on Payee.** Distributions of property other than money are measured for an individual shareholder by the fair market value of the property received. That value becomes his basis in the property [Section 301(d)]. For a corporate shareholder, however, the amount of the distribution is measured by the lesser of (1) the fair market value of the property, or (2) the adjusted basis of the property to the corporation making the distribution plus any gain recognized to that corporation on the distribution [Section 301(b)(1)(B)]. The basis of the property to the receiving corporation is equal to the amount of the distribution as so measured [Section 301(d)(2)].

19.44   The special tax treatment of property distributions to corporate shareholders prevents tax avoidance by related corporations. If a corporation took property dividends into income at fair market value and treated that value as its depreciable basis in the property, the following tax consequences would result:

   1. Related companies could pay dividends in appreciated property that, because of the dividends-received deduction, would be taxable to the

receiving corporation at only 15 percent of the property's value (see paragraph 4.7).

2. The receiving corporation would get a new basis in the property equal to its full fair market value.
3. The resulting increase or "step-up" in basis of the dividend property could be substantially more than the net dividend income of the payee resulting from the distribution.

Not surprisingly then, the rules concerning property distributions received by corporations limit the amount of a property distribution to the basis of the property received.

Effect on Distributing Corporation. As a general rule, the distributing corporation will recognize no income on the distribution of property; however, there are several exceptions to this general rule. If the property distributed consists of LIFO inventory, gain will be recognized to the extent the inventory amount valued under the lower-of-cost-or-market method (or retail method if otherwise used by the corporation) exceeds the LIFO amount. If the property distributed is depreciable property or other property subject to recapture and with value in excess of adjusted basis, gain may be recognized in the form of recapture of depreciation or other deductions. If the property is subject to a debt in excess of basis, the distributing corporation will recognize gain to the extent of such excess debt [Sections 311(b), 311(c), 1245, 1250, 1251, and 1252].   19.45

Effect on Earnings and Profits of Distributing Corporation. Corporations that distribute property as dividends ordinarily reduce earnings and profits by the adjusted basis of the property less any liabilities to which the property is subject and other liabilities assumed by the transferee-shareholders. When inventory assets and unrealized receivables or fees are distributed as a dividend, earnings and profits of the corporation (but not taxable income) are increased by the excess of fair market value of such assets over their inventory value (adjusted basis). Earnings and profits are then reduced, but not below zero, by the fair market value of the assets distributed. This adjustment assures that appreciation in value of distributed inventory and unrealized receivables will be included in earnings and profits for purposes of measuring dividend income of the shareholders receiving that inventory. Unrealized receivables and fees for this purpose include rights to receive payment for goods delivered or to be delivered and services rendered or to be rendered that have not previously been included in income (exclusive of amounts reportable as capital gains) [Section 312(b)]. On the distribution of property on which depreciation and other deductions are recaptured, the regulations are not clear, but it would appear that earnings and profits should be reduced by the adjusted basis of such property distributed plus the recapture gain recognized.   19.46

Stock Dividends

19.47 **General Rule—Nontaxable.** As a general rule distributions to share-holders paid in additional shares of stock or rights to acquire stock of the corporation are not taxable to the shareholder (Section 305). (For background, refer back to paragraphs 5.33–5.35.) For a number of years this general rule has been subject to the exception that if a distribution in stock is subject to the election of any shareholder to receive property (including cash) in lieu of stock, that distribution is taxable to all shareholders.

19.48 **Exceptions—Taxable.** In 1969 the Treasury issued new regulations under Section 305 that substantially broadened the scope of what constituted an election by shareholders to receive property or money in lieu of a stock dividend. Although those regulations met vigorous resistance from the business community, the Tax Reform Act of 1969 amended Section 305 to include the substance of most of those disputed regulations. As amended, subsections (b) and (c) of Section 305 provide that the following distributions of stock are taxable to shareholders:

1. Distributions in lieu of money—distributions that, at the election of any of the shareholders (exercised before or after the dividend declaration), are payable either in stock or in property (including money).
2. Disproportionate distributions—distributions that have the result of some shareholders receiving property (including money) and other shareholders receiving an increase in their proportionate interest in the assets or earnings and profits of the corporation.
3. Distributions of common and preferred stock—distributions that have the result of some common shareholders receiving preferred stock and other common shareholders receiving common stock.
4. Distributions on preferred stock—distributions to holders of preferred stock, other than an increase in the conversion ratio of convertible preferred stock that is made solely to take into account a stock dividend or stock split with respect to the stock into which such convertible stock is convertible. This exception also makes distributions of stock in payment of preferred dividends taxable.
5. Distributions of convertible preferred stock—any distribution of convertible preferred stock, unless it is established to the satisfaction of the Treasury Department that such distribution will not have the result of a disproportionate distribution.
6. Other transactions covered by regulations[10A]—any other transaction which under regulations to be prescribed by the Treasury Department has the effect of increasing the proportionate interest of any shareholder in the earnings and profits or assets of the corporation by reason of a change in conversion ratio or redemption price of stock or securities, a difference between redemption price and issue price, a redemption of stock that is treated as a distribution to shareholders under Section 301, or any other transaction including a recapitalization that has a similar effect on the interest of any shareholder.

10A. Reg. 1.305–7 was proposed March 18, 1971, and was revised March 8, 1972, but in early 1973 was not yet final.

Obviously, the above exceptions to the general rule of Section 305   19.49
are quite broad. They are broadened even further by the rule of Section 305(d) to the effect that the term "stock" includes rights to acquire stock, and the term "shareholder" includes a holder of rights or of convertible securities. The following examples illustrate some of these exceptions.[11]

A corporation has two classes of common, A and B, having equal rights   EXAMPLE 1
except that A pays only cash dividends and B only equivalent stock dividends. Since the stock dividend increases the B shareholder's proportionate interest, it will be taxable under exception (2) above.

A corporation has outstanding common and convertible debentures. It   EXAMPLE 2
pays cash interest on the debentures and distributes a stock dividend on common. The distribution of the stock will be taxable since the equity of the shareholders increases and the corporation is considered to have two classes of stock outstanding, the debentures being treated as stock for this purpose [exception (2)].

A corporation distributes convertible preferred stock to the holders of its   EXAMPLE 3
outstanding common stock. The common stock is the only issue outstanding. No shareholders have any election to take cash, and since common stock was the only stock outstanding the proportionate interests of shareholders do not change; therefore exceptions (1) and (2) do not apply. Because only preferred stock is distributed, exception (3) does not apply. Since no preferred stock is outstanding, exception (4) does not apply. However, since convertible preferred stock was distributed, exception (5) will apply unless the Treasury can be satisfied that such distribution does not have the result of a disproportionate distribution. If the conversion period is short, those shareholders who wish to increase their investment will convert, and those who prefer to obtain cash will sell; thus the Treasury might take the position that a disproportionate distribution has occurred which is taxable. On the other hand, if the conversion period is long (say twenty years), such an effect seems unlikely and the Treasury may agree that the distribution is not taxable.

Under exception (6), redemptions of stock, changes in conversion   19.50
ratios, recapitalizations of the corporation, changes in redemption prices, and other transactions that do not involve actual distributions to shareholders may alter their proportionate interests. The Treasury is directed to issue regulations to impose dividend treatment in these situations [Section 305(c)]. Obviously, great care must be exercised to determine the taxability or nontaxability of any distribution of stock that under any circumstances may alter the proportionate interests of shareholders in the assets or earnings and profits of the corporation.

Basis and Holding Period of Nontaxable Dividend Stock. If stock is   19.51
received as a nontaxable stock dividend, it takes as its basis a portion of the basis of the stock on which received. If the stock received is of the same class as that previously held, the basis of such stock is

11. Examples 1, 2, and 3 were taken substantially from *Tax Reform Act of 1969— Concise Explanation* (Englewood Cliffs, N.J.: Prentice-Hall, Inc., 1970).

determined by dividing the basis of the old shares by the total number of old and new shares held after the dividend [Section 307(a)].

EXAMPLE   Smith owned ten shares of XYZ Corporation, which he had purchased in 1965 at $100 per share for a total of $1,000. In 1971 he receives one share as a stock dividend. His total basis of the eleven shares now held is still $1,000. The basis of each share held after the dividend is $90.91 ($1,000 ÷ 11 = $90.91).

If the stock received as a dividend is of a class different from that previously held, the basis of the old shares is allocated over both the old and new shares held after the dividend in relation to their relative fair market values [Reg. 1.307–1(a)].

19.52   The holding period of the new shares is deemed to begin on the same date the old shares were acquired. See paragraph 12.64.

Redemptions of Stock

19.53   Redemption of a corporation's own stock represents a form of distribution to shareholders. Such redemptions invariably raise questions of whether they represent sales of stock by shareholders and thus capital-gain transactions, or distributions of property (including money) to shareholders and thus dividend transactions. These questions have been the subject of extensive litigation and legislative study.

19.54   **Taxation of Shareholder.** The general rule of the Code now is that any redemption of stock will be treated as a distribution to shareholders and thus as a dividend unless it qualifies under one of several exceptions set forth in the Code [Section 301(a) and 302(d)]. Such exceptions are found in Sections 302(a), 302(b), 303, and 331 and treat the following types of payments to shareholders in exchange for shares as capital-gain transactions:

1. Redemptions made in connection with the complete liquidation of a corporation [Section 331(a)(1)].
2. Redemptions made in connection with a corporation's partial liquidation as defined in Section 346 [Section 331(a)(2)].
3. Redemptions which, under all existing facts and circumstances, are not substantially equivalent to the distribution of dividends by the corporation [Section 302(b)(1)].
4. Redemptions which constitute substantially disproportionate redemptions as defined in Section 302(b)(2), of stock of particular shareholders.
5. Any redemption which results in the complete termination of the shareholder's interest in the corporation [Section 302(b)(3)].
6. Distributions in redemption of stock to pay death taxes, funeral bills, and estate-administration expenses as provided and subject to the limitations contained in Section 303.

19.55   If a redemption of stock is treated as a dividend, the full amount of the redemption proceeds is the amount of the dividend income (assuming, of course, that there are sufficient earnings and profits to cover it), and no deduction is allowable for the basis of the shares surrendered.

Assuming ample earnings and profits, redemption proceeds will be treated as dividend income in the first three of the following examples and as capital gain in the fourth.

EXAMPLE 1

An individual owns all of the 1,000 shares of the outstanding stock of a corporation. He transfers 200 of his shares to the corporation for redemption in the amount of $20,000. His dividend income is $20,000, and his basis for the shares surrendered (whether more or less than $20,000) is added to the basis of his remaining 800 shares.

EXAMPLE 2

Assume the same facts as in Example 1, except that 510 of the outstanding shares are owned by him and 490 by his wife. The redemption of 400 of the husband's shares or 400 of the wife's shares, or both, will again result in dividend income. By reason of Section 302(c)(1), the constructive-ownership rules of Section 318 apply, and under Section 318(a)(1)(A)(i) the wife is considered at all times to own the shares owned by her husband and vice versa.

EXAMPLE 3

Upon organization of a corporation, an individual paid in cash and property in exchange for all of its stock consisting of 1,000 shares of voting common stock and 500 shares of nonvoting preferred stock. If the corporation redeems any or all of the preferred stock from him, he will have dividend income. The exception of Section 302(b)(2) pertaining to disproportionate redemptions will not apply, because immediately after the redemption he will not own "less than 50 percent of the total combined voting power of all classes of stock entitled to vote" [Section 302(b)(2)(B)].

EXAMPLE 4

Smith, Jones, Green, and Brown each own 500 shares in a corporation, and the 2,000 shares constitute all of the outstanding stock. Smith is not related to any of them and is not a partner with any of them in any other venture. He turns in 200 shares for redemption and receives $20,000. This is a disproportionate redemption because immediately after the transaction he owns 16.67 percent of the 1,800 outstanding shares and this percentage is less than 80 percent of the 25 percent of the outstanding shares he owned immediately before the redemption. He has capital-gain income in the amount of the difference between the $20,000 he received and his basis for the 200 shares surrendered.

Exception 3 listed in paragraph 19.54 involves a "facts and circumstances" test to determine whether the redemption is essentially equivalent to the distribution of a dividend. Prior to 1970 a number of Circuit Courts of Appeal applied that exception and allowed capital gain treatment where (1) there was a bona fide business purpose for the redemption and (2) the transaction was not arranged to avoid tax. The cases concerned closely held corporations so that, because of the rules of attribution of stock ownership contained in Section 318 (discussed in paragraph 19.59), there was neither a disproportionate redemption (exception 4) nor a complete termination of the shareholder's interest in the corporation (exception 5, assuming the conditions of Section 302(c) were not applicable). In effect, the Circuit Courts disregarded the rules of attribution. In *U.S. v. Maclin P. Davis*,[12]

12. 397 U.S. 301 (1970), 70–1 USTC ¶9289, 25 AFTR 2d 70–827.

the U.S. Supreme Court held in 1970 that the attribution rules of Section 318 must be given effect, although it did not go so far as to say the mathematical tests of exceptions 4 and 5 (Sections 302(b)(2) and (3)) must always be met. It held that a pro-rata redemption of shareholders' stock will always be a dividend distribution under Sections 301 and 316, whether or not a business reason exists for the redemption. In the event of a non-pro-rata redemption, it said there must be a "meaningful reduction" in the particular taxpayer's proportionate interest in the corporation. As a result of this Supreme Court decision, exception 3 (Section 302(b)(1)) has little present vitality.

19.58   Because of the complexities involved in applying the rules of the cited exceptions, great care is always necessary to determine the exact tax consequences of a redemption of stock. Frequent and careful reference to the Code and regulations is mandatory.

19.59   **Attribution Rules for Stock Ownership.** In dealing with questions of termination of shareholder interests, disproportionate redemptions, and questions of "control" of a corporation, it often is necessary to consult Section 318 that provides extensive and complex rules concerning constructive ownership of stock. Under these rules, commonly referred to as rules of attribution, the ownership of stock may be attributed from one family member to another, from shareholder to corporation and vice versa, from partnerships to partners and vice versa, and from estates and trusts to beneficiaries and vice versa. Furthermore, stock options are considered stock, and stock actually owned by one person but attributed to another under these rules may, in some cases, be further attributed from that person to still another. The need for caution in working with Section 318 cannot be overemphasized.

19.60   **Taxation of Distributing Corporation.** It was noted earlier in this chapter that corporations ordinarily do not recognize gain or loss on property distributed to shareholders unless that property constitutes LIFO inventory, property subject to liabilities in excess of basis, or certain types of recapture property. Although a redemption of stock is a form of distribution to shareholders, Section 311(d), enacted by the Tax Reform Act of 1969, provides that gain *is* recognized by a corporation on the transfer of property in redemption of its stock if the property has a value in excess of its adjusted basis. However, this gain is not recognized if the redemption is in connection with a partial liquidation, a complete liquidation, or a reorganization of the corporation under Section 368. Further, Section 311(d)(2) enumerates several other rather involved situations in which gain or loss is not recognized. Examples are certain redemptions of all the stock of shareholders owning at least 10 percent in value of the outstanding stock, certain distributions of stock of operating subsidiaries, and distributions to pay death taxes under Section 303(a).

Section 306 Stock

Ordinarily, a shareholder's sale (as opposed to a redemption) of   19.61
stock in a corporation results in a capital gain or loss for tax purposes
unless the shareholder is a dealer in stocks. Section 306 provides a
notable exception to this rule by designating certain circumstances
under which proceeds from the sale or redemption of preferred stock
will be treated as ordinary income rather than capital gain. Section
306 closes what was thought to be a loophole in prior law called a
"preferred-stock bailout" which was publicized in the famous case
of *Chamberlin* v. *Com.*[13]

In the *Chamberlin* case, the shareholders of a corporation caused   19.62
the corporation to distribute to holders of common stock a stock dividend in redeemable preferred stock. The shareholders immediately
sold the preferred stock to two insurance companies. The Internal
Revenue Service tried to tax the proceeds from sale of the preferred
stock as dividends to the selling shareholders. The Sixth Circuit
Court of Appeals held that the distribution of the preferred-stock
dividend was not taxable, and each shareholder's basis in his preferred stock and its holding period was properly determined by reference to his basis and holding period of his common stock. The court
also held that the sale of the preferred stock to the insurance companies was a bona fide sale to bona fide investors; therefore, the entire
series of transactions resulted in capital gain to the selling shareholders rather than dividend income. In rendering this decision, the
court recognized that the economic result to the taxpayers was the
same as though they had received cash dividends from their corporation; nevertheless, it held that under the law as it then existed, the
gain realized was capital gain.

Section 306 was new in the 1954 Code and changed the law as it   19.63
existed at the time of the *Chamberlin* case. Under Section 306, proceeds from the sale or redemption of preferred stock generally are
ordinary income if the preferred stock was received as a dividend on
common stock, or if it was received in a nontaxable transaction yield-
ing results substantially similar to the receipt of a stock dividend.
To prevent hardship, however, the code provides certain exceptions
in Section 306(b) to this ordinary-income treatment where the taxpayer's receipt of the preferred stock and his sale thereof does not
yield a result to him equivalent to a dividend. For example, if the
payment of a cash dividend in lieu of the stock dividend would not
have been taxable to the shareholder because of an absence of earnings and profits in the corporation, then the proceeds from the sale of
the preferred stock are not treated as ordinary income. Likewise, if
the preferred stock is redeemed and the corporation has no earnings
and profits at date of redemption, the proceeds from the redemption
are not treated as ordinary income. Furthermore, if the sale or redemp-

13. 207 F.2d 462 (6th Cir. 1953), 53–2 USTC ¶9576, 44 AFTR 494.

tion of the preferred stock results in a complete termination of the shareholder's interest in the corporation, or if the preferred stock is redeemed in connection with the complete liquidation of the corporation, the ordinary-income treatment will not apply.

19.64   Section 306 operates as an effective barrier against the "preferred-stock bailout" device. The provisions of Section 306 are so broad that any prospective seller of preferred stock should determine carefully in advance whether his proceeds will be treated as dividends or proceeds from sale of a capital asset. When in doubt, a ruling should be requested.

PARTIAL LIQUIDATIONS—SECTION 346

19.65   It was indicated in paragraph 19.54 that a distribution in partial liquidation of a corporation is treated by the shareholder as a sale or exchange of his stock and not as the receipt of a dividend. Also, if the corporation distributes property in partial liquidation, it does not recognize gain even though such property has a value in excess of its adjusted basis [paragraph 19.59]. The determination of whether or not a distribution is in connection with a partial liquidation is made under Section 346. Regulation 1.346–1 explains a partial liquidation as follows:

(a) *General*—This section defines a partial liquidation. If amounts are distributed in partial liquidation such amounts are treated under Section 331(a)(2) as received in part or full payment in exchange for the stock. A distribution is treated as in partial liquidation of the corporation if:

(1) the distribution is one of a series of distributions in redemption of all of the stock of the corporation pursuant to a plan of complete liquidation, or

(2) the distribution:

(i) Is not essentially equivalent to a dividend

(ii) Is in redemption of a part of the stock of the corporation pursuant to a plan, and

(iii) Occurs within the taxable year in which the plan is adopted or within the succeeding taxable year.

An example of a distribution which will qualify as a partial liquidation under subparagraph (2) of this paragraph and section 346(a) is a distribution resulting from a genuine contraction of the corporate business such as the distribution of unused insurance proceeds recovered as a result of a fire which destroyed part of the business causing a cessation of a part of its activities. On the other hand, the distribution of funds attributable to a reserve for an expansion program which has been abandoned does not qualify as a partial liquidation within the meaning of section 346(a). ...

19.66   This regulation indicates the importance of a *plan* of partial liquidation. The plan must be adopted by the corporation and the distributions pursuant to the partial liquidation must occur within the year in which the plan is adopted or within the succeeding taxable year.

19.67   The other requirement for a partial liquidation is that distributions pursuant thereto must not be "essentially equivalent to a dividend." Ordinarily, in order for a distribution not to be essentially equivalent to a dividend, it must be in connection with a genuine contraction of the corporate business. This is a subjective requirement, which depends for its satisfaction upon the effect of all facts and circumstances surrounding the distribution. To assist taxpayers in meeting these subjective requirements, Section 346(b) sets forth some specific circumstances that will be deemed to meet the requirements of a partial liquidation; however, subsection (b) is not all-inclusive. Regulation 1.346–1(b) describes these circumstances as follows:

(b) *Special requirements on termination of business.* A distribution which occurs within the taxable year in which the plan is adopted or within the succeeding taxable year and which meets the requirements of subsection (b) of section 346 falls within paragraph (a)(2) [that is, a partial liquidation] of this section and within section 346(a)(2). The requirements which a distribution must meet to fall within subsection (b) of section 346 are:

(1) Such distribution is attributable to the corporation's ceasing to conduct, or consists of assets of, a trade or business which has been actively conducted throughout the five-year period immediately before the distribution, which trade or business was not acquired by the corporation within such period in a transaction in which gain or loss was recognized in whole or in part, and

(2) Immediately after such distribution by the corporation it is actively engaged in the conduct of a trade or business, which trade or business was actively conducted throughout the five-year period ending on the date of such distribution and was not acquired by the corporation within such period in a transaction in which gain or loss was recognized in whole or in part.

A distribution shall be treated as having been made in partial liquidation pursuant to Section 346(b) if it consists of the proceeds of the sale of the assets of a trade or business which has been actively conducted for the five-year period and has been terminated, or if it is a distribution in kind of the assets of such a business, or if it is a distribution in kind of some of the assets of such a business and of the proceeds of the sale of the remainder of the assets of such a business ...

This requirement of Section 346(b) is generally referred to as the "five-year-business-requirement." Although it is required that the business being distributed have been conducted for five years, that conduct need not have been by the distributing corporation. On the other hand, if that business has not been conducted for at least five years by the distributing corporation, that corporation must not have acquired the business within that period in a taxable transaction. Thus, the business can qualify for distribution in a partial liquidation if it has been conducted by a predecessor of the distributing corporation, and the distributing corporation acquired the business in a tax-free transaction. 19.68

It also should be noted that the distributing corporation must continue to be actively engaged in the conduct of a trade or business after the distribution, which trade or business must have been actively conducted throughout the five-year period ending on the date of such distribution. Again, this business need not have been conducted during this period by the distributing corporation, but, if not, it must have been acquired during that period in a nontaxable transaction. 19.69

19.70   Sometimes a tax problem arises in connection with the sale of the assets of a business shortly after their distribution in partial liquidation of a corporation. Sometimes this sale is contemplated before the distribution by the corporation, and the tax problem involves whether the corporation or the shareholder in substance made the sale. If a business is sold by a corporation, the corporation will pay a tax on the gain from the sale. Then, if the corporation distributes the proceeds from the sale in a partial liquidation, the distributee-shareholder will pay another tax on the liquidating distribution. To avoid this double tax, the assets of a business often are distributed in partial liquidation of the corporation, and the receiving shareholder then sells such assets. The shareholder reports a capital gain on the liquidating distribution, but he takes a basis in the assets equal to their fair market value and realizes no further gain on the sale of those assets. In this situation, Reg. 1.346–3 provides as follows:

> The determination of whether assets sold in connection with a partial liquidation are sold by the distributing corporation or by the shareholder is a question of fact to be determined under the facts and circumstances of each case.

Thus, if a part of a corporation's business is to be sold and the proceeds distributed in partial liquidation, significant tax savings often can be realized by distributing the assets and letting the shareholders make the sale. However, considerable care must be exercised to make sure that the sale is in fact, as well as in form, negotiated and consummated by the shareholders after the distribution. Any transaction of this type will be closely scrutinized by the Internal Revenue Service to make sure the sale was not in substance made by the corporation and thus taxable to it.

COMPLETE LIQUIDATIONS

General Rules

19.71   Complete liquidations of corporations usually involve few tax controversies. The shareholders treat the transaction as a sale or exchange of their stock (Section 331) and ordinarily recognize capital gain or loss to the extent of any difference between the amounts received and the adjusted basis of their stock (Section 1001). When a corporation is being liquidated by a series of distributions, the shareholders apply the first distributions to the recovery of adjusted basis in their stock. Gain is reported when receipts exceed adjusted basis. Losses are reported when it is determinable with reasonable certainty that receipts will be less than adjusted basis of stock.[14] When an individual shareholder receives property other than money, his basis in the property is usually equal to the property's fair market value at the date received [Section 334(a)].

19.72   The liquidating corporation generally recognizes no gain or loss

14. Rev. Rul. 68–348, 1968–2 C.B. 141.

on its distributions of property (Section 336). Exceptions to this rule are (1) the recapture of depreciation and other deductions on distribution of depreciable and other types of recapture property and (2) the income required to be recognized under Section 453(d) on dispositions of installment obligations. However, the rules of Section 311 requiring corporations to recognize gain on the distribution of LIFO inventory and certain other appreciated properties distributed in redemption of stock do not apply to distributions in partial or complete liquidation [Reg. 1.311–1(a)].

One-Month Liquidations—Section 333

Section 333 offers substantial relief to shareholders of a liquidating corporation which owns property that has a substantial amount of unrealized appreciation in value. If a sufficient number of qualified shareholders elect the benefits of Section 333, their gain on the liquidation attributable to the unrealized appreciation will not be recognized.   **19.73**

Under Section 333, the gain of a qualified electing shareholder is recognized as follows: **19.74**

(1) Shareholders other than corporations—a noncorporate shareholder's gain, to the extent of his share of the earnings and profits of the corporation, is taxable to him as a dividend for all purposes. Any remaining gain is taxable as a long-term or short-term capital gain, as the case may be, to the extent that money and the fair market value of stock or securities acquired by the corporation after December 31, 1953, which he receives, exceed his share of the corporation's earnings and profits. Any remaining gain is not recognized.

(2) Corporate shareholders—a corporate shareholder's gain is recognized to the extent of the greater of (a) its share of the earnings and profits of the liquidating corporation or (b) the value of the assets received consisting of money, and stock and securities acquired by the liquidating corporation after December 31, 1953. The corporate shareholder's recognized gain is treated as a long-term or short-term capital gain, as the case may be.

The benefits of Section 333 can be very substantial in situations where liquidating corporations have substantial amounts of appreciated property but a relatively small amount of earnings and profits accumulated after February 28, 1913. However, the price paid for not recognizing gain attributable to this unrealized appreciation is the requirement that the noncorporate shareholder recognize his gain as a dividend to the extent of his share of the corporation's earnings and profits.   **19.75**

The basis of property received by a shareholder in a Section 333 liquidation is equal to the adjusted basis of his stock in the liquidated corporation plus any gain recognized and minus any money received. The basis so determined is allocated over the properties received on the basis of their relative fair market values.   **19.76**

The benefits of Section 333 are available only to "qualified electing shareholders." Such benefits are then available only if (1) the liquidation of the corporation is made pursuant to a plan of liquidation adopted on or after June 22, 1954, (2) the distribution is in complete   **19.77** cancellation or redemption of all the stock of the corporation, and (3) the transfer of all property under the liquidation occurs within one calendar month. This one calendar month need not be the month the plan of liquidation is adopted; however, when the first liquidating transfer of property is made, all other liquidating transfers must be made within the same calendar month.

19.78   Qualified electing shareholders are determined by dividing all shareholders into three groups. First, any corporation that has owned stock possessing 50 percent or more of the total combined voting power of stock at any time between January 1, 1954 and the adoption of the plan of liquidation is considered an "excluded corporation" and is not entitled to the benefits of Section 333. Shareholders other than excluded corporations are then divided into two groups. The first group consists of shareholders who are corporations. If shareholders in this group who possess at least 80 percent of the total voting power of all stock held by this group elect in writing to receive the benefits of Section 333, all shareholders so electing will be "qualified electing shareholders." The third group of shareholders is composed of shareholders other than corporations. If shareholders in this group possessing at least 80 percent of the total voting power of stock owned by the group elect in writing to have the benefits of Section 333, all shareholders so electing will be qualified electing shareholders. The written elections of all shareholders must be filed, pursuant to the regulations, within thirty days after the date of the adoption of the plan of liquidation.

19.79   The benefits of Section 333 are elective, because some shareholders (for example those having large capital losses) may prefer to report their total gain on the liquidation as a capital gain rather than to report a lesser amount of gain, part as a capital gain and another part as a dividend.

19.80   Like all relief provisions, the requirements of Section 333 are meticulous, and they must be strictly observed. Furthermore, Section 333 does not apply at all if the corporation is a collapsible corporation to which Section 341(a) applies. That section treats gain on the liquidation of a collapsible corporation as ordinary income.

Twelve-Month Liquidations—Section 337

19.81   Section 337 is a relief provision that applies at the corporate level, in contrast to Section 333 that applies at the shareholder level. It is useful where corporations propose to sell part or all of their properties and completely liquidate. Under Section 337, if a corporation adopts a plan of complete liquidation and within twelve months after the adoption of the plan distributes all its assets in complete liquidation, less assets retained to meet claims, then no gain or loss is recognized to the liquidating corporation from the sale or exchange of property within such twelve-month period. Section 337 does not apply to sales of inventory and other property held by the corporation primarily for sale to customers in the ordinary course of its business or to installment obligations acquired in respect of *such sales* unless such properties are sold or exchanged to one person in one transaction. Section 337 also does not exempt the corporation from tax on recapture income under Sections 1245, 1250, 1251 and 1252. It will be recalled that those recapture provisions apply irrespective of the nonrecognition provisions of other sections of the Code.

19.82

Section 337 was enacted to eliminate controversies over whether property sold by shareholders immediately after its receipt in complete liquidation of a corporation was actually sold by the corporation or by the shareholders. The leading case in this area was *Com.* v. *Court Holding Co.*,[15] in which the United States Supreme Court held in effect that whether such properties were sold by the shareholders or by the liquidating corporation was a question of fact to be decided on the circumstances in each case. (See discussion of tax consequences at paragraph 19.69). Much litigation resulted from transactions such as this, and, to minimize these controversies, Section 337 was enacted in the Internal Revenue Code of 1954.

19.83

Section 337 does not apply to a corporation that meets the definition of a collapsible corporation in Section 341(b), and it does not apply to liquidations to which Section 333 applies. Further, if at least 80 percent of the stock of the liquidating corporation is owned by another corporation that is not taxable on the distribution under Section 332 (paragraph 19.85), then Section 337 does not apply to sales of assets by the liquidating corporation. However, in this last situation, a minority shareholder whose liquidating gain is subject to tax can obtain some relief under Section 337(d) in the form of a tax credit equal to his pro rata share of the corporation's tax applicable to the sale of property during the twelve-month liquidation period.

19.84

If a corporate shareholder's basis in property received from the liquidating corporation is determined under Section 334(b)(2) (see paragraph 19.87), then special calculations are required and a partial benefit of Section 337 may be available to the liquidating corporation.

19.85

In any twelve-month liquidation, time is of the essence. The twelve-month period within which liquidation must be completed begins with the date the plan of liquidation is adopted. This period cannot be extended (Reg. 1.337–1).

Intercorporate Liquidations of Subsidiaries—Section 332

19.86

If a corporation owns less than 80 percent of the stock of a liquidating corporation, its tax consequences from the receipt of property in the liquidation are the same as an individual's, and the basis of any property received is its fair market value [Section 334(a)]. If it owns 80 percent or more of the voting stock and at least 80 percent of the shares of nonvoting stock (other than nonvoting preferred), then under Section 332 no gain or loss is recognized to the parent corporation upon receipt of property in complete liquidation of the subsidiary. However, such liquidation must be completed within three years from the date a plan of liquidation is adopted by the corporation. Further,

15. 324 U.S. 331 (1945), 45–1 USTC ¶9215, 33 AFTR 593.

the parent corporation must maintain its 80 percent ownership throughout the period between the adoption of the plan and the receipt of the liquidating distribution.

19.87 **Carry-over of Basis.** The basis of property received by a parent corporation in a complete liquidation of a subsidiary under Section 332 depends upon how long the parent owned, and how it acquired, its stock in the subsidiary. If the stock has been owned for more than two years, the adjusted basis of the subsidiary in each asset transferred carries over and becomes the basis of the parent [Section 334(b)(1)]. If the stock in the subsidiary was acquired in a nontaxable transaction, such as in a reorganization, and has been held either more or less than two years, again basis carries over [Section 334(b)(1)].

19.88 **Step-up in Basis—Section 334(b)(2).** If the stock has been owned for two years or less and if at least 80 percent of the voting stock and at least 80 percent of the shares of nonvoting stock (other than nonvoting preferred) was acquired by purchase, then the parent corporation's aggregate basis of the assets received in the liquidation becomes an amount equal to its adjusted basis in its stock in the subsidiary plus liabilities assumed or taken over and plus any increase or minus any decrease in earnings and profits of the subsidiary between the date of purchase of the stock and the date of liquidation [Section 334(b)(2); Reg. 1.334–1(c)]. In such a liquidation the purchase of the subsidiary's stock is treated, in substance, as a purchase of its underlying assets. Section 334(b)(2) is a codification of a judge-made rule made famous in the case of *Kimbell–Diamond Milling Company.*[16] The Tax Court there held that if a corporation's sole intention at the time of the purchase of all the stock of another corporation was to acquire its assets and to liquidate it as soon as practicable, and the liquidation was carried out expeditiously, the two transactions of purchase and liquidation in substance were one and must be treated as a purchase of assets.

REORGANIZATIONS

19.89   When businesses are conducted in the corporate form, situations often arise that call for a rearrangement of the corporate structure of the business. In many cases, these transactions do not change the economic position of the corporations or the relationships between the shareholders and the corporate businesses sufficiently to justify the imposition of an income tax. In recognition of this fact, to keep the income tax from being an undue burden on the normal conduct of business, and to encourage the mobility of capital, the Code provides rules under which certain transactions of this kind can be carried out tax-free. Thus, under certain circumstances, gain or loss is not recognized on (1) exchanges of stock and securities by shareholders in connection with "reorganizations" [Sections 354 and 368], and (2) exchanges of property by corporations for stock and securities in

16. 14 T.C. 74 (1950), affirmed *per curiam* 187 F.2d 718 (5th Cir. 1951), 51–1 USTC ¶9201, 40 AFTR 328, cert. den.

other corporations in connection with "reorganizations" [Sections 361 and 368]. For this purpose, the term "reorganization" includes certain types of mergers, acquisitions, and divisions of corporations as well as certain types of recapitalizations and mere changes in name or state of incorporation.

19.90 Because the nonrecognition of gain or loss on any exchange of stock or property is contrary to the general rules of taxation, the rules of the Code concerning these tax-favored transactions are very specific. Taxpayers participating in these transactions must observe the appropriate rules strictly in order to avoid recognition of gain; furthermore, the true substance of the transaction must be in accord with the form utilized to effect the reorganization. It is quite common, now, for taxpayers to request rulings on the consequences of proposed reorganizations and recapitalizations.

19.91 Before considering the types of transactions that constitute reorganizations, this and the next few paragraphs will review the overall statutory scheme under which these transactions can be effected tax-free. First, transactions that constitute corporate "reorganizations" are described in detail in Section 368. Section 354 then provides that no gain or loss is recognized by shareholders (individuals or corporate) who exchange stock or securities *solely* for stock or securities of corporations that are parties to reorganizations. If shareholders receive not only stock or securities but also other property or money ("boot"), the transaction is part tax-free and part taxable under Section 356. The amount of the boot is taxable up to the amount of the gain realized and will usually be treated as dividend income. As will be seen shortly, there are only a few types of reorganizations that can qualify even in part as tax-free if any boot is distributed. If a particular reorganization is not one of those types and if boot is distributed, then the entire reorganization is taxable under Section 1002, and Section 356 does not apply.

19.92 Except for a recapitalization, every reorganization involves two or more corporations. An individual, partnership, estate, or trust can never be a "party to a reorganization" as that term is defined in Section 368(b), but, of course, it can and does participate as a shareholder. Section 361 provides that no gain or loss is recognized to a corporation that is a party to a reorganization on the exchange of property solely for stock or securities in another corporation that is also a party to the reorganization.

19.93 If the recipient corporation, in addition to the permitted stock or securities, also receives money or other property from another corporation, the amount of such boot is taxable to the extent of the gain realized on the reorganization exchange; but such boot is not taxable if distributed to shareholders of the recipient corporation pursuant to the plan of reorganization [Section 361(b)]. Section 357 provides that only under certain circumstances will liabilities assumed in reorganizations be treated as boot, and Section 358 sets forth rules for the determination of the basis of property, stock, or securities received in reorganizations. Before a foreign corporation can be considered a corporation for tax-free reorganization purposes, Section 367 requires that an advance ruling be obtained from the Treasury Department to the effect that a proposed exchange is not in pursuance of a plan having as one of its principal purposes the avoidance of federal income taxes.

The Six Types of Reorganizations

19.94   Six types of reorganizations are defined in paragraphs (A) through (F) of Section 368(a)(1). These are customarily referred to by tax practitioners by paragraph letter. Thus, an A type reorganization is a statutory merger or consolidation; a B type reorganization is an exchange solely of stock for stock in which one corporation acquires stock of another corporation solely in exchange for its own voting stock; a C type reorganization is sometimes referred to as a practical merger in which one corporation acquires substantially all the properties of another corporation in exchange solely for all or a part of the acquiring corporation's voting stock; a D type reorganization includes two types of transactions: (1) a division of one corporation into two or more corporations controlled by the same shareholders, and (2) a transfer of substantially all of the assets of one corporation to another corporation controlled by the transferor or its shareholders followed by the complete liquidation of the transferor corporation; an E type reorganization is a recapitalization; and an F type is a mere change in identity, form, or place of incorporation.

19.95   To have a nontaxable reorganization under Section 368 it is necessary also to have present three factors developed by the courts:

1. continuity of business enterprise;
2. continuity of an equity (stock) interest by the transferors as a group (more than 50 percent in value of their prior holdings according to the Service); and
3. corporate business purpose.

19.96   For discussion purposes reorganizations are divided into five groups: asset acquisitions (A and C types), stock acquisitions (B type), corporate divisions (D type), recapitalizations (E type), and mere changes in form (F type).

Asset Acquisitions

19.97   When one corporation wishes to acquire the assets and business of another, it often can do so through a statutory merger or consolidation. The word "statutory" means there must be an available corporation law of the United States, a state, the District of Columbia or a territory permitting the merger or consolidation, and all of the provisions of that corporation law must be complied with. If the requirements of corporation law make a statutory merger or consolidation impractical, a technique sometimes referred to as a "practical merger" is utilized. This practical merger involves the acquisition by one corporation of substantially all the properties and business of the other corporation solely in exchange for voting stock of the first corporation.

Statutory Mergers and Consolidations—A Type. From a tax stand-   19.98
point a statutory merger or consolidation is one of the simpler types
of reorganizations. In a statutory merger all the assets, liabilities, and
business of one or more corporations are transferred to another existing corporation. As a practical matter, the transferor corporation then
ceases to exist, but in a theoretical legal sense it is said to continue
to live inside the corporate body of the surviving corporation. The
transferee corporation, called the surviving corporation, issues its
stock to the shareholders of the first corporation(s), and thereafter
the businesses of all corporations are carried on under the charter of
the surviving corporation.

In a statutory consolidation, the assets, liabilities, and businesses   19.99
of two or more existing corporations are transferred to a new corporation, and the old corporations cease to exist. The new corporation
issues its stock to shareholders of the old corporations, and the new
corporation then carries on the business of all the old corporations.

The corporation laws of Delaware and some other states permit a   19.100
wholly owned subsidiary corporation, by use of its parent's stock, to
acquire a stranger corporation through a statutory merger into the subsidiary. The mechanics are, first, the parent creates the subsidiary
(unless it already exists); secondly, the parent transfers its stock to the
subsidiary as a contribution to capital or in exchange for new stock
of the subsidiary; and, thirdly, the subsidiary transfers its investment,
consisting of stock of its parent, for all of the net assets of the stranger
corporation. This is known as a triangular merger and was permitted
to be tax-free for the first time in late 1968 by reason of new subparagraph (D) of Section 368(a)(2). This relatively new technique is a
bonanza for acquisition minded conglomerates because it eliminates
the expense of a special shareholders' meeting to approve a proposed
acquisition through a statutory merger into the conglomerate parent.
Further, the new provision is also helpful to closely held corporations
where the family, perhaps for estate tax reasons, wishes to sell out to a
large listed corporation to obtain readily marketable securities. There
are two requirements for tax-free treatment: (1) the transaction would
have qualified as a reorganization if the merger had been into the parent corporation, and (2) no stock of the acquiring corporation is used.

Since 1971 there also has been a provision in the Code permitting   19.101
a tax-free reverse triangular statutory merger (Section 368(a)(2)(E)).
Here, a controlled subsidiary of a parent corporation is merged into a
stranger corporation, the stranger corporation survives, and the stock
issued in the merger is that of the parent corporation of the subsidiary
which ceases to exist. The House Ways and Means Committee Report
on P.L. 91–693, which added subparagraph (E) to Section 368(a)(2),
reads in part as follows:

Thus, under existing law [Sec. 368(a)(2)(D)] corporation X (an unrelated
corporation) may be merged into corporation S (a subsidiary) in exchange for
the stock in corporation P (the parent of S) in a tax-free statutory merger. However, if for business and legal reasons (wholly unrelated to Federal income

taxation) it is considered more desirable to merge S into X (rather than merging, X into S), so that X is the surviving corporation—a "reverse merger"—the transaction is not a tax-free statutory merger.

. . .

Your committee believes that there is no reason why a merger in one direction (S into X in the above example) should be taxable, when the merger in the other direction (X into S), under identical circumstances, is tax-free. Moreover, it sees no reason why in cases of this type the acquisition needs to be made solely for stock. For these reasons the amendment makes statutory mergers tax-free in the circumstances described above. [If the following conditions prevail:]

First, the corporation surviving the merger must hold substantially all of its own properties and substantially all of the properties of the merged corporation (except stock of the controlling corporation distributed in the transaction).

Second, in the transaction, former shareholders of the surviving corporation must receive voting stock of the controlling corporation in exchange for an amount of stock representing control in the surviving corporation. Control for this purpose (defined in sec. 368(c)) means that the amount of stock in the surviving corporation surrendered for voting stock of the controlling corporation must represent stock possessing at least 80 percent of the total combined voting power (in the surviving corporation), and also stock amounting to at least 80 percent of the total number of shares of all other classes of stock (in the surviving corporation). If voting stock of the controlling corporation is used in the exchange to the extent described, additional stock in the surviving corporation may be acquired for cash or other property (whether or not from the shareholders who received voting stock). Of course, this additional stock in the surviving corporation need not be acquired by the controlling corporation.

19.102 In professional and financial literature another term is sometimes encountered—a "downstream" merger. This is a statutory merger of a parent into a subsidiary accompanied by a transfer by the parent of shares of stock in the subsidiary in exchange for shares in the parent. The purpose usually is to simplify the corporate structure.

19.103 **Stock for Assets—C Type.** If the particular state laws involved do not lend themselves to a statutory merger or consolidation of two or more corporations, the same result may be obtained by using a C type reorganization. In a C type reorganization, one corporation acquires substantially all of the properties of another corporation in exchange solely for all or a part of its voting stock (or in exchange solely for all or a part of the voting stock of a corporation that is in control of the acquiring corporation). In a transaction of this kind, it seldom is practicable for one corporation to transfer all or substantially all of its assets to another without also transferring its liabilities. Accordingly, Section 368(a)(1)(C) provides that in determining whether or not an acquisition of this type is in exchange solely for voting stock, the assumption by the acquiring corporation of a liability of the other, or the fact that property of the other corporation is acquired subject to a liability, shall be disregarded.

19.104 In a simple C type reorganization, the acquiring corporation exchanges solely voting stock for the properties of the other corporation. Section 368(a)(2)(B), however, does permit the acquiring corporation to issue not only its voting stock but also to pay a small amount of cash or to transfer a minor amount of property to acquire the assets of the other corporation. This mitigating provision is more illusory than real. If the corporation being acquired is one with fairly substantial operations, then as a practical matter the acquiring corporation will be able to transfer nothing other than its voting stock. The reason is that operating corporations usually have sizable amounts of accounts payable and other liabilities. To have a tax-free "C" type reorganization fit within the exception of Section 368(a)(2)(B), the acquiring corporation's voting stock which it issues must be for at least 80 percent of the fair market value of the *gross* assets of the other corporation and the aggregate of money paid, property transferred, *and* liabilities assumed or taken over cannot be more than 20 percent of the fair market value of the gross assets acquired.

19.105   If the exception of Section 368(a)(2)(B) is not available because the liabilities of the corporation to be acquired are too large in amount, but it is necessary to buy out a dissident shareholder for cash, there may be another way to achieve the desired result. As mentioned previously, Section 368(a)(1)(C) requires the acquisition of substantially all of the properties of another corporation. For ruling purposes, the Service holds that the "substantially all" requirement is met if there is a transfer of assets representing at least 90 percent of the fair market value of the net assets and at least 70 percent of the fair market value of the gross assets held by the corporation immediately prior to the transfer.[17] This should mean that the corporation to be acquired can use its *own* cash to redeem shares of one of its own shareholders provided that the cash paid out does not exceed 10 percent of the value of its gross assets immediately prior to the redemption. The redemption date is probably the test date because of the step transaction principle mentioned in paragraph 19.109.

19.106   In a C type reorganization it is not uncommon for the corporation that transfers all of its assets thereafter to be liquidated. If this liquidation is a part of the plan of reorganization adopted by both corporations, the exchange by the shareholders of the liquidating corporation of their stock in exchange for stock of the acquiring corporation will be tax-free under Section 354 as an exchange of stock for stock pursuant to a reorganization. If the liquidating corporation distributes any property other than stock of the acquiring corporation, the shareholders will recognize gain, assuming a gain is realized, to the extent of the value of that other property or money. The income recognized will probably be treated as a dividend unless the facts and circumstances are such that it is not substantially equivalent to a dividend [Section 356(a)(2)].

17. Rev. Proc. 66–34, 1966–2 C.B. 1232, amplified by Rev. Proc. 67–13, 1967–1 C.B. 590.

Stock Acquisitions—B Type

19.107   If one corporation wishes to acquire control of another corporation, or if it already has control and wishes to acquire additional stock, this can be done tax-free by an exchange of stock under Section 368(a)(1)(B). A reorganization of the B type involves the acquisition by one corporation, in exchange solely for all or a part of its voting stock (or its parent corporation's voting stock), of stock of another corporation if, immediately after the acquisition, the acquiring corporation has control of the other corporation.

19.108   "Control" for all purposes of corporate reorganizations under Section 368 means the ownership of stock possessing at least 80 percent of the total combined voting power of all classes of stock entitled to vote and at least 80 percent of the total number of shares of all other classes of stock.

19.109   In a B type reorganization it is not necessary that control of the acquired corporation be obtained in the reorganization transaction. It is required that the acquiring corporation be in control of the acquired corporation immediately after the acquisition. Thus, if a corporation is the owner of 30 percent of the stock of another corporation, and it later acquires an additional 50 percent of the stock of that corporation in a transaction completely unrelated to its acquisition of its first 30 percent, the second acquisition of stock, if solely in exchange for voting stock of the acquiring corporation, is a tax-free reorganization. On the other hand, if the acquisition of the first 30 percent of the stock and the acquisition of the additional 50 percent are separate steps of a single overall plan for the acquisition of control of the second corporation, both acquisitions would have to meet the test of Section 368(a)(1)(B) in order for either to be tax-free. If both acquisitions are part of a single plan, they are referred to as step transactions and the overall effect of step transactions must be considered for tax purposes rather than the separate effects of each step. Thus, if pursuant to such an overall plan the first 30 percent of the stock were acquired for cash and the next 50 percent were acquired solely for voting stock, neither acquisition would qualify as a reorganization because the overall acquisition would not be "solely for voting stock."[18]

19.110   The most difficult problem generally encountered in B reorganizations is the requirement that the acquisition be "solely" for voting stock of the acquiring corporation or a corporation in control of it. If dissident shareholders of the acquired corporation refuse to take stock and demand cash for their stock, it will not be possible to effect the transaction as a B type reorganization, unless as a first step the shares of the dissidents are eliminated by redemption or purchase. Perhaps the dissident shares can first be redeemed by the corporation about to be acquired by the use of its own funds.[19] Somewhat more certainly, an individual shareholder, either of the acquiring cor-

18. Rev. Rul. 69–48, 1969–1 C.B. 106.
19. Bittker and Eustice, *Federal Income Taxation of Corporations and Shareholders*, 3rd ed. (Boston, Warren, Gorham & Lamont, Inc., 1971) pp. 14–35.

poration or of the corporation to be acquired, acting in his individual capacity and outside the plan of reorganization, could purchase the dissident shares and then at the later time of voting on the plan could vote in favor of it and exchange his newly purchased shares for shares of the acquiring corporation.[20] Likewise, if the acquiring corporation pays legal and other expenses of the acquired corporation or its shareholders in connection with the transaction, the payment of such expenses probably will be considered consideration for the acquisition, thus preventing it from being "solely for voting stock." However, the acquiring corporation is permitted to pay cash in lieu of transferring fractional shares to shareholders of the acquired corporation.[21]

Corporate Divisions—D Type

Whereas the A, B, and C type reorganizations involve corporate mergers and acquisitions, the D type reorganization more often than not involves the division of one corporation into two or more corporations. A D type reorganization requires two steps. First, the corporation transfers all or part of its assets to another corporation that is controlled immediately after the transfer by the transferor corporation, one or more of its shareholders, or some combination of both. Shareholders for this purpose include those who may cease to be shareholders during the reorganization. Second, the transferor corporation then distributes to its shareholders, pursuant to the plan of reorganization, all of its stock or securities of the corporation to which the assets were transferred and such distribution must meet the requirements of Section 354, 355, or 356.   19.111

If the corporation transferring the property or its shareholders control the transferee corporation before the transfer, the transfer of property need not be in exchange for stock or securities of the transferee. If the necessary control does not exist before the transfer, then of course the transfer must be in exchange for sufficient stock to vest control in the transferor corporation, its shareholders, or a combination of both.   19.112

All stock and securities of the transferee controlled corporation that are held by the transferor corporation after the transfer must be distributed to the shareholders of the transferor. If the purpose of the transaction is to effect a division of the corporate business, this distribution must qualify under Sections 355 and 356, and the separate-business and other requirements of Section 355 must be met. If the purpose is not to divide the corporation, then the distribution will be made under Sections 354 and 356. In this event, Section 354 requires that the transferor corporation in the reorganization must transfer substantially all its properties to the controlled corporation and then it must distribute its remaining properties along with its stock and securities of the controlled corporation pursuant to the plan of reorganization. The overall effect of these combined requirements of Sections 368(a)(1)(D), 354, 355, and 356 is to force all di-   19.113

---

20. Rev. Rul. 68–562, 1968–2 C.B. 157, involving a shareholder of the acquiring corporation.
21. Rev. Rul. 66–365, 1966–2 C.B. 116.

visive reorganizations to meet the separate-business and other requirements of Section 355. The requirements of Sections 354 and 355 will be discussed later.

19.114   A common D type reorganization can be illustrated as follows:

EXAMPLE   Corporation A, owned equally by individuals X and Y, has operated a men's clothing store and a ladies' ready-to-wear store in separate locations in the same city for more than five years. The men's store is transferred to Corporation B in exchange for all of B's stock which is then distributed pro rata to A's shareholders. Assuming all requirements of Section 355 are met, there will be a reorganization. This type of transaction is often referred to as a "spin-off."

Recapitalizations—E Type

19.115   A recapitalization is a rearrangement of the capital structure of a corporation, such as the issuance of common stock in exchange for preferred stock previously outstanding; the issuance of preferred stock in exchange for common stock previously held by certain shareholders; the issuance of preferred stock or common stock in discharge of bonds; or the issuance of one class of preferred stock in exchange for another class of preferred stock. Ordinarily, the issuance of bonds or other evidences of indebtedness in redemption of common stock or preferred stock will not constitute a tax-free recapitalization. Furthermore, if the issuance of common stock or preferred stock in redemption of preferred stock with dividends in arrears is made solely for the purpose of effecting the payment of dividends upon the preferred stock for the current and immediately preceding taxable years, an amount equal to the value of the stock issued in lieu of such dividend will be treated as a distribution of property to the shareholders and not as a part of the recapitalization [Reg. 1.368–2(e)(5)].

Changes in Form—F Type

19.116   The F type reorganization is the simplest type of all reorganizations and involves a mere change in identity, form, or place of organization of a corporation. This type of reorganization most commonly involves either the change in name of a corporation or the change in state of incorporation. Changing the state of incorporation requires the formation of a new corporation in the new state followed by either a statutory merger of the old corporation into the new one or a C type reorganization in which properties are transferred to the new corporation and the old corporation is liquidated. A change in name usually involves the issuance of new stock certificates bearing the new name in cancellation of the certificates bearing the old name. However effected, if the substance of the transaction is a mere change in identity, form, or place of organization it will qualify as an F type reorganization.

Further Requirements of Reorganizations

19.117   In addition to meeting the definitional requirements of Section

368(a), tax-free exchanges pursuant to reorganizations must meet certain other requirements.

Party to a Reorganization. Stocks or securities involved in the exchanges must be those of corporations that are *parties to the reorganization* in order that their receipt may be tax-free to the recipients. Section 368(b) defines a party to a reorganization as a corporation resulting from a reorganization and both corporations involved in those cases of a reorganization resulting from the acquisition by one corporation of stock or properties of another. Also, in A, B, or C type reorganizations if the stock exchanged for stock or properties of another corporation is stock of a corporation controlling the acquiring corporation, the term "party to a reorganization" includes the corporation so controlling the acquiring corporation.

19.118

Plan of Reorganization. The exchanges of stocks or securities must also be *pursuant to the plan of reorganization.* A plan of reorganization includes an interdependent series of acts that taken together constitute a consummated transaction specifically defined in Section 368(a). Ordinarily the plan should be put in writing and properly adopted by the boards of directors and frequently by the shareholders of both corporations.

19.119

Nonstatutory Requirements. The requirements discussed so far have been requirements set by statute. In addition, other requirements have developed over the years as a result of judicial interpretation of the purposes of the reorganization provisions. In a reorganization there must be continuity of business enterprise, a continuity of interest on the part of the owners of the businesses involved in the reorganization, and the reorganization must be pursuant to a bona fide purpose that is germane to the business of the corporations involved. These nonstatutory requirements are described in Reg. 1.368–1 as follows:

19.120

(b) ... The purpose of the reorganization provisions of the Code is to except from the general rule certain specifically described exchanges incident to such readjustments of corporate structures, made in one of the particular ways specified in the Code, as are required by business exigencies and which effect only a readjustment of continuing interest in property under modified corporate forms. Requisite to a reorganization under the Code are a continuity of the business enterprise under the modified corporate form, and [except as provided in Section 368(a)(1)(D)], a continuity of interest therein on the part of those persons who, directly or indirectly, were the owners of the enterprise prior to the reorganization. The Code recognizes as a reorganization the amalgamation (occurring in a specified way) of two corporate enterprises under a single corporate structure if there exists among the holders of the stock and securities of either of the old corporations the requisite continuity of interest in the new corporation, but there is not a reorganization if the holders of the stock and securities of the old corporation are merely the holders of short-term notes in the new corporation. In order to exclude transactions not intended to be included, the specifications of the reorganization provisions of the law are precise. Both the terms of the specifications and their underlying assumptions and purposes must be satisfied in order to entitle the taxpayer to the benefit of the exception from the general rule ...

(c) Scope ... A plan of reorganization must contemplate the bona fide execution of one of the transactions specifically described as a reorganization in Section 368(a) and for the bona fide consummation of each of the requisite acts under which nonrecognition of gain is claimed. Such transaction and such acts must be an ordinary and necessary incident of the conduct of the enterprise and must provide for a continuation of the enterprise. A scheme which involves an abrupt departure from normal reorganization procedure in connection with a transaction on which the imposition of tax is imminent, such as a mere device that puts on the form of a corporate reorganization as a disguise for concealing its real character, and the object and accomplishment of which is the consummation of a preconceived plan having no business or corporate purpose, is not a plan of reorganization.

Exchanges Pursuant to Corporate Reorganizations

19.121   Involved in corporate reorganizations are, first, exchanges by shareholders of stock and securities, and second, exchanges by corporations of property for stock or securities in other corporations.

19.122   **Exchanges by Shareholders.** Under Section 354, no gain or loss is recognized if stock or securities in a corporation that is a party to a reorganization are, pursuant to the plan of reorganization, exchanged solely for stock or securities in such corporation or in another corporation that is a party to the reorganization. Securities for this purpose include evidences of indebtedness other than mere short-term notes and similar documents more comparable to cash than to investments. When securities are involved in a reorganization exchange, if the securities received exceed the principal amount of securities surrendered, any gain realized will be recognized to the extent of the excess.

19.123   It will be remembered, that in reorganizations of the A, C, and D types, corporations sometimes transfer not only stock and securities but also other property or money (boot). When such boot is received by a shareholder, any gain realized is recognized to the extent of the boot received. Furthermore, this gain recognized will be treated as a dividend, unless it can be demonstrated that it is not essentially equivalent to a dividend (Section 356).

19.124   In the B type reorganization no boot is allowed; accordingly, if any boot is paid by the acquiring corporation, there will be no tax-free reorganization and the total transaction will be taxable to the shareholders exchanging stock.

19.125   **Exchanges by Corporations.** When corporations transfer property in connection with A, C, or D type reorganizations, Section 361 provides that no gain or loss shall be recognized on the transfer if it is pursuant to a plan of reorganization and is in exchange solely for stock or securities in another corporation that is a party to the reorganization. Under Section 361(d), if property other than stock or securities is received in connection with a reorganization, and if such other property is not distributed pursuant to the plan of reorganization, any gain realized will be recognized to the extent of the other property or money received and not distributed. When a corporation transfers property subject to a liability or when the transferee assumes a liability of the transferor, as long as the liabilities do not disqualify the transaction as a reorganization, such liabilities generally will not be considered other property or money; hence they will not cause gain to be recognized [Section 357(a)]. However, it should be remembered that in a C type reorganization in which other property or money is transferred, if the other property or money and the liabilities together equal more than 20 percent of the value of the transferor corporation's properties, the transaction will not qualify as a reorganization; therefore, the total gain realized on the transaction will be recognized. Further, if the transfer of property subject to liabilities, or the assumption of liabilities, has as its principal purpose the avoidance of federal income tax or any other purpose that is not a bona fide business purpose, such liabilities will be treated as money and gain will be recognized accordingly [Section 357].

Distributions Under Section 355

Section 355 covers the tax-free division of a corporation under certain circumstances with or without being pursuant to a reorganization. Under Section 355, a corporation may distribute to its shareholders the stock or securities of an existing corporation or it may distribute stock of a new corporation that it has just acquired in exchange for property transferred down to it pursuant to a D type reorganization. In both cases, the distribution must meet the following tests: 19.126

1. The distribution must consist of stock or securities of a corporation that the distributing corporation controls immediately before the distribution.
2. The transaction must not be used principally as a device for the distribution of the earnings and profits of the distributing corporation or the controlled corporation or both.
3. The distributing corporation must distribute all of the stock and securities it holds in the controlled corporation or it must establish to the satisfaction of the Treasury that its retention of stock or securities in the controlled corporation is not in pursuance of a purpose to avoid federal income tax. In any event, stock representing control within the meaning of Section 368(c) must be distributed.
4. Both the distributing corporation and the controlled corporation must be engaged immediately after the distribution in the active conduct of a trade or business. In this connection, a trade or business must have been actively conducted throughout the five-year period preceding the distribution. If it was not conducted during that period by the distributing corporation, it must have been acquired by the distributing corporation in a nontaxable transaction.

Obviously, the requirements of Section 355 are quite specific and must be observed very carefully in any corporate division. The pur-   19.127

pose of these rules is to prevent the distribution of earnings and profits in the guise of a reorganization or a distribution of stock and securities. For example, if the five-year-business requirement did not exist, it would be possible for a corporation's cash earnings to be invested in a controlled subsidiary and the stock of such subsidiary distributed tax free under Section 355. The shareholders would then be in a position to sell the stock of the controlled corporation and thereby realize the benefits of their cash earnings and profits in the form of a capital gain. All distributions under Section 355 can expect close scrutiny from the Internal Revenue Service. If stock received in a Section 355 distribution is disposed of shortly after it is received, the disposition will make the distribution suspect as a device to distribute earnings and profits and thus not a tax-free distribution.

Carry-over of Corporate Attributes

19.128   The tax-free treatment of transfers in connection with corporate reorganizations is based on the premise that such reorganizations affect only rearrangements of continuing interests in property under modified corporate form. Accordingly, where gain or loss is not recognized, it is only appropriate that no change occur in other tax attributes, such as adjusted basis in property transferred, basis in stocks or securities exchanged, accounting methods, and net operating losses.

19.129   **Basis.** When stocks or securities are exchanged for other stocks or securities and gain or loss is not recognized, the basis of the stocks or securities received is determined in a manner somewhat similar to that used in connection with tax-free exchanges of like-kind properties discussed in chapter 11. The basis of the stock or securities received is equal to the adjusted basis of the stock or securities transferred, increased by the amount of gain recognized, and decreased by the amount of (1) loss recognized to the taxpayer, (2) the fair market value of any other property or money received by the taxpayer, and (3) the amount of any liabilities of the taxpayer assumed by the other party to the exchange and the amount of any liabilities to which property transferred by the taxpayer was subject. If other property is received by the taxpayer in connection with a reorganization exchange, the basis of that property will be its fair market value. In a tax-free exchange where stock or securities of several types are received in exchange for stock or securities of a single type, the basis of the several types of stock or securities received must be allocated among them, ordinarily on the basis of their relative fair market values.

19.130   When stock or securities are received in a distribution under Section 355 that does not involve an exchange, the basis of the stock or securities received as well as the basis of the stock or securities previously held must be determined by allocating the taxpayer's basis in the stock or securities originally held over those shares of stock or securities plus those received in the distribution. Such allocation is

normally made on the basis of relative fair market values [Reg.
1.358–2(a)(2)].

Where property is acquired by a corporation in connection with the
reorganization, the basis of that property is the same as its adjusted
basis in the hands of the transferor corporation increased by the
amount of any gain recognized to the transferor on the transfer
[Section 362(b)].

The effect of these rules, like similar rules applicable to other nontaxable exchanges, is to cause the postponement of tax on gain realized on these exchanges. Such gains will be taxed at the time the
property received is sold or exchanged in a taxable transaction. Theoretically, this will occur at a time when the sale or exchange effects
a change in the economic position of the taxpayer or in his relationship to his property sufficient to justify the imposition of an income
tax.

Other Tax Attributes—Section 381. In those reorganizations in which
the business of one or more corporations is carried on by a successor
corporation, the Code provides that certain tax attributes of the original corporation will carry over to the successor corporation. This
carry-over of tax attributes applies in the following types of reorganizations:

1. A statutory merger or consolidation (A type).
2. The acquisition of substantially all the properties of another corporation in exchange solely for voting stock of the acquiring corporation or
   voting stock of its parent (C type).
3. The transfer by a corporation of substantially all of its assets to a controlled corporation followed by the liquidation of the transferor corporation (D type).
4. A mere change in identity, form, or place of organization (F type).

The carry-over rules also apply where a controlled corporation is
liquidated by its parent corporation in a transaction in which gain or
loss is not recognized if the parent's basis in properties of the subsidiary is determined by reference to the subsidiary's basis in such
properties instead of by reference to the parent's basis in its stock of
the subsidiary under Section 334(b)(2).

The tax attributes that carry over are set forth in Section 381(c). The
regulations indicate only the items listed in Section 381(c) carry over.
The application of these various carry-over provisions often involves
special rules set forth in the code and regulations, discussion of
which is not practicable in this text. However, the better-known items
that carry over are: (1) net operating-loss carry-overs, (2) earnings and
profits (including deficits in earnings and profits to the extent of earnings and profits accumulated after the date of transfer), (3) capital-loss
carry-overs, (4) methods of accounting, (5) inventories, (6) methods of
computing depreciation allowances, (7) installment method of accounting, (8) amortization of bond discount or premium, (9) contribu-

tions to pension plans, employees' annuity plans, and stock-bonus and profit-sharing plans, (10) carry-overs of excess charitable contributions, (11) carry-overs of unused pension trust deductions, (12) pre-1954 adjustments from changes in accounting method, and (13) investment credits under Section 38.

SPECIAL LIMITATIONS ON NET OPERATING LOSS CARRY–OVERS

19.136   Section 382 provides a significant limitation on the carry-over of a net operating loss in a reorganization, and it provides a different limitation applicable in the case of certain changes of ownership of a single corporation other than as a result of a reorganization. Section 269 also applies whether or not Section 382 is applicable.

19.137   In the case of a reorganization, if the shareholders of the loss corporation, as a result of owning stock of the loss corporation, own as much as 20 percent of the fair market value of the stock of the acquiring corporation immediately after the reorganization, then the net operating loss carryover from the loss corporation is not reduced. [Section 382(b)]. However, if the shareholders of the loss corporation receive less than 20 percent in value of the surviving corporation's stock, the carryover is reduced in direct proportion to the difference between 20 percent and the percentage of the total stock of the surviving corporation received by the loss corporation's shareholders. For example, if the loss corporation's shareholders become the owners of only 10 percent of the stock of the successor corporation, the loss carry-over is reduced by 50 percent. If the loss corporation's shareholders receive 15 percent of the successor corporation's stock, the carry-over is reduced by $\frac{5}{20}$ths or 25 percent. If the loss corporation's shareholders receive only 5 percent of the successor corporation's stock, the loss carry-over is reduced by $\frac{15}{20}$ths or 75 percent [Section 382(b)]. This limitation does not apply if the transferor and the transferee corporations are owned substantially by the same persons in the same proportion.

19.138   The other limitation contained in Section 382 applies whenever there is a substantial change in the ownership of a corporation and the corporation does not continue to carry on its same trade or business [Section 382(a)]. If at the end of any taxable year of a corporation, (1) any one or more of the ten largest shareholders owns a percentage of the total fair market value of the stock that is at least fifty percentage points more than that person or persons owned at the beginning of that taxable year or the beginning of the previous taxable year, (2) the increase in stock ownership is attributable to a taxable transaction or to a decrease in the amount of stock outstanding, and (3) such corporation has not continued to carry on a trade or business substantially the same as that conducted before any change in the percentage ownership of the stock, then the net operating loss carryover from years prior to the taxable year is not allowed. In determining the ten largest shareholders, the attribution rules of Section 318 are applicable. For purposes of this limitation, any person may ignore, however, any increases in his stock ownership attributable to an acquisition from a person whose stock would be attributed to him under these attribution rules.

Corporation A engages in the manufacture and sale of mobile homes. All of its stock is owned by individual X. A uses a calendar year for tax purposes, and on December 31, 1969, it has a net operating-loss carry-over of $100,000. During 1970, individual X sells his stock in A to individual Y, an unrelated person, for cash. During 1970, A incurs an additional operating loss of $25,000, making its carry-over to 1971 $125,000. In February, 1971, A sells its manufacturing business and uses the proceeds to acquire a machine shop which it operates from July, 1971 on. A's net operating-loss carry-over from 1970 and earlier years is not deductible by A because Y's ownership of stock at December 31, 1971, was 100 percentage points more than it was at the beginning of 1970, the beginning of A's preceding taxable year, the increase was attributable to a purchase of stock, and A had not continued to operate the same trade or business as that operated before the change in ownership.

19.139

Section 269 provides an even more far-reaching limitation on net operating-loss carryovers than Section 382. Furthermore, the limitations of Section 269 apply not only to net-operating losses but also to all other deductions, credits, or allowances that are beneficial to taxpayers. Space does not allow a discussion of Section 269 here, but the entire section should be read by every student of taxation. Briefly it provides that if (1) any person or persons (including other corporations) acquire control of a corporation (directly or indirectly), or (2) any corporation acquires property from another corporation which neither the acquiring corporation nor its shareholders control, and the basis of the property carries over to the acquiring corporation, and (3) the principal purpose of the acquisition is to avoid federal income tax by securing the benefit of some deduction, credit, or other allowance not otherwise available, then such deduction, credit, or allowance may be disallowed in whole or in part.

PENALTY SURTAXES ON CERTAIN CORPORATIONS

Personal Holding Companies

19.140

The penalty tax on personal holding companies is designed to discourage individual taxpayers from allowing investment income and income from certain personal-service contracts to accumulate in a closely held corporation subject only to corporation income taxes. A personal holding company has at times been described as an *incorporated pocketbook*. The definition of a personal holding company is rather complex; however, it can be described generally as a corporation that (1) derives more than 60 percent of its gross income, after certain adjustments, from investment sources such as dividends, interests, rents, royalties, etc., and from certain personal service contracts, and (2) which has more than 50 percent of its stock owned by five or fewer individuals (Section 542).

19.141　　The rate of the personal-holding-company penalty tax is 70 percent and is in addition to the regular normal tax and surtax. It is applied to the corporation's taxable income less distributions to shareholders, income taxes, and certain other adjustments (Sections 541 and 545). For the purpose of this penalty tax, a personal holding company is not allowed any dividends-received deduction, and the carry-over of any net operating loss is extremely limited.

19.142　　Because of its severity, the personal-holding-company tax operates as a rather effective barrier against the use of a closely held corporation for the avoidance of personal taxes on investment and personal service income.

Unreasonable Accumulation of Earnings

19.143　　Even though a corporation is not classified as a personal holding company, it still is subject to a penalty tax if it is used to avoid personal income taxes on its shareholders by allowing its earnings to accumulate beyond the reasonable needs of its business (Section 532).

19.144　　The accumulated-earnings penalty tax is equal to $27\frac{1}{2}$ percent of the first $100,000 of income subject to such tax and $38\frac{1}{2}$ percent of any additional income subject to such tax. This penalty tax is applied only to income of the year accumulated beyond the reasonable needs of the business (Sections 531 and 535). In this connection, every corporation is allowed to accumulate over the years of its existence a minimum of $100,000 before becoming subject to the tax. This is known as the "$100,000 accumulated-earnings credit." If earnings are allowed to accumulate beyond this amount, a corporation should be prepared to show (1) its accumulation of earnings is for the "reasonable needs of its business," and (2) the purpose for accumulating such earnings is not "the avoidance of income tax with respect to its shareholders."

SUBCHAPTER S CORPORATIONS

19.145　　For many years the double tax on corporate taxable income discussed earlier in this chapter has been a significant deterrent to use of the corporate form of organization by small businesses. Subchapter S, containing Sections 1371 through 1377, was added to the Code in 1958 to relieve this double-tax burden on closely held corporations and their shareholders who elect, and qualify, to come under its provisions. If the election and qualification provisions are met, the corporation's taxable income (except some long-term capital gains) is not taxed to it. Instead, the shareholders are taxed on the corporation's income or can deduct their proportionate shares of its losses, somewhat like partners are taxed on income of, or deduct losses of, their partnership. Qualifying corporations are referred to in the Code as "small business corporations."[22] Corporations that elect the benefits of Subchapter S are referred to as "electing small business corporations," although a better descriptive term is "Subchapter S corporations."

19.146 Corporations qualifying for Subchapter S treatment have been referred to also as "corporations taxable as partnerships." This reference is misleading, because the differences between the Subchapter S rules of taxation and the partnership rules of taxation outnumber the similarities. If the Subchapter S treatment is terminated either voluntarily or involuntarily, the corporation becomes subject to the usual rules of taxation applicable to corporations.

Stock and Shareholder Requirements

19.147 In order for a corporation and its shareholders to obtain the benefits of Subchapter S, the corporation must meet the following requirements of a "small business corporation" imposed by Section 1371:

1. It must not have more than ten shareholders.
2. All shareholders must be individuals or estates.
3. It must have only one class of stock.
4. No shareholder can be a nonresident alien.
5. It must not own 80 percent or more of the stock of any subsidiary corporation which has begun business activities or had taxable income.

These qualifications of a small business corporation do not refer particularly to its size. Although the requirements are such that corporations satisfying them are for the most part engaged in small businesses, the actual size of the business has nothing to do with the qualification.

Income Requirements

19.148 In addition to the above stock and shareholder requirements, in order for a Subchapter S corporation to remain qualified, it must meet the following requirements:

1. The corporation must not derive more than 80 percent of its gross receipts from sources outside the United States.
2. Other than during the first two years of its active existence, the corporation cannot receive passive investment income in any year amounting to more than 20 percent of its gross receipts, or in excess of $3,000.

The term "passive investment income" means gross receipts derived from royalties, rents, dividends, interest, annuities, and gains from the sale or exchange of stock or securities. If there is a loss on the sale

22. "Small business corporations" under Subchapter S have no relation to and should not be confused with "small business corporations" under Section 1244.

of a particular share or bond, there are no gross receipts from the sale, but the amount of the loss does not offset gains realized on other sales. Rent received is not passive investment income if significant services are rendered to the occupant, such as for the use or occupancy of rooms or other quarters in hotels or motels [Reg. 1.1372–4(b)].

Election and Shareholder Consents

19.149   If a corporation meets the requirements recited in paragraphs 19.147 and 19.148, if it files a proper election, and if the shareholders unanimously consent, the corporation and its shareholders will be taxed under Subchapter S. The election and consents must be filed with the local District Director during either (1) the first calendar month of the taxable year for which this special status is desired, or (2) during the calendar month preceding that calendar month. Once made the election remains in effect for all subsequent years unless (1) revoked by the shareholders, (2) a new person becomes a shareholder and does not file a consent, or (3) the corporation ceases to qualify. If a trust becomes a shareholder, the corporation will cease to qualify.

How Income Is Taxed to Shareholders

19.150   A Subchapter S corporation computes its taxable income generally in the same manner as an ordinary business corporation, but there are three exceptions: (1) the special corporate deductions of Sections 241–47, particularly the 85 percent dividends-received deduction, are not allowed; (2) no net operating-loss carry-over or carry-back from another year is allowed; and (3) deductions for contributions to pension and profit-sharing plans for the benefit of employee shareholders are limited in a manner similar to those of self-employed individuals. Return form 1120-S rather than 1120 is used. Except for certain net long-term capital gains realized in the amounts and under the circumstances specified in Section 1378, the corporation is exempt from all federal income taxes—normal tax, surtax, surcharge, tax on unreasonably accumulated earnings, and tax on undistributed personal-holding-company income.

19.151   The corporate income is taxed to the shareholders, whether distributed or not. To the extent distributed, it is taxed to the shareholder who received it. To the extent not distributed, it is taxed as a constructive dividend ratably to those who are shareholders on the last day of the corporation's taxable year. Distributions of money during the first two and one-half months after the close of the taxable year are treated as distributions of the undistributed taxable income of the taxable year to the extent that the recipient shareholder is required to include such income in his gross income. To the extent so treated, the distribution is not a dividend, is tax-free to the shareholder, and does not reduce earnings and profits. Nor does it reduce undistributed income of the current year taxed to the shareholders at the end of the current year.

In the calendar year 1970 a Subchapter S corporation had taxable income and earnings and profits of $10,000, none of which was distributed during the year. A is its sole shareholder. Its income and earnings and profits for 1971 are $12,000. On January 15, 1971, the corporation distributes $9,000 to A and on June 15, 1971, it distributes another $1,500.

In his return for 1970, A must include the $10,000 of undistributed taxable income existing on December 31, 1970, as being a constructive dividend. The $9,000 distributed on January 15, 1971, is tax-free to A and does not reduce the earnings and profits of 1971. The $1,500 is an ordinary taxable dividend, and the undistributed earnings taxable in 1971 to A are $10,500 ($12,000 − $1,500).

19.152 If a corporation has net long-term capital-gain income, that amount less the tax paid thereon by the corporation retains its character as net long-term capital gain in the hands of the shareholder whether distributed or not. All other items at the corporate level lose their identity when passed through to the shareholder. For example, a charitable contribution by a corporation merely reduces corporate taxable income and does not become a charitable contribution for the shareholder.

Treatment of Net Operating Losses

19.153 Any net operating loss of a Subchapter S corporation is passed through and deducted as a business loss by the shareholders. If it exceeds a shareholder's other income for the year, a net operating loss for him is created which he may carry back for three years and carry forward for five years under the general rules for net operating losses. The shareholder's deduction cannot exceed the adjusted basis of the stock owned by him plus the amount of any indebtedness of the corporation to him. His share of the loss in excess of these amounts is forever lost as a deduction. The corporation's loss for the year is allocated to shareholders on the basis of their shares held on each day of the year.

Qualified Pension and Profit Sharing Plans for Shareholder-Employees

19.154 As mentioned in paragraphs 19.9–19.12, professional corporations have been set up by physicians, dentists, certified public accountants, and other professional men primarily to enable their shareholder-employees to obtain the tax benefits of qualified pension and profit-sharing plans. While considering the Tax Reform Act of 1969, Congress rejected a proposal to limit deductions and benefits to amounts similar to those imposed on self-employed individuals (see paragraphs 17.60 –17.68). However, Congress did impose limits of that nature on Subchapter S corporations to the extent the deductions and benefits pertain to shareholder-employees. For that reason, although most professional corporations can elect Subchapter S status, few do. The new section is 1379 and became effective with taxable years beginning in 1971.

19.155   As provided in Section 1379(d), a shareholder-employee is an employee or officer of a Subchapter S corporation who owns, actually or constructively, on any day during the taxable year of such corporation, more than 5 percent of its outstanding stock.

19.156   In paragraph 17.21, it was pointed out that in every pension plan forfeitures must be used to reduce future contributions of the employer and cannot be allocated to other participants. This is also true as to the pension plan of a Subchapter S corporation. With respect to profit-sharing and stock bonus plans of "regular" corporations, it is customary to allocate forfeitures to other participants. However, if such a plan is set up by a Subchapter S corporation, no forfeitures can be allocated to shareholder employees but can be to common law employee participants.

19.157   Theoretically but not practically, there is no ceiling on the amount that a Subchapter S corporation can contribute to a qualified plan. To the extent that a contribution deductible by such a corporation for the benefit of a shareholder-employee exceeds the lesser of (a) 10 percent of his compensation or (b) $2,500, such excess is includible in the income of such shareholder-employee.

Pros and Cons of Electing Subchapter S

19.158   The small businessman has available to him the following benefits of Subchapter S status:

1. The legal benefit of conducting business in corporate form so as not to be personally liable for corporate debts.
2. The tax benefit of being able to deduct his share of a corporate net operating loss to the extent of his investment in stock and debt receivables of the corporation.
3. Group life insurance.
4. Wage continuation plan in the event of sickness.
5. Qualified pension or profit-sharing plan subject to the restrictions mentioned in paragraph 19.157.
6. Avoidance of corporate surtax imposed by Section 531 on earnings which might otherwise unreasonably accumulate (see also paragraphs 19.139–19.140).
7. Timing of income taxation to the shareholders if the corporation can use a fiscal year (see also paragraphs 13.6 and 13.17).

On the other hand, the shareholders of a growing profitable corporation which needs to accumulate its earnings to expand, will find Subchapter S status not advantageous.

WESTERN HEMISPHERE TRADE CORPORATIONS

19.159   In order to encourage foreign trade with countries in the Western Hemisphere, it has long been the policy of the United States to allow a special income-tax deduction to corporations utilized for this purpose. A Western Hemisphere Trade Corporation is a domestic corporation engaged in trade or business in countries in North, Central, or South America or in the West Indies that derives substantially all of its gross income from sources outside the United States (Section 921). The special deduction allowed such a corporation is a fraction of its taxable income, the numerator of which is 14 percent and the denominator is that percentage which equals the sum of the normal tax rate and the surtax rate for the taxable year, 48 percent for 1973 (Section 922). Many companies engaged in trade or business outside the United States in the Western Hemisphere have found it advantageous to transfer that trade or business into a United States subsidiary corporation that can meet the tests of a Western Hemisphere Trade Corporation.

INSURANCE COMPANIES AND CERTAIN OTHER FINANCIAL INSTITUTIONS

Because of the peculiar circumstances applicable to their operations, certain financial institutions such as insurance companies,[23] banks,[24] domestic building and loan associations,[25] and regulated investment companies[26] are subject to various special tax rules and regulations. Most of these special rules involve accounting methods, the allowance of special deductions, capital gains and losses, and special rules relating to the reserve for bad debts.

19.160

MULTIPLE CORPORATIONS

Limitation on Multiple Surtax Exemptions and Accumulated Earnings Credits

As explained in chapter 4 (paragraph 4.16), the first $25,000 of a corporation's taxable income is exempt from the surtax portion of the income tax. To a corporation having more than $25,000 of taxable income, this surtax exemption for 1965 and later years has been worth $6,500 (26% × 25,000). To prevent groups of commonly controlled corporations from multiplying the benefits of these surtax exemptions by increasing the number of corporations through which they operate their businesses, some extremely complicated rules were placed into the Code by Sections 1561 through 1563. These rules limit the members of a "controlled group" of corporations to only one surtax exemption.

19.161

Whether or not a particular corporation is a member of a controlled group and thus subject to these rules is determined as of December 31 of each year, irrespective of the taxable year of the corporation or the group. A corporation is deemed to be a member of a controlled group

19.162

23. Code Sec. 801 through 844 (Subchapter L).
24. Code Sec. 581 through 601 (Subchapter H).
25. Code Sec. 591 through 596.
26. Code Sec. 851 through 855 (Subchapter M, part 1).

Corporations   on December 31, if (1) it actually was a member on that date and had been for at least one-half of the days in its taxable year that precede December 31, or (2) it was not a member on December 31, but had been for at least one-half of the days in its taxable year that precede such December 31.

19.163   The general rule is that a controlled group of corporations is entitled to only one surtax exemption of $25,000 to be apportioned between them as they see fit. If no apportionment is elected, the single surtax exemption is divided equally among all members of the group. However, until taxable years beginning in 1975, an election is given so that each corporation can claim a separate surtax exemption. When a group makes this election, the amount of each exemption in excess of one allowed to the group is $25,000 for all taxable years that include the date of December 31 falling within the calendar years 1964 through 1969. However, starting with the date of December 31, 1970, Section 1564 provides that each year the exemption is to be reduced by $4,167 so that by December 31, 1975, it will be zero and this multiple exemption election will cease to exist.

19.164   Each corporation electing to take an additional exemption pays additional tax at the rate of 6 percent on taxable income equal to the additional exemption. The first election can be made or revoked retroactively within a three-year period and may be lost through certain events. Once revoked or lost, the election cannot be made again for six years.

19.165   These limitations and this election on multiple surtax exemptions also apply to the $100,000 accumulated earnings credit allowed in connection with the penalty tax on accumulation of surplus (paragraph 19.144), and to the small business deductions allowed life insurance companies.

19.166   For the purpose of the provisions relating to multiple surtax exemptions, there are two classes of "controlled groups of corporations." The first consists of parent–subsidiary controlled groups having one or more chains of corporations connected through stock ownership with a common parent, where the chains are connected within themselves and with the common parent through ownership of at least 80 percent of the total combined voting power of all classes of stock, or at least 80 percent of the total value of all classes of stock. The second consists of brother–sister controlled groups. A brother–sister group consists of two or more corporations of which five or fewer persons who are individuals, estates, or trusts own (1) 80 percent or more of the total combined voting power or the total value of all classes of stock and (2) more than 50 percent of the total voting power or the total value of all classes of stock taking into account only the stock ownership of each person that is identical to his ownership in each such corporation. For these purposes, nonvoting stock that is limited and preferred as to dividends, treasury stock, and excluded stock (consisting in general of stock owned by a deferred compensation trust, a principal shareholder, or certain employees) is disregarded. Furthermore for determining ownership of stock, the attribution rules of Section 1563(e) are applicable.

Shareholders A, B, and C own the stock of corporations X and Y as follows: EXAMPLE

SHAREHOLDERS	CORPORATIONS	
	X	Y
A	60%	10%
B	30%	20%
C	10%	70%
Total	100%	100%

X and Y do not constitute a controlled group. Although they satisfy the 80-percent test, they do not meet the 50-percent test. Under the 50-percent test shareholder A considers only 10 percent of the stock of X and Y, shareholder B considers only 20 percent, and C considers only 10 percent, a total of only 40 percent.

In some instances, a parent–subsidiary controlled group must be combined with a brother–sister controlled group. Exceptions are made for certain corporations owned jointly by a manufacturer and its distributor and for an insurance company where there are no other insurance companies in the group. The application of these tests for determining controlled groups can get extremely complex. This is particularly true when three or more corporations are involved and the attribution rules of Section 1563(e) are applicable. 19.167

Disallowance of Multiple Surtax Exemptions and Accumulated Earnings Credits

Section 1551 completely disallows the surtax exemption and the accumulated earnings credit under certain circumstances where a corporation receives property from controlling shareholders and is unable to show that a major purpose for receiving the property was not the securing of the exemption or credit. Since multiple surtax exemptions will be phased out by about 1975 in any event, this disallowance under Section 1551 is of only limited significance; therefore it is not discussed further here. 19.168

Consolidated Returns

Some tax provisions relating to multiple corporations are advantageous to taxpayers. If a group of corporations constitutes an affiliated group as defined in Section 1504, they may file a consolidated tax return provided all members of the group consent to be bound by the regulations concerning consolidated returns (Section 1501). If a consolidated tax return is filed, the income tax is based on the consolidated taxable income of the group and only one surtax exemption. In this connection, income and deductions from intercompany transactions generally are not recognized until they are realized in transactions with parties outside the affiliated group. Also, in general, net 19.169

losses incurred by members of the group are offset against taxable income of other members of the group in determining consolidated taxable income. Sections 1501 through 1505 set forth certain requirements for consolidated returns; however, the vast majority of the rules relating to consolidated returns are prescribed by the regulations. Since one of the requirements for filing a consolidated return is that all members of the affiliated group consent to be bound by the regulations, these consolidated regulations, from a practical standpoint, represent the law governing consolidated returns.

100 Percent Dividends Received Deduction

19.170   Corporations that qualify for the filing of a consolidated return but do not wish to file on a consolidated basis can elect to be allowed 100 percent dividends received deductions with respect to intercompany dividends received from within the affiliated group [Section 243(a)(3)]. In effect then, an affiliated group claiming the 100 percent dividends received deduction is in somewhat the same tax position as a group filing a consolidated return, except that the members do not have the privilege of setting off the losses of one company against income of another, and income and deductions from intercompany transactions are recognized.

19.171   The 100 percent dividends received deduction generally is not allowed for years in which a multiple surtax election is effective. During the years 1970 through 1975, while the multiple surtax election is being phased out, an exception is made for certain corporations that had made the multiple surtax election prior to April 23, 1969. These corporations may qualify for dividends received deductions ranging from 87½ percent to 97½ percent of dividends paid before 1978 from earnings and profits accumulated during these transition years [Section 1564(b)].

OTHER TRANSACTIONS BETWEEN CORPORATIONS AND SHAREHOLDERS

19.172   Many transactions between a corporation and its shareholders involve no unusual tax consequences as long as the transactions are bona fide; but to discourage manipulation of transactions between corporations and shareholders for the purpose of avoiding taxes, the courts and the Code have laid down a number of special rules.

19.173   One of these rules is basic to all income taxation, but it applies particularly to corporations and their shareholders: if the form of a transaction does not reflect its true substance, the tax consequences are determined by the substance and not by the form.[27] Thus, if a corporation sells property to a shareholder at less than fair market value, the excess of such value over the price paid by the shareholder

27. *Gregory* v. *Helvering*, 293 U.S. 465 (1935), 35–1 USTC ¶9043, 14 AFTR 1191; *Com.* v. *Court Holding Co.*, 324 U.S. 331 (1945), 45–1 USTC ¶9215, 33 AFTR 593.

is treated for tax purposes as a distribution of property to that shareholder. If the corporation has earnings and profits, the distribution is a dividend.

QUESTIONS AND PROBLEMS

1. Name the six more significant characteristics of a corporation. Explain how they are applied in determining whether an unincorporated organization is taxable as a corporation.

2. During 1973 individual A and corporation X decide to form a corporation (corporation N) to operate a mobile-home park. On July 1, 1973, A contributes to the new corporation a 40 acre tract of land valued at $50,000. A's basis in this land which he purchased in 1967 is $30,000, and it is subject to a purchase money mortgage of $10,000 which corporation N assumes. Corporation X contributes $30,000 cash to corporation N. A and X each receive 400 shares of N's common stock (all that is issued) and A also receives N's 8% promissory note for $10,000 payable on January 1, 1975.

   How much gain or loss, if any, is recognized on the transfer by A? By X? What is the basis of A and X respectively in their common stock of N? What is A's basis in the note? What is N's basis in the land?

3. Shareholders of corporation X decide to liquidate. After paying all known liabilities, the corporation has assets to be distributed to shareholders as indicated by the balance sheet below. Earnings and profits before the liquidation are equal in amount to the earned surplus.

	ADJUSTED TAX BASIS	FAIR MARKET VALUE
Cash	$ 25,000	$ 25,000
Inventory (first in, first out)	75,000	100,000
Machinery and equipment	300,000	300,000
Land	50,000	200,000
Total	$450,000	$625,000
Capital stock	$100,000	
Earned surplus	350,000	
Total	$450,000	

How much gain or loss will be recognized to each shareholder, and what will be the basis of each shareholder in the assets received under the following circumstances? Will the gain or loss be capital or ordinary? Assume Sections 333 and 337 do not apply:

(a) Individual A is the sole shareholder and his adjusted basis in his stock is $100,000. A has held the stock 10 years.

(b) Corporation Y is the sole shareholder and its adjusted basis in its stock is $500,000. Y has held the stock 10 years.

(c) Individual A owns 40 percent of the stock and corporation Y owns 60 percent. A's adjusted basis in his stock is $40,000 and Y's adjusted basis is $300,000. Assets are distributed ratably. Each

shareholder has held the stock 10 years.
4. Assume the same facts as in problem 3(a).
   (a) How much gain or loss is recognized to individual A if he elects the benefits of Section 333 and qualifies therefor by liquidating X within one calendar month?
   (b) Is the gain or loss capital or ordinary?
   (c) Do you believe it would be advisable in these circumstances for A to make the Section 333 election? Discuss your answer.
5. A corporation commenced business on January 2, 1972, and had net income from operations for the calendar year 1972 of $125,000 after taxes of $100,000. On December 15, 1972, it distributed to its sole shareholder securities owned by it having a market value of $150,000, which cost the corporation $135,000. The shareholder's basis for his stock is $140,000. What is the income tax effect of this distribution to: (a) The distributing corporation? (b) The sole shareholder, assuming the shareholder is an individual? (c) The sole shareholder, assuming the shareholder is a corporation?
6. B owns certain real estate which cost him $50,000 in 1950, but which in 1973 has a fair market value of $125,000. In 1973 B transfers the property to Swap Corporation for 245 shares of treasury stock having a fair market value of $125,000. Swap Corporation originally had 300 shares issued; and in 1969 Swap had purchased the 245 shares from another shareholder for $110,000, leaving 55 shares outstanding. (a) Did Swap realize a taxable gain upon the transfer of the stock to B? (b) What is Swap's basis in the real estate? (c) What was B's taxable gain on the transfer of real estate to Swap? Explain.
7. X, an individual, bought 500 shares of ABC Company for $54,000 on January 1. On May 15 of the same year, ABC paid a dividend of $4,800 on these shares, 25 percent of which was a return of capital. Also on the same day ABC Company issued a 20 percent stock dividend. On July 31 ABC Company effected a two-for-one stock split. On September 15, X sold 1,000 shares of ABC for $45,000. What is the gain or loss on the September 15 sales of ABC stock?
8. Discuss what is meant by a "partial liquidation" and the tax consequences to shareholders when they receive distributions in partial liquidation.
9. John Smith is the sole shareholder of a small manufacturing company which has been operating since 1964. He has had several proposals from larger companies to buy his business for cash, the last being a tentative offer of $1,000,000.

   At June 30,   the assets and liabilities of Smith's company are as follows:

	ADJUSTED BASIS	FAIR MARKET VALUE
Cash	$ 50,000	$ 50,000
Receivables	200,000	200,000
Inventory	100,000	125,000
Manufacturing equipment (net of reserve for depreciation of $175,000)	450,000	550,000
Goodwill	—	375,000
Total	$800,000	$1,300,000

Accounts payable	100,000	100,000	
Long-term notes	200,000	200,000	
Net worth	$500,000	$1,000,000	

Discuss the tax consequences of the following alternatives, considering the possible application of Sections 337 and 333.

(a) Smith sells his stock, in which his basis is $100,000, for $1,000,000 cash.

(b) The buying company insists on buying Smith's company's assets for $1,300,000 cash. Smith's company would then pay its liabilities and liquidate.

10. A corporation, the common stock of which was owned by three individuals, declared a dividend on its common stock payable in $100 par value preferred stock, one share of preferred for each share of common. The preferred stock had a fair market value of $85 per share, and the adjusted basis of each share of the common stock in the hands of each of the shareholders was $35 per share. At the time of this distribution and at all times during the year, the corporation's accumulated earnings and profits exceeded the par value of the stock distributed. The shareholders immediately sold the preferred stock to an investment trust for $85 per share, and three months afterwards the preferred stock was redeemed at par value by the corporation. On their tax returns the shareholders declared and paid capital gains tax on the sale of the preferred stock to the investment trust. Why and under what Code section would the Internal Revenue Service object to capital-gains treatment?

11. Corporation X owned shares (adjusted basis, $4,000; fair market value, $10,000) in Corporation Y (an unrelated corporation). Corporation X had accumulated earnings and profits of $25,000. In 1970, B, owner of all the stock in Corporation X, purchased from the latter the stock which it held in Corporation Y, the purchase price being $4,000. B held this stock for seven months and toward the end of 1970 sold it for $12,000. Corporation X made no distributions during the year. Assuming B had no other income or transactions, discuss the type and amount of income reportable by B on his income tax return.

12. On March 1 a taxpayer purchased land for $150,000. On October 1 he sold this land at its fair market value of $200,000 to the ABC Corporation, which was 85 percent owned by him. What is the nature and amount of taxpayer's taxable income on the sale?

13. XYZ Manufacturing Company has developed a good product but is badly in need of expansion capital. It has $500,000 worth of assets of which $10,000 is in cash. Liabilities are $300,000. Shareholders Y and Z want to merge the company with the ABC Corporation which is well financed and can provide adequate capital for expansion. Shareholder X is tired of the business, however, and he insists on some kind of deal which will provide him with $20,000 in cash for his 10 percent of the XYZ stock. ABC proposes to give XYZ $30,000 cash and 16,000 shares of its voting common stock, which is readily marketable at $10 per share, and assume all of XYZ's liabilities in exchange for all of its property except cash. XYZ can then liquidate by distributing ABC stock to Y and Z and $20,000 cash to X. It will have $20,000 to pay its expenses of liquidation. Can this transaction

be effected free of tax to all parties except shareholder X? If so, why? If not, why not? Is there any other way of arranging this deal to achieve the desired economic result without tax to anyone but X?

14. Corporation M has outstanding 100,000 shares of $10 par, 8 percent nonvoting preferred stock and 300,000 shares of $10 par common stock. To conserve cash for operating purposes it proposes to issue 75,000 shares of the additional common stock in exchange for the 100,000 outstanding shares of preferred. Will M or its shareholders incur any tax on this transaction? Discuss.

15. Corporation S, a Subchapter S corporation, has 2 equal shareholders, T and O. During its taxable years ending January 31, 1971, 1972, and 1973 it has taxable net income and losses (which are all of its earnings and profits or deficits) as follows:

1971	$50,000
1972	30,000
1973	(10,000) loss

Dividends were paid as follows:

March 15, 1971	$10,000
December 15, 1971	10,000
June 15, 1972	10,000

On July 31, 1972, shareholder T sells his stock to W who immediately files a consent to the Subchapter S election of S.

How much does each shareholder include in his gross income as a result of his ownership of S stock during the taxable years (calendar years) 1971, 1972, 1973? Assume S has no capital gains. Further, assume that the fiscal year ended January 31, 1971 was the first taxable year of the corporation.

20

TRUSTS
AND ESTATES

NATURE OF TRUSTS AND ESTATES . . . 720
TAXATION OF TRUST AND ESTATE INCOME IN
GENERAL . . . 721
TAXATION OF THE TRUST OR ESTATE . . . 722

Accounting Methods and Periods . . . 722
Gross Income and Deductions . . . 722

CHARITABLE CONTRIBUTIONS . . . 722
DEPRECIATION AND DEPLETION . . . 723
NET OPERATING LOSSES AND EXCESS DEDUCTIONS . . . 724
ADMINISTRATIVE EXPENSES OF ESTATE . . . 724
DEDUCTIONS FOR AMOUNTS TAXABLE TO BENEFICIARIES . . . 724

DISTRIBUTABLE NET INCOME . . . 724
TRUST OR ESTATE INCOME TAXABLE TO BENEFICIARIES . . . 726

Simple Trusts . . . 726
Complex Trusts and Estates . . . 727

THE TIER SYSTEM . . . 727
THE SEPARATE-SHARE RULE . . . 729

ACCUMULATION DISTRIBUTIONS FROM TRUSTS . . . 730
TRUST INCOME TAXABLE TO GRANTORS AND OTHERS . . . 731
TRUSTS CLASSIFIED AS CORPORATIONS . . . 732

NATURE OF TRUSTS AND ESTATES

20.1   Trusts and estates are entities through which title to property is held in the name of a fiduciary (the trustee, executor, or administrator) for the benefit of another (the beneficiary or heir). The property so held is referred to as the property, the corpus, or the principal of the trust or estate.

20.2   The types of trusts with which we are here concerned are "express" trusts, that is, those brought into existence by means of a written document. There are also "implied" trusts, that is, those imposed by general legal principles of equity. An express trust can be created by a written instrument during life, called an *inter vivos* or living trust, or by a provision in a will, called a testamentary trust. An *inter vivos* trust usually does not come into existence until there has been a transfer of money or property to the trustee named in the trust instrument. Similarly, a testamentary trust does not come into existence until the estate transfers money or property to the trustee.

20.3   The trust instrument sets forth the conditions of the trust. These conditions usually identify the beneficiaries, designate the term of the trust, define the authority of the trustee, and instruct the trustee concerning the distribution of income and property during the term of the trust and at termination of the trust. If the trust instrument does not provide adequate instructions concerning administration of the trust, the trustee looks to local law for instructions. In all respects, the governing instrument and local law are binding on the trustee in all matters concerning the trust property and income.

20.4   An estate comes into existence upon the death of an individual. All of his property subject to probate, which frequently is less than the amount of the gross estate for estate-tax purposes, is turned over to the custody of the executor or administrator upon his appointment by the appropriate court. He then administers the property, settles all claims against the estate, and distributes the property in accordance with the terms of the will or the applicable laws of descent. The right of any devisee, legatee, or heir to receive income during the administration of the estate is governed by local law. Most frequently a court order is obtained by the executor or administrator to authorize distribution of any income.

20.5   Since income beneficiaries and corpus beneficiaries are not necessarily the same persons, it is mandatory that fiduciaries correctly classify all amounts they receive as either income or corpus. The fiduciaries are then accountable for such amounts to the respective beneficiaries. Instructions for the classification of these receipts between income and corpus are often contained in the governing instrument. In the absence of adequate instructions in the governing instrument, the provisions of local law control.

20.6   It should be understood that the concept of income for legal and fiduciary accounting purposes is not the same as the concept of income for tax purposes. When the single term *income* is used in discussing trusts and estates, its legal or fiduciary accounting meaning is intended [Section 643(b)]. When the terms *gross income, taxable income,* and *distributable net income* are used, their meanings as defined by the Code and regulations are intended.

TAXATION OF TRUST AND ESTATE INCOME IN GENERAL

The taxation of income of trusts and estates requires consideration   20.7
of three or more possible taxpayers, the grantor of the trust or the decedent of the estate, the trust or estate represented by the fiduciary, and one or more beneficiaries. Subchapter J of the Code sets forth a comprehensive plan for the taxation of trust and estate income. This overall plan contemplates that all taxable income of trusts and estates will be taxed when earned, and this tax may be borne by any one or in part by all of these possible taxpayers. The allocation of the taxable income of a trust or estate among the possible taxpayers is one of the primary problems dealt with in Subchapter J. When trusts accumulate taxable income and distribute it in a later year, the income may be taxed to the trust in the year earned and again to the beneficiary in the year distributed. However, to avoid a double tax the beneficiary will be allowed a credit against his tax for the tax previously paid by the trust.

In some instances, the grantor of a trust retains such dominion and   20.8
control over part of the income and property of the trust that he is treated for tax purposes as its substantial owner. In these cases, the grantor is taxable on the income of that part of the trust, and the tax rules otherwise applicable to trusts never come into play with respect to such income (Section 671). Where the grantor is not considered a substantial owner, the trust income is taxed either to the trust or to the beneficiaries.

The income of an estate consists of two types: "income in respect   20.9
of a decedent" and income earned by the estate itself. In the final return of a decedent all gross income realized by him prior to his death is reported under his established method of accounting. As stated in Reg. 1.691(a)–1(b), "the term 'income in respect of a decedent' refers to those amounts to which a decedent was entitled as gross income but that were not properly includible in computing his taxable income for the taxable year ending with the date of his death or for a previous taxable year under the method of accounting employed by the decedent." It includes all accrued income and income to which the decedent had a contingent claim at the time of his death. Some items of income in respect of a decedent will be received by the estate and other items by his heirs. Each such amount is taxable to the estate or person who acquires a right to receive it and must be reported in the year when actually received [Section 691(a); Reg. 1.691(a)–2(a)]. If any estate tax was paid for the value of the right to

receive this income at the date of decedent's death, the estate or other person reporting the gross income is allowed a deduction for the estate tax attributable to such value [Section 691(c)].

20.10   The allocation of taxable income between a trust or estate and the beneficiaries is accomplished by treating all gross income attributable to trust or estate property as gross income of the trust or estate and then granting to it a deduction for amounts taxable currently to the beneficiaries. By this overall plan, all taxable income of the trust or estate is taxed in effect only once to the parties in the trust or estate arrangement.

20.11   Tax rates applicable to trusts and estates are the same as those applicable to individual taxpayers filing separate returns [Section 641(a)]. In determining taxable income, as noted in chapter 1, trusts and estates are allowed deductions for personal exemptions similar to those allowed individuals. An estate is allowed $600; a trust that is required to distribute all its income currently is allowed $300; and all other trusts are allowed a deduction of $100 [Section 642(b)].

TAXATION OF THE TRUST OR ESTATE

Accounting Methods and Periods

20.12   Trusts and estates are separate entities for tax purposes, and thus they must establish their own accounting methods and accounting periods. Unlike partnerships, they are allowed to establish fiscal years for tax purposes regardless of the taxable years of their beneficiaries. The accounting method and the accounting period are established in the first return of an estate or trust; and once established, they cannot be changed without permission from the Commissioner. Trusts and estates are also required to make whatever elections are appropriate to the determination of taxable income.

20.13   When a beneficiary's taxable year does not coincide with that of the trust or estate, the beneficiary reports his share of taxable income distributable from the trust or estate in his taxable year with, or within, which, the taxable year of the trust or estate ends [Section 652(c)].

Gross Income and Deductions

20.14   Gross income of an estate or trust is determined in the same way as that of an individual. In the area of allowable deductions, however, several special rules apply.

20.15   **Charitable Contributions.** A trust or estate is allowed to deduct for tax purposes any part of its gross income that, under terms of the governing instrument, is paid out for charitable, religious, scientific, or other similar purposes set forth in Section 642(c). This deduction ordinarily is allowed without limitation. Since it is allowed only for portions of "gross income" paid out for the prescribed purposes, no deduction is allowed to the extent tax-exempt income is so used. Similarly, if any part of a long-term capital gain is paid out for the enumerated purposes, the charitable deduction is reduced by a proportionate part of the deduction allowed for 50 percent of the excess of net long-term capital gains over net short-term capital losses [Reg. 1.642(c)–3]. If the income used for the charitable purpose is not specified by the governing instrument, it is presumed that the charitable contribution comes proportionately out of all items of trust or estate income. If any part of such income is exempt from tax, the charitable deduction is reduced proportionately [Reg. 1.642(c)–2].

20.16 In the case of estates, deductions are allowed not only for amounts paid out for qualifying charitable purposes but also for amounts *permanently set aside* for such purposes and for amounts *to be used exclusively for* certain such purposes. These set-aside deductions are also allowed to certain trusts created before October 9, 1969, provided the explicit requirements of Section 642(c)(2) are met. Generally, for an *inter vivos* trust the set-aside deduction is allowed only (1) for the transfer of an irrevocable remainder interest to charity or (2) when the grantor of the trust was under a mental disability to change the trust after October 9, 1969. For a testamentary trust, the set-aside deductions generally are allowed only where the testator did not have the right to change the trust after October 9, 1969, or it was not changed before October 9, 1972, and the testator was at all times thereafter unable to change it because of death or mental disability. Further, charitable trusts that qualify as pooled-income funds under Section 642 qualify for set-aside deductions in connection with long-term capital gains that are permanently set aside for charitable purposes pursuant to their governing instruments.

20.17 In order that a trustee or administrator may determine the trust or estate net income before paying out a charitable contribution, he may elect to treat any amount so paid out before the end of the next taxable year as if it were paid in the first such year.

20.18 **Depreciation and Depletion.** Deductions for depreciation and depletion attributable to income-producing property are calculated for trusts, estates, and their beneficiaries in the same manner as for other taxpayers. If any part of the income from the property is distributable or distributed to beneficiaries, the related depreciation and depletion deductions must be allocated between the trust or estate and the beneficiaries [Sections 167(h) and 611(b)]. The allocation is made in accordance with the provisions of the governing instrument, or in the absence of such provisions the allocation is made in proportion to the allocation of income between the trust or estate and the beneficiaries. In the case of a trust, but not an estate, if the trustee is required or allowed to maintain a reserve for depreciation or depletion, the deduction is allocated to the trust to the extent of such reserve [Reg. 1.167(h)–1(b), 1.167(h)–1(c), and 1.611–1(c)(4)]. Any deduction in excess of the amount allocated to the reserve is then allocated between the trust and the beneficiaries in proportion to the income, in excess of that set aside for the reserve, allocable to each.

20.19 **Net Operating Losses and Excess Deductions.** Trusts and estates both are allowed deductions for net operating loss carry-backs and carry-overs [Section 642(d)]. If a net operating loss carry-back reduces the amount of income properly reportable by a beneficiary for a prior year, the beneficiary is entitled to an appropriate adjustment of his taxable income for such prior year.

20.20 In the final year of an estate or trust, any unused net operating loss carry-overs, unused capital-loss carry-overs, and any excess of certain deductions over gross income for the final year may be carried over and deducted by the beneficiaries succeeding to the property of the estate or trust [Section 642(h); Reg. 1.642(h)–1 and 1.642(h)–2]. The unused net operating losses and capital losses will constitute carry-overs to each of such beneficiaries. The excess deductions of the final year of the trust or estate will be deductible by the beneficiaries in their taxable years with which, or within which, the final year of the trust or estate ends.

20.21 **Administrative Expenses of Estate.** Administrative expenses and losses from casualties and theft incurred during the administration of an estate are deductible in calculating either federal estate tax or federal income tax. However, such amounts are not deductible for income tax purposes, unless the estate files a waiver of its right to have such deductions allowed for estate tax purposes [Section 642(g)].

20.22 **Deductions for Amounts Taxable to Beneficiaries.** As indicated previously, in order to achieve the proper allocation of the tax burden between a trust or estate and the beneficiaries, a deduction is allowed to the trust or estate for amounts currently taxable to the beneficiaries. The amount of this deduction and the comparable amount currently taxable to beneficiaries are based on amounts of income and property distributed or required to be distributed to beneficiaries [Sections 651 and 661]. The trust or estate is allowed a deduction for all income that under the terms of the governing instrument is required to be distributed currently—whether or not actually distributed—plus any other amounts of income or corpus that are properly paid, credited, or required to be distributed during the taxable year. The total deduction allowed for these items is limited to the amount of *distributable net income* of the trust or estate for the taxable year.

DISTRIBUTABLE NET INCOME

20.23 If income for trust-accounting purposes and income for tax purposes were always the same, and if trusts and estates distributed all income in the year received, it would be a simple matter to allocate taxable income between the trust or estate and the beneficiaries on the basis of the trust income allocable to each. Because income for these two purposes is not always the same, special tax rules are necessary. Provision is needed to avoid taxing an income beneficiary on a distribution of income in the trust-accounting sense that is not gross income or taxable income for tax purposes. Provision also must be made to avoid taxing both the beneficiary and the trust on income that is received by the trust in one year and distributed to a beneficiary in later years.

20.24 To accomplish these objectives, the Code has adopted the concept of "distributable net income." The Code uses distributable net income to measure the amount of distributions that are deductible by an estate or trust and includible in the gross income of beneficiaries.

20.25 Distributable net income of a trust or estate is defined in the Code and represents a modified version of taxable income. For the most part, the modifications represent items included in gross income for tax purposes but not considered income for trust-accounting purposes, and other items considered income for trust-accounting purposes, but not considered gross income for tax purposes. Distributable net income may be determined by starting with the taxable income of the trust or estate and making the following modifications:

1. Exclude the deduction for distributions to beneficiaries.
2. Exclude the deduction for the personal exemption.
3. Exclude capital gains that for trust-accounting purposes are allocated to corpus and not actually distributed, and exclude capital losses except to the extent they have been used to reduce the amount of capital gains distributed during the year.
4. Include tax-exempt interest less any deductions disallowed because attributable to such exempt interest.
5. Include any dividends excluded from gross income under the $100 dividend exclusion provision of Section 116.
6. In the case of trusts that distribute current income only, exclude any extraordinary dividends and taxable stock dividends allocated to corpus and not distributed to any beneficiary.
7. Make certain additional modifications for income attributable to foreign trusts [Section 643(a)].

For purposes of limiting the deduction of the estate or trust for distributions to beneficiaries, distributable net income is computed without including tax-exempt income and any other items of income that are not included in gross income of the trust or estate. No deduction is allowed for amounts distributed or required to be distributed currently that are not included in gross income for tax purposes [Sections 651(b) and 661(c)].

TRUST OR ESTATE INCOME TAXABLE
TO BENEFICIARIES

20.26   Trusts and estates are treated to some extent as conduits for tax purposes. Just as the trust or estate is allowed a deduction for its distributable net income that is distributed or required to be distributed currently, the beneficiaries of the trust or estate are required to treat their respective shares of such distributable net income as their own gross income [Sections 652(a) and 662(a)]. Each beneficiary includes his share of the distributable net income of the trust or estate in his gross income for his taxable year with which, or within which, the taxable year of the trust or estate ends.

20.27   The conduit theory of trust and estate taxation also applies in determining the nature of the beneficiary's gross income. The nature of each beneficiary's share of trust or estate income is determined by the nature of the various income items making up distributable net income [Sections 652(b) and 662(b)]. Thus, if distributable net income includes tax-exempt interest or long-term capital gains that are distributed to beneficiaries, the amounts received by the beneficiaries are considered to include a part of that tax-exempt interest or long-term capital gains. Unless the governing instrument or local law allocates income in a particular way, each beneficiary's share is considered to be composed proportionately of all items of distributable net income. To determine the makeup of distributable net income for this purpose, all deductions of the trust or estate are allocated to the various kinds of income entering into the determination of distributable net income. Deductions directly related to particular income items are allocated to those items. All other deductions, along with any excess of the deductions previously allocated over the income to which they are related, are then allocated to income items in a manner selected by the fiduciary. The fiduciary is free to allocate these deductions to any items of income he chooses, except that a proportionate part of such deductions must be allocated to any tax-exempt income. In the absence of any specific allocation of these deductions by the fiduciary, they are allocated proportionately to all items of income included in the distributable net income of the trust or estate [Reg. 1.652(b)–3].

20.28   Further discussion of the taxation of beneficiaries can be simplified by considering separately beneficiaries of so-called "simple trusts" and beneficiaries of so-called "complex trusts" and estates.

Simple Trusts

20.29   Trusts that by the terms of their governing instruments are required to distribute all income currently, that are not required to set aside or use any amounts for charitable, etc., purposes, and that do not distribute corpus during the taxable year, are called simple trusts

[Reg. 1.651(a)–1]. Beneficiaries of simple trusts are required to treat their respective shares of all trust income of the taxable year, whether or not distributed, as gross income to the extent of the trust's distributable net income. If two or more beneficiaries are involved and the income required to be distributed currently exceeds distributable net income, each beneficiary's share of distributable net income is proportionate to his share of the trust income required to be distributed currently [Reg. 1.652(a)–2]. As discussed above, each beneficiary's gross income attributable to the trust has the same nature for tax purposes as the income items that make up distributable net income of the trust.

Complex Trusts and Estates

All trusts that are not simple trusts are referred to as complex trusts [Reg. 1.661(a)–1]. These include trusts that distribute corpus during the taxable year and trusts with governing instruments that permit them to accumulate income or pay out, set aside, or use income for charitable purposes.　　20.30

Beneficiaries of estates are treated the same for tax purposes as beneficiaries of complex trusts.　　20.31

Beneficiaries of complex trusts and estates are required to include in gross income not only the trust or estate income required to be distributed currently but also any other amounts *properly paid, credited, or required to be distributed* during the taxable year. For this purpose, amounts properly paid or credited during the first sixty-five days of a taxable year may be elected by the fiduciary to be treated as paid or credited during the preceding year. The total amount so included in gross income is limited to the distributable net income of the trust or estate. These other amounts paid, credited, or required to be distributed by complex trusts or estates may include current income, income accumulated in prior years, or corpus. Furthermore, they may include items such as capital gains, which represent corpus for trust-accounting purposes but gross income for tax purposes. Beneficiaries of these other amounts may be corpus beneficiaries, income beneficiaries, or both; and each beneficiary will not necessarily share ratably in all amounts.　　20.32

When the sum of the income required to be distributed currently and these other amounts exceeds distributable net income, the distributable net income must be allocated to beneficiaries. This will determine the extent to which each beneficiary is taxable on that year's income of the trust or estate. Obviously, this allocation should consider not only the amount of each beneficiary's participation but also the nature of that participation. The Code provides for this allocation to be made under the so-called "tier system" or the "separate-share rule," whichever is applicable.　　20.33

The Tier System. Under the tier system, distributable net income is allocated to beneficiaries in two steps or tiers. In the first tier, dis-　　20.34

tributable net income is allocated to beneficiaries of all income required to be distributed currently [Section 662(a)(1)]. If the distributable net income exceeds such income required to be distributed currently, the excess is allocated in the second tier. In the second tier, the remaining distributable net income is allocated to beneficiaries of the other amounts paid, credited, or required to be distributed in the taxable year [Section 662(a)(2)]. Distributable net income allocated in each tier is allocated proportionately among all beneficiaries in that tier. Thus, income required to be distributed currently is included in gross income of its beneficiaries to the extent of current distributable net income. Other amounts distributed or required to be distributed are included in gross income of beneficiaries only to the extent that distributable net income exceeds income required to be distributed currently. Under the tier system, distributions of corpus and of income accumulated in prior years are treated as second-tier distributions. They are included in gross income of beneficiaries only to the extent that trust or estate distributable net income for the current year, and for previous years subject to the throw-back rules discussed later, exceed income required to be distributed currently.

EXAMPLE[1]   A trust requires the distribution annually of $8,000 of income to A. Any remaining income may be accumulated or distributed to B, C, and D in the trustee's discretion. He may also invade corpus for the benefit of A, B, C, or D. During its first year, the trust has $20,000 of income after deducting expenses. Distributable net income is $20,000. The trustee distributes $8,000 of income to A. He also distributes $4,000 each to B and C, $2,000 to D, and an additional $6,000 to A. The amounts taxable to A, B, C, and D are determined as follows:

Distributable net income	$20,000
Less: First-tier distribution to A	8,000
Excess available for second-tier distributions	$12,000
Other amounts paid during year — second-tier distributions	$16,000
Amounts of second-tier distributions included in gross income of beneficiaries:	
A — 6,000/16,000 × $12,000	$ 4,500
B — 4,000/16,000 × $12,000	$ 3,000
C — 4,000/16,000 × $12,000	$ 3,000
D — 2,000/16,000 × $12,000	$ 1,500
	$12,000

The distributable net income of the year will be included in gross income of the beneficiaries as follows:

A includes $12,500 in gross income ($8,000 first-tier distribution plus $4,500 second-tier distribution). B and C each include $3,000 in gross

1. Example reprinted by permission from Prentice-Hall Federal Tax Handbook, 1970, page 392.

income. D includes $1,500. Since this was the first year of the trust, the amounts distributed in excess of distributable net income are not taxable to the beneficiaries. If the trust had had distributable net income in prior years in excess of amounts recognized as income by its beneficiaries (undistributed income), the taxability of this year's excess distributions to beneficiaries would be determined by the throw-back rules discussed later.

The Separate-share Rule. In lieu of the tier system for allocating distributable net income to beneficiaries, the "separate-share rule" is applied when the interest of any beneficiary in the income and corpus of a trust can be determined as a separate and independent share [Section 663(c)]. Regulation 1.663(c)–3 gives the following example of an instance in which the separate-share rule will be applicable:

20.35

If an instrument directs a trustee to divide the testator's residuary estate into separate shares (which under local law do not constitute separate trusts) for each of the testator's children and the trustee is given discretion, with respect to each share, to distribute or accumulate income or to distribute principal or accumulated income, or to do both, separate shares will exist under section 663(c).

EXAMPLE
FROM REG.

This rule applies only to trusts, not to estates. Under the separate-share rule, the distributable net income of each beneficiary's share of the trust is calculated as though that share were a separate trust. The deductions allowed the trust and the gross income of the beneficiary are then determined separately for each share. It should be noted that this separate treatment applies only to the determination of the deductions allowable to the trust and the gross income taxable to the beneficiary. This rule alone does not allow the trust to be treated as two or more trusts for purposes of the personal exemptions, the filing of returns, and other purposes. This separate-share rule avoids the inequity that otherwise might occur when a beneficiary receives a distribution of corpus, reducing his separate share of the trust. Under the tier system, if the income beneficiary's share of income for that year is neither distributed nor required to be distributed currently, the distributable net income of the trust would be allocated to the corpus distribution. This would subject the corpus beneficiary to tax on income actually accumulated for the income beneficiary.

From the above rules it can be seen that, generally, all distributions are treated as coming first out of distributable net income. To that extent they are deductible by the trust or estate and constitute gross income to the beneficiaries. An exception to this rule applies in the case of certain gifts and bequests of specific property or specific sums of money [Section 663(a)]. Where such specific gifts or bequests are not payable solely out of income of the trust or estate and are paid in not more than three installments, they are not treated as distributions of distributable net income. They are not deductible by the estate and are not treated as gross income to the beneficiary.

20.36

ACCUMULATION DISTRIBUTIONS FROM TRUSTS

20.37   Standing alone, the rules discussed above concerning complex trusts would leave an opportunity for tax avoidance by means of timing distributions to beneficiaries. This avoidance could be accomplished by the trustee's accumulating income in years when beneficiaries' tax rates are higher than the trust's rates, and distributing that accumulated income along with current income in subsequent years when beneficiaries are subject to lower tax rates. A special rule minimizes this tax-avoidance possibility. This special rule is sometimes referred to as the "throw-back rule." Although the same opportunity exists for estates, the throw-back rule does not apply to them.

20.38   The throw-back rule applies whenever the income distributed or required to be distributed currently plus other amounts paid, credited, or required to be distributed exceed the distributable net income of the current year [Section 665(b)]. This excess is called an accumulation distribution, and it is included in gross income of the beneficiaries to whom distributed to the extent that distributable net income of certain preceding years has not previously been included in gross income of beneficiaries. In other words, these accumulation distributions are "thrown back" and treated as though they were distributed in prior years to the extent that distributable net income of prior years was not previously taxed to beneficiaries. Any income taxes previously paid by the trust on this income are treated as additions to the accumulation distribution. Each beneficiary is then given credit against his tax for his proportionate share of taxes paid by the trust [Sections 666 and 668(b)].

20.39   The beneficiaries report their gross income attributable to accumulation distributions in their taxable year with which or within which the distribution year of the trust ends; however, the amount of that gross income and its nature depends upon the amount and nature of the trust's distributable net income in each of the prior years to which the accumulation distributions are thrown back.

20.40   For trust years beginning before 1969, the throw-back rule extended only to undistributed net income of the five years preceding the year of distribution. This rule continues to apply for all trust years beginning before 1974. For trust years beginning in 1974 and later, the Tax Reform Act of 1969 extended the throw-back rule to reach all trust years beginning after 1968. Thus accumulation distributions made in trust years beginning before 1974 will be included in gross income of beneficiaries to the extent that distributable net income of the five preceding years has not previously been included in their gross incomes. Accumulation distributions made in trust years beginning in 1974 and after will be included in gross income of beneficiaries to the extent that distributable net income of all years beginning after 1968 has not previously been included. Accumulation distributions made in years beginning in 1970 and later are deemed to come first from the earliest years reached by the throw-back rule [Section 666(a)]. Accumulation distributions made in trust years beginning in 1969 and earlier will be treated as coming from the five preceding years in inverse order.[2]

20.41

For trust years beginning before 1969, beneficiaries were not subject to tax on undistributed capital gains under the throw-back rules. For trust years beginning in 1969 and later, undistributed capital gains will be subject to the throw-back rules if accumulation distributions exceed ordinary income of previous years. The throwback of capital gains, however, is calculated separately from the throw-back of ordinary income.

20.42

The tax of a beneficiary attributable to an accumulation distribution is calculated separately from his tax on other income. Such tax is equal to the excess of (1) the additional taxes that would have been paid by the beneficiary if the accumulation distributions had actually been distributed in the years to which thrown back over (2) the tax paid on such income by the trust. The tax cannot exceed, however, an amount calculated under a special shortcut averaging method. Under this method the average yearly gross income for the throw-back years recognized under the throw-back rule is added to the beneficiary's actual taxable income for each of the three years preceding the year of the accumulation distribution. The average of the additional tax computed for those three years is then multiplied by the number of throw-back years involved in the calculation to arrive at the shortcut tax.

20.43

For years beginning before 1969, Code Section 665(b) provided several exceptions to the throw-back rule. Such exceptions involved distributions accumulated before a beneficiary attained age twenty-one, distributions for emergency needs of a beneficiary, amounts paid under certain circumstances on the beneficiary's attaining a specified age or ages, and final distributions made more than nine years after the last transfer of property to the trust.

20.44

These exceptions were eliminated by the Tax Reform Act of 1969, but a transitional rule provides they can still apply to distributions made in trust years beginning before 1974 to the extent of income accumulated in trust years beginning before 1969 if the exceptions would have applied to the distributions if made during those years.

TRUST INCOME TAXABLE TO GRANTORS AND OTHERS

20.45

When a grantor retains certain powers of dominion and control over trust property and income, he is considered the substantial owner of that property and is taxable on its income [Section 671]. The powers might be retained over all or only part of the trust property and income. In that event the gross income, deductions, and credits ap-

---

2. Section 331(d)(2)(B) of Tax Reform Act of 1969.

plicable to such part of the trust property or income are treated as gross income, deductions, and credits of the grantor. Although the trust is required to file a tax return, these items of the grantor are not included in that return as such but are shown on a separate schedule attached to the return [Reg. 1.671–4].

20.46 Sections 671 through 677 specify the circumstances under which a grantor is taxable on trust income. These provisions contain numerous qualifications and exceptions, and they have led to extensive litigation. In general the grantor is taxed whenever:

1. The grantor has a reversionary interest in the property or the income of the trust that might reasonably take effect within ten years from the date the property is transferred to the trust. However, the grantor is not taxable if the reversionary interest takes effect only after the death of the income beneficiary [Section 673].
2. The grantor retains the right to control the ultimate enjoyment of the income or the corpus of the trust without the consent of an adverse party [Section 674].
3. The grantor reserves any power over the administration of trust property that is exercisable in a nonfiduciary capacity or that represents the right to deal with trust property on other than an arm's-length basis. Examples are (1) the power to borrow funds from the trust without adequate interest or collateral or (2) to purchase property from the trust for less than full and adequate consideration [Section 675].
4. The grantor or a nonadverse party has the right to revoke the trust and revest the title of the trust property in the grantor (Section 676).
5. Without the consent of an adverse party, the income of the trust is, or may be, distributed to the grantor or his spouse, held for future distribution to him or his spouse, or may be used to pay premiums on life insurance policies on the life of the grantor or his spouse [Section 677].

20.47 If a person other than a grantor of the trust has the power to vest title to the trust property or income in himself, he is treated as the owner of that trust property or income and is taxed on its income. If the person releases part of this power but retains any of the powers discussed in the preceding paragraph, he is taxed in substantially the same manner as a grantor of the trust (Section 678). Furthermore, if trust income or property is used to satisfy the legal obligation of any person, the amount so used is treated as a distribution to him, and he is treated as a beneficiary in respect to such distribution [Reg. 1.662(a)(4)].

TRUSTS CLASSIFIED AS CORPORATIONS

20.48 It was indicated at the beginning of chapter 19 that the classification of organizations for tax purposes does not always follow the classification of those organizations for legal purposes. Accordingly, although an arrangement may be set up in the form of a trust, if it resembles a corporation more than a trust, it will be treated as a corporation for tax purposes. This result happens most often when a trust is set up to run a business enterprise. When a trust is taxed as a corporation, it is not allowed any deduction for amounts distributed to beneficiaries. Instead, the distributions are treated as dividends and are taxable to the beneficiaries to the extent of the trust's earnings and profits. The resulting double tax on trust earnings can be quite burdensome to beneficiaries.

QUESTIONS AND PROBLEMS

1. Are the following statements true or false? If any part of the statement is incorrect, it should be called false. Assume that the taxable years of the beneficiaries are the same as those of the trusts or estates.
   (a) The grantor of a trust is taxable on the income from any part of a trust in which he reserves a reversionary interest.
   (b) If the distributable net income of a trust exceeds the amount of its income that is required to be distributed currently, the beneficiaries entitled to receive the income required to be distributed currently are required to include such amount in gross income even if it is not distributed during the year.
   (c) Except when the throw-back rule applies, the amount of trust income includible in gross income of beneficiaries is limited to the trust's distributable net income for that year as computed for that purpose.
   (d) Under the throw-back rule, beneficiaries of trusts and estates may be taxed in one year on more than the distributable net income of the trust or estate for that year.
   (e) Trusts and estates are allowed deductions for personal exemptions as follows:

Estates	$600
Trusts which are required to distribute income currently	300
Trusts which are not required to distribute income currently	100

   (f) Trusts and estates may adopt taxable years different from the taxable years of their beneficiaries without obtaining permission from the Commissioner.
   (g) A trust or estate may deduct for income tax purposes any amount paid or permanently set aside for charitable purposes described in Section 642(c).
   (h) A net operating loss of a trust or estate is never deductible by the beneficiaries.
   (i) Capital gains are included in distributable net income if they are distributed to beneficiaries or if they are allocated to trust income under appropriate state law or the terms of the governing instrument.
   (j) Tax-exempt interest is always included in distributable net income because it constitutes income under state law.
   (k) The character or nature of a beneficiary's gross income attributable to a trust or estate is determined by the character or nature of the income items making up the trust or estate distributable net income.

2. Explain what is meant by the term "income in respect of a decedent." By whom is it reported for Federal income tax purposes?

3. Explain the significance of the taxable year of an estate or trust on the beneficiary's time for reporting income attributable to the estate or trust.

4. Trust A is established in 1972 as a complex trust. The trustee is not required to distribute income but may do so in his discretion to meet the reasonable needs of the beneficiary. The trust adopts a calendar year for tax purposes. Distributable net income is $15,000 in each of the years 1972, 1973, and 1974. Discuss when the following distributions should be reported as gross income by the lone beneficiary:

December 25, 1972	$10,000
February 5, 1973	8,000
December 15, 1973	10,000

5. Explain the purpose and concept of distributable net income.

6. What is the "separate-share rule"?

7. Grantor A establishes a trust from which all income is to be distributed to A's invalid father for the rest of his life. The father dies after $2\frac{1}{2}$ years and the property of the trust is returned to A. To whom is the trust income taxable during the life of the trust? Explain. What would be your answer if the trust had been set up for a period of twelve years or life of father, whichever was shorter?

8. Grantor X establishes a trust with income-producing securities. Terms of the trust provide that all property and accumulated income of the trust are to be distributed to X's daughter when she becomes thirty years of age. The terms also provide for the trustee to purchase and maintain a life insurance policy on the life of X's wife with the trust named as beneficiary. During the first year of the trust, taxable net income before personal exemption is $3,000; distributable net income is $3,000; insurance premium paid on life of X's wife is $1,000; and $2,000 is accumulated for future distribution to the daughter. Who is taxable on the net income of the trust?

9. John Smith died in October, 1970, leaving all his property in trust for his daughter and his son. The trustee was required to distribute $5,000 of income each year to each child, and he was given complete discretion on further distributions of income or corpus to both children. Distributable net income for taxable years of the trust ending September 30, and distributions to the children were as follows:

	YEARS ENDED SEPTEMBER 30		
	1971	1972	1973
Distributable net income	$14,100	$15,100	$10,000
Federal income tax paid by trust	800	1,000	-0-
Distributions to:			
Son	5,000	5,000	5,000
Daughter	5,000	5,000	15,000

Calculate each beneficiary's gross income attributable to the trust. Show the year of the trust to which it is applicable and the calendar year of the beneficiary in which he reports such income.

10. The XYZ trust received income and incurred expenses in 1973 as shown below. Terms of the trust give the trustee complete discretion whether to distribute or accumulate income during the life of the beneficiary. The trust terminates and all accumulated income and corpus are to be distributed to the beneficiary in 1977 when he becomes twenty-five years of age. During 1973 the trustee distributes $5,000 to the beneficiary. Under applicable law capital gains are added to corpus. The trustee makes no specific allocation of expenses. The trust requires the trustee to provide a reserve for depreciation equal to the amounts allowable each year for income tax purposes. Calculate (1) taxable net income of the trust, (2) the trust's tax liability, (3) distributable net income of the trust, and (4) the gross income of the beneficiary attributable to the trust.

Income:

Interest on corporate bonds	$3,000
Interest on New York City school bonds	1,200
Dividends on common stocks	5,000
Rent from warehouse building	3,600
Gain on sale of common stock purchased in 1967	4,500

Expenses:

Trustees fees	$2,000
Maintenance and repairs on rental property	600
Depreciation on warehouse	900
State property taxes on warehouse	800

INDIVIDUAL INCOME TAX RETURN PREPARATION PROBLEM

GENERAL DATA AND INSTRUCTIONS . . . 737
INFORMATION FROM PRIOR RETURNS AND CLIENT . . . 738

GENERAL DATA AND INSTRUCTIONS

James L. and Martha G. Snyder (taxpayer identification numbers 831–65–4188 and 831–65–4189) live at 1905 Blackmere Avenue, Wilmette, Illinois, with their son Jack, age 12 and daughter Mary, age 17. Their oldest son Bill, age 23, is a full-time student at Tulane University Medical School.

Mr. Snyder operates a sole proprietorship under the name Lucky Sales Company, located at 1300 Central Street, Skokie, Illinois, 60076. His employer I.D. number is 74–1358317. Mr. Snyder acts as a commission agent for machine tool parts. The Snyders also have various investment assets. They report their income on a calendar year basis and use the cash method of accounting.

The Snyders furnished more than half the support of the two youngest children. As to Bill, he is single, earned $1,600 during the summer and had $400 of interest income from a savings account. During the year he spent $500 of the $2,000 ($1,600 + $400) for clothes and banked the balance. The son had a non-taxable scholarship of $3,000 for the year, and the father paid $1,000 towards his support.

Both of the Snyders are less than 65 years of age, and neither is blind. Mr. Snyder, your client, has just brought his information to your office for preparation of the Snyders' joint Federal Income Tax Return for 1972. From the following information prepare and submit the following:

(1) Letter of transmittal to Mr. and Mrs. Snyder.
(2) Return form 1040 together with supporting schedules which may include some or all of the following official schedules:

    A&B – Itemized deductions and dividend and interest income
    C   – Profit (or loss) from business or profession
    D   – Capital gains and losses
    E&R – Supplementary income schedule and retirement income credit computation
    SE   – Computation of Social Security self-employment tax
    1116 – Computation of foreign tax credit
    3468 – Computation of investment credit
    4684 – Casualties and thefts
    4797 – Supplemental schedule of gains and losses
    4832 – CLADR
    Other longhand schedules, to the extent deemed appropriate should also be submitted.

(3) Memorandum listing tax planning points to be discussed with client which may have significance for the current and future years.
(4) Descriptive list (optional with you) of assumptions made in solving the problems which pertain to facts given in the problems and which you believe are ambiguous or not sufficiently

737

complete. (Do not invent new circumstances, and do not change the facts explicitly given.)

In solving this problem, the goal is to prepare a return which will show the least income tax liability for the year—all in accordance with the law and permissible alternatives.

INFORMATION FROM PRIOR RETURNS AND CLIENT

(1) Snyder paid $10,000 for 500 shares of Mound Company in January, 1967. He received $8,000 in April, 1971, as the first of several liquidating distributions under a plan of complete liquidation adopted by the Mound Company in March, 1971.

(2) Various shares of stock held as investments were sold during the year as follows:

STOCK	DATE PURCHASED	PURCHASE PRICE	DATE SOLD	GROSS SALES PRICE	COMMISSION PAID ON SALES	NEW YORK TRANSFER TAX PAID ON SALES
Corn Products (100 Shares)	12/3/69	$5,100	8/27/72	$8,300	$65.00	$5.00
Tennessee Gas (100 Shares)	1/8/70	2,200	12/23/72	2,500	44.50	5.00
Horseback Insurance (200 Shares)	6/15/72	1,500	8/21/72	1,100	34.80	5.00

(3) The 1971 return of the Snyders shows that for that year there was an excess of a net long-term capital loss over a net short term capital gain of $4,000 and that $1,000 of that amount was claimed as an ordinary deduction in 1971.

(4) The Snyders' home is mortgaged with the First Federal Savings and Loan Association of Wilmette. During the year 1972 they made twelve equal monthly payments totalling $5,176.00, consisting of $2,618.40 for principal and interest, $405.60 for insurance, and $2,152.00 for real estate taxes. The amounts paid in for insurance and taxes are deposited in an escrow account by the association. Then, as the bills become due, the association pays them. In January, 1973, the Snyders received the following information from the association regarding their mortgage:

Loan balance at 12/31/72	$28,789.44
Escrow credit balance at 12/31/72	130.00
Interest paid during 1972	2,046.03
Taxes paid during 1972	2,050.00
Insurance premiums paid during 1972	395.00

(5) The following information was extracted from U.S. Government information forms received by the Snyders pertaining to the taxable year 1972:

FORM NUMBER	RECEIVED FROM	INFORMATION REPORTED
1099L	Mound Company	$5,000 paid on 500 common shares— 2nd liquidating distribution
1099	Commonwealth Edison Co. Bonds	$1,400 interest paid to James Snyder
1099	El Paso, Texas, School District Municipal Bonds	$960 interest paid to Mrs. Snyder
1099	Bell Savings & Loan	$800 interest paid to James Snyder
1099	American Telephone & Telegraph	$340 dividends paid to Martha Snyder
1099	Corn Products	$112.50 dividends paid to James Snyder
1099	Tennessee Gas Transmission	$110 dividends paid to James Snyder
1099*	Canadian Utilities	Canadian $140 dividends paid to Martha Snyder. Mrs. Snyder commented that she received only U.S. $107.10 from Canadian Utilities.

*Form received from U.S. transfer agents.

(6) Canada withholds a 15 percent tax on dividends paid to non-residents. Also, any dividends paid in Canadian funds are subject to exchange at $.90 U.S. for one Canadian dollar.

(7) Mr. Snyder's information also included receipts and other documentation in support of $100.00 gambling losses.

(8) Interest of $160.00 was received from Jack Farmer on his $2,000.00, 8 percent note.

(9) A dividend check in the amount of $360.00 was received by Mrs. Snyder on January 3, 1973, from U. S. Gypsum Company. The check was dated December 31, 1972 and was mailed to her on that date.

(10) In 1969, Mr. Snyder loaned one of his corporate customers $5,000.00 on its unsecured 7 percent promissory note due in 1973. The corporation was adjudicated a bankrupt in early 1972, and the trustee in bankruptcy in December, 1972, announced that there would be no money available to pay unsecured creditors. Mr. Snyder made the loan to help the customer stay in business.

(11) State gasoline taxes were incurred in the use of a non-business auto. It was driven 8,000 miles in Illinois during the year.

(12) Illinois state sales tax was incurred during the year on non-business purchases. The Snyders' said to claim the amount set forth in the instructions for return form 1040 (pages 26, 10, and 11.).

(13) The Snyders also paid $116.00 for personal property tax and a $50.00 village assessment for sidewalk and curb improvements.

(14) Mr. Snyder commented that a windstorm had damaged a sign on his business office on December 5, 1972. Harry's Sign Shop esti-

mated that it will cost $50.00 to repair the sign. The sign had an adjusted basis of $120.00, and the loss was not insured.

(15) During the year the Snyders made payments of Illinois State Income Tax as follows:

SNYDER'S ILLINOIS STATE INCOME TAX:

1-15-72	¼ of 1971 estimated tax	$100.00
4-10-72	Balance of 1971 tax	$ 90.00
4-10-72	¼ of 1972 estimated tax	$150.00
6-15-72	¼ of 1972 estimated tax	$150.00
9-15-72	¼ of 1972 estimated tax	$150.00

During 1971, $300.00 had also been paid as installments on the 1971 estimated tax.

(16) The following cash donations were made during the year:

Boy Scouts	$ 200.00
Church of St. John the Divine	$1,500.00
United Fund	$ 200.00
American Red Cross	$ 150.00
Republican National Committee	$ 200.00
Wilmette Garden Club (a social organization)	$ 10.00
Individual beggars (Estimated)	$ 20.00

(17) Mrs. Snyder gave an old refrigerator to the Salvation Army on February 11, 1972. She had paid $550.00 for it in 1962. Similar used refrigerators could be purchased for $75.00 in 1972.

(18) Mrs. Snyder lost her new fur coat (only two weeks old) at a charity ball. Two other fur coats of other women also disappeared that night. The incident was reported to the police. The purchase price of the coat was $1,800. Of that sum, $900.00 was paid in 1972, and the balance is due at the end of 1973. No insurance recovery is available.

(19) Mr. Snyder borrowed $10,000.00 on May 4, 1972, from the Continental Illinois National Bank, but received only $9,100.00. Mr. Snyder states that the $900 balance is interest. The note is due on May 4, 1973 and has not yet been paid.

(20) The following medical bills were paid:

Dr. Frank James, M.D.	$ 250.00
Dr. Gerald Crain, M.D.	$1,250.00
Dr. James Morgan, D.D.S.	$ 222.00
T.S.O. Contact Clinic (contact lenses for Mary)	$ 175.00
Blue Cross premiums	$ 310.00
Drugs from Ridge Pharmacy	$ 312.00

As to the payments to the two physicians, a claim for reimbursement was filed in November, 1972, with Blue Cross and a check was received from it in February, 1973, for $1,200.00.

(21) During 1972, the Snyders drove 150 miles in visiting doctors. A deduction equal to $.06 per mile is allowed for medical travel according to Rev. Proc. 70-24, 1970-2 C. B. 505.

(22) Miscellaneous items paid from Mr. Snyder's personal funds:

The Wall Street Journal	$35.00
Fortune Magazine	$10.00
Safe deposit box rental	$15.00

(23) The Snyders paid $4,000.00 as estimated 1972 Federal Income Tax.

(24) A 1970 Chevrolet was sold to an unrelated individual on August 17, 1972, for $1,500. The auto originally cost $3,500.00 when purchased on January 5, 1970. Examination of Mr. Snyder's retained copies of his 1970 and 1971 returns discloses that depreciation of $1,166.67 was deducted on each of those returns. The auto was used for business purposes only.

(25) The following information was obtained from the invoice for a 1972 Dodge Dart, purchased on August 10, 1972, from Jerry Motors, Incorporated, by Mr. Snyder for use as a business car:

List price	$3,626.90
Sales tax	156.64
Title certificate	10.00
Illinois license plates	18.00
	$3,811.54
Cost of financing	$ 493.63
Cost of insurance (credit life for benefit of Jerry Motors, Inc.)	34.57
TOTAL	$4,339.74
Settlement:	
Discount from price of auto	$ 494.10
Cash payment	607.44
Payments due (36 at $89.95 commencing September 10, 1972)	3,238.20
	$4,339.74

(26) An office calculator purchased July 10, 1963, for $550.00 was traded in for a new one on July 1, 1972. The reserve for depreciation at December 31, 1971, was $467.50 calculated under the facts and circumstances life system and the straight-line method.

(27) In computing depreciation, Snyder has used the facts and circumstances life system in 1971 and prior years. For 1972, he is willing

to use whatever life systems and methods that are available. He made no application in 1972 to change any depreciation or other accounting method. With respect to 1971 and prior years' additions and retirements, he followed the practice of claiming depreciation according to the number of months in use in the year. In determining what constitutes a month, an asset acquired during the first 15 days of a calendar month was considered to have been acquired on the first day of that month, and an asset disposed of during the first 15 days of a month was considered to have been disposed of on the last day of the preceding month. Transactions occurring on the sixteenth or later day of a month were treated as occurring on the first day of the following month. He has estimated that his assets under the facts and circumstances life system have a 10 percent salvage value at the end of their useful life. All assets except automobiles, are assigned a ten-year life. Automobiles are assigned a three-year life.

(28) Besides the calculator, Lucky Sales Company has the following office equipment:

ITEM	COST	12-31-71 RESERVE	METHOD
Desks and chairs	$1,500.00	$500.00	10 yr. – S.L.
File cabinets	1,000.00	600.00	10 yr. – 150% DB
Miscellaneous fixtures	500.00	200.00	10 yr. – DDB
Typewriters	450.00	300.00	10 yr. – S.L.

(29) Under Rev. Proc. 72–10, as amended by Rev. Proc. 73–2, pertaining to the Class Life Asset Depreciation Range System: Class 70.13 "Data Handling Equipment, Except Computers," covers assets such as calculators, adding and accounting machines, copiers, duplicating equipment, and typewriters – class life of 6 years, (range of 5 to 7 years); Class 70.11, "Office Furniture, Fixtures, and Equipment," covers assets such as desks, files, safes, and some communication equipment – class life of 10 years (range of 8 to 12 years); Class 00.22 "Automobiles, Taxis" – class life of 3 years (range of 2.5 to 3.5 years).

(30) In their 1971 return, the Snyders claimed a non-business bad debt of $300.00 for money loaned their handyman in 1970. In early 1971, he was jailed for automobile stealing and was given a two year sentence. Due to time off for good behavior, he was released on parole in early 1972. During the latter part of 1972, he commenced repaying the $300.00 loan (no interest), and by the end of the year, he had repaid $150.00. Taxable income shown on the Snyders' 1971 return was in excess of $20,000.00.

(31) The following cash summary for Lucky Sales Company was supplied by Mr. Snyder:

LUCKY SALES COMPANY
CASH RECEIPTS AND DISBURSEMENTS
1972

Beginning cash balance		$10,000.00
Receipts:		
Commissions	$50,000.00	
Sale of 1970 Chevrolet	1,500.00	
Irish Sweepstakes net winning	200.00	51,700.00
		$61,700.00
Disbursements		
Car note payments	$ 359.80	
Salaries — secretary	4,697.52°	
Social Security	624.00	
Federal and Illinois Income Taxes		
Withheld on Salaries	990.48	
Federal and Illinois Unemployment Tax	134.40	
Office Rent	3,000.00	
1972 Dodge Dart purchased	607.44	
Travel and Entertainment	600.00	
Gasoline	1,200.00	
Repairs	300.00	
Calculator purchased°°	500.00	
Luncheon Club Dues	135.75	
Business Magazines	50.00	
Contributions (United Fund)	100.00	
Accounting and legal	500.00	
Withdrawals by Snyder	18,000.00	
Telephone and utilities	500.00	
Insurance (fire and theft)	100.00	$32,399.39
Ending cash balance		$29,300.61

°Net of $312.00 social security tax withheld, $864.00 Federal Income Tax withheld, and $126.48 Illinois Income Tax Withheld.
°°I traded my old one in on a new $600.00 calculator on July 1, 1972.

TABLE OF CASES

Cases that are digested or quoted in the text are set in *italic* type. Others, which are merely cited in the text or footnotes, are set in roman type. Where the Commissioner, the United States, or Helvering is the plaintiff, the title of the case is given under the name of the defendant.

NUMBERS REFER TO PAGES

A

Abegg, Werner, 670
Acro Mfg. Co., 451
Alderson v. Com., 423
Allen, Mary Frances, 336
All-Steel Equipment, Inc., 574
Aluminum Castings Co., v. Routzahn, 556
American Automobile Association v. U.S., 555
American Can Co. v. Com., 605
American Chicle Co., 371
American Chicle Co., Helvering v., 136
American Dental Co., Helvering v. 136
Amoroso, 529
Anderson v. Helvering, 304
Anderson, Charles N., Com. v., 189
Anderson, et al., P. Chauncey, U.S. v., 555
Andrews, Curtis B., 401, 564
Appelman v. U.S., 332

Armstrong v. Phinney, 191
Armstrong Cork Co., 556
Arnold v. U.S., 118, 189, 191
Artnell v. Com., 549
Ashby, Paul K., 450
Astoria Marine Construction Co., 137
Atlantic Coast Realty Co., 571
Atlantic Oil Co. v. Patterson, 160
Atzingen-Whitehouse Dairy Co., 208
Automatic Heating & Cooling Co., 250
Automobile Ins. Co. of Hartford, Conn. v. Com., 544
Auerbacher, William, 230
Avery, Sewell L. v. Com., 521, 529
Avery & Sons, Inc., B. F., 137

B

Babin, Sr., Alphonse L., 440
Bacon, Inc., 361

Badgley v. Com., 599
Baird Publishing Co., J. H., 423
Ball, Edmund F., 224, 368
Banigan, 333
Bardahl Manufacturing Corp., 625
Barrett, U.S., v., 333
Barrett, W. Stanley, 424
Barron, Herman, 201
Batten v. U.S., 224
Beacon Coal Co., 557
Bear Film Co., 570
Becken, Jr., Albert C., 565
Bedell, Alfred M., v. Com., 401
Bell Electric Co., 536
Bent Co., R. G., 599
Bercaw, 332
Bessemer Invest. Co. v. Com., 119
Bibb Mfg. Co. v. Rose, 576
Birdsboro Steel Foundry &Machine Co. v. U.S., 340
Birmingham News Co. v. Patterson, Jr., 250
Bishop v. Com., 368

Bishop, Charles Kay, 610
Bissett & Son, F.D., 520
Bixler, 226
Black, Limited, E. E., v. J. M. Alsup, 600
Blair, Inc., Algernon, 249
Blanton, George L., v. Com., 611
Blum's Incorporated, 587, 589, 590
Boe v. Com. 251
Boehm v. Com., 343
Bogardus v. Com., 165
Bogene, 179
Bolling et al. v. Com., 350
Borax, Estate of Herman, v. Com., 61
Boston American League Baseball Club, 440
Boston Elevated Railway Co., 327
Boudreau v. Com., 401
Boykin, J. Melvin, v. Com., 190
Boylston Market Assn., Com. v. 530
Bradford, Robert L., 341
Bridges v. Com., 363
Briggs v. Hofferbert, 450
Briggs v. U.S., 191
Brodie, Renton K., 524
Bromley v. McCaughn, 114
Broussard, Estelle, 529
Brown Company, H. H., 537
Brown Shoe Co. v. Com., 187
Brush-Moore Newspapers v. Com., 217
Bruun, Helvering v., 118
Bryan, L. M., 571
Buckley, Estate of Daniel, 61, 362
Budget Credits, Inc. v. Com., 351
Buist v. U.S., 333
Burnet v. Logan, 404
Burno v. U.S., 332
Burns v. Gray, 226
Buttrey Stores, Inc. v. U.S., 630

C

Caldwell v. Com., 603
Callan v. Westover, 335

Camilla Cotton Oil Co., 200
Camp Wolters Enterprises, Inc. v. Com., 672
Campbell v. Charles N. Prothro, 380
Campbell, Estate of Ira A., 346
Canelo III, Adolph B., 183
Canton Cotton Mills v. U.S., 556
Carboloy Company, Inc., 250
Carkhuff, John R., 205
Carp, Jacob, 442
Carpenter, W. K., v. U.S., 236
Carroll, James A., 213
Carroll Pressure Roller Corp., 478
Carter, G. S., 634
Carter, Susan J., 405
Castner Co., Inc., George L., 404
Celina Mfg. Co. v. Com., 530
Central Foundry Co., 235
Cesarini v. U.S., 133
Chadick v. U.S., 130
Chamberlin v. Com., 683
Champion Spark Plug Co., Com. v., 219
Chapin, S. C., 210
Chicago, R.I. & P. Ry. Co. v. Com., 114
Chicago Stoker Corp., 220
Chock Full O'Nuts Corp., v. U.S., 482
City Stores Co. v. Smith, 589
Clark, Edward H., 151
Clover, J.B., 598
Coastal Terminals, Inc. v. U.S., 423
Cohen, Edward L., 561
Collector v. Day, 115
Collier, U.S. v., 360
Comeaux, C. A., 209
Commercial Solvents Corporation, 539
Commerford, U.S. v., 130
Conner, 191
Consoer, Older & Quinlan, Inc. v. Com., 544
Consolidated Edison

Company of New York, Inc., U.S. v., 559
Continental Tie and Lumber Co. v. U.S., 557
Cooper, Frank B., 249
Cooper Tire & Rubber Co. Employees' Retirement Fund v. Com., 22
Corn Exchange Bank v. U.S., 543
Corn Products Refining Co. v. Com., 450, 457
Correll v. U.S., 227
Coulter, John M., 7.134
Court Holding Co., Com. v., 689, 714
Covington, George W., et al., Com. v., 456
Cowden, Sr., Frank, v. Com., 402, 403
Cowell, I. M. 201
Cox, Alfred M., 335
Crane v. Com., 401, 409
Crews, A. D., 230
Croker, Bula, 209
Cuba R. Co., 543
Curtis, James F., 327

D

Dairy Queen of Oklahoma, Inc. v. Com., 479
Daley v. U.S., 598, 599
Dally, Charles F., v. Com., 539
Dalriada Realty Co., 596
Davey, W. M., 440
Davis, Marlin P., U.S. v., 681
Davis, T. C., U.S. v., 142, 236, 400, 409
Daytona Marine Supply Co., et al. v. U.S., 365
Dearborn Gage Co., 573
Decision, Inc., 609
Denise Coal Co. v. Com., 562
Deputy v. du Pont, 201, 204
Detroit Edison Co. v. Com., 187
Devereux, Estate of, 411

746

Table of Cases

Dial, Robert J., 401, 525
Dickason, W. S., 209
Dickinson, 332
Diggs, Robert M., 334
Divine, Jr., T. M., 593
Dixie Pine Products Co. v. Com., 559
Dixon v. U.S., 36
Doak, Com. v., 191
Dobson v. Com., 183
Dorzback v. Collison, 360
Dow, Richard A., 332
Dravo Corp. v. U.S., 559
Dreymann, Carl G., 477
Droge, Christian H., 130
Drysdale, Robert M., v. Com., 120
Duberstein et al., Com. v., 164, 166
Ducros v. Com., 160
Dunn & McCarthy, Inc. v. Com., 202
Durden, 333
Duryea, 233
Dyer, J. Raymond, 234

E

Earle v. W. J. Jones & Son, 366
Eckert v. Burnet, 342
Edison Bros. Stores, Inc., Helvering v., 110
Edwards v. Cuba R.R. Co., 186
Edwards, E. W., 137
Ehret-Day Co., 600
Eisner v. Macomber, 110, 111, 115, 116
Electric Reduction Co. v. Lewellyn, 317
Eliot v. Robinson, 220
Ellis, James C., 599
Empey, U.S. v., 669
Engel, James J., 212
Ennis, Nina J., 401, 403
Eskimo Pie Corporation, 361
Estate Planning Corp., 361

F

Fackler, J. D., 531
Fahs v. John W. Martin, et al., 560

Fall River Electric Co., 171
Farley Realty Corp. v. Com., 361
Farmers & Ginners Cotton Oil Co., Com. v., 456
Farmers' and Merchants' Bank of Cattletsburg v. Com., 153
Farmers & Merchants National Bank of Nacoma, Tex., 341
Fay v. Helvering, 333
Federated Department Stores, Inc., 541
Fifth Avenue Coach Lines, Inc., 219
Fifth Ave.–14th St. Corp. v. Com., 137
Finkenberg's Sons, Inc., A., 587
Finn, Russell G., 599
First National Co., 361
First Savings & Loan Assn., 403
Fischer, 31
Fischer, L. M., 524
Fisher, Wilson J., 230
Flint, W. W., 529
Flowers, Com. v., 226
Forman Co., Inc., B. v. Com., 127
Forshay, Stewart, 123
Fort Pitt Bridge Works, 598
Foster Frosty Foods v. Com., 350
Fox, Maurice, v. Com., 523
Franc Furniture Co., 587
Frank, Morton, 233
Fraser Brick Co., 557
Fribourg Navigation Company, Inc. v. Com., 253
Friedman, S. M., v. Com., 125
Fruehauf Trailer Co., 606
Fulton Bag & Cotton Mills, 456
Fulton Gold Corp., 138

G

Garber, Inc., S., 552
Garlock, F., 226
Garlove, Frank A., 346

Garrett, W. O., 593
General American Investors Co., Inc. v. Com., 111, 152
Geometric Stamping Co., 574
Giblin v. Com., 346
Giffin, E. A., 593
Gilbert, Ida Mae, 142
Gillis, J. D., 528
Gilmore, U.S. v., 235
Glenshaw Glass Co., Com. v., 111, 112, 152
Globe Corporation, 542
Godwin, Arthur M., 114
Golden State Towel and Linen Service, Ltd. v. U.S., 251
Goldman, Douglas, 380
Golsen, 35
Goodman, C. 524
Gordon, Alice V., 329
Gould Securities Co. v. U.S., 409
Gowdey's Estate v. Com., 479
Grace Bros., Inc. v. Com., 450, 453
Graf Company, John, 538
Graham, R. Walter, v. Com., 234
Grant v. Com., 333
Great Island Holding Corp., 559
Green Bay and Western R.R. Co. v. Com., 366
Greenspon, Louis, 585
Gregory v. Helvering, 714
Gulf Power Co., 317
Gulledge, Sr., Edmund Thomas, 339
Gunderson Bros. Engineering Corp., 540

H

Haden Co., 137
Hagen Advertising Displays, Inc., 552
Hansen, et al., Com. v., 541
Harden v. Com., 603
Harmon D. Allan, U.S. v., 540
Harrold v. Com., 562
Harry Co., S. J., 539

Hartman Co., W. H., 423
Harvey, John J., v. Com., 226
Hawkins, C. A., 153
Hazeltine Corp. v. U.S., 329
Hellmers, M. J., 317
Hemingway, W. S., 126
Henke v. Jarecki, 209
Herter, Louise K., 530
Hertz Corp. v. U.S., 255
Hervey, W. R., 320
Hiatt, 138
Higgins v. Com., 204, 231
Highlands, Evanston—Lincolnwood Subdivision, 593
Hightower v. Com., 220
Hill, H. B., 250
Hirsch v. Com., 137,
Hodges, Hugh H., 250
Hoffman, U.S. v., 349
Holden, William, 442
Holley v. U.S., 171
Home Sales Co., The, 217
Hopka v. U.S., 319
Hopkins, J. R., 360
Hopkinson, Com. v., 478
Horrmann, William C., 237
Horst, Helvering v., 124
Hort v. Com., 116, 318
Horton, Rodney B., 454
Howell v. Com., 348
Hubbell Son & Co., F. M., v. Burnet, 249
Hubert, 169
Hudson, Calvin, et al., 473
Hudson, E. J., 403
Humphrey, Dudley T., 401
Humphreys v. Com., 130
Hunt Engineering Co., Inc., C. A., 598
Hunter v. Com., 440
Hutcheson, Palmer, 318
Hyde v. Continental Trust Co. of City of New York, et al., 4

I

Idaho Lumber & Hardware Co., 365
Illinois Terminal Railroad Co. v. U.S., 224
Imeson, 335

Independent Life Ins. Co., Helvering v., 197
Indiana Broadcasting Corp., Com. v., 250
Industrial Union Oil Co., 123
International Boiler Works, 318
International Trading Co. v. Com., 203
Interstate Drop Forge Co. v. Com., 217
Iowa Southern Utilities Co., 210
Ives Company, The H. B., Com. v., 555

J

Jackson, Howard A., v. Com., 122
Jacobson, Com. v., 136
Jacobson, Bernhard H., 224
Jamaica Water Supply Co., 558
James v. U.S., 130
James Petroleum Corp., 303
Jantzer v. Com., 451
Jerpe, J. P., 595
Jewell Ridge Coal Sales Co., Inc., 217
Jewel Tea Co. v. U.S., 361
Johns, Lee, 546
Johnson v. Com., 361
Johnson, G. M., 524
Jones Beach Theatre Corp., 329
Jones & Co., Paul, v. Lucas, 292
Jones Lumber Co., Inc. v. Com., 404, 543
Jones Syndicate, A. R., v. Com., 360
Jordan Marsh Co. v. Com., 423
Joseph, Inc., David J., v. Com., 562

K

Kahler, C. F., 524
Kahler Corp., 127
Kaufman, Estate of Leo P., 179
Keeney, Albert F., 571
Kehaya v. U.S., 36

Keller, Charlotte, 170
Kelley Company, John, 367
Kerry Investment Co., 127
Killiam Co., A. L., Helvering v., 137
Kimbell-Diamond Milling Company, 690
Kimble Glass Co., 477
Kintner, U.S. v., 669
Kirby Lumber Co., U.S. v. 136
Kiro, Inc., 258
Kleberg, Alice G. K., 401
Kliks v. U.S., 337
Knetsch v. U.S., 362
Knowlton v. Moore, 6
Koerner, Ernest, 209
Koppers Co., 441
Kornhauser v. U.S., 209
Koshland, 54
Kurzner v. U.S., 669

L

Lacy Contracting Co., 520
Lakeland Grocery Co., 137
Lake, Inc., P. G., et al., Com. v., 454
Landfield Finance Co. v. U.S., 159
La Pointe, Elmer John, 152
Larkin, 179
Layton, L. O., 539
Leach Corporation, 366
Leamington Hotel Co., 557
LeBlanc, U.S. v. 226
LeGierse, Helvering v., 160
Lenox Clothes Shops, Inc., 586, 590
Leslie, J. E., v. Com., 224
Leslie, Sr., Warren, 237
Lester, Com. v., 142
Lewis Corp., 329
Liebes & Co., H., v. Com., 537
Lincoln Electric Co., The, Com. v. 202
Lloyd, Ernest E., 317
Lo Bue, Com. v., 636
Locke Manufacturing Companies v. U.S., 235

Table of
Cases

Loewy Drug Company of
Baltimore City v.
U.S., 219
Logan Lumber Co., 217
Lorillard Co. v. U.S., 94
Lounsbury, Alton F., 141
Lucas v. Earl, 124
Lucas v. Ox Fibre Brush
Co., 217
Luhring Motor Company,
Inc., 541
Lukens Steel Co., 571
Lutz v. Com., 559
Lyeth v. Hoey, 170
Lykes v. U.S., 235
Lyman v. Com., 333

M

Macabe Co., 253
Maddas, Frank A., 209
Main & McKinney Bldg.
Co. of Houston,
Texas v. Com., 531
Malat et ux. v. Riddell,
452
Manhattan Co. of Vir-
ginia, Inc., 251
Mantell, John, 546
*Marshall Drug Co. v.
U.S.,* 136
Martin, John S., 327
Masser, Harry G., 427
Massillon-Cleveland-
Akron Sign Com-
pany, 152
Matchette, F. J., v. Hel-
vering, 129
Matheson et al. v. Com.,
333
Mathey v. Com., 152
May Department Stores
Co., 423
Mayson Manufacturing
Co. v. Com., 218
McCoy, L. W., 131
McDonald, L., 152
McFeely, Nancy K., v.
Com., 472
McGuirl, Inc., Patrick,
441
McIntosh, Sam F., 403
McKenna, James P., 130
*McKinley Mortuaries,
Utter,* 202
McNeil Machine & Engr.
Co. v. U.S., 574
*McWilliams, John P., et
al. v. Com.,* 320

Merchants' Loan &
Trust Co. v. Smie-
tanka, 109
Meridian & Thirteenth
Realty Co., Com. v.,
365, 367
Merrill, U.S. v., 610
*Metropolitan Laundry
Co. v. U.S.,* 251
Meyer, Henry Von L.,
Com. v., 172
Meyer, Madelon W., v.
U.S., 153
Meyer, Sr., Estate of
Rollin E., 419
Meyers, Edward C., 478
Michaels, Aaron, 454
Michaels, Emil J., 226
Midland-Ross Corpora-
tion, U.S. v., 36
Mifflin, Charles D., 603
Miller v. U.S., 419
Miller, Thomas 336
Millsap, Jr. v. Com., 191
*Milwaukee & Suburban
Transport Corp.,
Com. v.,* 562, 565
Minneapolis, St. Paul &
Saulte Ste. Marie
Railroad Company v.
U.S., 343
Mississippi River Fuel
Corp., 630
Missouri Public Service
Co. v. U.S., 254
Mitchell v. U.S. 210
Mitchell, Clinton H., 384
Mitnick, Moses, 227
Moberg, T. E., v. Com.,
479
Moberg, V. E., 479
Moberg, V. H., v. Com.,
479
Modernaire Interiors,
Inc., 552
*Moline Properties, Inc. v.
Com.,* 120
Moore, Fay Harvey, v.
Com., 439
Moran, Com. v., 191
Morgan's Est. v. Com.,
210
Moro Realty Holding
Corp., 123
Morrisdale Coal Mining
Co., 566
Morrissey v. Com., 668
Morse Co., A. H., v. Com.,
250

Morton, Sterling, 331
Motorlease Corp. v.
U.S., 253
Muhle, H. M. N., 593
Mulholland, Samuel E.,
209
Munroe Land Co., 200
Musselman Hub-Brake
Co. v. Com., 530

N

National Bread Wrapping
Machine Co., 564
*National Investors Corp.
v. Hoey,* 122
National Ry. Time Ser-
vice Co., 114
National Weeklies, Inc. v.
Reynolds, 251
Nesler, Estate of Jacob,
441
New Colonial Ice Co.,
Inc. v. Helvering,
197
Newberry, Anna C., 237
Newlin Machinery Corp.,
172
Nickerson Lumber Co. v.
U.S., 217, 219
Nitterhouse v. U.S., 441
Noonan Estate, Cato, 213
North American Oil Con-
solidated v. Burnet,
609
Norton v. Com., 336
Norwich Pharmacal Co.,
292

O

*O. Liquidating Corp.,
Com. v.,* 605
Oberman Mfg. Co., 200
O'Brien, Pat, 405
Odell Hardware Co., 570
Old Colony R.R. Co. v.
Com., 109, 360
Old Colony Trust Com-
pany, Exr. v. Com.,
112
Oliver, A. Y., 143
O'Malley v. Ames, 400
O'Neill v. U.S., 669
Oppenheimer Casting
Co., 217
Oswald, Vincent E., 218,
611
Overlakes Corp., The,
562

Oxford Development Corp., 361

P

Pacific Grape Products Co. v. Com., 563
Pacific National Co. v. Welch, 593
Palm Beach Tr. Co., 171
Palmer v. Bender, 304
Papineau, 191
Pappenheimer v. Allen, 143
Parker, C. T., 233
Parrott, John A., 165
Patrick, U.S. v., 235
Patterson v. Anderson, 130
Patterson v. Belcher, et al. 451
Peninsula Properties Co., Ltd., 134
Pennroad Corp., 210
Peoples Bank & Trust Co. v. Com., 555
Peoples-Pittsburgh Trust Co., Exr. v. Com., 210, 211
Persia Chevrolet, Inc., Mike, 350
Peter Pan Seafoods, Inc. v. U.S., 136
Peters, Martha R., 530
Peurifoy v. Com., 227
Philadelphia Park Amusement Co., 409
Phillips, Percy W., Com. v., 475
Photo-Sonics, Inc. v. Com., 573
Pittsburgh Milk Co., 208
Polacheck, Frank B., 233
Pollock v. Farmers' Loan & Trust Co., 4, 114, 115
Poorman, Jr., Samuel, 334
Portland General Electric Co. v. U.S., 253
Price, Julian, Helvering v., 529
Prichard Funeral Home, Inc., 547
Priddy, 226
Pulvers v. Com., 332
Putnam, Max, v. Com., 348
Putnam, Estate of, v. Com., 128

Q

Quality Roofing Co., 598

R

Ratterman, 220
Raytheon Production Corp. v. Com., 153
Real estate – Land Title & Trust Co., 291
Realty Operators, Inc., 328
Reynolds Tobacco Co., R. J., 217
Rice, Barton & Fales, Inc. v. Com., 600
Rickard, George L., 130
Riddell v. Callan, 335
Riddle, Theodore Pope, 171
Riker, Jr., Samuel, 327
Roberts v. Com., 169
Roberts & Porter, Inc. v. Com., 371
Robinson, John, 67
Robinson, Robert M., 598
Robinson, T., v. Com., 191
Rodney, Henry M., 254
Rogers, U.S. v., 333
Rogers, Inc., Robert, v. U.S., 218
Rose, Robert M., 386
Rosenberg, 333
Ross, Lewis H., v. Com., 520
Roth, Louis M., 230
Rowan v. U.S., 365, 366
Royal Oaks Apartments, Inc., 527
Runyon, Jr. v. U.S., 153
Russell v. Com., 603
Russell Manufacturing Co. v. U.S., 630
Ruwitch, Lee, 454

S

S. & A. Company, U.S. v., 253
Sand, 226
Scalish, Sam, 251
Schiffman, Allen, 209
Schlude v. Com., 548
Schnietzer, Sam, 341
Scholl Co., 598
Schuman Piano Co., 317
Schultz, Neils, 546
Schuessler, E. W., v.

Com., 564
Scott-Nickels Bus Co., 337
Seaboard Finance Co., Com. v., 251
Security Flour Mills Co. v. Com., 558
Seed, Harris W., 233
Shamberg, 172
Shapleigh Hardware Co. v. U.S., 562
Shearer v. Anderson, 333
Sheldon & Co., E. H. 566
Shopmaker v. U.S., 333
Shuster v. Helvering, 549
Sico Foundation v. U.S., 556
Silberblatt, Solomon, 442
Simon, William H., 361
Skeeles v. U.S., 337
Skemp v. Com., 222
Smith, Estate of T. E. G., v. Com., 129
Smith, Richard F., 211
Smith-Bridgman & Co., 127
Smith Motors, Inc. v. U.S., 541
Smithback, 179
South Western Electric Power Co. v. U.S., 223
Southwest Exploration Co., Com. v., 305
Spiegel, et al., Estate of M. J., 524, 528
Spring Canyon Coal Co. v. Com., 562
Spring City Foundry Co. v. Com., 339, 543
Sprunt & Son, Inc., Alexander, v. Com., 209
Stacey Mfg. Co. v. Com., 35
Standard Envelope Mfg. Co., 423
Standard Lumber Co., 539
Stephens, O. E., 524
Stern, Com. v., 114
Stern, Karl, v. Carey, 332
Stevens v. Com., 334
Stidger, Com. v., 226
Stoll, C. W., 332
Stratmore v. U.S., 348
Streight Radio & Television, Inc., 564
Strother v. Com., 153
Suffolk & Berks, 543

Table of Cases

Super Food Services, Inc. v. U.S., 251
Superior Garment Co., 361
Swastika Oil & Gas Co. v. Com., 152
Swoby Corp., 366

T

Talbot Mills v. Com., 368
Tampa & Gulf Coast R.R. v. Com., 561
Tampa Tribune Publishing Co. v. Tomlinson, 603
Tank Truck Rentals, Inc. v. Com., 207
Teleservice Company of Wyoming v. Com., 186
Tellier, Com. v., 210
Tennessee-Arkansas Gravel Co. v. Com., 127
Tennessee Consolidated Coal Co., 566
Tex-Penn Oil Co., Helvering v., 409
Texas & Pacific Ry Co., 333
Texas Company (South America) Ltd., The, 557
Thoene, John J., 385
Thomas Shoe Company, The, 607
Thomason, S. E., 375, 530
Thompson, Willard J., 334
Thompson-King-Tate, Inc. v. U.S., 600
Thrifticheck Service Corp. v. Com., 251
Tilles, Cap Andrew, 375
Titus, Louis, 528
Toledo Blade Co., 250
Toledo Newspaper Co., 454
Towne v. Eisner, 110, 115
Trent v. Com., 346
Turner, Reginald, 131
Twin Bell Oil Syndicate, Helvering v., 306
2 Lexington Avenue Corp., 439
Tyler, Grover, 337

U

Union Investment Co., 210

U.S. Trust Co. of N.Y. v. Anderson, 171
Unterman, John J., 61
Utility Trailer Mfg. Co. v. U.S., 360, 361
Uvalde Co., 598

V

Vaira, Peter, 83
Van Zandt v. Com., 221
Vander Poel, Francis & Co., Inc., 526
Vigilante, Vincent P., 596
Virginia Iron Coal & Coke Co. v. Com., 440

W

Waldheim Realty & Investment Co. v. Com., 530
Walet, Jr., Eugene H., 233
Walz, F. R., 143
Wampler, U.S. v., 130
Ward, Dwight A., 233
Washington Post Co. v. U.S., 571
Waterman v. Mackenzie, 477
Watson, Orla E., et al. v. U.S., 477
Webb Recess Co., Ltd., 538
Wedgwood & Sons, Ltd., Josiah, 218
Weiler, J. L. 212
Weiner, L., 130
Weingarten, Saul M., 336
Weinstein, Godfrey M., 49
Weir, E. T., v. Com., 324, 471
Weiss v. Wiener, 109
Welch v. Helvering, 201
Weller v. Com., 361
Wells Construction Co., L. A., 598
Wellston Company, The, 335
Wernentin, U.S. v., 479
Westervelt, George C., 233
Westinghouse Broadcasting Co., 250
Westover v. Smith, 405
Weyenberg Shoe Mfg. Co., 217, 219
Wharton, U.S. v., 54

Whipple v. Com., 204, 345
White, 172
White, David C., v. Brodrick, 380
White Dental Mfg. Co., S. S., U.S. v., 324
Wiggin Terminals, Inc. v. U.S., 360
Wikstrom & Sons, Inc., Frank G., 574
Wikstrom, Inc., A. S., 601
Wilcox, Com. v., 130
Wild, Ruth K., 236
Wilkins Pontiac v. Com., 350
Williams v. McGowan, 450
Williams v. U.S., 441
Williamson, Harry W., 530
Willicuts v. Bunn, 171
Willoughby Camera Stores, Inc. v. Com., 570
Wills, Maurice M., v. Com., 131
Wilmington Trust Co., Helvering v., 204
Wilshire and Western Sandwiches, Inc. v. Com., 365
Wineland, J. D., et al., 209
Winter, Com. v., 181
Wisconsin Cheeseman, Inc. v. U.S., 224
Witt Est., Eli B., v. Fahs, 529
Wolf Manufacturing Co., 556
Wood v. Com., 249
Wood Preserving Corp. of Baltimore, Inc. v. U.S., 200

Y

Yeomans, B. L., 230
Your Health Club, Inc., 547

Z

Zimmerman Steel Co. v Com., 560

FINDING LISTS

INTERNAL REVENUE CODE

Section	Paragraph
1	3.64
4	3.70
11	4.16
33	3.98–3.105, 4.11
37	3.94
38	3.107, 8.159–8.184
39	3.106
41	3.108
46	8.159–8.184
46–48	3.107
47	8.159–8.184
48	8.159–8.184
49	8.159–8.184
50	8.159–8.184
56–58	3.112–3.116
57	12.51–12.53
61	2.3–2.4, 5.17–5.37
62	3.10
62(2)(C)	7.96
71	5.100
72	5.115
72(d)	5.124
72(e)(2)	5.126
74	5.72
83	17.81–17.86
101	6.1–6.16
102	6.27
102(a)	6.17
103	6.36–6.37
103(a)(1)	6.30–6.37

Section	Paragraph
104	6.42–6.62
105	6.42–6.62
106	6.42–6.62
108	5.87
109	5.36, 8.92–8.94
111	6.63–6.68
116(a)	6.69–6.72
117	5.76
118	6.73–6.77, 19.14
119	6.78–6.89
121	11.123–11.126
123	6.90
141–144	3.30–3.47
143	3.38–3.40
151–153	3.48–3.62
162	7.4–7.108
162(a)(2)	7.89–7.95
162(a)(3)	7.67
162(e)	7.80
162(e)(2)	7.79
162(f)	7.30
163	12.54–12.55
163(a)	10.4–10.33
163(b)	10.30–10.33
163(d)	10.29
164	3.98, 4.11, 10.38–10.47
165	9.1–9.59
165(c)(2)	7.121
165(c)(3)	9.49–9.56
165(d)	9.57–9.59
165(g)(1)	9.33
166	9.65–9.104
166(g)	9.99

Section	Paragraph
167	8.1–8.184
167(d)	8.67
167(f)	8.14, 8.117
167(i)	8.36
167(j)	8.38–8.42
167(k)	8.43
170	10.48–10.80
171	8.155–8.157
172	9.60–9.64
177	8.152
178	8.153
179	8.44
183	7.24–7.26
186	5.133
212	7.109–7.137
213	10.81–10.88
214	10.89–10.91
215	5.100
216	10.92–10.95
217	7.98–7.103
243	4.9
243(a)(3)	19.170–19.171
247	4.10
248	8.158
262	6.88
264	10.29
265	7.81–7.84
265(2)	10.29
266	8.6, 10.29, 10.47
267	5.111, 9.12–9.17
267(a)(2)	10.29, 15.84–15.86
274	7.52–7.57
274(b)	6.14–6.16

Finding Lists

Section	Paragraph	Section	Paragraph	Section	Paragraph
275	10.47	481	16.57–16.60	1001(b)	9.8, 11.5
276(c)	7.79	481(a)(2)	16.51	1001(c)	9.8
301	19.39–19.40, 19.43	483	11.27–11.36	1001(e)	11.64
305	19.47–19.52	501	2.16	1002	9.8
305(a)	5.27	501(a)	17.7	1013	11.45
306	19.61–19.64	501(c)(3)	2.18	1014(a)	11.46–11.49
311(d)	19.60	512	2.21	1014(b)	11.50–11.51
311(d)(2)	19.19	514	2.22	1014(c)	11.54
312	19.41–19.42	521	2.16	1015	11.56–11.61
316	19.40	526	2.16	1016	11.39
318	19.59	532	19.143–19.144	1016(a)(2)	8.12
331	19.71–19.72	541	19.140–19.142	1016(b)	11.67
332	19.86–19.88	611	8.185–8.202	1017	5.87
333	19.73–19.80	613(a)	8.200	1031	11.71–11.84
334(b)(1)	19.87	613(b)	8.196	1032	11.89–11.90, 19.18
334(b)(2)	19.88	613(c)(4)	8.197	1033	11.91–11.110
337	19.81–19.85	614	8.202	1034	11.111–11.122
346	19.65–19.70	642(b)	4.36	1035	11.85–11.87
351	19.20–19.31	642(c)	20.15	1036(a)	11.88
354	19.122–19.124	642(d)	20.19	1038	11.131–11.136
355	19.126–19.127	643(b)	20.6	1039	11.127–11.130
358	19.30	652	4.37–4.38	1053	11.66
361	19.92, 19.125	652(a)	20.26	1071(a)	11.93
362(a)	11.93, 19.29	652(c)	20.13	1091	12.105–12.107
362(c)	6.76–6.77, 19.17	662	4.37–4.38	1201(b)	12.24
368	19.89–19.135	662(a)	20.26	1202	
368(a)(1)(A)	19.98–19.102	663(a)(1)	6.28		12.24–12.29, 12.30–12.33
368(a)(1)(B)		663(c)	20.35	1211(a)	12.47–12.50
	19.107–19.110	665(b)	20.37–20.38	1211(b)	12.37–12.46
368(a)(1)(C)		671		1212(a)	12.47–12.50
	19.103–19.106		4.33, 20.8, 20.45–20.47	1212(b)	12.40–12.46
368(a)(1)(D)		691(a)	20.9	1221	2.5, 12.6–12.19
	19.111–19.114	703	4.25	1223(1)	12.62
368(a)(1)(E)	19.115	703(a)	18.16	1223(4)	12.65
368(a)(1)(F)	19.116	704(a)	18.26	1223(5)	12.64
368(b)	19.118	704(b)	18.27	1223(6)	12.64
381	19.133–19.135	705(a)	18.13	1223(7)	12.62
382	19.136–19.139	706(a)	18.17	1231	12.108–12.112
385	10.15–10.28	707(a)	18.29	1232	12.68, 12.92–12.99
401	17.6–17.43	707(b)	18.33	1233	12.104
401(c)(3)	17.63	707(c)	18.30–18.31	1234	12.100
404	17.31–17.37	708(b)	18.19	1235	12.73–12.84
421	17.73–17.74	721	18.8–18.10	1239	12.161–12.165
422	17.75	723	18.11	1241	12.102
423	17.73	731	18.42	1244	19.32–19.38
441	13.1–13.25	732(a)(2)	18.45	1245	12.117–12.127
442	13.11–13.18	735(b)	12.63	1245(a)(3)	8.101
443	13.19–13.25	741	18.12, 18.36	1250	
446	14.3	751	18.37–18.40		8.101, 12.128–12.141
451(a)	11.137	751(b)	18.43	1251	12.142–12.156
452	15.29	761	18.4–18.6	1252	12.157–12.160
453	16.5–16.41	901–905	4.11–4.14	1253	12.86–12.90
461	14.23–14.33	901(b)(1)	3.99	1301–1304	3.76–3.82
461(a)	15.49	904	3.103	1311	2.42
461(f)	15.64	921	19.159	1348	3.83–3.89
462	15.29	960	4.11	1371–1377	19.145–19.158
471	14.3	1001(a)	9.7, 11.4	1379	19.154

Section	Paragraph	Section	Paragraph	Section	Paragraph
1401–1403	3.109–3.111	1.104–1(c)	6.45	1.167(a)–4	8.153
1501	19.169	1.105–5(a)	6.52	1.167(a)(8)	9.26
1551	19.168	1.108(a)–1(b)	5.98	1.167(a)–8(a)	8.55, 8.57
1561–1563	19.161–19.167	1.111–1(a)	6.64	1.167 (a)–8(b)	8.62
4940	2.20	1.111–1(b)	6.68	1.167(a)–8(c)(3)	8.51
6012	3.117	1.116–1(c)	6.70	1.167(a)–8(d)	8.55
6013	3.65, 3.70	1.117–1,–3,–4	5.76–5.81	1.167(a)–9	8.145
6015	3.124	1.118–1	6.74–6.75	1.167(a)–10(a)	8.12, 8.21
6072(a)	4.31	1.119–1(b)	6.82	1.167(a)–10(b)	8.64
6152(a)(2)	4.31	1.119–1(c)(1)	6.83	1.167(a)–11	
6154	4.20	1.119–1(c)(2)	6.85		8.87, 8.94–8.143
6212	2.35	1.121–5(g)	11.126	1.167(a)–11(g)(1)(i)	8.149
6315	3.92	1.144–2	3.43	1.67(a)–12	8.84–8.86
6501	2.41	1.152–1(a)(2)(i)	3.59	1.167(b)–0(c)	8.47
6511(d)	9.102	1.152–2(d)	3.55	1.167(b)–3(a)(2)	8.27
6653	3.67	1.152–4	3.60	1.167(f)–1	8.14
6654	3.127	1.162–1	7.5	1.170–1(b)	14.29
6655	4.20	1.162–2	7.51	1.171–2(c)	8.156
7502	3.121, 4.4, 4.5	1.162–4	7.9	1.172–5(a)	3.15
7503	3.121	1.162–5	7.45		
7701	2.12	1.162–7	7.58–7.65	1.183–1(b)(2)(ii)	7.24
		1.162–11(a)	8.154	1.212–1(b)	7.114, 7.132
Regulations		1.162–15(c)	7.49	1.212–1(d)	7.113
		1.162–17(b)(1)	7.87	1.212–1(h)	7.133
1.1–2(d)	3.73	1.162–20(a)(2)	2.19, 7.78	1.212–1(k)	7.131
1.47–1	8.175–8.178	1.162–20(c)(2)	7.80	1.212–1(l)	7.137
1.61–1(a)	5.20, 5.83	1.162–20(c)(3)	7.50	1.213–1(e)(1)(i), (ii)	10.83
1.61–2	6.86	1.162–20(c)(4)	7.79	1.262–1(b)(7)	7.129
1.61–2(a)(1)	6.24	1.163–1(b)	10.7	1.274–2(a)	7.53
1.61–2(d)	5.84	1.163–2(c)(5)	8.198–8.199	1.274–5	7.55–7.56
1.61–3(a)	5.30, 16.13	1.163–3(c)(2)	10.35	1.346–1	19.65
1.61–6(a)	5.31, 11.2	1.164–1(a)	10.40	1.346–1(b)	19.67
1.61–7(d)	5.67	1.164–6(b)(3)	10.45	1.346–3	19.70
1.61–8(b)	15.32	1.165–1(b)	9.4, 9.18	1.368–1	19.120
1.61–9(c)	5.64	1.165–1(d)	9.20	1.401–1(b)(1)	17.14–17.19
1.61–12(c)	5.88	1.165–1(d)(2)	9.52	1.401–1(b)(2)	17.17
1.61–14(a)	5.69	1.165–2	9.29	1.401–3(a)(3)	17.11
1.62–1(d)	3.13, 3.17	1.165–3	9.32	1.404(a)–6(a)(2)	17.34
1.62–1(f)(2)	3.18	1.165–7(a)(2)(ii)	9.51	1.404(a)–12	17.47
1.62–1(g)	7.96	1.165–7(a)(3)	9.44	1.404(b)–1	3.85
1.62–1(h)	7.97	1.165–7(b)(1)	9.47	1.421–1(a)(1)	17.70
1.72–2(b)(2)	5.118	1.165–7(b)(2)	9.48	1.421–6	17.79
1.72–4(a)(2)	5.115	1.165–7(c)(iv)	9.50	1.441–1(b)	13.6
1.72–4(b)	5.117	1.165–8	9.54–9.56	1.441–2(a)	13.4
1.72–5(a)	5.122	1.165–9(c)	9.22	1.442–1	13.16
1.72–6(a)	5.119	1.165–11	9.19	1.442–1(b)(1)	13.13
1.72–7(b)(4)	5.121	1.166–1(b)	9.103	1.442–1(b)(2)(i)	13.8
1.72–9	5.121	1.166–1(c)	9.70	1.442–1(c)(2)	13.17
1.72–11	5.127	1.166–2	9.75	1.446–1(a)(1)	14.5, 16.61
1.73–1	5.129	1.166–3	9.74	1.446–1(b)(2)	14.6
1.74–1(a)	5.72	1.166–5(b)	9.78	1.446–1(c)(1)(i)	14.8
1.101–1(a)(1)	6.1	1.166–5(d)	9.79	1.446–1(c)(1)(ii)	15.3
1.101–1(b)	6.10	1.167(a)–1	8.2	1.446–1(e)	16.53
1.101–1(b)(5)	6.11	1.167(a)–1(b)	8.65	1.446–1(e)(1)	14.7
1.101–4(a)(2)	6.8	1.167(a)–1(c)	8.13	1.451–1	15.57
1.103–1	6.33	1.167(a)–2	8.6	1.451–1(a)	15.6
1.104–1(e)	6.47	1.167(a)–3	8.7	1.451–2(a)	14.11

Finding Lists

Section	Paragraph
1.451–2(b)	14.13
1.451–3(a)	16.43
1.451–3(b)(1)	16.46
1.451–3(b)(2)	16.49
1.451–5	15.44–15.48
1.453–1	16.6
1.453–1(a)(1)	16.8
1.453–1(b)(1)	16.10
1.453–1(c)	16.25
1.446–1(c)(1)(ii)	11.151
1.453–2	16.8–16.9
1.453–2(a)(2)	16.14
1.453–2(b)(1)	16.7
1.453–4(c)	16.34
1.453–6(a)(1)	11.21
1.453–7	16.17–16.21
1.453–8(a)(2)	16.16
1.453–8(b)(1)	16.30
1.453–9	16.41
1.461–1(a)	15.50
1.461–1(a)(1)	14.23
1.461–1(a)(2)	15.56
1.471–1	15.92
1.471–2(d)	15.111
1.471–2	15.93
1.471–3	15.97
1.471–3(c)	15.102
1.471–4	15.108
1.472–1(c)	15.107
1.561–2	14.16
1.611–1(a)(1)	8.193
1.611–1(b)(1)	8.191
1.612–3(a)	8.199
1.613–3(a)	8.197
1.613–4(a)	8.200
1.631–1(d)(2)	5.85
1.651(a)–1	20.29
1.661(a)–1	20.30
1.663(a)–1(b)(2)	6.28
1.663(c)–3	20.35
1.691(a)	4.34
1.691(a)–1	11.55
1.702–1(a)(8)(ii)	18.22
1.703–1(b)	18.21
1.736–1(a)(1)(ii)	18.18
1.761–1(a)(1)	18.5
1.761–1(a)(2)	18.6
1.901–1(c)	3.102
1.1001–1(a)	11.8
1.1012–1	11.41–11.44
1.1013(d)–1	11.82
1.1014–1(a)	11.48
1.1014–4(a)(3)	11.49
1.1014–6(a)(3)	11.53
1.1031(a)–1	11.72
1.1031(b)–1(b)	11.74
1.1031(d)–2	11.78
1.1033(a)–2(c)(2)	11.108

Section	Paragraph
1.1033(a)–2(c)(3)	11.99
1.1033(a)–2(c)(9)	11.103
1.1034–1(i)	11.122
1.1035–1	11.86
1.1233–1(a)	12.103
301.7701–1(a)	2.12
301.7701–1(b), (c)	19.3
601.204(a)	13.15

ANNOUNCEMENTS

Number	Paragraph
71–76	8.92

FORMS

W–2	3.91
503	4.4
870	2.32
870–AD	2.34
960	15.112
982	5.99
1040	2.14, 3.1
1040A	3.2
1040ES	3.126
1041	4.30
1065	4.21–4.24
1118	4.11
1120	2.14, 4.2
1128	13.12
2440	6.61
3115	8.19, 9.103
4868	3.120
7004	4.3

GENERAL COUNSEL'S MEMORANDA

1162	16.6
1342	15.70
10557	6.35
21503	11.155
21890	6.31
22682	16.42
23587	14.36
23698	11.95
25298	15.63

INCOME TAX RULINGS

1748	6.32

Number	Paragraph
1852	5.134
1867	10.58
2305	16.33
2704	15.91
2767	6.75
2888	7.105
3447	5.130
3555	10.21
3564	7.78
3581	7.78
3633	15.76
3634	7.105
3662	5.130
3767	7.60
3835	11.156
3856	5.114
3918	10.80
3956	15.78
3957	16.22
3985	12.58
4001	5.113
4007	5.66
4018	5.95

I.R.S. PUBLICATIONS

778	17.9

MIMEOGRAPHS

3853	5.42
5897	15.57

OFFICE DECISIONS

14	5.23
514	6.86
684	15.91
712	10.79
933	16.47
1028	11.156

REVENUE PROCEDURES

57–1	6.61
62–21	8.3, 8.68–8.86
64–15	10.80
64–16	16.66
64–51	9.104
65–4	2.24
65–13	8.79, 8.83
65–32	16.66
66–6	13.14

Number	Paragraph	Number	Paragraph	Number	Paragraph	Finding Lists
66–34	2.24, 19.105	57–130	10.84	65–57	6.4	
67–27	2.31	57–135	10.79	65–287	16.70	
67–40	8.19	57–143	7.108	65–297	16.30	
69–6	2.24	57–198	10.5, 10.36	66–6	12.58	
70–21	15.43	57–244	11.83	66–7	12.58	
70–24	10.80	57–314	11.93–11.94	66–15	17.12	
70–25	7.96	57–377	8.10	66–330	7.44	
70–27	16.66–16.68	57–389	13.10	66–365	19.110	
71–2	7.100	57–418	7.121	67–1	7.125	
71–21	15.43	57–481	10.7	67–221	5.111	
71–25	8.87–8.93	57–562	10.58	67–272	8.16	
72–3	2.24, 2.57	58–42	6.33	67–297	10.6	
72–10	8.128–8.143	58–90	6.46	67–316	15.17	
72–18	7.83	58–91	6.59	68–37	11.95	
73–2	page 742	58–178	6.56	68–54	10.21	
		58–209	7.78	68–348	19.71	
		58–234	11.156	68–562	19.110	
		58–240	10.80	68–606	11.13	
REVENUE RULINGS		58–279	10.80	68–631	15.63	
		58–321	5.103	68–643	14.38	
		58–402	11.8	68–650	10.6	
79	9.40	58–418	5.134	69–48	19.109	
141	15.105	58–462	6.56	69–93	11.138	
162	10.79	59–64	6.55	69–102	5.56	
53–61	5.82	59–86	12.59	69–115	7.63, 16.76	
53–80	6.88	59–92	5.22	69–140	6.23	
54–97	11.48	59–170	6.56	69–154	6.49	
54–111	16.7, 16.14	59–343	16.20	69–243	10.35	
54–190	7.105	59–361	11.96	69–292	7.48	
54–421	8.189	59–383	17.48	69–336	15.63	
54–496	6.35	59–398	9.38	69–368	6.23	
54–580	10.51	59–416	12.60	69–369	6.23	
54–581	9.30	59–518	6.58	69–373	15.106	
54–608	15.78	60–31	17.59	69–462	16.28	
54–625	6.15	60–43	11.83	69–482	12.84	
55–75	6.35	60–53	16.15	69–582	10.6	
55–76	6.35	60–177	6.71	69–649	17.59	
55–85	6.55	60–189	7.91	69–650	17.59	
55–138	10.69	60–203	6.56	70–183	17.12	
55–212	6.15	60–248	6.35	70–279	3.71	
55–263	6.56	60–330	7.66	70–346	15.105	
55–275	10.69	60–358	8.33	70–367	15.68	
55–278	6.41	61–27	15.89	70–435	17.59	
55–283	6.56	61–131	6.6	70–474	7.107	
55–313	6.4	62–102	6.16	70–559	7.96	
55–327	9.41	62–156	7.80	71–295	17.16	
55–410	10.64	62–210	10.84	71–412	7.87	
55–446	15.89	62–214	9.98	71–446	17.10	
55–531	10.69	63–127	11.108	72–34	15.90	
55–540	7.73	63–219	6.55	72–77	6.32	
56–60	11.46	63–232	9.42	72–508	7.87	
56–169	10.90	63–239	7.95	73–35	11.96	
56–326	6.56	64–104	6.41			
56–484	5.44	64–224	7.32			
56–511	7.116	64–236	7.123	**SOLICITOR'S MEMORANDA**		
56–514	6.55	64–237	11.104			
56–520	8.10	64–279	17.59	1298	10.7	
57–49	6.31	65–5	12.58			

Finding Lists

Number	Paragraph	Number	Paragraph

SOLICITOR'S OPINIONS

Number	Paragraph
46	5.67
132	5.134

TREASURY DECISIONS

Number	Paragraph
7128	8.94
7159	8.95

TECHNICAL INFORMATION RELEASE

Number	Paragraph
747	10.68
756	16.30
1019	19.11

SUBJECT INDEX

A

Abandoned spouse,
    standard deduction
    of, 3.39
Abandonment losses,
    9.24–9.31
Accident and health
    benefits for em-
    ployees, 6.48–6.62
Accounting methods (see
    also particular
    type):
accrual method, 15.1–
    15.113
adoption of method,
    14.7
books, what are, 14.5–
    14.6
cash, 14.8–14.38
changes in:
    accounting practices
      and methods,
      16.66–16.68
    accrual to install-
      ment, 16.17–16.21
    adjustment under
      Sec. 481, 16.57–
      16.60
    bad debts, 9.103,
      16.54
    billing practices,
      16.69–16.71
    cash to accrual, 16.54

consent of Commis-
    sioner, 16.52–16.55
construction con-
    tracts, long-term,
    16.45
depreciation, 8.19–
    8.20, 8.109, 16.54
right of Commis-
    sioner to require
    change, 16.56
completed contract,
    16.48–16.50
definition, 16.61–16.65
hybrid, 16.1–16.4
installment, 16.5–16.41
restrictions on adop-
    tion, 14.3–14.4
trusts and estates, 20.12
Accounting periods, 13.1–
    13.25
annualized income for
    short periods,
    13.19–13.25
change of taxable year,
    13.11–13.18
fiscal year, 13.3–13.4
partnerships, 13.8–13.9
proprietors, 13.10
taxable year, 13.1–13.10
trusts and estates, 20.12
Accounting practice,
    change in, 16.66–
    16.68
Accrual method of ac-

counting, 15.1–
    15.113 (see also
    particular item):
claim of right doctrine,
    16.72–16.76
deductions, 15.49–
    15.90
    bonuses, year-end,
      15.87–15.90
    bookkeeping entries,
      15.55–15.83
    contested amounts,
      15.63–15.64
    estimated amounts,
      correction of,
      15.56–15.57
    expenses and in-
      terest owed to re-
      lated persons,
      15.84–15.86
    liability and deter-
      minable amount,
      15.50–15.55
    probable inability to
      pay, 15.65–15.68
    reserves for esti-
      mated future ex-
      penses, 15.69–
      15.77
    reserves for quantity
      discounts, 15.76–
      15.77
    subsequent events,
      15.58–15.62

Subject
Index

Accrual method of accounting *(continued)*
vacation pay, 15.78–15.83
description of, 15.1–15.4
inventories, 15.91–15.113
cost, 15.97–15.103
goods unsalable at normal prices, 15.107
identification, 15.111–15.113
market, 15.103–15.105
valuation, 15.95–15.96
prepaid income, 15.28–15.49
advance payments for:
future services, 15.35–15.43
merchandise, 15.44–15.48
rentals and royalties, 15.32–15.34
sales and exchanges, 11.20–11.22
uncollected income, 15.5–15.27
collectible amount, 15.21–15.27
determinable amount, 15.20
unconditional right to receive, 15.7–15.19
construction contracts, 15.12–15.15
dealers' reserves, 15.19
finance charges, 15.16–15.18
Accumulated earnings, surtax on unreasonable amount of, 19.143–19.144
Adjusted basis, 2.9, 11.38
Adjusted gross income, 3.3, 3.9–3.27
bad debts, nonbusiness, 3.10
business expenses, 3.10, 3.13–3.19
employees, 3.17–3.19

moving expenses, 3.10, 7.98–7.103
outside salesman, 3.10, 7.97
reimbursed expenses, 3.10 3.18, 7.86–7.89
transportation costs, 3.10, 7.85, 7.96
travel expenses, 3.10, 7.51–7.57 7.89–7.95
nonemployees, 3.13–3.16
net operating loss carry-over or carry-back, 3.15, 9.60–9.64
partners, 3.14
capital gains and losses, 3.10, 3.21–3.23
depletion, 3.10, 3.27, 8.185–8.202
income beneficiaries, 3.27
life tenants, 3.27
depreciation, 3.10, 3.27, 8.1–8.144
income beneficiaries, 3.27
life tenants, 3.27
losses from sales or exchanges of property, 3.10, 3.24–3.25
pension plan forfeitures, 3.10, 3.20
pension plan payments, self employed, 3.10, 3.16
profit sharing plan forfeitures, 3.10, 3.20
Section 1231 losses, 3.10
trade or business expenses, 3.10, 3.13–3.19
Administrative remedies on audit, 2.27–2.34
Advance payments:
future services, 15.35–15.43
insurance premiums, 14.35–14.36
interest, 14.38 (see also Interest)
merchandise, 15.44–15.48

rentals and royalties, 14.37, 15.32–15.34
Advertising expenses, 7.78–7.79
Agents, 5.39
Alimony:
deductions, 5.100–5.114
gross income, 5.100–5.114
indirect payments, 5.113–5.114
legal fees of wife, 5,114, 7.128–7.130
payments to support minor children, 5.109
periodic payments, 5.104–5.108
property settlements, 5.110–5.112
Allocation of income, 5.59–5.62
Allowances:
army, 6.47, 6.86
discounts on sales, 7.35
expense, adjusted gross income, 3.18
low-income, 3.34
uniformed forces, 6.47, 6.86
Amortization (see also Depreciation):
bond premium paid, 8.155–8.157
corporate organizational expenditures, 8.158
leased property, 8.153–8.154
recapture, 12.115
trade marks, 8.152
trade names, 8.152
Annuities, 5.115–5.126, 14.20
amount received as, 5.118
employees' as gross income, 5.124–5.125
exclusion ratio, 5.116
expected return, 5.122–5.123
income from assignment of policy by employer, 14.20
interest paid on policy loans, 10.29
investment in contract, 5.119

Annuities *(continued)*
 life insurance pro-
  ceeds, 6.9
 lump sum proceeds
  received, 5.126
 refund feature adjust-
  ment, 5.120–5.121
 refunds received, 5.126
 starting date, 5.117
Antitrust actions:
 damages as gross in-
  come, 5.133
 deductions for pay-
  ments, 7.31–7.33
 legal expenses, 7.44
Appellate Division, 2.34
Armed Forces:
 allowances for:
  injuries or illness,
   6.47
  quarters, 6.86
Assessments of tax:
 interest, 2.43
 limitation periods,
  2.41–2.42
 penalties, 2.43
Assessments, special, 8.6
Assignments of income,
 5.53–5.58
Associations:
 dues paid, deducti-
  bility of 7.49–7.50
 taxable as corporations,
  19.4–19.8
Authority, weight of,
 2.53–2.64
Automobiles:
 per diem mileage al-
  lowance, 7.90,
  7.96, 10.80
 trade-in, 11.71–11.83
Awards as gross income,
 5.72–5.75

B

Bad debts, 9.65–9.104
 basis, 9.78
 change in method,
  9.103–9.104
 charge-off, 9.72
 defaults on install-
  ment sales, 16.22
 definition of debt,
  9.70–9.72
 distinguished from
  losses, 9.65
 guarantors, 9.83–9.97
 indemnitors, 9.83–997

 loans by shareholders,
  9.71
 methods of deduction,
  9.66–9.69
 nonbusiness, 9.77–9.82
 adjusted gross in-
  come, 3.10
 recovery of, 6.66, 9.67
 reserve for, 9.67
  installment sales,
   16.22
 reserves for certain
  guaranteed debt
  obligations, 9.98–
  9.101
 statute of limitations,
  9.102
 sureties, 9.83–9.97
 types of deductions,
  9.66–9.69
 worthlessness, 9.74–
  9.76

Bankruptcy:
 gross income from dis-
  charge, 5.87, 5.92
Bargain purchases and
 sales:
 basis from donor, 11.61
 purchase by share-
  holder, 19.173
Basis, 11.37–11.68
 adjusted, definition of,
  2.9, 11.38
 bargain purchase from
  donor, 11.61
 contributions to capital
  from:
  nonshareholders,
   19.17
  shareholders, 19.15
 cost, 11.41–11.44
  (see also Cost)
 definitions, 2.9, 11.37–
  11.40
 income in respect of a
  decedent, 11.54–
  11.55
 inventory items, 11.45
 joint tenants, 11.52–
  11.53
 life estates and re-
  mainders, 11.62–
  11.65
 property acquired:
  before March 1, 1913,
   11.66
  corporate reorgani-
   zations, 19.129–
   19.132

 decedent, from,
  11.46–11.55
 gift, 11.56–11.61
 gift in contemplation
  of death, 11.51
 intercorporate liqui-
  dations, 19.87–
  19.88
 mortgage assumed or
  taken over, 11.42
 nontaxable ex-
  changes:
  insurance policies,
   11.87
  involuntary con-
   versions, 11.109–
   11.110
  low income hous-
   ing projects,
   11.130
  property held for
   productive use
   or investment,
   11.80–11.82
  repossessed real
   property, 11.132
  residence, 11.112,
   11.126
  stock for property,
   11.90
  stock for stock of
   same corpora-
   tion, 11.88
  one-month liquida-
   tion, 19.76
 real estate taxes al-
  located, 11.43
 shares of stock, 11.44
 substituted, 11.67–
  11.68
 tenancy by the entirety,
  11.52–11.53
 unadjusted, definition
  of, 2.9, 11.38
Beneficiaries (see Trusts
 and estates)
Bequests, 6.26–6.29
Billing practice, change
 in, 16.69–16.71
Board of Tax Appeals,
 2.35
Bonds (see also Securi-
 ties):
 amortization of pre-
  mium paid, 8.155–
  8.157
 arbitrage, 6.37
 gain on cancellation of
  indebtedness (see
  Gross income)

Subject
Index

Bonds*(continued)*
industrial develop-
ment, 6.36
interest when sold be-
tween payment
dates, 5.67–5.68
municipal:
arbitrage, 6.37
expenses relating to,
7.81–7.84
industrial develop-
ment, 6.36
interest paid on debt
to purchase, 10.29
interest received,
6.30–6.37
original issue discount,
12.94–12.99
treatment by holder,
12.94–12.98
treatment by issuer,
12.99
premium on redemp-
tion, 10.34–10.35
purchase by issuer,
5.88 (see also Gross
income – gain on
cancellation of in-
debtedness)
retirement as sale or
exchange, 12.92–
12.99
U.S., 6.37–6.40
U.S. savings, 6.38–6.40
Bonuses, 7.62, 7.64
Bribes, deductibility of,
7.34–7.36
Buildings:
demolition of, 9.32
depreciation restric-
tions, 8.35–8.42
Bulk sales, 12.9
Bureau of Internal Reve-
nue, 2.23 (see also
Internal Revenue
Service)
Business expenses, or-
dinary and neces-
sary (also see Non-
business expenses,
production of
income):
adjusted gross income,
3.10, 3.13–3.19
advertising, 7.78–7.79
antitrust damage pay-
ments, 7.31–7.33
association dues, 7.49–
7.50

bribes and kickbacks,
7.34–7.36
discounts distin-
guished, 7.35
business gifts, 6.14–
6.16, 7.54
capital expenditures,
7.8–7.12
carrying on trade or
business, 7.18–
7.21
cattle breeding, 7.23–
7.26
checks issued under
cash method,
14.27–14.29
compensation paid,
7.58–7.64 (see also
Compensation)
educational expenses,
7.45–7.48
employees:
clothing, 7.108
compensation paid
to, 7.58–7.64
death benefits, 7.65
fringe benefits, 7.66
moving expenses,
7.98–7.103
outside salesmen,
7.97
reimbursed ex-
penses, 3.10, 3.18,
7.86
tools, 7.106
transportation costs,
7.96
travel expense, 7.89–
7.95
uniforms, 7.107
union dues, 7.105
entertainment ex-
penses, 7.51–7.57
farms, 7.23–7.26
fines, 7.30
hobbies, 7.22–7.26
illegal business, 7.37
investment expenses,
7.20–7.21
legal expenses, 7.38–
7.44
(see also Legal ex-
penses):
antitrust proceed-
ings, 7.44
criminal defense,
7.43
expense or capital
expenditure, 7.39–

7.42
lobbying, 7.79–7.80
notes under cash
method, 14.30–
14.33
ordinary and neces-
sary, definition of,
7.13–7.15
payments to widows,
6.14–6.16
penalties, 7.30
profit v. pleasure,
7.22–7.26
proxy contest expenses,
7.123, 7.125
public policy viola-
tions, 7.27–7.37
reasonable amounts,
7.16–7.17
relating to tax-exempt
income, 7.81–7.87,
10.29
rentals, 7.67–776
lease with option to
purchase, 7.69–
7.74
related parties, 7.75–
7.76
repairs, 7.9–7.12
royalties, 7.77
trade or business:
defined, 7.19–7.26
hobbies, 7.22–7.26
promoters, 7.21
traders in securities,
7.20
travel expenses, 7.51–
7.57
Business gifts, 6.14–6.16,
7.54
Business investigation
expenses, 7.120–
7.122
Business property (see
Section 1231 prop-
erty)

C

Capital:
contributions to, 19.14–
19.17
recovery of net gross
income, 5.29
Capital assets:
assignments of antici-
pated ordinary in-
come, 12.14–12.16
bulk sales, 12.9
commodity futures and

Capital assets *(continued)*
hedging, 12.17–12.19
covenant not to compete distinguished from, 12.13
defined, 2.5, 12.6–12.8
good will, 12.12
holding period, 12.56–12.66
inventories distinguished from, 12.10–12.11
patents, 12.73–12.84 (see also Patents)
stock in trade distinguished from, 12.10–12.11
Capital expenditures, 7.8–7.12
business investigation, 7.120–7.122
legal expenses, 7.39–7.42
television:
F.C.C. license, 8.10
network affiliation contracts, 8.10
Capital gains and losses, 2.5–2.7, 12.1–12.107
(see also Capital assets, Sales and exchanges, Securities)
adjusted gross income, 3.10, 3.21–3.23
alternative tax, 3.23, 12.24–12.34
bulk sales, 12.9
corporate liquidations (see Corporations)
depreciable property sold between related taxpayers, 12.161–12.165
depreciation, recapture of, 12.113–12.141 (see also Depreciation)
dispositions treated as sales or exchanges, 12.91–12.102
cancellations of leases and distributor agreements, 12.102
failure to exercise option, 12.100–

12.101
retirement of bonds, 12.92–12.99
excess investment interest, 12.54–12.55
holding period, 2.5
long-term defined, 12.20
minimum tax on tax preferences, 3.112–3.116, 12.51–12.53
net long-term gain:
alternative tax:
corporations, 12.30–12.34
individuals, 12.24–12.29, 12.34
net loss, 2.7, 12.37–12.50
corporations, 12.47–12.50
carryover, 12.47–12.50
individuals, 12.37–12.46
carryovers, 12.40–12.46
net Section 1201 gain, 12.34
nonbusiness bad debts, 9.77–9.82
partnerships, 4.26, 18.23
property used in trade or business, 12.108–12.112
redemption of stock, 19.53–19.60
sale or exchange, 12.67–12.72
Section 306 stock, 19.61–19.64
Section 1231 property, 12.108–12.112
short sales, 12.103–12.104
short-term defined, 12.20
tax preferences, minimum tax on, 3.112–3.116, 12.51–12.53
transfer taxes, 10.40
transfers of franchises, trademarks, and trade names, 12.85–12.90
wash sales, 12.105–

12.107
Carrying charges:
interest and taxes during construction, 10.29
Cash method of accounting, 14.8–14.38
advance payments:
insurance premiums, 14.35–14.36
interest, 14.38
rents, 14.37
annuities, 14.20
charitable contributions, 14.27–14.29
checks:
deduction, 14.27–14.29
gross income, 14.18
claim of right, 16.72–16.76
constructive payment, no, 14.25–14.26
constructive receipt, 14.11–14.16
contractual rights to receive compensation, 14.19–14.20
deductions, 14.23–14.38
dividends, year-end, 14.14–14.16
interest, year-end, 14.13
nonqualified plans of deferred compensation, 17.44–17.59
notes:
deduction, 14.30–14.33
gross income, 14.21–14.22
payments, when made, 14.23
pension, profit-sharing, and stock bonus plans, qualified, 17.6–17.43 (see also that subject)
property and its value, 14.17–14.22
sales and exchanges, 11.11–11.19
Casualty losses, 9.37–9.53
accidental, 9.46
automobile accidents, 9.38, 9.44–9.45
corrosion, 9.41

Subject Casualty losses
Index *(continued)*
definition of casualty,
9.40–9.46
disasters, 9.53
Dutch elm disease,
9.41
measure of, 9.47–9.51
moths, 9.41
mysterious disappear-
ance, 9.46
property of another,
9.38
property used in trade
or business,
12.108–12.112
reimbursement for liv-
ing expenses, 6.90
termites, 9.42
thefts, 9.54–9.56
year of deductibility,
9.52
Cattle breeding as busi-
ness or hobby,
7.22–7.26
Charitable contributions,
10.48–10.80
accrual basis corpora-
tions, 10.67
cash, 10.68
expenses, unreim-
bursed, 10.80
foundations, private
operating, 10.55–
10.59
individual recipient,
10.49–10.50
limitations:
appreciated property,
10.69–10.77
percentage overall,
10.52–10.53
calculation,
10.61–10.62
methods of making,
10.68–10.80
partnerships, 18.16
period to deduct, 10.67,
14.27–14.29
personal services,
10.79–10.80
pledges, 10.64–10.66
property, 10.69–10.78
qualifying benefici-
aries, 10.54–10.60
rental value of prop-
erty, 10.78
trusts and estates,
20.15–20.17

Charitable organizations
(see Tax-exempt
organizations)
Checks:
income from, 14.18
deductions for, 14.27–
14.29
Child care expenses,
10.89–10.91
Children (see Minors)
Circulation list, depreciation of, 8.11
Claim of right doctrine,
16.72–16.76
Claims for refund,
2.41–2.42, 3.122
Closing agreement, 2.32
Committee reports, 1.35
Commodity futures,
12.17–12.18
Compensation:
annuity policies, 14.20
bonuses, 7.62, 7.64
bonuses, year-end,
15.87–15.90
contractual rights to
receive, 14.19–
14.20
death benefits, 6.13–
6.16
deferred, 17.1–17.86
nonqualified funded
plans, 17.44–
17.56
nonqualified non-
funded plans,
17.57–17.59
pension, profit-
sharing, and stock
bonus plans,
qualified, 17.6–
17.43 (see also that
subject)
retirement plans for
the self-employed,
17.60–17.68
stock options:
nonstatutory,
17.76–17.86
statutory, 17.73–
17.75
injuries or sickness,
6.42–6.62
payments to widows,
6.14–6.16
property, in form of,
5.83–5.85, 14.17–
14.22
reasonable amount,

7.61–7.63
services necessary,
7.59–7.60
Condemnation:
award, 11.95
definition, 11.94
interest received, 6.32
severance damages,
11.95
when gain or loss real-
ized, 11.149–
11.150
Conference:
Appellate, 2.31–2.34
District, 2.30
Consolidated returns,
19.169
Constitution:
Article 1, 1.4
gross income, exclu-
sions by, 5.25
Sixteenth Amend-
ment, 1.12
Construction contracts:
long-term, 16.42–
16.50
accounting method
rules, 16.44–16.45
accrual method,
15.12–15.15
books, 16.44
completed contract
method, 16.48–
16.50
definition, 16.43
percentage of com-
pletion method,
16.46–16.47
retained amounts as
income, 15.13–
15.15
short-term, 15.12
Constructive receipt,
14.11–14.16
Contracts, depreciation
of, 8.9
Contributions to capital,
19.14–19.17
Cooperative housing cor-
porations, tenant
stockholders of,
10.92–10.95
Corporations:
accumulated earnings:
dividends, year-end,
14.16
unreasonable
accumulation,
19.143–19.144

Corporations *(continued)*
credit, 19.144
limitation on
credit, 19.161–
19.168
associations taxable as,
19.4–19.8
consolidated returns,
19.169
contributions to capital,
6.73–6.77, 19.14–
19.17
cooperative housing,
10.92–10.95
credit for gasoline ex-
cise taxes, 4.15
definition, 19.3–19.12
dividend distributions,
4.10, 19.40–19.52
cash, 19.40–19.42
property, 19.43–
19.46
stock, 19.47–19.52
dividend paid deduc-
tion:
accumulated earn-
ings surtax, 4.10,
19.143–19.144
personal holding
companies, 19.141
utility companies,
4.10
dividends received de-
duction, 4.9
electing small busi-
ness, 19.145–
19.158
estimated tax, 4.18–
4.19
penalty for under-
payment, 4.20
foreign income tax
credit, 4.11–4.14
hybrid securities,
10.24–10.28
income tax return, 4.1–
4.20
insurance companies,
19.160
investment companies,
transfers to, 19.31
investment credit, 4.15,
8.159–8.184
liquidations:
complete, 19.71–
19.88
intercorporate,
19.86–19.88
one-month, 19.73–

19.80
partial, 19.65–19.70
twelve-month,
19.81–19.85
minimum tax on tax
preferences, 4.38
multiple, 19.161–
19.171
net operating loss
carry-overs, 9.60–
9.61
limitations, 19.136–
19.139
nonprofit, 2.17
organization expendi-
tures, amortization
of, 8.158
organization of, 19.20–
19.31
personal holding com-
panies, 19.140–
19.142
preferred Sec. 306
stock, 19.61–19.64
professional, 19.9–
19.12
real estate, dummy,
5.48–5.52
redemption of stock,
19.53–19.60
reorganizations, 19.89–
19.135
asset acquisitions,
19.97–19.106
carryover of basis,
19.129–19.132
carryover of corpo-
rate attributes,
19.128–19.135
change in form,
19.116
divisive, 19.107–110
downstream merger,
19.102
exchanges, 19.121–
19.125
nonstatutory require-
ments, 19.120
party to, 19.118
plan, 19.119
recapitalizations,
19.115
spin-off, 19.114,
19.126–19.127
statutory mergers
and consolidations,
19.98–19.102
stock for assets,
19.103–19.106

stock for stock,
19.103–19.106
triangular statutory
mergers, 19.100–
19.101
types, 19.93–19.95
returns, 4.1–4.20
Section 306 stock,
19.61–19.64
separate entity, 5.45–
5.52
small business stock,
losses on, 19.32–
19.38
spin-off, 19.114,
19.126–19.127
stock for property,
issuance of, 11.89–
11.90
Subchapter S, 19.145–
19.158
surtax exemption, 4.16
disallowance, 19.168
limitation on con-
trolled group,
19.161–19.168
tax rates, 4.16–4.17
taxable income, 4.6
thin capitalization,
10.21–10.23
transfers to, 19.13–
19.38
treasury stock, sales of,
19.18–19.19
trusts treated as, 20.48
unreasonable accumu-
lation of earnings,
19.139–19.140
credit, 19.140
limitation on credit,
19.161–19.168
Western Hemisphere
Trade, 19.159
Cost, determination of,
11.41–11.44
Courts, 2.35
Covenant not to compete:
capital asset, distin-
guished from,
12.13
depreciation of, 8.8
Credits:
estimated tax pay-
ments, 3.92, 4.18–
4.19
excess Social Security
taxes, 3.93
excise tax on gasoline,
3.106, 4.15

Subject
Index

Credits (*continued*)
foreign income taxes:
corporations, 4.11–
4.14
income tax withheld,
3.91
individuals, 3.98–
3.105
investment, 3.107,
4.15, 8.159–8.184
political contributions,
3.108
retirement income,
3.94–3.97
unreasonable accumu-
lation of earnings,
19.144
limitation on,
19.161–19.168
Customer lists, deprecia-
tion of, 8.11
Customs duties, 1.6
Community property,
3.65, 5.42–5.43
Commuters' expenses,
7.96

D

Damages:
alienation of affection,
5.134
antitrust:
deductions for pay-
ments, 7.31–7.33
gross income, 5.133
legal expenses, 7.44
breach of promise to
marry, 5.134
capital, return of, 5.138
goodwill, 5.137
loss of personal rights,
5.134–5.136
loss of profits, 5.132
nontaxable, 5.134–
5.138
patent infringement,
5.132
personal injury, 6.45,
6.49
interest on award for
by state, 6.32
right of privacy, inva-
sion of, 5.135
severance, 11.95
slander and libel, 5.134
taxable, 5.132–5.133
Death benefits:
deductibility, 7.65

exclusion from gross
income, 6.1–6.16
Decedents:
basis of property ac-
quired from,
11.46–11.55
income in respect of,
4.33, 20.9
basis, 11.54–11.55
surviving spouse, re-
turn of, 3.66
Declarations (see Estimated tax)
Deductions (see also
Business expenses,
ordinary and nec-
essary; see also
particular item)
accrued (see Accrual
method)
cash method (see Cash
method)
exemptions, personal,
3.48–3.63
itemized, 3.3
summary of, 3.28–
3.29
political contributions,
3.108
standard, 3.5, 3.30–3.47
abandoned spouse,
3.39
dependents, un-
earned income of,
3.35–3.37
election, 3.41–3.43
considerations in
making, 3.44–
3.47
low-income allow-
ance, 3.34
marital status, 3.40
percentage, 3.33
separate returns of
married persons,
3.38–3.40
Deficiencies:
administrative reme-
dies, 2.30–2.34
judicial remedies,
2.35–2.40
limitation periods,
2.41–2.42
Delinquency amounts,
recovery of, 6.63–
6.68
Dependents, 3.52–3.63
gross income test,
3.61–3.63

limitation on unearned
income, 3.35–3.37
relationship, 3.53–3.55
support test, 3.56–3.59
Depletion, 3.10, 3.27,
8.185–8.202
economic interest,
8.190–8.192
estates, 3.10
income beneficiaries,
3.27
life tenants, 3.10, 3.27
methods:
cost, 8.194–8.195
percentage, 8.196–
8.201
property, the, 8.202
trusts, 3.10
Depreciation, 3.10, 3.27,
8.1–8.144 (see also
Amortization)
accounting, 8.45–8.64
additional first year,
8.44
allowed or allowable,
8.12
asset accounts, types of,
8.45–8.47
item, 8.45
multiple asset, 8.45–
8.47
classified, 8.45
composite, 8.45
group, 8.45
open-end, 8.46
vintage, 8.46, 8.98
years of acquisi-
tion, 8.46
Asset Depreciation
Range life system,
8.87–8.93
averaging conventions,
8.64, 8.114–8.116
bonus, 8.44
buildings, restrictions
on accelerated de-
preciation of, 8.35–
8.42
Class Life Asset De-
preciation Range
system, 8.87–8.144
asset depreciation
period, 8.110–8.112
asset guideline class
repair allowance,
8.126
averaging conven-
tions, 8.114–8.116
bases, 8.113

Depreciation (continued)
  changes in methods, 8.109
  comparison with Facts and Circumstances life system, 8.144
  definitions, 8.98
  election, 8.102–8.103
  eligible property, 8.99–8.101
  enactment, 8.94–8.95
  exclusions:
    mandatory, 8.100
    optional, 8.101
  history, 8.87–8.93
  leased property, 8.112
  methods of depreciation, 8.108
  record keeping requirements, 8.104–8.107
  repairs and improvements, 8.123–8.132
  reserve for depreciation:
    gain recognized, 8.140
    loss recognized, 8.141
  retirements:
    abnormal or extraordinary, 8.137–8.139
    normal or ordinary, 8.113, 8.136
    salvage and removal costs, 8.117–8.122
    special basis vintage account, 8.139
    summary, 8.96
    vintage account, 8.98
    special basis, 8.139
  composite rates, 8.50–8.51
  construction costs, 8.6
  contracts, 8.9
  covenant not to compete, 8.8
  customer lists, 8.11
  definition, 8.1–8.4
  depreciable property, types of, 8.5–8.11
    intangibles, 8.7–8.10
    mass assets, 8.11
    tangibles, 8.6
  estates, 3.10
  Facts and Circum-

stances life system, 8.65–8.67
Federal Communications Commission license, 8.10
franchises, 8.9
Guideline life system, 8.68–8.86
  reserve ratio test, 8.80–8.84
housing property rehabilitated, 8.43
income beneficiaries, 3.27
intangibles, 8.7–8.10
land improvements, 8.6
life tenants, 3.10, 3.27
mass assets, 8.11
methods, 8.18–8.44
  additional first year, 8.44
  application to change, 8.19–8.20, 8.109
  buildings, restrictions on accelerated depreciation of, 8.35–8.42
  comparison of, 8.34
  declining balance:
    150%, 8.23
    125%, 8.40
    200%, 8.24
  expense capitalized, 8.21
  income forecast, 8.33
  job basis, 8.32
  machine hour, 8.29
  rehabilitation of housing property, 8.43
  retirement, 8.31
  straight-line, 8.22
  sum of the years-digits, 8.25–8.27
  unit of production, 8.30
network affiliation contract, 8.10
obsolescence, 8.145–8.149
recapture of, 12.113–12.141
  Section 1250 property, 12.128–12.141
  Section 1245 property, 12.117–12.127
rehabilitation of

housing property, 8.43
reserve for, 8.48
reserve ratio test, 8.80–8.84
retirements, 8.52–8.63, 8.133–139
salvage value, 8.13–8.17
  under CLADR, 8.117–8.122
tangible property, 8.6
television stations, 8.10
trusts, 3.10
useful life systems, 8.65–8.144
  Class Life Asset Depreciation Range, 8.87–8.144
  Facts and Circumstances, 8.65–8.67
  Guideline life for pre-1971 assets:
    years 1962 through 1970, 8.68–8.83
    years 1971 and later, 8.84–8.86
Devise, 6.26–6.29
Disaster losses, 9.53
Discount:
  distinguished from kickbacks, 7.35
  original issue on bonds, 12.94–12.99
Distributor agreements, cancellation of as sale or exchange, 12.102
District conference, 2.30
Dividends:
  applied to purchase price of shares, 11.142
  bargain purchase from own corporation, 19.173
  cash, 19.40–19.42
    year-end, 14.14–14.16
  distribution of, 19.40–19.52
  endowment policies, 5.127
  exclusion for individuals, 4.8, 6.69–6.72
  income, 5.63–5.66
  interest, distinguished from, 10.15–10.28
  life insurance policies,

Subject Index

Dividends (continued)
5.127
paid deduction:
accumulated earnings surtax, 4.10, 19.143–19.144
personal holding companies, 19.141
utility companies, 4.10
property, 19.43–19.46
received by partnerships, 4.28
received deduction:
corporations, 4.7, 4.9
individuals, 4.8, 6.69–6.72
stock, 5.33–5.35, 19.47–19.52
Divorce (see Alimony and Exemptions, personal)
Doctrines:
claim of right, 16.72–16.76
concept of capital, 5.29
constructive receipt, 14.11–14.16
convenience of employer, 6.78–6.87
fruit and tree, 5.53–5.58
realization, 5.4, 5.33–5.36
recognition of realized gains and losses, 9.6–9.8, 11.69
tax benefit, 6.63–6.65
violations of public policy, 7.27–7.37, 9.10–9.11
Dummy real estate corporations, 5.48–5.52

E

Earned income, maximum tax on, 3.83–3.89
Earnings and profits, 19.41
Economics:
gross income, 5.6–5.8
structure of tax system, 1.25–1.30
Educational expenses, 7.45–7.48
Employees (see Business expenses, ordinary and necessary)

Employment taxes, 1.22–1.24
Endowment policies:
dividends received, 5.127
interest credited, 5.128
interest paid on debt to purchase, 10.29
sale of, 12.70
surrender, 12.69
Entertainment expenses, 7.51–7.57
Escrows, 11.152–11.153
Estate taxes, 1.17–1.19
marital deduction, 1.18
Estates, 20.1–20.48 (see also Trusts and estates)
administrative expenses, 20.21
depletion, 3.10
depreciation, 3.10
income in respect of decedent, 4.33, 11.54–11.55, 20.9
tax rates, 4.35
Estimated tax:
corporations, 4.18–4.19
credit for payment, 4.18–4.19
penalty for underpayment, 4.20
individuals, 3.124–3.127
credit for payments, 3.92
penalty for underpayment, 3.127
Excess investment interest, 12.54–12.55
Excess profits tax, 1.14
Exchanges, nontaxable:
corporate reorganizations, 19.88–19.131 (see also Corporations)
insurance policies, 11.85–11.87
intercorporate liquidations, 19.86–19.88
involuntary conversions, 11.91–11.110
property held for productive use or investment, 11.71–11.84
repossessions of real property, 11.131–11.136

stock for property, 11.89–11.90
stock for stock, 11.88
Excise taxes:
Excise Tax Reduction Act of 1965, 1.16
history of, 1.6–1.8
nonhighway use of gasoline and lubricating oil, credit for, 3.102, 4.15
tax-exempt organizations, 2.20
Exempt income (see Gross income, exclusions from)
Exemptions, personal, 3.48–3.63
dependents, 3.52–3.63
gross income test, 3.61–3.63
relationship, 3.53–3.55
support test, 3.56–3.60
spouse, 3.50–3.51
trusts and estates, 4.35
Expense allowances, 3.18
Expenses, business (see Business expenses, ordinary and necessary)
Extensions (see Returns)

F

Farms:
business or hobby, 7.22–7.26
recapture of losses, 12.142–12.156
Federal bonds, 6.37–6.40
Federal Insurance Contributions Act, 1.22–1.23
Federal Unemployment Tax Act, 1.24
Fellowship grants, 5.76–5.81
Fiduciaries (see Trusts and estates)
Fines not deductible, 7.30
Foreign income taxes:
credit:
corporations, 4.11–4.14
individuals, 3.98–3.105

Foreign income taxes (*continued*)
deduction, 3.98, 4.11
partnerships, 4.28
Forms (see table of forms)
Foundations (see tax-exempt organizations)
Franchises, transfer of, 12.85–12.90
Fruit and the tree doctrine, 5.53–5.58

G

Gain on cancellation of indebtedness (see Gross income)
Gain or loss (see Capital gains and losses, Sales and exchanges)
Gambling:
business expenses, 7.37
gross income, 5.71
losses, 9.57–9.59
Gift taxes, 1.20–1.21
Gifts:
basis of property acquired by, 11.51, 11.56–11.61
bargain purchases, 11.61
gifts in contemplation of death, 11.51, 11.59
business expense, 7.54
gross income, exclusion from, 6.17–6.25
minors, to, 5.44
payments to widows, 6.14–6.16
Goodwill:
capital asset, 12.12
damages received, 5.137
definition, 12.12
Gross income (see also Gross income, exclusions from; see also particular item):
adjusted (see Adjusted gross income)
agents, 5.39
alimony (see also Alimony), 5.100–5.114

allocation between related taxpayers, 5.59–5.62
annuities, 5.115–5.126 (see also Annuities)
assignment of income, 5.53–5.58
awards, 5.72–5.75
benefit, form of, 5.18–5.19
benefit, source of, 5.20
capital, concept of, 5.29
capital gain (see Capital gains and losses)
checks, income from, 14.18
children, earnings of, 5.129
community property, 5.42–5.43
compensation (see Compensation)
constructive receipt, 14.11–14.16
contractual rights to receive compensation, 14.19–14.20
corporation v. shareholders, 5.45–5.52
damages, 5.131–5.138 (see also Damages)
definitions, 5.1–5.37
economic, 5.6–5.8
financial, 5.9–5.11
taxable, 2.3–2.8, 5.12–5.37
dividends, 19.40–19.52 (see also Dividends)
decedents, 5.65
endowment policies, 5.127
life insurance policies, 5.127
pertinent dates, 5.63–5.66
property, 19.43–19.46
received in stock, 5.33–5.35, 19.47–19.52
year-end, 14.14–14.16
embezzlement, 5.70
exclusions (see Gross income, exclusions from)

fellowship grants, 5.76–5.81
fruit and tree doctrine, 5.53–5.58
gain on cancellation of indebtedness, 5.86–5.99
election to exclude, 5.97–5.99
gifts, 5.90–5.91
insolvency, 5.92
no personal liability, 5.96
purchase of own obligations, 5.88
reduction of purchase price, 5.93–5.95
gains from illegal activity, 5.69–5.71
gifts, 6.17–6.25
interest (see Interest)
joint tenants, 5.40–5.41
minors, 5.44
nominees, 5.39
notes, 14.21–14.22
prizes, 5.72–5.75
property and its value, 14.17–14.22
purchase price, reduction of, 5.87, 5.93–5.95
real estate corporations, dummy, 5.48–5.52
realization doctrine, 5.4, 5.33–5.36
receipts in kind, 5.83–5.85
recovery of bad debts, prior taxes, and delinquency amounts, 6.63–6.68
scholarship grants, 5.76–5.81
separate maintenance payments (see also Alimony), 5.100–5.114
Social Security benefits, 5.130
stock redemption of, 19.54–19.59
tenancy in common, 5.40–5.41
tips and honoraria, 6.24–6.25
treasure finders, 5.82
widows, payments to,

Subject
Index

Gross income
(continued)
6.14–6.16
Gross income, exclusions from, 6.1–6.90
bequests, 6.26–6.29
compensation for injuries or sickness, 6.42–6.62
contributions to capital, 6.73–6.77
death benefits, 6.1–6.16
dividend exclusion, 6.69–6.72
employee death benefits, 6.13–6.16
gifts, 6.17–6.25
inheritances, 6.17, 6.26–6.29
interest:
  federal securities, 6.38–6.41
  local government securities, 6.30–6.37
life insurance proceeds, 6.1–6.12
meals or lodging, 6.78–6.89
recovery of bad debts, prior taxes, and delinquency amounts, 6.63–6.68
tips and honoraria, 6.24–6.25
widows, payments to, 6.14–6.16

H

H.R. 10 plans, 17.60–17.68
Head of household tax rates, 3.67–3.69
Hedging, 12.19
Heirs (see Trusts and estates)
History of taxation, 1.1–1.24
Constitution, 1.4
customs duties, 1.6
employment taxes, 1.22–1.24
estate taxes, 1.17–1.19
excess profits tax, 1.14
Excise Tax Reduction Act of 1965, 1.16
excise taxes, 1.6–1.8
gift taxes, 1.20–1.21

income tax, birth of, 1.9
Internal Revenue Code:
  of 1939, 1.13
  of 1954, 1.13
Revenue Act of 1909, 1.11
Revenue Act of 1913, 1.12
Revenue Act of 1971, 8.93, 8.160
Sixteenth Amendment, 1.12
Social Security taxes, 1.22–1.23
Tax Adjustment Act of 1966, 1.16
Tax Reform Act of 1969, 1.16
Unemployment tax, 1.24
Hobbies:
cattle breeding, 7.22–7.26
expenses, 7.25, 7.113
farms, 7.22–7.26
Honoraria, income from, 6.24–6.25
House of Representatives, 1.32–1.33
Household and dependent care services, 10.89–10.91
Housing projects, sales of, 11.127–11.130
Hybrid method of accounting, 16.1–16.4

I

Illegal business:
deductible expenses, 7.37
gross income, 5.69–5.71
Illness, compensation for, 6.42–6.62
Income (see Gross income, Gross income, exclusions from, Adjusted gross income, Taxable income)
Income averaging, 3.76–3.82
Innocent spouse, 3.67–3.69

Indebtedness, gain on cancellation of (see Gross income)
Inheritance taxes (see Estate taxes)
Inheritances not income, 6.17, 6.26–6.29
Injuries, compensation for, 6.42–6.62
Installment method, 16.5–16.41
dealers in personal property, 16.6–16.23
bad debts, 16.22
change from accrual method, 16.17–16.21
computation of income, 16.10–16.15
defaults and repossessions, 16.22–16.23
eligible dealers, 16.6
eligible sales, 16.7–16.9
initial adoption of method, 16.16
revolving credit plans, 16.8–16.9
installment obligations:
basis, 16.22, 16.41
disposition, 16.41
interest deductible by purchaser, 10.30–10.33
real estate and casual sales of personal property, 16.24–16.38
computation of income, 16.31–16.36
defaults and repossessions, 11.131–11.136, 16.39–16.40
election of method, 16.29–16.30
eligible sales, 16.25–16.28
lease with option to purchase, 7.70
subsequent reduction of selling price, 16.37–16.38
Insurance:
accident, 6.46
health, 6.46

Insurance *(continued)*
life (see Life insurance)
medical premiums, 10.85
policies, exchange of, 11.85–11.87
premiums prepaid, 14.35–14.36
reimbursement for living expenses, 6.90
Interest, 10.4–10.33
annuity policy loans, 10.29
assessments, payable on, 2.43
bonds sold between payment dates, 5.67–5.68
carrying charges, 10.29
deductions specifically prohibited, 10.29
definition, 10.5–10.6
distinguished from dividends, 10.15–10.28
excess investment, 12.54–12.55
federal securities, 6.38–6.41
hybrid securities, 10.24–10.28
imputed, 10.33, 11.27–11.36
indebtedness, 10.7
installment purchases, 10.30–10.33
investment indebtedness, 10.29
life insurance loans, 10.29
life insurance policy dividends, 5.128
municipal bonds, 6.30–6.37
arbitrage bonds, 6.37
industrial development bonds, 6.36
no tax preference, 3.115
original issue discount, 12.94–12.99
paid on debt to purchase municipal bonds, 10.29
penalties, on, 4.20
points on loans, 10.6
prepaid as a deduction, 14.38

prepayment penalty, 10.36
related taxpayer debts, 10.29
risk capital, 10.20
thin capitalization, 10.21–10.23
underpayments of tax, 4.20
U.S. savings bonds, 6.39–6.41
year-end, 14.13
Internal Revenue Code:
of 1939, 1.13
of 1954, 1.13
Internal Revenue Service, 2.23–2.24
Inventories, 15.88–15.108 (see also Accrual method)
Investment companies, transfers to, 19.31
Investment credit, 3.107, 4.15, 8.159–8.184
CLADR life controls, 8.142
financial statements, 8.183–8.184
recapture of, 8.174–8.182
Investment indebtedness, interest on, 10.29
Investors' expenses, 7.20–7.21, 7.115–7.119
Involuntary conversions, 11.91–11.110 (see also Condemnation)
residences, 11.120
Itemized deductions, 3.3, 3.28–3.29

J

Joint returns, 3.65–3.70
Joint tenancy, 5.40–5.41
Judicial remedies, 2.35–2.40

K

Keogh plans, 17.60–17.68
Kickbacks, deductibility of, 7.34–7.36

L

Land clearing expenses, recapture of,

12.157–12.160
Leases (see also Rentals):
cancellation of as sale or exchange, 12.102
with purchase option, 7.69–7.74
Legal expenses:
antitrust proceedings, 7.44
capital expenditure, 7.39–7.42
criminal defense, 7.43
divorce actions, 7.128–7.130
production of income, 7.126–7.130
tax determinations, 7.137
Legislative process, 1.31–1.38
Committee reports, 1.35
House of Representatives, 1.32–1.33
Ways and Means Committee, 1.32–1.33
Senate, 1.33–1.34
Senate Finance Committee, 1.33–1.34
Letters:
90 day, 2.35
30 day, 2.31
Life estates and remainders, basis of, 11.62–11.65
Life insurance:
dividends received, 5.127
interest credited, 5.128
interest deductibility on policy loans, 10.29
proceeds, 6.1–6.12
transfers of policies, 6.10–6.12
Limitation, unearned income of dependents, 3.35–3.37
Limitation periods, 2.41–2.42
bad debts, 9.97
worthless securities, 9.36
Lobbying expenses, 7.80
Lodging furnished:
convenience of employer, 6.78–6.87

Subject Index

Lodging furnished (*continued*)
  partners and proprietors, 6.88–6.89
Losses:
  abandonment, 9.24–9.31
    depreciable property, 9.25–9.27
    nondepreciable property, 9.29–9.31
  basis necessary, 9.5
  business or profit motivated transactions of individuals, 3.24–3.25, 9.21–9.23
  capital (see Capital gains and losses)
  casualties, 9.37–9.58 (see also Casualty losses)
  definition, 9.2–9.4
  demolition of buildings, 9.32
  disaster, 9.53
  embezzlement, 9.19, 9.54
  loss of useful value, 9.28
  trusts and estates, 20.19–20.20
  net operating losses, 9.60–9.64
    individuals, 3.15, 9.62–9.64
    limitations on corporate carryovers, 19.136–19.139
  realization and recognition, 9.6–9.8
  residential property, 9.22
  restrictions, 9.9–9.17
    public policy, 9.10–9.11
    related parties, 9.12–9.17
  small business stock, 19.32–19.38
  stock in club, 9.23
  theft, 9.19, 9.54–9.56
  wagering, 9.57–9.59
  worthless securities, 9.33–9.36
  year of deductibility, 9.18–9.20
Low-income allowance, 3.34

M

Marital deduction:
  estate taxes, 1.18
  gift taxes, 1.21
Marital status:
  exemptions, personal, 3.51
  standard deduction, 3.40
Mathematical errors in returns, 2.25
Maximum tax on earned income, 3.83–3.89
Meals furnished:
  convenience of employer, 6.78–6.87
  partners and proprietors, 6.88–6.89
Medical expenses, 10.81–10.88
  distinguished from personal, 10.84
  insurance premiums, 10.85
  limitations, 10.85–10.87
  qualifying expenditures, 10.82–10.83
  reimbursements for, 6.43, 6.52–6.53, 10.86, 10.88
Merchandise, advance payments received for, 15.44
Minimum tax on tax preferences, 3.112–3.116, 4.38, 12.51–12.53
Minors:
  earnings of, 5.44, 5.129
  gifts to, 5.44
Mortgages:
  cost, as part of, 11.42
  gain on satisfaction, 5.96
  sale of property, 11.9
Movie films, depreciation of, 8.33
Moving expenses, 3.10, 7.98–7.103

N

Net income, 3.3
Net operating loss carryovers and carrybacks, 9.60–9.64

individuals, 3.15, 9.62–9.64
limitations on corporate carryovers, 19.136–19.139
trusts and estates, 20.19–20.20
Nominees, gross income of, 5.39
Nonbusiness expenses:
  production of income, 7.109–7.136
    business investigation, 7.120–7.122
    hobbies, 7.22–7.26, 7.113
    investors, 7.115–7.119
    legal, 7.126–7.131
    proxy contests, 7.123–7.125
    real estate investments, 7.132
    residential property, 7.133–7.136
    tax determinations, 7.137
Nondeductible items, list of, 7.3
Non-profit organizations (see Tax-exempt organizations)
Notes:
  gain by debtor on settlement, 5.96
  income from collection, 11.23–11.26, 12.92–12.99
  issuance as payment, 14.30–14.33
  receipt of as gross income, 11.15–11.19, 14.21–14.22

O

Obsolescence, 8.145–8.149
Office audit, 2.30
Options:
  failure to exercise as sale or exchange, 12.100–12.101
  payments received for, 11.145
  purchase option in lease, 7.69–7.74
Outside salesmen's expenses, 3.10, 7.97

P

Partners and partnerships:
adjusted gross income, 3.14
basis of partner's interest, 18.12–18.14
basis of property, 18.11
capital gains and losses, 4.26, 18.23
contribution of property to, 18.8–18.10
definition, 18.4–18.6
distributions from, 18.41–18.46
distributive shares, 18.25–18.28
dividends received, 4.28
elections, 18.21
family, 18.48–18.49
foreign income taxes, 4.28
formation, 18.7–18.14
guaranteed payments, 18.30–18.31
inventory items, 18.37–18.40
liquidating distributions, 18.41–18.46
losses, limit on deductibility, 18.28
meals and lodging received, 6.88–6.89
operations, 18.15–18.35
partners' salaries, 18.30–18.31
partnership interest, sale or exchange of, 18.36–18.40
pass-through of special items, 18.22–18.24
principal partner, 18.17
property sales from or to partner, 18.32–18.35
return, 4.21–4.23
Section 1231 property, 4.27
spread sheet, 18.50–18.62
taxable income, determination of, 4.24, 18.16–18.24
taxable year, 4.21, 18.17–18.18
termination, 18.19–18.20

unrealized receivables, 18.37–18.40
Patents:
definition, 12.73
depreciation, 8.7
holding period, 12.76
infringement damages received, 5.132
license distinguished from sale, 12.78–12.80
sales of, 12.73–12.84
Payment:
checks, 14.27–14.29
constructive, no, 14.25–14.26
date of, 14.23
Payroll taxes (see Social Security taxes, Withholding)
Penalties:
deductibility, 7.30
estimated tax, underpayment of:
corporations, 4.20
individuals, 3.127
innocent spouse, 3.67–3.69
interest payable on, 4.20
types of, 2.43
Pension, profit-sharing, and stock bonus plans, qualified, 17.6–17.43
advantages, 17.43
benefits, 17.23–17.30
taxation of, 17.38–17.42
deductions, 17.31–17.37
distinctions between qualified plans, 17.13–17.19
forfeitures and vesting, 17.20–17.22
fund holder, 17.6–17.8
nondiscrimination and coverage, 17.10–17.11
plan, 17.9
self-employed, 3.10, 3.16
Subchapter S corporations:
forfeitures, 3.10, 3.20
limitations, 19.154–19.157

Person, definition of, 2.12
Personal exemptions (see Exemptions, personal)
Personal holding companies, 19.140–19.142
Political contributions, 3.108
Preferences, tax, 3.107–3.111
Prepaid income under accrual method, 15.28–15.49 (see also Accrual method)
Prizes as gross income, 5.72–5.75
Profit-sharing plans (see Pension, profit-sharing, and stock bonus plans, qualified)
Property (see also Real property)
basis of (see Basis)
community, 3.63, 5.42–5.43
held for productive use or investment, exchange of, 11.71–11.84
joint tenants, 5.40–5.41
life estates and remainders, basis of, 11.62–11.65
receipt of as gross income, 5.83–5.85, 14.17–14.22
repossessions of real, 11.131–11.136
Section 1250, 12.128–12.141
Section 1245, 12.117–12.127
tenants in common, 5.40–5.41
used in trade or business, sales of, 12.108–12.112 (see also Section 1231 property)
value of, 14.17–14.22
Proprietors:
accounting methods, 14.2, 14.6
meals and lodging, 6.88–6.89
self-employed pension

Proprietors (*continued*)
    contributions,
      17.60–17.68
Protests, 2.30–2.31
Proxy contest expenses,
    7.126–7.128
Public policy violations,
    7.27–7.37, 9.10–
    9.11
Puts and calls, 11.156

R

Railroad retirement bene-
    fits not gross in-
    come, 5.130
Real property:
    dummy corporations,
      5.48–5.52
    expenses, 7.132
    repossessions, 11.131–
      11.136
    taxes:
      allocation on sales,
        10.45–10.46
      effect on basis,
        11.43
      deduction, 10.37
Recapture:
    depreciation, 12.113–
      12.141
    farm losses, 12.142–
      12.156
    investment credit,
      8.174–8.182
    land clearing expenses,
      12.157–12.160
    soil and water conser-
      vation expendi-
      tures, 12.157–
      12.160
Recovery of bad debts,
    prior taxes, and
    delinquency
    amounts, 6.63–6.68
Refunds of federal in-
    come tax:
    claims for, 2.28, 2.32
    limitation periods,
      2.41–2.42
    overpayment shown on
      return, 3.119
    suits for, 2.38
Regulations, in general,
    2.60–2.61
Related parties:
    bargain purchase from
      own corporation,
      19.173
    expenses and interest,

10.29, 15.81–15.83
losses between, 9.12–
    9.17
rentals, 7.75–7.76
sales of depreciable
    property between,
    12.161–12.165
Rentals:
    advance:
      deduction, 14.37
      income, 14.37, 15.32–
      15.34
    deduction, 7.67–7.76
    lease with option to
      purchase, 7.69–
      7.74
    related parties, 7.75–
      7.76
    expenses of receiving,
      adjusted gross in-
      come, 3.10, 3.26
    security deposits, 15.34
Reorganizations (see Cor-
    porations, reorgan-
    izations)
Repairs, 2.27, 7.9–7.12,
    8.123–8.132
Repossessions:
    installment sales,
      16.23, 16.39–16.40
    personal property,
      16.39
    real property, 11.131–
      11.136
Reserves:
    bad debts, 9.67
    installment sales by
      dealers in personal
      property, 16.22
    dealers', 15.19
    depreciation, 8.48
    estimated future ex-
      penses, 15.69–
      15.77
    guaranteed debt obli-
      gations, 9.98–9.101
    quantity discounts,
      15.76–15.77
    self-insurance, 15.70
Residence:
    conversion to rental
      use, 9.22
    expenses, 7.133–7.136
    gain on sale, exemption
      of, 11.111–11.122
    after age 64, 11.123–
      11.126
    basis of new, 11.112
    husband and wife,

special rule for,
    11.119
replacement period,
    11.116–11.117
reporting, 11.121–
    11.122
involuntary conversion,
    11.120
loss on sale, 9.22
Retirement income
    credit, 3.94–3.97
Retirement of assets,
    8.52–8.63, 8.133–
    8.139 (see also
    Depreciation)
Retirement plans (see
    Compensation, de-
    ferred)
Returns:
    consolidated, 19.169
    corporation income,
      4.1–4.20
    examination of, 2.29–
      2.34
    field audit, 2.31
    Form 1040, 3.1–3.2
    Form 1120, 4.1–4.20
    forms, types of, 2.24
    individuals, 3.117–
      3.123
      due date, 3.119
      extensions of time,
        3.120
      joint, 3.65–3.70
      surviving spouse,
        3.70
      signatures, 3.123
      when and where to
        file, 3.119–3.123
      who must file, 3.117–
        3.118
    married persons:
      separate returns
      standard deduc-
        tion, 3.38–3.40
    mathematical errors,
      2.25
    office audit, 2.30
    partnerships, 4.21–4.23
    trusts and estates,
      4.29–4.30
Revenue Act:
    of 1909, 1.11
    of 1913, 1.12
Revenue agents' exami-
    nations, 2.27–2.34
Revenue Proc. 70–27,
    16.66–16.68
Royalties:

Royalties *(continued)*
  advance:
    deduction, 14.37
    income, 14.37, 15.32–
      15.34
  deductions, 7.77
  expenses of receiving,
    adjusted gross in-
    come, 3.26
Rulings, 2.56–2.59

S

Sales and exchanges (see
    also Corpora-
    tions, liquidations,
    organization of,
    and reorganiza-
    tions; also Capital
    gains and losses)
  amount realized, 11.5–
    11.36
  automobile trade-in,
    11.71–11.83
  bargain price:
    basis from partial
      donor, 11.61
    purchase by share-
      holder, 19.173
  basis of property (see
    Basis)
  bonds, retirement of,
    12.92–12.99
  collection of debt,
    11.23–11.26,
    12.92–12.99
  contract to sell, 11.140
  deferred payments,
    11.10–11.26
    accrual method,
      11.20–11.22
    cash method, 11.11–
      11.19
      contractual rights,
        11.12–11.14
      negotiable notes,
        11.15–11.16
      nonnegotiable
        notes, 11.17–
        11.19
    imputed interest,
      11.27–11.36
    income from collec-
      tion, 11.23–11.26
  depreciable property:
    between related tax-
      payers, 12.161–
      12.165
    recapture of depreci-

ation, 12.113–
  12.141
determination of gain
  or loss, 11.4
endowment policies,
  sale of, 12.70
fair market value de-
  fined, 11.6
mortgages of seller,
  11.9
nontaxable exchanges,
  11.69–11.136 (see
  also Exchanges,
  nontaxable)
insurance policies,
  11.85–11.87
involuntary conver-
  sions, 11.91–11.110
low income housing
  projects, 11.127–
  11.130
property held for pro-
  ductive use or in-
  vestment, 11.71–
  11.84
repossessions of real
  property, 11.131–
  11.136
residence, sale of,
  11.111–11.122 (see
  also Residence)
residence by person
  65 or over, 11.123–
  11.126
stock for property,
  11.89–11.90
stock for stock, 11.88
notes received (see de-
  ferred payments in
  this heading)
patents, 12.73–12.84
  (see also Patents)
puts and calls, 11.156
Section 306 stock,
  19.61–19.64
stock exchange trans-
  actions, 11.154–
  11.155
treasury stock, 19.18–
  19.19
when gain or loss is re-
  alized, 11.143–
  11.153
  casual sales of prop-
    erty, 11.143–11.150
  escrows, 11.152–
    11.153
  goods, 11.151
when sale occurs,

11.138–11.142
Salesman, outside, 3.10,
  3.17
Salvage value, 8.13–8.17,
  8.117–8.122
Scholarship grants, 5.76–
  5.81
Section 306 stock, 19.61–
  19.64
Section 1231 gains and
  losses, 2.8, 12.108–
  12.112
  adjusted gross income,
    3.10
  partnerships, 4.27
Securities (see also
    Bonds, Corpora-
    tions)
  bonds:
    amortization of orig-
      inal issue discount,
      12.94–12.99
    amortization of pre-
      mium paid, 8.155–
      8.157
    premium on redemp-
      tion, 10.34–10.35
    retirement as sale or
      exchange, 12.92–
      12.99
  commissions paid,
    7.119
  cost of shares, 11.44
  hybrid, 10.24–10.28
  investors' expenses,
    7.20–7.21, 7.115–
    7.119
  preferred stock:
    defined, 10.25
    Sec. 306 stock, 19.61–
      19.64
  proxy contest expenses,
    7.123–7.125
  redemption of stock,
    19.54–19.59
  short sales of stock,
    12.103–12.104
  transfer taxes, 7.118
  stock dividends and
    rights, 19.47–19.51
  wash sales, 12.105–
    12.107
  worthless, 9.33–9.36
Self-employed (see topic,
    e.g., adjusted
    gross income, busi-
    ness expenses,
    partnerships, pen-
    sion plans)

Subject
Index

Self-employment tax, 3.109–3.111
Senate, 1.33–1.34
Senate Finance Committee, 1.33–1.34
Services, receipts for future, 15.35–15.43
Severance damages, 11.95
Sick pay plans, 6.53–6.61
Sickness, compensation for, 6.41–6.61
Smith, Adam, 1.25
Social Security benefits not gross income, 5.130
Social Security taxes, 1.23
credit for excess payments, 3.93
self-employment tax, 3.109–3.111
Soil and water conservation expenditures, recapture of, 12.157–12.160
Sources of tax law, 2.44–2.52
Special assessments, 10.38, 10.47
Spouse, innocent, 3.67–3.69
Standard deduction, 3.5, 3.30–3.47
abandoned spouse, 3.39
dependents, unearned income of, 3.35–3.37
election, 3.41–3.47
considerations in making, 3.44–3.47
low-income allowance, 3.34
marital status, 3.40
percentage, 3.33
separate returns of married persons, 3.38–3.40
Statute of limitations, 2.41–2.42
Stock (see Corporations, Securities, Sales and exchanges)
Stock exchange transactions, 11.154–11.155
Stock options, 17.69–17.86
definition, 17.70

nonstatutory, 17.76–17.86
statutory, 17.73–17.75
employee stock purchase plans, 17.73–17.74
qualified, 17.75
restricted, 17.73–17.74
Subchapter S corporations, 19.145–19.158
pension plan forfeitures, 3.10, 3.20
Subscription list, depreciation of, 8.11
Supper money, 6.85
Surtax:
personal holding companies, 19.140–19.142
unreasonable accumulation of earnings, 19.143–19.144
Surtax exemption, 4.16
disallowance, 19.168
limitation on controlled group, 19.161–19.168
Surviving spouse, 3.70

T

Tax Court of the United States, 2.35
Tax credits (see Credits)
Tax determination fees, 7.137
Tax, estimated (see Estimated tax)
Tax-exempt organizations, 2.16–2.21
excise taxes, 2.20
private foundations, 2.19–2.21
private operating, contributions to, 10.55–10.56, 10.58–10.59
unrelated business income, 2.21–2.22
Tax preferences, minimum tax on:
corporations, 4.38, 12.53
individuals, 3.112–3.116, 12.52
trusts and estates, 4.38

Tax rates:
corporations, 4.16–4.17
estates and trusts, 4.35
individuals, 3.64–3.75
head of household, 3.71–3.73
income averaging, 3.76–3.82
joint returns, 3.65–3.79
maximum tax on earned income, 3.83–3.85
optional tax tables, 3.74–3.75
minimum tax on tax preferences, 3.112–3.116, 4.38, 12.52–12.53
Taxable income defined:
corporations, 4.6
individuals, 3.4
partnerships, 4.24
trusts and estates, 4.31–4.37
Taxable year (see Accounting periods)
Taxes, 10.37–10.47
cooperative housing corporation, 10.92–10.95
customs duties, 1.6
deductible types, 10.38–10.44
direct, 1.4–1.5
excise:
history of, 1.6–1.8, 1.15–1.16
nonhighway use of gasoline and lubricating oil, credit for, 3.106, 4.15
federal income (see also Tax rates)
history of, 1.9–1.14
foreign income:
credit:
corporations, 4.11–4.14
individuals, 3.98–3.105
deduction, 3.98, 4.11
partnerships, 4.28
nondeductible types, 10.47
real property:
allocation or sales, 10.45–10.46
effect on basis,

Taxes: real property
(*continued*)
11.43
deduction, 10.37
recovery of prior taxes
deducted, 6.67
refund from state, in-
terest on, 6.32
sales or use, 10.41
Social Security, deduc-
tibility of, 10.43
special assessments,
10.38, 10.47
transfer, 10.40
Taxpayers:
classification, 2.14
definition, 2.12
Television, deprecia-
tion of:
F.C.C. license, 8.10
network affiliation con-
tracts, 8.10
tapes, 8.33
Tenants:
by the entirety, 11.52–
11.53
cooperative housing
corporations,
10.92–10.95
in common, 5.40–5.41
joint, 5.40–5.41, 11.52–
11.53
Theft losses, 9.19, 9.54–
9.56
Tips, income from, 6.24–
6.25
Trade names, transfers
of, 12.85–12.90
Trademarks, transfers
of, 12.85–12.90
Transportation ex-
penses, 3.10, 7.96
Travel expenses, 3.10,
7.51–7.57, 7.89–
7.95
home, definition of,
7.90–7.94
necessity of overnight
trip, 7.95

Treasure finders, 5.82
Treasury stock, sales of,
19.18–19.19
Trusts and estates, 20.1–
20.48
accounting methods
and periods, 20.12–
20.13
accumulation distribu-
tions from trusts,
20.37–20.44
administrative ex-
penses of estates,
20.21
beneficiaries:
taxable income, 4.36–
4.37
charitable contribu-
tions, 20.15–20.17
complex trusts, 20.30–
20.36
deduction for distribu-
tions, 20.22
depreciation and de-
pletion, 3.10, 20.18
distributable net in-
come, 20.23–20.25
estimated tax, 4.30
excess deductions,
20.19–20.20
grantor trusts, 4.32,
20.45–20.47
income taxable to bene-
ficiaries, 20.26–
20.36
minimum tax on tax
preferences, 4.38
nature of, 20.1–20.6
net operating losses,
20.19–20.20
personal exemptions,
4.35
returns, 4.29–4.30
simple trusts, 20.29
taxable income, 4.31–
4.37
taxation in general,
4.31–4.35, 20.7–
20.11

throw-back rule, 20.37–
20.44
trusts treated as cor-
porations, 20.48

U

Unadjusted basis, 2.9,
11.38
Unemployment taxes,
1.24
Uniform expenses, 7.107
Uniformed forces:
allowances for:
injury or illness, 6.47
quarters, 6.86
Union dues, 7.105
Unreasonable accumu-
lation of earnings,
19.143–19.144
Unrelated business in-
come (see Tax-
exempt organiza-
tions)

V

Vacation pay deduction,
15.78–15.83
Value defined, 11.6

W

Wage continuation plans
for illness, 6.53–
6.61
Wash sales, 12.105–
12.107
Ways and Means Com-
mittee, 1.32–1.33
Weight of authority,
2.53–2.64
Western Hemisphere
Trade corpora-
tions, 19.159
Widows:
payments to, 6.14–6.16
Withholding of income
tax, credit for, 3.91
Workmen's compensa-
tion, 6.44

343.73
M 116
96770

McCarthy, C.F.

Federal income tax - sources & appls.

DATE DUE